Routledge Handbook of Foreign Policy Analysis Methods

The disintegration and questioning of global governance structures and a re-orientation toward national politics combined with the spread of technological innovations such as big data, social media, and phenomena like fake news, populism, or questions of global health policies make it necessary for the introduction of new methods of inquiry and the adaptation of established methods in Foreign Policy Analysis (FPA). This accessible handbook offers concise chapters from expert international contributors covering a diverse range of new and established FPA methods. Embracing methodological pluralism and a belief in the value of an open discussion about methods' assumptions and diverging positions, it provides new, state-of-the-art research approaches, as well as introductions to a range of established methods. Each chapter follows the same approach, introducing the method and its development, discussing strengths, requirements, limitations, and potential pitfalls while illustrating the method's application using examples from empirical research. Embracing methodological pluralism and problem-oriented research that engages with real-world questions, the authors examine quantitative and qualitative traditions, rationalist and interpretivist perspectives, as well as different substantive backgrounds. The book will be of interest to a wide range of scholars and students in global politics, foreign policy, and methods-related classes across the social sciences.

Patrick A. Mello is Assistant Professor of International Security at Vrije Universiteit Amsterdam. His most recent book is *Qualitative Comparative Analysis: An Introduction to Research Design and Application* (Georgetown University Press, 2021) and he has published, among other journals, in the *European Journal of International Relations*, *Foreign Policy Analysis*, and the *European Political Science Review*.

Falk Ostermann is Lecturer at Kiel University. He studies the domestic contestation of foreign policy with a focus on military interventions. He is the author of *Security, Defense Discourse and Identity in NATO and Europe. How France Changed Foreign Policy* (Routledge, 2019) and of *Die NATO* (UVK/UTB, 2020). He has published, among others, in the *European Political Science Review*, *Foreign Policy Analysis*, or *West European Politics*.

Routledge Handbook of Foreign Policy Analysis Methods

Edited by
Patrick A. Mello and Falk Ostermann

LONDON AND NEW YORK

Designed cover image: © Getty Images/Stellalevi

First published 2023
by Routledge
4 Park Square, Milton Park, Abingdon, Oxon OX14 4RN

and by Routledge
605 Third Avenue, New York, NY 10158

Routledge is an imprint of the Taylor & Francis Group, an informa business

© 2023 selection and editorial matter, Patrick A. Mello and
Falk Ostermann; individual chapters, the contributors

The right of Patrick A. Mello and Falk Ostermann to be identified as the authors of the editorial material, and of the authors for their individual chapters, has been asserted in accordance with sections 77 and 78 of the Copyright, Designs and Patents Act 1988.

With the exception of Chapter 4, 25 and 32 no part of this book may be reprinted or reproduced or utilised in any form or by any electronic, mechanical, or other means, now known or hereafter invented, including photocopying and recording, or in any information storage or retrieval system, without permission in writing from the publishers.

Chapters 4, 25 and 32 of this book are available for free in PDF format as Open Access from the individual product page at www.routledge.com. It has been made available under a Creative Commons Attribution-Non Commercial-No Derivatives 4.0 license.

Trademark notice: Product or corporate names may be trademarks or registered trademarks and are used only for identification and explanation without intent to infringe.

British Library Cataloguing-in-Publication Data
A catalogue record for this book is available from the British Library

Library of Congress Cataloging-in-Publication Data
Names: Mello, Patrick A., editor. | Ostermann, Falk, editor.
Title: Routledge handbook of foreign policy analysis methods / edited by Patrick A. Mello and Falk Ostermann.
Other titles: Handbook of foreign policy analysis methods
Description: First Edition. | New York : Routledge, 2023. | Includes bibliographical references and index.
Identifiers: LCCN 2022031680 (print) | LCCN 2022031681 (ebook) | ISBN 9780367689766 (Hardback) | ISBN 9780367689803 (Paperback) | ISBN 9781003139850 (eBook)
Subjects: LCSH: International relations—Research—Methodology. | International relations—Handbooks, manuals, etc.
Classification: LCC JZ1234 .R68 2023 (print) | LCC JZ1234 (ebook) | DDC 327.1072—dc23/eng/20221108
LC record available at https://lccn.loc.gov/2022031680
LC ebook record available at https://lccn.loc.gov/2022031681

ISBN: 978-0-367-68976-6 (hbk)
ISBN: 978-0-367-68980-3 (pbk)
ISBN: 978-1-003-13985-0 (ebk)

DOI: 10.4324/9781003139850

Typeset in Bembo
by codeMantra

Contents

List of Figures	ix
List of Tables	xi
List of Contributors	xiii
Foreword: The Conduct of Inquiry in Foreign Policy Analysis	xxi
Patrick Thaddeus Jackson	
Acknowledgments	xxv

PART I
Introduction   1

1 Methods of Foreign Policy Analysis: Charting Ground, Engaging Traditions, and Opening Up Boundaries   3
   Falk Ostermann and Patrick A. Mello

PART II
Perspectives on Foreign Policy   19

2 Ideas and Identity from Rationalism to Theories of Recognition   21
   Stefano Guzzini

3 Ethnography   39
   Iver B. Neumann

4 Norms and Norm Contestation   51
   Phil Orchard and Antje Wiener

5 Feminism   67
   Alexis Henshaw

6 Political Geography   82
   Luis da Vinha

v

Contents

PART III
Language and Interpretive Methods 99

7 Discourse Analysis and Discourse Theories 101
   Falk Ostermann and Roxanna Sjöstedt

8 Narrative Analysis 117
   Kai Oppermann and Alexander Spencer

9 Frame Analysis 133
   Sabine Mokry

10 Visual Analysis 150
   Bernhard Stahl and Julian Ignatowitsch

11 Emotion Discourse Analysis 168
   Simon Koschut

PART IV
Psychology, Roles, and Leaders 185

12 Role Theory 187
   Marijke Breuning

13 The Political Psychology of Threat Assessment 202
   Janice Gross Stein

14 Measuring Perceptions: Combining Low and High Inference
   Approaches to Data Analysis in International Political Communication 218
   Natalia Chaban, Linda Jean Kenix, Svetlana Beltyukova, and Christine Fox

15 Leadership Trait Analysis 238
   Klaus Brummer

16 Operational Code Analysis 255
   Mark Schafer and Stephen G. Walker

17 Groupthink, Polythink, and Con-Div: Identifying Group
   Decision-Making Dynamics 269
   Kasey Barr and Alex Mintz

PART V
Quantitative and Comparative Approaches — 289

18 Comparative Foreign Policy — 291
    Huiyun Feng and Kai He

19 Quantitative Content Analysis — 306
    Gordon M. Friedrichs

20 Statistical Analysis — 321
    Sibel Oktay

21 Experimental Methods — 338
    Danielle L. Lupton and Clayton Webb

22 Game Theory — 354
    Scott Wolford

23 Public Opinion Surveys — 370
    Katja B. Kleinberg

24 Qualitative Comparative Analysis — 385
    Patrick A. Mello

PART VI
Qualitative Methods and Historical Approaches — 403

25 Process Tracing: An Analyticist Approach — 405
    Hilde van Meegdenburg

26 Interviews — 421
    Delphine Deschaux-Dutard

27 Historical Analysis — 435
    Payam Ghalehdar

28 Oral History — 450
    Michal Onderco

29 Archival Research — 463
    Anne Kerstin Friedrich

Part VII
New Technology, Social Media, and Networks   **483**

30 Big Data Analysis   485
Sebastian Cujai

31 Analyzing Twitter   502
Andrea Schneiker

32 Discourse Network Analysis   516
Franz Eder

33 Text as Data   536
Valerio Vignoli

34 Conflict Event Data   551
Clionadh Raleigh and Roudabeh Kishi

Index   *567*

Figures

1.1	Publication Trends (Google Scholar and Web of Science)	5
2.1	A Rationalist Theory of Action	22
2.2	Influence Attempts in a Rationalist Theory of Action	23
2.3	The Endogenization of Preference and Interest Formation	24
8.1	The Narrative Turn in International Relations and FPA	118
8.2	Elements of a Narrative	124
9.1	Overview of the Frame Analysis Process	138
9.2	Shifts in Relative Salience in Chinese Constructions of National Interest	143
9.3	Shifts in Relative Salience in U.S. Constructions of National Interest	143
9.4	Distribution of Constructions of National Interests in Chinese Foreign Policy Statements	144
9.5	Differences in Relative Salience Between Statements by General Secretary and State Council Information Office	144
9.6	Differences in Relative Salience Between Statements by Foreign Minister and Premier	145
9.7	Distribution of Constructions of National Interest in U.S. Foreign Policy Statements	145
10.1	Single Image Analysis – *Spiegel* Cover Image of 12 November 2001	157
10.2	*Spiegel* Cover Images on Afghanistan, 2001–2013	159
10.3	*Spiegel* Cover Images on Afghanistan, 2021	163
14.1	Visibility of EU in Terms of Intensity (Centrality) of EU Crisis Coverage by News Source and Country	227
14.2	Visibility of the EU in Terms of Intensity (Centrality) Compared Across Western News Sources	228
14.3	Local Resonance (Domesticity Focus) of EU Crisis Coverage by News Source and Country	231
14.4	Visibility of EU in Terms of Local Resonance (Domesticity Focus) of EU Crisis Coverage by Western News Source and Country	231
14.5	Evaluation of EU Crisis Coverage by News Source and Country	232
14.6	Evaluation of EU Crisis Coverage by Western News Source and Country	233
14.7	Rasch Visibility Map for Four Countries	234
14.8	Rasch Visibility Map for India	234
17.1	The Group Decision-Making Continuum	270
17.2	Expanded Group Decision-Making Continuum	274
20.1	Are Women More Supportive of the UN?	331
22.1	A Game in the Extensive and Strategic Forms	359

Figures

22.2	A Game of Limited Information	360
22.3	Coordination and Limited War	361
22.4	The Prisoner's Dilemma	362
22.5	Subgame Perfect Equilibria in the Deterrence Game	363
22.6	Perfect Bayesian Equilibria in the Game of Limited Information	364
24.1	Fuzzy-Set Membership in Solution and Outcome	397
25.1	Schematic Causal Mechanism as Understood in the Regularity Understanding	406
25.2	Scope Conditions and Generalization in the Regularity Understanding	407
25.3	Schematic Process of a Hypothetical Concatenation of Mechanisms	411
29.1	Telex 418 from Mogadischu on October 4th, 1985, see Annotations "VS - Vertraulich" (Confidential) and "Citissime" (Very Urgent)	468
29.2	Telex on the Topic of Monetary Questions on the French-German Summit of 1972	475
29.3	Telex on the Topic of Monetary Questions on the French-German Summit of 1972	476
30.1	Information Retrieval Using Implicit Entity Networks (see Spitz 2019)	488
30.2	Intensity Trend of Russian and Georgian Conflict Actions from 1995 to 2019	493
30.3	The Most Frequently Occurring Relations Between State Leadership and Potential Topics	495
30.4	Appearances of Relations Over Time	497
32.1	Affiliation Network with Actors (a) Agreeing to Certain Claims (c). The Edgeweights (Displayed by the Line Width) Provide Information about the Extent of Agreement Towards Claims	521
32.2	Congruence Networks. (a) Actor-Congruence Network. (b) Claim-Congruence Network	522
32.3	Dynamic Affiliation Network. (a) Network at t_0. (b) Network at t_1	523
32.4	Dynamic Actor Congruence Network	523
32.5	Overall Agreement/Disagreement Toward Claims in 2002	526
32.6	Overall Agreement/Disagreement Toward Claims in 2003	527
32.7	Affiliation Network of Most Active Speakers and Central Claims. Black Edges Indicate Agreement with, Grey Edges Indicate Rejection of a Claim	528
32.8	Congruence Network between Most Active Speakers Via Shared Claims in 2002	528
32.9	Congruence Network between Most Active Speakers Via Shared Claims in 2003	529
32.10	Dendrogram of Organizations and their Distance to Each Other via Shared Claims in 2003	530
34.1	Conflict in Syria in 2017 by Source Type	558
34.2	Top 20 Countries Exhibiting Conventional Force in 2019, per ACLED Data	561

Tables

8.1	Coding Scheme for Foreign Policy Narratives	121
9.1	Operationalization of Frame Functions	136
9.2	Chinese Foreign Policy Statements Analyzed	140
9.3	U.S. Foreign Policy Statements Analyzed	141
14.1	Newspapers, Volume of News on EU and EU Migration Crisis, and News Sources by Country	225
14.2	Mapping High Inference Variables vs. Low Inference Data	226
14.3	Distribution of Western Sources	227
14.4	Visibility of EU in Terms of Article Length and Visual Support of EU Crisis Coverage by News Source and Country	229
14.5	Visibility of the EU in Terms of Article Length and Visual Support by Western News Sources and Country	230
15.1	Leadership Traits and Behavioral Expectations	241
15.2	Indicators for Different Manifestations of Leadership Traits	243
15.3	LTA's "Norming Group of World Leaders"	244
15.4	LTA's Full Analytical Framework	247
15.5	Binaries Men/Masculinity—Women/Femininity	248
15.6	Sample of Decision Makers	250
15.7	Leadership Traits of Female and Male Decision Makers	250
17.1	Publications Utilizing the Continuum Framework	272
17.2	Case 1, Groupthink, Con-Div, and Polythink	278
17.3	Case 2, Groupthink, Con-Div, and Polythink	282
19.1	Types of Leadership Roles	312
19.2	National Identity Conception Types and Foreign Policy Preferences	313
19.3	Key Comparison Other(s) of Trump	315
19.4	National Identity Conceptions of North Korean Leaders Over Time	316
20.1	Do Gender and Military Experience Influence Support for the UN?	329
20.2	Do Gender and Military Experience Influence Support for the UN? Results from Ordinal Logit Regression	330
21.1	Illustrative Examples Research Design	348
24.1	Democratic Leaders, Conditions, and Outcome Raw Data	393
24.2	Democratic Leaders, Conditions, and Outcome (Calibrated Data)	394
24.3	Truth Table for the Outcome Early Withdrawal (Abbreviated)	395
24.4	Solution for the Outcome Early Withdrawal	396
29.1	Elements of a Diplomatic Document Following Best Practices of the International Editors of Diplomatic Documents	474

Tables

29.2	Entities of a Diplomatic Document Following Best Practices of the International Editors of Diplomatic Documents	474
30.1	Selections of Identified Relations Sorted by Source Document or Weighting	494
30.2	A Selection of Identified Sentences	496
33.1	Example of a Document-Feature Matrix	538
33.2	Categories of Automated Text Analysis and Some Examples	539

Contributors

Barr, Kasey
Kasey Barr completed her PhD in Political Science at the Hebrew University of Jerusalem in 2021 and is currently a postdoctoral teaching and research fellow with the Behavioral Political Science Lab of Reichman University.

Beltyukova, Svetlana
Svetlana Beltyukova, PhD, is Professor in Research and Measurement at the University of Toledo, Ohio, USA. She has published in top tier journals advocating for increasing the rigor of research with psychometric evidence from the use of the measurement models and has been instrumental in introducing the Rasch method in a variety of disciplines nationally and internationally.

Breuning, Marijke
Marijke Breuning is Professor of Political Science at the University of North Texas. She specializes in Foreign Policy Analysis, especially role theory. Her work focuses on development cooperation, small states, women/gender and politics, international children's rights (specifically intercountry adoption), and the sociology of the profession. She has published numerous refereed journal articles and book chapters, as well as several books.

Brummer, Klaus
Klaus Brummer holds the chair of International Relations at the Catholic University of Eichstätt-Ingolstadt, Germany. He served as co-editor-in-chief of *Foreign Policy Analysis* (2018–2020) and as president of the Foreign Policy Analysis section of the International Studies Association (2015–2016). He has published in peer-reviewed journals, including *British Journal of Politics and International Relations*, *Foreign Policy Analysis*, *International Affairs*, *International Studies Review*, and *Journal of European Public Policy*.

Chaban, Natalia
Natalia Chaban is Professor in the Media and Communication Department, University of Canterbury, New Zealand. She is Director of the Public Diplomacy and Political Communication Forum at UC. She focuses her interdisciplinary research on cognitive and semiotic aspects of political and media discourses, image and perceptions studies within the EU and IR contexts, and public diplomacy and political communication. She leads multiple transnational research projects supported by the EU and NATO.

Contributors

Cujai, Sebastian
Sebastian Cujai studied Political Science, History, and Sociology in Heidelberg, Aachen, and Nottingham. Since 2018, he is a doctoral candidate at the Institute of Political Science (IPW) at Heidelberg University. Sebastian has worked at the IPW Heidelberg as Associate Lecturer and Contract Teacher in International Relations and Didactics. His research interests include mechanisms of conflict escalation, political psychology, and computational social science.

Deschaux-Dutard, Delphine
Delphine Deschaux-Dutard is Associate Professor in Political Science at the University Grenoble Alpes, France, and Vice-Dean for International Relation of the Faculty of Law at that university. She holds a PhD from Sciences Po Grenoble (2008) dedicated to the role of French and German diplomatic and military actors in the development of European defense policy since the 1990s. She has published several articles, books, and chapters on security and defense and method issues.

Eder, Franz
Franz Eder is Associate Professor of International Relations at the University of Innsbruck. He focuses on Foreign Policy Analysis, foreign/security policy, (counter)terrorism, and methodological questions of the study of international relations. His recent publications include "Making Concurrence-Seeking Visible: Groupthink, Discourse Networks, and the 2003 Iraq War" in *Foreign Policy Analysis*, and "Contesting Counter-terrorism: Discourse Networks and the Politicisation of Counter-terrorism in Austria" in the *Journal of International Relations and Development*.

Feng, Huiyun
Huiyun Feng is Associate Professor in the School of Government and International Relations at Griffith University. Her recent publications include a co-authored book *Contesting Revisionism: China, the United States, and the Transformation of International Order* (Oxford University Press, 2021) and a co-edited volume *China's Challenges and International Order Transition: Beyond Thucydides's Trap* (University of Michigan Press, 2020).

Fox, Christine
Dr. Christine Fox is Professor in Research and Measurement at the University of Toledo, Ohio, USA. She specializes in measuring perceptions for high-stakes decisions across a variety of academic, government, and corporate settings. She is best known for co-authoring one of the most influential books on the Rasch measurement model, which has helped revolutionize the way in which quantitative inferences can be made from perception data across multiple disciplines.

Friedrich, Anne Kerstin
Anne Kerstin Friedrich is a PhD candidate at Catholic University Eichstätt-Ingolstadt, Germany. She holds a master double-degree in Political Sciences and European Politics from KU Eichstätt-Ingolstadt, Sciences Po Rennes, and Sciences Po Strasbourg. Her doctoral thesis analyzes diplomacy and negotiation practices. Conducting research in FPA, world order, and European Studies, she works as Communications Director in the private sector and previously served in the French Ministry of Foreign Affairs.

Friedrichs, Gordon M.
Gordon M. Friedrichs is Postdoctoral Researcher and Lecturer in the Department of Political Science at University of Freiburg. He specializes in International Relations, comparative Foreign Policy Analysis, and mixed methods. His research focuses on the impact of polarization and populism on democracies' foreign policy making; resilience and transformation of global governance; and international relations of East Asia and the Asia-Pacific.

Ghalehdar, Payam
Payam Ghalehdar is a Fellow at the Henry A. Kissinger Center for Global Affairs of the Johns Hopkins University School of Advanced International Studies (SAIS) and in the Centre for International Security at the Hertie School. His research interests span US foreign policy, grand strategy, military intervention, and the role of emotions in foreign policy decision-making.

Gross Stein, Janice
Janice Gross Stein is Belzberg Professor of Conflict Management and Founding Director of the Munk School of Global Affairs and Public Policy at the University of Toronto. She is a Fellow of the Royal Society of Canada and an Honorary Foreign Member of the American Academy of Arts and Sciences. Her most recent publications are *Threat Perception in International Relations*, forthcoming, and "Deterrence as Performance" in *The Journal of Strategic Studies* (2020).

Guzzini, Stefano
Stefano Guzzini is Professor at Uppsala University and PUC-Rio de Janeiro, and Senior Researcher at the Danish Institute for International Studies. His publications include *The Return of Geopolitics in Europe? Social Mechanisms and Foreign Policy Identity Crises*, and *Power, Realism and Constructivism*, winner of the 2014 ISA Theory Section Best Book Award. He is currently co-editor of *International Theory*.

He, Kai
Kai He is Professor of International Relations and Director of the Centre for Governance and Public Policy, Griffith University, Australia. He was an Australian Research Council (ARC) Future Fellow (2017–2020). His books include *Institutional Balancing in the Asia Pacific: Economic Interdependence and China's Rise* (Routledge, 2009), *China's Crisis Behavior: Political Survival and Foreign Policy after the Cold War* (Cambridge University Press, 2016).

Henshaw, Alexis
Alexis Henshaw is Assistant Professor of Political Science at Troy University. She is the author of *Why Women Rebel: Understanding Women's Participation in Armed Rebel Groups* (Routledge 2017) and co-author of *Insurgent Women: Female Combatants in Civil* Wars (Georgetown University Press 2019). Her research examines gender and conflict as well as the institutionalization of the Women, Peace, and Security agenda.

Ignatowitsch, Julian
Julian Ignatowitsch completed his Master's degree in Governance and Public Policy with a focus on International Politics at the University of Passau, Germany. During his studies, he began conducting research on the importance of visual content and text-image-constellations

in the media coverage of foreign policy issues. As a journalist for German public broadcasters, he continues to be involved in media and visual analysis.

Jackson, Patrick Thaddeus
Patrick Thaddeus Jackson is Professor of International Studies in the School of International Service at American University in Washington, DC. His scholarly interests include the philosophy and sociology of science, relational social theory, and the practices of legitimation and authority globally.

Kenix, Linda Jean
Linda Jean Kenix is Professor in the Media and Communication Department at the University of Canterbury in New Zealand. She is also the Head of the School of Language, Social, and Political Sciences. She explores the representation of marginal groups in the news of mass and alternative media.

Kishi, Roudabeh
Roudabeh Kishi is Director of Research & Innovation at the Armed Conflict Location & Event Data Project (ACLED) and has worked at a number of organizations around the nexus of conflict, development, and data. Her work focuses on violence targeting women, far-right extremism, and data methodology and conflict research more broadly. She has published in various academic journals and media outlets.

Kleinberg, Katja B.
Katja B. Kleinberg (PhD, University of North Carolina, Chapel Hill, 2009) is Associate Professor of Political Science at Binghamton University, State University of New York. Her research focuses on public opinion on foreign economic and security policy, international political economy, and economic statecraft. Her work has appeared in *International Organization*, *The Journal of Politics*, *International Studies Quarterly*, *Journal of Conflict Resolution*, among others.

Koschut, Simon
Simon Koschut holds the Chair for International Security Policy at Zeppelin University Friedrichshafen. His research interests lie at the intersection of regional security governance, norms, and emotions in world politics. Previously, he held positions at Freie Universität Berlin, Harvard University, and the University of Erlangen-Nürnberg. His most recent book is *The Power of Emotions in World Politics* (Routledge, 2020).

Lupton, Danielle L.
Danielle L. Lupton is Associate Professor of Political Science at Colgate University. She received her PhD from Duke University. Her research interests include foreign policy, public opinion, and political methodology. Her book was published with Cornell University Press. Her work has been featured in journals such as *Political Analysis*, *International Studies Quarterly*, and *International Interactions*.

Meegdenburg, Hilde van
Hilde van Meegdenburg is Assistant Professor of International Relations at the Institute of Political Science, Leiden University. Her research focuses on international security and state foreign policy making, adopting an interpretivist and narrative-based approach. She also

works on and teaches process tracing methods. Her work has been published in *Cooperation and Conflict*, *Journal of European Public Policy*, and *Contemporary Security Policy*, among others.

Mello, Patrick A.
Patrick A. Mello is Assistant Professor of International Security at Vrije Universiteit Amsterdam. His most recent book is *Qualitative Comparative Analysis: An Introduction to Research Design and Application* (Georgetown University Press, 2021) and he has published, among other journals, in the *European Journal of International Relations*, *Foreign Policy Analysis*, and the *European Political Science Review*.

Mintz, Alex
Alex Mintz is Director of the Computerized Decision-Making Lab and former Provost of Reichman University (formerly IDC) and past President of the Israeli Political Science Association. He is the recipient of the 1993 ISA's Karl Deutsch Award and the 2005 Distinguished Scholar Award in Foreign Policy Analysis. Mintz served as Dean of the Lauder School of Government, Diplomacy and Strategy at IDC from 2008 to 2014.

Mokry, Sabine
Sabine Mokry is a PhD candidate at Leiden University's Political Science Department and a Visiting Researcher at the German Institute for Global and Area Studies (GIGA) in Hamburg. In her dissertation, she investigates when, how, and how much Chinese societal actors, specifically think-tankers and scholars, influence the construction of China's national interest.

Neumann, Iver B.
Iver B. Neumann is Director of The Fridtjof Nansen Institute, Norway. He holds doctorates in Politics (Oxford) and Social Anthropology (Oslo). He previously served as Professor at the University of Oslo and the London School of Economics. Neumann's main areas of expertise are social theory, qualitative methods, diplomacy, and Russian foreign policy. His three books *At Home with the Diplomats* (Cornell University Press, 2012), *Diplomatic Sites* (Hurst, 2013), and *Diplomatic Tenses* (Manchester University Press, 2020) draw, among others, on the ethnographic method.

Oktay, Sibel
Sibel Oktay is Associate Professor of Political Science at the University of Illinois at Springfield. She studies how domestic political institutions affect foreign policy, the impact of foreign policy on public opinion and voting behavior, and how leaders influence these relationships. Her most recent book is *Governing Abroad: Coalition Politics and Foreign Policy in Europe* (University of Michigan Press, 2022). She is the 2022–2023 recipient of the Jefferson Science Fellowship from the U.S. Department of State.

Onderco, Michal
Michal Onderco is Associate Professor of International Relations at Erasmus University Rotterdam. His research interests include nuclear politics and the domestic politics of foreign policy. Michal Onderco received his PhD from VU University Amsterdam, and he has held fellowships at the European University Institute and Stanford University's Center for International Security and Cooperation. His works include *Networked Nonproliferation* (Stanford University Press, 2021) and *Extending the NPT* (Wilson Center, 2020).

Contributors

Oppermann, Kai
Kai Oppermann is Professor of International Politics at the Chemnitz University of Technology. He has previously held positions at the University of Sussex, King's College London, and the University of Cologne. His work has been published in journals such as the *European Journal of International Relations, Foreign Policy Analysis, Journal of European Public Policy*, and *British Journal of Politics and International Relations*.

Orchard, Phil
Phil Orchard is Associate Professor of International Relations at the University of Wollongong, Australia, and Co-Director of the UOW Future of Rights Centre (FoRC). His books include *Protecting the Internally Displaced: Rhetoric and Reality* (Routledge, 2018) and *A Right to Flee: Refugees, States, and the Construction of International Cooperation* (Cambridge University Press, 2014).

Ostermann, Falk
Falk Ostermann is Lecturer at Kiel University. He studies the domestic contestation of foreign policy with a focus on military interventions. He is the author of *Security, Defense Discourse and Identity in NATO and Europe. How France Changed Foreign Policy* (Routledge, 2019) and of *Die NATO* (UVK/UTB, 2020). He has published, among others, in the *European Political Science Review, Foreign Policy Analysis*, or *West European Politics*.

Raleigh, Clionadh
Clionadh Raleigh is Professor of Political Violence and Geography in the School of Global Studies at the University of Sussex. She is also Executive Director of the Armed Conflict Location & Event Data Project (ACLED). Her primary research interests are the dynamics of conflict and violence, African political environments, and elite networks.

Schafer, Mark
Mark Schafer is Professor of Political Psychology at the University of Central Florida. His research interests include the operational code, groupthink, and psychological correlates of foreign policy. His published research is in journals such as *International Studies Quarterly* and *Journal of Conflict Resolution*. He received the Erik Erikson Award for Early Career Achievement from ISPP in 2003, and the Distinguished Scholar Award from the FPA section of ISA in 2021.

Schneiker, Andrea
Andrea Schneiker (she/her) is Full Professor of Global Governance at Zeppelin University in Friedrichshafen, Germany. She received her PhD in Political Science from the University of Münster, after which she worked as Assistant Professor at the Leibniz University of Hannover and the University of Bremen and as Junior Professor of Political Science at the University of Siegen. She was also visiting scholar at New York University, Radboud University Nijmegen, and the Graduate Institute in Geneva.

Sjöstedt, Roxanna
Roxanna Sjöstedt is Associate Professor of Political Science at Lund University. Her research is centered on International Relations, international security, and Foreign Policy Analysis, with a specific interest in securitization, socialization, and discourse analysis. She has published on these topics in different outlets such as the *European Journal of International Security*,

International Relations, Foreign Policy Analysis, Security Studies, Nationalism and Ethnic Politics, and the *Oxford Research Encyclopedia of Politics*.

Spencer, Alexander
Alexander Spencer holds the Chair for International Relations at the Otto-von-Guericke-University Magdeburg. In his research, he focuses on non-state violent actors and discourse-analytical methods. His work on narratives and politics has been published in a number of journals including the *Journal of European Public Policy*, *European Journal of International Relations*, *International Politics*, and *Cambridge Review of International Affairs*.

Stahl, Bernhard
Bernhard Stahl is Professor of International Politics at the University of Passau, Germany. His research interests cover European foreign policies (including German, French, Italian, Serbian) and EU foreign policy, in particular with regard to South-Eastern Europe. Current research projects deal with renewed great power rivalry in the Balkans and the silencing of mass atrocities in foreign policy.

Vignoli, Valerio
Valerio Vignoli is Postdoctoral Researcher in Political Science at the University of Milan, Italy. His research interests span over International Relations, Foreign Policy Analysis, and quantitative methods. He has published articles in various journals including *West European Politics*, *Foreign Policy Analysis*, and *Government and Opposition*.

Vinha, Luis da
Luis da Vinha is Lecturer in International Relations and Coordinator of the Master of International Relations at Flinders University, Adelaide, Australia. He received his PhD in IR from the University of Coimbra (Portugal). He is the author of *Geographic Mental Maps and Foreign Policy Change* (De Gruyter Oldenbourg, 2017) and *Three Approaches to Presidential Foreign Policy-Making in the Twenty-First Century* (Peter Lang, 2021).

Walker, Stephen G.
Stephen G. Walker is Professor Emeritus at Arizona State University and does research on conflict dynamics, Foreign Policy Analysis, and political psychology. His publications include *U.S. Presidents and Foreign Policy Mistakes* (2011), *Role Theory and Role Conflict in U.S.-Iran Relations* (2017), and *Operational Code Analysis and Foreign Policy Roles* (2021), plus numerous papers in journals and edited volumes. He received the Distinguished Scholar Award from the FPA Section of ISA (2003).

Webb, Clayton
Clayton Webb is Associate Professor of Political Science at the University of Kansas. He received his PhD from Texas A&M University. His research interests include political methodology, foreign policy, and international political economy. His work has been featured in journals such as *Political Analysis*, *The American Journal of Political Science*, and *International Studies Quarterly*.

Wiener, Antje
Antje Wiener is Professor of Political Science especially Global Governance at the University of Hamburg and By-Fellow of Hughes Hall at Cambridge University. Her books include

The Invisible Constitution of Politics: Contested Norms and International Encounters (Cambridge University Press, 2008) and the *Contestation and Constitution of Norms in Global International Relations* (Cambridge University Press, 2018).

Wolford, Scott

Scott Wolford (PhD, Emory University) is Professor of Government and Fellow of the Patterson-Bannister Chair at the University of Texas at Austin, Editor of *Conflict Management and Peace Science*, and Co-Director of the Correlates of War Project.

Foreword

The Conduct of Inquiry in Foreign Policy Analysis

Patrick Thaddeus Jackson

Foreign Policy Analysis, or FPA, has a long and distinguished history as a component part of academic international studies. Despite the classic efforts of scholars like J. David Singer and Kenneth Waltz to separate "international politics" from "foreign policy" in order to enable a more purely structural account of international affairs, the nearness between international studies scholarship and international-political practice—and the fact that many students in international studies aim to become international affairs practitioners themselves!—keeps blurring that boundary-line again and again. And since the day-to-day material of international affairs involves people doing stuff, acting either in their private capacities or as public representatives, the core FPA commitment to centering individual human beings and their decisions is perennially and perpetually held to be in order. So the tussle between individualist and holist modes of analysis continues, and likely will keep doing so unless and until the field collectively transcends the agent-structure problem in favor of some radical alternative.

The challenge, of course, is that simply saying that individuals and their decisions *matter* in international affairs doesn't tell us enough to go on with the conduct of actual scholarly research. For one thing, a focus on individuals and their decisions doesn't tell us what an "individual" is, or what a "decision" is. For that, we need a more refined scientific ontology, or a theory: are individuals rational actors? Bundles of psychological drives and desires? Meaning-makers or utility-maximizers? Expressers of established codes or problem-solving innovators? Do decisions arise from cognitive, emotional, sociological, or environmental sources? Do individuals *decide*, or is a "decision" an emergent product of events, yoked into a narrative form? All of those flavors and variants are compatible with a broad commitment to center individual human beings and their decisions, and thus in principle any or all of them could be part of FPA.

Theory alone, of course, does not make for a practical research strategy. At a minimum, a researcher also needs a methodological commitment, a broad sensibility about how knowledge is to be produced and what kind of knowledge counts as valid (and by what criteria knowledge-claims ought to be evaluated). There is certainly a well-established neopositivist methodological sensibility in the field, emphasizing nomothetic generalizations and transferrable metrics, but there are (in my view) at least three others: a scientific realist sensibility (not to be confused with "realism" as an IR theory!) emphasizing unobservable dispositional properties and causal mechanisms rather than general laws; an analyticist sensibility focusing on developing abstract models and using them in the singular causal analysis of how particular cases play out; and a critical or reflexive sensibility emphasizing the positionality of the researcher and the possibilities for progress engendered by a systematic reflection on the status and character of knowledge—both scholarly knowledge and the often-tacit knowledge informing expert professional practice.

But theory and methodology *still* aren't enough for an actual research strategy. That takes a third component, which we might call "method": specific procedures for turning observations into data and data into valid claims. In a broadly social-scientific context, many of those claims are explanatory claims, whether causal claims about why a certain outcome occurs rather than some other outcome, or interpretive claims about how to "go on" in some socially meaningful context. That said, we should also appreciate the value of a good descriptive claim, not just as a way-station on the road to explanation, but as a valuable good in itself: sometimes we simply want to know what something is, and to have a solid basis in evidence for that determination. Methods are the concrete steps that take a researcher up that ladder toward valid claims, and in doing so, interact and intersect with theory and methodology in a variety of ways.

So the basic equation might be something like

research strategy = theory + methodology + method

except that this is entirely too simplistic. For one thing, it assumes that the various commitments that a researcher might make on any of the three registers are always clearly defined in advance, or that it is always apparent just what commitments of theory, methodology, and method a given researcher is in fact making. But there are as many ways of sketching the possible commitments in theory, methodology, and method as there are people characterizing them. Indeed, the perennial debates about whether a particular scholar or piece of scholarship belongs in one or another category within each of these three registers should quickly indicate that this issue is far from being settled.

In addition, it assumes that theory, methodology, and method are hermetically sealed boxes, when in actuality, commitments on each register bleed into one another, displaying a variety of elective affinities and family resemblances. Rationalist theory is usually combined with a neopositivist or an analyticist methodology and quantitative methods; constructivist theory is frequently combined with a critical methodological sensibility and qualitative methods. That said, there is no categorically compelling reason why these combinations *have to* exist; instead, theory, methodology, and method can in principle be combined in a number of different ways, even if in practice we only find certain combinations as actually existing lines of scholarship. The reasons for the existence of certain combinations rather than others are *sociological* and *historical* rather than conceptual or philosophical: the scholarly field that we have did not have to look the way that it does, and how things presently stand does not exhaust all possible options.

To put this another way: the combinations of theory, methodology, and method that we have in the field at any given moment are better thought of as active, living *research traditions* than as a priori absolutes. These research traditions provide scholars with ways of orienting themselves, both in the course of a specific research project and vis-à-vis other scholars and scholarship. It is almost certainly the case that whenever we engage in discussions about exactly what "ethnography" or "liberalism" or whatever else "really are," we are doing both of these things at once, providing ourselves and others with a way of locating our work as we justify the choices and commitments we are making.

This brings us to a handbook like this one. The editors and contributors could have set out to define FPA as a single research tradition, and established parameters and signposts that would clearly indicate whether something was or was not part of FPA. After all, one reaction to the diversity of work that people call FPA would be to reject some of that work and police a boundary defined by theory, methodology, or method—or some combination thereof. That would have been a *canonical* approach, intended to produce a fixed canon for the future. But the editors and contributors adopted a *pluralist* approach instead, eschewing any firm definition of FPA in favor of a showcase of the variety of research traditions aiming to center individual human beings and their decisions in international studies. Instead of a canon, we get a compendium: a cookbook of thriving options which scholars can use to formulate their own tasty recipes and dishes. This makes for a book that is extremely useful for the practicing researcher, even as it is frustrating for the would-be canonizer of any One True Approach to FPA.

While in some ways it might be a useful hermeneutic exercise to spell out the specific commitments in theory, methodology, and method that are on display in this handbook, I am going to leave that as an exercise for the reader. The chapters themselves do an admirable job explicating their ways of producing knowledge, so the clues are there for anyone who wants to follow up on them. But if you do so, bear in mind that what is on offer here is not an exhaustive compilation of every possible flavor of FPA that there might ever be. Combinations of theory, methodology, and method—as well as the various commitments on each of those registers—are in important ways always unstable and incomplete, and scholarly innovation in international studies comes from precisely this incompleteness and instability. After all, the task of the practicing scholarly researcher is not to mechanically reproduce firmly established doctrine, but to produce new knowledge. The pluralist, compendium-oriented ethos of this handbook is a positive contribution to that ongoing endeavor.

Acknowledgments

This handbook has come a long way since our original idea to develop a concise edited volume on methods in Foreign Policy Analysis (FPA). We are grateful to the colleagues who encouraged us to pursue a more far-reaching publication project, which looked like a Sisyphean task initially (in addition to being like "herding cats," as one of our contributors cautioned us). Special thanks go to our editor Rob Sorsby at Routledge for embracing the idea of a handbook from the get-go and for putting the trust in us to develop this volume. Moreover, the three anonymous reviewers chosen by Routledge have been incredibly helpful for improving the structure of the handbook and pointing us at additional chapters and experts that we had not thought of ourselves. We are also grateful for initial institutional support and funding from the University of Erfurt, the Willy Brandt School of Public Policy—thanks to Achim Kemmerling, Heike Grimm, and Lena Kiesewetter—and the Foreign and Security Policy Group of the German Association of Political Science (DVPW), which facilitated the organization of a workshop in Erfurt in September 2019. Furthermore, we would like to express our gratitude to Eugénia da Conceição-Heldt and Helmut Breitmeier for their support while we have been working on this project at the Technical University of Munich and the Justus Liebig University Giessen, respectively.

While this handbook has grown in scope throughout the editorial process, we are aware that further additions could have been made and hence we look forward to suggestions for future editions. It was certainly challenging to work on this handbook and with our international group of 44 authors during a pandemic that prohibited personal meetings and the organization of a workshop with all contributors. Behind this handbook, too, there are stories of overburdened colleagues thrown back on extensive care responsibilities because of interrupted childcare during pandemic lockdowns, separations from family and friends, nerve-wracking online/hybrid teaching creating further workload, Covid-19 infections—all of which, as far as we know, have been cured without lasting disabilities – and even some surgeries, all gone well—all along the usual pandemic stress that all of us faced anyway. That said, we are extremely happy about the quality of our contributors' chapters and the way the handbook has come together as a coherent volume despite the challenging circumstances.

Therefore, our greatest thanks go to our amazing flock of authors from all over the world who continued to work on their chapters nevertheless. You had to live through three cycles of revisions with at times detailed comments and suggestions for improvement from either one or both of us, while tailoring chapter structures (and therefore, your arguments) and style to our suggestions and the necessity of having some cohesion in a common handbook project. We truly appreciate the professional attitude and kindness you all kept during this process, contributing to our common goal of putting together this volume. Thank you! You

Acknowledgments

all were—and are—a real academic *community* during this journey, and we look forward to meeting up as a group on some future occasion.

Several other people have made this handbook possible. We are indebted to the work of our competent and engaged student/research assistants Elisabeth Alm and Julia-Felicitas Günther at Justus Liebig University Giessen—the place Falk worked at for 75% of the handbook's journey, next to Catholic University Eichstätt-Ingolstadt and Kiel University in the end—for going over the delivered manuscripts, unifying bibliographies, headers, abstracts, and bios. We cannot express enough gratitude for having worked so thoroughly on the chapters, a job we could not have done but for the price of seriously running behind schedule. This being said, all mistakes remain, of course, our own. We are also grateful to our wives Katharina Monaco and Tanja Mello for their cheerful support throughout the work on this handbook.

Last but not least, we also want to extend our thanks and appreciation to the team at Routledge. Aneta Byzdra, Claire Maloney, and Rob Sorsby have always been available for help and advice with an enabling attitude during the writing and publication process. We are also grateful to Assunta Petrone for copy-editing this manuscript of considerable length so thoroughly, in the same way as to the type-setting team of CodeMantra for ultimately producing the handbook. A book like this—any book—is always the work of many, and we are grateful to having been a part of this journey.

Patrick A. Mello & Falk Ostermann
Amsterdam and Kiel, October 2022

Part I
Introduction

1
Methods of Foreign Policy Analysis
Charting Ground, Engaging Traditions, and Opening Up Boundaries

Falk Ostermann and Patrick A. Mello

Introduction

Contemporary politics faces a disintegration and questioning of global governance structures and a re-orientation toward national politics (Zürn 2014; Hooghe, Lenz, and Marks 2019). At the same time, geopolitics is on the rise again, certainly since Russia's war of aggression against Ukraine, but the re-emergence of geopolitical thinking can indeed be traced back to the end of the Cold War (Guzzini 2012, 2017; Mérand 2020). The liberal international order, which had never been universal and uncontested but nevertheless structured global politics for the past seven decades, has come under pressure not only from its main stakeholders, the U.S. and Western democracies, but also from autocratic challenger states (Mead 2017; Cooley and Nexon 2020; Adler-Nissen and Zarakol 2021; Börzel and Zürn 2021). Political decision-makers and institutions are forced to accommodate these shifts, either on their own or in cooperation with others, and to scale down or reform global governance and the policies that shape it (Fioretos and Heldt 2019; Debre and Dijkstra 2021).

While foreign policy analysts, in a conscious departure from systemic theories of world politics, have always highlighted the considerable variation in national foreign policies and pointed at the relevance of domestic-level variables for explaining this behavior (Legro 1996; Elman 2000; Beasley et al. 2013; Kaarbo 2015), the current level of domestic and transnational politicization of world politics in areas as broad as trade, climate change, or security, and the resulting contestation of policies seems unprecedented. Exploring some of these dimensions, recent work has begun to examine the shifting context of foreign policy decision-making (Aran, Brummer, and Smith 2021), the influence of multi-party cabinet dynamics (Kesgin and Kaarbo 2010; Kaarbo and Kenealy 2016; Vignoli 2020; Oktay 2022), the party-political contestation of foreign policy (Wagner et al. 2017; Haesebrouck and Mello 2020; Raunio and Wagner 2020), the role of leaders, their reputations, and personal characteristics (Brummer et al. 2020; Lupton 2020), the rise of populist parties and their impact on foreign policy (Chryssogelos 2017; Verbeek and Zaslove 2017; Plagemann and Destradi 2019; Jenne 2021; Ostermann and Stahl 2022), the involvement, politicization, and influence of parliaments in security policy (Raunio and Wagner 2017; Mello and Peters 2018; Oktay 2018; Strong 2018), and the role of emotions for foreign policy-making (Eberle 2019; Koschut 2020; Ghalehdar 2021).

Yet, it is not only the increasing amount of pressure from below that is challenging foreign policy-making, but it has also become harder to forge and implement coherent national foreign policy agendas given the multitude of partially conflicting demands – i.e., between economic, climate, and welfare policies –, leading to increased volatility and instability. Adding to this, on a societal level, increased digitalization and technological innovations such as big data, social media, and related phenomena like fake news and outside interference in domestic affairs further complicate foreign policy-making (Schneiker et al. 2018; Fisher 2020). Clearly, this goes beyond established conceptions of two-level games or multilevel interactions in foreign policy (Putnam 1988; Oppermann 2008; Strong 2017; Conceição-Heldt and Mello 2018; Friedrichs 2022). Consequently, these phenomena make it necessary to direct analytical attention toward new arenas for understanding the making of foreign policy, while impelling traditional methods and approaches to analyzing foreign policy to address increasing complexity and, if necessary, to adapt their methods. This handbook is committed to providing space for this two-fold endeavor while also catering to those readers that are interested in learning substantially about a certain method for its prospective use.

Disciplinary Development of Foreign Policy Analysis

During the past two decades, Foreign Policy Analysis (FPA) has developed into a thriving subdiscipline of International Relations (IR). If that were any measure for its existence or, if you wish, success, since 2005, FPA has had its own disciplinary journal – *Foreign Policy Analysis* –, and at the time of writing, the FPA section is the second largest sub-unit of the International Studies Association (ISA), with more than 1,000 members in 2022.[1] Recent years have also seen a host of seminal publications, including the magisterial *Oxford Encyclopedia of Foreign Policy Analysis* (Thies 2018), new FPA textbooks (Morin and Paquin 2018; Beach and Pedersen 2020), and new editions that have added to a growing canon of established FPA textbooks (Breuning 2007; Hill 2016; Smith, Hadfield, and Dunne 2016; Alden and Aran 2017; Brummer and Oppermann 2019; Hudson and Day 2019). Just to highlight two of these, *Foreign Policy: Theories, Actors, Cases* (Smith, Hadfield, and Dunne 2016) and *Foreign Policy Analysis: Classic and Contemporary Theory* (Hudson and Day 2019) have both already been published in their third editions. There have also been new handbooks focusing on the foreign policies of single countries, like Austria, Japan, and Russia, among others (McCarthy 2018; Tsygankov 2018; Senn, Eder, and Kornprobst 2022). Moreover, there have been recent initiatives to foster connections between FPA and other strands of research, including bridges toward *ethnography* (Hopf 2002; Neumann 2002, 2011; Kuus 2013, 2014; MacKay and Levin 2015; Cornut 2018), *feminist theory* (Hudson et al. 2008; Aggestam and True 2020; Okundaye and Breuning 2021), *public policy* (Oppermann and Spencer 2016; Brummer et al. 2019; Haar and Pierce 2021) and *history* (Brummer and Kießling 2019), as much as there has been new work on enduring topics such as *foreign policy change* (da Vinha 2017; Chryssogelos 2021; Joly and Haesebrouck 2021).

When looking at publication trends, it is apparent that the number of FPA-related books has been following an upward trajectory since the year 2008 (Google Books Ngram data).[2] Similar trends can be gleaned from journal-based data. During the first ten years since its formation, *Foreign Policy Analysis* published on average 21 articles per year. Since then, the number of articles in *FPA* increased substantially to an average of 35 articles per year (2015 to 2021). At the time of writing, *FPA* had published 471 articles in its lifetime. Data from Google Scholar (GS) and the Web of Science yield similar trends, as summarized in Figure 1.1. On GS, we conducted yearly searches for "Foreign Policy Analysis" (excluding citations). The results show a clear upward trend, from about 500 yearly publications in 2005 to nearly

3,000 publications in 2021. While GS is fairly inclusive in its count of publications and should thus be taken with a grain of salt, the Web of Science database only lists publication outlets that are included in the Social Sciences Citation Index (SSCI). Here, we searched for journal articles related to "Foreign Policy". The results show that the number of journal articles has been growing at a steady pace between the years 2005 and 2019, from about 329 articles to a peak of 1,085 articles. Notably, there has been a dip in the numbers since then, which is also reflected in the total number of articles published in IR journals that are covered in the Web of Science (these reach their highest value in the year 2019, at 9,864 articles, and have dropped to 8,853 and 5,411 articles in the years 2020 and 2021, respectively). It is apparent that the observed decrease in the years 2020–2021 coincides with the coronavirus pandemic. Hence, this may be an indication of the pandemic's impact on academic publishing, especially the increased burdens on authors, editors, and reviewers. Notably, this trend is not visible from the GS data, possibly because GS also includes conference papers and other types of unpublished manuscripts that have not gone through peer review and the editorial process.

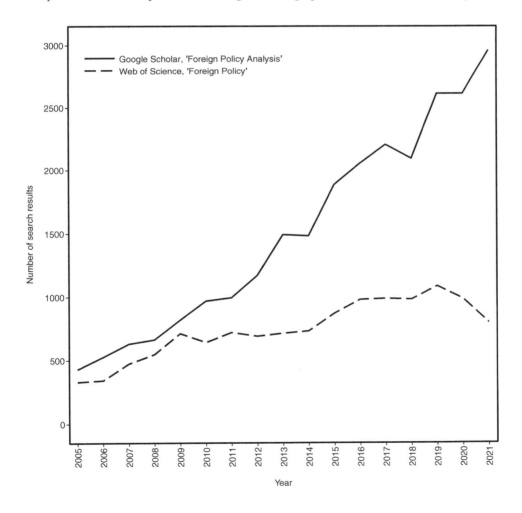

Figure 1.1 Publication trends (Google Scholar and Web of Science).

The situation within the past two years notwithstanding, FPA-related scholarly output has increased considerably since 2005.

Despite its relative youth, the birth of FPA is usually attributed to the 1950s and 1960s when work on public policy, decision-making, and on sub-state aspects of world politics emerged (Hudson 2005, 5ff.; Carlsnaes 2013, 300ff.; Hudson 2016, 13ff.). Starting from both individualist and group-based theories on organizational behavior (March and Olsen 1998), bureaucratic politics (Allison 1971), decision-making and political psychology in general (Snyder, Bruck, and Sapin 1962; Jervis 1976, 1978; Kahneman and Tversky 1979; Jervis, Lebow, and Welch Larson 1985; Welch Larson 1985), or leadership in particular (Leites 1951; Sprout and Sprout 1957; George 1969; Walker 1977; Hermann 1980), since the 1980s, FPA scholars have invested considerable efforts into developing foreign policy applications of major IR theories and approaches like constructivism (Risse-Kappen 1994; Buzan, Waever, and Wilde 1998; Finnemore and Sikkink 1998; Risse and Wiener 1999; Acharya 2004), feminism (Hudson et al. 2008; D'Aoust 2017), institutionalism (Putnam 1988; Holsti 2004), liberalism (Doyle 1986; Moravcsik 1997; Beasley et al. 2013; Kaarbo 2015), post-colonialism (Barkawi and Laffey 2006), neorealism (Grieco 1995; Elman 1996), or neoclassical realism (Rose 1998; Schweller 2003; Lobell, Ripsman, and Taliaferro 2009; Meibauer et al. 2021). These efforts had considerable impact on both IR and FPA scholarship because on the one hand, they stirred debate on theoretical underspecification, omitted variables, and problems of grand theories (Guzzini 1993; Vasquez 1997; Elman and Elman 2003), while on the other hand, they provided the "microfoundations" (Moravcsik 1997) for many IR theories' grander interpretive schemes of world politics, like patterns of cooperation and conflict, the occurrence of balancing and bandwagoning behavior, the impact of democracy and liberalism on peace and conflict, or the role of identity in foreign policy.

Today, FPA theories, approaches, and scholarship can be found across the globe, albeit to varying degrees and building on different traditions (Brummer and Hudson 2015). FPA's strongest institutional footing can still be found *in* the U.S. and academic systems that are close to the Anglo-Saxon tradition,[3] in the same way as its empirical scholarship often focuses *on* the U.S. (Brummer and Hudson 2015), similar to what has been observed for IR at large (Waever 1998; Schmidt 2002). Nonetheless, despite a continuing need for theoretical, methodological, and regional diversification, FPA as a field has become more pluralist during the last decades, acknowledging an increasing number of different approaches as valid means for the analysis of foreign policy. While there are still differences in the pervasiveness of certain methods or methodologies among regions – with, for instance, interpretive and small-N qualitative ("understanding" in the nomenclature of Hollis and Smith 1990)[4] approaches having a stronger footing outside the U.S. with its comparative, large-N "explaining" (ibid.) tradition (see the various contributions in Brummer and Hudson 2015; also Hudson 2016, 28f.) –, scholarly debate, conferences, journals, and other publications have become more multi-faceted or are in the process of becoming so.

To be sure, one may question whether a differentiation between *qualitative* and *quantitative* approaches does justice to the existing plurality of methods and approaches in the social sciences more broadly, but also within FPA. The idea of "two cultures" gained currency not least because it can be a useful shorthand to distinguish research traditions that are predominantly oriented toward the quantitative template from those that are not (Mahoney and Goertz 2006; Goertz and Mahoney 2012). Yet, this binary distinction also prompted pushback and initiatives to move "beyond" the qualitative-quantitative divide (Tarrow 1995; Rihoux and Grimm 2006; Prakash and Klotz 2007; Collier, Brady, and Seawright 2010; Cooper et al. 2012). Moreover, recent empirical research confirms what "qualitative" researchers have often highlighted, namely that there is much more diversity under the qualitative tent than the common label suggests (Kuehn and Rohlfing 2022). In light of these debates, as editors of this handbook, we firmly embrace the value of *methodological pluralism* rather than privileging certain methods and approaches over others. We side with Patrick Thaddeus Jackson who called for a "pluralist science of IR" and urged us to "stop worrying so much about the ultimate status of our knowledge-claims and get on with our primary task of producing knowledge about world politics" (Jackson 2011, 189). The contributions collected in this handbook differ in their methodological assumptions and their understandings of the scientific endeavor and the study of foreign policy. To the extent feasible in concise handbook chapters, we have pushed our contributors to make these assumptions explicit. Depending on their research aims and substantive interests, readers may find certain methods and approaches more suitable than others. Indeed, it was our aim to give readers a wide-ranging selection of contributions, all of which engage with foreign policy and international politics, but often from very different angles and with strikingly different tools. Therefore, this handbook is also a contribution to unite methods and perspectives whose use varies across world regions because of different institutional and scholarly traditions and historically developed research agendas (for an overview see Brummer and Hudson 2015). We are convinced that such pluralism promises to further both a methodically sound analysis of foreign policy across various fields, topics, and regions, on the one hand, and disciplinary exchange and understanding, on the other. In doing so, it is a contribution to providing the "nuts and bolts" (Elster 1989) for a methodically informed analysis of foreign policy.

That said, we are aware that our volume is not comprehensive in the sense that every existing perspective and method is equally represented. While it was our aim to cover the diversity of FPA in the 34 chapters that make up this handbook – rather than privileging one conception of FPA over another – we are aware that any such compilation has to remain selective. Future efforts should aim to further enhance diversity along several dimensions – topical, methods-wise, regional, and gender-related.

From Theoretical Diversity to Methods

Reflecting its behavioralist heritage (Stuart 2008; Carlsnaes 2013), FPA maintains a strong comparative component (Kaarbo 2003; Hudson 2005; Beasley et al. 2013), but methodological approaches are far more diverse today and draw on academic disciplines as varied as ethnography, geography, history, linguistics and semiotics, (social) psychology, or feminism. FPA at present-day can be strongly individualist and "actor-specific" (Hudson 2005, 1), as in leadership trait analysis (Brummer, Chapter 15) and operational code analysis (Schafer and Walker, Chapter 16); it can be group-focused as in groupthink approaches (Barr and Mintz, Chapter 17), intersubjective as in discourse analysis (Ostermann and Sjöstedt, Chapter 7) or research on emotions (Koschut, Chapter 11); and it can be comparative in a small-N sense (Feng and He, Chapter 18), in medium to large-N settings (Mello, Chapter 24), as well as case and process-oriented (van Meegdenburg, Chapter 25). Approaches and methods relying on other sciences such as ethnography (Neumann, Chapter 3), geography (da Vinha, Chapter 6), and political psychology (Stein, Chapter 13; Chaban, Kenix, Beltyukova, and Fox, Chapter 14) further complement and complete this picture of an analytically rich subfield of IR. All these approaches and methods contribute to understanding challenges to global governance and world politics from the bottom-up agency of national foreign policy actors and institutions, often starting with a specific case but also investigating domestic politics' impact on world politics comparatively, across time and space.

Although some publications, such as the aforementioned *Oxford Encyclopedia of Foreign Policy Analysis* edited by Cameron Thies (2018), contain dedicated methods chapters, most textbooks do not place special emphasis on questions of method and methodology. Exceptions are Jean-Frédéric Morin and Jonathan Paquin's (2018) *Foreign Policy Analysis. A Toolbox*, the French language *La politique étrangère. Théories, methods et références* by Morin (2013), or the German-language volume *Methoden der sicherheitspolitischen Analyse* (Methods for Analyzing Security Policy), edited by Alexander Siedschlag (2014). Most of these books or collections, however, adopt a two-fold approach by debating substantial theoretical concepts – such as the role of culture, rationalism, or bureaucracies – and how to analyze them jointly. While these are valuable contributions that foster debate and application, we believe that a dedicated methods volume can make an important contribution in its own right.[5] This is the approach we take in this handbook.

As editors of this handbook, it was our intent to reflect the field's diversity by proposing a wide, yet, in all honesty, still incomplete guide to methods of FPA. One challenge that may be particularly pronounced in FPA is the linkage between certain approaches (such as large-*N* research), their preferred methods (statistical analysis), and shared theoretical assumptions within certain research traditions (i.e., rationalism). Our emphasis in this handbook lies on *methods* but we adopt a broad conception that includes approaches that could rather be seen as *perspectives* than genuine methods in a narrow sense of the term. Hence, Part II of the handbook contains several contributions that evolve around certain perspectives on foreign policy and international politics (such as the chapters on *ideas and identity* by Stefano Guzzini and on *norms and norm contestation* by Phil Orchard and Antje Wiener). While one may object that these contributions stray from what a methods handbook should be expected to focus on – and some of our colleagues may also regard it as a mischaracterization if we labeled their contributions "methods chapters" – we believe it is vital to delineate a variety of foundational perspectives before diving deeper into specific methods of inquiry.

Outline of the Handbook

The handbook's chapters are divided into seven parts that loosely group methods by research traditions. To further the goals of both disciplinary discussion and practical orientation for prospective users of certain methods, where feasible and reasonable, the chapters follow the same structure. After introducing the respective method or approach in relation to foreign policy puzzles, the chapters engage in a literature review to familiarize readers with the empirical application and development of a method. The chapters proceed by discussing key terms and concepts that are central to a method's analytical endeavor while often presenting strategies and advice for implementation and broader questions of methodology. We encouraged our contributors to make the discussion of the method in question more palatable by either including a dedicated section that shows concrete empirical applications on real-world foreign policy puzzles or illustrating the method's key terms and proceedings with concrete analytical examples *en passant*. The chapters close by examining the assets and pitfalls in a method's application – the *dos and don'ts* –, giving practical advice, and reflecting on the past, present, and future use of an approach.

Following this introduction, Part II contains what we have referred to above as broader perspectives on foreign policy. To start with, in Chapter 2, Stefano Guzzini discusses one of the central debates of FPA when engaging with the role of *ideas and identity* in foreign policy and, ex negativo, rationalism. Among others, Guzzini uses great power confrontation, concepts of self and otherness, and ontological security to demonstrate the value of constructivism for FPA. Continuing the bottom-up perspective of constructivists, Chapter 3 by Iver B. Neumann presents *ethnography* as an interactive approach to analyzing diplomacy, based on participatory observation. Neumann centrally discusses the perspective's focus on observing, doing, and talking, while also debating issues of field access, cultural competence, and situatedness that are key for conducting ethnographically inspired FPA. Chapter 4, by Phil Orchard and Antje Wiener, introduces one of the major research programs of IR during the past decades – research on *norms and norm contestation* – and lays out its relevance for FPA. Orchard and Wiener argue that the turn toward studies of norm contestation and norm conflicts provides a useful entry point for understanding agency in the domestic politics of foreign policy. Chapter 5 on *feminism* by Alexis Henshaw presents the methodologically pluralist tradition of feminist, gender, and intersectional analysis in IR and FPA. Henshaw covers quantitative, qualitative, and mixed-methods approaches while examining central aspects like gendered power relations, meaning-making, patriarchy, and resulting gendered practices that impact on the conduct of foreign policy and international politics. The final contribution of Part II, Chapter 6, deals with another science that has been put into the service of FPA, *political geography*. Luis da Vinha discusses various traditions of political geography, including critical geopolitics. He demonstrates how concepts of space (like distance) and place (socially constructed locations) and leaders' resulting mental maps have important consequences for foreign policy-making.

Part III consists of five chapters that evolve around language and interpretive methods. Chapter 7 by Falk Ostermann and Roxanna Sjöstedt provides an introduction to *discourse analysis and discourse theories*. Ostermann and Sjöstedt discuss both key concepts that are central to all discursive approaches (like productive power) and a range of interpretive micro-methods, while they also present dedicated schools that provide more encompassing frameworks for the analysis of meaning-making in politics. In Chapter 8, Kai Oppermann and Alexander Spencer introduce *narrative analysis* to the study of foreign policy. Using congressional debates on the Iran nuclear deal as empirical example, Oppermann and Spencer demonstrate narratives' quality as fundamental form of human expression and how they structure discourse in a way that contextualizes and justifies foreign policy decision-making socially and culturally. Chapter 9 by Sabine Mokry is about *frame analysis*. Adopting a cognitive approach to frames that emphasizes their quality of structuring reality, Mokry specifies both quantitative and qualitative perspectives on how to make use of frames for analyzing the politics of foreign policy. She explicates the usefulness of the method on a study looking at the Chinese and U.S. communication of foreign policy intentions. The part closes with two chapters on issues that have recently seen increased insterest: images and emotions. Chapter 10 by Bernhard Stahl and Julian Ignatowitsch introduces *visual analysis* as method for making sense of visual representations of foreign policy. The authors discuss the particular way in which pictures code political messages between universalism and cultural particularities, how they structure perception of foreign policy issues, and how they try to persuade. Their chapter analyzes various cover images of the German weekly political magazine *Der Spiegel* and its coverage of the Afganistan deployments of the *Bundeswehr*. Finally, Chapter 11 by Simon Koschut presents *emotion discourse analysis* as an approach to shed light on the emotive side of foreign policy-making. He examines the methodological challenges when analyzing subjective emotions with an interest in group-based processes like foreign policy-making and turns toward a specific form of discourse analysis of social representations of emotions to make this work. Koschut illustrates this framework on the Russian invasion of Crimea and NATO's discursive reaction to it.

Part IV focuses on psychology, roles, and leaders. Chapter 12 by Marijke Breuning introduces *role theory* as one of the definitive approaches of FPA. Debating both the historical development of role-theoretical analysis and newer approaches, more structuralist and more agent-centered, individualist and interactive ones, the chapter delves into role patterns, national role conceptions, the importance of socialization, role contestation, and expectations in order to understand leaders' constructions and perceptions of foreign policy challenges. Breuning also discusses various methods to go about implementing a role-theoretical research agenda. Chapter 13 by Janice Gross Stein engages with the *political psychology of threat assessment*. From an intelligence studies perspective, Stein's contribution centrally considers how to assess actors' capabilities and the probabilities of certain foreign policy behaviors under conditions of uncertainty. Tapping into various psychological approaches like prospect theory or cognitive heuristics like representativeness and anchoring, and using the example of Saddam Hussein's weapons of mass destruction programs, she discusses how assessments made at the time of the threat, afterward, and by academics differed from each other and how assessment failures occurred. In Chapter 14, Natalia Chaban, Linda Jean Kenix, Svetlana Beltyukova, and Christine Fox deal with *measuring perceptions*. Specifically, their approach focuses on combining low inference (observational) and high inference (interpretive) approaches to data analysis in the context of international political communication. They show how various methods like the Rasch Measurement Model or frame analysis can be employed to analyze international media communication about EU foreign policy. Chapter 15, by Klaus Brummer, introduces *leadership trait analysis* (LTA) as a systematic and software-driven, at-a-distance approach aimed at comprehending leaders' more stable psychologic traits and leadership styles that fundamentally inform their decision-making, substance, and the conduct of foreign policy. Brummer illustrates the usefulness of LTA focusing on women as foreign policy leaders and the importance of gender for leadership traits/styles, while also discussing new developments in LTA like the possibilities of non-English language analysis. The second contribution on leadership profiling is Chapter 16 on *operational code analysis* (OCA) by Mark Schafer and Stephen G. Walker. Focusing on the Verbs in Context System (VICS), Schafer and Walker demonstrate how instrumental and philosophical beliefs about cooperation and conflict can be studied comparatively and in a quantitative fashion to assess leaders' psychology. The authors' empirical cases shed light on how to compare two different leaders' operational codes, how to go about large-N statistical analysis, or how to integrate game theory into OCA. Finally, Chapter 17 by Kasey Barr and Alex Mintz focuses on *groupthink, polythink, and con-div* as patterns of group decision-making dynamics and their central problems of cohesion and divergence. Starting out from the long-established groupthink model that puts collective decision-making processes and its inter and intra-group dynamics into perspective, Barr and Mintz present various theoretical developments in the literature, and they illustrative each of them with an empirical foreign policy case: convergence-divergence with the killing of bin Laden; polythink with the Syrian war *red line* issue; and groupthink with the Iranian nuclear program negotiations.

Part V entails seven contributions that examine foreign policy from a comparative and/or quantitative angle. In Chapter 18, Huiyun Feng and Kai He lay out the tradition of *comparative foreign policy*. From a critical review of early efforts at developing FPA grand theories from a comparative angle, Feng and He continue by introducing, on the one hand, three traditions of comparative FPA – geographic area studies, middle-range theories drawing on a variety of academic disciplines, and actor-specific studies focusing on decision-making properly – and three methodical approaches to implement comparative FPA – comparative cases, comparative theory, and comparative method (also know as mixed methods) – on the other hand. Chapter 19, by Gordon Friedrichs, introduces an approach to *quantitative content analysis* (QuantCA), focusing on role theory. Discussing parallels with and advantages of combining QuantCA with qualitative approaches and mixed-methods designs, Friedrichs develops QuantCA as a tool to measure national identity and role conceptions and to compare them cross-case and within-case. He illustrates the argument on a study using human coding of leaders' national identity messages. Chapter 20, by Sibel Oktay, introduces *statistical analysis* in FPA. Oktay presents statistical approaches as bedrock tool for finding out about generalizable patterns of foreign policy-making, and as an opportunity to work creatively with datasets to generate new insights into patterns of foreign policy. She brings out main descriptive usages of statistical analysis and introduces various analytical models while going in-depth with regression models of various kind. She illuminates the workings of statistical analysis with a study on the attitudes toward international organizations among the U.S. foreign policy elite. In Chapter 21, Danielle Lupton and Clayton Webb introduce *experimental methods* and their methodology. They emphasize the controlled environment and random variation procedures that make experiments a great way to study microfoundational aspects of foreign policy decision-making and public opinion. At the same time, Lupton and Webb extensively discuss methodological issues related to the conduct of experiments, such as internal/external validity or sampling, while explaining these issues with two empirical examples on leaders' reputation for resolve, on the one hand, and public attitudes toward terrorism on the other. Chapter 22, by Scott Wolford presents a concise introduction to *game theory* and its application in FPA. He advances the approach as prime way of modeling strategic interaction between foreign policy agents under certain informational and decisional conditions. Wolford familiarizes the reader with the game-theoretical theory of choice, concepts of equilibrium and solution, and various models used to analyze strategic interaction, such as the famous prisoner's dilemma, games of limited information, or the deterrence game. Chapter 23 by Katja Kleinberg introduces the study of *public opinion surveys*. She lays out how individual attitudes measured in surveys are central to politics, what is characteristic about public opinion on foreign policy, and how it affects foreign policy outcomes. Kleinberg then exposes the various methodological choices involved in designing the survey instrument (question wording, response options, etc.), the overall survey design (cross-sectional, panel surveys, experiments), and issues of population choice or sampling. Finally, Chapter 24, by Patrick A. Mello introduces the set-theoretic method of *qualitative comparative analysis* (QCA) and its empirical application in FPA. He discusses the strengths of QCA in addressing causal complexity in medium-N settings, often combined with explanatory conditions being located at multiple levels. Mello also illustrates QCA's flexibility in tailoring the method to the specific needs of a given research design. He illustrates the method with examples from a study on coalition defection during the Iraq War.

Part VI comprises five chapters on qualitative methods and historical approaches. In Chapter 25, Hilde van Meegdenburg presents an analyticist approach to *process tracing*. Her chapter lays out the regularity understanding of process tracing and discusses its fit for the analysis of foreign policies. Van Meegdenburg then develops an interpretive version of process tracing based on explanatory mechanisms as analytical, Weberian, ideal-typical constructs that she uses to explain the Danish decision not to employ private military/security contractors in peace operations. Chapter 26 by Delphine Deschaux-Dutard focuses on *interviews* as an important methodological tool to gather information on foreign policy decisionmaking processes and elite attitudes. She presents the up and downsides of various interview strategies and reviews their useability in the context of own experiences when researching sensitive military and defense issues with their culture of secrecy. In this context, Deschaux-Dutard also addresses the insider/outsider dilemma when engaging in interviews with policymakers, the social-interactionist aspects of the method, and gender issues. In Chapter 27, Payam Ghalehdar introduces *historical analysis* as a specific perspective on FPA. He deliberates on the role of history as data source, on the one hand, and as explanatory concept on the other (i.e., as in analogies, institutionalism, or learning). Ghalehdar then presents various ways of using historical data in case-oriented or theory-oriented research settings, engages in a debate about the usefulness and appropriateness of primary and secondary data sources, while providing concrete guidelines for either use. Similarly, Chapter 28 by Michal Onderco focuses on (critical) *oral history* as a specific form of practiced historicism that is focused on bringing out individual experiences of foreign policy agents, such as ambassadors, to reconstruct the unfolding of political events in the lack of otherwise recorded information or issues of secrecy. Onderco demonstrates the use, assets, and challenges of the method on two levels: individual interviews with foreign policy agents, and a conference project between practitioners and academics held to understand the accomplishment of the indeterminate extension of the Non-Proliferation Treaty (NPT) in 1995. He also elaborates on practical and conceptual issues of this direct method of engagement with history and/or historical figures, reliability issues, and triangulation efforts. Finally, in Chapter 29, Anne Kerstin Friedrich introduces the basics of *archival research* and its use on foreign-policy related topics. Focusing on diplomatic archives and giving examples from several countries, Friedrich explains the particularities of different sorts of diplomatic documents and how they can be used for tracing decision-making processes in, for instance, government departments concerned with foreign policy. She also discusses how archival research can be combined with other methods such as content analysis and certain coding procedures to understand diplomatic practice.

The handbook is completed by five chapters on new technology, social media, and networks, which together constitute Part VII. Chapter 30, by Sebastian Cujai, presents an approach to *big data analysis* in foreign policy that takes advantage of the increase of availability of large amounts of electronic data as a remedy to the traditionally scarce informational environment in foreign policy processes. Cujai cuts through different characteristics of the big data phenomenon before turning toward a form of script-based network analysis that distills relationships out of large amounts of textual data. He exemplifies the method's workings with a salience analysis across many years (2004–2008) of the Russia-Georgia conflict. Chapter 31, by Andrea Schneiker, shifts emphasis to *social media* and specifically to Twitter as a platform that has arguably gained a reputation for discourse-forming exchanges on foreign policy. Schneiker discusses the challenge of analyzing the platform's enormous amounts of content and metadata with various text mining methods and whether social media exchanges can count as public opinion. She then provides guidance on how to make research design decisions on actors, data selection, and data access with a particular focus on sentiment analysis, which she illustrates with a variety of studies from the realm of security and conflict issues. Chapter 32 by Franz Eder complements our other chapters on textual analysis with a specific approach to *discourse network analysis*. The methods combines a qualitative content analysis of agents' foreign policy preferences with a network analysis that is interested in change through time. Eder explains how discursive data are coded content-wise and further categorized to enable the construction of affiliation and congruence/conflict networks. He illustrates the method on UK House of Commons debates on Iraq war participation in 2003. Chapter 33 by Valerio Vignoli provides a concise introduction to *text as data*. He presents the development of automated text analysis methods and programs and gives an overview of the panoply of different approaches, such as qualitative, dictionary, (un)supervised classification methods, or scaling while examining the methods' potentials and challenges for FPA. Finally, Chapter 34, by Clionadh Raleigh and Roudabeh Kishi, provides an introduction to *conflict event data* based on the Armed Conflict Location and Event Data (ACLED) project database. Raleigh and Kishi take stock of different machine-based and researcher-led datasets (ACLED being one of the latter) and present the construction of ACLED as real-time source on conflict data that can be used to investigate shifts in subnational conflicts, local conflict actors, or the effectiveness of conflict prevention policies. They illustrate their dataset's use in FPA with data from Syria and on conventional warfare. Raleigh and Kishi also present thoughts on current limitations of datasets and crucial aspects for their construction.

Notes

1 Data communicated by the ISA's FPA Section leadership. Annual reports on the section's activities, financial status, and membership can be accessed at: https://www.isanet.org/ISA/Sections/FPA/Reports
2 The Google Books Ngram Viewer can be accessed at: https://books.google.com/ngrams
3 This academic tradition also finds an expression in the pervasiveness of distinct IR programs that are separate from, albeit still related to more generic political science curricula.
4 We deem this distinction problematic to the extent that it has been used to disqualify certain methods on scientific grounds.
5 Notably, the open access edited volume by Andreas Kruck and Andrea Schneiker (2017) provides introductions to a broad range of methods and approaches. However, the substantive emphasis of that volume lies on non-state actors in international security and is thus (mostly) outside the realm of FPA.

References

Acharya, Amitav. 2004. "How Ideas Spread: Whose Norms Matter? Norm Localization and Institutional Change in Asian Regionalism." *International Organization* 58 (2): 239–275.
Adler-Nissen, Rebecca, and Ayşe Zarakol. 2021. "Struggles for Recognition: The Liberal International Order and the Merger of Its Discontents." *International Organization* 75 (2): 611–634.
Aggestam, Karin, and Jacqui True. 2020. "Gendering Foreign Policy: A Comparative Framework for Analysis." *Foreign Policy Analysis* 16 (2): 143–162.
Alden, Chris, and Amnon Aran. 2017. *Foreign Policy Analysis: New Approaches*. Oxon: Routledge.
Allison, Graham T. 1971. *Essence of Decision: Explaining the Cuban Missile Crisis*. Boston, MA: Little & Brown.
Aran, Amnon, Klaus Brummer, and Karen E Smith. 2021. "Introduction: New Directions in Foreign Policy Analysis." *International Affairs* 97 (2): 261–265.
Barkawi, Tarak, and Mark Laffey. 2006. "The Postcolonial Moment in Security Studies." *Review of International Studies* 32 (2): 329–352.
Beach, Derek, and Rasmus Brun Pedersen. 2020. *Analyzing Foreign Policy*. London: Red Globe Press.
Beasley, Ryan K., Juliet Kaarbo, Jeffrey S. Lantis, and Michael T. Snarr, eds. 2013. *Foreign Policy in Comparative Perspective: Domestic and International Influences on State Behavior*. Los Angeles, CA: Sage.
Börzel, Tanja A., and Michael Zürn. 2021. "Contestations of the Liberal International Order: From Liberal Multilateralism to Postnational Liberalism." *International Organization* 75 (2): 282–305.
Breuning, Marijke. 2007. *Foreign Policy Analysis: A Comparative Introduction*. Basingstoke: Palgrave.
Brummer, Klaus, Sebastian Harnisch, Kai Oppermann, and Diana Panke, eds. 2019. *Foreign Policy as Public Policy? Promises and Pitfalls*. Manchester: Manchester University Press.
Brummer, Klaus, and Valerie M. Hudson, eds. 2015. *Foreign Policy Analysis Beyond North America*. Boulder, CO: Lynne Rienner.
Brummer, Klaus, and Friedrich Kießling, eds. 2019. *Zivilmacht Bundesrepublik? Bundesdeutsche Außenpolitische Rollen Vor Und Nach 1989 Aus Politik- Und Geschichtswissenschaftlichen Perspektiven*. Baden-Baden: Nomos.
Brummer, Klaus, and Kai Oppermann. 2019. *Außenpolitanalyse*. Berlin: De Gruyter.

Brummer, Klaus, Michael D. Young, Özgur Özdamar, Sercan Canbolat, Consuelo Thiers, Christian Rabini, Katharina Dimmroth, Mischa Hansel, and Ameneh Mehvar. 2020. "Forum: Coding in Tongues: Developing Non-English Coding Schemes for Leadership Profiling." *International Studies Review* 22 (4): 1039–1067.

Buzan, Barry, Ole Waever, and Jaap de Wilde. 1998. *Security: A New Framework for Analysis*. Boulder, CO: Lynne Rienner.

Carlsnaes, Walter. 2013. "Foreign Policy." In *Handbook of International Relations*, edited by Walter Carlsnaes, Thomas Risse and Beth A. Simmons. London *et al.*: Sage, 298–326.

Chryssogelos, Angelos. 2017. "Populism in Foreign Policy." In *Oxford Research Encyclopedia of Politics*, edited by William R. Thompson. Oxford: Oxford University Press. https://doi.org/10.1093/acrefore/9780190228637.013.467

Chryssogelos, Angelos. 2021. *Party Systems and Foreign Policy Change in Liberal Democracies. Cleavages, Ideas, Competition*. London and New York: Routledge.

Collier, David, Henry E. Brady, and Jason Seawright. 2010. "Outdated Views of Qualitative Methods: Time to Move on." *Political Analysis* 18 (4): 506–513.

Conceição-Heldt, Eugénia da., and Patrick A. Mello. 2018. "Two-Level Games in Foreign Policy Analysis." In *Oxford Encyclopedia of Foreign Policy Analysis*, edited by Cameron G. Thies. New York: Oxford University Press, 770–789.

Cooley, Alexander, and Daniel H. Nexon. 2020. *Exit from Hegemony: The Unraveling of the American Global Order*. Oxford: Oxford University Press.

Cooper, Barry, Judith Glaesser, Roger Gomm, and Martyn Hammersley. 2012. *Challenging the Qualitative-Quantitative Divide: Explorations in Case-Focused Causal Analysis*. London: Continuum.

Cornut, Jérémie. 2018. "Diplomacy, Agency, and the Logic of Improvisation and Virtuosity in Practice." *European Journal of International Relations* 24 (3): 712–736.

D'Aoust, Anne-Marie. 2017. "Feminist Perspectives on Foreign Policy." In *Oxford Research Encyclopedia of International Studies,* edited by Nukhet Sandal. Oxford: Oxford University Press. https://doi.org/10.1093/acrefore/9780190846626.013.179

da Vinha, Luis. 2017. *Geographic Mental Maps and Foreign Policy Change. Re-Mapping the Carter Doctrine*. Berlin and Boston, MA: de Gruyter Oldenbourg.

Debre, Maria Josepha, and Hylke Dijkstra. 2021. "Institutional Design for a Post-Liberal Order: Why Some International Organizations Live Longer Than Others." *European Journal of International Relations* 27 (1): 311–339.

Doyle, Michael W. 1986. "Liberalism and World Politics." *American Political Science Review* 80: 1151–1170.

Eberle, Jakub. 2019. *Discourse and Affect in Foreign Policy. Germany and the Iraq War*. London and New York: Routledge.

Elman, Colin. 1996. "Horses for Courses: Why Not Neorealist Theory of Foreign Policy?" *Security Studies* 6 (1): 7–53.

Elman, Colin, and Miriam Fendius Elman, eds. 2003. *Progress in International Relations Theory: Appraising the Field*. Cambridge, MA: MIT Press.

Elman, Miriam Fendius. 2000. "Unpacking Democracy: Presidentialism, Parliamentarism, and Theories of Democratic Peace." *Security Studies* 9 (4): 91–126.

Elster, Jon. 1989. *Nuts and Bolts for the Social Sciences*. Cambridge, New York: Cambridge University Press.

Finnemore, Martha, and Kathryn Sikkink. 1998. "International Norm Dynamics and Political Change." *International Organization* 52 (4): 887–917.

Fioretos, Orfeo, and Eugénia C. Heldt. 2019. "Legacies and Innovations in Global Economic Governance Since Bretton Woods." *Review of International Political Economy* 26 (6): 1089–1111.

Fisher, Aleksandr. 2020. "Trickle Down Soft Power: Do Russia's Ties to European Parties Influence Public Opinion?" *Foreign Policy Analysis* 17 (1): oraa013.

Friedrichs, Gordon M. 2022. "Conceptualizing the Effects of Polarization for Us Foreign Policy Behavior in International Negotiations: Revisiting the Two-Level Game." *International Studies Review* 24 (1): viac010.

George, Alexander L. 1969. "The 'Operational Code': A Neglected Approach to the Study of Political Leaders and Decision-Making." *International Studies Quarterly* 13 (2): 190–222.

Ghalehdar, Payam. 2021. *The Origins of Overthrow: How Emotional Frustration Shapes Us Regime Change Interventions*. New York: Oxford University Press.

Goertz, Gary, and James Mahoney. 2012. *A Tale of Two Cultures: Qualitative and Quantitative Research in the Social Sciences*. Princeton, NJ: Princeton University Press.

Grieco, Joseph M. 1995. "The Maastricht Treaty, Economic and Monetary Union and the Neo-Realist Research Programme." *Review of International Studies* 21 (1): 21–40.

Guzzini, Stefano. 1993. "Structural Power: The Limits of Neorealist Power Analysis." *International Organization* 47 (3): 443–478.

Guzzini, Stefano, ed. 2012. *The Return of Geopolitics in Europe? Social Mechanisms and Foreign Policy Identity Crises*. Cambridge, New York et al.: Cambridge University Press.

Guzzini, Stefano. 2017. "Militarizing Politics, Essentializing Identities: Interpretivist Process Tracing and the Power of Geopolitics." *Cooperation and Conflict* 52 (3): 423–445.

Haar, Roberta N., and Jonathan J. Pierce. 2021. "Foreign Policy Change from an Advocacy Coalition Framework Perspective." *International Studies Review* 23 (4): 1771–1791.

Haesebrouck, Tim, and Patrick A. Mello. 2020. "Patterns of Political Ideology and Security Policy." *Foreign Policy Analysis* 16 (4): 1–22.

Hermann, Margaret G. 1980. "Explaining Foreign Policy Behavior Using the Personal Characteristics of Political Leaders." *International Studies Quarterly* 24 (1): 7–46.

Hill, Christopher. 2016. *Foreign Policy in the Twenty-First Century*. Second edition. London and New York: Palgrave.

Hollis, Martin, and Steve Smith. 1990. *Explaining and Understanding in International Relations*. Oxford: Clarendon Press.

Holsti, Kalevi J. 2004. *Taming the Sovereigns: Institutional Change in International Politics*. Cambridge: Cambridge University Press.

Hooghe, Liesbet, Tobias Lenz, and Gary Marks. 2019. "Contested World Order: The Delegitimation of International Governance." *The Review of International Organizations* 14 (4): 731–743.

Hopf, T. ed. 2002. *Social Construction of International Politics: Identities & Foreign Policies. Moscow, 1955 and 1999*. Ithaca, NY: Cornell University Press.

Hudson, Valerie M. 2005. "Foreign Policy Analysis: Actor-Specific Theory and the Ground of International Relations." *Foreign Policy Analysis* 1 (1): 1–30.

Hudson, Valerie M. 2016. "The History and Evolution of Foreign Policy Analysis." In *Foreign Policy. Theories, Actors, Cases*, edited by Steve Smith, Amelia Hadfield and Tim Dunne. Oxford: Oxford University Press, 13–34.

Hudson, Valerie M., Mary Caprioli, Bonnie Ballif-Spanvill, Rose McDermott, and Chad F. Emmett. 2008. "The Heart of the Matter: The Security of Women and the Security of States." *International Security* 33 (3): 7–45.

Hudson, Valerie M., and Benjamin S. Day. 2019. *Foreign Policy Analysis: Classic and Contemporary Theory*. Lanham, MD: Rowman & Littlefield.

Jackson, Patrick Thaddeus. 2011. *The Conduct of Inquiry in International Relations: Philosophy of Science and Its Implications for the Study of World Politics*. London: Routledge.

Jenne, Erin K. 2021. "Populism, Nationalism and Revisionist Foreign Policy." *International Affairs* 97 (2): 323–343.

Jervis, Robert. 1976. *Perception and Misperception in International Politics*. Princeton, NJ, and Chichester: Princeton University Press.

Jervis, Robert. 1978. "Cooperation Under the Security Dilemma." *World Politics* 30 (2): 167–214.

Jervis, Robert, Richard Ned Lebow, and Deborah Welch Larson. 1985. *Psychology and Deterrence*. Baltimore, MD: Johns Hopkins University Press.

Joly, Jeroen K., and Tim Haesebrouck, eds. 2021. *Foreign Policy Change in Europe since 1991*. Cham: Palgrave Macmillan.

Kaarbo, Juliet. 2003. "Foreign Policy Analysis in the Twenty-First Century: Back to Comparison, Forward to Identity and Ideas." *International Studies Review* 5 (2): 156–163.

Kaarbo, Juliet. 2015. "A Foreign Policy Analysis Perspective on the Domestic Politics Turn in IR Theory." *International Studies Review* 17 (2): 189–216.

Kaarbo, Juliet, and Daniel Kenealy. 2016. "No, Prime Minister: Explaining the House of Commons Vote on Intervention in Syria." *European Security* 25 (1): 28–48.

Kahneman, Daniel, and Amos Tversky. 1979. "Prospect Theory: An Analysis of Decision Under Risk." *Econometrica* 47 (2): 263–291.

Kesgin, Baris, and Juliet Kaarbo. 2010. "When and How Parliaments Influence Foreign Policy: The Case of Turkey's Iraq Decision." *International Studies Perspectives* 11 (1): 19–36.

Koschut, Simon, ed. 2020. *The Power of Emotions in World Politics*. London and New York: Routledge.

Kruck, Andreas, and Andrea Schneiker, eds. 2017. *Researching Non-State Actors in International Security: Theory & Practice*. Oxon: Routledge.

Kuehn, David, and Ingo Rohlfing. 2022. "Do Quantitative and Qualitative Research Reflect Two Distinct Cultures? An Empirical Analysis of 180 Articles Suggests 'No'." *Sociological Methods & Research* (31 March).

Kuus, Merje. 2013. "Foreign Policy and Ethnography: A Sceptical Intervention." *Geopolitics* 18 (1): 115–131.

Kuus, Merje. 2014. *Geopolitics and Expertise. Knowledge and Authority in European Diplomacy*. Hoboken, NJ: Wiley Blackwell.

Legro, Jeffrey W. 1996. "Culture and Preferences in the International Cooperation Two-Step." *American Political Science Review* 90 (1): 118–137.

Leites, Nathan. 1951. *The Operational Code of the Politburo*. New York: McGraw-Hill.

Lobell, Steven E., Norrin M. Ripsman, and Jeffrey W. Taliaferro, eds. 2009. *Neoclassical Realism, the State, and Foreign Policy*. Cambridge: Cambridge University Press.

Lupton, Danielle L. 2020. *Reputation for Resolve: How Leaders Signal Determination in International Politics*. Ithaca, NY: Cornell University Press.

MacKay, Joseph, and Jamie Levin. 2015. "Hanging Out in International Politics: Two Kinds of Explanatory Political Ethnography for IR1." *International Studies Review* 17 (2): 163–188.

Mahoney, James, and Gary Goertz. 2006. "A Tale of Two Cultures: Contrasting Quantitative and Qualitative Research." *Political Analysis* 14 (3): 227–249.

March, James G., and Johan P. Olsen. 1998. *Rediscovering Institutions: The Organizational Basis of Politics*. New York: Free Press.

McCarthy, Mary M., ed. 2018. *Routledge Handbook of Japanese Foreign Policy*. Abingdon: Routledge.

Mead, Walter Russell. 2017. "The Jacksonian Revolt. American Populism and the Liberal Order." *Foreign Affairs* 96 (2): 2–7.

Meibauer, Gustav, Linde Desmaele, Tudor Onea, Nicholas Kitchen, Michiel Foulon, Alexander Reichwein, and Jennifer Sterling-Folker. 2021. "Forum: Rethinking Neoclassical Realism at Theory's End." *International Studies Review* 23 (1): 268–295.

Mello, Patrick A., and Dirk Peters. 2018. "Parliaments in Security Policy: Involvement, Politicisation, and Influence." *British Journal of Politics and International Relations* 20 (1): 3–18.

Mérand, Frédéric. 2020. *Coping with Geopolitical Decline. The United States in European Perspective*. Montreal et al.: McGill-Queen's University Press.

Moravcsik, Andrew. 1997. "Taking Preferences Seriously: A Liberal Theory of International Politics." *International Organization* 51 (4): 513–553.

Morin, Jean-Frédéric. 2013. *La Politique Étrangère. Théories, Méthodes Et Références*. Paris: Armand Colin.

Morin, Jean-Frédéric, and Jonathan Paquin. 2018. *Foreign Policy Analysis: A Toolbox*. Houndmills: Palgrave Macmillan.

Neumann, Iver B. 2002. "Returning Practice to the Linguistic Turn: The Case of Diplomacy." *Millennium - Journal of International Studies* 31 (3): 627–651.

Neumann, Iver B. 2011. *At Home with Diplomats. Inside a European Foreign Ministry*. Ithaca, NY: Cornell University Press.

Oktay, Sibel. 2018. "Chamber of Opportunities: Legislative Politics and Coalition Security Policy." *British Journal of Politics and International Relations* 20 (1): 104–120.

Oktay, Sibel. 2022. *Governing Abroad. Coalition Politics and Foreign Policy in Europe*. Ann Arbor, MI: The University of Michigan Press.

Okundaye, Gabriela, and Marijke Breuning. 2021. "Is the Expansion of Women's Access to Political Leadership Rewarded? Evidence from the Allocation of Us Foreign Aid." *Journal of Women, Politics & Policy* 42 (3): 225–242.

Oppermann, Kai. 2008. "Salience and Sanctions: A Principal-Agent Analysis of Domestic Win-Sets in Two-Level Games - the Case of British European Policy under the Blair Government." *Cambridge Review of International Affairs* 21 (2): 179–197.

Oppermann, Kai, and Alexander Spencer. 2016. "Studying Fiascos: Bringing Public and Foreign Policy Together." *Journal of European Public Policy* 23 (5): 643–652.

Ostermann, Falk, and Bernhard Stahl. 2022. "Theorizing Populist Radical-Right Foreign Policy: Ideology and Party Positioning in France and Germany." *Foreign Policy Analysis* 18 (3): orac006.

Plagemann, Johannes, and Sandra Destradi. 2019. "Populism and Foreign Policy: The Case of India." *Foreign Policy Analysis* 15 (2): 283–301.

Prakash, Deepa, and Audie Klotz. 2007. "The Forum: Should We Discard the 'Qualitative' Versus 'Quantitative' Distinction?" *International Studies Review* 9: 753–770.

Putnam, Robert. 1988. "Diplomacy and Domestic Politics: The Logic of Two-Level Games." *International Organization* 42 (3): 427–460.

Raunio, Tapio, and Wolfgang Wagner. 2017. "Towards Parliamentarisation of Foreign and Security Policy?" *West European Politics* 40 (1): 1–19.

Raunio, Tapio, and Wolfgang Wagner. 2020. "The Party Politics of Foreign and Security Policy." *Foreign Policy Analysis* 16 (4): 515–531.

Rihoux, Benoît, and Heike Grimm, eds. 2006. *Innovative Comparative Methods for Policy Analysis: Beyond the Quantitative-Qualitative Divide*. Boston, MA: Springer.

Risse-Kappen, Thomas. 1994. "Ideas Do Not Float Freely: Transnational Coalitions, Domestic Structures, and the End of the Cold War." *International Organization* 48 (2): 185–214.

Risse, Thomas, and Antje Wiener. 1999. "Something Rotten and the Social Construction of Social Constructivism: A Comment on Comments." *Journal of European Public Policy* 6 (5): 775–782.

Rose, Gideon. 1998. "Neoclassical Realism and Theories of Foreign Policy." *World Politics* 51 (1): 144–172.

Schmidt, Brian C. 2002. "On the History and Historiography of International Relations." In *Handbook of International Relations*, edited by Walter Carlsnaes, Thomas Risse and Beth A. Simmons. London: Sage, 3–22.

Schneiker, Andrea, Magnus Dau, Jutta Joachim, Marlen Martin, and Henriette Lange. 2018. "How to Analyze Social Media? Assessing the Promise of Mixed-Methods Designs for Studying the Twitter Feeds of PMSCs." *International Studies Perspectives* 20 (2): 188–200.

Schweller, Randall L. 2003. "The Progressiveness of Neoclassical Realism." In *Progress in International Relations Theory. Appraising the Field*, edited by Colin Elman and Miriam Fendius Elman. Cambridge, MA: MIT Press, 311–347.

Senn, Martin, Franz Eder, and Markus Kornprobst, eds. 2022. *Handbuch Außenpolitik Österreichs*. Wiesbaden: Springer VS.

Siedschlag, Alexander, ed. 2014. *Methoden Der Sicherheitspolitischen Analyse*. Wiesbaden: Springer VS.

Smith, Steve, Amelia Hadfield, and Tim Dunne, eds. 2016. *Foreign Policy: Theory, Actors, Cases*. Oxford: Oxford University Press.

Snyder, Richard C., Henry W. Bruck, and Burton M. Sapin, eds. 1962. *Foreign Policy Decision Making: An Approach to the Study of International Politics*. New York: Free Press.

Sprout, Harold, and Margaret Sprout. 1957. "Environment Factors in the Study of International Politics." *Journal of Conflict Resolution* 1 (4): 309–328.

Strong, James. 2017. "Two-Level Games Beyond the United States: International Indexing in Britain During the Wars in Afghanistan, Iraq and Libya." *Global Society* 31 (2): 293–313.

Strong, James. 2018. "The War Powers of the British Parliament: What Has Been Established and What Remains Unclear?" *British Journal of Politics and International Relations* 20 (1): 19–34.

Stuart, Douglas T. 2008. "Foreign-Policy Decision Making." In *The Oxford Handbook of International Relations*, edited by Christian Reus-Smit and Duncan Snidal. Oxford: Oxford University Press, 576–593.

Tarrow, Sidney. 1995. "Bridging the Quantitative-Qualitative Divide in Political Science." *American Political Science Review* 89 (2): 471–474.

Thies, Cameron G., ed. 2018. *Oxford Encyclopedia of Foreign Policy Analysis*, Oxford Encyclopedia of Foreign Policy Analysis. New York: Oxford University Press.

Tsygankov, Andrei P., ed. 2018. *Routledge Handbook of Russian Foreign Policy*. Abingdon: Routledge.

Vasquez, John A. 1997. "The Realist Paradigm and Degenerative Versus Progressive Research Programs: An Appraisal of Neotraditional Research on Waltz's Balancing Proposition." *American Political Science Review* 91 (4): 899–912.

Verbeek, Bertjan, and Andrej Zaslove. 2017. "Populism and Foreign Policy." In *The Oxford Handbook of Populism*, edited by Cristóbal Rovira Kaltwasser, Paul Taggart, Paulina Ochoa Espejo and Pierre Ostiguy. Oxford and New York: Oxford University Press, 384–405.

Vignoli, Valerio. 2020. "The Barking Dogs: Junior Coalition Partners and Military Operations Abroad in Italy." *Italian Political Science Review/Rivista Italiana di Scienza Politica*— 51: 25–21.

Waever, Ole. 1998. "The Sociology of a Not So International Discipline: American and European Developments in International Relations." *International Organization* 52 (4): 687–727.

Wagner, Wolfgang, Anna Herranz-Surrallés, Juliet Kaarbo, and Falk Ostermann. 2017. "The Party Politics of Legislative-Executive Relations in Security and Defence Policy." *West European Politics* 40 (1): 20–41.

Walker, Stephen G. 1977. "The Interface between Beliefs and Behavior: Henry Kissinger's Operational Code and the Vietnam War." *Journal of Conflict Resolution* 21 (1): 129–168.

Welch Larson, Deborah. 1985. *Origins of Containment: A Psychological Explanation*. Princeton, NJ: Princeton University Press.

Zürn, Michael. 2014. "The Politicization of World Politics and Its Effects: Eight Propositions." *European Political Science Review* 6 (1): 47–71.

Part II
Perspectives on Foreign Policy

2
Ideas and Identity from Rationalism to Theories of Recognition

Stefano Guzzini

Introduction

Henry Kissinger once remarked that

> An exact balance is [...] chimerical, above all, because while powers may appear to outsiders as factors in a security arrangement, they appear domestically as expressions of historical existence. No power will submit to a settlement, however well balanced and however "secure", which seems totally to deny its vision of itself.
>
> (Kissinger 1957, 146)

In his view, states have visions of themselves, and any security arrangement that does not sufficiently recognize them is bound to fail. The balance of power only works with a balance of identities.

Yet, for scholars of foreign policy, Kissinger's practical lead of diplomatic experience was left unfollowed until the arrival of constructivism. 'Vision of itself' does not figure prominently in realist and liberal institutionalist Foreign Policy Analysis (FPA). In fact, it cannot. Integrating identity and our relational self, constituted in social recognition, asks for an ontology other than individualism and for a theory of action other than utilitarianism, both of which became prevalent for the two main paradigms. In contrast, Kissinger's insight was explicitly taken up and further developed by both constructivist (Kratochwil 1978, 201) and poststructuralist scholars (Wæver 1995) working on identity and foreign policy. More generally, this scholarship understood identity as a process of identification in national biographies and also pointed to the phenomenon of *ontological security*, which refers to the idea that security is not only about defending oneself against different physical threats but also about defending a certain continuity of a self-understanding and self-esteem that provides an actor with an identity with which to be at ease.

As the chapter will show, the main issue is hence not that some theories deal with ideas and identity whereas others do not; the issue is *how* they do so. The underlying theory of action, from utilitarianism to discursive ontologies and theories of recognition, provides the methodological assumptions of their respective analyses. In the following, I will first show how the methodology of utilitarian approaches like recent versions of realism and liberalism deals with ideas, norms, and identity, yet in a way that is unsatisfactory to account for Kissinger's insight. A second section will then show how identity has been more coherently applied in constructivist FPA, including in approaches to ontological security. They meet however a different set of problems, such as its often homeostatic assumptions, its more acute problem with anthropomorphization and not least the pathologies of turning an observational theory into a nationalist foreign policy apology.

Rationalist Analysis of Ideas and Identity and Its Limits

Among other pernicious effects of the underlying binary of realism–idealism in International Relations (IR), there is a persistent misunderstanding that ideas are the stuff of liberals, whereas realists are mainly focused on power. Putting it this way already makes clear how unfair this is for realists, even if some of them may use that very argument. Realists know the power of ideas perfectly well, being certainly aware of propaganda and indoctrination. No good realist foreign policy strategist would be foolish enough to leave the battle of hearts and minds to the other side. No good realist observer would exclude such ideational factors from an analysis of power. The issue is, rather, *how* to combine the ideational with other factors in an analysis. Here, the more open rationalist move of US IR in the 1980s has helped to clarify the theoretical positions – and their limits.

Rationalist Theories of Action

Rationalist explanations follow a triangle made powerful by the rationality assumption. Rational choice entails an individualist theory of action. It makes two main assumptions about human behavior. First, humans are self-interested utility maximizers; and second, humans choose rationally on the basis of a consistent (transitive) preference ranking. If A is preferred to B and B to C, A should be preferred to C. A straightforward and parsimonious theory of action derives from this basic depiction of self-interest and rationality. Once we know the desires of individuals (their preferences), as well as their beliefs about how to realize them, we can deduce their rational behavior. Indeed, as Keith Dowding (1991, 23) has succinctly put it:

> The three go together in a triangle of explanation and given any two of the triumvirate the third may be predicted and explained [...] This is a behaviouralist theory of action, since it is studying the behaviour of individuals that allows us to understand their beliefs (by making assumptions about their desires) or their desires (by making assumptions about their beliefs). We may understand both by making assumptions about different aspects of each.

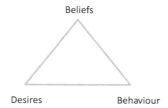

Figure 2.1 A rationalist theory of action.

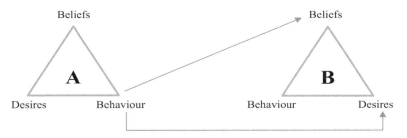

Figure 2.2 Influence attempts in a rationalist theory of action.

When information is limited, realist analysts (and others) will rely on an explanation that infers beliefs from the other two factors on the basis of the consistency between the three parts provided by rationality: behavior is the visible starting point and preferences are assumed to be known through realist theory, so the only variable to be inferred is (shifts in) beliefs (Figure 2.1).[1] In this way, the analysis is truly behavioralist, since it does away with any information on the *actual* process of how the decision and behavior have come about. It is a form of rationalism where foreign policy decision-making is left in an analytical black box, a mere conduit between an input (stimulus) and an output (response).

Accordingly, a rationalist foreign policy strategy can affect the behavior of other actors by trying to influence their beliefs, also by signaling a certain 'image' (Jervis 1970), or, and this is more complicated, their desires (preferences) (Figure 2.2).

Clearly, a black box model cannot really work; if anything, FPA became prominent for opening up that box. One path was adding more process factors. Over the years, and generally staying within a rationalist picture, it added factor after factor that would inform the national interest (preferences, desire): anything from individual psychology (operational code, see Schafer and Walker in this volume), public opinion (see Kleinberg in this volume), party preferences, to lobbies and bureaucracies, and more, would do. This led to fragmentation and increasing theoretical frustration, since comparative FPA became the analysis of 'everything but the kitchen sink' with little capacity to find more general regularities (see also Feng and He in this volume).

Another strategy therefore consisted in lifting the theoretical argument to a higher level of abstraction and inquiring into the origins of beliefs and desires more generally. Obviously, beliefs and preferences are neither idiosyncratic nor reducible to a single utilitarian calculation. But that does not mean they are arbitrary. Neoliberal institutionalists have oriented some of their research in FPA to the normative context and shared practices (*regimes*) within which actors form their beliefs, define their interests, and decide their action. Hence, rather than seeing this as influenced by another actor or domestic factors, the analysis moves to a higher level in which shared ideas are prime influencers. Although this sounds antithetical to realists, there is not much to oppose it once a rationalist setup is followed: ideas do not just fall from heaven, and they resonate because of a shared ideational and normative context (see also Orchard and Wiener in this volume). Hence, Stephen Krasner had no real choice but to admit the place of regimes as not only intervening but also as autonomous variables in structural explanations (see, respectively, Krasner 1982a, b), the 'neo-neo synthesis' of neorealism and neoliberalism (Wæver 1996).[2] All seems set. Having ideas and norms now as autonomous variables that influence beliefs, they may also influence preferences, since beliefs and preferences may not be independent of each other (Figure 2.3).

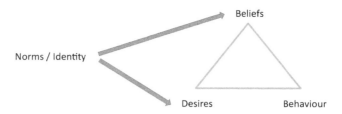

Figure 2.3 The endogenization of preference and interest formation.

But, as we will see, such moves would undermine the neopositivist methodologies and meta-theory on which established IR rationalism relies. In the end, the latter imposes a straitjacket on how to think beliefs and their effects: It narrows the ontology to individualism, conceives of ideas as objects, and imposes a vision of ideas as relevant only if causally efficient.

The Contradictions of Rationalist Analysis

In their programmatic statement, Judith Goldstein and Robert Keohane (1993) establish the model for the rationalist analysis of ideas in foreign policy. They define ideas as beliefs, that is, mental states. And they see them as necessary to overcome problems that rational action may face:

> Our argument is that ideas influence policy when the principled or causal beliefs they embody provide road maps that increase actors' clarity about goals or ends–means relationships, when they affect outcomes of strategic situations in which there is no unique equilibrium, and when they become embedded in political institutions.
> *(Goldstein and Keohane 1993, 3)*

In other words, there is simply no rational action without beliefs, neither for the actors themselves, nor for their observers. Yet, in setting up the analysis, they insist that the null hypothesis is an interest-based explanation of action, which is defined as autonomous from any role of beliefs. This is meant to isolate the specific causal effect that beliefs can have. This constitutes a surely curious move when a pragmatic argument about operationalization is meant to prime a meta-theoretical one: while we know that beliefs can influence interests and that both are intrinsically connected, let's just test them against each other as if they were not. Also, despite writing that beliefs are mental states, we can then ascribe efficient causality to them, as if there were external factors, like billiard balls. Finally, although allowing for the social embeddedness of beliefs (and norms), their content is analyzed in an individualist setup as if that very social nature were of no relevance. All opening acknowledgments of the intrinsic problems of the rationalist model in dealing with beliefs are eventually taken back in the actual approach.

The inconsistency between meta-theory and methodology was already exposed for regime theory. Friedrich Kratochwil and John Ruggie (1986) had welcomed regime theory for its move to include normative factors into the more general structural understanding of international order and yet found it wanting in its attempt to reduce them to external objects. They saw this move as being prompted by a positivist understanding of reality where the analysis needs to be purely causal and not also constitutive, and where causality is understood in the relation of mutually external units or factors. Mark Laffey and Jutta Weldes (1997) see this reinforced by the 'ideas as commodities' metaphor, in which ideas can be acquired, exchanged, and sold. An idea is just a different form of object or good, and hence subsumable under the external and causal analysis used for material factors.

But beliefs do not just hit actors and force them to do things. That type of causality simply does not work for this phenomenon. Beliefs are not external causes, but at best internal reasons for action. Those reasons may or may not be conscious to the actors; they are multiple, heterogeneous, and potentially conflicting. After all, it was exactly for these subjective effects that beliefs have been often reduced to material or objective needs, as proposed by both utilitarianism and (some form of) Marxism, which reduce actors to through-puts. Hence a dilemma: either they are important, but then not reducible, and so both theoretical and methodological consequences ensue; or they are reducible, but then, despite all statements to the contrary, they return to being only secondary for the analysis, playing the role of a residual or ad hoc variable to explain instrumentally unexplained outcomes. Rationalism needs to go the latter way: by trying to stick to a positivist and utilitarian setup, whether scholars acknowledge it or not, all openings are withdrawn again.

But, most importantly, beliefs are not just mental states. There is a significant difference between a belief that is understood as some individual mental state leading to action and beliefs that are social by definition since they are embedded in wider normative or other ideational systems to which actors attach meaning and act. Let me use both Max Weber and the rationalist idea of 'common knowledge' as ways to show that beliefs are not about subjectivity, but intersubjectivity, with both theoretical and methodological consequences.[3]

Weber famously distinguished between *instrumental rationality* and *value rationality* or rationality of ultimate ends. The former is the classical utilitarian understanding in which an actor tries to achieve a cost-efficient usage of means to reach an end, while comparing and choosing between alternative options. The latter refers to a different type of consistent, hence rational, behavior in which actors choose their action in terms of reaching certain values, potentially independent of any concerns of other consequences; the aim informs the choice of means, irrespective of costs (but not all means are necessarily justified; that depends on the end).

In the utilitarian setup, whenever the cost–benefit calculation goes wrong, besides incomplete information and other circumstances, one can refer to erroneous beliefs or ideologies that lead to 'irrational' action. Value rationality hence becomes the residual explanation when instrumental rationality does not work. But the underlying instrumental and utilitarian frame is preserved as the default explanation. In this way, the theory can never go wrong, since it can always be tweaked in this way to conform to the behavioral outcome (Allison 1971; Steinbruner 1974, 47; Pizzorno 2007, chapter 4).

But Weber would not have spent what feels like several thousands of pages on world religions and cosmologies were it not fundamental for his sociological theory. For him, the relationship is the other way round: value rationality is not the exception, but the default. Here, instrumental rationality is but the form value rationality takes in a specific cultural or social environment where utilitarian efficiency becomes the overarching value. It is a special case that cannot just be assumed, but needs to be justified through an analysis of the social and normative context.

This reversal can also be illustrated through the closest that rationalist theory gets to the idea of intersubjectivity, namely *common knowledge*. Game theorists have met the problem that some coordination problems, irresolvable by independent individual calculation in theory, are resolved in practice, namely through a kind of knowledge that A knows that B knows that A knows that B… (see also Wolford in this volume). Indeed, common knowledge is based on a logically infinite regress of anticipation of the others' beliefs, where agent A in an interaction believes something that others believe, too, and that they believe A also believes, who, in turn, and so on. As Wendt puts it, 'Common knowledge requires "interlocking" beliefs, not just everyone having the same beliefs' (Wendt 1999, 160). Knowing that others know what you know, also about them, hence provides a common backdrop against which coordination can happen. Tom Schelling has given famous examples of this, including where to meet in a city without having given any previous information about it. When there is common knowledge, actors will coordinate blindly.

No doubt this scheme is a very helpful and welcome inclusion of wider ideational concerns. Yet, it is still severely limited for our concerns about Kissinger's 'vision of itself'. First, the setup remains one of strategic interaction, where all that is varied is the belief that then affects behavior. Interests or identities are untouched in this analysis. The amount of socialization into a set of ideas is hence purely limited to beliefs, not 'character', to use Kissinger's term.

Also, the origins of this background knowledge are not clear. Yet they may be the relevant issue. Take the following example. You are invited to a dinner and the host expresses the intention to serve fish. You know that the host assumes you know that this implies that you should bring the wine, white wine to boot. This is taken for granted, and goes without saying, as background knowledge does. Yet, recently, having met new friends, the host prefers different beer types to be paired with the food, preferably from some hip micro-brewery, and may have assumed you to know this. So, when you arrive with the wine, the coordination functioned, since there is wine for the food. But then, also it did not. One could now argue that the relevant common knowledge should have included the 'vision of itself', here informed by the host's identification with a certain social group with a distinctive taste. It cannot take for granted that we all share the same social environment with the same norms. What this amounts to, however, is that in this game of mutual anticipation, one needs to think about preferences and interests in terms of the 'circles of recognition', to use Alessandro Pizzorno's (1986, 367) term, that constitute (not cause) them in the first place. The analysis is only about beliefs – but those beliefs include a constitutive link between norms and/or identity and interests that the very approach neglects. Apparently, actors know more about the thicker social role of ideas than their rationalist observers.

Also, we can easily agree that reducing this encounter to a mere coordination game may miss that which is relevant for understanding the (future) social relation between those agents. Common meals are rituals. What if the host decides to go with the wine this time, rather than priggishly parading the fancy beer, hence humiliating the guest? What if the guest cannot be bothered, let alone humiliated, since she could not care less about the host and accepted the invitation only out of some form of politeness? We move from a theory of instrumental action to one of symbolic action and social recognition. Behavior is understood as a practice informed by the tacit, ritualized, and open rules of recognition in their respective spheres and social fields. Identity is always part of a relation, and that relation part of wider fields within which we learn to distinguish ourselves by constructing a biography of ourselves (the 'vision of itself') that narrates identity across time as well as identification with and difference to others.

Identity in Constructivist and Poststructuralist Foreign Policy Analysis

Constructivism is often amalgamated with the analysis of the role of norms. But for FPA, a second constructivist research program has also been important, one focusing on the link between identity and interests and behavior, which is central for thinking 'visions of itself'.

In the following section, an early study by Audie Klotz will serve as an initial background to provide a link between the two. After that, this section discusses a series of theoretical research programs that move from the external and domestic relations of identity formation to the study of national biographies, and finally to the poststructuralist reversal and studies of ontological security, where identity practices are to be understood as ways to see an always precarious identification (de)stabilized.[4]

Constructivist Takes on Foreign Policy Analysis

Why would a US right-wing government obsessed with the Cold War competition in all parts of the world decide to abandon a highly reliable Western ally? Why would the Reagan administration end up undermining the South African apartheid government? By putting the question in this manner, Klotz (1995) de facto follows the setup envisaged by Goldstein and Keohane: the interest explanation (Cold War competition) is the null hypothesis that defines the puzzle, and an ideational analysis is meant to fix it. Her explanation shows how anti-apartheid norms trumped strategic interests. But the analysis shows more. She insists that apartheid was a practice simply no longer acceptable within US domestic politics. It harked back to and justified racial discrimination when the US had moved on to a self-understanding in which this was no longer defensible. However racist parts of the US public and government may have been, apartheid was not just an informal, but a legal form of segregation, and such segregation was no longer publicly justifiable in race politics. It stood for the race politics of a US that the US had officially left behind. What the US *stood for* was driven by what the by now different *US* stood for.

This is the main inspiration for constructivism-inspired FPA centering on identity: identity and norms are not independent of, if residual to, interests, but they inform and constitute the latter in the first place (Jepperson, Wendt, and Katzenstein 1996). Here, Goldstein and Keohane's point that the very counterposition of ideas and interests is ontologically untenable is not just acknowledged but also followed up. As a result, rationalism may well have a place in the explanation, but 'a core constructivist research concern is what happens *before* the neo-utilitarian model kicks in' (Ruggie 1998, 867, original emphasis). Norms and ideas are not

> Just congealed rational responses to an objectively present material or organizational obstacle course. Thus the debate about the constitutive nature of norms, ideas, or identities is a debate not about static properties but about why people ended up with particular norms, ideas, or identities.
>
> *(Abdelal, Blyth, and Parsons 2010, 19)*

As a result, the burden of justification is turned around: ideational factors are not only relevant when they provide residual explanatory power to utilitarianism. Instead, if one does start with utilitarianism, one needs to carefully justify why it can do without understanding ideas through their wider social context and without endogenizing identity formation in the explanation. That justification is, in turn, necessary to justify the selection of a rationalist theory as the general framework to start with. It is perhaps hardly surprising that some rationalists shy away from this implication of being a special case in need of constant justification. It is much nicer if rationalism provides the null hypothesis.

Jutta Weldes and Ted Hopf have provided the textbook research approaches of two complementary constructivist foreign policy traditions: one addressing more the practices of identification with regard to the relational other abroad, and the other addressing them more through identification practices within a society. In an enviably clear approach, Weldes (1999) builds up her research puzzle. She shows how Cuban, Soviet, and US understandings of the Cuban missile crisis differ. This is not simply meant to show that all countries see the world through their lenses or how they deem fit, but to raise the issue why the Cuban interpretation was so easily dismissed. In the aftermath of the botched Bay of Pigs invasion, the Cuban justification for having Soviet missiles was that it was for sheer defense: not being able to trust the US to respect Cuba's sovereignty, given the US-supported invasion attempt to topple the regime, a credible deterrence was needed. A Soviet coupling and a nuclear deterrence was arguably the best strategy for this, if achieved as a *fait accompli*. In Weldes' close reading of the documents of the ExComm responsible for deciding the US response, that particular justification and rationale for the missile installation never seriously figures, however, even in a discussion which did not address a public audience. 'How come?' (her research question is not 'why?', since it refers to a process-focused version of causation).

Weldes uses discourse analysis (see also Ostermann and Sjöstedt in this volume) to reconstruct the foreign policy identity of the US as it appears in these documents and in the wider social context. According to her, that particular reading *could not* seriously figure in the discussion since it would have profoundly contradicted the US's vision of itself, to use Kissinger's term. Identity discourses hence inform what and how we understand. She argues, in her wording, how that particular understanding would have 'interpellated' a US identity as an imperialist power bound to invade smaller and relatively speaking defenseless countries when it saw fit. Accepting the Cuban justification of a necessary defense would portray the US in a manner that is excluded from the latter's self-identification, its identity discourses. That discourse has several scripts. It is not homogeneous. There are interventionists and isolationists, for instance, America First or the multilateral liberal order (much of this discussion is already foreshadowed in Hoffmann 1978). But the underlying implicit consensus or *doxa* is about a certain US exceptionalism.

Hence, discourse analysis cannot predict in a generic manner which script will become dominant and inform the understanding of world affairs. It is not deterministic in this sense. It answers *how possible?* questions, not *why?* questions, if by the latter we imply an efficient causal explanation (Doty 1993; Vennesson 2008). But, once fitted with the historical and empirical detail of the specific case, it can exclude certain understandings, since they would be outside the boundaries of existing identity discourses. These identity discourses can originate in three different environments. Critical geopolitics (see da Vinha in this volume) distinguishes between the formal, practical, and popular levels, i.e. the discursive fields of the observers, the practitioners, and civil society that inform the way state identity is conceived and through this also constituted and negotiated (Ó Tuathail and Dalby 1998).

Ted Hopf (2002), in particular, opened up this constructivist analysis by including societal discourses such as novels or movies. His approach also aimed to distinguish and compare the respective importance of (external) role recognition and (internal) self-identifications for informing the understanding of the leading decision-makers, showing that, for the majority of his cases, the domestic discourses prevailed, therefore prompting him to call his approach societal constructivism (for a similar design, see also Hopf 2012). This may not necessarily be persuasive, though, since role recognition is often included or anticipated in societal discourses and surely so when the analysis focuses on state decision-makers. In other words, although it makes sense to assume that such a relational practice as identity formation needs to be approached by analytically distinguishing the different spheres of relations and circles of recognition, in this case domestic and foreign relations, the very moment one moves to the level of the actor exposed to these discursive fields, the multiple spheres are mediated and no longer separated. Still, the approach has the advantage of clearly showing that identity discourses are never homogeneous, nor do they have only one single script. It is within the identity discourse that the different specific identity scripts are related, and are often set against each other.

Identification or Identity as Process

From here, the analysis of identity in FPA made two significant steps forward. First, it specified identity in that all identity discourses are relational and are both national biographies that diachronically construct continuity over time and synchronically constitute distinctions that define the self with regard to an Other (Pizzorno 1986, 368).[5] Second, the poststructuralist twist reversed the explanatory arrow: whereas constructivism tends to read from existing identity discourses to foreign policy behavior, poststructuralism takes the always precarious identity formation as its very core of analysis and looks into how foreign practices do not just express a certain identity, but actually intervene in its very constitution and (de)stabilization (for early interventions, see e.g. Doty 1993; 1996; for more recent ones, see e.g. Ostermann 2019).

Identity is constituted over time. Narratives are there to construct a continuity that can be called a self (see Oppermann and Spencer in this volume). In this way, a prominent way to understand identity discourses is to treat them as national biographies (Berenskoetter 2014b; for an analysis of Ricoeur's approach to memory and identity in IR, see Kopper 2012), constantly updated, if not rewritten, with multiple competing scripts. In this biographical practice, the self is re-constituted through that which it is not over time. Hence, any identity discourse is systematically connected to an Other (see e.g. Neumann 1996, 1999). This Other, however, does not need to be an enemy (Hansen 2006). Indeed, in an interesting twist, also friends are others who inform identity narratives in significant ways (Roshchin 2006; Berenskoetter 2007, 2014a).

Finally, such othering may not only be primarily geopolitical but can also be temporal. As Ole Wæver remarked, 'Europe's other is Europe's own past which should not be allowed to become its future' (Wæver 1998, 90), an identity discourse whose content closely overlaps with Germany's foreign policy identity. When then Secretary of Defense Rumsfeld tried to divide Europe, enlisting 'new' Europe for the Bush administration's war in Iraq, Germany was faced with a difficult choice: continue to be a friend of the US, also in recognition of the US effort for German security, or accept that this friend was undermining the EU, which is intrinsically related to German identity. Given the centrality of the EU in Germany's own temporal othering, it becomes more easily understandable why the Schröder government decided for the (old) EU and against the US (besides the strategic misconception of this war, lacking moreover legal and political (UNSC) legitimacy). Obviously, geopolitical and temporal othering cannot always be distinguished so clearly (Rumelili 2004; Prozorov 2010). But it is an interesting twist that othering in identity discourses can be self-reflexive (Diez 2004, 321), which produces, in particular for the EU, a very provisional sense of identity.

The other major research path consists in the poststructuralist reversal: rather than seeing identity discourses as informing certain understandings and hence predisposed to a limited set of foreign policy actions, it looks back on how these very understandings lead to actions which re-inscribe certain identity scripts. Or put more strongly, it looks at how action fixes (or not) an always precarious identity in search of recognition. Identity is not the start of an analysis of action, but the analysis of action (or practices) has the purpose of understanding identity processes.

The starting point is the 'dangerous liaison' between constructivist theorizing and the very nature of identity (Zehfuss 2001). Identity is always in the process of being re-inscribed. Hence, one cannot simply assume that in any given situation there is a stable identity from which the explanation originates. In contrast, the process in which the identity discourses are affected by events and actions may become the privileged focus for the analysis. This reversal, famously introduced by David Campbell (1990, 1992), starts the analysis from the practices that provide continuity to an ever-unaccomplished identity, and sees understandings and actions as potential ways to stabilize these processes. Jutta Weldes also sees the US reaction to the Cuban missile installations as an attempt to return credibility to a particular masculinist and macho US role in international affairs, trying not to appear 'weak' (see also Weldes 1996, 46). Rather than seeing the Cuban missile crisis as a (given) security crisis, she sees it primarily as an identity crisis that prompted its own security concerns.

In this context, the analysis moves toward the very identity discourses themselves, their history, their composition in multiple scripts, what will constitute threats to them, and how actions and understandings not only fix but also undermine them. In an almost complete reversal of the usual understanding of the national interest as being driven by given physical security concerns, there *can* be moments in which states' identities are so much accustomed to an enemy other that its disappearance induces insecurity. Giorgy Arbatov, Director of the Institute for USA and Canada Studies and advisor to Mikhail Gorbachev, is widely quoted for saying in an interview to a US journalist in 1988 that '[w]e are going to do a terrible thing to you—we are going to deprive you of your enemy'. In such cases, states are looking for matches of pre-defined danger and threats, looking for an enemy other that stabilizes the self: 'On a deep level, they prefer conflict to cooperation, because only through conflict do they know who they are' (Mitzen 2006, 361). There can hence be a national (identity) interest in insecurity. In an echo of Kissinger's concern with identity and absolute security, this specifies why peace-building and diplomacy may turn out to be far more complicated (Rumelili 2015b).

The work by Mitzen and Rumelili also provides a further example of the analysis of identity in FPA, namely Ontological Security Theory (OST). Initially inspired by social psychology and Anthony Giddens' social theory (Giddens 1991, chapter 2), ontological security refers to the idea that 'human beings need relatively stable expectations about the natural and especially social world around them' (Wendt 1999, 131). It 'entails having a consistent sense of self and having that sense affirmed by others' (Zarakol 2010, 6) so as to be able to sustain a coherent autobiographic narrative. Since this 'pushes human beings in a conservative, homeostatic direction, and to seek out recognition of their standing from society' (Wendt 1999, 131), '[o]ntological security does not presuppose a threat to identity but underlines an ongoing concern with its stability' (Rumelili 2015a, 58).

The analysis of ontological security initially targeted what one could call status anxieties and foreign policy pathologies. A major research issue is the study of the systematic ontological insecurity for those whose integration into international society is deferred and/or comes from the outside of that which is considered the civilizational 'standard', those 'forced … to rearticulate their new state identities around the anxiety of "demonstrable" inferiority and the goal of catching up with the West by following its "standards"' (Zarakol 2011, 62). This makes ontological security studies particularly fruitful for analyzing foreign policies at the periphery of the international order (Ejdus 2017; Vieira 2017). Indeed, some countries may get stuck in identity discourses that offer different scripts which are alternatively mobilized to meet crises without ever being able to provide a stabilized self, such as in the case of Turkey (Bilgin 2012) or Russia (Astrov and Morozova 2012; Morozov 2015).

Methodological/Theoretical Problems: Anthropomorphization, Homeostasis, and Reflexivity

Anthropomorphization is underlying all rationalist analysis where actors are assumed to have interests, ideas, aims, indeed a 'character', as Kissinger called it. But it is arguably more pronounced for discursive methodologies and theories of social recognition when applied to IR. There are three proposed solutions to this problem, none perfect (for a good discussion, see also Narozhna 2020).

One consists in arguing that states are persons in international society (Wendt 2004). Here, anthropomorphization is not metaphorical, but ontological in the figure of a (social) person. That is an ambitious take, and one that has met resistance (Jackson 2004; Neumann 2004; Wight 2004; yet see also the discussion in Lerner 2021). A second solution consists in focusing on the actual decision-makers and hence not scaling up at all. Yet, for this to work, some collective ideas and identifications need to enter the picture. Hopf (2002, chapter 1) achieves this by positing that identity is a cognitive device that stabilizes human orientations and understandings in their social environment. This creates societally shared discursive formations composed of different identity scripts. Decision-makers, as members of the same society, rely on these when understanding the situations in foreign policy. Alternatively, this link can be made by using other forms of social psychology, as in the study of nationalist mobilization (Kinnvall 2004, 2017), or, put slightly differently, by focusing on the ways and processes/institutions that provide ontological security to members of a society (Zarakol 2017), i.e. defending not the self but the wider social context (Pratt 2017).

Finally, there is the possibility of seeing a state's identity not as being scaled up but as being the ascription of international and/or domestic society. Hence, anthropomorphization is not an attribute assigned by the observer who imposes an anthropomorphic grid when analyzing a collective actor; it is the various social contexts that attribute such anthropomorphic traits to collective actors, while accordingly making sense of their acts, something the observer then registers and analyses (Guzzini 2012b). States, then, *are* what their circles of recognition make of them, to reuse Pizzorno's term mentioned above. Put into a more narrative approach to identity (Somers 1994), Erik Ringmar writes that: 'States too can be intentional, interest-driven, actors, we may conclude, provided that we tell stories which identify them as such' (Ringmar 1996, 75). This solution has the advantage of overcoming the paradox that, although observers and practitioners routinely declare that states are not persons, they refer to them as such in ways that influence their understanding and actions, and not only in terms of legal personality and liability. It also allows an empirical check on such attributions by analyzing practices of recognition (in its many meanings) within domestic and international society.[6] Yet it may miss the social psychological component that links it to domestic national identity practices (Guzzini 2017). De facto, most analyses, depending on whether they concentrate more on the domestic or external social context, will use versions of the last two, with their respective limitations, and often explore the tensions between the two (e.g. Subotić and Zarakol 2013).

There are more specific problems with OST. The major unease stems from the 'conservative, homeostatic direction' noted by Wendt above that tends to provide functionalist analyses that, in turn, favor securitization strategies for re-establishing an 'identity equilibrium' and hence have the usual problems with understanding both agency and change. If all starts from anxiety and its fixing, then ontological security pays a similar price to that paid by constructivist FPA earlier when it took identity discourses as stable (Bucher and Jasper 2016). Whereas the poststructuralist twist of reversing the focus from action to identity processes is taken seriously, the parallel insistence of the openness of such processes has been partly lost.

There have been different ways of dealing with this fundamental problem, but almost all of them open up for more contingency in the re-articulation of narratives and identity scripts. Rather than a functionalist fix, it becomes an open process. One line consisted in finding in the initial inspirational literature – be it Laing or Giddens, but also the existentialist takes in Hobbes and then in Heidegger and Kierkegaard – indications that anxiety not only induces crises to be fixed, but also generates opportunities to be explored (Gustafsson and Krickel-Choi 2020; Kinnvall and Mitzen 2020; Rumelili 2020), where securitization would not be the default coping strategy (Browning and Joenniemi 2017). This allows for a conceptualization of agency that can be more emancipatory (Berenskötter 2020) and may also involve desecuritization moves that bring ontological security closer to classical peace research concerns (Browning and Joenniemi 2017). As Lupovici's (2012) point about ontological dissonance implies, there is no necessity that crises be resolved rather than being constantly patched up and their solution hence adjourned.

In the analysis of identity crisis, the greater openness of the process is achieved by including more process factors in the analysis, not only for the link between interpretations and behavior, but already for establishing the contours of the narrative struggles. Such factors include the analysis of the hierarchies, habitus, and practices in the foreign policy expert field, the ideational path dependency of political cultures, and the struggles within the political field itself (Guzzini 2012b). The idea of an 'identity crisis' hence does not refer to an external event that hits identity discourses, but to the predispositions of identity discourses that may find it difficult to keep consistency in the interpretation of events. The end of the Cold War unsurprisingly unsettled identity scripts in Russia, but also oddly in Italy, and not in Germany and the Czech Republic, which were, however, states newly constituted in this form (Guzzini 2012a). As seen, an international crisis, even a war, may stabilize identity scripts. To constitute the event and assess its effects, the analysis is from the discursive field via scripts and interpretations to the event, an *interpretivist process-tracing*, not the other way round (see van Meegdenburg in this volume).

Last but not least, it is important to highlight a reflexive element so important for constructivist scholarship. What happens when an observational theory is re-translated into a political doctrine and policy justification, as also happened to democratic peace theory (see also Ish-Shalom 2006, 2013)? What happens when ideas about identity mechanisms travel into the world of practice; when the search for recognition is not simply a long-standing practice of international politics, but becomes implicitly justified through our social theories; and when practitioners (or scholars), aware of this justification, use it to defend as untouchable an identity script of their predilection, any infringement of which would count as undermining a vital interest?

This ontologically reflexive twist is a temptation, in particular with ontological security; however, much observers of ontological security have warned about it. It is not too hard to see how ontological security can move from being an observational concept to a practical one. Just as the idea of a sphere of interest, ontological security, if used as a doctrine, defines a red line. But it is a specific red line, since it does not allow for much of a compromise. Indeed, as Maria Mälksoo (2015, 223) has argued, the problem is that such a move normalizes and makes inevitable 'a state's need to seek and sustain the intactness and consistency of its identity [which] could dangerously depoliticize the act of protecting a biographical narrative of the state', normalizing, in turn, strategies of securitization.

The wider practical implications of normalizing ontological security have to do with a similar twist, namely that it is the country itself which can define the legitimate red line of its 'vision of itself'. Yet all of the classical international practices, such as spheres of influence, only work when they are recognized by others. Unilateral actions can be part of their establishment, but not more. However, whereas shared rules that define the acceptance of such practices have been established over time, which 'visions of itself' would be legitimate and which not is more difficult to establish. If actors decide that there is a completely untouchable 'vision of itself', based for instance on a historical status of victimhood (Lerner 2019), that any security arrangement will have to accept, a world order can easily become impossible.

It is therefore important to note that although great power status and recognition involve the privilege to make fewer compromises, the 'vision of itself' is objectively never the property of an actor alone; it is social. Its invocation for foreign policy purposes is hence always contestable. If ontological security is erroneously translated into a self-centered doctrine to justify uncompromising foreign policy action, it leads to diplomatic pathologies. It expresses, metaphorically speaking, a form of narcissism (see also the discussion in Hagström 2021). In fact, in this case, it is not that a given ontological insecurity justifies uncompromising behavior; uncompromising behavior serves to essentialize a certain definition of the vision of oneself. Such a temptation is visible in many political justifications of foreign policies, as analyzed, for instance, in research on foreign policy discourses in Central and Eastern European countries, and in particular in Russia (see, for instance, Hansen 2016; Akchurina and Della Sala 2018; Kazharski 2019; Freire 2020; Narozhna 2022).

Conclusion

Kissinger's concern with 'vision of the self' cannot be consistently accommodated in a rationalist framework of analysis because of its individualist understanding of beliefs, its objectivation as external cause, and the exogenization of interest formation that neglects the constitutive role of ideas and identity. The constructivist and then poststructuralist research agenda on identity remedies this situation by framing the role of ideas within a more appropriate sociological theory, yet meeting problems of their own. In this process, the question of identity has not only moved center stage but also shifted beyond Kissinger's take.

For Kissinger, that vision of itself was surely contingent to some extent, but it was something given that could be threatened by events and decisions. Seeing how particular events may pose problems for such identities (and identity discourses) is surely part of the previously mentioned research programs (and also for the concept of societal security, as introduced by Wæver 1993). But there has been a further twist, in that such identity discourses are intrinsically unstable and in need of fixes. Identities are relational and hence part of continuous recognition practices for an identity that *is*, by being, always *in the making*. No actor ever has an identity that is guaranteed to be at one with the 'vision of itself'. Hence – and this is different from Kissinger's take – there is not only a given identity registering tensions with the outside world, be they in self-identifications or role recognitions. Instead, identities are part of processes that have autonomous effects on that very mediation between self and the world. In particular, the search for recognition informs identity practices that intervene in this world. It gives meaning to our actions. Following the trail of an increasingly thicker account of ideas and identities leads us to a theory of action that is not utilitarian, but symbolic, and where the search for recognition, not value maximization, becomes the main underlying logic.

Acknowledgments

I am gratefully indebted to careful readings and suggestions, not all of which I was able to integrate, to Fernanda Alves, Andreas Behnke, Teresa Cravo, Bernardo Fazendeiro,

Stephanie Hofmann, Ted Hopf, Magdalena Kozub-Karkut, Halvard Leira, Patrick Mello, Clara Oliveira, Falk Ostermann, Tomasz Pugacewicz, David Welch, and Anna Wojciuk. The usual disclaimers apply. A slightly longer version has appeared as '"Vision of itself" in Foreign Policy Analysis: From the role of ideas to identity and recognition', *Teoria Polityki*, September 2022.

Notes

1 They do so even though (other) realist theorists argued early that no such given set of preferences can be assumed: the effects of international anarchy are indeterminate (Wolfers 1962), and individual aims are not reducible to one that could express a maximization of utility (Aron 1962).
2 In his forceful critique of such systemic approaches, Andrew Moravcsik presented a liberal theory based on the domestic determinants of state preferences, including 'social identity' (Moravcsik 1997, 525 ff.), defined, in turn, by a set of shared preferences, whose origins are exogenous to the theory.
3 The study of belief-systems has been an important precursor of this turn. As the different contributions to Little and Smith (1988) however show, it mixes diverse methodologies that go from those undergirding cognitive psychology, social psychology to more sociological and discursive approaches. Important research also looked at the institutional underpinnings of norm and beliefs diffusion. See, just as an example, the studies on the end of the Cold War by Risse-Kappen (1994), Checkel (1997) and Evangelista (1999). Evangelista (2015) has later reflected on how ideas enter a more open process-tracing approach.
4 As Juliet Kaarbo (2003) rightly noted, role-theory has been a closely related research program. For this, see Breuning in this volume. For a socio-psychological approach, see Sucharov (2005).
5 This is closely connected to the research agenda on collective memories in Foreign Policy Analysis. For cases in Central and Eastern Europe, this has been analyzed by, for instance, Elizaveta Gaufman (2017), Maria Mälksoo (2009, 2015) and Jelena Subotić (2020a, b). This, in turn, relates to the materiality of many practices of 'commemoration' that feed into the scripts of national biographies. See e.g. Heath-Kelly (2016).
6 This position is hence exactly not metaphorical 'as if'. The state is a person and real, yet 'only because we act as if it were and consequently *make it so*' (Jackson 2004, 283). See also the discussion in Fleming (2017) which fruitfully does not start from the ontology of the state as such but on the implications of our practice of ascribing actions (or properties) to states.

References

Abdelal, Rawi, Mark Blyth, and Craig Parsons. 2010. "Introduction: Constructing the International Economy." In *Constructing the International Economy*, edited by Rawi Abdelal, Mark Blyth and Craig Parsons. Ithaca, NY: Cornell University Press, 1–19.
Akchurina, Viktoria, and Vincent Della Sala. 2018. "Russia, Europe and the Ontological Security Dilemma: Narrating the Emerging Eurasian Space." *Europe-Asia Studies* 70 (10): 1638–1655.
Allison, Graham T. 1971. *Essence of Decision: Explaining the Cuban Missile Crisis*. Boston: Little Brown.
Aron, Raymond. 1962. *Paix et guerre ente les Nntions*. Paris: Calmann-Lévy.
Astrov, Alexander, and Natalia Morozova. 2012. "Russia: Geopolitics from the Heartland." In *The Return of Geopolitics in Europe? Social Mechanisms and Foreign Policy Identity Crises*, edited by Stefano Guzzini. Cambridge: Cambridge University Press, 192–216.
Berenskoetter, Felix. 2007. "Friends, There Are No Friends? An Intimate Reframing of the International." *Millennium: Journal of International Studies* 35 (3): 647–676.
Berenskoetter, Felix. 2014a. "Friendship, Security and Power." In *Friendship and International Relations*, edited by Simon Koschut and Andrea Oelsner. Houndmills: Palgrave Macmillan, 51–71.
Berenskoetter, Felix. 2014b. "Parameters of a National Biography." *European Journal of International Relations* 20 (1): 262–288.
Berenskötter, Felix. 2020. "Anxiety, Time, and Agency." *International Theory* 12 (2): 273–290.
Bilgin, Pinar. 2012. "Turkey's 'Geopolitics Dogma'." In *The Return of Geopolitics in Europe? Social Mechanisms and Foreign Policy Identity Crises*, edited by Stefano Guzzini. Cambridge: Cambridge University Press, 151–173.

Browning, Christopher S., and Pertti Joenniemi. 2017. "Ontological Security, Self-Articulation and the Securitization of Identity." *Cooperation and Conflict* 52 (1): 31–47.

Bucher, Bernd, and Ursula Jasper. 2016. "Revisiting 'Identity' in International Relations: From Identity as Substance to Identifications in Action." *European Journal of International Relations* 23 (2): 391–415.

Campbell, David. 1990. "Global Inscription: How Foreign Policy Constitutes the United States." *Alternatives* XV (3): 263–286.

Campbell, David. 1992. *Writing Security: United States Foreign Policy and the Politics of Identity*. Minneapolis, MN: University of Minnesota Press.

Checkel, Jeffrey T. 1997. *Ideas and International Political Change: Soviet/Russian Behavior and the End of the Cold War*. New Haven, London: Yale University Press.

Diez, Thomas. 2004. "Europe's Others and the Return of Geopolitics." *Cambridge Review of International Affairs* 17 (2): 319–335.

Doty, Roxanne Lynn. 1993. "Foreign Policy as a Social Construction: A Post-Positivist Analysis of U.S. Counterinsurgency Policy in the Philippines." *International Studies Quarterly* 37 (3): 297–320.

Doty, Roxanne Lynn. 1996. *Imperial Encounters*. Minneapolis, London: University of Minnesota Press.

Dowding, Keith. 1991. *Rational Choice and Political Power*. Hants: Edward Elgar.

Ejdus, Filip, ed. 2017. *Memories of Empire and Entry into International Society: Views from the European Periphery*. Abingdon: Routledge.

Evangelista, Matthew. 1999. *Unarmed Forces: The Transnational Movement to End the Cold War*. Ithaca: Cornell University Press.

Evangelista, Matthew. 2015. "Explaining the Cold War's End: Process Tracing All the Way Down?" In *Process Tracing: From Metaphor to Analytic Tool*, edited by Andrew Bennett and Jeffrey T. Checkel. Cambridge: Cambridge University Press, 153–185.

Fleming, Sean. 2017. "Artificial Persons and Attributed Actions: How to Interpret Action-Sentences About States." *European Journal of International Relations* 23 (4): 930–950.

Freire, Maria Raquel. 2020. "EU and Russia Competing Projects in the Neighbourhood: An Ontological Security Approach." *Revista Brasileira de Política Internacional* 63 (1): e013.

Gaufman, Elizaveta. 2017. *Security Threats and Public Perception: Digital Russia and the Ukraine Crisis*. Cham: Palgrave Macmillan.

Giddens, Anthony. 1991. *Modernity and Self-Identity: Self and Society in the Late Modern Age*. Cambridge: Polity Press.

Goldstein, Judith, and Robert O. Keohane. 1993. "Ideas and Foreign Policy: An Analytical Framework." In *Ideas and Foreign Policy: Beliefs, Institutions, and Political Change*, edited by Judith Goldstein and Robert O. Keohane. Ithaca, NY: Cornell University Press, 3–30.

Gustafsson, Karl, and Nina C. Krickel-Choi. 2020. "Returning to the Roots of Ontological Security: Insights from the Existentialist Anxiety Literature." *European Journal of International Relations* 26 (3): 875–895.

Guzzini, Stefano, ed. 2012a. *The Return of Geopolitics in Europe? Social Mechanisms and Foreign Policy Identity Crises*. Cambridge: Cambridge University Press.

Guzzini, Stefano. 2012b. "Social Mechanisms as Micro-Dynamics in Constructivist Analysis." In *The Return of Geopolitics in Europe? Social Mechanisms and Foreign Policy Identity Crises*, edited by Stefano Guzzini. Cambridge: Cambridge University Press, 251–277.

Guzzini, Stefano. 2017. "Militarizing Politics, Essentializing Identities: Interpretivist Process Tracing and the Power of Geopolitics." *Cooperation and Conflict* 52 (3): 423–445.

Hagström, Linus. 2021. "Great Power Narcissism and Ontological (In)Security: The Narrative Mediation of Greatness and Weakness in International Politics." *International Studies Quarterly* 65 (2): 331–342.

Hansen, Flemming Splidsboel. 2016. "Russia's Relations with the West: Ontological Security Through Conflict." *Contemporary Politics* 22 (3): 359–375.

Hansen, Lene. 2006. *Security as Practice: Discourse Analysis and the Bosnian War*. London, New York: Routledge.

Heath-Kelly, Charlotte. 2016. *Death and Security: Memory and Mortality at the Bombsite*. Manchester: Manchester University Press.

Hoffmann, Stanley. 1978. *Primacy or World Order: American Foreign Policy since the Cold War*. New York: McGraw Hill.

Hopf, Ted. 2002. *Social Construction of International Politics: Identities and Foreign Policies, Moscow, 1955 and 1999*. Ithaca, NY: Cornell University Press.

Hopf, Ted. 2012. *Reconstructing the Cold War: The Early Years, 1945–1958*. Oxford: Oxford University Press.
Ish-Shalom, Piki. 2006. "Theory as a Hermeneutical Mechanism: The Democratic Peace and the Politics of Democratization." *European Journal of International Relations* 12 (4): 565–598.
Ish-Shalom, Piki. 2013. *Democratic Peace: A Political Biography*. Ann Arbor: The University of Michigan Press.
Jackson, Patrick Thaddeus. 2004. "Hegel's House, or 'People Are States Too'." *Review of International Studies* 30 (2): 281–287.
Jepperson, Ronald L., Alexander Wendt, and Peter J. Katzenstein. 1996. "Norms, Identity and Culture in National Security." In *The Culture of National Security*, edited by Peter J. Katzenstein. New York: Columbia University Press, 33–75.
Jervis, Robert. 1970. *The Logic of Images in International Relations*. Princeton: Princeton University Press.
Kaarbo, Juliet. 2003. "Foreign Policy Analysis in the Twenty-First Century: Back to Comparison, Forward to Identity and Ideas." *International Studies Review* 5 (2): 156–202.
Kazharski, Aliaksei. 2019. "Civilizations as Ontological Security? Stories of the Russian Trauma." *Problems of Post-Communism* 67 (1): 24–36.
Kinnvall, Catarina. 2004. "Globalization and Religious Nationalism: Self, Identity, and the Search for Ontological Security." *Political Psychology* 25 (5): 741–767.
Kinnvall, Catarina. 2017. "Feeling Ontologically (in)Secure: States, Traumas and the Governing of Gendered Space." *Cooperation and Conflict* 52 (1): 90–108.
Kinnvall, Catarina, and Jennifer Mitzen. 2020. "Anxiety, Fear, and Ontological Security in World Politics: Thinking with and Beyond Giddens." *International Theory* 12 (2): 240–256.
Kissinger, Henry A. 1957. *A World Restored*. Boston: Houghton Mifflin.
Klotz, Audie. 1995. *Norms in International Relations: The Struggle Against Apartheid*. Ithaca: Cornell University Press.
Kopper, Ákos. 2012. "The Oppressive Totality of the Past." *Alternatives* 37 (2): 121–132.
Krasner, Stephen D. 1982a. "Regimes and the Limits of Realism: Regimes as Autonomous Variables." *International Organization* 36 (2): 497–510.
Krasner, Stephen D. 1982b. "Structural Causes and Regime Consequences: Regimes as Intervening Variables." *International Organization* 36 (2): 185–205.
Kratochwil, Friedrich. 1978. *International Order and Foreign Policy: A Theoretical Sketch of Post-War International Politics*. Boulder, CO: Westview Press.
Kratochwil, Friedrich, and John Gerard Ruggie. 1986. "International Organization: A State of the Art on an Art of the State." *International Organization* 40 (4): 753–775.
Laffey, Mark, and Jutta Weldes. 1997. "Beyond Belief: From Ideas to Symbolic Technologies in the Study of International Relations." *European Journal of International Relations* 3 (2): 193–237.
Lerner, Adam B. 2019. "The Uses and Abuses of Victimhood Nationalism in International Politics." *European Journal of International Relations* 26 (1): 62–87.
Lerner, Adam B. 2021. "What's It Like to Be a State? An Argument for State Consciousness." *International Theory* 13 (2): 260–286.
Little, Richard, and Steve Smith, eds. 1988. *Belief Systems and International Relations*. Oxford: Basil Blackwell.
Lupovici, Amir. 2012. "Ontological Dissonance, Clashing Identities, and Israel's Unilateral Steps Towards the Palestinians." *Review of International Studies* 38 (4): 809–833.
Mälksoo, Maria. 2009. "The Memory Politics of Becoming European: The East European Subalterns and the Collective Memory of Europe." *European Journal of International Relations* 15 (4): 653–680.
Mälksoo, Maria. 2015. "'Memory Must Be Defended': Beyond the Politics of Mnemonical Security." *Security Dialogue* 46 (3): 221–237.
Mitzen, Jennifer. 2006. "Ontological Security in World Politics: State Identity and the Security Dilemma." *European Journal of International Relations* 12 (3): 341–370.
Moravcsik, Andrew. 1997. "Taking Preferences Seriously: A Liberal Theory of International Politics." *International Organization* 51 (4): 513–555.
Morozov, Viatcheslav. 2015. *Russia's Postcolonial Identity: A Subaltern Empire in a Eurocentric World*. Houndmills: Palgrave Macmillan.
Narozhna, Tanya. 2020. "State–Society Complexes in Ontological Security-Seeking in IR." *Journal of International Relations and Development* 23 (3): 559–583.
Narozhna, Tanya. 2022. "Misrecognition, Ontological Security and State Foreign Policy: The Case of Post-Soviet Russia." *Australian Journal of International Affairs* 76 (1): 76–97.

Neumann, Iver B. 1996. "Self and Other in International Relations." *European Journal of International Relations* 2 (2): 139–174.

Neumann, Iver B. 1999. *Uses of the Other: The 'East' in European Identity Formation*. Minneapolis: University of Minnesota Press.

Neumann, Iver B. 2004. "Beware of Organicism: The Narrative Self of the State." *Review of International Studies* 30 (2): 259–267.

Ó Tuathail, Gearóid, and Simon Dalby, eds. 1998. *Rethinking Geopolitics*. London and New York: Routledge.

Ostermann, Falk. 2019. *Security, Defense Discourse and Identity in NATO and Europe: How France Changed Foreign Policy*. Abingdon: Routledge.

Pizzorno, Alessandro. 1986. "Some Other Kinds of Otherness: A Critique of 'Rational Choice' Theories." In *Development, Democracy and the Art of Trespassing: Essays in Honor of Albert O. Hirschman*, edited by Alejandro Foxley, Michael S. McPherson and Guillermo O'Donnell. Notre Dame: Notre Dame University Press, 355–373.

Pizzorno, Alessandro. 2007. *Il velo della diversità. Studi su razionalità e riconoscimento*. Milano: Feltrinelli.

Pratt, Simon Frankel. 2017. "A Relational View of Ontological Security in International Relations." *International Studies Quarterly* 61 (1): 78–85.

Prozorov, Sergei. 2010. "The Other as Past and Present: Beyond the Logic of 'Temporal Othering' in IR Theory." *Review of International Studies* 37 (3): 1273–1293.

Ringmar, Erik. 1996. *Identity, Interest and Action: A Cultural Explanation of Sweden's Intervention in the Thirty Years War*. Cambridge: Cambridge University Press.

Risse-Kappen, Thomas. 1994. "Ideas Do Not Float Freely: Transnational Coalitions, Domestic Structures, and the End of the Cold War." *International Organization* 48 (2): 185–214.

Roshchin, Evgeny. 2006. "The Concept of Friendship: From Princes to States." *European Journal of International Relations* 12 (4): 599–624.

Ruggie, John Gerard. 1998. "What Makes the World Hang Together? Neo-Utilitarianism and the Social Constructivist Challenge." *International Organization* 42 (4): 855–886.

Rumelili, Bahar. 2004. "Constructing Identity and Relating to Difference: Understanding EU's Mode of Differentiation." *Review of International Studies* 30 (1): 27–47.

Rumelili, Bahar. 2015a. "Identity and Desecuritisation: The Pitfalls of Conflating Ontological and Physical Security." *Journal of International Relations and Development* 18 (1): 52–74.

Rumelili, Bahar. 2015b. "Ontological (In)Security and Peace Anxieties: A Framework for Conflict Resolution." In *Conflict Resolution and Ontological Security: Peace Anxieties*, edited by Bahar Rumelili. Abingdon: Routledge, 10–29.

Rumelili, Bahar. 2020. "Integrating Anxiety into International Relations Theory: Hobbes, Existentialism, and Ontological Security." *International Theory* 12 (2): 257–272.

Somers, Margaret R. 1994. "The Narrative Constitution of Identity: A Relational and Network Approach." *Theory and Society* 23 (5): 605–649.

Steinbruner, John D., Jr. 1974. *The Cybernetic Theory of Decision: New Dimensions of Political Analysis*. Princeton, NJ: Princeton University Press.

Subotić, Jelena. 2020a. "Foreign Policy and Physical Sites of Memory: Competing Foreign Policies at the Jasenovac Memorial Site." *International Politics* 57 (6): 1012–1029.

Subotić, Jelena. 2020b. *Yellow Star, Red Star: Holocaust Remembrance after Communism*. Ithaca, NY: Cornell University Press.

Subotić, Jelena, and Ayşe Zarakol. 2013. "Cultural Intimacy in International Relations." *European Journal of International Relations* 19 (4): 915–938.

Sucharov, Mira. 2005. *The International Self: Psychoanalysis and the Search for Israeli-Palestinian Peace*. Albany: SUNY Press.

Vennesson, Pascal. 2008. "Case Studies and Process Tracing: Theories and Practices." In *Approaches and Methodologies in the Social Sciences: A Pluralist Perspective*, edited by Donatella della Porta and Michael Keating. Cambridge: Cambridge University Press, 223–239.

Vieira, Marco A. 2017. "(Re-)Imagining the 'Self' of Ontological Security: The Case of Brazil's Ambivalent Postcolonial Subjectivity." *Millennium: Journal of International Studies* 46 (2): 142–164.

Wæver, Ole. 1993. "Societal Security: The Concept." In *Identity, Migration and the New Security Agenda in Europe*, edited by Ole Waever, Barry Buzan, Morten Kelstrup and Pierre Lemaitre. London: Pinter, 17–40.

Wæver, Ole. 1995. "Power, Principles and Perspectivism: Understanding Peaceful Change in Post-Cold War Europe." In *Peaceful Changes in World Politics*, edited by Heikki Patomäki. Tampere: Tampere Peace Research Institute, 208–282.

Wæver, Ole. 1996. "The Rise and Fall of the Inter-Paradigm Debate." In *International Theory: Positivism and Beyond*, edited by Steve Smith, Ken Booth and Marysia Zalewski. Cambridge: Cambridge University Press, 149–184.

Wæver, Ole. 1998. "Insecurity, Security and Asecurity in the Western European Non-War Community." In *Security Communities*, edited by Emanuel Adler and Michael Barnett. Cambridge: Cambridge University Press, 69–118.

Weldes, Jutta. 1996. "The Cultural Production of Crises: U.S. Identity and Missiles in Cuba." In *Cultures of Insecurity: States, Communities, and the Production of Danger*, edited by Jutta Weldes, Hugh Gusterson and Raymond Duvall. Minneapolis: University of Minnesota Press, 35–62.

Weldes, Jutta. 1999. *Constructing National Interests: The United States and the Cuban Missile Crisis*. Minneapolis: University of Minnesota Press.

Wendt, Alexander. 1999. *Social Theory of International Politics*. Cambridge: Cambridge University Press.

Wendt, Alexander. 2004. "The State as Person in International Theory." *Review of International Studies* 30 (2): 289–316.

Wight, Colin. 2004. "State Agency: Social Action without Human Activity?" *Review of International Studies* 30 (2): 269–280.

Wolfers, Arnold. 1962. *Discord and Collaboration: Essays on International Politics*. Baltimore, London: The Johns Hopkins University Press.

Zarakol, Ayşe. 2010. "Ontological (in)Security and State Denial of Historical Crimes: Turkey and Japan." *International Relations* 24 (1): 3–23.

Zarakol, Ayşe. 2011. *After Defeat: How the East Learned to Live with the West*. Cambridge: Cambridge University Press.

Zarakol, Ayşe. 2017. "States and Ontological Security: A Historical Rethinking." *Cooperation and Conflict* 52 (1): 48–68.

Zehfuss, Maja. 2001. "Constructivism and Identity: A Dangerous Liaison." *European Journal of International Relations* 7 (3): 315–348.

3
Ethnography
Iver B. Neumann

Introduction

The shortest possible description of ethnography is furnished by Fredrik Barth: ethnography is watching and wondering (see Eriksen 2015). Bronislaw Malinowski (1922) famously spoke about the ethnographer's data as the imponderabilia of native life, and the material from which one could identify cultural patterns.[1] Barth and Malinowski were both social anthropologists. In the professionalization of the social sciences that took place in the late 1800s and early 1900s, anthropology made off with the pre-modern and the non-modern, hence Malinowski spoke of 'native' life. With few textual sources at hand, anthropologists evolved ethnography as a new method. The basic idea was to interact with people to understand what they do and wonder about why they do things the way they do it, and which effects it has that they do it this way, or not that. So much for the *ethos* (Greek for *people*) in ethnography. The other part of the word hails from the Greek verb *graphein*, to write. Typically, ethnographers would live with their interlocutors, try to learn some of their language, put themselves in situations similar to those they saw that *the natives* were in, and then write a so-called community study – a well-rounded account of life in a specific village. More specialized studies, say of religious practices or of kinship structures, might follow.

Drawn by the pull of studying other groups of people by drawing on the same method, and by the push of an increasing dearth of *natives*, the method spread. Seeing that this was an apt method for capturing social forms, how people actually live and how their way of life is a determinant of their life chances, other professions began to draw on the method of ethnography as well. Geographers have long been keen on it, cultural sociologists have grown fond of it, and it has a presence in a number of other disciplines as well. Foreign Policy Analysis should be no exception.

Literature Review

There are no full-length monographs on foreign policy making based on relations between different agents using the ethnographic method. General works of particular importance include Riles (2001); Shore, Wright, and Però (2011); Mullers (2013); and Niezen and Sapignoli

(2017). We have a clutch of ethnographies of organizations whose work is key to foreign policy-making processes. These include international organizations (Garsten and Jacobsson 2011) like the European Space Agency (Zabusky 1995), the European Union (Shore 2000; Kuus 2014; Adler-Nissen and Drieschova 2019), and Association of Southeast Asian Nations (ASEAN; Nair 2019) as well as Foreign Ministries (Neumann 2012; Lequesne 2017), and non-governmental organizations (NGOs; Hopgood 2006; Hall 2022) as well as other state organizations (a nuclear weapons lab; Gustersen 1998). We also have some autobiographically based works written by people in the field on how foreign policy-relevant processes worked on them (Barnett 1997, 2003 on genocide; Dauphinée 2013 on war), and some books that draw more sporadically on ethnographic data (Pouliot 2010 on delegations to NATO; Adler-Nissen 2014 on the Danish foreign ministry, see Adler-Nissen in this volume). We also have so-called multi-sited work (Schia 2018 on UN peace and reconciliation work regarding Liberia). All of these are methodologically explicit, empirically exemplary, and highly recommended. I will return to most of them below, in order to illustrate certain points.

Three literatures in particular include a number of works that are not directly on foreign policy, but that often have indirect bearings thereon. They are, first, the literature on development (see references in Schia 2018), identity (see Guzzini in this volume) and migration (see Inglis, Li and Kadria 2019, part four). Note that we have little ethnographic work on diplomacy at postings, or on the corps diplomatique. Here, we have low-hanging fruit for a burgeoning ethnographer, for such studies could capture interaction from the point of view of field-working diplomats and also interaction between diplomats representing different countries who are all working in the field. These would complement studies of home-working diplomats, and so make for a thicker ethnographic description of diplomacy at work.

The geographer Merje Kuus (2013), herself perhaps the most prolific writer on the issue of ethnography and diplomacy, has noted that most interventions about ethnography on foreign policy had by then been programmatic rather than extant. It may be added that these programmatic interventions have not really caused much debate. The exception, which also served as Kuus's launching pad, was the debate in the London School of Economics and Political Science (LSE)-based International Relations journal *Millennium,* where the issue was what kind of political agendas ethnography have, have not, should, and should not serve (Vrasti 2008; Rancatore 2010; Sande Lie 2013). These debates basically concern the politics of situatedness, and are useful as such.

Key Terms and Concepts, Methodology

There are two key preconditions for doing ethnography: field access and cultural competence. When we talk about ethnography, a *field* means where you garnish your data. If you have no field to watch and wonder about, you cannot do ethnography. If you do not have field access, then other methods will have to be used to have any data at all. Foreign policy making tends to be an elite pursuit, and often elites have something to lose by being studied, so gaining access to the field is harder than gaining access to, say, the homeless, who rarely have anything to lose but often have something to gain by letting an outsider in (Nader 1972; Gustersen 1997; Shore and Nugent 2002; Holmes and Marcus 2005; Kuus 2020). With some elites, their secrets are theirs to give away. Not so with state officials, who by definition do their work on behalf of somebody or something else; a King, perhaps, or a state. Access to a ministry of foreign affairs (MFA) is, therefore, not any one official's to give, but will involve a complex bureaucratic procedure. It is no coincidence that the only two book-length ethnographies on a central locus of foreign policy making, MFAs that exist to date are both done by citizens of the state whose MFA they have studied (Neumann 2012 on Norway; Lequesne 2017 on France). Those two researchers were also insiders, in the sense that they were known to key people in the field beforehand, and so more easily trusted. The first key to field access lies here, in making yourself known to the keepers of the keys. Acquaintances help. So do the right professional institutional affiliations. My own way in was to make it known that I wanted a job on the inside. Half a year later, an offer to become a foreign policy planner materialized, and I was able to negotiate a deal where I was allowed to write something about my experience afterward, as long as I did not give details about substantial work pertaining to other states.

Having a job is an advantage for field access, but it is a disadvantage in the sense that you actually have to carry out work that may not be readily recognized as field work. To put it differently, your time is not your own. Note that there is also an ethical side to this. Observation should be open, that is, people should know that they are being studied. We do not talk about active acquiescence here, in the sense that you need written permissions all the time. It is rather a case of avoiding hidden observation. In practice, I told people that I was there also because I was interested in what they were doing and wanted to write about it as a researcher. As we got acquainted, they all forgot about this, which meant that I had access to most if not all the information I wanted. The main challenge turned out to be not the practical one of playing by the book, but the ethical one of using the material in a responsible manner (more on this below).

The fact that field access is so much easier to attain for citizens than for others, is in and of itself a methodological challenge, for the forgers of the ethnographic method, anthropologists, have traditionally been wary of picking fields that belong to the ethnographer's home culture. It is a fact that it is easy to become home blind, that is, you cannot get a holistic and detailed grasp on a society because what you see seems obvious, and so you do not really see it. There are, however, two central counter arguments to this. First, it is problematic to talk about *one's own culture*. To most citizens, the organizational cultures that surround foreign policy making will appear as partly foreign. One may certainly be a stranger in what is ostensibly *one's own* culture. A second argument in favor of doing ethnography in a field in which you have extensive cultural capital hails from the philosophy of science. It is impossible to sense social phenomena directly, if that means without some kind of prejudice, for without categories, sensing is not social, and so cannot be applied to the social. It takes a certain pre-understanding to organize what you see. The optimal relation between researcher and field is not, therefore, the greatest possible distance, with the researcher being a *tabula rasa* or clean slate relative to that which is to be observed. The optimal relation will be close enough to sort out and organize different kinds of information, and distant enough to afford analytical distance. To put it differently, ethnographers cannot be fully culturally competent, for then everything will be taken for granted, but neither can they be culturally illiterate (Dunn and Neumann 2016: 83–86). Cultural competence simply means that you understand enough of what you see to make proper data out of it. On the obvious side, in a tight environment like the MFA, it is impossible to use an interpreter, and it is very hard to be taken seriously if your command of the everyday language spoken as well as of English is not up to speed. A bit less obviously, you have to know something about general ministerial work, and on how to carry yourself. Not knowing what a demarche is, is OK. Not knowing how you write a text in an impersonal voice is not. In order to fit in and have conversations that may yield interesting data, you also have to know something about the political traditions of the state whose foreign policy making you are studying, and of the general global environment to which that foreign policy is pitched. The main point here is that it is your own autobiography that determines how much work is needed to classify and analyze what you experience. This calls for reflection on the significance of autobiographical *situatedness* (see below), and not for an outright ban on doing ethnography in *your own* culture.

There *are* ways of gaining field access to foreign policy making without actually setting foot in a state ministry. One of them is to work on a foreign posting to the country where you are, say, at the Nigerian High Commission to the Court of St. James (that is, in London) or the German General Consulate to Shanghai. Such posts are fully legitimate sites through which to access the foreign policy field.

Another possibility is to secure a job in an international organization, where state members' foreign policies may be observed as they are put into effect by the national delegations thereto (Kuus 2014). It is also possible to take up residence in an organization that works on and lobbies for specific foreign policy questions, say a developmental organization or a human rights NGO. All these are fine as long as you flag what you are doing. What is definitely not OK, however, is to take a job, say, as a cleaner, and then hang around a relevant site to engage in hidden observation.

There is also the possibility of doing a so-called multi-sited field work, where some kind of logic is used to identify more than one site which together will make up your field, and then "study it through" (Nyqvist 2013). Niels Schia (2018) did this in his study of UN peace and reconciliation. The logic here was processual, so Schia began by studying policy making in the UN Security Council (politicians) and at UN headquarters (bureaucrats), and then followed the process as it played out at UN headquarters in Monrovia, Liberia as well as in a Liberian state ministry and in the countryside.

A final word of advice on field access: if at all possible, get your permission to observe in writing. Unexpected situations that make you vulnerable may easily arise. For example, at one point during my second field work at the Norwegian MFA, where it had simply slipped my mind to get permission in writing, a high-ranking police officer who was working at the Norwegian embassy in Washington published an op-ed from which the MFA distanced itself. A journalist found out that I had written a scholarly article on diplomacy while I was working in the MFA, and asked why the MFA did not censor that. Given the lack of a written permit, the MFA was seemingly left caught looking inconsistent. That is not to any MFA's liking. I escaped unscathed because of my goodwill account, but it was a close shave.

Crucially, ethnography builds on what people say, what they do, and the difference between the two. As a discipline, social anthropology is skeptical to methods that only build on what people say, and more so the more what they say is decontextualized. Survey methods are considered especially dodgy. Interviews, particularly when done in the field, are considered much less dodgy, since the context is there. However, interviews still tend to capture only what people say, and what they say they do. Without interaction data that may complement data garnished by interviews, we cannot speak of the ethnographic method. A famous example concerns Margaret Mead's (1928) work on sexuality in Samoa, which highlighted how sexual practices there were much less shackled by social restrictions than were sexual mores in Mead's native contemporary America. Mead celebrated this, and went on to draw on her own work in order to argue for more sexual freedom in the west. However, in 1983, anthropologist Derek Freeman (1983) also did field work in Samoa, and documented a number of practices that were rather more restrictive than those noted by Mead (Freeman was also able to demonstrate that the practices in question were not new, but had also existed when Mead was in the field). He also demonstrated how certain power-laden practices, for example males crawling in to engage in sex with sleeping females, were systematically absent in Mead's account. A fracas ensued, and it has yet to be settled.

The Mead/Freeman debates may be used to demonstrate two key characteristics of the ethnographic method. First, given that ethnographers use themselves as their own research tools (it is they who pick out observations, decide which to note down, and then what will go into published texts), their understandings and explanations of phenomena cannot easily be separated from who they themselves are. This lends special poignancy to what kind of philosophy of science wagers (see Introduction to this volume) that an ethnographer places on his research. If the wager is social, and individuals are seen primarily as a result of their societies, then the ethnographer will tend to explain agency as following what March and Olsen (1995) refer to as a logic of appropriateness: people act in what they consider to be the appropriate fashion given their self-understanding and their understanding of the context of action. If the wager is on the individual understood as an interest-maximizing agent, on the other hand, then the ethnographer will tend to explain agency as following a logic of consequence, and Mead and Freeman may serve as illustrations.

Note the parallel between socially minded ethnographers and practitioners of the method called *memory work* here. Memory work understood as a scientific method was trail-blazed by feminists, and rests on the structural precondition that individuals are spawned by social structures. Some of those individuals go on to become researchers. If that is so, then introspection with a view to understanding how the researcher became the way she is, will be a good starting point from which to garner insights about the structure that made her (Haug n.d.). The method is built on introspection, the methodology is structural.

The Mead/Freeman debates also highlight another key issue in the philosophy of science, namely reproducibility. Freeman reproduced Mead's study in the sense that he drew on the same method and focused on the same phenomena. Other factors differed: he was male where Mead was female, he tended to explain things more in terms of a logic of consequence than a logic of appropriateness, etc. As a result, Freeman's account of sexuality in Samoa differed widely from Mead's. Given that ethnographers are not much given to the method of the natural experiment (see Lupton and Webb in this volume), there is little to do about this beyond highlighting the importance of explicit situatedness when ethnography is used, and the importance of putting field notes on display (one of the reasons why this case is so instructive is that Mead had archived her field notes). Situatedness, then, is an important part of the methodology of ethnography, that is, of thinking about how the data produced by the ethnographic method may be made to say something about more than those data themselves.

To be situated is to be placed or positioned (a related term is positionality) relative to contexts and other people: to one's own personal history, to the groups to which one belongs, in relation to other groups and other persons.[2] The first question to ask is what one is situated *as*. Physiology is an obvious place to start. In many cases, gender and ethnicity shows. The issue here is not self-identification, but how one is represented by interlocutors, and then looks are important. Then there is class, which is visible if not physiologically, then socially; the social shaping that appears in the body's form through walk, gesticulations, mimicry and sometimes also name and dress. Social scientists from Marcel Mauss (1979 [1936]) and Norbert Elias (1994 [1936]) to Pierre Bourdieu (1977) have done useful work in theorizing this as *habitus*. In addition to physiology and social factors, one may also be situated according to experiences that have left their traces in the psyche. In a classic essay on body techniques, anthropologist Marcel Mauss argued that the body is the place where three social systems meet: the physiological system, the social system, and the psychological system (Mauss 1979 [1936]). To situate oneself autobiographically is not only about the physiological (sex, physical handicap) and the social (e.g. class, gender), but also about psychological situating.

Situatedness is not only about reflecting on how others see you, but it is also about knowing yourself, for as a field-working ethnographer, you use yourself as a generator of data. You are, as it were, your own research tool, and researchers have to know their tools to know their trade. A field-working ethnographer cannot avoid forming relations with her interlocutors. The very idea that you should be able to stand on the outside of the relation, or not engage in any relation at all, and simply be a neutral and objective observer that would not influence your informants and the field of research, is founded on false assumptions (cf. Smith 2005, Harding 2015). Furthermore, since human interaction is by definition open ended, you cannot know what will happen during an interview or in the field beforehand, no matter how well prepared you are. The need for improvisation is therefore always there. If everything was simply there ready-made, social research would be like picking mushrooms or collecting firewood. It is not. Data are created, not collected.

This simple insight has wide-reaching implications. The informant will be affected by the presence of the researcher, influenced by your way of being, impressed by your way of posing questions. In some situations, you will be challenged intellectually and emotionally in ways you may not have anticipated. Informants will frequently, and often out of the blue, ask for your personal point of view on a specific question, ask you to comment on a difficult situation in the field or criticize one of your angles.[3] In situations like these, it is standard to experience departure from or even a break with some idea that you are somehow simply an objective observer. It is of course often crucial to keep one's own opinions, personal experiences, likes and dislikes in the background, in order to generate good empirical data. On the other hand, you have no choice but to bring your own perspectives, history, and points of view to the table. You may take solace from the philosopher Hans-Georg Gadamer, who argues that this situation is what he calls hermeneutically productive. Here we have arrived at a methodological question.

Understanding and interpreting social phenomena are in fundamental ways about the awkward meeting of different standpoints. When *the other* appears to be different from me, it means at the same time that I become aware of my own particularity. The ideal of objectivity thereby runs counter to the possible.

A second characteristic of hermeneutic productivity is how it is exactly by twisting questions and taking advantage of situations that you may be able to extract the most relevant data. It is right to strive toward bringing out the other person's viewpoints and perspectives, but the way in which it happens is precisely not by staying in the background, but instead by stressing certain topics, guiding the conversation toward the research questions, bringing out the informant's opinions by alluding to one's own and so on (cf. Brigg and Bleiker 2010). Here we come up against that old chestnut, that a lack of objectivity spells relativity. On this point, American feminist Sandra Harding offers help. Harding writes:

> In an important sense, our cultures have agendas and make assumptions that we as individuals cannot easily detect. Theoretically unmediated experience, that aspect of a group's or an individual's experience in which cultural influences cannot be detected, functions as a part of the evidence for scientific claims. [...] If the goal is to make available for critical scrutiny all the evidence marshalled for or against a scientific hypothesis, then this evidence too requires critical examination within scientific research processes. In other words, we can think of strong objectivity as extending the notion of scientific research to include systematic examination of such powerful background beliefs.
>
> *(Harding 1991, 150)*

To sum up so far, it is important for an ethnographer to situate oneself in relation to one's data creation, for the simple reason that ethnographers are their own research tools, and a good craftsman knows his tools. If researchers cannot effortlessly claim an objective *view from nowhere* from which to observe an unmediated reality, but have to factor in how the data used are mediated by a number of factors, then they also owe it to their readers to account for as much of that mediation as possible.

Empirical Illustration: Applying the Method

Once in the field, the main task is to transform observations into data. Given the personal nature of this process, it would be counter-productive to draw up a one-size fits all-formula for how this should be done. The most important thing is to immerse oneself in interactions while at the same time maintaining the bird's-eye perspective on those interactions. It is a good idea to seek out the widest possible range of interlocutors, contexts and situations. An organization cannot function without its heads, but interaction with administrators, errand-boys and data engineers will often open new vistas of investigation and reveal new kinds of integration and tension within the organization. Field work which is based mostly on the ethnographer's peers will by definition be inferior to a more widely based one, simply because the latter will be based on a wider and therefore more solid sample of interaction data. By the same token, an ethnographer should be open to all kinds of data. One may be looking for material on a specific topic — say, consensus-building — but it is important to be open to the possibility that other lines of inquiry may present themselves and be followed.

One way to make oneself available to new kinds of situation is by joining some of the organization's trade unions, sports clubs and other clubs. Another is to entertain guests at home. Chances are that there will be return invitations, which will open the door to interaction with diplomats in a new kind of context, namely *en famille*. A third is to volunteer for chores that bring you into contact with new parts of the organization.

If the creation of interaction is an idiosyncratic affair, what comes next is a mandatory part of all ethnographic work, namely the writing down of notes. As soon as possible after something has happened, it should be written down. Some ethnographers take to the hallway or even the lavatory to write down their notes, others do it in bed at day's end. If at all possible, it should be done the same day. Initial notes will often be taken by hand, and then ordered and creased out when put on a computer. It is important to write down more than what you think is of obvious importance, for in light of future experiences, recursive epiphanies may occur. When I feel a whiff of incomprehension about the proceedings I am enveloped in, I always write down the sequence of events and a couple of quotes, on the assumption that, when the reason for my incomprehension eventually comes to light, the sequence leading to that moment may serve as a story line when data are to be transformed into text.

It is my experience that scholars speak too little about text production. This has been a topic in the social sciences since the late 1960s, when poststructuralists like Roland Barthes and Michel Foucault problematized the death of the author. Poststructural anthropologists followed up in the 1970s by asking who produced ethnographic data. Autobiographical concerns were firmly tied to textual situatedness and produced a string of works on the matter, with the locus classicus being James Clifford and George Marcus's (1986) *Writing Culture: The Poetics and Politics of Ethnography*. Michael Shapiro formulated the main issue at stake as follows:

> Here is the epistemological rub: the idea that lives are "represented" by an obtrusive, scientifically oriented form of discourse. With this idea, central to a bankrupt version

> of empiricism, comes a failure to appreciate that biographers are writers who participate in representational practices, and that their texts impose meaning on lives. When one recognizes the existence of these practices, the knowledge problematic shifts from the accumulation of so-called facts about a life to the writing itself.
>
> (Shapiro 1988, 72)

There is certainly an element of 'what happens to me when I write in this and that fashion' in all textual production. There is also an intersubjective element in textual situatedness. Every writer has one of more implied readers or imagined personae that they expect will read the text. These readers will not coincide with actual readers, for who knows by whom and in which contexts a given text will be read. Still, the more one thinks through who the implied readers may be, the better one situates the text for the implied reader.

As to the writing itself, I am always worried when students say that they are almost finished with a project and 'just have to write it up'. To me, comprehension does not antecede the writing process. On the contrary, it resides in that process. I therefore try to shape my field notes as bits of fairly finished text, and to find opportunities while in the field to sit down and try out certain story lines. Once I have some text, it almost always becomes clear that I need interaction data to round out the story. This is a nice stimulus to further work when one is actually in the field. If it happens after field work, it may also be highly frustrating, for access to the MFA may by then be limited, or even closed. A stop-gap may then be to interview already established interlocutors, but this alternative method will usually yield somewhat different data than would interaction.

The historian Hayden White (1973: 1–42) has drawn attention to certain narrative characteristics that cannot be avoided. One is the choice of protagonists. Histories will often have a hero. In ethnographies, that hero is quite often the ethnographer her or himself (Sontag 1994 [1963]; Hartman 2007). One particularly good example of this is Michael Barnett's (1997) article about how he, as an instant Rwanda expert in the UN during the 1994 genocide, was socialized into defending non-action by the system within which he served. Barnett's exemplary text may also serve to illustrate another key point made by White, which is that any history will belong to a genre, say comedy or tragedy, and genre conventions will in and of themselves shape the history in question. Barnett's text is a tragedy: things go south. In ancient Greek tragedy, events are tragic not only because they end badly, but also because they have to end badly; once a certain train of events is in motion, they cannot be stopped. This sense of inevitability is part and parcel of the tragic genre's history, and so the question of whether or not events discussed are to be understood as inevitable or not will be activated by anyone who chooses the tragic genre. By the same token, in text written in the comic genre, where the ethnographer chooses a happy ending, there is a tendency for the hero (that is, the ethnographer himself) to look somewhat bumbling (see Neumann 2007 for an example of what van Maanen 2001 calls a 'confessional tale'; see also Kušić and Záhora 2020).

A trick that has come in handy for me on a number of occasions is to ask main interlocutors to read drafts. The comments they offer will often turn out to be highly useful new data, either because their readings will be at loggerheads with your own in interesting ways, or because they will foreground and background quite different things than you have yourself. Anthropologist Hugh Gusterson (1998) even invited key informants to write their own retorts to his ethnography and published them as an appendix to his book.

One last point on the writing up of an ethnographic text concerns the ethics of the matter. Where there are elites, there is secrecy. In most state bureaucracy, it is actually illegal to publish documents pertaining to decision making. Rather a lot of the information that an ethnographer will gain will have been given in confidence. The problem is not as great as someone with no experience of field work might imagine, for the simple reason that the lion's share of secret information will only remain secret for a relatively short time. Documents are often stamped 'secret' simply because their authors want them to appear more attractive, so that the chances that they will be read and perhaps be influential will increase. Still, one will do well to consider what kind of material that may be published, and what not.

A particularly pressing problem is that of anonymity. A text that contains material that will make it possible to identify diplomats, is potentially damaging to the careers of those diplomats, and so should not be published. Again, in practice this problem often turns out to be less pressing than someone who has no experience with writing up ethnographic research may imagine. The reason is that the ethnographic method is particularly apt to capture practices, identities and social forms. This may be done with scant attention to political substance. It is my experience that details which look potentially compromising and at the same time hard to avoid to begin with, tend to crease out as the writing up proceeds. Again, it is often useful to let one or more of your main interlocutors look at your draft texts, for diplomats will be highly tuned to what kind of things that may prove damaging to their kind, and will often be prickly about things that even a seasoned student of diplomacy would not expect.

Ethics does not only concern the care of the other, but also the care of the self. You want to do right by your interlocutors, but you also want to live by your scholarly professional ethics. For the student of foreign policy making, this involves a balancing act between spelling out the logics of the organizations that participate therein as a social form on the one hand, and of maintaining your ties to your interlocutors on the other. When you hold back on details about delicate matters, you do so to defend your informants, but you also do so to defend your own future access to the field.

Conclusion

Ethnography is a nice – in my view, the best available – method when it comes to capturing the social form of the organizations active in the foreign policy process. We have some fine work on this which typically pertain to international organizations and foreign ministries. We lack relevant ethnographic studies of state organizations such as parliamentarian foreign affairs committees and diplomatic postings, as well as of party secretariats, NGOs and networks (but see Constantinou 2006, 2021; Bleiker and Butler 2016). It is also a highly apt way of studying what different kinds of foreign policy does to the respective life chances of different groups of people who have to live with their effect. While we have some ethnobiographical studies of how effects of foreign policies such as genocide and war affect scholars themselves, the many extant studies that look at the effects of foreign policies do so without linking those effects to the actual foreign policies in question. Here we have a research question that is ripe for the picking, either in the form that foreign policy scholars re-read such studies and link them back to their own areas of expertise, or in the form that new work is undertaken.

Let me end by wishing students and colleagues who intend to study these and other issues by drawing on ethnographic methods well, and offer these final pieces of advice in the spirit of Micawber and Douglas Adams (1979): Do not despair when it comes to field access. There are more ways than one to skin a cat. Do not despair when it comes to interpreting your notes. Something will jump out on you. And do not despair of getting your material published. Sooner or later, your ship will come in.

Acknowledgment

I would like to thank Rebecca Adler-Nissen, Stefano Guzzini, Niels Nagelhus Schia, and the editors of this volume for help with this chapter.

Notes

1 The best full-length introduction to ethnographic method in general remains van Maanen (2011 [1988]). For foreign policy purposes, Garsten and Nyqvist (2013) is also very valuable. For even more specialized purposes, see de Guevara and Bøås (2020).
2 The discussion of situatedness, also called positionality, draws on Neumann and Neumann 2018; see also Kuus 2018; Mc Cluskey and Charalambous 2021.
3 Anthropologists often talk about the importance of not *going native*, that is, of maintaining one's distance to how one's interlocutors see things and not be socialized by them to see that as an obvious thing. See Okely and Callaway (2002); Brady (2017).

References

Adams, Douglas. 1979. *The Hitchhiker's Guide to the Galaxy*. London: Pan.
Adler-Nissen, Rebecca. 2014. *Opting Out of the European Union: Diplomacy, Sovereignty and European Integration*. Cambridge: Cambridge University Press.
Adler-Nissen, Rebecca, and Alena Drieschova. 2019. "Track-Change Diplomacy: Technology, Affordances, and the Practice of International Negotiations." *International Studies Quarterly* 63 (3): 531–545; including the online appendix "Ethnographic Methods: Participant Observation, Documents and Interviews". Doi: 10.1093/isq/sqz030 (last accessed 27 January 2021).
Barnett, Michael. 2003. *Eyewitness to a Genocide: The United Nations and Rwanda*. Ithaca, NY: Cornell University Press.
Barnett, Michael N. 1997. "The UN Security Council, Indifference, and Genocide in Rwanda." *Cultural Anthropology* 12 (4): 551–578.
Bleiker, Roland, and Sally Butler. 2016. "Radical Dreaming: Indigenous Art and Cultural Diplomacy." *International Political Sociology* 10 (1): 56–74.
Bliesemann de Guevara, Berit, and Morten Bøås, eds. 2020. *Doing Fieldwork in Areas of International Intervention: A Guide to Research in Violent and Closed Contexts*. Bristol: Bristol University Press.
Bourdieu, Pierre. 1977. *Outline of a Theory of Practice*. Cambridge: Cambridge University Press.
Brady, Ivan. 2017. "Other Places and the Anthropology of Ourselves: Early Fieldwork in Tuvalu." *Qualitative Inquiry* 23 (3): 179–191.
Brigg, Morgan, and Roland Bleiker. 2010. "Autoethnographic International Relations: Exploring the Self as a Source of Knowledge." *Review of International Studies* 36 (3): 779–798.
Clifford, James, and George Marcus. 1986. *Writing Culture: The Poetics and Politics of Ethnography*. Berkeley, CA: University of California Press.
Constantinou, Costas M. 2006. "On Homo-Diplomacy." *Space and Culture* 9 (4): 351–364.
Constantinou, Costas M. 2021. "Around the Broken Chair." *Hague Journal of Diplomacy* 16 (1): 120–132.
Dunn, Kevin C., and Iver B. Neumann. 2016. *Undertaking Discourse Analysis for Social Research*. Ann Arbor, MI: University of Michigan Press.
Elias, Norbert. 1994 [1939]. *The Civilizing Process*. Oxford: Blackwell.
Eriksen, Thomas Hylland. 2015. *Fredrik Barth – An Intellectual Biography*. London: Pluto.
Freeman, Derek. 1983. *Margaret Mead and Samoa*. Cambridge: Harvard University Press.
Garsten, Christina, and Kerstin Jacobsson. 2011. "Transparency and Legibility in International Institutions: The UN Global Compact and Post-political Global Ethics." *Social Anthropology* 19 (4): 378–393.
Garsten, Christina, and Anette Nyqvist, eds. 2013. *Organisational Anthropology: Doing Ethnography in and among Complex Organisations*. London: Pluto Press.
Gustersen, Hugh. 1997. "Studying up Revisited." *Political and Legal Anthropology Review* 20 (1): 114–119.
Gusterson, Hugh. 1998. *Nuclear Rites: A Weapons Laboratory at the End of the Cold War*. Berkeley, CA: University of California Press.

Hall, Nina. 2022. *Transnational Advocacy in the Digital Era, Think Global, Act Local*. Oxford: Oxford University Press.

Harding, Sandra. 1991. *Whose Science? Whose Knowledge? Thinking from Women's Lives*. Ithaca, NY: Cornell University Press.

Harding, Sandra. 2015. *Objectivity and Diversity. Another Logic of Scientific Research*. Chicago, IL: University of Chicago Press.

Hartman, Tod. 2007. "Beyond Sontag as a Reader of Lévi-Strauss: 'Anthropologist as Hero'." *Revisited Anthropology Matters Journal* 9 (2): 1–11.

Haug, Frigga. No date. *Memory-work as a Method of Social Science Research: A Detailed Rendering of Memory-Work Method*. Available from http://www.friggahaug.inkrit.de/documents/memorywork-researchguidei7.pdf (last accessed 15 January 2021).

Holmes, Douglas R., and George E. Marcus. 2005. "Culture of Expertise and the Management of Globalization: Towards the Re-functioning of Ethnography." In *Global Assemblages: Technology, Politics and Ethics as Anthropological Problems*, edited by Aihwa Ong and Stephen J. Collier. Oxford: Blackwell, 235–252.

Hopgood, Stephen. 2006. *Keepers of the Flame: Understanding Amnesty International*. Ithaca, NY: Cornell University Press.

Inglis, Christin, Wei Li, and Binod Khadria, eds. 2019. *The SAGE Handbook of International Migration*. London: SAGE.

Kuus, Merje. 2013. "Foreign Policy and Ethnography: A Sceptical Intervention." *Geopolitics* 18 (1): 115–131.

Kuus, Merje. 2014. *Geopolitics and Expertise: Knowledge and Authority in European Diplomacy*. Hoboken, NJ: Wiley Blackwell.

Kuus, Merje. 2018. "Transnational Institutional Fields: Positionality and Generalization in the Study of Diplomacy." *Political Geography* 67 (4): 156–165.

Kuus, Merje. 2020. "Professions and their Expertise: Charting the Spaces of 'Elite' Occupations." *Progress in Human Geography* 45 (2). Available from https://doi.org/10.1177/0309132520950466.

Kušić, Katarina, and Jakub Záhora, eds. 2020. *Fieldwork as Failure: Living and Knowing in the Field of International Relations*. Bristol: E-International Relations.

Lequesne, Christian. 2017. *Ethnographie du Quai d'Orsay. Les Pratiques des Diplomats Français*. Paris: CNRS éditions.

Malinowski, Bronislaw. 1961 [1922]. *Argonauts of the Western Pacific: An Account of Native Enterprise and Adventure in the Archipelagoes of Melanesian New Guinea*. New York: Dutton.

March, James G., and Johan P. Olsen. 1995. *Democratic Governance*. New York: Free Press.

Mauss, Marcel. 1979 [1936]. "The Notion of Body Techniques." In *Sociology and Psychology: Essays*, edited by Marcel Mauss. London: Routledge & Kegan Paul, 95–123.

Mc Cluskey, Emma, and Constadina Charalambous, eds. 2021. *Security, Ethnography and Discourse: Transdisciplinary Encounters*. London: Routledge.

Mead, Margaret. 1928. *Coming of Age in Samoa: A Psychological Study of Primitive Youth for Western Civilisation*. New York: William Morrow. Available from https://archive.org/details/comingofageinsam-00mead (last accessed 4 January 2021).

Mullers, Birgit. 2013. *The Gloss of Harmony: The Politics of Policy Making in Multilateral Organizations*. New York: Pluto.

Nader, Laura. 1972. "Up the Anthropologist: Perspectives Gained From Studying Up." In *Reinventing Anthropology*, edited by D. E. Hymes. New York: Pantheon, 284–311.

Nair, Deepak. 2019. "Saving Face in Diplomacy: A Political Sociology of Face-to-face Interactions in the Association of Southeast Asian Nations." *European Journal of International Relations* 25 (3): 672–697.

Neumann, Iver B. 2007. "'A Speech that the Entire Ministry May Stand for', or: Why Diplomats Never Produce Anything New." *International Political Sociology* 1 (2): 183–200.

Neumann, Iver B. 2012. *At Home with the Diplomats: Inside a European Ministry of Foreign Affairs*. Ithaca, NY: Cornell University Press.

Neumann, Cecilie Basberg, and Iver B. Neumann. 2018. *Situated Research Methodology – Autobiography, Field, Text*. London: Palgrave Pivot.

Niezen, Ronald, and Maria Sapignoli, eds. 2017. *Palaces of Hope – The Anthropology of Global Organizations*. Cambridge: Cambridge University Press.

Nyqvist, Anette. 2013. "Access to All Stages? Studying Through Policy in a Culture of Accessibility." In *Organizational Anthropology – Doing Ethnography in and among Complex Organizations,* edited by Christina Garsten and Anette Nyqvist. London: Pluto, 91–119.

Okely, Judith, and Helen Callaway, eds. 2002. *Anthropology and Autobiography.* London: Routledge.

Pouliot, Vincent. 2010. *International Security in Practice: The Politics of NATO-Russia Diplomacy.* New York: Cambridge University Press.

Rancatore, Jason P. 2010. "It *is* Strange: A Reply to Vrasti." *Millennium* 39 (1): 65–77.

Riles, Annelise. 2001. *The Network Inside Out.* Ann Arbor, MI: University of Michigan Press.

Sande Lie, Jon Harald. 2013. "Challenging Anthropology: Anthropological Reflections on the Ethnographic Turn in International Relations." *Millennium* 41 (2): 201–220.

Schia, Niels Nagelhus. 2018. *Franchised States and the Bureaucracy of Peace.* London: Palgrave Macmillan.

Shapiro, Michael J. 1988. *The Politics of Representation: Writing Practices in Biography, Photography, and Policy Analysis.* Madison, WI: University of Wisconsin Press.

Shore, Cris. 2000. *Building Europe: The Cultural Politics of European Integration.* London: Routledge.

Shore, Chris, and Stephen Nugent, eds. 2002. *Elite Cultures: Anthropological Perspectives.* New York: Routledge.

Shore, Cris, Susan Wright, and Davide Però, eds. 2011. *Policy Worlds: Anthropology and the Analysis of Contemporary Power.* Oxford: Berghahn.

Smith, Dorothy E. 2005. *Institutional Ethnography: A Sociology for the People.* Lanham, MD: Alta Mira Press.

Sontag, Susan. 1994 [1963]. *Against Interpretation.* London: Vintage.

Van Maanen, John. 2011 [1988]. *Tales of the Field: On Writing Ethnography.* Second edition. Chicago, IL: University of Chicago Press.

Vrasti, Wanda. 2008. "The Strange Case of Ethnography and International Relations." *Millennium* 37 (2): 279–301.

White, Hayden. 1973. *Metahistory: The Historical Imagination in Nineteenth-Century Europe.* Baltimore, MD: Johns Hopkins University Press.

Zabusky, Stacia E. 1995. *Launching Europe: An Ethnography of European Cooperation in Space Science.* Princeton, NJ: Princeton University Press.

4
Norms and Norm Contestation
Phil Orchard and Antje Wiener

Introduction

Can International Relations (IR) theory, particularly constructivism, and Foreign Policy Analysis (FPA) work together? It has long been argued that there is a disconnect between FPA and IR theory. Juliet Kaarbo, in particular, has argued that this occurs because "domestic and decision-making factors and conceptions of agency are undertheorized and underdeveloped in contemporary IR theory" Kaarbo 2015, 189). And, while Valerie Hudson and Benjamin Day acknowledge that "bridges seem more easily built between FPA and constructivist schools of IR" they also argue that ideational forces alone cannot be an explanation: "That FPA critique is simple: only human beings have ideas… It isn't 'ideas all the way down'; it is *human agents* all the way down" (Hudson and Day 2019, 9, 11).

However, if, as Valerie Hudson has argued, FPA has "an actor-specific focus, based upon the argument that all that occurs between nations and across nations is grounded in human decision makers acting singly or in groups" (Hudson 2005, 1), we would argue that constructivism and FPA have actually become if not theoretically entwined then two complementary theoretical perspectives to understand decision-making at the international, transnational, and domestic levels. These critiques, as we argue below, reflect rather early constructivist theorizing which has been addressed in more recent work (Acharya 2004; Betts and Orchard 2014). Particularly important is the development of norm contestation, which reflects societal practices in which rules, regulations, or procedures are critically questioned. Contestation specifically focuses on how societal actors gain access to shaping these norms in ways that can have both negative and positive effects on how a norm is understood (Wiener 2014, 2018). This argument is rooted in the principle of contestedness which

> Reflects the agreement that, in principle, the norms, rules and principles of governance are contested. They therefore require regular contestation in order to work. To that end, it is suggested to establish organizing principles (type 2 norms) at an imagined intermediary level of governance. Thus, the legitimacy gap between fundamental

norms (type 1) and standardized procedures (type 3 norms) is filled by access to regular contestation (as opposed to ad-hoc contestation) for all involved stakeholders.

(Wiener 2014, 1)

It follows that enhancing access to regular contestation increases legitimacy. In light of this principle, "only a contested norm can ever be a good norm" (Wiener 2020: 197).

This chapter explores these developments in three stages. We begin by examining how norm research has developed over the past 30 years, framed around three specific moves that have added layers to constructivist theorizing: a focus on the *social* in global politics, the adaptation of norms in processes of policymaking, and finally a renewed focus on the role that politics plays in processes of norm contestation. We then focus specifically on exploring how norm contestations can lead to behaviorally induced changes in norms (either improving them or undermining them and potentially leading to violations) through processes of proactive, reactive, and interpretive contestations. To better explore how norm contestations link to foreign policy decision-making, we end the chapter with an illustration of the case of the US response to Syria's use of chemical weapons during the Obama and Trump administrations, including air strikes against the Syrian military in 2017 and 2018.

The Development of Norm Research in Three Moves

Constructivism first emerged in IR in the late 1980s and early 1990s, and is today "firmly established in mainstream IR theory" (Adler 2013, 112). But – as a relatively new approach – it has also continued to evolve. Thus, many of the critiques that FPA scholars have exposed it to, particularly around its neglect of human agency, *were* true of early norm research. Thus, Kaarbo, for instance, argues that constructivism pays too little attention to how "the social is constructed," that it fails to conceptualize how norms are contested and negotiated and ignores domestic processes, and that it presumes a too strong connection between culture and policymaking (Kaarbo 2015, 201–203). But let us briefly explore how constructivism has changed in ways that already address many of these criticisms.

In other work, we have argued that norm research within constructivism has gone through three distinct conceptual moves (Orchard and Wiener forthcoming). Each of these moves was integral to the development of norm research, but each one has also introduced its own set of issues and limitations. The first introduced a focus on the *social* in global politics, the second the adaptation of norms in processes of policymaking, and the third has been a renewed focus on the role that politics plays in processes of norm contestation.

The above critiques tend to focus on the first move, which introduced a focus on the social in global politics. This focus included two important developments: exploring the role of 'social facts' alongside material facts at the international level, including norms, standards, regulations, rules, and ideas (Ruggie 1993; Searle 1995); and a move away from an agent-centered perspective to instead focus on agents and structures existing in a mutually constitutive manner (Wendt 1999). These shifts were critically important, but much of this early work still sought to "bracket" agents and structures (Finnemore 1996, 25), focusing on the effects one had on the other.

For instance, in Martha Finnemore and Kathryn Sikkink's three-stage norm life cycle model (Finnemore and Sikkink 1998) norm entrepreneurs play a critical role in the initial stage of norm emergence in placing issues on to the international agenda. However, following the emergence of a new norm, early adopting states become norm leaders and socialize other states to follow them through a variety of mechanisms including legitimation effects, self-esteem effects, and pressure for conformity. Once a critical mass of states adopts a new norm, it passes a threshold or tipping point. After this point, the new norm is so widely accepted that it is "internalized by actors and achieve a 'taken-for-granted' quality that make conformance with the norm almost automatic" (Risse and Sikkink 1999, 15; see also Finnemore and Sikkink 1998).

The problem with this model is that it creates both a limited understanding of agency and of how norms are actually understood. With respect to agency, the model treats norm entrepreneurs as both being present only at the early stages of norm emergence and being treated as part of an outside-in process, with the goal to influence states as unitary actors. It neglects the possibility that states can be norm entrepreneurs (Orchard 2014; Davies and True 2017). It also discounts the capacity of actors within government, such as the US President, to be norm entrepreneurs with their own sources of legitimacy, authority, and persuasion (Orchard and Gillies 2015, 491). A similar issue exists with the life cycle culminating in a norm that is presumed to have a fixed identity, a "stability assumption" in other words, when it is institutionalized at the international level (McKeown 2009, 9; Wiener 2014, 23). Further, the model also sees domestic factors drop out as the life cycle runs its course: "domestic influences are strongest at the early stage of a norm's life cycle, and domestic influences lessen significantly once a norm has become institutionalized in the international system" (Finnemore and Sikkink 1998, 893). Combined, these remove the capacity of societal agents to understand, challenge, and re-create a given norm in different forms rather than just being norm takers. And, by focusing only on norms that exist and shape state behavior, it also "necessarily brackets the international ethics question of whether or not a norm is 'good' or 'bad', 'just' or unjust'" a problem that Havercroft (2018, 117) has referred to as *cryptonormativism*.

These problems led to a *second move* exploring how international norms were adapted in processes of policymaking. Beginning with Amitav Acharya's work (2004, 247–249) on localization – a process through which agents build congruences between international norms and local beliefs and practices – this move focused on how individual actors – particularly at the domestic level – were able to alter norms to fit their own cultural and institutional contexts. This includes processes of domestic implementation and local translation that can also see national-level legal and constitutional frameworks and domestic political institutions playing important roles (Simmons 2009; Busby 2010; Betts and Orchard 2014; Zimmermann 2017). Regional level institutions can also shape domestic interpretations of international norms (Checkel 2005).

This move also expanded our understandings of norm entrepreneurs, seeing them compete against alternative frames put forward by different sets of actors, winning such framing contests when states accept these new understandings (Payne 2001; Krebs and Jackson 2007, 44–45). *Antipreneurs* may not put forward new understandings, but instead seek to "defend the entrenched normative status quo against challenges" by seeking to refute claims and undermining any new norms (Bloomfield 2016, 321). Thus, Alan Bloomfield identifies Russia as an antipreneur with respect to the Responsibility to Protect (R2P) doctrine by implacably resisting the "accumulation of precedents which would otherwise strengthen a new norm" (Bloomfield 2016, 324). Alternatively, *norm saboteurs* may seek to undermine efforts to adhere to existing norms and thereby undermine the existing status quo, as Andrea Schneiker has argued the Trump administration did with respect to multilateral organizations such as the UN Human Rights Council or the World Trade Organization (Schneiker 2021, 107, 111). Such efforts may mean that wins are not possible. Opposition may cause potential changes to be stymied, stalled, or blocked (Bob 2012, 32).

Even with these developments, this move introduced its own issues by inadvertently leading to an *ontologization* of norms which focused on the structural effects of norms rather than their socially constructed quality – agents were viewed as shaping the norms, rather than engaging with their underlying legitimacy. This has led into the *third move*, one which focuses on norms as processes which are subject to interpretation and contestation, and which will be explored in the next section.

Norm Contestation: Key Terms and Concepts

Contestation allows us to understand norms in two key ways. The first is that contestation highlights the importance of conceiving of norms as both indicators of *normality* (i.e. indicating standards of appropriate behavior) and of *normativity* (i.e. indicating moral principles that ought to be applied). The second is that it highlights the "dual quality of norms," that norms "are both structuring and socially constructed through interaction in a context. While stable over particular periods, they always remain flexible by definition" (Wiener 2007, 49).

Today's norms researchers especially take account of practices of norm contestation and ask how contestation affects norm-change or stability, whether and if so how contestation affects normative order, as well as more fundamentally how contestation contributes to norm-generation and change, and who has access to contestation? These questions are approached by a research operationalization that distinguishes between practices of contestation and validation, and which begins by identifying norm conflicts to then follow the conflict to local sites of contestation, then identify the involved societal agents, and their opportunities of access to contestation.

The practice of norm contestations generates norm conflicts, which are distinguishable according to two distinct takes of how agents interact amongst each other and vis-à-vis specific norms. The first take considers the challenge-change relationship to take place between a given agent (A) and a given norm (N1) which produces a specific understanding of that norm for that agent – this is the A-N1 relationship. While this interaction may be repeated, it is always between one or more agents (A+1) and a given norm and may reflect two types of contestation: one that is deliberate or one that is interpretive. By contrast, the second take considers the challenge-change relation to take place between a variety of agents (A1, A2, and so on) who are part of a conflictive encounter. During that encounter, norms are challenged and changed. And it is expected that as a norm-generative practice, contestation generates mutually recognized norms or normative meaning, as it were, in addition to normality. Here, the distinction between reactive contestation (objection to norm violation or to compliance with a norm) and proactive contestation (critical engagement with a norm) is helpful. All agents bring individual "normative baggage" to international encounters (Wiener 2010, 203) which may result in consensus or dissensus in a negotiation. In addition, it has been demonstrated that reactive contestation includes both discursive and behaviorally expressed disagreement (i.e., protest, resistance or contention) whereas proactive contestation is performed through iterated discursive interaction. According to the quod omnes tangit principle, proactive contestation ideally includes the highest number among the multitude of affected stakeholders (Wiener 2018, 217). This latter type of contestation is therefore key for generating norm(ative) change such as, for example, shared meanings-in-use about extant, emerging, or changing norms and thereby enable compromise.

As Anette Stimmer and Lea Wisken (2019, 516–519) have shown, the practice of contestation can be either a deliberate or an inadvertent process. Therefore, contestation should be understood as including "any differences in the understanding of norms, no matter what the source."

Deliberate contestations reflect societal agents knowingly contesting different understandings of a norm's validity, which leads to a norm conflict. But agents can also have *unknowingly* adopted different interpretations of what a given norm means. Societal agents reflect a notion of a corporate actor: they are composed of many individuals, whether in a state, organization, or other agglomeration. Particularly as a given norm moves downwards through the meso and micro-levels, it will primarily be subject to contestations by societal agents within the state (or within large organizations). Specific implementation processes, during which formal legal and policy mechanisms are introduced in order to routinize compliance, will be particularly prone to these forms of contestation (see Betts and Orchard 2014, 22).

The key issue here is that this domestic implementation process (as it occurs not only across the micro-level sites, such as within formal domestic institutions such as legislatures or the Courts, but also through more informal processes in government) may incorporate both visible factors – such as formal constitutional functions – and invisible factors – including "expectations of norms and the interpretation of their respective meanings derived from the historical and cultural contingency." These constitutional functions are "crucial for the interpretation of norms and yet may remain hidden or opaque to actors beyond the state (Wiener 2008, 7, 23). Thus, in 2013 UK Prime Minister David Cameron moved a motion in the House of Commons to support a potential military intervention following the Syrian government's use of chemical weapons. Despite no constitutional requirement to do so (involvement in the 2011 Libyan intervention was authorized only post-hoc, while involvement in Afghanistan was not subject to a vote), Kaarbo and Kenealy note that Cameron's action here was an indication "of changing norms and efforts to strengthen parliamentary authority in security policy…" (Kaarbo and Kenealy 2016, 35–36; Mello 2017). In this case, Cameron's decision was ill-fated, with Parliament voting against the government and blocking any further action.

Three types of contestations are possible. *Reactive contestations* tend to occur at the implementing stage and are indicated primarily as an objection to compliance with or violation of a norm. Typical for this practice are contestations of norm violation in cases where fundamental (type 1) norms such as the prohibition of torture or sexual violence against women and girls during wartime are targeted (Wiener 2018, chs. 6 and 7, respectively). *Proactive contestations* tend to occur at the constitutive state of norm implementation, and are indicated primarily as efforts to constructively engage with a norm. Typical for this practice are contestations in the process of detailing the emergence of an organizing principle (type 2 norm) such as for example the R2P or the common but differentiated responsibility norms, respectively (Wiener 2018, 2014). Finally, *interpretive contestations* reflect that any given agent may have interpretive variance on how they understand a given norm. Such variances may not be readily apparent without direct application of the norm and, in theory, can exist between any agent and any norm. Thus, interpretive contestations have a distinctly different character than other types; they may be inadvertent rather than deliberate and more likely to appear in the form of applicatory contestations rather than validity contestations as the agent believes their understanding of the norm is the same as others (Orchard and Wiener forthcoming). In 2008, when Myanmar sought to limit international humanitarian aid after being hit by Cyclone Nargis, French Minister of Foreign Affairs Bernard Kouchner suggested the UN Security Council use the R2P to authorize assistance without the consent of the government. This view was widely rejected internationally, with the UN Special Advisor on R2P Ed Luck noting that "it would be a misapplication of responsibility to protect principles to apply them at this point to the unfolding tragedy in Myanmar" (Bellamy 2011, 58).[1] As Eglantine Staunton demonstrates, however, Kouchner's argument reflected how France had conceived of human protection since the 1980s as "not restricting it to specific populations or sources of emergency" (Staunton 2020, 125).

These types of contestation take on the second form of challenge-change relation, between a specific norm and a variety of agents (A1, A2, and so on). During such encounters, norms are challenged and changed. And it is expected that as a norm-generative practice, contestation generates mutually recognized norms or normative meaning, as it were, in addition to normality. While the conflict is likely to be ignited through contested universal validity claims of a fundamental norm – such as human rights, the rule of law, or the ban on landmines – it is expected to settle the ground rules or the organizing principles according to which these universal validity claims are sensibly implemented. These ground rules reflect a compromise considering constraints and opportunities of sustainable normativity in a given context. The central research question is the effect on the meaning of the involved norm/s: does the contestation only take effect at the implementing stage (reactive contestation), or does it imply a more substantive impact at the constitutive stage of norm implementation (proactive contestation)?

The first take assumes that agents no longer consider a norm as appropriate (*applicatory contestation*) or do not agree with its value (*validity contestation*). When a norm such as the torture taboo is no longer taken for granted, increased reactive contestation indicates the change. In this case, agents object to the implementation of the norm (Price and Sikkink 2021). The key interaction at the offset for empirical research is therefore the reaction of agent A *to* norm N1, which is most likely to be substantiated by further reactions of agent B (+1) to norm N1. In turn, the second take on the situation of contestation involves agents who clash with others in international encounters. Based on reconstructive discourse analysis of these contestations, this take reveals the norms that are at stake, the conditions of access, and the emerging changed normative meaning. For example, while a norm such as say the right to fish is defined by the statutes of the United Nations Convention on the Law of the Sea (UNCLOS), it is interpreted differently by the involved agents who do not share the same national roots. Upon these agents' encounter in international contexts, the contested implementation of the norm comes to the fore. The key interaction is a norm conflict between agents A and B (or more) about which norm (N1 or N2) to refer to, in order to warrant proper implementation, or what the norms' hierarchical orderings are. Here, the key question is whether the contesting agents agree on the authority of one norm N1 (the right to fish according to the rule of law under UNCLOS) or another norm N2 (sustainable fisheries according to regional experience in the North West Atlantic Ocean). Agreement on which norm to follow requires engagement and a struggle over the recognition of a shared ground rule to guide further common action.

A final question relates to how norms are validated. Norm validation takes on three distinct forms relating to both the scale of global order and the stage of norm implementation: *formal validation, habitual validation*, and *cultural validation*. In the context of international relations, *formal validation* is expected in negotiations involving committee members of international organizations, negotiating groups, ad-hoc committees or similar bodies involving high-level representatives of states and/or governments. It entails validity claims with regard to formal documents, treaties, conventions or agreements. *Habitual validation* is practiced habitually and therefore depends on the context of social groups. It entails validity claims that are constituted through regular interaction within a social environment. The higher the level of integration among the group, the more likely uncontested habitual validation of norms becomes. Different from formal validation where validity claims are explicitly negotiated, habitual validation reflects mediated access to validity claims qua prior social interaction within a group. *Cultural validation* is an expression of an individual expectation mediated by individually held background experience. Importantly, the qualifier 'cultural' is used to distinguish individual from group practices. It refers to background experience derived through everyday practice and as such carries a thin rather than a thick meaning of culture (Wiener 2014, 9).

Norm clashes indicate where to zoom in on local sites. The cycle-grid model features nine ideal-typical sites which are distinguished with relation to their situation in the process of norm implementation on the one hand, and their location on distinct scales of global order, on the other. Following sensitizing reading to identify norm contestation, the "cycle-grid model" (Wiener 2018, 44, Figure 2.1) allows for empirical research to map contestations with reference to the grid which indicates three 'scales of global order' and 'stages of norm implementation' on the one hand, and then to evaluate 'conditions of access' with reference to the validation cycle, on the other (Wiener 2018, Ibid.). The grid allows the identification of, first, the groups of affected stakeholders involved in contestations and, second, the rules of engagement that condition their access to political participation. Following this step of mapping contestations, which typically occur in cases of contested compliance with norms or violations of fundamental norms on local sites, the conditions of access to contestation are evaluated with reference to the cycle. For instance, do stakeholders have access to proactive contestation and hence engaging with negotiations about normative meanings-in-use, or is their access restricted to reactive contestation, i.e. mere objection to implementing a norm as such? At this stage the research moves toward normative evaluation. Here, the validation cycle facilitates the distinction between access to formal, social, and/or cultural validation. It indicates the power differential of affected stakeholders by distinguishing for instance those agents with access to all three practices (typically agents on site 1 involved in proactive contestation about normative substance with regard to a selected fundamental or *type 1* norms) on the one hand, from those who are excluded from full access to participation and whose impact on shaping normative meanings-in-use is fairly limited due to their exclusion from formal validation (most typically agents on site 9 involved in reactive contestation with regard to a selected regulatory standard or *type 3* norm), on the other (Wiener 2018, 58–59). The approach enables norms researchers to determine which practices of norm validation are available under the rules of engagement that enable and/or constrain affected stakeholders at these sites. The model is therefore helpful for studying the exploration of the opportunities and constraints of agency in global governance. Following the leading questions of practice-based norm research, i.e. 'whose practices count' and 'whose practices ought to count' in global IR (Wiener 2018, 1), it also opens up important empirical questions including: what is the highest set of *type 2* norms (i.e. organizing principle) that is aggregated through cultural validation of type 3 norms (i.e. standardized procedures and regulations)?

The arrow on the spinning cycle indicates the normative condition for the best-case scenario, namely that each of the three practices of norm validation become available for the stakeholders affected by a norm. They therefore help localize empirically where and when *reactive* contestation stands to be expected in the process of norm implementation. Relatedly, they also point to the sites where facilitative conditions for *proactive* contestation ought to be established. Sociological research on norms has generated manifold data to map distinct patterns of access to contestation on behalf of the variety of stakeholders. They can be distinguished with reference to type of actor (i.e. state vs. non-state), role in the process of norm implementation (i.e. designated norm-setter or designated norm-follower), and socio-cultural background experience (i.e. individual background experience). While the former two have been thoroughly studied by social constructivists over the past two decades, the latter have been predominantly addressed by more recent pragmatist and Bourdieusian research (Adler-Nissen and Pouliot 2014; Kornprobst and Senn 2016; McCourt 2016; Sending 2016).

The empirical challenge consists in both identifying *and* facilitating the institutional means for access to proactive contestation. Proactive contestation depends on the normative structure of the environment. To establish this precondition, research begins from instances of norm conflict. These are often, if not exclusively, based on diverging stakeholder expectations. A good example is the 'Turbot War' in fisheries governance when Canadian fishing folk considered the fundamental norm guiding their action to be 'sustainable fisheries', whereas the Galician fishing folk referred to the 'right to fish' in international waters which is formally granted by UNCLOS. Similarly, post-conflict and post-enlargement situations represent environments in which the likelihood of international encounters where norms are contested is particularly high (Tully 2004; Wiener 2008, 64). For example, the rule of law is most likely to be contested in contexts that involve recent political change: post-conflict and post-enlargement contexts involve the transition from one political regime to another including the reform of political institutions (Sedelmeier 2014; Müller 2015). Conflictive encounters in these contexts shed light on stakeholder access to distinct practices of norm validation. The argument holds that by identifying which of the three practices of norm validation (if any) are accessible to the involved stakeholders, the cycle model can offer a framework for explaining stakeholder involvement and alienation with regard to selected norms of global governance.

Foreign Policy and Norm Contestations: Chemical Weapons Use in Syria[2]

How do norm contestations occur in practice? This section explores contestations over the US response during the Obama and Trump administration to Syria's use of chemical weapons, including air strikes against the Syrian military in 2017 and 2018. This was a norm conflict marked by two distinct sets of contestations. First, the US government proactively contested the prohibition on the use of chemical weapons (CW), a fundamental norm, by linking CW use to punitive international actions. Second, there were also contestation between two different forms of response. Both US administrations prioritized the prohibition of CW use [3] against an alternative set of norms based around the R2P doctrine which could have also been invoked and potentially provided a clearer legal basis for air strikes. The R2P, which was endorsed by the United Nations at the 2005 World Summit, creates a threefold set of responsibilities on states to prevent war crimes, crimes against humanity, and genocide against their own populations; to assist other states in upholding their responsibilities, and, in the case where a state is manifestly failing its own responsibility, for the UN Security Council to take action under Chapter VII of the UN Charter. Thus, the cases focus *primarily* on how formal validation occurs at international/macro-level through negotiations at the United Nations (site 2 of the cycle-grid model Wiener 2018, 44, Figure 2.1) but it also reflects how habitual validation – particularly the recurring invocations of the prohibition against CW use – can be used to support a particular understanding.

The first major event which triggered a contestation was Syria's use of CW against Ghouta, a Damascus suburb, in August 2013, which killed at least 734 people. US President Barack Obama was bound by declarations he had made the previous year when he noted that, "a red line for us is we start seeing a whole bunch of chemical weapons moving around or being utilized. That would change my calculus" around military engagement (Obama 2012).

Obama was generally viewed as a strong proponent of the R2P doctrine. His administration had been instrumental in ensuring the Security Council took action against the Libyan government of Muammar Gaddafi in 2011. This was the first (and, to the present, only) time that the UN Security Council authorized non-consensual military action for humanitarian reasons without the consent of the state (Glanville 2013). Consensus for that intervention, was enabled, as Alex Bellamy and Paul Williams (2011, 825) put it, "by several exceptional factors, in particular a putative regional consensus and the poor international standing of Qaddafi's regime, as well as the clarity of the threat and short timeframe for action."

Even so, Obama was initially not in favor of following a French proposal to create a no-fly zone over Libya (Watt 2011). In a meeting of his national security team, he noted "based on what I'm hearing, here's the one thing we're *not* going to do – we're not going to participate in some half-assed no-fly zone that won't achieve our objective" (Obama 2020, 657). At the same time, he was concerned over the potential that "tens of thousands or more would be starved, tortured, or shot in the head" and focused in meetings on seeking to "gauge the likelihood of mass killings" (Lewis 2012; Power 2019, 299–300; Obama 2020, 658–659). Because of this, he did move to support a broader mandate, one that would enable the protection of Libyan civilians but which would also allow the US to quickly step back and hand off the bulk of the operation (Obama 2020, 658–659). Libya also sparked a wider commitment to the R2P. Soon after the Libyan intervention began, Obama introduced a Presidential Study Directive on Mass Atrocities in which he defined "preventing mass atrocities and genocide is a core national security interest and a core moral responsibility of the United States" (White House 2011). The Directive created an Interagency Atrocities Prevention Board, one tasked with coordinating a whole of government approach to preventing mass atrocities and genocide.

Thus, when the Syrian government used CW in 2013, the R2P could well have framed the US response. The use of CW constituted both crimes against humanity and war crimes under the International Criminal Court's Rome Statute given their widespread and systematic use. Following the release of a US Government assessment on 30 August 2013, which asserted "with high confidence that the Syrian government" had carried out the attacks (White House 2013),[4] Obama stated he had:

> Decided that the United States should take military action against Syrian regime targets. This would not be an open-ended intervention…. But I'm confident we can hold the Assad regime accountable for their use of chemical weapons, deter this kind of behavior, and degrade their capacity to carry it out.
>
> *(New York Times 2013)*

These actions, however, were not framed as falling within the R2P.[5] Obama instead framed action around the idea that the prohibition on CW itself "represents a conclusive international norm" based around the Chemical Weapons Convention, even though Syria was not yet a party (Price 2013; Nahlawi 2016, 79–80). In this sense, not only did Obama prioritize one norm – the prohibition on CW use – over another set – the R2P – but US entrepreneurship led this to become the default international position.

Having made the decision to take military action, however, Obama ran into significant issues gaining authorization from the US Congress and then lost the support of the UK when the House of Commons voted against authorizing strikes as discussed above. Privately,

Obama viewed this as undermining the chance to take action to combat mass atrocities in general. As Ben Rhodes recounts:

> 'Maybe we never would have done Rwanda' Obama said. The comment was jarring. Obama had written about how we should have intervened in Rwanda… 'You can't just stop people from killing each other like that… I'm just saying, maybe there's never a time when the American people are going support this kind of thing…
>
> *(Rhodes 2019, 239)*

The Red Line crisis ended not with a Congressional vote, but with a Syrian chemical weapons disarmament deal, negotiated between US Secretary of State John Kerry and Russian Foreign Minister Sergei Lavrov. The deal led to Security Council Resolution 2118. In their deliberations, Council members reinforced this as a violation of non-use of CW norm and did not reference the R2P doctrine at all. Kerry noted that the agreement required the Assad regime to "get rid of its tools of terror" and that "the world carried the burden of doing what it must to end mass killing by other means." Jean Asselborn, the Foreign Minister of Luxembourg, stated that "for the first time the Security Council has determined chemical weapons use is a threat to international peace" (United Nations 2013). Price argues these debates demonstrated the robustness of the norm against chemical weapons use: "the violator did not offer any justifications that outright rejected the norm. What's more, no party attempted to justify the violation as an exception to the norm, and no one attempted to redefine what could count as a violator" (Price 2019, 41).

The disarmament deal, unfortunately, did not end Syria's CW use. The Trump Administration engaged in two sets of air strikes against the Syrian government in 2017 and 2018 in response to new incidents. In both cases, the Trump Administration continued to focus on the violation of the norm against CW use, and in particular on the need for air strikes to have a deterrent effect. This is in spite of the Trump administration continuing to support efforts to prevent atrocities, with the 2017 National Security Strategy noting that "we will hold perpetrators of genocide and mass atrocities accountable" (White House 2017). Trump himself noted in remarks at the United States Holocaust Memorial Museum in 2017 that "we will never, ever be silent in the face of evil again…" (Trump 2017). And his administration supported the Elie Wiesel Genocide and Atrocities Prevention Act of 2018 which enshrined the Atrocities Prevention Board into US legislation. Further, alternative arguments were made including by Harold Hongju Koh, the Legal Adviser to the State Department under Obama, that the R2P could provide a level of legal protection for the strikes (Koh 2017).

The first air strike was launched by the US against a single military base following a CW attack by the Syrian government on the town of Khan Shaykhun in April 2017, which killed at least 80 civilians.[6] President Trump adopted very similar language to Obama's around the need to deter CW use, arguing the strikes were justified as being in the "vital national security interest of the United States to prevent and deter the spread and use of deadly chemical weapons" (Gordon et al. 2017).

International deliberations also continued to reflect such a framing and the notion that CW use constituted a mass atrocity, which required an international response. In a UN Security Council debate following the strike, US Ambassador Nikki Haley justified the strike by arguing that "the moral stain of the Assad regime could no longer go unanswered. His crimes against humanity could no longer be met with empty words" (UNSCOR 2017, 17). Matthew Rycroft, the UK representative, noted that "impunity cannot be the norm… war crimes have consequences…" (UNSCOR 2017, 5). But the US also sought to justify the strike by arguing that it was in violation of the earlier agreement and that Russia was blocking action, with Haley arguing "when the international community consistently fails in its duty to act collectively, there are times when States are compelled to take their own action. The indiscriminate use of chemical weapons against innocent civilians is one of those times" (UNSCOR 2017, 17).

Vladimir Safronkov, the Russian representative, responded to these arguments by suggesting that the attack was "a flagrant violation of international law and an act of aggression" (UNSCOR 2017, 10, 11). Other states, however, were more balanced in their response. The representative of Bolivia, for instance, while noting the "extremely serious violation of international law" stated "we unequivocally condemn chemical attacks…" (UNSCOR 2017, 3, 5). The Chinese response was also muted, with Representative Liu Jieyi simply noting that "China has always advocated for dialogue and consultations… a political solution is the only way out of the situation. A military solution will not work" (UNSCOR 2017, 10).

A more significant series of strikes were undertaken by the US in partnership with the UK and France on 13 April 2018 following another chemical attack on the town of Douma which killed at least 40 people. Trump again argued that "Chemical weapons are uniquely dangerous… the purpose of our actions tonight is to establish a strong deterrent against the production, spread and use of chemical weapons. Establishing this deterrent is a vital national security interest of the United States" (New York Times 2018).[7] National Security Adviser John Bolton echoed this focus on the need to deter CW use:

> The US opposed anyone's use of WMD… A crucial question in the ensuing debate [of what action to take] was whether reestablishing deterrence against using weapons of mass destruction inevitably mean greater US involvement in Syria's civil war. It did not.
> *(Bolton 2020, 46)*

The UN Security Council deliberations following the strikes included the same set of issues as those the previous year. Speaking on behalf of the US, Haley framed the attacks as limited, legitimate, and proportionate designed to deter future CW use in response to the violation of resolution 2118 (UNSCOR 2018, 5). Both the UK and French representatives echoed similar points (UNSCOR 2018, 6–8). The Russian representative again stated that the attack demonstrated "a flagrant disregard for international law" and that the US, UK, and France were "undermining the Council's authority" (UNSCOR 2018, 3–4). Other responses, however, were more tempered. The Chinese representative simply noted that "any unilateral military action that circumvent the Security Council contravene" the Charter (UNSCOR 2018, 10). Other states simply called for restraint (UNSCOR 2018, 10, 16) and an effort by Russia to pass a resolution condemning the aggression failed with only three votes (from Bolivia, China, and Russia) in favor (UN, 2018).

Thus, in all three instances, two different normative understandings could have been invoked, framing the government of Syria's actions as either a violation of the prohibition on CW use or a violation of the R2P doctrine. In each case, the Obama and Trump administrations framed it as a violation of the norm against CW use, even while also using language that framed the attacks as atrocities. As such, these states appear to be hierarchically rank-ordering norms, treating the non-use of CW norm as the primary norm of concern. They also sought to link violations of the norm to the need for international action, particularly through the retaliatory air strikes of 2017 and 2018. It is clear from the Council deliberations that many countries were leery of these arguments due to their lack of legal foundation. It should also be noted that if the air strikes were designed to deter subsequent use, they do appear to have had some success- while there was no decline in use following the Khan Sheykhoun attacks, the Global Public Policy Institute found that there was a pause in use following the April 2018 Douma attacks until September 2019, when the US again alleged CW use (CNBC 2019; Global Public Policy Institute 2019).

Conclusions

FPA has long had concerns with constructivist approaches to the study of norms, particularly viewing them as not providing a sufficient examination of agency at the domestic level. We have sought to demonstrate that while these concerns were justified in terms of the initial first move constructivist theorizing, the approach has evolved considerably. The second move has explored how norms functioned in policymaking, while the third move has layered on top of these understandings a renewed focus on the role of agents through the process of norm contestation. As such, in our view norm contestation provides an important theoretical framing to support FPA, particularly by exploring at the micro- and meso-levels how state-based decision making and norm entrepreneurship can not only lead to norm emergence and change but also proactively create clearer and more legitimate normative understandings. While in the best-case scenario contestations will take place across the cycle-grid, in most cases they happen unevenly, marked by issues with stakeholder access and a power balance that is frequently tipped in favor of actors such as states with privileged access. Even so, highlighting the moments when proactive contestations are able to occur (whether between states, or between states and other actors) is critical for understanding normative legitimacy.

Thus, an important empirical challenge consists in identifying *and* facilitating the means by which stakeholders can gain access to proactive contestations, to study *whose practice counts*. In any situation of norm conflict, the first step will be to identify the affected stakeholders, then to determine where the specific site of contestation is occurring per the cycle-grid model, and finally, to examine whether they are able to access the contestation process. In some situations, this is quite easy- as with our case above where the main stakeholders were state representatives engaging in formal processes, which we mapped onto Site 2 of the cycle-grid. In other cases, this may involve studying a conflict carefully in order to map out what is occurring and to examine what forms of access are possible. This can be done through a series of questions: What norm (or norms) is involved? What is the central claim of the conflict? Do contestations focus on the norm's validity or its application? Or is it a conflict around the application of different norms? What are the claims of affected stakeholders? Do affected stakeholders have access? Do they have reactive access only (the ability to object to the norm) or also proactive access (the ability to critically engage with the norm's substantive values)? These questions can be used to identify both access *opportunities* and *restrictions* and then used to shape and create opportunities for proactive access (Wiener 2018, 30, 44–45).

Potential assets and pitfalls for future norms research include the importance of distinguishing between norms research that considers a norm as promoting stability within a given order (i.e. the liberal international order, or a regional order, or similar) and whether a norm is discussed with regard to the larger goal of addressing justice or inequality in world society (i.e. gender justice, climate justice, or similar). This choice is of vital importance with regard to identifying the guiding research questions. For example, when focusing on single norms research questions typically address the stability, robustness, recognition, or in fact, the violation of norms. In turn, research that studies how norm bundles evolve and work with regard to a particular policy sector, research questions typically target multiple policy and/or political activities.

Acknowledgments

Phil Orchard is grateful for funding by the Australian Research Council (Discovery Project Number DP200100750). Antje Wiener thanks for funding by the Deutsche Forschungsgemeinschaft (DFG, German Research Foundation) under Germany's Excellence Strategy – EXC 2037 *CLICCS - Climate, Climatic Change, and Society* –, project number: 390683824.

Notes

1 While Kouchner's argument was dismissed at the time, the UN Security Council would take such action in 2014 with respect to the Syrian government's similar efforts to block assistance. See Orchard (2017, 177–179).
2 This section draws in part on Orchard (2020).
3 Significant evidence exists that not only is there a proscriptive norm and even a taboo against the use of CW, (Price 1995): "despite widespread use in World War I, the use of CW has been exceedingly rare in warfare since that time, making the CW taboo an unusually robust norm of warfare" (Price 2019, 38).
4 Other reports subsequently came to similar conclusions, with the Independent International Commission of Inquiry on the Syrian Arab Republic concluding the perpetrators "likely had access to the chemical weapons stockpile of the Syrian military, as well as the expertise and equipment necessary to manipulate safely large amounts of chemical agents," and with Human Rights Watch noting evidence strongly suggests it was "carried out by government forces" (UNHRC 2014; Human Rights Watch 2014).
5 One reason to not invoke R2P may have been a lack of clear international law: "our lawyers also had concerns. There was no firm international legal basis for bombing Syria – no argument of self-defense, which justified our actions against al-Qaeda; no UN resolution such as we had had in Libya" (Rhodes 2019, 232–233). The UK did argue that a "doctrine of humanitarian intervention" did allow these steps under international law, but did not explicitly mention the R2P (United Kingdom 2013).
6 An OPCW-UN investigation subsequently stated the government was responsible for the attack (UN Security Council 2017). Five days after the strikes, the White House declassified an intelligence report that stated it was "confident that the Syrian regime conducted a chemical weapons attack, using the nerve agent sarin…" However, it is unclear when the report was prepared (New York Times 2017).
7 The same day as the strike, the White House stated "with confidence that the Syrian regime used chemical weapons in the eastern Damascus suburb of Duma on April 7, 2018" (White House 2018). A subsequent investigation by the OPCW concluded the attacks had included the use of a 'toxic chemical' containing chlorine" but did not assign blame (Al-Jazeera 2019).

References

Note: All electronic sources have been last accessed on 4 February 2022.

Acharya, Amitav. 2004. "How Ideas Spread: Whose Norms Matter? Norm Localization and Institutional Change in Asian Regionalism." *International Organization* 58 (2): 239–275.

Adler, Emanuel. 2013. "Constructivism in International Relations: Sources, Contributions, and Debates." In *Handbook of International Relations*, edited by Walter Carlsnaes, Thomas Risse and Beth A. Simmons. London: Sage, 112–144.

Adler-Nissen, Rebecca, and Vincent Pouliot. 2014. "Power in Practice: Negotiating the International Intervention in Libya." *European Journal of International Relations* 20 (4): 889–911.

Al Jazeera. 2019. Chlorine likely used in attack on Syria town Douma, says OPCW. 2 Mar. Available from https://www.aljazeera.com/news/2019/3/2/chlorine-likely-used-in-attack-on-syria-town-douma-says-opcw

Bellamy, Alex J. 2011. *Global Politics and the Responsibility to Protect: From Words to Deeds*. Milton Park: Routledge.

Bellamy, Alex J., and Paul D. Williams. 2011. "The New Politics of Protection? Côte D'ivoire, Libya and the Responsibility to Protect." *International Affairs* 87 (4): 825–850.

Betts, Alexander, and Phil Orchard. 2014. "Introduction: The Normative Institutionalization-Implementation Gap." In *Implementation and World Politics: How International Norms Change Practice*, edited by Alexander Betts and Phil Orchard. Oxford: Oxford University Press.

Bloomfield, Alan. 2016. "Norm Antipreneurs and Theorising Resistance to Normative Change." *Review of International Studies* 42 (2): 310–333.

Bob, Clifford. 2012. *The Global Right Wing and the Clash of World Politics*. Cambridge: Cambridge University Press.

Bolton, John. 2020. *The Room Where It Happened: A White House Memoir*. New York: Simon and Schuster.

Busby, Joshua W. 2010. *Moral Movements and Foreign Policy*. Cambridge: Cambridge University Press.

Checkel, Jeffrey T. 2005. "International Institutions and Socialization in Europe: Introduction and Framework." *International Organization* 59 (4): 801–826.

CNBC. 2019. Pompeo says Syrian government used chlorine in May chemical weapon attack, 26 Sep. Available from https://www.cnbc.com/2019/09/26/pompeo-says-syria-government-used-chlorine-in-may-chemical-weapon-attack.html

Davies, Sara E., and Jacqui True. 2017. "Norm Entrepreneurship in Foreign Policy: William Hague and the Prevention of Sexual Violence in Conflict." *Foreign Policy Analysis* 13 (3): 701–721.

Finnemore, Martha. 1996. *National Interests in International Society*. Ithaca, NY: Cornell University Press.

Finnemore, Martha, and Kathryn Sikkink. 1998. "International Norm Dynamics and Political Change." *International Organization* 52 (4): 887–917.

Glanville, Luke. 2013. "Intervention in Libya: From Sovereign Consent to Regional Consent." *International studies perspectives* 14 (3): 325–342.

Global Public Policy Institute. 2019. Nowhere to Hide: The Logic of Chemical Weapons Use in Syria. Available from https://www.gppi.net/media/GPPi_Schneider_Luetkefend_2019_Nowhere_to_Hide_Web.pdf

Gordan, Michael R., Helene Cooper, and Michael D. Shear. 2017. "Dozens of U.S. Missiles Hit Air Base in Syria," The New York Times, 6 Apr. Available from https://www.nytimes.com/2017/04/06/world/middleeast/us-said-to-weigh-military-responses-to-syrian-chemical-attack.html?_r=0%3E

Havercroft, Jonathan. 2018. "Social Constructivism and International Ethics." In *Routledge Handbook on Ethics in International Relations*, edited by Brent J. Steele and Eric A. Heinze. London: Routledge, 116–129.

Hudson, Valerie M. 2005. "Foreign Policy Analysis: Actor-Specific Theory and the Ground of International Relations." *Foreign Policy Analysis* 1 (1): 1–30.

Hudson, Valerie M., and Benjamin S Day. 2019. *Foreign Policy Analysis: Classic and Contemporary Theory*. Lanham, MD: Rowman & Littlefield.

Human Rights Watch. 2014. Attacks on Ghouta: Analysis of Alleged Use of Chemical Weapons in Syria. Available from https://www.hrw.org/report/2013/09/10/attacks-ghouta/analysis-alleged-use-chemical-weapons-syria

Kaarbo, Juliet. 2015. "A Foreign Policy Analysis Perspective on the Domestic Politics Turn in IR Theory." *International Studies Review* 17 (2): 189–216.

Kaarbo, Juliet, and Daniel Kenealy. 2016. "No, Prime Minister: Explaining the House of Commons' Vote on Intervention in Syria." *European Security* 25 (1): 28–48.

Koh, Harold Hongju. 2017. "Not Illegal: But Now the Hard Part Begins," *Just Security*, 7 April, https://www.justsecurity.org/39695/illegal-hard-part-begins/.

Kornprobst, Markus, and Martin Senn. 2016. "Introduction: Background Ideas in International Relations." *The British Journal of Politics and International Relations* 18 (2): 273–281.

Krebs, Ronald R., and Patrick Thaddeus Jackson. 2007. "Twisting Tongues and Twisting Arms: The Power of Political Rhetoric." *European Journal of International Relations* 13 (1): 31.

Lewis, Michael. 2012. "Obama's Way." *Vanity Fair*. October. Available from https://www.vanityfair.com/news/2012/10/michael-lewis-profile-barack-obama

McCourt, David M. 2016. "Practice Theory and Relationalism as the New Constructivism." *International Studies Quarterly* 60 (3): 475–485.

McKeown, Ryder. 2009. "Norm Regress: US Revisionism and the Slow Death of the Torture Norm." *International relations* 23 (1): 5–25.

Mello, Patrick A. 2017. "Curbing the Royal Prerogative to Use Military Force: The British House of Commons and the Conflicts in Libya and Syria." *West European Politics* 40 (1): 80–100.

Müller, Jan-Werner. 2015. "Should the EU Protect Democracy and the Rule of Law inside Member States?" *European Law Journal* 21 (2): 141–160.

Nahlawi, Yasmine. 2016. "The Responsibility to Protect and Obama's Red Line on Syria." *Global Responsibility to Protect* 8 (1): 76–101.

New York Times. 2013. "Text of President Obama's Remarks on Syria," 31 Aug. Available from https://www.nytimes.com/2013/09/01/world/middleeast/text-of-president-obamas-remarks-on-syria.html?ref=middleeast&_r=0

New York Times. 2017. "Declassified U.S. Report on Chemical Weapons Attack," 11 Apr. Available from https://www.nytimes.com/interactive/2017/04/11/world/middleeast/document-Syria-Chemical-Weapons-Report-White-House.html

New York Times. 2018. "President Trump on Syria Strikes: Full Transcript and Video," 13 Apr. Available from https://www.nytimes.com/2018/04/13/world/middleeast/trump-syria-airstrikes-full-transcript.html

Obama, Barack. 2012. "Remarks by the President to the White House Press Corps," 20 Aug. Available from https://obamawhitehouse.archives.gov/the-press-office/2012/08/20/remarks-president-white-house-press-corps

Obama, Barack. 2020. *A Promised Land*. New York: Penguin Viking.

Orchard, Phil. 2014. *A Right to Flee: Refugees, States, and the Construction of International Society*. Cambridge: Cambridge University Press.

Orchard, Phil. 2017. "Transnational Humanitarian Action and Regime Complexity: The Case of Syria." In *Transnational Actors in War and Peace: Militants, Activists, and Corporations in World Politics*, edited by David Malet and Miriam J. Anderson. Washington DC: Georgetown University Press, 168–184.

Orchard, Phil. 2020. "Contestation, Norms and the Responsibility to Protect as a Regime." In *Constructing the Responsibility to Protect: Contestation and Consolidation*, edited by Charles T. Hunt and Phil Orchard. London: Routledge, 28–49.

Orchard, Phil, and Jamie Gillies. 2015. "Atypical Leadership: The Role of the Presidency and Refugee Protection, 1932–1952." *Presidential Studies Quarterly* 45 (3): 490–513.

Orchard, Phil, and Antje Wiener. forthcoming. "Introduction: Norm Research in Theory and Practice." In *Contesting the World: Norm Research in Theory and Practice*, edited by Phil Orchard and Antje Wiener.

Payne, Rodger A. 2001. "Persuasion, Frames and Norm Construction." *European Journal of International Relations* 7 (1): 37–61.

Power, Samantha. 2019. *The Education of an Idealist: A Memoir*. New York: Dey St.

Price, Richard. 1995. "A Genealogy of the Chemical Weapons Taboo." *International Organization* 49 (1): 73–103.

Price, Richard. 2013. "No Strike, No Problem." *Foreign Affairs*. 5 September. Available from https://www.foreignaffairs.com/articles/syria/2013-09-05/no-strike-no-problem

Price, Richard. 2019. "Syria and the Chemical Weapons Taboo." *Journal of Global Security Studies* 4 (1): 37–52.

Price, Richard, and Kathryn Sikkink. 2021. *International Norms, Moral Psychology, and Neuroscience*. Cambridge: Cambridge University Press.

United Kingdom. 2013. "Chemical weapon use by Syrian regime: UK government legal position," 29 Aug. Available from https://www.gov.uk/government/publications/chemical-weapon-use-by-syrian-regime-uk-government-legal-position/chemical-weapon-use-by-syrian-regime-uk-government-legal-position-html-version

United Nations (UN). 2013. "Security Council Requires Scheduled Destruction of Syria's Chemical Weapons, Unanimously Adopting Resolution 2118 (2013)," SC/11135, 27 Sep. Available from https://www.un.org/press/en/2013/sc11135

UN. 2018. "Following Air Strikes against Suspected Chemical Weapons Sites in Syria, Security Council Rejects Proposal to Condemn Aggression," SC/13296, 14 Apr. Available from https://www.un.org/press/en/2018/sc13296.doc.htm

UN Human Rights Council (UNHRC). 2014. "Report of the independent international commission of inquiry on the Syrian Arab Republic," A/HRC/25/65, 12 Feb.

UN Security Council (UNSC). 2017, "Letter dated 26 October 2017 from the Secretary-General addressed to the President of the Security Council," S/2017/904, 26 Oct.

UN Security Council Official Records (UNSCOR). 2017. 7919th meeting, 7 April, S/PV.7919.

UNSCOR. 2018. 8233rd meeting, 14 Apr, S/PV.8233.
Rhodes, Ben. 2019. *The World as It Is: A Memoir of the Obama White House*. London: Vintage.
Risse, Thomas, and Kathryn Sikkink. 1999. "The Socialization of International Human Rights Norms into Domestic Practice." In *The Power of Human Rights: International Norms and Domestic Change*, edited by Thomas Risse, Stephen C. Ropp and Kathryn Sikkink. Cambridge: Cambridge University Press: 1–38.
Ruggie, John Gerard. 1993. "Territoriality and Beyond." *International Organization* 47(1): 139–174.
Schneiker, Andrea. 2021. "Norm Sabotage: Conceptual Reflection on a Phenomenon That Challenges Well-Established Norms." *International Studies Perspectives* 22 (1): 106–123.
Searle, John R. 1995. *The Social Construction of Reality*. London: Free Press.
Sedelmeier, Ulrich. 2014. "Anchoring Democracy from Above? The European Union and Democratic Backsliding in Hungary and Romania after Accession." *JCMS: Journal of Common Market Studies* 52 (1): 105–121.
Sending, Ole Jacob. 2016. "Agency, Order, and Heteronomy." *European Review of International Studies* 3 (3): 63–75.
Simmons, Beth A. 2009. *Mobilizing for Human Rights: International Law in Domestic Politics*. Cambridge: Cambridge University Press.
Staunton, Eglantine. 2020. *France, Humanitarian Intervention and the Responsibility to Protect*: Manchester: Manchester University Press.
Stimmer, Anette, and Lea Wisken. 2019. "The Dynamics of Dissent: When Actions Are Louder Than Words." *International Affairs* 95 (3): 515–533.
Tully, James. 2004. "Recognition and Dialogue: The Emergence of a New Field." *Critical Review of International Social and Political Philosophy* 7 (3): 84–106.
Trump, Donald J. 2017. Remarks at the United States Holocaust Memorial Museum's Days of Remembrance Ceremony, 25 Apr. Available from https://www.presidency.ucsb.edu/node/326682
Watt, Nicolas. 2011. "Libya no-fly zone call by France fails to get David Cameron's backing," *The Guardian*, 24 Feb. Available from https://www.theguardian.com/world/2011/feb/23/libya-nofly-zone-david-cameron
Wendt, Alexander. 1999. *Social Theory of International Politics*. Cambridge: Cambridge University Press.
Wiener, Antje. 2007. "The Dual Quality of Norms and Governance Beyond the State: Sociological and Normative Approaches to 'Interaction'." *Critical Review of International Social and Political Philosophy* 10 (1): 47–69.
Wiener, Antje. 2008. *The Invisible Constitution of Politics*. Cambridge: Cambridge University Press.
Wiener, Antje. 2010. "Normative Baggage in International Encounters: Contestation All the Way." In *On Rules, Politics and Knowledge: Friedrich Kratochwil, International Relations, and Domestic Affairs*, edited by Rodney Bruce Hall, Nicholas Onuf, Cecelia Lynch and Oliver Kessler. Basingstoke: Palgrave Macmillan, 202–212.
Wiener, Antje. 2014. *A Theory of Contestation*. Heidelberg: Springer.
Wiener, Antje. 2018. *Contestation and Constitution of Norms in Global International Relations*. Cambridge: Cambridge University Press.
Wiener, Antje. 2020. The Concept of Contestation of Norms - An Interview. In: Reder, Michael et al. (eds.) Yearbook on Practical Philosophy in a Global Perspective (YPPGP-JPPGP). 4th Edition, Munich: Karl Alber Publishing, 196-206.
White House. 2011. Presidential Study Directive on Mass Atrocities/PSD-10, 4 Aug. Available from https://obamawhitehouse.archives.gov/the-press-office/2011/08/04/presidential-study-directive-mass-atrocities
White House. 2013. Government Assessment of the Syrian Government's Use of Chemical Weapons on August 21, 2013, 30 Aug. Available from https://obamawhitehouse.archives.gov/the-press-office/2013/08/30/government-assessment-syrian-government-s-use-chemical-weapons-august-21
White House. 2017. National Security Strategy of the United States of America. Available from https://trumpwhitehouse.archives.gov/wp-content/uploads/2017/12/NSS-Final-12-18-2017-0905.pdf
White House. 2018. United States Government Assessment of the Assad Regime's Chemical Weapons Use, 13 Apr. Available from https://www.whitehouse.gov/briefings-statements/united-states-government-assessment-assad-regimes-chemical-weapons-use/
Zimmermann, Lisbeth. 2017. *Global Norms with a Local Face: Rule-of-Law Promotion and Norm Translation*. volume 143. Cambridge: Cambridge University Press.

5
Feminism
Alexis Henshaw

Introduction

Feminist approaches to Foreign Policy Analysis (FPA) and work on gender in foreign policy are receiving greater recognition than in the past. Bolstered by years of feminist research and reflection on methodologies in International Relations (IR), Security Studies, and other related fields, feminist work arises as a natural and necessary corollary to emergent discourses on Feminist Foreign Policy (FFP) and related efforts to change the dynamics of world politics by reaching women.

The academic enterprise of feminist FPA is first and foremost about interrogating the role of gender in process and outcomes. As discussed further below, "gender" refers to the social and cultural characteristics that are generally associated with biological sex, are transmitted by processes of socialization, and are institutionalized in ways that structure and reinforce a hierarchy which, in turn, interacts with other power relationships (Paxton, Hughes, and Barnes 2020). As this definition implies, feminism is by extension concerned with power relationships more broadly, including how race/ethnicity, class, sexuality, age, ability/disability, and a variety of other factors combine with gender in an intersectional process of meaning-making. By this enterprise, feminists seek not only to expose the working of gender but also to produce research that has the potential to improve the lives of women and other marginalized groups.

Doing feminist FPA may be of interest not only to anyone researching policy that seeks to forefront gender—like the explicitly named FFPs addressed in this chapter—but also to anyone looking to better understand how the social environment produces–and, in turn, is produced by inequalities and power dynamics (on power and language see also Ostermann and Sjöstedt in this volume). It is of interest to anyone who wishes to interrogate how power relationships and social hierarchies impact foreign policy. It is not, however, for those who look to use "gender" as a simple proxy for "sex" or "women" or for those who fail to recognize gender as a complex, diverse concept. Doing feminist research entails recognizing that gender itself is a concept that varies over space and time, creating distinct outcomes that require deeply contextual analysis.

Literature Review

Before proceeding to a review of literature on gender and foreign policy, it is worth taking a moment to situate feminism in the context of political science research more broadly. The understanding of gender as a social and cultural system in which we as researchers are embedded demands that we understand its relevance both as a topic for analysis and as a practical issue within our field (Henshaw 2021). This leads us to two interrelated concerns. The first is that scholarship on gender tends to be disproportionately—although not exclusively—produced by women, and the second is that scholarship by women tends to receive less recognition in the field as a whole.

Examining each of these points in greater detail, data from professional organizations broadly illustrate the gender imbalance in gender-focused scholarship. The Feminist Theory and Gender Studies section of the International Studies Association, according to organizational figures, is over 80% women, while the Women and Politics Research section of the American Political Science Association (APSA) is over 90% women (Breuning and Sanders 2007; Hidalgo et al. 2018). Compare this, for example, to the gender distribution within APSA's foreign policy section, which is approximately 70% men (Hidalgo et al. 2018). Given that the discipline of political science as a whole is estimated to be approximately 60% male at the graduate student level, with inequality tilted further toward men at more senior ranks of the professoriate (Teele and Thelen 2017), the preponderance of women identifying themselves primarily as gender scholars is notable. It further tracks with observations from feminist political scientists, who point out the role lived experience plays in determining what questions are deemed valuable, important, and necessary for research (Randall 2002; Weldon 2006).

In spite of growing gender diversity in the profession, scholarship both by women and about gender remains marginalized in many ways. Scholars have noted that women tend to publish fewer peer-reviewed journal articles at every career stage, a trend that is likely amplified by the concentration of women in high teaching- and service-load positions as well as greater care-work demands (Hesli and Lee 2011; Hesli, Lee, and Mitchell 2012; Mitchell and Hesli 2013). Even when women are publishing scholarship, research has found that their work—broadly—is less likely to be cited, to appear on syllabi, and to yield invitations to publish in projects like edited volumes or compilations (Mitchell, Lange, and Brus 2013; Maliniak, Powers, and Walter 2013; Dion, Sumner, and Mitchell 2018; Sumner 2018; Scola, Bucci, and Baglione 2020).[1] Research further suggests that these differences are at least equally pronounced for research about gender, which is less likely to be integrated into course syllabi or readers and less likely to be cited than work on more mainstream topics, like terrorism or international security (Han and Heldman 2019; M. Davis, McGrath, and Super 2019; Scola, Bucci, and Baglione 2020; J. Davis, West, and Amarasingam 2021). This apparent bias against feminist work and/or work focused on gender may be entangled with questions of methodological bias. Work by women authors as well as studies about gender are more likely to use qualitative methods; this makes such work less likely to appear in the pages of prestigious political science journals, many of which are far more likely to publish quantitative studies (Caprioli 2004; Breuning and Sanders 2007; Teele and Thelen 2017; Djupe, Smith, and Sokhey 2019). Where feminist scholarship is discussed in detail, authors have further argued that a kind of "big name" bias leads to a small number of senior (women) scholars dominating citations at the expense of broader, more comprehensive engagement with work on gender (Duriesmith 2020; Davis, West, and Amarasingam 2021). The persistence of these problems, insofar as they reflect gendered power dynamics in the field at large, has led some to call for deeper reflections on problems in the peer-review, publication, and citation processes (Duriesmith 2020).

This portrait of the field may tempt some readers to set aside this section and rush to another chapter of the volume. However, as the remainder of this piece will show, feminist FPA is an established, growing, and even exciting area that is developing in tandem with the practice of gender mainstreaming in the policy realm (Aggestam, Bergman Rosamond, and Kronsell 2019). As a research tradition that is inclusive, intersectional, and methodologically pluralistic, feminist inquiry may provide a welcoming home for an array of scholarship that sees gender as relevant to foreign policy. In the context of FPA research, scholars have noted that gender and feminist perspectives have been underrepresented (Hudson 2013; Achilleos-Sarll 2018; Smith 2020). This is true, although not the entire story. A longer tradition of feminist work in IR, security studies, and comparative politics has intersected with the study of foreign policy for the past few decades. The cross-cutting nature of scholarship across these silos and levels of analysis, rather than within FPA-focused outlets specifically, may reflect feminist beliefs about the overarching nature of gender and the impossibility of disentangling, for example, the individual from the larger sociocultural fabric.

Early work applying gender to foreign policy took a specific interest in women's roles within bureaucratic structures related to foreign policymaking, including the realm of national security. Cohn (1987) represents one such canonical piece, employing participant observation and narrative analysis to highlight the masculinized nature of nuclear security discourse in the Cold War era. Her work further interrogates the androcentric qualities of discussions that erase the potential human costs of nuclear war and the gendered impact on the civilian population. Other contemporary works develop similar themes in their analyses about women in foreign policymaking (Crapol 1992; McGlen and Sarkees 1993). In particular, the interview-based work of McGlen and Sarkees (1993) positioned women in Cold War-era U.S. foreign policymaking within the broader context of gendered institutions, norms, and beliefs. Such work points to another trend in the literature, toward recognizing and highlighting the role of men and masculinities in constructing foreign policy. Weber (1999), for instance, draws connections between masculinity, patriarchy, and heteronormative views in assessing late Cold War-era moves, such as the reassertion of U.S. hegemony in the Western Hemisphere during the Reagan Administration. More broadly, Enloe (1983; 1999; 2014) situates militarism and war-making within a superstructure of gender that intertwines sexuality, conflict, empire, economy, consumerism, and family—among other things.

Feminist approaches find greater prominence in the study of IR through the late 1990s into the early 2000s, as reflected by the production of new and influential work in feminist IR, new international policies aimed at mainstreaming gender, and the emergence of new data sources that—for some—made the study of gender issues seem more accessible. The books *Gendering World Politics* (Tickner 2001) and *War and Gender* (Goldstein 2001) have been influential in developing discourse about gender in international security, while the emergence of the *International Feminist Journal of Politics* in 1999 as a publication seeking to forefront diverse and critical scholarship offered a new outlet for voices that struggled to enter the mainstream (Youngs, Jones, and Pettman 1999). Such work further helped to crystallize the project of feminist security studies in the early 2000s, creating an academic community that sought to broaden the definition of security (i.e., to include personal/communal as well as national security), expose androcentrism, interrogate the role of gender, question intersectional hierarchies, and move beyond state-centered conceptualizations of security (Sjoberg 2009; Stern and Wibben 2014; Wibben 2014b).

At the same time, gender was acquiring greater prominence in international policy, a combined result of longstanding feminist advocacy, the high-profile occurrence of gender-based violence in post-Cold War conflicts, and the increasing recognition of the gendered impacts of transnational concerns like the HIV-AIDS pandemic. United Nations Security Council Resolution (UNSCR) 1325 on Women, Peace, and Security (WPS) drew upon earlier documents including the Namibia Plan of Action (2000) for gender mainstreaming in peace operations (also known as the Windhoek Declaration) and the Beijing Platform for Action (1995), to create a larger international agenda seeking to mainstream gender perspectives in security policy. UNSCR 1325 is the first of, as of this writing, ten resolutions constituting the core of the WPS Agenda. Coinciding with the development of this resolution, the United Nations rolled out the Millennium Development Goals (2000) as a development agenda that engaged multistakeholder action in pursuit of eight key objectives—many of which implicitly or explicitly dealt with the status of women. Combined, these initiatives brought recognition and resources to bear upon the types of concerns that feminist advocacy had long called upon governance structures to address, including women's health, gender-based violence, inequality in education, and the need to promote both women and gender perspectives.

With new goals come new mandates and new challenges, some of which bring gender into direct conversation with FPA. Current work on gender in foreign policy is diverse but tends to center around a few key lines of inquiry. First, there has been a continuation and growth of earlier research on women's representation in foreign policy bureaucracies. Second, an interest in domestic implementation of the WPS agenda has emerged, centered in IR but with points of dialogue in foreign policy. Finally, the emergence of FFP as an act of policy entrepreneurship has opened a new line of research and dialogue that brings feminism directly into contact with foreign policy.

As noted above, work on women in foreign policy bureaucracies builds upon a mature line of inquiry. It further intersects with feminist analysis, comparative politics, and lines of FPA that explore both the roles of individuals and of political/bureaucratic process in policymaking. The work of Bashevkin (2018) represents a noteworthy contribution in this area, not only for the quality of analysis but simply because such a work—comparing multiple case studies of women at the highest levels of U.S. foreign policy, including UN Ambassadors and three former Secretaries of State—can exist, there now having been enough women in these positions to warrant a comparative study. The same could be said of the work of Barnes and O'Brien (2018), whose project offers an overview of female defense ministers and the characteristics of the states and governments who appoint them. An analysis of gender in the context of defense bureaucracies continues with work on gender mainstreaming in NATO (Bastick and Duncanson 2018; Hurley 2018a; Wright, Hurley, and Ruiz 2019; Hardt and von Hlatky 2020). Such work variously examines the experiences of women and men as gendered individuals navigating the organization as well as the mainstreaming of gender perspectives in the work of NATO, including the adoption of the WPS agenda. In the diplomatic arena, work on gender and diplomacy has drawn on quantitative data, first-hand reflections, and interviews to offer a more complete picture of women's advancement in the diplomatic corps—including the experiences of women from ethnic/religious minorities and members of the LGBTQI community (Towns and Niklasson 2017; Cassidy 2019). Collectively, these projects highlight the ongoing underrepresentation of women and gender perspectives, the resilience of masculinity in foreign policy institutions, and the tensions between entrenched political processes and the transformative goals of gender mainstreaming.

The incorporation of the WPS agenda represents one specific challenge for gender mainstreaming and has been another topic of interest in feminist research. Though much of this research grounds itself in feminist IR, there is substantive overlap with FPA. One such example is the institutionalization of WPS through National Action Plans (NAPs). While these plans are considered an important tool for creating actionable goals and state-level accountability (as well as civil society consultation), scholars have noted that—especially for developed states—they frame WPS distinctly as a foreign policy issue. In particular, the focus of many NAPs in the Global North on plans to mainstream gender in fragile and conflict-affected states of the Global South is regarded with suspicion insofar as it both overlooks the existence of gendered insecurity within the Global North and legitimizes militaristic interventions (Shepherd 2016; Kirby and Shepherd 2016; Achilleos-Sarll 2020; Basu and Kirby 2020; Haastrup and Hagen 2020). How best to monitor and assess the impact of gendered interventions is another challenge for the many stakeholders engaged in gender mainstreaming. As discussed below, monitoring and assessment efforts that have often reduced outcomes to easily quantified metrics have reinvigorated larger methodological debates about feminist research (Hamilton, Naam, and Shepherd 2020; Shepherd 2021). Beyond the study of NAPs, analyses on gender mainstreaming and the institutionalization of WPS has connected with work on gender and representation, discussed above. The position of women and men "doing gender" within bureaucracies at the national, regional, and international levels has been a focus of inquiry (Hurley 2018a; Bastick and Duncanson 2018; Wright 2020; Shepherd 2021).

A review of feminist work would not be complete without discussing the emergence of an explicitly named FFP in states including Sweden, Canada, and Mexico. Sweden's announcement of its FFP in 2014 marked a moment of policy entrepreneurship that built upon aspects of the WPS agenda—including calls for greater representation—while also expanding the agenda to encompass a broader, normative discourse about rights, resources, and the need to mainstream gender more comprehensively into policy on development, climate change, and other issues (Aggestam and Bergman Rosamond 2019). The emergence and spread of FFP has fostered the developments of new lines of inquiry that highlight contested claims to "feminism" in foreign policy while simultaneously leveraging and expanding the domain of FPA (Achilleos-Sarll 2018; Aggestam and True 2020). Work in this area is discussed in greater detail *infra* with an eye toward examining how the feminist analysis of FFP advances methodological and analytical innovations for FPA.

Key Terms and Concepts, Methodology

Researchers seeking to engage in feminist analysis of foreign policy may wish to familiarize themselves with some key concepts and debates from work in feminist theory and feminist political science.

Distinctions between sex and gender: As defined above, *gender* refers to the set of cultural characteristics that may be associated with biological *sex*, including ways of dressing, behaviors, roles within the family, etc. Gender can also be more broadly ascribed to objects, institutions, ideas, and even places based on their perceived association with biological sex and whether they are valorized or devalorized (Runyan and Peterson 2013; P. Paxton, Hughes, and Barnes 2020). Feminists note the ways in which gender and sex are used to enforce binary categorizations as well as hierarchical ordering of that which is considered "masculine" above that which is considered "feminine" (Runyan and Peterson 2013). This practice of *dichotomization* is problematic not only because of the power dynamic it creates, but also because it precludes the existence of those who fail to conform to the binary. Outside of Western culture, many states and populations extend legal and cultural recognitions to third (or more) genders, while intersex individuals account for an estimated 1.7% of the global population (Free and

Equal 2017). Seeing beyond the binary, therefore, is an important aspect of dismantling power dynamics.

Essentialist arguments and intersectional experiences: Essentialist logics are used to undercut or conceal the social construction of gender by painting aspects of gender as normal, natural, or immutable. *Essentialist* thinking, which promotes the notion that "all women or all men or all those within a given race or class share the same experiences and interests" (Runyan and Peterson 2013, 16) is used to deny difference, reinforce stereotypes about how men and women should behave, and to preclude arguments in favor of change. Essentialism is also frequently connected to *heteronormative* views, which see opposite-sex relationships and male-headed households as standard. One possible outcome of essentialist arguments are *universalist* approaches to analysis or policymaking, which predict that because all men or women share the same traits and experiences, they are likely to benefit from the same policies promising empowerment, liberation, etc. (Runyan and Peterson 2013). Such logics are undercut by variations in cultural concepts of gender but also by the experience of *intersectionality*, which speaks to the differences among women based on their interlinked identities of gender, race/ethnicity, religion, class, sexuality, dis/ability, age, and so on. As described by Paxton and Hughes (2013, 245), intersectionality "acknowledges complexity" and the varied experiences of women who live in a world shaped by multiple and interlocking hierarchies.

Logics of patriarchy and their impact on researchers: Patriarchy, the social system of male domination, is deeply ingrained in the social, political, and economic practices of modern societies (Paxton and Hughes 2013). One impact of this pattern of domination is that male experiences—which are more closely associated with power and the public sphere—may be seen as the default, while the experiences of women—devalorized and confined to the private sphere—are rendered invisible or unimportant. This male-as-default perspective is also known as *androcentrism*. Scholars have pointed out that, beyond gender, androcentric practices may extend beyond gender to encapsulate the experience of only elite males as the default, for instance those of white males in the United States (Runyan and Peterson 2013). For researchers, understanding the impact of patriarchy is important because we ourselves are embedded within patriarchal systems, a fact which shapes our worldviews and analytical approaches. As discussed below, methodological and epistemological disagreements among feminists and between feminist researchers and those from other paradigms often center around this notion of positionality. While the appellation of "science" to political science was meant to imply rigor, systematization, and a value-neutral approach to analysis, feminist researchers have pointed out that the male-dominated nature of the field has in fact often elevated inquiry centered on the male experience at the expense of knowledge about women (Weldon 2006; Zalewski 2006). As discussed below, moves in the discipline toward mainstreaming analysis about gender are regarded with caution in part because of the historical biases evident in academia.

Debates in methodology, epistemology, and ontology: The understanding of gender as a social construction, combined with an interest in the lived experience of women, means that feminist research has often gravitated toward qualitative forms of inquiry (Randall 2002). Positivist and empirical traditions, which claim to be value neutral, tend to be regarded with suspicion by feminist researchers. On the one hand, feminist work views such research as at odds with the normative goals of feminism (i.e., to improve the lives of women and marginalized groups) (Tickner 2006). At the same time, there is also an understanding that claims to scientific neutrality have at times masked the way in which gendered power relations within the academy either dismissed or disregarded the importance of gender as a framework for analysis (Weldon 2006; Zalewski 2006). These debates have been reinvigorated in the context of moves within political and academic communities to understand gender outcomes through the production and analysis of quantitative data. In addition to data collection by the United Nations and other international agencies, connected to the mandates established through the WPS agenda, the Millennium Development Goals, and the subsequent Sustainable Development Goals, projects like the WomanStats database and the WPS Index have sought to fill gaps in the global availability of gender disaggregated data (GIWPS/PRIO 2019; WomanStats n.d.). While some feminist scholars have expressed an openness toward the possibility of quantitative, empirical, feminist research produced via inclusive and ethically collected data (Caprioli 2004; Tickner 2006; Hudson et al. 2014), others express concern that the heavy focus on metrics risks producing reductive or exclusionary analysis (Henshaw 2020; Shepherd 2021). For instance, at least some of these projects purporting to produce gender disaggregated data are only producing data *about women*, leaving relevant gaps in our knowledge about nonbinary populations and the experience of men.

In IR, work declaring gender to be at the "cutting edge" of the discipline primarily because it could be empirically and systematically studied sparked backlash among critical scholars who were already deeply engaged in feminist research for decades (Reiter 2014; 2015; Sjoberg, Kadera, and Thies 2018). The resulting call for methodological pluralism and engagement across the epistemological/ontological divide has ramifications for feminist work in FPA, a topic addressed in greater detail below.

Taken together, what do these concepts and principles mean for researchers interested in conducting feminist FPA? Historically, feminist researchers may have found their research questions and/or methodological options limited by the types of data available for analysis. The emergence of new data projects with a qualitative or mixed-methods focus may mitigate these limitations—though it does not eliminate them entirely. Similarly, the discussion calls upon researchers to reflect on their own axiological stance, i.e., how their values shape their research. Feminist researchers have argued that what makes research feminist—as opposed to being about gender or about women—is that such work both understands the importance of gender and seeks to improve women's lives (Tickner 2006). While methodological debates are likely to continue within the feminist research community, the examples in the following section illustrate how FFP research has grown as well as provide possible directions for the future.

Empirics

An openness to methodological pluralism in feminist work means that feminist FPA can proceed via multiple pathways. This section offers examples of just a few approaches—narrative and discourse analysis, quantitative research, and feminist fieldwork—deployed in recent work (for details on these methods and approaches see the other chapters in this volume).[2] This is not intended to represent an exhaustive list of methodologies but, rather, to highlight how feminist research is produced by the application of research methods in tandem with a feminist ethic and the application of gendered lenses.

Discourse and Narrative Analysis

A special issue of *Foreign Policy Analysis* (16:2) on Gender and Foreign Policy Analysis illustrates some of these dynamics at work. Editors Jacqui True and Karin Aggestam use their introduction to highlight the many points of agreement between feminist theory and FPA, including their mutual interest in bridging the domestic and international units of analysis, their focus on the interplay of agency and structure, and their openness to multiple methods of inquiry (Aggestam and True 2020). In the case of critical FPA, there are even more linkages to explore including a shared interest in the role of norms, nonstate actors and social movements, and national role conceptions (Holsti 1970; Checkel 1999; S. Smith, Hadfield, and Dunne 2012; Aggestam and True 2020). Work in the issue draws heavily on comparative analysis, engaging both the notion of national roles (all countries explored in the issue are so-called "middle powers," i.e., states that wield influence primarily through soft power and reputational interest) and normative orientation. In doing so, the editors advance a definition of what they call "pro-gender" norms in foreign policy, including a commitment to gender mainstreaming, international development assistance aimed at transformative gender relations, a commitment to women's security (as evidenced by support for the WPS agenda), and internal institutional reforms such as the establishment of ambassadors for gender empowerment (Aggestam and True 2020). The remainder of the issue explores these themes in the context of case studies of Australia, Canada, Norway, Sweden, and South Africa. The majority of these pieces incorporate content or discourse analysis, understanding the conceptualization and implementation of foreign policy via official government documents and statements from foreign policy elites (Bergman Rosamond 2020; Haastrup 2020; Lee-Koo 2020; Parisi 2020). Such an approach, common within both FPA and feminist research, allows researchers to track change and contestation in the shared understandings of policy, as well as how cultural and social factors shape policy outcomes (Hudson 2013).

In their contribution to the special issue, Skjelsbæk and Tryggestad (2020) further offer a narrative analysis of interviews with foreign policy elites, using these interviews to understand how values, interests, and perceptions of the relevance of gender are shaped by experiences within the foreign policy bureaucracy. Shepherd (2021, 31) describes narratives as "sticky arrangements of discourse" that concatenate actors' experiences and events into stories used to conjure and convey meaning (Bal 2017; Shepherd 2021). Feminist work embraces narrative analysis as a means of exploring research questions that are often left out of empirical political science inquiry (see also Oppermann and Spencer in this volume). Narrative analysis is seen as a way of interrogating and deconstructing meaning, exploring the relevance of lived experience, and understanding how rhetorical moves may serve and reinforce power relationships (Wibben 2011; 2014a). In this sense, narrative analysis aligns with feminist epistemological and ethical interests. The extent to which it also aligns with FPA is, perhaps, an underexplored topic. The notion of narrative and lived experience as formative to the construction of meaning and the actions of foreign policy elites would seem to represent an opportunity for engagement between feminist research and psychological approaches to FPA. The role of belief systems, schemas, or "associative networks," for example, similarly emphasize the importance of lived experience, social and psychological construction, and analogy in the attachment of meaning to concepts and situations (Larson 1994; McGraw 2000; Brunk 2008). Feminist narrative analysis may also speak to work on the role of culture in FPA, which further sees culture as a force for defining preferred processes and pathways (Hudson and Sampson 1999).

Feminist Quantitative Approaches

The existence of feminist quantitative work in FPA speaks directly to debates within feminist research, as noted above. Feminist researchers who argue in favor of the possibilities for such work argue that it is not solely the research method but also the methodological perspectives with which it is applied that matter (Caprioli 2004; Tickner 2006). In IR, an array of cross-national data projects over the past two decades has demonstrated how data collection may shed light on the lived experiences of women (See, inter alia, Cohen and Nordås 2014; Hudson et al. 2014; Henshaw 2017; Wood and Thomas 2017; Haer and Böhmelt 2018; GIWPS/PRIO 2019). At the same time, feminists working in data science have interrogated with it means to do feminist data analysis. D'Ignazio and Klein (2020) offer a list of potential principles to guide feminist data work, including the need to examine and challenge power relationships, to elevate emotion and embodiment, to rethink binaries and hierarchies, to embrace pluralism, to consider context, and to make visible the labor of data production.

The research of Towns and Niklasson (2017) demonstrates some of these principles at work. Drawing on a new data set of nearly 7,000 ambassador appointments, they interrogate where men and women are positioned and how gendered trends in appointments are determined by interstate power relationships, culture, and gender hierarchies. Their conclusions note that: (1) Women remain broadly underrepresented in ambassadorial appointments, with men holding 85% of all appointments, (2) patterns of appointments are shaped by cultural and normative commitments, for example with Nordic countries leading in appointments of women, and (3) economic and military power in recipient states impact gender patterns, with men more likely to hold "high status" postings (Towns and Niklasson 2017).

From a methodological perspective, this work demonstrates the application of several feminist principles. First, it creates data with the intent of rendering visible women's lived experience within the foreign policy elite. It further applies and analyzes that data in such a way as to examine and confront power relationships within the diplomatic realm and on the global stage. The authors are transparent in discussing their coding choices and in discussing the limitations of their work—for example, the question of whether the mere appointment of women as ambassadors has any substantive effect on the outcomes of diplomatic activity. In doing do, they implicitly reinforce the methodological pluralism associated with feminist analysis by citing and engaging with qualitative feminist and critical work.

Doing Feminist Fieldwork

This final methodological vignette explores how feminist fieldwork may be leveraged in FPA. As demonstrated above, interview-based research can offer important insights into gender policy analysis and FPA. Participant-observation and first-hand reflection from practitioners (see also Neumann in this volume) have also added richness to recent projects on gender in foreign and security policy (See, e.g., Cassidy 2019; Basu, Kirby, and Shepherd 2020). The rise in microfoundational and experimental research in political science has further provoked wider disciplinary conversations about fieldwork methods, ethics, and the limitations of such research. One outcome of this conversation is the recognition that fieldwork is not possible for all researchers, and the accessibility of fieldwork projects may reflect power dynamics in our profession. Researchers who are disabled, ill, or experiencing physical impairments may be unable to complete fieldwork projects, or may find their research outcomes impacted by these conditions (Ortbals and Rincker 2009; Perry 2020). The racial or ethnic identity of researchers may also impact fieldwork outcomes (Bouka 2015; King 2020; Nobles 2020). Such issues may be particularly pronounced for women, who have historically been underrepresented among researchers in the field (Kapiszewski, MacLean, and Read 2015, 48). Considerations like pregnancy, care work responsibilities, or the structural and resource limitations associated with high teaching- and service-load work can inhibit the capacity for women interested in feminist research to spend prolonged periods abroad. Gender dynamics in fieldwork contexts can also shape outcomes and access (Bouka

2015; Kapiszewski, MacLean, and Read 2015). In this sense, feminist researchers engaged in fieldwork must approach their work with the knowledge that the field is not level and reflect upon the impact of their own positionality.

Katherine A.M. Wright and Matthew Hurley are researchers who each independently conducted fieldwork and completed research projects on gender mainstreaming in NATO (Wright 2016; Hurley 2018a; 2018b; Wright, Hurley, and Ruiz 2019). In a reflection piece comparing their experiences, they note the various ways in which identity and power dynamics shaped their fieldwork experiences (Wright and Hurley 2017). Each express the sense their gender identity shaped their interactions with participants. The dynamics associated with elite interviewing also produced tensions, with the researchers both intimidated by the elite environment of NATO headquarters and at times—albeit unwittingly—intimidating research subjects who were afraid of being perceived as not knowledgeable enough.

In my own research experience, speaking to foreign policy elites in and around military bases and government facilities, I have also observed the dynamics of gender, race, seniority, and place (Henshaw 2021a). During successive rounds of fieldwork between 2018 and 2020 on gender and U.S. foreign policy, my personal networks and institutional affiliations unquestionably opened doors that may have been closed to others, while my gender (and, in some cases, familiarity with my work on the part of interviewees) helped build trust and rapport. Like Wright and Hurley (2017), I experienced the intimidation of place at interview sites as well as the tension of being "tested" by some subjects, who may have felt tested in turn. In some cases, the siting of fieldwork activities may heighten or mitigate tensions, depending on whether the setting renders power dynamics more or less visible (Cohn 2006; Fujii 2017). In any context, though, engaging in the field remains a relational activity—a *pas de deux* in which both researcher and subjects engage, but with the researcher ultimately privileged in both process and presentation of research outcomes (Fujii 2012).

Conclusions

This chapter has offered a brief glimpse into the possibilities for feminist FPA. In the space available, it has presented an overview of a few lines of inquiry and methodological approaches; however, the pluralism of feminist research should be a takeaway of this discussion. While feminist methodological debates exist, what makes work feminist is not its application of a specific method but, rather, its methodological, epistemological, and ethical stance. Seeing diverse experiences of gender, reflecting on one's own positionality, and engaging with the normative commitment to respect and—ideally—improve women's lived experience, are all best practices in feminist research. Future research in gender and FPA may build on a variety of other topics aside from those addressed here—for example, masculinity and foreign policy, Global South perspectives, and queer perspectives on FPA. One hopes that the engagements between feminist scholarship and FPA will continue to grow and yield new innovations.

Note

1 Academics interested in seeing how their own syllabi fare in terms of inclusion can use the Gender Balance Assessment Tool (GBAT), available at https://jlsumner.shinyapps.io/syllabustool/ (Sumner 2018).

References

Achilleos-Sarll, Columba. 2018. "Reconceptualizing Foreign Policy as Gendered, Sexualised, and Radicalised: Toward a Postcolonial Feminist Foreign Policy." *Journal of International Women's Studies* 19 (1): 34–49.

Achilleos-Sarll, Columba. 2020. "'Seeing' the Women, Peace and Security Agenda: Visual (Re)Productions of WPS in UK Government National Action Plans." *International Affairs* 96 (6): 1643–1663. https://doi.org/10.1093/ia/iiaa168.

Aggestam, Karin, and Annika Bergman Rosamond. 2019. "Feminist Foreign Policy 3.0: Advancing Ethics and Gender Equality in Global Politics." *SAIS Review of International Affairs* 39 (1): 37–48.

Aggestam, Karin, Annika Bergman Rosamond, and Annica Kronsell. 2019. "Theorising Feminist Foreign Policy." *International Relations* 33 (1): 23–39. https://doi.org/10.1177/0047117818811892.

Aggestam, Karin, and Jacqui True. 2020. "Gendering Foreign Policy: A Comparative Framework for Analysis." *Foreign Policy Analysis* 16 (2): 1–20. https://doi.org/10.1093/fpa/orz026.

Bal, Mieke. 2017. *Narratology: Introduction to the Theory of Narrative, Fourth Edition*. 4th Edition. Toronto Buffalo London: University of Toronto Press, Scholarly Publishing Division.

Barnes, Tiffany D., and Diana Z. O'Brien. 2018. "Defending the Realm: The Appointment of Female Defense Ministers Worldwide." *American Journal of Political Science* 62 (2): 355–368.

Bashevkin, Sylvia. 2018. *Women as Foreign Policy Leaders: National Security and Gender Politics in Superpower America*. New York: Oxford University Press.

Bastick, Megan, and Claire Duncanson. 2018. "Agents of Change? Gender Advisors in NATO Militaries." *International Peacekeeping* 25 (4): 554–577. https://doi.org/10.1080/13533312.2018.1492876.

Basu, Soumita, and Paul Kirby, eds. 2020. "Women, Peace and Security: A Critical Cartography." In *New Directions in Women, Peace and Security*, edited by Soumita Basu, Paul Kirby and Laura J. Shepherd, 1st Edition, 1–28. Bristol: Policy Press.

Basu, Soumita, Paul Kirby, and Laura Shepherd, eds. 2020. *New Directions in Women, Peace and Security*. 1st Edition. Bristol: Policy Press.

Bergman Rosamond, Annika. 2020. "Swedish Feminist Foreign Policy and 'Gender Cosmopolitanism.'" *Foreign Policy Analysis* 16 (2): 217–235. https://doi.org/10.1093/fpa/orz025.

Bouka, Yolande. 2015. "Researching Violence in Africa as a Black Woman: Notes from Rwanda." *Research in Difficult Settings*. Hamilton, NY: Colgate University/Conflict Field Research. http://conflictfieldresearch.colgate.edu/wp-content/uploads/2015/05/Bouka_WorkingPaper-May2015.pdf.

Breuning, Marijke, and Kathryn Sanders. 2007. "Gender and Journal Authorship in Eight Prestigious Political Science Journals." *PS: Political Science & Politics* 40 (2): 347–351. https://doi.org/10.1017/S1049096507070564.

Brunk, Darren C. 2008. "Curing the Somalia Syndrome: Analogy, Foreign Policy Decision Making, and the Rwandan Genocide." *Foreign Policy Analysis* 4 (3): 301–320. https://doi.org/10.1111/j.1743-8594.2008.00071.x.

Caprioli, Mary. 2004. "Feminist IR Theory and Quantitative Methodology: A Critical Analysis." *International Studies Review* 6 (2): 253–269.

Cassidy, Jennifer A., ed. 2019. *Gender and Diplomacy*. 1st Edition. London: Routledge.

Checkel, Jeffrey T. 1999. "Norms, Institutions, and National Identity in Contemporary Europe." *International Studies Quarterly* 43 (1): 83–114.

Cohen, Dara Kay, and Ragnhild Nordås. 2014. "Sexual Violence in Armed Conflict: Introducing SVAC Dataset 1989-2009." *Journal of Peace Research* 51 (3): 418–428.

Cohn, Carol. 1987. "Sex and Death in the Rational World of Defense Intellectuals." *Signs* 12 (4): 687–718.

Cohn, Carol. 2006. "Motives and Methods: Using Multi-Sited Ethnography to Study U.S. National Security Discourses." In *Feminist Methodologies for International Relations*, edited by Brooke A. Ackerly, Maria Stern and Jacqui True, 1st Edition, 91–107. New York: Cambridge University Press.

Crapol, Edward P. 1992. *Women and American Foreign Policy: Lobbyists, Critics, and Insiders*. 2nd Edition. Wilmington, Del: Rowman & Littlefield Publishers.

Davis, Jessica, Leah West, and Amarnath Amarasingam. 2021. "Measuring Impact, Uncovering Bias? Citation Analysis of Literature on Women in Terrorism." *Perspectives on Terrorism* 15 (2): 58–76.

Davis, Megan, Erin McGrath, and Betsy Super. 2019. *2017–2018 APSA Departmental Survey: Enrollments and Curriculums*. Washington DC: American Political Science Association. https://www.apsanet.org/Portals/54/APSA%20Files/Data%20Reports/Enrollment%20Data/APSA%20Departmental%20Survey_Enrollment%20and%20Curriculum_FINAL.pdf?ver=2019-05-21-113745-243.

D'Ignazio, Catherine, and Lauren F. Klein. 2020. *Data Feminism*. Cambridge, Massachusetts: The MIT Press.

Dion, Michelle L., Jane Lawrence Sumner, and Sara McLaughlin Mitchell. 2018. "Gendered Citation Patterns across Political Science and Social Science Methodology Fields." *Political Analysis* 26 (3): 312–327. https://doi.org/10.1017/pan.2018.12.

Djupe, Paul A., Amy Erica Smith, and Anand E. Sokhey. 2019. "Explaining Gender in the Journals: How Submission Practices Affect Publication Patterns in Political Science." *PS: Political Science & Politics* 52 (1): 71–77.

Duriesmith, David. 2020. "Friends Don't Let Friends Cite the Malestream: A Case for Strategic Silence in Feminist International Relations." *International Feminist Journal of Politics* 22 (1): 26–32. https://doi.org/10.1080/14616742.2019.1700818.

Enloe, Cynthia. 1999. *Maneuvers*. Berkeley, CA: University of California Press.

Enloe, Cynthia. 2014. *Bananas, Beaches and Bases: Making Feminist Sense of International Politics*. 2nd Edition, Completely Revised and Updated. Berkeley, CA: University of California Press.

Enloe, Cynthia H. 1983. *Does Khaki Become You?: The Militarisation of Women's Lives*. London: Pluto Press.

Free and Equal. 2017. *Fact Sheet: Intersex*. New York: United Nations Office of the High Commissioner on Human Rights. https://www.unfe.org/wp-content/uploads/2017/05/UNFE-Intersex.pdf.

Fujii, Lee Ann. 2012. "Research Ethics 101: Dilemmas and Responsibilities." *PS: Political Science & Politics* 45 (4): 717–723. https://doi.org/10.1017/S1049096512000819.

Fujii, Lee Ann. 2017. *Interviewing in Social Science Research: A Relational Approach*. London: Routledge.

GIWPS/PRIO. 2019. "Women, Peace, and Security Index." *Women, Peace, and Security Index*. 2020, 2019. https://giwps.georgetown.edu/the-index/.

Goldstein, Joshua. 2001. *War and Gender*. Cambridge: Cambridge University Press.

Haastrup, Toni. 2020. "Gendering South Africa's Foreign Policy: Toward a Feminist Approach?" *Foreign Policy Analysis* 16 (2): 199–216. https://doi.org/10.1093/fpa/orz030.

Haastrup, Toni, and Jamie Hagen. 2020. "Global Racial Hierarchies and the Limits of Localization via National Action Plans." In *New Directions in Women, Peace and Security*, edited by Soumita Basu, Paul Kirby and Laura J. Shepherd, 1st Edition, 133–153. Bristol: Policy Press.

Haer, Roos, and Tobias Böhmelt. 2018. "Girl Soldiering in Rebel Groups, 1989–2013: Introducing a New Dataset." *Journal of Peace Research* 55 (3): 395–403. https://doi.org/10.1177/0022343317752540.

Hamilton, Caitlin, Nyibeny Naam, and Laura Shepherd. 2020. *Twenty Years of Women, Peace and Security National Action Plans: Analysis and Lessons Learned*. Sydney, Australia: University of Sydney. https://www.wpsnaps.org/app/uploads/2020/03/Twenty-Years-of-Women-Peace-and-Security-National-Action-Plans_Report_Final_Web.pdf.

Han, Lori Cox, and Caroline Heldman. 2019. "Teaching Women/Gender and Politics: Current Trends and Challenges." *PS: Political Science & Politics* 52 (3): 531–535. https://doi.org/10.1017/S1049096519000155.

Hardt, Heidi, and Stéfanie von Hlatky. 2020. "NATO's About-Face: Adaptation to Gender Mainstreaming in an Alliance Setting." *Journal of Global Security Studies* 5 (1): 136–159. https://doi.org/10.1093/jogss/ogz048.

Henshaw, Alexis. 2021a. "Gendered Labor in the Making of U.S. Policy on Women, Peace, and Security: An Interagency Perspective." *International Feminist Journal of Politics*. https://doi.org/10.1080/14616742.2021.2011762

Henshaw, Alexis. 2021b. "Mainstreaming Gender in Research Methods." In *Teaching Research Methods in Political Science*, edited by Jeffrey Bernstein, 222–237. Cheltenham, UK: Edward Elgar.

Henshaw, Alexis Leanna. 2017. *Why Women Rebel: Understanding Women's Participation in Armed Rebel Groups*. New York: Routledge.

Henshaw, Alexis Leanna. 2020. "Female Combatants in Postconflict Processes: Understanding the Roots of Exclusion." *Journal of Global Security Studies* 5 (1): 63–79. https://doi.org/10.1093/jogss/ogz050.

Hesli, Vicki L., and Jae Mook Lee. 2011. "Faculty Research Productivity: Why Do Some of Our Colleagues Publish More than Others?" *PS: Political Science & Politics* 44 (2): 393–408. https://doi.org/10.1017/S1049096511000242.

Hesli, Vicki L., Jae Mook Lee, and Sara McLaughlin Mitchell. 2012. "Predicting Rank Attainment in Political Science: What Else Besides Publications Affects Promotion?" *PS: Political Science & Politics* 45 (3): 475–492. https://doi.org/10.1017/S1049096512000364.

Hidalgo, F. Daniel, Suzanna Linn, Margaret Roberts, Betsy Sinclair, and Rocio Titiunik. 2018. *Report on Diversity and Inclusion in the Society for Political Methodology*. Washington DC: American Political Science Association.

Holsti, K. J. 1970. "National Role Conceptions in the Study of Foreign Policy." *International Studies Quarterly* 14 (3): 233–309. https://doi.org/10.2307/3013584.

Hudson, Valerie M. 2013. *Foreign Policy Analysis: Classic and Contemporary Theory*. 2nd Edition. Lanham: Rowman & Littlefield Publishers.

Hudson, Valerie, Bonnie Ballif-Spanvill, Mary Caprioli, and Chad Emmett. 2014. *Sex and World Peace*. Revised Edition. New York: Columbia University Press.

Hudson, Valerie M., Mary Caprioli, Chad F. Emmett, Rose McDermott, Matthew Stearmer, and Bonnie Ballif-Spanvill. 2014. *WomanStats Codebook*. http://www.womanstats.org/CodebookCurrent.htm.

Hudson, Valerie M., and Martin W. Sampson. 1999. "Editor's Introduction: Culture Is More than a Static Residual: Introduction to the Special Section on Culture and Foreign Policy." *Political Psychology* 20 (4): 667–675.

Hurley, Matthew. 2018a. "The 'Genderman': (Re)Negotiating Militarized Masculinities When 'Doing Gender' at NATO." *Critical Military Studies* 4 (1): 72–91. https://doi.org/10.1080/23337486.2016.1264108.

Hurley, Matthew. 2018b. "Watermelons and Weddings: Making Women, Peace and Security 'Relevant' at NATO Through (Re)Telling Stories of Success." *Global Society* 32 (4): 436–456. https://doi.org/10.1080/13600826.2018.1440195.

Kapiszewski, Diana, Lauren M. MacLean, and Benjamin L. Read. 2015. *Field Research in Political Science: Practices and Principles*. New York: Cambridge University Press.

King, Desmond. 2020. "'Why Are You Interested in That?': Studying Racial Inequality in the United States from the Outside." In *Stories from the Field: A Guide to Navigating Fieldwork in Political Science*, edited by Peter Krause, and Ora Szekely, 245–253. New York: Columbia University Press.

Kirby, Paul, and Laura J. Shepherd. 2016. "The Futures Past of the Women, Peace and Security Agenda." *International Affairs* 92 (2): 373–392. https://doi.org/10.1111/1468-2346.12549.

Larson, Deborah Welch. 1994. "The Role of Belief Systems and Schemas in Foreign Policy Decision-Making." *Political Psychology* 15 (1): 17–33. https://doi.org/10.2307/3791437.

Lee-Koo, Katrina. 2020. "Pro-Gender Foreign Policy by Stealth: Navigating Global and Domestic Politics in Australian Foreign Policy Making." *Foreign Policy Analysis* 16 (2): 236–249. https://doi.org/10.1093/fpa/orz029.

Maliniak, Daniel, Ryan Powers, and Barbara F. Walter. 2013. "The Gender Citation Gap in International Relations." *International Organization* 67 (4): 889–922. https://doi.org/10.1017/S0020818313000209.

McGlen, Nancy E., and Meredith Reid Sarkees. 1993. *Women in Foreign Policy: The Insiders*. New York: Routledge.

McGraw, Kathleen M. 2000. "Contributions of the Cognitive Approach to Political Psychology." *Political Psychology* 21 (4): 805–832.

Mitchell, Sara McLaughlin, and Vicki L. Hesli. 2013. "Women Don't Ask? Women Don't Say No? Bargaining and Service in the Political Science Profession." *PS: Political Science & Politics* 46 (2): 355–369. https://doi.org/10.1017/S1049096513000073.

Mitchell, Sara McLaughlin, Samantha Lange, and Holly Brus. 2013. "Gendered Citation Patterns in International Relations Journals." *International Studies Perspectives* 14 (4): 485–492. https://doi.org/10.1111/insp.12026.

Nobles, Melissa. 2020. "Race and the Study of a Racial Democracy." In *Stories from the Field: A Guide to Navigating Fieldwork in Political Science*, edited by Peter Krause and Ora Szekely, 238–244. New York: Columbia University Press.

Ortbals, Candice D., and Meg E. Rincker. 2009. "Embodied Researchers: Gendered Bodies, Research Activity, and Pregnancy in the Field." *PS: Political Science & Politics* 42 (2): 315–319. https://doi.org/10.1017/S1049096509090635.

Parisi, Laura. 2020. "Canada's New Feminist International Assistance Policy: Business as Usual?" *Foreign Policy Analysis* 16 (2): 163–180. https://doi.org/10.1093/fpa/orz027.

Paxton, Pamela M., and Melanie M. Hughes. 2013. *Women, Politics, and Power: A Global Perspective*. 2nd Edition. Thousand Oaks, CA: SAGE Publications, Inc.

Paxton, Pamela, Melanie M. Hughes, and Tiffany D. Barnes. 2020. *Women, Politics, and Power: A Global Perspective*. 4th Edition. Lanham: Rowman & Littlefield Publishers.

Perry, Ravi. 2020. "Shingles on the Campaign Trail." In *Stories from the Field: A Guide to Navigating Fieldwork in Political Science*, edited by Peter Krause and Ora Szekely, 335–339. New York: Columbia University Press.

Randall, Vicky. 2002. "Feminism." In *Theory and Methods in Political Science*, 2nd Edition, 109–130. New York: Palgrave MacMillan.

Reiter, Dan. 2014. "The Positivist Study of Gender in International Relations." *Journal of Conflict Resolution* December 2014: 1–26.

Reiter, Dan. 2015. "Gender in IR, Now at the Cutting Edge." *Duck of Minerva* (blog). 2015. https://duckofminerva.com/2015/04/gender-in-ir-now-at-the-cutting-edge.html.

Runyan, Anne Sisson, and Spike Peterson, V. 2013. *Global Gender Issues in the New Millennium*. 4th Edition. Boulder, CO: Westview Press.

Scola, Becki, Laura C. Bucci, and Lisa Baglione. 2020. "'Pale, Male, and Stale'? An Analysis of Introductory Readers in Political Science." *Journal of Political Science Education* 0 (0): 1–24. https://doi.org/10.1080/15512169.2020.1818574.

Shepherd, Laura J. 2016. "Making War Safe for Women? National Action Plans and the Militarisation of the Women, Peace and Security Agenda:" *International Political Science Review*, March. https://doi.org/10.1177/0192512116629820.

Shepherd, Laura J. 2021. *Narrating the Women, Peace and Security Agenda: Logics of Global Governance*. 1st Edition. New York,: Oxford University Press.

Sjoberg, Laura. 2009. "Introduction to Security Studies: Feminist Contributions." *Security Studies* 18 (2): 183–213.

Sjoberg, Laura, Kelly Kadera, and Cameron Thies. 2018. "Reevaluating Gender and IR Scholarship: Moving beyond Reiter's Dichotomies toward Effective Synergies." *Journal of Conflict Resolution* 62 (4): 848–870.

Skjelsbæk, Inger, and Torunn Lise Tryggestad. 2020. "Pro-Gender Norms in Norwegian Peace Engagement: Balancing Experiences, Values, and Interests." *Foreign Policy Analysis* 16 (2): 181–198. https://doi.org/10.1093/fpa/orz028.

Smith, Karen E. 2020. "Missing in Analysis: Women in Foreign Policy–Making." *Foreign Policy Analysis* 16 (1): 130–141. https://doi.org/10.1093/fpa/orz019.

Smith, Steve, Amelia Hadfield, and Tim Dunne. 2012. *Foreign Policy: Theories, Actors, Cases*. 2nd Edition. Oxford: Oxford University Press.

Stern, Maria, and Annick Wibben. 2014. "A Decade of Feminist Security Studies Revisited." *Security Dialogue* Special Virtual Issue: 1–6.

Sumner, Jane Lawrence. 2018. "The Gender Balance Assessment Tool (GBAT): A Web-Based Tool for Estimating Gender Balance in Syllabi and Bibliographies." *PS: Political Science & Politics* 51 (2): 396–400. https://doi.org/10.1017/S1049096517002074.

Teele, Dawn Langan, and Kathleen Thelen. 2017. "Gender in the Journals: Publication Patterns in Political Science." *PS: Political Science & Politics* 50 (2): 433–447. https://doi.org/10.1017/S1049096516002985.

Tickner, J. Ann. 2001. *Gendering World Politics*. New York: Columbia University Press.

Tickner, J. Ann. 2006. "Feminism Meets International Relations: Some Methodological Issues." In *Feminist Methodologies for International Relations*, edited by Brooke A. Ackerly, Maria Stern and Jacqui True, 1st Edition. New York: Cambridge University Press.

Towns, Ann, and Birgitta Niklasson. 2017. "Gender, International Status, and Ambassador Appointments." *Foreign Policy Analysis* 13 (3): 521–540. https://doi.org/10.1093/fpa/orw039.

Weber, Cynthia. 1999. *Faking It: U.S. Hegemony in a "Post-Phallic" Era*. University of Minnesota Press.

Weldon, S. Laurel. 2006. "Inclusion and Understanding: A Collective Methodology for Feminist International Relations." In *Feminist Methodologies for International Relations*, edited by Brooke A. Ackerly, Maria Stern and Jacqui True, 1st Edition. Cambridge University Press.

Wibben, Annick T. R. 2011. *Feminist Security Studies: A Narrative Approach*. 1st Edition. Routledge.

Wibben, Annick T. R. 2014a. "On Narrative, Metaphor and the Politics of Security." In *Warring with Words: Narrative and Metaphor in Politics*, edited by Michael Hanne, William D. Crano and Jeffery Scott Mio, 118–136. New York: Psychology Press.

Wibben, Annick T. R. 2014b. "Researching Feminist Security Studies." *Australian Journal of Political Science* 49 (4): 743–755. https://doi.org/10.1080/10361146.2014.971100.

WomanStats. n.d. *The WomanStats Project*. n.d. http://www.womanstats.org/aboutoverview.html.
Wood, Reed M., and Jakana L Thomas. 2017. "Women on the Frontline: Rebel Group Ideology and Women's Participation in Violent Rebellion." *Journal of Peace Research* 54 (1): 31–46. https://doi.org/10.1177/0022343316675025.
Wright, Hannah. 2020. "'Masculinities Perspectives': Advancing a Radical Women, Peace, and Security Agenda?" *International Feminist Journal of Politics* 22 (5): 652–674.
Wright, Katharine A. M. 2016. "NATO'S Adoption of UNSCR 1325 on Women, Peace and Security: Making the Agenda a Reality." *International Political Science Review* 37 (3): 350–361. https://doi.org/10.1177/0192512116638763.
Wright, Katharine A. M., and Matthew Hurley. 2017. "Navigating Gender, Power and Perceptions When Researching NATO: A Conversation." *International Feminist Journal of Politics* 19 (3): 390–392. https://doi.org/10.1080/14616742.2017.1324096.
Wright, Katharine A. M., Matthew Hurley, and Jesus Ignacio Gil Ruiz. 2019. *NATO, Gender and the Military: Women Organising from Within*. New York: Routledge.
Youngs, Gillian, Kathleen B. Jones, and Jan Jindy Pettman. 1999. "New Spaces, New Politics." *International Feminist Journal of Politics* 1 (1): 1–13. https://doi.org/10.1080/146167499360013.
Zalewski, Marysia. 2006. "Distracted Reflections on the Production, Narration, and Refusal of Feminist Knowledge in International Relations." In *Feminist Methodologies for International Relations*, edited by Brooke A. Ackerly, Maria Stern and Jacqui True, 1st Edition. Cambridge University Press.

6
Political Geography
Luis da Vinha

Introduction

Foreign policy and geography have a long and complicated relationship. In particular, the role of geography in foreign policymaking has either been wholly overstated or completely neglected. Political, cultural, and scientific developments, particularly since the mid-twentieth century have greatly contributed to shaping this tumultuous relationship. However, after a time of disengagement, the last few decades have witnessed a renewed disposition for reconciling these two complementary bodies of knowledge. Currently, there is a shared acknowledgement that Geography is essential to understanding international politics and, more specifically, foreign policy (Pickering 2018).

Geography has traditionally differentiated itself from other scientific disciplines, particularly in the social sciences, by arguing that it provides a unique framework for understanding the complex inter-connections underscoring political problems from the local to the global scales (Jackson 2006). As the French geographer Jean Gottman (1951, 153) keenly argued over seven decades ago, "If the earth were uniform – well polished, like a billiard ball – there probably would not be any such science as geography, and international relations would be much simpler."

As the understanding of the concept *political* developed in recent decades, the complicity between International Relations (IR) and Geography was increasingly recognized by scholars in both disciplinary fields. As a result, a renewed Political Geography has re-established itself as a credible academic endeavor, particularly in relation to international political phenomena. Over the past few decades, the academic endeavors of authors such as John Agnew (2003a), Simon Dalby (2002), Colin Flint (2005), Colin Gray (1988), and Gearóid Ó Tuathail (1996), among many others, have reenergized the field of Political Geography, placing it once again at the center of the debates on the most pressing issues in international politics. Today, political geographers of all strands are at the forefront answering questions as diverse as how changes to the international distribution of power are affecting international order (Newman and Visoka 2021), how economic dynamics are reshaping regional and global interactions (Solingen 2021), what is the appeal of human rights and democratic governance in a period of growing authoritarianism (Regilme Jr. 2021), how global environmental issues are transforming international relations (Dalby 2020), and how governments engage with the challenges presented in cyberspace (Kamarck 2011). Ultimately, Political Geography's subtle use of concepts such as *space* and *place* help improve our understanding of the complex relationship between geographical and political phenomena.

To be sure, despite this recent convergence, Political Geography and Political Science, particularly Foreign Policy Analysis (FPA), still diverge in many aspects. Conceptual, theoretical, and methodological issues contrast as both disciplinary areas continue to differ in varying degrees. In fact, not much has changed in the two decades since John O'Loughlin (2000, 126) identified the "import-export imbalance of information" between Political Geography and Political Science. According to the author, while political geographers incorporated many of the theoretical and methodological innovations of Political Science, political scientists for their part did not reciprocate by expanding their understanding of Geography. This is particularly true in the field of IR, which continues to espouse an archaic conception of Geography and its main conceptual elements. While IR scholars have increasingly embraced Geography, according to Flint, Diehl, Scheffran, Vasquez, and Chi (2009, 827), they have "not developed a sophisticated understanding of the term."

In fact, as John Agnew (2003b) and John O'Loughlin (2018) have argued in their reflections on the status of the field, much of the scholarly work labeled Political Geography is either not very political or very geographical. Today claims of intellectual exclusivity would be considered ludicrous as interdisciplinarity is celebrated rather than disparaged. However, while Political Geography as an academic discipline has increasingly embraced different theoretical and methodological approaches over time, it is united by a set of research questions and key concepts – such as space, place, and environment – that have defined Geography since its institutionalization as a body of scientific knowledge. More precisely, Political Geography employs these concepts as analytical frameworks for studying how geography and political issues interact, with a particular emphasis on understanding how the former affects the latter.

This chapter provides an overview of how Political Geography has engaged with foreign policy issues over time. While risking oversimplification, I provide a cursory account of the historical relationship between political geography and foreign policy, as well as an assessment of the main conceptual and methodological issues contributing to the development of the discipline. I also provide an empirical example using geographical mental maps as an analytical concept to illustrate how Political Geography can contribute to improving our understanding of foreign policy decision-making. The chapter concludes with a brief reflection on the challenges and opportunities facing Political Geography in its relationship with FPA.

Political Geography and Foreign Policy: A Complex Relationship

Providing a precise account of the development of Political Geography is a daunting task. As O'Loughlin (2018, 144) recently acknowledged, as a sub-discipline of Human Geography, it "is chaotic and is lacking internal cohesion, agreement on core tenets, and is characterized by faddism and dilettantism." Ultimately, Political Geography manifests many of the problems that geographers have faced in defining the discipline as a whole since its institutionalization as a distinct field of scientific knowledge. Since its academic foundations in the first half of the nineteenth century, scholars and practitioners alike have struggled to provide a definitive answer to "what geographers *are*, what geographers *do*, or *how* they should study the world" (Hubbard et al. 2005, 10). Geography's unique position as a mediator between the physical and social sciences inherently hindered the development of a strict homogenous intellectual endeavor. Even the split between Physical and Human Geography has not helped to clarify these questions.[1]

Just like its parent discipline, Political Geography also has a convoluted history. To begin with, when surveying the scholarly literature, one is immediately befuddled by the diverse nomenclature employed by different scholars. It is common to find some scholars making reference to Political Geography and Geopolitics as if they are synonymous. In fact, upon reflecting on the importance of espousing a geographical perspective for understanding international affairs, Colin Flint (2013) claims that there are no significant distinctions between the two concepts. According to the author, in recent years "the distinction between geopolitics and political geography has become blurred, and arguably meaningless" (ibid, 159). In contrast several other scholars argue that Political Geography and Geopolitics are two distinct fields of intellectual inquiry (see Kuus 2009; Martin 1959). This conceptual perplexity results from the tumultuous historical development of Political Geography. Its meaning has changed substantially as political, social, cultural, and scientific developments have generated profound introspection among political geographers regarding the objects, theories, and methodological underpinnings of their discipline (Agnew and Muscarà 2012).

In reality, the two terms – Political Geography and Geopolitics – were indeed one and the same until the early twentieth century. The sub-discipline was founded in the political context of the late nineteenth-century imperial competition among the Great Powers. The works of scholars such as Rudolf Kjellén, Friedrich Ratzel, Halford Mackinder, Karl Haushofer, and Nicholas Spykman shaped the early years of Political Geography. While each scholar contributed to the field in different ways, there are several distinct features that characterized what has become commonly designated as *classical geopolitics*. To begin with, the geographical features of the Earth were seen to determine the political world since it was believed that "in geography lie the clues to the problems of military and political strategy" (Spykman 2007 [1942], 41). Accordingly, Political Geography presented itself as the science that could identify and explain how geography dictates global political interactions.

Equally important, the nation-state was the key political reference for the sub-discipline. Since geographical information and knowledge was produced on behalf of the state, it was assumed that statesmen needed to have a firm grasp of the Earth's main geographical features in order to develop policies that could guarantee their political and economic success over rivals. Underlying this rationale was a racially oriented geographical perspective that justified and legitimized the "civilizing missions" of the imperial powers (Mackinder 1996 [1942]). Therefore, during this period, as Agnew, Mamadouh, Secor, and Sharpe (2015, 3) argue, "political geographical analysis thus involved explaining the success and actions of states and their elites based on their physical locations and resources."

However, by the end of the first half of the twentieth century, Political Geography – particularly in its geopolitical garb – found itself under siege. Its association with Nazi politics and Germany's territorial expansionism tarnished its reputation and delegitimized its standing as an academic field of inquiry. Whereas some of the concepts central to classical geopolitics continued to inform foreign policymaking in many national capitals, the work that continued to be conducted under the banner of Political Geography in academia, focused on more technical issues dealing with spatial planning and electoral districts, and disengaging from political issues (Flint 2013).

Geographers began re-engaging with politics in the late-1960s and the 1970s, particularly through a growing intellectual affinity with Marxist theories that emphasized issues of unequal distribution of economic and political power. As a result, Geography began placing greater importance on studying the spatial distribution and production of power relationships (Unwin 1992). This trend was bolstered in the 1980s by the broader changes to Human Geography's ontological and epistemological foundations brought about by postmodern philosophies. Postmodernism realigned the discipline with mainstream social theories that rejected the epistemological foundations of positivism and refocused the discipline on issues of power. Michael Dear accurately identified the destabilizing effect of postmodernism in Human Geography (1998) by highlighting its role in challenging any claims to authority and identifying its commitment to resist any attempts to build hegemonic claims to knowledge.

The natural result of this new approach was that Human Geography, along with its many subdisciplines, increasingly focused on political issues. In particular, urban geographers, cultural geographers, and environmental geographers, among others, centered their research on small "p" politics such as identity, gender, sexuality, environment, and other non-traditional political issues (Flint 2003). Many of the assumptions underscoring postmodernism were also embraced by many political geographers, leading to a revitalization of Political Geography. In contrast to other subfields of Geography, political geographers continued to place an emphasis on large-*P* politics which continue fixated on the political interactions among states and other themes of "high politics" (ibid).

Thus, after decades of ignominy, after the end of the Cold War, Political Geography once again recovered its academic standing and established itself as one of the most vibrant and prominent fields of geographical research. As Pickering (2018, 775) enthusiastically notes, "we are now in a position where a whole generation of geographers coming from many different perspectives are taking back the term 'geopolitics,' recognizing its history and applying it in new and useful ways."

One of the main schools of thought in the rejuvenated field of Political Geography embraced a critical approach. *Critical Geopolitics*, as this school of thought has become known, incorporates many of the theoretical assumptions of the post-positivist theories in IR to address the international political challenges of the post-Cold War world. More specifically, geographers began to address issues of how certain geographical representations gained an institutional and political preeminence and how these representations were used to legitimize certain policies. While a precise definition of Critical Geopolitics remains unsurprisingly elusive (see Ó Tuathail et al. 2010), since the early 1990s, research under its banner has grown to a position of preeminence in Political Geography (Dalby 2010). Over the years, this research has sought to expose the structures of power and knowledge underlying hegemonic geopolitical narratives. Critical Geopolitics, therefore, focused its attention and scholarly enterprise on contextualizing traditional geopolitical narratives and exposing the biases and political agendas of classical geopoliticians and their political heirs. Ultimately, Critical Geopolitics tries to speak *truth to power* by confronting the geopolitical narratives driving the foreign policy of major international powers.

Research in critical geopolitics swelled as U.S. interventionism increased after the Cold War. Critical geopolitical scientists challenged American foreign policy and its increased militarism, as well as the growing securitization of non-traditional threats such as development (Dalby 2010). America's response to the terrorist attacks of 11 September 2001 further invigorated Critical Geopolitics. In particular, the war in Iraq spurred a vast amount of research seeking to deconstruct the American geopolitical narratives of the *war on terror* and expose the imperial strategy underscoring U.S. foreign policy (see Coward 2005; Dalby 2008; Elden 2007; Gregory 2004).

However, while commentators such as Agnew (2000) are correct to point out that Critical Geopolitics has shifted Political Geography from advocates of state policy to critical commentators of international events, they tend to overlook its underlying agenda of political transformation. In other words, we cannot sever Critical Geopolitics' agenda from the larger commitment of critical theory to political emancipation from hegemonic power. As Richard Devetak (1995, 37) pointedly explains, critical theory seeks to move beyond merely enlightening us to the oppressive structures of domination, but rather to concentrate our efforts on "transcending the present system by specifying the historical conditions under which the dominant order might give way to 'alternative oppositional coalitions'."

The failure to achieve this objective has been the basis for many of the recent indictments against Critical Geopolitics (see Kelly 2006). Scholars have highlighted how the normalization and institutionalization of critical research in geography has led it, in their view, to lose its progressive edge, increasingly running the risk of "becoming uncritical" (Blomley 2006, 88). These critiques might be exaggerated if we are to be humble in evaluating the role that academic research actually plays in driving social revolutions. That said, we cannot fail to point out that by focusing its efforts on exposing the structures of power underlying geographical discourses, critical geopolitics "tells us how but not why geopolitical knowledge is constructed where it is and by whom" (Agnew 2000, 98).

To address these latter issues, another, more understated, school of thought in Political Geography developed alongside critical geopolitics. Cognitive Geopolitics, as David Criekemans (2010) has labeled this school of thought, diverges from its critical counterpart by placing its main focus on understanding foreign policy decision-makers' perceptions of their geopolitical environment. While some initial studies developed these themes under the research agenda of the environmental perception movement, these studies only gained traction in Political Geography with the dissemination of constructivist theories across the social sciences. Constructivism's emphasis on the socially constructed nature of individuals' interests and identities allowed geographers to analyze how political and geographical phenomena are dynamic and interconnected (Flint 2013).

Cognitive Geopolitics differs from its critical counterpart in several important aspects. The most important distinction, however, is that it does not assume that political decision-makers have *a priori* grand designs of exploitation. In other words, while critical geopoliticians' main focus "is on exposing the plays of power involved in grand geopolitical schemes" (Ó Tuathail 1992, 438), cognitive geopolitical scientists are more concerned with how geography influences foreign policy decision-makers understanding of the political world, and particularly how it contributes to define the "problem representation" underscoring foreign policy decision-making (da Vinha 2019). Accordingly, by focusing on policymaker's perceptions of the international political environment, Cognitive Geopolitics is much more aligned with the key tenets of the FPA research agenda. By placing individuals and the decision-making process at the center of its analysis, FPA tends to reject unbounded rationalist explanations of foreign policy by seeking to identify "the definition of the situation created by the human decisionmakers" (Hudson and Day 2020, 8).

Over the years, cognitive geopoliticians have used several different analytical concepts, such as cognitive maps (O'Loughlin and Grant 1990), image plans (Henrikson 1980), geographical images (Kolossov 2003), geographical mental maps (da Vinha 2017), and geopolitical codes (Dijkink 1998), to analyze foreign policymakers' geographical representations. This has contributed to making cognitive geopolitics a heterogeneous field of research. The lack of agreement on basic theoretical and methodological issues hinders the development of a more consistent approach and has contributed to cognitive geographers assuming a less pronounced role than their critical counterparts in driving developments in Political Geography.

Conceptual and Methodological Issues in Political Geography

As mentioned above, Political Geography encompasses a broad array of conceptual, theoretical, and methodological approaches. However, we can contextualize the main concepts and methods employed by the different schools of thought in Political Geography. Geography is structured around several key central concepts of which *space* and *place* are the most important (Massey 1994; Matthews and Herbert 2004). The different schools of thought in Political Geography have embraced these two concepts to different degrees, with significant methodological implications (see O'Loughlin 2018). Since the second half of the twentieth century we have witnessed a proliferation of different methods that have generated a rift within the discipline, particularly evident in Political Geography (Herbert and Matthews 2004). More to the point, we can identify a stark division between what has been dubbed the "spatial analysts" and the "social theorists."

While risking oversimplification, traditional geopolitical theories focused on spatial phenomena to explain politics. This yielded a rudimentary and deterministic approach to *space*, based essentially on how the Earth's physical features determined states' foreign policies. More recently, a neoclassical school of geopolitics has surfaced employing spatial theories and models to explain international events.[2] While space has become a highly contested concept, neoclassical geopoliticians tend to continue to employ a simplified concept of it in their analyses. Rather than viewing space as a product of complex social, economic, and political processes, neoclassical geopolitical scholars build on the legacy of the spatial quantitative revolution and view geographical space as being an essentially tangible, immutable, and deterministic variable that can be quantified and measured. More importantly, they seek to generate law-like statements that can explain international political phenomena. As a result, they tend to concentrate their analyses on spatial primitives such as location, distance, sequence and order, and connection (Cox, Murray, and Robinson 2008).

The most basic spatial variable emphasized in this line of research is *distance*. For instance, while realism has traditionally assumed that distance hinders the ability of states to project power, Markowitz and Fariss (2013) employ a negative binomial regression model and a generalized estimation equation (GEE) model of spatial analysis to assess how technological innovations and economic wealth affect states' ability to project power abroad.[3] More precisely, the authors measure the distance between the capitals of belligerent states and the location of the militarized interstate disputes (MIDs) throughout a long time series. Subsequently, the conflicts are assigned to a distance cohort based on the distance traveled by the states engaging in the MIDs. The research concludes that states are more prone to project power abroad as technology reduces costs and as their economies grow, confirming that "more economically powerful states are likely better able to afford the technologies that reduce the cost of projecting power" (ibid, 139). According to this model, the authors suggest that the economic growth of China, India, and Brazil makes it more likely that they will project power globally, redefining the relationships among powers in the international system.

In a similar vein, Buhaug, Gates, and Lujala (2009) use a contest success function (CSF) model to explain why some armed civil conflicts last longer than others. The authors employ geo-referenced conflict data to analyze the military capability of governments to overcome military challenges from rebel groups by measuring it as a function of the distance between governmental resources and the conflict region. The models calculated by the authors confirm their basic hypothesis that geography plays a substantial role in determining the duration of civil conflicts. The research concludes that the further away a conflict occurs from a state's center, the longer its likely duration. Also, the study finds that "conflicts where rebels have access to an international border are twice as durable as other conflicts" (ibid, 546).

There are countless other studies employing spatial variables and spatial analysis methods to explain international affairs (for an overview on geospatial analyses see De Juan 2017). Despite the diversity of their research, neoclassical geopolitics share a common element in elevating the concept of space over that of place in an attempt to explain international politics through the use of formal theory and statistical modeling (see Johnston and Sidaway 2016). However, this approach has generated significant criticism for its lack of attention to the historical and geographical contexts in which politics play out. And it neglects FPA's emphasis on an agency-oriented approach which places decision-makers at the center of the research agenda. Therefore, it is not surprising that some geographers have reproached those espousing a spatial analytical approach as engaging in "political geometry" rather than political geography (O'Loughlin 2018). As a result, the concept of place has been devalued in many studies.

However, the concept of *place* is central to geographical knowledge and our understanding of the world. In fact, over one century ago, the founder of the French school of geography, Paul Vidal de la Blache (1913, 299), defined the discipline of Geography as the "science of places." For de la Blache and his disciples, the concept of place was essential to understanding the unique qualities of each particular region. While it is also a contested concept, most conceptualizations of place imbue it with social meaning. Therefore, places are understood to be socially constructed since they do not possess a "true" reality independent of the observer(s). Rather, meaning is ascribed in accordance with particular social contexts, beliefs, and experiences. Ultimately, as Jones, Jones, and Woods (2004, 99) claim, the use of place "provides a context for the formation of political identities and the identification of political interests."

John O'Loughlin (2000, 133) has cogently delineated the difference between these two critical concepts, arguing that "Space is associated with abstractness, quantitative modeling (the spatial approach), freedom, movement, formality and impersonal location; while place is associated with familiarity, security, home, intimacy, historical tradition, social-cultural relations, context, and geo-sociological effects." However, the concept of place does not deny the existence and value of geography's spatial features. Rather the two concepts are related and complementary. Ultimately, place assumes that space only gains meaning and significance within the context of individuals' cognitive and social experiences (da Vinha 2019). Moreover, conceptualizing place as a social process is particularly important for the study of foreign policy since it highlights the fluid and volatile nature of geographical space in which meaning can always be disputed and contested.

In contrast to their spatial analyst counterparts, political geographers embracing the concept of place tend to employ more qualitative methods in their research projects and many of these scholars frame their work within the post-positivist paradigm that rejects would be pretensions to an objective external *reality* and a value-free social science (Smith 2002). For instance, research under the banner of Critical Geopolitics has embraced methods that focus on discursive practices in an attempt to deconstruct hegemonic geopolitical constructs and theories. As Colin Flint (2017, 5) argues, over the decades, Critical Geopolitics has employed discourse analysis to

> Highlight the role of language in creating taken-for-granted assumptions about terrorism, Islam, the Middle East, etc. and expose unquestioned narratives about parts of the world, and the people that populate them, that justify military action and other foreign policy agendas.

That is, critical geopoliticians use an assortment of different geographical concepts, from the macro-level – e.g., "geopolitical imagination" – to the meso-level – e.g., "geopolitical traditions," "geopolitical visions" – to the micro-level – "geopolitical codes" – to differentiate the different approaches to political discourses (Mamadouh and Dijkink 2006).

Much of the early research focused on the political geography of the Cold War and the geopolitical representations guiding U.S. foreign policy in that era. For instance, in their highly referenced paper *Geopolitics and Discourse*, Ó Tuathail and Agnew (1992) use discourse analysis (see also Ostermann and Sjöstedt in this volume) to identify the geopolitical representations used by American officials to justify U.S. foreign policy throughout the Cold War. To do so, the authors analyze George Kennan's renowned *Long Telegram* and *The Sources of Soviet Conduct*, arguing that these portray the Soviet Union in accordance with three distinct features: (1) U.S.S.R. as Oriental, (2) U.S.S.R. as a potential rapist, and (3) Soviet foreign policy and communism as a flood. By conceptualizing Kennan's texts as a discourse that forged American thinking about postwar international politics, the authors argue that it impeded any reasonable attempts to develop a more cooperative relationship between the two Great Powers since the Soviet Union's character was represented as historically and geographically determined *a priori*. For the authors, the Cold War geopolitical discourse developed and codified by Kennan, was detrimental to the U.S. since "The irony of practical geopolitical representations of place is that, in order to succeed, they actually necessitate the abrogation of genuine geographical knowledge about the diversity and complexity of places as social entities" (Ó Tuathail and Agnew 1992, 202).

The events of 11 September 2001 further bolstered the focus of critical geopoliticians on discourses used to justify America's "Global War on Terror" and its foreign policy of neoliberal accumulation by dispossession (see Dalby 2007; Sparke 2007). Many of these studies focused on exposing how U.S. foreign policy promoted a callous political and economic project of imperial dominance that sought to expunge specific regional and local realities (i.e., place) by forcefully integrating them into an amorphous space of global capitalist transactions.

However, despite the proliferation of this line of research, several issues have been raised regarding the methodological robustness of critical geopolitical studies being carried out under the label of discourse analysis. Despite some theoretical developments in recent years, the concern highlighted over a decade ago by Martin Müller (2010) that "explicit attempts at a discourse analysis which lays out its methodological assumptions and is candid about the process of constructing a methodology are still comparatively rare" is still valid today as many studies are lacking precision in terms of describing and justifying the sources used and techniques employed to analyze them.

More importantly, several scholars have also criticized Critical Geopolitics' focus in analyzing foreign policy. As Phil Kelly (2006, 48) points out,

> Linking an understanding of foreign policy to elite scripts and discourse ignores the complexity of decisionmaking, because to me a vast assortment of types and levels of groups and inputs contribute to state actions and goals that are not contained in the words of leaders.

In fact, while critical geopoliticians distinguish between formal geopolitics (i.e., grand geopolitical narratives), popular geopolitics (i.e., public geopolitical images), and practical geopolitics (i.e., geopolitical reasonings involved in decision-making), their research fixates predominantly on the first two types (Mamadouh and Dijkink 2006). As mentioned above, this deviates from FPA's focus on decision-making processes and, particularly, as to how decision-makers construct the definition of the situation (Hudson and Day 2020; Ripley 1993). In this sense, Cognitive Geopolitics, with its emphasis on understanding how decision-makers understand their political environment, is more aligned with FPA's main theoretical commitments.

Cognitive geopoliticians also employ a host of different concepts and methods to analyze foreign policy policymakers' cognitive representations. For example, several scholars have used content analysis to identify the "geographical codes" and "worldviews" of American presidents over time (Flint, Adduci, Chen, and Chi 2009; O'Loughlin and Grant 1990; see also Brummer or Schafer and Walker in this volume). By analyzing the geographical references in the State of the Union addresses, these studies reveal the dynamic geographical foci of U.S. foreign policy, as certain *places* acquire more or less prevalence over time. The research employs a sound methodological framework, highlighting the textual sources (i.e., State of the Union address), as well as the coding protocol employed for the analysis. The methodological consistency of this line of research allows for an accumulation of knowledge and for a greater longitudinal assessment of presidents' geographical representations. More precisely, it demonstrates how U.S. geopolitical representations have expanded since the end of the Cold War and embraced a more global perspective.

Other researchers use the concept of geographical *mental maps* to explain how particular decision-makers' geographical representations are constructed and influence their political decisions. More precisely, this line of research seeks to understand how foreign policy is influenced by policymakers' perceptions of different *places* around the world. The research on mental maps diverges in terms of its focus, as well as methods employed. However, most scholars have predominantly relied on qualitative historical analysis (see also Ghalehdar in this volume) as their method of choice. For instance, several studies use biographical sources to explain how decision-makers "life-stories" contributed to shaping their mental maps (see da Vinha 2015a; Henrikson 2008; Wolff 2020). Other studies highlight how individuals' mental maps are shaped and influenced by an individual's socialization in broader institutional (Henrikson 1980), societal (Erforth 2016), and political (Brown 2015) contexts. By emphasizing the socially constructed nature of geographical place, the research on geographical mental maps has also focused on how foreign policymakers create shared meanings through their regular interactions in the decision-making processes (da Vinha 2017). The diversity of approaches in the mental map research agenda is patent in the multi-volume collections edited by Steven Casey and Jonathan Wright (2008, 2011, 2015) and Martin Thomas (2011, 2012) which bring together the research of historians, political scientists, and geographers.

Cognitive geopolitics has also been subject to several critiques. Critical geopoliticians have denounced these studies for helping legitimize geographical representations that perpetuate artificial boundaries between "Us" and the "Others" (Dodds 1994). However, the most significant limitations of cognitive geopolitics are the diverse theoretical and methodological approaches espoused by scholars (see da Vinha 2012). In other words, for Cognitive Geopolitics to provide a genuine contribution to FPA further theoretical work is required to explain how geographical representations actually influence foreign policymaking – i.e., explain the causal mechanisms. Enlarging the methodological scope for analyzing the mental map's influence on foreign policy is also imperative. Also, just like its critical counterpart, cognitive geopolitical research needs to be more precise in describing and justifying the sources and techniques used in its analyses.

In the following section, I present an abridged example of the methodical considerations and specific strategies involved in applying geographical mental maps in the analysis of foreign policymaking.[4] The case presented focuses on explaining how the Carter administration's geographical representations contributed to a wholesale transformation of its Middle East policy and to the development of the Carter Doctrine.

Using Geographical Mental Maps to Explain the Carter Doctrine

The Carter Administration arrived in Washington in the wake of several years of détente. Carter's predecessors Nixon and Ford had sought to improve U.S.-Soviet relations by emphasizing a constructive engagement between the two superpowers. Upon assuming the presidency, Carter sought to maintain the course. Since both superpowers had expanding global interests, the president and his main foreign policy advisors shared the belief that managing U.S.-Soviet relations was crucial to avoid a devastating military conflict between the two states. In particular, Carter identified several areas in which the U.S. and the Soviets could cooperate to reduce the risk of nuclear proliferation. He informed his Soviet counterparts that he believed that the two countries could contribute to promoting a peaceful settlement to the Middle Eastern conflict since there was a general conviction within the administration that the time was ripe for a comprehensive peace settlement in the region. Accordingly, in early 1977, the interagency debate settled on the decision to seek a comprehensive settlement to the Middle East conflict (Brzezinski 1983; Vance 1983). After the initial meetings with Arab and Israeli leaders, President Carter (1982, 288) was optimistic: "After meeting with these key Arab leaders, I was convinced that all of them were ready for a strong move on our part to find solutions to the long-standing disputes and that with such solutions would come their recognition of Israel and the right of Israelis to live in peace."

However, less than three years later, Carter would announce the culmination of a sweeping reorientation of U.S. foreign policy in his State of the Union address, stating that

> An attempt by any outside force to gain control of the Persian Gulf region will be regarded as an assault on the vital interests of the United States of America, and such an assault will be repelled by any means necessary, including military force.
> *(Carter 1980)*

Hence, any further attempts to secure a comprehensive peace agreement in the Middle East and retain a cooperative relationship with the U.S.S.R. were abandoned. Going forward, the U.S. renewed a confrontational posture with the Soviets, increased its military capabilities, and transformed the Middle East into a critical strategic region second only to that of Europe. The significance of the policy change was aptly captured by Lawrence Freedman (2009, 94) who argues that "the cold war, which earlier in the 1970s had appeared to be effectively over, to be replaced by an era of negotiation and détente, returned with a vengeance."

Traditional accounts of the Carter Doctrine tend to attribute this change in policy to the fall of the Shah in Iran (January 1979), the Soviet invasion of Afghanistan (December 1979), or a combination of both. However, a more judicious assessment of the administration's foreign policy decision-making reveals that Carter and his foreign policy team had long been reassessing the situation in the Middle East and continuously reconstructing the challenges and opportunities facing the U.S. in the region. In the early years of the Carter presidency, political developments in the Middle East and the neighboring regions had already begun transforming the president and his national security team's understanding of the political challenges facing the U.S. in the region (da Vinha 2015b).

In order to assess the dynamic and emergent nature of the Carter administration's mental maps of the Middle East, I conducted a longitudinal case design using a process tracing technique to help identify

> What stimuli the actors attend to; the decision process that makes use of these stimuli to arrive at decisions; the actual behavior that then occurs; the effect of various institutional arrangements on attention, processing, and behavior; and the effect of other variables of interest on attention, processing, and behavior.
>
> *(George and McKeown 1985, 35)*

Process tracing (see also van Meegdenburg in this volume) relies heavily on a careful description of the trajectories of change and causation. This called for the use of numerous primary and secondary materials acquired and collected from a wide array of sources associated with the Carter administration such as memoirs and biographies, Presidential Directives, Policy Review Memoranda, official minutes or records of meetings, memoranda, official public statements, official transcripts, oral history transcripts, official publications, and official reports. These documents were collected from various different institutions and entities.[5]

I used these sources to analyze the communicative interactions among the administrations main foreign policy decision-makers and assess how they constructed and reconstructed shared meaning and beliefs about the challenges and opportunities facing the U.S. in the Middle East. In other words, the documental analysis allowed for the creation of a narrative of how the administration created the definition of the situation and the adequate policy response throughout their tenure. For analytical purposes, this narrative was separated into several discrete policy debates which occurred within the Carter Presidency regarding the Middle East. By parsing the communicative interactions into distinct foreign policy episodes, we can better appreciate how the administration's mental maps were reconstructed as well as their relationship to other interaction processes.[6]

Therefore, as new challenges and threats surfaced in the Middle East and beyond (e.g., Sub-Saharan Africa), the region was increasingly viewed as a place of danger and potential conflict. While diplomacy and cooperation were still political options, the administration gradually assumed a more assertive policy towards regional events, particularly towards Soviet involvement in the Middle East. Ultimately, small-scale, continuous adjustments to policy transformed America's engagement with the Middle East. Thus, by the time Iranian revolution unfolded and the Soviets invaded Afghanistan, the Carter administration had long altered its view regarding the potential for a comprehensive peace in the region and cooperation with the Soviets. In fact, the administration had long been working to check Soviet power, namely by ratcheting up the international promotion of human rights, rebuffing Soviet influence in the Shaba and Ogaden regions, cooperating with China on intelligence, aiding Afghani insurgents and the Pakistani intelligence services, and strengthening U.S. military capabilities to project military power in the Persian Gulf (da Vinha 2021).

Accordingly, by employing geographical mental maps as an analytical concept, we could gain a better understanding of the role of geography in foreign policymaking. While the approach also has several shortcomings which we discuss in the final section, it does broaden the contributions of Political Science to FPA. More precisely, it provides an opportunity to understand the complex social dynamics involved in constructing shared cognitive maps, as well as the dynamic nature of the geopolitical representations.

Conclusion

As the preceding sections confirm, Political Geography has a long and complex history. It has oscillated between being the central focus of geographical inquiry and being an academic chagrin that faded into scholarly obscurity. However, in recent decades, Political Geography has again captured the interest of geographers and political scientists alike. Whereas geography was traditionally understood as determining the political, this relationship is now inverted (Agnew 2019).

Currently, Political Geography engages with a broad array of actors and has a vast research agenda. However, despite this diversity, international political phenomena continue to occupy a central place. Recent developments in critical and cognitive geopolitics, as well as their neoclassical counterparts, have provided political geographers with a broad assortment of conceptual, theoretical, and methodological tools to help them explain international politics. Neoclassical geopoliticians continue to emphasize quantitative methods and their associated statistical analyses and formal models to explain how spatial features determine political behavior. In contrast, critical and cognitive geopoliticians tend to espouse qualitative methods that are more in agreement with those typically employed in FPA (see Potter 2017).

For some, the profusion of approaches thwarts the development of Political Geography as a unified, coherent field of research. I disagree with this perspective, knowing that there is no reasonable prospect or justification to try to impose any conceptual and methodological orthodoxy on political geographers. In fact, as Agnew (2003b, 603) argues, this diversity should be seen favorably for "it finds contention, critique, and disagreement to be sources of intellectual invention and the enemies of complacency."

There are indubitably several challenges facing political geographers. For instance, the overwhelming number of themes and issues studied under the banner of Political Geography makes it difficult to pinpoint the discipline's main research agenda and further adds to the conceptual quagmire that currently characterizes the field. Also, we still struggle with clear theoretical and methodological issues that help us determine *how* geographical phenomena actually influence foreign policy decision-making – i.e., identifying and explaining the causal mechanisms. Moreover, the lack of communication among the different approaches in Political Geography thwarts attempts to address these and other challenges.

However, rather than debating the merits and flaws of these different approaches, we are better served by thinking about how Political Geography can address the paramount political challenges facing us today and in the near future. To begin with, political geographers can begin by extending a warmer welcome to physical geographers since environmental and political issues are increasingly intertwined and a more holistic approach is needed to study how they interact and define one another. Also, the changing international system and the reorganization of the loci of global power provide an opportunity for Political Geography to again engage with how we understand issues of systems change and international order. This naturally implies providing greater opportunities to broaden the scope of the research beyond the traditional confines of the U.S. and Europe and expand the authorship as well as the geographical focus of analyses. Moreover, the changes to the international political environment also provide an opportunity for Political Geography to sever its affiliation with the early geopolitical theories of empire and belligerency. In other words, it can refute Yves Lacoste's (2014 [1976]) renowned claim that "la géographie, ça sert, d'abord, à faire la guerre" ["geography serves, first and foremost, to wage war"] and endeavor to provide a discipline that can place peace at the core of its research agenda.

Notes

1 In fact, it may have contributed to making it even more difficult to define the object of geographical inquiry. As Nigel Thrift (2003, 295) notes, whereas human and physical geographers once shared a common language, particularly in terms of its methods, "now this only rarely exists."
2 I use the term neoclassical geopolitics as a broad categorization to include scholars that focus on spatial features to explain international politics and not on the recent resurgence of scholars that have been identified by Megoran (2010) and others that embrace the deterministic approach of classical geopoliticians.
3 For two notable examples of how distance has traditionally been articulated by realists see the work by Stephen Walt (1985) and John Mearsheimer (2003).
4 I define geographical mental maps as cognitive constructs that encompass "an individual or group's beliefs about the geographical character of a particular place or places and their relationship to other places or spatial phenomena" (da Vinha 2017, 115).
5 Sources were collected at the Jimmy Carter Presidential Library and Museum, *American Foreign Policy Basic Documents, 1977–1981*, Central Intelligence Agency website, Commission on Presidential Debates website, *Foreign Relations of the United States, 1977–1980* (Volumes II, VI, and VIII), Jimmy Carter Presidential Library and Museum website, Miller Center of Public Affairs website, Office of the Historian of the U.S. Department of State, American Presidency Project, National Security Archive at the George Washington University, and Public Papers of the Presidents of the United States (see da Vinha 2017).
6 The policy episodes focused on the early review of U.S. Middle East policy, Middle East Peace Process, the review of U.S. strategy vis-à-vis the U.S.S.R., the Shaba crises and Ogaden war, the Iranian Revolution, the Iranian hostage crisis, and the Soviet invasion of Afghanistan.

References

Agnew, John. 2000. "Global Political Geography Beyond Geopolitics." *International Studies Review* 2(1): 91–99.
Agnew, John. 2003a. *Geopolitics: Re-Visioning World Politics*. London: Routledge.
Agnew, John. 2003b. "Contemporary Political Geography: Intellectual Heterodoxy and Its Dilemmas." *Political Geography* 22 (2): 603–606.
Agnew, John. 2019. "Political Geography." In *The International Encyclopedia of Geography*, edited by Douglas Richardson, Noel Castree, Michael Goodchild, Audrey Kobayashi, Weidong Liu and Richard Martson. John Wiley & Sons, 1–21. Available from https://doi.org/10.1002/9781118786352.wbieg0382.pub2
Agnew, John, Virginie Mamadouh, Anna Secor, and Joanne Sharpe. 2015. *The Wiley Blackwell Companion to Political Geography*. Malden, MA: Wiley Blackwell.
Agnew, John, and Luca Muscarà. 2012. *Making Political Geography*. New York: Rowman & Littlefield Publishers.
Blomley, Nicholas. 2006. "Uncritical Critical Geography" *Progress in Human Geography* 30(1): 87–94.
Brown, Archie. 2015. "Mikhail Gorbachev." In *Mental Maps in the Era of Detente and the End of the Cold War 1968–1991*, edited by Steven Casey and Jonathan Wright. New York: Palgrave-Macmillan, 216–235.
Brzezinski, Zbigniew. 1983. *Power and Principle: Memoirs of the National Security Adviser, 1977–1981*. New York: Farrar, Straus, & Giroux.
Buhaug, Halvard, Scott Gates, and Päivi Lujala. 2009. "Geography, Rebel Capability, and the Duration of Civil Conflict." *Journal of Conflict Resolution* 53 (4): 544–569.
Carter, Jimmy. 1980. *The State of the Union Address Delivered Before a Joint Session of the Congress*. Available from https://www.presidency.ucsb.edu/documents/the-state-the-union-address-delivered-before-joint-session-the-congress.
Carter, Jimmy. 1982. *Keeping Faith: Memoirs of a President*. New York: Bantam Books.
Casey, Steven and Jonathan Wright. 2008. *Mental Maps in the Era of Two World Wars*. New York: Palgrave Macmillan.
Casey, Steven and Jonathan Wright. 2011. *Mental Maps in the Early Cold War Era, 1945–1968*. New York: Palgrave Macmillan.

Casey, Steven and Jonathan Wright. 2015. *Mental Maps in the Era of Détente and the End of the Cold War 1968–1991*. New York: Palgrave Macmillan.
Cox, Kevin, Murray Low, and Jennifer Robinson. 2008. "Introduction. Political Geography: Traditions and Turns." In *The Sage Handbook of Political Geography*, edited by Kevin Cox, Murray Low and Jennifer Robinson. London: Sage Publications, 1–14.
Coward, Martin. 2005. "The Globalisation of Enclosure: Interrogating the Geopolitics of Empire." *Third World Quarterly* 26 (6): 855–871.
Criekemans, David. 2010. "Réhabilitation et Rénovation en Matière de Pensée Géopolitique." *L'Espace Politique. Revue en Ligne de Géographie Politique et de Géopolitique* 13 (3): 2–13.
Dalby, Simon. 2002. *Environmental Security*. Minneapolis, MN: University of Minnesota Press.
Dalby, Simon. 2007. "Regions, Strategies and Empire in the Global War on Terror." *Geopolitics* 12 (4): 586–606.
Dalby, Simon. 2008. "Imperialism, Domination, Culture: The Continued Relevance of Critical Geopolitics." *Geopolitics* 13 (3): 413–436.
Dalby, Simon. 2010. "Recontextualising Violence, Power, and Nature: The Next Twenty Years of Critical Geopolitics?" *Political Geography* 29 (5): 280–288.
Dalby, Simon. 2020. *Anthropocene Geopolitics: Globalization, Security, Sustainability*. Ottawa: University of Ottawa Press.
da Vinha, Luis. 2012. "Charting Geographic Mental Maps in Foreign Policy Analysis: A Literature Review." *Human Geographies* 6 (1): 5–17.
da Vinha, Luis. 2015a. "Ronald Reagan." In *Mental Maps in the Era of Detente and the End of the Cold War 1968–1991*, edited by Steven Casey and Jonathan Wright. New York: Palgrave-Macmillan, 195–215.
da Vinha, Luis. 2015b. "The (Not So) Rapid Deployment Force: Bureaucratic and Political Barriers to Implementing Strategic Change." *Nação e Defesa*. 141: 156–174.
da Vinha, Luis. 2017. *Geographic Mental Maps and Foreign Policy Change: Remapping the Carter Doctrine*. Berlin: De Gruyter.
da Vinha, Luis. 2019. "Maps of War and Peace: Rethinking Geography in International Affairs." *The Brown Journal of Word Affairs* 25 (2): 73–89.
da Vinha, Luis. 2021. "Dangers on the Edge of the Map: Geographic Mental Maps and the Emergence of the Carter Doctrine." In *Geopolitics and International Relations: Grounding World Politics Anew*, edited by David Criekemans. Leiden: Brill Publisher, 258–286.
De Juan, Alexander. 2017. "Geospatial Analyses of Non-State Actors in Violent Conflicts." In *Researching Non-State Actors in International Security*, edited by Andreas Kruck and Andrea Schneiker. Oxon: Routledge, 143–158.
de la Blache, Paul Vidal. 1913. "Des Caractères Distinctifs de la Géographie." *Annales de Géographie* 22 (124): 289–299.
Dear, Michael. 1988. "The Postmodern Challenge: Reconstructing Human Geography." *Transactions of the Institute of British Geographers* 13(3): 262–274.
Devetak, Richard. 1995. "The Project of Modernity and International Relations Theory." *Millennium* 24 (1): 27–51.
Dijkink, Gertjan. 1998. "Geopolitical Codes and Popular Representations." *GeoJournal* 46 (4): 293–299.
Dodds, Klaus. 1994. "Geopolitics and Foreign Policy: Recent Developments in Anglo-American Political Geography and International Relations." *Progress in Human Geography* 18 (2): 186–208.
Elden, Stuart. 2007. "Terror and Territory." *Antipode* 39 (5): 821–845.
Erforth, Benedikt. 2016. "Mental Maps and Foreign Policy Decision-Making: Eurafrique and the French Military Intervention in Mali." *European Review of International Studies* 3 (2): 38–58.
Flint, Colin. 2003. "Dying For a 'P'? Some Questions Facing Contemporary Political Geography." *Political Geography* 22 (6): 617–620.
Flint, Colin. 2005. *The Geography of War and Peace: From Death Camps to Diplomats*. Oxford: Oxford University Press.
Flint, Colin. 2013. "Geopolitics and Political Geography: Why a Geographic Perspective Is Essential in Defining the Field of Geopolitics." *International Studies Journal* 10 (2): 143–164.
Flint, Colin. 2017. *Introduction to Geopolitics*. New York: Routledge.
Flint, Colin, Michael Adduci, Michael Chen, and Sang-Hyun Chi. 2009. "Mapping the Dynamism of the United States' Geopolitical Codes: The Geography of the State of the Union Speeches, 1988–2008." *Geopolitics* 14 (4): 604–629.

Flint, Colin, Paul Diehl, Juergen Scheffran, John Vasquez, and Sang-Hyun Chi. 2009. "Conceptualizing ConflictSpace: Toward a Geography of Relational Power and Embeddedness in the Analysis of Interstate Conflict." *Annals of the Association of American Geographers* 99 (5): 827–835.

Freedman, Lawrence. 2009. *A Choice of Enemies: America Confronts the Middle East*. London: Phoenix.

George, Alexander, and Timothy McKeown. 1985. "Case Studies and Theories of Organizational Decision Making." *Advances in Information Processing in Organizations* 2: 21–58.

Gottmann, Jean. 1951. "Geography and International Relations." *World Politics* 3 (1): 153–173.

Gray, Colin. 1988. *The Geopolitics of Super Power*. Lexington, KY: The University of Kentucky Press.

Gregory, Derek. 2004. *The Colonial Present: Afghanistan. Palestine. Iraq*. Malden, MA: Blackwell Publishing.

Henrikson, Alan. 1980. "The Geographical 'Mental Maps' of American Foreign Policy Makers." *International Political Science Review* 1 (4): 495–530.

Henrikson, Alan. 2008. "FDR and the 'World-Wide Arena'." In *FDR's World: War, Peace, and Legacies*, edited by David Woolner, Warren Kimball and David Reynolds. New York: Palgrave Macmillan, 35–61.

Herbert, David, and John Matthews. 2004. "Geography: Roots and Continuities." In *Unifying Geography: Common Heritage, Shared Future*, edited by John Matthews and David Herbert. Oxfordshire: Routledge, 3–18.

Hubbard, Phil, Rob Kitchen, Brendan Barteley, and Duncan Fuller. 2005. *Thinking Geographically: Space, Theory and Contemporary Human Geography*. New York: Continuum Books.

Hudson, Valerie, and Benjamin Day. 2020. *Foreign Policy Analysis: Classic and Contemporary Theory*. Lanham, MD: Rowman & Littlefield.

Jackson, Peter 2006. "Thinking Geographically." *Geography* 91 (3): 199–204.

Johnston, Ron, and James Sidaway. 2016. *Geography and Geographers: Anglo–American Human Geography Since 1945*. New York: Routledge.

Jones, Martin, Rhys Jones, and Michael Woods. 2004. *An Introduction to Political Geography: Space, Place and Politics*. New York: Routledge.

Kamarck, Elaine. 2011. "The Cybersecurity Policy Challenge: The Tyranny of Geography." In *Cybersecurity: Public Sector Threats and Responses*, edited by Kim Andreasson. Boca Raton, FL: CRC Press, 109–125.

Kelly, Phil. 2006. "A Critique of Critical Geopolitics." *Geopolitics* 11 (1): 24–53.

Kolossov, Vladimir. 2003. "'High' and 'Low' Geopolitics: Images of Foreign Countries in the Eyes of Russian Citizens." *Geopolitics*, 8 (1): 121–148.

Kuus, Merje. 2009. "Political Geography and Geopolitics." *The Canadian Geographer* 53 (1): 86–90.

Lacoste, Yves. 2014. *La géographie, Ça sert, D'abord, à Faire la Guerre*. Paris: La Découverte.

Mackinder, Halford. 1996. *Democratic Ideals and Reality: A Study in the Politics of Reconstruction by the Right Honourable Sir Halford J. Mackinder*. Washington, DC: National Defense University Press.

Mamadouh, Virginie, and Gertjan Dijkink. 2006. "Geopolitics, International Relations and Political Geography: The Politics of Geopolitical Discourse." *Geopolitics* 11 (3): 349–366.

Markowitz, Jonathan, and Christopher Fariss. 2013. "Going the Distance: The Price of Projecting Power." *International Interactions* 39 (2): 119–143

Martin, Geoffrey. 1959. "Political Geography and Geopolitics." *Journal of Geography* 58 (9): 441–444.

Massey, Doreen. 1994. "Introduction: Geography Matters." In *Geography Matters! A Reader*, edited by Doreen Massey and John Allen. Cambridge: Cambridge University Press, 1–11.

Matthews, John, and David Herbert. 2004. "Unity in Geography: Prospects for the Discipline." In *Unifying Geography: Common Heritage, Shared Future*, edited by John Matthews and David Herbert. Oxfordshire: Routledge, 369–393.

Mearsheimer, John. 2003. *The Tragedy of Great Power Politics*. New York: W.W. Norton & Co.

Megoran, Nick 2010. "Neoclassical Geopolitics." *Political Geography* 29 (4): 187–189.

Müller, Martin. 2010. "Doing Discourse Analysis in Critical Geopolitics." *L'Espace Politique. Revue en Ligne de Géographie Politique et de Géopolitique* 12(3): 1–19.

Newman, Edward, and Gëzim Visoka. 2021. "The Geopolitics of State Recognition in a Transitional International Order." *Geopolitics*: 1–28. Available at https://doi.org/10.1080/14650045.2021.1912018.

O'Loughlin, John. 2000. "Geography as Space and Geography as Place: The Divide Between Political Science and Political Geography Continues." *Geopolitics* 5 (3): 126–137.

O'Loughlin, John. 2018. "Thirty-Five Years of Political Geography and *Political Geography*: The Good, the Bad, and the Ugly." *Political Geography* 65 (1): 143–151.

O'Loughlin, John, and Richard Grant. 1990. "The Political Geography of Presidential Speeches, 1946–1987." *Annals of the Association of American Geographers* 80 (4), 504–530.

Ó Tuathail, Gearóid. 1992. "The Bush Administration and the 'End' of the Cold War: A Critical Geopolitics of U.S. Foreign Policy in 1989." *Geoforum* 23 (4): 437–452.

Ó Tuathail, Gearóid. 1996. *Critical Geopolitics: The Politics of Writing Global Space*. London: Routledge.

Ó Tuathail, Gearóid, and John Agnew. 1992. "Geopolitics and Discourse: Practical Geopolitical Reasoning in American Foreign Policy." *Political Geography* 11 (2): 190–204.

Ó Tuathail, Gearóid, Jennifer Hyndman, Fraser MacDonald, Emily Gilbert, Virginie Mamadouh, Laura Jones, and Daniel Sage. 2010. "New Directions in Critical Geopolitics: An Introduction." *GeoJournal* 75 (4): 315–325.

Pickering, Steve. 2018. "Geography and Foreign Policy." In *The Oxford Encyclopedia of Foreign Policy Analysis (Volume 1)*, edited by Cameron Thies. New York: Oxford University Press, 775–793.

Potter, Philip. 2017. "Methods of Foreign Policy Analysis." *Oxford Research Encyclopedia of International Studies*. Available at https://oxfordre.com/view/10.1093/acrefore/9780190846626.001.0001/acrefore-9780190846626-e-34.

Regilme Jr., Salvador. 2021. "Contested Spaces of Illiberal and Authoritarian Politics: Human Rights and Democracy in Crisis." *Political Geography* 89: 1–12.

Ripley, Brian. 1993. "Psychology, Foreign Policy, and International Relations Theory." *Political Psychology* 14 (3): 403–416.

Smith, Steve. 2002. "Positivism and Beyond." In *International Theory: Positivism and Beyond*, edited by Steve Smith, Ken Booth and Marysia Zalewski. Cambridge: Cambridge University Press, 11–44.

Solingen, Etel. 2021. *Geopolitics, Supply Chains, and International Relations in East Asia*. Cambridge: Cambridge University Press.

Sparke, Matthew. 2007. "Geopolitical Fears, Geoeconomic Hopes, and the Responsibilities of Geography." *Annals of the Association of American Geographers* 97 (2): 338–349.

Spykman, Nicholas. 2007. *America's Strategy in World Politics: The United States and the Balance of Power*. London: Transaction Publishers.

Thomas, Martin. 2011. *The French Colonial Mind, Volume 1: Mental Maps of Empire and Colonial Encounters*. Lincoln, NE: University of Nebraska Press.

Thomas, Martin. 2012. *The French Colonial Mind, Volume 2: Violence, Military Encounters, and Colonialism*. Lincoln, NE: University of Nebraska Press.

Thrift, Nigel. 2003. "The Future of Geography." *Geoforum* 33 (2): 291–298.

Unwin, Tim. 1992. *The Place of Geography*. Essex: Pearson Education.

Vance, Cyrus. 1983. *Hard Choices: Critical Years in Americas Foreign Policy*. New York: Simon and Schuster.

Walt, Stephen. 1985. "Alliance Formation and the Balance of World Power." *International Security* 9 (4): 3–43.

Wolff, Larry. 2020. *Woodrow Wilson and the Reimagining of Eastern Europe*. Stanford, CA: Stanford University Press.

Part III
Language and Interpretive Methods

7
Discourse Analysis and Discourse Theories

Falk Ostermann and Roxanna Sjöstedt

Introduction

Discourse approaches to Foreign Policy Analysis (FPA) are generally interested in understanding how language – or social practices of speaking and writing in a certain political arena – shapes foreign policy. A discourse is an "ensemble of ideas, concepts, and categories" (Hajer 2005, 300) that meaningfully constructs a political issue, i.e. national security. Thus, a discourse represents a certain state of debate on a political issue (*object* in discourse-analytical language); it designates what is considered appropriate to say (or not) on a certain topic according to the agents (*subjects*) involved in it; and, in doing so, it *creates political reality* (Fierke 2002; Zehfuss 2004, 153; on the limitation of this construction see below). Hence, what is (not) included in discourses is always subject to relations of power and hegemony (Cox 1983) among its participants. Accordingly, in a constructivist spirit (Adler 2013), discursive analyses aim at comprehending *how* foreign policy is rendered socially meaningful through constitutive practices of speaking and writing, i.e. in the context of parliamentary debate or public speech by the executive (cf. also Ripley 2017). There are more materialist and more ideational, more structuralist and more poststructuralist approaches under the big tent of discourse analysis. (That is why we will speak of discourse approaches or discourse analysis if we are talking about the totality of approaches applying some sort of discourse-analytical procedure.) However, what these approaches all have in common is the interest in revealing the political ideas and linguistic practices that constitute policies from a bottom-up perspective, and they want to understand the power relations and the sociopolitical structures behind on the grounds of some sort of sociolinguistic analysis of public texts. Within the above variation, all discourse approaches will also be interpretive by nature (what does not mean subjective!) and have a more or less explicit relationship with critical theory and thinking (Devetak 2013; Ripley 2017).

This densely interpretive, *thick* understanding of politics pursued in discourse approaches comes with considerable ideational, linguistic, and sociological ballast and complexity when analyzing foreign policy, often demanding extensive documentary and sometimes linguistic analysis. The benefits of discourse approaches can certainly be found, however, in their ability to understand and explain the social foundations of foreign policy, its construction, and the meanings and ideas attached to it. With their sophisticated concept of power, discourse approaches are also able to show *how* social structures (i.e. gender, money, power, violence) influence (foreign) policy-making, rather than taking their influence for granted. Hence, they allow for an interactive, integrated analysis of agency and structures instead of focusing analytical attention to one of them only (i.e. Parsons 1966; Wendt 1987).

On the following pages, we will first discuss how FPA literature has made use of discursive approaches and what questions these works address. We will then introduce key concepts of discourse approaches and their methodologies. Finally, we will debate possible strengths, limitations, and pitfalls when using the method. For illustrative purposes, we will make use of examples from empirical scholarship along the way.

Literature Review: Discourse Approaches and Foreign Policy

Discourse approaches have made their way into International Relations (IR) and FPA in the wake of two streams of literature that have developed during the 1980s as alternatives to and criticism of mainstream positivist theorizing: the poststructuralist turn, on the one hand (Ashley 1984; Fierke 2002), and critical (Linklater 1996) and feminist scholarship (Bergman Rosamond 2020; D'Aoust 2017; Shepherd 2006) on the other. In FPA, discursive scholarship has started to sprawl since the early 1990s with the path-breaking works of David Campbell (1992, 1993) and Roxanne L. Doty (1993). Scholarship has then taken a leap forward in the 2000s in terms of quantity and establishment (i.e. Cox 2005; Diez 1999; Hansen 2006; Jackson 2006; Sjöstedt 2007, Stahl 2006). Today, discursive contributions to FPA deploy sophisticated theoretical frameworks and related methods from a variety of traditions (e.g. linguistics, Interpretive Policy Analysis, or framing, cf. Yanow and Schwartz-Shea 2006; Entman 1993; Rein and Schön 1993) to provide thick textual analyses of foreign policy matters (Epstein 2010; Erdogan 2017; Fanoulis 2014; Nabers 2015; Ostermann 2019; overviews in Ripley 2017; Stengel and Nabers 2019). Recent days have also seen a surge in scholarship on populism and foreign policy that at times strongly builds on discourse approaches (e.g. Burai 2016; Chryssogelos 2021; De Sá Guimarães and De Oliveira E Silva 2021; Glencross 2020; Jenne 2021; Stengel, MacDonald, and Nabers 2019; Wojczewski 2019, 2021).

Until today, however, the establishment of discourse approaches in relation to FPA shows strong regional differences. Discourse analysis remains marginalized in U.S. scholarship, where it still suffers issues of acceptance in a discipline that is dominated by positivist methodology, while there is more discursive scholarship in Europe, South America, and elsewhere (Aydın-Düzgit 2014; Giacalone 2015, 131f.; Groppo 2009; Hadfield and Hudson 2015, 150ff.; Ratuva 2016; Sandrin and Hoffmann 2018). During the last decade, however, FPA as a discipline has let discourse approaches sink in and settle.

Understanding and explaining *hard* international security issues and the policies of handling conflict – in terms of preventing, pursuing, or putting an end to it – lie at the core of FPA. The aforementioned studies by Campbell (1992) and Doty (1993) are pioneering attempts to explain security policy through discourse and *identity* (see also Guzzini in this volume), in particular with regard to *self/other constructions* (Neumann 1996; Weldes 1996). Several studies have continued this way of approaching FPA, exploring different empirical contexts, such as Soviet and Russian foreign policy (Hopf 2002), Western debates on the Bosnian War (Hansen 2006), the longstanding UK-U.S. special relationship (Vucetic 2011), or Turkey's foreign policy turn toward the West after 1919 (Coş and Bilgin 2010). Identity constructions are also central in studying the re-orientation of U.S. foreign policy after 9/11 (Nabers 2009), when explaining the French reintegration into NATO's military command structures (Ostermann 2019), or changes in U.S. grand strategy under President Obama (Löfflmann, 2017). Other studies have examined the role discourse plays in understandings of conflict and the resulting foreign policy consequences, i.e. the effect of (Somalia) analogies for approaching the Rwanda war in the U.S. (Brunk 2008), the Cold War or the war on terror (Sjöstedt 2007; Solomon 2014), the British decision to join the U.S. in the Iraq War (Hayes 2016) or Germany's positioning on it (Eberle 2019), Turkish discourses on humanitarian intervention (Erdogan 2017), and small-state participation in international military intervention (Noreen, Sjöstedt, and Ångström 2017; Sjöstedt and Noreen 2021). Another vibrant group of critical studies on the discourse-conflict nexus is concerned with the study of identity in relation to the construction of and responses to terrorism, often with a focus on the U.S. (Jackson 2005; Jarvis 2009) but also from comparative (Holland 2012) or global perspectives (Herschinger 2011).

With regard to foreign policy and institutions more broadly, scholars have employed discourse approaches to get a more fine-tuned comprehension of states' behavior in the international arena. Europe and the EU are often the unit of analysis here. Henrik Larsen (1997), for instance, has examined British and French foreign policy behavior vis-à-vis Europe in the 1980s. Thomas Diez (1999, 2001) has explored the role discourse plays in European integration. Different discourse approaches have been employed to understand the EU's foreign policy practices (Carta and Morin 2016). Foucault's concept of *governmentality* has been used to investigate the EU's Common Security and Defence Policy (e.g. Merlingen 2011; Fanoulis 2014) and the consequences of EU-China cooperation (Fanoulis and Song 2022). Similarly, Milja Kurki (2011) has looked into how EU democracy and human rights policies promote specific visions of democracy.[1] Thorsten Wojczewski (2018, 2019, 2021) has investigated populist foreign policy identity constructions under Trump and the German *Alternative für Deutschland* party, or Indian foreign policy discourses about world order. In the African context, Dereck Becker (2010) uses discourse analysis and metaphors to explain post-apartheid South African foreign policy legitimacy. These studies demonstrate that the investigation of both *hard* foreign policy issues and more routine interactions between states clearly benefit from a discourse approach. Here, foreign policy outcomes are not seen as the *natural* result of given external threats or the behavior of other states. Rather, the formation of domestic discourses makes a certain foreign policy (outcome), i.e. the Iranian nuclear negotiation strategy (Rivera 2016), *possible*. In turn, once established, the foreign policy behavior helps to constitute and reproduce political and societal identities (Marcussen et al. 2001).

Key Terms and Concepts in Discourse-Analytical Scholarship on FPA

Some Remarks on Methodology

Conducting a discourse analysis of whatever kind means engaging in the analysis of language. The depth of linguistic analysis varies across approaches, but they will always analyze language and *meaning-making* (semiosis) in some way. This core interest comes with at least two methodological strings attached. First, *ontologically* speaking, discourse approaches are on the *ideas side* of IR/FPA scholarship (Goldstein and Keohane 1993; Parsons 2003; Risse-Kappen 1994). We understand ideas as "symbolic technologies" (Laffey and Weldes 1997, 209) that represent certain social, intersubjectively available meanings (i.e. about collective defense or humanitarian aid). This does not mean that discourse approaches deny the influence of material explanatory factors on behavior. Except for some very structuralist analyses (as in CDA-inspired work), however, for a discourse analyst, material factors have no automatic causal powers but only through the way people *think* (or rather: speak) about money, economics, or weapons, and how they conceptualize their impact on a discourse's topic or a political problem to solve (Wendt 1999, 24). At the post-structuralist end of the spectrum, therefore, the very distinction between ideas and matter becomes futile (Diez 2001, 12). As the doyen of discourse analysis, Michel Foucault, puts it: discourses are "practices that systematically form the objects of which they speak" (Foucault 1972, 49). Ideas about the world, the social, and politics provide the material for these discursive practices of meaning-making (Laffey and Weldes 1997, 209ff.; Yee 1996, 95ff.).

The second methodological consequence of this is that discourse analysis usually comes with a *post-positivist epistemology*. Because of the constitutive relationship between language and reality, the concepts we use (like cause-effect relations, power, hegemony) to explain social/political phenomena are subject to linguistic construction, too. Hence, they depend on mutual agreement within an epistemic community (e.g. academia, or IR/FPA) that accepts certain knowledge claims as a valid way to do science (Guzzini 2000, 160; Wendt 1999, 24f., 77ff.). This means that linguistic construction in politics meets the reconstruction of these discourses by researchers, entailing double hermeneutics: "We interpret an already interpreted social world" (Guzzini 2000, 162). The feasibility of objective observation, the (neo)positivist grail, is, therefore, impossible in a discursive epistemology (cf. also Jackson 2011, 33ff.). On these epistemologically cautious grounds toward large-T truth claims, discourse analysis forwards explanations emphasizing the constitutive effects of a certain discourse or identity construction (or, in CDA, social mechanism) for foreign policy behavior. However, for the most part, discourse analysis rejects any claims of discourses being the direct *cause* of a certain foreign policy behavior (Hansen 2006, 18ff.; similarly Campbell 1992, 4ff.). Rather, post-positivism follows "a discursive research agenda focused on the construction of identity and policy and the way in which the two are linked within political discourses" (Hansen 2006, 28).

Consequently, discourse analysis does not put a strong weight on generalizability or prediction but wants to understand specific constructions of the national interest or identity and their effects on politics at precise moments. Thus, discourse analysts are better at "negative predictions" about things that most likely won't happen given a certain articulated foreign policy identity (Wæver 2002, 32). However, the less a foreign policy discourse (e.g. for going to war in Libya, cf. Ostermann 2016) is opposed, the greater is its predictive power for behavior, as strongly hegemonic discourses serve as "heuristics" (Hopf 2002, 4) for action. The rejection of causality in discourse analysis (Hansen 2006) has also been criticized though as self-inflicted limitation, strengthening the neopositivist hegemony in the field (Kurki 2008). The distinction between *explanation* (supposedly objective) and *understanding* (supposedly interpretive, Hollis and Smith 1990) is today widely perceived as not useful (Humphreys 2017, 659).

Instead, we can think of discursive explanation as a narrative (see Oppermann and Spencer in this volume) or *causal story* (Hellmann 2017; Patterson and Monroe 1998) that underscores certain causal factors (like hegemony or relational power) while neglecting others. Hence, if explanation is understood as providing a *model* – like a Weberian ideal-type (Jackson 2011, 114f.) – that structures reality for the sake of a practical gain of comprehension, then a structured, theoretically informed discourse analysis is providing an explanation as causal as others. It is merely a *different* concept of causality than the temporal cause-effect one from neopositivism or the mechanistic one of scientific realism (Jackson 2017, 17; Ostermann 2019, 29ff.) – it is *constitutive*: Without the German foreign policy identity of self-restraint, induced by the formative experiences of having brought about two world wars, we cannot explain German non-engagement in the Gulf or Iraq wars in 1990 and 2003. We cannot explain

German participation in the Kosovo War in 1999 without the discursive re-signification of *Never again Auschwitz!*, reinterpreting the post-1945 German mantra against war to an argument in favor of protecting Kosovars against the threat of genocide. These factors did not cause German non-participation in the Middle East or participation on Kosovo in a linear sense but, speaking with constructivism, they made them *possible* (Laffey and Weldes 1997, 201ff.; Wendt 1987, 362ff.). While there are other approaches using discourse for quantitative analyses of larger corpora of text (see Eder or Vignoli in this volume; similarly Lustig 2016), any discourse analysis relying on the interpretation of the processes of intersubjective (political) meaning-making will necessarily be post-positivist in its epistemology (see also Koschut in this volume). It's a methodological necessity that comes with taking the role of language for society, politics, and science seriously for formulating coherent questions and research designs when analyzing discourses. It's nothing to be afraid of, but to be aware of. Beyond these foundational commitments of discourse-analytical scholarship, there are many roads leading to Rome, aka to getting a discourse analysis done.

Discourse-Analytical Tools

In line with what has been discussed above, there is general agreement that discourse can be defined as a system of statements and practices bound together in a web of *intertextuality* (Kristeva 1980). This means that a discourse entails the construction and reconstruction of certain claims/topics by a number of different actors with regard to a particular social phenomenon, for instance, military intervention. This intertextuality means that when we analyze discourses, we do not limit the investigation to a single actor or text. To the contrary, as Lene Hansen's (2006), Ted Hopf's (2002), or Ted Hopf and Bentley Allan's (2016) studies demonstrate, using a wide array of different sources, i.e. from opposition figures or parties, is crucial to capture positionings that reach beyond the ultimate hegemonic claims. The final choice of documents must be made in accordance with the specific research question (cf. also Ripley 2017).

Discursive statements do not merely describe reality, but they actually shape and construct it in terms of creating meaning and establishing norms and standards for what is possible and acceptable to say and do in a certain situation (and what is not). Speech is neither neutral nor objective since "all language has a basic binary structure such that almost every noun, adjective and verb has its direct opposite" (Jackson 2005, 21). These types of dichotomies always favor one over the other, i.e., through normatively constructed binaries such as good-evil; love-hate; primitive-modern. Thus, as the content of statements is loaded with certain connotations, speech has implications on human cognition, emotions, and behavior. Along with speech, different forms of practices – e.g., routines, traditions, rituals (Adler and Pouliot 2011; Adler-Nissen and Pouliot 2014) – as well as symbols can contribute to the establishment of a discourse.

There are different ways of conducting a discourse analysis to capture the different aspects described above. Studying U.S. counterinsurgency policies in the Philippines in the 1950s, Roxanne Doty (1993) proposes a framework that structures the analysis and demonstrates how a particular foreign policy behavior was made possible. The so-called *presuppositions* articulated by discursive agents provide background knowledge to a phenomenon and establish dominant truths. What discursive agents take for granted or not is an important element in understanding the social/political stakes in a problem and consensus or conflict around it. *Predication* establishes qualities to different subjects and objects by connecting certain adjectives and adverbs to them, such as when calling the former Libyan head of state,

Muammar Gaddafi, *insane* or *criminal* when the French argued in favor of intervention in 2011 (Ostermann 2016, 79). Predication can also be linked to objects, i.e., when referring to the Russia-Ukraine war of 2022 as *Putin's war*. Such a predication indicates that one does not hold the Russian people accountable for the war but the president, which can have major implications for how to deal with the conflict. Finally, *subject positioning* places these subjects and objects in relation to one another. These categories, or discursive mechanisms (in the sense of explanatory tools), organize the analysis of texts and they highlight what meaning is associated with different discursive elements. For example, Russian decision-makers attached a wide array of often contradictory subject positionings – such as partner, ally, competitor, bully – to the relationship between the U.S. and other Western identities, on the one hand, and Russia on the other as regards the AIDS pandemic (Sjöstedt 2008).

The concept of *discursive nodal points (DNPs)* is another tool that helps to systematize the discourse analysis by identifying central concepts (i.e., governance) in relation to a particular policy area (i.e., European integration), their connotations, and the meta-narratives they tie into (Diez 2001). This type of unpacking central terms provides us with a deeper understanding of how and why different discourses establish, contest, and legitimize key ideas that policies are built upon.

Another way of analyzing discursive constructions of meaning is to look into *frames* (or framing moves) and *narratives* as more encompassing representations of culture and identity. Frames (see also Mokry in this volume)[2] are "a way of selecting, organizing, interpreting, and making sense of a complex reality to provide guideposts for knowing, analyzing, persuading, and acting" (Rein and Schön 1993, 146; similarly Entman 2004). For instance, when France wanted to reintegrate the NATO command structures (unsuccessfully in 1997, successfully in 2009), "more influence", and accepting reality "as it is" were frames constantly used to persuade people of the appropriateness of the policy (Ostermann 2019, 51).

The influence frame was also part of a larger historical *narrative* on the relevance of *Gaullism*, former President de Gaulle's positioning of France as an independent, influential global power. Narratives (see also Oppermann and Spencer in this volume) extend frames sequentially through time by providing a coherent story about past events, interpreting their relevance for present times, and taking the audience to the future, i.e., the attempted policy, to persuade them about its legacy and larger meaning (Tilly 2002). Narratives knit history, culture, identity, and politics together in a culturally ingrained messaging effort (Miskimmon, O'Loughlin, and Roselle 2013; Patterson and Monroe 1998). They are a powerful tool deployed (consciously or not) to make opposition harder. Hence, when the Sarkozy government argued in favor of intervention in Libya, the presentation of the war as extension of the French fight for human rights, republicanism, and enlightenment practically silenced criticism (Ostermann 2016).

Finally, *metaphors* (and other tropes) are another means of molding discursive objects and directing subjects toward accepting certain representations. Deeper than frames – because culturally embedded, often standardized, and therefore more difficult to manipulate (in the sense of use, not deception), but less encompassing than narratives because they are highly condensed/short –, metaphors influence discourses by the analogies and "Figure[s] of Thought" (Lakoff 1986) they create (Cienki and Yanow 2013). For instance, speaking of the *house of Europe* in a discourse on the EU evokes family and home and therefore creates a particularly powerful idea of belonging. Hence, metaphors can inform us about the salience of foreign policy issues by the concepts they invoke (Oppermann and Spencer 2013). Analyzing metaphors exposes the cultural significance attributed to certain discursive elements. Thus, they are crucial for comprehending the importance of arguments and hence the persuasive power their use shall convey.

Power is a central analytical category for discourse analysts. Power is not just a repressive force when actor A forces B to do something it otherwise would not have done (Aron 2003[1966]). For Foucault (1984, 61) conversely, power is an intersubjective "productive network which runs through the whole social body", ruling what can or cannot be said or done, or what we consider to be normal or *true*. Thus, it manifests in conventions, rules, knowledge, or institutions (like the state and its organizations) that we take for granted. It is a relational concept that does not only need an agent deploying it but also people accepting the imposition of a meaning or opinion as hegemonic, generally accepted interpretation of, for instance, democracy, war, or the content of a certain policy. Therefore, power has who can make her ideas prevail in politics. Even hierarchically superior people, like presidents or prime ministers, only have power when the subjects of a discourse are accepting them as competent speakers in a certain foreign policy discourse. Although, due to her exposed position, the head of state might have a larger ability to *influence* discourse, whether her framings of an issue and visions of the world are accepted depends on at least tacit acceptance by the audience (Foucault 2002, 340ff.). Thus, for power to work it must move both ways! It is, therefore, never total (although it can be quite stable and vested) but a temporal establishment of discursive hegemony on a political issue that enables the conduct of policies (Cox 1983, 54, 57; Laclau 2000). Although this definition renders power ubiquitous, it also enables freedom through people's ability to question conventionality and truths. When researching power, therefore, we do not only have to look at repression, but also at institutions and taken-for-grantedness to fully comprehend who exerts and has power in a society or over a certain discourse. In this sense, discourse analysis is intrinsically critical because, ultimately, it aims at revealing the contingent construction of social relations, making the supposedly natural or unchangeable a product of history and, therefore, agency (cf. also Hacking 2000, 6f.).

Discourse-Analytical Schools

Whereas the aforementioned steps of linguistic and power analysis are central to any discourse analysis as a method, some studies adhere more closely to the theoretical assumptions of different discourse-analytical schools.[3] *Securitization theory*, for example, combines an interest in foreign policy matters with a discursively informed theoretical structure (i.e. Lupovici 2016; Stritzel 2014, Wilhelmsen 2021; overview in Sjöstedt 2019). Building on speech act theory (Austin 1962), speech is considered to be central in the construction of reality. Hence, "The way to study securitization is to study discourse" (Buzan, Wæver, and de Wilde 1998, 25). Adding to the role of speech, "practices, context, and power relations" (Balzacq 2011, 1) play also important performative functions in showing how an issue is moved away from more routine decision-making to so-called extraordinary politics (Roe 2012). The key actor in a securitization process is the so-called securitizing actor who usually is someone with some degree of power and influence like a president (i.e., Sjöstedt 2007), a government (Hayes 2016), or an organization (Léonard and Kaunert 2020). The threat construction offered by the securitizing actor is called the *securitizing move*. It can concern either military or non-military issues and can either be linked to an antagonistic actor or constitute more general threatening processes such as environmental degradation (i.e., Diez, Von Lucke, and Wellmann 2016; Floyd 2010; Rothe 2015) or epidemics (Kirk and McDonald 2021; Sjöstedt 2011). Correspondingly, the *referent object* – or what is being threatened – can vary from being society, the nation, a region, or the global community. Roxanna Sjöstedt (Sjöstedt 2007), for example, demonstrates how violent Islamism and Communism respectively, and the actors associated with these ideologies were constructed as threats to national security in the U.S. political and societal discourses. Jef Huysmans (2000, 2006) shows how migration is securitized (economically, militarily, and societally) in relation to the European referent object. The final entity of the securitization framework, and which has to accept the securitizing move in order for an issue to move up on the security agenda, is the *audience*. The audience is often paired with the securitizing actor: if the latter is the head of government, the audience could be the broader political elite in parliament (Hayes 2016), the general public, or both (Roe 2008).

Critical Discourse Analysis, for its part, is more strongly informed by Marxist conceptions of society and politics dominated (or at least strongly influenced) by capitalist mechanisms of hegemony and exploitation. CDA "studies the way social power abuse, dominance, and inequality are enacted, reproduced, and resisted by text and talk in the social and political context" (Van Dijk 2001, 352; similarly Fairclough 2007). In this conception, discourses are but one social practice among others that exert causal power on politics (Chouliaraki and Fairclough 1999, 28ff., 125; Forchtner and Wodak 2017). While CDA emphasizes the possibility of agency and change, this weight given to non-discursive practices can come with flavors of structuralist analysis that is difficult from a methodological perspective because the mechanism through which extra-discursive practices influence discourse is not always clearly elaborated. Nevertheless, CDA stands out for its level of sophistication of textual analysis that serves as a guidepost for concrete tools of sociolinguistic analysis until today (Fairclough 1992). The above-mentioned study of Richard Jackson (2005) is a good demonstration of how CDA is performed in relation to foreign policy issues. By a close analysis of political and bureaucratic discourses, Jackson demonstrates how power is constructed, exercised, and abused in enabling the war on terror. Another example is the study by Daniel McCarthy (2011) who has combined CDA and narrative analysis to explain U.S. internet policies abroad.

Building on CDA's conceptual legacy, another important discourse-analytical school can be found in the work by Ernesto Laclau and Chantal Mouffe (Laclau 2005, 2000) and the discourse theory of the *Essex School* (Glynos and Howarth 2007; Howarth, Norval, and Stavrakakis 2000; Torfing and Howarth 2005). These scholars adopt a poststructuralist methodology by conceptualizing discourse as the totality of social practices, studying the sociolinguistic processes that create and fix meanings and truth (Foucault 1984, 51ff.). This means analytically that for making statements on causal effects of social/political/cultural structures they must be *perceived* as such (as in *formulated*) by discursive agents. This poststructuralist approach enables the inclusion of structural factors (like capital, culture, or institutions) into an explanatory model by analyzing their discursive manifestations phenomenologically, in written or spoken text (Jackson 2011, 88). Thus, structures are considered to have power over discourses if they appear as such, i.e. have meaning for discursive subjects. A research design that uses a wide variety of sources, including opposition and other deviant agents, will usually capture these tacit/structural levers on discourse (Ostermann 2019, 17ff.; Stengel and Nabers 2019, 254f.). This framework can be used to understand how foreign policy change is initiated through the establishment of new *hegemonic discourses* (Laclau and Mouffe 1985; Laclau 2000) that, in a constructivist spirit, *enable* political change.

Building on Antonio Gramsci's thoughts on hegemony as unstable, temporal fixation of power relations (Cox 1983; Gramsci 1971), Laclau and Mouffe pay particular attention to investigating what they call the political and social *logics* of discourse, which they conceive as constructed explanatory mechanisms. The *social logic* characterizes a certain discourse, its subjects (agents), objects (topics), and rules and norms. The *political logic* focuses on the struggle for meaning between subjects of the discourse that try to forge relations and barriers between the discourse's various objects (or its signifiers). This also means to comprehend who is included or excluded in this discursive struggle, entailing constructions of self and otherness that define politics socially (Neumann 1996). Laclau and Mouffe also investigate *floating* and *empty signifiers* – concepts that are debated in discourses among different groups (floating) and filled with new and more meanings than they originally had, becoming sort of an empty shell that represents something new (like *Europe* referring to the EU). Once settled (temporarily), discourses fill a political void that fixes a new hegemonic understanding of politics, like in U.S. foreign policy (Nabers 2009). Additionally, Essex School scholars have conceptualized a third logic, the *fantasmatic* one that describes the concrete means of persuasion that are deployed in a discourse. As mentioned above, these means can be culturally significant metaphors and other tropes, concrete frames, or larger historical or political narratives that convey importance and authority in a specific sociocultural community (Hajer, 1997; also Mokry or Oppermann and Spencer in this volume; Ostermann 2019, 23ff.).

In sum, discourse-analytical scholarship is a broad research approach that consists of different schools, concepts, logics, and tools. This scholarship shares nonetheless a common foundation in recognizing the importance of ideas, meanings, and productive power and how they make certain behaviors and actions possible.

Conclusion

This chapter has probed how different discourse approaches can be successfully employed to FPA. In particular, discourse analysis helps us to detect the meanings, processes, assumptions, and ideas underlying foreign policy-making that might be omitted in a more traditional form of analysis, but which nonetheless play important roles in how foreign policy is made possible, or constructed, from a social, intersubjective perspective. This approach is opposed to an individualist methodology while not being ignorant toward contextualized individual agency (Bevir 1999). Hence, discourse approaches provide the grounds for understanding foreign policy from a bottom-up perspective that is sensitive to both domestic and international influences on policy-making – and actually able to show *how* these influences are made sense of and processed in politics rather than assuming that they have automated causal powers. Therefore, we would confidently locate discourse approaches to FPA in the constructivist camp of IR scholarship while holding that they provide distinct tools/concepts (hegemony, intertextuality, logics, power analysis), theoretical schools, and coherent methodological approaches to make constructivist/ideational analysis work.

Discourse approaches to analyzing foreign policy are well-established today while the field continues to develop and innovate. Contemporary challenges lie, for instance, in the way new technologies like social media platforms (see Schneiker in this volume) can be approached to investigate important discursive arenas of modern politics. The increasing availability of large corpora of text (see Cujai or Vignoli in this volume) rekindles debates about the merits of qualitative vs quantitative ways of analyzing texts and its discursive elements, making it necessary to think about a refinement of discourse approaches' analytical toolkit while maintaining their theoretical and methodical asset in the thick, contextual analysis of language. Discourse approaches also relate to conceptions and processes of international politics discussed in scholarship on the *practice turn* (Adler and Pouliot 2011; Bueger and Gadinger 2014), creating interesting avenues and perspectives for research.

First time or prospective users of discourse approaches might be advised that they are conceptually demanding and take time to implement. They necessitate deep cultural knowledge (and often language skills) of the chosen discursive arena and a thorough understanding of how agents interact. Put differently, discourse analyses need a clear communicative model!

Choosing some but not other actors for a study with a specific focus is okay but one must be crucially aware what influences this choice has on the discourse(s)/political process one is trying to grasp, and hence on the conclusions one wants to draw. (Hansen (2006) provides one of the best guides for getting this process right.) It is hardly ever possible to re-construct a discourse in its entirety, but discourse analyses will usually field large documentary apparatuses for reliability and validity reasons. Depending on the precise research question, these can cover longer/shorter periods and more/less agents – *but never a single agent only*, as a discourse only exists in intersubjectivity, and so does its analysis of meaning, power, and hegemony. Therefore, careful calibration of the analyzed topics, periods, and agents is necessary to keep investigations manageable. The coding or analytical dissection of discourse(s) and their reconstruction is usually conducted manually for validity reasons that derive from discourse analysis' linguistic ontology and the not flatly quantifiable character of the production of meaning (for a discussion of the reliability of manual discursive coding, see Ostermann 2019, 33ff.).[4] The researcher must also decide on whether she wants to approach the discourse under investigation with pre-defined categories or in an entirely inductive way. Both approaches have not only merits (e.g. the straightforwardness of categorical proceedings, also time-wise) but also trade-offs (such as confirmation bias from overly selective readings of discourses). As social scientists, we are usually not free from assumptions that influence our work, but it is crucial to be aware of them and to reflect how they might impact our approach to a certain discourse. This is not a way of saying that discourse analysis is subjective but rather a call for self-reflexive and rule-driven hermeneutic analysis.

If the researcher handles the difficult aspects of complexity, analytical reconstruction, and reflexivity successfully, discourse approaches can make a unique contribution to explaining foreign policy from a social and intersubjective, bottom-up perspective. Such a perspective provides theoretical and analytical beef to major FPA research agendas on the influence of ideas and domestic politics on foreign policy or the pathways through which system-level influences make their way into foreign policy-making (or don't).

Acknowledgments

We are grateful for documentary support from our research assistant Elisabeth Alm at Justus Liebig University Giessen, Germany, where Falk Ostermann has worked prior to switching to Kiel University.

Notes

1 Governmentality covers a lot more concepts outside the realm of discourse analysis so that we cannot discuss it here properly. Governmentality models the interaction of discourses, practices, institutions, and processes through which governing agents co-opt other subjects, impose their views, and conduct their policies. The concept is particularly useful for analyzing processes of governance as a whole, including other domains than speech (Foucault 1989, years 1977–1978; Sending and Neumann 2006, 655ff.).
2 Mokry presents frames in a quantitative research design that, in opposition to an interpretive logic, assigns equal values to every frame's occurrence for analyzing frequency.
3 The *discourse-coalition theory* by Hajer (1997) is another school touching on foreign policy issues, often used for explaining environmental politics.
4 The frequency of certain discursive elements can be an indicator of their importance but at the same time, even little mentioned concepts may carry significant explanatory burden if they are socioculturally meaningful. As Hansen (2006, 86f.) argues, frequency measurements are but a good point of departure for discursive investigations but they must never stop there.

References

Adler, Emanuel. 2013. "Constructivism in International Relations: Sources, Contributions, and Debates." In *Handbook of International Relations*, edited by Walter Carlsnaes, Thomas Risse and Beth A. Simmons. London *et al.*: Sage, 112–145.

Adler, Emanuel, and Vincent Pouliot, eds. 2011. *International Practices*. Cambridge, UK and New York: Cambridge University Press.

Adler-Nissen, Rebecca, and Vincent Pouliot. 2014. "Power in Practice: Negotiating the International Intervention in Libya." *European Journal of International Relations* 20(4): 889–911.

Aron, Raymond. 2003[1966]. *Peace and War. A Theory of International Relations*. London and New York: Routledge.

Ashley, Richard K. 1984. "The Poverty of Neorealism." *International Organization* 38(2): 225–286.

Austin, John Langshaw. 1962. *How to Do Things with Words*. Oxford: Clarendon Press.

Aydın-Düzgit, Senem. 2014. "Critical Discourse Analysis in Analysing European Union Foreign Policy: Prospects and Challenges." *Cooperation and Conflict* 49(3): 354–367.

Balzacq, Thierry, ed. 2011. *Securitization Theory. How Security Problems Emerge and Dissolve*. London and New York: Routledge.

Becker, Derick. 2010. "The New Legitimacy and International Legitimation: Civilization and South African Foreign Policy." *Foreign Policy Analysis* 6(2): 133–146.

Bergman Rosamond, Annika. 2020. "Swedish Feminist Foreign Policy and "Gender Cosmopolitanism"." *Foreign Policy Analysis* 16(2): 217–235.

Bevir, Mark. 1999. "Foucault and Critique. Deploying Agency against Autonomy." *Political Theory* 27(1): 65–84.

Brunk, Darren C. 2008. "Curing the Somalia Syndrome: Analogy, Foreign Policy Decision Making, and the Rwandan Genocide." *Foreign Policy Analysis* 4(3): 301–320.

Bueger, Christian, and Frank Gadinger. 2014. *International Practice Theory. New Perspectives*. Houndmills and New York: Palgrave Macmillan.

Burai, Erna. 2016. "Parody as Norm Contestation: Russian Normative Justifications in Georgia and Ukraine and Their Implications for Global Norms." *Global Society* 30(1): 67–77.

Buzan, Barry, Ole Wæver, and Jaap de Wilde. 1998. *Security: A New Framework for Analysis*. Boulder, CO, and London: Lynne Rienner.

Campbell, David. 1992. *Writing Security: United States Foreign Policy and the Politics of Identity*. Revised edition. Minneapolis, MN: University of Minnesota Press.

Campbell, David. 1993. *Politics Without Principle. Sovereignty, Ethics, and the Narratives of the Gulf War*. Boulder, CO, and London: Lynne Rienner.

Carta, Caterina, and Jean-Frederic Morin. 2016. *EU Foreign Policy Through the Lens of Discourse Analysis: Making Sense of Diversity*. London and New York: Routledge.

Chouliaraki, Lilie, and Norman Fairclough. 1999. *Discourse in Late Modernity: Rethinking Critical Discourse Analysis*. Edinburgh: Edinburgh University Press.

Chryssogelos, Angelos. 2021. *Party Systems and Foreign Policy Change in Liberal Democracies. Cleavages, Ideas, Competition*. London and New York: Routledge.

Cienki, Alan, and Dvora Yanow. 2013. "Why Metaphor and Other Tropes? Linguistic Approaches to Analysing Policies and the Political." *Journal of International Relations and Development* 16(2): 167–176.

Coş, Kıvanç, and Pinar Bilgin. 2010. "Stalin's Demands: Constructions of the "Soviet Other" in Turkey's Foreign Policy, 1919–1945." *Foreign Policy Analysis* 6(1): 43–60.

Cox, M. 2005. "Beyond the West: Terrors in Transatlantia." *European Journal Of International Relations* 11(2): 203–233.

Cox, Robert W. 1983. "Gramsci, Hegemony and International Relations: An Essay in Methods." *Millennium - Journal of International Studies* 12(2): 162–175.

D'Aoust, Anne-Marie. 2017. Feminist Perspectives on Foreign Policy. In *Oxford Research Encyclopedia of International Studies,* edited by Nukhet Sandal. Oxford: Oxford University Press. https://doi.org/10.1093/acrefore/9780190846626.013.179

De Sá Guimarães, Feliciano, and Irma Dutra De Oliveira E Silva. 2021. "Far-Right Populism and Foreign Policy Identity: Jair Bolsonaro's Ultra-Conservatism and the New Politics of Alignment." *International Affairs* 97(2): 345–363.

Devetak, Richard. 2013. "Critical Theory." In *Theories of International Relations*, edited by Scott Burchill and Andrew Linklater. Houndmills and New York: Palgrave Macmillan, 162–186.

Diez, Thomas. 1999. "Speaking 'Europe': The Politics of Integration Discourse." *Journal of European Public Policy* 6(4): 598–613.

Diez, Thomas. 2001. "Europe as a Discursive Battleground: Discourse Analysis and European Integration Studies." *Cooperation and Conflict* 36(1): 5–38.

Diez, Thomas, Franziskus Von Lucke, and Zehra Wellmann. 2016. *The Securitisation of Climate Change: Actors, Processes and Consequences*: London and New York: Routledge.

Doty, Roxanne Lynn. 1993. "Foreign Policy as Social Construction: A Post-Positivist Analysis of U.S. Counterinsurgency Policy in the Philippines." *International Studies Quarterly* 37(3): 297–320.

Eberle, Jakub. 2019. *Discourse and Affect in Foreign Policy. Germany and the Iraq War*. London and New York: Routledge.

Entman, Robert M. 1993. "Framing: Toward Clarification of a Fractured Paradigm." *Journal of Communication* 43(4): 51–58.

Entman, Robert M. 2004. *Projections of Power. Framing News, Public Opinion, and U.S. Foreign Policy*. Chicago, IL, and London: The University of Chicago Press.

Epstein, Charlotte. 2010. "Who Speaks? Discourse, the Subject and the Study of Identity in International Politics." *European Journal of International Relations* 17(2): 327–350.

Erdogan, Birsen. 2017. *Humanitarian Intervention and the Responsibility to Protect. Turkish Foreign Policy Discourse*. Cham: Palgrave Macmillan.

Fairclough, Norman. 1992. *Discourse and Social Change*. Cambridge, UK and Malden, MA: Polity.

Fairclough, Norman. 2007. "The Contribution of Discourse Analysis to Research on Social Change." In *Discourse and Contemporary Social Change*, edited by Norman Fairclough, Giuseppina Cortese and Patrizia Ardizzone. Bern et al.: Peter Lang, 25–47.

Fanoulis, Evangelos. 2014. "Understanding the Social Construction of the Democratic Deficit in Csdp: A Foucauldian Approach." *European Security* 23(4): 466–483.

Fanoulis, Evangelos, and Weiqing Song. 2022. "Cooperation between the EU and China: A Post-Liberal Governmentality Approach." *Review of International Studies* 48(2): 346–363.

Fierke, Karin M. 2002. "Links across the Abyss: Language and Logic in International Relations." *International Studies Quarterly* 46(3): 331–354.

Floyd, Rita. 2010. *Security and the Environment: Securitisation Theory and Us Environmental Security Policy*. Cambridge, UK: Cambridge University Press.

Forchtner, Bernhard, and Ruth Wodak. 2017. "Critical Discourse Studies." In *The Routledge Handbook of Language and Politics*, edited by Ruth Wodak and Bernhard Forchtner. London and New York: Routledge, 135–149.

Foucault, Michel. 1972. *The Archaeology of Knowledge*. London: Tavistock.

Foucault, Michel. 1984. *The Foucault Reader*. New York and Toronto: Pantheon Books.

Foucault, Michel. 1989. *Résumé Des Cours. 1970–1982*. Paris: Julliard.

Foucault, Michel. 2002. "The Subject and Power" In *Power*, edited by James D. Faubion. London, New York et al.: Penguin Books, 326–348.

Giacalone, Rita. 2015. "Latin American Foreign Policy Analysis." In *Foreign Policy Analysis Beyond North America*, edited by Klaus Brummer and Valerie M. Hudson. Boulder, CO: Lynne Rienner, 121–138.

Glencross, Andrew. 2020. "'Love Europe, Hate the EU': A Genealogical Inquiry into Populists' Spatio-Cultural Critique of the European Union and Its Consequences." *European Journal of International Relations* 26(1): 116–136.

Glynos, Jason, and David R. Howarth. 2007. *Logics of Critical Explanation in Social and Political Theory*. London and New York: Routledge.

Goldstein, Judith, and Robert O. Keohane. 1993. *Ideas and Foreign Policy: Beliefs, Institutions, and Political Change*. Ithaca, NY: Cornell University Press.

Gramsci, Antonio. 1971. *Selections from the Prison Notebooks*. London: Lawrence and Wishart.

Groppo, Alejandro J. 2009. *Los Dos Príncipes: Juan D. Perón Y Getulio Vargas*. Cordoba: Eduvim.

Guzzini, Stefano. 2000. "A Reconstruction of Constructivism in International Relations." *European Journal of International Relations* 6(2): 147–182.

Hacking, Ian. 2000. *The Social Construction of What?* Cambridge, MA: Harvard University Press.

Hadfield, Amelia, and Valerie M. Hudson. 2015. "North American and European Foreign Policy Analysis." In *Foreign Policy Analysis Beyond North America*, edited by Klaus Brummer and Valerie M. Hudson. Boulder, CO, and London: Lynne Rienner, 139–168.

Hajer, Maarten A. 1997. *The Politics of Environmental Discourse: Ecological Modernization and the Policy Process*. Oxford: Oxford University Press.

Hajer, Maarten A. 2005. "Coalitions, Practices, and Meaning in Environmental Politics: From Acid Rain to Bse." In *Discourse Theory in European Politics. Identity, Policy and Governance*, edited by David R. Howarth and Jacob Torfing. Houndmills and New York: Palgrave Macmillan, 297–315.

Hansen, Lene. 2006. *Security as Practice. Discourse Analysis and the Bosnian War.* London and New York: Routledge.

Hayes, Jarrod. 2016. "Identity, Authority, and the British War in Iraq." *Foreign Policy Analysis* 12(3): 334–353.

Hellmann, Gunther. 2017. "Linking Foreign Policy and Systemic Transformation in Global Politics: Methodized Inquiry in a Deweyan Tradition." *Foreign Policy Analysis* 13(3): 578–598.

Herschinger, Eva. 2011. *Constructing Global Enemies. Hegemony and Identity in International Discourses on Terrorism and Drug Prohibition.* London and New York: Routledge.

Holland, Jack. 2012. *Selling the War on Terror : Foreign Policy Discourses after 9/11.* New York: Routledge.

Hollis, Martin, and Steve Smith. 1990. *Explaining and Understanding in International Relations.* Oxford: Clarendon Press.

Hopf, Ted. 2002. *Social Construction of International Politics: Identities & Foreign Policies. Moscow, 1955 and 1999.* Ithaca, NY: Cornell University Press.

Hopf, Ted, and Bentley B. Allan. 2016. *Making Identity Count. Building a National Identity Database.* New York: Oxford University Press.

Howarth, David R., Aletta J. Norval, and Yannis Stavrakakis, eds. 2000. *Discourse Theory and Political Analysis. Identities, Hegemonies and Social Change.* Manchester and New York: Manchester University Press.

Humphreys, Adam R. C. 2017. "Introduction: Problems of Causation in World Politics." *Journal of International Relations and Development* 20(4): 659–666.

Huysmans, Jef. 2000. "The European Union and the Securitization of Migration." *Journal Of Common Market Studies* 38(5): 751–777.

Huysmans, Jef. 2006. *The Politics of Insecurity: Fear, Migration and Asylum in the EU.* London and New York: Routledge.

Jackson, Patrick Thaddeus 2006. *Civilizing the Enemy: German Reconstruction and the Invention of the West.* Ann Arbor, MI: University of Michigan Press.

Jackson, Patrick Thaddeus 2011. *The Conduct of Inquiry in International Relations: Philosophy of Science and Its Implications for the Study of World Politics.* London and New York: Routledge.

Jackson, Patrick Thaddeus 2017. "Causal Claims and Causal Explanation in International Studies." *Journal of International Relations and Development* 20(4): 689–716.

Jackson, Richard. 2005. *Writing the War on Terrorism: Language, Politics, and Counter-Terrorism.* Manchester, NY: Manchester University Press.

Jarvis, Lee. 2009. *Times of Terror: Discourse, Temporality and the War on Terror.* Houndmills and New York: Palgrave Macmillan.

Jenne, Erin K. 2021. "Populism, Nationalism and Revisionist Foreign Policy." *International Affairs* 97(2): 323–343.

Kirk, Jessica, and Matt McDonald. 2021. "The Politics of Exceptionalism: Securitization and Covid-19." *Global Studies Quarterly* 1 (3): ksab024.

Kristeva, Julia. 1980. "Word, Dialogue, and Novel." In *Desire in Language: A Semiotic Approach to Literature and Art*, edited by Leon S. Roudiez. New York: Columbia University Press, 64–91.

Kurki, Milja. 2008. *Causation in International Relations. Reclaiming Causal Analysis.* Cambridge, UK and New York: Cambridge University Press.

Kurki, Milja. 2011. "Governmentality and EU Democracy Promotion: The European Instrument for Democracy and Human Rights and the Construction of Democratic Civil Societies1." *International Political Sociology* 5(4): 349–366.

Laclau, Ernesto. 2000. "Identity and Hegemony: The Role of Universality in the Constitution of Political Logics." In *Contingency, Hegemony, Universality. Contemporary Dialogues on the Left*, edited by Ernesto Laclau, Chantal Mouffe and Slavoj Zizek. London and New York: Verso, 44–89.

Laclau, Ernesto. 2005. *On Populist Reason.* London and New York: Verso.

Laclau, Ernesto, and Chantal Mouffe. 1985. *Hegemony & Socialist Strategy. Towards a Radical Democratic Politics.* London and New York: Verso.

Laffey, Mark, and Jutta Weldes. 1997. "Beyond Beliefs: Ideas and Symbolic Technologies in the Study of International Relations." *European Journal of International Relations* 3(2): 193–237.

Lakoff, George. 1986. "A Figure of Thought." *Metaphor and Symbolic Activity* 1(3): 215–225.

Larsen, Henrik 1997. *Foreign Policy and Discourse Analysis: France, Britain and Europe*. London and New York: Routledge.

Léonard, Sarah, and Christian Kaunert. 2020. "The Securitisation of Migration in the European Union: Frontex and Its Evolving Security Practices." *Journal of Ethnic and Migration Studies*: 1–13.

Linklater, Andrew. 1996. "The Achievements of Critical Theory." In *International Theory: Positivism and Beyond*, edited by Steve Smith, Ken Booth and Marysia Zalewski. Cambridge, UK *et al.*: Cambridge University Press, 279–298.

Löfflmann, Georg. 2017. *American Grand Strategy under Obama. Competing Discourses*. Edinburgh: Edinburgh University Press.

Lupovici, Amir. 2016. "Securitization Climax: Putting the Iranian Nuclear Project at the Top of the Israeli Public Agenda (2009–2012)." *Foreign Policy Analysis* 12(3): 413–432.

Lustig, Carola M. 2016. "Soft or Hard Power? Discourse Patterns in Brazil's Foreign Policy Toward South America." *Latin American Politics and Society* 58(4): 103–125.

Marcussen, Martin, Thomas Risse, Daniela Engelmann-Martin, and Joachim Knopf. 2001. "Constructing Europe? The Evolution of Nation-State Identities." In *The Social Construction of Europe*, edited by Thomas Christiansen, Knud Erik Jørgensen and Antje Wiener. London *et al.*: Sage, 101–120.

McCarthy, Daniel R. 2011. "Open Networks and the Open Door: American Foreign Policy and the Narration of the Internet." *Foreign Policy Analysis* 7(1): 89–111.

Merlingen, Michael. 2011. "From Governance to Governmentality in Csdp: Towards a Foucauldian Research Agenda." *Journal of Common Market Studies* 49(1): 149–169.

Miskimmon, Alister, Ben O'Loughlin, and Laura Roselle. 2013. *Strategic Narratives. Communication Power and the New World Order*. London and New York: Routledge.

Nabers, Dirk. 2009. "Filling the Void of Meaning: Identity Construction in U.S. Foreign Policy after September 11, 2001." *Foreign Policy Analysis* 5(2): 191–214.

Nabers, Dirk. 2015. *A Poststructuralist Discourse Theory of Global Politics*. Houndmills and New York: Palgrave Macmillan.

Neumann, Iver B. 1996. "Self and Other in International Relations." *European Journal of International Relations* 2(2): 139–174.

Noreen, Erik, Roxanna Sjöstedt, and Jan Ångström. 2017. "Why Small States Join Big Wars: The Case of Sweden in Afghanistan 2002–2014." *International Relations* 31(2): 145–168.

Oppermann, Kai, and Alexander Spencer. 2013. "Thinking Alike? Salience and Metaphor Analysis as Cognitive Approaches to Foreign Policy Analysis." *Foreign Policy Analysis* 9(1): 39–56.

Ostermann, Falk. 2016. "The Discursive Construction of Intervention: Selves, Democratic Legacies, and Responsibility to Protect in French Discourse on Libya." *European Security* 25(1): 72–91.

Ostermann, Falk. 2019. *Security, Defense Discourse and Identity in Nato and Europe. How France Changed Foreign Policy*. London and New York: Routledge.

Parsons, Craig. 2003. *A Certain Idea of Europe*. Ithaca, NY and London: Cornell University Press.

Parsons, Talcott. 1966. *Societies. Evolutionary and Comparative Perspectives*. Englewood Cliffs: Prentice-Hall.

Patterson, Molly, and Kristen Renwick Monroe. 1998. "Narrative in Political Science." *Annual Review of Political Science* (1): 315–331.

Ratuva, Steven. 2016. "Subalternization of the Global South: Critique of Mainstream 'Western' security Discourses." *Cultural Dynamics* 28(2): 211–228.

Rein, Martin, and Donald Schön. 1993. "Reframing Policy Discourse." In *The Argumentative Turn in Policy Analysis and Planning*, edited by Frank Fischer and John Forester. Durham, NC and London: Duke University Press, 145–166.

Ripley, Charles G. 2017. "Discourse in Foreign Policy" In *Oxford Research Encyclopedia of Politics*, edited by William R. Thomson. Oxford: Oxford University Press. Available from https://oxfordre.com/politics/view/10.1093/acrefore/9780190228637.001.0001/acrefore-9780190228637-e-411.

Risse-Kappen, Thomas. 1994. "Ideas Do Not Float Freely: Transnational Coalitions, Domestic Structures, and the End of the Cold War." *International Organization* 48(2): 185–214.

Rivera, William Anthony. 2016. "Discursive Practices of Honor: Rethinking Iran's Nuclear Program." *Foreign Policy Analysis* 12(3): 395–412.

Roe, Paul. 2008. "Actor, Audience(S) and Emergency Measures : Securitization and the UK's Decision to Invade Iraq." *Security dialogue Security Dialogue* 39(6): 615–635.

Roe, Paul. 2012. "Is Securitization a 'Negative' Concept? Revisiting the Normative Debate over Normal Versus Extraordinary Politics." *Security Dialogue* 43(3): 249–266.

Rothe, Delf. 2015. *Securitizing Global Warming: A Climate of Complexity*. London and New York: Routledge.

Sandrin, Paula Orrico, and Andrea Ribeiro Hoffmann. 2018. "Silences and Hierarchies in European Union Public Diplomacy." *Revista Brasileira de Política Internacional* 61 (1): e011.

Sending, Ole Jacob, and Iver B. Neumann. 2006. "Governance to Governmentality: Analyzing Ngos, States, and Power." *International Studies Quarterly* 50(3): 651–672.

Shepherd, Laura J. 2006. "Veiled References: Constructions of Gender in the Bush Administration Discourse on the Attacks on Afghanistan Post-9/11." *International Feminist Journal of Politics* 8(1): 19–41.

Sjöstedt, Roxanna. 2007. "The Discursive Origins of a Doctrine. Norms, Identity, and Securitization Under Harry S. Truman and George W. Bush." *Foreign Policy Analysis* 3(3): 233–254.

Sjöstedt, Roxanna. 2008. "Exploring the Construction of Threats: The Securitization of Hiv/Aids in Russia." *Security Dialogue* 39(1): 7–29.

Sjöstedt, Roxanna. 2011. "Health Issues and Securitization: Hiv/Aids as a Us National Security Threat." In *Securitization Theory. How Security Problems Emerge and Dissolve*, edited by Thierry Balzacq. Milton Park: Routledge.

Sjöstedt, Roxanna. 2019. Securitization and Foreign Policy Analysis. In *Oxford Research Encyclopedia of Politics: World Politics*, edited by Cameron Thies. Oxford: Oxford University Press.

Sjöstedt, Roxanna, and Erik Noreen. 2021. "When Peace Nations Go to War: Examining the Narrative Transformation of Sweden and Norway in Afghanistan." *European Journal of International Security* 6(3): 318–337.

Solomon, Ty. 2014. *The Politics of Subjectivity in American Foreign Policy Discourses*. Anna Arbor, MI: University of Michigan Press.

Stahl, Bernhard. 2006. *Frankreichs Identität und außenpolitische Krisen. Verhalten und Diskurse im Kosovo-Krieg und der Uruguay-Runde des GATT*. Baden-Baden: Nomos.

Stengel, Frank A., David B. MacDonald, and Dirk Nabers, eds. 2019. *Populism and World Politics: Exploring Inter- and Transnational Dimensions*. Cham: Palgrave Macmillan.

Stengel, Frank A., and Dirk Nabers. 2019. "Symposium: The Contribution of Laclau's Discourse Theory to International Relations and International Political Economy - Introduction." *New Political Science* 41(2): 248–262.

Stritzel, Holger. 2014. *Security in Translation: Securitization Theory and the Localization of Threat*. Houndmills and New York: Palgrave Macmillan.

Tilly, Charles. 2002. *Stories, Identities, and Political Change*. Lanham, MD et al.: Rowman & Littlefield.

Torfing, Jacob, and David R. Howarth, eds. 2005. *Discourse Theory in European Politics. Identity, Policy and Governance*. Houndmills and New York: Palgrave Macmillan.

Van Dijk, Teun A. 2001. "Critical Discourse Analysis." In *Handbook of Discourse Analysis*, edited by D. Tannen, D. Schiffrin and H. Hamilton. Oxford: Blackwell.

Vucetic, Srdjan. 2011. "A Racialized Peace? How Britain and the Us Made Their Relationship Special." *Foreign Policy Analysis* 7(4): 403–422.

Wæver, Ole. 2002. "Identity, Communities and Foreign Policy: Discourse Analysis as Foreign Policy Theory." In *European Integration and National Identity. The Challenge of the Nordic States*, edited by Lene Hansen and Ole Wæver. London and New York: Routledge, 20–49.

Weldes, Jutta. 1996. "Constructing National Interest." *European Journal of International Relations* 2(3): 275–318.

Wendt, Alexander E. 1987. "The Agent-Structure Problem in International Relations Theory." *International Organization* 41(3): 335–370.

Wendt, Alexander E. 1999. *Social Theory of International Politics*. Cambridge, UK et al.: Cambridge University Press.

Wilhelmsen, Julie. 2021. "Spiraling toward a New Cold War in the North? The Effect of Mutual and Multifaceted Securitization." *Journal of Global Security Studies* 6(3): ogaa044.

Wojczewski, Thorsten. 2018. *India's Foreign Policy Discourse and Its Conceptions of World Order: The Quest for Power and Identity*. London and New York: Routledge.

Wojczewski, Thorsten. 2019. "Trump, Populism, and American Foreign Policy." *Foreign Policy Analysis* 16(3): 292–311.

Wojczewski, Thorsten. 2021. "Conspiracy Theories, Right-Wing Populism and Foreign Policy: The Case of the Alternative for Germany." *Journal of International Relations and Development* 25: 130–158.

Yanow, Dvora, and Peregrine Schwartz-Shea. 2006. *Interpretation and Method. Empirical Research Methods and the Interpretive Turn*. Armonk, NY and London: M. E. Shape.

Yee, Albert S. 1996. "The Causal Effects of Ideas on Policies." *International Organization* 50(1): 69–108.

Zehfuss, Maja. 2004. *Constructivism in International Relations. The Politics of Reality*. Cambridge, UK et al.: Cambridge University Press.

8
Narrative Analysis

Kai Oppermann and Alexander Spencer

Introduction

Storytelling, or rather the analysis of storytelling, may not look like a serious academic endeavor at first sight, as we generally associate stories or narratives as something done for private entertainment. Narrative analysis is commonly considered the realm of literary studies and does not seem an appropriate tool to investigate important issues in international affairs, such as diplomatic negotiations, economic sanctions, or military interventions, which are commonly the concern of Foreign Policy Analysis (FPA). Yet this chapter will show that the analysis of narratives is, in fact, quite central to the study of foreign policy as narratives can be considered one of the most basic means of sense making. We understand the world in which we live through narratives as they give meaning to context, actors, and events. Narratives are essential in all areas of social interaction in which there is a need to elaborate, justify, and explain actions, decisions, and behavior. Foreign policy is no different in this regard.

This chapter will outline a method of narrative analysis that understands narratives as a form of organizing discourse. Based on many assumptions of other discourse analytical approaches, narrative analysis focuses on how the world is said to be. How is the international order constructed in the form of narratives, and what do these narratives do politically? In pursuit of outlining the method and highlighting its merits, the chapter will be structured as follows. The next part will give a brief overview of the research conducted on narratives in International Relations (IR) and FPA. Part three will suggest a method of narrative analysis which emphasizes the aspects of setting, characterization, and emplotment as three essential yet overlapping elements of a narrative. Part four will turn to a short empirical illustration of how we have applied the method in previous research on US congressional debates around the 2015 *Iran nuclear deal*. The conclusion will reflect on the strengths and limits of narrative analysis as a method as well as highlight some of the potential pitfalls of using such an approach in FPA. It will also outline recent trends in the analysis of narratives in political science and indicate where research might be going in the future.

The Narrative Turn in Political Science and FPA

The analysis of storytelling has moved from the margins of political science to the mainstream and an increasing number of scholars have started to engage with narratives as an important aspect of (international) politics worthy of scientific investigation. While narratives have played a major role in other disciplines such as psychology and history for some time (White 1973; Sarbin 1986), and discourse analysis has become a common sight in research, the narrative turn in IR is a fairly recent phenomenon (Roberts 2006; Subotić 2016). As Figure 8.1 shows, when analyzing the most relevant publications in Google Scholar using the search terms *narratives* AND *international relations* OR *foreign policy* between 1990 and 2016, there has been a sustained interest in narratives only since the early 2000s.

Within the narrative turn in political science, and IR and FPA more specifically, one can identify two major, though overlapping, strands of research. While the first focuses on the strategic use of narratives by political elites, the second is more concerned with the implications or consequences of narratives for politics. It is less interested in the intentions of those articulating the narrative, but more in the power of the narrative itself.

The first group of scholars works with the concept of *strategic narratives*, which was made prominent in IR by Alister Miskimmon, Ben O'Loughlin, and Laura Roselle (2013, 2017). They understand strategic narratives as

> A means for political actors to construct a shared meaning of the past, present, and future of international politics to shape the behaviour of domestic and international actors. Strategic narratives are a tool for political actors to extend their influence, manage expectations, and change the discursive environment in which they operate.
>
> *(Miskimmon et al., 2013, 2)*

The aim here is to analyze narratives as a form of soft power that focuses on the intentional use of narratives by actors. Narratives are seen as a form of communication predominantly

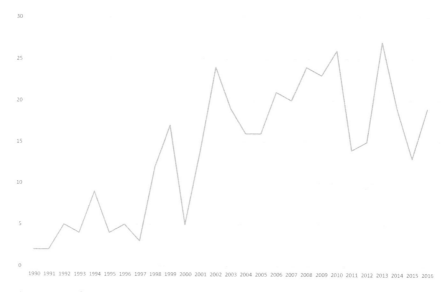

Figure 8.1 The narrative turn in international relations and FPA.

spread through the media in order to influence and change beliefs about political issues (Roselle et al., 2014). The ideas discussed by Miskimmon, O'Loughlin, and Roselle have also been considered by others who have focused on certain specific elements of narratives. This has included, for example, the relationship between strategic narratives and public opinion and how attitudes toward political decisions can be effectively influenced (Ringsmose and Børgesen 2011; De Graaf et al., 2015; Schmitt 2018) and how such narratives impact policy adoption (Van Noort and Colley 2021). In particular, research on strategic narratives has been interested in the intersection between narratives, public opinion, and war, for example, the role of strategic narratives in the war in Afghanistan in a range of Western countries (see De Graaf et al., 2015).

On an empirical level, some have continued to examine the relationship between strategic narratives and the acceptance of military and humanitarian interventions in conflicts around the world (Coticchia and De Simone 2016; Waldmann 2019), while others have turned to single or comparative case studies which examine the use of strategic narratives in specific states or geographic locations, by looking, for example, at China, Russia, or the Indo-Pacific region (Hinck and Kluver 2018; Lams 2018; Barthwal and Chacko 2020). On a theoretical level, the discussions around strategic narratives at first concentrated on critical reflections on the concept itself and have more recently moved to distinguishing strategic narratives from other concepts such as rhetoric, frames, or ideology (Hanska 2015; Livingston and Nassetta 2018; Coticchia and Catanzaro 2020). This is paralleled by the analysis of the role of news media in influencing public opinion (Szostek 2018; Khaldarova 2021) and the issue of competing strategic narratives (Irvin-Erickson 2017; Chaban et al., 2019).

In contrast to strategic narrative approaches, which consider narratives an intentional tool used by political actors to gain political influence, a second perspective on narratives in IR and FPA is more concerned with what narratives do in politics (Berenskoetter 2014; Subotić 2016). The intentionality in using narratives is far less relevant here, and the focus shifts away from actors to narratives themselves and to the audiences to which they are being told. This zooms in on discursive dynamics as well as the acceptance and hegemony of certain narratives. While approaches which are concerned with strategic narratives are more embedded in the literature on media studies and psychology, the second group feels more comfortable in the disciplines of history and literary studies. Historical narratives play an important role here as they can give insights into the power of narratives and the question of why certain narratives become established and others not (Krebs 2015; Gustafsson et al., 2019; Klymenko 2020). This includes questions regarding the structure of narratives (Oppermann and Spencer 2016, 2018), the notion of intertextuality, and the connection between past and present narratives (Hansen 2006; Spencer 2016) or the role of genres such as tragedy, romance, satire, and comedy and expectations of how stories should be told (Spencer 2019; Spencer and Oppermann 2020). More recently, research on strategic narratives and those less interested in the intentionality of the narratives have come together to reflect on aspects which seem vital for both strands, including the role of emotions in narratives (Clément et al., 2017; Holland and Fermor 2017) and the functions of visualization in the telling of stories (Heck 2017; Freistein and Gadinger 2020; Wright and Bergman-Rosamond 2021).

Narrative Analysis: Concepts and Methodology

Narrative analysis constitutes a particular method to guide the study of political discourse. The method is compatible with both major research strands on narratives detailed above and will be as useful for scholars interested in the strategic use of narratives as for research into the political consequences and power of narratives. It starts out from insights in cognitive linguistics and literary studies which show that narratives are fundamental to social and political meaning-making (Sarbin 1986; White 1987; Fludernik 2009). Human beings make sense of the world in the form of narratives and use narratives to negotiate intersubjective understandings in political discourse (Shenhav 2015). Narratives are constitutive of political discourse and central to the discursive construction of social and political facts. We are all "story-telling beings" (Devetak 2009, 795) who think, understand, and communicate through narratives.

Specifically, as a discourse analytical method in FPA, narrative analysis aims at identifying and reconstructing narratives in foreign policy discourse (see also Ostermann and Sjöstedt or Eder in this volume). To that purpose, it is useful to adopt a fairly minimal structural definition of narratives as a particular form of political discourse that consists of three interrelated elements: setting, characters, and emplotment (Spencer 2016). While narratives can be conceptualized in different ways (see Shenhav 2006), at their core, they involve a cast of characters who enact a particular plot that develops in a specific setting. The setting can be understood like the stage set of a theater play, providing the context in which a narrative unfolds (Toolan 2001, 41). The narrative characters are the agents who put the story on the stage and drive it forward (Fludernik 2009, 46). Finally, the emplotment scripts what happens in the narrative, making the story intelligible and orientating it toward some form of resolution (Ricoeur 1981, 167).

One can distinguish here between temporal and causal emplotment (Bridgeman 2007, 52). *Temporal emplotment* refers to the dimensions of order, duration, and frequency (Genette 1990). The order or sequence of events presented in the text as well as the logical order of events in time is important for IR and FPA as

> [a]ll reading is a combination of memory and anticipation. Our focus on whatever moment in the text we have reached will invariably be colored by our memory of what has gone before and our anticipation of what is to come. The order in which events are presented in the text is therefore crucial to our temporal experience of narrative.
>
> *(Bridgeman 2007, 57)*

Duration is concerned with the extent of time an event is supposed to take and the amount of space given to the presentation of that event in the text. The focus on duration can not only give us an insight into the emphasis, but also on the silences and untold aspects of a narrative. Frequency refers to the relationship between "how often something happens in story compared with how often it is narrated in text" (Toolan 2001, 43). Overall, the temporal elements of a narrative are important as they emphasize or foreground certain events and limit or silence others.

Causal emplotment, as the name suggests, elaborates on the causal relationship between the settings, characters, events, and actions (Paterson and Renwick Monroe 1998). It is through the causal emplotment of events and the actions of characters in front of a setting that they gain a narrative meaning. Emplotment "allows us to *weight* and *explain* events rather than just list them, to turn a set of propositions into an intelligible sequence about which we can form an opinion" (emphasis in original, Baker 2006, 67). The notion of causal emplotment illustrates how events hang together.

The main advantage of focusing on these three structural elements of narratives is that they provide a clear methodological template to explore narratives in political discourse. Along these lines, applying the method of narrative analysis in FPA proceeds in two steps. The first is to disaggregate the discourse under study into the narrative elements of setting, characterization, and emplotment. The second step involves re-assembling these elements as distinct narratives. Like a modular construction system, these two core analytical steps can be complemented with other methods to pursue different research angles in FPA. In particular, they provide the raw material for a narrative framework to study the construction, projection, or resonance of foreign policy narratives in political discourse (Miskimmon et al., 2013). First, the method can be used to probe narrative meaning-making in foreign policy and to map out the meaning(s) attributed to foreign policy issues in political discourse. This can shed light, for example, on the representation of foreign policy problems by decision-makers, the range of foreign policy decisions that are made possible by narrative constructions (Oppermann and Spencer 2013), as well as patterns of contestation between competing foreign policy narratives (Shenhav 2006; Ostermann 2019). Second, narrative analysis can zoom in on how foreign policy narratives are told and projected. This foregrounds the storytelling of "narrative entrepreneurs" (Subotić 2016, 615) and how they seek to develop convincing and powerful foreign policy narratives (Hülsse 2009). Third, the objective can be to explore how foreign policy narratives resonate and why some narratives gain traction in foreign policy discourse while others fail to catch on (Oppermann and Spencer 2018). This centers on the audiences of foreign policy narratives and may focus, for example, on how such narratives are taken up by the media or shape domestic or foreign public opinion.

In any case, however, the first task is to tease out the structural narrative elements of setting, characterization, and emplotment from the foreign policy discourse under study. This involves the coding of representations of the three elements by way of a qualitative content analysis of the source material. The coding scheme can be developed inductively, from a close reading of a representative sample of the material, or deductively, from a theoretical knowledge of key concepts and arguments in the relevant discourse. While the specific shape of the coding scheme will depend on the topic of the discourse under study, it needs to capture the general aspects that constitute the narrative setting, characterization, and emplotment in the respective discourse. In addition, the coding has to document the speakers in the foreign policy discourse who tell particular stories, that is, the narrators. This is because the identity of the narrators will often be relevant for understanding the intended meaning, political purpose, or broader resonance of different narratives. Table 8.1 summarizes the main elements of a general coding scheme to analyze foreign policy narratives.

On the dimension of the setting, the analysis focuses on references that speak to the background against which a narrative is being told. The setting gives important cues about the story that is about to unfold and the meaning it is meant to convey (Roselle et al., 2014).

Table 8.1 Coding Scheme for Foreign Policy Narratives

Narrator: Who Tells the Story?

Setting	Characterization	Emplotment
Against what background does the story take place?	Who are the characters of the story and how are they like?	How and why does the story unfold the way it does?
Elements of the setting: Decision-making situation Stakes involved Pointers to appropriate and inappropriate behaviors Historical analogies	Elements of characterization: Labeling characters Describing character behavior Associating characters with other characters Describing the decision-making process	Elements of emplotment: Reasons for foreign policy Objectives of foreign policy Means to achieve objectives Explaining success or failure to achieve objectives and attributing credit or blame

In the context of foreign policy, in particular, the setting sketches the decision-making situation, indicates the stakes involved, and places the narrative in a greater discursive context. This points audiences to the challenges, opportunities, or dilemmas decision-makers face and gives hints to what foreign policy behaviors should be seen as appropriate, possible, desirable, or normal in a given setting. For example, settings that embed a foreign policy narrative in the realms of gain/loss, cooperation/conflict, necessity/choice, or emergency/business-as-usual will likely invite different interpretations of what the main characters of the narrative do or say. The settings of foreign policy narratives also often involve historical analogies (Khong 1992; Kaarbo and Kenealy 2017) as intertextual linguistic figures to portray current decisions in light of particular historical reference points.

As for the dimension of characterization, the analysis maps how the cast of characters in a foreign policy narrative is being characterized. This helps audiences understand the motives, interests, abilities, and behaviors of narrative actors and gives further clues about the overall meaning of the story. To grasp the narrative element of characterization, the coding of the source material must distinguish between relevant groups of individual or collective characters in the narrative, for instance proponents or opponents of a foreign policy, government or opposition actors, elite decision-makers or the general public, international or domestic actors, and categorize how the narrative imbues them with particular character traits. In particular, the coding scheme needs to map out how the narratives constitute the characters of their different protagonists, for example, as powerful/weak, good/bad, friend/enemy, knowledgeable/ignorant, sincere/hypocritical, or competent/incompetent. This can be achieved through four complementary discursive techniques.

First, narratives may give their characters certain labels, nicknames, or shorthands which shape the opinions audiences form of them. As cases in point, referring to the Soviet Union as the *evil empire* or calling the former US President George W. Bush a *cowboy* constitutes these actors in a particular way, invoking certain images of their intentions, capabilities, and qualities. Second, characterization can take the form of describing and judging what the protagonists of a story say or do (Herman and Vervaeck 2007, 227). For example, depicting Boris Johnson's decision to campaign for Brexit as an opportunistic, cynical, and reckless ploy to advance his own political career or as a principled and fearless fight for British freedom and democracy will cast his character in a negative or positive light (Spencer and Oppermann 2020). Third, the protagonists of a story can be characterized by placing them in relation to other actors. Such *characterization by association* works by prompting audiences to transfer onto the protagonists the same traits, reputation, and qualities which they attribute to the characters the protagonists become associated with (Fludernik 2009, 44–45). For example, by casting Iraq, Iran, and North Korea as members of an *axis of evil*, George W. Bush closely associated the three countries with each other, inviting similar characterizations of each of them as rogue states and sponsors of international terrorism. Fourth, actors in foreign policy narratives can be characterized through descriptions of the decision-making process. By painting this process in a particular way, for instance as orderly or chaotic, open or closed, rational or irrational, narratives can shape how audiences view the quality and legitimacy of foreign policy decisions as well as the characters of the protagonists that the narratives implicate in decision-making (Marsh and McConnell 2010). As a case in point, narrating the decision-making of the Blair government in the UK on the European single currency as ad-hoc "policymaking in the pub" (Daddow 2018) serves to undermine the integrity both of the policy and of the key characters involved in making the policy.

As regards the temporal or causal emplotment, finally, the analysis focuses on how narratives put what happens in a story into an intelligible order of events (Ricoeur 1981, 167). The narrative emplotment scripts the behavior of the characters and puts the individual events of a story into a meaningful relationship. These events only become understandable for the audience as part of a plot with a sequence that links them to other events (Baker 2010, 353). Such narrative meaning-making centrally involves a temporal structure which sees a story unfold from a beginning toward an end (Gadinger, Jarzebski and Yildiz 2014, 72–74). What is more, emplotting events in a temporal order also suggests a causal relationship between them that explains how past events have led to future events (Ewick and Silbey 1995, 200; see also van Meegdenburg in this volume).

Generally speaking, the emplotment of foreign policy narratives can revolve around four questions that are central to how narratives attribute meaning to foreign policy (see Oppermann and Spencer 2018). While foreign policy narratives will not always speak to all these questions, they can guide the coding of the source material in order to fully grasp the narrative emplotment. First, how does the narrative construct the reasons for a particular foreign policy? For example, foreign policy can be narrated as a response of the characters to an immediate crisis, threat, or challenge or as part of a long-term agenda. In particular, narratives may situate the reasons for foreign policy either in the realms of strategic calculus or identity and foreground the role of individual beliefs and perceptions, domestic politics, or international factors. Second, how does the narrative construe the objectives of a foreign policy? For example, foreign policy narratives may include targets to be achieved, relationships to be improved, or dangers to be averted. In other words, the emplotment orientates the story toward a desired ending. Third, how does the narrative envisage the objectives to be realized? Specifically, the narrative emplotment may advocate for certain decisions, policies, and instruments that are believed to lead to the desired ending and warn against others that threaten to deflect from such an ending. Finally, how does the narrative explain success or failure in moving toward the desired ending of the story? In particular, the causal emplotment of foreign policy narratives is deeply entwined with allocating responsibility and blame for foreign policy problems that need to be overcome as well as credit and praise for moving the story in the desired direction.

The purpose of the coding scheme (see Table 8.1) is to provide the analysis with a template to capture the main discursive elements that constitute the setting, characterization, and emplotment of the narrative(s) in the discourse under study. After a first draft of such a template has been developed, it should be trialed with a subset of the source material to identify possible blind spots or inconsistencies and be revised if necessary. The consolidated coding scheme is then to be applied to the full source material. The coding can be supported by using qualitative data analysis software, such as MAXQDA or NVivo which help processing the coded material and making the coding decisions transparent. It is important to note, however, that the purpose of the coding scheme is not to neatly assign parts of the discourse to precisely one of the three constitutive narrative elements. Rather, the same part of the discourse can simultaneously speak to more than one of these elements, for example the setting and the emplotment, and may therefore have to be coded in terms of different narrative elements at the same time. This is because the three structural elements will often overlap empirically (see Figure 8.2), as elements of the setting or characterization, for example, can be important aspects in the causal or temporal emplotment. The analytical framework provided is meant to be used as a fishing net which makes sure that the most important elements of a narrative are captured, and it is less central if a phrase is coded as either setting, characterization, or emplotment. While researchers will always have some discretion in how they code their source material, the coding scheme must make sure that coding decisions have been transparent. The contribution of the suggested tri-partite structure of

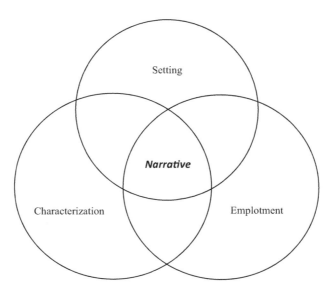

Figure 8.2 Elements of a narrative.

narratives is, therefore, less descriptive than analytical. In other words, it should be seen as a methodological device to guide the study of narratives in political discourse.

The coding of the source material provides the building blocks to carve out the foreign policy narratives that are being told. To that end, the second step of the analysis re-assembles the coded material into one or more foreign policy narratives that are discernible in the discourse. The analytical task, therefore, is to bring together interrelated representations of the setting, characterization, and emplotment that have been identified through the coding and to represent them as distinct narrative constructions of foreign policy. This results in a mapping of narrative meaning-making in the discourse under study. To illustrate, a narrative analysis of the German foreign policy discourse may come to distinguish two competing narratives that are told by different narrators: one that places German foreign policy in the historical setting of the lessons learned from World War II, portrays decision-makers as having internalized a foreign policy culture of restraint, and follows a plot of upholding Germany's role as a civilian power; and another that describes the setting of German foreign policy in terms of Germany's increased international power position, characterizes decision-makers as seeking a more active role for Germany in international affairs, and follows a plot of the *normalization* of German foreign policy (see Gaskarth and Oppermann 2021). What this simplified example shows is how the suggested method of narrative analysis can be used to reconstruct, and to compare and contrast, the foreign policy narratives in a particular political discourse.

Building on the mapping of foreign policy narratives in political discourse, which forms the core of the method, the analysis can be further developed in at least three directions, depending on the research interest. First, the analysis may zoom in on the patterns of narrative meaning-making. In particular, the mapping of foreign policy narratives may point to three such patterns. One possibility is that the narrative analysis identifies only one main foreign policy narrative that is dominant in the discourse under study. This represents a "settled" narrative situation (Krebs 2015, 33), in which the meaning of foreign policy is largely uncontested, the scope for legitimate and successful challenges to the foreign policy consensus small, and foreign policy change unlikely. A case in point would be the dominant US narrative of Cold War threats during the Reagan administrations (Krebs 2015, 66–121). Alternatively, the narrative analysis may point to a range of different foreign policy narratives in a particular discourse. In this case, the narratives may be either complementary or competing. Complementary foreign policy narratives do not suggest mutually exclusive constructions of meaning, but may emphasize different aspects of a foreign policy or address different audiences. Such narratives can be mutually supportive if they include intertextual references to each other, for example in the form of similar terminology and concepts (Hagström and Gustafsson 2019, 388). To an extent, this can be observed in some of the narratives the UK government tells about Britain's post-Brexit role in international politics, for example, *Global Britain* and *Great Power* (Oppermann, Beasley and Kaarbo 2020). Competing narratives, in contrast, advance conflicting constructions of meaning and are drawn into narrative struggles over the interpretation of foreign policy. Such struggles often pitch narratives against counter-narratives in a contest over narrative dominance in the foreign policy discourse. This can be seen in the example of the discourse in the US Congress over the *Iran nuclear deal* during the Obama administration (Oppermann and Spencer 2018).

Second, the research may focus on the level of storytelling and explore how foreign policy narratives are being told and projected. Narratives do not normally stand on their own but are usually embedded in broader storytelling conventions or narrative genres. Such genres provide established frameworks for constructing narratives that involve certain expectations about how a story develops (Baumann 1999). This is because genres are "intertextual concept[s]" (Wales 1989, 259) with which audiences are already familiar from previous encounters and which can therefore shape how competent audiences make sense of a narrative (McQuail 1987). Specifically, a well-known canon of narrative genres in literary studies distinguishes the ideal types of tragedy, comedy, satire, and romance (White 1973) which all include a range of characteristic features and storytelling techniques (see Frye 1957, 1963). The assumptions, therefore, are that foreign policy narratives will often be told in a way that resembles a literary genre and that they will be easier understood and resonate better the more consistent they are with one of the genres. Along these lines, the analysis may seek to match the setting, characterization, and emplotment of foreign policy narratives to the literary genres and establish how much they conform to any of the ideal types.

Third, the research interest may be to examine how different foreign policy narratives resonate in broader discourse. Specifically, this calls for a research strategy that examines to what extent foreign policy narratives which have been identified in one particular discourse, for example government discourse, impact on foreign policy debates in other arenas. To that purpose, narrative analysis can be combined with media content analyses to establish the salience of foreign policy narratives in media reporting (Oppermann and Spencer 2013). In particular, such analyses can explore to what extent the media take up the settings, characterizations, and emplotments of one or more foreign policy narratives under study. Moreover, the focus can also be on the resonance of foreign policy narratives with domestic or international public opinion. Here, the method of narrative analysis can usefully be complemented with survey experiments which are increasingly popular in FPA (e.g., Busby et al., 2020; Guimarães et al., 2020; cf. also the chapter on public opinion surveys in this volume) and which enable research designs that isolate the effects of foreign policy narratives on selected audiences.

More generally, empirical research into the resonance of foreign policy narratives in the media or in public opinion speaks to the broader question of why some narratives catch on more with relevant audiences than others. While this question remains largely unresolved, possible answers can be found on three levels of analysis. On the level of the speaker, the resonance of foreign policy narratives comes from attributes of the narrator, for example its authority, reputation, credibility, likeability, or prominence (see Sharman 2007). As a case in point, the impact of public diplomacy narratives on foreign publics has been shown to be shaped by the credibility of their source (Schatz and Levine 2010). On the level of the narrative, the focus shifts to the structure and content of the foreign policy narratives themselves. The argument is that foreign policy narratives should resonate most if they are structurally complete, weaving together a clear setting, rich characterizations of the main actors, and a consistent and well-developed emplotment. For example, the strong resonance in German public discourse of the narrative construction of Germany's decision in March 2011 to abstain on UN resolution 1973 authorizing military force in Libya into a major foreign policy failure has been linked to the finding that this narrative was much more fully developed than the rudimentary counter-narrative (Oppermann and Spencer 2016). On the level of the audience, finally, the resonance of foreign policy narratives is related to their intertextuality. In other words, such narratives are expected to resonate better if they reference pre-existing intersubjective understandings and familiar, culturally embedded symbols, events, or texts (Spencer 2016), including established literary genres (see above). As a case in point, public diplomacy narratives have been shown to leave a stronger imprint on target audiences if they speak to prevailing cultural values and beliefs (Chapman and Gerber 2019).

A Narrative Analysis of US Congressional Debates on the Iran Nuclear Deal

The application of narrative analysis in FPA can be illustrated with our previous research on the narrative contestation over the 2015 *Iran nuclear deal* in the US Congress during the Obama administration (see Oppermann and Spencer 2018). The agreement between the five permanent members of the UN Security Council (plus Germany) and Iran—the Joint Comprehensive Plan of Action (JCPOA)—put in place a regime to limit and monitor Tehran's nuclear activities to prevent its development of nuclear weapons in exchange for relief from international sanctions that targeted Iran's nuclear program (MacFarlane 2015). The deal represents a cornerstone of President Obama's foreign policy record and was a highly controversial issue in US political debate. In fact, the JCPOA pitched the Obama administration and most Democrats who hailed the agreement as "a very good deal" (Obama 2015) against most Republicans, including Donald Trump who branded it as "the worst deal ever negotiated" (Reuters 2016) and who subsequently withdrew from the agreement when he became US president. This partisan divide was embedded in a highly fluid discursive environment which was marked by uncertainty about how the deal would work in practice and in which no intersubjective consensus about how the JCPOA should be judged had emerged. We have argued that this debate between supporters and opponents of the nuclear agreement in the US took the shape of a discursive struggle between competing narratives that tried to constitute the JCPOA as a major US foreign policy success or failure. To develop this argument, our research followed the two core steps of a narrative analysis of foreign policy discourse as described in the previous section. Our source material consisted of the main debates about the agreement in the US Senate and House of Representatives in September 2015.

In the first step, we coded the three narrative elements of setting, characterization, and emplotment in the discourse under study. We started out from the general coding scheme for foreign policy narratives (see Table 8.1), but adapted the scheme to capture the specific representations of these three elements in narratives of foreign policy success and failure (see Oppermann and Spencer 2018). To this purpose we relied on existing insights about the social construction of political failures and successes (e.g., Bovens and 't Hart 1996; McConnell 2011). For example, narratives of foreign policy failure are embedded in settings that give space for viable alternatives which are denied by the counter-narratives; on the dimension of characterization, failure narratives use the discursive techniques identified in the general coding scheme to portray the decision-makers and the decision-making process in a negative light, whereas success narratives involve positive characterizations; as for the emplotment, narrative struggles between stories of foreign policy failure and success revolve around why the objectives of a policy have (not) been met, what the consequences of the policy are, and who is to blame or deserves credit. We used the adapted coding scheme to draw out and categorize the parts of our source material that speak to the different narrative elements constituting the setting, characterization, and emplotment of failure and success narratives. This led to a MAXQDA data set which included all (parts of) sentences in the discourse under study that we judged contributed to the representation of the different narrative elements on each of the three narrative dimensions.

In the second step, our research used the data set to reconstruct the competing narratives of success or failure of the JCPOA. This enabled us to compare the narratives and to show how stories of foreign policy success and failure are being told. We presented our results as a kind of *collage* that retold the two narratives by weaving in diverse direct quotations from our coded material to bring to life their respective setting, characterization, and emplotment. The key finding of our narrative analysis was that the competing stories about the JCPOA displayed a close structural resemblance. While the content of the setting, characterization and emplotment of the failure and success narratives stood in direct contrast, the narratives gave similar prominence to the different narrative elements on all three narrative dimensions. We argued that these structural similarities on the level of the narratives explain why at the time of our research neither of the two narratives had emerged as a clear winner in the US debate about the meaning of the Iran nuclear deal. More broadly, we hypothesized that narratives of foreign policy success and failure are structurally bound to rely on similar storytelling elements.

Conclusion

Traditionally, every narrative is said to have a beginning, a middle, and an end. While fairy tales commonly begin with *once upon a time* and end with *the end*, the conclusion of this chapter reflects on some of the strengths, limitations, and pitfalls for users of narrative analysis in FPA and indicates some recent trends in the literature.

We believe that one of the major strengths of the suggested method of narrative analysis is that it provides the researcher with a simple analytical roster (setting, characterization, and emplotment) which helps structure the analysis. It provides a guideline for what to look for when examining the empirical material and prevents being overwhelmed by the sheer magnitude of examining such a vast phenomenon as discourse. Furthermore, as narrative analysis is based on the insights of literary studies and narratology, it provides theoretical arguments why narratives are important to comprehend the world both on an individual and a collective level.

A further advantage of the kind of narrative analysis we articulated in this chapter is that its constructivist meta-theoretical assumptions stand between hard positivism and radical post-positivism. The method starts out from a constructivist ontology and holds that meaning is constituted through narratives, but adopts an epistemological position that is compatible with positivist research and argues that the tripartite analytical roster enables privileged and systematic insights into the main structural features of narratives. It takes a *middle ground* perspective that rejects both *objectivist* and purely *relativist* understandings of foreign policy. Foreign policy does not speak for itself, but what it means is also not completely in the eye of the beholder. In other words, while the meaning of foreign policy is discursively constructed through narratives, not all possible meanings have an equal chance to become intersubjectively accepted. Rather, which meanings – if any – become dominant in political discourse is shaped by the attributes of foreign policy narratives which the suggested method of narrative analysis brings into focus. The method can therefore also be read as a form of bridge-building across the positivist versus post-positivist divide.

At the same time, narrative analysis has several limits and potential pitfalls researchers should be aware of. First, narrative analysis is only really helpful for certain kinds of research questions. Its main strength lies in its ability to reveal *how things are considered to be*. It is less suited to questions concerned with investigating *how things really are*. Its strength lies on the level of perceptions and discourse, as it is less likely to be helpful with *why questions* and more at home with *how possible* questions concerned with the construction of social phenomena.

Second, being caught between positivism and post-positivism, the suggested method of narrative analysis faces criticism from both sides. On the one hand, positivists may be skeptical of the scientific value of the method and disregard it as too subjective and mere opinion:

> Because storytelling is commonly associated with fiction, fantasy and pretending, some critics are sceptical about the use of the narrative as a model for thought and action. For the serious scientist, storytelling is related to immaturity and playfulness.
>
> *(Sarbin 1986, 12)*

On the other hand, more radical post-positivists may be quick to highlight the contradictory nature of a constructivist ontology and a more positivist epistemology. We believe that narrative analysis can stand its ground with reference to its desire to reveal not subjective but intersubjective understandings, its ability to provide transparency and verifiability of the findings, and its employment of verisimilitude as a backbone of how the narrative is read, dissected, and retold.

Beyond these strengths and limits of the method, the more recent engagement with narratives in IR and FPA, as already indicated above, has started to reveal two general research trends which are bound to be expanded on in the future. The first is concerned with the role of visualization in and of narratives and is connected to the visual turn in IR (Bleiker 2001; Crilley et al., 2020; see also Stahl and Ignatowitsch in this volume). How do images contribute to the establishment of narratives and how are they interconnected? A number of scholars have recently turned their attention to the role of visuality in narratives concerning, for example, the Iran nuclear deal (Miskimmon and O'Loughlin 2020), China's Maritime Silk Road Initiative (Van Noort 2020), or populism (Freistein and Gadinger 2020). A second trend is concerned with the role of narrative genres (Kuusisto 2018; Spencer and Oppermann 2020). The question is how do these storytelling conventions influence our ability to tell, accept, and comprehend (new) stories? While some have investigated the genres of tragedy or romance (Spencer 2019), others have looked at the genres of comedy and satire in international politics and foreign policy (Crilley and Chatterje-Doody 2020; Beck and Spencer 2021; Chernobrov 2021). What role do humor narratives play in the constitution of politics not only as a form of critique and resistance but also as a means of legitimation of power? In any case, narrative analysis stands to remain a vibrant field in IR and FPA, and the ending of the method's story has not yet been written.

References

Baker, Mona. 2006. *Translation and Conflict: A Narrative Account*. London: Routledge.
Baker, Mona. 2010. "Narratives of Terrorism and Security: Accurate Translations, Suspicious Frames." *Critical Studies on Terrorism* 3(3): 347–364.
Barthwal-Datta, Monika, and Priya Chacko. 2020. "The Politics of Strategic Narratives of Regional Order in the Indo-Pacific: Free, Open, Prosperous, Inclusive?" *Australian Journal of International Affairs* 74(3): 244–263.
Baumann, Richard. 1999. "Genre." *Journal of Linguistic Anthropology* 9(1/2): 84–87.
Beck, Daniel, and Alexander Spencer. 2021. "Just a Bit of Fun: The Camouflaging and Defending Functions of Humour in Recruitment Videos of the British and Swedish Armed Forces." *Cambridge Review of International Affairs* 34(1): 65–84.
Berenskoetter, Felix. 2014. "Parameters of a National Biography." *European Journal of International Relations* 20(1): 262–288.
Bleiker, Roland. 2001. "The Aesthetic Turn in International Political Theory." *Millennium* 30(3): 509–533.
Bovens, Mark, and 't Hart, Paul. 1996. *Understanding Policy Fiascoes*. London: Transaction Publishers.
Bridgeman, Teresa. 2007. "Time and space". In *The Cambridge Companion to Narrative*, edited by David Herman. Cambridge: Cambridge University Press, 52–65.
Busby, Joshua, Craig Kafura, Jonathan Monten, and Jordan Tama. 2020. "Multilateralism and the Use of Force: Experimental Evidence on the Views of Foreign Policy Elites." *Foreign Policy Analysis* 16(1): 118–129.
Chaban, Natalia, Alister Miskimmon, A., and Ben O'Loughlin. 2019. "Understanding EU Crisis Diplomacy in the European Neighbourhood: Strategic Narratives and Perceptions of the EU in Ukraine, Israel and Palestine." *European Security* 28(3): 235–250.
Chapman, Hannah S., and Theodore P. Gerber. 2019. "Opinion-Formation and Issue-Framing Effects of Russian News in Kyrgyzstan." *International Studies Quarterly* 63(3): 756–769.
Chernobrov, Dmitry. 2021. "Strategic Humour: Public Diplomacy and Comic Framing of Foreign Policy Issues." *The British Journal of Politics and International Relations*, Online First:https://eprints.whiterose.ac.uk/173575/1/Chernobrov%20BJPIR%20submitted%20version.pdf.
Clément, Maéva, Thomas Lindemann, and Eric Sangar. 2017. "The 'Hero-Protector Narrative': Manufacturing Emotional Consent for the Use of Force." *Political Psychology* 38(6): 991–1008.
Coticchia, Fabrizio, and Andrea Catanzaro. 2020. "The Fog of Words: Assessing the Problematic Relationship between Strategic Narratives, (Master) Frames and Ideology." *Media, War & Conflict*, Online First: https://doi.org/10.1177/1750635220965622.
Coticchia, Fabrizio, and Carolina De Simone. 2016. "The War that Wasn't there? Italy's 'Peace Mission' in Afghanistan, Strategic Narratives and Public Opinion." *Foreign Policy Analysis* 12(1): 24–46.
Crilley, Rhys, and Precious N. Chatterje-Doody. 2020. "From Russia with Lols: Humour, RT, and the Legitimation of Russian Foreign Policy." *Global Society*, Online First: https://doi.org/10.1080/13600826.2020.1839387.
Crilley, Rhys, Ilan Manor, and Corneliu Bjola. 2020. "Visual Narratives of Global Politics in the Digital Age: An Introduction." *Cambridge Review of International Affairs*, 33(5): 628–637.
Daddow, Oliver. 2018. "Policymaking in the Pub: New Labour's European Policy Failure." In *Political Mistakes and Policy Failures in International Relations*, edited by Andreas Kruck, Kai Oppermann and Alexander Spencer. London: Palgrave, 101–119.
De Graaf, Beatrice, George Dimitriu, and Jens Ringsmose, eds. 2015. *Strategic Narratives, Public Opinion and War: Winning Domestic Support for the Afghan War*. London: Routledge.
Devetak, Richard. 2009. "After the Event: Don DeLillo's White Noise and September 11 Narratives." *Review of International Studies* 35(4): 795–815.
Ewick, Patricia, and Silbey, Susan S. 1995. "Subversive Stories and Hegemonic Tales: Towards a Sociology of Narrative." *Law and Society Review* 29(2): 197–226.
Fludernick, Monika. 2009. *An Introduction to Narratology*. London: Routledge.

Freistein, Katja, and Frank Gadinger. 2020. "Populist Stories of Honest Men and Proud Mothers: A Visual Narrative Analysis." *Review of International Studies* 46(2): 217–236.

Frye, Northrop. 1957. *Anatomy of Criticism*. Princeton, NJ: Princeton University Press.

Frye, Northrop. 1963. *Romanticism Reconsidered: English Institute Essays*. New York: Columbia University Press.

Gadinger, Frank, Frank Jarzebski, and Taylan Yildiz. 2014. "Vom Diskurs zur Erzählung: Möglichkeiten einer politikwissenschaftlichen Narrativanalyse." *Politische Vierteljahresschrift* 55(1): 67–93.

Gaskarth, Jamie, and Kai Oppermann. 2021. "Clashing Traditions: German Foreign Policy in a New Era." *International Studies Perspectives* 22(1): 84–105.

Genette, Gérard. 1990. "Fictional Narrative, Factual Narrative". *Poetics Today* 11(4): 755–774.

Guimarães, Feliciano, Ivan F. Fernandes, and Gerardo Maldonado. 2020. "Domestic Attitudes Toward Regional Leadership: A Survey Experiment in Brazil." *Foreign Policy Analysis* 16(1): 98–117.

Gustafsson, Karl, Linus Hagström, and Ulv Hanssen. 2019. "Long Live Pacifism! Narrative Power and Japan's Pacifist Model." *Cambridge Review of International Affairs* 32(4): 502–520.

Hagström, Linus, and Karl Gustafsson. 2019. "Narrative Power: How Storytelling Shapes East Asian International Politics." *Cambridge Review of International Affairs* 32(4): 387–406.

Hansen, Lene. 2006. *Security as Practice: Discourse Analysis and the Bosnian War*. London: Routledge.

Hanska, Jan. 2015. "From Narrated Strategy to Strategic Narratives." *Critical Studies on Security* 3(3): 323–325.

Hinck, Robert S., Randolph Kluver, and Skye Cooley. 2018. "Russia Re-envisions the World: Strategic Narratives in Russian Broadcast and News Media During 2015." *Russian Journal of Communication* 10 (1): 21–37.

Heck, Axel. 2017. "Images, Visions and Narrative Identity Formation of ISIS." *Global Discourse* 7(2–3): 244–259.

Herman, Luc, and Bart Vervaeck. 2007. "Ideology." In *The Cambridge Companion to Narrative*, edited by David Herman. Cambridge: Cambridge University Press, 217–230.

Holland, Jack, and Ben Fermor. 2017. "Trump's Rhetoric at 100 Days: Contradictions within Effective Emotional Narratives." *Critical Studies on Security* 5(2): 182–186.

Hülsse, Rainer. 2009. "The Catwalk Power: Germany's New Foreign Image Policy." *Journal of International Relations and Development* 12(3): 293–316.

Irvin-Erickson, Douglas. 2017. "Genocide Discourses: American and Russian Strategic Narratives of Conflict in Iraq and Ukraine." *Politics and Governance* 5(3): 130–145.

Kaarbo, Juliet, and Daniel Kenealy. 2017. "Precedents, Parliaments, and Foreign Policy: Historical Analogy in the House of Commons Vote on Syria," *West European Politics* 40(1): 62–79.

Khaldarova, Irina. 2021. "Brother or 'Other'? Transformation of Strategic Narratives in Russian Television News during the Ukrainian Crisis." *Media, War & Conflict* 14(1): 3–20.

Khong, Yuen F. 1992. *Analogies at War*. Princeton, NJ: Princeton University Press.

Klymenko, Lina. 2020. "The Role of Historical Narratives in Ukraine's Policy Toward the EU and Russia." *International Politics* 57(6): 973–989.

Krebs, Roland R. 2015. *Narrative and the Making of US National Security*. Cambridge: Cambridge University Press.

Kuusisto, Riikka. 2018. "Comparing IR Plots: Dismal Tragedies, Exuberant Romances, Hopeful Comedies and Cynical Satires." *International Politics* 55(2): 160–176.

Lams, Lutgard. 2018. "Examining Strategic Narratives in Chinese Official Discourse under Xi Jinping." *Journal of Chinese Political Science* 23(3): 387–411.

Livingston, Steven, and Jack Nassetta. 2018. "Framing and Strategic Narratives: Synthesis and Analytical Framework." *SAIS Review of International Affairs* 38(2): 101–110.

MacFarlane, Philip. 2015. *The Iran Nuclear Agreement: An Assessment Under U.S. and International Law*. Houston, TX: University of Houston Law Center.

Marsh, David, and Allen McConnell. 2010. "Towards a Framework for Establishing Policy Success." *Public Administration* 88(2): 564–583.

McConnell, Allen. 2011. *Understanding Policy Success*. Basingstoke: Palgrave.

McQuail, Denis. 1987. *Mass Communication Theory: An Introduction*. London: Sage.

Miskimmon Alister, and Ben O'Loughlin. 2020. "The Visual Politics of the 2015 Iran Deal: Narrative, Image and Verification." *Cambridge Review of International Affairs* 33(5): 778–798.

Miskimmon, Alistair, Ben O'Loughlin, and Laura Roselle. 2013. *Strategic Narratives. Communication Power and the New World Order*. New York: Routledge.

Miskimmon, Alistair, Ben O'Loughlin, and Laura Roselle, eds. 2017. *Forging the World. Strategic Narratives and International Relations.* Ann Arbor: University of Michigan Press.

Obama, Barack. 2015. "Remarks by the President on the Iran Nuclear Deal." 5 August 2015. Available from https://obamawhitehouse.archives.gov/the-press-office/2015/08/05/remarks-president-irannuclear-deal, last access on 26 July 2017.

Oppermann, Kai, Ryan Beasley, and Juliet Kaarbo. 2020. "British Foreign Policy after Brexit: Losing Europe and Finding a Role." *International Relations* 34(2): 133–156.

Oppermann, Kai, and Alexander Spencer. 2013. "Thinking Alike? Salience and Metaphor Analysis as Cognitive Approaches to Foreign Policy Analysis." *Foreign Policy Analysis* 9(1): 39–56.

Oppermann, Kai, and Alexander Spencer. 2016. "Telling Stories of Failure: Narrative Constructions of Foreign Policy Fiascos." *Journal of European Public Policy* 23(5): 685–701.

Oppermann, Kai, and Alexander Spencer. 2018. "Narrating Success and Failure: Congressional Debates on the 'Iran Nuclear Deal'." *European Journal of International Relations* 24(2): 268–292.

Ostermann, Falk. 2019. *Security, Defense Discourse and Identity in NATO and Europe. How France Changed Foreign Policy.* London: Routledge.

Paterson, Molly, and Kristen Renwick Monroe. 1998. "Narrative in Political Science". *Annual Review of Political Science* 1: 315–331.

Reuters. 2016. "Trump Election Puts Iran Nuclear Deal on Shaky Ground." 9 November, 2016. Available from https://www.reuters.com/article/us-usa-election-trump-iran-idUSKBN13427E, last access on 25 May 2021.

Ricoeur, Paul. 1981. "Narrative Time." In *On Narrative*, edited by W. J.T Mitchell. Chicago, IL: Chicago University Press, 165–186.

Ringsmose, Jens, and Berit Kaja Børgesen. 2011. "Shaping Public Attitudes Towards the Deployment of Military Power: NATO, Afghanistan and the Use of Strategic Narratives." *European Security* 20(4): 505–528.

Roberts, Geoffrey. 2006. "History, Theory and the Narrative Turn in IR." *Review of International Studies* 32(4): 703–714.

Roselle, Laura, Alister Miskimmon, and Ben O'Loughlin, 2014. "Strategic Narrative: A New Means to Understand Soft Power." *Media, War & Conflict* 7(1): 70–84.

Sarbin, Theodore R. 1986. "The Narrative as a Root Metaphor for Psychology." In *Narrative Psychology. The Storied Nature of Human Conduct*, edited by Theodore R. Sarbin. New York: Praeger, 3–21.

Schatz, Edward, and Renan Levine. 2010. "Framing, Public Diplomacy, and Anti-Americanism in Central Asia." *International Studies Quarterly* 54(3): 855–869.

Schmitt, Olivier. 2018. "When Are Strategic Narratives Effective? The Shaping of Political Discourse through the Interaction between Political Myths and Strategic Narratives." *Contemporary Security Policy* 39(4): 487–511.

Sharman, J. C. 2007. "Rationalist and Constructivist Perspectives on Reputation." *Political Studies* 55(1): 20–37.

Shenhav, Shaul R. 2006. "Political Narratives and Political Reality." *International Political Science Review* 27(3): 245–262.

Shenhav, Shaul R. 2015. *Analyzing Social Narratives.* New York: Routledge.

Spencer, Alexander. 2016. *Romantic Narratives in International Politics: Pirates, Rebels and Mercenaries.* Manchester: Manchester University Press.

Spencer, Alexander. 2019. "Narratives and the Romantic Genre in IR: Dominant and Marginalized Stories of Arab Rebellion in Libya." *International Politics* 56(1): 123–140.

Spencer, Alexander, and Kai Oppermann. 2020. "Narrative Genres of Brexit: The Leave Campaign and the Success of Romance." *Journal of European Public Policy* 27(5): 666–684.

Subotić, Jelena. 2016. "Narrative, Ontological Security, and Foreign Policy Change." *Foreign Policy Analysis* 12(4): 610–627.

Szostek, Joanna. 2018. "News Media Repertoires and Strategic Narrative Reception: A Paradox of Dis/Belief in Authoritarian Russia." *New Media & Society* 20(1): 68–87.

Toolan, Michael J. 2001. *Narrative. A Critical Linguistic Introduction.* London: Routledge.

Van Noort, Carolijn. 2020. "Strategic Narratives, Visuality and Infrastructure in the Digital Age: The Case of China's Maritime Silk Road Initiative." *Cambridge Review of International Affairs* 33(5): 734–751.

Van Noort, Carolijn, and Thomas Colley. 2021. "How Do Strategic Narratives Shape Policy Adoption? Responses to China's Belt and Road Initiative." *Review of International Studies* 47(1): 39–63.

Waldman, Thomas. 2019. "Strategic Narratives and US Surrogate Warfare." *Survival* 61(1): 161–178.

Wales, Katie. 1989. *A Dictionary of Stylistics*. London: Longman.
White, Hayden. 1973. *Metahistory: The Historical Imagination in Nineteenth-Century Europe*. Baltimore, MD: Johns Hopkins University Press.
White, Hayden. 1987. *The Content of the Form: Narrative Discourse and Historical Representation*. Baltimore, MD: Johns Hopkins University Press.
Wright, Katharine A. M., and Annika Bergman-Rosamond. 2021. "NATO's Strategic Narratives: Angelina Jolie and the Alliance's Celebrity and Visual Turn." *Review of International Studies*, Online First: https://doi.org/10.1017/S0260210521000188.

9
Frame Analysis
Sabine Mokry

Introduction

In the context of Foreign Policy Analysis (FPA), as introduced in this chapter, frame analysis is a systematic, versatile, and economical approach for analyzing text. It is a systematic approach, because it strictly separates the identification of frames in the material from the actual analysis of identified frames. It is a versatile approach, because it allows analyzing any type of text issued by any actor involved in the foreign policy process of any state. Finally, since the version of frame analysis introduced here facilitates a quantitative and a qualitative assessment of frames based on the same coding effort, the approach is fairly economical.

Initially developed in communications research, frame analysis describes the systematic identification and examination of frames. As schemata of interpretation (Goffman 1974, 21), frames are "cognitive tool[s] that help actors organize information in a complex environment" (Lenz 2018, 32). Frames are generated by actors who engage in framing processes. Entman (2007) describes framing as a "process of culling a few elements of a perceived reality and assembling a narrative that highlights connections among them to promote a particular interpretation" (Entman 2007, 164). According to Entman, each frame performs at least one of four functions: defining a problem, diagnosing its causes, evaluating it morally, or suggesting remedies (Entman 1993). Since frames are the result of framing processes, frames from different points in time differ from each other, allowing researchers to examine changes over time.

Frame analysis offers three main benefits for studying foreign policy: first, frame analysis can render an abstract, multifaceted theoretical concept, such as the construction of a state's national interest, applicable to the analysis of individual foreign policy statements. Second, it enables researchers to draw on data that are easily available. Foreign policy statements, ranging from speeches by the head of government/state over policy papers to speeches by the foreign minister, are generally easy to obtain. Data availability is particularly important in authoritarian states where access to (foreign) policy processes is often restricted. Since similar data are available for all political systems, comparative assessments across different polities become feasible. Third, frame analysis can be applied to different actors involved in the foreign policy process. It is particularly well suited to examine the role of sub- and non-state actors even when the researcher does not have direct access to them, as long as they contribute to foreign policy debates and foreign policy rhetoric.

In its empirical part, this chapter shows that frame analysis can reveal changes in emphasis and substantive shifts in how two fundamentally different states, the U.S. and the People's Republic of China (PRC), convey their foreign policy intentions. The empirical analysis reveals how different actors within each state, from the head of state to the foreign minister, express the national interest of their respective countries. The national interest is thereby understood as constructed: it needs to be defined before a state can pursue it. Defining the national interest can occur through socialization at the international level (Finnemore 1996, 2) and/or through interpretation processes within the state. In the latter, the focus of this chapter, state officials try to understand the state's situation and respond to it (Weldes 1999, 4). These constant interpretation processes lead to different definitions of the national interest. For conceptualizing these different constructions of the national interest, I link Nuechterlein's conception of national interests, which distinguishes defense interests, economic interests, world order, and ideological interests (Nuechterlein 1976, 248), to more recent empirical accounts of states' national interest in International Relations (IR). The quantitative component of the analysis will show how prominent these different constructions of national interest feature over time. The qualitative assessment will uncover substantive shifts within each construction.

The next section illustrates how frame analysis has been used in FPA. Then, foundational concepts and the broad contours of the frame analysis approach are introduced. Finally, the hands-on explanation of how to apply the version of frame analysis introduced in this chapter illustrates the benefits the approach brings to FPA by examining how the U.S. and the Chinese government convey their foreign policy intentions in official statements.

Literature Review

In the study of foreign policy, frame analysis has been mainly employed to analyze how states articulate their foreign policy goals and to assess the impact of non- and substate actors on foreign policy decision-making. Studies of frames in official communication have focused on EU-China relations (Smith 2016), China's changing policy toward Taiwan (Li 2015), Australia's approach to the war on terror (Holland 2010), and Russian and Norwegian approaches toward the European Arctic (Jensen and Skedsmo 2010). U.S. foreign policy receives the most scholarly attention, with researchers examining communication around particular instances, such as the aftermath of terrorist attacks (Entman and Stonbely 2018), and frames that relate broadly to the country's national interest (Brewer 2006). However, the EU, in particular, its attempts to shape the foreign policy discourses of its member states (Kratochvil, Cibulkova, and Benik 2011), and its external relations have also been addressed (Rudolph 2018; Smith 2016). Moreover, frame analysis has made some inroads into the analysis of foreign policy decision-making, for example, in examining how presidential advisors shape policy definitions and signals toward China (Garrison 2007). Some of the investigations into the influence of non-state actors on foreign policy bring frame analysis back to its roots in social movements research. Kim (2017), for example, shows how "framing battles between activists and the media" expanded political opportunities for anti-base movements (2017, 309). Voltolini (2016) investigates how the lobbying efforts of non-state actors influence EU-Israel relations by contributing to the "emergence and codification of new frames that underpin EU external policies" (2016, 1502).

Frame analysis is well suited to draw on different data sources, from official communication over newspapers to social media posts. For example, to capture official communications, speeches by the head of state/government and white papers are frequently used sources (Hur 2018; Jensen and Skedsmo 2010; Li 2015; Panayirci and Iseri 2014; Smith 2016). How foreign policy issues are framed in the media is another important strand of research. While most analyses of media framings use newspaper articles as their data sources (Dimitrova and Strömbäck 2008; Entman and Stonbely 2018; Fong and Chia 2017; Golan and Lukito 2015; Kim 2017; Kratochvil, Cibulkova, and Benik 2011; Rudolph 2018), recently, Facebook has also come into the focus of researchers working with frame analysis (Liang 2019).

Frame analysis covers a wide spectrum from quantitative approaches that rely on fully automated coding to interpretative approaches. Automated variants of frame analysis are based on word frequencies. Examining the use and omission of certain words requires large amounts of text. Greussing and Boomgaarden (2017), for instance, analyzed more than 10,000 articles from Austrian newspapers to identify the most dominant frames used in the coverage of the arrival of refugees in Europe in 2015 (Greussing and Boomgaarden 2017). Nicholls and Culpepper (2021) provide an in-depth assessment of the promises and difficulties of employing automated text analysis to frame analysis (Nicholls and Culpepper 2021). On the other end of the spectrum, interpretative approaches draw on frame analysis to analyze discursive practices (For example, Ostermann 2019).

Since frames play an important role in the study of foreign policy, more reflection about its foundational concepts and a more detailed discussion about how to implement it is necessary. In their investigation into Israel's response to the Arab uprisings, Aran and Fleischmann (2019, 3) describe framing as "constitutive of the foreign policy process". According to them, through framing, foreign policy actors define plausible, possible, responsible, and moral foreign policy options (Aran and Fleischmann 2019, 3). Besides, there is a consistent focus on mapping frames in foreign policy debates and media coverage and an increasing number of attempts to examine the influence of frames on the foreign policy process. Futák-Campbell and Pütz (2021, 10), in their analysis of changes in German policy toward refugees, find, for example, that the relationship between foreign policy decision-makers, public opinion, and media framing can quickly shift the basis for foreign policy decisions because they prioritize certain events and thereby shape the agenda. Hur (2018) details the reciprocal relationship between the President, the National Assembly, and South Korean media. He finds that who influences whom among these key foreign policymakers depends on foreign policy goals and the nature and urgency of policy enforcement (ibid., 153). However, often researchers do not explain how they conceptualize frames and framing. Hence, more reflection about the foundational concepts underpinning frame analysis is necessary and more debate about how best to implement the approach and its many variants.

Foundational Concepts and Methodology

Frames are "cognitive tool[s] that help actors organize information in a complex environment" (Lenz 2018, 32). They are the result of framing, which Entman describes as the "process of culling a few elements of a perceived reality and assembling a narrative that highlights connections among them to promote a particular interpretation" (Entman 2007, 164). In the context of this chapter, "particular interpretation" refers to the respective official construction of national interest. When expressing their intentions through official foreign policy statements, governments select and convey what they deem important, hence engage in framing. Out of the many definitions of frames in the communications literature, the specificity of Entman's framing definition makes it useful for conceptualizing and operationalization frames (Jecker 2017, 13).

Entman's distinction of the four functions frames can perform enables researchers to identify and analyze frames in official foreign policy statements. According to Entman, "to frame is to select some aspects of a perceived reality and make them more salient in a communicating text, in such a way as to promote a particular problem definition, causal interpretation, moral evaluation, and/or treatment recommendation" (Entman 1993, 52). Table 9.1 describes each of these four functions by summarizing Matthes and Kohring's operationalization of Entman's definition (Matthes and Kohring 2008, 264). First, Entman describes the diagnosis of causes as "identify[ing] the forces creating the problem" (Entman 1993, 52). Frames that perform the function of moral evaluation "evaluate causal agents and their effects" (ibid.). Entman's third frame function is the suggestion of remedies to "offer and justify treatments for the problems and predict their likely effects" (ibid.). According to Entman, a frame can perform several of these functions simultaneously. Most frames that appear in official foreign policy rhetoric perform one of the above functions and the frame function problem definition. In Entman's words, this frame function allows identifying "what a causal agent is doing with what costs and benefits" (ibid.). Following Matthes and Kohring, I operationalize this frame function as "issues and actors" (Matthes and Kohring 2008, 264).

Since frames result from framing processes, frames from different points in time differ from each other. Comparing frames across time can reveal shifts in the government's intentions. Tracing these changes is the focus of the analysis of substantive shifts. In order to get an initial grasp of how much the frames changed, each frame is categorized into one of the following four categories: stable, new, faded, or modified. *Stable frames* appear multiple times across the foreign

Table 9.1 Operationalization of Frame Functions

Frame function based on Entman	Operationalization Following Matthes and Kohring	Application to Constructions of National Interest	Example from Analyzed Foreign Policy statements
Diagnosis of causes	Benefit attribution	Indicates who/what causes policy success	U.S. government regard a certain way containing the spread of deadly disease in the countries of origin is a vital U.S. national security interests
	Risk attribution	Indicates who/what cause policy failure	U.S. government come up against a situation hackers who shut down networks, steal trade secrets
Moral evaluation	Benefit	Describes the positive effects of a policy	U.S. government is catalyst for global prosperity
	Risk	Describes the negative effects of a policy	world faces global development challenges
Suggestion of remedies	Positive judgment	Calls for adopting a certain measure	International community need construct structure capacity for states that are in distress
	Negative judgment	Calls for avoiding certain measures	U.S. government refuses rushing into war
Problem definition	Actor	Describes what a causal actor is doing	Co-occurs with other frame functions
	Topic		

policy statements in exactly the same form. *Faded frames* have not appeared in a previously specified time frame, while *new frames* have only appeared once in the respective time frame. The researcher needs to choose this time frame based on several factors inherent to her research project, including the overall time frame of the analysis, the research question, and polity-related features, such as if elections are held and how long terms are. *Modified frames* change across the documents. Assessing the overall distribution of new, stable, faded, and modified frames shows how much change there is across the foreign policy statements. However, the modified frames are most interesting for analyzing substantive shifts. Since each frame consists of a frame object and a frame verb, there are three possible *modification scenarios*: change in frame object, change in frame verbs, change in both. First, a change in the frame object introduces a change in the issue a frame describes. For example, changes in frame object appeared in the U.S. president addressing the military. The 2014 speech referred to "faster changes in the world", while the 2019 speech mentioned "a lot of changes". Second, changes in the frame verb mainly describe changes in degree. For instance, the following frame was identified in the 2017 U.S. National Security Strategy: "the U.S. government will increase the confidence in ourselves as a nation". A year later, in the speech by the U.S. government's representative at the Munich Security Conference, this changed into "the U.S. government will not be deprived of confidence because of repressive and revisionist powers". In the Chinese government's foreign policy statements, there was a shift from participating in global governance (GWR 2012) to reforming it (19th PCR). Finally, changes in issue and degree can be detected if both frame object and frame verb change. Since the frame verb determines the function a frame performs, a change in the verb can change the frame function, which constitutes a major change.

Entman's framing definition puts actors who engage in framing front and center. In the study of foreign policy, the frames of any actor who shapes or contributes to a country's foreign policy can be analyzed. This chapter focuses on actors that express a state's foreign policy intentions. I draw on Robertson's framework to identify and classify relevant sources (Robertson 2017), distinguishing the strategic from the policy planning level. The *strategic level* refers to the most authoritative level of policy-making. It describes broad, conceptual, and long-term directions. In most polities, the strategic level is represented by the head of state or government. On the other hand, the *policy planning level* describes more focused communication related to an immediate context, such as ministerial speeches. In most polities, the policy planning level in foreign policy is mainly represented through the Ministry of Foreign Affairs.

The version of frame analysis introduced in this chapter is particularly suited to uncover changes in official foreign policy statements. Based on the theoretical framework, one's study is built on one can group frames into themes and then trace shifts in the relative salience of different themes. Such quantitative assessments of shifts in relative salience can showcase changes in overall emphasis and provide insights into how consistent a state is in its communicated foreign policy intentions over time, across different policy levels, and between different policy actors. After examining these general trends in how states communicate their foreign policy intentions, frame analysis also allows us to trace subtle shifts in policy substance across different foreign policy statements.

In the study of foreign policy, this version of frame analysis inspired by Entman can help researchers develop an in-depth understanding of different states' policy positions, how these positions have evolved, and what possible inconsistencies exist between the foreign policy actors of a state. Moreover, as shifts in rhetoric can predate changes in policy behavior, frame analysis can point researchers toward areas in which changes in foreign policy behavior are likely.

In the following, I describe how to identify and analyze frames step by step. The basic idea is to code frame fragments in the material, retrieve them, and combine them into frames in a structured manner. After identifying frames, one can describe how they evolve across the selected foreign policy statements. Finally, since each construction of national interest comprises several themes, and every identified frame is subsumed under one theme, one can calculate how prominently the different constructions of national interest appear over time. Figure 9.1 provides an overview of these steps.

The first step for identifying frames is to code the frame fragments. Codes that cover the frame fragments are developed inductively on the material. While I suggest developing the codes manually by going through the material, software tools used for content analysis, such as MAXQDA or NVivo, can be of great help. MAXQDA's dictionary function, for example, allows applying predefined codes to the material automatically, which makes it easy to identify word combinations that appear multiple times in the material. For frame analysis, as introduced in this chapter, there needs to be a code for every frame fragment, meaning codes need to be exhaustive, and every frame fragment needs to be coded with only one code, meaning the codes need to be exclusive. I recommend going through the material several times to ensure that all codes are exhaustive and exclusive (Neuendorf 2017, 131). This step is complete once all the material is coded.

The coded frame fragments are the building blocks for the frame components, which will later be assembled into frames. For turning frame fragments into frame components, one first retrieves the coded frame fragments; then subsumes each frame fragment under one of the structural components that a frame consists of: actors, verbs, qualifiers, and objects. Frame actors describe who is doing something. Frame verbs express policy action and direction. The degree of policy action is described by qualifiers that modify frame verbs. Frame objects describe the policy dimensions. Frame components that appear within a sentence are then combined into frames. The final step in identifying frames is to discern which function(s) a frame performs. Since the frame verb describes a frame's action, it determines which frame function(s) the frame performs.

For the quantitative part of the analysis, one examines how prominently certain themes that emanate from the theoretical framework appear across the selected foreign policy statements and to what extent there are differences based on addressed audiences, policy levels,

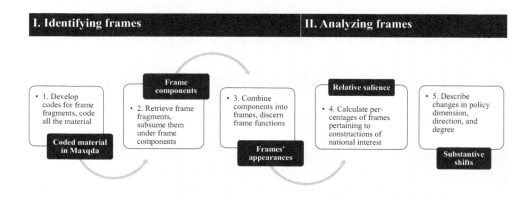

Figure 9.1 Overview of the frame analysis process.

and institutional authors. For this, one compares the percentages of frames that pertain to different themes with each other. Thus, to examine overall changes in prominence over time, one calculates the percentages of frames that pertain to each theme per year and compares the results. Likewise, to examine differences between institutional authors, one calculates percentages of frames pertaining to each theme for each author and compares the results.

Once the frames are identified in the material, one can analyze how they evolve over time, thus adding a qualitative assessment. MAXQDA's Code-Matrix-Browser, for example, shows in which of the analyzed documents the identified frames appear. This graphical representation is the starting point for describing changes in frames based on the categorization of possible changes introduced above. One can now see which frames were stable, new, faded, or modified. Researchers will closely examine how the modified frames changed over time in their attempts to trace incremental changes in policy substance.

Empirical Illustration

The following section illustrates how one can apply the frame analysis approach to map changes and differences in how the U.S. and China communicate their foreign policy intentions. The empirical illustration draws on the construction of the national interest as a theoretical framework to reveal how the two governments express their intentions through official foreign policy statements. After introducing the theoretical framework and the framing actors that matter in the Chinese and the U.S. context, the section maps changes in relative salience and substantive shifts in how the governments express their countries' national interest.

Theoretical Framework and Framing Actors in the U.S. and Chinese Context

For conceptualizing official constructions of the national interest, I link the basic needs Nuechterlein describes in his seminal conception of the national interest to more recent empirical accounts from IR literature. Hence, I distinguish six constructions of the national interest: first, it is in a state's interest to *defend its territory, political system, and citizens* (Def, for short). Second, it is in a state's interest to *grow its external economic relations* (Econ). Moreover, it is in a state's interest to *lead global governance* (Gov) and *promote its values* (Val). Reviews of the empirical literature on states' national interest suggest that Nuechterlein overlooks states' role in the region in which they are situated and the importance of providing global public goods. Finally, for great powers at least, it is in the state's interest to *control the region* (Reg) and *provide global public goods* (Publ).

In both states, several foreign policy actors are located at different policy-making levels. Statements at the strategic level are most authoritative and outline broad and long-term directions. In the U.S. context, this applies to statements by the President; in the Chinese context, it applies to statements by the Chinese Communist Party (CCP) General Secretary/State President. The policy planning level describes more focused communication related to a particular context. This includes speeches by the Vice-President and Secretary of State in the U.S. context. In the Chinese context, this includes the Premier representing China at international summits, the State Council Information Office, closely linked to the Propaganda Department (Brady 2008), publishing White Papers explaining the Chinese government's position to the outside world, as well as the Foreign Minister and the Head of the Office of the Central Foreign Affairs Commission. For each analyzed statement, I assess whether it is primarily directed toward a domestic or an international audience (Tables 9.2 and 9.3).

Table 9.2 Chinese Foreign Policy Statements Analyzed

Target Audience	Type of foreign Policy Statement	Institutional Author	Frequency	Occasions Covered by this Article	n
Strategic level					
Domestic	CCP General Secretary's Political Work Report to Party Congress	CCP General Secretary, but reflects party leadership's consensus	Every five years	• 18th Party Congress • 19th Party Congress	2
Domestic	Speeches by CCP General Secretary/State President in front of a domestic audience	CCP General Secretary/State President	Regularly, no specific schedule	• Central work conferences • Politburo study sessions	7
International	Speeches by CCP General Secretary/State President in front of an international audience	CCP General Secretary/State President[a]	Regularly, no specific schedule	• AIIB • Arab League • Asian-Africa Summit • Belt and Road Forum • Boao Forum • BRICS Summit • CDAC • CELAC • China-Africa Cooperation Forum • China-Arab Cooperation Forum • CICA • G20 Summit • Import Export Expo • SCO Summit • Sino-French Symposium on global governance • UN General Assembly • UNESCO	47
Policy planning level					
Domestic	Government Work Reports	Chinese Premier delivers to NPC	Annually	NPC Annual Session 2013–2019	7
Domestic	Five-Year Plan	CCP Central Committee and State Council	Every five years	Five-Year Plan from 2016	1
Domestic	Foreign Minister's domestic speeches	Ministry of Foreign Affairs	Annually	Annual symposium for international affairs 2013–2019	7

	Policy Papers and Defense White Papers	State Council Information Office	Regularly No specific schedule	• Africa policy • Arab policy • Arctic policy • Asia-Pacific security • China and the world • Defense White Papers • EU • Foreign aid and development assistance • Latin America policy • WTO	14
International	Premier's international speeches	Premier	Regularly No specific schedule	• Boao Forum • UNGA • WEF	5
	Foreign Minister's international speeches	Ministry of Foreign Affairs	Regularly No specific schedule	• UNGA • WEF	6

^aThis category includes one speech by Wang Qishan, Vice-President of the PRC at the WEF 2019.

Table 9.3 U.S. Foreign Policy Statements Analyzed

Target Audience		Type of Foreign Policy Statement	Institutional Author	Frequency	Occasions Covered by this Article	n
Strategic level	Domestic	National security strategy	U.S. President	Regularly, no specific schedule	• NSS 2017 • NSS 2015	2
		State of the Union address	U.S. President	Annually	State of the Union Address 2013–2019	7
		Presidential speech	U.S. President	Regularly, no specific schedule	• Meetings with members of the military • Programmatic foreign policy speeches	7
	Inter-national	Presidential speech	U.S. President	Regularly, no specific schedule	• UN General Assembly 2013–2019 • WEF 2018	8

(Continued)

Sabine Mokry

Table 9.3 U.S. Foreign Policy Statements Analyzed (Continued)

Target Audience		Type of Foreign Policy Statement	Institutional Author	Frequency	Occasions Covered by this Article	n
Policy planning level	Domestic	Foreign Minister's domestic speeches	Secretary of State	Regularly, no specific schedule	• Rice University 2019 • Ceraweek 2019 • Kansas State University 2019 • American Legion 2019 • Claremont College 2019 • Grand Challenges Meeting 2017 • Naval Academy 2017 • CGA 2016 • CAP 2013	9
	International	Foreign Minister's international speeches	Secretary of State	Regularly, no specific schedule	• GMF 2018 • WEF 2016 • MSC 2016	3
		Other leaders' international speeches	Vice-President, Secretary of Defense, Military Leaders	Regularly, no specific schedule	• MSC 2019 • MSC 2018 • MSC 2017 • WEF 2017 • MSC 2015 • MSC 2013	6

Changes in Relative Salience

Throughout the time frame, *lead global governance* appears as one of the, at times, even as the most prominent construction of national interest in U.S. and Chinese foreign policy statements. While the U.S. government mostly tries to balance this ambition only with *defending its territory, political system, and citizens*, the Chinese government's attention is spread more widely between the different constructions of national interest. Both countries spend hardly any attention on *controlling the region*. In the Chinese statements, *lead global governance* is constantly gaining prominence. In the U.S. statements, it lost prominence around 2014 and then regained it slowly until 2019. The prominence of the construction of national interest *defend territory, political system, and citizens* is shifting significantly in Chinese statements. In U.S. statements, it experienced a substantial increase and decline in prominence between 2014 and 2018. *Offer global public goods, expand economic relations, and promote one's values* appear more prominently in Chinese than U.S. statements. Around 2018, *expand economic relations* became more prominent in both countries. *Promote China's values* had a spike in prominence in 2014. In U.S. statements, *promote U.S. values* first lost prominence then gained it again between 2017 and 2019. *Control the region* continually experienced sharp drops in Chinese statements and is almost inexistent in U.S. statements (Figures 9.2 and 9.3).

Differences between policy levels reveal inconsistencies in a country's foreign policy rhetoric. In Chinese statements, the most significant differences between the strategic and the policy planning level appear in *control the region*. In U.S. statements, the most significant differences appear in *expand economic relations*. In Chinese statements, *control the region* was first

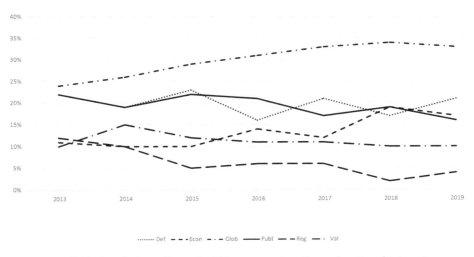

Figure 9.2 Shifts in relative salience in Chinese constructions of national interest.

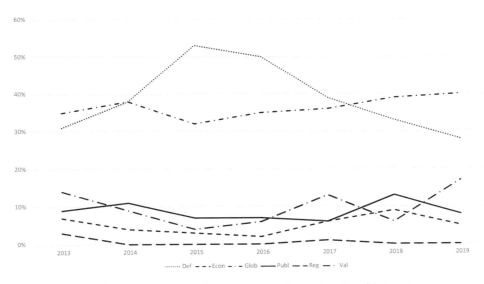

Figure 9.3 Shifts in relative salience in U.S. constructions of national interest.

highly salient on the strategic level and played hardly any role on the policy planning level. Then, it lost prominence on the strategic level and gained prominence on the policy planning level until around 2015, after which it was more salient on the policy planning level than on the strategic level. In U.S. statements, *expand economic relations* was highly salient on the strategic level and played hardly any role on the policy planning level in 2014 and 2018. In contrast, foreign policy rhetoric is more consistent in *lead global governance* and in *promote U.S. values*. In Chinese statements, the smallest differences appear in *lead global governance*. Except for 2016, when *lead global governance* was much more salient on the policy planning level, the two policy levels were always closely aligned. The smallest differences overall appeared in the construction of national interest *promote U.S. values*.

The two policy-making levels are composed of various institutional authors who highlight different aspects of their countries' foreign policy rhetoric. As Figure 9.4 illustrates, differences in how prominently the six constructions of national interest appear in statements by different Chinese authors are negligible, which suggests a high degree of consistency in China's foreign policy rhetoric. However, important differences emerge when tracing how prominently the constructions of national interest feature in different authors' statements. The most pronounced differences appear between the General Secretary and the State Council Information Office (SCIO, see Figure 9.5). Most importantly, the trends in relative salience often point in different directions: *Expand China's economic relations, control the region*, and *promote China's values* all first became more important in statements issued by the SCIO and less important in the General Secretary's statements, then it is the other way round. This hints at fundamental differences between the two institutions. Figure 9.6 illustrates the more subtle differences in relative salience of different constructions of national interest between the foreign minister and the Premier, because the trends often point in the same direction.

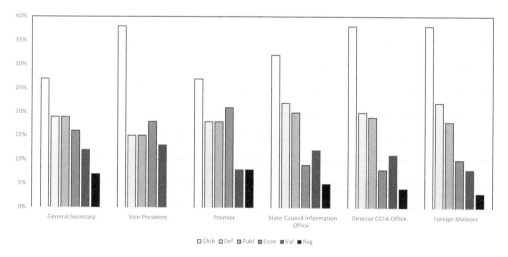

Figure 9.4 Distribution of constructions of national interests in Chinese foreign policy statements.

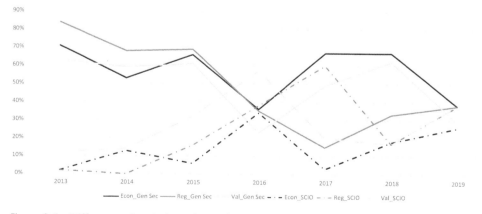

Figure 9.5 Differences in relative salience between statements by General Secretary and State Council Information Office.

Frame Analysis

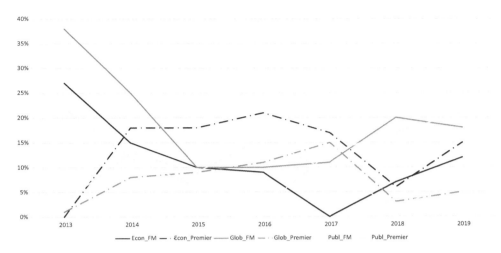

Figure 9.6 Differences in relative salience between statements by Foreign Minister and Premier.

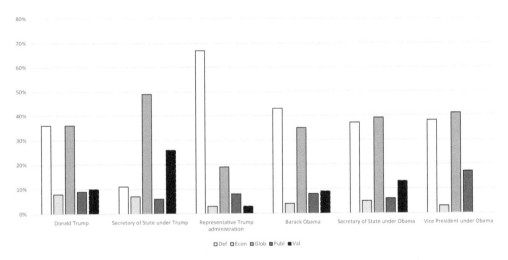

Figure 9.7 Distribution of constructions of national interest in U.S. foreign policy statements.

In the U.S., differences between the Obama and the Trump administration are not as significant as one might expect. In all statements by the representatives of the Obama administration, *defend territory, political system, and citizens* are equally as prominent as *lead global governance*. While this also holds for Donald Trump himself, *lead global governance* and *promote U.S. values* appear much more prominently in statements by his Secretaries of State, which reveals an important difference in the Trump administration's foreign policy (Figure 9.7).

The analysis of differences and changes in the relative salience of the different constructions of national interest in U.S. and Chinese foreign policy statements showed that frame analysis can uncover broad shifts in emphasis over time in previously delimited areas, such as the construction of a country's national interest. Moreover, frame analysis can illustrate how much dynamic there is in foreign policy statements over time. Besides, it can give a good

145

impression of how close statements from different actors across different policy-making levels within a state are aligned and where potential fault lines could be.

Substantive Shifts

With its focus on substantive shifts, frame analysis can reveal subtle changes in how countries describe the security challenges they face. Over time, the U.S. government highlighted different areas it must secure: In 2013, the focus was on those who serve their country abroad (Union 2013).[1] In 2015, technologies that have unleashed untold opportunities (Union 2015), the international financial system (NSS 2015), and free speech (Union 2015) were singled out as important challenges. In contrast, the 2017 National Security Strategy focused on protecting national borders. Then, at the U.N. General Assembly, Trump highlighted citizens' values as worth protecting. Frame analysis shows that the description of challenges the U.S. is facing has become more specific over time. Initially, severe challenges to national security were mentioned (NSS 2015), then challenges were described as intertwined and long-term (NSS 2017, CGA 2016). From 2017 onward, concrete issue areas were identified, first, escalating challenges to cybersecurity (NSS 2017), then illegal immigration (UNGA 2019).

With frame analysis, one can also trace subtle shifts in how states intend to respond to security challenges. For example, the Chinese government mentioned more concrete measures to protect Chinese citizens when they travel abroad. Since 2012, all authors have claimed that they wanted to secure Chinese citizens' and businesses' legitimate rights and interests (PCR 2012, GWR 2014, 2015, Arab policy 2016, Symposium 2015, 2016). In 2018, this was replaced by a stronger frame put forward by the foreign minister that described the Chinese government as fighting back when citizens' rights and interests were infringed upon (Symposium 2018). The foreign minister has long been concerned with guaranteeing Chinese citizens' safety during visits abroad. Over time, these frames have become more specific: from ensuring that citizens are treated well (Symposium 2015) over making their trips safer and smoother (Symposium 2016) to introducing "procedures to ensure the safety of Chinese citizens traveling abroad" (Symposium 2018). Since 2017, he has referred to the "system for the protection of Chinese nationals overseas" (Symposium 2017, 2019).

Even more important for international politics are the U.S. and China's changing approaches to international institutions and the international order that frame analysis helps uncover. The U.S. government first described itself as conforming to historic institutions (Union 2017), then as partly responsible for institutions that they believe can be improved (GMF 2018). While in 2014, the U.S. government explained that it cared deeply about the promise of the United Nations (UNGA 2014), in 2018, the foreign minister mentioned that the U.S. government would not reduce the strength of international institutions (GMF 2018). Besides, there was a change in policy direction regarding the international order: in 2014, the U.S. government announced that it would improve the international order (Mil Acad 2014). In 2018, it specified that it would change the liberal international order, working with others toward the peaceful, liberal order each citizen deserves (GMF 2018).

The Chinese government also voiced more forcefully how they intended to change the international order and how they wanted to reform global governance. In 2014, the SCIO put forward that China wanted to construct a peaceful, stable, equitable, and orderly development environment for all countries (EU policy 2014); it described it as pursuing a more just and equitable international order (GWR 2014, 2015, EU policy 2014, Africa policy 2014) and as publicly supporting a more just and reasonable international order (CELAC 2014, LatinAmerica 2015, Politburo Study Session 2015). Regarding the reform of global governance, the SCIO first pointed to flaws in the existing global governance system in its Africa policy paper, mainly since it has not fully accommodated changes in the international system. Then, Xi spelled out his vision of a fairer, more reasonable global governance system in front of domestic audiences (Politburo Study Session 2013, 2015, Central Work Conference 2014). In international speeches, he assured his audience that this would reflect the interests of most countries (FOCAC 2018, UNGA 2017). Regarding the reform process, the foreign minister first mentioned its keen sense of responsibility in shaping the reform of the global governance system. Regarding reform details, first, many authors claimed that China would work together with others (PCR 2017, BRICS 2013, GWR 2017, 2019, CN in the world 2019). Then, in front of domestic audiences, Xi described China as taking on a leadership role (Politburo Study Session 2015, Central Work Conference 2018). Finally, at the Boao Forum, Xi underlined that states needed to accelerate the global governance system's reform (Boao 2019).

Conclusion

The most important strength of the version of the frame analysis approach introduced in this chapter is that it combines a qualitative assessment of substantive shifts in foreign policy intentions with a quantitative assessment of changes in how salient different aspects are. The empirical illustration shows that this allows painting a comprehensive picture of changes in different states' constructions of national interest. Moreover, since similar foreign policy statements are available for almost all states and because computer-assisted coding facilitates the use of a fairly large amount of text, the approach allows an in-depth comparison of different states' constructions of national interest while also covering incremental changes in policy substance within each state. Moreover, the approach is fairly economical since the qualitative and quantitative assessments are based on the same coding efforts.

However, depending on the number of texts researchers want to incorporate, the coding can become very resource-intensive. The manual coding work required can limit the applicability of the frame analysis approach as introduced in this chapter, because it limits the number of documents that can be processed. In this case, one would need to go one step further to link the conceptual considerations raised here to automated variants of text analysis and big data analysis (see other chapters in this volume).

Frame analysis, as introduced in this chapter, is well suited if one wants to detail different states' policy positions but, at the same time, also does not want to lose sight of broader changes in states' foreign policy intentions. First-time users of frame analysis should be aware that coding the frame fragments is fairly time-intensive. Therefore, one should carefully select the material one wants to include in the analysis to avoid unnecessary coding. As the approach allows to draw on data from different polities, it is important to always keep in mind differences that result from regime type. Recent advances in automatic translation make cross-country comparisons more feasible. While researchers should pay attention to possible differences between the foreign policy statements and their official English translations and be able to check the translations themselves, automatic translations can offer help along the way (Mokry, 2022).

Acknowledgments

The author wishes to thank participants of the workshop on FPA methods organized by the Foreign Policy and Security Studies Group of the German Political Science Association (DVPW) for their valuable suggestions. This chapter emerged from the research for the author's PhD dissertation which is funded by Cusanuswerk Scholarship Foundation.

Note

1 For space reasons and to improve readability, the respective foreign policy statements are referenced in an abbreviated version. A full list of the documents used is available on the author's personal website. Link: https://www.sabinemokry.com/frame-analysis.

References

Aran, Amnon, and Leonie Fleischmann. 2019. "Framing and Foreign Policy—Israel's Response to the Arab Uprisings." *International Studies Review* 21(4): 614–639.

Brady, Anne-Marie. 2008. *Marketing Dictatorship: Propaganda and Thought Work in Contemporary China*. Lanham, MD: Rowman & Littlefield Publishers.

Brewer, Paul R. 2006. "National Interest Frames and Public Opinion about World Affairs." *Harvard International Journal of Press-Politics* 11(4): 89–102.

Dimitrova, Daniela V., and Jesper Strömbäck. 2008. "Foreign Policy and the Framing of the 2003 Iraq War in Elite Swedish and US Newspapers." *Media, War and Conflict* 1(2): 203–220.

Entman, Robert M. 1993. "Framing: Towards Clarification of a Fractured Paradigm." *Journal of Communication* 43(4): 51–58.

Entman, Robert M. 2007. "Framing Bias: Media in the Distribution of Power." *Journal of Communication* 5(1): 163–173.

Entman, Robert M., and Sarah Stonbely. 2018. "Blunders, Scandals, and Strategic Communication in U.S. Foreign Policy: Benghazi vs. 9/11." *International Journal of Communication* 12: 3024–3047.

Finnemore, Martha. 1996. *National Interests in International Society*. Ithaca, NY: Cornell University Press.

Fong, Yang Lai, and Teoh Yong Chia. 2017. "Framing Diplomatic Relations: A Comparative Analysis of Malaysian and Chinese Newspaper Coverage on Premier Li Keqiang's Visit to Malaysia." *China Report* 53(4): 467–489.

Futák-Campbell, Beatrix, and Mira Pütz. 2021. "From the 'Open Door' Policy to the EU-Turkey Deal: Media Framings of German Policy Changes during the EU Refugee 'Crisis.'" *International Relations* 36(1): 61–82.

Garrison, Jean. 2007. "Constructing the 'National Interest' in U.S.–China Policy Making: How Foreign Policy Decision Groups Define and Signal Policy Choices." *Foreign Policy Analysis* 3(2): 105–126.

Goffman, Erving. 1974. *Frame Analysis - An Essay on the Organization of Experience*. Cambridge, MA: Harvard University Press.

Golan, Guy J., and Josephine Lukito. 2015. "The Rise of the Dragon? Framing China's Global Leadership in Elite American Newspapers." *International Communication Gazette* 77 (8): 753–771.

Greussing, Esther, and Hajo Boomgaarden. 2017. "Shifting the Refugee Narrative? An Automated Frame Analysis of Europe's 2015 Refugee Crisis." *Journal of Ethnic and Migration Studies* 43(11): 1749–1774.

Holland, Jack. 2010. "Howard's War on Terror: A Conceivable, Communicable and Coercive Foreign Policy Discourse." *Australian Journal of Political Science* 45(4): 643–661.

Hur, Jaeyoung. 2018. "Frame Contest of Foreign Policy: Who Influences Whom in South Korea?" *Pacific Focus* 33(1): 141–174.

Jecker, Constanze. 2017. *Entmans Framing-Ansatz - Theoretische Grundlegung und empirische Umsetzung*. Köln: Herbert von Halem Verlag.

Jensen, Leif Christian, and Pål Wilter Skedsmo. 2010. "Approaching the North: Norwegian and Russian Foreign Policy Discourses on the European Arctic." *Polar Research* 29(3): 439–450.

Kim, Claudia J. 2017. "War over Framing: Base Politics in South Korea." *Pacific Review* 30(3): 309–327.

Kratochvil, Petr, Petra Cibulkova, and Michael Benik. 2011. "The EU as a 'Framing Actor': Reflections on Media Debates about EU Foreign Policy." *Jcms-Journal of Common Market Studies* 49(2): 391–412.

Lenz, Tobias. 2018. "Frame Diffusion and Institutional Choice in Regional Economic Cooperation." *International Theory* 10(1): 31–70.

Li, Chien pin. 2015. "New Leaders with Old Lenses? China's Conflict Frames Toward Taiwan, 2003–2013." *Journal of Chinese Political Science* 20(1): 67–85.

Liang, Fan. 2019. "The New Silk Road on Facebook: How China's Official Media Cover and Frame a National Initiative for Global Audiences." *Communication and the Public* 4(4): 261–275.

Matthes, Jörg, and Mattias Kohring. 2008. "The Content Analysis of Media Frames: Toward Improving Reliability and Validity." *Journal of Communication* 58: 258–279.

Mokry, Sabine. 2022. "What Is Lost in Translation? Differences between Chinese Foreign Policy Statements and Their Official English Translations." *Foreign Policy Analysis* 18(3): 1–17.

Neuendorf, Kimberley A. 2017. *The Content Analysis Guidebook*. 2nd edition. Los Angeles, CA: SAGE.

Nicholls, Tom, and Pepper D. Culpepper. 2021. "Computational Identification of Media Frames: Strengths, Weaknesses, and Opportunities." *Political Communication* 38(1–2): 159–181.

Nuechterlein, Donald E. 1976. "National Interests and Foreign Policy: A Conceptual Framework for Analysis and Decision-Making." *British Journal of International Studies* October (2): 246–266.

Ostermann, Falk. 2019. *Security, Defense Discourse and Identity in NATO and Europe - How France Changed Foreign Policy*. London: Routledge.

Panayirci, Ugur Cevdet, and Emre Iseri. 2014. "A Content Analysis of the AKP's 'Honorable' Foreign Policy Discourse: The Nexus of Domestic-International Politics." *Turkish Studies* 15(1): 62–80.

Robertson, Jeffrey. 2017. "More than Old Friends? Narrative in Australia's Relationship with Korea." *Australian Journal of Politics and History* 63(1): 15–30.

Rudolph, Rachael M. 2018. "Framing Sino-American Military Relations: The Power and Problem of Perception in Preventing Geostrategic Security Cooperation between China and the United States." *Asia and the Pacific Policy Studies* 5(2): 182–195.

Smith, Michael. 2016. "EU Diplomacy and the EU-China Strategic Relationship: Framing, Negotiation and Management." *Cambridge Review of International Affairs* 29(1): 78–98.

Voltolini, Benedetta. 2016. "Non-State Actors and Framing Processes in EU Foreign Policy: The Case of EU-Israel Relations." *Journal of European Public Policy* 23(10): 1502–1519.

Weldes, Jutta. 1999. *Constructing the National Interest - The United States and the Cuban Missile Crisis*. Minneapolis, MI and London: University of Minnesota Press.

10
Visual Analysis
Bernhard Stahl and Julian Ignatowitsch

Introduction

The academic grasp of foreign policy started with historical narratives, mainly nation-state centered institutional descriptions. Pictures merely served to embellish these works – portraying famous politicians, illustrating sites of conflicts and battlefields, showing maps, or exemplifying chosen glories of respective national histories. Analyses of such visual elements are practically non-existent in the field of foreign policy. This did not change with the advent of Foreign Policy Analysis (FPA) as a discipline, since FPA focuses on decision-making, favoring text-based analyses of political processes. In addition, research designs with causal pathways prefer factual information to complex and often ambiguous information assemblages that happen in and with images. But the wind changes when it comes to analyzing how foreign policy is legitimized. Competing narratives, arguing in the public sphere, convincing the public, explaining crises – all of these actions call for methods that deliver *a broader picture* of the foundations on which foreign policy rests. By linking visual analysis to social constructivist foreign policy research, the interdisciplinary followability can be stressed and further enhanced. Findings from other fields – such as film and media sciences, history of arts, cultural studies, and semiotics – may find their way into FPA and enable common research endeavors.

Today, the use of images has gained ground considering, first, that images are omnipresent under the condition of unlimited reproduction in the digital age.[1] Second, images can be seen as "asset items" structuring our perceptions, triggering actions, and (re-)constructing reality (Paul 2008, 28).[2] Third, images can also have a special impact and persuasive power (visual persuasiveness, Burri 2008, 349 et seq), possibly leading to political mobilization (Casas and Webb Williams 2019)[3]; and fourth, they can be universally employed (cf. Bulmer and Buchanan-Oliver 2006, 50 for studies on advertisement). Moreover, images have an impact on identity, linking practical politics, population, and academia (Carver 2010, 425). Theoretically speaking, conceiving of images as "iconic acts" means that "a powerful relation between the producer, the image and the spectator [is constituted]. This relation regulates "how we see what we see" (Schlag 2016, 187).

This chapter aims to show how visual analysis can offer a new methodological perspective that complements established approaches to analyzing foreign policy. Text-based methods such as discourse analysis, narrative analysis, interviews, or historical analysis (see the chapters by Sjöstedt and Ostermann, Oppermann and Spencer, Deschaux-Dutard, or Ghalehdar in this volume) can be complemented and amended by image analysis without any problems (e.g., Freistein et al. 2020 for a "visual narrative analysis" or Jungblut and Zakareviciute 2019 for a "multimodal frame analysis"). This is why visual analysis is well suited to serve mixed methods or triangulation research designs.

The aim of this chapter, therefore, is to establish how visual analysis can be made prolific for FPA. Empirically, the chapter looks at covers of the German news magazine *Der Spiegel* on the Afghanistan involvement (2001–2021) to provide an example of how images may constitute a powerful counter-discourse in the political sphere. By doing so, we are offering a constitutive argument that stresses the formative power of images conveyed by the media. The discursive meaning of images is generally seen as being under-researched, particularly because the interpretation of images is more challenging than interpreting texts. Images – as (visual) signs in the broader sense – belong to discourse and are therefore easily connected to the theoretical assumptions of social constructivism. The structure of this article is as follows: after a brief view on the literature, we focus on basic insights regarding images (Key concepts and terms). Subsequently, we apply a model of visual analysis to the German Afghanistan operation, which looks very suitable due to 20 years of military and political commitment and its disruptive end in 2021. We thus aim to portray how images in scientific work can be epistemologically analyzed and – regarding contents – what they can ontologically say about German foreign policy.

Literature Review

The arrival of social constructivism in IR (cf. Adler 2013) is the result of the linguistic turn of the social sciences, the core of which is the ontological assumption that the world is primarily defined by language (Rorty 1968). As a methodological consequence, qualitative methods such as discourse analysis or content analysis were established as research tools, thus cementing the primacy of language.

When the visual or pictorial turn for IR was called out (Mitchell 1994), many scientists expected a far-reaching change challenging the dominance of verbal texts and their reconstructions of meanings (Ahäll 2009; Hebel and Wagner 2011; Kirkpatrick 2015). Yet, mainstream theories of IR such as the realist and liberal schools of thought remained rather unimpressed by the turn, and visual studies remain marginal until today. For instance, while different authors analyzed the infamous image of the situation room in the White House during the raid on Bin Laden as an impressive image from a journalistic, pedagogic, sociological, and psychological perspective, the IR view was missing (Przyborski and Haller 2014).

So far, only post-structural analyses on the basis of French philosophical work (Deleuze 1968; Virilio 1989 and his works on cinema; Barthes 1989)[4] have looked at 'visuality' and reflected on the 'power of images' in the background of dominating discourses (e.g. Campbell 2007, 230; Der Derian 2000; Fairclough 2001, 23; Shapiro 1988). The analysis of images and 'the visual' found inroads to Critical Security Studies (Heck and Schlag 2020; Schlag 2016), Critical Geopolitics (Dodds 2010), Popular Culture (Grayson et al. 2009) and 'aesthetic IR' (Bleiker 2015). Inter-textuality and the 'circulability' of images, for example, are a common theme in Critical Security Studies (Hansen 2011; Heck und Schlag 2013; Moeller 2007; Van Veeren 2011). The common thread of all of these studies is to criticize established theories (e.g., Andersen and Moeller 2013; Williams 2003) in the hope that image critique would gain traction after centuries of mere text critique (Beuthner and Weichert 2003, 13).

While visual analysis has not yet found its way into foreign policy studies, such critical accounts of IR come close.

Two examples of visual analyses in the critical school of IR may serve as an example. In Lene Hansen's "How images make world politics: International icons and the case of Abu Ghraib" (2015), the author deals with iconic images[5] which are commonly held to be very important[6] but without any consent "on what 'importance' is and how to study it" (ibid., 4). Iconic images may serve different functions for the study of foreign policy, but their meaning remains ambiguous in the first place: "the icon does not 'speak' foreign policy on its own. It is drawn upon by discursive agents to constitute events, threats, subjects, and identities, to defend policies taken or promote alternatives not pursued" (ibid., 3). It is media, the political elites, and the text in which pictures are embedded which give meaning to the images (ibid., 12) – or better suggest what the most plausible meaning could be.

In their study on "The female body and the war in Afghanistan", Axel Heck and Gabi Schlag (2013) demonstrate how images can be analyzed in Critical Security Studies. They embed their argument within Securitization theory (Buzan et al. 1998) which provides a framework for understanding how political reaction to security threats leads to excessive politicization and 'emergency politics'. By "theorizing the image as an iconic act" (ibid., 7), the authors examine the *TIME* cover 'Aisha', a female victim of physical violence (her ears and nose were cut off) of the Taliban regime. The cover was published in 2010 supporting the US-administration's claim to stay in Afghanistan after serious setbacks of the coalition forces there (ibid., 10). Within the context of this debate, the authors pursue a three-step iconographic analysis of the cover (ibid., 12f., cf. below). In their subsequent interpretation, they demonstrate how the image detaches from the text in the volume, or the possible motives of the photographer, securitizing the Afghanistan intervention: "The securitization of gender and the body as it is performed in this image leads to a moral hierarchy among different discourse positions, legitimizing those who justify a military intervention and delegitimize those who articulate a critique" (ibid., 15). By doing so, they state, a Western identity construction consisting of a dualism of humanity and barbarism is strengthened (ibid., 16).

The two examples demonstrate the usefulness of analyzing images in IR. The critical impetus of the authors serves an enlightening and illustrating purpose, which aims at revealing hegemonic orders. Yet image analysis, as this article aims to show, can also serve re-constructing purposes. The toolbox offered here may be used for all types of theoretical approaches, which aim at explaining foreign policy phenomena (such as neoclassical realism, new liberalism, discourse-bound identity theory).

Key Terms and Concepts

While 'picture' denotes the concrete artifact (which may hang on a wall), 'image' is the broader term used in the humanities also comprising projections, metaphors, appearances, memories, and designs (Mitchell 1984, 505). Visual studies, in turn, limit images to what can be seen while emphasizing the meaning of them (Prosser 2013, 177). The spectrum of gaining knowledge regarding images is abundant. And, to make things even more complicated: "All media is mixed media" (Mitchell 2005, 215). Hence, images do not come across on a *tabula rasa*, they are always laden with context. Usually, images illustrate texts, are published in specific media outlets such as news, and their production stems from a specific conflict, event, or issue area. This also applies to covers of journals and weekly magazines where images are complemented by headlines and other text fragments (Tseronis 2021). Such "image-text constellations" (Mitchell 2005, 5) are typical for images in the political sphere in general and for foreign policy in particular. As Heck and Schlag (2013) point out in their analysis of the cover 'Aisha' (cf. above), the political debates of the time give the image its primary meaning (without knowing what the recipients make of it). Typically, cover images and lead stories fulfill the characteristic of a 'key image' in the media, with the potential to become even iconic images. In Hansen's example 'The Hooded Man', on the cover of the 8 May 2004 issue of *The Economist*, the headline 'Resign, Rumsfeld' alluded to the horrific events which took place in the Abu Ghraib prison during the US occupation of Iraq. Hansen (2015, 277) recommends a "three tiered analytical and methodological strategy" in order to examine such iconic images:

Step 1: The iconic image itself which consists of the formal composition of the image, the attributed factual meaning, its "inter-iconicity" (i.e. its implicit reference to previous similar images), and its rise to iconic status.

Step 2: The international status and political impact of the icon, which consists of the icon's circulation (foreign policy, regional or global), internationally attributed discursive meanings, and its possible impact on politics.

Step 3: Appropriations of the icon, which consists of the range of appropriations, possible critical interventions, alternative readings, and limits to appropriation.

Following Aby Warburg (cited in Paul 2008, 30), key and iconic images work with symbolic and emblematic clichés and stereotypes, with allegorical concentration in order to fulfill their function as an assault on the public consciousness. Of particular resonance are war images, for they let the imaginations of war become alive in a peaceful community: "Only wars that produce mass medial evidence, are wars that stay in the memory of peoples" (Müller and Knieper 2005, 7). They thereby do not only stay in the collective memory of a nation, or rather influence their national identity, but they are also more likely asset items that structure ideas and perceptions of the past and present, trigger actions, and (de-)legitimize as well as constitute reality:

> The vast shaping power of war images and the interest for them, has shaped the images themselves to weapons. With them it is possible to legitimize wars and prepare societies for wars. The homeland gets involved in the events through images. Yet images can also persuade troops to retreat.
>
> *(Paul 2009, 39)*

Admittedly, the so-called *CNN-effect* – when an image triggers a specific political decision – seems exaggerated (Jakobsen 2000) but the role of images for the politics of history of a nation looks self-evident.

Political magazines with their covers are publicly visible at newsstands; they are cited and reproduced in other media and are part of the public sphere. Based on business calculations they not only represent a way of thinking about the society but also aim at polarizing and provoking. In any case, they are part of a societal discourse. With no doubt, this applies to covers of the *Spiegel*, which is the most important political weekly magazine in the German speaking part of Europe with six million readers. Following the assumption of medialization, the magazine accounts for a "privileged storyteller" (Milliken 1999) and serves as a political, independent constructor of reality.

Some caveats are in order here. First, visual analysis calls for humility. Considering Rose's (2016) proposition to differentiate between production, content, circulation, and audiencing of images, the analyst cannot do justice to all. In the case here, one may want to know what the *Spiegel*-board of editors and the cover designer had in mind when they drafted the covers. Second, one might be interested in the circulation and reception of the audience – what the analyst 'sees' might be miles away from a viewer's take.[7] Third, a model based on Panofsky's ideas might be considered outdated for experts of the history of arts and insufficient for communication and media analysts. So admittedly, the following model only serves as a first inroad to "visual interpretation competence" (Müller 2008).

An Illustration – The Model

The four-stage model presented here is based on Panofsky's work (Hasenmueller 1978; Panofsky 1978) and rather conventional, considering that it is used in similar forms in the history of arts, cultural studies, as well as communication studies. It has already found its way into Critical Security Studies in IR (Heck and Schlag 2013) and has been applied in identity studies (Heinrich and Stahl 2012) and European affairs (i.e. the Euro-debt crisis: Heinrich and Stahl 2017). Here, it is proposed as a traveling concept, as a tool to examine foreign policy legitimation – be it to support executive policies or to express contestation against the government (as the illustration in this text does). This chapter is based on a pluralistic understanding of methods to deal with the legitimation, contestation, and expression of politics.[8] It is more modest than Hansen's methodological steps sketched above considering that her analytical tool-kit aims at comprehending iconic images. Here, we will present a model for image analysis which is based on a classic, the iconological method of Panofsky (1978) amended by Marotzki and Stoetzer (2006) and inspired by the above sketched visual analyses in IR.

The four steps of the model are:

1. Pre-iconographic description
2. Iconographic analysis (universal and culture-specific meanings)
3. Analysis of pictorial arrangement (orchestration, mise-en-scène)
4. Interpretation and theoretical contextualization

ad 1. Pre-Iconographic Description

The first step of image interpretation demands for identification in terms of purely recognizing immediately visible pictorial objects: Subjects, people, events, and actions that can be seen in the picture are labeled (Marotzki and Stoetzer 2006, 17). The denotative meaning, that is, the simple meaning of what we see, can thus be determined. This happens in a context-independent manner. Panofsky (1978, 50) calls this descriptive part "pre-iconographic description". It deals with the primary or natural subject, whereby a distinction is made between factual and expressive appearance. The sense of this approach is in avoiding an unconsciously, overhasty identification – "a colonising view" (Marotzki and Stoetzer 2006, 18). Furthermore, it allows for a common start of interpretation, since all viewers may agree on what they see before possibly disagreeing on what it means.

ad 2. Iconographic Analysis (Universal and Culture-Specific Meanings)

The second step that Panofsky (1978, 50) describes as "iconographic analysis" engages the correlations of meaning and sense. This step is therefore about the cultural, specific meaning of the objects and, if applicable, even about the narrative dimension of an image. Besides useful information around the production of the image, the prior description can be linked here to human universals that can be named easily, such as family, food, or communication. It is imperative on the level of connotation to ask for the additional, context-independent meanings that are dependable on the text's internal and external contexts. The crucial point of this interpretation step is to make the historical and cultural perceptions susceptible to reflection (Marotzki and Stoetzer 2006, 21). So, what does the picture mean? Here, different cultural backgrounds have to be considered. In order to do this, we can use a multitude of sources and material to get closer to the artist's intention to create imaginative or empirical comparative cases, or to present information regarding the image's date and location of origin (ibid., 22). It means that in the case of analyzing media images, as we are intending to do, we have to include image signatures, titles, and even the continuous text, as they essentially contribute to the semantization and illustrate the first and most important image external sources.

Moreover, in order to deconstruct implicit characteristics, the cultural historic context and the identification of semantic relations are vital. Therefore, implementing cultural knowledge is central. Panofsky (1978, 37) typifies this by using the known example of the man on the street lifting his hat (description): Most viewers raised in Western cultures would attribute this gesture to greeting – maybe the younger generations less so since the hat as headdress is no longer à la mode. This action on an image would be a typical culture-specific connotation, bound to a specific culture and even bound to a specific time.

As a matter of fact, these hermeneutic findings should not be arbitrarily and subjectively interpreted into the image: one has to be careful with the attribution of universal and culture-specific meaning and motives. That is why motive assumptions are only unproblematic if the meaning is institutionalized or communicatively generalized (Bohnsack 2006, 53), as an image of the UN general secretary could be attributed to motives of world peace and the principles of the UN charter, for instance.

ad 3. Analysis of Pictorial Arrangement (Orchestration, mise-en-scène)

The question of orchestration touches upon the level of illustration. While in the preceding steps we looked at what can be seen in an image, we will now be looking at how it is presented (orchestration).[9] The image composition is called *mise-en-scène* in film science. It essentially deals with the three determinants color, line, and form yet includes open and closed forms, image limitations, image framings, 'margins', foreground – middle ground – background, dominance of lines, forms, symmetries, image divisions, position of the object/figure to each other, sharpness, depth of focus, color codes, light, and lighting. In addition, the camera distance (e.g., close-up, long shot, panorama) and the perspective (e.g., line of sight angle, horizontal angle) as well as the interaction of the pictured objects with the viewer (e.g., eye contact) are included. The reconstruction of the perspective has to literally be determined as the insight into the perspective of the pictured image producer and in his view of the world. This step contributes to the analysis by allowing additional interpretations such as hierarchical elements (upper-under; big-small, etc.) and normative implications (e.g., light-dark color).

ad 4. Interpretation and Theoretical Contextualization

The final step of image interpretation carves out "the societal content of the image" (Marotzki and Stoetzer 2006, 26). The point is to synthesize the findings gained so far and to put them into the socio-historical context. Panofsky (1978, 50) calls this step the "iconological interpretation". It develops the actual meaning of an artwork that creates the symbolic value. The image therefore gets a meaning that can be accounted as for a person, an environment, a society, or culture-bound, historically contingent mentality (Marotzki and Stoetzer 2006, 26). By doing so, the overall image analysis climbs "the ladder of abstraction" (Sartori 1970, 1040ff.): from a most probably undisputed description of what we see via possibly low contested areas of analysis (connotation and orchestration) to ambiguous levels of interpretation. It is this last step, which makes visual analysis so rewarding, that is, by connecting the results of this interpretation of visual data with IR and foreign policy questions (Schlag 2016, 194). A first resource of interpretation lies in an inter-iconic approach integrating more images of the same genre, the same time, the same producer, or the same *sujet*. A second resource would respect the image's interdependence with the era, the *Zeitgeist*, considering political, societal, and scientific debates of the time. Third, one could embed the image analysis in other methods such as discourse or narrative analysis, contents analysis, expert interviews, surveys, etc. (cf. the respective chapters in this volume). Finally, the visual analysis can be linked to an IR or a foreign policy theory. Theory gives the overall analysis sense and direction, points to why-questions, and may even take a normative stance (cf. Heck and Schlag's approach to Critical Security Studies above).

Case study: 2001 *Spiegel* Cover on the Afghanistan War

By the means of a single image analysis of a *Spiegel* cover image, we will now show which argumentation pattern can be visually detected and to which element of identity it can be referred to (Figure 10.1).

Pre-Iconographic Description

The image depicts two sawn-off logs of wood, or branches, assembled to a cross in an angle of 90 degrees. The longer, vertical branch is red; the shorter, horizontal branch is green. It is birchwood. The wood is scarred in various places. A soldier's helmet is placed on the top end of the vertical, red log. The background is white. The heading of the image is (translated): "Bundeswehr [the German armed forces, the authors] to be deployed to Afghanistan (Title) – case of emergency for Red-Green (Subtitle)".

Iconographic Analysis (Universal and Culture-Specific Meanings)

Taken together, the illustrations just described present an iconographic motive, the 'soldier's grave'. This cross is a Latin cross (a.k.a. high cross or passion cross), in which the stringer is longer than the cross-piece, crossing it above the center. In the Christian tradition, this symbolizes the sacrificing death of Jesus Christ on the one hand and the connection between earth and heaven, or rather between humans and god on the other. It has been the symbol commemoration for graves, or rather for death since the early modern age. In this respect, it symbolizes, in reference to the crucifixion of Jesus Christ, death and the hope of resurrection of the deceased. In this context, it is interesting that the cross, as a religious icon, represents the Jewish-Christian tradition of Europe and is semantically loaded as a symbol of collective identity through the historic context of, among others, the crusades or contemporary debates on the role of religious symbols in public (e.g., Esser 2000).

Visual Analysis

Figure 10.1 Single image analysis – *Spiegel* cover image of 12 November 2001.

The helmet on top of the high cross is the combat helmet of the Bundeswehr (made of the synthetical material Aramid), as used in Afghanistan. In connection with the cross, it commonly symbolizes the grave of a soldier killed in action. Usually, the gravesites in this form are anonymous and temporary. This is underlined by the scarred piece of wood and the absence of a significant sign for the identification of the (allegedly) dead person. In the European cultural knowledge, the soldier's grave is mainly connected to the institutionalized military cemeteries and memorials of the First and Second World Wars. These take on a special reminder function: "War graves urge us to peace and remind us of war, displacement, captivity, home coming" (Nowey 2009).

Certainly, the colors of the branches that form the cross are significant in this correlation. The heading of the image makes it unambiguously clear. "Case of Emergency for Red-Green" refers to the linguistic usage of the German (red-green) coalition government of the Social-Democrats (SPD) and the *Bündnis 90/Die Grünen* (Green Party), in power from 1998 to 2005. As the cross, or rather the grave, is colored in the colors of the coalition, it allows us to identify two interpretations that result from the correlation of the connotations of 'death' and 'coalition government': On the one hand, the code of colors assigns the responsibility of the soldier's grave. On the other hand, the possible end of the coalition is symbolized through the connotation of the cross with death. In this context, the word 'Emergency' may allude to the possible death of the Red-Green coalition but it could just as well have been 'for German/our soldiers' or 'for Germany'. The verbal text thereby presents the coalition as an actor in the center of attention, whereby the non-verbal text, or rather the image, focuses on the dead soldier. The title image foregrounds the decision of the coalition for a mission in Afghanistan and its causal (deadly) outcome. In doing so, the image at the same time presents a reference to the clearly stated people responsible, or rather perpetrators, that is, the government, as well as their anonymous victims – the soldiers. Following the argumentation logic of the *Spiegel*, the perpetrators can also rapidly become (political) victims of the Afghanistan mission, in the sense of the end of the coalition.

Analysis of Pictorial Arrangement (Orchestration, mise-en-scène)

The orchestration of the image is very canny. Yet, especially in the reduced form, we find the most important stylistic device in the way of representing: namely the focus on the substantial statement of the few image elements. The historical level is supposed to be emphasized additionally by the depicted discourse. This is underlined by the choice of perspective. The close-up of the soldier's grave explicitly shows what the focus is on – and only that. Consequently, we can explain the white background, not wanting to distract from the meaningful foreground, yet aiming to create the biggest possible contrast and highlighting it with the most clinical precision unchanged.

Interpretation and Theoretical contextualization

The cover was published two months after 9/11 when the German public discussed sending troops to Afghanistan assisting the US operation to fight the Taliban. It is remarkable that the *Spiegel* used these negative depictions even at the very early stage (long before any German soldiers had died in Afghanistan). A first question of interest may be whether this cover is an outlier. A quick inter-iconic argument, that is, analyzing further title images of the *Spiegel* (frames 2–7), shows that the chosen title image is a typical one for the news coverage by this magazine on Afghanistan, in the time between 2001 and 2013 (between 2014 and 2020, there were no Afghanistan-related covers anymore). This means that the topic largely disappeared from the political agenda, in other words, the intervention became uncontested in the political elite (Figure 10.2).

Visual Analysis

2 The Abyss of Afghanistan – Deployment at the Hindukush

3 Pitfall Afghanistan – America's forlorn bomb war and the ghost of Vietnam

4 Germans on all fronts – The overwhelmed army

5 "Germans have to learn to kill" – How Afghanistan became an emergency

6 When are Germans allowed to kill? The Bundeswehr, Afghanistan and War in the 21st Century

7 Afghanistan: The 200 year war – Cemetery of the Superpowers

8 At War – German Soldiers on the Killing and Dying in Afghanistan

9 TASK FORCE 373 – The Afghanistan Protocols: America's secret war

10 When Germany went to war – Afghanistan: The History of a Fallacy

Figure 10.2 Spiegel cover images on Afghanistan, 2001–2013.

Inter-Iconic Contextualization

Overall, the *Spiegel* denies the mission in Afghanistan any form of legitimacy right from the beginning, both within the limits of the US-led Operation Enduring Freedom (OEF) and NATO's International Security Assistance Force (ISAF). The magazine manages this by using the paradigms of 'risk' and of 'death', both of which the title covers on the Afghanistan mission are filled with. The war in Afghanistan appears as either a soldier's grave, alternatively an abyss, a trap, a graveyard (according to covers no. 2, 3, 7), or a "hopeless bombing war" (no.3). The Bundeswehr is portrayed as weak, overstrained, and as a force that cannot live up to the requirements of the mission. All of the images add up to a clear distinction into 'us' and the 'others'. The construction of 'us' unfolds predominantly through the definition of the others (namely that, which we are not) and less through the self-definition (namely that, what we are). The other, 'Afghanistan' or rather the Afghans, are depicted as alien, scary, and volatile, and evidently show post-colonial traits; it contradicts the 'us' and has hostile characteristics attributed to it; the other people are illustrated as holy warriors and barbarians (no. 2 and 7). Through these characteristics, the images practically create a threat, the supremacy of the other on their own territory – and an inferiority to the US. The US, though, is only to some extent equated with the Western allies in NATO, as there is a dividing line between Germany and the US. As a result, Germany is partially separated from its transatlantic partner, explicitly identified in the title "America's [...] bombing war" and its formal orchestration (no. 3). In this respect, Germany is assigned a special or rather an island position within the coverage of the *Spiegel*.

Regarding the motives and causes of the mission in Afghanistan, religion has an important significance (no. 1). Religion correlates with violence and irrationality in general and in particular with war, terrorism, and fanaticism. The mission in Afghanistan, as part of the War on Terror, is synonymous with the war of religion(s) and equates to the "Clash of civilizations". Paradoxically, the *Spiegel* often uses religious emblems of death allegories for its construction of meaning, for example, the cross/grave (no. 1), the cemetery (no. 7), or the abyss (no. 2); yet at the same time, it promotes its degradation. While religion is perceived as being the key cause of the war, the history is an unprecedented warning sign. On the one hand, image no. 3 refers directly to the Vietnam War with the traumatic effects it had and on the other hand indirectly refers to the First and Second World Wars with its anonymous mass graves (no. 1). Furthermore, the mission becomes related to the Afghanistan War of the USSR during the Cold War in the 1980s and – showing a downed Soviet helicopter as prime object on the cover – is set on the same image level (especially intriguing!) without further indication (no. 7).

The resolute skepticism concerning military intervention is very prominent within the coverage of the *Spiegel* in 2001. 'Danger' and 'Death' related to Afghanistan are omnipresent. According to image no. 7, Afghanistan is "a cemetery of superpowers". A "fiasco at the Hindukush" (*Spiegel* 5 November 2001, 140) seems to be looming, visualized through a huge mushroom detonation cloud. Kabul is designated as "pandora's box" (*Spiegel* 3 December 2001, 178), Masar-i-Sharif (the German-run mission headquarters) as the "terrain of death" (ibid., 182).

While the TIME cover 'Aisha' and the pictures from Abu Ghraib point to universal values – of course in one way or another –, the *Spiegel* rather adheres to a particularistic worldview: "Our world is different to yours" (title in *Spiegel* 8 October 2001). To demonstrate this, there is a specific image of a refugee camp and of a bazar, as an image of the Other, or rather the 'strange' (ibid., 147 et seq.). The same edition underlines this with the title "Religious insanity.

The return of the Middle Ages" in the usual manner of (anti) religious rhetoric. Through the use of icons, among them the crescent, Osama bin Laden, crusaders, and the burning towers of the World Trade Center, Islam and Christianity are visualized under the paradigm of "violence" (ibid., 1). The edition of 22 December 2001 (*Spiegel* 22 December 2001, 1) contrasts "religious insanity", "dignity", and "intellectual tradition" of the "Belief of the Non-Believers" with icons such as the writer Johann Wolfgang von Goethe, Marilyn Monroe, and the female national emblem of the French Republic (Marianne) from Eugène Delacroix's famous painting "For the liberty of the people". The ideal point of reference is hereby formed though enlightenment, humanity, and the secularity of Western culture. To underline this, the magazine says: "Her [the Western culture's] intellectual tradition is worth being defended – even against Islam" (ibid., 50). At the point where religion and politics form a symbiosis, they turn irrational and justify wars. Then they become a part of the other. Yet, the separation of the two stands for peace, reason, and knowledge and is therefore essential for the construction of 'us' in the *Spiegel*.

This inter-iconicity – making use of other covers from the magazine on the same topic – already provides a lot of additional insights, all the more so, if one takes other academic sources regarding the deployment of German troops to Afghanistan into account. For instance, the results of the image analysis here complement Bulmahn, Fiebig, and Sender's study (2008, 109f.), which examines the media coverage of 2006 concluding that it has been widely negative about the Bundeswehr in Afghanistan. This corresponds with the analysis of the "Tagesschau" (the prime news on German TV) between October 2006 and October 2008, which also has "a consistently negative image of the international ISAF Operation, yet also of the German ISAF-Mission" (Jungbauer 2010, 114).

Zeitgeist, Political Rhetoric, and Theoretical Contextualization

Any interpretation of the findings is dependent on the theory used. It is not the place here to introduce a specific theory, be it IR theories, for example, strategic culture, neo-liberal intergovernmentalism, critical security studies or foreign policy approaches, for example, civilian power, discourse-bound identity theory, neo-classical realism. Though all of them would certainly refer to some analytical features of German foreign policy, which are recurrent themes in the literature, be it 'pacifism' or Germany as a power of peace (*Friedensmacht*). The main tendency of pacifism in Germany can be traced back to the lost Second World War and the mental and physical destruction that it caused, not only in the world but also in Germany itself. Pacifist statements always had their place in the debates about German foreign policy after the rearmament debate – for instance, the "ferocity of anti-war mood in Germany" (Bredow 2008, 150) surged on the occasion of the second Gulf War 1990/1991, when three quarters of the population rejected a military participation of Germany (Kaiser and Becher 1992, 48). Pacifist arguments became more defensive in the late 1990s since non-intervention and humanitarian assistance could not prevent genocide in Rwanda (1994) and Srebrenica (1995) and the Responsibility to Protect evolved as an emerging norm from the Kosovo war.

The US militarily intervened in Afghanistan in order to fight Al Qaida and capture Osama bin Laden. Therefore, the "unconditional solidarity with the US" prevailed in 2001 (for the 'War on Terror', OEF and ISAF). Between 2002 and 2005, 'security for Germany', as formulated by Germany's minister of defense, Struck, 'humanitarian commitment' (2006–2009), and since the end of 2009 'security in Afghanistan', have become the dominant elements of the discourse (Müller and Wolff 2011, 213ff.). Over time, issues of state-building, humanitarian assistance, and the peace process were also raised (Leithner 2009). Overall, the political discourse on the Afghanistan mission has been rather homogenous and continuous throughout the twenty years of commitment. One can merely identify a slight shift of emphasis in the legitimization in the first decade (Harnisch 2011, 244). Yet overall, the statements in parliament give an uninspired impression[10]: "The politically intended weak commitment corresponds accurately with the weak statement" (Müller and Wolff 2011, 217). The overwhelming majority of German Members of Parliament agreed with the commitment of the Bundeswehr in Afghanistan but avoided more extensive debates on the mission (Lagassé and Mello 2018). Merely a small pacifist formation, mainly represented in parliament by the Left Party (*Die Linke*), issues criticism toward the government's promise of 'unconditional solidarity' and in the progress of the conflict, openly criticizes the US and NATO. As an opponent to the mission, *Die Linke* follows the catch phrase 'No more War!', criticizes the 'logic of war' of the other parties, and bemoans the civilian casualties and the human rights abuses. It was only when the Alternative für Deutschland (AfD) entered the Bundestag in 2017 that critical voices regarding the mission increased.[11] While the supporters are clearly in the majority in the political debate and therefore the arguments for a legitimacy of the mission are hegemonic, the *Spiegel* is clearly and permanently an adversary of the mission from the beginning. This oppositional public sphere to the hegemonic pro-intervention discourse of the political class is exemplarily formed by the *Spiegel*. Formative arguments of the pro-camp in the political debate, such as "humanitarian aid", "human rights", "state-building" or "democratization" (Leithner 2009, 51ff.), are practically nonexistent in the media discourse on Afghanistan. Furthermore, a certain ignorance is shown by the *Spiegel* discourse toward international institutions and treaties, for example, toward the UN, NATO, and international law. Rather, the magazine follows (national) pacifist arguments, which are represented in parliament by members of *Die Linke* only, which is clearly in the minority. Hence, the *Spiegel* takes on an oppositional control function in this respect (Strohmeier 2004, 72 et seq). The pacifist reporting of the *Spiegel* correlates with the increasingly dismissive attitude in the public (Miller 2010, 1), which could motivate further research on the relationship between the media and foreign policy.[12]

The medial form of illustration follows typical enemy image constructions. This is prototypical for the *Spiegel* in the case of Afghanistan and can be seen in similar ways in the coverage of magazines such as *Focus*, *Stern* and in the *Bild* newspaper (Becker 2002, 148 et seq):[13] "These print editions function through a mix of image language and symbols, with threatening masses of people, angry men, veiled women" (Becker 2002, 149). Particularities of the medial discourse that have been hinted at in this analysis and that are commonly known in the media sciences can be summarized under the catchwords 'emotionalization', 'personalization', 'dramatization', 'eventization'. Even the *Spiegel* follows boulevard typical forms of illustration, which comes as a surprise, as the *Spiegel* is commonly not known to be a boulevard magazine.

In the seven years after 2013, no other picture related to Afghanistan made it on the cover. Only when the Taliban took over the country in the summer of 2021, the disastrous withdrawal of German forces became a top media *sujet* again (cf. below). In "The return of fear" (*Spiegel* 21 August 2021), the bearded Taliban warriors make it on the title again – the othering construction of the *Spiegel* remains intact. Yet surprisingly, the cover of 28 August 2021 partly breaks with the particularistic and orientalist impressions: for the first time, there are victims on the cover and the people's dress as well as the traffic around could be attributed to any modern city. "The abandoned" look stupendously universal. But the othering of the US remains; the cover text does not refer to Germany at all, it is not Merkel's but "Joe Biden's fiasco" (Figure 10.3).

Visual Analysis

11 The return of fear.

12 Afghanistan – THE HORRIBLE ENDGAME – The new terror. The Abandoned. Joe Biden's fiasco.

Figure 10.3 *Spiegel* cover images on Afghanistan, 2021.

Conclusion

The article started from the premise that the "iconic turn" has established visuality as a promising research program in the social sciences in general and IR in particular. Yet, the main inroads are in the field of Critical Security Studies while foreign policy by and large remained untouched. The arguments presented here propose to make use of visual studies as they can be a valuable tool for analyzing foreign policy legitimation and contribute to a more critical understanding of FPA (Brummer 2022). The introduced model may serve to analyze various kinds of 'text-image constellations' which are typical not only in political reporting (news) but also in political protests (posters in mass demonstrations, graffiti, etc.). The hermeneutical process of the four-step model presented here can be used for re-constructing and critical purposes alike, that is, a better understanding of in- and exclusion processes, friend-foe dichotomies, clichés, etc. Another asset concerns the interdisciplinary followability and the model's openness for method triangulation. Regarding contents, the article deals with the German military intervention in Afghanistan, as depicted by the prestigious news magazine, the *Spiegel*. By doing so, a significant counter-discourse in the media could be revealed representing a large part of the public, who were unconvinced by the arguments of the political elite. In theoretical terms, the *Spiegel* covers demonstrate Germany's foreign policy identity of pacifism. What is more, as a side effect, important features of the *Spiegel*'s reporting on foreign policy issues came to the fore: from the objection to universal values to clichés of orientalism.

Notes

1 Paul (2008) speaks of "a century of images" and Diers (2006, 12, our translation from German) adds: "Never before were there as many images".

2. Images serve immanent functions of structuring and memorizing for human memory as Social Psychology (e.g., Welzer 2001) and Neurobiology (e.g., Hüther 2004) note.
3. The argument of 'the power of images' is also omnipresent in academic discourses (cf., Bredar 2011; Krings 2006).
4. It has to be recalled that Foucault spent his first chapter on an extensive visual analysis in his ground-breaking study "The order of things" (1970).
5. Iconic images are world pictures that are widely disseminated and 'made history' (Hansen 2015, 6). She (ibid., 3) gives the following examples of "iconic images":

> the raising of the flag at Iwo Jima (1945), the shooting of a suspected Vietcong in Saigon during the Tet Offensive (1968), the naked girl fleeing the napalm bombing in Vietnam (1972), the Bosnian prisoners behind barbed wire (1992), the falling World Trade Center Towers on 11 September (2001), the toppling of Saddam Hussein's statue (2003), the charred, lynched contractors from Fallujah (2004), and the dying Iranian activist Neda Agha Soltan (2009).

6. The attribution of importance is also shared by politicians. For instance, US President Obama blocked the release of up to 2,000 photographs of alleged prisoner abuse (in Abu Ghraib) on the grounds that they would "inflame anti-American public opinion and put our troops in greater danger" (cf. Hansen 2015, 3)
7. Please note that studies on the reception of collages are difficult since they can hardly construct an experimental situation: What contextual information should experimental reviewers owe to 'properly understand' the image?
8. Bleiker (2015) has called for an "assemblage approach", in this respect.
9. Panofsky is often accused of having neglected the third step of this model, the reconstruction of the images' formal structure (Imdahl 1994, 300).
10. Jacobi et al. (2011) assess this as "a case of failing security communication".
11. AfD Party leader Alexander Gauland's first speech in the parliament was exactly on Afghanistan denouncing the engagement on nationalist, Bismarck-prone grounds (Gauland 2017).
12. Regarding the relationship between mass media and politics, the findings would support the interdependence thesis (cf. Reiser 1994, 341).
13. Following his findings, only the *Frankfurter Allgemeine Zeitung* is excluded from this assessment.

References

Primary Sources

Der Spiegel. 2001. "11. September 01: Was wirklich geschah", No. 49, 3 December.
Der Spiegel. 2001. "Abgrund Afghanistan", No. 40, 1 October.
Der Spiegel. 2001. "Der Glaube der Ungläubigen", No. 52, 22 December.
Der Spiegel. 2001. "Der religiöse Wahn", No. 41, 8 October.
Der Spiegel. 2001. "Ernstfall für Rot-Grün", No. 46, 12 November.
Der Spiegel. 2001. "Falle Afghanistan: Amerikas heilloser Bombenkrieg und das Gespenst von Vietnam", No. 45, 5 November.
Der Spiegel. 2002. "Deutsche an allen Fronten", No. 11, 11 March.
Der Spiegel. 2006. "Die Deutschen müssen das Töten lernen", No. 47, 20 November.
Der Spiegel. 2009. "Wann dürfen Deutsche töten?", No. 49, 30 November.
Der Spiegel. 2010. "Friedhof der Supermächte", No. 4, 25 January.
Der Spiegel. 2010. "Im Krieg – Deutsche Soldaten über das Töten und Sterben in Afghanistan", No. 16, 19 April.
Der Spiegel. 2010. "Task Force 373 – Die Afghanistan-Protokolle: Amerikas geheimer Krieg", No. 30, 26 July.
Der Spiegel. 2011. "Als Deutschland in den Krieg zog – Afghanistan: Die Geschichte eines Irrtums", No. 36, 5 September.
Der Spiegel. 2021. "Afghanistan – Das schreckliche Finale – Der neue Terror. Die Zurückgelassenen. Das Fiasko des Joe Biden", No. 35, 28 August.
Der Spiegel. 2021. "Die Rückkehr der Angst", No. 34, 21 August.
The Economist. 2004. "Resign, Rumsfeld", 8 May.
Time. 2010. "What Happens if We Leave Afghanistan", 9 August.

Secondary Sources

Adler, Emanuel. 2013. "Constructivism in International Relations: Sources, Contributions, and Debates". *Handbook of International Relations* 2: 112–144.
Ahäll, Linda. 2009. "Images, Popular Culture, Aesthetics, Emotions – The Future of International Politics?" *Political Perspectives Graduate Journal* 3(1): 1–44.
Andersen, Rune S., and Frank Möller. 2013. "Engaging the Limits of Visibility: Photography, Security, and Surveillance." *Security Dialogue* 44(3): 203–221.
Barthes, Roland. 1989. *Die helle Kammer. Bemerkungen zur Photographie*. Frankfurt am Main: Suhrkamp.
Becker, Jörg. 2002. "Afghanistan: Der Krieg und die Medien." In *Medien zwischen Krieg und Frieden*, edited by Ulrich Albrecht and Jörg Becker. Baden-Baden: Nomos, 139–172.
Beuthner, Michael, and Stephan A. Weichert. 2003. "Zur Einführung: Bilder des Terrors – Terror der Bilder." In *Bilder des Terrors - Terror der Bilder? Krisenberichterstattung am und nach dem 11. September*, edited by Michael Beuthner, Joachim Buttler, Sandra Fröhlich, Irene Neverla and Stephan A. Weichert. Köln: von Halem, 10–25.
Bleiker, Roland. 2015. "Pluralist Methods for Visual Global Politics." *Millenium* 43(3): 872–890.
Bohnsack, Ralf. 2006. "Die Dokumentarische Methode der Bildinterpretation in der Forschungspraxis." In *Bildinterpretation und Bildverstehen. Methodische Ansätze aus Sozialwissenschaftlicher, Kunst- und Medienpädagogischer Perspektive*, edited by Winfried Marotzki and Horst Niesyto. Wiesbaden: VS Verlag für Sozialwissenschaften, 45–75.
Bredar, John. 2011. *Die Macht der Bilder – Amerikanische Präsidenten und ihre Inszenierung*. Hamburg: National Geographic Deutschland.
Bredow, Wilfried von. 2008. *Die Außenpolitik der Bundesrepublik Deutschland*. Wiesbaden: VS Verlag für Sozialwissenschaften.
Brummer, Klaus. 2022. "Toward a (More) Critical FPA". *Foreign Policy Analysis* 18(1): orab031.
Bulmer, Sandy, and Margo Buchanan-Oliver. 2006. "Visual Rhetoric and Global Advertising Imagery." *Journal of Marketing Communication* 12(1): 49–61.
Bulmahn, Thomas, Rüdiger Fiebig, and Wolfgang Sender. 2008. *Sicherheits- und Verteidigungspolitisches Meinungsklima in der Bundesrepublik Deutschland. Ergebnisse der Bevölkerungsbefragung 2006, Research Report 84*. Strausberg: Sozialwissenschaftliches Institut der Bundeswehr.
Burri, Regula V. 2008. "Bilder als soziale Praxis: Grundlegungen Einer Soziologie des Visuellen." *Zeitschrift für Soziologie* 4: 342–358.
Buzan, Barry, Ole Wæver, and Jaap de Wilde. 1998. *Security: A New Framework for Analysis*. Boulder: Lynne Rienner.
Campbell, David. 2007. "Poststructuralism". In *International Relations Theories. Discipline and Diversity*, edited by Tim Dunne, Milja Kurki and Steve Smith. Oxford: Oxford University Press, 203–228.
Carver, Terrell. 2010. "Cinematic Ontologies and Viewer Epistemologies: Knowing International Politics as Moving Images." *Global Society* 24(3): 421–431.
Casas, Andreu, and Nora Webb Williams. 2019. "Images that Matter: Online Protests and the Mobilizing Role of Pictures." *Political Research Quarterly* 72(2): 360–375.
Der Derian, James. 2000. "Virtuous War/Virtual Theory." *International Affairs* 76(4): 771–788.
Deleuze, Gilles. 1968. *Différence et Repetition*. Paris: PUF.
Diers, Michael. 2006. *Fotografie. Film. Video. Beiträge zu einer kritischen Theorie des Bildes*. Hamburg: Philo&Philo Fine Arts.
Dodds, Klaus. 2010. "Popular Geopolitics and Cartoons: Representing Power Relations, Repetition and Resistance." *Critical African Studies* 2(4): 113–131
Esser, Sonja M. 2000. *Das Kreuz – ein Symbol kultureller Identität? Der Diskurs über das "Kruzifix-Urteil" (1995) aus kulturwissenschaftlicher Perspektive*. Münster and München: Waxmann.
Fairclough, Norman. 2001. *Language and Power*. London: Pearson Education Limited.
Freistein, Katja, Frank Gadinger, and Christine Unrau. 2020. *From the Global to the Everyday: Anti-Globalization Metaphors in Trump's and Salvini's Political Language*. (Global Cooperation Research Papers 24). Duisburg: Käte Hamburger Kolleg / Centre for Global Cooperation Research.
Gauland, Alexander. 2017. Rede im Deutschen Bundestag am 21. November 2017 zum Tagesordnungspunkt 4: "Antrag der Bundesregierung: Fortsetzung der Beteiligung bewaffneter deutscher Streitkräfte am NATO-geführten Einsatz Resolute Support für die Ausbildung, Beratung und Unterstützung der afghanischen nationalen Verteidigungs- und Sicherheitskräfte in Afghanistan". *Deutscher Bundestag – Stenografischer Bericht, 2. Sitzung, 19. Wahlperiode, Plenarprotokoll 19/2*, 63A. Available from: http://dipbt.bundestag.de/doc/btp/19/19002.pdf.

Grayson, Kyle, Matt Davies, and Simon Philpott. 2009. "Pop Goes IR? Researching the Popular Culture–World Politics Continuum." *Politics* 29(3): 155–163.

Hansen, Lene. 2011. "Theorizing the Image for Security Studies: Visual Securitization and the Muhammed Cartoon Crisis." *European Journal of International Relations* 17(1): 51–74.

Hansen, Lene. 2015. "How Images Make World Politics: International Icons and the Case of Abu Ghraib." *Review of International Studies* 41(2): 263–288.

Harnisch, Sebastian. 2011. "Deutschlands Rolle in Afghanistan: State-Building Dilemmata einer Zivilmacht." In *Zehn Jahre Deutschland in Afghanistan*, edited by Klaus Brummer and Stefan Fröhlich. Wiesbaden: VS Verlag für Sozialwissenschaften, 223–252.

Hasenmueller, Christine. 1978. "Panofsky, Iconography, and Semiotics." *The Journal of Aesthetics and Art Criticism* 36(3): 289–301.

Hebel, Udo J., and Christoph Wagner. 2011. *Political Cultures and Political Iconographies: Approaches, Perspectives, Case Studies from Europe and America*. Berlin: De Gruyter.

Heck, Axel, and Gabi Schlag. 2013. "Securitizing Images: The Female Body and the War in Afghanistan." *European Journal of International Relations* 19(4): 891–913.

Heinrich, Horst-Alfred, and Bernhard Stahl. 2012. "Uroš Predić' Kosovo Mädchen – Sterben und Töten für das Gute". In *Jahrbuch für Politik und Geschichte* (3), edited by Claudia Fröhlich and Harald Schmid. Stuttgart: Steiner, 221–238.

Heinrich, Horst-Alfred, and Bernhard Stahl. 2017. "Pictorial Stereotypes and Images in the Euro debt Crisis." *National Identities* 19(1): 109–127.

Hüther, Gerald. 2004. *Die Macht der inneren Bilder. Wie Visionen das Gehirn, den Menschen und die Welt verändern*. **Göttingen**: Vandenhoeck & Ruprecht.

Imdahl, Max. 1994. "Ikonik. Bilder und ihre Anschauung." In: *Was ist ein Bild?*, edited by Gottfried Boehm. München: Fink, 300–324.

Jacobi, Daniel, Gunther Hellmann, and Sebastian Nieke. 2011. "Deutschlands Verteidigung am Hindukusch: Ein Fall Misslingender Sicherheitskommunikation." In *Zehn Jahre Deutschland in Afghanistan*, edited by Klaus Brummer and Stefan Fröhlich, Wiesbaden: VS Verlag für Sozialwissenschaften, 171–196.

Jakobsen, Peter Viggo. 2000. "Focus on the CNN Effect Misses the Point: The Real Media Impact on Conflict Management Is Invisible and Indirect." *Journal of Peace Research* 37(2): 131–143.

Jungbauer, Stefan. 2010. *Die Bundeswehr in Afghanistan. Die Innerstaatlichen Restriktionen des Deutschen ISAF-Einsatzes*. Hamburg: Dr. Kovac.

Jungblut, Marc, and Ieva Zakareviciute. 2019. "Do Pictures Tell a Different Story? A multimodal Frame Analysis of the 2014 Israel-Gaza Conflict." *Journalism Practice* 13(2): 206–228.

Kaiser, Karl, and Klaus Becher. 1992. "Germany and the Iraq Conflict." In *Western Europe and the Gulf : A Study of West European Reactions to the Gulf War Carried out Under the Auspices of the Institute for Security Studies of Western European Union*, edited by Nicole Gnesotto and John Roper. Paris: The Institute for Security Studies, 39–70.

Kirkpatrick, Erika. 2015. "Visuality, Photography and Media in International Relations Theory: A Review." *Media, War and Conflict* 8(2): 199–212.

Krings, Annette. 2006. *Die Macht der Bilder. Zur Bedeutung der Historischen Fotografien des Holocaust in der politischen Bildungsarbeit*. Berlin: LIT-Verlag.

Lagassé, Philippe, and Patrick A. Mello. 2018. "The Unintended Consequences of Parliamentary Involvement: Elite Collusion and Afghanistan Deployments in Canada and Germany." *British Journal of Politics and International Relations* 20(1): 135–157.

Leithner, Anika. 2009. *Shaping German Foreign Policy. History, Memory and National Interest*. Boulder, CO: First Forum Press.

Marotzki, Winfried, and Katja Stoetzer. 2006. "Die Geschichte Hinter den Bildern. Annäherungen an Eine Methode und Methodologie der Bildinterpretation in Biographie- und Bildungstheoretischer Absicht." In *Bildinterpretation und Bildverstehen. Methodische Ansätze aus Sozialwissenschaftlicher, kunst- und medienpädagogischer Perspektive*, edited by Winfried Marotzki and Horst Niesyto. Wiesbaden: VS Verlag für Sozialwissenschaften, 15–44.

Miller, Charles A. 2010. *Endgame in Afghanistan? Explaining the Decline in Support for the War in Afghanistan in the United States, the United Kingdom, Canada, Australia, France and Germany*. US Army War College: Letort Papers. Available from: https://press.armywarcollege.edu/cgi/viewcontent.cgi?article=1345&context=monographs.

Milliken, Jennifer. 1999. "The Study of Discourse in International Relations: A Critique of Research and Methods." *European Journal of International Relations* 5(2), 225–254.
Mitchell, W. J. T. 1984. "What Is an Image?" *New Literary History* 15(3): 503–537.
Mitchell, W. J. T. 1994. *Picture Theory: Essays on Verbal and Visual Representation.* Chicago: Chicago University Press.
Mitchell, W. J. T. 2005. *What Do Pictures Want? The Lives and Loves of Images.* Chicago and London: The University of Chicago Press.
Moeller, Frank. 2007. "Photographic Interventions in Post-9/11 Security Policy." *Security Dialogue* 38(2): 179–196.
Müller, Harald, and Jonas Wolff. 2011. "Demokratischer Krieg am Hindukusch? Eine kritische Analyse der Bundestagsdebatten zur deutschen Afghanistanpolitik 2001–2011." In *Zehn Jahre Deutschland in Afghanistan*, edited by Klaus Brummer and Stefan Fröhlich. Wiesbaden: VS Verlag für Sozialwissenschaften, 197–222.
Müller, Marion G. 2008. "Visual Competence: A New Paradigm for Studying Visuals in the Social Sciences." *Visual Studies* 23(2): 101–112.
Müller, Marion G., and Thomas Knieper. 2005. "Krieg ohne Bilder?" In *War Visions. Bildkommunikation und Krieg*, edited by Marion G. Müller and Thomas Knieper. Köln: von Halem, 7–21.
Nowey, Waldemar. 2009. *Kriegsgräber Mahnen zum Frieden und Erinnern an Krieg, Vertreibung, Gefangenschaft, Heimkehr: Nachdenkliches zwischen Krieg und Frieden.* Mering bei Augsburg.
Panofsky, Erwin. 1978. *Sinn und Deutung in der Bildenden Kunst.* Köln: DuMont.
Paul, Gerhard. 2008. "Das Jahrhundert der Bilder. Die visuelle Geschichte und der Bildkanon des kulturellen Gedächtnisses." In *Das Jahrhundert der Bilder. Band II: 1949 bis Heute*, edited by Gerhard Paul. Bonn: Bundeszentrale für Politische Bildung, 14–39.
Paul, Gerhard. 2009. "Kriegsbilder – Bilderkriege." *Aus Politik und Zeitgeschichte* 31: 39–46.
Prosser, Jon D. 2013. "Visual Methodology. Toward a More Seeing Research." In *Collecting and Interpreting Qualitative Materials*, edited by Norman K. Denzin and Yvonna S. Lincoln, London: Sage, 177–212.
Przyborski, Aglaja, and Günther Haller, eds. 2014. *Das politische Bild. Situation Room: Ein Foto – vier Analysen. Sozialwissenschaftliche Ikonologie: Qualitative Bild- und Videointerpretation (6).* Opladen: Verlag Barbara Budrich.
Reiser, Stefan. 1994. "Politik und Massenmedien im Wahlkampf, Thematisierungsstrategien und Wahlkampfmanagement." *Media Perspektiven* (7): 341–348.
Rorty, Richard. 1968. *The Linguistic Turn: Recent Essays in Philosophical Method.* Chicago, London: University of Chicago Press.
Rose, Gillian. 2016. *Visual Methodologies: An Introduction to Researching with Visual Materials.* Los Angeles, et al.: Sage.
Sartori, Giovanni. 1970. "Concept Misformation in Comparative Politics." *The American Political Science Review* 64(4): 1033–1053.
Schlag, Gabi. 2016. "Imagining Security: A Visual Methodology for Security Studies." In *Transformations of Security Studies: Dialogues, Diversity and Discipline*, edited by Gabi Schlag, Julian Junk and Christopher Daase. London and New York: Routledge, 173–189.
Schlag, Gabi, and Axel Heck, eds. 2020. *Visualität und Weltpolitik. Praktiken des Zeigens und Sehens in den Internationalen Beziehungen.* Wiesbaden: VS Verlag für Sozialwissenschaften.
Shapiro, Michael J. 1988. *The Politics of Representation: Writing Practices in Biography, Photography, and Policy Analysis.* Madison, WI: The University of Wisconsin Press.
Strohmeier, Gerd. 2004. *Politik und Massenmedien. Eine Einführung.* Baden-Baden: Nomos.
Tseronis, Assimakis. 2021. "From Visual Rhetoric to Multimodal Argumentation: Exploring the Rhetorical and Argumentative Relevance of Multimodal Figures on the Covers of The Economist." *Visual Communication* 20(3): 374–396.
Van Veeren, Elspeth. S. 2011. "Captured by the Camera's Eye: Guantánamo and the Shifting Frame of the Global War on Terror". *Review of International Studies*, 37(4): 1721–1749.
Virilio, Paul. 1989. *War and Cinema: The Logistics of Perception.* New York: Verso.
Welzer, Harald, ed. 2001. *Das soziale Gedächtnis. Geschichte, Erinnerung, Tradierung.* Hamburg: Hamburger Edition.
Williams, Michael C. 2003. "Words, Images, Enemies: Securitization and International Politics." *International Studies Quarterly* 47(4): 511–531.

11
Emotion Discourse Analysis
Simon Koschut

Introduction

The growth of research on emotion in International Relations (IR) has produced a significant body of literature in recent years. This body of literature has raised a number of interesting questions, debates, and theoretical positions regarding the agentic properties of foreign policy actors and how they are embedded in international structures. A major challenge in the study of emotions in foreign policy is methodological. Emotions represent subjectively perceived ephemeral phenomena, the recording and effect of which can be hard to trace. In the realm of politics, we have neither direct access to emotional feeling states and intentions, nor can we adequately retrieve the felt emotional reception and experience of foreign policy actors. The study of emotion discourse in Foreign Policy Analysis (FPA) involves a project that seeks to systematically integrate emotions within FPA. I propose that the problem of the subjective ontology of emotion can be resolved by shifting the analytical focus from their internal phenomenological appraisal by individuals to their representational and intersubjective articulation and communication within social spheres. Emotion Discourse Analysis (EDA) is concerned with how foreign policy actors talk about emotions and how they employ emotion categories when talking about subjects, events, or social relations. Emotionalized language can be strategically used to construct social hierarchies by, for example, assigning praise or blame to actions or attributes and by verbally contrasting various emotions with alternative emotion categories within the discursive construction of reality. Theoretically, such an understanding views emotions as socially constructed representations of meaning that are linked to conceptions of identity and power. The chapter is structured as follows: after a brief review of the literature, I will present a methodological framework for studying emotions in foreign policy discourses. The framework will then be empirically illustrated using NATO's foreign policy discourse vis-à-vis Russia over the annexation of Crimea. The chapter closes with some reflections on the strengths and limitations of this approach.

Emotions in Foreign Policy Analysis

Even though war, nationalism, and international conflict are almost intuitively associated with strong emotions, FPA has only recently integrated them more systematically into its theories. This is even more surprising since classical FPA explicitly referred to emotions as key analytical variables. For example, Hans Morgenthau (1948, 78) claimed that fear is what drives nation-states into war: "(P)ersonal fears are thus transformed into anxiety for the nation". In a similar way, Arnold Wolfers (1952, 498) suggested that part of the reason why nations pursue policies is "because they satisfy their pride, heighten their sense of self-esteem or reduce their fears". Early realist and liberal theories acknowledged the role of emotions but generally assigned them a "taken-for-granted-status" (Crawford 2000). Despite their obvious relevance, emotions were completely sidelined when the rational actor paradigm took hold of IR in the 1960s. There were important exceptions, however. Emerging in the 1970s, some studies in Political Psychology as well as in Strategic Studies took emotions seriously, exploring the relationship between cognitive and emotional factors in political decision-making affecting security policy (Allison 1971; Janis 1972; Jervis 1976; Jervis et al. 1985; Schelling 1960; Welch Larson 1985).

Building on this tradition of studies in Political Psychology and Strategic Studies as well as recent neuroscientific research, a first major strand in FPA seeks to understand the role that emotions play in diplomacy and foreign policy decision-making (Alexieva 2016; Dolan 2016; Fettweis 2013; Markwica 2018; McDermott 2014; Mercer 2013; Reinke de Buitrago 2016; Sasley 2010; Schilling 2015; Stein 2013). Another line of scholarship engages with the role of emotions in face-to-face diplomacy (Hall 2015; Holmes 2018; Jones and Clark 2019; Keys and Yorke 2019; Liberman 2006; Rosen 2005; Wong 2016). Some scholars have recently widened the concept of interpersonal trust by exploring its emotional basis (Michel 2012; Rathbun 2012; Wheeler 2018). Yet another strand of literature investigates how foreign policy leaders and the general public emotionally react to events (Clément et al. 2017; Edney-Browne 2019; Graham 2014; Hall 2017; Hall and Ross 2019; Small and Lerner 2008; Van Hoef and O'Connor 2019; Widmaier 2010). These and other studies have made important contributions to our understanding of the role of emotions in FPA. They have demonstrated how emotions play an intrinsic role in the process of rational decision-making as well as in the construction of intergroup identities relating to questions of war and peace and thus challenged many traditional assumptions of FPA by suggesting that foreign policy actors behave rationally *because* they are emotional actors, not despite of it (Crawford 2000; Mercer 2013).

Building on a rich tradition of contributions from sociological and cultural theories, a second major strand in FPA research investigates how emotion structures and shapes political identities, communities, and practices (Bially Mattern 2011; Crawford 2014; Hall 2015; Hymans 2006; Koschut 2014; Pace and Bilgic 2019). Some of these have focused on the role of emotional language and discourse in foreign policy making (Ahäll and Gregory 2015; Danchev 2006; Eberle 2019; Eroukhmanoff 2019; Fattah and Fierke 2009; Hutchison 2016; Koschut 2017, 2020; Leep 2010; Saurette 2006; Solomon 2015; Van Rythoven 2015). Yet, there has been strikingly little elaboration of appropriate methods and criteria for studying emotion discourse in FPA, understood as the words, phrases, narratives, expressions, and representations that in some way symbolically refer to emotion and anything that is visual such as photographs, artwork, and images. This raises an important methodological question: if the power of language includes an affective dimension, then the question is how can researchers analytically extract the emotion potential and emotionalizing effects built into foreign policy discourse? When I say "potential", I mean that emotions in texts and other forms of discourses do not automatically generate political effects. This depends on a number of other factors, such as audience reception, situational awareness, or social norms.

Emotion Discourse Analysis

In a step toward fostering methodological engagement and dialogue on this issue, I propose a framework for empirical research of emotional discourse in FPA. The goal is to offer more specific ways to integrate the consideration of emotion into existing research, particularly that of a constructivist vein. A social constructivist perspective emphasizes the importance of the intersubjective and sociocultural character of emotions (Averill 1980; Harré 1986). In line with this view, it is argued here that emotions involve institutionalized responses that allow foreign policy actors to participate in world politics using shared meaning structures, or as Fattah and Fierke (2009, 70) put it, "emotions (are) socially meaningful expressions, which depend on shared customs, uses and institutions". In short, a social constructivist perspective argues that individual emotions and their expressions are cultural products that owe their meaning and purpose to learned social rules. What we feel often depends on what our social environment tells us that we should feel.

Why is it necessary to study emotions through discourse analysis? Emotions play an important role in language-based processes at the international level. Take the example of naming and shaming: if language power is able to inflict social suffering (the loss of social status or ontological insecurity) upon agents, such discursive identity constructions implicate an affective dimension. For, if an actor can be shamed into changing its behavior through non-physical power, it must *feel* the negative social implications of such power in order to be persuaded or forced into compliance. Otherwise, these discursive mechanisms would be useless. If emotions underpin the meanings within and effects of foreign policy discourses, they need to be identified and made accountable for based on empirical research. For reasons of analytical clarity and due to limited space, I will focus on the textual dimension of discourse in this chapter. I am not concerned here with the non-verbal and visual dimension of discourse, although I recognize that this is an important area of research (see e.g., Bleiker 2009; Hansen 2011, and Stahl in this volume). This chapter takes discourses, understood as "framings of meaning and lenses of interpretation" (Hansen 2006, 7), as a point of entry for the study of emotion in FPA (see also Ostermann and Sjöstedt in this volume). I propose three criteria that the study of emotion discourse must answer to, which revolve around (1) selecting appropriate texts, (2) mapping the verbal expression of emotions (emotion potential of texts), and (3) interpreting and contextualizing their political effects (emotionalization effects of texts).

Step One: Developing Research Questions and Making Text Selections

The point of departure for any EDA is to compile a dossier of sources produced by the actor(s) under study. The focus should be on emotions that are either explicitly expressed or tacitly implied over a range of sources and within or across a coherent time period. This may include a variety of textual sources, including (but not limited to) official statements (speeches, press releases, parliamentary debates), legal texts (treaties, conventions, agreements), biographical texts (diaries, autobiographies, personal notes), media texts (newspaper articles, interviews, editorials), and even popular culture (poems, novels, songs). While the selection of texts ultimately depends on the research question, there are some things to consider when studying the emotions within these texts.

To begin with, one would assume that the more formal and official the character of the text the more implicit and circumscribed emotional expressions are likely to be. Hence, a biographical text or a novel is more likely to contain more explicit and outspoken emotional statements than say a legal text. That, however, should not mislead researchers to conclude that legal texts do not contain emotional meanings at all, only that these are more concealed behind legal prose and style. It is widely recognized that legal cultures are not emotion-free spaces but deeply intertwined with emotional norms, rules, experience, and expectations (Nussbaum 2003; Posner 1999). In some cases, legal texts may, for example, even prescribe specific emotions, such as the legal practice of dueling, which is based on the emotion of honor. Still, some texts in FPA may be more emotionally loaded than others. A clever way to conduct an EDA is thus to combine different textual genre to get a more comprehensive picture of and better access to the emotions involved. This may not be confined to single actors but includes a collection of different sources of text as well as spontaneous material or interviews. It should be pointed out again that EDA is rooted in a social, representational ontology of emotions rather than aiming at the individual level of analysis. It is, thus, less interested in emotions *within* individual political leaders but more inclined to trace emotional patterns *between* individual political leaders and the societies they represent.

The researcher should then search for a small number of canonical texts by charismatic authorities that may serve as emotional "landmarks" (Laclau and Mouffe 1985). Such landmark texts usually involve foundational or transformative moments or crises during which emotions are likely to be more prevalent and outspoken. This is not to say that emotions cannot be studied under *normal* circumstances. Rather, the focus on foundational or transformative moments represents a pragmatic move to study emotions at times when they become most acutely visible (Crawford 2000, 130; Ross 2006, 211). Moreover, dramatic events challenge and often transform established emotional attachments and meanings, which arguably makes them more relevant to FPA (Bleiker and Hutchison 2008, 129; see also Hansen 2006).

While the initial focus on a small number of texts from dramatic and uprooting points in time may be useful from a research perspective, it nevertheless creates problems for the study of emotion discourse. As I have pointed out elsewhere, the focus on charismatic foreign policy actors delimits the study to the emotional expressions of a particular group of people, which may or may not be representative of a larger collective (Koschut 2016). This selection bias needs to be addressed, either by delimiting the research question or by extending the data material. A more sophisticated way to do this would be to develop a theory for why the emotional expressions by foreign policy leaders are worth looking at, for example by pointing to their accentuated social status and power within their respective group.

Another problem results from the temporal framing of texts. Emotional expressions during crises are likely to be very different from those expressed during more stable periods. For example, in the aftermath of 9/11, the Cuban government temporally abandoned its previous antagonistic emotional rhetoric vis-à-vis the United States in favor of official emotional expressions of sympathy and condolence (Hall 2015, 171). It is, thus, sometimes necessary to extend or at least consider the time frame beyond a period of crisis. Finally, the meaning of emotions themselves is highly contingent on their historical and cultural embedding. For example, the philosophers of the Enlightenment period employed the term *passion* when referring to emotions, which has very little to do with the modern usage of the word *passion*. It is thus important to include a larger text-based analysis from the relevant time period under study as well as secondary sources or interviews to confirm or disconfirm the findings and/or to detect changes in emotional meanings and expressions.

Step Two: Mapping the Emotion Potential of Texts

The second step concentrates on the analysis of the emotion potential of texts and how identities and meanings are discursively constructed through specific emotional expressions. The main purpose of mapping emotions within the data material in this way is to analytically separate the descriptive meaning of written words from their connotative emotional meaning (Abu-Lughod and Lutz 1990, 5). From a methodological perspective, researchers need to show *what kind* of emotional meanings are linked to exactly *which* textual components to fully grasp the emotion potential and, subsequently, the emotionalizing effects of texts (see step three). For example, one might be able to make a reasonable case that Ronald Reagan's *Evil-Empire-speech* was an emotionalized foreign policy speech, characterized by an aggressive, hard-line stance toward the former Soviet Union. But that hardly answers the question of what kind of textual items actually make such a discursive performance emotional. A key assumption of social constructivism is that emotions are linked to identities rooted in sociocultural structures. In addition to establishing the frequencies of specific emotion terms and words through a simple word count, the analysis needs to observe which emotions are the most fundamental and prevalent to their styles of expression. This dimension concerns, for example, whether emotions refer to the self-image of a group or to the outside-image of other groups. It differentiates between those emotion categories, which are both inward and reserved for members of a group, on the one hand, and those emotion categories that are directed outward (Hutchison 2016; Koschut 2014). Consider how intergroup conflict is often linked to positive emotions of pride and self-esteem for the in-group ("proud Self"), on the one hand, and negative emotions of contempt and inferiority toward particular out-groups ("disgusting Other"), on the other hand (Leep 2010, 335). Conversely, some groups may display emotions of sympathy toward likeminded others. Accounting for the large range of linguistic features that serve to express emotion, it is helpful to distinguish between at least four ways of communicating emotions in foreign policy discourse: emotion terms, connotations, metaphors, as well as comparisons and analogies.

First, emotional meaning may be conveyed explicitly by establishing a direct reference to an emotional feeling through emotion terms. With nouns like *fear, anger, love, hate, pride, shame*; verbs like *to fear, to love, to hate*; adjectives like *afraid, loving, hateful, angry*; or adverbs like *sadly, regrettably* words refer directly to emotions in foreign policy discourse. It is necessary and important, however, to keep in mind the lexical and semantic variation of emotion terms in and among different languages and cultures. Some emotion concepts are so unique in their cultural meaning that they cannot be translated into English at all, such as the German *schadenfreude*, or the Japanese emotion term *amae*. Hence, some emotions get *lost in translation* and researchers should be fully aware of this by gaining a considerable degree of cultural and historical background knowledge.

Second, emotional meanings may be communicated implicitly through connotations. An emotional connotation contains a context-invariant value judgment or opinion that conveys the emotional attitude of the speaker (Schwarz-Friesel 2013). Certain words are affectively *loaded* in the sense that their semantic utterance can be linked to emotional meaning in foreign policy discourse. Some affective items such as *genocide, terrorist, rogue state, outlaw, massacre* often carry a negative appeal because they refer indirectly to specific emotion concepts of disapproval, such as anger, contempt, or even hate (though some may also take pride in being labeled a *terrorist* or *outlaw*). By contrast, other emotional connotations with a more positive appeal such as *peaceful, freedom fighter, hero, honest broker, responsible member of the international community* typically indicate emotional connotations of admiration such as pride, respect, joy, or sympathy. Further, the emotional value expressed in texts can be raised or lowered by linguistic markers of duration and intensity. Speaking of the "horror of an *endless conflict*" or the "*never-ending* fear of nuclear war", for example, adds a temporal dimension to an emotional connotation like *horror* or an emotion term like *fear*, thereby communicating the enduring presence of an emotional disposition. As to intensity, verbal means such as *very, utterly, somewhat, lightly, deeply, heavily, exceedingly* denote a high or low level of emotional intensity, respectively. Conversely, words may be stripped off their negative emotional connotation in foreign policy discourse, for example, by coding them as *ethnic cleansing* instead of *genocide* or *collateral damage* in order to trivialize the killing of innocent civilians. Needless to say, the meanings resulting from emotional connotations are often sociocultural constructs and may thus resonate differently from culture to culture. Conversely, it is equally important to read the silence: which emotional terms and connotations are avoided in which contexts and toward which actors? For example, one might think about how German politicians painfully attempted to avoid the words *war* or *war-fighting* in the context of the military intervention in Afghanistan. This also had legal implications, but its main purpose was to avoid its highly emotionally charged content given Germany's history.

Finally, a typical characteristic of emotional language is that it is highly figurative. Bleiker (2009), for example, shows how the metaphor of *balance of power* produces emotional poetic images in foreign policy discourse. Figures of speech, particularly metaphors, comparisons, and analogies, play an important role in encoding emotional expressions. For example, a metaphor is supposed to illustrate an emotional state (e.g., *waves or floods of refugees* may express anxiety or fear). Metaphors are usually employed to express emotions that are difficult to articulate otherwise (Kövecses 2000; Wierzbicka 1999). Emotional comparisons and analogies construct comparative categories by either employing historical references that are widely known and shared and thus evoke similar emotional responses ("He is the greatest war criminal since Adolf Hitler") or conceptualizing emotional expressions through mental imagery (Khong 1992; Kaarbo and Kenealy 2017). For example, comparisons such as *feel like in heaven, problem from hell, dark abyss*, and *beacon of democracy* conceptualize emotions through the image of light and darkness, which many people associate with moral hope and mortal fear, respectively.

Step Three: Interpreting and Contextualizing the Emotionalization Effects of Texts

This final move shifts attention to larger and interdependent textual structures to show that emotions are not only expressed in foreign policy discourse but also produce political effects. The researcher's task here is to explicitly state how emotional expressions have implications for foreign policy behavior. Even though the prevailing assumption among mainstream constructivists in IR is that social norms and ideas are "a property of intentional actors that generate motivational and behavioral dispositions" (Wendt 1999, 224), it is questionable to claim that ideas and knowledge have motivational force of their own. Simply knowing about *self* and *other* may influence thought processes and mindsets but it does not alone motivate to act in a certain way. It is when one gets angry at the *Other* that one feels inclined to seek revenge and embark on retaliatory acts. Likewise, if one sympathizes with members of a group, one will likely be more trustful and behave in a conciliatory way toward that group. Cognition that lacks emotional input fails to produce a sense of obligation or loyalty necessary for collective action. Conversely, emotion that lacks cognition has no object, so there is nothing to get angry or sympathetic about. In short, it is the socio-psychological link between mental and emotional categories that constitutes a motivational resource for foreign policy behavior (Mercer 2013).

One particular way of interpreting political effects in emotional discourse is to look for cases of emotional Othering in foreign policy discourses. Social identity not only involves cognitive commitments in terms of *knowing* to belong to a particular group but, crucially, also entails emotional attachments in terms of the connection one *feels* toward other people, sensitivity to their opinions, feelings, and expectations. Analyzing the way emotional expressions refer to "the Other" in foreign policy discourses is to search for the construction of chains of connotations between words or pairs of concepts and their emotional meaning. For example, the social construction of an *Arian identity* in Nazi Germany was deeply rooted in the collective establishment and experience of ritualized and institutionalized emotions of pride and confidence in the German *Herrenvolk* accompanied by foreign policy projections of collective feelings of contempt and disgust toward the Slavic Other or *Untermensch*, which served to legitimate war and mass atrocities. It is important to remember, however, that there is rarely a single Self/Other dichotomy but rather different degrees of Otherness in discourse. It is thus necessary to show "how the Other is situated within a web of identities rather than in a simple Self-Other duality" (Hansen 2006, 36). In the next section, I will illustrate how emotional Othering may be traced in and underpins the current relationship between NATO and Russia. Besides Othering, there are many more ways to study emotions in foreign policy discourse. These include, for example, intertextuality (interconnection and cross-links of emotional meanings between different texts), performativity (deliberate emotional construction of subjects), or interpellation (identification with ideological emotional states) (Koschut 2020, 12). In sum, EDA aims to provide a way of studying emotions in foreign policy discourses to further methodological progress. By methodological "progress", I mean the need to adapt traditional methodological tools of analyzing discourses to make them more sensitive to emotions. The idea of using these diverse tools to trace the emotional construction of intersubjectivity adds to our understanding of discourses in FPA because it allows researchers to examine questions that are not amendable in conventional discourse analysis.

Empirical Illustration: NATO's Emotional Construction of Russia as the New *Radical Other*

The methodological framework developed above will be empirically illustrated using NATO's foreign policy discourse vis-à-vis Russia following the annexation of Crimea. The case is chosen to offer an empirical window into the emotional underpinnings of foreign policy discourse. Its purpose is to give the reader a more detailed empirical account of the emotion potential and emotionalization effects of a particular foreign policy discourse. Specifically, I will look at how NATO's construction of Russia as the *radical Other* during the Crimean crisis was significantly underpinned by emotional meanings, resulting in the suspension of most of NATO's cooperation with Russia and a (re)construction of the Russian Other from being a partner of the West to becoming the enemy.

Text Selection

As pointed out above, a fruitful way to study emotions in foreign policy discourse is to initially focus on a small number of texts from dramatic and uprooting points in time, involving charismatic authorities that carry significance for foreign policy audiences. Due to limited space and for illustrative purposes, I will put the analytical focus on the study of a single, exemplary text. The text that I have chosen is an official press release by NATO, issued on 1 April 2014 (NATO 2014a). Why did I choose this particular text? The press release includes a joint statement by the foreign ministers of NATO member states following their meeting in Brussels, the first such meeting after the Russian annexation of Crimea. In this statement, NATO member states articulate their position pertaining to the Crimean crisis, which makes the text a formidable source to study how NATO members initially constructed the Russian Other in the face of a crisis. Furthermore, the fact that this statement was adopted by all NATO members makes it a representative sample of NATO foreign policy discourse as opposed to, for example, a statement by single member state. As I will argue, NATO emotionally constructed Russia as the *radical Other* following the Crimean crisis, resulting in a shift in foreign policy behavior. This is significant, because it differs fundamentally from previous emotion discourse in which NATO depicts its relationship with Russia in much more amicable terms. For example, as the NATO-Russia Founding Act of 1997 states:

> NATO and Russia do not consider each other as adversaries. They share the goal of overcoming the vestiges of earlier confrontation and competition and of strengthening mutual trust and cooperation. (…) They intend to develop, on the basis of common interest, reciprocity and transparency a strong, stable and enduring partnership.
> *(NATO 1997)*

In addition to an analysis of the emotions underpinning this process of constructing Russia as the *radical Other*, I will consult additional sources and the political context surrounding the event.

Mapping Emotional Expressions

Having selected a textual source, I will now map the textual components that create emotional (inter)subjectivity between NATO and Russia. For reasons of analytical clarity and space limitation, I will confine the empirical analysis to relatively simple emotion terms and connotations rather than more complex metaphors and comparisons/analogies as well as to the immediate implications of NATO's foreign policy discourse for its member state leaders rather than its reception among wider audiences.

Below, I will highlight the emotional expressions in the text in *italics* and denote their meaning using a short commentary in [cling squares], focusing on the parts of the statement that explicitly deal with Russia. The insertions written into the text have the merits of making the assumed emotional meanings of relevant textual components more explicit and transparent to the reader. Nevertheless, this represents my own subjective reading of the text and I am certainly not claiming that this analysis constitutes the only way of emotionally reading the text. By making the emotion potential of the text explicit and transparent via text insertion, the reader may either ascribe to my particular reading of the text or reach an alternative conclusion and, in the latter case, may wish to empirically challenge the analysis put forward here.

In early March 2014, tensions increased between NATO and Russia following Russia's move to annex Crimea. On 1 April 2014, NATO foreign ministers gathered for the first time since the Russian occupation of Crimea had touched off one of the worst crises in NATO-Russian relations since the end of the Cold War. As a result of the meeting, NATO foreign ministers suspended all practical cooperation with Russia, issuing the following statement to justify its reaction:

> We, the Foreign Ministers of NATO, are
> *united* [emotional reference to mutual sympathy/we-feeling]
> in our

condemnation [intensification of the prior 'we-feeling' by contrasting it with a negative emotion encoding of anger and projection of guilt/blame on an outsider]
of Russia's
illegal [emotional expression of anger for breaking a taboo]
military intervention in Ukraine and Russia's
violation [emotional reference to a perceived moral breach]
of Ukraine's sovereignty and territorial integrity. We
do not recognize [withholding respect]
Russia's
illegal and illegitimate [repeated and extended emotional expression of anger for breaking a taboo]
attempt to
annex [intensification of the emotional expression of anger by making explicit the perception of unlawfully taking possession of something]
Crimea. We
urge [emotional expression of hope/desire]
Russia to take immediate steps, as set out in the statement by the NATO-Ukraine Commission, to return to compliance with international law and its international obligations and responsibilities, and to engage immediately in a
genuine [emotional reference to honesty and truthfulness]
dialogue towards a political and diplomatic solution that
respects [specific categorization of a positive emotion through an emotion term]
international law and Ukraine's internationally recognized borders. We support the deployment of an OSCE monitoring mission to Ukraine.

A conventional FPA discourse analyses would take this emotional content for granted without making it explicit. The analytical focus on emotion employed in this case seeks to correct this imbalance and extends discourse analysis by proposing a framework for empirical research on emotion discourse in FPA. The goal is to identify a way to specifically examine emotional expressions that come to the fore in these discourses. The next step is to study their political implications.

Interpreting and Contextualizing Emotionalization Effects

Having identified emotional expressions and meanings in the text, the next step is to gain insights pertaining to their political implications. This is based on the assumption that NATO members do not express emotions randomly but as part of a carefully crafted foreign policy script that seeks to emotionally construct intersubjectivity between NATO and Russia in a particular way. In other words, we need to search for a "structure of feeling" – a set of emotions that show a regular pattern – built into the text that arguably constrains and compels the affective experience among NATO members on the inside and Russia on the outside (Williams 1961, 47). How do emotions underpin and structure this insider/outsider dualism?

The discourse (re)constructs the relationship between NATO and Russia as, once again, rooted in antagonistic identities of the Cold War by constructing radically different categories of *self* and *other*, *us* and *them*. This represents a sharp discursive shift from previous NATO statements, such as one from March 2012: "NATO and Russia are not adversaries or enemies. We are committed to being strategic partners and we are working on it together (NATO 2012)".

A mere two years later, NATO's identity is constructed as the in-group, based on liberal values in a peaceful transatlantic space. Russia, by contrast, is constructed as the out-group, challenging and violating liberal values through its actions in the Ukraine and, as a consequence, threatening the peaceful order and *way of life* of the transatlantic area. These antagonistic identities establish an insider/outsider dualism that draws a sharp psychological line between NATO and Russia. The identity politics behind this construction of antagonistic intersubjectivity is reinforced by NATO's Secretary General Anders Fogh Rasmussen, who sets the tone in his remarks to NATO's foreign ministers, shortly before their meeting on 1 April: "NATO's open door policy (...) erase(d) many of the painful dividing lines on our continent. (...) the crisis in Ukraine risks creating new dividing lines" (NATO 2014b). This is what a conventional discourse analysis might come up with (see Ostermann and Sjöstedt in this volume). However, such a conventional discourse analysis, while compelling, arguably draws only a partial picture of the identity politics at play here. The antagonistic identities linked to the insider-outsider dualism between NATO and Russia are not only discursively constructed through cognitive knowledge about *us* and *them* but also simultaneously underpinned by corresponding emotions of sympathy for *us* and anger toward *them*.

In the case of NATO and Russia, the sympathy/anger dualism arguably constitutes the discursive structure of feeling that facilitates group cohesion among NATO member state leaders on the inside as well as social distance vis-à-vis Russia on the outside through emotional Othering. This can be empirically traced, for example, in the statement by NATO foreign ministers on Russia when they stand "united in our condemnation of Russia's illegal military intervention in Ukraine and Russia's violation of Ukraine's sovereignty and territorial integrity". Here, an implicit emotional reference to mutual sympathy between NATO members ("united") is contrasted to the divisive acts by Russia that are accompanied by emotional expressions of anger ("condemnation", "illegal", "violation"). Another example is the juxtaposition between, on the one hand, the transatlantic area that aims to be "whole, free, and at peace", which again implies unity, belonging, and mutual sympathy among NATO members, and, on the other hand, emotional expressions of anger with Russia for "fundamentally challenging" this goal. One can find similar sympathy/anger dualisms in several other places in the text. Emotion words and terms that denote sympathy, such as "closer cooperation", "trust", "solidarity", "Alliance cohesion", "indivisibility", or "assurance", and emotion words that imply anger, such as "condemnation", "violation", "illegal and illegitimate", "gravely breached", or "threat of aggression", are placed in stark contrast to each other and thus underpin an emotionally attuned cognitive separation between the 'in-group' and the 'out-group', 'us' and 'them'. Importantly, this has behavioral implications and motivates collective action, as NATO enhanced its air policing in the Baltic States, deployed: Airborne Warning & Control System (AWACS) aircraft to improve surveillance of Poland and Romania, and increased its naval presence in the Black Sea following the meeting.

This, of course, is not to say that anger and sympathy are the only emotions present in NATO discourse, only that anger and sympathy are viewed here as *master emotions* in this particular discourse because they drive the political implications of the discourse. NATO discourse also employs alternative emotional expressions such as hope and desire that appear to express NATO's plea for reconciliation. For example, when NATO foreign ministers "urge Russia to take immediate steps (...) to return to compliance", "engage in a genuine dialogue", and "respect international law", they are effectively building an emotional bridge to leave the door open for future cooperation. A similar emotional bridge-building through hope and desire can also be found in the inaugural remarks by NATO's Secretary General minutes before the foreign ministers meeting: "We continue to urge Russia to pull back its troops; live up to its international obligations and engage in a constructive dialogue with Ukraine" (NATO 2014c).

To sum up, the foreign policy discourse constructs the relationship between NATO and Russia as rooted in antagonistic identities by constructing cognitive categories of *self* and *other*, *us* and *them*. These antagonistic identities are simultaneously underpinned by corresponding emotional expressions of sympathy and anger that motivate certain types of behavior (suspension of NATO-Russia cooperation), thereby establishing and reproducing a new insider/outsider dualism. This dualism, however, is not total. There are also mixed emotions that display a desire for reconciliation. The case illustrates how the discursive construction of Russia as the Other was facilitated and underpinned by emotions. One could easily think of other cases where this might be relevant as well, such as Brexit, Trump, or the European reactions to migration.

Conclusion

This chapter concludes by reflecting on some of the gains and limitations of integrating EDA within FPA, specifically speaking to the significance, originality, and limitations of the use of EDA as a method of data collection. In addition to outlining the specific value of the analysis for FPA, I identify three sets of concerns that researchers need to address. The chapter will conclude by tentatively exploring possible synergies and cross-links with other methodological approaches.

The idea of using EDA to construct the emotional representation of social reality adds to our understanding of discourse analysis in FPA, because it allows researchers to examine questions that are not amendable in conventional discourse analysis. It underlines the need to adapt traditional methods in FPA to make them more sensitive to emotions. Emotions are no more private than language and their expression and effects within political spheres adds explanatory value to the construction of social meanings and foreign policy behavior. Moreover, EDA develops insights into the social nature of feelings that are not easily accessible by traditional interpretive methods and aims to trace the political effects of emotional expressions in discourse and how this might change over time. As with any method, there are limitations attached to using EDA as a data collection tool. While these limitations do not negate the usefulness of EDA, they need to be acknowledged in order for future researchers to identify strategies that can potentially ameliorate these difficulties.

One difficulty concerns the wide range of phenomena that potentially fall into the category of emotions, such as short-term bodily reactions, undifferentiated moods and sensations, affects, feeling states, or relatively stable emotional dispositions. How can we differentiate analytically between these different phenomena simply by studying texts? The short and unsatisfactory answer is we cannot (at least not by looking at a small selection of texts). The best we can do is to search for possible indicators that may be able to approximate the type of emotion potential in texts and triangulate between different sources, for example, by conducting interviews with relevant decision makers or by watching video footage (if available) to trace the tone and facial expression of speaker and audience over time.

A second concern relates to the difficulty of analytically separating the individual level from the collective level of emotional expression. For example, when NATO's Secretary General speaks about "painful dividing lines", is he referring to his own subjective feeling of bodily pain or to the collective feeling of pain experienced by NATO as a body politic? From a social constructivist perspective, the straightforward answer would be that culturally influenced patterns of emotions impact deep inside people as they are emotionally socialized into communities. Hence, the link between emotion and language is necessarily a social one. Yet, we do not have "emotional x-ray machines" (Wilce 2009, 25). EDA claims no access to the inner emotional world of human beings but instead targets their intersubjective expression and collective representation within social spheres. While this may come at the risk of homogenizing the emotions of groups, it, nevertheless, offers generalizable patterns that allow FPA researchers to study and compare emotions in intergroup relations. Some social groups in IR may be more expressive than others in their use and articulation of emotions in the international realm. For example, diplomats tend to conceal their emotions during political negotiations, whereas members of NGOs tend to employ emotions openly as a strategy to achieve political ends.

A third challenge stems from the problem of subjectivity. As pointed out above, EDA outlines a hermeneutic procedure for interpreting emotions. It is based on the assumption that emotional reality is not objective but is shaped by human experience and social context. From this viewpoint, a *neutral* observer can hardly exist. This draws critical attention to the role of the individual researcher. First, it requires critical self-reflection on behalf of the researcher as her specific role and perspective must be made explicit to avoid personal bias. Moreover, it requires analytical rigor in terms of deep contextual knowledge. As a result, the research findings may not be easily replicated or generalized. Finally, this type of analysis is usually very time-consuming in data collection since too little data may lead to premature or prejudiced conclusions. Despite these challenges, EDA has unique advantages for tapping into the implicit emotions *hidden* in texts where conventional methods would only be able to obtain explicit emotional references. Since international actors rarely express their emotions in such explicit ways, EDA is often the best way to achieve meaningful and context-sensitive results.

Finally, the goal of identifying generalizable patterns of emotion discourse necessitates the construction of ideal-type emotional categories for analytical purpose. This does not negate the fact that emotions constitute a mixed and oftentimes messy object of inquiry. While emotions are indeed fluid and shifting, EDA argues that they also display a high degree of attachment and entanglement, resulting in relatively stable patterns of emotional meanings and webs of interconnections. Emotional meanings overlap with, mutually influence, and conflict with other emotional meanings. Importantly, emotions can also change and vary significantly in their historical meaning and sociocultural expression. In my view, the crucial factor is to determine the dominant emotion meanings by which hierarchies and identities are underpinned relative to other, less prevalent emotion meanings. In short, emotions underpin the discursive construction of foreign policy by framing what is possible to say and what is not. As pointed out above, whether this emotion potential generates political effects depends on situational awareness, audience reception, and social norms.

While EDA adds considerable strength to traditional discursive methods, it also allows for possible synergies and cross-links with other methodological approaches such as visual analysis (see Stahl in this volume) and narrative analysis (see Oppermann and Spencer in this volume). Since narrative analysis equally emphasizes the historical, cultural, and social contextualization of language, the way emotions impact, enrich, and enable certain narratives to *stick* with audiences as well as how emotions become the subject of storytelling can be easily combined with EDA (Kleres 2010). For example, in the case above, NATO foreign policy discourse was arguably embedded in a larger narrative of separation and difference rooted in historical conceptions of Russia as the "semibarbarian state" that despite its material power and social adaptations could not be fully ascribed "great power status" by the established European great powers (Neumann 2014, 102). Furthermore, EDA may also be combined with visual analysis, particularly if the aim of the researcher is to link emotions in texts with bodily movements, gestures, or emotionalized imagery (Adler-Nissen et al. 2020).

Acknowledgments

Research for this chapter has been generously funded by the German Research Council (DFG). A previous version of this chapter has been published as "Speaking From the Heart: Emotion Discourse Analysis in International Relations" in *Researching Emotions in International Relations*, edited by Maéva Clément and Eric Sangar (Palgrave Macmillan, 2018), 277–301. It is presented here in much revised form.

References

Abu-Lughod, Lila, and Catherine A. Lutz. 1990. "Introduction." In *Language and the Politics of Emotions*, edited by Catherine A. Lutz and Lila Abu-Lughod. Cambridge: Cambridge University Press, 1–23.
Adler-Nissen, Rebecca, Katrine Emilie Andersen, and Lene Hansen. 2020. "Images, Emotions, and International Politics: The Death of Alan Kurdi." *Review of International Studies* 46(1): 75–95.
Ahäll, Linda, and Thomas Gregory, eds. 2015. *Emotion, Politics, and War*. New York: Routledge.
Alexieva, Assia. 2016. "The Role of Emotions in Foreign Policy Decision Making: Embarrassment from the Bay of Pigs." In *Emotions in International Politics: Beyond Mainstream International Relations*, edited by Yohan Ariffin, Jean-Marc Coicaud and Vesselin Popovski. Cambridge: Cambridge University Press, 221–253.
Allison, Graham. 1971. *Essence of Decision: Explaining the Cuban Missile Crisis*. Boston, MA: Little, Brown.
Averill, James R. 1980. "A Constructivist View of Emotion." In *Emotion: Theory, Research and Experience: Vol. I. Theories of Emotion*, edited by Robert Plutchik and Henry Kellerman. New York: Academic Press, 305–339.
Bially Mattern, Janice. 2011. "A Practice Theory of Emotion for International Relations." In *International Practices*, edited by Emanuel Adler and Vincent Pouliot. New York: Cambridge University Press, 63–86.
Bleiker, Roland. 2009. *Aesthetics and World Politics*. New York: Palgrave Macmillan.
Bleiker, Roland, and Emma Hutchison. 2008. "Fear No More. Emotions and World Politics." *Review of International Studies* 34: 115–135.
Clément, Maéva, Thomas Lindemann, and Eric Sangar. 2017. "The 'Hero-Protector Narrative': Manufacturing Emotional Consent for the Use of Force." *Political Psychology* 38(6): 991–1008.
Crawford, Neta C. 2000. "The Passion of World Politics. Propositions on Emotion and Emotional Relationships." *International Security* 24(4): 116–156.
Crawford, Neta C. 2014. "Institutionalizing Passion in World Politics: Fear and Empathy." *International Theory* 6(3): 535–557.
Danchev, Alex. 2006. "'Like a Dog!': Humiliation and Shame in the War on Terror." *Alternatives: Global, Local and Political* 31 (3): 259–283.
Dolan, Thomas M. 2016. "Emotion and Strategic Learning in War." *Foreign Policy Analysis* 12(4): 571–590.
Eberle, Jakub. 2019. *Discourse and Affect in Foreign Policy: Germany and the Iraq War*. New York: Routledge.
Edney-Browne, Alex. 2019. "The Psycho-social Effects of Drone Violence: Social Isolation, Self-objectification and De-politicisation." *Political Psychology* 40(6): 1341–1356.
Eroukhmanoff, Clara. 2019. *The Securitization of Islam: Covert Racism and Affect in the United States Post 9/11*. Manchester: Manchester University Press.
Fattah, Khaled, and Karin M. Fierke. 2009. "A Clash of Emotions: The Politics of Humiliation and Political Violence in the Middle East." *European Journal of International Relations* 15(1): 67–93.
Fettweis, Christopher J. 2013. *The Pathologies of Power: Fear, Honor, Glory, and Hubris in US Foreign Policy*. Cambridge: Cambridge University Press.
Graham, Ellen Sarah. 2014. "Emotion and Public Diplomacy: Dispositions in International Communications, Dialogue, and Persuasion." *International Studies Review* 16(4): 522–539.

Hall, Todd H. 2015. *Emotional Diplomacy: Official Emotion on the International Stage*. Ithaca, NY: Cornell University Press.
Hall, Todd H. 2017. "On Provocation: Outrage, International Relations, and the Franco–Prussian War." *Security Studies* 26(1): 1–29.
Hall, Todd H., and Andrew A. G. Ross. 2019. "Re-thinking Affective Experience and Popular Emotion: World War I and the Construction of Group Emotion in International Relations." *Political Psychology* 40(6): 1357–1372.
Hansen, Lene. 2006. *Security as Practice: Discourse Analysis and the Bosnian War*. London: Routledge.
Hansen, Lene. 2011. "Theorizing the Image for Security Studies: Visual Securitization and the Muhammad Cartoon Crisis." *European Journal of International Relations* 17(1): 51–74.
Harré, Rom. 1986. "An Outline of the Social Constructionist Viewpoint." In *The Social Construction of Emotions*, edited by Rom Harré. Oxford: Blackwell, 2–14.
Holmes, Marcus. 2018. *Face-to-Face Diplomacy. Social Neuroscience and International Relations*. Cambridge: Cambridge University Press.
Hutchison, Emma. 2016. *Affective Communities in World Politics*. Cambridge: Cambridge University Press.
Hymans, Jacques E. 2006. *The Psychology of Nuclear Proliferation. Identity, Emotions and Foreign Policy*. Cambridge: Cambridge University Press.
Janis, Irving. 1972. *Groupthink: Psychological Studies of Foreign Policy Decisions and Fiascoes*. Boston: Houghton Mifflin.
Jervis, Robert. 1976. *Perception and Misperception in International Politics*. Princeton, NJ: Princeton University Press.
Jervis, Robert, Richard N. Lebow, and Janice Gross Stein. 1985. *Psychology and Deterrence*. Baltimore, MD: John Hopkins University Press.
Jones, Alun, and Julian Clark. 2019. "Performance, Emotions, and Diplomacy in the United Nations Assemblage in New York." *Annals of the American Association of Geographers* 109(4): 1262–1278.
Kaarbo, Juliet, and Daniel Kenealy. 2017. "Precedents, Parliaments, and Foreign Policy: Historical Analogy in the House of Commons Vote on Syria." *West European Politics* 40(1): 62–79.
Keys, Barbara, and Claire Yorke. 2019. "Personal and Political Emotions in the Mind of the Diplomat." *Political Psychology* 40(6): 1235–1249.
Khong, Yuen Foong. 1992. *Analogies of War: Korea, Munich, Dien Bien Phu and the Vietnam Decisions of 1965*. Princeton, NJ: Princeton University Press.
Kleres, Jochen. 2010. "Emotions and Narrative Analysis: A Methodological Approach." *Journal for the Theory of Social Behaviour* 41(2): 182–202.
Koschut, Simon. 2014. "Emotional (Security) Communities: The Significance of Emotion Norms in Inter-allied Conflict Management." *Review of International Studies* 40(3): 533–558.
Koschut, Simon. 2016. "The Structure of Feeling: Emotion Culture and National Self-Sacrifice." *Millennium – Journal of International Studies* 45(2): 174–192.
Koschut, Simon. 2017. "The Power of (Emotion) Words: On the Importance of Emotions for Social Constructivist Discourse Analysis in IR." *Journal of International Relations and Development* 21(3): 495–522.
Koschut, Simon, eds. 2020. *The Power of Emotions in World Politics*. New York: Routledge.
Koschut, Simon, Todd H. Hall, Reinhard Wolf, Ty Solomon, Emma Hutchison, and Roland Bleiker. 2017. "Introduction to Forum: Discourse and Emotions in International Relations." *International Studies Review* 19(3): 481–508.
Kövecses, Zoltan. 2000. *Metaphor and Emotion*. Cambridge: Cambridge University Press.
Laclau, Ernesto, and Chantal Mouffe. 1985. *Hegemony and Socialist Strategy*. London: Verso.
Leep, Matthew C. 2010. "The Affective Production of Others. United States Policy Towards the Israeli-Palestinian Conflict." *Cooperation and Conflict* 45(3): 331–352.
Liberman, Peter. 2006. "An Eye for an Eye: Public Support for War against Evildoers." *International Organization* 60(3): 687–722.
Markwica, Robin. 2018. *Emotional Choices. How the Logic of Affect Shapes Coercive Diplomacy*. Oxford: Oxford University Press.
McDermott, Rose. 2014. "The Biological Bases for Aggressiveness and Nonaggressiveness in Presidents." *Foreign Policy Analysis* 10(4): 313–327.
Mercer, Jonathan. 2013. "Emotion and Strategy in the Korean War." *International Organization* 67(2): 221–252.

Michel, Torsten. 2012. "Time to Get Emotional: Phronetic Reflections on the Concept of Trust in International Relations." *European Journal of International Relations* 18(1): 1–22.

Morgenthau, Hans J. 1948. *Politics among Nations: The Struggle for Power and Peace*. New York: Knopf.

NATO. 1997. *Founding Act on Mutual Relations, Cooperation and Security between NATO and the Russian Federation*. Paris, 27 May 1997. Last modified 12 October 2009. Available from http://www.nato.int/cps/en/natohq/official_texts_25468.htm (last accessed 17 June 2021).

NATO. 2012. *Remarks by NATO Secretary General Anders Fogh Rasmussen at a Press Conference with Moscow-based Journalists*. Moscow, 26 March 2012. Last modified 30 March 2012. Available from http://www.nato.int/cps/en/natohq/opinions_85625.htm?selectedLocale=en (last accessed 17 June 2021).

NATO. 2014a. *Statement by NATO Foreign Ministers on Russia*. Press Release 062, 1 April 2014. Last modified 1 April 2014. Available from http://www.nato.int/cps/en/natohq/news_108501.htm (last accessed 17 June 2021).

NATO. 2014b. *Remarks by NATO Secretary General Anders Fogh Rasmussen*. Ceremony to Mark the NATO Enlargement Anniversaries, 1 April 2014. Last modified 1 April 2014. Available from http://www.nato.int/cps/en/natolive/opinions_108509.htm (last accessed 17 June 2021).

NATO. 2014c. *Doorstep Statement by NATO Secretary General Anders Fogh Rasmussen*. Start of the NATO Foreign Ministers Meeting, 1 April 2014. Last modified 1 April 2014. Available from http://www.nato.int/cps/en/natolive/opinions_108502.htm (last accessed 17 June 2021).

Neumann, Iver B. 2014. "Status is Cultural Durkheimian Poles and Weberian Russians Seek Great-Power Status." In *Status in World Politics*, edited by Deborah Welch Larson, T.V. Paul and William C. Wohlforth. Cambridge: Cambridge University Press, 85–114.

Nussbaum, Martha. 2003. *Upheavals of Thought. The Intelligence of Emotions*. Cambridge: Cambridge University Press.

Pace, Michelle, and Ali Bilgic. 2019. "Studying Emotions in Security and Diplomacy: Where We Are Now and Challenges Ahead." *Political Psychology* 40(6): 1407–1417.

Posner, Richard A. 1999. "Emotion versus Emotionalism in Law." In *The Passions of Law*, edited by Susan A. Bandes. New York: New York University Press, 309–329.

Rathbun, Brian C. 2012. *Trust in International Cooperation. International Security Institutions, Domestic Politics and American Multilateralism*. Cambridge: Cambridge University Press.

Reinke de Buitrago, Sybille. 2016. "The Role of Emotions in US Security Policy Towards Iran." *Global Affairs* 2(2): 155–164.

Rosen, Stephen P. 2005. *War and Human Nature*. Princeton, NJ: Princeton University Press.

Ross, Andrew. 2006. "Coming in from the Cold. Constructivism and Emotions." *European Journal of International Relations* 12(2): 197–222.

Ross, Andrew. 2014. *Mixed Emotions. Beyond Fear and Hatred in International Conflict*. Chicago, IL: Chicago University Press.

Sasley, Brent E. 2010. "Affective Attachments and Foreign Policy: Israel and the 1993 Oslo Accords." *European Journal of International Relations* 16(4): 687–709.

Saurette, Paul. 2006. "'You Dissin Me?' Humiliation and Post 9/11 Global Politics." *Review of International Studies* 32(3): 495–522.

Schelling, Thomas C. 1960. *The Strategy of Conflict*. Cambridge: Harvard University Press.

Schilling, Christopher L. 2015. *Emotional State Theory: Friendship and Fear in Israeli Foreign Policy*. Lanham, MD: Lexington Books.

Schwarz-Friesel, Monika. 2013. *Sprache und Emotion*. Tübingen and Basel: UTB.

Small, Deborah A., and Jennifer S. Lerner. 2008. "Emotional Policy. Personal Sadness and Anger Shape Judgments About a Welfare Case." *Political Psychology* 29(2): 149–168.

Solomon, Ty. 2015. *The Politics of Subjectivity in American Foreign Policy Discourses*. Ann Arbor: University of Michigan Press.

Stein, Janice Gross. 2013. "Psychological Explanations of International Decision Making and Collective Behavior." In: *Handbook of International Relations*, edited by Walter Carlsnaes, Thomas Risse and Beth A. Simmons. London: SAGE, 195–219.

Van Hoef, Yuri, and Ryan O'Connor. 2019. "Sentimental Utility Theory: Interpreting the Utilization of Collective Emotions by the Political Elite Through the Erdoğan-Obama Friendship." *Political Psychology* 40(6): 1217–1233.

Van Rythoven, Eric. 2015. "Learning to Feel, Learning to Fear? Emotions, Imaginaries, and Limits in the Politics of Securitization." *Security Dialogue* 46(5): 458–475.

Welch Larson, Deborah. 1985. *Origins of Containment: A Psychological Explanation*. Princeton, NJ: Princeton University Press.
Wendt, Alexander. 1999. *Social Theory of International Politics*. Cambridge: Cambridge University Press.
Wheeler, Nicholas J. 2018. *Trusting Enemies. Interpersonal Relationships in International Conflict*. Oxford: Oxford University Press.
Widmaier, Wesley W. 2010. "Emotions Before Paradigms: Elite Anxiety and Populist Resentment from the Asian to Subprime Crises." *Millennium: Journal of International Studies* 39(1): 127–144.
Wierzbicka, Anna. 1999. *Emotions Across Languages and Cultures*. Cambridge: Cambridge University Press.
Wilce, James M. 2009. *Language and Emotion*. Cambridge: Cambridge University Press.
Williams, Raymond. 1961. *The Long Revolution*. Westport, CT: Greenwood.
Wolfers, Arnold. 1952. "'National Security' as an Ambiguous Symbol." *Political Science Quarterly* 67(4): 481–502.
Wong, Seanon S. 2016. "Emotions and the Communication of Intentions in Face-to-Face Diplomacy." *European Journal of International Relations* 22(1): 144–167.

Part IV
Psychology, Roles, and Leaders

12
Role Theory
Marijke Breuning

Introduction

Role theory in Foreign Policy Analysis (FPA) has seen a resurgence over the past decade (Breuning 2011, 2017, 2019; Thies 2010). This renewed attention coincides with the rediscovery of the individual level of analysis, which has always been central to FPA, in the broader discipline of International Relations (IR) (Chiozza and Goemans 2011; Hafner-Burton et al. 2017; Horowitz et al. 2015; Hudson 2005). Role theory in FPA can be traced back to the seminal article of Holsti (1970), who used it to study foreign policy from the perspective of the decision maker. His work is an early effort to take the agent-structure problem seriously (Carlsnaes 1992), albeit with an emphasis on structural constraints. Holsti's (1970) effort fits well within the FPA tradition pioneered by Snyder et al. (2002 [1962]). The latter were agent-centered, arguing that "the key to the explanation of why the state behaves the way it does lies in the way its decision-makers as actors define their situation" (Snyder et al. 2002 [1962], 59).

The concept of the definition of the situation deserves explication. It is often operationalized in terms of a *specific* occasion for decision (Hudson 2005, 2002; Hudson and Vore 1995; Ozkececi-Taner 2006). However, actors also define their situation in general terms. Role theory pursues the latter. National role conceptions reflect a general framing of foreign policy commitments and behaviors that decision makers perceive as appropriate to their state (Holsti 1970).

A strength of role theory as originally introduced to FPA is its focus on patterns in how a state's decision makers perceive the range of possible actions vis-à-vis the international environment. Contemporary role theory differs in that it examines roles in the context of interactions between relevant actors and in specific issue areas, rather than the comprehensive perspective of the first generation of role theory in FPA. This has entailed a move away from larger-scale approaches like Holsti's (1970) that seek to classify the foreign policies of countries into one or more role patterns, such as regional leader, active independent, or faithful ally. Instead, recent empirical work first emphasizes specific issue areas and events and second develops generalizable theory with well-specified scope conditions. In essence, role theory is quintessentially a mid-level theory, grounded in comparative method, and anticipating knowledge cumulation across studies and over time.

In sum, role theory enables researchers to understand how decision makers make sense of the foreign policy environment generally and in specific issue areas. Role theory facilitates understanding of the logic of foreign policy decisions from the perspective of the relevant decision makers. For instance, although Russia seeks to cast the states that were formerly part of the Soviet Union in the role of client state (or protectees in Holsti's language), the citizens of these states differ in their views of country's role vis-à-vis Russia: a large proportion of Armenian citizens perceives their state's role as that of faithful ally to Russia, Georgian citizens are split between an adversarial and a faithful ally role, and the most common role among Belarusian citizens is that of dependent (Breuning and Ishiyama 2021). Decision makers in these states take cues from the predominant national role conceptions among their citizens, which explains the differences in foreign policy toward Russia.

In what follows, this chapter first outlines the genesis and current state of role theory in FPA. Subsequently, the chapter introduces the concepts and methodologies, as well as the empirical strategies employed in role theory. The chapter concludes with some guidance for researchers who wish to use role theory in their work.

Role Theory in FPA

The revitalization of role theory over the past decade has been accompanied by a change in its use in FPA (Breuning 2019, 2017, 2011; Thies 2010). The introduction hinted at this. To better understand it, let's start at the beginning – the first generation of role theory in FPA.

Holsti (1970) introduced role theory to the discipline. He observed that IR scholars "made references to national roles as possible causal variables," but also that they did so without defining the concept (Holsti 1970, 234). He explored role theory in other social sciences to determine whether FPA and IR could profit from it. His main interest was in explaining the interactions between states in the international system. He defined roles in terms of the (kind of) foreign policy *commitments* and *behaviors* that decision makers deem appropriate to their state (Holsti 1970, 245ff.). He focused primarily on how the external environment shapes national role conceptions, rather than the impact of domestic influences or decision makers' experiences (or preferences) on role conceptions. This is not surprising: Holsti's work takes important cues from structural role theory.

A short detour will clarify this claim. Role theory builds on two related research traditions in sociology and social psychology, which both investigate what IR scholars call the agent-structure problem (Carlsnaes 1992; Wendt 1987). The concern is: does the international environment compel states and their decision makers to enact specific foreign policies, or do decision makers have the capacity to shape their state's role in the international environment – and perhaps even reshape (actors in) that international environment? Evidence of the first demonstrates the impact of structure, whereas the second supports the importance of agency.

In sociology and social psychology, this debate is represented by the interconnected research programs of role theory and symbolic interactionism. Both originate in the work of George Herbert Mead (1934). Stryker and Statham (1985, 312; see also Stryker 2008, 2001) comment that both "analyze social phenomena from the perspectives of participants in social processes." In sociology, role theory emphasizes that society constrains human agency. Individuals are socialized to perceive certain behaviors as acceptable, and to act within the bounds of social rules and conventions. Hence, role theory emphasizes the weight of existing social structures on human behavior. In contrast, symbolic interactionism places greater emphasis on the ability of individuals to subvert social convention, shape their roles in society, and, in the process, modify the societal structure. Symbolic interactionism suggests that the relationship between social structure and human agency is, as the name suggests, interactive. Compared to role theory, symbolic interactionism places greater weight on human agency.

Role theory in FPA relies on both role theory and symbolic interactionism in sociology. The emphasis has shifted across time. The first generation of role theory research was closely connected to the structural interpretation (Holsti 1970; Hollis and Smith 1986; Jönsson and Westerlund 1982; Shih 1988; Walker 1987, 1981, 1979; Wish 1987, 1980), whereas more recent – second generation – role theory scholarship draws increasingly on insights from symbolic interactionism (Breuning 1995; Harnisch 2012, 2011a; McCourt 2012; Walker 1992; Wehner 2016, 2015; Wehner and Thies 2014).

This brief detour through the interconnected origins of role theory and symbolic interactionism explains the shifting emphasis between first- and second-generation role theory scholarship in FPA. Note that Schafer and Walker (2021) describe the development of role theory in FPA differently. They identify a first, second, and third wave, and place their work on binary role theory in the third. Their first wave consists of the metaphorical use of roles in historical narratives, which I identify as a *precursor* to role theory. Therefore, this chapter employs a distinction between a first and second generation of role theory scholarship, with the first drawing primarily on structural role theory and the second connecting to symbolic interactionism and exhibiting a stronger emphasis on human agency. The second is highly differentiated and the core focus of this chapter. The remainder of this section illustrates the differences between the first and second generation of role theory in FPA in more detail.

As mentioned in the introduction, role theory in FPA can be traced back to Holsti (1970), who noticed that scholars employed the idea of roles without defining the concept. These scholars used roles metaphorically rather than as a theoretical concept. Hence, before Holsti's (1970) seminal article, we cannot genuinely speak of role theory in FPA. Holsti's work generated followers. Walker (1987, 1981, 1979) and Wish (1987, 1980) most closely mirrored the quantitative empirical approach pioneered by Holsti (1970), whereas Hollis and Smith (1986) and Shih (1988) utilized case studies. The former most clearly imply that decision makers' national role conceptions were shaped primarily by their state's position in the international environment. The case studies presented more nuanced conclusions but remained grounded in a hierarchical understanding of international politics.

The presence of hierarchy in this early role theory scholarship is best illustrated with Holsti's (1970) foundational work – in part because the roles he enumerated continue to influence (some) empirical efforts in role theory. Consider the role of regional leader, which describes a state whose leaders perceive "special responsibilities" in relation to other states "in a particular region with which it identifies" (Holsti 1970, 261). Or, alternatively, consider the role of protectee, which describes a state which leaders lack "any particular orientation, tasks, or functions toward the external environment" (Holsti 1970, 270). Leaders who perceive their state in these terms conceptualize their state as powerless and dependent on other, more powerful states for protection.

Interestingly, Holsti (1970) wondered whether protectee should be considered a role rather than a position in the international hierarchy of states, implying that a role cannot be passive. This seems odd: roles are not defined by whether they are passive or active, nor by whether they are positive or negative. Instead, roles are defined by decision makers' conceptions of the foreign policy commitments and behaviors that are – or are not – appropriate for their state. Rather than positioning their state as a protectee, decision makers might have chosen the role of isolate and minimized external contacts (Holsti 1970, 270).

Hence, despite the overlap between a state's position in the international system and the identified role conceptions, Holsti (1970) does imply some level of agency. That said, agency was not emphasized in early role theory work in FPA. This is understandable in the context of the time period: IR, especially in the US, was dominated by structural – or system level – theories (e.g., Singer 1961; Waltz 2010 [1979]). However, the hold of system-level analysis on the discipline also hampered role theory: if it was merely structural IR presented at a different level of analysis and with a different set of concepts, then what was the added explanatory value?

Second-generation role theorists have given serious thought to this question. The process of reevaluation was facilitated by two developments. First, there was a resurgence of interest in the individual level of analysis in IR after the Cold War (Hafner-Burton et al. 2017; Hudson 2005, 2002; Hudson and Vore 1995; Kaarbo 2015, 2003). Second, around the same time, the constructivist approach became prominent in IR (Matthews and Callaway 2017; Thies 2013). Despite differences in emphasis, constructivist scholars (e.g., Finnemore and Sikkink 2001; Hopf 1998; Jepperson et al. 1996; Wendt 1992) share several core assumptions with role theorists. These assumptions include, first, the idea that interests are defined by actors. Second, in order to develop an understanding of actor interests, scholars need to understand these actors' norms, values, and beliefs. Third, agent and structure actively shape one another – and are shaped by one another. This is called co-constitution.

Constructivism's core assumptions fit well with those of role theory (Breuning 2017). First, both agree with Simon (1985, 298) that it is important to evaluate foreign policy situations as they appear "subjectively to the actors." Second, constructivism and role theory accept the notion of *bounded rationality* – the core assumption that, to make sense of foreign policy behavior (or role enactment), analysts need to understand not only what the relevant decision makers knew, but also their objectives, their capacity to "draw inferences from the information" they had, and the problem representation (or definition of the situation) they formulated (Simon 1985, 294). Third, the influence of constructivism prompted a move away from structural role theory and toward symbolic interactionism. Put differently, whereas the agent had been cast as constrained by the international structure in first-generation role theory, there was now more attention paid to the ways in which agents affect structure. First-generation role theorists, including Holsti (1970), did recognize this possibility, but their empirical work did not pay particular attention to it.

Not all second-generation role theorists focus on empirical cases where decision makers representing smaller states are able to defy international structural constraints, but Guimarães (2021) provides an excellent example. He empirically demonstrates under what circumstances small states can influence more powerful neighbors. I will discuss his comparative case study in more detail in the section on empirical strategies later in the chapter.

Second-generation role theory in FPA has benefited from both the return to the individual level of analysis and the emergence of constructivism in IR. It has also strengthened its theoretical frameworks through interdisciplinarity. Renewed connections to social psychology and sociology allowed FPA scholars to consider the applicability of new developments in role theory, symbolic interactionism, and other related work in those fields to revitalize role theory in FPA (Breuning 2019, 2017, 2011; Harnisch et al. 2011; McCourt 2012; Walker 1992; Walker et al. 2011; Wehner and Thies 2014).

These new conceptual developments are addressed in greater detail in the next section. Before moving on to key terms, concepts, and methodology, I note that there are additional approaches to role theory. The most prominent of these is the attempt to formalize role theory, using a game-theoretic approach called *binary role theory* (Malici and Walker 2017; Walker 2016, 2013; Walker et al. 2011). The ambition of this effort is to create a "general theory of symbolic and strategic interaction" (Walker 2011a, 272). This quest for a general theory stands in contrast to the prevailing trend in second-generation role theory scholarship. The latter focuses on theory-driven empirical analysis, often using comparative methods, to better understand how role conceptions are constituted, change over time, and influence foreign policy behavior (or: role enactment). This will become increasingly evident in the next sections.

Concepts and Methodology

Role theory in FPA has its own terminology and concepts, as well as methodological preferences for its empirical work. This section addresses these in some detail. To start, Holsti provided a definition of *national role conceptions*, which he described as consisting of

> the policymakers' own definitions of the general kind of decisions, commitments, rules and actions suitable to their state, and of the functions, if any, their state should perform on a continuing basis in the international system or in subordinate regional systems. It is their 'image' of the appropriate orientations or functions of their state toward, or in, the external environment.
>
> *(Holsti 1970, 245ff.)*

Although role conceptions are only one part of role theory's conceptual apparatus, Holsti's definition provides a useful starting point; it contains elements that remain relevant today. First, Holsti's definition centers on decision makers' *perceptions*. It seeks to determine how a decision maker understood a specific situation. Second, the definition implies that decision makers may perceive their state to play *multiple roles*. Just like individuals can simultaneously identify as professor and parent, states can simultaneously identify as, for example, a regional power and a faithful ally. Third, (some of) these roles may pertain to specific *relationships* or classes of relationships. For instance, a state that adopts the role of regional power within its geographic region may serve as a faithful ally to a global power.

Holsti's (1970) discussion of role theory was not comprehensive, as will become evident. The literature reviewed in the previous section referenced George Herbert Mead's (1934) work as providing the origins of role theory (and symbolic interactionism). Mead theorized about the relationship between the individual and society. Role theory in FPA extends this thinking to the relationship between the state and the international environment. Of course, there are differences between individuals and states, and this necessitated the development of concepts that acknowledge this. Let's start with role theory's foundational concepts.

In Mead's (1934) view, the development of the (individual) self requires interaction with others in a *society*. In other words, the self is inherently a social creature. Through interactions with others starting very early in life, humans have the opportunity to try a variety of roles – for example, young children often mimic the role behavior of adults as they play parent, cook, waiter, teacher, doctor, and so on – and to learn socially appropriate behavior – for example, by absorbing social conventions. Mead (1934) employs the terms *ego* (self) and *alter* (other) and argues that the self emerges out of both mimicking of and feedback from others in society.

Harnisch (2011a) translates Mead explicitly to FPA and writes that state A's "self" consists of *national role conception(s)*, which are defined as the role(s) that its decision makers perceive as appropriate for their state. The "other" has *role expectations*, defined as the role(s) that decision makers representing the relevant other state(s) perceive as appropriate for state A.

For convenience, I will refer to the one or more "others" as B. Important to note is that A's role conceptions and B's role expectations need not be congruent. Assuming that state A acts on the basis of its role conception, its *role enactment*, defined as its actual foreign policy behavior, may or may not correspond to state B's expectations of A. In the example in the introduction, Russia expected former Soviet republics to take the role of client state. In fact, these states differ in their national role conceptions. Some see themselves as a faithful ally and expect Russia to treat them as sovereign equals, rather than as clients.

This is where the concept of *role socialization* (Thies 2013, 2012) becomes useful. Role socialization addresses the process through which state A's role enactment is brought into alignment with state B's role expectations. A tacit underlying assumption of Thies' (2013, 2012) conceptualization of the role socialization process is that states get socialized by more powerful states. This process has most often been studied in the context of the socialization of new states, although Thies (2013, 2012) is careful to point out that socialization processes continue across time and interactions.

Thies' (2013) *socialization game* is a theory of role modification that plays out across a sequence of moves. These moves represent a careful dance of adjustments between emerging state A and its socializer(s) B. Over the course of the moves, A takes on a role that both it and the other (B) view as acceptable. Thies' (2013, 2012) socialization game represents a symbolic interactionist approach: rather than B socializing A into its "proper" role, the game leaves open the possibility that B adjusts its role expectations to bring them a bit closer to A's role conception. The interactions between Russia and the former Soviet republics can be understood in terms of an ongoing socialization game.

Thies' (2013, 2012) conceptualization differs from Mead's (1934) original formulation, which presumed that an actor's role conceptions were the end result of socializing encounters with others. That original formulation is now called *structural role theory*. As defined earlier, this version of role theory privileges social structures and expects new actors to be socialized into them. Translated to FPA, this means that state A's role conceptions (and role enactment) are driven primarily by what the preexisting international structure (and the more powerful B's in it) will allow. The problem that emerges, both at the societal and international level, is that this formulation cannot account for change. Symbolic interactionism (Stryker 2008, 2001; Stryker and Statham 1985), on the other hand, recognizes that actors can – and do – influence societal structure.

Although the description to this point has recognized that decision makers perceive and act in the name of the state, the careful reader will have noticed the slip into state-centric language. As conveyed above, the first generation of role theory scholarship in FPA recognized the importance of the perspective of decision makers, yet it also tended to see decision makers as synonymous with the state. Second-generation role theory scholarship has begun to question this implicit unitary actor perspective. Do decision makers generally agree on the state's role conception(s)? Do decision makers and the domestic public agree on the state's role in international politics?

These questions have led to the conceptualization of *domestic role contestation*, which is defined as disagreement within the state regarding the role(s) the state should play on the international stage. Cantir and Kaarbo (2016, 2012; see also Wehner and Thies 2014) define this in terms of horizontal and vertical role contestation. *Horizontal role contestation* captures debate about the state's role(s) between decision makers, both within the government and also between governing and opposition elites (Cantir and Kaarbo 2016, 11ff.). For instance, in the mid-1990s, Belgium's coalition government contested whether their state should enact the role of trading state or that of generous aid donor (Breuning 2016). *Vertical role contestation* captures differences between decision makers and the domestic public regarding the state's role(s) (Cantir and Kaarbo 2016, 9ff.). Belgian decision makers did not face pressure from their domestic public acquiesces, indicating an absence of vertical role contestation (Breuning 2016).

The conceptualization of these two types of domestic role contestation not only recognizes that the state is a *composite self*, but also allows role theory in FPA to ask new questions about the domestic sources of national role conceptions, as well as query the interaction between domestic and international sources. This not only makes models more complex but also serves to improve explanations of foreign policy behavior. For instance, Breuning and Ishiyama (2021) leverage survey data to show that the citizenry in eight states that were formerly part of the Soviet Union converge to different degrees on a shared conception of their state's role vis-à-vis Russia. They theorize that the more fragmented the citizenry, the more difficult it is for decision makers to persuade the public regarding chosen foreign policy behaviors. Conversely, if there is solid convergence around a specific role, then it is easier for decision makers to get "buy-in" from the public – as long as foreign policy role enactment is in line with that role conception.

I have also alluded to the fact that states can have multiple roles, as was also recognized in the earliest work on role theory in FPA. More recently, these multiple roles have been conceptualized as forming a system of roles, with states having a *master role* as well as *auxiliary roles* (Breuning and Pechenina 2020; Thies 2013; Wehner 2015). A master role is defined as a state's most salient attribute (Wehner 2015). It can range from global or regional power to simply having acquired sovereignty (Breuning and Pechenina 2020). The master role need not be one that mirrors the state's position in a presumed international hierarchy, but it must be its most salient role. All other roles are defined as auxiliary roles and are usually issue or geographically specific. These auxiliary roles may be congruent with the master role, but need not be. For instance, Russia's leaders perceive a master role as a big power, which conflicted with its auxiliary role as a sending country in international child adoption (Breuning and Pechenina 2020). When auxiliary and master roles are dissonant (i.e., not congruent), this may lead to *role conflict* (Breuning and Pechenina 2020; Thies 2013). The circumstances under which *role dissonance* generates role conflict – and how this is managed – were explored by Breuning and Pechenina (2020), but more empirical exploration of this dynamic is warranted.

Role theory has developed from a relatively simple set of concepts that prompted researchers to investigate how decision makers perceive and frame the foreign policy environment to become quite conceptually rich. It has maintained (and strengthened) the core assumption that decision makers are boundedly rational (Simon 1985). A key tenet is that to understand foreign policy behavior (or role enactment), the researcher must understand what the relevant decision makers knew, as well as their goals, their capacity to "draw inferences from the information," and their definition of the situation (Simon 1985, 294). Hence, role theory is inherently constructivist, in the sense that it accepts that international politics is defined by what states and their decision makers make of it (Wendt 1992).

This core assumption of role theory has consequences for empirical study. Role theory fits within the FPA perspective, which posits that the interactions between states are "grounded in *human decision makers acting singly or in groups*" (Hudson 2005, 1, italics in original; see also Snyder et al. 2002 [1962]).

Content analysis was the dominant empirical strategy in first-generation role theory analysis. It generally aggregated statements of decision makers and/or foreign policy elites together to represent the state's collective (set of) national role conception(s) (Holsti 1970; Walker 1987, 1981, 1979; Wish 1987, 1980). As role theory's conceptual apparatus developed further, there was a shift to a wider range of empirical strategies in its second generation. Content analysis remains part of role theory's toolkit, although it is less likely to be aggregated to a unified national role conception. Instead, more recent work tends to be interested in the relative prevalence of related or competing role conceptions among decision makers (Breuning 1995; Hansel and Möller 2015).

In addition to content analysis, role theorists now also employ narrative analysis, which has the advantage of being able to trace shifts that occur as a result of interaction. Work that employs narrative analysis leans clearly toward the symbolic interactionist perspective (McCourt 2012; see also Oppermann and Spencer in this volume; Wehner 2016, 2015). Other scholars employ case study analysis. Some case study-based analysis approximates narrative analysis as it carefully traces the process of, for instance, role socialization (Guimarães 2021; Thies 2013, 2012). Other work employs case studies in a more traditional manner, working inductively or demonstrating the plausibility of theoretical propositions (Akbaba and Özdamar 2019; Harnisch et al. 2016).

Each of these empirical approaches represents the kind of "painstaking empirical research" that Simon (1985, 303) advocated and that has been a core aspect of FPA research. The appropriateness of an empirical strategy often depends on the specific question the role theorist seeks to evaluate, as well as on data availability. Even though content analysis remains attractive now that automated analysis can code large volumes of text, such programs are not always suitable (see also Vignoli in this volume). Most automated content analysis requires the text to be in (or translated into) English. Translations can be excellent, but there is always the risk that the original meaning is distorted or that nuance is not captured adequately. This may be less of a problem in the future, as there are ongoing efforts to code text in other languages (Brummer et al. 2020). In addition, researchers may at times prefer interpretive narrative analysis to be able to discern subtle shifts that machine coding might not easily capture.

In sum, each of these empirical strategies has its own benefits and offers its own contribution to the advancement of knowledge regarding specific research questions in role theory. The next section will provide some brief illustrations of the key three empirical strategies employed by role theorists: content analysis, narrative analysis, and case study analysis.

Empirical Strategies

The previous section described content analysis, (interpretive) narrative analysis, and case study research as the most prevalent empirical strategies associated with second-generation research in role theory. I discuss these here in some detail. In doing so, I use existing studies, with a focus on smaller and emerging states. This choice is deliberate. First, the study of these types of states highlights the strengths of role theory, which is well-suited to empirically evaluate questions and puzzles related to states that take on outsized roles in terms of their "place" in the international hierarchy. Second, scholars focusing beyond the "usual suspects" have often asked interesting questions that are also relevant to improving our understanding of the foreign policies of more powerful states.

Content analysis was at the heart of Holsti's (1970) empirical strategy and remains a methodological approach that is often used in role theoretical work in FPA. It is a flexible methodology and there are many variations (Breuning 2010; see also Friedrichs in this volume). Content analysis was traditionally performed by human coders, but there are now many computer programs that can assist in the task. Automated (or machine-coded) content analysis generally relies on vocabularies that look for specific words and/or phrases. It has the advantage that it can process large volumes of text quickly and accurately. The validity of its measures depends on a well-designed coding scheme, which is also true of manual content analysis. The latter continues to rely on human coders who read, evaluate, and code text according to rules specified in a codebook. The use of human coders is labor and time intensive. Human coders get tired and lose focus, which can lead to inconsistencies and/or errors in their work. However, human coders have greater capacities to evaluate nuances in language and are better at coding tasks that call for a more interpretive approach.

Quite often, researchers who employ human coders will ask multiple coders to evaluate the same text, using the same coding rules. An excellent example is Hansel and Möller's (2015) study of the foreign policy role conceptions of Indian decision makers. Their study was inductive and initially employed basic guidelines, requiring that: "the word 'India' (or a substitute term such as 'We', 'Us', or 'Our') had to be present, and there had to be an indication of particular responsibilities or functions India performs in the international system" (Hansel and Möller 2015, 82). These very basic criteria allowed them to identify the role conceptions Indian decision makers verbalized about their country's *self*. Hansel and Möller (2015) followed this initial effort with two more rounds of coding all materials, employing a revised codebook that included the role conceptions identified in the first round. They then triangulated between the three efforts, keeping only the text that "at least two of our three coders categorized in the same way" (Hansel and Möller 2015, 82). The authors then used the resulting data, which revealed the presence of multiple role conceptions (eight in all) that varied in salience, to evaluate questions about India's puzzling foreign policy role enactment (or: behavior) regarding international humanitarian norms.

Well-designed content analysis coding schemes provide careful guidance to facilitate consistent coding decisions and, hence, contribute to reliable measurement. At the same time, the coding scheme must be designed to capture those elements of speech or text that most accurately represent the role concepts in which the researcher is interested. This ensures the validity of the measures. Hansel and Möller's (2015) strategy may seem quite laborious, but their process also ensured both validity and reliability. Other examples of content analysis-based role theory research include Holsti (1970), Breuning (1995), and Mello (2019).

Narrative analysis is a relatively more recent empirical strategy (see also Oppermann and Spencer in this volume). It has gained ground as role theory in FPA has become more interactionist in its approach. Narrative analysis, like content analysis, employs speech and text as its source. However, narrative analysis is more distinctly interpretive than content analysis. Wehner (2020, 368) argues that narrative analysis "enables researchers to make robust interpretations of the events that constitute foreign policy traditions and dilemmas – thus intimately portraying the role relationship process." It is a technique to gather and interpret data (Wehner 2020, 360).

Before the researcher can analyze the narrative, however, she must first meticulously collect the information necessary to reconstruct the interactions and/or contestations at the heart of the study. Wehner (2020, 368) describes this as similar to the data collection process in which historians engage. A wide variety of sources may be employed, including not only what is recorded in official documents and the press, but also secondary sources. Interviews with relevant decision makers, if feasible, are quite useful as well. That said, Wehner (2020, 368) cautions that triangulation of source materials is desirable. He also notes that researchers should assume that the evidence is never fully complete and only provides fragments rather than a complete story (Wehner 2020, 370).

The researcher will need to assemble these fragments, like an incomplete puzzle. This requires the researcher to evaluate the most plausible (re)construction of the fragments, as the pieces might be fitted together in multiple ways. The fragments become "reference points" to identify the key narrators and the ruling narrative regarding the emergence of, or contestation about, role conceptions and role expectations, as well as shifts and changes as states engage in a socialization game (Wehner 2020, 371). The objective is to give a "voice to the actors" (both *self* and *other(s)*) by reconstructing the narrative "from their point of view" (Wehner 2020, 370).

In order to perform a narrative analysis, then, after the relevant information has been collected, the analyst will need to discern the time period across which the analysis must stretch, as well as the main location(s) of action and the key actor(s). The puzzle that prompted the inquiry will often point the way regarding the time period, location(s), and the actor(s), but the analyst should be careful to look beyond the obvious. A foreign policy debate may seem to be primarily driven by domestic debate, but perhaps there is a significant international dimension as well, or vice versa. Wehner (2020) illustrates the methodology with a study of Hugo Chávez. Although he is the main actor, Wehner is careful to point out that other points of view both domestically and internationally must be considered to construct a well-rounded narrative. Narrative analysis is not only a simple reconstruction of events but also a vehicle for discerning patterns in decision makers' role conceptions and role enactment. The latter may not see these patterns, as they focus on addressing the situations in front of them in real time (Wehner 2020, 370).

In his work on the methodology of narrative analysis in role theory, Wehner (2020, 360) focuses on "ruling narratives," which he defines as the "stories that actors in decision-making positions employ to frame their world." In earlier work, he used narrative analysis to explore the role expectations that the decision makers of secondary powers in South America had of Brazil (Wehner 2015), as well as role conflict in the relationship between Chile and Brazil (Wehner 2016). McCourt (2012, 2011) has used a similar approach to study the Suez Crisis of 1956 and Britain's decision to recapture the Falklands in 1982.

In sum, narrative analysis is an interpretive methodology that explicitly takes the point of view of the relevant decision makers. Wehner (2020) describes some aspects of this type of analysis as akin to the craft of historians. However, narrative analysis also shares commonalities with case study analysis. Narrative analysis might be seen as similar to process tracing (see van Meegdenburg in this volume), albeit with the caveat that the latter need not take the point of view of the relevant decision makers.

Case studies are another popular research methodology employed by role theory scholars. These are not wholly separate from the previous two empirical strategies. Some case study designs employ content analysis (Breuning 1995) or narrative analysis (Wehner 2015), which can facilitate structured comparison and/or process tracing. Case study-based research can use either a single case or a small number of cases to develop hypotheses, explore causal mechanisms, or test a theory (George and Bennett 2005). Some case study analysis is inductive, whereas other case studies aim to test a theory that has been developed separately. Some studies explore a single case, whereas others provide a structured and focused comparison of a small number of carefully chosen cases (George and Bennett 2005; Gerring 2007). Single case studies often employ process tracing to facilitate the identification of causal mechanisms (Collier 2011; George and Bennett 2005). Comparative case study designs – that is, studies using a small to medium number of cases – often aim to test hypotheses (Gerring 2007; see also Mello in this volume).

Guimarães' (2021) provides an excellent example of comparative case study analysis. He starts by questioning the widely cited Melian Dialogue from the *History of the Peloponnesian War* by Thucydides, which is invariably used to convey that small and weak states are at the mercy of big powers. As a counter, Guimarães (2021) offers a compelling story from

Jonathan Swift's *Gulliver's Travels*, which plausibly suggests that small powers can sometimes successfully stand up to bigger states. Solidly grounded in role theory, Guimarães (2021) then conceptualizes ongoing processes of state socialization, which he terms *role learning* to distinguish them from the initial socialization of new states. He carefully justifies a set of four conditions that should be present for a small state to be able to cause role change in a larger neighbor. He then presents five case studies of small state interactions with a more powerful neighbor. By choosing his cases carefully, Guimarães (2021) is able to demonstrate that small states can not only influence their larger neighbors but also that this happens only when all four theorized factors are present. He employs an interactionist approach to carefully trace the role learning process. By employing both cases in which the small state was and was not successful in achieving change in the foreign policy behavior (or role enactment) of its more powerful neighbor, and showing that the lack of success occurred when one of the four conditions was absent, Guimarães (2021) is able to effectively leverage his comparative case study analysis to empirically demonstrate the value of his theory.

Other role theory-based studies that employ case study designs include Thies (2013), Harnisch et al. (2016), Akbaba and Özdamar (2019), and Breuning and Pechenina (2020). Case study-based research has long been a staple of role theory, FPA, IR, and is also quite prevalent in comparative politics. As the descriptions show, these three types of empirical analysis are distinct and have different strengths, but also share points of connection. They each offer valuable empirical strategies for role theory research.

Conclusion

Role theory's name suggests a conceptual approach to studying foreign policy. However, from its earliest use in FPA, it has also been tied to empirical analysis. Because a variety of empirical strategies have been employed, others have claimed that role theory is conceptually rich but methodologically poor (Thies 2017; Walker 2016, 1987). This chapter offers an alternative view and argues that role theory's methodological diversity is appropriate. First, role theory in FPA is conceptually rich and has gradually shifted from a structural to a symbolic interactionist interpretation. This has influenced researchers' preferences regarding empirical strategies. Second, the three most prevalent empirical strategies share commonalities, which means that the methodological diversity of role theory research may be overstated.

Role theory, especially as it increasingly takes seriously the interactive nature of foreign policy interactions, benefits from careful, theoretically driven analysis of single – or small to medium numbers of – cases to build cumulative knowledge. In contrast, IR has often eschewed this approach in favor of the bird's eye view provided by system-level analysis, although it has recently rediscovered the value of state- and individual-level analysis (Hafner-Burton et al., 2017). Hence, this may be a fortuitous time for role theory: its focus on "painstaking empirical research" (Simon 1985, 303) may be more readily understood as advantageous as IR scholars begin to realize that the individual is indeed the ground of the field (Hudson 2005).

Role theory has sought to facilitate a bridging of the divide between FPA and IR (Wehner and Thies 2021; Kaarbo 2015). Recent work in role theory endeavors to "unpack" national role conceptions. This has led to research on both *horizontal* and *vertical role contestation* (Cantir and Kaarbo 2016, 2012). A new development is the effort to leverage survey data to better understand the degree to which the domestic public does (or does not) converge around a single role conception regarding the relations with important foreign policy interlocutors (Breuning and Ishiyama 2021). Unpacking national role conceptions in these ways facilitates better understanding of the two-level game foreign policy decision makers face as they navigate between the expectations of their domestic public and of the decision makers of relevant other countries.

Methodologically, role theory will benefit from further developments in automated coding of text for content analysis, which makes possible a move from small-N to medium-N comparative case study designs. The inclusion of more cases will increase the confidence in the findings of comparative studies, although they will not eliminate the need for careful process-tracing of causal mechanisms through single or small-N studies.

Substantively, the increasingly prevalent focus on the role conceptions and role enactment of smaller and emerging states is beginning to pay off. These studies demonstrate that foreign policy behavior is guided by ideational factors as well as material power. Moreover, these studies show that role theory enhances FPA's capacity to offer insight into both the ideational and material aspects of foreign policy behavior.

Finally, researchers diving into role theory analysis for the first time will want to avoid resorting to the metaphorical use of roles and instead familiarize themselves with role theory's theoretical assumptions and concepts. The best role theory research is carefully grounded in conceptual precision of relevant role templates, transparency and clarity about how the empirical work is conducted, and how the researcher arrived at conclusions.

References

Akbaba, Yasemin, and Özgur Özdamar. 2019. *Role Theory in the Middle East and North Africa: Politics, Economics, and Identity*. New York: Routledge.

Breuning, Marijke. 1995. "Words and Deeds: Foreign Assistance Rhetoric and Policy Behavior in the Netherlands, Belgium, and the United Kingdom." *International Studies Quarterly* 39(2): 235–254.

Breuning, Marijke. 2010. "Content Analysis." In *21st Century Political Science: A Reference Handbook*, edited by John Ishiyama and Marijke Breuning. Thousand Oaks, CA: Sage, 490–496.

Breuning, Marijke. 2011. "Role Theory Research in International Relations: State of the Art and Blind Spots." In *Role Theory in International Relations: Approaches and Analyses*, edited by Sebastian Harnisch, Cornelia Frank and Hanns W. Maull. New York and London: Routledge, 16–35.

Breuning, Marijke. 2016. "Contesting Belgium's Role in Development Cooperation." In *Domestic Role Contestation, Foreign Policy, and International Relations*, edited by Cristian Cantir and Juliet Kaarbo. London and New York: Routledge, 72–88.

Breuning, Marijke. 2017. "Role Theory in Foreign Policy." In *Encyclopedia of Foreign Policy Analysis/Oxford Research Encyclopedia of Politics*, edited by Cameron Thies. New York: Oxford University Press. DOI:10.1093/acrefore/9780190228637.013.334.

Breuning, Marijke. 2019. "Role Theory in Politics and International Relations." In *Oxford Handbook of Behavioral Political Science*, edited by Alex Mintz and Lesley Terris. New York: Oxford University Press. DOI: 10.1093/oxfordhb/9780190634131.013.29.

Breuning, Marijke, and John Ishiyama. 2021. "Confronting Russia: How Do the Citizens of the Near Abroad Perceive their State's Role?" *Communist and Post-Communist Studies* 54(3): 97–118.

Breuning, Marijke, and Anna Pechenina. 2020. "Role Dissonance in Foreign Policy: Russia, Power, and Intercountry Adoption." *Foreign Policy Analysis* 16(1): 21–40.

Brummer, Klaus, Michael D. Young, Özgur Özdamar, Sercan Canbolat, Consuelo Thiers, Christian Rabini, Katharina Dimmroth, Mischa Hansel, and Ameneh Mehvar. 2020. "Coding in Tongues: Developing Non-English Coding Schemes for Leadership Profiling." *International Studies Review* 22(4): 1039–1067.

Cantir, Cristian, and Juliet Kaarbo. 2012. "Contested Roles and Domestic Politics: Reflections on Role Theory in Foreign Policy Analysis and IR Theory." *Foreign Policy Analysis* 8: 5–24.

Cantir, Cristian, and Juliet Kaarbo. 2016. "Unpacking Ego in Role Theory: Vertical and Horizontal Role Contestation and Foreign Policy." In *Domestic Role Contestation, Foreign Policy, and International Relations*, edited by Cristian Cantir and Juliet Kaarbo. New York: Routledge, 1–22.

Carlsnaes, Walter. 1992. "The Agency-Structure Problem in Foreign Policy Analysis." *International Studies Quarterly* 36(3): 245–270.
Chiozza, Giacomo, and H. E. Goemans. 2011. *Leaders and International Conflict*. New York: Cambridge University Press.
Collier, David. 2011. "Understanding Process Tracing." *PS: Political Science and Politics* 44(4): 823–830.
Finnemore, Martha, and Kathryn Sikkink. 2001. "Taking Stock: The Constructivist Research Program in International Relations and Comparative Politics." *Annual Review of Political Science* 4: 391–416.
George, Alexander, and Andrew Bennett. 2005. *Case Studies and Theory Development in the Social Sciences*. Cambridge, MA: MIT Press.
Gerring, John. 2007. *Case Study Research: Principles and Practices*. New York: Cambridge University Press.
Guimarães, Feliciano de Sá. 2021. *A Theory of Master Role Transition: Small Powers Shaping Regional Hegemons*. New York: Routledge.
Hafner-Burton, Emilie, Stephen Haggard, David A. Lake, and David G. Victor. 2017. "The Behavioral Revolution and International Relations." *International Organization* 71(Suppl. 1): S1–S31.
Hansel, Mischa, and Miriam Möller. 2015. "Indian Foreign Policy and International Humanitarian Norms: A Role-Theoretical Analysis." *Asian Politics and Policy* 7(1): 79–104.
Harnisch, Sebastian. 2012. "Conceptualizing in the Minefield: Role Theory and Foreign Policy Learning." *Foreign Policy Analysis* 8: 47–69.
Harnisch, Sebastian. 2011a. "'Dialogue and Emergence': George Herbert Mead's Contribution to Role Theory and His Reconstruction of International Politics." In *Role Theory in International Relations: Approaches and Analyses*, edited by Sebastian Harnisch, Cornelia Frank and Hanns W. Maull. New York and London: Routledge, 36–54.
Harnisch, Sebastian, Sebastian Bersick, and Jörn-Carsten Gottwald, eds. 2016. *China's International Roles: Challenging or Supporting International Order?* New York: Routledge.
Harnisch, Sebastian, Cornelia Frank, and Hanns W. Maull, eds. 2011. *Role Theory in International Relations: Approaches and Analyses*. London and New York: Routledge.
Hollis, Martin, and Steve Smith. 1986. "Roles and Reasons in Foreign Policy Decision Making." *British Journal of Political Science* 16(3): 269–286.
Holsti, K. J. 1970. "National Role Conceptions in the Study of Foreign Policy." *International Studies Quarterly* 14(3): 233–309.
Hopf, Ted. 1998. "The Promise of Constructivism in International Relations Theory." *International Security* 23(1): 171–200.
Horowitz, Michael C., Allan C. Stam, and Cali M. Ellis. 2015. *Why Leaders Fight*. New York: Cambridge University Press.
Hudson, Valerie M. 2002. "Foreign Policy Decision-Making: A Touchstone for International Relations Theory in the Twenty-First Century." In *Foreign Policy Decision-Making (Revisited)*, edited by Richard C. Snyder, H. W. Bruck and Burton Sapin. New York: Palgrave, 1–20.
Hudson, Valerie M. 2005. "Foreign Policy Analysis: Actor-Specific Theory and the Ground of International Relations." *Foreign Policy Analysis* 1(1): 1–30.
Hudson, Valerie M., and Christopher S. Vore. 1995. "Foreign Policy Analysis Yesterday, Today, and Tomorrow." *Mershon International Studies Review* 39: 209–238.
Jepperson, Ronald L., Alexander Wendt, and Peter J. Katzenstein. 1996. "Norms, Identity, and Culture in National Security." In *The Culture of National Security: Norms and Identity in World Politics*, edited by Peter J. Katzenstein. New York: Columbia University Press, 33–75.
Jönsson, Christer, and Ulf Westerlund. 1982. "Role Theory in Foreign Policy Analysis." In *Cognitive Dynamics and International Politics*, edited by Christer Jönsson. New York: St. Martin's Press, 122–157.
Kaarbo, Juliet. 2003. "Foreign Policy Analysis in the Twenty-First Century: Back to Comparison, Forward to Identity and Ideas." *International Studies Review* 5(2): 156–202.
Kaarbo, Juliet. 2015. "A Foreign Policy Analysis Perspective on the Domestic Politics Turn in IR Theory." *International Studies Review* 17(2): 189–216.
Malici, Akan, and Stephen G. Walker. 2017. *Role Theory and Role Conflict in U.S.-Iran Relations*. New York: Routledge.
Matthews, Elizabeth G., and Rhonda L. Callaway. 2017. *International Relations Theory: A Primer*. New York: Oxford University Press.
McCourt, David M. 2011. "Role-Playing and Identity Affirmation in International Politics: Britain's Reinvasion of the Falklands, 1982." *Review of International Studies* 37: 1599–1621.

McCourt, David M. 2012. "The Roles States Play: A Meadian Interactionist Approach." *Journal of International Relations and Development* 15(3): 370–392.

Mead, George H. 1934. *Mind, Self, and Society*. Chicago, IL: University of Chicago Press.

Mello, Patrick A. 2019. "Von der Bonner zur Berliner Republik: Die 'Zivilmacht' Deutschland im Spiegel parlamentarischer Debatten zu Auslandseinsätzen der Bundeswehr, 1990 bis 2018." In *Zivilmacht Bundesrepublik? Bundesdeutsche außenpolitische Rollen vor und nach 1989 aus politik- und geschichtswissenschaftlichen Perspektiven*, edited by Klaus Brummer and Friedrich Kießling. Baden-Baden: Nomos, 295–316.

Ozkececi-Taner, Binnur. 2006. "Reviewing the Literature on Sequential/Dynamic Foreign Policy Decision Making." *International Studies Review* 8(3): 545–554.

Schafer, Mark, and Stephen G. Walker, eds. 2021. *Operational Code Analysis and Foreign Policy Roles: Crossing Simon's Bridge*. New York: Routledge.

Shih, Chih-yu. 1988. "National Role Conception as Foreign Policy Motivation: The Psychocultural Bases of Chinese Diplomacy." *Political Psychology* 9(4): 599–631.

Simon, Herbert A. 1985. "Human Nature in Politics: The Dialogue of Psychology with Political Science." *American Political Science Review* 79(2): 293–304.

Singer, J. David. 1961. "The Level-of-Analysis Problem in International Relations." *World Politics* 14(1): 77–92.

Snyder, Richard C., H. W. Bruck, and Burton Sapin. 2002 [1962]. *Foreign Policy Decision-Making (Revisited)*. New York: Palgrave.

Stryker, Sheldon. 2001. "Traditional Symbolic Interactionism, Role Theory, and Structural Symbolic Interactionism: The Road to Identity Theory." In *Handbook of Sociological Theory, Handbooks of Sociology and Social Research*, edited by John H. Turner. Boston, MA: Springer. https://doi.org/10.1007/0-387-36274-6_11.

Stryker, Sheldon. 2008. "From Mead to a Structural Symbolic Interactionism and Beyond." *Annual Review of Sociology* 34: 15–31.

Stryker, Sheldon, and Anne Statham. 1985. "Symbolic Interactionism and Role Theory." In *Handbook of Social Psychology*, volume 1, 3rd edition, edited by G. Lindzey and E. Aronson. New York: Random House, 311–378.

Thies, Cameron. 2010. "Role Theory and Foreign Policy." In *The International Studies Encyclopedia*, edited by Robert A. Denemark. Oxford: Blackwell; Blackwell Reference Online.

Thies, Cameron. 2012. "International Socialization Processes vs. Israeli National Role Conceptions: Can Role Theory Integrate IR Theory and Foreign Policy Analysis?" *Foreign Policy Analysis* 8(1): 25–46.

Thies, Cameron. 2013. *The United States, Israel, and the Search for International Order: Socializing States*. London: Routledge.

Thies, Cameron. 2017. "Role Theory and Foreign Policy Analysis in Latin America." *Foreign Policy Analysis* 13(3): 662–681.

Walker, Stephen G. 1979. "National Role Conceptions and Systemic Outcomes." In *Psychological Models in International Politics*, edited by Lawrence Falkowski. Boulder, CO: Westview Press.

Walker, Stephen G. 1981. "The Correspondence Between Foreign Policy Rhetoric and Behavior: Insights from Role and Exchange Theory." *Behavioral Science* 26: 272–280.

Walker, Stephen G. 1987. *Role Theory and Foreign Policy Analysis*. Durham, NC: Duke University Press.

Walker, Stephen G. 1992. "Symbolic Interactionism and International Politics." In *Contending Dramas: A Cognitive Approach to International Organizations*, edited by Martha Cottam and Chih-yu Shih. New York: Praeger, 19–38.

Walker, Stephen G. 2011a. "The Integration of Foreign Policy Analysis and International Relations." In *Rethinking Foreign Policy Analysis*, edited by Stephen G. Walker, Akan Malici and Mark Schafer. New York: Routledge, 267–282.

Walker, Stephen G. 2013. *Role Theory and the Cognitive Architecture of British Appeasement Decisions*. New York: Routledge.

Walker, Stephen G. 2016. "Role Theory as an Empirical Theory of International Relations." In *The Oxford Research Encyclopedia of Empirical International Relations Theory*, edited by William Thompson. New York: Oxford University Press.

Walker, Stephen G., Akan Malici, and Mark Schafer. 2011. *Rethinking Foreign Policy Analysis*. New York: Routledge.

Waltz, Kenneth N. 2010 [1979]. *Theory of International Politics*. Long Grove, IL: Waveland Press.

Wehner, Leslie E. 2015. "Role Expectations as Foreign Policy: South American Secondary Powers' Expectations of Brazil as a Regional Power." *Foreign Policy Analysis* 11(4): 435–455.

Wehner, Leslie E. 2016. "Inter-Role Conflict, Role Strain and Role Play in Chile's Relationship with Brazil." *Bulletin of Latin American Research* 35(1): 64–77.

Wehner, Leslie E. 2020. "The Narration of Roles in Foreign Policy Analysis." *Journal of International Relations and Development* 23(2): 359–384.

Wehner, Leslie E., and Cameron G. Thies. 2014. "Role Theory, Narratives, and Interpretation: The Domestic Contestation of Roles." *International Studies Review* 16: 411–436.

Wehner, Leslie E., and Cameron G. Thies. 2021. "Leader Influence in Role Selection Choices: Fulfilling Role Theory's Potential for Foreign Policy Analysis." *International Studies Review* 23: 1424–1441. https://doi.org/10.1093/isr/viab014.

Wendt, Alexander. 1987. "The Agent-Structure Problem in International Relations Theory." *International Organization* 41(3): 335–370.

Wendt, Alexander. 1992. "Anarchy Is what States Make of It: The Social Construction of Power Politics." *International Organization* 46(2): 391–425.

Wish, Naomi B. 1980. "Foreign Policy Makers and their National Role Conceptions." *International Studies Quarterly* 24(4): 532–554.

Wish, Naomi B. 1987. "National Attributes as Sources of National Role Conceptions: A Capability-Motivation Model." In *Role Theory and Foreign Policy Analysis*, edited by Stephen G. Walker. Durham, NC: Duke University Press, 94–103.

13
The Political Psychology of Threat Assessment

Janice Gross Stein

Introduction

There is no more studied subject in international politics and political psychology than threat. When politicians perceive a threat, at first intuitively and then more formally, they assess both its gravity and its likelihood. This assessment of threat is the critical intermediate step between perception and response. The chapter deals with the conceptual and methodological challenges of threat assessment.

I pay particular attention to the methodological challenges at three different stages with three different groups: first, the methods that policy makers use in assessing threats in real time, then the judgments about the adequacy of assessment methods that review panels make with the benefit of hindsight, and finally the methods scholars use when they evaluate both the methods of policy makers at the time and those of review panels after the fact. Each of these three groups use somewhat different methodologies, or practices, shaped in part not only by differences in time pressures and degrees of uncertainty but also by history and culture (see also Oktay, Kleinberg, or Lupton and Webb in this volume). I look at the largely quantitative methodologies used by all three groups to assess capabilities and the survey and experimental methods used by at least two of the groups to assess estimates of probability under conditions of uncertainty. I also look at the qualitative methods academics used to assess the causes of failure to assess threats accurately. I find significant differences in methodologies across the three groups and conclude that no methodology ensures agreement even when people assess evidence with the benefits of time and hindsight. Threat assessment has proven to be a *wicked* problem.

Key Terms and Methodology

Threats can be verbal and physical. Verbal threats are conditional statements designed to signal the capacity and intention to inflict harm if desired results are not forthcoming. Leaders do not always threaten verbally; they can also use non-verbal signals to communicate the seriousness of their intent to punish undesirable behavior. In international politics, they may withdraw their ambassadors, kidnap and hold hostages, or move forces to contested borders.

The accumulation of economic, military, and technological power is at times perceived as threatening by others, even if that is not its principal or even intended purpose. It is because threats do not unambiguously speak for themselves that the analysis of threat perception is so important (Stein 2023).

Perception is the process of apprehending by means of the senses and recognizing and interpreting what is processed. Psychologists think of perception as a single unified awareness derived from sensory processes when a stimulus is present. It is quick and is experienced physically before we are fully aware. Giving content and meaning to threat perception is a cognitive and emotional process that is generally, although not always, triggered by physiological processes. The content of threat perception then provides the framing and structure for the assessment and the responses that follow.

There is increasing bi-partisan sentiment in Washington, for example, that China is now a threat to the United States. The term *threat* conceals three different dimensions that can be separated analytically but often bleed into each other, which makes threat assessment an analytically challenging process. The overarching question is one of *intentions*. Intention is determined largely, though not exclusively, through processes of perception. In this chapter, I bracket the question of intention, which I have examined elsewhere, and focus on the analytical and methodological challenges of assessing the other two dimensions, capabilities and probabilities (Stein 2023).

The first dimension of threat assessment is the assessment of *capabilities*. Leaders can perceive states or non-states as threatening. They can also perceive *actorless threats*, such as climate change, or pandemics, or meltdowns from nuclear plants. In those cases where a state or non-state actor is the source of threat, the first stage of threat assessment asks if the threatener has the capacity to inflict harm. If the actor's capacity is relatively limited, then even though the intent to threaten is significant, the threat can become less urgent although this is increasingly less the case in an age of asymmetrical warfare where a broad range of capabilities becomes relevant. When a threat is actorless, such as COVID-19, leaders will still ask for assessments of its capability to cause death, overwhelm health infrastructure, and disrupt the economy. Capabilities matter, and assessing those capabilities, how they can be used, and how much harm they can inflict for how long are all essential components of threat assessment. Assessing capabilities generally involves quantitative methods, but, as I argue, these are often not sufficient.

The second category of threat assessment is the *likelihood* that a threat will occur. Epidemiologists stressed for decades that a viral pandemic was a serious threat, capable of inflicting terrible harm directly through infection and death and indirectly through the associated economic and social costs. They could not estimate the probability that a pandemic would occur within a specified period of time because pandemics occur so infrequently that it is impossible to construct their probability distribution. As a result, preventing and preparing for a pandemic did not rise to the top of the policy agenda before 2020. Even in the wake of COVID-19, scientists struggle to estimate the likelihood of another pandemic in the next five years and default to claims that it is *more* likely than it has been in the past. Similarly, when actors intend to inflict harm and have the capacity to do so, decision makers still have to grapple with the likelihood of the threat. How important is inflicting harm to a potential adversary? How likely is an adversary to proceed? Sophisticated methods for updating probabilities can draw on formal Bayesian models that explicitly ask people to update their prior estimates in the face of new evidence. These formal models are rarely used in a systematic way by policy analysts or review panels (Stein and Tanter 1980).

Assessing capabilities and probabilities once people perceive threats raises difficult methodological challenges. First, assessment often takes place in an environment of uncertainty, where probability distributions are unknown, rather than in an environment of risk. Second, in international politics, political leaders tend to rely, in the first instance, on the estimates of professional analysts. These analysts operate in a bureaucratic and political environment and these dynamics are not well captured by methods that focus on individuals. Despite these challenges, analysts have to generate assessments for political leaders in real time.

Intelligence analysts focus their attention on both estimates of capabilities and likelihoods and have established methods that they use to gather evidence and to analyze the evidence to identify and minimize bias. Evidence is subject to interpretation through embedded practices that always occur within preexisting subjective frames. The methodological challenges that analysts, reviewers, and scholars face are formidable, because the evidence is incomplete, although to different degrees at the three stages, and because even the most careful methodologies do not eliminate differences in interpretation. Historiographers have always understood that *truth* is contested and contingent, to be investigated again and again in different times and in different ways.

Assessing Capabilities

Assessing capabilities should be the easier challenge. In the first instance, it involves using all available means of intelligence to gather good information on the assets an adversary has. This appears to be a largely technical problem that culminates in *counting* the assets and assessing how well they can be used and the harm they can inflict.

The challenge is not as simple as it appears. It is easiest to assess capabilities when they are visible and, in some roughly defined way, related to the outcome. In an era when tank warfare dominated the battlefield, roughly from 1940 to 1975, let us assume that tanks are parked in open fields, as they were at times. With access to the results of good aerial surveillance, the analyst counts the tanks and, knowing the number of tanks her own country has, estimates their likely impact on the battlefield. Even these stylized conditions – a single weapons system that is totally visible – diminish but do not resolve the methodological challenges of analyzing relative capabilities. The analyst has no quantitative tools to measure the relative skill of tank commanders, their capacity to adapt to the demanding conditions of mobility on the battlefield, their trust in their commanding officers, and their ability to adapt to changing battlefield conditions in real time. There are no formal models that can estimate the impact of these factors individually and their interaction effects cumulatively, so analysts use their background knowledge, established practices, and ultimately their subjective experience and judgment to develop these largely qualitative estimates. Try as they might, it is here that what cognitive psychologists call embedded patterns of thinking and practice shape the analysis.

Measuring relative capability in tank warfare is a fairly easy problem. Assessing weapons of mass destruction – chemical, biological and nuclear – is far harder and the methodological challenges are greater. It is harder because many of the components that go into the production of unconventional weapons are used in civilian manufacturing processes. When analysts review evidence that an adversary has purchased these dual-use technologies, they are more likely to make worst-case assumptions although when a friendly country makes the same purchases, they are likely to assess these purchases as benign, intended for civilian uses. Assessing the capabilities of an adversary to deploy weapons of mass destruction is hard, because some facilities are built deep underground where they are hidden from satellites and aircraft overflying the sites. And it is hard because governments seeking to develop these capabilities sometimes go to great lengths to conceal what they are doing. At other times, they deliberately exaggerate their capabilities in an effort to reap the reputational and deterrent benefits.

Review panels that examine failures after the fact also face methodological challenges. They have all the information from multiple sources that departments across the government received and they know the outcome. In reviewing the processes and methodologies analysts used before the fact, they have to be very careful not to use criteria of evaluation that rely on information that analysts working at the time did not have. Political psychologists call this error the *hindsight bias* (Fischoff and Beyth 1975). A few review panels meet these methodological criteria and most oversimplify, quite unfairly, the challenges that analysts faced at the time.

Finally, scholars, who also have access to that information and possibly more, have to *think* themselves back into the shoes of analysts at the time and develop explanations and make recommendations based on what was then possible for analysts. They have to make clear their criteria of evaluation, be transparent about their standards of evidence, and be explicit about the methodologies they use to make inferences. These methodologies are likely to be qualitative, given the nature of the problem, and criteria of logic, argument, and inference need to be clear. Scholars also need to think carefully about the counter-intuitive consequences of organizational solutions they recommend, since the evidence is strong that every institutional reorganization produces a new set of challenges. These are demanding methodological standards to meet.

Assessing Probabilities

A second critical component of threat assessment is the estimation of the probability that the threat will occur. Intentions matter most when capabilities are present. Once a judgment is made that an adversary is capable, probability comes to the fore. How likely is the threat to materialize? Foreign policy decision makers face special challenges because many of the threats they consider occur in an environment where underlying probability distributions are not available. Foreign policy decision makers generally live in a world of uncertainty, not risk.

To make matters worse, even when probability distributions are robust, people are generally not intuitive probability thinkers. Experimental evidence (see also Lupton and Webb in this volume), a great deal of it with undergraduate students but some of it with retired foreign policy experts (Tetlock 2005), as well as survey analysis (see also Kleinberg in this volume) are the most frequently used methodologies to establish patterns of thinking about probability. Studies relying largely on these two methodologies find that people depart systematically from what objective probability calculations or even Bayesian models would dictate in the estimates they make (Kahneman and Tversky 1979; Friedman et al. 2018). There is also vigorous debate about how well evidence generated from rigorously designed experimental studies under controlled conditions travels into a messy world.

Foreign policy decision makers tend to use cognitive short cuts to estimate the likelihood of threats and, like decision makers in general, tend to be loss averse and, under specific conditions, overweight the likelihood of a threatening loss. To make matters worse, people tend to be overconfident in the estimates that they generate.

"Human performance suffers," argues Tetlock, "because we are, deep down, deterministic thinkers with an aversion to probabilistic strategies that accept the inevitability of error" (Tetlock 2005: 40). Within these general patterns, there is variation across individuals.

Likely states of the world are very difficult to estimate in world politics. It is this extraordinary difficulty that is a significant contributor to the ordinariness of intelligence failures. Analysts in other fields – medicine, epidemiology, economics – can draw on repeated trials with large numbers. Leaders responsible for estimating threat in international politics generally do not live in a world of risk, where the probability distributions are known and the task is to estimate the likelihoods. They do not have probability distributions of attacks by militants against civilian infrastructure in the United States or the United Kingdom. Nor do they have a large data base on the number of attacks by great powers on offshore islands close to their territory. There are a small number of cases where organized military forces like the Taliban move through a country and capture a capital city. There have been too few such attacks to generate a probability distribution.

When intelligence agencies in western capitals were asked in July of 2021 to estimate how long it would take the Taliban to sweep through the country and occupy Kabul, many estimated that it would take at least a year if not more. In early August, the intelligence community in the United States updated their estimate to December 2021. Political leaders in most western capitals were surprised by the rapidity of the Taliban advance, were caught unprepared, and struggled to evacuate their citizens once the Taliban entered the city on August 15, 2021. This world of structural uncertainty without probability distributions is one that is particularly uncomfortable psychologically and it is under these conditions that leaders, just like experts, are most likely to seek security of the self, often expressed through the search for order and control. Sociologists and philosophers label this pattern the search for ontological security (Mitzen 2006).

Thinking about probability through cognitive short cuts. An analysis of the probability estimates of foreign policy experts shows that they do surprisingly poorly. This evidence is derived not from experimental evidence but from a carefully designed survey. It finds that highly educated specialists in foreign affairs approached only 20% of the ideal across all exercises (Tetlock 2005: 77). They performed poorly because they thought causally and did not pay attention to the frequencies with which events occurred. Experts tend to overestimate the likelihood of the threat of war, for example, because they can easily imagine the causal pathways to war, a highly salient occurrence that they have experienced or studied (Tversky and Kahneman 1983; Koehler 1996). They pay less attention to the threats that did not lead to war and to the frequency of threats over an extended period of time.

In laboratory experiments, cognitive psychologists have identified heuristics and cognitive patterns that people use in environments of both risk and uncertainty that can impair processes of probability estimation and threat perception (Tversky and Kahneman 1973; Nisbett and Ross 1980; Kahneman, Slovic and Tversky 1982; Jervis 1986; Johnson et al. 2012). Heuristics are convenient short cuts or rules of thumb for processing information. Two of the best documented heuristics directly related to estimating the likelihood of threats are *representativeness* and *anchoring*. The heuristic of representativeness refers to people's proclivity to exaggerate similarities between one event and a prior class of events, typically leading to significant errors in probability judgments (Kahneman and Tversky 1972; 1973; Tversky and Kahneman 1973, 1982). The heuristic of anchoring refers to an estimation of magnitude or degree by comparing it with an *available* initial value as a reference point and making a comparison. In a world of uncertainty, leaders search for the relevant reference classes to anchor their judgments. Initial judgments or prior beliefs serve as a conceptual anchor on the processing of new information and the revision of estimates. Evidence from cognitive psychology suggests that processes of information processing are weighed down by prior beliefs and initial estimates (Tversky and Kahneman 1982). The implications for the estimation of the likelihood of a threat are considerable: once an estimate of the likelihood of a threat is generated, it anchors subsequent rates of revision so that revision tends to be slower and less responsive to diagnostic information. Anchoring leads to estimates of the probability of threats that can be too low or too high, in part because they become embedded and resistant to change.

Although scholars will have to do painstaking research, I suspect that it is likely that the initial estimate of at least a year before the Taliban took control *anchored* the subsequent estimate. Analysts then failed to update in response to the large number of provincial districts in Afghanistan that fell to the Taliban with no fighting, especially to the fall of capitals of two northern provinces that in the past had been the sites of significant opposition to the Taliban. Had they updated their estimates at the time, the United States and others would have had some time to pull some of their nationals and loyal Afghans out before the Taliban took control of the capital.

These conservative processes of information processing are present in almost all intelligence failures. Josef Stalin ignored evidence that was inconsistent with his belief that Adolf Hitler would not turn away from the western front and attack the Soviet Union. Similarly, in the United States, although a few very senior officials warned of the intention of *al-Qa'eda* to strike the United States before 2001, officials generally failed to update their estimates as they received disconnected pieces of information before September 11. Similar conservatism in updating estimates explains the failure of leaders to update their assessment of a likely pandemic even though there was strong evidence by early January of 2020 that something extraordinary was happening in the city of Wuhan in China.

Non-linearity. Conservative updating is not the only obstacle to better estimates. There is good evidence from experiments that people tend to be non-linear in the way they weight probabilities (Kahneman and Tversky 1979; Tversky and Kahneman 1992). When the probability of a consequence is low, people will tend to systematically underweight that probability; at the extreme, they will treat low probability consequences as impossible. When the probability of a consequence is high, they will overweight these probabilities and treat high probabilities as certain. Economists have advanced their knowledge of the threshold at which non-linear probability weighting shifts (Barberis 2013).

Loss aversion. Foreign policy decision makers, like people generally, are not neutral about risk. Prospect theory is among the most influential theories of risk propensity and while it is a primarily a theory of response to risk, it also speaks to estimating the likelihood and valuation of threatening losses under conditions of uncertainty. To diminish the psychological discomfort of uncertainty, people tend to convert uncertainty to subjective estimates of risk. Daniel Kahneman and Amos Tversky argue first that the pain of a loss is greater than the pleasure of an equivalent gain. People frame choice around a reference point and give more weight to losses from that reference point than to comparable gains in constructing their assessments of risk. Because losses are far more painful than gains, people are risk-averse with respect to gains and risk-acceptant with respect to losses when probability estimates are high (Kahneman and Tversky 1979; Tversky and Kahneman 1992).

Within this general pattern, there is variation. Domain has an impact not only on the weighting of loss but also on the estimation of its likelihood. The tendency toward risk-seeking is greater in human life problems than in money problems (Mandel 2001). Prospect theory is more likely to be relevant, therefore, to estimation of the likelihood of security threats than it is to threats arising from international trade or finance (Kanner 2004; McDermott 2009; Stein 2017). When their survival or the survival of those they represent is at risk, decision makers tend to weigh that threat as very costly and overestimate its probability (Johnson 2020).

The impact of loss aversion on threat assessment is considerable (Jervis 1992; Farnham 1994; Levy 1997; McDermott 1998; Davis 2000). Leaders are likely to be more sensitive to the likelihood of threats to what they already have, because they tend to value what they have – the *endowment effect* – more than comparable assets that they do not have (Kahneman et al. 1990; Jervis 1992). Prospect theory, although primarily a theory of decision, is, nevertheless, a very useful screen for analysts to assess the likelihood of threat. In 1973, Egypt's President Sadat, who had never normalized for the loss of the Sinai in 1967, chose as his reference point not the status quo but Egyptian possession of the Sinai. He was consequently in the domain of loss and extraordinarily risk-acceptant in his choices. He designed around Israel's deterrence – its superiority in the air and on the ground – and his generals planned a limited strike across the Suez Canal under the protection of a missile shield. Israel's analysts systematically underestimated the threat from Egypt because they missed the impact of loss aversion on Sadat's calculation of risk and subsequent decision (Stein 1985). Prospect theory would have been a far more useful theoretical screen for Israel's analysts to assess the likely threat from Egypt than a rational model of deterrence based on net assets and a balance of military capabilities. The argument and the evidence suggest that leaders need to be especially vigilant in their threat assessment when their adversary is in the domain of loss (Levy 2003). Under these circumstances, leaders need to correct for the risk of underestimating rather than overestimating the likelihood of threat (Stein and Sheffer 2019).

Overconfidence amplifies the impact of forecasting errors (Arkes 2001; Johnson and Fowler 2011). People who are overconfident tend, by definition, to be more confident than they are accurate; they exaggerate the true likelihood of an outcome (Johnson 2020: 51; Tetlock 2005). Overconfidence is a tendency toward optimism that neuroscientists locate in specific areas of the brain that block disconfirming evidence (Moore and Healy 2008; Sharot 2011; Johnson 2020: 52). Accuracy is a function of the ability of people to make predictions and then get feedback so that they can adjust their future estimates (Agrawal et al. 2018). In world politics, feedback is generally slower and more ambiguous, leaving greater scope for people to reinforce rather than adjust their prior beliefs and avoid revising their estimates. In this domain, decision makers are likely to remain overconfident far longer than in domains where feedback comes quickly and is undisputable. Only after their estimates of likelihood have been proven wrong do leaders acknowledge that they were overconfident. There is strong evidence that decision makers tend to be overconfident both in their estimation of the likelihood of threats and in their capacity to prevail should they choose to use force to respond to the perceived threat (Levy 1983). Overconfidence varies significantly across individuals, genders, domains, and cultures.

These patterns of thinking and heuristics are drawn from experimental evidence, but they have proven to be useful in the interpretation of events that are anomalous in the context of alternative theoretical interpretations. Do these results explain what would otherwise be difficult to explain with existing theory? Intelligence analysts overestimated the likelihood that Saddam had weapons of mass destruction. They resorted to the language of certainty in their estimates and never systematically calculated the cumulative probabilities that would have led them to revise their estimates of probability downward rather than upward. Almost 30 years later, they underestimated how quickly Kabul would fall and updated these estimates too little and too late in response to new information.

These systematic errors provide strong explanations of both failures, but the evidence also shows that there is variation in the ways individuals estimate probability (Schaub 2004; McDermott et al. 2008; Stein and Sheffer 2019). That is true for academics and review panels as well as for policy makers and analysts. It is conceivable, although by no means demonstrated, that careful articulation of methodologies and attention to procedures and practices explain the variation that leads to success. We do not know because these patterns have not been investigated in cases of success, largely because these cases have not been systematically identified.

Assessing Estimates of Capabilities and Likelihood: U.S. Assessment of Saddam Hussein's Programs of Chemical, Biological, and Nuclear Weapons

Discussions of methodology are often abstract and difficult to relate to concrete cases. Careful examination of the assessments of whether or not Saddam Hussein had weapons of mass destruction illustrates the methodological challenges faced by analysts in real time, after the fact by review panels, and finally by academics who have the luxury of time and much better evidence. Other things being equal, we would expect analysts in real time facing the greatest uncertainty to fare most poorly, reviewers to do somewhat better, and academics free from institutional bias with access to better evidence to do to best.

Analysts Assessments at the Time

A great deal of evidence is now publicly available about how analysts assessed capabilities and likelihoods at the time, how the reviews and commissions of inquiry assessed these assessments, and how academics assessed the assessors as well as the original assessments (Butler Report 2004; Cirincione et al. 2004; Kennedy 2004; SSCI Report 2004; Davies 2005; WMD Report 2005; Jervis 2006; Department of Defense Inspector-General 2007; Rovner 2011). These overlapping assessments provide a unique opportunity to evaluate methodologies across time and space.

Robert Jervis, in his review of all these post-mortems, makes the important methodological point that intelligence failures are ordinary. They are ordinary, he says, because intelligence is "a game between hiders and finders, and the former usually have the easier job" (Jervis 2006: 11). This point is so important because it suggests that intelligences failures are routine. How routine? For scholars or anyone else to answer this question, we would need a careful coding of all intelligence investigations as either successes or failures before we could make that inference (Robarge 2005). The obstacles to doing that kind of analysis are obvious. Intelligence agencies rarely release any information about their successes, often because they do not wish to discuss either sources or methods of operation that can be inadvertently exposed. Review panels and scholars alike consequently draw on a set of cases that are heavily biased toward failure. As a result, they cannot systematically discriminate whether the patterns they find in intelligence failure are also present when intelligence analysis succeeds. This is a pervasive methodological challenge that not only frames scholarly research but the findings of review panels as well.

The general point that capabilities are easier to hide than to find applies even more strongly to programs to develop weapons of mass destruction. In the case of Saddam's capabilities, there was a serious shortage of reliable information. United Nations' inspectors, who had provided eyewitness reports based on their inspections, left the country in 1998. Neither the United States nor the United Kingdom had high-level agents in the country, and overhead photography could not reveal what was hidden. Until the summer of 2002, intelligence agencies in both the United States and the United Kingdom estimated that Iraq had a small number of unconventional weapons but could not be much more precise. There was considerable disagreement among U.S. intelligence agencies about the scope and speed of programs in the three different areas – chemical, biological, and nuclear. A ground-level methodological challenge, then, was the poor quality of information that intelligence agencies had.

A new source, codenamed *Curveball*, became active in 2,000 and provided German intelligence with estimates that Iraq had accelerated its efforts to deploy mobile laboratories to produce biological agents (SSCI Report 2004: 144). Intelligence agencies in the United States were only given direct access to the source very late and only once. In April 2001, the CIA learned that Iraq was trying to buy 60,000 high-strength aluminum tubes from Hong Kong that, the agency suspected, could be used as uranium enrichment centrifuges. That estimate was challenged by the Department of Energy that insisted the specifications of the tubes were inconsistent with known centrifuge designs (Jervis 2010: 143ff).

After the al-Qaeda attacks on September 11, 2001, the sensitivity to threat increased dramatically, as did the prominence of the CIA in the threat assessment process. Still agencies across the government could not agree on whether the new evidence suggested an increased pattern of activity at chemical plants and whether the allegation that Iraq was trying to acquire uranium ore (*yellowcake*) from Niger was reliable and whether it indicated that Saddam was restarting his nuclear program. Analysts at the State Department rejected the theory (SSCI Report 2004: 37–38). These disagreements reflect the deep methodological challenges of making inferences in a context of uncertainty and ambiguity. Agencies across the government generally continued to emphasize the poor quality of the evidence.

In the summer of 2002, intelligence analysis abruptly changed and began to sound a growing note of alarm. This change in their estimates coincided with much closer questioning by senior policy makers about the conclusions they were presenting, a subtle form of pressure that signaled that decision makers were not hearing what they expected – or wanted – to hear. Asked to assess Saddam's unconventional weapons programs, the CIA delivered a comprehensive estimate that concluded that Iraq was actively producing chemical weapons and considerably increased the estimate of the tonnage of chemical agents (SSCI Report 2004: 195–204). Even though internal disagreements about the significance of a white tanker truck at a chemical complex were not resolved, the estimate reflected worst-case assumptions (Rovner 2011; WMD Commission, 125–126).

The public version of the National Intelligence Estimate that was released on October 4 reached the alarming conclusion that Iraq was expanding all its programs of unconventional weapons (NIE 2002). It stated definitively that Iraq had biological weapons, that it had grown its stockpile of lethal chemicals, and that international controls were too weak to prevent a determined Iraq from acquiring a nuclear weapon by the end of the decade. At the same time, the CIA issued a declassified paper which, in unequivocal language, concluded that Iraq was expanding its WMD capabilities and, ignoring disagreements, concluded that the aluminum tubes were part of a program to enrich uranium (CIA 2002). This was not an updating of estimates in response to new evidence, as Bayesian methodologies recommend, but a reinterpretation of existing evidence using worst-case assumptions. After the attack against Iraq, none of these estimates was confirmed by analysts searching for evidence in the field (Duelfer Report 2004).

Review Panel Assessments in the Immediate Aftermath

Why did analysts exaggerate the likelihood of unconventional weapons and minimize the uncertainty in their estimates? What methodologies did they use to generate their assessments, what errors did they make, and were these errors of methodology? That they were wrong does not necessarily indicate methodological failure, because they worked in a context of subjective probability – where there is always some chance that they could be wrong – and the inherent ambiguity of evidence when technologies are dual-use.

Review panels in both the United States and the United Kingdom were asked to provide explanations for the intelligence failures and to make recommendations on how this kind of failure could be avoided in the future. These panels had the power to call witnesses and had access to classified information across departments and agencies. The methodologies these panels used were clear: established techniques of evidence-gathering and forensic examination to assess cause and explain the failure. These reviews were clearly operating in a highly charged political context where intelligence agencies were accused of distorting evidence and downplaying disagreement and governments were accused of manipulating intelligence for political purposes.

The reviews generally conclude that the poor quality of information and very limited time explain the flawed estimates. This judgment is reasonable, given that analysts working in real time were scanning thousands of pieces of information and trying to make sense of inconsistent evidence. Some of the reviews went beyond the situational constraints of evidence and time and focused on common patterns of psychological inference that can impair judgment. The Butler Report in particular concluded that analysts leaned toward worst-case analysis, because they feared underestimating more than they feared overestimating the threat (Butler Report 2004: 139). Analysts worried more about underestimating Saddam's unconventional capabilities in large part, because they had missed these programs in 1990 and were surprised when Saddam's son-in-law revealed them several years later. They were biased against making the error they had made in the past and their judgments reflected that bias. Overcompensation for past mistakes is a methodological error that reflects a common pattern of inference. As I will argue in the next section, it is extraordinarily difficult to determine which of these explanations was the most important.

All three major reports made judgments about whether the intelligence agencies did the best that could be expected given the limited information and time that they had. There are significant differences among the reports – the *Report of the Select Committee on Intelligence on the U.S. Intelligence Community's Prewar Intelligence Assessments on Iraq* (SSCI Report) is most critical, followed by the *Commission on the Intelligence Capabilities of the United States Regarding Weapons of Mass Destruction, Report to the President of the United States* (WMD Report), and the *Review of Intelligence on Weapons of Mass Destruction* (Butler Report) that is the most restrained. They all cite systematic bias against underestimation of the threat, the expression of judgments with excessive certainty, a failure to report continuing dissent and disagreement, and lack of care in reporting levels of certainty to policy makers. Analysts also failed to recognize that evidence of purchase of specific dual-use items that was consistent with their interpretations was also consistent with other arguments. The reports made especially strong arguments about the sloppy estimates of probability and the layering of uncertainties that violated basic calculation of cumulative probabilities (Butler Report 2004: 13; SSCI Report 2004: 22). The reports identified these as methodological failures that produced predictable errors in assessments.

How methodologically sound were these reports? The review panels generally avoided the well-established methodological error of *hindsight bias*, where they knew what evidence was significant and so unfairly faulted analysts for not finding the needle in the haystack when the reviewers knew – but the analysts did not – where the needle was (Fischoff and Beyth 1975). None of the major reports, however, deals with the *ordinariness* of intelligence failure, and none makes a systematic attempt to test the patterns they find against cases of intelligence success that they may have known about.

The reports were not significantly better at systematically exploring alternative explanations of Saddam's behavior even though they faulted analysts for not doing exactly that. We know now from Saddam's detailed interviews with the FBI after he was captured by American forces that he was worried about his ongoing capacity to deter Iran and was reluctant, therefore, to disclose the fact that he had not restarted his nuclear program (Battle 2004). Although that argument was not advanced by any agency before the war, not even by country experts outside the government, the failure by the review panels to consider alternative explanations is not consistent with the methodological rules of drawing inferences from qualitative evidence that they recommended to analysts (Jervis 2006: 15–16).

Finally, none of the three reviews deals with the anomaly that almost all allied intelligence agencies came to roughly the same conclusions, although there were differences in degree. That there was widespread agreement among agencies working in different political and institutional contexts suggests that differences in politics or institutional design are not sufficient methodological explanations of the widespread failure.

Academic Assessments After the Fact

Academic analysts handled the methodological challenges of explaining an intelligence failure differently than either analysts or reviewers. Like reviewers, they have the advantage of hindsight, time, and far better evidence, but the best scholars were far better in actively considering alternative explanations and testing them meticulously against the evidence, at times using counterfactual logic. Although they were far more sophisticated methodologically, scholars, nevertheless, reached different conclusions on what was the most important explanation of the failure. Good methodology and good evidence do not necessarily resolve the challenges of adjudicating among competing claims.

Joshua Rovner and Robert Jervis, two of the very best scholars of intelligence who each had policy experience as well as deep academic expertise, disagreed on the degree of the politicization of the intelligence process in the United States and on how important that politicization was in explaining the failure. What methodological strategies did each use to arrive at his conclusions?

All the major reviews rejected the proposition that intelligence failed because they were subject to political pressure by leaders who had already made up their minds to go to war. Joshua Rovner disagrees and challenges that interpretation by systematically reviewing alternative explanations, looking at the evidence, and rejecting the alternatives to polarization as unconvincing. To cite only one example, Rovner observes that the reviews in both the United States and the United Kingdom speculated that perhaps *groupthink* had been at work in both (t'Hart et al., 1997, see also Barr and Mintz in this volume). Yet, he notes the evidence shows considerable disagreement in both countries through to December 2002.

Rovner argues that neither changes in the evidence or time pressures, nor routine bureaucratic politics or psychological biases are sufficient explanations of the failure to assess Saddam's unconventional weapons more accurately (Rovner 2011: 156–162). He traces the increasing alarm in the intelligence estimates in the summer of 2002 to the politicization of the relationship with the intelligence community by the White House. The most senior Administration officials – Vice-President Cheney, Secretary of Defense Donald Rumsfeld, and National Security Advisor Condoleezza Rice – all spoke with increasing frequency about Saddam as a threat and warned that he was pursuing unconventional capabilities. Behind closed doors, policy makers repeatedly questioned analysts, subtly signaling their displeasure at what they were hearing and hinting that they wanted different answers.

In London as well as in Washington, already committed political leaders and their advisers used intelligence information to persuade skeptical political opponents and doubting publics. By bringing intelligence evidence into the public debate, Rovner concludes, both governments were able to forge a policy consensus and overcome domestic opposition. The two governments politicized intelligence by downplaying dissent within their agencies, exaggerating the certainty of threats, and claiming that intelligence overwhelming supported their preferred policy options (SSCI 2004; Rovner 2011). He carefully sifts through the evidence to establish why his argument of politicization covered more instances and worked better across both countries than did alternative explanations.

Robert Jervis rejected the explanation of politicization as the primary explanation of the failure. He began with a detailed summary of the arguments *for* politicization of intelligence and provided additional evidence in support of the argument, which the review panels missed. He noted that the failure of U.S. forces to search for WMD as they moved through Iraq during the attack was troubling. Had these weapons been stockpiled, they could have fallen into the hands of adversaries. The evidence he cited was inconsistent with his preferred interpretation but unlike analysts or reviewers, he was candid in saying that he could not explain the anomaly and scrupulous in citing that evidence (Jervis 2006: 33, n7).

In support of his preferred interpretation, Jervis then cited confidential interviews where analysts did not blame the errors they made on political pressure (Jervis 2006: 35). He observed as well that agencies in all the major countries, even those that actively opposed the war, concluded that Iraq had active WMD programs (cf. Barnes 2020). There is no evidence of political pressure in several of the countries that reached the same conclusion. Moreover, the CIA was able to resist political pressure throughout 2002 and into 2003 right up to the attack when it consistently denied that there was significant evidence that Saddam might turn over WMD to al-Qaeda. There was consistent pressure, Jervis argues, but it was not determining in driving intelligence estimates of Iraq's weapons of mass destruction.

Jervis then qualified his own conclusion and acknowledged that, at the least, political pressure encouraged judgments of excessive certainty and worked against critical analysis (Jervis 2006: 36). Using counterfactual reasoning as a key methodological tool, he concluded that the Review Panels ignored the most compelling evidence *for* politicization "…probably because it was something that did not happen" (Jervis 2006: 37). Intelligence analysts did not update their estimates of probability after the UN inspections resumed and found no evidence of WMD. The failure to do so, Jervis reasoned, is because it was then obvious that both governments were bent on war and would dismiss any revisions to the estimates. Nevertheless, he claimed that the fundamental drivers of error were the overlearning from their previous error and the strength of the belief in the intelligence community that Saddam was consistent, coherent, and unchanging in his determination to acquire WMD (Jervis 2006: 22, 23). These assumptions, he concluded, "…were reasonable, much more so than the alternatives" (Jervis 2006: 42).

Both these analyses use methodologies that are more rigorous than both the review panels and the intelligence analysts in their attention to alternative explanations, to evidence that would discriminate among these explanations, and in the willingness of both authors to challenge their own explanations and acknowledge where others might be more plausible. Academics, of course, do their work at a distance and at leisure and are free from the political pressures of the moment, but academics too bring preexisting beliefs to their work of analysis and interpretation. That both resist that trap is testimony to their rigorous scrutiny of the evidence, to their openness to disconfirming evidence, and to their willingness to confront logical flaws in their own arguments. What separates their methodology is their willingness to argue against themselves.

It is not obvious, however, what methodologies scholars could use to adjudicate between these competing explanations of the most important cause of the failure. Each acknowledged the factors that the other identified, so the disagreement between them was on the relative weight of different explanatory variables. When scholars use quantitative methods, there are a variety of methods that they can use to establish the relative weights of contributing factors. When the evidence is not suited for quantitative analysis, the challenges of adjudication are much harder.

What options do scholars have? They could test arguments against comparative cases and make inferences about necessary but not sufficient conditions. They can also acknowledge that the outcome is often overdetermined, pay attention to the top two or three without claiming primacy, and pay special attention to the interaction effects among the most important drivers. When evidence and methodologies are qualitative, it is especially challenging to adjudicate claims about which variable provides the strongest explanation. It is not by chance that, 100 years later, there is no consensus on the causes of World War I and that interpretation changes as the context changes.

Conclusion: Improving Assessment

I have identified systematic patterns of assessing capabilities and estimating probabilities that characterize many people much of the time. Scholars have found that these assessments are remarkably difficult to improve, largely because people generally tend to be anchored in their beliefs and poor at estimating probabilities. But there is individual variation. Some people do much better than others at both tasks. How can we improve the performance of analysts and policy makers and what role does methodology play?

Some scholars have encouraged decision makers to systematically consider alternative explanations for the indicators that are most diagnostic in shaping their estimates (Arkes 2001; Jervis 2010). In a related recommendation, others recommend institutionalizing challengers, suggesting that decision makers build in *red teams* or *devil's advocates* who can challenge estimates early enough in the process, before these assessments become deeply embedded. There is value in these recommendations, because they build in the equivalent of methodological checks, but in real time. When they work best, they challenge analysts to consider alternative explanations and to make explicit the indicators that they are using in their assessments. Heightening awareness of the indicators that guide judgment can be especially valuable, because analysts are then predisposed to pay attention to changes in the indicators that they have identified. Some of these recommendations have been tried and have been successful, but they have proven difficult to institutionalize and sustain over time.

A second approach is centered in the benefits of machine learning and text analysis as complements to decision making (see also Cujai or Vignoli in this volume). Using text and sentiment analysis of diplomatic cables and documents from Washington to the U.S. Embassy in Teheran and back in 1979, scholars found that officials underestimated the likelihood of the fall of the Shah until it was too late (Connelly et al. 2021). Monitoring of large amounts of texts for changes in sentiment could alert officials to changing public moods earlier. We are at the very beginning of the use of machine learning and artificial intelligence as aids to official processes of assessment.

By far the most sustained attempt to improve estimates and forecasts of geopolitical events is the *Good Judgment Project* that, in a four-year tournament, consistently outperformed intelligence analysts who had access to classified data. The development of rigorous methodological processes and training, combined with the selection of individuals who have certain traits, produces significantly better forecasts. The primary attributes of *superforecasters* are open-minded thinking and the belief that forecasting is a skill to be cultivated (Tetlock and Gardner 2015). Training can improve performance in forecasting, as people become better at distinguishing signals from noise. Encouraging decision makers and analysts to use clearer, more precise, and quantifiable probability estimates that are consistent with natural language-based descriptions also improves performance as does making frequent, small updates to estimates (Friedman et al. 2018; Atanasov et al. 2020).

While these methodologies are encouraging, it is important that we remain modest. As human beings, we evolved a very long time ago to address immediate threats that put our survival at risk. The threats that we face today in our complex, uncertain, fragile, and networked world are very different in nature and scope. The human machinery that we have inherited must adapt to the challenges that we face today and are likely to face in the future. Methodology matters at all three levels – the analyst, the reviewer, and the scholar – because it can increase awareness of our patterns of thinking and the methodological tools that we can use to improve assessment. Even as we work to improve our methodologies, it is important that we remain aware of the contextual and contingent nature of what we know and how we know what we know.

References

Agrawal, Ajay, Joshua Gans, and Avi Goldfarb. 2018. *Prediction Machines: The Simple Economics of Artificial Intelligence*. Boston, MA: Harvard Business Review Press.

Arkes, Hal. R. 2001. "Overconfidence in Judgmental Forecasting." Principles of Forecasting: A Handbook for Research and Practitioners, Edited by J. S. Armstrong. Boston, MA: Springer, 30: 495–515.

Atanasov, Pavel, Jens Witowski, Lyle Ungar, Barbara Mellers, and Philip E. Tetlock. 2020. "Small Steps to Accuracy: Incremental Belief Updaters are Better Forecasters." Organizational Behavior and Human Decision Processes 160(September): 19–35.

Barberis, Nicholas C. 2013. "Thirty Years of Prospect Theory in Economics: A Review and Assessment." Journal of Economic Perspectives 27(1): 173–196.

Barnes, Alan. 2020. "Getting it Right: Canadian Intelligence Assessments on Iraq, 2002–2003." Intelligence and National Security 35(7): 925–953.

Battle, Joyce, ed. 2004. Saddam Hussein Talks to the FBI: Twenty Interviews and Five Conversations with "High Value Detainee # 1 in 2004. National Security Archive Electronic Briefing Book No. 279. https://nsarchive2.gwu.edu/NSAEBB/NSAEBB279/index.htm.

Butler Report. 2004. Report of a Committee of Privy Counselors. Review of Intelligence on Weapons of Mass Destruction. London: The Stationary Office.

CIA. 2002. Director, Iraq's Weapons of Mass Destruction Programs, October 4. https://www.cia.gov/library/reports/general-reports-1/iraq_wmd/Iraq_Oct_2002.htm#01

Cirincione, Joseph N., Jessica T. Matthews, and George Perkovich, with Alexis Orton. 2004. WMD in Iraq: Evidence and Implications. Washington, DC: Carnegie Endowment for International Peace 2(1): 51–55.

Connelly, Matthew, Raymond Hicks, Robert Jervis, and Arthur Spirling. 2021. "New Evidence and New Methods for Analyzing the Iranian Revolution as an Intelligence Failure." Intelligence and National Security 36(6): 781–806.

Davies, Philip H. J. 2005. "A Critical Look at Britain's Spy Machinery: Collection and Analysis on Iraq." Studies in Intelligence 49(4): 47–48.

Davis, James. 2000. Threats and Promises. Baltimore, MD: John Hopkins University Press.

Department of Defence Inspector-General. 2007. Review of the Pre-Iraqi War Activities of the Under Secretary of Defense for Policy, February 9. http://www.dodig.mil/fo/Foia/pre-iraqi.htm.

Duelfer Report. 2004. Comprehensive Report of the Special Advisor to the DCI on Iraq's WMD, with Addendums. https://www.govinfo.gov/app/details/GPO-DUELFERREPORT.

Farnham, Barbara. 1994. Taking Risks/Avoiding Losses. Ann Arbor, MI: University of Michigan Press.

Fischoff, Baruch and Ruth Beyth. 1975. I Knew it Would Happen: Remembered Probabilities of Once-Future Things. Washington, DC: National Technical Information Service 13(1): 1–16.

Friedman, Jeffrey A., Joshua D. Baker, Barbara A. Mellers, Philip E. Tetlock, and Richard Zeckhauser. 2018. "The Value of Precision in Probability Assessment: Evidence from a Large-Scale Geopolitical Forecasting Tournament." International Studies Quarterly 62(2): 410–422.

Jervis, Robert. 1986. "Representativeness in Foreign Policy Judgments." Political Psychology 7(3): 483–505.

Jervis, Robert. 1992. "Political Implications of Loss Aversion." Political Psychology 13(2): 87–204.

Jervis, Robert. 2006. "Reports, Politics, and Intelligence Failures: The Case of Iraq." The Journal of Strategic Studies 29(1): 3–52.

Jervis, Robert. 2010. Why Intelligence Fails: Lessons from the Iranian Revolution and the Iraq War. Ithaca, NY: Cornell University Press.

Johnson, Dominic D. P. 2020. Strategic Instincts: The Adaptive Advantages of Cognitive Biases in International Politics. Princeton, NJ: Princeton University Press.

Johnson, Dominic D. P., and James H. Fowler. 2011. "The Evolution of Overconfidence." Nature 477(7364): 317–320.

Johnson, Dominic D. P., Rose McDermott, Jon Cowden, and Dustin Tingley. 2012. "Dead Certain: Confidence and Conservatism Predict Aggression in Simulated International Crisis Decision-Making." Human Nature 23(1): 98–126.

Kahneman, Daniel, Jack L. Knetsch, and Richard H. Thaler. 1990. "Experimental Tests of the Endowment Effect and the Coase Theorem." Journal of Political Economy 98(6):1325–1348.

Kahneman, Daniel, and Amos Tversky. 1972. "Subjective Probability: A Judgment of Representativeness." Cognitive Psychology 3(3): 430–454.

Kahneman, Daniel, and Amos Tverksy. 1973. "On the Psychology of Prediction." Psychological Review 80(4): 237–251.

Kahneman, Daniel, and Amos Tversky. 1979. "Prospect Theory: An Analysis of Decision Under Risk." Econometrica 47(2): 263–291

Kahneman, Daniel, Paul Slovic, and Amos Tversky eds. 1982. Judgement Under Uncertainty: Heuristics and Biases. Cambridge: Cambridge University Press.

Kanner, Michael D. 2004. "Framing and the Role of the Second Actor: An Application of Prospect Theory to Bargaining." Political Psychology 25(2): 213–239.

Kennedy, Donald. 2004. "Intelligence Science: Reverse Peer Review?" Science 203 (5666): 1945.

Koehler, Derek J. 1996. "A Strength Model of Probability Judgments for Tournaments." Organizational Behavior and Human Decision Processes 66(1):16–21.

Levy, Jack. 1983. "Misperception and the Causes of War: Theoretical Linkages and Analytical Problems." World Politics 36(1): 76–99.

Levy, Jack. 1997. "Prospect Theory, Rational Choice, and International Relations." International Studies Quarterly 41(1): 87–112.

Levy, Jack. 2003. "Political Psychology and Foreign Policy." In Oxford Handbook of Political Psychology, edited by David O. Sears, Leonie Huddy and Robert Jervis. New York: Oxford University Press, 253–284.

Mandel, David R. 2001. "Gain-Loss Framing and Choice: Separating Outcome Formulations from Descriptor Formulations." Organizational Behavior and Human Decision Processes 85(1): 56–76.

McDermott, Rose. 1998. Risk Taking in International Relations. Ann Arbor, MI: University of Michigan Press.

McDermott, Rose. 2009. "Prospect Theory and Negotiation." In Negotiated Risks, edited by Rudolf Avenhaus, and Gunnar Sjostedt. Berlin: Springer, 87–109.

McDermott, Rose, James H. Fowler, and Oleg Smirnov. 2008. "On the Evolutionary Origin of Prospect Theory Preferences." The Journal of Politics 70(2): 335–350.

Mitzen, Jennifer. 2006. "Ontological Security in World Politics: State Identity and the Security Dilemma." European Journal of International Relations 12(3): 341–370.

Moore, Don A., and Paul J. Healy. 2008. "The Trouble with Overconfidence." Psychological Review 115(2): 502–517.

National Intelligence Estimate 2002-16HC. 2002. Iraq's Continuing Programs for Weapons of Mass Destruction, October 1. Edited version published in the Washington Post in April 2004. http://www.washingtonpost.cm/wp-srv/nation/nationalsecurity/documents/nie_iraq_wmd.pdf

Nisbett, Richard E., and Lee Ross. 1980. Human inference: Strategies and Shortcomings of Social Judgment. Englewood Cliffs, NJ: Prentice-Hall.

Robarge, David. 2005. "Getting it Right: CIA Analysis of the 1967 Arab-Israeli War." Studies in Intelligence 49(1): 1–8.

Rovner, Joshua. 2011. Fixing the Facts: National Security and the Politics of Intelligence. Ithaca, NY: Cornell University Press.

SCCI Report. 2004. Report of the Select Committee on Intelligence on the U.S. Intelligence Community's Prewar Intelligence Assessments on Iraq, July 9. http://www.gpoaccess.gov/serialsecretreports/ira.html

Schaub, Gary. 2004. "Deterrence, Compellence, and Prospect Theory." Political Psychology 25(3): 389–411.

Sharot, Tali. 2011. The Optimism Bias: A Tour of the Irrationally Positive Brain. New York: Pantheon.

Stein, Janice G. 1985. "Calculation, Miscalculation, and Conventional Deterrence, II: The View from Jerusalem." In Psychology and Deterrence, edited by Robert Jervis, Richard N. Lebow and Janice G. Stein. Baltimore, MD: John Hopkins University Press, 60–85.

Stein, Janice G. 2017. "The Micro-Foundations of International Relations Theory: Psychology and Behavioral Economics." International Organization 71(S1): S249–263.

Stein, Janice G. 2023. "Perceiving Threat: Cognition, Emotion and Judgment." In The Oxford Handbook of Political Psychology, edited by Leonie Huddy, David O. Sears and Jack Levy. Third edition. Oxford: Oxford University Press.

Stein, Janice G., and Lior Sheffer. 2019. "Prospect Theory and Political Decision Making." In The Oxford Handbook of Behavioral Political Science, edited by Alex Mintz and Lesley Terris. Oxford: Oxford University Press. DOI:10.1093/oxfordhb/9780190634131.013.31.

Stein, Janice G., and Raymond Tanter. 1980. Rational Decision Making: Israel's Security Choices, 1967. Columbus, OH: Ohio State University Press.

Tetlock, Philip E. 2005. Expert Political Judgment: How Good Is it? How Can We Know? Princeton, NJ: Princeton University Press.

Tetlock, Philip E., and Dan Gardner, D. 2015. Superforecasting: The Art and Science of Prediction. New York: Random House.

t'Hart, Paul, Eric Stern, and Bengt Sundelius. 1997. Beyond Groupthink: Political Group Dynamics and Foreign Policy-Making. Ann Arbor, MI: University of Michigan Press.

Tversky, Amos, and Daniel Kahneman. 1973. "Availability: A Heuristic for Judging Frequency and Probability." Cognitive Psychology 5(2): 207–232.

Tversky, Amos, and Daniel Kahneman. 1982. Judgement Under Uncertainty: Heuristics and Biases. New York: Cambridge University Press.

Tversky, Amos, and Daniel Kahneman 1983. "Extensional vs. Intuitive Reason: The Conjunction Fallacy in Probability Judgment." Psychological Review 90(4): 293–315.

Tversky, Amos, and Daniel Kahneman. 1992. "Advances in Prospect Theory: Cumulative Representation of Uncertainty." Journal of Risk and Uncertainty 5(4): 297–323.

WMD Report. 2005. Commission on the Intelligence Capabilities of the United States Regarding Weapons of Mass Destruction, Report to the President of the United States, March 31. http://www.gpoaccess.gov/wmd/.

14
Measuring Perceptions
Combining Low and High Inference Approaches to Data Analysis in International Political Communication

Natalia Chaban, Linda Jean Kenix, Svetlana Beltyukova, and Christine Fox

Introduction

Information revolution, new media ecology, and infodemics continue to mark the twenty-first century decision and policy making, including foreign policy. Understanding – and conquering – the complexity of information flows is paramount in the world marked by ongoing multiple crises, such as growing multipolarity with increased competition and contestation, challenged multilateralism and return of power politics, environmental and climate catastrophes, technological breakthroughs twinned with technological disasters, mass migration triggered by human-made and natural calamities, and the most recent crisis of the Covid pandemic. The multitude and magnitude of crises that cross national borders beg a critical insight into the nature and peculiarities of information flows and meaning formation behind perceptions that may impact foreign policy formulation, projection, and conduct at times of uncertainty. When there is a crisis on an international scale, how do different media systems frame the crisis and form public perceptions of all involved actors and how do they combine/associate/relate meanings from a different origin?

Perception data are often used to influence policy decisions and drive high-stakes decision making, both domestically and in foreign policy arenas. Since the data represent a range of opinions shared by a range of individuals, it is critical to explore multiple methodological approaches to extract maximum meaning from such data. This chapter presents several approaches to analyzing perceptions data, discusses their appropriate uses and limitations, and demonstrates how they can be used to complement one another to improve the quality of our inferences. The Rasch Measurement Model (RMM) is used as a methodology for analyzing high inference approaches to perceptions data (Rasch 1960, 1980; Bond and Fox 2013). So far, the RMM has only occasionally been used in IR perceptions studies (for an exception see Chaban, Beltyukova and Fox 2017).

We define low inference variables as directly observable, descriptive, and factual. They are objectively quantified with little room for varying interpretations. High inference variables, on the other hand, are open to the subjective interpretation of the observer. We begin by highlighting the difference between low and high inference variables, with descriptive and non-parametric as appropriate analyses for low inference variables, and the RMM as appropriate for investigating high inference variables. Combining these approaches with construct definition and operationalization will illuminate the extent to which each is appropriate and useful, either separately or in combination, to further our theoretical understanding. We argue that it is the alignment of construct definition, data coding, and analysis that allows researchers to extract maximum meaning from their perception data.

The combination of low and high inference approaches in our method allows us to test the theories that provide explanations to how images and perceptions are spread and activated among foreign policy actors and international relations, and to understand them in a more complex way. The theoretical novelty of this chapter is in its critical revision of the *cascading activation framing model* (Entman 2003, 2004). According to this model, news media are a mechanism that spreads ideas on foreign policy and international relations down the cascade from elites to the general public. This model argues that news media also pump up the feedback from the public to the decision-makers. The model has been empirically informed by the US media system, which traditionally relies on its own, local reporters to report foreign policy. As such, the model has overlooked the importance of news sources (local vs. international) in its theorization. Proposed in the early twenty-first century, the model also under-addresses the proliferation of new media, which has changed the entire media ecology leading to a weaker agenda setting effect within (Western-type) liberal media environments (see also Schneiker in this volume).

These media systems – the focus of our study – are open on one side due to new media influences, and, on the other side, to a range of news sources, the choice of which is often based on cost-effective and bottom-line imperatives. In the revision of his earlier model, Entman states that media frames are no longer nation-originated or nation-specific (Entman and Usher 2018). We add that in the coverage of international affairs, Western-type liberal media have been traditionally open to inputs of international reputable news sources for cost-savings, as international newsmaking is expensive. These media resort to a range of strategies to cope with high costs on international news: from foreign location-based correspondents and parachute assignments (the most expensive) to cooperation with stringers, freelancers, and international news agencies, and finally, desk work using a range and combination of international sources. Arguably, when a major international crisis takes place, local media will use all types of sources as an international crisis is ultimately a sexy topic that sells the news. Given how media rely on international wire services for news content about international crises, we share the assumption that media framing is not happening exclusively within the nation state (here we are building on Entman and Usher's (2018) notion that media frames do not move in national systems exclusively), but rather through a network of shared meanings of different origin that later form relations and associations between each other.

For empirical illustrations, the chapter draws upon large datasets from a comparative transnational research project on EU external perceptions (*Analysis of EU perceptions abroad and its policies*, PPMI/NCRE/NFG 2015) demonstrating a multidisciplinary potential of the combined low and high inference data analysis approach to the media images of international actors vis-à-vis news sources. This chapter seeks to examine whether the nature of news sources – local versus international – acts as a filter in shaping views and perceptions of key foreign policy partners, at times of uncertainty and crisis. We argue that news sources should be factored into the understanding of and interpreted as a *cultural filter* in foreign actors' framing. Cultural filters are "based on the interplay between the construction of knowledge and the creation of social and political identity" (Manners 2002:245).

A debate on globalization versus localization of news flows informs this interpretation. Advocates of the former approach argue that "news is becoming homogenized at a global level [and] the development of a global media network is often tacitly equated with an increasing cultural homogenization" (Giddens 1990, 1991; Lash and Urry 1994; Robertson 1992 as cited in Archetti 2008:464). The proponents of the latter approach oppose the idea of global news and argue that the "same information is framed differently at the national level by news producers, who adapt it to the taste and interests of local audiences" (Clausen 2003, 2004; Gurevitch et al. 1991 as cited in Archetti 2008:464). The perceptions of a major internal crisis presented through different media lenses – local versus international – can serve as "road maps" and "focal points" (Goldstein and Keohane 1993), prompting the general public and policy-makers in countries around the world to consider how best to define the crisis, how to relate to it, how to assess key actors involved, and how to respond.

We engage with a particular case – the major humanitarian crisis of irregular migration to the EU that started in 2015 and has continued to test Europe ever since, with its peak in 2015–2016, when about 1 million arrivals were estimated (Chaban and Lucarelli 2021). The magnitude of the crisis has attracted major international attention to the EU. This chapter focuses on five EU strategic partners that experienced Europe as post-colonial subjects – Brazil, Mexico, Canada, India, and South Africa. With our novel methodology, we examine the consequences of source selection on an international actor representation (the EU in our case) among the key partners, given that sources are fundamental in shaping news content (Manning 2001). This chapter contributes to the studies of EU external perceptions, a dynamic field within EU foreign policy studies (for reviews of the field see Chaban and Elgström 2021; Chaban and Lucarelli 2021; Chaban et al. 2020). We add a systematic insight into correlations between EU media images in international media vis-à-vis EU news sources currently missing in the relevant scholarship. With the focus on external perceptions, we also add to the "decentring" trend in EU foreign policy studies, which aims to overcome EU-centrism in the scholarship (Gstöhl and Schunz 2021).

The key terms that we use in this chapter – media systems and media framing and flows – are discussed below, followed by a detailed presentation of the method. We then engage with our case study and conclude with several points about how analytical tools we develop in this chapter could be used by public diplomacy practitioners.

Key Terms

Media Systems

Typologies of media systems "describe typical patterns of how journalism cultures, media policy, media markets, and media use are connected in a given society" (Brüggemann et al. 2014:1038). Hallin and Mancini (2004) put forth three models of media systems in Western democracies:[1] the Polarized Pluralist Model of Southern Europe, the Democratic Corporatist Model of Northern Europe, and the Liberal Model of the North Atlantic. Their work has been examined against broader international regions, such as South America and Asia, with varying degrees of success (Hallin and Mancini 2012).

The four dimensions used in the analysis of media systems are: media market, journalistic professionalism, political parallelism, and the role of the state (Hardy 2012). *Media market*, or the "inclusiveness of the press market" (Brüggemann et al. 2014:1040), is the degree that a media system reaches and includes traditionally marginalized groups. *Political parallelism* measures the degree to which political advocacy is thought to be essential to the journalistic mission, whether on the part of the reporter or the reader. This includes political parties, perceived political bias in the media (and consumption of media in accordance with political beliefs), and the degree of financial dependence of media on local government. *Journalistic professionalism* is measured by the degree of professional autonomy, the level of professionalism within journalism, and the propensity of journalists toward ethically serving the public interest. The last dimension, *role of the state*, can be measured according to the strength of public broadcasting, the level of ownership regulation by the state, and the amount of press subsidies available.

These dimensions can and have been successfully used to assess media systems models. The original *Polarized Pluralist Model*, for example, was found to have low levels of the press market and journalistic professionalism dimensions, but high levels of political parallelism and role of the state dimensions (Hallin and Mancini 2012:287). The *Liberal Model* is the opposite and has high levels of the press market and journalistic professionalism dimensions, and low levels of political parallelism and the role of the state dimensions. The third *Democratic Corporatist Model* has high levels of all four dimensions. Thus, these four dimensions help flesh out the original model in a more contextual and more descriptive way. Arguably, the media system of the five cases in this study – Canada, Brazil, Mexico, India, and South Africa – belongs to the Liberal Model. This may be why their leading national news providers rely heavily on international sources when reporting key foreign policy counterparts. The use of internationally sourced reports may be seen as the most cost-efficient way to gather international news and thus serve bottom line imperatives, which reflect the press market dimension typical in a Liberal Model. This research examines that possibility and takes it further by testing the news sources not only against local but also against international reporting outlets.

Media Framing and News Flows

In our inquiry into the influence of the origin of news sources on representation of foreign policy actors, we engage with framing theory (see also Mokry in this volume). Almost two decades ago, Gitlin defined frames as "persistent patterns of cognition, interpretation, and presentation, of selection, emphasis, and exclusion, by which symbol-handlers routinely organise discourse" (1980:7). This early definition has continued to hold scholarly attention, as it alludes to the both the pragmatic process of framing and the power of frames in society. Frames are formed through the repeated use of an extensive interconnected nexus of lexical choices, as well as the recurrent selections of news sources (Blum 2005) that are combined to form a thematic impression. Despite the importance of news sources to media framing, they remain "widely overlooked, if not completely ignored, by studies of international communication" (Archetti 2008: 466; see also Ostermann 2019).

Public understanding of the social world derives, in large part, from a selectively framed construction of meaning provided by media over time (Jakubowicz 2007). Research has consistently linked framing to power and ideology (Hardy 2012). This linkage is due to the intrinsic relationship between framed representations in the media and societies' general understanding of the social world. A consequence of dominant media framing from a particular perspective is that audiences may not have "adequate opportunity to learn all sides" of an event in order "to resist any single dominant interpretation" (Fahmy 2010:711). An exploration of audience reception is outside of the scope of this research. However, examining sources used and how they are situated within larger media frames can, indeed, shed light on the gatekeeping processes involved beforehand. By examining a range of media content systemically and cohesively, analysts can expose critical gatekeeping choices that might not otherwise be immediately apparent when examining individual texts (Entman 1993:52).

To better understand how news frames travel across different media and different networks, Entman (2003) put forth the *cascading activation model* of framing. He argued that the US White House, in his case study, put forth frames that were then picked up by other elites (members of Congress, experts) who perpetuated those frames to the news media. The latter crafted specific news frames to reflect the original frames of the White House. Entman's exploration of how networks of association can work to spread activation of these frames in the form of a framing hierarchy offers a "conceptual framework for predicting the extent to which counterframes will be triggered or ignored within the press" (2012). Framing is thus "the central process by which government officials and journalists exercise political influence over each other and over the public" (Entman 2003:415). Entman states, however, that there is an opportunity for variance at every level of the model, and the model helps illuminate information that is "critical to politics and policy-making" (Entman 1993:52). In addition, another strength of the model is the ability to analyze the feedback of information that cascades back up to elites, also in the form of frames.

Cascading activation research has had a continued and important influence on developing a theory of framing processes. However, the cascade model developed from empirical material originating in the US press does not address the role of local and international reporting sources in framing foreign actors. Other research has argued that both the source and content of political frames deeply matter in determining which frames manifest in the press (Brüggemann et al. 2014:1038). Yet research exploring both news flows and the cascading activation model has not fully explored the role of international sources as contrasted against local sources. This research attempts to fill this gap and expands the explanatory power of the cascading activation model to environments beyond those of the US democratic news media. Factoring the new media ecology of the twenty-first century, Entman and Usher (2018) share the assumption that media framing is not happening exclusively within the nation state, but rather through a network of shared meanings of different origin that later form relations and associations between each other. We also follow the revision of this framing model proposed by these authors.

Two hypotheses guide this research. The debate on localized versus globalized news flows informs the first hypothesis, which predicts that locally sourced news about an international actor will project different frames of the actor than internationally sourced news. Locally sourced news is expected to highlight issues and themes of immediate relevance to the location and profile of local interpretations of international relations. This research predicts that international reporters will present more generic frames of the international actor produced to be sold globally as many times as possible. We also argue that differentiation *within* international news sources is needed for a more nuanced understanding of framing. This analysis predicts differentiation between international news reporting sources.

Methodological Approach: Combining Low and High Inference Analysis Approaches

Recognizing the importance of images and perceptions in IR/FPA's conception and conduct, our chapter highlights the importance of differentiating between and considering analyses of both low and high inference variables that are frequently of interest in the studies of international political communication. Low inference variables are easy to measure and analyze using traditional statistical methods, including descriptive statistics. However, if the research involves complex phenomena, such as perceptions, high inference variables are critical and should be properly constructed. Conceptually, this involves combining a set of low inference variables into composite high inference variables and testing whether the data are meaningful when the responses are summed. Let's take as an example the measurement of public perceptions about an elected official. We can survey respondents and just ask one question of whether or not they believe a candidate was telling the truth about a specific issue. Taking their responses and interpreting them at face value would be an example of using a low inference variable. If a common understanding of "telling the truth" is shared, and if both the researcher and respondents agree what a "yes" means and what a "no" means, then a simple frequency/count of occurrences would most likely suffice in summarizing these data.

However, it is very likely that a researcher would want to capture how the public perceives the *trustworthiness* of the candidate as well. Trustworthiness is a construct that is abstract and not easy to measure. We could, for example, ask a series of ten statements about a particular candidate that represent different critical issues and obtain a total score for each respondent that would indicate the number of issues on which they believe the candidate was telling the truth. Would this number represent, however, each respondent's perceived level of trustworthiness? That seems like quite a stretch, doesn't it? Would it really be that easy to operationalize such a complex construct in such a simplistic way? What if another researcher attempted to do the same, used a different set of ten issues, and claimed that his/her total score was also a measure of trustworthiness? How could we make any sense of the resultant *measure*, given it was not grounded in any theoretical meaning, was arbitrarily coded, and could change meaning at any time? Yet, this is exactly what many social science researchers do all the time, that is, they assume, rather than empirically test, whether or not their definitions and operationalizations are sufficient for representing their construct of interest (Michell 1999; Bond and Fox 2013).

The construct of trustworthiness can be referred to as a *high inference variable*. High inference variables, therefore, are the source of our richest inferences. Other examples of high inference questions include: How *engaged* were the respondents? What is *important* to them? What is the *strength of their conviction*? How much *knowledge* do they have about the material? These variables are typically of the greatest interest to researchers, and they must be deliberately and methodically constructed from a set of responses to the *low inference* questions that are included on surveys. We recommend that after low inference survey data are collected (how we decide which of these to use is an issue addressed later in this chapter), researchers employ a measurement analysis to properly transform these low inference responses into a high inference variable. Simply adding up ordinal raw scores is not a hallmark of scientific rigor. Instead, a falsifiable hypothesis about the theoretical structure of the high inference variable must be tested and the empirical results from the measurement analysis should be examined to support or refute that hypothesis.

Ordinal survey data in their raw form are, however, *sufficient* for estimating the extent to which data from low inference variables can be transformed into a meaningful high inference quantitative structure. Even though the raw numbers themselves do not possess a mathematical meaning, they possess all the information necessary for constructing equal-interval measures. This means that we can take responses to all trustworthiness items and instead of summing them into a total score that does not have qualitative meaning, we should transform them into equal-interval units using a measurement model, specifically the RMM.

The RMM combines rigorous statistical methods with rich qualitative descriptions to provide meaningful measures that can be used to compare attributes, perceptions, and attitudes across any subgroup or time period of interest. The RMM is a family of models that are appropriate for different types of data. The most commonly used models are the Rasch Dichotomous Model (for yes/no, right/wrong, present/absent type of data), the Rasch Rating

Scale Model (for survey items that respondents are asked on a scale, such as agreement or frequency), and the Partial-Credit Model for items where multiple ratings are given to different items (e.g., some items are worth four points, other worth two points). All RMM models transform ordinal raw data into equal-interval units on a log-odd scale (called logits) and provide an array of diagnostics that we evaluate to determine the extent to which the resultant high inference variable structure can be interpreted meaningfully using the construct theory. Once the evidence of the meaningful high inference variable structure is obtained, the transformed data can be validly used in traditional statistical analyses. The value in pre-processing low inference survey data using RMM is that the resulting high inference variables are not only *quantitative* but also possess a rich *qualitative* meaning.

RMM, although most powerful when used in conjunction with strong theory, can also be used post-hoc to investigate the extent to which meaningful linear patterns exist in the data. If such meaningful measures are found, and supported both empirically and qualitatively, they can help further enhance our understanding of the construct and advance perception theory. Thus, theory not only informs data analysis and interpretation, but new analytic findings can also help advance theory (see Bond and Fox 2013 for an illustration). In other words, construct theory, substantive expertise, and RMM diagnostics should be used together to construct meaning and adjust hypotheses for multiple analyses and interpretations of the data. We highlight this methodological integration in our case study in this chapter.

Case Study

For the case study, we used the data from daily content analyses of 15 leading opinion-forming agenda-setting newspapers with a national outreach in Brazil, Mexico, Canada, India, and South Africa (Table 14.1). Data collection continued from April 1 to June 30, 2015 prescribed by the framework of a multinational research project, *Analysis of Perceptions of the EU and EU's Policies Abroad* (PPMI/NCRE/NFG 2015), and included the beginning of the EU's major migration crisis. Where possible, newspapers were chosen to represent the political continuum. One of the selected newspapers in each country was a business newspaper, since the business community is one of the target groups of EU public diplomacy.

The key search words used to locate content in the PressReader news engine included: European Union/EU, European Commission/EC, European Parliament/EP, European Court of Justice/ECJ, European Central Bank/ECB, the European Council, and Eurozone. Trained coders examined media content performing manual coding, with double coder reliability check undertaken by the trained project data managers.

The construct theory that we used is the cascading activation model which argues differentiation between frames that had more capability to "stimulate support of or opposition to the sides in a political conflict" (Entman 2003:417) and other frames that failed to stir such an activation of ideas. According to this model, the more *capable* frames are the ones that resonate culturally within and across different levels in the network (meaning they are *noticeable, understandable, memorable,* and *emotionally charged*); and they are characterized by magnitude (including *prominence* and *repetition,* ibid.). Respectively, our research identified frames that were more visible, locally understood, and emotionally charged, and it examined if they correlated with the type of news source (local vs. international). Media coverage was assessed in terms of *visibility, local resonance*, and *emotive charge* (all high inference variables) assigned to the images of an international actor (the EU in our case). Each high inference variable was unpacked through sets of the low inference variables (Table 14.2). In this chapter, the RMM was employed to extract the most stable *visibility* profiles from the data and examine how these profiles compared across the five countries. The RMM allowed for understanding the unique contribution that each indicator made to the overall construct of *visibility* of the EU in local media in this study. This model allowed for examining the indicators that comprised the variable of visibility in combination, as opposed to analyzing each indicator separately. Using the RMM also allowed us to extract the most dominant and stable patterns from the data and describe profiles of EU visibility for each country as well as compare the profiles across the countries. The RMM transformed raw data into interval measures and produced standardized scores of visibility of the EU in each country. The WINSTEPS software was used to run a series of analyses using the Rasch Partial-Credit Model to accommodate a different number of response options

Table 14.1 Newspapers, Volume of News on EU and EU Migration Crisis, and News Sources by Country

Country	# Articles Sampled*	# Articles Reporting EU Migration Crisis	News Source**	
			Local	Int'l
Brazil		62	15	17
O Globo	212			
Folha de São Paulo	148			
Valor Econômico	213			
Canada		65	24	38
The Globe and Mail	257			
National Post	241			
La Presse	100			
India		13	3	10
The Times of India	97			
The Hindu	92			
The Economic Times	121			
Mexico		48	12	36
El Universal	175			
La Jornada	198			
El Financiero	178			
South Africa		28	3	25
The Times	24			
The Star	86			
Business Day	141			
Total	1,970	216	57	126

* These numbers represent the # articles sampled from 1 April to 30 June 2015.
** These numbers represent the news sources in the articles that reported EU migration crisis. There were several instances where the news source could not be identified

Table 14.2 Mapping High Inference Variables vs. Low Inference Data

	High Inference Variables		
	Visibility	*Local Resonance*	*Emotive Charge*
Low inference data	Volume (# of articles) Degree of centrality • major • secondary • minor Length • long • medium • short Use of visual support (yes/no)	Presence of local actors (yes/no) EU domesticity • if the EU was presented to act with a 'local hook' (i.e., in some relation to the country of the reportage), • if the EU's actions were reported without any 'local hooks' the EU acting within its borders and/or with EU Member States with a 'third-country hook' (neither the country of the reportage nor the EU) globally (e.g., in international multilateral fora)	• positive • neutral-to-positive • neutral • neutral-to-negative • negative • mixed

for each of the indicators (e.g., some of the indicators were measured as yes/no, while others were ranked). In addition to the RMM, for those variables where the number of the observed indictors was small – local resonance and emotive charge – descriptive statistics and non-parametric tests (e.g., chi-square tests of independence) were used to examine patterns in the data at the level of low inference variables.

Low Inference Analysis

This analysis involved examining the frequency distribution of each low inference variable as well as conducting non-parametric tests, where a sample size was sufficiently large. The following results were obtained:

Visibility – VOLUME. Despite the varying volume of news in the monitored period, all locations demonstrated a high dependency on international sources in covering the EU in the beginning of the irregular migration crisis compared with local sources (from 90% in South Africa to 50% in Brazil). The news gatekeepers in the five locations preferred to consult Western sources for information in covering the migration crisis, even though there were many internationally recognized media voices reporting on the EU in the migration crisis from the other side of the Mediterranean (e.g., *Al Jazeera*). The pool of those Western news sources was rather limited, with most of them being of Anglo-Saxon origin, with the exception of French *AFP*. South Africa and India used more sources from the UK than the other three countries. Overall, Brazil, Canada, and South Africa had a tendency to use more sources from the US than India and Mexico (Table 14.3). The linguistic background of Canada, India, and South Africa may explain such choices. However, taking into account the linguistic profiles of Brazil and Mexico, it was interesting that continental European sources reporting about the EU's reactions to the migration crisis in Portuguese and Spanish were

Table 14.3 Distribution of Western Sources

Country	Western News Source*							
	UK only	US only	Mixed UK/US	Mixed UK/US/EUR	Mixed UK/EUR	Mixed US/EUR	EUR
Brazil	2	8	0	0	0	0	1
Canada	6	14	4	1	1	0	9
India	4	1	0	0	0	0	5
Mexico	1	1	0	3	2	6	5
South Africa	14	6	1	0	1	0	3
Total	26	30	5	4	4	6	23

*These numbers are not additive, as they represent some overlapping categories

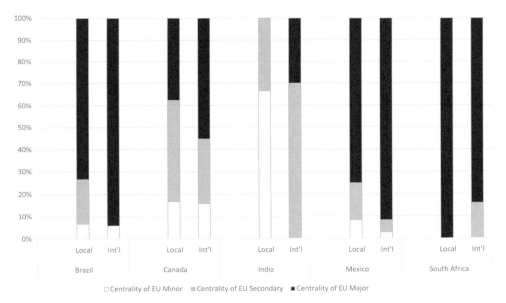

Figure 14.1 Visibility of EU in terms of intensity (centrality) of EU crisis coverage by news source and country.

ignored in those locations. Due to the relatively small number of Western sources in this sample, no statistical comparisons could be made, yet patterns could be detected.

Visibility – DEGREE OF CENTRALITY. EU representations were further assessed in terms of their *degree of centrality* and according to the news source. The EU holding major centrality was most visible in the locally-sourced news in Brazil, South Africa, and Mexico (Figure 14.1), where the EU was cast as a main actor in the unfolding drama of the fleeing refugees. In contrast, in India and Canada, EU centrality was not major in locally-sourced news. In India, minor centrality and the total lack of major centrality was characteristic of the EU's portrayals by the local sources.

This lack of emphasis on the EU in India was not only found in their locally-sourced news but also observed in India's internationally-sourced news where secondary centrality was the most predominant (Figure 14.1). In contrast, the other four countries gave the EU major centrality through the chosen internationally-sourced news. Overall, international agencies turned out to be the dominant voices in presenting the EU's nascent migration crisis across all five countries, with 68.9% of content from international sources, and there were statistically significant differences in the centrality of EU representations from internationally-sourced news ($\chi^2=99.62$, $p<.0001$). However, the local and international sources could not be statistically compared due to the small sample sizes.

Comparison of the frames in terms of *visibility* across the three groups of Western sources revealed that sources from each geographic region (the UK, the US, and continental Europe) framed the EU somewhat differently. In general, these three groups of international sources were eager to profile the EU as one of the leading protagonists in the unfolding drama. However, the EU was cast by the news coming from the US and European Continental sources as a major actor more often than in the UK-sourced news (Figure 14.2). There were some location-specific peculiarities in how visibility was conveyed, for example, Indian editors preferred stories where the EU was cast in a secondary role even though the same sources provided information for many other articles casting the EU in a major role as demonstrated in the four other cases.

Visibility – USE OF VISUAL SUPPORT. The 'projection' effect by international sources was further intensified by the editors' choice to support the internationally-sourced news with *visual support* more frequently than locally-sourced news (Table 14.4). Visual support was noted in approximately one third of the locally-sourced news about EU migration crisis in Brazil, India, and Mexico and in approximately half of the Canadian articles. None of the locally-sourced news articles in South Africa had visual support. In comparison, visual support was noted in approximately half of the internationally-sourced news in Brazil, Canada, India, and Mexico and in one quarter of the South African articles. Overall, there were

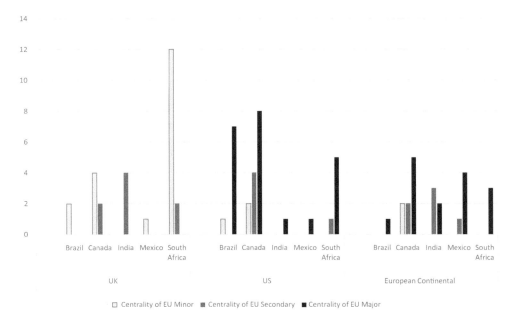

Figure 14.2 Visibility of the EU in terms of intensity (centrality) compared across Western news sources.

no statistically significant differences in visual support in the internationally-sourced news across the five countries. The local and international sources could not be statistically compared due to the small sample size of the locally sourced news.

Visibility – LENGTH AND VISIBILITY. To further assess visibility, this research also examined *length* and *visual support*. These were location-specific features that revealed choices made by local gatekeepers (Table 14.5). Reflecting on the patterns of *length*, locally-sourced EU news on the crisis tend to be longer than internationally-sourced (Table 14.4), and according to the chi-square test (all countries combined) the difference was significant (χ^2=6.79, p<.05). This difference might be connected to the financial side of the news production, where local authors may be paid according to the word count. Overall, significantly more articles from US sources were long (χ^2=11.86, p<.02).

Local resonance. In terms of local resonance, we found that despite migration being a leading topic in the EU's strategic dialogue with the five countries, as defined by EU Global Strategy (European Union, 2016), almost all locally and internationally-sourced news in our analysis was about the EU acting within its continent (Figure 14.3). Only in Canada and Mexico did local authors use a local angle to tell the story of the EU's migration crisis. Keeping in mind that the number of locally-sourced news was very low in India and South Africa, the absence of *local hooks* in Brazilian locally-sourced news is of note. Local authors in the five countries refrained from linking the EU's emerging migration crisis to their own local actors or contexts, which arguably sent a message to local readers about a lack of immediate resonance of the event to local concerns.

In contrast, Brazilian authors were the most willing to report the EU reacting to the crisis in global or third-country contexts. Such positioning frames the EU as an actor performing in a drama that takes place on a remote stage, without local involvement and with local readers as distant spectators. The involvement of local actors was extremely limited and virtually non-existent in this major humanitarian crisis. No local actor interaction with the EU was observed in Indian, Mexican, and South African media. A local actor was mentioned in one Brazilian article and in eight Canadian articles.

Table 14.4 Visibility of EU in Terms of Article Length and Visual Support of EU Crisis Coverage by News Source and Country

Country	News Source	Article Length			Visual Support	
		Short	Medium	Long	Present	Absent
Brazil	Local	5	7	3	5	10
	International	6	6	5	9	8
Canada	Local	2	12	10	13	11
	International	8	20	10	18	20
India	Local	0	2	1	1	2
	International	0	8	2	6	4
Mexico	Local	1	9	2	4	8
	International	17	19	0	17	19
South Africa	Local	0	0	3	0	3
	International	3	16	6	7	8
Total		42	99	42	80	103

Table 14.5 Visibility of the EU in Terms of Article Length and Visual Support by Western News Sources and Country

Western News Source	Country	Article Length			Visual Support	
		Short	Medium	Long	Present	Absent
UK						
	Brazil	1	0	1	0	2
	Canada	1	4	1	3	3
	India	0	4	0	2	2
	Mexico	1	0	0	0	1
	South Africa	2	11	1	4	10
US						
	Brazil	3	3	2	5	3
	Canada	3	7	4	5	9
	India	0	0	1	1	0
	Mexico	1	0	0	0	1
	South Africa	0	1	5	2	4
European Continental						
	Brazil	0	1	0	0	1
	Canada	3	5	1	4	5
	India	0	4	1	3	2
	Mexico	3	2	0	0	5
	South Africa	1	2	0	0	3
Total		19	44	17	29	51

It is only logical that the internationally-sourced news did not have *local anchors* grounding the news to the location-specific context, thus revealing the presence of the *globalization* tendency in EU news coverage. However, some differences were observed between stories from Anglo-Saxon and European Continental sources (Figure 14.4). Across the five locations, the UK- and US-sourced stories about the EU handling the migration crisis focused mostly on the EU acting within its borders. European Continental sources seemed to lead in reporting the EU's actions in relation to its neighbors to the South.

Emotive charge. And finally, our analysis of the emotive charge at the low inference level revealed that the negative evaluations of the coverage of the EU's migration crisis varied in the news sampled. Some articles criticized EU policies on migration and critiqued proposed action plans to solve the crisis. These articles described the EU as under enormous pressure to confront the human-trafficking crisis and noted the scaling-back of the sweeping seaborne rescue campaign because of a lack of EU financial and moral support. Strong anti-immigrant sentiments on the continent also attracted negative comments that extensively focused on the individual EU Member States portrayed as obstructing the EU's common response. Examples include Hungary and Bulgaria, who were seen to have contributed to the tragedy of migrants' deaths at the Mediterranean Sea after announcing plans to build barbed walls to contain immigrants, or Italy, who ended its search and rescue mission Mare Nostrum. A more positive tone was found in the news reporting of EU leaders who committed new resources to save lives in the Mediterranean at an emergency summit convened after hundreds of migrants drowned in the space of a few days. There were positive evaluations of

Measuring Perceptions

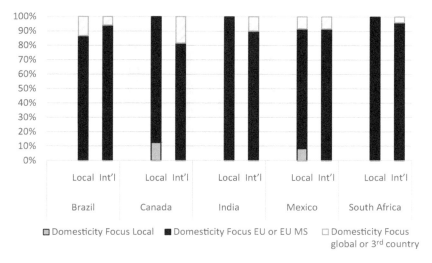

Figure 14.3 Local resonance (domesticity focus) of EU crisis coverage by news source and country.

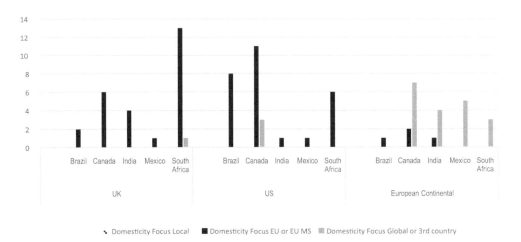

Figure 14.4 Visibility of EU in terms of local resonance (domesticity focus) of EU crisis coverage by Western news source and country.

the EU in their actions to destroy vessels that could be used for trafficking. The EU was cast in a positive light by the EU nations that approved plans for a naval operation to battle the human-trafficking networks. Positive tones were also found in the news that EU foreign policy chief Federica Mogherini asked for help from the international community to save migrants in the Mediterranean.

Turning to the news sources, very few locally-sourced articles had a positive or even positive-neutral evaluation of the EU in dealing with the migration crisis (Figure 14.5). Less than 4% of coverage from locally-sourced news across all five countries was positive or positive-to-neutral; 40% was negative; and 56% was mixed, negative-to-neutral, or neutral.

231

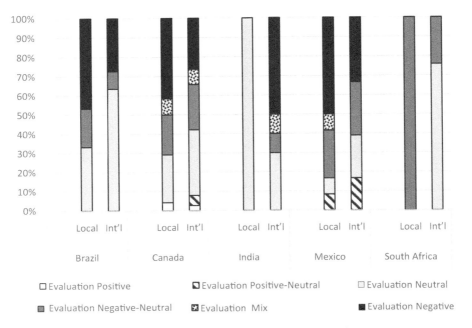

Figure 14.5 Evaluation of EU crisis coverage by news source and country.

With the exception of India, locally-sourced EU news tended to significantly be more negative than internationally-sourced news ($\chi^2=14.88$, $p<.02$).

Evaluations of the EU and its actors in the internationally-sourced articles revealed a very limited positive coverage (6%), with no positive or even somewhat positive evaluations in internationally-sourced news in Brazil and South Africa, and some positive tones only in mixed evaluations in India.

Turning to the origin of the news source, the sampled UK sources tended to present the EU in a neutral-to-negative light. All the articles in four of the five countries sampled, with reporters from the UK, were equally distributed across the "negative" and "neutral" evaluation categories. The only exception was South Africa, where 86% of the UK-sourced articles had neutral evaluation of the EU and its actors. No positive evaluations were observed.

The US and European Continental sources featured some positive perspectives on the EU. The pattern of evaluations for the articles with US-sourced news revealed that the majority of the articles in Brazil had neutral evaluations of the EU and its actors. More than half of the articles in Canada were to some extent negative, and 10% of the articles across the five countries had positive or positive-neutral evaluations of the EU and its actors. The pattern of evaluations for the articles with European Continental-sourced news was somewhat similar to that of US-sourced news in that 9% of the articles across the five countries had somewhat positive evaluations of the EU and its actors. More than 50% of the remaining 90 articles had either negative or negative-neutral evaluations of the EU and its actors (Figure 14.6).

Our analysis revealed differences in framing the EU in its response to the migration crisis by local correspondents vis-à-vis international news sources: locally-sourced articles seemed to be more negative in EU representations (except of India) and with a more diluted profile of the EU (articles were longer on average yet less inclined to present the EU as a major actor,

Measuring Perceptions

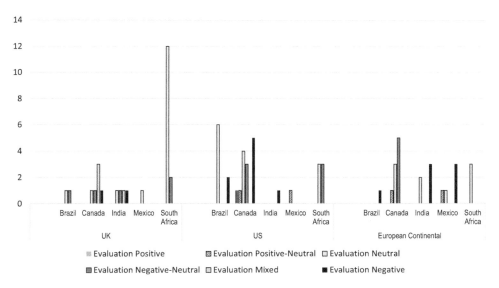

Figure 14.6 Evaluation of EU crisis coverage by Western news source and country.

except South Africa) and with less visual support. However, due to small sample size, it was impossible to explore those differences statistically.

In summary, our first hypothesis which predicted that international news sources for the EU migration crisis would present more generic frames of the EU was supported. Our second hypothesis which predicted a difference in framing between internationally sourced news was partially confirmed. The differentiation *within* international news sources demonstrated a difference in *centrality* and *evaluation* – the UK-sourced news did not frame the EU as a major actor and was more Euro-skeptic (dominated by negative views on the EU, all five countries, with positive tones appearing only alongside the negative ones, in articles with mixed evaluations).

High Inference Analysis: RMM Analysis of Visibility

Importantly, it was not only local sources by themselves that produced diverse frames of the EU but also a *combination* of local reporters and international news sources that resulted in location-specific frames of the EU in terms of visibility, local hooks, and evaluation. The results of the RMM analysis of the *visibility* of the EU provided additional insights into the profiles of visibility when the three indicators (*centrality, visual support,* and *article length*) were considered together. This analysis revealed the resultant framing of the EU as the combination of the two reporting sources. The RMM analysis showed that the construct of visibility was defined similarly in all the countries, except India. This is visually depicted through the ordering of the indicators on the Rasch Visibility Map, which shows the relative weight or contribution of each indicator to the overall visibility score (Figure 14.7).

This ordering of the three visibility indicators produced by RMM points to the EU centrality as the most frequently observed indicator while visual support is the most rarely observed indicator. The lines on the Rasch map correspond to the average visibility score for each country (defined by the combination of EU *centrality*, *article length*, and *visual support*) and are quite close, suggesting that visibility was statistically comparable across the four countries and had the same pattern, with the majority of the articles having major EU centrality, being medium, and lacking visual support, with the exception of South Africa where the indicator of visual support was more likely to be observed.

In contrast, in the sampled Indian media, the definition of visibility was quite unique and the pattern was reversed. In India, visibility of EU in the local media means first of all visual support (Figure 14.8). Following the line that shows the average visibility score for India suggests that, on average, we would expect the local media in India to have visual support, have secondary centrality, and be medium in length. We would not expect the articles in India to be short or have minor centrality, as evidenced by the absence of those codes on the map.

This finding supports the *localization* argument in conceptualizing news flow, which occurs when the "same information is framed differently at the national level by news producers, who adapt it to the taste and interests of local audiences" (Archetti 2008:464).

In summary, the results of the RMM analysis of high inference data allowed us to conclude that the cascading model may be expanded to include news sources within the range of influences on the cascade of information. This revision would account for media systems that tend to be more open to and rely more on international news sources than other systems. Originally, this distinction was not considered by Entman, who modeled his theory on the US news media that tend to produce their own news about international events and actors.

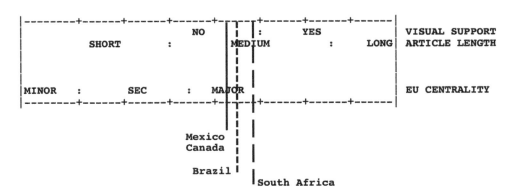

Figure 14.7 Rasch visibility map for four countries.

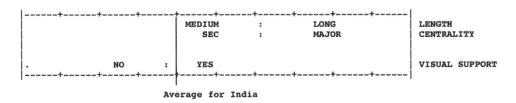

Figure 14.8 Rasch visibility map for India.

Conclusions

Whether explicated or not, we all intuitively understand the properties of the physical measures we use on a daily basis (e.g., time, temperature, height, weight, distance, currency). All of these measures adhere to the same strict properties: they represent a less-to-more continuum and are deliberately demarcated into equal-interval units for the convenience of addition, subtraction, comparison, and ultimately, objectivity and validity. Additionally, each measure represents only one attribute at a time. For example, we can qualitatively describe a tree, but to measure it we must separate it into separate attributes of trunk circumference, height, and average crown spread.

Thus, all measurement systems are *deliberately* constructed to objectively quantify attributes while at the same time maintaining a rich qualitative meaning. In other words, anyone can describe what it means qualitatively to be 10 minutes late, own $100, or have the room temperature increase by 10 degrees. Yet these units are also quantitatively defensible because they adhere to the strict measurement principles. Proper development of standard measurement units allows for comparisons across time, distance, and objects, and these comparisons represent qualitative attributes in a fair and transparent way.

We want to reiterate – and specifically for the first users of the method – when developing measures for psychological data in Foreign Policy Analysis, the Rasch model serves as a mathematical representation of the properties of physical measures. As such, it gives researchers the same quantitative rigor and allows them to construct meaningful units for psychological rating scale data extracted from provided response options. In practical terms, by testing the fit of the psychological data to the RMM and examining the extent to which the response patterns fit the data, researchers then construct statistically defensible and meaningful units for their psychological data. What follows is an objective framework for comparing different attributes in a common frame of reference to enhance theory building in commonly understood units.

The methodological approach demonstrated in this chapter allowed for a deeper understanding of the EU perceptions by incorporating the analysis of both low and high inference variables. This analysis focused on five countries that arguably belong to the liberal news system, where media are more open to using and publishing internationally-sourced news alongside locally-reported news. In these locations, both localization and globalization of the news flows complemented each other. As such, frames of foreign policy actors diffused by domestic influential news media were a function of endogenous and exogenous news sources working in *combination* with each other. Importantly, this combination was similar in four of the five countries and quite unique in India (as demonstrated by the RMM). Future studies must account for both tendencies – not in isolation or in opposition – but *in interaction* with each other: media frames are no longer nation-originated or nation-specific (Entman and Usher 2018). In this light, applying a combined method of low and high inferences analyses may provide public diplomacy practitioners with clues for concrete effective strategies to communicate with their actor. The application of the RMM to the high inference variable of *visibility* – visibility being one of the priorities of public diplomacy actions in a host society – gives informed leads for strategic communicators to fine-tune the impact of their messages: for some societies, it is visual images that would translate into higher visibility (India in our case), while for others it is the intensity of representation that shapes the message about visibility (the other four locations).

Our results also highlighted that the UK-sourced EU news tended to focus on the EU as a secondary or minor actor (not major) and was more negative about the EU than news produced by other Western international sources. This is of concern to the EU's public diplomacy. Over the past decade, the UK sources have been used more frequently than other sources to report the EU in the third countries, especially in the Asia-Pacific (Chaban and Holland 2019). The UK news sources will remain popular due to their global reputation, as well as domestic institutional practices and individual outlet arrangements in place. Future, post-Brexit research into EU media images outside EU borders should pay more attention to the UK news sources reporting about the EU and account for potential biases of popular international sources vis-à-vis geo-political priorities of their home states.

Our case also demonstrated that there were location-specific editors' decisions to choose certain internationally-sourced news stories and ignore others from the same pools of international news (Indian editors chose very different news about the EU from the same international sources used in other four locations). Future research should explore a set of factors behind editors' decisions, which are expected to be a complex combination of system-, location-, outlet-, and personality-specific factors.

Note

1 This original model typology of media systems being criticized for its focus only on the Western world (Brüggemann et al. 2014:1038) and a lack of focus on digital communication (Brüggemann et al. 2014:1038).

References

Archetti, Cristina. 2008. "News Coverage of 9/11 and the Demise of the Media Flows, Globalization and Localization Hypotheses." *The International Communication Gazette* 70(6): 63–485.

Blum, Roger. 2005. "Bausteine zu einer Theorie der Mediensysteme (Building Blocks for a Theory of Media Systems)." *Medienwissenschaft Schweiz* 16(2): 5–11.

Bond, Trevor G., and Christine M. Fox. 2013. *Applying the Rasch Model: Fundamental Measurement in the Human Sciences*. Third edition. New York: Taylor and Francis.

Brüggemann, Michael, Sven Engesser, Florin Büchel, Edda Humprecht, and Laia Castro-Herrero. 2014. "Hallin and Mancini Revisited: Four Empirical Types of Western Media Systems." *Journal of Communication* 64(6): 1037–1065.

Chaban, Natalia, Svetlana Beltyukova, and Christine Fox. 2017. "Communicating NATO in the Asia-Pacific Press: Comparative Analysis of Patterns of NATO's Visibility, Capability, Evaluation, and Local Resonance." *Asian Security* 14(1): 66–81.

Chaban, Natalia, and Ole Elgström. 2021a. *The Ukraine Crisis and EU Foreign Policy Roles: Images of the EU in the Context of EU–Ukraine Relations*. Cheltenham, UK and Northampton, MA: Edward Elgar Publishing.

Chaban, Natalia, and Ole Elgström. 2021b. "Theorizing External Perceptions of the EU." In *Studying the EU's External Action: Concepts, Approaches, Theories*, edited by Sieglinde Gstöhl and Simon Schunz. London: Red Globe Press/Macmillan International, 265–277.

Chaban, Natalia, and Martin Holland, eds. 2019. *Shaping the EU's Global Strategy: Partners and Perceptions*. Cham: Palgrave Macmillan.

Chaban, Natalia, and Sonia Lucarelli. 2021. "Reassessing External Images of the EU: Evolving Narratives in Times of Crisis." *European Foreign Policy Review* 26(1): 177–196.

Chaban, Natalia, Arne Niemann, and Johanna Speyer, eds. 2020. *Changing Perceptions of the EU at Times of Brexit: Global Perspectives*. Abingdon and New York: Routledge.

Clausen, Lisbeth. 2003. *Global News Production*. Copenhagen: Copenhagen Business School.

Clausen, Lisbeth. 2004. "Localizing the Global: 'Domestication' Processes in International News Production." *Media, Culture and Society* 26 (1): 25–44.

Entman, Robert. 1993. "Framing: Toward Clarification of a Fractured Paradigm." *Journal of Communication* 43(4): 51–58.

Entman, Robert. 2003. "Cascading Activation: Contesting the White House's Frame after 9/11." *Political Communication* 20(4): 415–432.

Entman, Robert. 2004. *Projections of Power: Framing News, Public Opinion, and U.S. Foreign Policy.* Chicago, IL: University of Chicago Press.

Entman, Robert M., and Nikki Usher. 2018. "Framing in a Fractured Democracy: Impacts of Digital Technology on Ideology, Power and Cascading Network Activation." *Journal of Communication* 68(2): 298–308.

European Union. 2016. Shared Vision, Common Action: A Stronger Europe. *A Global Strategy for the European Union's Foreign And Security Policy*, June 2016. Available at http://eeas.europa.eu/archives/docs/top_stories/pdf/eugs_review_web.pdf. Accessed 23 September 2019.

Fahmy, Shahira. 2010. "Contrasting Visual Frames of our Times: A Framing Analysis of English- and Arabic-Language Press Coverage of War and Terrorism." *The International Communication Gazette* 72(8): 695–717.

Giddens, Anthony. 1990. *The Consequences of Modernity.* Stanford, CA: Stanford University Press.

Giddens, Anthony. 1991. *Modernity and Self-Identity: Self and Society in the Late Modern Age.* Stanford, CA: Stanford University Press.

Gitlin, Todd. 1980. *The Whole World is Watching: Mass Media in the Making and Unmaking of the New Left.* Berkeley, CA: University of California Press.

Goldstein, Judith, and Robert O. Keohane. 1993. "Ideas and Foreign Policy: An Analytical Framework." In *Ideas and Foreign Policy*, edited by Judith Goldstein and Robert Keohane. Ithaca and London: Cornell University Press, 3–30.

Gstöhl, Sieglinde, and Simon Schunz, eds. 2021. *Studying the EU's External Action: Concepts, Approaches, Theories.* London: Red Globe Press/Macmillan International.

Gurevitch, Michael, Mark R. Levy, and Itzhak Roeh. 1991. "The Global Newsroom: Convergences and Diversities in the Globalization of Television News." In *Communication and Citizenship*, edited by Peter Dahlgren and Colin Sparks. London: Routledge, 195–217.

Hallin, Daniel, and Paolo Mancini. 2004. *Comparing Media Systems: Three Models of Media and Politics.* New York: Cambridge University Press.

Hallin, Daniel C., and Paolo Mancini, eds. 2012. *Comparing Media Systems Beyond the Western World.* Cambridge: Cambridge University Press.

Hardy, Jonathan. 2012. "Comparing media systems." In *Handbook of Comparative Communication Research*, edited by Frank Esser and Thomas Hanitzsch. London: Routledge, 185–207.

Jakubowicz, Karol. 2007. "Introduction: The Eastern European/Post Communist Media Model Countries." In *European Media Governance: National and Regional Dimensions*, edited by Georgios Terzis. Bristol: Intellect, 303–313.

Lash, Scott, and John Urry. 1994. *Economies of Signs and Space.* London: Sage.

Manners, Ian. 2002. "Normative Power Europe: A Contradiction in Terms?" *Journal of Common Market Studies* 40(2): 235–258.

Manning, Paul. 2001. *News and News Sources: A Critical Introduction.* London: Sage.

Michell, Joel. 1999. *Measurement in Psychology: A Critical History of a Methodological Concept.* Cambridge: Cambridge University Press.

Ostermann, Falk. 2019. *Security, Defense Discourse and Identity in NATO and Europe. How France Changed Foreign Policy.* London and New York: Routledge.

PPMI/NCRE/NFG. 2015. *Analysis of EU Perception of the EU and EU's Policy of the EU.* http://ec.europa.eu/dgs/fpi/showcases/eu_perceptions_study_en.htm.

Rasch, Georg. 1960. *Probabilistic Models for Some Intelligence and Attainment Tests.* Copenhagen: Danmarks Paedagogiske Institute.

Rasch, Georg. 1980. *Probabilistic Models for Some Intelligence and Attainment Tests.* Expanded edition. Chicago, IL: University of Chicago Press.

Robertson, Roland. 1992. *Globalization: Social Theory and Global Culture.* London: Sage.

15
Leadership Trait Analysis
Klaus Brummer

Introduction

Leadership Trait Analysis (LTA) places individual decision makers front and center. Actors like presidents or prime ministers are considered key drivers of foreign policy processes and outcomes. This is not to suggest that structural or environmental factors are irrelevant. However, the latter become meaningful only based on leaders' perception and handling of them (Sprout and Sprout 1957). Indeed, the example of U.S. presidents Trump and Biden and their handling of the Coronavirus pandemic at home or their policies toward certain allies (e.g., Germany) and international institutions and agreements (e.g., climate change) abroad illustrates that actors can behave and act rather differently in very similar contexts.

Contrary to other leadership approaches, LTA does not focus on situation-specific conditions or "states" of leaders as does Integrative Complexity (e.g., Suedfeld, Guttierei and Tetlock 2005) or on more time- and context-dependent political beliefs, as does Operational Code Analysis (see the chapter by Mark Schafer in this volume). Rather, LTA zooms in on more durable leadership traits as well as the ensuing overarching leadership styles of decision makers (e.g., Hermann 1980a, 2005a). Traits and styles are held to exert a significant impact on the way that leaders address the challenges and dilemmas of foreign policy decision making and, in the final analysis, impact the conduct as well as the substance of foreign policy.

The remainder of this chapter proceeds in four steps. The next section offers a review of the LTA literature. This is followed by a discussion of LTA's core substantive and methodological assumptions. Next comes a brief original illustration which shows how LTA can be used in empirical analysis, focusing on the issue of gender in foreign policy. The conclusion summarizes the strengths and weaknesses of the approach.

Literature Review

Since the 1980s, LTA has been widely used in empirical analysis. Rather than summarizing individual pieces of work, the following discussion highlights five patterns and trends in the vibrant LTA literature. First, LTA has been used to analyze a diverse set of foreign policy outcomes. Those include: leaders' use of analogies during foreign policy making processes

(Dyson and Preston 2006); the use of military force (Keller and Foster 2012; Foster and Keller 2014; Keller, Grant, and Foster 2020); foreign policy change (Yang 2010); foreign policy fiascos (Brummer 2016); the violation of international norms (Shannon and Keller 2007); peace processes (Mastors 2000); and the support of free trade (Crichlow 2002).

Second, LTA studies cover a broad array of actors, in form of state and non-state actors as well as Western and non-Western leaders. The typical focus is on state actors, especially presidents and prime ministers (e.g., Keller and Foster 2014; Van Esch and Swinkels 2015; Cuhadar et al. 2017b) and, albeit more rarely, foreign or defense ministers (e.g., Dyson 2009; Rabini et al. 2020a, b), lower-ranking officials (Shannon and Keller 2007), or legislators (Crichlow 2002), In addition, authors have analyzed non-state actors, which range from central bankers (Thies 2009) to leaders from political parties such as Sinn Fein's Gerry Adams (Mastors 2000) to leading representatives of international organizations, in form of presidents of the European Commission (Brummer 2014) and secretary generals of the United Nations (Kille and Scully 2003; Kille 2006) respectively.

Relatedly, empirical works have covered both Western and non-Western political leaders. The former comprises numerous post-World War II U.S. presidents (e.g., Hermann 2005b; Dyson and Preston 2006; Keller and Foster 2014; Siniver and Featherstone 2020) and various heads of government of European states (e.g., Dyson 2006, 2007; Van Esch and Swinkels 2015; Rabini et al. 2020a). In turn, among the non-Western leaders who have been analyzed are members of the Soviet Politburo (Hermann 1980b), leaders from sub-Sahara Africa (Hermann 1987), Iraq (Hermann 2005c), and Iran (Taysi and Preston 2001; Brummer et al. 2020), as well as several Turkish presidents and prime ministers (Kesgin 2013; Cuhadar et al. 2017a, b).

Third, LTA is often used for comparative analyses. True, a few studies address individual leaders (e.g., Mastors 2000; Taysi and Preston 2001; Hermann 2005b, c; Dyson 2006; Kesgin 2020a). Having said that, it is much more common in the LTA literature to find empirical works that zoom in on pairs of leaders (e.g., Dyson 2007; Yang 2010; Cuhadar et al. 2017a) or even larger groups of leaders (e.g., Kesgin 2013, 2020b; Brummer 2016; Cuhadar et al. 2017b; Rabini et al. 2020a). Indeed, the existence of a "norming group" of world leaders (see below) renders LTA particularly well-suited for comparative studies.

Fourth, most studies do not use the LTA framework in full but rather focus on specific aspects of it. As outlined in greater detail in the next section, LTA features a three-tiered analytical framework which comprises individual leadership traits, intermediary dimensions, and overarching leadership styles. In terms of empirical analysis, the majority of studies focuses on one, several, or all of the seven traits covered by LTA (e.g., Dyson 2006; Keller and Yang 2008; Yang 2010; Foster and Keller 2014; Brummer 2016) rather than on leadership styles (for exceptions, see Hermann 2005b, c; Brummer 2014). Arguably this is the case for two reasons. On the one hand, it is typically more intuitive and plausible to connect individual traits, and specific manifestations thereof, with specific foreign policy phenomena of interest, such as foreign policy change or foreign policy fiascos, rather than to establish such connections based on the broader leadership styles. On the other hand, the aggregation of individual traits into overarching styles is not really straightforward and, more problematically, still can lead to inconclusive results (i.e., a leader exhibiting more than one style), as outlined in the next section.

The final trend relates to the coding of speech acts. As outlined in greater detail below, LTA profiles of leaders are based on the latter's verbal utterances. Initially, those utterances were coded manually, which was very time-consuming. In addition, hand-coding raised the issues of coding reliability for individual publications and the comparability of findings across different publications. The aforementioned challenges have been addressed through the development of a computer-based coding scheme for LTA which runs on the Profiler Plus text analysis platform (Levine and Young 2014).[1]

In terms of language, the LTA coding scheme was originally confined to utterances in English. More recently, additional partial coding schemes (i.e., schemes which focus on just a few of the seven traits contained in LTA) or full coding schemes have been developed (Brummer et al. 2020). Those schemes, which are in place for Spanish, Persian, and German, allow for the profiling of many more leaders in their own language. The advent of those schemes has not only further expanded the analytical scope of LTA in general but also put analyses of non-Western leaders on firmer methodological ground more specifically (Brummer 2021, 415–420). That is, for the aforementioned languages it is no longer necessary to resort to translations of leaders' statements into English whose accuracy may be questionable—provided that such translations do exist in the first place, of course, which is often not the case. Similarly, it is no longer necessary to rely on original English-language statements by leaders whose first language is not English. For many leaders such statements are few and far between to begin with, and even if they do exist in quantities required for LTA profiling (see next section), they can be challenged on the grounds that nuances in speech are lost when leaders do not speak in their native tongue. Overall, LTA is a well-established analytical framework for leadership profiling in Foreign Policy Analysis (FPA) that has been widely used in empirical analyses for both Western and non-Western leaders and that is particularly conducive to comparative analysis.

Key Substantive and Methodological Assumptions

LTA comprises three inter-related levels. Those pertain to leadership traits, intermediary dimensions, and leadership styles. This section discusses the three levels in turn.

Leadership Traits

The first level entails seven specific leadership traits (on the selection of those traits, see Hermann 2005, 181–187). Those are:

- *Belief in the ability to control events* (BACE) assesses the extent to which leaders perceive of having control and influence over situations and developments.
- *Need for power* (PWR) aims at leaders' aspiration to control, influence, or impact other actors.
- *Conceptual complexity* (CC) identifies leaders' ability to perceive nuances in their political environment and to differentiate things and people in their environment.
- *Self-confidence* (SC) gets at leaders' sense of self-importance as well as perceived ability to cope with their environment.
- *Task focus or orientation focus* (TASK) explores whether leaders focus on problem solving or group maintenance /relationships.
- *Distrust of others* (DIS) ascertains leaders' tendency to suspect or doubt the motives and deeds of others.
- Finally, *in-group bias* (IGB) appraises leaders' tendency to value (socially, politically, etc. defined) groups and to place their group front and center.

As mentioned in the previous section, the majority of LTA studies confine themselves to (one, a few, or all of) those traits rather than moving on to incorporate also the two subsequent levels of the LTA framework in their analyses. Arguably, the key reason for this is that it is both possible and sufficient to connect those traits, and specific manifestations thereof, with a large number of foreign policy outcomes of interest. This is because distinct behavioral expectations are associated with specific manifestations of the individual traits (see Table 15.1). To give but one example: Yi Edward Yang (2010) has argued that a leader's propensity to change his or her country's foreign policy can be conceived as a function of his or

Table 15.1 Leadership Traits and Behavioral Expectations

Leadership Traits	General Meaning	Exemplary Behavioral Expectation Based on a...	
		...High Manifestation of the Leadership Trait	...Low Manifestation of the Leadership Trait
Belief in the ability to control events (BACE)	Perception of having control and influence over situations and developments	• Active involvement in decision-making processes • Low willingness to delegate tasks	• Rather hesitant and wait-and-see behavior • Low tendency to take initiative
Need for power (PWR)	Aspiration to control, influence, or impact other actors	• Focus on maximizing own benefit • Little consideration for others	• Willingness to fit into decision-making groups • Focus on balance and fairness
Conceptual complexity (CC)	Ability to perceive nuances in one's political environment, differentiate things and people in one's environment	• Consideration of situations from different points of view • Openness to new information and advice	• Own intuition essential • Stereotypical ideas of facts and/or people
Self-confidence (SC)	Sense of self-importance as well as perceived ability to cope with one's environment	• Little inclination to critically examine oneself and/or facts • Ignoring or reinterpreting "inappropriate information	• Reluctance to commit oneself; third parties have great influence on decision making • Erratic and inconsistent positions
Task focus or orientation focus (TASK)	Focus on problem solving or group maintenance / relationships	• Focus on tasks and/or issues • Groups serve primarily as a means to process or solve problems	• Focus on relationships • Relationships between group members and group cohesion central
Distrust of others (DIS)	Tendency to suspect or doubt the motives and deeds of others	• Categorical suspicion of actions and motivations of third parties (esp. adversaries) • Expectation of high loyalty from members of own group	• More unbiased perception/ image of third parties • Distrust not excluded but situation-specific
In-group bias (IGB)	Tendency to value (socially, politically, etc. defined) groups and place a specific group front and center	• Preservation of own group's independence central • Shifting of blame to other groups	• No categorical demarcations from other groups • Less tendency to hold other groups responsible for one's own problems

Source: Own depiction based on Hermann (2005a) and Brummer et al. (2020, 1041).

her level of conceptual complexity. Using the example of U.S. foreign policy toward China under the presidencies of respectively Bill Clinton and George W. Bush, Yang showed that "high-complexity leaders" (in this case: Clinton) are more likely to redirect their country's foreign policy than "low-complexity leaders" (in this case: Bush) and that the latter "require more dramatic external stimuli to trigger [foreign policy change] than do high-complexity leaders" (Yang 2010, 426).

The aforementioned leadership traits represent the basis for any LTA study in that they provide the substantive foundation for the other two levels. Accordingly, it is those traits that scholars using LTA need to ascertain first. The ensuing question is how this can be accomplished, that is, how to establish the characteristics of leaders without "hav[ing] direct access to [them] in a way that would allow for traditional psychological analysis" (Schafer 2000, 512)? Like other "at-a-distance assessment techniques" (see Post 2005), LTA relies on quantitative content analysis to ascertain leaders' characteristics.

More specifically, LTA draws on verbal utterances of leaders, which allows for the latter's systematic profiling without requiring direct access to them. However, not any statement can or rather should be used in this regard. Rather, LTA stipulates several quantitative and qualitative requirements concerning source material that should be adhered to when profiling a leader (Hermann 2005a, 2008).

First, a minimum of 50 verbal statements (ideally: 100 statements or more) must be collected for every leader under examination. Second, each of those statements must contain at least 100 words (ideally: 150 words or more). Thus, each LTA profile is based on at least 5,000 words. Mind you, though, that those quantitative requirements hail from a period when the coding was still done manually. With the advent of automated coding using Profiler Plus (see previous section), profiles nowadays can and typically do draw on much larger amounts of leaders' statements.

Third, moving from quantitative to qualitative requirements, the source material must contain spontaneous statements only. As Hermann (2005, 179) suggests,

> [I]nterviews are the material of preference. In the interview, political leaders are less in control of what they say and, even though still in a public setting, more likely to evidence what they, themselves, are like than is often possible when giving a speech.

Conversely, non-spontaneous statements like scripted speeches should not be incorporated in the text corpus. Fourth, leaders' statements should have been uttered in different contexts, that is, in front of different audiences such as parliament or the press.

While variation across "time, audience, and topic" (Hermann 2005a, 180) is not ruled out,[2] LTA typically assumes that leadership traits, which are considered as being deeply ingrained in leaders' personalities rather than representing mere situation-dependent states of leaders, as well as the ensuing leadership styles are essentially stable over time as well as similar across issue areas. The final two requirements on source material follow from those substantive assumptions. Thus, fifth, verbal statements should cover the leader's entire tenure in office rather than just a specific period (e.g., a leader's first or second term). Finally, the statements should focus on different substantive areas, spanning not only different areas of foreign policy but also domestic issues.

A leader's LTA profile is based on the automated content analysis of source material (i.e., verbal utterances) assembled in accordance with the aforementioned requirements. More specifically, the LTA coding scheme as contained in Profiler Plus generates results for the seven leadership traits. As shown in Table 15.2, every trait is associated with a particular set of words or expressions (ranging from some 200 for self-confidence up to some 1,500 for distrust of others) that indicate the existence of either high or low manifestations of the respective trait.

For all seven traits, the range for the score is between 0 and 1. The lower the score, the weaker is the manifestation of the respective trait, and vice versa. For instance, U.S. Secretary of State Hillary Clinton's score for self-confidence was .51 (see the next section for details). At face value, this score suggests that Clinton was essentially average on that trait when measured against the full spectrum from 0 to 1. However, the more interesting question is how Clinton's level of self-confidence fares *compared* with other foreign policy leaders. There are two ways of answering this question. The first option is to develop additional profiles of other leaders on top of Clinton's to generate a group for comparison, which for obvious reasons would be rather time-consuming. The second and much more "user-friendly" option is to use LTA's pre-existing "norming group of world leaders" as point of reference. As shown in Table 15.3, the norming group currently contains close to 300 foreign policy leaders

Table 15.2 Indicators for Different Manifestations of Leadership Traits

Leadership Trait	Exemplary Indicators for a...	
	...High Manifestation of the Leadership Trait	...Low Manifestation of the Leadership Trait
Belief in the ability to control events (BACE)	Carry out, initiate, tackle, set in motion, work out, go ahead, conceive, reshape, get the ball rolling	Regret, hope, wish, doubt, reconsider, lament, fret
Need for power (PWR)	Fight, attack, hold accountable, win, threaten, punish, retaliate, snatch, intervene	Residual rule (all remaining verbs that are used in reference to the leader or his in-group but which have not been evaluated as "high power" automatically become "low power")
Conceptual complexity (CC)	Dependent on, conditional, on the one hand . . . on the other hand, differentiate, particularity, probability, tendency, open to interpretation	Absolute, by no means, unequivocal, inevitable, without alternative, eternal, irrevocable, at any price, indisputable, unlimited
Self-confidence (SC)	Implement, take charge of, single-handedly, direct, set the course, know, vision	Pay a lesson, get your fingers burned, powerless, have your hands tied, not in my power, not allowed, see with concern
Task focus or orientation focus (TASK)	Achieve, against all odds, efficiency, implementation, increase possibilities, decisiveness, design, solution concept, overcome	Understanding, assistance, award, cohesion, confidence, hope, loyalty, unity, empathy
Distrust of others (DIS)	Criminal, unlawful, deceitful, subversive, behind our/my back, set-up, deception, exploit, undermine	Partnership, relationship of trust, solidarity
In-group bias (IGB)	World-class, prestige, light-years ahead, can't be brought down, prove yourself, don't back down, X denies us, X takes advantage of us	Residual rule (all in-group references in whose context no indicator with a high in-group favoritism is connected, are counted as "low" in terms of in-group bias)

Source: Own depiction based on Hermann (2005a) and Rabini et al. (2020a): Chapter 2.

Table 15.3 LTA's "Norming Group of World Leaders"

Leadership Traits	World Leaders (n=284)
Belief in the ability to control events (BACE)	.35 (.05)
Need for power (PWR)	.26 (.05)
Conceptual complexity (CC)	.59 (.06)
Self-confidence (SC)	.36 (.10)
Task focus (TASK)	.63 (.07)
Distrust of others (DIS)	.13 (.06)
In-group bias (IGB)	.15 (.05)

Source: Own depiction based on Cuhadar et al. (2017): 47 (average scores for world leaders; standard deviations in parentheses).

(presidents, prime ministers, and foreign ministers) from around the globe.[3] This norming group renders possible meaningful comparisons between leaders without having to create the profile of more than one leader, thereby helping to put into context the scores of one's own analysis.

Returning to our example: Hillary Clinton's score for self-confidence was .51. The norming group shows that the average score for this particular trait among close to 300 world leaders is .36, with a standard deviation of .10.[4] Hence, Clinton's trait score is more than one standard deviation above the world average. This is not only a finding in itself but also becomes all the more pertinent when considering possible behavioral expectations that are associated with a high manifestation in that trait (see Table 15.1), which include little inclination to critically examine oneself and/or facts as well as ignoring or reinterpreting "inappropriate" information. Not accidentally, leaders with a high manifestation in that trait have been shown, for instance, to exhibit a greater likelihood of ending up with foreign policy fiascos (Brummer 2016).

Intermediary Dimensions

On the second level of the LTA framework, certain traits are combined to provide information on three more general "questions." Those relate to leaders' responsiveness to constraints, openness to information, and motivation for office-seeking respectively (Hermann 2005a, 181–184):

- *Responsiveness to constraints:* Whether leaders respect or challenge constraints results from their belief in the ability to control events (BACE) and their need for power (PWR).
- *Openness to information:* Whether leaders are open or closed to information can be inferred from their conceptual complexity (CC) and self-confidence (SC).
- *Motivation for office-seeking:* Whether leaders' motivation for office is driven by problems or relationships follows from their focus on tasks or rather on group maintenance (TASK), their general distrust or suspiciousness of others (DIS), and their in-group bias (IGB).

The automated coding procedure outlined above is restricted to the identification of the seven individual traits. This is to say that the interaction of certain traits to get answers to the aforementioned more general questions needs to be done "manually" by the researcher since the coding scheme does not contain an automated procedure for that purpose. At times, this interaction is anything but straightforward which, as suggested in the previous section, is arguably one of the key reasons why most LTA studies do not move beyond the level of individual traits. Indeed, problems arise when leaders exhibit average manifestations of individual traits.

This "aggregation problem" will be illustrated based on leaders' responsiveness to constraints which, as just mentioned, is a function of BACE and PWR. Leaders with both a low belief in the ability to control events and a low need for power are supposed to respect constraints (low BACE/low PWR). Conversely, leaders with low BACE/high PWR, high BACE/low PWR, and high BACE/high PWR are supposed to challenge constraints. In all instances, what counts as low or high is typically ascertained by comparing a leader's trait scores with the mean scores of the aforementioned norming group of world leaders. The problem emerges when leaders exhibit "moderate" manifestations of traits. Thus, when he or she scores average (i.e., less than one standard deviation above or below the mean) in one or even both traits, it is impossible to ascertain whether the leader will challenge or respect constraints since both could happen "depending on the nature of the situation" (Hermann 2005a, 187). Fair enough, but the problem is that a definite answer—in the sense of either challenging or respecting constraints—is required at this point in order to arrive at clear evaluations with respect to leaders' styles on the third and final level of LTA, as discussed below.

Similar challenges can arise with respect to assessing leaders' motivation based on task focus (TASK), in-group bias (IGB), and distrusts of others (DIS). While all three traits provide answers to whether leaders are problem or relationship oriented respectively, TASK assesses why leaders seek office whereas IGB and DIS zoom in on leaders' "need to preserve and secure the group they are leading" (Hermann 2005a, 197). The evaluation of TASK is straightforward as long as leaders score high or low, which suggests that they are driven by problems or relationships respectively. However, when leaders exhibit moderate scores, they can be motivated by either problems or relationships depending on context. A similar problem associated with moderate scores emerges with respect to the interaction of IGB and DIS since in those cases leaders can also be motived by either problems or relationships. Conversely, low IGB/low DIS and low IGB/high DIS are suggestive for a relationship focus whereas high IGB/low DIS and high IGB/high DIS point to a problem focus. Of course, the aforementioned problems of moderate scores do not go away when trying to come up with an overall evaluation of a leader's motivation that takes into account the assessments for both TASK and IGB/DIS.

It is only for the question on leaders' openness to information, which is based on conceptual complexity (CC) and self-confidence (SC), where the interaction of traits is unproblematic. Leaders are open to information when CC is higher than SC or when leaders are high on both traits. Conversely, leaders are closed to information when SC is higher than CC or when leaders score low on both traits (Hermann 2005a, 194).

Of course, alternative combinations of the seven traits that cut across the aforementioned clustering and accordingly also provide answers to questions different from the three mentioned before (i.e., constraints, information, motivation) are also possible. For instance, Keller and Foster (2012) combine the belief in the ability to control events (BACE) and self-confidence (SC) to what they call "locus of control," which they, in turn, connect to leaders' propensity to engage in diversionary action. They suggest that leaders with an "internal locus of control" (i.e., high scores in both traits) are most likely to resort to military force abroad in order to distract from domestic political problems. While such novel combinations of traits enable researchers to address additional research questions, they effectively prohibit moving forward to the third level of the LTA framework pertaining to leadership styles which are necessarily based on the aforementioned interactions of the seven traits.

Leadership Styles

The third and final level of the LTA framework relates to leadership styles. The latter are defined as "the ways in which leaders relate to those around them—whether constituents, advisers, or other leaders—and how they structure interactions and the norms, rules, and principles they use to guide such interactions" (Hermann 2005a, 181). Based on the preceding assessment of the three intermediary questions, it is up to the researcher (rather than it being done by LTA's automated coding scheme) to establish which of the eight leadership styles contained in LTA a leader exhibits.

When the assessment on the intermediary level leads to unequivocal conclusions (which, however, is not always the case as just discussed), establishing a leader's style is straightforward. For instance, a leader who challenges constraints, is open to information, and focuses on problems is called "actively independent." Conversely, a leader who respects constraints, is open to information, and focuses on relationships is called "collegial." And a leader who challenges constraints, is closed to information, and focuses on problems is called "expansionistic."

Having said that, when leaders exhibit moderate/average manifestations of individual traits (level I) which, in turn, lead to inconclusive answers on the intermediary level (level II), it is impossible to establish a single specific leadership style for a leader. Therefore, at times one can find in the literature ascriptions of more than one style to individual leaders, for instance to several Turkish prime ministers (Kesgin 2013, 149). Since the different leadership styles come with different and often competing behavioral expectations, the inability to come to unequivocal assessments is quite problematic. Table 15.4 depicts the full analytical framework of LTA.

Empirical Illustration

This section offers a brief original illustration for the use of LTA in empirical analysis. FPA scholarship has paid limited attention to women as foreign policy leaders (for exceptions, see Hudson and Leidl 2015; Ankel 2020). In this sense, Karen Smith (2020, 130) recently noted that women are "missing in analysis" and suggested that there is a need for further "gendering FPA," including on the level of individual decision makers. Against this background, this section explores whether female foreign policy leaders exhibit systematically different leadership traits compared with their male counterparts. The question is addressed from two perspectives: one pertaining to sex and the other to gender.

The first perspective (sex) focuses on alleged biological differences between men and women. From this vantage point, "'men' and 'women' [are] assumed to be distinct personality types embodying stereotypically 'masculine' and 'feminine' traits and characteristics en mass" (Hooper 2001, 23). Indeed, feminist IR scholarship has shown that mainstream conceptions of international politics are infused by ascriptions of different characteristics and attributes to female and male decision makers respectively (e.g., Tickner, 1992, 2001; Hooper, 2001; Shepherd, 2010; Enloe, 2014; see also the chapter by Henshaw in this volume).[5] It is argued that mainstream IR theory is based on the experience and behavior of men, such as violence, combat, and war-fighting which is conducted by soldiers who are (or

Table 15.4 LTA's Full Analytical Framework

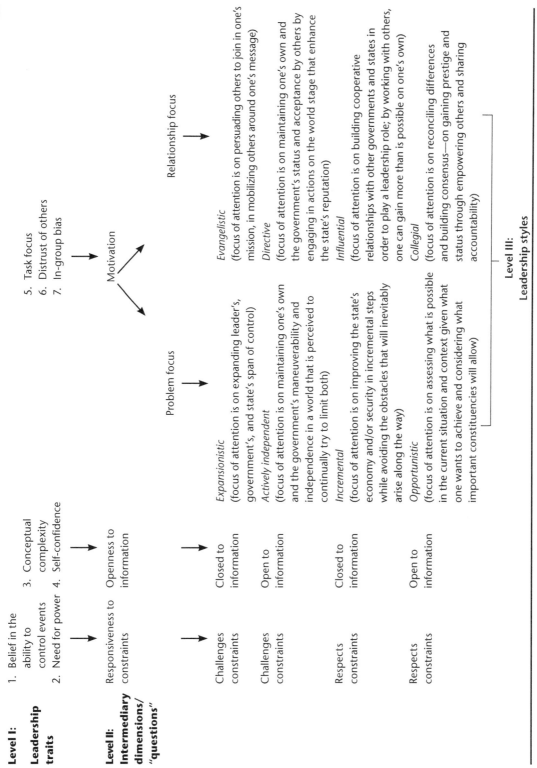

Source: Own depiction based on Hermann (2005a) (behavioral expectations associated with leadership styles are quoted from Hermann 2005a, 185).

at least have used to be) almost exclusively male (Sjoberg 2009, 196; for details, see Goldstein 2001, Chapter 2). As a result, mainstream conceptions of international politics are heavily influenced by gender stereotypes as well as gender dichotomies and binaries (see Table 15.5).

A gender perspective rejects the aforementioned essentialist perspective pertaining to biologically-rooted differences between the sexes (Steans 2013, 11). Instead, gender can be understood as "characteristics (or learned attributes) associated with maleness (masculinity) and characteristics associated with femaleness (femininity)" (Sjoberg 2012, 8). Thus, from a critical perspective, the above-mentioned dichotomies are considered mere social constructions whose purpose is to prolong the dominance of men and masculine characteristics as well as the subordination of women and feminine characteristics. By extension, not all men and women must necessarily exhibit the attributes associated with their respective sex: "Women can be *masculinist*, that is, they can express a social preference for masculinity and subordinate and/or exclude femininity. Correspondingly, men…can be *feminized*, that is, they can be subordinated by association with values perceived as feminine" (Sjoberg 2012, 8; emphasis in the original). Hence, both male and female decision makers could exhibit either masculine or feminine attributes. A female decision maker who exhibits strong masculine attributes is thus no contradiction in terms.

The next question is whether the above-mentioned binaries can be plausibly associated with the traits covered by LTA—or, more precisely, with certain manifestations of the respective traits. One of the more obvious linkages is that male/masculine decision makers, who are supposedly power-seeking and strive for dominance, should exhibit a higher need for power (i.e., higher PWR score) than female/feminine decision makers. Similarly, male/masculine decision makers should be more self-confident (i.e., higher SC score) than their weaker and more vulnerable female/feminine counterparts. Moreover, male/masculine decision makers should be more task-oriented (i.e., higher TASK score) than female/feminine decision makers who, based on their focus on cooperation and communication, should be more concerned about relationships.

Regarding the remaining traits, possible correlations to sex or gender are harder to come by. One could, for instance, argue that male/masculine decision makers are more likely to

Table 15.5 Binaries Men/Masculinity—Women/Femininity

Men/Masculinity	Women/Femininity
Rational	Irrational, intuitive, emotional
Strong, powerful	Weak, vulnerable
Courageous	Fearful
Aggressive	Compassionate
Violent	Nurturant
Autonomous, independent	Dependent
Public life	Private life
Use of force	Cooperative
Physical strength	Communicative, compromise-seeking
Power-seeking	Restraint
Domination	Subordination

Source: Own compilation based on Tickner (1992, 2001); Hooper (2001); Connell (2009); Gerber and Stiegler (2009); Sjoberg (2012); Steans (2013); Kronsell (2016).

consider themselves capable of controlling events (i.e., higher BACE score) than female/feminine decision makers due to their rational, rather than emotional or intuitive, approach to decision making. This could also be the reason why male/masculine decision makers might exhibit a higher conceptual complexity (i.e., higher CC score) than their female/feminine counterparts. Moreover, male/masculine decision makers, who rely more on themselves rather than on a certain group, could possibly exhibit a higher distrust of others (i.e., higher DIS score) as well as a lower in-group bias (i.e., lower IGB score) than female/feminine decision makers. However, this is admittedly rather speculative and not really grounded in the literature.

In short, then, a perspective that focuses on sex would expect male leaders to exhibit masculine characteristics and female leaders to exhibit feminine characteristics. Conversely, a gender perspective would move beyond such stereotypes and expect to see greater variation, in the sense that both male and female leaders can exhibit masculine and/or feminine attributes. After establishing the research question, the following paragraphs illustrate the specific steps that are required for an LTA analysis.

First, the leaders to be profiled have to be selected. The following discussion examines seven female leaders (four prime ministers and three foreign ministers) from four different countries, all of whom belong to the English-speaking world (i.e., Australia, New Zealand, United Kingdom, United States). The "Anglo-American" bias in this illustration results from the fact that I did not want to use translated speech acts but rely on original statements of leaders in order to get as authentic representations of their traits as possible and, relatedly, that LTA stipulates a set of quantitative and qualitative requirements concerning source material that cannot be easily met (and in many cases cannot be met at all) for non-English speaking leaders if one relies on original English-language statements. Future research could and should expand the sample to include a broader sample of leaders, both Western and non-Western.

To ascertain whether there are systematic differences between the female leaders on the one hand and male leaders on the other, a second sample brings together male decision makers from the same four countries. In order to keep the domestic and international context as constant as possible, the sample only includes the immediate predecessor and the immediate successor of the respective female leader. Since two female leaders (Shipley and Rice) were succeeded by other female leaders (Clark and Clinton), the sample comprises nine male decision makers. Hence, the overall sample comprises a total of 16 people (seven female and nine male) (see Table 15.6).

Next, for the selected leaders, verbal utterances were compiled in accordance with LTA's requirements pertaining to source material outlined above. Thus, for every decision maker 50 spontaneous statements of at least 100 words each that cover the entire time in office and address different substantive issues were compiled. Sources for the spontaneous speech acts included question times in parliamentary debates, statements from press conferences or "doorstep interviews," and transcripts from media (primarily television) interviews. Overall, 800 spontaneous statements totaling more than 157,000 words were used to identify the leadership traits of the 16 prime minister and foreign ministers covered in the analysis.

Finally, this source material was processed using the LTA coding scheme contained in the Profiler Plus platform. As outlined above, Profiler Plus performs frequency counts for the text corpuses that are inputted in the program based on which indices for the seven leadership traits are constructed. Table 15.7 shows the results.

The results offer little support for the biologically-rooted assumption that female leaders exhibit systematically different manifestations of leadership traits compared with their male counterparts in general, or more feminine traits in particular. Indeed, there is just a single

Table 15.6 Sample of Decision Makers

Country	Leader	Office	Tenure
Australia	**Julia Gillard**	Prime Minister	2010–2013
	Kevin Rudd	Prime Minister	2007–2010
	Tony Abbott	Prime Minister	2013–2015
New Zealand	**Jenny Shipley**	Prime Minister	1997–1999
	Jim Bolger	Prime Minister	1990–1997
	Helen Clark	Prime Minister	1999–2008
New Zealand	**Helen Clark**	Prime Minister	1999–2008
	Jenny Shipley	Prime Minister	1997–1999
	John Key	Prime Minister	2008–2016
The United Kingdom	**Margaret Thatcher**	Prime Minister	1979–1990
	James Callaghan	Prime Minister	1976–1979
	John Major	Prime Minister	1990–1997
The United States	**Madeleine Albright**	Foreign Minister	1997–2001
	Warren Christopher	Foreign Minister	1993–1997
	Colin Powell	Foreign Minister	2001–2005
The United States	**Condoleezza Rice**	Foreign Minister	2005–2009
	Colin Powell	Foreign Minister	2001–2005
	Hilary Clinton	Foreign Minister	2009–2013
The United States	**Hilary Clinton**	Foreign Minister	2009–2013
	Condoleezza Rice	Foreign Minister	2005–2009
	John Kerry	Foreign Minister	2013–2017

Source: Own compilation. The table shows first the female prime minister or foreign minister (in bold), followed by her predecessor and successor.

Table 15.7 Leadership Traits of Female and Male Decision Makers

Decision Makers Trait	**Female** Decision Makers (n=7)	**Male** Decision Makers (n=9)
Belief in the ability to control events (BACE)	.30 (SD: .02)	**.33*** (SD: .04)
Need for power (PWR)	.20 (SD: .04)	.22 (SD: .05)
Conceptual Complexity (CC)	.63 (SD: .03)	.64 (SD: .05)
Self-confidence (SC)	.51 (SD: .12)	.50 (SD: .08)
Task focus (TASK)	.68 (SD: .04)	.67 (SD: .05)
Distrust of others (DIS)	.09 (SD: .05)	.12 (SD: .08)
In-group bias (IGB)	.12 (SD: .02)	.10 (SD: .03)

Source: Own compilation. * $p < .10$ (one-tailed t-tests).

trait (BACE) in which the two groups do differ significantly, and the direction of the difference (i.e., a higher belief in the ability to control events on part of male leaders) is also in accordance with the above-mentioned expectations. Other than that, female and male leaders exhibit very similar manifestations of traits.

Conversely, there is greater support for a gendered perspective in that both male and female decision makers exhibit either masculine or feminine attributes (see Table 15.5).[6] For instance, the profile of former U.S. Secretary of State Madeleine Albright shows a (feminine) low need for power and task orientation while at the same time suggests a (masculine) high level of self-confidence and a low level of in-group bias. Other examples for masculine attributes on part of female leaders are former Australian Prime Minister Julie Gillard's high need for power and the two former Prime Ministers of New Zealand's, Helen Clark and Jenny Shipley, high levels of conceptual complexity. Conversely, the scores for former Australian Prime Minister Tony Abbott point to a (masculine) high belief in the ability to control events, a high need for power, and a high level of distrust of others while at the same time suggest a (feminine) a high level of in-group bias. Other examples for feminine attributes on part of male leaders are former U.S. Secretary of State Colin Powell's low belief in the ability to control events and former British Prime Minister James Callaghan's low level of self-confidence.

The main purpose of this brief illustration has been to show LTA *in action*. Concerning the specific substantive issue under examination, follow-up research is required that moves beyond the somewhat smaller and clearly Western-biased sample of leaders to arrive at more robust findings. Still, heeding the above-mentioned call by Smith (2020), what the discussion ideally has shown is that leadership profiling can be fruitfully employed to contribute to the "gendering of FPA."

Conclusion

Representing an "at-a-distance" assessment technique, Leadership Trait Analysis (LTA) develops personality profiles of decision makers based on their verbal utterances. LTA offers a three-tiered conceptual framework which comprises seven leadership traits, three intermediary dimensions, and ultimately eight leadership styles. It has been widely used in empirical analysis, covering a broad range of foreign policy processes and outcomes. The advent of automated coding schemes has rendered the identification of traits both more reliable and efficient. Indeed, nowadays the collection of source material, for which LTA offers a clearly defined set of requirements, is much more time-consuming than the actual coding procedure. The availability of a "norming group" of close to 300 world leaders makes LTA an ideal tool for comparative analyses.

Having said that, LTA also exhibits certain shortcomings. For example, the aggregation of individual traits to overarching styles can lead to inconclusive results. Further, automated coding schemes are currently available for only a few languages, which means that a large number of leaders cannot be profiled based on statements in their native tongue, and often not at all in case no sufficient amount of translated statements is available. Finally, LTA has little to say about why leaders exhibit specific manifestations of traits in the first place. Recent scholarship has looked in the possibly formative effect of war experience, or lack thereof, in this regard (Rabini et al. 2020, 146–154) but more needs to be done also in this regard. Still, on balance the strengths of the approach clearly outweigh the challenges, which is why LTA continues to be one of the most widely used approach in FPA for profiling leaders.

Notes

1 The LTA coding scheme is available on the Profiler Plus website (profilerplus.org).
2 Accordingly, more targeted samples with respect to issue areas and/or time periods are not categorically excluded.
3 The latest norming group overview together with information on, for the most part, geographically-defined sub-groups (Western Europe; Eastern Europe; Middle East and Northern Africa; Pacific Rim; Latin America; and Anglo-America) can be obtained through the Profiler Plus website (profilerplus.org).
4 However, Clinton's self-confidence score is less exceptional for the sub-group of "Anglo-American" leaders (n=15) whose average score is .45 with a standard deviation of .08.
5 References to "feminist IR scholarship" are not meant to imply that this strand of IR theorizing is homogenous but rather that works in this tradition share certain "foundational arguments" that also distinguish this literature from other critical perspectives (Sjoberg 2009).
6 Yet most of the scores are within the range of one standard deviation above or below the mean.

References

Ankel, Danae. 2020. *Angela Merkels Überzeugungen in der Eurokrise. Eine Operational Code-Analyse.* Wiesbaden: Springer VS.
Brummer, Klaus. 2014. "Die Führungsstile von Präsidenten der Europäischen Kommission." *Zeitschrift für Politik* 61(3): 327–345.
Brummer, Klaus. 2016. "'Fiasco Prime Ministers'. Beliefs and Leadership Traits as Possible Causes for Policy Fiascos." *Journal of European Public Policy* 23(5): 702–717.
Brummer, Klaus. 2021. "Advancing Foreign Policy Analysis by Studying Leaders from the Global South." *International Affairs* 97(2): 405–421.
Brummer, Klaus, Michael D. Young, Özgur Özdamar, Sercan Canbolat, Consuelo Thiers, Christian Rabini, Katharina Dimmroth, Mischa Hansel, and Ameneh Mehvar. 2020. "Forum: Coding in Tongues: Developing Non-English Coding Schemes for Leadership Profiling." *International Studies Review* 22(4): 1039–1067.
Connell, Raewyn. 2009. *Gender in World Perspective.* 2nd edition. Cambridge: Polity.
Crichlow, Scott. 2002. "Legislators' Personality Traits and Congressional Support for Free Trade." *Journal of Conflict Resolution* 46(5): 693–711.
Cuhadar, Esra, Juliet Kaarbo, Baris Kesgin, and Binnur Ozkececi-Taner. 2017a. "Examining Leaders' Orientations to Structural Constraints: Turkey's 1991 and 2003 Iraq War Decisions." *Journal of International Relations and Development* 20(1): 29–54.
Cuhadar, Esra, Juliet Kaarbo, Baris Kesgin, and Binnur Ozkececi-Taner. 2017b. "Personality or Role? Comparisons of Turkish Leaders Across Different Institutional Positions." *Political Psychology* 38(1): 39–54.
Dyson, Stephen Benedict. 2006. "Personality and Foreign Policy: Tony Blair's Iraq Decisions." *Foreign Policy Analysis* 2(3): 289–306.
Dyson, Stephen Benedict. 2007. "Alliances, Domestic Politics, and Leader Psychology: Why Did Britain Stay Out of Vietnam and Go into Iraq?" *Political Psychology* 28(6): 647–666.
Dyson, Stephen Benedict. 2009. "'Stuff Happens': Donald Rumsfeld and the Iraq War." *Foreign Policy Analysis* 5(4): 327–347.
Dyson, Stephen Benedict, and Thomas Preston. 2006. "Individual Characteristics of Political Leaders and the Use of Analogy in Foreign Policy Decision Making." *Political Psychology* 27(2): 265–288.
Enloe, Cynthia. 2014. *Bananas, Beaches and Bases. Making Feminist Sense of International Politics,* 2nd edition. Berkeley et al.: University of California Press.
Foster, Dennis, and Jonathan W. Keller. 2014. "Leaders' Cognitive Complexity, Distrust, and the Diversionary Use of Force." *Foreign Policy Analysis* 10(3): 205–223.
Gerber, Elisabet, and Barbara Stiegler. 2009. *Gender an der Macht? Über die Bedeutung von Geschlecht in politischen Spitzenpositionen am Beispiel von Deutschland, Chile, Argentinien und Spanien.* Bonn: Friedrich-Ebert-Stiftung.
Goldstein, Joshua S. 2001. *War and Gender. How Gender Shapes the War System and Vice-Versa.* Cambridge: Cambridge University Press.

Hermann, Margaret G. 1980a. "Explaining Foreign Policy Behavior Using the Personal Characteristics of Political Leaders." *International Studies Quarterly* 24(1): 7–46.

Hermann, Margaret G. 1980b. "Assessing the Personalities of Soviet Politburo Members." *Personality and Social Psychology Bulletin* 6: 332–352.

Hermann, Margaret G. 1987. "Assessing the Foreign Policy Role Orientations of Sub-Saharan African Leaders." In *Role Theory and Foreign Policy Analysis*, edited by Stephen G. Walker. Durham: Duke University, 161–198.

Hermann, Margaret G. 2005a. "Assessing Leadership Style: Trait Analysis." In *The Psychological Assessment of Political Leaders. With Profiles of Saddam Hussein and Bill Clinton*, edited by Jerrold M. Post. Ann Arbor: University of Michigan Press, 178–212.

Hermann, Margaret G. 2005b. "William Jefferson Clinton's Leadership Style." In *The Psychological Assessment of Political Leaders. With Profiles of Saddam Hussein and Bill Clinton*, edited by Jerrold M. Post. Ann Arbor: University of Michigan Press, 313–323.

Hermann, Margaret G. 2005c. "Saddam Hussein's Leadership Style." In *The Psychological Assessment of Political Leaders. With Profiles of Saddam Hussein and Bill Clinton*, edited by Jerrold M. Post. Ann Arbor: University of Michigan Press, 375–386.

Hooper, Charlotte (2001) *Manly States. Masculinities, International Relations, and Gender Politics.* New York: Columbia University Press.

Hudson, Valerie M., and Patricia Leidl. 2015. *The Hillary Doctrine: Sex and American Foreign Policy.* New York: Columbia University Press.

Keller, Jonathan W., and Dennis M. Foster. 2012. "Presidential Leadership Style and the Political Use of Force." *Political Psychology* 33(5): 581–598.

Keller, Jonathan W., Keith A. Grant and Dennis M. Foster. 2020. "Presidential Risk Propensity and Intervention in Interstate Conflicts." *Foreign Policy Analysis* 16(3): 272–291.

Keller, Jonathan W., and Yi Edward Yang. 2008. "Leadership Style, Decision Context, and the Poliheuristic Theory of Decision Making. An Experimental Analysis." *Journal of Conflict Resolution* 52(5): 687–712.

Kesgin, Baris. 2013. "Leadership Traits of Turkey's Islamist and Secular Prime Ministers." *Turkish Studies* 14(1): 136–157.

Kesgin, Baris. 2020a. "Turkey's Erdoğan: Leadership Style and Foreign Policy Audiences." *Turkish Studies* 21(1): 56–82.

Kesgin, Baris. 2020b. "Features of Foreign Policy Birds: Israeli Prime Ministers as Hawks and Doves." *Cooperation and Conflict* 55(1): 107–126.

Kille, Kent J. 2006. *From Manager to Visionary. The Secretary-General of the United Nations.* New York and Basingstoke: Palgrave Macmillan.

Kille, Kent J., and Roger M. Scully. 2003. "Executive Heads and the Role of Intergovernmental Organizations: Expansionist Leadership in the United Nations and the European Union." *Political Psychology* 24(1): 175–198.

Kronsell, Annica. 2016. "The Power of EU Masculinities: A Feminist Contribution to European Integration Theory." *Journal of Common Market Studies* 54(1): 104–120.

Levine, Nick, and Michael D. Young. 2014. "Leadership Trait Analysis and Threat Assessment with Profiler Plus." In *Proceedings of ILC 2014 on 8th International Lisp Conference. Association for Computing Machinery Digital Library*, August 2014, pp. 50–59. https://doi.org/10.1145/2635648.2635657.

Mastors, Elena. 2000. "Gerry Adams and the Northern Ireland Peace Process: A Research Note." *Political Psychology* 21(4): 839–846.

Post, Jerrold M. ed. 2005. *The Psychological Assessment of Political Leaders. With Profiles of Saddam Hussein and Bill Clinton.* Ann Arbor: University of Michigan Press.

Rabini, Christian, Katharina Dimmroth, Klaus Brummer, and Mischa Hansel. 2020a. *Entscheidungsträger in der Deutschen Außenpolitik. Führungseigenschaften und Politische Überzeugungen der Bundeskanzler und Außenminister.* Baden-Baden: Nomos.

Rabini, Christian, Katharina Dimmroth, Klaus Brummer, and Mischa Hansel. 2020b. "Profiling Foreign Policy Leaders in Their Own Language: New Insights into the Stability and Formation of Leadership Traits." *British Journal of Politics and International Relations* 22(2): 256–273.

Schafer, Mark. 2000. "Issues in Assessing Psychological Characteristics at a Distance: An Introduction to the Symposium." *Political Psychology* 21(3): 511–527.

Shannon, Vaughn P., and Jonathan W. Keller. 2007. "Leadership Style and International Norm Violation: The Case of the Iraq War." *Foreign Policy Analysis* 3(1): 79–104.

Shepherd, Laura J. 2010. "Sex or Gender? Bodies in World Politics and Why Gender Matters." In *Gender Matters in Global Politics. A Feminist Introduction to International Relations*, edited by Laura J. Shepherd. London and New York: Routledge, 3–16.

Siniver, Asaf, and Christopher Featherstone. 2020. "Low Conceptual-complexity and Trump's Foreign Policy." *Global Affairs* 6(1): 71–85.

Sjoberg, Laura. 2009. "Introduction to Security Studies: Feminist Contributions." *Security Studies* 18(2): 183–213.

Sjoberg, Laura. 2012. "Gender, Structure, and War: What Waltz Couldn't See." *International Theory* 4(1): 1–38.

Smith, Karen E. 2020. "Missing in Analysis: Women in Foreign Policy–Making." *Foreign Policy Analysis* 16(1): 130–141.

Sprout, Harold, and Margaret Sprout. 1957. "Environmental Factors in the Study of International Politics." *Journal of Conflict Resolution* 1(4): 309–328.

Steans, Jill. 2013. *Gender and International Relations. Theory, Practice, Policy*, 3rd edition. Cambridge: Polity.

Suedfeld, Peter, Karen Guttieri, and Philip E. Tetlock. 2005. "Assessing Integrative Complexity at a Distance: Archival Analyses of Thinking and Decision Making." In *The Psychological Assessment of Political Leaders. With Profiles of Saddam Hussein and Bill Clinton*, edited by Jerrold M. Post. Ann Arbor: University of Michigan Press, 246–273.

Taysi, Tanyel, and Thomas Preston. 2001. "The Personality and Leadership Style of President Khatami: Implications for the Future of Iranian Political Reform." In *Profiling Political Leaders. Cross-Cultural Studies of Personality and Behavior*, edited by Ofer Feldman and Linda O. Valenty. Westport and London: Praeger, 57–77.

Thies, Cameron G. 2009. "The Conceptual Complexity of Central Bankers and the Asian Financial Crisis." *Political Psychology* 30(3): 445–464.

Tickner, J. Ann. 1992. *Gender in International Relations. Feminist Perspectives on Achieving Global Security*. New York: Columbia University Press.

Tickner, J. Ann. 2001. *Gendering World Politics. Issues and Approaches in the Post-Cold War Era*. New York: Columbia University Press.

Van Esch, Femke, and Marij Swinkels. 2015. "How Europe's Political Leaders Made Sense of the Euro Crisis: The Influence of Pressure and Personality." *West European Politics* 38(6): 1203–1225.

Yang, Yi Edward. 2010. "Leaders' Conceptual Complexity and Foreign Policy Change: Comparing the Bill Clinton and George W. Bush Foreign Policies toward China." *Chinese Journal of International Politics* 3(4): 415–446.

16
Operational Code Analysis
Mark Schafer and Stephen G. Walker

Introduction

Writing a chapter on *the* method of operational code analysis (OCA) is impossible because there have been many different ones used in the research program since its inception. However, in recent times, one approach has become the most commonplace, the Verbs In Context System (VICS), which is the primary focus of this chapter. Our intention is to make the reader familiar with the basic quantitative content analysis methods for OCA using VICS. That system provides benefits in the form of quantitative indicators of an actor's cognitive beliefs about other actors and about the actor's own best strategies and tactics. These quantitative indicators may be used to profile or compare leaders; to assess changes in beliefs over time; to fit actors to game-theoretical models; or to model conflict behavior in conjunction with large-n data sets.

OCA: A Brief History. The history of OCA is important in understanding where we are today, and the earlier methods deserve some attention. As Lewis Carroll's King said, therefore, let us begin at the beginning. Here we provide a brief historical overview of OCA extending back to the qualitative method of content analysis in the seminal studies of the Bolshevik operational code by Leites (1951, 1953) and trace forward to the more modern quantitative methods in most of the current contributions to the literature. The first operational code study in the field of Foreign Policy Analysis was *The Operational Code of the Politburo* (1951) by the sociologist Nathan Leites. He applied a psychoanalytical form of the *verstehen* method of putting oneself in another's shoes by reading the writings of Lenin and Stalin to identify their conscious beliefs and infer their subconscious fears and motivations. Leites also became steeped in the cultural context of the Bolshevik movement in Russia (Geertz 1973), tracing Lenin's operational code in *A Study of Bolshevism* (1953) to his experience as a Marxist revolutionary in Tsarist Russia.

Leites employed psychoanalysis as a method to interpret the results of his qualitative content analysis of Lenin's writings. He reported that Lenin's cognitive beliefs included the conscious diagnosis of politics as dominated by conflict rather than cooperation, in which the key question was "kto-kovo?" (who-whom?) in Russian, that is, who dominates, destroys, controls whom in the exercise of power in politics (Leites 1951: 78–81, 1953: 27–29). Lenin's main unconscious fear was the fear of annihilation as the result of miscalculations about power relations in a hostile political universe. His primary motivation was the pursuit of power so that the answer to the kto-kovo question would be a favorable one for him.

To ensure this outcome, Lenin's prescriptions for strategies, tactics, and calculating risks were expressed as favoring conflict over cooperation strategies in the pursuit of power and employing flexible tactics of advance and retreat in implementing conflict strategies, in order to avoid the risk of annihilation (Leites 1951). The methodological assumption by the Leites analysis was that Lenin had left his personal stamp on the central beliefs of his successors (Josef Stalin and Nikita Khrushchev) as well as in the enduring strategic culture of the Soviet Politburo (Leites 1964). Reviews of the Leites studies by Alexander George and others prompted attempts to develop more reliable methods of observation and adopt a mode of interpretation more accessible to political scientists than psychoanalysis for identifying and interpreting the operational codes of other world leaders (George 1969; Holsti 1977; Walker 1977).

Three major methodological advances include the development of a list of research questions to identify operational code beliefs (George 1969); the specification of a set of operational code types based on the answers to these questions (Holsti 1977; Walker 1983); and the creation of quantitative indices of the answers from a systematic analysis of a leader's public statements (Walker, Schafer, and Young 1998). George's research questions were organized into five questions about a leader's philosophical beliefs diagnosing the nature of the political universe plus five questions about instrumental beliefs prescribing the best means for the effective use of political power (George 1969). The two sets of beliefs constituted a belief system unified as a theory of cognitive consistency, in which the philosophical beliefs constrain the instrumental beliefs so that together a leader's operational code specifies a model of "bounded rationality" regarding the exercise of power in world politics (Simon 1957, 1985; George 1969).

Several scholars initially employed the ten questions as guides for profiling a series of US and foreign leaders based on a qualitative content analysis of a leader's speeches and other documents attributed to them (Walker 1990, 409–410). These single-case studies included analyses of US leaders John Foster Dulles (Holsti 1970), Dean Acheson (McLellan 1971), Arthur Vandenberg (Anderson 1973), J. William Fulbright (Tweraser 1974), Mark Hatfield (Caldwell 1976), Frank Church (Johnson 1977), and Henry Kissinger (Walker 1977). There were also studies of foreign policymakers, including German leaders Kurt Schumacher and Willy Brandt (Ashby 1969), and the British leader Ramsey MacDonald (Kavanagh 1970).

Holsti (1977) developed a method for identifying the possible answers to George's questions as a six-fold typology of belief systems, which was refined by Walker (1983, 1990). The revised typology specified a leader's master belief about the nature of the political universe (P-1) as friendly or hostile. Depending on the answer to P-1, the leader's other philosophical beliefs were constrained as (P-2) optimistic or pessimistic about the prospects for realizing fundamental political values; (P-3) more or less confident about the predictability of the future; (P-4) high or low control over historical development; and (P-5) a high or low role to chance in deciding political outcomes. The answers to the questions about instrumental beliefs were specified as (I-1) the direction of strategies as cooperation or conflict; (I-2) the intensity of tactics as low or high; (I-3) the orientation toward risk-taking as low or high; (I-4) the flexibility of tactics and strategies as low or high; and (I-5) the relative utility of different means for exercising power as low or high.

The evidence from subsequent studies indicated that the ideal types identified by Holsti (1977) and revised by Walker (1983) were simply instances of possible operational codes; they are better understood as "states of mind" that can even co-exist in the same individual and be applied as schemata to diagnose the definition of different situations in the political universe and prescribe the exercise of power in different situations (Stuart 1979; Starr 1984; Walker and Falkowski 1984; Walker 1995). Such hybrid operational codes are commensurable with a "bottom-up" or "building blocks" pattern represented by middle-range, attribution, and schema theories from the cognitive revolution in psychology, which has partly replaced the "top-down," or "holistic" approach represented earlier by cognitive consistency theory (George 1979; Herrmann 1988; Fiske and Taylor 1991).

An individual's actions are still consistent with personal beliefs, but the beliefs are not always organized hierarchically as a single system (Jervis 1976; Dennett 1989; Fiske and Taylor 1991). Beliefs are also not necessarily recognized or acknowledged by the individual. They may simply be abstractions constructed as a schema (pattern) of attributions recorded from observations of the individual by third-party observers (Dennett 1989; Fiske and Taylor 1991). The source of these observations may be the actions (words or deeds) by the individual directly observed by a third party, or they may be "text-actions," that is, words or deeds recorded in audio or visual records and observed indirectly by a third party (Schafer 2006).

In sum, George (1979) and Holsti (1976) argued that the beliefs of leaders are important under different conditions singly or in combination, for example, when decision-making is centralized under the control of a single leader or small group; information about the decision-making situation is scarce or unreliable; time is short for a decision; the occasion for decision is not anticipated (Hermann 1976; Holsti 1976). Under these conditions, beliefs (old information) can become substitutes for new information that is missing or unreliable or not recognized as legitimate.

VICS: An Overview. While the early OCA qualitative contributions were important in developing operational code analysis as an approach and in applying the construct to a number of leaders, they also had limitations. The qualitative nature of those studies – built upon the subjective interpretations of the researchers – limited the extent to which subjects could be meaningfully compared. There were no explicit measurements; rarely was more than one leader studied at a time; it was unwieldy to do such things as systematically analyze temporal effects or conduct larger-n studies. Recognizing these limitations, Walker, Schafer, and Young (1998) developed a system to generate quantitative indicators of operational code beliefs.

As the operational code has focused on cognitive beliefs since George (1969), the Verbs In Context System (VICS) also has the same focus. The VICS assumes that cognitive beliefs are manifested in the spoken or written words of individuals. Systematic content analysis then allows for the creation of indices – measurements – that provide quantitative indicators of the subject's beliefs. This assumption – that spoken words can provide indicators of some components of a subject's psychology – is a well-grounded approach in the field of political psychology, theoretically-driven, but also born out of necessity. It is virtually impossible to directly access and assess a leader's psychology through clinical observation or self-responses to questionnaires. Few if any living leaders would agree to such assessments, and many historical subjects of interest are no longer alive. Thus, researchers needed to develop methods that allow for psychological assessment "at-a-distance" (Hermann 1980; Winter et al. 1991; Schafer 2000).

At its core, VICS assesses the subject's beliefs about cooperation versus conflict. This is done by looking at the verbs in the context of other words used by the speaker. A leader who uses many conflict-oriented verbs (e.g., fight, attack, bomb) compared with cooperation-oriented words (e.g., help, assist, support) is displaying an orientation toward conflict. A simple ratio of these two kinds of words gives a measurement of a leader who can be compared with others. The system also scales the verbs which are used to construct some of the indices.

This instrument is a six-point scale of Baldwin's (1978, 1980) negative (−) and positive (+) sanctions, with the two ends of the scale (-3 and +3) anchored by present- or past-tense action verbs, which we label as "punish" (-3) and "reward" (+3). The next two categories are future-tense verbs, where the actor says they will (may) take the action. We label these verbs as "threaten" (-2) and "promise" (+2). The final two categories include verbs where the actor states a for-or-against position, without a corresponding physical action. We label these verbs as "oppose" (-1) and "support" (+1).

As noted, George (1969) posited two broad sets of beliefs as comprising the operational code: philosophical beliefs and instrumental beliefs. In general, the former are those beliefs the actor holds about others in the political universe, while the latter are those the actor holds about himself/herself and her/his own tactics and strategies. While the verbs provide an indication of conflict versus cooperation, we use the grammatical subject of the sentence to code whether the verb belongs with the philosophical or the instrumental beliefs. As an example, in the phrase "you attacked us," the verb "attacked" is a conflict term, and the grammatical subject "you" refers to others. If the subject has a high ratio of such phrases, s/he would be holding more conflictual (vs. cooperative) views of others, which is the first philosophical belief (P-1).

If we re-phrase the example slightly to be "I will attack you," the verb base is still conflict, but the grammatical subject is different ("I"), meaning it would be categorized as an instrumental belief. A ratio of these verb constructions provides the measurement for the first instrumental belief (I-1). We end up with indicators of the leader's core philosophical beliefs (P-1 and P-2), with the latter using the scaled version of the verbs and the leader's instrumental beliefs (I-1 and I-2) and with the latter using the scaled verbs about the relative utility of conflictual or cooperative tactics and strategies for self to use.

There are also several other less-commonly used indices that are, nonetheless, insightful and helpful. The third philosophical index (P-3) assesses how predictable the actor sees the political universe. The formula for calculating it is a measure of variability across all categories of verbs when others are the grammatical subject; more variability means there is less predictability. P-4 is fairly commonly used in the literature and is central to many of the game-theoretical approaches using VICS. It assesses how much control the actor thinks he or she has in the political universe. The measure is a ratio of verb constructions that the actor attributes to self versus other. As the ratio goes up, it indicates that self is taking more of the action, is more in control; as the ratio goes down, it indicates that others are doing more, and, therefore, that self has less control. The fifth index (P-5) looks at the subject's beliefs about the role of chance. It is a combination of P-3 and P-4, indicating that as the political universe is more predictable and as self has more control, the role of chance is lower.

The instrumental indices focus on the utility of conflict versus cooperation that the actor sees for self. I-3 assesses the actor's risk orientation by looking at the variability in the verb categories when the grammatical subject is the self. This indicates the extent to which the actor metaphorically puts all their eggs in one (or a few) basket(s), as opposed to varying them across baskets; the former is riskier than the latter. The fourth instrumental index (I-4) looks at the role of timing in the actor's strategies and tactics, focusing on the flexibility of actions across conflict versus cooperation tactics (I-4a) or across word versus deed categories (I-4b). And finally, the I-5 indices are the individual percentages of the actor's use of each of the six verb categories when the actor is the grammatical subject of the construction. Thus, high scores on "punish" indicate that the actor sees utility in conflict-oriented actions, whereas high scores on "promise" indicate that the actor finds utility in promising cooperative actions.

These indices provide benefits in the form of many different research applications. The VICS provides a set of reliable, quantitative indicators of an actor's cognitive beliefs, particularly in terms of conflict and cooperation. They may be used to profile a leader or a set of leaders, to look for changes and trends in one or more leaders over time, to compare groups or types of leaders, as independent variables in larger-n studies of foreign policy behavior or group decision-making processes, or as indicators for game-theoretical moves or the enactment of roles in formal models of rule-based approaches (Schafer and Walker 2021; see also Walker 1977; Hudson and Day 2020: 199–203). We turn now to a review of these applications of OCA with VICS methods.

Literature Review

The incentive to employ profiles of leaders today in FPA is the same one that motivated the original Leites study of Bolshevik leaders. It is desirable to include the personal characteristics of some leaders in order to describe, explain, and anticipate the decisions and actions of some states. Since foreign policy decisions and actions are reported indirectly as "text-actions" in event chronologies retrieved from public sources such as newspapers and archival sources such as government documents, these sources are also codable with the VICS method and its metrics for retrieving and identifying transitive verbs from them, which indicate the exercise of social power by the state (Walker, Schafer, and Young 1998). It is then possible with this information to compare the VICS cognitive profiles of leaders and the VICS behavioral profiles of states to see if they are congruent (match up) in a single case of one leader and one state or covary together over time or across a group of leaders and states.

These two research designs test a psychological explanation of a state's foreign policy through the methods of a structured-focused comparison of a small number of cases or the statistical analysis of a large number of cases. The complexity of these research designs can be expanded to include other variables, such as additional personality traits of leaders or other background characteristics of states and societies, such as their material power, wealth, and culture (Walker, Malici, and Schafer 2011; Schafer, et al. 2021). It is also not necessary to specify and measure operational code beliefs and foreign policy characteristics with the same metrics.

It is possible to correlate VICS operational code indices with membership in international organizations, for example, alliances or IGOs, the involvement in militarized international disputes (MIDS), or with other dependent variables that the analyst considers relevant expressions of a state's foreign policy. Conversely, it is possible to correlate the national characteristics of a state or society with the operational codes of leaders. For example, do the leaders of autocracies have different types of operational codes than democracies? Do the leaders of less-developed economies have different operational codes than the leaders of more-developed economies in the Global North?

OCA employing the VICS method has expanded to investigate many of these possibilities. There are profiles of individuals and foreign policies, for example, Vladimir Putin (Dyson 2001; Dyson and Parent 2018); Tony Blair and the democratic peace (Schafer and Walker 2001); stability and change in the operational codes of Jimmy Carter (Walker, Schafer, and Young 1998) and George W. Bush (Robison 2006; Renshon 2011); Evo Morales and the Chilean-Bolivian rivalry (Thiers 2021). There are also comparisons of pairs of leaders as conflict managers, such as George H. W. Bush and Bill Clinton (Schafer, Young, and Walker 2002), Theodore Roosevelt and Woodrow Wilson (Walker and Schafer 2007), George W. Bush and Barack Obama (Macdonald and Schneider 2017), and Hillary Clinton and Donald Trump (Walker, Schafer, and Smith 2018).

Larger groups of leaders and their foreign policy decisions have also been profiled: discord among NATO and EU members (Malici 2011, 2015); generations of China's leaders in the United Nations (Feng and Kai 2013); US presidents and the initiation of NAFTA economic disputes (Stevenson 2006); democratic leaders and the democratic peace (Schafer and Walker 2006b); international bankers and beliefs in the Asian financial crisis (Thies 2006); foreign policy beliefs of populist leaders in European democracies (Ozdamar and Ceydelik 2019); terrorist leaders and extremist tactics in the Middle East and North Africa (Canbolat 2021); the operational codes of leaders in civil conflicts (Smith 2021); and US presidents and the initiation of militarized disputes (Schafer, et al. 2021).

The expansion of large-n studies has facilitated more rigorous statistical analyses in several ways. They include assessing the separate effects of beliefs on foreign policy decisions and actions as well as the interaction effects between beliefs and environmental sources of foreign policy decisions, actions, and outcomes. The inclusion of more variables in a study permits controlling for the effects of other variables on the relationship between beliefs and foreign policy. More observations of a single case over time also provides the opportunity to analyze as dependent variables the beliefs of leaders as they "learn" (experience belief-change) in response to changes in external stimuli and conditions, for example, changes in the actions of other states and changes in wealth or power distributions between them (Lambert, Schafer, Walker, and Kazazis 2021; see also Marfleet and Simpson 2011; Malici 2008; Walker, Schafer and Marfleet 2012). The inclusion of more cases extends the ability to investigate the nexus of beliefs and foreign policy decisions across cases (leaders or states), for example, do leaders from the same type of political system have different operational code beliefs (Schafer and Walker 2006b; Bakker and van Willigen 2021; Canbolat 2021; Kazazis 2021)?

Finally, the introduction of the VICS method and large-n samples has facilitated the use of statistical interaction and formal computation models as methods of analysis in identifying and isolating the effects of operational codes on foreign policy actions and outcomes. Statistical interaction models explain emergent properties (outcomes) as the product of interaction between or among variables, for example, the interaction between a leader's beliefs and the power position of the state may condition the initiation and escalation of a militarized dispute (Schafer et al. 2021). Or the interaction between the beliefs of two leaders and their respective preferences for different foreign policy outcomes may alter the temporal direction and sequence of moves as foreign policy actions and outcomes between them. These results can be generated either with statistical models of strategic interaction (Lambert, Schafer, Walker, and Kazazis 2021) or by formal models of strategic interaction (Walker and Schafer 2011; Walker 2013; Malici and Walker 2017: Walker and Malici 2021; Walker, He, and Feng 2021).

The use of game theory models to represent the link between operational code beliefs and the foreign policy strategies of bandwagoning, appeasement, balancing, and bullying involves the inference of a leader's ranked preferences for the foreign policy outcomes of mutual cooperation, mutual conflict, domination, or submission between members of a foreign policy dyad from VICS indices for the key operational code beliefs attributed to Self and Other regarding the strategies of Self (I-1) and Other (P-1), plus (P-4) the control over historical development attributed to Self and Other (Schafer and Walker 2006). Recent examples of this kind of research are the profile of the Russian leader Vladimir Putin by Schafer, Nurmanova, and Walker (2021); the comparison of American leaders Donald Trump and Hillary Clinton by Walker, Schafer, and Smith (2018); and the evolution of games of strategic interaction between Iran and the USA represented by the operational codes of their leaders and strategic interactions during crucial historical episodes between them (Malici and Walker 2017; Walker and Malici 2021).

Key Terms, Concepts, and Methodological Considerations

In this section, we elaborate on some of the methodological advances in the VICS research tradition that are beneficial and helpful to researchers. We have already discussed the two most important terms in the research tradition, Operational Code Analysis (OCA) and the Verbs In Context System (VICS). Others shall be addressed as we further discuss issues of research design, helpful resources available to those scholars new to OCA and VICS, and some additional advances in OCA. Operational code analysis employs both statistical and rule-based theoretical models to provide psychological explanations of foreign policy decisions and actions. The VICS can provide the data for both statistical and rule-based explanations.

The VICS indices function as quantitative variables. They may be used as dependent variables in designs that profile an individual, investigate cognitive change over time (learning or adjustment models), compare individuals or groups of individuals, or do some combination of them. They may also be used as independent variables intended to help explain foreign policy behavior. This may involve a small number of cases, such as two individuals in similar circumstances who behave differently, with the hypothesis that their operational codes predict the different behaviors. It may also involve large-n statistical modeling, where the indices may be used in multivariate models to explain, for example, different patterns of conflict behavior in a large sample of states or cases. Finally, the indices may be used in conjunction with game-theoretical models to explain moves made monadically by a state or dyadically by two states.

There are several important elements of research design that need to be conducted to generate appropriate VICS scores. The sample must be specified along with an appropriate unit of analysis. Each actor considered for the sample must have verbal material available that will allow for the generation of the indices. We recommend a minimum total word count of 4000 for each unit of analysis, though in some circumstances smaller word counts can work (as small as 2500). The unit of analysis should be appropriate for the research question at hand. Examples include the individual, the individual at different time periods, the leader-year or leader-quarter, or others.

Once the verbal material is gathered, it must be prepped for running through a specialized software program used by VICS called Profiler Plus (Levine and Young 2014).[1] Material must be in a digitally readable format and must be cleaned up to remove words spoken by others or parenthetical notes (such as "applause"), leaving only the words spoken by the subject. Profiler Plus is an automated, full-language parser that content analyzes verbal material in conjunction with VICS linguistic requirements discussed above. Profiler Plus produces raw counts per speech act, which can then be converted to VICS index scores. In some cases, depending upon the unit of analysis, researchers will first have to combine the raw counts from multiple speech acts and then convert those summed scores to VICS indices.[2]

Any kind of verbal material (spoken or written) may be used, but the material should be chosen carefully with some consideration of several factors. Most VICS projects in the literature have used spoken words by subjects. These may include press conferences, speeches, interviews, transcribed conversations or phone calls, or testimony before committees. Sources for verbal material include government websites, archival collections, and news reports. Written material may include autobiographies, personal diaries, personal correspondence, or academic writings. In general, the type of material used should be consistent across one's units of analysis, which is why the most common types of verbal material found in the literature are speeches.

There is some debate in the literature, though no definitive answer, over the value of using spontaneous comments (such as press conferences or interviews) versus prepared, formal speeches. Again, research projects should be consistent across units of analysis and provide explanation for the choices made. The literature includes contributions that have used many different languages. Most of the verbal material for these projects went into Profiler Plus as translations into English, but today the software has modules for several languages (Arabic, German, Spanish, and Turkish) with others likely to come in the future (Brummer and Young 2020).

One helpful resource is a newly released data set called the Psychological Characteristics of Leaders (PsyCL).[3] This is the first publicly available large data set of psychological characteristics of many different actors. The data set includes over 130 leaders from 34 different countries, virtually every US president (using 100% of their verbal material), a nearly complete set of British Prime Ministers, and good-sized collections from some other countries. It has over 46,000 speech acts, all of which are already coded with VICS raw counts that can be aggregated to a researcher's specified unit of analysis. PsyCL also has pre-aggregated versions of the data: leaders, leader-years, leader-quarters, and leader-months (Schafer et al. 2021).

Empirical Illustrations

In this section, we shall present three different empirical examples from the literature, each one demonstrating a different approach using VICS. The first is a comparison of two leaders and how their operational codes changed over time in a way that predicted their changing behavior. The two subjects are Patrick Pearse and James Connolly, the leaders of the Easter Rising in Ireland in 1916.[4] The puzzle presented by the researchers (Schafer, Robison, and Aldrich 2006) is what caused these two leaders to suddenly escalate the situation with the United Kingdom in 1916 by declaring Irish independence, which quickly led to the violent suppression of the Rising by the British, the deaths of nearly 500 people, and the execution of 16 Irish rebels. The researchers hypothesized that the sudden escalation by Pearse and Connolly was caused by rising frustration levels – a test of the frustration-aggression hypothesis – particularly for Pearse, who had previously been working peacefully for change.

The concept of frustration was operationalized by a combination of three OCA indexes: P-1 (view of others), P-2 (optimism), and P-4 (control), with higher levels of frustration being indicated by lower levels of all three: an actor is frustrated when s/he sees others as hostile, is pessimistic about the future, and perceives a low level of control. Schafer, Robison, and Aldrich (2006) used samples of speeches made by Pearse and Connolly across two different periods, a baseline period of 1913–1914, and the period in the run-up to the Rising, 1915–1916, and compared their scores with a sample of other leaders. They found that Connolly had a high baseline of frustration that continued into the second period: he was always ready to take aggressive action, but he and his organization could not do it alone. Pearse's level of frustration in the baseline period was about average compared with the sample of other leaders. However, in the second period, his frustration level rose notably. It was then that he led his organization to join with Connolly and to initiate the Rising. The answer to the puzzle is the changing frustration level for Pearse as demonstrated by his operational code.

Our second example demonstrates the use of operational code indices in a large-n statistical design, where the leader's OCA is hypothesized to affect the state's conflict behavior.

Kazazis (2021) selected several of the philosophical indices to investigate their effects on US foreign policy decisions to use force. The dependent variable comes from Meernik's (2004) Use of Force data set, in which the unit of analysis is the opportunity for the US to use force. It is a dichotomous variable: given the opportunity to use force, either the US did or did not do so. The data cover all cases of US opportunities to use force from 1948 to 1998 and resulted in 555 cases for the analysis. With the unit of analysis as the case, Kazazis (2021) collected verbal material for the president for a three-month period to coincide with each case, and, to avoid the endogeneity problem, he used the three-month period before the onset of the case.

In addition to the OCA variables, Kazazis (2021) also controlled for several situational factors that may affect foreign policy decisions: the Composite Indicator of National Capability (CINC, an indicator of power), the popularity of the president at the time, and if the situation posed a direct threat to US economic interests. In the probit statistical tests, the operational code indices were significant both in a bivariate model and after controlling for the three situational variables. In fact, while all the control variables were also significant, the min-max predicted probabilities analysis demonstrated that the operational code variables produced the highest percent change in the dependent variable of all the independent variables in the analysis: a president's cognitive beliefs as measured by the operational code indices proved to be very strong predictors of a president's decision to use force.

Our third example links three key operational code beliefs with sequences of foreign policy behavior (moves) using concepts associated with game theory (Walker, Malici, and Schafer 2011). The dependent variable of behavior is measured as one of four kinds of rule-based strategies as exercises of social power: (1) unconditional or (2) conditional cooperation behavior and (3) unconditional or (4) conditional conflict behavior. The independent variable is a combination of VICS indices for a leader's I-1, P-1, and P-4 beliefs that define the cooperation roles of (1) friend or (2) partner and the conflict roles of (3) enemy or (4) rival. The main hypothesis is that different configurations of beliefs dispose a leader to choose different strategies of cooperation or conflict behavior as roles. Leaders with more asymmetrical net distributions of positive (+) and negative (−) sanctions for the I-1 and P-4 indices in their public statements are more likely to follow the unconditional rule (don't reciprocate) with strategies of cooperation (+) as friends or conflict (−) as enemies. Conversely, leaders with more balanced (less asymmetrical) distributions for their I-1 and P-4 indices are more likely to follow the conditional rule (do reciprocate) with strategies of cooperation (+) as partners or conflict (−) as rivals (Walker, Malici, and Schafer 2011, 27–41).

A test of this hypothesis measured the strategies of the US and Iraq in the Persian Gulf conflict and the strategies of the US and Serbia in the Kosovo conflict and compared them with the configurations of the three VICS indices for the roles of George H. W. Bush and Saddam Hussein in the first case and for Bill Clinton and Slobodan Milosovic in the second case (Walker and Schafer 2011, 240–241; see also Brams 1994). The results showed that the subjective role games constructed from the VICS indices predicted the next moves (n =76) by each state in the two conflicts an average of 75% of the time and final outcomes an average 69.3% of the time. In contrast, the objective games defined by their respective distributions of material power and interests predicted the next moves (n = 76) an average of 45.6% of the time and final outcomes 33.5% of the time. More recently, multiple tests of different subjective role games during three crucial historical episodes in US-Iran relations showed similar average levels of predictability ($>$ .70) for next moves between them (Walker and Schafer 2021: 351, 365–366).

Conclusion

In this section, we summarize some of the strengths and limitations of OCA with VICS, some of the recent trends in this research tradition, and some general suggestions to researchers as they undertake OCA research with VICS. The strengths of using VICS are clear. First, VICS provides meaningful conceptual insights into the cognitions of one or more actors, particularly in terms of orientations toward conflict, something that is eminently helpful in FPA. Second, quantitative indicators are useful for providing meaningful comparisons of actors, larger-n studies of foreign policy behavior, and categories that may be used with game-theoretical analyses. Third, and importantly, VICS is a user-friendly and very doable research method that is easily learned and applied. If one has verbal material for the subjects of interest, VICS (and the software program Profiler Plus) can easily be used to generate research projects that are highly relevant to FPA.

Of course, there are limitations with VICS as an OCA method as well. Quantitative indicators simply do not provide the rich, thicker analyses associated with the qualitative methods of OCA used early in the research program. And, while much more data are now publicly available than in the past – both as raw verbal material and as already-processed VICS values in the PsyCL data set – there are still many actors of interest for whom there are no data available, which, of course, will limit some research designs. Finally, there are unresolved debates in the literature regarding several topics, such as the appropriateness of prepared versus spontaneous verbal material, and the use of translated versus original-language material. Some of these limitations are inherent with quantitative indicators, while others will continue to be investigated as more empirical projects are conducted.

One important trend in VICS OCA research is its expansion as a scientific research program. As discussed, early OCA studies were typically qualitative single-case studies. Even after VICS was created, the early studies using it continued to be single-case, or very small-n studies, due in part to the hand-coding bottleneck that existed before automated coding was developed. However, two important breakthroughs have contributed to the advancement of VICS as a scientific method. First, Profiler Plus automated coding software broke through the bottleneck and allowed for many more actors to be analyzed much more quickly. Second, the development of the PsyCL data set is now making large amounts of data readily available to all researchers. This not only makes it much easier to start with VICS and OCA as one's primary research program, but it also makes it much easier for any researcher interested in FPA or IR to include these cognitive variables at least as controls in large-n studies. We are now seeing VICS data used in conjunction with events data and large-n conflict data sets such as MID (Schafer et al. 2021), ICB (Schafer, Butler, and Hartmann 2011), Meernik's Use of Force (Kazazis 2021), Evolution of Peace (Smith et al. 2019), and others.

A second important trend has been the conceptual and empirical advances connecting VICS metrics to game theory and role theory. This has been important in its own right as contributing new empirical insights into OCA and FPA. But it has also been important in linking the field of FPA to the broader field of international relations. Game theory and role theory together with OCA provide conceptual and methodological tools to "cross Simon's bridge" and link the disciplines of psychology and political science (Lupia et al. 2000: 12; see also Simon 1985; Schafer and Walker 2021).

In terms of suggestions to new researchers in this area, nothing is more important than developing a sound research design. There will always be challenges with that: nonexistent verbal material for some actors, a learning curve with VICS and Profiler Plus, decisions about data availability and data limits, and others. But if one puts together sound research ideas by specifying a clear unit of analysis, an appropriate sample, a dependent variable, primary explanatory variables, and appropriate control variables, then VICS makes it possible to conduct the research and get valuable results. And, to paraphrase a saying by Voltaire, do not let the pursuit of the *perfect* get in the way of the *good*: remember that samples are never perfect, not all appropriate controls are readily available, timeframes often need to be adjusted to work. But there is great satisfaction in designing a good project, conducting the research, and reporting the results to the larger research community. The cognitions of leaders are critically important in understanding foreign policy behavior. Today, much more so than in the past, VICS, Profiler Plus software, and the PsyCL data set readily facilitate rigorous OCA research with VICS that will make important contributions to FPA.

Notes

1. More information on Profiler Plus may be found at SocialScienceAutomation.com.
2. It is helpful to have a base spreadsheet that already has the VICS formula embedded in it. Then, one simply needs to cut and paste the formula to correspond to the raw counts. A version of this spreadsheet may be obtained from the first author of this chapter at mark.schafer@ucf.edu. It may also be found at the following website: https://www.psycldataset.com/faq/.
3. See psycldataset.com. For a fuller discussion of PsyCL, see Schafer et al. (2021).
4. Pearse and Connolly were, respectively, the leaders of the two largest independence organizations in Ireland at the time. The two had not worked together at all prior to the Rising, because there were major differences between them and their strategies for achieving independence.

References

Anderson, Joel. 1973. The Operational Code Approach: The George Construct and Senator Arthur H. Vandenberg's Operational Code Belief System. *Presented at the Annual Meeting of the American Political Science Association*, New Orleans, LA.

Ashby, Ned. 1969. *Schumacher and Brandt: The Divergent Operational Codes of two German Socialist Leaders*. Stanford University mimeo.

Bakker, Femke, and Niels van Willigen. 2021. Policy Documents and the Beliefs of Foreign Policy Decision-makers. In *Operational Code Analysis and Foreign Policy Roles,* ed. Mark Schafer and Stephen Walker, 111–128. New York: Routledge.

Baldwin, David. 1978. Power and Social Exchange. *American Political Science Review* 27: 1229–1242

Baldwin, David. 1980. Interdependence and Power. *International Organization* 34: 491–506.

Brams, Steven. 1994. *Theory of Moves*. Cambridge, UK: Cambridge.

Brummer, Klaus, and Michael Young. 2020. Introduction: Decentering Leadership Profiling. *International Studies Review* 22: 2–7.

Caldwell, Dan. 1976. *The Operational Code of Senator Mark Hatfield*. Stanford University mimeo.

Canbolat, Sercan. 2021. Deciphering Deadly Minds in their Native Language. In *Operational Code Analysis and Foreign Policy Roles,* ed. Mark Schafer and Stephen Walker, 69–92. New York: Routledge.

Dennett, Daniel. 1989. *The Intentional Stance*. Cambridge: MIT.

Dyson, Stephen. 2001. Drawing Policy Implications from the 'Operational Code' Of a 'NewPolitical Actor: Russian President Vladimir Putin. Policy Sciences 34(3/4): 329-346.

Dyson, Stephen, and Matthew Parent. 2018. The Operational Code Approach to Profiling Political Leaders.*Intelligence and National Security* 33(1): 84-100.

Fiske, Susan, and Shelley Taylor. 1991. Social Cognition. 2nd Edition. New York: McGraw-Hill.

Geertz, Clifford (ed.). 1973. Thick Description. In *The Interpretation of Culture*, 13–30. New York: Basic Books.

George, Alexander. 1969. The 'Operational Code'. *International Studies Quarterly* 23: 190–222.

George, Alexander. 1979. The Causal Nexus Between Cognitive Beliefs and Decision-Making Behavior. In *Psychological Models in International Politics*, ed. Lawrence Falkowski, 93–124. Boulder: Westview.

He, Kai, and Huiyun Feng. 2013. Xi Jinping's Operational Code Beliefs and China's Foreign Policy. *The Chinese Journal of International Politics* 6: 209–231.

Hermann, Margaret. 1976. Circumstances under which Leader Personality will affect Foreign Policy. In *In Search of Global Patterns*, ed. James Rosenau, 326–333. New York: Free Press.

Hermann, Margaret. 1980. Explaining Foreign Policy Behavior using the Personal Characteristics of Political Leaders. *International Studies Quarterly* 24: 7–46.

Herrmann, Richard. 1988. The Empirical Challenge of the Cognitive Revolution. *International Studies Quarterly* 32: 175–204.

Holsti, Ole. 1970. The Operational Code Approach to the Study of Political Leaders. *Canadian Journal of Political Science* 3: 123–157

Holsti, Ole. 1976. Foreign Policy Viewed Cognitively. In *The Structure of Decision*, ed. Robert Axelrod, 18–54. Princeton: Princeton.

Holsti, Ole. 1977. The 'Operational Code' as an Approach to the Analysis of Belief Systems. *Report to the National Science Foundation*, Grant SOC 75–15368. Durham: Duke.

Hudson, Valerie, and Benjamin Day. 2020. *Foreign Policy Analysis*. Lanham: Rowman and Littlefield.

Jervis, Robert. 1976. *Perception and Misperception in International Politics*. Princeton: Princeton.

Johnson, Loch. 1977. Operational Codes and the Prediction of Leadership Behavior. In *A Psychological Examination of Political Leaders*, ed. M. Hermann, 89–109. New York: Free Press.

Kavanagh, Dennis. 1970. *The Operational Code of Ramsey MacDonald*. Stanford University mimeo.

Kazazis, Collin. 2021. Operational Code Beliefs and Threat Perceptions by U.S. Presidents. In *Operational Code Analysis and Foreign Policy Roles*, ed. Mark Schafer and Stephen Walker, 176–195. New York: Routledge.

Lambert, Joshua., Mark Schafer, Stephen Walker, and Collin Kazazis. 2021. Presidential Personalities and Operational Codes. In *Operational Code Analysis and Foreign Policy Roles*, ed. Mark Schafer and Stephen Walker, 196–219. New York: Routledge.

Leites, Nathan. 1951. *The Operational Code of the Politburo*. New York: McGraw-Hill.

Leites, Nathan. 1953. *A Study of Bolshevism*. New York: Free Press.

Leites, Nathan. 1964. *Kremlin Moods*. RM-3535–ISA (January). Santa Monica: Rand.

Levine, Nick, and Michael Young. 2014. Leadership Trait Analysis and Threat Assessment with Profiler Plus. In *Proceedings of ILC 2014 on 8th International Lisp Conference, Montreal, QC, Canada — August 14 - 17, 2014*. Association for Computing Machinery Digital Library: 50–59.

Lupia, Arthur, Mathew McCubbins, and Samuel Popkin. Eds. 2000. *Elements of Reason*. New York: Cambridge.

Macdonald, Julia, and Jacquelyn Schneider. 2017. Presidential Risk Orientation and Force Deployment Decisions. *Journal of Conflict Resolution* 61: 511–536.

Malici, Akan. 2008. *When Leaders Learn and When They Don't*. Albany: SUNY.

Malici, Akan. 2011. Alliances and Their Microfoundations. In *Rethinking Foreign Policy Analysis*, ed. Stephen Walker, Akan Malici and Mark Schafer, 130–150. New York: Routledge.

Malici, Akan. 2015. *The Search for a Common European Foreign and Security Policy*. New York: Palgrave.

Malici, Akan, and Stephen Walker. 2017. *Role Theory and Role Conflict in U.S.-Iran Relations*. New York: Routledge.

Marfleet, B. Gregory, and Hannah Simpson. 2011. Cognitive Responses by U.S. Presidents to Foreign Policy Crises. In *Rethinking Foreign Policy Analysis*, ed. Stephen Walker, Akan Malici and Mark Schafer, 205–220. New York: Routledge.

McLellan, David. 1971. The Operational Code Approach to the Study of Political Leaders. *Canadian Journal of Political Science* 4: 52–75.

Meernik, James David. 2004. *The Political Use of Military Force in US Foreign Policy*. Aldershot, UK: Ashgate (now Routledge).

Ozdamar, Ozgur, and Erdem Ceydelik. 2019. European Populist Radical Right Leaders' Foreign Policy Beliefs. *European Journal of International Relations* 26: 137–162.

Renshon, Jonathon. 2011. Stability and Change in Political Belief Systems. In *Rethinking Foreign Policy Analysis*, ed. Stephen Walker, Akan Malici and Mark Schafer, 169–188. New York: Routledge.

Robison, Samuel. 2006. Experiential Learning by U.S. Presidents. In *Rethinking Foreign Policy Analysis*, ed. Stephen Walker, Akan, Malici and Mark Schafer, 189–205. New York: Routledge.

Schafer, Mark. 2000. Issues in Assessing Psychological Characteristics at a Distance. *Political Psychology* 21: 511–527.

Schafer, Mark, John Butler, and Steven Hartmann, Jr. 2011. Leader Psychology and State Behavior in Crisis Situations. Paper delivered at the annual meetings of the International Studies Association, Montreal, Canada.

Schafer, Mark, Didara Nurmanova, and Stephen Walker. 2021. Revisiting the Operational Code of Vladimir Putin. In *Operational Code Analysis and Foreign Policy Roles,* ed. Mark Schafer and Stephen Walker, 45–68. New York: Routledge.

Schafer, Mark, and Stephen Walker. 2001. Political Leadership and the Democratic Peace. In *Profiling Political Leaders,* ed. Ofer Feldman and Linda Valenty, 21–37. Westport, CN: Praeger.

Schafer, Mark, and Stephen Walker. 2006a. Operational Code Analysis at a Distance. In *Beliefs and leadership in world politics,* ed. Mark Schafer and Stephen Walker, 25–52. New York: Palgrave.

Schafer, Mark, and Stephen Walker. 2006b. Democratic Leaders and the Democratic Peace. *International Studies Quarterly* 50: 561–584.

Schafer, Mark, and Stephen Walker. Eds. 2021. *Operational Code Analysis and Foreign Policy Roles.* New York: Routledge.

Schafer, Mark, Stephen Walker, Clayton Besaw, Paul Gill, and Gary Smith. 2021. Psychological Correlates and U.S. Conflict Behavior. In *Operational Code Analysis and Foreign Policy Roles,* ed. Mark Schafer and Stephen Walker, 151–174. New York: Routledge.

Schafer, Mark, Michael Young, and Stephen Walker. 2002. U.S. Presidents as Conflict Managers. In *Political Leadership for the New Century,* ed. Linda Valenty and Ofer Feldman, 51–64. Westport, CN: Praeger.

Simon, Herbert. 1957. *Models of Man.* New York: John Wiley.

Simon, Herbert. 1985. Human Nature and Politics. *American Political Science Review* 79: 293–304.

Smith, Gary. 2021. Operational Code Analysis and Civil Conflict Severity. In *Operational Code Analysis and Foreign Policy Roles,* ed. Mark Schafer and Stephen Walker, 93–110. New York: Routledge.

Smith, Gary, Stephen Walker, Mark Schafer, and Collin Kazazis. 2019. Testing Reality: U.S. Presidential Belief Systems and the Evolution of Peace in the International System. Paper presented at the Annual Meeting of the International Society of Political Psychology, San Antonio, TX.

Starr, Harvey. 1984. *Henry Kissinger.* Lexington, KY: University Press of Kentucky.

Stevenson, Mark. 2006. Economic Liberalism and the Operational Code beliefs of U.S. Presidents. In *Beliefs and Leadership in World Politics,* ed. Mark Schafer and Stephen Walker, 201–218. New York: Palgrave.

Stuart, Douglas. 1979. *The Relative Potency of Leader Beliefs as a Determinant of Foreign Policy: John F. Kennedy's Operational Code.* University of Southern California Doctoral Dissertation (January).

Thies, Cameron. 2006. Bankers and Beliefs. In *Beliefs and Leadership in World Politics,* ed. Mark Schafer and Stephen Walker, 218–236. New York: Palgrave.

Thiers, Consuelo. 2021. One Step Forward, Two Steps Back. In *Operational Code Analysis and Foreign Policy Roles,* ed. Mark Schafer and Stephen Walker, 129–148. New York: Routledge.

Tweraser, Kurt. 1974. Changing Patterns of Political Beliefs. *Sage Professional Papers in American Politics* Number 04-016.

Walker, Stephen. 1977. The Interface Between Beliefs and Behavior. *Journal of Conflict Resolution* 21: 129–168.

Walker, Stephen. 1983. The Motivational Foundations of Political Belief Systems. *International Studies Quarterly* 27: 179–201.

Walker, Stephen. 1995. Psychodynamic Processes and Framing Effects in Foreign Policy Decision-Making. *Political Psychology* 16: 697–717.

Walker, Stephen. 1990. The Evolution of Operational Code Analysis. *Political Psychology* 11: 403–418.

Walker, Stephen. 2013. *Role Theory and the Cognitive Architecture of British Appeasement Decisions.* New York: Routledge.

Walker, Stephen, and Lawrence Falkowski. 1984. The Operational Codes of U.S. Presidents and Secretaries of State. *Political Psychology* 5: 33–51.

Walker, Stephen, Kai He, and Huiyun Feng. 2021. Binary Role Theory and the Evolution of World Politics. In *Operational Code Analysis and Foreign Policy Roles,* ed. Mark Schafer and Stephen Walker, 245–270. New York: Routledge.

Walker, Stephen, and Akan Malici. 2021. An Operational Code Analysis of Foreign Policy Roles in U.S.-Iran Strategic Dyads. In *Operational Code Analysis and Foreign Policy Roles,* ed. Mark Schafer and Stephen Walker, 339–370. New York: Routledge.

Walker, Stephen, and Mark Schafer. 2000. The Political Universe of Lyndon B. Johnson and his Advisors. *Political Psychology* 21: 529–544.

Walker, Stephen, and Mark Schafer. 2007. Theodore Roosevelt and Woodrow Wilson as Cultural Icons of U.S. Foreign Policy. *Political Psychology* 28 (6): 747–776.

Walker, Stephen, and Mark Schafer. 2011. Dueling with Dictators. In *Rethinking Foreign Policy Analysis*, ed. Stephen G. Walker, Akan Malici, and Mark Schafer, 223–244. New York: Routledge.

Walker, Stephen, Akan Malici, and Mark Schafer. 2011. *Rethinking Foreign Policy Analysis*, ed. Stephen Walker, Akan Malici and Mark Schafer, 223–244. New York: Routledge.

Walker, Stephen, Mark Schafer, and B. Gregory Marfleet. 2012. The British Strategy of Appeasement. In *When Things Go Wrong*, ed. Charles Hermann, 111–141. New York: Routledge.

Walker, Stephen, Mark Schafer, and Gary Smith. 2018. The Operational Codes of Hillary Clinton and Donald Trump. In *The Oxford Handbook of Behavioral Political Science,* ed. Alex Mintz and Lesley Terris. New York: Online Publication Date: Aug 2018. DOI: 10.1093/oxfordhb/9780190634131.013.4.

Walker, Stephen, Mark Schafer, and Michael Young. 1998. Systematic Procedures for Operational Code Analysis. *International Studies Quarterly* 43: 173–188.

Winter, David, Margaret Hermann, Walter Weintraub, and Stephen Walker. 1991. The Personalities of Bush and Gorbachev Measured at a Distance. *Political Psychology* 12: 215–245.

17

Groupthink, Polythink, and Con-Div

Identifying Group Decision-Making Dynamics

Kasey Barr and Alex Mintz

Introduction

The psychological dynamics and processes of small groups at the apex of foreign policy and national security decision-making have intrigued social scientists and policy makers since Irving Janis (1972) introduced his Groupthink model. Subsequently, researchers have been engaged in an ongoing search for the proper way to identify and analyze the impact of the circle of individuals informing the decision-making of leaders around the world. Foreign policy advisors play a key role in guiding decisions related to international negotiations and agreements, matters of trade and climate, war entry, escalation, and termination, imposing or removing sanctions, and other interactions in the global arena. Furthermore, the analysis of group processes plays a key role in understanding and improving foreign policy decision-making. Therefore, how one identifies and analyzes intra-group and inter-group dynamics and interactions is of great consequence.

Fifty years after the concept of Groupthink was introduced, a trove of research exists offering diverse explanations and models of group dynamics in decision-making. Paul 't Hart, Eric Stern, and Bengt Sundelius (1997) edited a book, *Beyond Groupthink*, presenting several alternate views and perspectives to Janis' Groupthink model. Garrison's (2003) review of the evolution of foreign policy concepts and models notes that, despite the many advances in scholarship, "the study of group decision making is still in its infancy [because], currently no coherent model or paradigm exits" that is able to cull together the many new models and expanding classifications and contradictions among various models (p. 182). How does one identify, categorize, and utilize intra-group dynamics in Foreign Policy Analysis? To answer this key question, we build upon the Group Decision-Making Continuum (Mintz and Wayne 2016a), a framework for conceptualizing the full array of intra-group dynamics. We demonstrate how the continuum, as we refer to it henceforth, contextualizes the vast corpus of scholarship and provides a means to conceptualize, utilize, and identify three leading models of group interaction patterns: Groupthink, Polythink, and Con-Div.

The foundational model of Groupthink (Janis 1972; 1982) anchors one end of the continuum and represents the vice of *excessive* cohesion and consensus seeking wherein the group is unable to benefit from a variety of viewpoints and policy options. This model has dominated

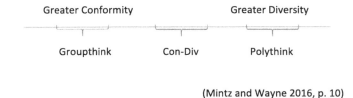

Figure 17.1 The group decision-making continuum.

the research agenda until recently. Counterbalancing this concept, at the opposite extreme of the continuum, is the Polythink model (Mintz, Mishal, and Morag 2005; Mintz and Wayne 2016a). Polythink represents the vice that is the *deficiency* of cohesion and consensus wherein the group is fragmented by a plurality of voices and opinions and, at its most extreme manifestation, the group is unable to engage in any meaningful and effective collective thinking and acting.

The central range on the continuum, between these two polar opposites, is represented by the Con-Div model (Mintz and Wayne 2016a) and is characterized by a decision unit that benefits from both the "convergence and divergence" of opinions. Such a decision unit has a common goal and can benefit from multiple viewpoints while still moving in a positive and productive process of decision-making wherein neither Groupthink nor Polythink dominates. This is visually demonstrated on the group decision-making continuum in Figure 17.1.

The group decision-making continuum zooms out from the microscopic to the panoramic in its broad conception of three main model types; yet it allows us to understand that there can also be minute degrees of variation. For example, some group dynamics can "lean" toward one type of model or another (Sofrin 2021). This allows for a straightforward comprehensible framework for analysis that facilitates and invites a greater level of nuance and identification of patterns of group dynamics between and under the three main models. In this chapter, we describe the three models and the relevant literature. We then introduce new terms to categorize dynamics that fall between the three main models, expanding upon the continuum. We then present three case studies which exemplify the three models, demonstrating how to analyze the full array of group decision-making dynamics.

Key Terms and Concepts: Identifying and Analyzing Intra-Group Dynamics

Groupthink, Janis' (1972; 1982) seminal work, enriched political science and FPDM literature in profound ways. Groupthink has become a ubiquitous term appearing in business, economics, medicine, media, and even in the day-to-day nomenclature of society as we deal with collective human decision-making. However, Janis' work was limited to the defectiveness of only one type of flawed decision-making – premature consensus seeking at the expense of a thorough decision-making process. It was innovative yet limited.

Groupthink exhibits specific symptoms, which include: the illusion of invulnerability, belief in inherent group morality, collective rationalization, stereotypes of outsiders, self-censorship, the illusion of unanimity, pressure on dissenters, and self-appointed mind-guards. These attributes lead to information processing defects, including an incomplete survey of alternatives and objectives, failure to re-examine preferred choices and to re-examine rejected alternatives, poor information search, selective bias in processing information, and the failure to develop contingency plans. The outcome is associated with a low probability of a success (Janis 1982).

Polythink represents a fragmented and divisive group dynamic

> whereby different members in a decision-making unit espouse a plurality of opinions and offer divergent policy prescriptions which can result in intragroup conflict, a disjointed decision-making process, and decision paralysis and inaction as each group member pushes for his or her preferred policy action.
>
> *(Mintz and Wayne 2016b, 4).*

The group is characterized by

> disparate worldviews, institutional and political affiliations, and decision-making styles, typically have deep disagreements over the same decision problem. Consequently, members of Polythink-type groups will often be unable to appreciate or accept the perspectives of other group members, and thus will fail to benefit from the consideration of various viewpoints.
>
> *(ibid, 3)*

Mintz and Wayne argue that this dysfunctional dynamic is no less common or destructive than the Groupthink dynamic.

The Polythink model explains much of the disconfirming evidence against Groupthink without detracting from its contributions and continuing importance. It offers another group type, opposite to Groupthink. Groups often perform poorly when there is a rush to consensus and a striving for cohesion at the expense of thorough investigation, but groups can also perform poorly when there is little to no consensus and a fragmented and conflicted process resulting from many "poly" views and opinions regarding the policy objectives.

There are a number of symptoms and consequences unique to Polythink which can be utilized by analysts as a diagnostic criterion. Mintz and Wayne outline these as a greater likelihood of (1) group conflict and turf battles, (2) leaks, (3) confusion and lack of communication, (4) framing and counter-framing, a (5) limited review of policy options due to extensive debate on options, (6) no room for reappraisal of previously rejected policy options for fear of rehashing battles, (7) adoption of positions with the lowest common denominator, and (8) decision paralysis (2016a, 7). Mintz and Wayne also conceived of a balanced central range in which neither Groupthink nor Polythink dominates and described a model of optimal decision-making processes that they termed Con-Div.

Con-Div is a pattern of group dynamics in which "group members are more balanced in the distribution of their opinions and so there is some *convergence* and *divergence* of opinions" (Mintz and Wayne 2016a, 17). The Con-Div dynamic is found at the center of the continuum where a group neither falls victim to Groupthink nor fosters the Polythink syndrome. "In this scenario", explain Mintz and Wayne, "the group is most likely to benefit from thorough yet productive decision-making process that consider a multitude of options but ultimately reach some sort of consensus or agreement and execute well-formulated policies and actions" (2016a, 7). Group members share a general vision of the organization or administration but do not all share the same viewpoints and opinions.

There are symptoms and consequences unique to Con-Div that analysts can utilize as a diagnostic criterion. Mintz and Wayne (2016a) outline these as: (1) clearer policy direction than in Polythink, with little or no confusion over direction, (2) fewer group information processing biases than in Groupthink, (3) less likelihood of ignoring critical information than in Groupthink, (4) operating in one voice, (5) too much harmony that may hinder real debate, (6) less likelihood of decision paralysis, and (7) greater likelihood of "good" decisions compared with decisions under Groupthink or Polythink" (pp. 26–27).

These three models – Groupthink, Polythink, and Con-Div, and the quasi-group dynamic models we introduce below, mark the main types of intra-group consensus/dissent. To identify the specific intra-group dynamics and model, researchers should analyze the symptoms associated with each model, in each case. In our view, this is an efficient and accurate method for identifying the pattern of intra-group dynamics associated with Groupthink, Polythink, Con-Div, and the quasi-Groupthink, quasi-Polythink, and quasi-Con-Div models. By utilizing this framework, inquiry into collective decision-making of groups is poised to vastly expand the scope of FPA. Table 17.1 lists numerous case studies utilizing this framework. Scholars have identified the presence or absence of symptoms and evaluated the decision-making process to determine which model best describes the group interaction patterns in a particular case

Table 17.1 Publications Utilizing the Continuum Framework

Year	Case	Actor	Group Dynamic	Citation
1962	Cuban missile crisis blockade decision	US	Con-Div	(Mintz and Barr, 2022)
1973	Yom Kippur war pre-war decisions	Israel	Groupthink	(Mintz and Schneiderman 2018)
1973	Yom Kippur war (October 6) mobilization decision	Israel	Polythink	(Mintz and Schneiderman 2018)
1976	Raid on Entebbe	Israel	Polythink (in the decision design group) Polythink (in the decision approval group)	(Sofrin 2021)
1978	Operation Litani (Israel)	Israel	Groupthink (in the decision design group) Groupthink (within the decision approval group)	(Sofrin 2021)
1994	Response to the abduction of corporal Wachsman	Israel	Groupthink (in the decision design group) Groupthink (within the inner circle)	(Sofrin 2021)
2001	September 11 attacks	US	Polythink	(Mintz and Wayne 2016a)
2002	Operation "defensive shield"	Israel	Groupthink (in the decision design group) Groupthink (in the decision approval group)	(Sofrin 2021)
2003	Afghanistan war initiation decision	US	Groupthink	(Mintz and Wayne 2016a)
2003	Iraq war invasion decision	UK	Groupthink	(Grube and Killick 2021)
2003	Iraq war invasion decision	US	Groupthink	(Mintz and Wayne 2016a)

Year	Decision	Actor	Type	Source
2006	Iraq war surge decision	US	Con-Div	(Mintz and Wayne 2016a)
2009	Afghanistan review and attempted withdrawal	US	Polythink	(Mintz and Wayne 2016a)
2010	Iran sanctions	US	Polythink	(Mintz and Wayne 2016a)
2011	Iraq war withdrawal decision	US	Polythink	(Mintz and Wayne 2016a)
2012	Decision not to sanction Syria	UN	Polythink	(Mintz and Wayne 2016a)
2013–2014	Israel and Palestinian peace talks	Israel	Polythink	(Greene 2019)
2013–2014	Israel and Palestinian peace talks	Israel	Polythink	(Mintz and Wayne 2016a)
2013–2014	Israel and Palestinian peace talks	Palestinian Authority	Polythink	(Mintz and Wayne 2016a)
2014	Strategic decisions in attacking the Islamic state	US	Groupthink	(Mintz and Wayne 2016a)
2014	Tactical decision in attacking the Islamic state	US	Polythink	(Mintz and Wayne 2016a)
2014	Response to Israel–Gaza conflict	UK	Polythink	(Greene 2019)
2016	Raqqa offensive policy formulation decisions	US	Con-Div	(Barr and Mintz 2018b)
2016	Raqqa offensive strategic decisions	US	Groupthink	(Barr and Mintz 2018a, 2018b)
2016	Raqqa offensive strategic decisions	Coalition forces	Groupthink	(Barr and Mintz 2018a, 2018b)
2016	2016 Raqqa offensive implementation/tactical decisions (US and coalition forces)	US	Polythink	(Barr and Mintz 2018a, 2018b)
2016	2016 Raqqa offensive implementation/tactical decisions	Coalition forces	Polythink	(Barr and Mintz 2018a, 2018b)
2016–2018	Decisions to maintain the JCPOA	US	Polythink	(Barr 2021)
2018	Decision to withdraw from the JCPOA	US	Groupthink	(Barr 2021)
2017–2018	Trump's early decision making	US	Polythink	(Lourie 2019)
N/a	Security decisions and business outcomes	US	Groupthink/Polythink	(Dall'Acqua 2021)
2021	Six Dunedin city council meetings	NZ	Groupthink/Polythink/Con-Div	(Garnyk and Gonnelli 2021)

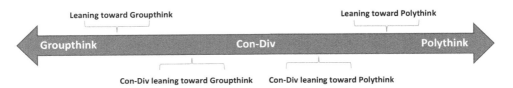

Figure 17.2 Expanded group decision-making continuum.

Expanding the Group Decision-Making Continuum

In this section, we introduce additional points to the Groupthink-Polythink continuum. We refer to these intra-group dynamics that deviate to some extent from the *pure* models of Groupthink and Polythink, as *quasi* group dynamic models. Specifically, we add:

(1) Quasi Groupthink; (2) Quasi Polythink; (3) Quasi Con-Div toward Groupthink; and (4) Quasi Con-Div toward Polythink. Below, we define each of these models, as follows:

The Quasi Groupthink Model: when there is a consensus among group members, with the exception of a tiny minority with different opinion/s.
The Quasi Polythink Model: when almost all group members have plurality of opinions, except for a tiny minority that shares the same opinion.
The Quasi Con-Div toward Groupthink Model: where there is some convergence among group members on the group's agendas/goals and some conformity of opinions.
The Quasi Con-Div toward Polythink Model: where there is some convergence among group members on the group's agendas/goals and some plurality of opinions.

The expanding continuum, presented in **Figure 17.2,** allows analysts to identify various configurations of group dynamics, and potentially study how they shape and influence the ultimate group or leader's choice. In the next section, we provide three case study examples of assessing foreign policy decision groups across the continuum. The three cases we have chosen occur during the Obama administrations. Each of the three models is exemplified in one of the following case illustrations: (1) Con-Div and the 2011 Killing of Bin Laden, (2) Polythink and the 2013 retreat from the Syrian "Red Line", and (3) Groupthink and the 2015 Joint Comprehensive Plan of Action (JCPOA). We have gathered evidence to assess the symptoms of each model by reviewing memoirs and transcripts of speeches and press releases by key decision makers. Additionally, we utilized information gathered from official government documents, media coverage, and secondary peer-reviewed sources.

Case Study 1: Con-Div and the 2011 Killing of Bin Laden

Below is an analysis of the symptoms associated with models of group dynamics with regard to the killing of Bin Laden:

Clear Policy Direction

In a presidential debate on October 7, 2008, Obama declared, "If we have Osama bin Laden in our sights and the Pakistani government is unable or unwilling to take them out, then I think we have to act and we will take them out". Leon Panetta recalls how, soon after he was confirmed to his position as director of the CIA, "president Obama made it clear that killing or capturing Osama bin Laden was to be the single most important mission for the CIA" (Panetta and Newton 2014, 290). President Obama and CIA Director Panetta maintained a clear line of communication within the administration. Panetta presented the intelligence information to the president at the beginning of September 2010 and subsequently met with other cabinet members and members of Congress to brief them of the steady progress in intelligence gathering (Panetta and Newton 2014, 298–299). The clear policy and open communication process are both hallmark indicators of a Con-Div dynamic, distinct from the obfuscated strategy and confused messaging characteristic of Polythink and dogmatism associated with the Groupthink model that resists skepticism.

Less Likelihood of Ignoring Critical Information than in Groupthink

In a Con-Div dynamic, it is less likely that the group will ignore critical information as is the case in Groupthink. While President Obama was clear about his objective to bring Bin Laden to justice, he invited and benefited from diverse and conflicting points of views within his heterogeneous team of advisors, including the Secretary of Defense Robert Gates, who was a republican and holdover from the George W. Bush administration, as well as democrats who, in contrast to the President, were known as liberal interventionists such as Secretary of State Hillary Clinton. Unlike in Groupthink, there was not a tendency toward close-mindedness, President Obama fostered communication and encouraged challenges from within the group.

Unlike the Groupthink dynamic, where the team engages in pressure toward uniformity, President Obama encouraged contrarian views. Two of the most verbal and persistent were Vice President Biden and Secretary Gates. However, Gates noted, "everyone was asking tough questions" (Gates 2014, 539). Biden preferred waiting for more intelligence and was primarily "concerned with the political consequences of failure" (Gates 2014, 539). Deputy National Security Advisor Ben Rhodes recollects how Biden "went on at length about the catastrophe that could ensue with Pakistan" (Rhodes 2018, 128). Gates was against any action in Pakistan, successful or unsuccessful, because it could upset US-Pakistan relations and endanger the war efforts in Afghanistan (Gates 2014, 539). Yet Gates affirmed how President Obama welcomed criticism: "I told him [President Obama] . . . my experience was doing him a disservice because it made me too cautious. He forcefully disagreed, saying my concerns were exactly what he needed to take into account as he weighed the decision" (Gates 2014, 542). Panetta, and Assistant to the President for National Security Affairs Tom Donilon recommended the special operations raid. Clinton concluded that "the risk of not going outweighed the risk of going" (Rhodes 2018, 128). Mullen McRaven, Deputy National Security Advisor, John Brennan, and the team from CIA supported a raid (Rhodes 2018, 128). President Obama respected the input from each advisor, expanding the scope and quality of deliberations. He encouraged debate and cross-examination of all options and alternatives. In addition to debating the value of the intelligence presented by the CIA, the national security team deliberated multiple responses. Evidence suggests that Obama was an impartial leader during deliberations, a symptom associated with the Con-Div model. He did not reveal his preference. Ben Rhodes reflected on the final meeting of April 28, "Obama didn't tip his hand, he just said he'd make his decision overnight" (Rhodes 2018, 130).

Most meetings were held in the utmost secrecy and were far less likely to fall victim to the Polythink syndrome of debates and multiple perspectives all vying for attention and traction. But how, if at all, did deliberations avoid the trappings of insulation associated with Groupthink? Panetta recalls, "We deliberately kept the circle of those involved in the bin Laden case extraordinarily small, even within the CIA" (Panetta and Newton 2014, 298). Any leaks could spell disaster for the mission. However strong the fear of leaks may have been, it did not override the group's commitment to bring in outsiders. Optimal decision-making is often linked to the presence of external experts and advisors who offer unique skills. Rhodes recalls how

> After weeks of secret meetings with Obama's closest advisors, when the time for the decision approached, he brought in "newcomers", including a 'red team' of intelligence analysts who had been brought on to review the case that it was bin Laden at the coumpound.
>
> *(Rhodes 2018, 127)*

This guarded against the isolation associated with Groupthink that may obscure the risks associated with a given decision.

Panetta played a role in promoting oversight of the decision-making. The CIA needed congressional funding to support continued and increased surveillance in Abbottabad. "I had promised to keep Congress abreast of our operation and I needed congressional support to pay for this increasingly complicated and costly undertaking", he disclosed (Panetta and Newton 2014, 298). Panetta had briefed ranking members of the intelligence and defense appropriations committee, as well as the congressional leaders in the Democratic Party and then the Republican leaders when they took control of the House of Representatives. This oversight provided continued funding and political support from both parties, despite the risks of potential leaks, which, in the end, never occurred.

Fewer Group Information Processing Biases than in Groupthink

In a Con-Div dynamic, the group is far less likely to be constrained by cognitive biases than groups with a Groupthink or Polythink dynamic. President Obama's team was diverse, including individuals with a long and distinguished career in foreign affairs. They referenced past decision failures for consideration which guarded against biases commonly associated with Groupthink such as "shooting from the hip" and "plunging in" which often result in suboptimal and potentially disastrous decision. Secretary Clinton recalled that "the failed intelligence process that concluded that Saddam Hussein possessed weapons of mass destruction" encouraged her to earnestly "sifted through the reports, listened to the experts, and weighted the probabilities on both sides" (Clinton 2014, 180). She eventually voted in favor of the mission. This was not the case for Gates. Assessing the same information, he called moving on such intelligence a "crapshoot" (Gates 2014, 540), directing everyone's attention to *Desert One*, the botched effort by Jimmy Carter to rescue the American hostages in Iran. "These were difficult and emotional discussions. . . . ", wrote Clinton (2014, 181). Consequently, the decision to raid the Abbottabad compound was reached through a decision-making process that did not foster group biases. These deliberations, and the utilization of national memory, were difficult yet did not descend into the paralyzing conflict associated with Polythink.

Planning for Contingencies

There was discussion of contingencies and penetrating scrutiny of each proposal. One option was to strike the compound with precision guided missiles. This option was dissected and debated. If there was a strike,

> who would call the Pakistanis and when? Who would call the Saudis and when? What happens if we caputre him alive? If he's dead, how can we verify that it's bin Laden? How should he be buried? What happens if it's not him? What happens if it all goes wrong?
> *(Rhodes 2018, 127)*

Another important contingency plan that proved invaluable to the operation was the addition of two backup helicopters. Without this contingency plan the mission may, have, indeed failed because the main helicopter did in fact go down and the special ops forces were able to utilize the backup helicopters in order to complete the mission.

Operating in One Voice

We find evidence of another important symptom of Con-Div, **operating in one voice.** There were intense debates and even conflict over tactical options, but the group was dedicated and united behind the president's strategic objective. In a Groupthink dynamic, there is often no disagreement on either the strategic or tactical level. In Polythink, there is often disagreement on both of these levels. However, in a Con-Div dynamic, there is agreement on the strategic level, but debate surrounding the best way of reaching the strategic outcome. This fosters discussions which are likely to yield the most optimal means of accomplishing the strategic objective. There was some disagreement – centered on the tactics (killing vs. capturing Bin Laden, the size of the SEAL team, etc.); nonetheless, the general mission was clear – killing or capturing bin Laden and bringing justice and closure for 9/11 attacks.

No Excessive Harmony that Hinders Real Debate

We do not find that all of the symptoms of Con-Div are present. Harmony was not so excessive that it hindered debate. Drawing from the above analysis, it is clear that there was disagreement over the quality of the intelligence and intense scrutiny of assessments from members within the group and specialists from outside. Once the intelligence estimates were understood and considered strong enough for some type of intervention by the president, the advisors also debated the appropriate way to target the compound in Abbottabad. Throughout the process, evidence suggests that the president encouraged debate and skepticism, yet kept the group steadily focused upon the strategic objective of his foreign policy, to kill or capture Bin Laden.

The Bottom Line

As this case study demonstrates, President Obama and his team of foreign policy advisors neither fell victim to Groupthink nor were plagued by the Polythink syndrome in deliberations on the Abbottabad raid. The presence of Con-Div symptoms – we find five of six symptoms – reveals that the group decision-making process operated in the mid-range on the group decision-making continuum, denoted by Con-Div. Table 17.2 presents the findings. As this case study showed, the group did not rush to a decision without a thorough

Table 17.2 Case 1, Groupthink, Con-Div, and Polythink

	Groupthink	Con-Div	Polythink
2011 Killing of Bin Laden	(1) Illusion of invulnerability (2) Unquestioned belief in the group's morality (3) rationalization to discount warnings (4) stereotyped views of enemy (5) Self-censorship (6) pressure on dissenters (7) self-appointed mind-guards (8) illusion of unanimity	**(1) a clearer policy direction than in Polythink** **(2) fewer group information processing biases than in Groupthink** **(3) less likelihood of ignoring critical information than in Groupthink** **(4) soliciting advice from outsiders** **(5) operating in one voice. Divergences are likely to be reconciled and fit into an overarching policy framework** (6) too much harmony that may hinder real debate	(1) Intragroup disagreements dissent and conflict (2) lack of communication and confusion **(3) leaks and fear of leaks** **(4) framing and counter-framing** (5) selective review of information (6) multiple gatekeepers (7) limited review of alternatives (8) failure to reapprise previously rejected alternatives
Score	0/8	**5/6**	2/8

Symptoms present are bolded and tallied for comparative assessment.

decision-making process. We do not find any symptoms of Groupthink associated with the decision-making process. President Obama allowed skepticism, debate, and deliberation over options and alternatives right up until the final meeting on the mission. He ultimately made a decisive choice, and his team supported that decision. Despite the presence of two symptoms of Polythink, debates did not descend into group conflict and fragmentation. The decision to approve the operation exhibited balanced and careful decision-making that harnessed the collective strengths in opposing and supporting views from individuals both internal and external to the group.

Case Study 2: Polythink and the 2013 Retreat from the Red Line in Syria

President Obama came into office with a promise to take the US off the perpetual war-footing. However, the president faced multiple dilemmas regarding the Syrian civil war. When asked about the potential use of chemical weapons by the Assad regime, President Obama responded saying, "a red line for us is we start seeing a whole bunch of chemical weapons moving around or being utilized . . . that would change my calculus" (White House, Office of the Press Secretary 2012).

In the year that followed, Assad engaged in small-scale chemical weapons attacks, culminating in a major attack on August 21, 2013. that killed nearly 1,500 Syrians, including hundreds of children.

The president decided to follow-through on his red-line and launch military strikes. He ordered Navy destroyers to the eastern Mediterranean and redirected additional carriers to the region. Chairman of the Joint Chiefs, General Dempsey, explained, "Our finger was on the trigger . . . we were just waiting for instructions to proceed" (Smith and Hirsch 2015). Two days before the planned strike, President Obama decided to postpone strikes and seek authorization for the use of force from Congress. Soon after, Obama seized on a proposal by Russian President Vladimir Putin which would allow Russia to oversee the destruction of all chemical weapons by 2014 (Gordon 2013). What might group dynamics within Obama's team of advisors explain about this decision? In the months between the president's red-line declaration and Assad's major attack on August 21, the foreign policy team exhibited a pattern of Polythink concerning the use of force in Syria. One journalist concluded that Obama "presided over a far more contentious debate among his advisors than previously known" and that this "reflected Mr. Obama's own conflicting impulses on how to respond" (Mazzetti, Worth, and Gordo 2013). The UK House of Commons vetoed military involvement – a decision that certainly also impacted upon Obama's calculus (not necessarily decisive, but certainly an important factor).

The Decision Unit

The main players in the decision unit included, but were not limited to, White House Chief of Staff Denis McDonough; National Security Advisor Tom Donilon; Deputy National Security Advisor Ben Rhodes; Ambassador to the UN and later National Security Advisor Susan Rice; White House Advisor, and later Ambassador to the UN, Samantha Power; Secretary of State John Kerry; Secretary of Defense Robert Gates; Chairman of the Joint Chiefs of Staff, Gen. Martin Dempsey; and Ambassador to Syria, Robert Ford. Below is an analysis of the group dynamic's symptoms.

Intra-Group Disagreement

Those skeptical about military intervention in Syria included National Security Council (NSC) advisor Susan Rice. She argued that intervention would "draw the United States into a murky conflict that could consume the agenda of the president's second" (Mazzetti, Worth, and Gordo 2013). Deputy National Security Advisor for Strategic Communications, Ben Rhodes, was against strikes, arguing that it is not easy to "impose order and solutions on very complicated situations in the Middle East" (Smith and Hirsch 2015). White House Chief of Staff Denis McDonough was against intervention in Syria, reasoning that the "status quo in Syria could keep Iran pinned down for years" (Mazzetti, Worth, and Gordo 2013). Chairman of the Joint Chiefs of Staff Gen. Martin Dempsey argued against intervention.

Those in the decision unit who favored strikes included Secretary of State Hillary Clinton, later John Kerry, Secretary of Defense Leon Panetta, followed by Chuck Hagel, Director of the CIA David Petraeus, and Ambassador to the UN Samantha Power. NSC Advisor Tom Donilon was against a strike but later supported it. US Ambassador to Syria, Robert Ford, strongly advocated for a retaliatory strike. A multitude of viewpoints does preclude a Groupthink dynamic and indicates a group plagued by Polythink.

Intra-group disagreement is perhaps the hallmark symptom of Polythink. Rhodes recounts the mood among campaign staffers as President Obama announced his incoming team of foreign policy advisors. "Bob Gates, the Secretary of Defense through Bush's surge was asked to stay on at the Pentagon. Hillary Clinton was named Secretary of state . . . I could see the rationale . . . But cumulatively, it felt like a punch in the gut" (Rhodes 2018, 35). There was a general distrust within the team. This changed somewhat as President Obama reengineered his team in the second term. However, the change may have initially exacerbated the Polythink dynamic. Secretaries Clinton and Gates left, but their replacements continued to argue for intervention. Kerry, as the new Secretary of State, became a fresh voice of support for the arming the rebels. Citing evidence from US Intelligence, he argued that failure to "impose consequences" would be interpreted as a "green light for continued CW use" (Mazzetti, Worth, and Gordo 2013). Heated debate continued, and one advisor noted that meetings regarding Syrian strategy always ended with "the president's aides deeply divided over how to respond" (Mazzetti, Worth, and Gordo 2013).

Lack of Communication, Confusion, Gatekeepers, and Leaks

There were several off-message comments by top officials. General Dempsey told reporters that even if Assad would use chemical weapons, the US would not "step into a hostile atmosphere, with or without Assad, to keep those chemicals under control" (Ackerman and Shachtman 2013). When reports of chemical weapons use began surfacing, top administration officials directly contradicted one another. White House spokesperson Jay Carney explained that the administration "is still treading cautiously in assigning blame" (Inskeep 2013). Kerry did not discuss "if" the US would strike, but rather explained that the campaign would be "carefully measured and not protracted" (Marcus 2013). In addition to off-messages, Polythink often leads to leaks and the fear of leaks. In this case, Defense Secretary Hagel explained how large, open NSC meetings created an atmosphere where people were reserved about sharing their opinions, complaining that "the more people you have in a room, the more possibilities there are for self-serving leaks" (de Luce 2015).

Framing Effects and Selective Use of Information

The conflicting messages point to two competing perspectives that framed the debate. One group of advisors believed strikes would drag the US down a slippery slope of increasing military intervention. The other group supported strikes on moral and humanitarian grounds, as well as to preserve presidential credibility. Ambassador Power argued for strikes on moral grounds. Secretary Hagel supported punitive strikes, arguing the importance of American credibility. "When a president of the United States says something", he argued, "the president and the White House has to understand that means something" (Smith and Hirsch 2016). In an unusual role reversal, state department officials urged limited strikes and the Pentagon played the skeptics. Military leaders cautioned the president, raising questions about the instability that would arise if Assad were forced from power (Landler 2016). Gen. Dempsey, an early critic of military intervention in the civil war, "helped take any military option 'off the table' by demonstrating that instituting a no-fly zone would require at least 70,000 US military personnel" (Mazzetti, Worth, and Gordo 2013). Some officials say the number was intentionally inflated to discourage the president from military intervention (Smith and Hirsch 2016).

Limited Review of Policy Alternatives, Objectives, Risks, and Contingencies

One symptom of Polythink is a limited review of policy alternatives. Unlike with Groupthink, alternative plans are not cast aside because of consensus on one choice, but because the options are too voluminous to be included in the choice set and there is no consensus on multiple alternatives. However, evidence suggests that a few, if any, alternatives were limited. Hagel, discussing NCS meetings directed by Susan Rice, recalled that "everybody had a chance to talk. We rarely got to a conclusion or a decision, [with] too many people talking, and I think that always leads to an ineffective process" (Michael, Wizer, and Gilmore 2016). An anonymous White House official confessed, "The thing I think is fundamentally wrong with the NSC process is that there's too much process. There's too much airing of every agency's view and recommendations, and not enough adjudicating" (DeYoung 2015). Exacerbating the Polythink dynamic, President Obama was not visibly engaged in the debate. Senior White House advisors agreed that President Obama "rarely voiced strong opinions during senior staff meetings . . . and often appeared impatient or disengaged while listening to debate" (Mazzetti, Worth, and Gordo 2013).

While there was an extensive review of options, one previously rejected alternative was not seriously reappraised: dramatically increasing aid to the rebels. Earlier in the Syrian civil war, the administration had been bogged down in decisions about whether to support rebel forces on the ground. Ambassador Ford pressed Washington to support moderate Rebels (Smith and Hirsch 2016). Clinton and Panetta both supported Petraeus' proposal, as well as Gen. Dempsey (Mazzetti, Worth, and Gordo 2013). After the first reports of chemical weapons use, the new director of the CIA, Michael Morell, updated the plan and presented it to President Obama. However, one anonymous advisor commented, "they could have tweaked this thing till kingdom come, it wouldn't have made any difference, he [President Obama] just didn't think it was a good idea".

Decision Paralysis and Lowest Common Decision-Making

A hallmark symptom of Polythink is decision paralysis, a major contributor to a status quo policy. Paralysis and delayed decision-making typified the NSC meetings in Syria. One senior defense official explained how policy debates were "sclerotic at best, constipated at worse", continuing that "Time seems to be all this process produces. More time, more meetings, more discussions" (DeYoung 2015). Another unnamed senior administration official bemoaned how paralysis in the group left them unprepared for the use of chemical weapons, "We spend so much damn time navel gazing, and that's the tragedy of it . . . [we] could have bolstered moderate forces battling Assad's troops for more than two years" (Mazzetti, Worth, and Gordo 2013). The president wanted some form of military intervention to uphold his red-line declaration. However, once he made the decision, Polythink within his circle of advisors led to pushback, resulting in retreat and a satisficing solution.

President Obama took the strike off the table and instead seized on Russia's proposal to oversee the removal of all chemical weapons. The decision was praised by some administration officials and international leaders, yet it was also highly criticized by both insiders and outsiders. Working through Assad undermined a key US policy; President Obama had declared that Assad had to go, now he was relying on Assad's cooperation for his foreign policy to succeed. Former Defense Secretary Gates argued that retreating once the red-line was crossed "impacted American credibility" and was a "serious mistake" (Engle 2016). Ambassador Ford resigned his position in 2014, reportedly frustrated over inaction (Landler 2016). Later, Secretary Kerry admitted the administration's failure to enforce the "red line" drawn for intervention in Syria against Assad in 2012 "cost" the US "significantly" in the Middle East (Bertrand 2016); however, he placed the blame on Congress for not voting to support the strikes. Analyzing the US and Russia with regard to the decision to dismantle Syria's chemical weapons arsenal, Mintz and Tal-Shir (2021) have shown that the decision-making followed "a two-step poliheuristic process consisting of (1) eliminating alternatives dissatisfactory on non-compensatory dimensions and (2) obtaining equilibrium for the reduced choice sets through a game-theoretic strategic interaction" (Mintz and Tal Shir 2021).

Table 17.3 Case 2, Groupthink, Con-Div, and Polythink

	Groupthink	Con-Div	Polythink
2013 Retreat from red-line in Syria	(1) Illusion of invulnerability (2) Unquestioned belief in the group's morality (3) Rationalization to discount warnings (4) Stereotyped views of enemy (5) Self-censorship (6) Pressure on dissenters (7) Self-appointed mind-guards (8) Illusion of unanimity	(1) A clearer policy direction **(2) Fewer group information processing biases than in Groupthink (3) Less likelihood of ignoring critical information than in Groupthink (4) Soliciting advice from outsiders** (5) Operating in one voice (6) Too much harmony that may hinder real debates	**(1) Intra-group disagreements, dissent, and conflict (2) Lack of communication and confusion (3) Leaks and fear of leaks (4) Framing and counter-framing (5) Selective review of information, because of overload (6) Multiple gatekeepers (7) Limited review of alternatives, because of excessive contension (8) Failure to reapprise previously rejected alternatives, because of contention**
Score	0/5	3/6	8/8

Symptoms present are bolded and tallied for comparative assessment.

Case Study 2: The Bottom Line

In this case study, we demonstrated evidence of eight out of eight symptoms of Polythink within President Obama's decision unit. Table 17.3 presents the findings. We found evidence of three of six symptoms associated with the Con-Div model and no evidence that the decision unit fell victim to Groupthink (see the Symptoms in Table 17.3). Evidence in this case suggests that the group was deeply fragmented and conflicted. Furthermore, President Obama was unwilling to override the conflict about the fundamental question of America's role in Syria which exacerbated the Polythink dynamic and effectively brought a retreat from President Obama's ultimatum.

Case Study 3: Groupthink and the 2015 Joint Comprehensive Plan of Action

The 2015 JCPOA between Iran and the P5+1 was a major policy change from the sanctions of 2010. Why was President Obama successful at driving policy change in 2015 and not in 2010? Group dynamics and the construct of President Obama's cabinet provide insights into answering this question. President Obama, particularly in his second term, became known for "concentrating decision making inside the White House by relying on close aids and distancing himself from more hawkish cabinet members" (Ignatius 2014). The inability to reach consensus within Obama's first-term circle of advisors made engagement with Iran politically risky. One scholar noted, "While Obama's extended hand to Iran had encountered outside opposition, the last thing the president could afford was opposition from his own immediate circle of advisors" (Parsi 2012, 62).

The Decision Unit

The main advisors included White House Chief of Staff Denis McDonough, National Security Advisor Susan Rice, Deputy National Security Advisor Ben Rhodes, Ambassador to the UN Samantha Power, Secretary of State John Kerry, and Secretary of Defense Ashton Carter. Previous advisors such as Hillary Clinton, Bob Gates, and Leon Panetta, who were skeptical of a nuclear deal with Iran, were replaced by Carter and Kerry, who led the diplomatic efforts. Those closest to the president, who supported his views on Iran, were promoted. Additionally, there are structural faults of Groupthink associated with this case. President Obama was not impartial. He had been pushing for change in US relations with Iran prior to becoming president. He engineered his second-term decision unit, replacing the team of rivals with a team of loyalists. Rhodes (2018) recalls how, in his final two years in office, "Obama finally had the national security team that he wanted in place" (p. 311). The divisive tensions and infighting eased with key staff changes, alleviating many Polythink symptoms. However, in the second term, decision making increasingly exhibited a pattern of Groupthink. Below, we analyze the symptoms.

Isolation and the Belief in the Inherent Morality of the Group

President Obama and his team shared an ambition to create a "legacy defining" agreement with Iran and end the enmity between the two nations (Koring 2015). Rhodes recalls "thinking that I was part of a movement that would remake the world order…we were doing something both historic and right" (Rhodes 2018, 19). The team viewed Iran as the "central arc" in their foreign policy strategy and that other foreign policy goals all "converged around Iran" (Samuels 2016). President Obama argued publicly, that the "deal will make America and the world safer and more secure" (White House Office of the Press Secretary, 2015). This led to increasing confidence in the morality of the policy objectives, quelling serious debate and the number of policy alternatives. Agreement within the White House allowed members to discount the apprehensions of allies such as Israel, Saudi Arabia, Jordan, and Egypt, each expressing concerns about the deal (Hubbard 2015).

Stereotyping and Uniformity Pressures

Stereotyping of dissenting opinions increased in the second. A senior White House official explained how the president began to view dissenters within his Cabinet, stereotyping them as Bush-era holdovers. The official explained that the president would discount arguments from dissenters, because he would "hear Dick Cheney in those arguments" (Samuels 2016). Rhodes was quick to blame poor policy outcomes and tragic global events on the "blob", which included former Secretaries of State Clinton and Defense Gates. He reasoned that "The buck stops with the establishment, not with President Obama, who was left to clean up their mess" (ibid).

Biased, Selective Information Processing

Secretary Panetta remarked in an interview that President Obama was so focused on his legacy of ending wars that any policy proposal that may bring friction was dismissed. Panetta discussed how Obama was concerned that "If you ratchet up sanctions, it could cause a war" (Samuels 2016, see also Panetta 2014). This caused the president to "lock into" his preferred course of action, ignoring what could go wrong, and focusing only on what could go right (Hersh 2004, 168–169). This led to ignoring critical information that contradicted their views, leading to the accusation that the president's administration was "failing to listen to his Middle East allies" (Hersh 2004, 168–169).

Mind-Guards and the Failure to Explore Alternatives and Previously Rejected Policy Options

Characteristic of a Groupthink dynamic, members act as mind-guards, blocking dissenting opinions. Panetta explained how White House staff prevented countering opinions from reaching the president. He recalled how

> "There were staff people who put themselves in a position where they kind of assumed where the president's head was on a particular issue, and they thought their job was not to go through this open process of having people present all these different options, but to try to force the process to where they thought the president wanted to be
>
> *(Samuels 2016)*

Panetta recalled the "increasing centralization of power at the White House" and a "penchant for control" that required him to submit all speeches and interview requests for White House approval" (DeYoung 2015).

This led to the failure to consider other options and proposals. The White House staff learned from their experience in the first term, the damage that dissenting advisors could have on the messaging and direction of foreign policy objectives. Panetta explained how a sub-group within the White House controlled the policy path. He explains how aids told him, "This is where we want you to come out' [on the decision]". He would respond, saying "that's not the way it works. We'll present a plan, and then the president can make a decision" (Samuels 2016). His views were echoed by others who discussed frustration with being top-level Cabinet officials prevented by lower-level staff from presenting information to the president (DeYoung 2015). In a Groupthink dynamic, the decision unit rejects advice from those who do not share the same worldview as the majority, leading to the illusion of unanimity. President Obama replaced most of the dissenting voices in his advisory unit.

Framing

Framing the message on the Iran Nuclear Deal became a massive White House operation in the second administration under the direction of Ben Rhodes. Staffer Chad Kreikemeir recalls that Rhodes would frame the nuclear deal as a choice between "peace and war" as his go-to-move to win support (Samuels 2016). Another frame that Rhodes utilized to give Americans confidence in the Nuclear Deal was to reference the 2013 Iranian elections as the catalyst for the renewed negotiations and a framework to lend credibility and support to the deal. However, the Obama team was deeply engaged in pushing for a deal in 2012, many months before the election of Rouhani. Rhodes also recounts how President Obama was concerned that the focus of the public would be on "Iran's non-nuclear behavior" and would delegitimize the deal. "We don't want to let the critics muddy the nuclear issue with other issues", President Obama explained to Rhodes (Rhodes 2018, 325). Rhodes created a "war room" to advance the administrations framing of the Iran Deal. By controlling the message, he admitted that he was able to "create an echo chamber" for positions the President held by

Table 17.4 Case 3, Groupthink, Con-Div, and Polythink

	Groupthink	Con-Div	Polythink
2015 Joint comprehensive plan of action	(1) **Illusion of invulnerability** (2) **Unquestioned belief in the group's inherent morality** (3) **Rationalization to discount warnings** (4) **Stereotyped views of enemy** (5) **Self-censorship** (6) **Pressure on dissenters** (7) **Self-appointed mind-guards** (8) **Illusion of unanimity**	(1) **A clearer policy direction than in Polythink** (2) Fewer group information processing biases than in Groupthink (3) Less likelihood of ignoring critical information than in Groupthink (4) Soliciting advice from outsiders (5) **Operating in one voice** (6) **Too much harmony that may hinder real debates**	(1) Intra-group disagreements, dissent, and conflict (2) Lack of communication and confusion (3) Leaks and fear of leaks (4) Framing and counter-framing (5) Selective review of information (6) Multiple gatekeepers (7) Limited review of alternatives (8) Failure to reapprise previously rejected alternatives
	8/8	3/6	0/3

Symptoms present are bolded and tallied for comparative assessment.

recruiting key supporters from relevant agencies (Department of Defense, State Department, the Delegation to the UN, among others) who would go on record supporting the president as an "unnamed" official of the respective agency leading to a picture of administrative unity (Samuels 2016).

Case Study 3: The Bottom Line

In this case study, we have demonstrated that a team of loyalists, operating with a Groupthink dynamic within President Obama's national security team, facilitated the reversal of US foreign policy on Iran. They fell victim to eight of the eight symptoms associated with the Groupthink model. Table 17.4 presents the findings. In contrast to the Polythink dynamic that plagued President Obama's first foreign policy team, evidence suggests that President Obama's closest advisors operated with a Groupthink dynamic within the White House, allowing him to make a major reorientation from sanctions and back to diplomacy and the eventual Nuclear Deal. President Obama's ability to engineer his decision unit was key in securing the Iran Deal. The case study reveals that the Iranian Nuclear Deal was possible because, at least in part, the advisors around the president blocked dissent, designed a powerful narrative, and crafted a press team throughout the executive agencies to operate in one voice to convey unanimity that was not fully representative of the reality. Additionally, we find evidence of three of six symptoms of Con–Div and no symptoms of Polythink.

Conclusion

In this chapter, we have added to the FPA toolbox by introducing a method for analyzing intra-group dynamics. We showed how to identify such dynamics, based on the "symptoms method". We also added several quasi models of group dynamics and three case studies. These cases illustrate how the three main models (Groupthink, Polythink, and Con-Div) can be identified in real-world situations. Each case has illustrated how to identify and analyze specific group dynamics as applied to major foreign policy decisions. Collectively, these three cases reveal the application of our framework and the possibilities of more nuanced and widely applicable comparative research, enriching foreign policy and national security analysis.

References

Ackerman, Spencer, and Noah Shachtman. 2013. "Top US General Says Stopping a Syrian Chemical Attack Is 'Almost Unachievable.'" Wired, January 10.
Barr, Kasey. 2021. Groupthink, Polythink, and Con-Div in US Foreign Policy in the Middle East. Doctoral Dissertation: Herew University of Jerusalem.
Barr, Kasey, and Alex Mintz. 2018a. "The Role of Groupthink and Polythink in Foreign Policy Change and Continuity." 2018 Annual Meeting. San Francisco, CA.
———. 2018b. "Public Policy Perspective on Group Decision-Making Dynamics in Foreign Policy." *Policy Studies Journal* 46 (May): S69–90.
Bertrand, Natasha. 2016. "Kerry: Not Enforcing Obama's Red Line in Syria 'Cost' the US Considerably in the Middle East." *Business Insider*, December 5.
Clinton, Hillary Rodham. 2014. *Hard Choices: A Memoir*. London: Simon & Schuste.
Dall'Acqua, Luisa. 2021. "Exploring Cognitive Biases, Groupthink, and Polythink Syndrome in Security Decisions and Business Outcomes." In *Transdisciplinary Perspectives on Risk Management and Cyber Intelligence*, 47–61. IGI Global. https://doi.org/10.4018/978-1-7998-4339-9.ch003.
DeYoung, Karen. 2015. "How the Obama White House Handles Foreign Policy." *Washington Post*, August 4.
Engel, Pamela. 2016. "Former US Defense Secretary: Obama Hurt US Credibility When He Backed Down From His Red Line on Syria." *Business Insider*, January 26, 2016. http://www.businessinsider.com/robert-gates-syria-red-line-obama-2016-1.
Garnyk, Anton, and Claudia Gonnelli. 2021. "Dynamics of Group Decision Making." *SIJAR* 1 (1): 50–60.
Garrison, Jean A. 2003. "Foreign Policymaking and Group Dynamics: Where We've Been and Where We're Going." *International Studies Review* 5 (2): 177–202.
Gates, Robert Michael. 2014. *Duty : Memoirs of a Secretary at War*. New York: Random House.
Gordon, Michael R. 2013. "US and Russia Reach Deal to Destroy Syria's Chemical Arms." *New York Times*, September 14.
Greene, Toby. 2019. "Foreign Policy Anarchy in Multiparty Coalitions: When Junior Parties Take Rogue Decisions." *European Journal of International Relations* 25 (3): 800–25.
Grube, D.C., and A. Killick. 2021. "Groupthink, Polythink and the Challenges of Decision-Making in Cabinet Government." *Parliamentary Affairs*. https://doi.org/10.1093/pa/gsab047
Hersh, Seymour M. 2004. *Chain of Command: The Road from 9-11 to Abu Ghraib*. New York: HarperCollins.
Hubbard, Ben. 2015. "Iran Nuclear Deal Provokes Sharp Reactions Across the Arab World." *New York Times*, July 15.
Ignatius, David. 2014. "New Blood Could Give Obama Lift," *Omaha World-Herald*. October 10.
Inskeep, Steve. 2013. "White House Sorts Out Syrian Chemical Weapons Allegation." National Public Radio.
Janis, Irving L. 1972. *Victims of Groupthink: A Psychological Study of Foreign Policy Decisions and Fiascoes*. Boston, MA: Houghington Mifflin.
———. 1982. *Victims of Groupthink: A Psychological Study of Foreign Policy Decisions and Fiascoes*. 2nd ed. Boston, MA: Houghton Mifflin.
Koring, Paul. 2015. "Iran Nuclear Deal Aims to End Decades of Antagonism." *The Globe and Mail*, July 14.
Landler, Mark. 2016. "51 US Diplomats Urge Strikes Against Assad in Syria," *New York Times*. June 16.
Lourie, Tom. 2019. "The Decision Calculus of Donald Trump", How Do Leaders Make Decisions? (Contributions to Conflict Management, Peace Economics and Development, Vol. 28A), Emerald Publishing Limited, Bingley, pp. 13–33. https://doi.org/10.1108/S1572-832320190000028004

Luce, Dan de. 2015. "Hagel: The White House Tried to Destroy Me." Foreign Policy, December 18.

Marcus, Jonathan. 2013. "Syria Chemical Weapons Attack Killed 1,429, Says John Kerry." *BBC*, August 20, 2013. /www.bbc.com/news/world-middle-east-23906913.

Mazzetti, Mark, Robert F. Worth, and Michael R. Gordo. 2013. "Obama's Uncertain Path Amid Syria Bloodshed." *New York Times*, October 22.

Michael, Kirk;, Mike Wizer Wizer, and Jim Gilmore. 2016. "The Secret History of ISIS." Frontline PBS, May 17.Mintz, Alex, and Eldad Tal-Shir. 2021. "Polihueristic Theory in Strategic Interactions: The United States and Russia on Syrian Chemical Weapons in 2013." In *The Oxford Handbook of Behavioral Political Science, edited by Alex Mintz and Lesley Terris*. Oxford: Oxford University Press. https://doi.org/10.1093/oxfordhb/9780190634131.013.10.

Mintz, Alex, and Kasey Barr. 2022. "Rethinking Group Dynamics: The Cuban Missile Crisis Revisited." In *Cambridge Handbook of Political Psychology*, edited by Chris Sibley and Danny Osborne. Cambridge: Cambridge University Press.

Mintz, Alex, Shaul Mishal, and Nadav Morag. 2005. Evidence of Polythink?: The Israeli Delegation at Camp David 2000. Discussion Paper: Yale University, UN Studies.

Mintz, Alex, and Itai Schneiderman. 2018. "From Groupthink to Polythink in the Yom Kippur War Decisions of 1973." ERIS - European *Review of International Studies* 5 (1): 48–66.

Mintz, Alex, and Carly Wayne. 2016a. *The Polythink Syndrome, US Foreign Policy Decisions on 9/11, Afghanistan, Iraq, Iran, Syria, and ISIS*. Stanford University Press.

———. 2016b. "The Polythink Syndrome and Elite Group Decision-Making." *Political Psychology* 37 (S1): 3–21.

Panetta, Leon E., and Jim Newton. 2014. *Worthy Fights : A Memoir of Leadership in War and Peace*. New York: Penguin Press.Parsi, Trita. 2012. *A Single Roll of the Dice: Obama's Diplomacy with Iran*. New Haven, CT: Yale University Press.

Rhodes, Ben. 2018. *The World as It Is: A Memoir of the Obama White House*. New York: Random House.

Samuels, David. 2016. "Through the Looking Glass with Ben Rhodes." *New York Times Magazine*, May 13, 2016.

Secretary, White House Office of the Press. 2012. "Remarks by the President to the White House Press Corps." [Press Release], August 20, 2012.

Smith, Martin, and Linda Hirsch. 2015. "Obama at War." *Frontline PBS*, May 26, 2015. https://www.pbs.org/wgbh/frontline/film/obama-at-war/.

Sofrin, Amnon. 2021. "Decision Making Processes in Counter-Terrorism Operations in Israel." *Journal of Political Science and International Relations* 4 (3): 112–124.

't Hart, Paul, Eric K. Stern, and Bengt Sundelius. 1997. *Beyond Groupthink: Political Group Dynamics and Foreign Policy-Making. Beyond Groupthink: Political Group Dynamics and Foreign Policy-Making*. Ann Arbor: University of Michigan Press.

White House Office of the Press Secretary. 2015. "Remarks by the President on the Iran Nuclear Deal." [Press Release], August 5.

Part V
Quantitative and Comparative Approaches

18
Comparative Foreign Policy

Huiyun Feng and Kai He

Introduction

Comparative foreign policy (CFP) used to be a distinctive and dominant research program in Foreign Policy Analysis (FPA) in the 1960s and the 1970s. CFP aimed to develop cross-national, generalizable grand theories to explain states' foreign policy behaviours through the application of statistical methodologies (Hermann, Kegley, and Rosenau 1987). It originated from the behavioural revolution in the social sciences in the 1960s (e.g., Easton 1953; Lipset 1960). CFP experienced serious theoretical setbacks because it failed to live up to its early promises of developing grand theories in FPA despite major scholarly attempts. Consequently, scholars gradually abandoned CFP as a desirable research program in FPA. The label of CFP has been discredited by FPA scholars and has even become "close to being pejorative in nature" (Kaarbo 2003, 157).

The decline of CFP as a research program encouraged scholars to adopt more eclectic approaches and pluralistic methodologies in FPA. Below, we identify three distinct approaches or schools related to the CFP research program in FPA: geographic-area studies, middle-range theories, and actor-specific studies (Smith 1986; Neack, Hey, and Haney 1995; Hudson and Vore 1995; Hudson 2005; Potter 2010). However, the explicitly *comparative* feature seems to have lost its edge in the contemporary FPA field. This is why many scholars have advocated that FPA should "bring the comparative back" (Breuning 2004) or get "back to comparison" (Kaarbo 2003). Some scholars have also renamed CFP the "Analysis of Foreign Policy in Comparative Perspective" (Kaarbo, Lantis, and Beasley 2012) and "Comparative Foreign Policy Analysis" (Lantis and Beasley 2017) as a new FPA approach in some scholarly works.

In this chapter, we intend to take stock of the evolution and transformation of CFP in FPA. First, we briefly discuss the rise and fall of CFP in the 1960s–1980s as well as the period of a "hundred-flowers-bloom" after the Cold War (Hudson and Vore 1995). We argue that three distinctive approaches—geographical-area studies, middle-range theory, and the actor-specific approach—have certain connections with CFP. However, there is still a lack of scholarly attention to *comparative* foreign policy as a distinctive analytical approach to FPA.

Therefore, we suggest that FPA should bring back the "comparative" to the field. We highlight three types of comparative approaches employed by these three schools: comparative case, comparative theory, and comparative methodology, to illustrate the CFP approach as a unique one in the FPA field. By drawing on empirical examples from current research studies, we elaborate on how scholars have conducted their FPA analyses by employing these three comparative methods in their research. In conclusion, we argue that FPA scholars should pay due respect to the CFP approach and improve the utility of the three types of comparison in their FPA research.

CFP: The Rise and Fall of a Research Program in FPA

CFP emerged in the 1960s with the promise to "generate the establishment of empirical generalizations" (Carlsnaes 1980, 3) on states' foreign policy behaviour. CFP as a research program was "one of the major growth areas in the study of international relations in the era of behaviouralism" (Smith 1986, 17). Together with the behavioural revolution in the 1960s–1970s and the scientific orientation in the study of international relations (IR), the early CFP featured efforts of generalizable theory-building toward a grand theory of foreign policy (Rosenau 1966; McGowan and Shapiro 1973). The CFP scholarship was predominantly American while it lagged relatively behind in Europe, but it was also emerging there by the 1970s. As Smith states, "A distinct CFP approach dominated the literature in the United States. In Britain, however, it was much less popular" (Smith 1986, 18).

As a behaviouralism-driven research program, CFP featured first the adoption of natural science's scientific methodology and design for the purpose of developing grand theories. CFP scholars worked under the assumption that all nations' foreign policy behaviours were comparable, and thereby hypotheses were developed to look for general patterns for a general theory of foreign policy. Early pioneers, such as James Rosenau and his 1966 seminal work on a pre-theory and adaptation framework, led the way theoretically and empirically to establish that CFP was not a fad or fashion but a research program or research field (Rosenau 1966, 1968). These scholars tried to "tease out cross-nationally applicable generalisations about the foreign policy behaviour of states in a systematic and scientific fashion" (Hudson and Vore 1995, 212).

The core unit of analysis in CFP is the "event," which is "simply a formalized observations of a conflictual or cooperative interaction between states" (Potter 2010, 4; see also Raleigh and Kishi in this volume). CFP scholars sought to collect and develop quantifiable events datasets to statistically analyse and empirically theorize a state's foreign policy behaviours. One major CFP project in America in the 1960s–1970s was the *Inter University Comparative Foreign Policy Project* (ICFP) and "it also provided the basis for the most extensive development of behavioural theory" (Smith 1986, 18). Other events-data-driven projects include the *World Event/Interaction Survey* (WEIS), the *Conflict and Peace Data Bank* (COPDAB), the *International Crisis Behavior Project* (ICB), and the *Correlates of War Project* (COW, Potter 2010).

Despite increasing intellectual efforts and financial support from the National Science Foundation, CFP as a research program in FPA started to decline in the late 1970s. There are many methodological and theoretical reasons for the decline of CFP (Caporaso 1987; Potter 2010). Steve Smith (1986) highlights three of them. First, the increasing role of economic factors in IR could not be explained well by the events-data-driven research of CFP scholars. Second, the rise of non-state actors in world politics posed an "identity crisis" for CFP scholars, who conceived states as the dominant actor in their research on foreign policy. Last and most important, "by the mid-1970s, despite the hopes and despite the claims, a general theory of foreign policy behaviour was simply not going to emerge" (Smith 1986, 20). Even Rosenau publicly recognized that the CFP program might "be grinding to a halt in the scientific study of foreign policy" (Rosenau 1976, 1–2).

The disappointment about the original CFP hope for a general theory of foreign policy led scholars to reflect and adopt more eclectic methodologies and pluralistic approaches in FPA. One popular approach after the decline of CFP in the United States was to conduct research on foreign policy by integrating it with the bourgeoning knowledge from area studies. As David Wurfel and Bruce Burton note, "the comparative study of foreign policy, which lagged in the 1970s, has been revived in recent years by a new focus on Third World states, with a leading role taken by specialists on Africa and the Middle East" (Wurfel and Burton 1990, 1).

In East Asia and Southeast Asia, many area-studies scholars focused on the economic and security challenges of these post-colonial countries in foreign policy by employing their rich area-study knowledge of the region. Some exemplary works include Sheldon Simon's work on ASEAN and Southeast Asian security issues (Simon 1982, 1983), Lowell Dittmer's work on China-Soviet relations (Dittmer 1981), and David Lampton's research on China's foreign policy (Lampton, Madancy, and Williams 1986; Lampton and Keyser 1988).

Major developments in the world politics of the 1980s and the 1990s brought in new players and new issue areas to the foreign policies of emerging economies and states. The triumph of anti-colonial movements in Third World countries guided new research agendas in IR and FPA, highlighting the significance of political economy for FPA. New theories, such as dependency theory and modern world systems theory, appeared as well in the studies of the developing world, especially Asia, Africa, and Latin America (Wallerstein 1987). Consequently, scholars in FPA started a new thematic focus on political economy, linking economics and foreign policy, particularly as a consequence of rising interdependence in the international system (Keohane and Nye 1973).

Although area-studies scholars indeed enriched FPA by integrating their thick local and area knowledge with the study of foreign policy, one key weakness is that their research findings appeared idiosyncratic and non-generalizable except for a specific country or a region. As Smith (1986, 21) points out, "even a quick glance through the literature will reveal that the vast majority of work on foreign policy consists of case studies of either a single country's foreign policy or an event or series of events." Consequently, "there is no uniformity on appropriate methods, nor on the variables to be studied." Compared with CFP in its attempt to develop a general theory of foreign policy, the area-studies school seemed to move to another narrow extreme in terms of theorization. In the United States, the scientific and behavioural movement in political science posed serious challenges to the field of area studies in general and the area-studies approach to foreign policy in particular (Shea 1997).

Another notable FPA approach after the decline of CFP is the rise of middle-range theory scholars, who advocate a middle ground in theory-building between CFP's early grand theory ambition and the narrow theoretical aim of the area-studies approach. These middle-range theory scholars draw theoretical insights from various sources and disciplines, such as IR, political psychology, and behavioural economics, and adopt both qualitative and quantitative methods to examine states' foreign policy behaviours and decision-making processes.

For example, Stephen Walt's balance of threat theory, built on Kenneth Waltz's balance of power theory in IR, explains under what conditions states form military alliances (Walt 1987). Borrowing insights from political psychology (see also Gross Stein or Chaban, Beltyokova, Fox, and Kenix in this volume), scholars explore how leaders' personality, cognitions, belief systems, perceptions, misperceptions, as well as images shape states' foreign policy behaviours (Holsti 1970; Jervis 1976; Walker 1987; Hermann 1980; Vertzberger 1990). In a similar vein, scholars employ prospect theory from behavioural economics to explore states' risk-taking behaviours in world politics (Levy 1992; Farnham 1994; McDermott 1998; He and Feng 2013).

This middle-range theory approach started to gain intellectual popularity in the 1980s, especially after the Cold War because the structural factors, like power and polarity, were no longer perceived as the only determinants in shaping states' foreign policies after the collapse of the Soviet Union and the end of bipolarity in the international system. The "constructivist turn" of IR after the Cold War (Checkel 1998), to a certain extent, also encouraged the rise of middle-range theorizing in the field of FPA. In addition, scholars started to look into multi-level variables to explain states' policy behaviour as well as to explore the micro-foundations of states' decision-making processes (Walker, Malici, and Schafer 2011). However, this type of theoretical and methodological pluralism is also criticized as evidence that "the subject-area of FPA as a *distinct* subfield of the discipline of international relations is in a state of disarray" (Smith 1987, 21). The proliferation of middle-range theories can somehow blur the boundary between FPA and IR and thereby erode the identity of FPA as a subfield of IR.

Since the mid-1990s, some leading FPA scholars, such as Valerie Hudson, have advocated an actor-specific approach to the study of foreign policy aiming to rebuild FPA's unique identity as the "ground of International Relations" (Hudson 2005, 1). This actor-specific approach suggests that "all that occurs between nations and across nations"—IR—"is grounded in human decision makers acting singly or in groups." Therefore, this actor-specific FPA approach aims to examine and understand "how humans perceive and react to the world around them and how humans shape and are shaped by the world around them" (Hudson 2005, 1). Compared with the "middle-range theory" approach that lacks a consensual theoretical focus, this actor-specific approach seems to put all the theoretical weight on the individual level of analysis. Variables from other levels, such as the system and domestic politics, might be examined but they will go through the perceptual or cognitive lenses of decision makers.

Another feature of this actor-specific approach is to focus on foreign policy decision making instead of foreign policy itself. In other words, the actor-specific approach aims to examine the "process" of making foreign policy, not what "policy" a state is more likely to adopt in IR (Carlsnaes 2016). The traditional IR approach to the study of foreign policy, treating states as a black box, is distinguished as an actor-general approach, which is more suitable to examine different "policies," not the "policy process," in the studies of foreign policy. To a certain extent, if we use a strict actor-specific approach to define the subfield of FPA, it seems that the traditional IR approach—actor-general theory—is largely excluded from the FPA subfield (Hudson 2005).

All three FPA approaches—the area-studies school, middle-range theory, and the actor-specific approach—are linked to the original CFP research program because all explicitly or implicitly rely on various comparative methods in their research. Unfortunately, the term "comparative foreign policy" has largely disappeared in contemporary FPA research as a distinctive research program or even as a specific research approach. There might be two reasons for this phenomenon in FPA. First, as Hudson argues, FPA as a subfield of IR has moved in the direction of actor-specific theorization, emphasizing a "concrete, contextual, and complex" explanation and understanding of the foreign policy decision-making process (Hudson 2005, 14). Consequently, the comparative approach, aiming to develop parsimonious, abstractive, elegant, and even grand theories, seems to be at odds with Hudson's actor-specific theorization of FPA although many scholars have constantly advocated returning to *comparative* as mentioned before.

The second reason might be rooted in the omnipresence of the comparative element in all FPA and IR research. In other words, most FPA and IR research is innately comparative in nature and the comparative approach is a natural method that many scholars consciously or subconsciously adopt to design their arguments/explanations. Almond (1966, 878) used to suggest, "if it is a science, it goes without saying that it is comparative in its approach." Although comparative is by no means the only way to understand science, it is a critical and even natural attribute for the studies of political behaviour and decision making in the general field of political science, including FPA. Therefore, it is hard to argue that comparative is a distinctive approach in FPA. However, as some scholars argue, "CFP also is a rather cohesive subfield, populated by several generations of scholars who sought to advance theoretical understanding of foreign policy-making in comparative perspective" (Lantis and Beasley 2017).

Therefore, some scholars advocate that FPA should return to the "comparative" method. The CFP approach has been relabelled as the "analysis of foreign policy in comparative perspective" (Kaarbo, Lantis, and Beasley 2012) or "comparative Foreign Policy Analysis" (Lantis and Beasley 2017). These scholars highlight the different "factors" or theoretical perspectives in explaining foreign policy. Differing from the actor-specific school of FPA, this new CFP school is more inclusive toward IR-oriented or actor-general theories in FPA. For example, regarding "the external factors and foreign policy," Lantis and Beasley discuss how different IR theories, such as realism, liberalism, constructivism, and Neo-Marxist theory, can contribute to the study of foreign policy. As mentioned before, according to the strict definition of FPA as actor-specific theorization, these IR-theory approaches should not be included in the FPA subfield. One potential problem of the current CFP school, therefore, is that it does not have a clear analytical demarcation on what the CFP approach is and what it is not.

The CFP Approach in FPA: Key Terms and Concepts

In this chapter, we have identified three types of CFP approaches to FPA from an analytical perspective, that is, how scholars conduct comparative foreign policy analyses in their research. Here, we adopt a broad definition of FPA in that FPA refers to a subfield of IR aiming to explain or understand states' foreign policy choices as well as the processes of foreign policy decision making. In other words, as long as the explanandum of research (or dependent variables in a positivist sense) is related to foreign policy and/or the foreign policy decision-making process, we can call it a study of FPA. As mentioned before, there are many approaches to FPA. CFP is just one of the analytical approaches that highlight the importance of "comparison" in academic inquiry. In particular, we have suggested three ways that scholars can conduct CFP research, including "comparative case," "comparative theory," and "comparative method." The common goal of the CFP approaches is to develop explanations of certain patterns of foreign policy behaviour or policy decision making under some specific conditions. Because the newer CFP approaches aim to develop middle-range theories, they have departed from the traditional CFP research program that relied on events data and statistical methodologies for the pursuit of grand theories of foreign policy.[1]

It is worth noting that the CFP's "comparative methods" approach is also different from the area-studies school in that CFP needs to make "comparison" explicitly in theory or research design while the area-studies approach normally focuses on the in-depth analysis of a "theory of the case" or a class of cases. CFP is also distinct from the agent-specific approach because CFP does not constrain its explanans (or independent variables) at any particular level of analysis. The agent-specific approach seems to focus on the "individual level" of analysis or "actors"; it also pays particular attention to the process of foreign policy decision making instead of policy itself (Carlsnaes 2016). In terms of its analytical goal, CFP's "comparative method" approach is close to the middle-range theory approach. It just explicitly emphasizes the role of comparison in theory-building, theory testing, and theory confirmation through different types of comparison. Below, we discuss the employment of the comparative method in each of the three new approaches to CFP that we have identified.

Comparative Case Approach

The comparative case approach is the prevailing CFP approach to FPA. Comparative politics scholars have traditionally employed this method to conduct comparative investigations. For example, Barrington Moore conducted a comparative study of modernization in Britain, France, the United States, China, Japan, and India in his famous 1966 book—*Social Origins of Dictatorship and Democracy: Lord and Peasant in the Making of the Modern World*. However, it is a mistake to think the comparative case study method is exclusively reserved for topics in comparative politics (He 2012).

The major utility of a comparative case study is to help scholars develop new middle-range theories to explain empirical puzzles. A "case" refers to a "phenomenon for which we report and interpret only a single measure on any pertinent variable" (Eckstein 1975). In plain language, a case means an event or an observation which can help researchers investigate their research questions. A case study, therefore, refers to the investigation of an event that scholars select for analysis (He 2012). One challenge for a comparative case study is how to select appropriate cases for conducting effective comparative analyses, because selection bias will lead to misleading and biased inference (King, Keohane, and Verba 1994; Collier and Mahoney 1996).

There are two types of comparative case method: cross-case comparison and within-case comparison. Cross-case comparison means to compare different cases to explore a better explanation for a research puzzle. Scholars can basically adopt two methods in their case selection following John Stuart Mill's methods of agreement and difference (Mill 1862). Mill's method of agreement is to select at least two cases that have the same outcome, that is, the same value for the dependent variable. The two cases should also be significantly different from one another, that is, the political background, geographical location, and even timeframe of these cases are completely different. For example, we can compare the same behaviour of the use of military force between two different states, like China and the United States, across different time periods. The method of agreement is called "the least similar" case comparison (George and Bennett 2005). Through comparing the two significantly different cases, if scholars can identify the same value for an independent variable across the cases, they can draw a causal inference from the independent variable to the dependent variable of interest.

For example, Steven Ward examines an empirical puzzle in the study of foreign policy on why rising powers sometimes adopt a radical revisionist strategy, that is, by waging wars, to challenge the foundation of international order even if it is in their interest to behave cautiously. To explore this empirical puzzle, Ward introduces a new hypothesis, called "status immobility," which suggests that "the belief that the rising state's status claim cannot be accommodated can produce preferences among individuals for politics that reject the status quo order" (Ward 2017, 33). In order to test this "status immobility" hypothesis, Ward (2017) adopts the "method of agreement" to examine three cases in which rising powers launched radical challenges to the existing international order: Wilhelmine Germany, Imperial Japan, and Weimar/Nazi Germany.² As mentioned before, the value of the dependent variable is the same across these three cases, namely, the radical revisionist strategy against the status quo order. Through this cross-case comparison, Ward examines how the belief about "status immobility"—the same value for the independent (belief) variable across the three cases—causes the leaders of these three rising powers to choose military conflicts to challenge the status quo powers with the aim of overthrowing the existing international order.

Differing from Mill's method of agreement, researchers can also choose the "method of difference" to select cases and test their hypotheses. They need to find at least two cases which have different and even opposite outcomes (dependent variables). The values for independent variables of the two cases should be almost identical with one variable as an exception. This exceptional variable, therefore, can be inferred as the causal variable leading to the different outcomes for the two cases. The method of difference is also called the "most similar" case comparison because the selected cases should ideally be identical in all respects except for the value of only one independent variable.

One example of choosing the "method of difference" in conducting the cross-case comparison is Michelle Murray's work, titled *The Struggle for Recognition in International Relations* (2018). The empirical puzzle that Murray asks is why some rising powers, like the United States, can rise peacefully while others, such as Germany, cannot. In order to explain this puzzle, Murray proposes a constructivism-based "struggle-for-recognition" argument, suggesting that "a rising power's revisionism is socially constructed through its interactions with others as it seeks to gain recognition of its identity as a major power" (Paul, Larson, Wohlforth 2014; Murray 2018, 26). In other words, if a rising power is recognized as a major power by the existing ruling powers or hegemon, its growing power strategy will be seen as legitimate and acceptable, leading to a peaceful power transition. However, if a rising power is not recognized, its growing power will be constructed as a threat, which will trigger military conflicts between the rising power and the existing hegemon.

In order to test her "struggle-for-recognition" hypothesis, Murray conducts a cross-case comparison between Germany and the United States. As Murray (2018) points out, these two cases have many aspects in common in that both Germany and the United States were rising powers on a global scale and both imposed challenges to the hegemonic power—the Great Britain of the late 19th century to the early 20th century. However, the dependent variable for these two cases has different values because Britain contained Germany's growing power but accommodated the US rise. It makes these two cases a "most similar" case comparison, which follows Mill's "method of difference" in selecting cases. Through examining the different social processes of Britain's recognition toward Germany and the United States respectively, Murray successfully tests her thesis on how the struggle for recognition shapes the different outcomes of power transitions between rising powers and existing ruling powers.³

In addition to the cross-case comparison method, scholars also employ within-case comparison to conduct research in CFP. The within-case comparison is to examine a single case but pays special attention to foreign policy variations within the case. This approach is beneficial for developing a middle-range theory to explain a single country's various foreign policy behaviours under different conditions. From this single case research design, scholars can control many factors, such as population, political regime, and culture, which are difficult to control in cross-case comparison. One challenge of the within-case comparison, however, is the weak external validity of the findings from the single case in that the arguments or theories developed from this single case will be difficult to generalize to other cases.

For example, a recent study by Scott Kastner, Margaret Pearson, and Chad Rector (2019) focuses on examining China's multilateral strategies after the Cold War. Since this research is only about China's foreign policy behaviours, it is a single case study. However, the empirical puzzle of the research is to ask why China adopts different strategies toward multilateral institutions. For example, China sometimes actively invests in revising and maintaining multilateral institutions, such as the Six Party Talks on North Korea's nuclear crises. At other times, China has played the role of spoiler, using its bargaining power to push for the restructuring of international institutions. One empirical example is China's role in reforming the rules and decision-making regulations of the International Monetary Fund (IMF). A third type of China's multilateral behaviour is to become a "free-rider" and let others pay the costs of sustaining international institutions and cooperation, which is illustrated by China's behaviour in the World Trade Organization (WTO).

To explore why and under what conditions China chooses each multilateral strategy, Kastner et al. conduct a within-case comparison by looking into China's policy choices in five multilateral institutions: the Shanghai Cooperation Organization, the Non-Proliferation Treaty, the Six Party Talks, the IMF, and the UN climate negotiations. Since all cases focus on China's multilateral behaviour, it could be seen as a single-case study in a strict sense (for different types of variation in case studies, see Gerring 2007). However, within this single case, Kastner et al. compare and contrast China's different institutional strategies, including "invest," "hold-up," and "accept" policies across different multilateral institutions. In conclusion, they suggest that two variables, the outside options and the perception of rising power indispensability, shape China's different multilateral strategies in the post-Cold War era. Although they argue that these two variables might be generalizable in explaining other rising powers' multilateral behaviours, more research is needed to test the external validity of their findings generated from the China case.

It is worth noting that the comparative case approach is normally a small-N case study, which has some inherent analytical problems, such as potentially confounding and missing variables as well as possible case selection bias. However, the advantage of a small-N case study lies in its theory development and innovation because scholars are more likely to conduct in-depth analyses and discover nuanced insights in a small-N research environment.[4]

Comparative Theory Approach

While the comparative case method is a major path to theory development (George and Bennett 2005), scholars can employ a comparative theory method to test the utility of different theoretical perspectives in explaining a state's foreign policy or decision making in FPA. One classic example of theoretical comparison is Graham Allison's *Essence of Decision: Explaining the Cuban Missile Crisis*, in which Allison examines three theoretical models—the rational actor model, the organizational behavioural model, and the governmental politics model in explaining US decision making during the Cuban missile crisis (Allison 1971). Although it is a single case study—the Cuban missile crisis, Allision compares and contrasts the possible explanations derived from the three models for US decision making during the crisis. In conclusion, Allison (1971) argues that the combination of these three models offers a clear picture of how the United States made decisions during the Cuban missile crisis.

In a similar vein with theoretical comparison, Barry Posen (2014) examines how military doctrine takes shape and the role it plays in grand strategy. Differing from Allison, Posen does not focus on a single case. Instead, he examines the military doctrine changes of France, Britain, and Germany during the interwar period. In particular, he examines three military doctrines: German Blitzkrieg, the British air defence system, and the French Army's defensive doctrine often associated with the Maginot Line. Like Allison, Posen (2014) compares and contrasts the explanatory power of two theoretical frameworks, organizational theory (e.g., Allison 1971) and balance of power theory (e.g., Waltz 1979), in explaining the changes in these military doctrines in France, Britain, and Germany between the two world wars. In conclusion, Posen suggests that balance of power theory does a better job in explaining how civilian leaders play a determinant role in shaping the overall changing features of military doctrines although organizational theory can also predict certain tendencies in military doctrine.

It is worth noting that devoting a whole study to conduct theoretical comparisons, as Allison and Posen do, seems to be out of fashion in FPA in recent years. As Kaarbo points out, "many studies of foreign policy seek to justify the conclusion of domestic or decision-making variables through a comparison to the grand theories of international relations, particularly realism" (2003, 158). However, this type of comparison seems to be an easy task, or even a strawman approach, because the rise of FPA is to challenge the grand theories of IR, especially realism, in the first place. Therefore, more serious theoretical comparisons should be conducted among some middle-range theories, not between a middle-range theory and a grand theory.[5]

Another reason for the lack of theoretical comparison in FPA is rooted in the rising standard of scholarship for innovation and theory-building. In other words, because all research intends to develop new theories or innovative arguments, merely comparing and testing the utility of existing theoretical frameworks become insufficient for the advancement of scholarship. However, it does not mean that theoretical comparison as a CFP method should be ignored or overlooked because it is an indispensable analytical step in developing any new or innovative theory. Therefore, most scholars have integrated theoretical comparison into their literature review in which they discuss how existing theoretical arguments have tried but failed to fully explain their research puzzles. Based on a critical review of these existing or rival explanations, scholars can then propose some new theoretical hypotheses to address their identified puzzles.

For example, David Edelstein introduces a novel theory of "time horizons" to explain why existing powers sometimes cooperate with emerging threats and why they sometimes compete. A leader's time horizon refers to "the value that the leader places on present as opposed to future payoffs," which is often called "the rate of intertemporal discounting" (Edelstein 2017, 5). By introducing the "time horizons" of political leaders as the key variable, he examines how state leaders tend to delay their responses to long-term threats hoping to gain profits from short-term cooperation as well as how uncertainty can create opportunity for pragmatic cooperation between existing powers and rising powers (Edelstein 2017). In order to test this "time horizon" theory, Edelstein conducts a comparative case study analysis by examining four historical cases: the rise of late 19th-century Germany, British reactions to the rise of the United States, the rise of interwar Germany in the 20th century, as well as US reactions to the rise of the Soviet Union in the wake of World War II (for another example of research on time in FPA, see Beasley and Hom 2021).

Before testing his "time horizon" theory, he critically discusses the weaknesses of two existing arguments, the buck-passing argument and engagement theory, in explaining states' foreign policy strategies in dealing with rising powers. In particular, he suggests that the buck-passing argument cannot explain cooperative behaviour between the existing power and rising powers, which can enrich the rising power, although it might explain the absence of balancing from the dominant powers. For the engagement argument, he suggests that it can explain cooperation between the existing hegemon and the rising powers, but it fails to account for when such efforts are abandoned or when more competitive strategies are adopted instead (Edelstein 2017). Unlike Allison and Posen, Edelstein does not employ these two alternative theories to examine the four case studies in detail. Instead, he evaluates these two existing arguments in the literature review section before the research design. It has become a normal practice for contemporary FPA research. As mentioned before, the high standard for theoretical innovations in FPA has encouraged scholars to forgo the mere theory testing exercise in their research. Instead, they treat "theoretical comparison" as an integral part of their literature review.

It is still a debatable question whether this trend toward a simple literature review in FPA research is a healthy development, because Allison's classic work is, indeed, based on his critical theoretical comparisons with detailed case studies. A short literature review on alternative explanations is necessary for scholars to propose their hypotheses. However, it might create a strawman phenomenon, in which scholars just pick some easy targets to criticize without any thorough theoretical considerations. Therefore, scholars should be encouraged to conduct detailed "theoretical comparisons," especially if they are proposing a new multi-disciplinary argument that challenges the conventional FPA theories.

Comparative Method Approach

The last type of comparative foreign policy approach is to compare different methods. It is also called the "multi-methods approach" or "mixed-methods" approach. The major purpose of methodological comparison is to strengthen causal inferences that scholars develop to explain states' foreign policy or decision making in FPA. As mentioned before, the case study approach inherently faces a weak external validity problem because of the potential case selection bias problem in a small-N research design. In a similar vein, a large-n statistical research sometimes cannot directly test innovative hypotheses and trace causal mechanisms if non-quantifiable variables, such as ideas and culture (for an exception of quantifying culture and identity variables, see Hopf and Allan 2016), are involved. Therefore, scholars advocate a mixed-methods approach or conduct methodological comparison through integrating both quantitative and qualitative analyses in their research so that their findings can be strengthened (Goertz 2017). However, as some scholars point out, in reality, a successful mixed-methods approach is "rarely used" (Thies and Nieman 2017, 39). The reason is simple: quantitative and qualitative methods produce two types of evidence. In particular, "a specific case may or may not conform to theoretical expectations [generated from quantitative models] because of its unique features. The findings from a large-n statistical analysis might not be observed in any single case" (Thies and Nieman 2017, 39).

Nevertheless, some scholars have skilfully employed the mixed-methods approach in their CFP research. One possible way to overcome the methodological incompatibility problem is to use different methods to test various aspects of the hypotheses. For example, through a multi-methods approach, including large-N statistics, network analysis, experiments, and case study methods, Jonathan Renshon (2017, 24) introduces a "status dissatisfaction" theory to suggest that "states are more likely to initiate violent military conflicts to shift beliefs about where they stand in a given hierarchy." In this "status dissatisfaction" theory, there are at least two aspects: the micro-foundation of individual behaviour and the macro-application of state foreign policy behaviour.

In order to test the behavioural foundation of "status dissatisfaction" theory—the linkage between status concern and behavioural response—Renshon employs two simultaneous field experiments to examine two fundamental tenets of his argument: "that status concerns vary predictably in response to contextual and dispositional factors, and once triggered, these concerns raise the value that actors are willing to pay for increased status" (Renshon 2017, 27). In particular, the first experiment is a well-known, *sunk cost* experiment that asks subjects to make a hypothetical investment decision. The second one is to introduce a newly developed experimental paradigm—the "Island Game"—to provide a behavioural measure of escalation. In the second experiment study, Renshon utilizes a unique sample of political and military leaders from the Senior Executive Fellows Program at the Harvard Kennedy School, which strengthens the external validity of his findings, compared with other similar experiments using college students as samples. Through both experimental studies, Renshon argues that individuals with a high status in hierarchy are most affected by status concerns and more likely to adopt escalating behaviours (Renshon 2017, 28).

The evidence between status concern and escalating behaviour for individuals in the experiments supports Renshon's major argument about state behaviour at the macrolevel: a state's status dissatisfaction is more likely to trigger military conflicts. He later tests this macrolevel argument through a comparative case study by examining some historical cases of rising powers fighting for status, including Germany before World War I, Russia's decision to back Serbia in the 1914 crisis, Britain's initiation of the 1956 Suez War, and Egypt's 1962 decision to intervene in the Yemen Civil War. It is worth noting that Renshon also employs the tools of network analysis to infer international status rankings and a large-N statistical analysis to test the relationship between status dissatisfaction and international conflict. Through this exemplary mixed-methods approach, Renshon firmly supports his "status dissatisfaction" argument and sheds new light on the studies of status and foreign policy behaviour in world politics.

Besides using different methods to test various aspects of one theory, some scholars innovatively combine quantitative and qualitative methods to examine the same cases. In their book titled *Rising Powers and Foreign Policy Revisionism*, Thies and Nieman (2017) integrate both qualitative and quantitative analyses to examine a state's role identity and behaviour. Based on structural realism (Waltz 1979) and role theory (Walker 1987; see also Breuning in this volume), they develop two competing arguments: the structural materialist hypothesis and the foreign policy hypothesis. The structural one is to suggest that the increases in material power are more likely for rising powers to adopt conflictual behaviours in both economic and military domains. The foreign policy one is to argue that the web of domestic constraints and international socialization pressures mediate changes in relative material power for rising powers, leading to more deliberate changes in national role conceptions as well as less conflictual behaviours (Thies and Nieman 2017, 38).

In order to test these two hypotheses, Thies and Nieman need to examine the relationship between a state's role identity and its behaviour. They employ a comparative case approach to examine the BRICS's (Brazil, Russia, India, China, and South Africa) role identities and their foreign policy behaviours. One key challenge for role theory scholars is to measure a state's national role conception or role identity. In contrast to Renshon, who uses different methods to test different aspects of one theory, Thies and Nieman employ both quantitative and qualitative methods to measure and test the relationship between a state's role identity and behaviour in these five BRICS cases.

On the one hand, Thies and Nieman use the qualitative approach, such as leaders' speeches, governmental statements, and press conferences, to gauge these BRICS states' national role conceptions as well as to examine the processes of role transition along with the increases of material power over time. On the other hand, they conduct a quantitative analysis on economic and militarized conflict behaviour of BRICS countries. By using Bayesian change-point modelling, they examine "the data-generating processes associated with economic and militarized conflicts to see whether any structural breaks occur in the data" (Thies and Nieman 2017, 40). They then examine whether the structural breaks in the data are associated with dramatic changes in material competition. If the answer is yes, they find evidence for the structural hypothesis. If the answer is no, then the more nuanced foreign policy hypothesis might better explain BRICS countries' behaviour. In conclusion, they suggest that the foreign policy hypothesis is better than the structural materialist one in explaining rising power behaviours because socialization and domestic political processes might "smooth out rough changes" of rising powers' identities and behaviours (Thies and Nieman 2017, 160).

It is worth noting that the mixed-methods approach or applying methodological comparison has made great strides in recent years in FPA in particular and in political science in general. However, as mentioned before, it is not an easy task not only due to the sophisticated methodological training required for researchers but also because it requires some innovative research designs to overcome the methodological gap between the quantitative and qualitative methods.

Conclusion

This chapter examines the evolution of CFP from a distinctive research program in the 1960s to an undervalued analytical approach in FPA after the Cold War. After briefly discussing the three FPA approaches related to the decline of the CFP: the area-studies school, middle-range theorization, and the actor-specific approach, we argue that CFP should be brought back to FPA as a valuable analytical approach.

We suggest that CFP as a distinctive analytical approach to FPA should emphasize the value of comparison in research by focusing on building middle-range theories. In particular, we propose three types of comparison in the CFP approach to FPA: case comparison, theoretical comparison, and methodological comparison. The case comparison approach refers to adopting a research design of cross-case comparison or/and within-case comparison to pursue new theoretical developments in FPA. The theoretical comparison is to test and compare the explanatory utility of at least two competing or rival explanations on a single case or a group of cases. The methodological comparison is also called a mixed-methods approach, through which scholars use different methodologies to test and confirm their findings. Scholars sometimes employ more than one CFP approach to conduct their research in FPA. For example, Renshon's research includes both the case comparison and the methodological comparison approaches. In a similar vein, Thies and Nieman combine all three types of CFP comparisons in their study of rising powers.

Scholars should take the CFP approach more seriously in FPA. Comparison is a natural feature of all scientific inquiries, including FPA. Although the original CFP research program has been discredited, it did not preclude scholars from employing different comparative approaches in their research. However, due to the negative reputation of CFP in the past, scholars hesitate to use the term "CFP" to define their analytical approach in FPA even though they have implicitly employed different types of comparative analyses. We suggest that CFP methods should be recognized as a distinctive analytical approach to FPA. This will encourage scholars to conduct more sophisticated comparative research with innovative research designs, which will, in turn, form an intellectual bridge between FPA and other sub-disciplines, especially Comparative Politics.

The future development of the CFP as a distinctive FPA approach should focus on addressing the weaknesses of the three types of comparison. For the case comparison approach, scholars should pay more attention to case selection in order to avoid possible biased findings from their case studies. Although the case comparison approach faces an inherent problem of limited external validity, scholars should maximize the generalizability of their findings within the scope of their middle-range theorizations. For the theoretical comparison, scholars need to avoid attacking the "strawman" by conducting superficial comparisons among different theoretical frameworks. More in-depth theoretical comparisons among various theoretical perspectives across different disciplines should be encouraged for scholars to pursue theoretical breakthroughs and innovation. Last, but not least, scholars are encouraged to employ the mixed-methods approach or conduct methodological comparisons to test and confirm their findings. However, along with the rapid emergence of new research methods, such as machine learning and computer simulation, how to integrate different methods effectively and efficiently in one study will become a tough challenge for FPA scholars.

Acknowledgements

This project is supported by the Australian Research Council (DP210102843).

Notes

1. In this chapter, we do not treat the event-data-based statistical research as a part of the CFP approach. On event data, see Raleigh and Kishi in this volume. We also do not include rational choice modelling because it is a distinct theoretical or methodological school in FPA and IR fields (Amadae and de Mesquita 1999).
2. It is worth noting that Ward also includes a "negative case"—the Anglo-American power transition—to explore why the rising United States did not choose a radical means to challenge Great Britain.
3. It is worth noting that the dependent variables of Murray's research not only include Britain's different foreign policy choices toward the United States and Germany, but also touch on the interactions between Britain on the one hand and the United States and Germany on the other. Therefore, Murray's research can be seen as an instance of foreign-policy-oriented IR research. For the purpose of this chapter, we focus on the foreign policy side of the research.
4. For the limitations on small-N comparison and analytical advantages of a medium-N research, see Patrick Mello, "Qualitative Comparative Analysis" in this volume.
5. For an example of comparing different middle-range, domestic-level arguments in explaining foreign policy choices, see Mello 2012.

References

Allison, Graham T. 1971. *Essence of Decision: Explaining the Cuban Missile Crisis*. Boston: Little, Brown and Company.
Almond, Gabriel A. 1966. "Political Theory and Political Science." *American Political Science Review* 60 (4): 869–879.
Amadae, Sonja M., and Bruce Bueno de Mesquita. 1999. "The Rochester School: The Origins of Positive Political Theory." *Annual Review of Political Science* 2 (1): 269–295.
Beasley, Ryan K. and Andrew R. Hom. 2021. "Foreign Policy in the Fourth Dimension (FP4D): Locating Time in Decision-Making". *Foreign Policy Analysis* 17 (2): https://doi-org.libraryproxy.griffith.edu.au/10.1093/fpa/oraa028
Breuning, Marijke. 2004. "Bringing 'Comparative' Back to Foreign Policy Analysis." *International Politics* 41 (4): 618–628.
Caporaso, James A. 1987. "The Comparative Study of Foreign Policy: Perspectives on the Future." *International Studies Notes* 13 (2): 32–46.
Carlsnaes, Walter. 1980. "The Concept of Foreign Policy Actions in Comparative Analysis." *Cooperation and Conflict* 15 (1): 3–20.

Carlsnaes, Walter. 2016. "Actors, Structures, and Foreign Policy Analysis." In *Foreign Policy: Theories, Actors, Cases*, edited by Steve Smith, Amelia Hadfield, and Tim Dunne, Third edition. Oxford: Oxford University Press, 113–129.

Checkel, Jeffrey T. 1998. "The Constructive Turn in International Relations Theory." *World Politics* 50 (2): 324–348.

Collier, David, and James Mahoney. 1996. "Insights and Pitfalls: Selection Bias in Qualitative Research." *World Politics* 49 (1): 56–91.

Dittmer, Lowell. 1981. "The Strategic Triangle: An Elementary Game-Theoretical Analysis." *World Politics* 33 (4): 485–515.

Easton, David. 1953. *The Political System: An Inquiry into the State of Political Science*. New York: Knopf.

Eckstein, Harry. 1975. "Case Study and Theory in Political Science." In *Handbook of Political Science, vol. 7, Strategies of Inquiry*, edited by Fred I. Greenstein and Nelson W. Polsby. Reading: Addison-Wesley Press.

Edelstein, David M. 2017. "Over the Horizon." In *Over the Horizon: Time, Uncertainty, and the Rise of Great Powers*. Ithaca, NY: Cornell University Press.

Farnham, Barbara. 1994. *Avoiding Losses/Taking Risks: Prospect Theory and International Conflict*. Ann Arbor, MI: University of Michigan Press.

George, Alexander, and Andrew Bennett. 2005. *Case Studies and Theory Development in Social Sciences*. Cambridge, MA: MIT Press.

Goertz, Gary. 2017. *Multimethod Research, Causal Mechanisms, and Case Studies*. Princeton, NJ: Princeton University Press.

He, Kai. 2012. "Case Study and the Comparative Method." In *Political Science Research in Practice*, edited by Akan Malici and Elizabeth S. Smith. New York: Routledge, 41–56.

He, Kai, and Huiyun Feng. 2013. *Prospect Theory and Foreign Policy Analysis in the Asia Pacific: Rational Leaders and Risky Behavior*. New York: Routledge.

Hermann, Charles F., Charles W. Kegley, and James N. Rosenau. eds. 1987. *New Directions in the Study of Foreign Policy*. Milton Park: Taylor & Francis.

Hermann, Margaret G. 1980. "Explaining Foreign Policy Behavior Using the Personal Characteristics of Political Leaders." *International Studies Quarterly* 24 (1): 7–46.

Holsti, Kalevi J. 1970. National Role Conceptions in the Study of Foreign Policy. *International Studies Quarterly* 14 (3): 233–309.

Hopf, Ted and Bentley Allan. eds. 2016. *Making Identity Count: Building a National Identity Database*. Oxford: Oxford University Press.

Hudson, Valerie M. 2005. "Foreign Policy Analysis: Actor-Specific Theory and the Ground of International Relations." *Foreign Policy Analysis* 1 (1): 1–30.

Hudson, Valerie M., and Christopher S. Vore. 1995. "Foreign Policy Analysis Yesterday, Today, and Tomorrow." *Mershon International Studies Review* 39 (Supplement 2): 209–238.

Jervis, Robert. 1976. *Perception and Misperception in International Politics*. Princeton, NJ: Princeton University Press.

Kaarbo, Juliet. 2003. "Foreign Policy Analysis in the Twenty-First Century: Back to Comparison, Forward to Identity and Ideas." *International Studies Review* 5 (2): 156–202.

Kaarbo, Juliet, Jeffrey S. Lantis, and Ryan K. Beasley. 2012. "The Analysis of Foreign Policy in Comparative Perspective." In *Foreign Policy in Comparative Perspective: Domestic and International Influences on State Behavior*, edited by Ryan K. Beasley, Juleit Kaarbo, Jeffrey S. Lantis and Michael T. Snarr. Thousand Oaks, CA: Sage, 1–23.

Kastner, Scott L., Margaret Pearson, and Chad Rector. 2019. *China's Strategic Multilateralism: Investing in Global Governance*. Cambridge: Cambridge University Press.

Keohane, Robert O., and Joseph S. Nye Jr. 1973. "Power and Interdependence." *Survival* 15 (4): 158–165.

King, Gary, Robert O. Keohane, and Sidney Verba. 1994. *Designing Social Inquiry*. Princeton, NJ: Princeton University Press.

Lampton, David M., and Catherine H. Keyser. eds. 1988. *China's Global Presence: Economics, Politics, and Security*. Washington, DC: American Enterprise Institute for Public Policy Research and the Institute of Southeast Asian Studies.

Lampton, David M., Joyce A. Madancy, and Kristen M. Williams. 1986. *A Relationship Restored: Trends in US-China Educational Exchanges, 1978–1984*. Washington, DC: National Academy Press.

Lantis, Jeffrey S., and Ryan K. Beasley. 2017. "Comparative Foreign Policy Analysis." In *Oxford Research Encyclopedia of Politics*, edited by William R. Thompson. Oxford: Oxford University Press (online version: https://doi.org/10.1093/acrefore/9780190228637.013.398).

Lipset, Seymour Martin. 1960. *Political Man: The Social Bases of Politics*. Baltimore, MD: The Johns Hopkins University Press.

Levy, Jack. S. 1992. "Prospect Theory and International Relations: Theoretical Applications and Analytical Problems." *Political Psychology* 13 (2): 283–310.

McDermott, Rose. 1998. *Risk-Taking in International Politics: Prospect Theory in American Foreign Policy*. Ann Arbor, MI: University of Michigan Press.

McGowan, Patrick J., and Howard B. Shapiro. 1973. *The Comparative Study of Foreign Policy: A Survey of Scientific Findings*. Beverly Hills, CA: Sage.

Mello, Patrick A. 2012. "Parliamentary Peace or Partisan Politics? Democracies' participation in the Iraq War." *Journal of International Relations and Development* 15 (3): 420–453.

Mill, John Stuart. 1862. *A System of Logic*, Fifth edition. London: Parker.

Moore, Barrington. 1966. *Social Origins of Dictatorship and Democracy: Lord and Peasant in the Making of the Modern World*. Boston, MA: Beacon Press.

Murray, Michelle. 2018. *The Struggle for Recognition in International Relations: Status, Revisionism, and Rising Powers*. Oxford: Oxford University Press.

Neack, Laura, Jeanne A.K. Hey, and Patrick J. Haney. 1995. "Generational Change in Foreign Policy Analysis." In *Foreign Policy Analysis. Contiguity and Change in its Second Generation*, edited by Laura Neack, Jeanne A.K. Hey, and Patrick J. Haney. Englewood Cliffs, NJ: Prentice Hall, 1–15.

Paul, T.V., Deborah Welsh Larson, and William C. Wohlforth. eds. 2014. *Status in World Politics*. Cambridge: Cambridge University Press.

Posen, Barry R. 2014. *The Sources of Military Doctrine*. Ithaca, NY: Cornell University Press.

Potter, Philip B. 2010. "Methods of Foreign Policy Analysis." In *Oxford Research Encyclopedia of International Studies*, edited by Nukhet Sandal, Nukhet and Renée Marlin Bennett. Hoboken, NJ: Wiley-Blackwell, 1–28.

Renshon, Jonathan. 2017. *Fighting for Status*. Princeton, NJ: Princeton University Press.

Rosenau, James N. 1966. "Pre–Theory and Theories of Foreign of Policy." In *Scientific Study of Foreign Policy*, edited by James N. Rosenau. New York: Free Press, 95–151.

Rosenau, James N. 1968. "Comparative Foreign Policy: Fad, Fantasy, or Field?" *International Studies Quarterly* 12 (3): 296–329.

Rosenau, James N. 1976. "Puzzlement in Foreign Policy." *Jerusalem Journal of International Relations* 1 (1): 1–2.

Shea, Christopher. 1997. "Political Scientists Clash Over Value of Area Studies." *Chronicle of Higher Education*, January 10.

Simon, Sheldon W. 1982. *The ASEAN States and Regional Security*. Stanford, CA: Hoover Institution Press.

Simon, Sheldon W. 1983. "Davids and Goliaths: Small Power-Great Power Security Relations in Southeast Asia." *Asian Survey* 23 (3): 302–315.

Smith, Steve. 1986. "Theories of Foreign Policy: An Historical Overview." *Review of International Studies* 12 (1): 13–29.

Thies, Cameron G., and Mark D. Nieman. 2017. *Rising Powers and Foreign Policy Revisionism: Understanding BRICS Identity and Behavior Through Time*. Ann Arbor, MI: University of Michigan Press.

Vertzberger, Yacoov Y.I. 1990. *The World in Their Minds: Information Processing, Cognition, and Perception in Foreign Policy Decision Making*. Stanford, CA: Stanford University Press.

Walker, Stephen G., Akan Malici, and Mark Schafer. 2011. *Rethinking Foreign Policy Analysis: States, Leaders, and the Microfoundations of Behavioral International Relations*. New York: Routledge.

Walker, Stephen J. 1987. *Role Theory and Foreign Policy Analysis*. Durham, NC: Duke University Press.

Wallerstein, Immanuel. 1987. "World-Systems Analysis." In *Social Theory Today*, edited by Anthony Giddens and Jonathan H. Turner. Stanford, CA: Stanford University Press, 309–324.

Walt, Stephen M. 1987. *The Origins of Alliances*. Ithaca, NY: Cornell University Press.

Waltz, Kenneth. 1979. *Theory of International Politics*. New York: McGraw-Hill.

Ward, Steven. 2017. *Status and the Challenge of Rising Powers*. Cambridge: Cambridge University Press.

Wurfel, David, and Bruce Burton. 1990. "Introduction: A Foreign Policy Framework for Southeast Asian States." In *The Political Economy of Foreign Policy in Southeast Asia*, edited by David Wurfel and Bruce Burton. New York: Palgrave Macmillan, 1–8.

19
Quantitative Content Analysis
Gordon M. Friedrichs

Introduction

Quantitative content analysis (QuantCA) can be briefly defined as a "systematic, objective, quantitative analysis of message characteristics" (Neuendorf 2017, 19). A more comprehensive definition describes it as

> a summarizing, quantitative analysis of messages that relies on the scientific method (including attention to objectivity-intersubjectivity, a priori design, reliability, validity, generalizability, replicability, and hypothesis tests) and is not limited as to the types of variables that may be measured or the contexts on which the messages are created or presented.
>
> *(Neuendorf and Skalski 2009, 203)*

Its application encompasses different kinds of messages, ranging from examining human interactions; character portrayals in media venues; computer-driven analysis of word usage in speeches and written statements; or the examination of interactive (commonly digital) content (Neuendorf 2017, 19). QuantCA includes both human-coded analyses and computer-aided text analysis. As such, QuantCA is neither limited "as to the types of variables that may be measured nor the contexts on which the messages are created or presented" (Neuendorf and Skalski 2009, 203).

More generally speaking, QuantCA can be applied to study manifest (i.e., intended, conscious, deliberate) and latent (i.e., unintended, unconscious) communications (Pashakhanlou 2017). Conducting a successful QuantCA involves "unitizing (segmenting the texts for analysis), sampling (selecting an appropriate collection of units to analyze), reliability (different researchers making codes consistently), and validity (using a coding scheme that adequately represents the specified phenomena)" (Coe and Scacco 2017, cf. Huxley 2020), making the method amenable to a variety of social science research areas (Weber 1990).

QuantCA is often combined with other types of measurement (Fink and Gantz 1996, Oleinik 2011, White and Marsh 2006), most prominently with qualitative content analysis (QualCA) in mixed-method research designs (Altheide and Schneider 2013, Mayring 2000,

Schreier 2012; 2013, Zhang and Wildemuth 2009). As a rule of thumb: Whereas QuantCA privileges manifest meaning, it is often assumed that qualitative content analysis (QualCA) privileges latent meaning (Pashakhanlou 2017, 449). This can result in higher reliability with QuantCA when establishing manifest meaning and higher validity with QualCA in determining latent meaning. On a general note, QuantCA is more applicable to answering "what" questions, whereas QualCA is more inclined to answer "how" and "why" questions (Ibid.). However, it should be noted that the dividing line between quantitative and qualitative can be rather arbitrary because even "quantitative research remains dependent on natural language (words), while most qualitative studies do contain some kind of quantitative information (numbers)" (Schedler and Mudde 2010, 418–419, quoted in Neuendorf 2017, 30). This often results in the usage of the more general term *content analysis*, in which both quantitative and qualitative measures are applied (Krippendorf 2004, Drisko & Maschi 2016). In QuantCA studies, numerical values, either counts or amounts, are commonly assigned to qualities of a phenomenon (framing, emotionality, etc.), whereas in QualCA studies, quantitative measures are often interpreted qualitatively (Neuendorf 2017, 30).

QuantCA offers a variety of promising research avenues to study foreign policy. Albeit QuantCA has been applied in various fashions to the study of foreign policy (e.g., operational code analysis; see Walker and Schafer 2018, Schafer and Walker 2021; see also their contribution to this volume), I argue here that a key benefit of adopting QuantCA to study foreign policy is its capacity to measure *collective identities* (Neuendorf and Skalski 2009) and particularly *national identity conceptions* (Harnisch and Friedrichs 2018, Hymans 2006), *national role conceptions* (Harnisch and Friedrichs 2022), as well as *foreign policy preferences* (Friedrichs 2022) on the individual or aggregate level. As will be shown throughout this chapter, the analytical strengths of QuantCA are the *measurement* and *comparison* (cross-case and within-case) of identity-related explanatory variables of foreign policy decision making of individuals or group actors (on identity see also the chapter by Guzzini in this volume).

There are several ways in which QuantCA can be conducted in identity research. Generally, QuantCA is conducted on the basis of three different categories of messages as well as three kinds of coding procedures (Neuendorf and Skalski 2009, 212 ff.). Messages are thereby not necessarily limited to text, for example, minutes of parliamentary debates or executive speeches, but can be derived from any form of communication, verbally, digitally, or written (Riffe et al. 2005). Neuendorf and Skalski (2009) distinguish between response-based messages (individuals generate messages in response to assigned identity-related tasks or prompts), assumed identity messages (naturally occurring messages that one might assume to constitute identity messages), and extracted identity messages (inspection or extraction of messages that are not wholly identity-related). Furthermore, there is human preset coding, computer preset coding, and computer emergent coding (see below). In this chapter, I focus on theoretical and empirical applications of assumed identity messages with a human preset coding, which is a coding scheme that is developed beforehand by the researchers and uses measures based on theory (see below).

However, despite its benefits, QuantCA is less capable of making causal inferences from the measurement of collective identities with regard to foreign policy implementation. Hence, QuantCA is particularly powerful analytically when applied in mixed-method research designs, combining quantitative measurement of message characteristics with qualitative assessments of cases. Within a mixed-method research design, QuantCA is prone to contribute to answering *why* and *how* questions as well, for example, understanding foreign policy decisions at a particular point in time in comparative perspective, or explaining foreign policy change from one leader to another.

In the remaining part of the chapter, I will first briefly reflect on the usage of QuantCA in the FPA and IR scholarship before I focus on one particular application of human preset coding of assumed identity messages related to collective identities originally developed by Hymans (2006). I continue with empirical illustrations of how QuantCA has been applied in different studies. The chapter closes by discussing some of the benefits but also the potential pitfalls for researchers when using QuantCA in their own research.

Quantitative Content Analysis in Foreign Policy Analysis Scholarship

Early approaches to events data generation focused predominately on the quantitative content of elite communication (Potter 2017). These approaches were largely in the tradition of 1940s International Relations (IR) scholars, who approached content analysis in predominantly quantitative terms, that is, word counts (cf. Dillard and Pevehouse 2017). QuantCA approaches to the study of foreign policy have focused primarily on computer-assisted statistical inferences based on events data sets that mainly comprise of newspaper reports on the interactions among nations following a previously defined set of criteria or codebook (Potter 2017, 4), for example, the World Event/Interaction Survey (McClelland 2006), the Conflict and Peace Data Bank (Azar 2009), International Crisis Behavior Project(Beardsley et al. 2020), or the Correlates of War Project (Sarkees and Wayman 2010). The Kansas Event Data System (Schrodt 2008) employs the latest machine coding technique to news reports and generate political event data that enables users to specify and create personalized events data sets with a variety of output options.[1] More recently, Walker developed a typology and QuantCA scheme for operational code analysis (Walker et al. 1998; 2018). The majority of this work follows a positivist epistemology and is interested in questions related to power and threat perception of leaders and their foreign policy decisions, as well as the international structural causes to states' foreign policy behavior (Larson 1988).

More recent quantitative work on identity construction, computing narratives, and social structures has contributed to this research by strengthening the methodological foundation of post-positivist approaches (i.e., social constructivism and critical theory, Barkin and Sjoberg 2017). Indeed, FPA scholarship offers a plethora of approaches to the study of national identity and foreign policymaking (cf. Abdelal et al. 2006, Vucetic 2010; 2017). Most studies exploring the relationship between identity and foreign policy hold the premise that states are social collectives marked by shared values and norms, which, in turn, predispose the state to certain foreign policy preferences (Kubalkova 2001). These studies have substantially contributed to our understanding why states deem certain foreign policies as inappropriate or decide to pursue strategies that run counter to their material capacities through emphasizing national identity and as a constitutive variable (Kaarbo 2003).

The most promising application of QuantCA to the study of foreign policy has drawn from psychological constructivism (Hymans 2010, Shannon and Kowert 2012) and particularly the theoretical model of identity-driven foreign policymaking developed by Jacques Hymans (2006). The model is based on the premise that individual state leaders hold certain *national identity conceptions* (NICs). NICs are defined as a leader's understanding of what their nation stands for (*solidarity dimension*) and how high it stands (*status dimension*) in *comparison* to (a) key comparative other(s). The solidarity dimension, on the one hand, reveals how the individual leader defines the nation's interests and values. This can either be similar to (sportsmanlike) or different from (oppositional) the key comparison other(s). The status dimension, on the other hand, highlights whether the leader defines its nation as equal, if not superior (nationalist) or as inferior (subaltern) to the key comparison other(s).

Via a human preset coding of assumed identity messages, Hymans quantitatively measured the NICs of state leaders from four different countries over time (France, Australia, India, and Argentina). This way, he assessed whether an NIC *type* (i.e., sportsmanlike subaltern, sportsmanlike nationalist, oppositional nationalist, oppositional subaltern) correlates with the individual country's decision point to pursue a nuclear weapons program. Following a mixed-method research design that combined QuantCA of NICs as well as (QualCA) (i.e., process-tracing), Hymans showed how and why different NIC types foreground a particular nuclear proliferation behavior. In short, oppositional nationalists proved to be most likely to pursue a nuclear weapons program for their country because they combine emotions of fear and pride as key elements in their conceptions of their own state and the key comparison other (Hymans 2006).

Hymans' theoretical model was further adapted and refined by Harnisch and Friedrichs (2022) to measure national role conceptions (NRCs), particularly conceptions by U.S. presidents of the U.S. global leadership role. Harnisch and Friedrichs (2022) introduced a methodological approach to the measurement of NRCs that can fit more neatly into the symbolic interactionism stream of role theory (Harnisch 2011). They adapted Hyman's original research design and modeled NRCs of U.S. global leadership along two dimensions: a functional (task allocation) and a relational (followership) dimension. So far, NRCs were primarily derived from the coding of primary sources, including public speeches, legislative debates, and press statements of foreign policy officials (Holsti 1970), or by relying solely on secondary source materials (Thies and Nieman 2017, 44).

By measuring and comparing the NRCs of Barack Obama and Donald Trump regarding the U.S. global leadership role, Harnisch and Friedrichs (2022) showed that Trump's NRC reveals a U.S. leadership role conception along the continuum of the self-centered and dominant leadership subtype. This, in turn, results in a unique functional leadership role allocation paired with a low incentive for broad, inclusive followership. In contrast, they identify Obama's NRC of U.S. leadership as the legitimate subtype with a strong sense of assimilation and a lesser degree of nationalism, although still noticeable yet directed at U.S. enemies and adversaries while identifying strongly with the international community of states. They further test changes in the U.S. leadership role conceptions in two case studies: U.S. alliance politics and U.S. trade policy, to see whether NRC foreground U.S. leadership role-taking. In both cases, the quantitative measurement and comparison of NRCs translated into commensurate role-taking in both administrations. This study underlined the methodological merit of QuantCA to measure and compare NRCs along two dimensions. Their findings further suggest that while both former friends and foes have resisted U.S. relative gains seeking policies, they have neither abrogated their relationship with the U.S. nor left international institutions established and traditionally upheld by various U.S. administrations.

Finally, Friedrichs (2022) applied QuantCA to comparatively study the foreign policy preferences of populist state leaders and their non-populist predecessors. The comparative analysis exposed populist leaders as oppositional nationalists, whereas non-populist leaders were identified as sportsmanlike nationalists. In addition, not only do populist leaders share the same NIC, but they also compare their nation to a similar key comparison other, that is, a generic foreign other. A "generic foreign other" is a reference to the unspecified outside world, for example, references to "foreign," "abroad," "overseas," "outside," "exterior," "external," national "independence," "sovereignty," "self-determination," "freedom," "autonomy," references to bilateral relations, negotiations, and conferences with "generic foreign others" (Hymans 2006, 230–231). A subsequent analysis of the selected states' position toward global governance under populist and non-populist rule presented further evidence that an oppositional nationalist NIC translates into foreign policy preferences of revisionism, but differ in their degree of contestation and issue saliency over time.

The Methodology of Quantitative Content Analysis in the Context of Human Preset Coding of Assumed Identity Messages: Key Terms and Concepts

The study of collective identities via QuantCA is based on three categories of messages as well as three kinds of coding procedures (Neuendorf and Skalski 2009, 212 ff.). We can distinguish between response-based messages, assumed identity messages, and extracted identity messages. Furthermore, there is human preset coding, computer preset coding, and computer emergent coding.

To begin with, human preset coding "is the application of a set of written rules for measurement to a set of messages by trained individuals" (Neuendorf and Skalski 2009, 212 ff.). Here, a coding scheme is developed beforehand as well as measures based on theory, including secondary sources or even pilot work. The coding scheme consists of a codebook, which entails instructions for each coder involved as well as a coding form into which coders protocol their assessments for the purpose of replicability and inter-coder reliability. Inter-coder reliability is further ensured due to the fact that the coding scheme (derived beforehand) is the most crucial analytical instrument instead of coder's personal expertise. This kind of human coding is thereby open to analysis of text, images, or symbols to measure collective identity (ibid.).

Furthermore, computer preset coding is an automated *machine* coding or computer-assisted text analysis (CATA). This coding form is built on preset dictionaries that entail lists of words and/or word combinations that are processed digitally. Dictionaries are either provided by a software (e.g., General Inquirer and Diction 5.0, which also comes with a mathematical algorithm that goes beyond simple word counts) or created by the researcher (ibid.).[2] Some CATA programs and software include dictionary building facilities (e.g., WordStat) to avoid command pitfalls when creating one's own dictionary that need to be consistent with conceptual definitions and include possible variants of root terms (antonyms, synonyms, similar terms, hypernyms, hyponyms, holonyms, ibid.). In any case, the researcher needs to be involved in these decisions as dictionary construction is not automatic.

Finally, CATA emergent coding describes a process in which dimensions or patterns of text are derived from the texts under investigation without any preset dictionaries (Neuendorf and Skalski 2009). A typical example of such a procedure is the visual representation of "the frequency of occurrence, cooccurrence, and/or correspondence of words and text segments through cluster analysis, multidimensional scaling, and neural networking" (ibid., 208), for example, in programs such as CATPAC, TextSmart, and TextAnalyst. The potential of CATA emergent coding is basically that the dimensions derived from emergent machine coding may be used in a second-stage, ordinary preset coding process.

These measures of collective identity – human preset coding, computer preset coding, and CATA emergent coding – can each be applied to three different types of messages: response-based messages (individuals generate messages in response to assigned identity-related tasks or prompts), assumed identity messages (naturally occurring messages that one might assume to constitute identity messages), and extracted identity messages (inspection or extraction of messages that are not wholly identity-related).

Human preset coding of assumed identity messages is particularly applicable to the study of individual actors' conceptions about their state's national identity as it involves an immediate link between the theorization of what drives leader foreign policy conceptions and the analysis of specific leader messages, such as speeches. In the context of FPA, this combination represents a reliable tool to identify foreign policy preferences and thus contributes to the literature studying the political psychology of world leaders (cf. Hudson and Day 2020, 40–42). These messages may be either at the individual or the aggregate level (i.e., an institution representing a collective entity). Concerning individual messages, the method assumes the collection and analysis of original speech or text either as it occurs naturally (e.g., transcripts; digital postings; letters) or in response to prompts (essays or open-ended responses to a questionnaire or interview protocol, Neuendorf and Skalski 2009). Aggregate messages (e.g., nation-level) might include official constitutions or law, news stories about a nation, official web sites, history textbooks, official political communications such as party platforms, speeches and debates, governmental annual reports, national leaders' vision statements, and other political documents (ibid.).

Focusing on QuantCA in the context of human preset coding of assumed identity messages requires proper theorization of what to code and why. A proper application of human preset coding to assumed identity messages is the research by Hymans (2006) and his study of NICs of state leaders and their decision to pursue a nuclear weapons program. NICs are a leaders' "deep-seated, essentially unfalsifiable beliefs about the 'true' nature of the nation, which are developed through comparison and contrast with the 'true' nature ascribed to certain external others." (ibid., 13) They reflect a state leader's "sense of *what the nation naturally stands for* and of *how high it naturally stands*, in comparison to others in the international arena" (ibid., emphasis in original). Such key comparison others are usually external others that are most present in the mind of the state leader and function as a point of comparison for self-identification as well as demarcation.

According to Hymans (2006, 21 ff.), NICs consist of two key dimensions: *solidarity* and *status*. The solidarity dimension reflects individuals' understanding of "what the national naturally stands for," whereas the status dimension refers to the understanding of "how high the nation naturally stands" (ibid., 21). The solidarity dimension of self-identification ranges from oppositional NICs, which derive the nation's identity in dichotomizing fashion via the key comparison other ("us against them"), to sportsmanlike NICs "that nest the us-them distinction within a broader, transcendent identity conception" (ibid., 23).

The status dimension, on the other hand, defines individuals' understanding whether the nation is naturally equal (or even superior) or inferior to the key comparison other(s). The status dimension is thereby considered supplemental to the solidarity dimension to predispose oppositional consciousness toward conflict with the "other" (Hymans 2006, 23). In other words, feeling superior and oppositional to the key comparison other can explain revisionist foreign policy preferences and actions. A key component of the status dimension is thereby an individual's sense of international efficacy, that is, whether "the nation can hold its head high in dealings with its key comparison other(s)" (Ibid., 24). On one end of the spectrum on the status dimension are nationalist NICs, meaning that the individual sees its nation equal in status to others. On the other end of the spectrum are subaltern NICs, which is an understanding that the nation is naturally below others.

Following a similar research design, Harnisch and Friedrichs (2022) see NRCs of U.S. leadership constituted by two central elements of ego and alter identification. On the ego side, they locate the degree of nationalism as a central marker for judging whether state leaders conceive of their state more self-centered or other-directed. The notion of nationalism corresponds with the functional dimension of leadership roles. The degree of nationalist tendencies, ranging from compassion to chauvinism, can than serve as a role cue for others whether their role expectations match with expectations. For the alter side of leadership roles, they locate the degree of oppositionalism as a measurement of how state leaders see their state in relation to significant others. They distinguish between inclusive and exclusive leadership roles when we think about the followership of leadership roles. More inclusive leadership roles require NRCs that have a low degree of oppositionalism and instead of self-identification with many significant others. They call that a sense of communitarianism (or other-directedness). In contrast, exclusive leadership roles are marked by a smaller group of followers as being essential for the self-identification as a leader. Here, dissimilation is a key driver because it is the demarcation from others that provides ontological security. Table 19.1 summarizes the model graphically.

Finally, Friedrichs (2022) derived four categories of foreign policy preferences that correspond to both dimensions of NIC (see Table 19.2). Whether leaders are sportsmanlike or oppositional determines if they prefer a competitive or an antagonistic foreign policy, respectively. The reason is that sportsmanlike types hold a transcendent identity conception vis-à-vis the key comparison other(s), which is less fearful of others. In addition, whether leaders are subaltern or nationalist determines if they prefer a more coalitional (aligned) foreign policy or singular (unilateral) foreign policy, respectively.

Combined, the assumption is that oppositional nationalists pursue revisionist foreign policy because they understand their nation to be equal if not superior to that key comparison other. In contrast, sportsmanlike subaltern NIC types favor status quo foreign policies due to their general sense of inferiority vis-à-vis the key comparison other(s). It is not expected from them to support the international status quo in order to eventually brake from it when the opportunity arises, but instead stick to it because they lack both "motivation and gumption" (Hymans 2006, 40).

Friedrichs (2022) locates the combinations sportsmanlike nationalists and oppositional subaltern in between both extremes. Sportsmanlike nationalists are less fearful of the key comparison other(s), which inclines them to pursue competitive foreign policies not aimed at revising international order, while at the same time, to be skeptical of aligning with the key comparison other(s). In short, they prefer a foreign policy of boosting their competitiveness within existing institutions as long as this is a possible strategy given the power relations within those very institutions.

Oppositional subaltern types, on the other hand, are inclined to pursue antagonistic foreign policies but at the same time, to be less skeptical of aligning with the key comparison other(s). Consequentially, the expectation is that oppositional subaltern leaders align with great powers vis-à-vis others they oppose, including international institutions and modes of global governance that they fear, while maintaining those they feel comfortable in.

Table 19.1 Types of Leadership Roles

		Functional (Task Allocation)	
		Singular	*Collective*
Relational (followership)	Exclusive	Self-centered leadership role	Hierarchical/dominant leadership role
	Inclusive	Legitimate/ascribed leadership role	Shared leadership role

Source: Harnisch and Friedrichs 2022.

Table 19.2 National Identity Conception Types and Foreign Policy Preferences

	Solidarity Dimension	
Status Dimension	*Sportsmanlike*	*Oppositional*
Subaltern	Status quo dependency	Status quo maintenance
Nationalist	Competitiveness boosting	Revisionism

Source: Friedrichs 2022 (cf. Hymans 2006, 25).

Empirical Illustration

Following Hymans (2006), I now illustrate the application of a QuantCA via a human preset coding of assumed identity messages and then describe the empirical results of applying this method in two different studies. To begin with, the collected messages include speeches of the selected individual state leaders that can be assumed to be representations of the individual's NRCs or NICs, respectively (cf. Neuendorf and Skalski 2009, 219). In order to account for as assumed representations of the individual's NRC or NIC, the selected speeches entailed an explicit foreign policy theme; consisted of at least 500 words; and have ideally taken place annually in the form of a major address (e.g., State of Union Speech). These messages are selected with the goal in mind that they reveal the intentions of the speakers. In both studies that serve as empirical illustrations here, I only included individual leaders' speeches instead of party manifestos. Although party manifestos are valid sources, I was primarily interested in individual state leaders' understanding of their nation and how these translate into NRCs or foreign policy preferences.

Once the speeches were selected, I prepared the data for coding. I started by identifying (i.e., counting and listing) the frequently occurring "key comparison other" as in each collected speech. These included any human community that is not primarily based inside the national territory of the respective leader's own state, although broader references to communities of which the state is in part a member (e.g., the United Nations) are counted, while explicit references to the state were ruled out (cf. codebook in Hymans 2006, 229).

In order to identify which external actors are referred to in how many paragraphs, I counted any referenced actor once in any paragraph, regardless of whether the actor is referred to multiple times within one paragraph (Hymans 2006, 230). Such a coding-by-hand technique allows qualitative choices, especially in instances where the leader might be hesitant to call out certain others as key comparison others. For instance, coding the speeches of Maduro revealed that he often implicitly called out the U.S. when describing foreign activities against Venezuela. Importantly, although references to wider communities of which the respective nation is a part (e.g., world community) are counted, a key comparison other has to be a "truly foreign other" (cf. Hymans 2006, 52). For example, references by Orbán to Europe could not count as *key* comparison other because Hungary is part of Europe (physically speaking).

Table 19.3 displays an illustration from the Obama/Trump study about how the counting and selection process looks like when using a spreadsheet. Trump's NRC entails a strong bias toward a generic, unspecified foreign other whereas Obama refers predominately to the world community. Interestingly, and in sharp contrast to Obama, it appears that in relative terms, the numeric values of the top-five most significant external actors in the Trump sample are equally distributed between U.S. allies, the world community of which the U.S. and all other countries are a part, and enemies of the U.S. (i.e., North Korea, but also China and Terrorism). The low number of references to the West appears significant for an American president, especially since the speeches we selected had this particular audience and thus can be seen as a sign of demarcation from this shared historic bonding narrative.

After listing all references to external others, the QuantCA is mainly interested in computing proportions between the key comparison other(s) in the speeches and the other references. The general idea is to quantitatively assess whether the key comparison other is referred to other external entities that are part of the same social group in the same context (IOs, alliances, world community, etc.) or the key comparison other is located outside of the social group. Accordingly, the studies by Harnisch and Friedrichs (2022) and Friedrichs (2022) computed the proportion of certain references to the key comparison other and other external entities along both pre-defined dimensions (see above).

As a rule of thumb and in accordance with Hymans (2006) original design, we can measure the level of oppositionalism by following Hymans and "take the total number of references to the other, divided by that number plus the total number of references to collective entities that include both our nation and the other" (Hymans 2006, 232). We thus compute the degree of opposition in each leader's NIC (oT) by dividing the total number of references to the most significant other (Σ) with Σ plus the number of combined collective entities (η) (cf. Harnisch and Friedrichs 2022, Friedrichs 2022). Hence:

$$oT = \frac{\Sigma}{(\Sigma + \eta)}$$

Results range between 0 and 1, whereas a value closer to 0 suggests that the leader sees – literally – zero distinction between its state's own identity and that of the key comparison other. This is because "an oppositional identity is hard to maintain if 'we' and 'they' are also understood to be connected under a strong transcendent identity that covers us both" (Hymans 2008, 262). In contrast to such a transcendent identity conception, a value closer to "1" suggests that the leader's NIC is highly dichotomous in which one's own state identity is regularly pitted in opposition to the identity of the key comparison other based on fear (Hymans 2006, 22 ff.). In general, the rough boundary between sportsmanlike and oppositional NICs is 0.5 for heuristic purposes.

After measuring the solidarity dimension, we can address the status dimension in leader's NICs. We take "the proportion of the number of references to the other, versus the number of paragraphs referring to the other that also include references to wider entities in which we, but not necessarily the other, take part" (Hymans 2006, 233). Thus, to calculate the degree of nationalism in leaders' NIC (nT), we compute references to the key comparison other (Σ) minus the number of paragraphs that entailed references to the key comparison other *and* references to those groups of external actors of which the leader is part of but not necessarily the other (β), which is then divided by the references to the key comparison other (Σ). In short:

$$nT = \frac{(\Sigma - \beta)}{\Sigma}$$

A value closer to 0 suggests that the leader holds a subaltern identity conception of its state with, literally, zero status assumption vis-à-vis the key comparison other(s). In contrast, a value closer to 1 suggests a conception in which the state is naturally at least of equal sovereign standing compared with its key comparison other(s) if not superior (Hymans 2006, 23–24).

Table 19.3 Key Comparison Other(s) of Trump

Other	Speech at the National Interest April 27, 2016	Speech on Trade June 28, 2016	Remarks to Poland July 2017	Remarks at UN GA September 19, 2017	UN GA Speech September 25, 2018	UN GA Speech September 25, 2019	Speech at National Assembly South Korea November 8, 2017	National Security Strategy Speech December 18, 2017	Missile Defense Review Speech January 17, 2019	SOTU January 30, 2018	SOTU February 5, 2019	SOTU 2020	Sum
Generic foreign other	14	23	15	38	47	25	8	32	8	20	20	12	262
World community	13	11	17	33	24	9	8	12	4	7	5	10	153
Allies/Friends	18	6	8	5	5	9	1	4	2	3	3	1	65
North Korea	1		1	5	5	1	29	2	1	7	2	1	53
Poland	1		41	1				1					47 (partial, as read)
China	7	14		1	3	7	2	1	2	3	3	3	44
Iran	5		1	7	6	8		2		2	4	2	39
Terrorists	6	1	3	5	4	1	2	6		4	3	4	39
Migrants	3			5	2			2	2	9	10	5	38
South Korea		2			2		23	1					28
Middle East Region	6	1		4	8	1		2		3	2	2	25
The West/Western Hemisphere	2	5	8	2	2	5						3	22
ISIS	7			2	1		1	2		4	2		19
Venezuela		5		4	3					1	2	3	18
Europe	1		11	2	1	1			1				17
Asia	2	9		2		1		1		2			16
Syria	2		1	2	5	1		1		1	2	1	16
Israel	3		1	2	4	1			1	1	1	1	14
Iraq	3			1	1			1		1	2	3	13
Russia	4		1	1	1	1	1	2		1	1		12
Cuba	1		2	2	1	2				1		2	10

It is assumed that a value closer to 1 is associated with a high sense of status by the individual state leader. This is because "a willingness to compare oneself directly with the key comparison other suggests high self-esteem, while a tendency to use a wider community as a screen to avoid that head-to-head comparison suggests low self-esteem" (Hymans 2008, 262). Again, the rough boundary between subaltern and nationalist NICs is 0.5 for heuristic purposes. Finally, results from the measurement of the solidarity and status dimension were reinforced by 95% confidence intervals calculated around each data point.

Table 19.4 summarizes some findings from a QuantCA study conducted by Harnisch and Friedrichs (2018) on North Korean leaders in continuation of a study by Hymans (2008). It illustrates how the QuantCA can help testing for within-case variance, that is, of North Korean state leaders' NICs over time. The findings show that there is initially no quantitative change in the naming of significant others compared with the Hymans sample: The reference group "generic foreign others" dominates with a total of 70 references. However, the development of the degree of opposition and nationalism in comparison to the phase under Kim Jong-Il is striking, because here the degree of opposition to the dominant significant other, "generic foreign others," averaged 0.85 between 1995 and 2008. According to the coding of the material for Kim Jong-Un, the degree of opposition is 0.7, which is comparable to

Table 19.4 National Identity Conceptions of North Korean Leaders Over Time

Count of Other	KIS 1975–1979	KIS 1980–1984	KIS 1985–1989	KIS 1990–1994	KJI 1995–1999	KJI 2000–2005	KJI 2006–2008	KJU 2013–2016
Generic foreign others	55	65	77	125	113	149	99	70
SK	31	24	118	107	61	60	22	51
U.S.	34	25	69	62	40	40	18	7
World community	19	20	66	62	22	33	14	30
Imperialist club	2	5	30	38	35	57	12	13
Communist community	8	6	30	21	6	0	0	16
Japan	12	6	16	8	9	16	2	2
Progressive community	9	8	17	7	10	2	2	5
Asia community	1	0	4	3	4	1	1	13

Leader	Generic foreign others	Level of opposition	Level of nationalism
KIS 1975–1979	55	0.74	0.78
KIS 1980–1984	65	0.76	0.82
KIS 1985–1989	77	0.54	0.75
KIS 1990–1994	125	0.67	0.66
KJI 1995–1999	113	0.84	0.79
KJI 2000–2005	149	0.82	0.89
KJI 2006–2008	99	0.88	0.89
KJU 2013–2016	70	0.7	0.8

the period in the early 1990s. When coding and scoring the degree of nationalism, the Kim Jong-Un sample is on par with the sample coded by Hymans for Kim Jong-Il (at about 0.8), so that neither identity expression shows significant changes for the new regime since 2012.

The study of populist and non-populist state leaders' NICs conducted by Friedrichs (2022) was able to show that although all leaders see their country of equal status compared with the key comparison other, only populist leaders share an oppositional identity conception vis-à-vis their key comparison other. In contrast, non-populist leaders are sportsmanlike nationalists. This results from an asymmetric relationship between the number of references to the key comparison other and external actors (or groups) of which the populist leader but not necessarily the generic foreign other is part of. Furthermore, Friedrichs (2022) tested whether oppositional nationalist NICs among populist leaders translate into revisionist foreign policy preferences in the form of voting patterns in the UN General Assembly. The findings suggest only a rather weak correlation between both, yet preferences for revisionism somewhat differ in their degree of contestation and issue saliency across and within cases. While across-case correlation between populists' oppositional nationalist NIC and a general contestation cannot be observed, some populists shared a critical stance towards the UN in the realm of disarmament and human rights (Friedrichs 2022).

Conclusion

This chapter discussed the method of QuantCA in the specific context of measuring and comparing state leaders' conceptions of their state's national identity as well as international role via a human preset coding of assumed identity messages. Based on the theoretical model developed by Hymans (2006), QuantCA can explore within-case (identity/role conceptions of different leaders of the same country over time) as well as cross-case (identity/role conceptions of different leaders of different countries over time) variance. It is, thus, most suitable in comparative research designs that measure and compare identity/role conceptions of state leaders.

Moreover, the chapter suggested that QuantCA of assumed identity messages via a human preset coding is less capable in establishing causal inference between identity conception types and foreign policy decisions. As the chapter exemplified by drawing from the original research by Hymans (2006) as well as subsequent, further developments by Harnisch and Friedrichs (2022) as well as Friedrichs (2022), the QuantCA of identity messages requires a qualitative analysis of leaders' decision making that reflect their NRC or NIC type. In the case of Hymans (2006), an in-depth qualitative study of nuclear proliferation choices via primary and secondary sources proved sufficient to show that oppositional nationalist leaders are more likely to pursue a nuclear weapons program. Harnisch and Friedrichs (2022) showed via case vignettes of Trump's alliance and free trade policy that oppositional nationalist role conceptions translated into a self-centered leadership role-taking. Friedrichs (2022) demonstrated that oppositional nationalist NICs translated in some policy realms into revisionist foreign policy preferences. Besides the benefit of embedding QuantCA into mixed-method research designs for the purpose of establishing causal inference, the chapter suggested that QuantCA requires proper theorization and typology of aspects of collective identities, such as status and solidarity dimensions, to function properly when utilized for measurement of text data sets.

Another benefit of QuantCA is its practical application and utility compared with other quantitative approaches to the study of foreign policy, such as computer-coding or survey research. This is mainly due to the data management. A key benefit is that researchers can start by collecting and coding only a small sample of speeches (i.e., messages) before deciding to expand on the data to achieve significant findings. This keeps data collection initially rather limited but can easily be expanded in a controlled and manageable way (e.g., adding more speeches within a year, increasing the time frame, or expanding the scope of potential speeches). Furthermore, quantitative referencing and proportion computing can easily be done on an Excel Sheet, as the data (speeches) are stored separately and are usually stored in printed form due to the necessity to code by hand (i.e., reading and marking). Finally, since the QuantCA approach presented in this chapter requires proper theorization and modeling prior, the method is handily applicable to other research questions of FPA that involve aspects of self-identification and otherness.

Overall, the theoretical model can examine how state leaders define the values, interests, and capabilities of their nations in comparison to others. This procedure not only allowed for the establishment of NICs as a fruitful variable in the study of individual state leaders' characteristics and personality that contributes to the literature on individual foreign policy decision makers; it also strengthened the FPA toolbox to study the language of state leaders that is synergetic to existing approaches.

However, given that the method relies on a coding-by-hand technique, researcher should not underestimate the labor and time necessary to conduct a replicable study. This implies that researchers need to focus on individual leaders instead of collectives (i.e., parties, bureaucracies, legislative branches), a manageable set of assumed messages (as a rule of thumb I suggest somewhat between five and twenty speeches, each of at least 500 words), and a comparative research design (addressing either within-case or cross-case variance, or both). Furthermore, the key comparison other category of a "generic foreign other" seems to appear more numerously after the end of the Cold War in Hymans' own research, and it certainly dominates the more contemporary leaders in this article. This suggests that state leaders today are more likely to compare their nation with a broader reference group, that is, international order in general. While this indicates a more general trend within the method toward capturing the effects of globalization, it also invites us to think about specifying the codebook developed by Hymans.

In addition to these methodological challenges, researchers need to be aware that QuantCA offers limited causal interference without proper case analysis that tracks the measured NICs, NRCs, or other forms of identity formation in action. This should underline the fact that QuantCA offers a solid within-case and cross-case comparison of explanatory variables, yet it lacks proper analysis of intervening variables. This should by no means discourage researchers from employing QuantCA but it should underscore its analytical limitation. Instead, QuantCA in the context of collective identities, as illustrated in this chapter, is of much more value when considered as a method to measure and compare constitutive variables for foreign policymaking (e.g., preferences, conceptions, perceptions, cf. Hymans 2010).

Notes

1 On Event Data Analysis, see also the chapter by Clionadh Raleigh and Roudabeh Kishi in this volume.
2 The software can be accessed at: http://www.mariapinto.es/ciberabstracts/Articulos/Inquirer.htm.

References

Abdelal, Rawi, Yoshiko M. Herrera, Alastair Iain Johnston, and Rose McDermott. 2006. 'Identity as a Variable', *Perspectives on Politics*, 4: 695–711.
Altheide, David, L., and Christopher J. Schneider. 2013. *Qualitative Media Analysis* (Sage: Thousand Oaks).
Azar, Edward E. 2009. Conflict and Peace Data Bank (COPDAB), 1948–1978. Inter-University Consortium for Political and Social Research, https://doi.org/10.3886/ICPSR07767.v4.

Barkin, J. Samuel, and Laura Sjoberg. 2017. *Interpretive Quantification: Methodological Explorations for Critical and Constructivist IR* (University of Michigan Press: Ann Arbor).

Beardsley Kyle, Patrick James, Jonathan Wilkenfeld, and Michael Brecher. 2020. The International Crisis Behavior Project. *Oxford Research Encyclopedias.* https://doi.org/10.1093/acrefore/9780190228637.013.1638.

Coe, Kevin, and Joshua M. Scacco. 2017. 'Content Analysis, Quantitative.' in C.S. Davis, J. Matthes and R.F. Potter (eds.), *The International Encyclopedia of Communication Research Methods*, 1–11. https://doi.org/10.1002/9781118901731.iecrm0045.

Dillard, Micah, and Jon C.W. Pevehouse. 2017. 'Quantitative Methods in Foreign Policy.' In William R. Thompson (ed.), *Oxford Research Encyclopedia of Politics* (Oxford University Press: Oxford).

Drisko, James W., and Tina Maschi. 2016. *Content Analysis* (Oxford University Press: Oxford).

Fink, Edward, and Walter Gantz. 1996. 'A content analysis of three mass communication research traditions: Social science, interpretive studies and critical analysis', *Journalism & Mass Communication Quarterly*, 73: 114–134.

Friedrichs, Gordon M. 2022. "Populist minds think alike? National identity conceptions and foreign policy preferences of populist leaders." *Foreign Policy Analysis*, 18(2): orac004. https://doi.org/10.1093/fpa/orac004.

Harnisch, Sebastian. 2011. ""Dialogue and emergence": George Herbert Mead's Contribution to Role Theory and His Reconstruction of International Politics." in Sebastian Harnisch, Cornelia Frank and Hanns W. Maull (eds.), *Role Theory in International Relations: Approaches and analyses*, 36–54 (Routledge: New York).

Harnisch, Sebastian, and Gordon M. Friedrichs. 2018. 'Nordkoreas neue Strategie zur Stabilisierung dynastischer Herrschaft: Nuklearwaffen und innenpolitische Säuberungen.' in Mischa Hansel, Sebastian Harnisch and Nadine Godehardt (eds.), *Chinesische Seidenstraßeninitiative und amerikanische Gewichtsverlagerung*, 125–156 (Nomos: Baden-Baden).

Harnisch, Sebastian, and Gordon M. Friedrichs. 2022. 'Shrinking the U.S. Leadership Role: Populism and the Change of Domestic and International "Others".' in Michael Grossman, Francis Schortgen and Gordon M. Friedrichs (eds.), *National Role Conceptions in a New Millennium: Defining a Place in a Changing World*, 25–39 (Routledge: London & New York).

Holsti, K.J. 1970. 'National Role Conceptions in the Study of Foreign Policy', *International Studies Quarterly*, 14: 233–309.

Hudson, Valerie M., and Benjamin S. Day. 2020. 'The Individual Decisionmaker: The Political Psychology of World Leaders.' in Valerie M. Hudson and Benjamin S. Day (eds.), *Foreign Policy Analysis: Classic and Contemporary Theory*, 39–74 (Rowman & Littlefield: Lanham).

Huxley, Katy. 2020. 'Content Analysis, Quantitative.' in Paul Atkinson, Sara Delamont, Alexandru Cernat, Joseph W. Sakshaug and Richard A. Williams (eds.), *SAGE Research Methods Foundations*. https://doi.org/10.4135/9781526421036880564.

Hymans, Jacques. 2006. *The Psychology of Nuclear Proliferation. Identity, Emotions, and Foreign Policy* (Cambridge University Press: New York).

—. 2008. Assessing North Korean nuclear intentions and capacities: A new approach, *Journal of East Asian Studies* 8: 259–292.

Hymans, Jacques E.C. 2010. 'The arrival of psychological constructivism', *International Theory*, 2: 461–467.

Kaarbo, Juliet. 2003. 'Foreign policy analysis in the Twenty-First Century: Back to comparison, forward to identity and ideas', *International Studies Review*, 5: 156–202.

Krippendorff, Klaus. 2004. *Content Analysis: An Introduction to Its Methodology* (Sage: Thousand Oaks).

Kubalkova, Vendulka. 2001. *Foreign Policy in a Constructed World* (M.E. Sharpe: Armonk, New York).

Larson, Deborah Welch. 1988. Systems, Problems of Content Analysis in Foreign-Policy Research: Notes from the Study of the Origins of Cold War Belief, *International Studies Quarterly*, 32: 241–255.

Mayring, Philipp. 2000. 'Qualitative content analysis', *Forum: Qualitative Social Research*, 1: 365–380.

McClelland, Charles. 2006. World Event/Interaction Survey (WEIS) Project, 1966–1978. Inter-University Consortium for Political and Social Research https://doi.org/10.3886/ICPSR05211.

Neuendorf, Kimberly A. 2017. *The Content Analysis Guidebook* (Sage: Thousand Oaks).

Neuendorf, Kimberly A., and Paul D. Skalski. 2009. 'Quantitative Content Analysis and the Measurement of Collective Identity.' in Rawi Abdelal, Yoshiko M. Herrera, Alastair Iain Johnston and Rose McDermott (eds.), *Measuring Identity: A Guide for Social Scientists*, 203–236 (Cambridge University Press: Cambridge).

Oleinik, Anton. 2011. 'Mixing quantitative and qualitative content analysis: Triangulation at work', *Quality & Quantity*, 45: 859–873.

Pashakhanlou, Arash Heydarian. 2017. 'Fully integrated content analysis in International Relations', *International Relations*, 31: 447–465.

Potter, Philip B.K. 2017. 'Methods of Foreign Policy Analysis.' in Nukhet Sandal (ed.), *Oxford Research Encyclopedia of International Studies* (Oxford University Press: Oxford).

Riffe, Daniel, Stephen Lacy, and Frederick G. Fico. 2005. *Analyzing Media Messages: Using Quantitative Content Analysis in Research* (Lawrence Erlbaum Associates: Mahwah, New Jersey).

Sarkees, Meredith Reid, and Frank Wayman. 2010. "The Correlates of War Project: COW War Data, 1816 - 2007 (v4.0)." https://correlatesofwar.org/data-sets/COW-war.

Schafer, Mark, and Stephen G. Walker. 2021. *Operational Code Analysis and Foreign Policy Roles: Crossing Simon's Bridge* (Routledge: New York).

Schedler, Andreas, and Cas Mudde. 2010. 'Data usage in quantitative comparative politics', *Political Research Quarterly*, 63: 417–433.

Schreier, Margrit. 2012. *Qualitative Content Analysis in Practice* (Sage: London).

—. 2013. 'Qualitative Content Analysis.' in Uwe Flick (ed.), *The SAGE Handbook of Qualitative Data Analysis*, 170–183 (Sage: Los Angeles).

Schrodt, Philip A. 2008. "Kansas Event Data System (KEDS)", https://doi.org/10.7910/DVN/EXX5RM.

Shannon, Vaughn P., and Paul A. Kowert. 2012. *Psychology and Constructivism in International Relations: An Ideational Alliance* (The University of Michigan Press: Ann Arbor).

Thies, Cameron G., and Mark Nieman. 2017. *Rising Powers and Foreign Policy Revisionism: Understanding BRICS Identity and Behavior Through Time* (University of Michigan Press: Ann Arbor).

Vucetic, Srdjan. 2010. 'Identity and Foreign Policy', Oxford Bibliographies in International Relations, Accessed June 18. https://oxfordre.com/politics/view/10.1093/acrefore/9780190228637.001.0001/acrefore-9780190228637-e-435.

—. 2017. 'Identity and Foreign Policy', Oxford Research Encyclopedia of Politics, Accessed June 18. https://oxfordre.com/politics/view/10.1093/acrefore/9780190228637.001.0001/acrefore-9780190228637-e-435.

Walker, Stephen G, and Mark Schafer. 2018. 'Operational Code Theory: Beliefs and Foreign Policy Decisions.' *Oxford Research Encyclopedias*. https://oxfordre.com/internationalstudies/view/10.1093/acrefore/9780190846626.001.0001/acrefore-9780190846626-e-411.

Walker, S.G., M. Schafer, and M.D. Young. 1998. 'Systematic procedures for operational code analysis: measuring and modeling Jimmy Carter's operational code', *International Studies Quarterly*, 42: 175–189.

Walker, Stephen G., Mark Schafer and Gary Smith. 2018. 'The Operational Codes of Donald Trump and Hillary Clinton.' in Alex Mintz and Lesley Terris (eds.), *The Oxford Handbook of Behavioral Political Science*.

Weber, Robert P. 1990. *Basic Content Analysis* (Sage: Los Angeles).

White, Marilyn Domas, and Emily E. Marsh. 2006. 'Content analysis: A flexible methodology', *Library Trends*, 555: 22–45.

Zhang, Yan, and Barbara M. Wildemuth. 2009. 'Qualitative Analysis of Content.' in Barbara Wildemuth (ed.), *Applications of Social Research Methods to Questions in Information and Library Science* (Libraries Unlimited: Westport).

20
Statistical Analysis
Sibel Oktay

Introduction

Statistical analysis lies at the heart of all quantitative research, including in Foreign Policy Analysis (FPA). This approach allows us to investigate large swathes of numerical and comparable data points to detect patterns and trends across time and space, identify relationships between variables, and make predictions. Ranging from basic descriptive work that recounts frequencies to more sophisticated regression models, statistical methods in FPA offer a wide array of tools to study the relationships between leaders, domestic political factors, and systemic dynamics on one hand and the foreign policy tools, processes, and outputs of states on the other. In so doing, statistical analysis brings us closer to making lean and generalizable claims about the ways in which foreign policy is made and enacted by actors of interest and received by audiences both at home and abroad. Finally, statistical analysis presents researchers novel opportunities to construct and analyze original datasets, leading them to generate new knowledge in creative ways.

Although the early quantitative contributions to the FPA literature used simpler statistical tools (East 1973), regression analysis has become a go-to method in the field for analyzing large-N, observational data. While earlier contributions utilized ordinary least squares (OLS) models (Schafer and Crichlow 2002), more recent research also adopts models such as logit, probit, and multilevel models (Clare 2010; 2014; Oktay 2014), as well as time-series cross-section models such as error correction or interrupted time series (Kisangani and Pickering 2015; Greene and Licht 2018). The resurgence of experimental methods in FPA scholarship similarly demonstrates several ways in which statistical methods are utilized, ranging from the more straightforward significance tests to multiple linear and ordinal logistic regression models in order to determine the causal effect of treatments on outcome variables (Lupton 2020; Tomz, Weeks, and Yarhi-Milo 2020; Lin-Greenberg 2021; Bayram and Thomson 2021, see also Lupton and Webb in this volume).

In the remainder of this chapter, I focus on regression analysis to demonstrate how this method can be utilized in the study of foreign policy. In the next section, I start by providing an overview of the literature. I argue that statistical analysis was the primary method of choice in FPA when the field began to flourish in the early 1960s. I survey the trends in the field by discussing how regression analysis has been used widely across a range of research programs such as the domestic politics of foreign policy, economic sanctions, and foreign aid, among others. Next, I present a number of key terms and concepts to familiarize readers with the regression analysis method, as well as some *decision rules* that researchers of FPA should keep in mind as they design their own projects that call for this method, including multiple linear regression, logistic regression, and multilevel modeling. In the third section, I provide an empirical example of regression analysis that illustrates not just the strengths of the method but also how some of the decisions pertaining to research design could impact the results of the analysis. I conclude with a discussion of the pros and cons of regression analysis for studying foreign policy and offer some tips for success when using this method.

Literature Review

FPA takes an 'actor-centric' approach to studying international politics (Hudson and Vore 1995; Hudson 2005). Contrary to mainstream International Relations (IR) theories that black-box the states and treat them as 'billiard balls' that interact in response to the forces that operate above and beyond them at the systemic level, FPA theorizes at the level of the decision itself. Explaining foreign policy processes and outputs, according to this view, should start with a focus on the individual decision-makers, the groups and organizations around them, and the domestic political factors that shape their constraints and opportunity structures as they make and enact these policies, in addition to international systemic factors.

This approach is encapsulated by what James Rosenau (1966) calls "middle-range" theorizing in FPA, juxtaposing the merits of FPA to the grand theories of IR. Importantly, mid-range theorizing can "tease out cross-nationally applicable generalizations about the foreign policy behavior of states in a systematic and scientific fashion" while developing explanations that span multiple levels of analysis (e.g., individual, domestic, as well as international systemic) and engage multiple causal pathways (Hudson and Vore 1995, 212–213). Doing so facilitates the emergence of a cumulative body of scientific knowledge about how and why states act the way they do at the international level.

It is hardly a coincidence that mid-range theorizing in foreign policy took off at the same time as the behavioral revolution was taking over the social sciences. Could we study human behavior and social phenomena the way we study natural phenomena in other disciplines—through an unbiased and objective observation of data? If we could study the behaviors of atoms, plants, and insects objectively, perhaps we could also study the behaviors of voters, leaders, and states in a similar fashion. We could collect information on how people vote, how leaders speak, and how states act at the international level. We could then investigate these data points over time and across the world, and against other variables at the individual, state, and international levels, to detect patterns of behavior in foreign affairs.

Comparative Foreign Policy was "the first major phase of FPA research that emerged from this crucible" that brought together an actor-centric approach to studying IR in an era of behavioral social science (Potter 2017, 3). Comparative Foreign Policy scholars had three key goals: (a) systematic and parsimonious investigation of foreign policy that leads to (b) generalizations (c) across national and temporal contexts. Statistical analysis, therefore, was a natural fit for this endeavor. As Potter (2017, 2) points out, "from its inception, FPA was an explicitly theoretical exercise aimed at uncovering the systematic elements of foreign policy interactions, and the methods deployed reflected this." Earlier work on foreign policy events datasets (see also Raleigh and Kishi in this volume) and subsequent analyses that used these datasets invariably relied on statistical methods to engage in exploratory work as well as hypothesis testing (Hermann et al. 1973; McClelland 1978; Azar 1980; Schrodt 1995).

Today, foreign policy scholarship frequently employs statistical analysis across a variety of research programs. Researchers who study the domestic politics of foreign policy using quantitative methods regress the characteristics of foreign policy behavior on a range of domestic institutional factors, including the parliamentary seat share of or the number of parties in government and its ideological composition in order to test the extent to which these variables explain extremity, commitment intensity, cooperation, or conflict (Prins and Sprecher 1999; Ireland and Gartner 2001; Leblang and Chan 2003; Palmer, London, and Regan 2004; Kaarbo and Beasley 2008; Clare 2010; Kaarbo 2012; Beasley and Kaarbo 2014; Oktay 2014; for a review, see Oktay and Beasley 2017). Others utilize statistical analysis to assess the role of national parliaments on military deployment decisions (Ostermann et al. 2021). Most recently, a burgeoning literature uses statistical methods to study the impact of political parties in foreign policy processes and outcomes and, in return, how foreign policy influences support for political parties (Wagner et al. 2017, 2018; Oktay 2018; Coticchia and Vignoli 2020; Haesebrouck and Mello 2020; Hofmann and Martill 2021; Onderco and Joosen 2021).

The FPA literature on economic sanctions also frequently uses statistical analysis (for a review of this literature, see Peksen 2019). This scholarship focuses, among other puzzles, on the impact of sanctions as a specific type of foreign policy tool on a variety of outcomes such as media freedom and human rights (Peksen 2009; Peksen, Peterson, and Drury 2014), the conditions under which target countries may respond to sanctions with counter-sanctions (Peksen and Jeong 2021), and how third-party sanctions-busters can mitigate the effectiveness of economic sanctions (Early 2011), testing their expectations using regression analysis.

Studies on foreign aid similarly utilize regression analysis as a key method (for a review, see Apodaca 2017). Greene and Licht (2018) test their "partisan theory of aid allocation," which claims that party ideology influences policy preferences over foreign aid distribution, by utilizing a large-N dataset of aid activity (Tierney et al. 2011) and using error correction models that take into account the time-series cross-sectional nature of their data. Kisangani and Pickering (2015, 221) use interrupted time-series models to demonstrate how a "discrete" event such as military intervention can have both short-term and long-term impacts on the state's "continuous" foreign policy behavior such as foreign aid allocation. The authors show that military intervention by a member of the OECD's Development Assistance Committee leads to both a short-term increase and a long-term upward trend in the amount of foreign aid that this member gives to the target state (Kisangani and Pickering 2015).

In addition to these research programs, recent studies at the intersection of leadership and foreign policy have increasingly been using regression analysis to assess the independent effect of leadership traits (see also Brummer in this volume) on foreign policy behavior, as well as to investigate whether these traits moderate existing relationships between institutions and foreign policy outcomes (Foster and Keller 2014; Keller and Foster 2016; Foster and Keller 2020; Arana Araya 2021). In sum, empirical research in FPA frequently employs regression analysis as a key method to investigate observational data. In the next section, I provide a brief introduction to this method. I explain what it is and how it analyzes data, the key terms and concepts that are associated with regressions, as well as the method's key assumptions.

Key Terms and Concepts

As a statistical estimation method, regression modeling explains phenomena by answering the following question: what is the predicted relationship between a dependent variable (DV) and an independent variable(s) (IV)? Does a change in the independent variable(s) account for the change in the dependent variable (Lewis-Beck 2004)? Regression models are mathematical equations, whereby "a dependent variable, commonly labeled Y, is a function of one or more independent variables, commonly labeled x_1, x_2, and so on" (Lewis-Beck 2004). Based on this general definition, researchers who plan to employ statistical analysis, and in particular regression analysis, should have a good understanding of the following concepts and terms.[1]

Independent variable: Regardless of which methodology we use, the goal of empirical analysis is to explain the relationship between two or more variables. Of these, the independent variables capture the factors that we expect to influence the outcome of interest. In statistical analysis, independent variables are represented by the *x* notation.

Dependent variable: The dependent variable, also known as the outcome variable or the outcome of interest, is the variable whose values are expected to be influenced by the variation in the independent variable. The dependent variable is represented by the *y* notation.

Unit of analysis: The unit of analysis is the basic element that we analyze in a study. In statistical analysis, the unit of analysis is the element that occupies the rows of a spreadsheet (and columns generally represent the variables). For example, in a study that investigates the relationship between government type and foreign policy behavior using foreign policy events data, the events constitute the unit of analysis. If the study focuses on the relationship between gender (independent variable) and parliamentary voting behavior on a specific military deployment proposal (dependent variable) at the level of the members of the parliament (MP), then the unit of analysis would be the individual MPs. Regression analysis requires enough observations (N) relative to the number of independent variables to achieve enough degrees of freedom for parameter estimation.[2] A general rule of thumb is to include a minimum 10–20 observations in the dataset per independent variable that is entailed in the model (Harrell 2015).

Null hypothesis: The null hypothesis assumes that there exists no relationship between our dependent variable and our key independent variable of interest. Regression analysis allows us to test whether we can reject the null (and therefore find support for our hypothesis) or fail to reject the null (and therefore fail to find support for our hypothesis).

Regression model: The regression model is an equation that serves as an abstraction of the relationship that we hypothesize to observe in the data. It includes the dependent variable on one side of the equation and the independent variables on the other side. A linear regression model is often captured by an equation that looks like the following: $y = a + b_1x_1 + b_2x_2 + \ldots + b_nx_n + e$, where y is the dependent variable, $x_1 \ldots x_n$ are the independent variables, and e is the error term.

Model intercept, coefficients, and the error term: In the equation above, the intercept, a, captures the expected value of the dependent variable when all other independent variables assume a value of 0. Each coefficient, $b_1 \ldots b_n$, reports the size of the effect on y that a unit increase in each independent variable $x_1 \ldots x_n$ is associated with. The error term in the model, represented by e, captures all other variation in the dependent variable that is not accounted for by the model's independent variables (Gujarati 2004).

Ordinary Least Squares: OLS is a regression estimation method that fits a linear relationship between the independent and dependent variables by minimizing the sum of the squared difference between the actual and the predicted value of the dependent variable (Wood and Park 2004). In other words, OLS predicts the relationship between the independent and dependent variables to be linear (as opposed to, say, curvilinear). It does so by fitting a line to the data such that the total sum of the squared distances between the line (i.e., the predicted value of the dependent variable) and each data point (e.g., the true value of the dependent variable) is minimized. (We take the squared sum of distances since some data points might fall below the regression line and some might be above it.) The slope of the fitted regression line gives us the regression coefficient, which captures the strength (size) and direction (positive or negative sign) of the relationship.

Multiple Linear Regression: Estimates the relationship between one dependent variable and two or more independent variables.

Interaction effect: In many instances, our theoretical models imply that a second independent variable influences the relationship between an independent and dependent variable. For example, the effect of coalition governments on foreign policy might be *further* altered by the degree of ideological cohesiveness inside the coalition (Oktay 2022). This relationship is conceptualized as the 'interaction effect.' In mathematical representation, this relationship calls for an interaction term in the regression model. The model with an interaction term would look like the following: $y = a + b_1 x_1 + b_2 x_2 + b_3 (x_1 \times x_2) + \ldots + b_n x_n + e$, where b_3 is the coefficient of the interaction effect. The interaction effect manipulates the slope of the regression model, therefore changing the strength of the relationship between the independent and dependent variables (for a different perspective on interaction and conjunctural causation, see also Mello in this volume).

Standard error (of the coefficient): Often included alongside the coefficient in a regression output, the standard error measures how dispersed the actual values are from the predicted value calculated by the regression model (we call this a regression line, since the model fits a linear relationship between the DV and the IVs). The smaller the standard error, the more concentrated the actual values are around the regression line, which suggests that the predicted relationship closely resembles the actual relationship between the variables (Little 2004). The bigger the standard error, the less so. The standard error of the coefficient is also used to calculate the confidence interval.

Confidence interval: Broadly speaking, the confidence interval is the range of predicted values that we think the true value of a parameter falls within. For example, we could say that the average age of a college freshman in the U.S. is 20 and that most college freshmen would be somewhere between 18 and 27 years old. That does not mean that there are college students who are younger than 18 or older than 27, but that it is quite probable that most students would still fall within this range in the U.S.

Similarly, in regression analysis we are interested in the confidence interval around a coefficient estimate since our goal is to find out whether there is a relationship between the dependent and independent variable (e.g., a coefficient that is different than zero), and, how similar the predicted relationship is to the actual relationship. Conventionally, we use 95% or 99% probability as our benchmark to construct the confidence interval. For example, imagine that the 95% confidence interval for a regression coefficient is [−0.324, 0.156]. Looking at this result, we would conclude that the true value of the coefficient between these variables would fall somewhere within this range 95% of the time. However, note that this interval includes zero. Having zero within the confidence interval suggests that *no relationship* is within the realm of possibility 95% of the time. (In other words, we cannot reject the null hypothesis.) The confidence interval, therefore, gives us a broader sense of the predicted relationship between the independent and dependent variable. The smaller the standard error relative to the coefficient estimate, the narrower the confidence interval. Therefore, the confidence interval also tells us how precisely the predicted relationship captures the true relationship (see also Smithson 2004).

P-value: The coefficient divided by its standard error gives the *t* statistic, which is used to find the p-value. The p-value denotes "the probability, calculated under the assumption that the null hypothesis is true, of obtaining a sample result as extreme as, or more extreme than, that observed in a particular direction" (Gibbons 2004). In other words, the p-value tells us the probability that the relationship predicted by the regression is due to random chance. The smaller the p-value of a coefficient (conventionally smaller than 0.05, 0.01, or 0.001), the more confidently we can claim that the size and direction (positive or negative) of the predicted relationship is not due to chance. The p-value helps us conclude whether the relationship is statistically significant.

Statistical significance: This notion captures how meaningful the predicted relationship is from a statistical standpoint. Statistical significance tells us that the coefficient estimate is statistically different from zero, allowing us to conclude that there does exist a relationship between the independent and dependent variables. Conventionally, coefficients with p-values that are smaller than 0.05 are considered statistically significant. This is different from *substantive significance*, which has to do with the size of the coefficient. It may well be that a coefficient is statistically significant but substantively not. In the absence of substantive significance, a unit change in the independent variable does not have a notable impact on the dependent variable.

P-hacking: This term describes the practice of 'torturing the data' using various measurement and estimation strategies to generate statistically significant results with p-values that are smaller than 0.05. Scholars may adopt this behavior in response to the perverse incentive structures in academic publishing, where null results are often deemed unworthy of making a contribution to scientific knowledge and therefore not published. For this reason, in a 2019 piece published in the journal *Nature* some 800 researchers from various disciplines have called for "retiring statistical significance" in favor of more nuanced interpretations of results (Amrhein et al. 2019). These include focusing on confidence intervals and pre-registering the study to prevent post-test manipulation of analyses, among others (Jacobs et al. 2020).

R-squared: Reported in the output of linear regression analysis, the R-squared provides the percentage of the variation in the dependent variable that is explained by the model. For instance, if the R-squared of the regression model *DefenseSpending* = $a + b_1 LeaderAge + b_2 LeaderGender + e$ returns an R-squared value of 0.5, then we can conclude that 50% of the variation in defense spending in our dataset is explained by just two independent variables, the age of the leader and their gender. In other words, R-squared is a measure of the model's goodness-of-fit. The value of the R-squared increases when the number of independent variables in the model increases. The *adjusted R-squared* accounts for the size of the dataset as well as the number of variables in the model and thus reports a better goodness-of-fit measure. The R-squared is a contentious measure among methodologists, however, since its size does not always provide a thorough sense of model fit (Nau n.d.).

Methodological Assumptions

After having clarified these key terms, it is important to identify some of the core assumptions that multiple linear regression rests on. First, this method assumes that the observations are independent of each other. In other words, the value of an observation is not influenced by the value of another observation. Second, the method assumes that the relationship between the dependent and independent variables is linear. Students must beware of fitting a linear model to estimate a nonlinear relationship for this reason. An easy way to detect the linearity of the relationship is to visualize it by building a simple scatterplot graph that plots the independent variable on the x-axis and the dependent variable on the y-axis. Third, multiple linear regression assumes that the residuals (i.e., the differences between the observed values in the sample and the model's predicted values) are normally distributed. Fourth, we assume that *multicollinearity* does not exist; in other words, independent variables are not strongly correlated with each other (Tacq 2004). (Building a correlation matrix of the independent variables should help detect multicollinearity.) Finally, we assume *homoskedasticity*, which means that the residuals are not correlated with the independent variables (Lewis-Beck 2004; Nau n.d.). In other words, the variance of the error terms should be constant. Otherwise, we would observe *heteroskedasticity*, which means that the variance of the error term is non-uniform at different levels of the independent variable. OLS regression, which fits a linear line to minimize the sum of squared errors, would therefore not be the best estimator when there is heteroskedasticity (Pollins 2004).

In addition to multiple linear regression, two other statistical estimation techniques are also frequently used in FPA research. These include logistic regression and multilevel regression.

Logistic Regression: This modeling technique is "the standard way to model binary outcomes (that is, data y_i that take on the values 0 or 1)" (Gelman and Hill 2006, 79). Logistic regression is used in FPA research that focuses on binary outcomes such as dispute initiation or voting behavior (Clare 2010; Oktay 2018). It fits a non-linear, logistic function to estimate the relationship between the dependent and independent variables.

Multilevel Regression: Most of the studies mentioned in the previous sections (with the exception of Oktay 2014; Oktay 2022) utilize pooled regression models. Pooled modeling carries an *a priori* assumption about the nature of the data; specifically, that the predicted relationship between the variables is uniform regardless of the contexts that the datapoints are drawn from. Take foreign policy events datasets, such as WEIS (McClelland 1978). These datasets compile events from across dozens of countries. In other words, these events are naturally grouped by the countries that initiate them. As a result, the events that are drawn from the same country (or even government) context might also be correlated due to various underlying reasons that are specific to that context (this is known as intra-class correlation). This would violate the OLS assumptions for linear models and may lead to biased results. Moreover, no-pooled analyses may be erroneous when sample sizes vary dramatically across groups (such as the countries in WEIS, see Gelman and Hill 2006, 8).

One solution to mitigate these pitfalls is to run no-pooled analyses by including group indicators into the models (such as country dummies when using WEIS). However, doing so forces us to exclude from the model any group-level (in this case, country-level) variables to avoid multicollinearity (Steenbergen and Jones 2002). For example, if we include country dummies in a model that investigates the WEIS data and takes events as the unit of analysis, then we cannot use the Composite Index of National Capabilities (CINC) score as an independent variable since these scores are country-level variables (Singer, Bremer, and Stuckey 1972; Singer 1988; Oktay 2022).

This is exactly where multilevel modeling helps foreign policy analysts conducting large-N statistical analysis. Rather than having to choose either a complete-pooling or no-pooling model, multilevel modeling uses partial pooling. This method relaxes the assumption that the relationship between the independent and dependent variables is constant across the different contexts that they exist in. It helps account for contextual variation (Steenbergen and Jones 2002). It allows researchers to include group-level variables in the model (such as countries and governments if the observations are foreign policy events) without committing multicollinearity. It also works better for datasets which have variation in group sample sizes (Gelman and Hill 2006, 254), which those of us working with foreign policy events datasets often must deal with. Indeed, these datasets often include more data points from great powers compared with middle or small powers, a bias that is caused by the reporting choices of media outlets from which we derive events datasets (Oktay 2022).

Empirical Illustration

Let's see regression analysis at work using a brief example that investigates the factors that shape U.S. foreign policy elites' attitudes toward international organizations.

An important question in foreign policy research concerns how individual-level factors such as gender (Bendix and Jeong 2020; Schwartz and Blair 2020), schooling (Dreher and Yu 2020), or military experience (Horowitz, Stam, and Ellis 2015) shape leaders' political attitudes and behavior (Gift and Krcmaric 2017; Grewal 2020; Krcmaric, Nelson, and Roberts 2020). More recent studies focus on international organizations as a specific context where leaders' attitudes matter (Gaxie and Hubé 2012; Dellmuth et al. 2021). To the extent that international organizations enjoy legitimacy as long as national leaders consider them to be legitimate, it is important for foreign policy scholars to identify if individual-level factors shape their attitudes toward these actors.

How about those who constitute the leader's inner circle? Do similar individual-level factors also shape the attitudes of legislative staffers, executive branch officials, think-tank leaders, and influential scholars toward international organizations? For example, in the United States, these foreign policy elites have the ears of key foreign policy decision-makers in Congress and the White House. If who they are shapes what they think about international organizations, then how they think could impact how they advise the leaders, thereby shaping how the U.S. engages with these organizations.

Scholars who focus on the influence of gender in foreign policy find that that women favor "communal" efforts over individualism and often have more dovish policy preferences than men (Post and Sen 2020; Bendix and Jeong 2020). If this is true, then women may favor international organizations more than men since, by definition, IOs operate based on cooperation toward facilitating peaceful outcomes between nations. Therefore, I expect U.S. foreign policy elites who identify as female to have greater support for IOs (H1).

The literature also suggests that leaders with military experience are less supportive of militaristic solutions to international disputes (Horowitz and Stam 2014). Having seen the devastation of war, these leaders may thus favor diplomatic solutions to international crises—precisely where we expect IOs to play a critical role. Therefore, I hypothesize that U.S. foreign policy elites with military experience should be more supportive of IOs (H2).

Between 2020 and 2021, we fielded a survey among U.S. foreign policy elites working in Congress, the executive branch, U.S. foreign policy think-tanks, and international relations departments across top U.S. colleges and universities to learn about their attitudes and opinions about a range of international affairs issues (Oktay et al. 2021). The survey generated nearly 600 responses. In what follows, I use this dataset to test whether the respondents' gender and military experience influence their attitudes toward the United Nations (UN), a key international organization that champions human rights, collective security, and diplomacy.

The dependent variable (DV) is *support for the UN*. I code this variable using the survey question "How much confidence do you have in the United Nations?" I assume that having confidence in the UN is a good proxy for capturing the respondent's support for this institution. The response values vary from 1 (not at all confident) to 5 (very confident). I regress the dependent variable on two key independent variables: being female and having military experience. The variable *female* assumes 1 for female, 0 for male. There are six respondents who did not identify themselves with either gender category. For the purposes of this analysis, I code those responses as missing data. The variable *military experience* assumes 1 for respondents who reported that they had served in the military, 0 for those with no military experience.

Attitudes toward the UN may be influenced by some other covariates. In particular, the respondent's political ideology and age might very well influence their attitudes toward the UN. Existing research shows that support for international organizations like the UN decreases as we move along the political spectrum from left to right (Busby et al. 2020). The variable *ideology* assumes 1 for Democrat, 2 for Independent, and 3 for Republican to measure the respondent's ideology. I code non-US citizens and 'others' in the sample that have been interviewed as missing. Older respondents might be more supportive of the UN, having lived long enough to observe the role of the UN in maintaining global security and peace on several occasions in the post-war era. The variable *age* ranges from 1 (18–29) to 5 (75+). I add *age* and *ideology* as control variables in the model, since I anticipate that these variables could also influence support for the UN and therefore should be accounted for in my model to demonstrate the independent effect of my key independent variables, *female* and *military experience*. I estimate the model using OLS regression because the dependent variable is continuous, and I want to fit a linear relationship. Table 20.1 presents the results.

The table reports the model intercept (Constant), the coefficients of each predictor in the model along with their standard errors in parentheses, the number of observations included in the analysis, and the legend that explains the statistical significance levels of the coefficients denoted by the asterisks. The model intercept captures the value of the dependent variable if all independent variables assume a value of zero. Conventionally, we do not interpret the model intercept since a meaningful value of zero may not exist for all independent variables in the model. In Table 20.1, for instance, the *Ideology* variable cannot assume a value of zero.

Now let's turn to interpreting the results. The findings suggest that women have a positive and statistically significant impact on elite support for the UN. Female respondents are more supportive toward the UN than male respondents. H1 is supported. Military experience, however, is not a statistically significant predictor of elite attitudes toward the UN.

Table 20.1 Do Gender and Military Experience Influence Support for the UN?

	OLS Model
Female (1: Female, 0: Male)	0.246*
	(0.095)
Military experience (1: Yes, 0: No)	−0.162
	(0.111)
Ideology (1: Dem, 2: Ind, 3: Rep)	−0.206**
	(0.064)
Age	−0.012
	(0.038)
Constant	3.149***
	(0.162)
N	482

Standard errors in parentheses.
*p < 0.05, **p < 0.01, ***p < 0.001

Therefore, H2 fails to receive support. Not surprisingly, political ideology of the respondent is a statistically significant predictor of UN support. As we move from the left to the right along the political spectrum, elite support for the UN decreases. Age, on the other hand, has no impact on how our respondents feel about the UN.

This is a preliminary analysis. The model needs further adjustments to ensure that the results are not biased. Potentially the most critical source of bias is the disconnect between the nature of the dependent variable and the estimation method we have used (for a useful discussion, see Potter 2017). OLS works best with continuous dependent variables that are measured at the interval-level. In other words, we want the dependent variable to have a meaningful zero and equal intervals between its units. In our example, the dependent variable is measured using a Likert scale, with response categories ranging from 1 to 5. One could argue that even though the scale looks like an interval-level variable (which is what I assumed to produce the results in Table 20.1), we cannot be sure that the distance between "not at all confident" (1) and "somewhat unconfident" (2) is equal to the distance between "somewhat unconfident" (2) and "neutral" (3), and so on. Even though the ascending order of these categories makes sense, in other words, we do not know how the respondent thinks about the distance between each pair.

Using ordered logistic regression instead of OLS would remedy this problem. The ordered logistic regression takes the dependent variable for what it really is—an 'ordinal-level' variable with ordered categories rather than an interval-level variable (like, say, the respondent's height or salary). The estimation method we choose to test the model must suit the nature of the dependent variable. Let's do a robustness check of our original findings by running the

Table 20.2 Do Gender and Military Experience Influence Support for the UN? Results from Ordinal Logit Regression

	Ordinal Logit Model
Female	0.497*
	(0.205)
Military experience (1: Yes, 0: No)	−0.319
	(0.243)
Ideology (1: Dem, 2: Ind, 3: Rep)	−0.482***
	(0.142)
Age	−0.005
	(0.083)
cut1	−3.669***
	(0.414)
cut2	−1.310***
	(0.360)
cut3	0.724*
	(0.359)
cut4	3.022***
	(0.440)
N	482

Standard errors in parentheses.
*p < 0.05, **p < 0.01, ***p < 0.001

same model using ordered logistic (also called 'ordinal logit') regression. Will our conclusions from Table 20.1 still hold? Check out Table 20.2.

Table 20.2 reports the results from the ordinal logit estimation of the same model. The coefficients have the same sign and significance levels as Table 20.1. *Female* is still a positive and significant predictor, *military experience* still has no significant effect, and identifying as right-wing still negatively impacts UN support.

So far, we can see that the relationships echo those in Table 20.1. However, ordinal logit coefficients are more complicated to interpret than OLS coefficients, since they report the ordered log-odds coefficients.[3] Looking at Table 20.2, we can say that being female leads to a 0.5 increase in the log-odds of being in a higher response category of 'UN support,' while holding all the other variables constant.[4]

Obviously, this interpretation is not intuitive. When we run logistic regression models, we often rely on predicted probabilities as a post-estimation technique to interpret the results. And when we run ordinal logistic regression, we use the cutoff points reported in Table 20.2 (e.g., cut1, cut2, cut3, cut4) to compute the predicted probability of observing each level of the dependent variable given a change in the independent variable. Put differently, then, predicted probabilities capture the marginal effect of a unit change in the independent variable on the likelihood of observing a change in the dependent variable. Figure 20.1 below uses the results from Table 20.2 and reports how being male or female changes the predicted probability of being in a specific category of *UN support*.

Figure 20.1 reports the change in the predicted probability of being in a specific category of *UN support* at different values of *female*, when all other variables in the model (age, military experience) are kept at their mean values. Remember that OLS predicts a linear

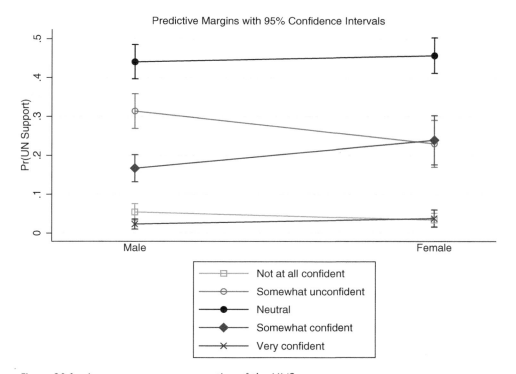

Figure 20.1 Are women more supportive of the UN?

relationship and assumes that as we move from 0 to 1 on the *female* variable, support for the UN uniformly increases. Figure 20.1 shows that the relationship is a little more complicated (and interesting!) than that. First of all, it shows that regardless of gender, respondents are most likely to have a neutral opinion toward the UN (the top line on Figure 20.1). In fact, we could verify this by simply tabulating *UN support*. Most folks in our sample are neutral toward the UN (225 out of 523), while very few respondents are either very confident (15) or not at all confident (28).

Now let's look more closely at Figure 20.1 to see the nuanced relationship between *gender* and *UN support*. The lines with the hollow square and circle markers denote the probability of the lowest categories of *UN support*, namely "not at all confident" and "somewhat unconfident," respectively. These lines show that the probability of being in these categories of opinions toward the UN *decreases* when the respondent is a woman. Meanwhile, the probability of having a "neutral," "somewhat confident," or "very confident" opinion toward the UN increases when the respondent is a woman. So indeed, we find that support for the UN does increase among U.S. foreign policy elites who identify as female. However, this support is not uniform at different response categories of our *UN support* variable. The likelihood of being somewhat unconfident of the UN goes from about 31% to 24% as we shift from men to women (a 7-point decline). Meanwhile, the likelihood of being "not at all confident" decreases from about 6% for men to 5% for women (a 1-point decline). Ordinal logit helps us identify these nuances.

To be sure, there are various ways in which this analysis can be improved. The marginal effects reported in Figure 20.1 were computed while keeping all other variables in the model at their mean values. This is a standard procedure to control for the other variables in the model and extract the predicted effect of the key variable of interest on the dependent variable. However, not all independent variables in our model have meaningful means, such as *Military experience* (it's either 0 or 1). When controlling for categorical independent variables at the post-estimation stage, we could use their modal value (instead of mean value) to generate even more meaningful results.

More significant improvements to the analysis can be made by asking what other factors (i.e., independent variables) might influence UN support (i.e., the dependent variable). Another potential explanation for *UN support* among our respondents is their profession: whether they are working for a government agency or Congress, a foreign policy think-tank, or in the academy could potentially have an independent effect on how they view the UN. Moving forward, we can add *profession* to the model as an independent variable to see whether our key variable of interest, *female*, remains a significant explanation of these elites' attitudes toward the UN. Indeed, it is important to highlight that our theoretical reasoning should always precede the data analysis. Why we are focusing on a specific independent variable, or variables, to explain the change in the dependent variable is a key question that shapes our research design strategy. After all, statistical methods such as regression analysis are tools for us to investigate the data.

Conclusion

Statistical methods are widely used in FPA—and researchers will no doubt continue to rely on them in the future. Methods like regression analysis are valuable as they provide insights that are lean, generalizable, easily visualizable, and multi-factorial. They offer us 'big picture' conclusions about why elites, masses, and institutions think and act the way they do in the foreign policy domain. Statistical methods allow us to test our theories across time and space using large spreadsheets of data and a few dozen lines of computer code.

Despite its many merits, statistical analysis in foreign policy also comes with its own warnings and pitfalls. First and foremost, statistical methods assume that the phenomena we intend to study are sufficiently quantifiable. Naturally, then, how we conceptualize, operationalize, and quantify these phenomena becomes directly consequential for testing our theories and generating findings. In the empirical illustration above, I assumed 'confidence' in the UN to proxy 'support for the UN.' Some might theoretically disagree with that assumption. That assumption has inevitably shaped my model and the results I have received. Researchers should therefore be intentional about establishing their decision rules pertaining to the operationalization and quantitative measurement of their variables. These decisions, made at the design stage of the research process, impact the availability, granularity, and comparability of the data as well as the findings.

Second, it must be noted that the generalizable quantitative findings that we retrieve using statistical analysis almost invariably come at the expense of nuance and in-depth contextual information that qualitative analysis provides. This is another reason why the deployment of fundamentally qualitative concepts (e.g., leadership, personality, foreign policy behavior, role conception, party ideology, or parliamentary procedure, to name a few) toward statistical analysis always starts with their thoughtful operationalization and measurement, but also followed by a strong understanding of the nature and shape of the data. Although capturing the substantive context in which foreign policy takes place might be challenging in quantitative studies, statistical techniques such as multilevel modeling offer useful solutions by accounting for the nested nature of the data that we often deal with in this subfield.

Acknowledgments

The author would like to thank Matthew Geras, Beyza Buyuker, Falk Ostermann, and Patrick Mello for their very helpful comments and suggestions.

Notes

1 For more tips and training on statistical analysis, I highly recommend Oscar Torres-Reyna's and Robert Nau's online manuals, available on their Princeton University and Duke University websites, respectively. Torres-Reyna: https://www.princeton.edu/~otorres/Stata/statnotes Nau: https://people.duke.edu/~rnau/411home.htm. I relied on these sources, among others cited in this chapter, while working on this chapter.
2 For an explanation of degrees of freedom in statistical analysis, see Lewis-Beck (2004).
3 The function that undergirds logistic regression is the natural logarithm of the odds ratio. For an explanation of the odds ratio and the logistic function, see the UCLA Statistical Consulting website (https://stats.oarc.ucla.edu/stata/faq/how-do-i-interpret-odds-ratios-in-logistic-regression/) as well as Han and Swicegood (2004).
4 The UCLA Institute for Digital Research and Education's Statistical Consulting website is an incredibly useful resource for both beginners and seasoned users of statistical methods. I used this website frequently in the making of this chapter, and, in particular, the ordinal logit test of the empirical example. https://stats.idre.ucla.edu/stata/dae/ordered-logistic-regression/.

References

Amrhein, Valentin, Sander Greenland, and Blake McShane. 2019. "Scientists Rise Up Against Statistical Significance." *Nature* 567: 305–307.
Apodaca, Clair. 2017. "Foreign Aid as Foreign Policy Tool." Oxford Research Encyclopedia of Politics. April 26, 2017. https://doi.org/10.1093/acrefore/9780190228637.013.332.
Arana Araya, Ignacio. 2021. "The Personalities of Presidents as Independent Variables." *Political Psychology* 42 (4): 695–712. https://doi.org/10.1111/pops.12722.

Azar, E.E. 1980. "The Conflict and Peace Data Bank (COPDAB) Project." *Journal of Conflict Resolution* 24 (1): 143–152.

Bayram, A Burcu, and Catarina P Thomson. 2021. "Ignoring the Messenger? Limits of Populist Rhetoric on Public Support for Foreign Development Aid." *International Studies Quarterly*, June, sqab041. https://doi.org/10.1093/isq/sqab041.

Beasley, R.K., and J. Kaarbo. 2014. "Explaining Extremity in the Foreign Policies of Parliamentary Democracies." *International Studies Quarterly* 58 (4): 729–740.

Bendix, William, and Gyung-Ho Jeong. 2020. "Gender and Foreign Policy: Are Female Members of Congress More Dovish than Their Male Colleagues?" *Political Research Quarterly* 73 (1): 126–140.

Busby, Joshua, Craig Kafura, Jonathan Monten, and Jordan Tama. 2020. "Multilateralism and the Use of Force: Experimental Evidence on the Views of Foreign Policy Elites." *Foreign Policy Analysis* 16 (1): 118–129.

Clare, J. 2010. "Ideological Fractionalization and the International Conflict Behavior of Parliamentary Democracies." *International Studies Quarterly* 54 (4): 965–987.

———. 2014. "Hawks, Doves, and International Cooperation." *Journal of Conflict Resolution* 58 (7): 1311–1337.

Coticchia, Fabrizio, and Valerio Vignoli. 2020. "Italian Political Parties and Military Operations: An Empirical Analysis on Voting Patterns." *Government and Opposition* 55 (3): 456–473. https://doi.org/10.1017/gov.2018.35.

Dellmuth, Lisa, Jan Aart Scholte, Jonas Tallberg, and Soetkin Verhaegen. 2021. "The Elite–Citizen Gap in International Organization Legitimacy." *American Political Science Review*, 1–18. https://doi.org/10.1017/S0003055421000824.

Dreher, Axel, and Shu Yu. 2020. "The Alma Mater Effect: Does Foreign Education of Political Leaders Influence UNGA Voting?" *Public Choice* 185 (1): 45–64.

Early, Bryan R. 2011. "Unmasking the Black Knights: Sanctions Busters and Their Effects on the Success of Economic Sanctions." *Foreign Policy Analysis* 7 (4): 381–402.

East, Maurice A. 1973. "Size and Foreign Policy Behavior: A Test of Two Models." *World Politics* 25 (4): 556–576. https://doi.org/10.2307/2009952.

Foster, Dennis M., and Jonathan W. Keller. 2014. "Leaders' Cognitive Complexity, Distrust, and the Diversionary Use of Force." *Foreign Policy Analysis* 10 (3): 205–223. https://doi.org/10.1111/fpa.12019.

———. 2020. "Single-Party Government, Prime Minister Psychology, and the Diversionary Use of Force: Theory and Evidence from the British Case." *International Interactions* 46 (2): 227–250. https://doi.org/10.1080/03050629.2020.1708741.

Gaxie, Daniel, and Nicolas Hubé. 2012. "Elites' Views on European Institutions: National Experiences Sifted through Ideological Orientations." In *The Europe of Elites*. Oxford: Oxford University Press. https://doi.org/10.1093/acprof:oso/9780199602315.003.0006.

Gelman, Andrew, and Jennifer Hill. 2006. *Data Analysis Using Regression and Multilevel/Hierarchical Models*. Cambridge: Cambridge University Press.

Gibbons, J. D. 2004. P Value, in Lewis-Beck, M.S., Bryman, A., & Liao, T.F., ed. *The SAGE Encyclopedia of Social Science Research Methods*. Sage Publications. Credo Reference: https://search.credoreference.com/content/entry/sagessrm/p_value/0?institutionId=3798

Gift, Thomas, and Daniel Krcmaric. 2017. "Who Democratizes? Western-Educated Leaders and Regime Transitions." *Journal of Conflict Resolution* 61 (3): 671–701.

Greene, Zachary D., and Amanda A. Licht. 2018. "Domestic Politics and Changes in Foreign Aid Allocation: The Role of Party Preferences." *Political Research Quarterly* 71 (2): 284–301. https://doi.org/10.1177/1065912917735176.

Grewal, Sharan. 2020. "From Islamists to Muslim Democrats: The Case of Tunisia's Ennahda." *American Political Science Review* 114 (2): 519–535. https://doi.org/10.1017/S0003055419000819.

Gujarati, D. N. 2004. Error, in Lewis-Beck, M.S., Bryman, A., & Liao, T.F., ed. *The SAGE Encyclopedia of Social Science Research Methods*. Sage Publications. Credo Reference: https://search.credoreference.com/content/entry/sagessrm/error/0?institutionId=3798

Haesebrouck, Tim, and Patrick A Mello. 2020. "Patterns of Political Ideology and Security Policy." *Foreign Policy Analysis* 16 (4): 565–586. https://doi.org/10.1093/fpa/oraa006.

Han, S., and Swicegood, C.G. 2004. Logistic Regression, in Lewis-Beck, M.S., Bryman, A., & Liao, T.F., ed. *The SAGE Encyclopedia of Social Science Research Methods*. Credo Reference: https://search.credoreference.com/content/entry/sagessrm/logistic_regression/0?institutionId=3798.

Harrell, Frank E. 2015. *Regression Modeling Strategies: With Applications to Linear Models, Logistic and Ordinal Regression, and Survival Analysis*. Vol. 3. London: Springer.

Hermann, C.F., M.A. East, M.G. Hermann, B.G. Salmore, and S.S. Salmore. 1973. *CREON, A Foreign Events Data Set*. Beverly Hills, CA: Sage.

Hofmann, Stephanie C, and Benjamin Martill. 2021. "The Party Scene: New Directions for Political Party Research in Foreign Policy Analysis." *International Affairs* 97 (2): 305–322. https://doi.org/10.1093/ia/iiaa165.

Horowitz, M.C., and A.C. Stam. 2014. "How Prior Military Experience Influences the Future Militarized Behavior of Leaders." *International Organization* 68: 527–559.

Horowitz, Michael C., Allan C. Stam, and Cali M. Ellis. 2015. *Why Leaders Fight*. Cambridge: Cambridge University Press.

Hudson, V.M., and C.S. Vore. 1995. "Foreign Policy Analysis Yesterday, Today, and Tomorrow." *Mershon International Studies Review* 39 (2): 209–238.

Hudson, V. M. (2005). "Foreign Policy Analysis: Actor-Specific Theory and the Ground of International Relations." *Foreign Policy Analysis*, 1 (1), 1–30.

Ireland, M.J., and S.S. Gartner. 2001. "Time to Fight Government Type and Conflict Initiation in Parliamentary Systems." *Journal of Conflict Resolution* 45 (5): 547–568.

Jacobs, Alan M., Colin Elman, John Gerring, and James Mahoney. 2020. "Pre-Registration and Results-Free Review in Observational and Qualitative Research." *The Production of Knowledge: Enhancing Progress in Social Science* (2020): 221–264.

Kaarbo, J. 2012. *Coalition Politics and Cabinet Decision Making: A Comparative Analysis of Foreign Policy Choices*. Ann Arbor, MI: University of Michigan Press.

Kaarbo, J., and R.K. Beasley. 2008. "Taking It to the Extreme: The Effect of Coalition Cabinets on Foreign Policy." *Foreign Policy Analysis* 4 (1): 67–81.

Keller, Jonathan W., and Dennis M. Foster. 2016. "Don't Tread on Me: Constraint-Challenging Presidents and Strategic Conflict Avoidance." *Presidential Studies Quarterly* 46 (4): 808–827. https://doi.org/10.1111/psq.12320.

Kisangani, Emizet F, and Jeffrey Pickering. 2015. "Soldiers and Development Aid: Military Intervention and Foreign Aid Flows." *Journal of Peace Research* 52 (2): 215–227. https://doi.org/10.1177/0022343314561363.

Krcmaric, Daniel, Stephen C. Nelson, and Andrew Roberts. 2020. "Studying Leaders and Elites: The Personal Biography Approach." *Annual Review of Political Science* 23: 133–151.

Leblang, D., and S. Chan. 2003. "Explaining Wars Fought by Established Democracies: Do Institutional Constraints Matter?" *Political Research Quarterly* 56 (4): 385–400.

Lewis-Beck, M.S. 2004. Degrees of Freedom, in Lewis-Beck, M.S., Bryman, A., & Liao, T.F., ed. *The SAGE Encyclopedia of Social Science Research Methods*. Credo Reference: https://search.credoreference.com/content/entry/sagessrm/degrees_of_freedom/0?institutionId=3798.

Lin-Greenberg, Erik. 2021. "Soldiers, Pollsters, and International Crises: Public Opinion and the Military's Advice on the Use of Force." *Foreign Policy Analysis* 17 (3): orab009. https://doi.org/10.1093/fpa/orab009.

Little, J. S. 2004. Standard Error, in Lewis-Beck, M.S., Bryman, A., & Liao, T.F., ed. *The SAGE Encyclopedia of Social Science Research Methods*. Sage Publications. Credo Reference: https://search.credoreference.com/content/entry/sagessrm/standard_error/0?institutionId=3798

Lupton, Danielle L. 2020. *Reputation for Resolve: How Leaders Signal Determination in International Politics*. Ithaca: Cornell University Press.

McClelland, C.A. 1978. *World Event/Interaction Survey (WEIS), 1966–1978*. Ann Arbor, MI: Inter-university Consortium for Political and Social Research. https://www.icpsr.umich.edu/web/ICPSR/studies/5211.

Oktay, S. 2014. "Constraining or Enabling? The Effects of Government Composition on International Commitments." *Journal of European Public Policy* 21 (6): 860–884.

———. 2018. "Clarity of Responsibility and Foreign Policy Performance Voting." *European Journal of Political Research* 57 (3): 587–614.

Oktay, S. 2022. *Governing Abroad: Coalition Politics and Foreign Policy in Europe*. Ann Arbor, MI: University of Michigan Press.

Oktay, S., and R. Beasley. 2017. "Quantitative Approaches in Coalition Foreign Policy: Scope, Content, Process." *European Political Science* 16 (4): 475–488.

Oktay, S., Paul Poast, Dina Smeltz, and Craig Kafura. 2021. "Treaty Allies Matter for US Foreign Policy Experts—but They Are Not Indispensable." *The Chicago Council on Global*

Affairs. https://www.thechicagocouncil.org/research/public-opinion-survey/treaty-allies-matter-us-foreign-policy-experts-they-are-not.

Onderco, Michal, and Rik Joosen. 2021. "Dimensionality of Party Politics of Foreign Policy: Spatial Modeling of Slovakia's National Council." *Foreign Policy Analysis* 17 (3): orab012. https://doi.org/10.1093/fpa/orab012.

Ostermann, Falk, Florian Böller, Flemming J Christiansen, Fabrizio Coticchia, Daan Fonck, Anna Herranz-Surrallés, Juliet Kaarbo, et al. 2021. "Voting on the Use of Armed Force: Challenges of Data Indexing, Classification, and the Value of a Comparative Agenda," in Deschaux-Dutard, D., ed. *Research Methods in Defence Studies: A Multidisciplinary Overview*, 170–188. London and New York: Routledge.

Palmer, G., T. London, and P. Regan. 2004. "What's Stopping You? The Sources of Political Constraints on International Conflict Behavior in Parliamentary Democracies." *International Interactions* 30 (1): 1–24.

Peksen, Dursun. 2009. "Better or Worse? The Effect of Economic Sanctions on Human Rights." *Journal of Peace Research* 46 (1): 59–77.

———. 2019. "When Do Imposed Economic Sanctions Work? A Critical Review of the Sanctions Effectiveness Literature." *Defence and Peace Economics* 30 (6): 635–647.

Peksen, Dursun, and Jin Mun Jeong. 2021. "Coercive Diplomacy and Economic Sanctions Reciprocity: Explaining Targets' Counter-Sanctions." *Defence and Peace Economics*, https://doi.org/10.1080/10242694.2021.1919831.

Peksen, Dursun, Timothy M. Peterson, and A. Cooper Drury. 2014. "Media-Driven Humanitarianism? News Media Coverage of Human Rights Abuses and the Use of Economic Sanctions." *International Studies Quarterly* 58 (4): 855–866.

Pollins, B.M. 2004. Homoskedasticity, in Lewis-Beck, M.S., Bryman, A., & Liao, T.F., ed. *The SAGE Encyclopedia of Social Science Research Methods*. Credo Reference: https://search.credoreference.com/content/entry/sagessrm/homoskedasticity/0?institutionId=3798

Potter, Philip B.K. 2017. "Methods of Foreign Policy Analysis," in Potter, Philip B.K., ed. *Oxford Research Encyclopedia of International Studies*. Oxford University Press. https://doi.org/10.1093/acrefore/9780190846626.013.34.

Prins, B.C., and C. Sprecher. 1999. "Institutional Constraints, Political Opposition, and Interstate Dispute Escalation: Evidence from Parliamentary Systems, 1946–1989." *Journal of Peace Research* 36 (3): 271–287.

Post, Abigail S., and Paromita Sen. 2020. "Why Can't a Woman Be More like a Man? Female Leaders in Crisis Bargaining." *International Interactions* 46 (1): 1–27. https://doi.org/10.1080/03050629.2019.1683008.

Rosenau, J. N. (1966). "Pre-theories and theories of foreign policy, " in Farrell, R.B., ed. *Approaches to Comparative and International Politics*, 27–92. Evanston, IL: Northwestern University Press.

Schafer, Mark, and Scott Crichlow. 2002. "The Process-Outcome Connection in Foreign Policy Decision Making: A Quantitative Study Building on Groupthink." *International Studies Quarterly* 46 (1): 45–68. https://doi.org/10.1111/1468-2478.00222.

Schrodt, P. 1995. "Event Data in Foreign Policy Analysis," in Neack, L., Hey, J.A., and Haney, P.J., ed. *Foreign Policy Analysis: Continuity and Change in Its Second Generation*, 145–166. Englewood Cliffs, NJ: Prentice Hall.

Schwartz, Joshua A., and Christopher W. Blair. 2020. "Do Women Make More Credible Threats? Gender Stereotypes, Audience Costs, and Crisis Bargaining." *International Organization* 74 (4): 872–895. https://doi.org/10.1017/S0020818320000223.

Singer, J.D. 1988. "Reconstructing the Correlates of War Dataset on Material Capabilities of States, 1816–1985." *International Interactions* 14 (2): 115–132.

Singer, J.D., S. Bremer, and J. Stuckey. 1972. "Capability Distribution, Uncertainty, and Major Power War, 1820–1965," in Russett, B., ed. *Peace, War, and Numbers*, 19–48. Beverly Hills, CA: Sage.

Smithson, M. 2004. Confidence Interval, in Lewis-Beck, M.S., Bryman, A., & Liao, T.F., ed. *The SAGE Encyclopedia of Social Science Research Methods*. Credo Reference: https://search.credoreference.com/content/entry/sagessrm/confidence_interval/0?institutionId=3798

Steenbergen, M.R., and B.S. Jones. 2002. "Modeling Multilevel Data Structures." *American Journal of Political Science* 46 (1): 218–237.

Tacq, J. 2004. Multicollinearity, in Lewis-Beck, M.S., Bryman, A., & Liao, T.F., ed. *The SAGE Encyclopedia of Social Science Research Methods*. Sage Publications. Credo Reference: https://search.credoreference.com/content/entry/sagessrm/multicollinearity/0?institutionId=3798

Tierney, Michael J., Daniel L. Nielson, Darren G. Hawkins, J. Timmons Roberts, Michael G. Findley, Ryan M. Powers, Bradley Parks, Sven E. Wilson, and Robert L. Hicks. 2011. "More Dollars than Sense: Refining Our Knowledge of Development Finance Using AidData." *World Development* 39 (11): 1891–1906.

Tomz, Michael, Jessica L.P. Weeks, and Keren Yarhi-Milo. 2020. "Public Opinion and Decisions About Military Force in Democracies." *International Organization* 74 (1): 119–143. https://doi.org/10.1017/S0020818319000341.

Wagner, W., A. Herranz-Surrallés, J. Kaarbo, and F. Ostermann. 2017. "The Party Politics of Legislative–Executive Relations in Security and Defence Policy." *West European Politics* 40 (1): 20–41.

Wagner, Wolfgang, Anna Herranz-Surrallés, Juliet Kaarbo, and Falk Ostermann. 2018. "Party Politics at the Water's Edge: Contestation of Military Operations in Europe." *European Political Science Review* 10 (4): 537–563. https://doi.org/10.1017/S1755773918000097.

Wood, B.D., and Park, S.H. 2004. Ordinary Least Squares (OLS), in Lewis-Beck, M.S., Bryman, A., & Liao, T.F., ed. *The SAGE Encyclopedia of Social Science Research Methods*. Sage Publications. Credo Reference: https://search.credoreference.com/content/entry/sagessrm/ordinary_least_squares_ols/0?institutionId=3798

21
Experimental Methods
Danielle L. Lupton and Clayton Webb

Introduction

An experiment is a research design where the researcher randomly assigns and controls the values of the independent variables to the participants (Kellstedt and Whitten 2018). Control and random assignment are the key features that distinguish experimental research designs from many of the observational studies discussed in this volume. While the researcher measures the amount of variation in the independent variable in an observational study, the researcher chooses the levels and amount of variation in an experimental study. Where a researcher uses auxiliary variables to control for potential confounding in observational studies, the experimental researcher is able to rule out confounding by design. Together, control and random assignment make experimental designs a powerful tool in the foreign policy analyst's toolkit.

In this chapter, we describe the use of experimental research designs in the conduct of Foreign Policy Analysis (FPA). While experiments are not well-suited to all topics in FPA, they are particularly useful for studying microfoundational questions related to public opinion and decision-making. In this chapter, we explain the primary ways experiments have been used by FPA scholars over time, describe the key concepts and terms used in experimental research, and provide examples of applied experimental work. In doing so, we delineate the key benefits and pitfalls in conducting experimental research and provide readers with key questions and issues to consider before employing experimental methods.

Literature Review

The use of experiments in FPA is not new, but their diffusion and sophistication have increased over time. For decades, scholars have recognized the value of experiments for testing the causal mechanisms underlying key theories of FPA. In their groundbreaking work, Snyder, Bruck, and Sapin (1954) laid the foundation for the use of experiments as a tool for studying foreign policy decision making. Yet, it wasn't until the late 1960s and early 1970s that a relatively small group of scholars began using experiments to test the cognitive models at the heart of foreign policy decision-making (e.g., Hermann and Hermann 1967; Hermann and Kogan 1968; Shapiro and Bonham 1973). These early works maintained a special focus on the influence of cognitive processes and individual versus group decision-making, relying primarily on in-person laboratory and gaming experiments. This focus on simulations and laboratory experiments to mimic and understand elite decision-making would continue throughout the 1980s (e.g., Beer et al. 1987).

In the late 1990s and early 2000s, a new wave of scholars expanded the substantive focus of experiments, while still maintaining an interest in the cognitive processes underlying foreign policy decision-making. Influential works from this period examine how images influence foreign policy preferences (Herrmann et al. 1997; Schafer 1997; McDermott, Cowden and Koopman 2002), the role of risk taking and prospect theory in FPA (Kowert and Hermann 1997; Boettcher 1995, 2004), the impact of advisors on the foreign policy process (Redd 2002), how individuals engage in dynamic decision-making during crises (Mintz et al. 1997; Geva, Mayhar and Skorick 2000; Mintz 2004), and how gender influences such decision-making (McDermott and Cowden 2001), among other topics. The diffusion of technology and the rise of the internet provided new avenues for the dissemination of survey experiments and expanded the boundaries of experimental work (see Mintz, Yang and McDermott 2011). This sparked such a strong interest in the use of experiments that scholars also began engaging in research on best practices in experimental methods, both in FPA and across political science more broadly (e.g., McDermott 2002a, b; Mintz, Redd and Vedlitz 2006; Mintz, Yang and McDermott 2011).

Since the late 2000s, the field has witnessed a veritable explosion in the use of experiments, and this interest in experimental methods has continued to accelerate in recent years. FPA scholars have expanded the types of questions and substantive focus of their experiments. Experimental methods have been particularly useful for understanding questions associated with audience costs (e.g., Tomz 2007; Levendusky and Horowitz 2012; Levy et al. 2015), casualty tolerance (e.g., Gartner 2008; Boettcher and Cobb 2009; Gelpi 2010; Kriner and Shen 2014), reputational considerations in foreign policy decision-making (Lupton 2018, 2020; Kertzer, Renshon and Yarhi-Milo 2021), and the sources of foreign policy preferences (e.g., Guisinger and Saunders 2017; Kertzer and Zeitzoff 2017; Lupton and Webb 2022), among other issues. Scholars have also found great success in using experiments to understand the influence of public opinion on a variety of foreign policy preferences, including support for military intervention (Johns and Davies 2014; Tomz and Weeks 2020), trade policy (Hiscox 2006; Ardanaz, Murillo and Pinto 2013), the use of economic sanctions (e.g., Heinrich, Kobayashi and Peterson 2017; McLean and Roblyer 2017; Sejersen 2021), and public perceptions of terrorism (e.g., D'Orazio and Salehyan 2018; Avdan and Webb 2019; Dvir, Geva and Vedlitz 2021).

The increased use of experimental methods to address questions across FPA has been met with increased scrutiny of experimental designs and some resistance. Experiments are not a panacea and not all questions are well-suited to experimental analysis. Lupton (2020, 40) explains that "experiments help us understand how people think, interpret information, and use this information to formulate their perceptions and assessments." In contrast, it is difficult to use experimental methods to test questions related to foreign policy outcomes or behavior. This is due, in part, to the fact that experiments are simplifications of the *real world* by design.

The problem here is three-fold. First, behavioral outcomes themselves can be difficult to employ as treatments. For example, one cannot randomly assign individuals to experience the effects of economic sanctions or foreign direct investments (FDI). Second, there are problems employing behavior or outcomes as the dependent variable of interest due to intermediary factors regarding how perceptions translate into actual behavior. For example, one cannot directly observe how different experimental treatments regarding foreign policy interventions actually influence an individual's behavior at the ballot box. In short, there are extenuating factors that affect how perceptions translate into behavior. Finally, there are practical and ethical factors that proscribe the manipulation of outcomes or behavior. Even if you could randomly assign terrorist attacks to cities to observe how people responded, you shouldn't want to and your university institutional review board would not approve such a project.

These limitations, however, do not undermine the value of experiments, as experiments can provide insight into questions of perceptions and decision-making. This is a critical methodological asset in the realm of FPA, where scholars are often interested in these issues. Given an appropriate question, there are several considerations scholars should take into account when designing their experiments. These include which samples to use, which type of experiment to employ, and how to analyze and present experimental data. We discuss each of these considerations in turn.

Key Concepts and Terms

In order to address each of these issues, we need to consider the issue of *validity*. The concept of validity is essential to any discussion of experimental design. Cook and Campbell (1979, 37) begin their seminal chapter on validity by differentiating validity, "the best available approximation to the truth" of a proposition from invalidity, the best available approximation of the falsehood of a proposition. They are primarily concerned about the truth or falsehood of causal claims, and they make a point of emphasizing the term *approximate* because one can never know whether a causal proposition is true or false. Our research designs are meant to get us as close to the truth as possible, but there is always a variety of factors that introduce uncertainty into the scientific process. Validity provides a means of conceptualizing the sources of these uncertainties; the sources and varieties of uncertainties encountered in the application of experimental designs are fundamentally different than those typically encountered in observational analyses.

We highlight three types of validity: *internal validity*, *external validity*, and *statistical conclusion validity* (Cook and Campbell 1979, 37ff.). These forms of validity are tied to other important concepts in experimental methods. Internal validity is relevant to experimental design; external validity is relevant to sampling; and statistical conclusion validity is relevant to the power and efficiency of statistical tests used in experimental analyses.

Internal Validity and Experimental Design

The primary advantage of experimental design over observational data analysis is internal validity. Internal validity is "the approximate validity with which we infer that a relationship between two variables is causal or that the absence of a relationship implies the absence of cause" (Cook and Campbell 1979, 37). There are three criteria for establishing a causal relationship: (1) the temporal precedence of the cause to the effect, (2) covariation between the cause and the effect, and (3) the exclusion of confounding explanations for the effect (Mutz 2011, 123). Experiments allow researchers to establish two of these three criteria by design, through treatment and random assignment.

A treatment is a stimulus that a researcher administers to an experimental unit (Cook and Campbell 1979, 4). The treatment in a conventional survey experiment is a vignette that the survey participant (the experimental unit) reads. In his audience cost experiment,

Tomz (2007, 824) asks participants to read about a foreign crisis where one country sends its military to take over another country; the U.S. President either responds by choosing not to send troops and saying nothing or by threatening to send troops but not following through. In their experiment on public perceptions of terrorism, Avdan and Webb (2019) ask U.S. participants to read a short vignette about a terrorist attack in one of four foreign countries: Canada, Mexico, Argentina, or the United Kingdom. These vignettes are essentially short stories, and the researcher is interested in how differences in the stories shape participant responses.

Random assignment is a means of applying treatments to experimental units where the treatments are applied to the units in a deliberately non-arbitrary fashion. The word *random* has become colloquially synonymous with arbitrary. Random assignment in an experimental context is systematically non-arbitrary. Classic examples of random assignment are the role of a fair die or the flipping of a fair coin. Today, random assignment is usually conducted via random number generation in the computer programs used to administer surveys. In the popular platform Qualtrics, one can randomly assign exposure to vignettes as part of a survey; random assignment occurs when participants access the survey through their email or through a survey link.

Avoiding systematic patterns in assignment ensures that the levels of the experimental treatments administered to the experimental units are independent of potential confounding variables. To confound an inference, an omitted variable must be correlated with the outcome variable and the independent variable. While it is possible for variables like race, sex, and partisanship to systematically influence participants responses to survey questions in a foreign policy experiment, random assignment into treatment conditions ensures that these variables are not correlated with the independent variables. If the number of subjects per group is sufficiently large, random assignment renders the average unit of any one treatment group comparable to the average unit in any other treatment group before the treatments are applied. This is why, with a sample of 1,127 U.S. adults Tomz (2007, 827) is able to evaluate the differences in reactions to empty threats to the reactions of the U.S. President saying nothing and staying out of the conflict without the use of any observational variables to *control for* confounding created by omitted variables, like education, sex, and race.

Treatment is always administered before measurement and randomization into treatment conditions obviates problems with potential confounding. This is why randomized experiments are the gold standard of causal inference. Given these features of randomized experiments, one can attribute a causal interpretation to any statistically significant covariation between the experimental treatment and the outcome variable.

The approach to treatment determines the nature of the experiment. There are two dimensions to treatment: how the subjects are compared and how the treatments are applied. *Between-subject* designs are the most common in FPA. Participants are randomly assigned into treatment conditions, and comparisons are made between groups. The audience cost experiment by times and the terrorism experiment by Avdan and Webb are both examples of between-subject designs; participants are only exposed to one treatment and inferences are drawn from their responses after this single treatment.

Within-subject designs are less common. In a within-subject experiment, all the participants receive treatment and the comparison is made between the levels of the outcome of interest before and after the treatment. In their experiment probing the microfoundations of democratic peace theory, Tomz and Weeks (2013, 854) conduct a within-subject experiment in the United States, evaluating how public support for conflict changes before and after participants are told whether the adversary is a democracy or an autocracy. One can also construct a hybrid of these two treatment schedules where the outcome is measured before and after the treatment, but the treatment is randomly applied to a subset of participants. In this case, a comparison is made between or among the before-and-after differences in the outcome between the treated and non-treated groups.

The two most common ways to apply experimental treatments in foreign policy experiments are *treatment-control* assignment and *factorial* assignment. In a treatment-control experiment, participants are randomized into a control condition, where the outcome is measured absent the stimuli, and a treatment condition where the stimuli is applied. In these studies, the researcher is looking for differences between the treatment and control groups. It is also possible for there to be multiple treatment groups. In these designs, the researcher can make comparisons between the treatment and control groups, between the treatment groups, or between the differences in the sizes of the treatment-control comparisons across treatment conditions. In the experiment discussed below, Lupton (2020) uses this kind of design; some participants are randomized into a control group while others are randomized into treatment conditions where they read different vignettes about an impending conflict with a foreign country. The features of the leader of the foreign country vary across conditions, so she is able to make a variety of theoretically relevant comparisons.

In a factorial experiment, participants are randomized into treatment conditions where they are exposed to multiple experimental factors simultaneously. Each factor has multiple levels. The dimensions of the experiment are determined by the number of factors and the number of levels of each factor. In a 3 × 2 factorial experiment, there are two factors: one has three levels, and one has two levels. Participants are randomized into one of six experimental conditions where they are exposed to unique combinations of the different factors. Comparisons are then made across the levels of the experimental factors, at a minimum, and perhaps across the combinations of experimental factors. Factorial experiments can also be combined with treatment-control experiments by setting one level of an experimental factor to a control condition that does not contain information about that factor. The Avdan and Webb (2019) experiment described below is a factorial design.

Before moving forward, the state of the discipline dictates that we highlight *conjoint* designs, a type of factorial survey experiment that has gained traction in recent years. Like other survey experiments, conjoints randomly assign participants to different treatments. Yet, what makes conjoint designs unique is that they allow "researchers to estimate the causal effects of multiple treatment components and assess several causal hypotheses simultaneously" by randomizing multiple attributes (or treatments) each with multiple levels (Hainmueller, Hopkins and Yamamoto 2014, 1). The main advantage of conjoints is their ability to "assess the effect of one factor and compare this effect to the effect of various other factors" (Knudsen and Johannesson 2019, 2). This makes conjoint designs particularly attractive for studying phenomena that have multiple contributing factors. This approach also mimics the way decisions are naturally made, with participants taking multiple factors or considerations into account at once. Within FPA, conjoint design experiments have been used to test a variety of issues, including (but not limited to) public support for foreign aid (Doherty et al. 2020; Heinrich and Kobayashi 2020), perceptions of resolve and credibility (Kertzer, Renshon and Yarhi-Milo 2021; Lupton 2021), public preferences of candidates' foreign policy positions (Horiuchi, Smith and Yamamoto 2018; Clary and Siddiqui 2021), and support for military intervention (Escriba`-Folch, Muradova and Rodon 2021). Conjoint designs are also valued for their statistical efficiency, and they do not necessarily require larger sample sizes than other types of survey experiments (Huertas-Garc´ıa, Nunez-Carballosa and Miravitlles 2016).[1]

There are different varieties of conjoint experiments. Many conjoint experiments—known as forced choice conjoints—require participants to choose between two profiles with randomized attributes (see Hainmueller, Hopkins and Yamamoto 2014). For example, participants might be asked about their preferences of two competing candidates with distinct policy positions (e.g., Clary and Siddiqui 2021). However, conjoints may also be more openended, treating participants with one profile at a time and measuring the variables of interest for each profile or set of attributes. These types of conjoint designs are similar to the types of factorial experiment employed by Auspurg and Hinz (2014), a close-cousin to the conjoint that is underutilized in political science but benefits from many of the same efficiency gains.

Regardless of whether one has participants evaluate multiple or single profiles at once, researchers must be careful in the interpretation of the results. As there is not a traditional control group in conjoint experiments, all results must be interpreted in comparison to a baseline—or *reference category*—which the researcher chooses at their discretion. Such decisions should be rooted in theory and hypotheses underlying the conjoint design, where applicable. In their analysis of support for foreign aid to "nasty regimes," Heinrich and Kobayashi (2020) make their baseline categories the smallest value. For example, one of their primary variables of interest is how the cost of the cost of each aid package influences public perceptions. Accordingly, the baseline category is "no cost" to which they compare costs of increasing value, such as $25 million, $50 million, or $75 million. In instances where there is no clear hierarchy or ordering of the levels of a factor, researchers should be mindful to keep the baseline consistent across their analyses.

External Validity and Sampling

External validity is "the approximate validity with which we can infer that the presumed causal relationship can be generalized to and across alternate measures of cause and effect and across different types of persons, settings, or times" (Cook and Campbell 1979, 37). The *persons* and *settings* of this quote have generated a considerable amount of debate in the context of experimental research. The type of inference one is attempting to make has important implications for the type of study one should conduct and the type of conclusions one can draw from that study. Said differently, the type of inferences you intend to make should inform your sampling decisions.

Sampling is a fundamental concept in survey research and experimental design. A sample is a subset of a population. A population is the universe of all possible cases, or individuals, that could be included in a sample. If a sample is drawn from a population, the sample is considered a random sample if each member of the population has an equal likelihood of being selected and the selection of one member of the population does not influence whether any other member will or will not be selected. When the sample is sufficiently large, we can draw inferences about the population parameters from the sample statistics. Population parameters could include a population mean (μ), the difference between two population means ($\mu_1 - \mu_2$), or a population regression parameter that describes the relationship between two variables (β). The sample mean ($\bar{X}$), difference between two means in a sample ($\bar{x}_1 - \bar{x}_2$), and the sample regression coefficient ($\hat{\beta}$) are the corresponding sample statistics. If one randomly draws a sample of the U.S. population and asks questions about public perceptions of the president and public perceptions of the economy to test a hypothesis about how the latter affects the former, there is a population effect (β) that the researcher cannot observe; the researcher is able to make inferences about β using $\hat{\beta}$, a quantity that describes the relationship in the sample. While there is a degree of uncertainty involved in this sample-to-population inference, we are often satisfied to draw conclusions this way because we can quantify the uncertainty created by sampling, the sampling error.

There are three types of samples worth considering in the context of experimental design. A *random probability sample* is a sample that meets the criteria outlined above: all individuals have the same probability of being selected, and there is no instance where the selection of one individual affects the probability that another will be selected. The plausibility of this sort of sampling strategy depends on the inferential target, what one is trying to learn from the sample, and the target population. If the population is well defined and easy to access, probability sampling might not be too onerous. If the population is very large and response rates are expected to be low, probability sampling is impractical. Indeed, most experimental designs in FPA, and political science more broadly, do not employ probability samples due to these constraints.

A *non-probability sample* is any sample that does not conform to the strictures of a random probability sample. There are many types of non-probability samples that might be valuable in applied work. An extensive review of different sample types and sampling methods is beyond the scope of this chapter (see Scheaffer et al. 2011; Kalton 2020). Instead, we focus on the two types of samples that are most often used in contemporary experimental research: quota samples and convenience samples.

A *quota sample* (or stratified sample) is a sample drawn so that certain features of the sample match those of the target population. The researcher selects strata, variables that are sometimes called "quota controls," that they believe are relevant to their outcome variable and the sample is selected so that the sample is proportionate to the population on these strata (Yang and Banamah 2014, 33).[2] Common strata in political science include sex, age, race, partisanship, and education. Many survey research firms like Dynata and YouGov maintain online panels of participants that can opt into studies for pay. These firms provide researchers samples that match their designated strata. When public opinion researchers and survey research firms report that their inferences are drawn from a *nationally representative sample*, this is usually what they are referring to, not random probability samples.

A *convenience sample* is a non-probability sample that is drawn based on, well, convenience. In other words, the researcher uses participants they can easily access. The most common types of convenience samples used in contemporary experiments are undergraduate students (Lupton 2018) and participants recruited through Amazon's Mechanical Turk (MTurk) (Mullinix et al. 2015).[3] Convenience samples are not without cost. Some social scientists are able to recruit undergraduate students through pools created by institutions or departments, but many must recruit students on a piecemeal basis. These students may be required to participate in surveys and experiments to receive course credit, extra credit, or financial remuneration. MTurk participants must be paid, and a small fee—calculated as a proportion of the payment given to the participants—is given to Amazon. While MTurk samples are not free, MTurk allows researchers to access a large number of participants at a fraction of the cost of what must be paid to research firms for national quota samples.

A recent trend in experimental research relevant to sampling and external validity—particularly in FPA research—pertains to the use of so-called *elite samples*. For example, Tomz, Weeks, and Yarhi-Milo (2020) evaluate competing theories about the role of public opinion in decisions to use military force by asking members of the Israeli parliament to evaluate plans about military strikes given information about differing levels of public support. Dietrich, Hardt, and Swedlund (2021) offer a strong case for the use of these kinds of elite samples. They argue that political elites are often the population of interest because many IR and FPA theories focus on the behavior of states. They also suggest that foreign policy elites are superior participants for foreign policy experiments because they "behave fundamentally differently" from the general public as they have more ability to make decisions, are less prone to loss aversion, have more information, and have different political attitudes (Dietrich, Hardt and Swedlund 2021, 598). While we agree that there are important insights that can be gained from the analysis of elite samples, we find this view of elite research overly enthusiastic.

Scholars should approach the study of elites and elite decision-making cautiously. First and foremost, the line of demarcation between elites and the general public is not always clear. Busby et al. (2020) enlist members of the prestigious Chicago Council of Global Affairs in their study of the importance of multilateral support for foreign policy intervention and find that this group is more responsive than members of the general public. This and the example highlighted by Tomz Weeks and Yarhi-Milo above seem like reasonable applications of elite sampling, but it is not clear that a sample of West-Point cadets, for example, is radically different from a standard group of undergraduates. Lupton and Webb (2022) note that elite status is a matter of one's expertise. A military officer may be an elite participant when it comes to matters of war and peace but they may not know much more about international monetary policy than many members of the general public. Furthermore, one must be careful about the assumptions made about the decision-making capabilities of different samples. Are we, for example, certain that elected officials are always capable of higher levels of decision-making than MTurk workers? The utility of elite samples is likely to vary from application-to-application. Along these lines, Kertzer (2022) conducts a meta-analysis comparing elite and public behavior in experiments and differences in elite and public responses to survey questions; he finds that the magnitude of the difference between members of the public and foreign policy elites is generally overstated and not related to specific experience or expertise. Given how difficult it can be to access elites and the low response rates of many elite surveys, we urge researchers to consider the specific benefits of applying their experiment to an elite sample before investing time and resources.

In sum, sampling decisions can be important for the external validity of one's study but external validity is not always of primary importance in foreign policy experiments. Sampling decisions should be guided by the study's inferential target. Accordingly, when making decisions about sample populations, researchers should keep several questions in mind: Is there a population parameter of interest (such as individuals from a specific background), or are you more interested in testing a theory? Is there more that can be learned by focusing on elite groups, or does your theory predict that most people should respond in a similar fashion to your treatments? Unless you have a strong theoretical reason to do otherwise, we suggest that you defer to convenience samples and focus on the form of validity more relevant to experimental design, internal validity.

Statistical Conclusion Validity and Analysis

Statistical conclusion validity is the approximate validity with which we infer that two variables are related, that the two variables covary. Cook and Campbell (1979, 37) identify three decisions that are potentially relevant to statistical conclusion validity: (1) whether the test is sensitive enough to detect an effect that exists, (2) whether an effect is detected given a test, and (3) the size of the effect. The first topic is relevant to statistical power, the second with the various statistical tests, and the third pertains to the substantive importance of the effect.

In our discussion of internal validity and experimental design, we explained why the primary advantage of experimental design over observational studies is the ability to control for confounding through design rather than relying on observational controls. If the sample size is sufficiently large, randomization into treatment conditions ensures that the average unit in any treatment group is comparable to the average unit in any other group. All of the other factors—sex, race, age, partisanship, education, etc.—that might be related to the outcome variable in an experimental study are orthogonal to the randomized treatment by design. This makes the analysis of experimental data relatively easy compared with the analysis of observational data.

Researchers can use analysis of variance (ANOVA) difference of means tests (t tests) or regression to analyze experimental effects. Some scholars prefer one approach to another, but these are just preferences. King (1986) shows how the standard ANOVA model used in experimental designs, difference-of-means t-tests, and ordinary least squares (OLS) regression are isomorphic to one another. These are just different ways of expressing the same information. Each of the tests is built on sums of squared deviations from the means, and each is equally likely to detect an effect. To argue against one approach is to argue against all three. In general, researchers should use the approach they are most comfortable with. However, as we will discuss in a moment, there are some reasons to prefer regression models to the more basic alternatives.

Statistical power is a measure of a hypothesis test's ability to reject a null hypothesis when the null hypothesis is false. The power of a statistical test depends on the significance level (α-level), the sample size (N), and the standardized effect size (d) (see also Oktay in this volume). The value of d depends on the type of test but a general formula for the calculation is the ratio of the effect to the variability in the data, the ratio of the signal (the effect) to the noise (the variability) (Cohen 2013). Despite the importance of the concept to all of applied statistics, power is often the source of a considerable amount of confusion in experimental research. As such, we believe it is important to address several points of confusion regarding statistical power.

First, there is no special threshold for statistical power. Whether a test is under powered or not depends on the signal-to-noise ratio in the data. If the effect is very large compared with the remaining variability in the data, one could detect an effect with ten observations. If the variability in the data is high compared with the size of the effect, one may not be able to detect an effect with 10,000 observations. Second, the power of a test depends on the type of effect you are trying to detect. This point is particularly important in the context of factorial designs. The power of tests for main effects (the levels of the experimental factors) are determined by the number of individuals that receive each level of each factor, not the number of participants per condition. The number of participants per condition only matters if one is interested in testing conditional hypotheses.

A final area of confusion that commonly arises in the analysis of experiments concerns *covariate balance across* experimental conditions. Covariates in experiments are variables that might explain a significant amount variation in the outcome variable. A covariate is *balanced* across treatment conditions if an equal or near equal levels of that covariate appear in the treatment and control groups or across the levels of the experimental factors. The concern that often arises with covariate balance in applied work is that some imbalance in the sample may confound the inference on the treatment effect. This concern is, generally, misplaced and seems to be born out of confusion about the meaning of balance.

However, balance is not something one should expect in any sample. Randomization balances all potential confounders, observed or unobserved, on average. That is, covariates are expected to be balanced in repeated sampling. In any individual sample, we should not expect to observe balance across all covariates. Morgan and Rubin (2012, 1263) explain that with "*k* independent covariates, the chance that at least one covariate showing a 'significant difference' between the treatment and control groups, at a significance level α, is $1 - (1 - α)$ *k*, so for an experiment with ten observed covariates and a 5% significance level, there is a 40% probability of observing some imbalance." Imai, King and Stuart (2014) note that using a *t*-test to evaluate imbalance in this way is fallacious, because the observed differences are not part of a population but simply a sample feature. Mutz, Pemantle, and Pham (2019) go so far as to say that presenting tables and formal tests of balance should be avoided in general. The exercise offers no useful insights and only serves to confuse and mislead readers. That some audiences, including reviewers, have come to expect these kinds of descriptive statistics highlights that their concern is founded. It is our position that covariate imbalance will, in most cases, be unimportant in most applied FPA experiments.

In some subfields of political science, it has become common practice for researchers to test, and for reviewers to demand tests, before large numbers of auxiliary hypotheses where the treatment effect is conjectured to depend on some other variable collected as part of the survey where the experiment was embedded. Does your treatment effect depend on the partisanship of the participant? Do participants provide different responses based on their propensity for empathy? When one starts conditioning treatments on observables, one is wandering into potentially murky waters. Researchers should never condition on variables that could be affected by the treatment. Montgomery, Nyhan and Torres (2018) show how conditioning on post-treatment variables can bias estimated treatment effects. That being said, not all potential variables present a risk of post-treatment confounding. The key to post-treatment bias is that the variable measured post-treatment could plausibly be affected by the treatment. Variables that we think of as innate features of a respondent's identity (e.g., sex, race, and partisanship) should not be affected by the reading of a 300-word vignette.[4]

This then begs the question of why researchers might ever want to include control variables in an experimental analysis if they could induce bias. To be sure, you never have to. As we previously explained, randomization into treatment conditions resolves most of the problems associated with potential confounding. One should be able to test their hypotheses using difference-of-means tests, ANOVA, or simple regression. This being said, there are some circumstances where including control variables may be useful. Mutz, Pemantle, and Pham (2019) explain how, while control variables are never necessary in an experimental analysis, the inclusion of control variables can increase the efficiency of your estimates. In the Avdan and Webb (2019) study we have been discussing throughout the chapter, one can see how the inclusion of controls increases efficiency of the estimates by carefully inspecting the results in Table 2 (Avdan and Webb 2019, Table 2). The first model is a simple regression where the outcome is regressed on the levels of the experimental factors alone. In the second model of Table 2, a series of demographic controls are included along with the treatment variables. The standard errors on the treatment coefficients decrease from moderately in model 2; including the control variables in the model improves the power of the coefficient *t*-statistics used to draw inferences about the experimental factors.

Conjoint designs are unique in that the standard method of analysis for conjoint design experiments is employing regression analysis to obtain average marginal component effects (AMCEs) (Hainmueller, Hopkins and Yamamoto 2014). As noted earlier, the results of conjoint design experiments must be interpreted in relation to each attribute's baseline category. As Leeper, Hobolt, and Tilley (2020, 207) explain, "By capturing the multidimensionality of target objects, the randomized conjoint design breaks any explicit, or implicit, confounding between these objects. This gives the AMCE a clear causal interpretation: the degree to which a given value of a feature increases, or decreases, respondents' favorably toward a packaged conjoint profile relative to a baseline." Scholars employing conjoint designs may also be interested in understanding subgroup preferences. Yet, recent research indicates such analyses warrant caution (see Montgomery, Nyhan and Torres 2018). Furthermore, special consideration should be taken if engaging in such analysis for conjoint designs when descriptive analysis or understanding causal interactions across attributes is the primary objective (Egami and Imai 2018; Leeper, Hobolt and Tilley 2020).

Illustrative Examples

To best illustrate these concepts, we provide two distinct examples from recent work: one which focuses on elite decision-making (Lupton 2020) and the other on public perceptions of terrorism (Avdan and Webb 2019). The key features of the research designs of each of these studies are highlighted in Table 21.1.

Lupton (2020) examines which factors influence leader-specific reputations for resolve and how these reputations change across interactions. Lupton argues that such reputations should not only be primarily driven by a leader's own statements and past behavior, such as whether a leader has stood firm in the past in similar situations, but may also be conditioned by key contextual factors, such as a pre-existing state reputation for resolve or signaled interest in an issue under dispute. To test her argument against competing theories, Lupton employs a factorial survey experiment in which participants are asked to take the role of a leader of an unnamed state and evaluate the resolve of an opposing leader from another state. Participants engage in multiple rounds of decision-making across three vignettes of increasingly high stakes: a diplomatic summit, extended negotiations, and a territorial crisis.

As the goal of the research is to understand how different factors identified by competing theories and approaches to reputations influence a leader's reputation for resolve, participants are randomly assigned to treatment groups in which they are exposed to different information about the opposing leader's characteristics or key state characteristics at each round of interaction. These treatments include the strength of the opposing leader's statements, the opposing leader's past behavior in similar situations, the regime type of the opposing leader's state, the relative military capability of the opposing leader's state, how the opposing leader's state has behaved in similar situations in the past, and the communicated level of state interest in the issue under dispute. The experiment also employs a control group in which participants aren't exposed to any treatments. As participants engage in multiple rounds of decision-making in a single session, the experimental design allows for both within- and between-subject comparisons. This provides insight into reputation development, as the

Table 21.1 Illustrative Examples Research Design

Attribute	Lupton (2020)	Avdan and Webb (2019)
Sample type	Convenience	Convenience
Subject pool	MTurk	MTurk
Sample size	3,198	306
Within-subjects design	Yes	No
Between-subjects design	Yes	Yes
Control condition	Yes	No
Analysis	ANOVA & regression	t-tests & regression
Control variables	Yes	Yes

researcher can examine the effects of treatments across participants (between-subjects design) as well as how each participant's decision-making changes across each round of the survey (within-subjects design). Accordingly, the survey design robustly tests the key question of interest: which factors influence perceptions of resolve and how these perceptions change across interactions. Through this design, Lupton finds that a leader's statements and past behavior are crucial to her reputation—leaders who make firm statements or who have stood firm in the past are perceived as more resolute in the current situation. While she finds further support that strategic interest in an issue under dispute influence perceptions of resolve, there is little evidence that regime type of relative military capability influences these perceptions. Furthermore, within-subject comparisons reveal that perceptions of resolve during the first round of decision-making significantly influence later perceptions of resolve.

Avdan and Webb (2019) examine public perceptions of terrorism. They argue that these perceptions will be driven by the personal and physical proximity of the attack: people will feel more vulnerable when an attack occurs closer in physical proximity to them and when the victims of the attack are more like them in terms of race and nationality. To test their argument, Avdan and Webb use a 2 × 2 factorial experiment where participants are randomized into treatment conditions where they read about similar terrorist attacks that occur in different countries. Participants are asked to rate the seriousness of the attack as a threat to the United States on an 11-point scale. The authors use a combination of OLS and t-tests to evaluate the effects of the treatments on this rating. Consistent with expectations, they find evidence that personal proximity and physical proximity of foreign terrorist attacks shape public perceptions of terrorism. People cared more about terrorist attacks in England and Canada than attacks in Mexico and Argentina and more about the attacks in Mexico and Canada than the attacks in Argentina and England.

Discussion and Conclusion

In this chapter, we provided a brief introduction to the use of experimental design as a research method for FPA. We outlined the many uses of experiments in FPA over the years, reviewed the key elements of experimental designs, and provided a brief description of some applied examples. In conclusion, we want to offer you, the reader, some rules of the road to follow when deciding if and how you want to use an experiment to answer a question about FPA. Before you dive headlong into experimental research, ask yourself the following questions.

What do you want to know? This question is relatively simple, but it has important implications. As we noted in the introduction, experimental designs are not well-suited for all topics in FPA. If you are interested in foreign policy outcomes or behaviors, you should consider the observational research methods discussed in the other chapters of this volume. You do not have the ability to, nor should you want to, manipulate foreign policy outcomes for the sake of social research. The answer to this question also has important implications for your sampling decisions. Is there an inferential target in the population or not? Avdan and Webb (2019) provide interesting insights into the factors that shape public perceptions of terrorism, but they are able to use a convenience sample because there is no coherent inferential target in the population. Avdan and Webb have a theory about the way people, in general, think. Their inferences are not limited or targeted to a particular population, so they do not need to expend the resources necessary for a nationally representative sample. If you have a coherent inferential target, the population treatment effect may be of interest but you should not waste your time and energy if it is not.

What comparisons are most meaningful? We outlined three types of experimental designs in this chapter: treatment-control, factorial, and conjoint. Having decided to field an experiment, you need to make decisions about which type of design is best suited to your question. Not every experiment needs a control. Avdan and Webb (2019) compare differences in public perceptions of hypothetical terrorist attacks. There is no control condition in this experiment, only the levels of the experimental factors. What would a control look like? You cannot ask participants to rate the threat of a terrorist attack if they do not read about one, so it doesn't make any sense to measure a "control" or "baseline" level of threat perception in that experiment. In contrast, Lupton (2020) does provide meaningful control comparisons. If you want to make a large number of comparisons at once, a conjoint experiment may be of interest, though these are somewhat more difficult to design, implement, and analyze than the other designs described in this chapter.

What doesn't your experiment tell you? We often feel pressure to draw broad conclusions from our research. While this can be a useful exercise, you need to be cognizant of the scope conditions of your study. Internal validity is the strength of experimental designs. What we gain from random assignment and control, we typically sacrifice in external validity. Foreign policy doesn't happen in a laboratory, and the decisions leaders make are often contingent on a great number of things that cannot be manipulated in an experimental study. This doesn't mean that experiments are not useful, but you need to be honest with yourself and your audience about the limitations of your experimental results. You are not limited to a single research design per project. You can use the experimental designs in your study to evaluate the microfoundations of your argument and pair those results with some of the observational designs discussed elsewhere in this book to evaluate the external validity of your findings.

Notes

1 As with all experiments, sample size for conjoint designs should be driven by considerations of statistical power.
2 This selection can be achieved through a variety of statistical methods, including ranking, matching, propensity weighting, or combinations of the different approaches. See Mercer, Lau, and Kennedy (2018) for a more in-depth discussion.
3 MTurk is not the only online convenience sample pool available, but it is one of the most commonly employed and has been the subject of much debate.
4 One may be an exceptional writer but it is unlikely that the researcher will be able to systematically induce identity crises among all of their respondents.

References

Ardanaz, Martin, M. Victoria Murillo, and Pablo Pinto. 2013. "Sensitivity to Issue Framing on Trade Policy Preferences: Evidence from a Survey Experiment." *International Organization* 67 (2): 411–437.

Auspurg, Katrin, and Thomas Hinz. 2014. *Factorial Survey Experiments*, Vol. 175. Los Angeles, CA: Sage Publications.

Avdan, Nazli, and Clayton Webb. 2019. "Not in My Back Yard: Public Perceptions and Terrorism." *Political Research Quarterly* 72 (1): 90–103.

Beer, Francis, Alice Healy, Grant Sinclair, and Lyle Bourne Jr. 1987. "War Cues and Foreign Policy Acts." *The American Political Science Review* 81 (3): 701–715.

Boettcher, William, III. 1995. "Context, Methods, Numbers, and Words: Prospect Theory in International Relations." *Journal of Conflict Resolution* 39 (3): 561–583.

Boettcher, William, III. 2004. "The Prospects for Prospect Theory: An Empirical Evaluation of International Relations Applications of Framing and Loss Aversion." *Political Psychology* 25 (3): 331–3 62.

Boettcher, William III, and Michael Cobb. 2009. "'Don't Let Them Die in Vain' Casualty Frames and Public Tolerance for Escalating Commitment in Iraq." *Journal of Conflict Resolution* 53 (5): 677–697.

Busby, Joshua, Craig Kafura, Jonathan Monten, and Jordan Tama. 2020. "Multilateralism and the Use of Force: Experimental Evidence on the Views of Foreign Policy Elites." *Foreign Policy Analysis* 16 (1): 118–129.

Clary, Christopher, and Niloufer Siddiqui. 2021. "Voters and Foreign Policy: Evidence from a Conjoint Experiment in Pakistan." *Foreign Policy Analysis* 17 (2): orab001.

Cohen, Jacob. 2013. *Statistical Power Analysis for the Behavioral Sciences*. New York, NY: Routledge Academic Press.

Cook, Thomas D., and Donald T. Campbell. 1979. *Quasi-Experimentation: Design and Analysis Issues for Field Settings*. Boston, MA: Houghton Mifflin Company.

Dietrich, Simone, Heidi Hardt, and Haley J. Swedlund. 2021. "How to Make Elite Experiments Work in International Relations." *European Journal of International Relations* 27 (2): 596–621.

Doherty, David, Amanda Clare Bryan, Dina Hanania, and Matthew Pajor. 2020. "The Public's Foreign Aid Priorities: Evidence from a Conjoint Experiment." *American Politics Research* 48 (5): 635–648.

Dvir, Rotem, Nehemia Geva, and Arnold Vedlitz. 2021. "Unpacking Public Perceptions of Terrorism: Does Type of Attack Matter?" *Studies in Conflict & Terrorism*, 1–21.

D'Orazio, Vito, and Idean Salehyan. 2018. "Who Is a Terrorist? Ethnicity, Group Affiliation, and Understandings of Political Violence." *International Interactions* 44 (6): 1017–1039.

Egami, Naoki, and Kosuke Imai. 2018. "Causal Interaction in Factorial Experiments: Application to Conjoint Analysis." *Journal of the American Statistical Association* 114: 529-40.

Escribà-Folch, Abel, Lala Muradova, and Toni Rodon. 2021. "The Effects of Autocratic Characteristics on Public Opinion toward Democracy Promotion Policies: A Conjoint Analysis." *Foreign Policy Analysis* 17 (1): oraa016.

Gartner, Scott. 2008. "The Multiple Effects of Casualties on Public Support for War: An Experimental Approach." *American Political Science Review* 102 (1): 95–106.

Gelpi, Christopher. 2010. "Performing on Cue? The Formation of Public Opinion toward War." *Journal of Conflict Resolution* 54 (1): 88–116.

Geva, Nehemia, James Mayhar, and J. Mark Skorick. 2000. "The Cognitive Calculus of Foreign Policy Decision Making: An Experimental Assessment." *Journal of Conflict Resolution* 44 (4): 447–471.

Guisinger, Alexandra, and Elizabeth Saunders. 2017. "Mapping the Boundaries of Elite Cues: How Elites Shape Mass Opinion across International Issues." *International Studies Quarterly* 61 (2): 425–441.

Hainmueller, Jens, Daniel Hopkins, and Teppei Yamamoto. 2014. "Causal Inference in Conjoint Analysis: Understanding Multidimensional Choices via Stated Preference Experiments." *Political Analysis* 22 (1): 1–30.

Heinrich, Tobias, and Yoshiharu Kobayashi. 2020. "How Do People Evaluate Foreign Aid to 'Nasty' Regimes?" *British Journal of Political Science* 50 (1): 103–127.

Heinrich, Tobias, Yoshiharu Kobayashi, and Timothy Peterson. 2017. "Sanction Consequences and Citizen Support: A Survey Experiment." *International Studies Quarterly* 61 (1): 98–106.

Hermann, Charles, and Margaret Hermann. 1967. "An Attempt to Simulate the Outbreak of World War I." *The American Political Science Review* 61 (2): 400–416.

Hermann, Margaret, and Nathan Kogan. 1968. "Negotiation in Leader and Delegate Groups." *Journal of Conflict Resolution* 12 (3): 332–344.

Herrmann, Richard, James Voss, Tonya Schooler, and Joseph Ciarrochi. 1997. "Images in International Relations: An Experimental Test of Cognitive Schemata." *International Studies Quarterly* 41 (3): 403–433.

Hiscox, Michael. 2006. "Through a Glass and Darkly: Attitudes toward International Trade and the Curious Effects of Issue Framing." *International Organization* 60 (3): 755–780.

Horiuchi, Yusaku, Daniel Smith, and Teppei Yamamoto. 2018. "Measuring Voters' Multidimensional Policy Preferences with Conjoint Analysis: Application to Japan's 2014 Election." *Political Analysis* 26 (2): 190–209.

Huertas-Garc´ıa, Rub´en, Ana Nunez-Carballosa, and Paloma Miravitlles. 2016. "Statistical and Cognitive Optimization of Experimental Designs in Conjoint Analysis." *European Journal of Management and Business Economics* 25 (3): 142–149.

Imai, Kosuke, Gary King, and Elizabeth A. Stuart. 2014. "Misunderstandings Between Experimentalists and Observationalists About Causal Inference." In *Field Experiments and Their Critics*, edited by Dawn Langan Teele. New Haven: Yale University Press, 196–227.

Johns, Robert, and Graeme Davies. 2014. "Coalitions of the Willing? International Backing and British Public Support for Military Action." *Journal of Peace Research* 51 (6): 767–781.

Kalton, Graham. 2020. *Introduction to Survey Sampling*, Vol. 35. Los Angeles, CA: Sage Publications.

Kellstedt, Paul M., and Guy D. Whitten. 2018. *The Fundamentals of Political Science Research*. New York, NY: Cambridge University Press.

Kertzer, Joshua D. 2022 "Re-Assessing Elite-Public Gaps in Political Behavior." *American Journal of Political Science* 66 (3): 539–553.

Kertzer, Joshua, Jonathan Renshon, and Keren Yarhi-Milo. 2021. "How Do Observers Assess Resolve?" *British Journal of Political Science* 51 (1): 308–330.

Kertzer, Joshua, and Thomas Zeitzoff. 2017. "A Bottom-up Theory of Public Opinion about Foreign Policy." *American Journal of Political Science* 61 (3): 543–558.

King, Gary. 1986. "How Not to Lie With Statistics: Avoiding Common Mistakes in Quantitative Political Science." *American Journal of Political Science* 30 (3): 666–687.

Knudsen, Erik, and Mikael Johannesson. 2019. "Beyond the Limits of Survey Experiments: How Conjoint Designs Advance Causal Inference in Political Communication Research." *Political Communication* 36 (2): 259–271.

Kowert, Paul, and Margaret Hermann. 1997. "Who Takes Risks? Daring and Caution in Foreign Policy Making." *Journal of Conflict Resolution* 41 (5): 611–637.

Kriner, Douglas, and Francis Shen. 2014. "Reassessing American Casualty Sensitivity: The Mediating Influence of Inequality." *Journal of Conflict Resolution* 58 (7): 1174–1201.

Leeper, Thomas, Sara Hobolt, and James Tilley. 2020. "Measuring Subgroup Preferences in Conjoint Experiments." *Political Analysis* 28 (2): 207–221.

Levendusky, Matthew, and Michael Horowitz. 2012. "When Backing Down Is the Right Decision: Partisanship, New Information, and Audience Costs." *The Journal of Politics* 74 (2): 323–338.

Levy, Jack, Michael McKoy, Paul Poast, and Geoffrey Wallace. 2015. "Backing Out or Backing In? Commitment and Consistency in Audience Costs Theory." *American Journal of Political Science* 59 (4): 988–1001.

Lupton, Danielle L. 2018. "Signaling Resolve: Leaders, Reputations, and the Importance of Early Interactions." *International Interactions* 44 (1): 59–87.

Lupton, Danielle L. 2020. *Reputation for Resolve: How Leaders Signal Determination in International Politics*. Ithaca, NY: Cornell University Press.

Lupton, Danielle L. 2021. "Rhetoric, Threat Construction, and Crisis Bargaining: How the Content of Threats Influences Coercive Credibility." Working Paper.

Lupton, Danielle L., and Clayton Webb. 2022. "Wither Elites? The Role of Elite Credibility and Knowledge in Public Perceptions of Foreign Policy." *International Studies Quarterly* 6 (3): sqac057.

McDermott, Rose. 2002a. "Experimental Methods in Political Science." *Annual Review of Political Science* 5 (1): 31–61.

McDermott, Rose. 2002b. "Experimental Methodology in Political Science." *Political Analysis* 10 (4): 325–342.

McDermott, Rose, and Jonathan Cowden. 2001. "The Effects of Uncertainty and Sex in a Crisis Simulation Game." *International Interactions* 27 (4): 353–380.

McDermott, Rose, Jonathan Cowden, and Cheryl Koopman. 2002. "Framing, Uncertainty, and Hostile Communications in a Crisis Experiment." *Political Psychology* 23 (1): 133–149.

McLean, Elena, and Dwight Roblyer. 2017. "Public Support for Economic Sanctions: An Experimental Analysis." *Foreign Policy Analysis* 13 (1): 233–254.

Mercer, Andrew, Arnold Lau, and Courtney Kennedy. 2018. "For Weighting Online Opt-in Samples, What Matters Most?" Washington, DC: Pew Research Center.

Mintz, Alex. 2004. "Foreign Policy Decision Making in Familiar and Unfamiliar Settings: An Experimental Study of High-Ranking Military Officers." *Journal of Conflict Resolution* 48 (1): 91–104.

Mintz, Alex, Nehemia Geva, Steven Redd, and Amy Carnes. 1997. "The Effect of Dynamic and Static Choice Sets on Political Decision Making: An Analysis Using the Decision Board Platform." *American Political Science Review* 91 (3): 553–566.

Mintz, Alex, Steven Redd, and Arnold Vedlitz. 2006. "Can We Generalize from Student Experiments to the Real World in Political Science, Military Affairs, and International Relations?" *Journal of Conflict Resolution* 50 (5): 757–776.

Mintz, Alex, Yi Yang, and Rose McDermott. 2011. "Experimental Approaches to International Relations." *International Studies Quarterly* 55 (2): 493–501.

Montgomery, Jacob, Brendan Nyhan, and Michelle Torres. 2018. "How Conditioning on Posttreatment Variables Can Ruin Your Experiment and What to Do about It." *American Journal of Political Science* 62 (3): 760–775.

Morgan, Kari Lock, and Donald B. Rubin. 2012. "Rerandomization to Improve Covariate Balance in Experiments." *The Annals of Statistics* 40 (2): 1263–1282.

Mullinix, Kevin J., Thomas J. Leeper, James N. Druckman, and Jeremy Freese. 2015. "The Generalizability of Survey Experiments." *Journal of Experimental Political Science* 2 (2): 109–138.

Mutz, Diana C. 2011. *Population-Based Survey Experiments*. Princeton, NJ: Princeton University Press.

Mutz, Diana C., Robin Pemantle, and Philip Pham. 2019. "The Perils of Balance Testing in Experimental Design: Messy Analyses of Clean Data." *The American Statistician* 73 (1): 32–42.

Redd, Steven. 2002. "The Influence of Advisers on Foreign Policy Decision Making: An Experimental Study." *Journal of Conflict Resolution* 46 (3): 335–364.

Schafer, Mark. 1997. "Images and Policy Preferences." *Political Psychology* 18 (4): 813–829.

Scheaffer, Richard L., William Mendenhall III, R. Lyman Ott, and Kenneth G. Gerow. 2011. *Elementary Survey Sampling*. Boston, MA: Cengage Learning.

Sejersen, Mikkel. 2021. "Winning Hearts and Minds with Economic Sanctions? Evidence from a Survey Experiment in Venezuela." *Foreign Policy Analysis* 17 (1): oraa008.

Shapiro, Michael, and G. Matthew Bonham. 1973. "Cognitive Process and Foreign Policy Decision-Making." *International studies quarterly* 17 (2): 147–174.

Snyder, Richard, Henry Bruck, and Burton Sapin. 1954. "Decision-Making as an Approach to the Study of International Politics. (Foreign Policy Analysis Series No. 3.)."

Tomz, Michael. 2007. "Domestic Audience Costs in International Relations: An Experimental Approach." *International Organization* 61 (4): 821–840.

Tomz, Michael, Jessica L.P. Weeks, and Keren Yarhi-Milo. 2020. "Public Opinion and Decisions about Military Force in Democracies." *International Organization* 74 (1): 119–143.

Tomz, Michael, and Jessica Weeks. 2020. "Public Opinion and Foreign Electoral Intervention." *American Political Science Review* 114 (3): 856–873.

Tomz, Michael R., and Jessica L.P. Weeks. 2013. "Public Opinion and the Democratic Peace." *American Political Science Review* 107 (4): 849–865.

Yang, Keming, and Ahmad Banamah. 2014. "Quota Sampling as an Alternative to Probability Sampling? An Experimental Study." *Sociological Research Online* 19 (1): 56–66.

22
Game Theory
Scott Wolford

Introduction

Strategic interaction suffuses international politics. War breaks out when one side chooses to fight and another gives battle, and both decisions depend on beliefs about third-party reactions. Incentives to cheat can complicate cooperation over environmental protection, tariff reductions, coalition war efforts, and intellectual property rights. Domestic publics watch UN Security Council votes to judge the attractiveness of military intervention, while other states watch them to inform balancing decisions. National leaders choose between war and peace with an eye to how domestic audiences like voters or regime insiders may punish or reward them. Foreign Policy Analysis (FPA) often concerns outcomes that depend on multiple actors, each of whom can influence each other's pursuit of their goals. Yet even when the rationale behind individual choices is clear, the outcome of interdependent choices isn't always obvious, and game theory can help sharpen our thinking about these situations.

Game theory is a branch of mathematics that analyzes strategic interaction. Its basic unit is the *game*, which describes strategic settings in terms of the relevant players, information and choices available to them, substantive outcomes produced by their choices, and players' preferences over those outcomes. Analysts make guesses about how games are likely to be played by identifying strategies that exist in *equilibrium*, a state at which no player can profit by switching to a different strategy given what they know about other players' strategies. Equilibrium is a social standard of explanation, requiring us to consider the interdependent choices and shared beliefs of multiple actors. Game-theoretic analyses define precise deductive relationships between a model's assumptions (the premises it uses to describe the social world) and conclusions (its equilibria), which facilitates the generation of valid—and the identification of invalid—arguments. Useful models provide parsimonious, transparent, and logically sound explanations that (a) clarify causal mechanisms; (b) challenge resonant but invalid arguments; (c) identify common strategic processes across ostensibly disparate phenomena; and (d) assist in the identification and interpretation of empirical models, whether quantitative or qualitative, observational or experimental.

In this chapter, I first review applications of noncooperative game theory to FPA, limiting my focus to the study of international conflict, where game theory has changed (a) how we explain war and (b) where and how we look for evidence.[1] I pay special attention to how strategic censoring shapes observational data on reputations and domestic audience costs and how models have improved research designs in each area. The second section gives a brief overview of the specification and analysis of games in the strategic and extensive forms, as well as three popular solution concepts—Nash, Subgame Perfect, and Perfect Bayesian Equilibrium—with examples drawn from the study of limited war, the challenges of cooperation, and the problem of deterrence. I close with a discussion of game theory's strengths and weaknesses in FPA and common mistakes that first-time users should avoid.

Game Theory in Foreign Policy Analysis

Game theory has contributed to broad swathes of IR, including international and civil conflict, international law and institutions, transnational politics, and international political economy. I focus here on international conflict, because it's easy to show a range of different contributions in a single substantive context.[2] I describe two types of contribution. First, *accounting work* checks the logical and substantive foundations of other models, identifying hidden assumptions or changing our understanding of their implications. Second, *positive work* explains stylized facts, collects multiple models under a single framework, or aids in the identification and interpretation of empirical models. Contrary to accounts that locate game-theoretic contributions in early American nuclear strategy, it began to influence the study of conflict only much later (O'Neill 1994). As such, I begin my survey with models developed in the early 1990s as a reaction to then-dominant "debates" between collections of incomplete arguments about international relations called "paradigms" by their advocates (Wagner 2007, Ch. 1).

Accounting work checks the assumptions and logic of other arguments. Game theory's treatment of structural realism, for example, led to numerous advances in the theory of war. Powell shows that many claims in structural realism, like the importance of "relative gains" (1991), the implications of anarchy (1994), and the link between the distribution of power and war (1996), don't follow in a straightforward way from realism's stated premises. Nalebuff (1991) shows that many informal discussions of signaling (e.g., Jervis 1970) depend on unstated—and often untenable—assumptions about responses to unexpected events; Kydd (1997) scrutinizes the unclear logic of the "spiral model" of conflict; and Wagner (2007, 24–27, 182–183) shows that many treatments of the "security dilemma" struggle to explain why both sides choose as they do. Morrow (2014, Ch. 2) shows that the distinction between power and ideas, the former associated with realism and the latter with constructivism, is often misplaced, because meaningful strategic interaction depends on shared beliefs about who acts and who doesn't, as well as the meaning of and likely responses to players' choices. And in one of the most influential pieces of accounting work, Fearon (1995) shows that many explanations for war fail a crucial substantive test: they can't explain why states would fight, which imposes death and destruction on all parties, rather than negotiate, which can (and very often does) produce the same distributive outcome less the costs of war.

Positive work often builds on accounting work, exploring causal mechanisms, explaining stylized facts, organizing other models, and aiding in the identification of empirical models.[3] Fearon (1995) complements his accounting exercise by identifying two bargaining frictions (private information and commitment problems) that can explain war between unitary states. Powell (2006) extends the analysis by showing how several mechanisms—preventive war, stakes that influence bargaining power, risk attitudes, and issue indivisibilities—are all special cases of commitment problems, and Leventoğlu and Tarar (2008) identify limitations of informational accounts of war. Other work explores interactions between leaders and their supporters, where war may not be Pareto inefficient, to explain how political institutions shape decisions for war (e.g., Debs and Goemans 2010) and communication between states with incentives to bluff (Debs and Weiss 2016, Fearon 1994, Schultz 1998). Others consider communication between unitary states aiming to signal both resolve (Favretto 2009, Sartori 2005, Slantchev 2005, Trager 2010) and restraint (Haynes and Yoder 2020, Kydd 2005, Wolford 2020). Finally, some models explore how costly fighting can solve information or commitment problems to end wars, explaining why (a) some wars are short and others long and (b) most wars end short of military defeat (Filson and Werner 2002, Langlois and Langlois 2009, Leventoğlu and Slantchev 2007, Powell 2004, Thomas et al. 2016, Wolford et al. 2011). These models inform analyses of the duration of peace between both former enemies (Fortna 2003, Lo et al. 2008, Werner 1999, Werner and Yuen 2005) and coalition partners (Phillips and Wolford 2021).

Other positive work explores variation in uncertainty, the costs of arming, and the number of actors. Meirowitz and Sartori (2008) show why states generate private information that boosts the risks of war; Arena and Wolford (2012) show how intelligence-gathering can increase the chances of war; and Bils and Spaniel (2017) show that how uncertainty influences war depends on the things over which players are uncertain. Modeling the costs of arming allows Slantchev to show that states may fight rather than arm enough to secure peace (2005) and that they may continue fighting to avoid debt repayment (2012). Coe and Vaynman (2020) and Fearon (2018) identify fundamental limits on arms control, while Coe and Vaynman (2015) and Carnegie and Carson (2018) analyze the nuclear nonproliferation regime using the same logic of costly conflict. Another group of models explores settings with more than two players (Krainin and Wiseman 2016), considering signaling in front of third parties (Trager 2015, Wolford 2020) and the relationship between bargains leaders strike with foreign states and (a) their own constituencies (Davis 2021) or (b) coalition partners (Phillips and Wolford 2021).

Game theory has also informed empirical work. First, games help distinguish between theories' observable and unobservable implications. Schultz (2001) shows that attempts to find evidence that leaders are punished for backing down from public threats are typically bound to fail, because leaders strategically avoid all but the smallest punishments. Rather than look for "audience costs" in the observable record, where they should be difficult to find, scholars have responded by pivoting to experiments to get closer to the proper counterfactual (e.g., Trager and Vavreck 2011). Wu and Wolford (2018) make a similar argument about reputations for resolve; leaders are unlikely to back down when the reputation costs will be most dire, which complicates the search for an observable link between backing down in the past and how other states treat them in the present. The model also generates observable implications, pointing to changing rates of dispute escalation over time, where reputations are more in evidence. Bueno de Mesquita and Tyson (2020) show that many causal identification strategies fail to distinguish the direct, payoff-relevant effect of some behaviors from indirect, informational effects on observed responses, in the process emphasizing the tight, even necessary, link between theoretical and empirical models of strategic interaction (see also Ashworth et al. 2021). Finally, Goemans and Spaniel (2016) discuss using game theory in qualitative work by treating the entire analytical structure—game, solution concept, and equilibrium—as the causal mechanism.

Part of game theory's usefulness comes from its formalization, which helps analysts get the logic of their arguments right and serves the goal of parsimony, keeping track of which elements of a theory are performing which function. Its concept of equilibrium entails a clear, consistent standard of explanation that takes seriously the social structure in which actors' "opportunities, beliefs, and desires" (Ashworth et al. 2021, 53) interact to produce outcomes. Its common theoretical vocabulary helps us to spot similar mechanisms in different contexts, like the strategic censoring that selects both audience costs and reputation costs out of observational data. Finally, it ensures that engagement with other work need not stop at accounting, pointing the way—as it did for the development of the bargaining model of war—to more substantively satisfying sets of assumptions and more informative empirical analyses. I turn next to a formal explication of how games are specified, solved, and interpreted.

Choice, Games, and Equilibrium

Modeling strategic interaction requires a baseline model of individual decisions, that is, a way to relate goals to actions in a consistent way that (a) doesn't do too much violence to how people make choices and (b) allows us to separate the effects of individual and collective processes in explaining politics—for example, separating the effects of individual cognitive processes from the effects of norms and institutions on collective choice. Game theory relies on the theory of expected utility, which is often (if not always helpfully) called the theory of "rational choice," for this purpose. After describing the theory of choice, I show how games represent strategic settings with examples from deterrence, cooperation, and limited war, then close by introducing Nash Equilibrium and two of its refinements as means of making guesses about how games are likely to be played.

The Theory of Choice

Our basic theory of choice entails an individual, or a *player*; a set of choices, or *actions*; a function determining the *state of the world*, which translates those choices into *outcomes*; and the player's *preferences* over those outcomes. We describe a player's preferences with a *utility function*, u_i for player i, that takes outcomes as its inputs (e.g., war or concessions) and translates them into real numbers (called *payoffs* or *utility*), where players prefer outcomes represented by higher numbers to outcomes represented by lower numbers. We make *no* assumptions about the content of preferences—materialist or otherwise, venal or altruistic, self- or other-regarding, etc.—only that they're complete and transitive over analyst-defined outcomes. This ensures that players can be goal-directed: (a) an optimal choice (or set of choices) exists and (b) our players can recognize it. We want nothing getting in the way of goal-directed action at the individual level, because we want to describe outcomes as the result of strategic interaction. Note that this implies nothing about players being omniscient or their choices being error-free, searching for all relevant information, or even that players will draw the same conclusions from looking at the same information. We sometimes build those features into models to isolate certain mechanisms, but this spare definition of rationality is a far cry from oft-caricatured *homo economicus*.

Representing preferences with real numbers lets us identify likely choices by maximizing utility functions. Players choose the action that gives them the highest payoff—that is, the one that maximizes their utility function—subject to constraints on their ability to achieve those goals. When players know the state of the world, they choose under *complete information*. When players are uncertain over the state of the world, they have *limited information*, and optimal choices maximize *expected utility*, which is a weighted average over all possible payoffs and players' subjective estimates of the probabilities of each outcome. Suppose that we have a player (or country) i who must choose whether to form a new alliance. Signing no alliance leaves i's security situation unchanged, so information is complete about the consequences of standing pat. But signing an alliance may provoke counterbalancing, depending on what enemies believe about the alliance's intent. Suppose that i is uncertain over the state of the world: will an enemy counterbalance, or won't it? To formalize the intuition, action NA ("no alliance") yields a payoff of 3, such that $u_i(\text{NA}) = 3$. If i chooses A ("alliance"), it escapes counterbalancing with probability p, yielding 4, but enemies counterbalance with probability $1-p$, yielding 2. Therefore, i's expected utility for A is $EU_i(\text{A}) = p \times 4 + (1-p) \times 2$, which it then compares with $u_i(\text{NA})$. In this non-strategic setting, i makes the choice that maximizes its utility function: A when p (the probability of getting 4) is high enough and NA when p is low enough (such that 2 is relatively more likely than 4). Formally, $EU_i(\text{A}) > u_i(\text{NA})$ when

$$p4 + (1-p)2 > 3, \text{ or when } p > \frac{1}{2}.$$

Our simple model shows that i signs the alliance only when it's optimistic enough that doing so won't provoke a reaction from its rivals. Expected utility theory is intentionally sparse—for example, it abstracts away from how players receive and process information—but as we'll see below, this helps isolate the effects of strategic processes.

Before continuing, two additional points about expected utility theory are in order. First, payoffs *represent* players' preferences, but they don't cause them. Players don't pursue certain actions because they yield more utility; rather, we try to write down payoff functions that represent what the actors whose behavior we're trying to explain value (Morrow 1994, 20–22). Second, players act to maximize their expected utility in models, but we don't take this to mean that people *actually* make these calculations; rather, defining and maximizing a utility function is an act of representation, of using the language of mathematics to tell a simple, coherent, and transparent story about how individuals make choices and that, if preferences are based on our substantive knowledge of what we're studying, can serve as a useful building block for a theory of strategic choice.

Games

A *game* describes strategic situations with five elements:

1 *Players*, who makes choices in pursuit of their goals.
2 *Strategies*, or contingency plans, available to each player.
3 *Outcomes* produced by combinations of players' actions.
4 *Preferences* by which players rank outcomes against their goals.
5 *Information* available to each player.

We also assume that the game itself is *common knowledge*: players know and agree on what game they're playing, even if they might be uncertain over things like each other's payoffs. This not only helps when it comes to solving the game—it's a minimum requirement for strategic interaction—but it also reflects the fundamentally social nature of strategic interaction and highlights a key substantive challenge in designing useful models: the game represents what players know about the strategic setting of interest.

Games come in one of two forms. First, as shown in the left panel of Figure 22.1, the *extensive form* describes the temporal sequence of moves, clarifying individual choices and

Game Theory

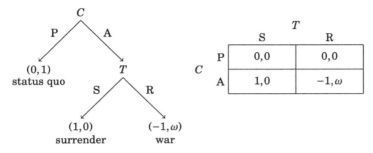

Figure 22.1 A game in the extensive and strategic forms.

stipulating what players know about previous moves at each *node*. In this game of complete information, player *C* chooses first between actions P and A, and if it chooses the latter, player *T* chooses between S and R. Payoffs are distributed at *terminal nodes*, which define the game's outcomes. In this representation of deterrence, the status quo prevails if *C* passes (P), but if *C* attacks (A), *T* chooses between surrender (S), which yields the goods in dispute to *C*, and resistance (R), which means war. Payoff functions are

$$u_C = \begin{cases} 0 & \text{if status quo} \\ 1 & \text{if surrender} \\ -1 & \text{if war} \end{cases} \text{ and } u_T = \begin{cases} 1 & \text{if status quo} \\ 0 & \text{if surrender} \\ \omega & \text{if war.} \end{cases}$$

C's most-preferred outcome is *T*'s surrender, its worst is war, and the status quo falls in between; *C* would like concessions, but not at the cost of war. For *T*, we fix the status quo at 1 and surrender at 0, but *T*'s war payoff is a variable *parameter*, $\omega < 1$. We assume that war is never as good as the status quo for *T* ($\omega < 1$), but it may be better than, equal to, or worse than surrender, which is fixed at 0. This lets us explore how different preferences—here, *T*'s war payoffs, which increase in its valuation for the issue at stake—affect its ability to deter attack. This restrictive set of preferences isolates cases where deterrence might work, stripping away less interesting cases in which *C* can't be deterred or *T* always resists.

The right panel of Figure 22.1 represents the same game in the *strategic form*, which collapses strategies into *strategy profiles*. For example, the strategy profile (A; S), read as "*C* attacks, *T* surrenders," leads to surrender, with payoffs (1, 0). The game has three outcomes, but the strategic form spreads them across four strategy profiles, because two profiles yield the status quo: (P; S), where *C* passes and *T* plans (but isn't called upon) to surrender, and (P; R), where *C* passes and *T* plans (but isn't called upon) to resist. The strategic form has some limitations, not least of which is that it allows players to pre-commit to actions that they wouldn't take if given the choice (see below), but it's useful when players make choices in ignorance of each other—say, if each fears a surprise attack or opportunistic ceasefire violation. The strategic form is also useful for defining a *strategy*: "a [complete] plan of action that specifies what actions a player will take based on beliefs about what actions other players will take" (Wolford 2019b, 32). In Figure 22.1, strategies entail one choice per player, but strategies can be arbitrarily complicated, including (a) intentional randomization in *mixed strategies*, where players try to obscure their plans (see Wolford 2019b, Ch. 8); (b) a potentially infinite number of iterations, like states complying with international law in the shadow of reciprocity (Gilligan and Johns 2012); or (c) choices along a continuum, like how much territory to demand of an enemy.

359

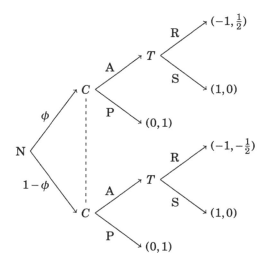

Figure 22.2 A game of limited information.

Finally, Figure 22.2 is a game of limited information. Suppose that C in our deterrence game is uncertain whether T will resist or surrender. To model this uncertainty, we introduce a non-strategic player called Nature, who chooses the value of ω according to a commonly known probability distribution and reveals that information only to T. Each possible value of ω (two, in this case) represents a potential *player-type* of T, such that C is uncertain over which type of T it faces. T's war payoff is *private information*, and the probability distribution over ω represents C's *beliefs* about T's type. Nature assigns T a resolute type, such that $\omega = 1/2$ with probability ϕ, and an irresolute type, such that $\omega = -1/2$, with probability $1-\phi$. The *information set* represented by the dotted line indicates that C doesn't know the result of Nature's move—that is, C can't distinguish one prior move from another. This allows us to retain the assumption of common knowledge while introducing C's uncertainty over T's preferences. T moves last in this model, which entails an expected utility calculation for C. But in *signaling models*, T moves first, which may allow a public threat to resist attack or costly military moves to reveal information about its type (see Fearon 1997). That said, games of limited information can be useful for thinking about the institution-sparse international system, but many causal mechanisms don't rest on uncertainty. Any such additional complication should be approached with care, if not outright skepticism (see, always, Healy 2017).

Equilibrium and Solution Concepts

With a game specified, we can ask how players are likely to play it. This requires a *solution concept*, which defines a set of rules about (a) what players know about previous moves and (b) when they're allowed to choose their actions. The most common solution concepts are variants of *Nash Equilibrium*, in which players choose strategies at which they do as well as they can, given what they know about what all other players are doing. Each player's strategy is a *best response* (or *best reply*) to all other players' strategies, and knowledge of those strategies rests on a *common conjecture* of shared ideas about norms, identities, and social roles—that is, who acts, who responds, and how others interpret and respond to others' actions (Morrow 2014, 28–33). In other words, equilibrium is a set of self-fulfilling social expectations.

The common conjecture is the very stuff of the social world, the basis of equilibrium reasoning in which players choose strategies in anticipation of what others are likely to do.

Nash Equilibrium. When a strategy profile constitutes a Nash Equilibrium, no player can benefit by switching to another strategy, given what it knows about other players' strategies. Formally, we say that no player has a *profitable deviation* from its stipulated strategy. Calculating Nash Equilibria is straightforward in the strategic form, so I begin with a *coordination game*, whose multiple equilibria highlight the importance of the common conjecture. Figure 22.3, adapted from Wolford's (2019b, Ch. 10) model of the naval war in the North Sea during World War I, represents the challenge of limiting the scale of fighting. Belligerents A and B consider whether to wage a "limited" war, of circumscribed scope or intensity, or a "total" war that doesn't observe these restraints. In World War I, this entailed the British and German navies waging a sporadic, relatively low-intensity surface war in the North Sea, each declining to force a decisive confrontation. Each side's best outcome is a limited conflict (4), allowing it to control escalation and invest resources elsewhere—like the land war for Germany and, for Britain, protecting its network of coaling stations—followed by going total while the other observes limits (3), a mutually total war (2), and worst, observing limits while the other goes total (1).

Figure 22.3 shows that there are two Nash Equilibria, one at (total; total) and another at (limited; limited). To verify this, we take a candidate strategy profile, then see whether any player can do better by deviating, holding the other's strategy constant. If *any* player has a profitable deviation, the strategy profile isn't a Nash Equilibrium. If *no* player has a profitable deviation, we have a Nash Equilibrium. At (total; total), each player receives 2, and given that the other is playing "total," deviating to "limited" yields a payoff of 1. This is true for both players; we have a Nash Equilibrium, and players reason like so: "Matching my enemy's total war strategy is better than allowing it to go total while I observe limits, so I'll wage a total war." Note that the comparison isn't to some other strategy profile, like the more attractive limited war, but to what a player could achieve with a single deviation. In this case, though, the strategy profile (limited; limited) is also a Nash Equilibrium; both players receive 4, and each prefers maintaining this limited war to going total while the other observes limits, which yields only 3. Each side is happy to maintain limits on the war if the other does, and only *because* the other does.

The common conjecture determines which equilibrium gets played. Players prefer to match the other's strategy—to keep the war limited if the other will, but to go total if the other will—but they can only play the limited-war equilibrium when they can make accurate guesses about each other's strategy. In World War I, the limited naval war depended on the crudeness of the available strategies: the British to maintain a distant blockade of German ports that was easily distinguishable from a much-feared coastal raid and the Germans to stay in port at Wilhelmshaven, launching only occasional sorties toward the British Isles (see Wolford 2019b, 261–271). Belligerents communicated their strategies tacitly, because

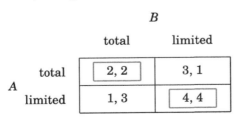

Figure 22.3 Coordination and limited war.

the "limited" option was clearly distinguishable from the alternative—that is, focal (see Schelling 1960, Ch. 3). This logic of coordination has also shed light on the roles of international law in maintaining limits on war (Morrow 2014, Wolford 2019a) and the United Nations in international conflict (Chapman and Wolford 2010; Voeten 2005).

Figure 22.4 presents another widely used game with a single, *unique* Nash Equilibrium. The Prisoner's Dilemma is inspired by situations in which players have incentives to exploit each other's cooperation. Like two suspects offered a chance to testify against the other for a lighter prison sentence, they can get their second-best outcome of a light sentence (3) by cooperating—that is, playing C and refusing to confess—but each one gets off with a slap on the wrist if the other cooperates while she defects, playing D by pointing the finger at the other. Staying silent while the other defects yields a player's worst payoff (1), and if both players confess, they each get heavy sentences, though not as heavy if they're the only one charged. In situations represented by the Prisoner's Dilemma, neither player can resist the temptation to defect if the other player will cooperate (4 > 3), nor can they afford to cooperate if the other will defect (2 > 1). Therefore, each player has a *dominant strategy* of playing D, which implies a single Nash Equilibrium at which both players defect and for which payoffs are (2, 2). Players fail to achieve the benefits of cooperation, represented by payoffs (3, 3) at strategy profile (C; C), because neither can credibly promise not to exploit the other's cooperation. The equilibrium is *inefficient*, since there's less to go around than there would be if the players chose differently, but their incentives and the structure of the interaction lead them to choose actions that they regret ex post. The underlying logic of the Prisoner's Dilemma has been used, often in more complicated models, to explain the breakdown of ceasefires (Fortna 2003; Werner and Yuen 2005), limits on arms control (Coe and Vaynman 2020; Fearon 2018), political incentives for protectionism (Bagwell and Staiger 2002), the duration of civil (Walter 2002) and interstate war (Reiter 2009), and the emergence of international anarchy (Kim and Wolford 2014).

Thinking harder about the strategic form highlights Nash Equilibrium's main limitation. In Figures 22.3 and 22.4, players move simultaneously because we want them to choose without observing the other's choice. This is a problem for Figure 22.1's deterrence game, because the strategic form obscures the fact that T moves in full knowledge that C has chosen to attack. Yet, Nash Equilibrium allows players to choose strategies ahead of time, to pre-commit to actions that might not be in their interest when given a choice. Suppose that $\omega < 0$, such that T prefers surrender to resistance. T would never choose R *if given the chance*, but T can make this *incredible* threat as part of a Nash Equilibrium because the threat is never called in. In other words, Nash Equilibrium allows T to choose a strategy as if it doesn't yet know whether C has attacked, even though neither (a) the game itself nor (b) the kind of deterrence interactions it represents entail such pre-commitments. Take the strategy profile (P; R), at which C passes and T resists. Since C is passing, T's only possible deviation is to play S, and it's indifferent over those options, so it has no profitable deviation; and since T is playing R, C can't profit by switching to A, because it would get −1 instead of 0. That's a Nash Equilibrium, but it rests on a patently incredible threat—a move that T wouldn't make

		B	
		C	D
A	C	3,3	1,4
	D	4,1	2,2

Figure 22.4 The Prisoner's Dilemma.

if we took the sequential nature of play seriously—so we'd like a way to find equilibria that *don't* rest on such shaky substantive foundations.

Subgame Perfect Equilibrium. We refine the set of Nash Equilibria with *Subgame Perfect Equilibrium* (SPE), which decomposes extensive-form games into *subgames* at which players condition their choices on the history of play. The extensive-form game in Figure 22.1 has two subgames: (1) T's terminal move, and then (2) the entire game beginning with C's move. For games of complete information, we calculate SPE with *backward induction*, beginning at the game's last move and working backward, identifying each player's best replies conditional on being given a choice. This ensures that we rule out incredible threats, such that while all SPE are Nash Equilibria, not all Nash Equilibria are subgame perfect.

Figure 22.5 returns to our basic model of deterrence for two examples, where we show how different values of ω, or T's war payoffs, condition C's decision to attack. At left, we let $\omega < 0$, such that T expects to do poorly enough in a war that it prefers surrender to resistance. T is sure to choose S, because $0 > \omega$, so we highlight that move with a bold line. Moving up the tree, C anticipates T's surrender, so it chooses to attack (also highlighted in bold) because $1 > 0$. Therefore, when $\omega < 0$, the only SPE is (A; S). The strategy profile (P; R) remains a Nash Equilibrium even when T's war payoff is so low, but it can't survive backward induction; as such, we'd say that T playing R can't be part of an SPE when $\omega < 0$. Next, $\omega > 0$ at right, such that T prefers resistance to surrender; T expects to do well enough in a war that it would rather fight than give up the prize to the challenger. Given the chance to resist, T plays R. Moving back up the tree, C passes rather than attacks, since it prefers the status quo to war ($0 > 1$).[4] Therefore, (P; R) *can* be an SPE, but only when T's threat to resist is credible. Otherwise, when $\omega < 0$, T wouldn't resist if given the chance, so under those conditions there can be no SPE in which T resists. Other work extends this basic deterrence interaction to include multiple players, for example, a third party that might come to the target's defense or otherwise intervene in an extended deterrence setting (Fang et al. 2014, Yuen 2009), and it can inform questions about the effectiveness of threats, the probability of war, and war outcomes.

Subgame perfection forces us to think carefully about how the data from which we sample (e.g., the historical record) are generated. It's useful for telling us where—and where not—to look for evidence. The equilibria of Figure 22.5 identify two distinct *paths of play*, (A; S) and (P; R), which identify sets of choices we observe in equilibrium. When $\omega < 0$, we observe

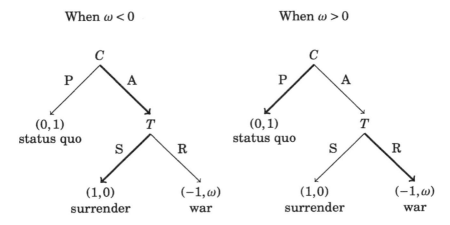

Figure 22.5 Subgame perfect equilibria in the deterrence game.

C attacking and T surrendering, but when $\omega > 0$, we observe C passing, precisely because it expects T to resist. The structure of the interaction is the same, yet the observable implications differ; precisely when T expects to do better in war, C avoids provoking a conflict. We call this *strategic censoring*, because states choose whether to select themselves into the sample of observed conflicts. Suppose that we'd like to estimate the relationship between a country's valuation of the issues at stake, which for T is correlated with ω, and its performance in war, which occurs only if C attacks and T resists. We only observe conflicts when C believes T's war payoff to be low ($\omega < 0$); otherwise, if ω were high enough that T would resist, war wouldn't occur. If we were to examine observed conflicts to make an inference about how issue salience affects war performance, we'd work from a biased sample: the very things that make T do poorly in a war are associated with *not* observing that war. Estimates of the relationship between ω and success in war would be biased toward zero, because the true relationship—that higher ω implies better war performance—is obscured in observational data.

Perfect Bayesian Equilibrium. Next, players are often uncertain over aspects of their strategic environment, and Perfect Bayesian Equilibrium (PBE) retains SPE's focus on sequential rationality but introduces the concept of *beliefs* over previous moves. Returning to Figure 22.2, recall that C can't distinguish Nature's initial choices from one another. Substantively, this means that C is uncertain over how T responds to an attack; it knows only that Nature assigns a resolute type ($\omega = 1/2$) with probability ϕ and an irresolute type ($\omega = -1/2$) with probability $1 - \phi$. Backward induction breaks down at C's information set, but beliefs allow us to describe a set of strategies that are sequentially rational and consistent with beliefs informed by common knowledge of each player's strategies. These *prior beliefs* also represent C's subjective uncertainty; C is relatively confident that T is irresolute when ϕ is close to 0, relatively confident that T is resolute when ϕ is close to 1, and maximally uncertain when $\phi = 1/2$.

Figure 22.6 describes two PBE of the limited-information deterrence game, where equilibrium actions are again bolded. First, we can use backward induction to show that T resists if resolute and surrenders if irresolute in any equilibrium; recall that, since its choice nodes aren't connected with the dotted line of an information set, T knows its own type. Second, C

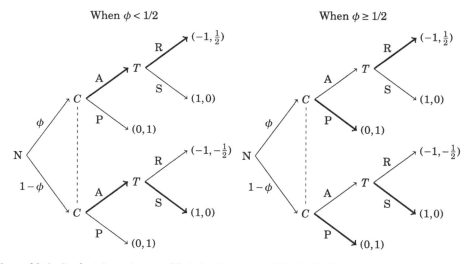

Figure 22.6 Perfect Bayesian equilibria in the game of limited information.

makes an expected utility calculation based on its knowledge of Nature's strategy. C attacks when $EU_C(A) > u_C(P)$, or when the expected utility for attacking is greater than the known payoff for passing, or

$$\phi(-1) + (1-\phi)(1) > 0,$$

and passes otherwise. Therefore, the game has two PBE. First, when C believes $\phi < 1/2$, it attacks, and T resists if resolute and surrenders if irresolute. Second, when C believes $\phi \geq 1/2$, it passes, and T resists if resolute and surrenders if irresolute. In equilibrium, (a) C attacks only when sufficiently optimistic that T is irresolute, and (b) T is a type that resists with probability ϕ. Comparing this with the SPE in Figure 22.5, we see that private information can cause war that wouldn't occur if players were fully informed.

Finally, players can't hold just any beliefs in PBE. On the path of play, they form beliefs about being at a given node with Bayes' Rule, ensuring that beliefs are consistent with the laws of probability. Beliefs are straightforward in our example, but if T were to have the first move after learning its type, it's possible that its choice—say, a threat to resist if C attacks—might reveal information that C can use to update its beliefs about the relative probability of facing a resolute or irresolute type of T. For example, if the resolute T were to take an action that an irresolute T would find too costly, perhaps making expensive military moves or staking one's political reputation on resistance, then C could use Bayes' Rule to form a *posterior belief* that raises its estimate of facing the resolute type if such a threat is made and lowers its estimate if no such threat is made. A similar exercise shows that, in situations like deterrence where an irresolute type has incentives to bluff about its willingness to fight, costless threats like simple diplomatic speech often can't reveal war-averting information (see Fearon 1995, 395–401). But recall that strategies are complete plans of action, so players must form beliefs about the history of play even in the event of unexpected moves; for example, if all types of T are supposed to make a verbal threat to resist, C must still know what to do if T makes no such threat, and T must know what happens if it doesn't make the threat. Perfect Bayesian Equilibrium places no restrictions on beliefs after zero-probability events, because Bayes' Rule is undefined (i.e., the denominator is zero). A substantial literature has developed around just how to refine PBE to handle these *out-of-equilibrium beliefs*. For more on refinements, see Morrow (1994, Ch. 8) and Cho and Kreps (1987).

Conclusion

Game theory's strengths for FPA include its explicitly strategic standard of explanation and the transparency of its assumptions and arguments. It helps us rationalize—that is, make sense of—actors' decisions by forcing us to think about how they understand their choices, the choices of others, and the consequences of those choices. Formalization helps ensure that our definitions and arguments are coherent, clear, and contestable—a set of features which has enabled notable theoretical and empirical progress in understanding international conflict, informing empirical work on both observational and experimental data.

But game theory has limits. First, preferences over outcomes are fixed over the course of the game, which means that games are often not a useful way of thinking about preference formation—for example, why the states in deterrence models disagree in the first place over how to divide the international pie. Models *can* explain changing preferences over means (actions) in a single game, but the game's ends (preferences) are, of necessity, fixed, requiring great care and greater substantive knowledge in choosing endpoints. Second, while games built on expected utility are useful for explaining how strategic incentives can induce risk-acceptant or risk-averse behavior (see, e.g., Goemans and Fey 2009), they're less useful for explaining the influence of idiosyncratic risk preferences, which may violate some rules of expected utility (Morrow 1994, 44–49; but see Druckman 2004). It's up to the analyst to choose what they wish to explain—the influence of social structures and institutions or of cognitive processes on collective choices and outcomes—and to choose the proper theoretical tools. Third, though this implicates analysts more than game theory itself, a bad fit between model and solution concept can impose (a) social structure or (b) informational access that's unavailable to the actors whose behavior we're trying to explain. In terms of social structure, countries interacting across different or changing international-legal regimes—like Japan and Korea in the 1870s (Park 2020)—might have less information about preferences and strategies than states in the same legal regime, necessitating relaxations of assumptions about common knowledge and even, in some cases, about the strength of the common conjecture (Coe and Wolford 2020, 271). When it comes to informational access, the median voter is often rationally ignorant of foreign policy (Berinsky 2009; Chapman 2011), which makes it problematic to assume that the voters who punish leaders draw equally important inferences from actions taken than from those not taken (Arena 2015; Enke 2020). All told, choosing solution concepts requires care and—I can't stress this enough—substantial case knowledge.

Finally, first-time users should be aware of a few common missteps. First, not all research questions require a new game. If it's possible to argue that a particular phenomenon is well-described by an extant game, then we're better served by learning about those similarities, by identifying the highest common factor across different contexts, than by the construction of a redundant or misleading game that complicates matters unnecessarily. Second, it's easy to (unwittingly) build an expected solution into the game. That temptation must be avoided. Very often, students will rule out logically possible choices because "the players would never do that," but that gets things backward. We want to explain why some choices—like war in the complete-information deterrence game—stay off the path of play, because paths not taken explain why other paths *are* taken. Finally, users should also resist the temptation to evaluate theoretical models in the way they evaluate empirical models. Accounting for every potential causal variable, for example, isn't useful when we're trying to isolate and explore a putative causal mechanism. The answer to why one factor causes an outcome need not depend on why another factor might also cause it. Nor does the idea of "controlling for" alternative explanations in a theoretical model make sense; that's important for identifying empirical models, where we hope that all-else-equal claims match those in our theoretical models (Ashworth et al. 2021), but it comes *after* the theoretical model tells us how the mechanism works and where to look for evidence. Ultimately, it's worth remembering Harrison Wagner's (2001, 4) advice on the topic: "The world is a messy and confusing place. We do not enhance our understanding of it by saying messy and confusing things about it."

Notes

1. On the distinction between noncooperative and cooperative game theory, see Morrow (1994, Ch. 4).
2. For recent game-theoretic work on international law, see Chapman (2011) on the informational role of the UN Security Council, Conrad and Ritter (2019) on dissent and repression in the shadow of human rights law, and for IPE, see Carnegie (2014) on how the WTO can solve political hold-up problems.
3. See Ashworth et al. (2021) and Clarke and Primo (2012, Ch. 4).
4. Both SPE exist when $\omega = 0$, and we typically make an assumption about what players do at indifference to reduce the number of equilibria.

References

Arena, Philip. 2015. "Crisis bargaining, domestic opposition, and tragic wars." *Journal of Theoretical Politics* 27(1): 108–131.

Arena, Philip, and Scott Wolford. 2012. "Arms, intelligence, and war." *International Studies Quarterly* 56(2): 351–365.

Ashworth, Scott, Berry, Christopher R., and Ethan Bueno de Mesquita. 2021. *Theory and Credibility.* Princeton University Press.

Bagwell, Kyle, and Robert Staiger. 2002. *The Economics of the World Trading System.* MIT Press.

Berinski, Adam J. 2009. *In Time of War.* University of Chicago Press.

Bils, Peter, and William Spaniel. 2017. "Policy bargaining and militarized conflict." *Journal of Theoretical Politics* 29(4): 647–768.

Bueno de Mesquita, Ethan, and Scott A. Tyson. 2020. "The commensurability problem: Conceptual difficulties in estimating the effect of behavior on behavior." *American Political Science Review* 114(2): 375–391.

Carnegie, Allison. 2014. "States held hostage: Political hold-up problems and the effects of international institutions." *American Political Science Review* 108(1): 54–70.

Carnegie, Allison, and Carson, Austin. 2018. "The spotlight's harsh glare: Rethinking publicity and international order." *International Organization* 72(3): 627–657.

Chapman, Terrence L. 2011. *Securing Approval.* University of Chicago Press.

Chapman, Terrence L., and Scott Wolford. 2010. "International organizations, strategy, and crisis bargaining." *Journal of Politics* 72(1): 227–242.

Cho, In-Koo, and David M. Kreps. 1987. "Signaling games and stable equilibria." *Quarterly Journal of Economics* 102(2): 179–221.

Clarke, Kevin A., and David M. Primo. 2012. *A Model Discipline.* Oxford University Press.

Coe, Andrew J., and Jane Vaynman. 2015. "Collusion and the nuclear nonproliferation regime." *Journal of Politics* 77(4): 983–987.

Coe, Andrew J., and Jane Vaynman. 2020. "Why arms control is so rare." *American Political Science Review* 114(2): 342–355.

Coe, Andrew J., and Scott Wolford. 2020. "East Asian history and international relations." In *East Asia in The World*, edited by Haggard, Stephan and David C. Kang. Cambridge University Press, 263–281.

Conrad, Courtenay R., and Emily Hencken Ritter. 2019. *Contentious Compliance.* Oxford University Press.

Davis, Jason S. 2021. "War as a redistributive problem." *American Journal of Political Science*, https://doi.org/10.1111/ajps.12623.

Debs, Aexandre, and Hein Goemans. 2010. "Regime type, the fate of leaders, and war." *American Political Science Review* 104(3): 430–445.

Debs, Alexandre, and Jessica Chen Weiss. 2016. "Circumstances, domestic audiences, and reputational incentives in international crisis bargaining." *Journal of Conflict Resolution* 60(3): 403–433.

Druckman, James N. 2004. "Political preference formation: Competition, deliberation, and the (ir)relevance of framing effects." *American Political Science Review* 98(4): 671–686.

Enke, Benjamin. 2020. "What you see is all there is." *Quarterly Journal of Economics* 135(3): 1363– 1398.

Fang, Songying, Johnson, Jesse C., and Brett Ashley Leeds. 2014. "To concede or resist? The restraining effect of military alliances." *International Organization* 68(4): 775–809.

Favretto, Katja. 2009. "Should peacemakers take sides? Major power mediation, coercion, and bias." *American Political Science Review* 103(2): 248–263.

Fearon, James D. 1994. "Domestic political audiences and the escalation of international disputes." *American Political Science Review* 88(3): 577–592.

———. 1995. "Rationalist explanations for war." *International Organization* 49(3): 379–414.

———. 1997. "Signaling foreign policy interests: Tying hands versus sinking costs." *Journal of Conflict Resolution* 41(1): 68–90.

———. 2018. "Conflict, cooperation, and the costs of anarchy." *International Organization* 72(3): 523–559.

Filson, Darren and Suzanne Werner. 2002. "A bargaining model of war and peace: Anticipating the onset, duration, and outcome of war." *American Journal of Political Science* 46(4): 819– 838.

Fortna, Virginia Page. 2003. "Scraps of paper? Agreements and the durability of peace." *International Organization* 57(2): 337–372.

Gilligan, Michael J., and Leslie Johns. 2012. "Formal models of international institutions." *Annual Review of Political Science* 15: 221–243.

Goemans, Hein, and Mark Fey. 2009. "Risky but rational: War as an institutionally induced gamble." *Journal of Politics* 71(1): 35–54.

Goemans, Hein, and William Spaniel. 2016. "Multimethod research: A case for formal theory." *Security Studies* 25: 25–33.

Haynes, Kyle, and Brandon K. Yoder. 2020. "Offsetting uncertainty: Reassurance with two-sided incomplete information." *American Journal of Political Science* 64(1): 38–51.

Healy, Kieran. 2017. "Fuck nuance." *Sociological Theory* 35(2): 118–127.

Jervis, Robert. 1970. *The Logic of Images in International Relations*. Princeton University Press.

Kim, Moonhawk, and Scott Wolford. 2014. "Choosing anarchy: Institutional alternatives and the global order." *International Theory* 6(1): 28–67.

Krainin, Colin, and Thomas Wiseman. 2016. "War and stability in dynamic international systems." *Journal of Politics* 78(4): 1139–1152.

Kydd, Andrew H. 1997. "Game theory and the spiral model." *World Politics* 49(3): 371–400.

———. 2005. *Trust and Mistrust in International Relations*. Princeton University Press.

Langlois, Catherina C., and Jean-Pierre P. Langlois. 2009. "Does attrition behavior help explain the duration of interstate wars? A game theoretic and empirical analysis." *International Studies Quarterly* 53(4): 1051–1073.

Leventoğlu, Bahar, and Ahmer Tarar. 2008. "Does private information lead to delay or war in crisis bargaining?" *International Studies Quarterly* 52(3): 533–553.

Leventoğlu, Bahar, and Branislav Slantchev. 2007. "The armed peace: A punctuated equilibrium theory of war." *American Journal of Political Science* 51(4): 755–771.

Lo, Nigel, Hashimoto, Barry, and Dan Reiter. 2008. "Ensuring peace: Foreign-imposed regime change and postwar peace duration, 1914–2001." *International Organization* 62(4): 717–736.

Meirowitz, Adam, and Anne E. Sartori. 2008. "Strategic uncertainty as a cause of war." *Quarterly Journal of Political Science* 3(4): 327–352.

Morrow, James D. 1994. *Game Theory for Political Scientists*. Princeton University Press.

———. 2014. *Order Within Anarchy*. Cambridge University Press.

Nalebuff, Barry. 1991. "Rational deterrence in an imperfect world." *World Politics* 43(3): 315–335.

O'Neill, Barry. 1994. "Game theory models of peace and war." In *Handbook of Game Theory with Economic Applications*, Vol. 2, Ch. 29, edited by Aumann, Robert. J. and Sergiu Hart. Elsevier.

Park, Saeyoung. 2020. "The death of Eastphalia, 1874." In *East Asia in The World*, edited by Haggard, Stephan and David C. Kang. Cambridge University Press, 239–259.

Phillips, Julianne, and Scott Wolford. 2021. "Collective deterrence in the shadow of shifting power." *International Studies Quarterly* 65(1): 136–145.

Powell, Robert. 1991. "Absolute and relative gains in international relations theory." *American Political Science Review* 85(4): 1303–1320.

———. 1994. "Anarchy in international relations theory: The neorealist-neoliberal debate." *International Organization* 48(2): 313–344.

———. 1996. "Bargaining in the shadow of power." *Games and Economic Behavior* 15(2): 255–289.

———. 2004. "Bargaining and learning while fighting." *American Journal of Political Science* 48(2): 344–361.

———. 2006. "War as a commitment problem." *International Organization* 60(1): 169–203.

Reiter, Dan. 2009. *How Wars End*. Princeton University Press.

Sartori, Anne. E. 2005. *Deterrence by Diplomacy*. Princeton University Press.

Schelling, Thomas. C. 1960. *The Strategy of Conflict*. Harvard University Press.

Schultz, Kenneth A. 1998. "Domestic opposition and signaling in international crises." *American Political Science Review* 92(4): 829–844.

———. 2001. "Looking for audience costs." *Journal of Conflict Resolution* 45(1): 32–60.

Slantchev, Branislav. 2005. "Military coercion in interstate crises." *American Political Science Review* 99(4): 533–547.

———. 2012. "Borrowed power: Debt finance and the resort to arms." *American Political Science Review* 106(4): 787–809.

Thomas, Jakana L., Reed, William, and Scott Wolford. 2016. "The rebels' credibility dilemma." *International Organization* 70(3): 477–511.

Trager, Robert F. 2010. "Diplomatic calculus in anarchy: How communication matters." *American Political Science Review* 104(2): 347–368.

———. 2015. "Diplomatic signaling among multiple states." *Journal of Politics* 77(3): 635–647.

Trager, Robert F., and Lynn Vavreck. 2011. "The political costs of crisis bargaining: Presidential rhetoric and the role of party." *American Journal of Political Science* 55(3): 526–545.

Voeten, Erik. 2005. "The political origins of the UN Security Council's ability to legitimize the use of force." *International Organization* 59: 527–557.

Wagner, R. Harrison. 2001. *Who's Afraid of Rational Choice Theory?* Typescript, University of Texas at Austin.

———. 2007. *War and the State*. The University of Michigan Press.

Walter, Barbara F. 2002. *Committing to Peace*. Princeton University Press.

Werner, Suzanne. 1999. "The precarious nature of peace: Resolving the issues, enforcing the settlement, and renegotiating the terms." *American Journal of Political Science* 43(3): 912–934.

Werner, Suzanne, and Yuen, Amy T. 2005. "Making and keeping peace." *International Organization* 59(2): 261–292.

Wolford, Scott. 2019a. "Neutrality regimes." *Security Studies* 28(4): 807–832.

———. 2019b. *The Politics of the First World War*. Cambridge University Press.

———. 2020. "War on the world stage: Crisis bargaining before third parties." *Journal of Theoretical Politics* 32(2): 235–261.

Wolford, Scott, Reiter, Dan, and Clifford J. Carrubba. 2011. "Information, commitment, and war." *Journal of Conflict Resolution* 55(4): 556–579.

Wu, Cathy X., and Scott Wolford. 2018. "Leaders, states, and reputations." *Journal of Conflict Resolution* 62(10): 2087–2117.

Yuen, Amy T. 2009. "Target concessions in the shadow of intervention." *Journal of Conflict Resolution* 53(5): 727–744.

23
Public Opinion Surveys
Katja B. Kleinberg

Introduction

Polling data are a ubiquitous feature of modern political life. The basic feature of this mode of inquiry is a standardized survey instrument, composed of carefully crafted questions and administered by one of several modes (face-to-face interviews, phone interviews, online modules) to a representative sample of a population of interest. Ideally, the data so gathered will allow inferences about the demographic characteristics, attitudes, beliefs, and preferences of the underlying population. Public opinion surveys are the primary source of information about the intensity and direction of the public will for policymakers, the media, and even the public itself.

For political scientists, including foreign policy scholars, public opinion survey data have several attractive features. People's attitudes and actions are the basic building block of politics: individuals organize, take up arms, engage in commerce, support or topple governments. And it is people and populations whose lives and livelihoods are directly affected by foreign policy, their own governments' or that of an adversary, a trading partner, or an international organization. Public opinion surveys promise to allow us to ascertain their attitudes and preferences directly, without having to infer them from individuals' behavior in elections, markets, or protests.

The public also play a role in many mid-range theories in international relations. Without public opinion survey data, testing predictions from these theories must rely on proxies and assumptions about what different types of publics—democratic and non-democratic ones in particular—want: from competent and steadfast leaders (bargaining model of war) to peace and cooperation with other democracies (democratic peace), income from international commerce or protection from adverse competition (international political economy of trade and investment), or protection of human rights abroad (humanitarian intervention). Surveys, and increasingly survey experiments, allow us to investigate directly whether the public (and which parts of the public) are willing and able to play the role our theories assign.

Finally, studies using public opinion data can speak to broader concerns about democratic governance in the context of foreign policy. This includes the extent to which democratic governance requires an informed and interested citizenry, how well the public are equipped and sufficiently 'prudent' to exercise a role in policymaking (Jentleson 1992; Fordham and Kleinberg 2020), and whether the will of the public is adequately and equally represented in policymaking (e.g., Page and Bouton 2006). A better understanding of the sources and dynamics of public opinion can inform longstanding normative debates over such thorny questions as whether policymakers should listen to the public in matters of foreign policy (e.g., Berelson 1952; Lippmann 1955).

This chapter provides an overview of the use of public opinion surveys in Foreign Policy Analysis (FPA). The following sections focus, respectively, on the research questions scholars have explored using surveys and survey experiments, select choices and challenges in designing public opinion surveys in FPA, and implications of recent trends in survey research.

Public Opinion Surveys in Foreign Policy Analysis

Systematic public opinion polling in the United States has its origins in the 1930s and 1940s, with the pioneering work of Elmo Roper, George Gallup, Paul Lazarsfeld, among others (Groves 2011). Almost from its inception, public opinion research was used to gauge the public's views on foreign affairs (Casey 2001). Coinciding with World War II and the emergence of the U.S.' role as the most powerful country in the international state system, early studies sought to ascertain the U.S. public's attitudes toward the war and, subsequently, toward continued engagement in Europe and the world (e.g., Lazarsfeld et al. 1948; Almond 1960). Since then, scholars of foreign policy have applied survey research methods to answer a wide range of questions concerning the shape and nature of foreign policy public opinion, democratic representation, and the role of the public in foreign policy outcomes.

Nature and Determinants of Foreign Policy Public Opinion. What does the public want and why? At the most basic level, survey data allow researchers to ascertain what the public think about foreign policy issues, what outcomes the public desire and how strongly they desire them, and what policies the public will support to obtain those outcomes. Classic studies have analyzed individual survey questions or sets of questions asked over several years (or decades) to describe patterns and trends in aggregate opinion and to investigate influences on the national mood (e.g., Almond 1960; Page and Bouton 2006; Owen and Quinn 2016). Aggregate survey data have also been employed as measures of country-level characteristics. Andrews et al. (2018), for example, use national Gallup polls from 2004 to 2012 about support for increased immigration to construct a U.S. state-year measure of ethnocentrism, a source of political risk that the authors argue deters inward foreign investment.

A more fundamental question is whether the public, individually and collectively, in fact have stable and predictable opinions on matters of foreign policy. Revisiting early survey research that characterized American public opinion as shallow, fickle, and inconsistent (e.g., Lippmann 1955; Almond 1960; Conserve 1964), more recent work has applied advanced statistical methods to a wider range of survey data to explore whether foreign policy public opinion is internally structured along distinct dimensions (e.g., Wittkopf 1990; Gravelle, Reifler, and Scotto 2017), organized into hierarchies (e.g., Hurwitz and Peffley 1987), or constrained by core values (e.g., Rathbun et al. 2016).

What influences foreign policy public opinion? A large and diverse body of scholarship investigates the sources of individual-level attitudes and preferences toward foreign policy. Most commonly, these studies examine correlations between survey responses to foreign policy questions and observational data on individual-level characteristics, such as respondents' levels of education, sex, industry of employment, geographic location, or other survey items designed to measure individual-level traits, such as personality type (e.g., Schoen 2007) or xenophobia (e.g., Mansfield and Mutz 2009). Finally, recent survey experimental work in this area focuses on the psychological processes involved in preference formation and survey response, respectively, including the role of knowledge (e.g., Rho and Tomz 2017), emotions (e.g., Fisk et al. 2019), and elite communication (e.g., Guisinger and Saunders 2017).

Democratic Representation and Foreign Policy Outcomes. How does public opinion affect foreign policy? The responsiveness of policymakers to the preferences of the public is an important factor in many theoretical arguments in international relations and a core concern of democratic theory (e.g., Dahl 1956). Researchers have employed public opinion surveys in a variety of ways to answer this question.

One approach has been to link longitudinal public opinion survey data to votes in legislatures or to changes in policy or policy outcomes, such as levels of defense spending (e.g., Bartels 1991; Soroka and Wlezien 2010) and election outcomes (for an overview of this work, see Aldrich et al. 2006). Other studies have used original survey experiments to probe the causal mechanisms underlying democratic accountability in different areas of foreign policy. For example, an influential study by Guisinger (2009) on the dynamics of representation in foreign economic policy shows not only that many voters are unaware of their representatives' positions on major trade policies, but also that even those who know where their representatives stand do not substantially adjust their voting behavior based on this information (see also Guisinger 2017).

A more indirect approach employs surveys of mass opinion and the opinions of societal elites and policymakers to investigate the extent of congruence in attitudes toward foreign policy. For example, Jacobs and Page (2005) examine evidence from eight pairs of surveys between 1974 and 2002 conducted by the Chicago Council on Foreign Relations (CCFR, now the Chicago Council on Global Affairs). Their findings suggest that mass opinion has only limited impact on policymakers' views compared with the impact of business elites and expert opinion, except on economic policy and highly salient issues like war (see also Page and Bouton 2006; Bartels 2016; for a critical assessment of these studies, see Kertzer 2020).

Microfoundations. Scholars are increasingly using public opinion surveys and survey experiments to reevaluate and refine game-theoretic models of international relations (Kertzer 2017). While many stipulate a role for the public—and democratic publics in particular—it has long been unclear whether the public can and will act in the ways these models suggest. Prime examples are the bargaining model and role that audience costs are assumed to play in making commitments credible (Fearon 1994). A growing number of studies have employed public opinion surveys methods to probe key assumptions about the public's propensity for punishing leaders who renege on threats or promises (e.g., Tomz 2007; Chaudoin 2014; Levy et al. 2015). By employing survey experiments, these studies can uncover individual-level dynamics and do so without concern for selection bias or confounding variables that plagued earlier efforts.

Drawing on insights from psychology, sociology, and American politics, scholars have used survey and experimental methods to uncover a range of causal mechanisms driving the responses of domestic and international audiences. These studies ask, for example, whether publics are more likely to punish belligerence or inconsistency (Kertzer and Brutger 2016), whether female leaders are more likely than male leaders to be punished by their publics (Schwartz and Blair 2020), whether some individuals are more likely than others to punish leaders for particular behaviors (Brutger and Kertzer 2018), and to what extent audience costs function differently in different national contexts (Weiss and Dafoe 2019). Others have used survey experiments involving political elites to investigate whether policymakers perceive costly signals in the way the bargaining model suggests (e.g., Yarhi-Milo, Kertzer, and Renshon 2018).

Broader Trends. The most notable trend in foreign policy research in recent years is the immense growth in studies using public opinion survey methods. This development can be credited to institutional initiatives (notably, the Cooperative Congressional Election Study and Time-Sharing Experiments in the Social Sciences), the proliferation of high-quality polls (including several regularly fielded, representative national and cross-national surveys), and technological innovations such as computer-administered surveys and online respondent pools, which have lowered the cost of public opinion research.[1] Fueled by a renewed interest in individual-level processes and the use of psychological approaches and models in FPA (for overviews, see Hafner-Burton et al. 2017 and Kertzer and Tingley 2018), survey experiments, in particular, have become increasingly popular.

While survey-based FPA is still heavily focused on the U.S. mass public, scholars are also increasingly moving beyond the narrow geographic domain of Western democracies. Some of this work probes whether existing insights about concepts like audience costs and the democratic peace travel to other national settings (e.g., Weiss and Dafoe 2019; Bell and Quek 2017). Other studies employ survey methods as part of complex research designs to investigate phenomena that are more common in other parts of the world, such as armed insurgency (e.g., Matanock and García-Sánchez 2018) and large-scale refugee flows (e.g., Ghosn et al. 2021). At the same time, the globalization of public opinion research has generated new and unique theoretical and methodological challenges (see Heath, Fisher, and Smith 2005; Lupu and Michelitch 2018).

Survey-based research has substantially increased our understanding of the shape of foreign policy public opinion, as well as of the individual-level characteristics and psychological dynamics that influence opinions and preferences on a wide range of issues. Yet the gain in knowledge has been uneven: the processes by which individual-level opinions and preferences are translated into votes, behaviors, and policy outcomes remain the least well-developed area of research on foreign policy public opinion. This leaves findings from survey-based studies open to the 'so what' question: Why should we care about what individuals claim to think and want? More broadly, survey-based FPA has yet to fully grapple with the question of how to integrate findings at different levels of aggregation (such as those arising from individual-level survey experiments and state-level observational data) and whether—in the extreme case—to discard or substantially revise an underlying theory if predictions derived from it are not borne out by individual-level evidence (for a critical discussion, see Pepinksy 2014).

Survey Methodology: Choices and Challenges

Public opinion surveys gather data about respondents by asking questions. While seemingly straightforward, this process requires scholars to make a series of choices, including what to ask (instrument design), who to ask (populations, sampling), and how to ask (survey design, survey mode). A complete accounting of survey design considerations and pitfalls is beyond the scope of this chapter. First-time users are encouraged to consult one or more of several widely used introductory texts, including Fowler (1995) on question design, Weisberg (2005) on the total survey error approach, and Groves et al. (2011) on general survey methodology.[2]

This section outlines some of the considerations that should inform researchers' choices. Note that while the discussion is aimed primarily at researchers considering the creation of an original survey, the concerns raised apply equally to studies using existing surveys.

Survey Instrument

In studying foreign policy through public opinion surveys, we make at least two assumptions. First, we assume that the public—specifically, our survey respondents—actually have opinions on foreign policy questions. Second, we assume that we can measure these opinions accurately and reliably using survey methods. Research on the nature of foreign policy public opinion and survey response raises concerns on both fronts, with direct implications for survey design.

For the mass public foreign policy often appears abstract and remote from one's direct experience. While foreign policy views may not necessarily resemble Converse's (1964) *non-attitudes*, prominent studies make a compelling case that most people 'simply do not possess preformed attitudes at the level of specificity demanded in surveys' (Zaller and Feldman 1992, 579). Instead, in answering survey questions respondents frequently draw on their predispositions as well as information made salient by recent events, elite discourse, and the survey instrument itself (Zaller 1992). This raises the possibility that what we measure and interpret as public opinion is substantially shaped by features of the survey instrument, including how our questions are worded, which answer options are offered, and the order in which both questions and response options are presented.

Question Wording. Writing good survey questions is difficult, writing the perfect question probably impossible. A good question should get the researcher the information she desires while being easy enough for the respondent to understand and answer. This can be an especially difficult balance to strike when we are asking about topics that most people do not ponder daily.

First and foremost, the researcher must decide what type of information she is trying to ascertain: facts about the respondent, such as basic demographics or more complex traits, relevant knowledge, attitudes, or preferences. For respondent traits, existing surveys can provide model questions. For other items, the literature suggests a few basic rules of thumb: keep it short, keep it simple, avoid double-barreled questions (such as 'Do you approve of the government's handling of terrorism and national security?'), avoid double-negatives (such as 'Do you oppose not going to war?'), and avoid politically loaded terms (e.g., 'radical Islamist'). As much as possible, researchers should refrain from using jargon. We might be interested in respondents' views on globalization, multilateral cooperation, or leaders' resolve, but it is important to remember that these terms may not have the same meaning for respondents—if they have any meaning at all. Poorly worded questions will produce unreliable and possibly biased public opinion data.

Framing effects are another source of concern. Alternative ways of presenting an issue can lead respondents to express distinctly different opinions about it. Studies have shown that even seemingly minor differences in question wording can call to the respondents' minds different aspects of an issue or generate different assessments of a given set of facts, even if the substantive content of the survey item does not change (e.g., Sniderman and Theriault 2004). Framing effects are especially problematic if they are correlated with other variables of interest. A study by Hiscox (2006), for example, suggests that opinions about international trade of respondents with lower levels of formal education are more sensitive to the framing of information about the effects of international trade. Because education is a widely used proxy for one of the key predictors of pro-trade sentiment in open economy models (skill-endowment), differential susceptibility to question framing can produce biased inferences about the determinants of public opinion on trade liberalization. At the same time, a growing number of studies actually exploit framing effects to investigate the effects of elite cues in debates about military intervention (e.g., Brownlee 2020), of competing narratives in legitimizing civil war (e.g., Corstange and York 2018), and similar phenomena.

Question Format. Survey questions generally take one of two forms: closed or open. Closed-ended questions give respondents a set menu of responses. While it might make sense to limit the range of possible responses to those the researcher finds most interesting—because they are suggested by a particular theoretical argument or because they dominate real-life policy debate at a given time—closed-ended question can be problematic. Respondents are effectively forced to choose among set options even if they would have preferred to give a different response. For respondents who know or care little about an issue, closed-ended questions also alleviate the need to engage in the cognitive work required to come up with a response that is closer to their 'true' preference or opinion (on *satisficing* in survey response, see Krosnick 1991). In either case, survey responses will likely misrepresent the actual distribution of attitudes in the sample.

Open-ended questions, in contrast, invite respondents to give an answer of their choosing in their own words. They can be used as stand-alone items or to follow up on a closed question, inviting respondents to explain their reasoning behind a particular response and allowing researchers to probe the causal mechanism expected to generate a particular response (for an example in the context of audience costs, see Tomz 2007). Open-ended questions can pose challenges of their own. First, they require survey respondents to be able to express opinions and rationales and researchers to be able to make sense of the responses in a systematic way. Second, especially for large samples coding several open-ended questions may not be feasible, though recent methodological advances promise to aid in this process (e.g., Roberts et al. 2014).

Response Options: DKNO. A separate decision is whether to offer a 'don't know'/'no opinion' (DKNO) answer option. DKNO options are intuitively appealing, especially on issues like foreign policy where levels of knowledge and salience are likely to be low among respondents. Without them, researchers might rightly worry that survey responses provide poor measures of true attitudes as respondents are forced to choose among substantive opinions they may not actually hold (or hold only weakly). In surveys on foreign policy topics that include such an option, the proportion of DKNO responses is often substantial.

Yet lack of knowledge or interest is not the only reason why respondents may choose a DKNO option when it is offered. Poorly or ambiguously worded questions can be difficult to answer even for respondents who have an opinion. Questions about controversial or sensitive issues, such as whether one supports local militant groups, can prompt DKNO responses from those reluctant to provide a more substantive response (social desirability). Alternatively, respondents may settle on DKNO as an easy way out of having to think harder to choose a more substantive response. In short, researchers need to at least consider the possibility that 'don't know' may not mean 'don't know.'[3]

One set of alternatives to providing a DKNO option to respondents is to ask screening questions or to include follow-up questions to ascertain how strongly respondents hold a particular view (Krosnick and Petty 1995). Questions about attitude strength provide important additional and potentially qualifying information about respondents' views. Another option is to ask questions that require less specific knowledge to answer or to ask several questions that can be aggregated into a single (but potentially multi-dimensional) measure of opinion (Berinsky 2017). Similarly, to reduce concerns about social desirability bias as a source of DKNO responses (or outright non-response), researchers can craft questions or experimental designs that will elicit potentially controversial opinions indirectly (for an example, see Blair et al. 2012).

Researchers who encounter DKNO responses in existing surveys need to carefully consider how to treat them in analyses. Most commonly, foreign policy researchers have dropped these responses, effectively treating them as missing data. Though defensible when the proportion of these responses is very small, this approach can be problematic when listwise deletion of DKNOs discards larger numbers of observations. More worryingly, DKNO responses are often not random; individual-level characteristics that predict item non-response are often the same ones that researchers draw on to predict substantive foreign policy attitudes, including gender, income, and education (e.g., Kleinberg and Fordham 2018). Discarding DKNO responses can then create biased samples and inferences. Where possible, researchers will want to model DKNO responses alongside other responses to gain a fuller understanding of the drivers of particular foreign policy attitudes (ibid., 445).

Order Effects. The order in which questions appear in a survey and the order in which response options are presented can influence respondents' answers. Questions can raise the salience of a particular foreign policy issue—or particular aspects of an issue—in the minds of respondents. With these considerations now top-of-mind, respondents may well answer the next question differently than they would have otherwise. For example, a survey question about support for the use of military force abroad might elicit a different response from the same person depending on whether or not it was immediately preceded by a question about perceived security threats. The ordering of responses to a question is similarly fraught: depending on how a survey is administered, such as visually (e.g., online) or verbally (e.g., in person or by phone), respondents may be more likely to choose answer options that are presented earlier (primacy effects) or later (recency effects) in a survey, respectively (Sudman et al. 1996). One means of alleviating concerns about order effects is to rotate the order of questions in a survey, and the order of response options for each question.

Pretesting the Survey Instrument. The most important piece of advice for developing an effective survey instrument is to pretest and refine it before putting it in the field. Ideally, a pretest will involve subjects who resemble the intended survey respondents and can provide feedback on readability and comprehension, on the time and effort required to complete the whole survey, and any other features of the instrument. Pretesting also allows the researcher to establish whether a survey item or set of items captures an opinion of interest reliably across subjects or over time. In the case of surveys that are self-administered online and involve branching or experiments, pretesting also provides an opportunity to find and fix programming or display errors. While repeated test runs used to be cost-prohibitive, the availability of online survey platforms and respondent pools has made this much more feasible even for smaller original studies.

Survey Designs

Public opinion surveys can take a variety of forms, allowing researchers to answer different types of questions about the content, shape, and determinants of public opinion on a given issue. *Cross-sectional designs* collect data about public opinion at one point in time, either in a single locality or cross-nationally. These surveys provide a snapshot of the prevalence of opinions within a population, as well as of the distribution of attitudes or preferences across subgroups of age, education, or political affiliation. They also allow the researcher to explore relationships between opinions and subgroup characteristics (e.g., gender and support for war, Eichenberg 2003) and assess correlations between opinions (e.g., economic protectionism and national pride, Mayda and Rodrik 2005).

One disadvantage of cross-sectional designs is that interpreting correlations as evidence of causal relationships—especially for relations between attitudes—requires strong theoretical assumptions and can raise suspicions about reverse or reciprocal causality, or even spurious relationships. Consider a situation where survey respondents who express more ethnocentric attitudes are also more likely to express the opinion that international trade has a negative impact on the country. One plausible inference to be drawn from this correlation is that ethnocentrism affects trade attitudes; yet it is also plausible that trade attitudes arising from income effects of trade influence the extent of a respondent's ethnocentrism. Without strong prior beliefs about the relationship between these attitudes, there is little we can say with confidence about its direction or substantive significance (for an example, see Fordham and Kleinberg 2012).

Repeated cross-sectional designs collect data on public opinion by asking the same question(s) repeatedly over time using similarly composed samples of new respondents. Researchers frequently pool responses from different waves of surveys to both increase the number of observations for analysis and ensure that findings are not driven by the peculiarities of any one survey. Moreover, if the samples used in each wave of the survey are representative of the same underlying population, it is possible to treat the data as longitudinal, allowing researchers to assess change over time in aggregate opinion (e.g., Almond 1960; Page and Bouton 2006), to assess the effect on public opinion of events that happened between different waves of the survey (e.g., Wlezien 2004 on defense appropriations and defense spending preferences), or to assess how changes in responses to different survey questions are correlated over time (e.g., Kertzer 2013 on subjective economic assessments and support for isolationism).

Panel surveys collect data on the same respondents repeatedly over time. Panel data allow the researcher to investigate the direction of changes in attitudes at the level of the individual (that is, within-unit), and to pinpoint how individual-level changes contribute to net changes in aggregate opinion. In contrast to cross-sectional designs, panel surveys can provide direct evidence of what drives attitude change and how persistent certain attitude changes are over time. In a recent study, Agerberg and Sohlberg (2021) take advantage of three waves of panel data surrounding a 2017 terrorist attack in central Stockholm to study the impact of respondents' geographic proximity to the event on emotions, rally effects, and attitudes toward outgroups. One wave of the survey had been conducted several months prior to the attack, another one on the day of the attack and during the following week, and a third several weeks later. Using data from all three waves, the authors investigate not only the effect on attitudes of physical and mental proximity to the event, but also whether the onset of such effects might be delayed for some respondents.

For all their advantages, panel surveys also present distinct challenges. The very process of reinterviewing respondents may affect the way they respond to questions (panel conditioning effects), which can bias inferences based on those responses. A recent study by DeJuan and Koos (2021) finds that survey participants in conflict zones who were interviewed multiple times were likely to differ from first-time respondents in their attitudes on a range of issues and often chose more extreme answer options. Another potential problem for panels is gradual erosion as respondents drop out of the sample for a variety of reasons (panel mortality).

Survey experiments represent the fastest growing segment of public opinion survey-based studies in FPA. Experiments generally involve the random assignment of subjects to different treatments, designed to allow the researcher to draw unbiased causal inferences about the effects of a treatment. Embedding experiments in public opinion surveys that employ representative samples of broader populations has several advantages (on population-based survey experiments, see Mutz 2011). For one, survey experiments can clarify potential causal relationships uncovered in standard public opinion surveys. Experimental findings drawn from representative samples will likely also have greater external validity than those drawn from convenience samples, such as local college students. Moreover, the large samples employed in many public opinion surveys can accommodate a greater number of treatments than typical lab experiments. For a more detailed discussion of the strengths and weaknesses of experiments in FPA, see the chapter by Lupton and Webb in this volume.

Populations, Survey Mode, and Sampling

Public opinion surveys, especially those trying to capture the views of the mass public, are usually unable to query everyone. Instead, researchers rely on representative samples from which they generalize to a broader population of interest. Many recent studies do not employ the probability sampling that was common in earlier polls; they instead increasingly use other techniques for generating representative samples, such as post-survey weighting. Understanding who is and isn't included in our samples and *why* is vitally important for the inferences we can draw from the responses to our survey questions. Two potential sources of bias arise from scholars' growing reliance on pools of online respondents and from declining response rates.

An important innovation over the past decades has been to move survey research online. Both major national surveys in the United States and many, if not most original surveys and survey experiments, are now self-administered, rather than conducted by interviewers, and disseminated over the internet to existing online panels or pools of respondents. Coupled with the opt-in nature of surveys offering respondents cash and incentives, this has raised questions about representativeness and the external validity of findings derived from them.

One basic concern is *coverage bias*. Those without access to the technology required to participate in the survey (computers, reliable internet access) have no opportunity to be represented in the sample. Similar challenges arose in connection with earlier changes in survey modes, such as the move from face-to-face interviews to telephone surveys and from landline phones to cell phones (e.g., Groves 2011).

A separate question is whether survey respondents drawn from existing pools or recruited via popular platforms (e.g., Amazon's MTurk or Prolific) differ systematically from the broader population of interest. On the one hand, studies suggest that online samples compare favorably with more established nationally representative survey samples such as the CCES and ANES in terms of demographic and political characteristics (e.g., Levay, Freese, and Druckman 2016). On the other hand, respondents on online platforms have been found to differ from the broader population on a range of traits not captured by basic demographics, such as attention, honesty, and the propensity to shirk or satisfice in answering questions (e.g., Berinsky, Margolis, and Sances 2014). Professional survey takers who populate online platforms may further bias nonprobability samples. Hillygus, Jackson, and Young (2014) find frequent survey takers to be less politically interested, engaged, or knowledgeable than infrequent or less experienced respondents. One recommendation for limiting bias from shirking behavior (such as 'clicking-through') in self-administered surveys is to include a variety of attention checks (e.g., Berinsky, Margolis, and Sances 2014).

Survey non-response raises additional concerns about representativeness. Response rates have been declining for some time across all types of surveys. A 2019 Pew Research Center report noted that the percentage of sampled households who were willing to be interviewed by phone had declined from 36% in 1997 to 6% in 2018 (Pew Research Center 2019). Changes in how surveys are administered have been cited as a possible cause, as has an overall drop in the willingness to participate (Holbrook, Krosnick, and Pfent 2008; Pew Research Center 2012). Low response rates do not automatically threaten representativeness, but problems for generalizability arise when respondents are missing from samples in a non-random fashion.

What influences systematic survey non-response? One factor might be growing political polarization. A recent study by Borgschulte, Cho, and Lubotsky (2019) found evidence of a 'political business cycle' in survey responses among U.S. respondents, with refusal rates among Republicans increasing after the election of Barack Obama and Democrats' refusal rates increasing after the election of Donald Trump in 2016 (2019, 2). Similarly, an analysis of polling limitations surrounding the 2016 and 2020 presidential elections in the United States suggests that Republican respondents, and specifically Republicans with lower levels of trust in others, were missing from samples at higher rates (Pew Research Center 2021). There is no a priori reason to believe that polarization effects are limited to the U.S. context.

Solutions to the problems just outlined are not obvious. At a minimum, users of survey methods need to be aware of their existence and think through possible implications for their work. Public opinion surveys require the voluntary cooperation of the people whose opinions and preferences make up our data. Societal trends like political polarization have the potential to shape the content of foreign policy public opinion; their effects might even trump those of other considerations in which we might have a theoretical interest. But they can also affect whose views show up in our samples and thus whether our survey results reflect the real views of the public. The cardinal virtue of public opinion survey methods is that they provide data at the ground level of political systems: individuals and aggregate publics. Our ability to use these methods effectively is also uniquely susceptible to societal forces that may differ across time and space. Research designs that include surveys and the conclusions drawn from the findings they generate need to reflect these potential limitations.

Advice to First-Time Users

The literature on survey methodology is nearly as large as the literature on public opinion itself. Beyond the guidance provided by the introductory texts noted at the beginning of this section, there are a few basic pieces of advice for scholars considering the use of public opinion survey data.

- Be clear about the purpose of the survey in your research design. What can survey data tell you that is relevant to the research question? Who is the public of interest? What role do the public play in the theoretical argument? More to the point: (Why) Do you need a survey?
- Decide what you want to know from (or about) the public. Designing informative and useful surveys requires a clear idea of the phenomena, such as attitudes or preferences, that you hope to capture. Consider developing multiple survey items to measure a single phenomenon, using different question formats and asking about different aspects of the concept of interest.
- Be prepared for tradeoffs. For example, while including multiple survey items can increase precision and reliability, doing so may strain respondents' willingness to cooperate. It will also increase the cost of administering the survey. You may have to choose between measuring one concept in depth or several more superficially.
- Pretest your survey instrument. Many subtle—and some not so subtle—sources of bias and measurement error in question wording and survey design become obvious only after first contact with the respondent. Write, test, revise as needed.

- Know both your sample and your population of interest. Consider the factors that might shape who becomes a survey respondent, including, but not limited to, basic demographic characteristics. Formulate any conclusions from your study accordingly.

Conclusion

Public opinion and surveys methods have seen a surge in popularity in the past two decades; FPA has not been exempted from this trend. A skeptic might note that this work has generated more questions than answers, and that the answers it has produced are often contradictory—if they speak to each other at all. The overall impact of the proliferation of public opinion surveys on foreign policy scholarship remains difficult to pin down. Scholars newly interested in using surveys might consider three avenues for future contributions.

One longstanding challenge is clarifying the link between individual-level attitudes and preferences on the one hand and state-level policymaking and political outcomes on the other hand. Arguably, this is what we primarily care about when studying foreign policy public opinion—even for studies investigating the shape and sources of public opinion, the 'so what' question usually looms large. Studies such as Guisinger (2009) on political accountability in trade policymaking and, more recently, Barnhart et al. (2020) on the 'suffragist peace' explicitly link foreign policy public opinion to policymaking, tracing its effect (or lack thereof) on politically relevant behavior, aggregation, and representation. This type of work, still fairly rare, provides a richer and more compelling account of how public opinion 'matters.'

Another promising recent development is the move toward investigating the attitudes and preferences of distinct publics. For some research questions, it may be preferable to consider subpopulations that are directly involved in decision-making or occupy some privileged position in the process (elites), or subpopulations who are disproportionately or most directly affected by a phenomenon of interest (such as combatants or refugees). While not without challenges for sampling and survey administration, studies using surveys of narrower, politically relevant populations may require fewer heroic assumptions about their impact on outcomes. Two recent examples of this type of work are Dietrich's (2018) study of preferences of foreign aid officials and Kaplan and Nussio's (2018) study of ex-combatants' decisions to demobilize rather than engage in illegal activity or rejoin armed groups.

Finally, future work should focus explicitly on the replication and extension of existing insights. Although there is now a wealth of studies considering public opinion and using survey data in FPA, there are still only small 'pockets' of cumulative knowledge (research on audience costs described in an earlier section being prominent example). Original surveys and especially survey experiments are often unique designs, administered once and only in one country, which raises concerns about the generalizability of findings beyond specific surveys, specific years, or specific national contexts. Most importantly, the lack of studies that truly speak to each other makes it difficult to know what we have learned and where we should go next.

Notes

1 In addition to longstanding projects such as the World Values Survey (first established in 1981), the European Values Study (1981), and the International Social Survey Programme (1984), scholars can now draw on Latinobarometro (1995), Afrobarometer (1999), the Pew Global Attitudes Project (2001), the AmericasBarometer (2004/5) of the Latin American Public Opinion Project (LAPOP),

as well as a wide range of regular single-country surveys. An especially valuable resource is the Roper Center's searchable iPoll database, which allows researchers to search for survey questions on specific topics from a wide collection of polls.
2 A more recent overview of survey methodology is provided by Stantcheva (2022).
3 Much of our understanding of the determinants of survey non-response derives from studies involving U.S. respondents. Here again, the expansion of survey research beyond Western democracies raises new and interesting challenges (e.g., Gengler et al. 2021).

References

Agerberg, Mattias, and Jacob Sohlberg. 2021. "Personal Proximity and Reactions to Terrorism." *Comparative Political Studies* 54(14): 2512–2545.
Aldrich, John H., Christopher Gelpi, Peter Feaver, Jason Reifler, and Kristin Thompson Sharp. 2006. "Foreign Policy and the Electoral Connection." *Annual Review of Political Science* 9: 477–502.
Almond, Gabriel A. 1960. *The American People and Foreign Policy.* New York: Praeger.
Andrews, Sarah, David Leblang, and Sonal S. Pandya. 2018. "Ethnocentrism Reduces Foreign Direct Investment." *The Journal of Politics* 80(2): 697–700.
Barnhart, Joslyn N., Robert F. Trager, Elizabeth N. Saunders, and Allan Dafoe. 2020. "The Suffragist Peace." *International Organization* 74(4): 633–670.
Bartels, Larry M. 1991. "Constituency Opinion and Congressional Policymaking: The Reagan Defense Buildup." *American Political Science Review* 85(2): 457–474.
———. 2016. *Unequal Democracy.* Princeton, NJ: Princeton University Press.
Bell, Mark S., and Kai Quek. 2018. "Authoritarian Public Opinion and the Democratic Peace." *International Organization* 72(1): 227–242.
Berelson, Bernard. 1952. "Democratic Theory and Public Opinion." *Public Opinion Quarterly* 16(3): 313–330.
Berinsky, Adam J., Michele F. Margolis, and Michael W. Sances. 2014. "Separating the Shirkers from the Workers? Making Sure Respondents Pay Attention on Self-administered Surveys." *American Journal of Political Science* 58(3): 739–753.
Berinksy, Adam. J. 2017. "Measuring Public Opinion with Surveys." *Annual Review of Political Science* 20: 309–329.
Blair, C. Graeme, Christine Fair, Neil Malhotra, and Jacob N. Shapiro. 2012. "Poverty and Support for Militant Politics: Evidence from Pakistan." *American Journal of Political Science* 57(1): 30–48.
Borgschulte, Mark, Heepyung Cho, and Darren Lubotsky. 2019. "Partisanship and Survey Refusal." NBER Working Paper No. 26433. URL: http://www.nber.org/papers/w26433.
Brownlee, Jason. 2020. "Cognitive Shortcuts and Public Support for Intervention." *Journal of Conflict Resolution* 64(2–3): 261–289.
Brutger, Ryan, and Joshua D. Kertzer. 2018. "A Dispositional Theory of Reputation Costs." *International Organization* 72(3): 693–724.
Casey, Steven. 2001. *Cautious Crusade: Franklin D. Roosevelt, American Public Opinion, and the War against Nazi Germany.* New York: Oxford University Press.
Chaudoin, Stephen. 2014. "Promises or Policies? An Experimental Analysis of International Agreements and Audience Reactions." *International Organization* 68(1): 235–256.
Converse, Philip E. 1964. "The Nature of Belief Systems in Mass Publics." In *Ideology and Its Discontents*, edited by David E. Apter. New York: Free Press, 206–261.
Corstange, Daniel, and Erin A. York. 2018. "Sectarian Framing in the Syrian Civil War." *American Journal of Political Science* 62(2): 441–455.
Dahl, Robert A. 1956. *A Preface to Democratic Theory.* Chicago: University of Chicago Press.
De Juan, Alexander, and Carlo Koos. 2021. "Survey Participation Effects in Conflict Research." *Journal of Peace Research* 58(4): 623–639.
Dietrich, Simone. 2018. "Donor Political Economies and the Pursuit of Aid Effectiveness." *International Organization* 70(1): 65–102.
Eichenberg, Richard C. 2003. "Gender Differences in Public Attitudes toward the Use of Force by the United States, 1990–2003." *International Security* 28(1): 110–141.
Fearon, James D. 1994. "Domestic Political Audiences and the Escalation of International Disputes." *American Political Science Review* 88(3): 577–592.

Fisk, Kerstin, Jennifer L. Merolla, and Jennifer M. Ramos. 2019. "Emotions, Terrorist Threat, and Drones: Anger Drives Support for Drone Strikes." *Journal of Conflict Resolution* 63(4): 976–1000.

Fordham, Benjamin O., and Katja B. Kleinberg 2012. "How Can Economic Interests Influence Support for Free Trade?" *International Organization* 66(2): 311–328.

Fordham, Benjamin O., and Katja B. Kleinberg. 2020. "Too Pacifist in Peace, Too Bellicose in War: Political Information and Foreign Policy Opinion." *Journal of Conflict Resolution* 64(10): 1828–1856.

Fowler, Floyd J. 1995. *Improving Survey Questions*. Thousand Oaks, CA: Sage.

Gengler, Justin J., Mark Tessler, Russell Lucas, and Jonathan Forney. 2021. "'Why Do You Ask?' The Nature and Impacts of Attitudes towards Public Opinion Surveys in the Arab World." *British Journal of Political Science* 51(1): 115–136.

Ghosn, Faten, Tiffany S. Chu, Miranda Simon, Alex Braithwaite, Michael Frith, and Joanna Jandali. 2021. "The Journey Home: Violence, Anchoring, and Refugee Decisions to Return." *American Political Science Review* 115(3): 1–17.

Gravelle, Timothy B., Jason Reifler, and Thomas J. Scotto. 2017. "The Structure of Foreign Policy Attitudes in Transatlantic Perspective: Comparing the United States, United Kingdom, France and Germany." *European Journal of Political Research* 56(4): 757–776.

Groves, Robert M. 2011. "Three Eras of Survey Research." *Public Opinion Quarterly* 75(5): 861–871.

Groves, Robert M., Floyd J. Fowler Jr, Mick P. Couper, James M. Lepkowski, Eleanor Singer, and Roger Tourangeau. 2011. *Survey Methodology*. Hoboken, NJ: John Wiley & Sons.

Guisinger, Alexandra. 2009. "Determining Trade Policy: Do Voters Hold Politicians Accountable?" *International Organization* 63(3): 533–557.

———. 2017. *American Opinion on Trade: Preferences without Politics*. New York: Oxford University Press.

Guisinger, Alexandra, and Elizabeth N. Saunders. 2017. "Mapping the Boundaries of Elite Cues: How Elites Shape Mass Opinion across International Issues." *International Studies Quarterly* 61(2): 425–441.

Hafner-Burton, Emilie M., Stephan Haggard, David A. Lake, and David G. Victor. 2017. "The Behavioral Revolution and International Relations." *International Organization* 71(S1): S1–S31.

Heath, Anthony, Stephen Fisher, and Shawna Smith. 2005. "The Globalization of Public Opinion Research." *Annual Review of Political Science* 8: 297–333.

Hillygus, D. Sunshine, Natalie Jackson, and M. Young. 2014. "Professional Respondents in Non-Probability Online Panels. " *Online Panel Research: A Data Quality Perspective* 1: 219–237.

Hiscox, Michael J. 2006. "Through a Glass and Darkly: Attitudes toward International Trade and the Curious Effects of Issue Framing." *International Organization* 60(3): 755–780.

Holbrook, Allyson L., Jon A. Krosnick, and Alison Pfent. 2008. "The Causes and Consequences of Response Rates in Surveys." In *Advances in Telephone Survey Methodology*, edited by Lepkowski, James M., Clyde Tucker, Michael Brick, Edith de Leeuw, E., Lilli Japec, Paul J. Lavrakas, Michael W. Link, and Roberta L. Sangster. Stanford, CA: Stanford University.

Hurwitz, Jon, and Mark Peffley. 1987. "How Are Foreign Policy Attitudes Structured? A Hierarchical Model." *American Political Science Review* 81(4): 1099–1120.

Jacobs, Lawrence R., and Benjamin I. Page. 2005. "Who Influences U.S. Foreign Policy?" *American Political Science Review* 99(1): 107–123.

Jentleson, Bruce W. 1992. "The Pretty Prudent Public: Post Post-Vietnam American Opinion on the Use of Military Force." *International Studies Quarterly* 36(1): 49–73.

Kaplan, Oliver, and Enzo Nussio. 2018. "Explaining Recidivism of Ex-combatants in Colombia." *Journal of Conflict Resolution* 62(1): 64–93.

Kertzer, Joshua D. 2013. "Making Sense of Isolationism: Foreign Policy Mood as a Multilevel Phenomenon." *The Journal of Politics* 75(1): 225–240.

———. 2017. "Microfoundations in International Relations." *Conflict Management and Peace Science* 34(1): 81–97.

———. 2020. "Re-Assessing Elite-Public Gaps in Political Behavior." *American Journal of Political Science* 66(3): 539–553.

Kertzer, Joshua D., and Ryan Brutger. 2016. "Decomposing Audience Costs: Bringing the Audience Back into Audience Cost Theory." *American Journal of Political Science* 60(1): 234–249

Kertzer, Joshua D., and Dustin Tingley. 2018. "Political Psychology in International Relations: Beyond the Paradigms." *Annual Review of Political Science* 21: 1–23.

Kleinberg, Katja B., and Benjamin O. Fordham. 2018. "Don't Know Much about Foreign Policy: Assessing the Impact of 'Don't Know' and 'No Opinion' Responses on Inferences about Foreign Policy Attitudes." *Foreign Policy Analysis* 14(3): 429–448.

Krosnick, Jon A. 1991. "Response Strategies for Coping with the Cognitive Demands of Attitude Measures in Surveys." *Applied Cognitive Psychology* 5(3): 213–236.

Krosnick, Jon A., and Richard E. Petty. 1995. "Attitude Strength: An Overview." In *Attitude Strength: Antecedents and Consequences*, edited by Richard E. Petty and Jon A. Krosnick. Mahwah, NJ: Lawrence Erlbaum Associates, 1–24.

Lazarsfeld, Paul F., Bernard Berelson, and Hazel Gaudet. 1948. *The People's Choice*. New York: Columbia University Press.

Levay, Kevin E., Jeremy Freese, and James N. Druckman. 2016. "The Demographic and Political Composition of Mechanical Turk Samples." *Sage Open* 6(1): 1–17.

Levy, Jack S., Michael K. McKoy, Paul Poast, and Geoffrey PR Wallace. 2015. "Backing Out or Backing In? Commitment and Consistency in Audience Costs Theory." *American Journal of Political Science* 59(4): 988–1001.

Lippmann, Walter. 1955. *Essays in the Public Philosophy*. New York: Little, Brown, and Company.

Lupu, Noam, and Kristin Michelitch. 2018. "Advances in Survey Methods for the Developing World." *Annual Review of Political Science* 21: 195–214.

Mansfield, Edward D., and Diana C. Mutz. 2009. "Support for Free Trade: Self-interest, Sociotropic Politics, and Out-group Anxiety." *International Organization* 63(3): 425–457.

Matanock, Aila M., and Miguel García-Sánchez. 2018. "Does Counterinsurgent Success Match Social Support? Evidence from a Survey Experiment in Colombia." *The Journal of Politics* 80(3): 800–814.

Mayda, Anna Maria, and Dani Rodrik. 2005. "Why are Some People (and Countries) More Protectionist than Others?" *European Economic Review* 49(6): 1393–1430.

Mutz, Diana C. 2011. *Population-Based Survey Experiments*. Princeton, NJ and Oxford: Princeton University Press.

Owen, Erica, and Dennis P. Quinn. 2016. "Does Economic Globalization Influence the U.S. Policy Mood? A Study of U.S. Public Sentiment, 1956–2011." *British Journal of Political Science* 46(1): 95–125.

Page, Benjamin I., and Marshall M. Bouton. 2006. *The Foreign Policy Disconnect. What Americans Want from Our Leaders but Don't Get*. Chicago and London: University of Chicago Press.

Pepinsky, Thomas B. 2014. "Surveys, Experiments, and the Landscape of International Political Economy." *International Interactions* 40(3): 431–442.

Pew Research Center. 2012. "Assessing the Representativeness of Public Opinion Surveys." Pew Research Center Report, May 15.

Pew Research Center. 2019. "Growing and Improving Pew Research Center's American Trends Panel." Pew Research Center Report, February 27.

Pew Research Center. 2021. "Confronting 2016 and 2020 Polling Limitations." Pew Research Center Report, April 8.

Rathbun, Brian C., Joshua D. Kertzer, Jason Reifler, Paul Goren, and Thomas J. Scotto. 2016. "Taking Foreign Policy Personally: Personal Values and Foreign Policy Attitudes." *International Studies Quarterly* 60(1): 124–137.

Rho, S. and Tomz, M. 2017. "Why Don't Trade Preferences Reflect Economic Self-interest?" *International Organization* 71(S1): S85–S108.

Roberts, Margaret E., Brandon M. Stewart, Dustin Tingley, Christopher Lucas, Jetson Leder-Luis, Shana Kushner Gadarian, Bethany Albertson, and David G. Rand. 2014. "Structural Topic Models for Open-Ended Survey Responses." *American Journal of Political Science* 58(4): 1064–1082.

Schoen, Harald. 2007. "Personality Traits and Foreign Policy Attitudes in German Public Opinion." *Journal of Conflict Resolution* 51(3): 408–430.

Schwartz, Joshua A., and Christopher W. Blair. 2020. "Do Women Make More Credible Threats? Gender Stereotypes, Audience Costs, and Crisis Bargaining." *International Organization* 74: 872–895.

Soroka, Stuart N., and Christopher Wlezien. 2010. *Degrees of Democracy: Politics, Public Opinion, and Policy*. New York: Cambridge University Press.

Sniderman, Paul M., and Sean M. Theriault. 2004. "The Structure of Political Argument and the Logic of Issue Framing." In *Studies in Public Opinion: Attitudes, Nonattitudes, Measurement Error, and Change*, edited by Willem E. Saris and Paul M. Sniderman. Princeton, NJ: Princeton University Press, 133–165.

Stantcheva, Stefanie. 2022. "How to Run Surveys: A Guide to Creating Your Own Identifying Variation and Revealing the Invisible." Working paper. Washington, DC: National Bureau of Economic Research. https://www.nber.org/papers/w30527

Sudman, Seymour, Norman M. Bradburn, and Norbert Schwarz. 1996. *Thinking about Answers: The Application of Cognitive Processes to Survey Methodology*. Hoboken, NJ: Jossey-Bass.

Tomz, Michael 2007. "Domestic Audience Costs in International Relations: An Experimental Approach." *International Organization* 61(4): 821–840.

Weisberg, Herbert F. 2005. *The Total Survey Error Approach. A Guide to the New Science of Survey Research.* Chicago, IL: University of Chicago Press.

Weiss, Jessica Chen, and Allan Dafoe. 2019. "Authoritarian Audiences, Rhetoric, and Propaganda in International Crises: Evidence from China." *International Studies Quarterly* 63(4): 963–973.

Wittkopf, Eugene R. 1990. *Faces of Internationalism: Public Opinion and American Foreign Policy*. Durham and London: Duke University Press.

Wlezien, Christopher. 2004. "Patterns of Representation: Dynamics of Public Preferences and Policy." *The Journal of Politics* 66(1): 1–24.

Yarhi-Milo, Keren, Joshua D. Kertzer, and Jonathan Renshon. 2018. "Tying Hands, Sinking Costs, and Leader Attributes." *Journal of Conflict Resolution* 62(10): 2150–2179.

Zaller, John R. 1992. *The Nature and Origins of Mass Opinion*. Cambridge and New York: Cambridge University Press.

Zaller, John, and Stanley Feldman. 1992. "A Simple Theory of the Survey Response: Answering Questions versus Revealing Preferences." *American Journal of Political Science* 36(3): 579–616.

24
Qualitative Comparative Analysis
Patrick A. Mello

Introduction

Foreign Policy Analysis (FPA) often seeks to account for outcomes that are rooted at different levels of analysis, bringing together a variety of potential causes. For instance, how to explain Russian President Putin's decision to attack Ukraine on February 24, 2022? Arguably, despite some warning signs, this egregious behavior was unexpected by international observers. Some have suggested to investigate leaders' personal characteristics to understand such policy decisions. In the case of Vladimir Putin, several psychological reasons may explain why he has become more risk-prone and intoxicated by power (Kaarbo 2022). Others point to a sweeping transformation of Putin's inner circle of advisers (Treisman 2022). What is clear, however, is that a comprehensive account requires the consideration of various factors and that there is no single explanatory variable to account for the observed outcome.

Qualitative Comparative Analysis (QCA) is a method that was designed to account for *causal complexity*, which entails the existence of multiple paths toward an outcome (*equifinality*), the combination of factors to jointly bring about an outcome (*conjunctural causation*), and asymmetry between the explanation of an outcome and its negation (*causal asymmetry*). As a comparative approach, QCA requires a certain minimum number of cases, but this can be as small as 12 or 15 cases. This means that QCA can also be applied in settings where large datasets are absent and researchers are working primarily with qualitative data they have gathered themselves, such as from interviews or focus groups (Pagliarin, La Mendola, and Vis 2022; see also Deschaux-Dutard in this volume). This makes QCA an amenable method for FPA, where researchers are often interested in phenomena that are relatively rare (e.g., wars, military coups, economic sanctions, foreign policy failures) but where the aim is to conduct comparisons and to achieve (moderate) generalization across cases. Moreover, QCA can also work in medium to large-N settings, especially when researchers draw on pre-existing datasets or when the method is utilized in larger, collaborative projects.

In this chapter, I start out with a review of QCA applications in the field of FPA. Since QCA can still be considered an emerging method, at least when compared with more prevalent statistical or case-study approaches, the number of empirical applications remains limited. This is even though the method's usage has been growing dynamically, especially when taking a broader conception of FPA into account. Hence, I will investigate IR applications more broadly, also because the dividing line between the fields of IR and FPA can be rather fuzzy. The second part of the chapter introduces QCA's methodological assumptions and key terminology. To be sure, this will not suffice to replace a full textbook introduction to the method (see Rihoux and Ragin 2009; Schneider and Wagemann 2012; Mello 2021), especially for those who are entirely new to the method, but the presentation in this chapter should serve to provide an understanding of how QCA works and how its results should be interpreted. Hence, the chapter should also be of use for those who simply want to understand how to read the results reported in QCA studies. The chapter proceeds with an empirical illustration to show how QCA works in practice. I close with a discussion of the method's strengths and limitations, together with recommendations on how to avoid frequently encountered mistakes and a brief look into prospective applications in FPA.

Qualitative Comparative Analysis in FPA

While QCA has been around since Charles Ragin published *The Comparative Method* (Ragin 1987) and the method can be considered firmly established in political science, sociology, and many other fields of the social sciences – the number of studies in International Relations (IR) and FPA is considerably smaller. In their recent review, Ide and Mello (2022) identify a total of 43 empirical applications of QCA published in IR journals that are indexed on the Web of Science. For FPA, the number will still be considerably smaller.[1] That said, the publication of QCA textbooks and the broader dissemination of the method, also through summer schools, training opportunities, and methods curricula at graduate schools, have led to a rapid increase in applications in recent years.

To be sure, a central question is how narrowly one defines the field of FPA. If one adopts a broad conception, then any "goal-oriented behavior of state actors across borders" could be considered as such (Brummer and Oppermann 2019, 1, own translation). A narrower definition places human agents and their decisions at the center of FPA (Hudson and Day 2019, 3). If we follow the first definition, then any study that focuses on foreign policy outcomes could be within the purview of FPA, whereas the latter definition would limit that scope to those studies that analyze foreign policy decision-making processes and individual or group decision-makers. In this chapter, I follow the former conception of FPA, if only to allow for a broader inclusion of studies in my literature review. Arguably, some of the authors of these studies may not self-identify their articles as FPA studies, but for the purposes of this chapter they are considered as such because they engage with substantive matters that fall within the realm of the discipline.

A first cut to distinguish QCA applications in FPA can be achieved by looking at the level of analysis. As in other fields of the social sciences, a majority of FPA studies using QCA are situated at the country level, comparing across a medium number of states. Examples include democracies' involvement and non-involvement in the Iraq War of 2003 (Mello 2012, 2014), countries' participation in the multilateral coalition against the "Islamic State" (Haesebrouck 2018; Mello 2022), NATO burden sharing in Libya (Haesebrouck 2017b), the role of junior partners in coalition warfare (Schmitt 2018), the political contestation of military missions (Haesebrouck and van Immerseel 2020), the implementation of sanctions against "Arab Spring" countries in the Middle East and North Africa (Boogaerts 2018; Boogaerts and Drieskens 2020), the occurrence of unintended consequences of UN sanctions in targeted states (Meissner and Mello 2022), and the allocation of the foreign ministry to junior partners in governing coalitions of parliamentary democracies (Oppermann and Brummer 2020).

Other studies operate at different levels, for instance examining the influence of ethnic identity groups on U.S. foreign policy (Rubenzer 2008), the inclusion of human rights in territorial peace agreements (Caspersen 2019), the conditions under which democratic leaders opted for defection from the multilateral Iraq War coalition (Mello 2020), the foreign policy behavior of Brazil in various international crises (de Sá Guimarães and de Almeida 2017), agency slack within UN organizations (Heldt et al. 2022), military intervention in Africa (Kisangani and Pickering 2022), conceptions of international order, as expressed in Australian and Chinese policy documents (van Nieuwenhuizen 2019), and even international arbitration under Hellenistic rulers in ancient times (Grynaviski and Hsieh 2015).

With its affinity toward medium-N comparisons of 20–30 cases, it is no surprise that QCA has frequently been applied on EU and NATO member states. In substantive terms, it is apparent that many QCA studies in FPA focus on matters of international security, including decisions on military interventions, burden sharing within alliances and among coalition partners, international sanctions in response to human rights violations, and decision-making on arms control agreements. On the latter, for example, Böller and Müller (2018) examine inter-branch dynamics between the U.S. Congress and the President in relation to military interventions and Böller (2021) investigates U.S. decisions on international arms control treaties. In sum, a review of empirical applications of QCA shows that the method has gained ground in FPA research. While QCA is still in its infancy in FPA, recent years indicate a dynamic growth in the number of publications, even more so if one takes a look at IR studies at-large (Ide and Mello 2022). One particular advantage of QCA, besides its ability to account for causal complexity, is that the method can be flexibly applied and tailored toward the specific needs of a research project. It is up to researchers to define their "cases" and to craft a comparative research design on that basis. That said, one major limitation is the availability of comparative data. I will return to this point in the final section of this chapter.

Methodological Assumptions and Key Terminology

The comparative approach of QCA rests on set theory and Boolean logic. This means that relationships are framed in the language of necessary and sufficient conditions. A *sufficient condition* is a condition that always leads to the outcome, whereas a *necessary condition* is a condition without which the outcome does not occur. Lately, set theory has made strong inroads into the social sciences, serving as the foundation for new frameworks of analysis (Goertz and Mahoney 2012; Schneider and Wagemann 2012; Mahoney 2021). Beyond this, QCA involves certain methodological assumptions and specific terminology, which will be introduced in this section. I should highlight that, for reasons of space, I will set aside debates about *ontology* – for instance, whether and under which conditions QCA can be a suitable method for a critical realist framework (e.g., Gerrits and Verweij 2014; Rutten 2020). I will also just touch upon recent exchanges about set theory and different theories of causation (Haesebrouck and Thomann 2021, Ch. 4; Mello 2021; Haesebrouck 2022).

Causal Complexity

A distinct strength of QCA is its ability to account for *causal complexity*. This overarching concept entails three components: conjunctural causation, equifinality, and causal asymmetry. *Conjunctural causation* means that two (or more) conditions may jointly bring about an outcome, but not individually in the absence of the other condition(s). For example, it may require both a leader with certain political preferences *and* a window of opportunity to implement an otherwise contentious policy. *Equifinality* means that the same outcome may be reached through multiple, different pathways. For instance, while many EU member states eventually decided to support Ukraine with arms deliveries in its self-defense against Russian aggression, the foreign policy decision-making processes through which this outcome was reached were markedly different across the EU. Finally, *causal asymmetry* indicates that the explanation for an outcome can usually not be mirrored to account for the non-outcome but requires a separate analysis.

The notion of causal complexity resonates with many phenomena that are of interest to FPA research. It also departs from commonly held assumptions, especially in quantitative research.[2] As such, conjunctural causation challenges the utility of exploring net effects of individual variables without examining their interaction, while equifinality calls into question the assumption that similar outcomes must be rooted in similar causes. Finally, causal asymmetry highlights the fact that symmetrical causation is an assumption that may also prove false. This departs from linearity assumptions frequently held in statistical analyses (Mello 2021, 69–70).

Calibration

QCA works with calibrated data. *Calibration* means that the researcher defines a target set (e.g., "aggressive foreign policy stance") and determines empirical anchors in the raw data (which may be quantitative or qualitative) to reflect a certain degree of membership in the target set. To take the example of an aggressive foreign policy stance, we may say that certain government statements or actions are considered to indicate set membership. Hence, these would be coded accordingly. This also allows for degrees of membership, which would translate into a *fuzzy set* that can take on any values from 0 to 1 (as opposed to *crisp sets* that are binary in nature). It is considered good practice to use adjectives for set labels because this indicates the qualitative direction (e.g., "*high* unemployment", "*low* aggressiveness", and the like). This reflects the fact that sets are always directed toward a qualitative state, which also distinguishes calibrated data from mere numerical scales where – lacking additional information – it is not possible to say whether a score is high or low in the given context.

Calibration can be conducted manually by assigning scores in a spreadsheet or – the more viable option for larger data sets – through an R function (for more on *software*, see below). In both cases, the researcher needs to decide about calibration criteria to be applied consistently across all the included cases. It is important to realize that calibration should not be exercised mechanically, as in transforming the raw data into calibrated data merely based on descriptive statistics like the mean, minimum, or maximum scores on a given condition. Instead, researchers should anchor their calibration decisions in substantive considerations and external criteria derived from their research area. For example, to distinguish between being poor and not poor, we may refer to the UN poverty line as an external criterion. The number could then be applied to the data as the cross-over (fuzzy score of 0.5) between being rather inside than outside the set *poor country*. Below, I describe examples in more detail, which may help to grasp how calibration works in practice.[3]

Consistency and Coverage

How to assess whether an individual condition or a combination of conditions is necessary and/or sufficient for an outcome? Similar to statistical analyses (see Oktay in this volume), QCA uses metrics to describe the fit between the empirical data and certain relationships.

In the case of QCA, this is about set-theoretic relationships of necessity and/or sufficiency. The primary measure of fit, *consistency* describes the extent to which an empirical relationship between a condition or a combination of conditions and the outcome approximates set-theoretic necessity and/or sufficiency. The secondary measure of fit, *coverage* describes the empirical importance or the relevance of a condition or combination of conditions (Ragin 2008; Mello 2021). These measures of fit are part of the computation the software conducts. They allow an easy assessment of whether the data fits a set-theoretic relationship. As a rule of thumb, truth table rows should have a minimum of 0.75 consistency to be included in the minimization procedure (more on this below). For necessary conditions, the conventional benchmark is 0.90 consistency. As for coverage, there is no firm rule, but the aim should always be to account for at least more than half the observations (the more the better). This means that coverage should usually be in the range of 0.60 and above.

Truth Tables

The core of QCA is entailed in the *truth table analysis*, which is about identifying combinations of conditions (*configurations*) that are sufficient for the outcome of interest. The *truth table* displays all logically possible configurations for a given research design and the number of conditions the researcher chose to include. The size of the truth table is calculated as 2^k, where k represents the included number of conditions. For instance, a study with four conditions would yield a truth table that comprises 16 rows (2^4), whereas five conditions would result in 32 truth table rows. Apart from displaying the different configurations, the truth table also links these to the included empirical cases and indicates whether and how consistently the rows are associated with the outcome. If all cases that share certain characteristics (indicated by their assignment to the same truth table row) also show the outcome, then this row would yield a high consistency (consistency can range from 0 to 1). Conversely, low consistency indicates that a considerable number of cases in the respective row do not show the outcome.[4] By convention, the minimum threshold for truth table rows to be considered "sufficient enough" to be included in the ensuing minimization is 0.75 consistency (Mello 2021).

Truth tables also provide information about configurations that are not filled with empirical cases (the phenomenon of *limited diversity*). These "empty rows" are *logical remainders* that can be incorporated as counterfactuals during the set-theoretic analysis. For example, in a study on U.S. presidents all combinations involving a female president would be empty because historically there has not (yet) been a case with this configuration. However, researchers could still explore the potential of such a configuration and what outcome it would be associated with. And even if the aims were more limited or a researcher would not want to engage in counterfactual reasoning, it is valuable to know which configurations are filled with empirical cases and which ones are not. The truth table makes this information immediately visible.

Boolean Minimization

Once a truth table has been constructed, the researcher needs to determine a consistency threshold for truth table rows to be included in the *Boolean minimization* that constitutes the next step in the QCA analysis. As mentioned, the conventional threshold is a minimum of 0.75 consistency, below which rows should not be included. Higher thresholds are quite common, but this ultimately depends on the nature of the empirical data. Rows that meet this threshold will undergo a software-based comparison based on the rules of Boolean algebra.

In simple terms, this means that all the included truth table configurations are compared with each other, and redundant elements are eliminated to reach a more concise solution. For example, in a simple research design with the conditions A and B we may come across two configurations that turn out to be sufficient for an outcome Y. The first comprises the presence of both conditions, while the second entails the absence of the second condition. Using Boolean operators (AND = ·, OR = +, NOT = ~), we can express this as such:

$$A \cdot B + A \cdot {\sim}B \rightarrow Y \tag{1}$$

In verbal terms, this means that *the presence of both A and B or the presence of A and the absence of B are sufficient for the outcome Y*. Hence, we can say that once A is present it does not matter whether it combines with the presence or with the absence of B – because both configurations are sufficient for the outcome. Therefore, we can apply the Boolean minimization rule and delete redundant elements B and ~B, respectively. This leaves us with:

$$A \rightarrow Y \tag{2}$$

In practice, Boolean minimization is more complicated because it will typically involve numerous conditions and configurations. There is also a consecutive step that allows for further minimization using *prime implicants* (see Mello 2021, Ch. 7). However, for our purposes, it must suffice that the truth table analysis applies the rules of Boolean algebra to logically simplify the sufficient configurations identified in the truth table. It is also important to underline that Boolean minimization merely deletes redundant information. If the first statement is true, then – by logical necessity – the second statement will also be true. But the second statement is more parsimonious.

Solution Terms

QCA results are summarized in *solution terms*. This can take the form of statement (1) or (2) shown above but often solution terms are more complex, involving various combination of conditions (conjunctions) that are linked by the Boolean operator OR. What is more, QCA entails three different types of solution terms, depending on the treatment of the logical remainders. The *conservative solution* (also called *complex solution*) works solely with the empirical rows. The *parsimonious solution* allows the algorithm to include logical remainders in the minimization, provided their use yields a simpler result. As the name implies, this solution is often more parsimonious because more Boolean comparisons can be made. The downside is that the parsimonious solution may rest on *implausible counterfactuals* (Mello 2021, 205). For example, we may know that a certain combination of our conditions is impossible in the social world. Hence, it would be erroneous to assume that the respective logical remainders would show a certain outcome if it existed (because it simply cannot exist and therefore cannot show the outcome). To be fair, such problems appear less often than one may think at first glance. But it is crucial to be aware of the potentiality of implausible counterfactuals and to assess this when working with the parsimonious solution. Finally, the *intermediate solution* enables the researcher to customize the treatment of logical remainders, to avoid working with implausible counterfactuals. For instance, the intermediate solution allows a researcher to exclude a certain logical remainder row in the truth table because it may be deemed implausible as counterfactual. Likewise, researchers can introduce "directional expectations" about which qualitative states of their conditions are assumed to be associated with the outcome.

Software

The analytical part of QCA is *software*-based, with a variety of different solutions on offer.[5] Depending on the subfield, the most popular software may still be fs/QCA (Ragin and Davey 2017) and TOSMANA (Cronqvist 2019), both of which are "click-and-point" programs that are easy to navigate also for beginners. While these two programs remain in use and may be a good entry point to explore how QCA works, a host of advanced functions for QCA are available within the R environment, where the package "QCA" (Dușa 2019) covers the analytical core of QCA and the complementary "SetMethods" package provides additional functions (Oana and Schneider 2018; see also Oana, Schneider, and Thomann 2021). Because these packages run under R, users can benefit from the vast opportunities that R provides. This means that researchers can easily combine QCA with statistical tests or conduct visualizations of their results with other packages such as the versatile "ggplot2" (Wickham 2016). That said, the entry barrier to conducting QCA in R can be quite steep, especially if one has not worked with R before.[6]

Empirical Illustration

This section provides an illustration of how QCA works in practice, drawing on a published study on military coalition defection during the Iraq War (Mello 2020). In that article, I sought to answer the question as to why some of the democratic coalition partners of the U.S. decided at various points between March 2003 and December 2008 to withdraw their country's forces, whereas others stayed until the end of the multinational mission. Overall, 29 democracies were militarily involved in the Iraq War, and these comprised 51 leaders who were in charge during their country's deployment. Out of these, 18 leaders announced their country's unilateral withdrawal before the end of the mission (Mello 2020, 56–58), while 33 leaders continued the military involvement throughout their tenure.

In my research design, I built an integrative theoretical framework that included factors that had been prominently suggested in the literature, such as arguments about electoral incentives and leadership changes (e.g., Tago 2009; Pilster, Böhmelt, and Tago 2013). Prior studies suggested that changes in an unpopular foreign policy, such as the Iraq War deployment, became more likely when a new leader came to power or when an incumbent faced an election. Apart from testing these general expectations on the specific case of the Iraq War, I also examined civilian and military casualties, the relative size of a country's military deployment (in relation to its military capabilities), and the political partisanship of the respective government (left-right placement on a one-dimensional scale). While all these factors were expected to be of relevance for democratic leaders' withdrawal decisions, I expected *combinations* of these conditions to be jointly sufficient for the outcome. For instance, one hypothesis was that "A change in the political leadership combined with leftist partisanship is a sufficient condition for early withdrawal from coalition operations" (Mello 2020, 50). This reflects the assumption that a substantive change in a country's foreign policy requires not just a window of opportunity (a newly elected leader) but also preferences that resonate with it (political partisanship). Likewise, it was also expected that multiple paths could lead toward the outcome, for example when leaders faced casualties and/or had made a small coalition commitment to begin with. These theoretical expectations resonated with QCA's emphasis on *causal complexity*, as discussed above.

The data collection for this study involved both qualitative and quantitative sources. In general, QCA can be used with all types of data, as long as a complete assignment of scores to cases is feasible, in the sense that there are no missing data.[7] The coding of the outcome early withdrawal was based on *qualitative* data, such as leaders' press statements, parliamentary speeches, and news coverage. This involved a labor-intensive cross-checking and verification of sources for the 51 leaders, to identify whether any announcements had been made, on which date these had been issued, and whether the statements had actually been official declarations that initiated the country's withdrawal from Iraq. For the explanatory conditions, I drew on *quantitative* information in existing databases, such as the Chapel Hill Expert Survey, the Rand Database of Worldwide Terrorism Incidents, and data from the Iraq Casualties Project, among other data sources (Mello 2020, 58–59).

Table 24.1 displays the uncalibrated *raw data* on a selection of 14 out of 51 leaders (abbreviated for reasons of space). The table indicates that some leaders made withdrawal announcements that did not qualify as early withdrawal announcements, because the statements were either indeterminate or involved partial withdrawals (dates set in italics). The table further includes information on the date of the next election. Decisions made within two months of the next election were coded as instances of an *upcoming election* (as a robustness test, I also checked for a six-month period, which led to substantively similar results). The left-right indicator of a government's placement in political space runs from 0 (extreme left) to 10 (extreme right). Data on the size of a country's deployment and military spending were used to inform the calculation of relative indicators of *fatalities* and *commitment*. Each of these had to be linked to the tenure of the respective leader (if there had been a withdrawal announcement, then the fatalities also had to have happened before that statement was issued).

As mentioned above, QCA requires calibrated data. This meant I had to transform the raw data listed in Table 24.1 into calibrated set-membership values. This can be done in a qualitative fashion, where the researcher defines calibration criteria for the target concepts and then assigns the respective scores by hand.[8] More commonly, the "direct method of calibration" is used, which is a software-run procedure that transforms numerical raw data into decimal-score fuzzy-set values based on a logarithmic function (Ragin 2008). For example, the measure of governments' political partisanship is based, among others, on data from the Chapel Hill Expert Survey. These data run from 0 to 10, where low scores indicate leftist partisanship. For the calibration procedure, the empirical anchors were set at 3.75 (full membership), 5 (crossover), and 6.25 (full non-membership). Hence, raw data scores of 3.75 and lower were coded as being "fully inside" the set *leftist partisanship*. For example, the leftist multi-party coalition of Prime Minister Romano Prodi received a left-right score of 3.49. This translated into a fuzzy score of 0.97 for leftist partisanship (almost fully in). Here, it should be highlighted that small differences in the decimal scores in QCA should not be overinterpreted. What is more important are the qualitative differences between cases with fuzzy scores above 0.5 (these are rather inside the set) and those below. Thus, it is also of no utility to report more than two decimals in QCA applications. Table 24.2 lists the calibrated data. The conditions upcoming elections and leadership change were coded in binary fashion as *crisp sets*. The outcome also largely followed a binary coding, but fuzzy sets allowed for further differentiation (e.g., when withdrawal announcements included caveats or no clear timeline was given, resulting in scores just above 0 and below 1, respectively). Finally, the conditions leftist partisanship, fatalities, and low commitment were calibrated with the direct method, resulting in fine-grained fuzzy scores.[9]

The first step in the QCA analysis proper involves testing for *necessary conditions*. In my analysis, none of the conditions turned out to be formally necessary for the outcome. However, the absence of upcoming elections turned out to be a condition that could be considered "almost necessary" for early withdrawal because its test for necessity comes close to

Table 24.1 Democratic Leaders, Conditions, and Outcome Raw Data

Country/Leader (Selection, 14 out of 51)	Withdrawal Announcement	Next Election	Left-Right	Fatalities per depl.	Fatalities Nominal	Commitment Depl./ME	Deployment Relative	Deployment Troops	Military Expenditure Relative	Military Expenditure Mil. USD
Australia (J.W. Howard)	17-Apr-03	9-Oct-04	7.46	0.19%	2	0.85	2.35	1,048	2.78	9,927
Australia (K. Rudd)	30-Nov-07	21-Aug-10	3.90	0.00%	0	0.62	2.98	1,330	4.81	17,185
Bulgaria (S. Sakskoburggotski)	31-Mar-05	25-Jun-05	5.62	2.06%	10	6.81	1.09	485	0.16	569
Czech Republic (M. Topolánek)	8-Oct-07	29-May-10	7.40	0.00%	0	0.36	0.25	110	0.69	2,450
Denmark (A.F. Rasmussen)	21-Feb-07	13-Nov-07	7.28	0.83%	4	1.16	1.08	480	0.93	3,333
Estonia (A. Ansip)	-	6-Mar-11	5.34	0.00%	0	0.75	0.09	40	0.12	444
Italy (S. Berlusconi)	19-Jan-06	9-Apr-06	7.33	1.00%	24	0.64	5.38	2,400	8.47	30,242
Italy (R. Prodi)	7-Jun-06	13-Apr-08	3.49	0.00%	0	0.31	2.91	1,300	9.35	33,408
Netherlands (J.P. Balkenende)	21-Oct-04	22-Nov-06	6.29	0.23%	3	1.24	2.89	1,288	2.34	8,356
Poland (D. Tusk)	23-Nov-07	9-Oct-11	5.94	0.00%	0	0.84	2.02	900	2.4	8,589
Portugal (J.M.D. Barroso)	-	20-Feb-05	6.50	0.00%	0	0.31	0.27	120	0.87	3,110
Slovakia (R. Fico)	18-Oct-06	10-Mar-12	4.51	1.18%	1	0.73	0.19	85	0.26	911
Spain (J.M. Aznar)	-	14-Mar-04	7.60	0.83%	10	0.75	2.71	1,208	3.61	12,881
Spain (J.L.R. Zapatero)	19-Apr-04	12-Apr-08	3.70	0.08%	1	0.68	2.91	1,300	4.27	15,262

Note: Italics indicate partial or indeterminate withdrawal announcements. Left-Right cores range from 0 (extreme left) to 10 (extreme right).

Table 24.2 Democratic Leaders, Conditions, and Outcome (Calibrated Data)

Country/Leader (Selection, 14 out of 51)	Outcome	Explanatory Conditions				
	Early Withdrawal	Upcoming Elections	Leadership Change	Leftist Partisanship	Fatalities	Low Commitment
Australia (J.W. Howard)	0.10	1.00	0.00	0.00	0.75	0.71
Australia (K. Rudd)	0.90	0.00	1.00	0.93	0.00	0.90
Bulgaria (S. Sakskoburggotski)	1.00	0.00	0.00	0.19	1.00	0.00
Czech Republic (M. Topolánek)	0.20	0.00	1.00	0.00	0.00	0.98
Denmark (A.F. Rasmussen)	0.90	0.00	0.00	0.00	0.99	0.28
Estonia (A. Ansip)	0.00	0.00	1.00	0.31	0.00	0.81
Italy (S. Berlusconi)	0.30	1.00	0.00	0.00	1.00	0.89
Italy (R. Prodi)	1.00	0.00	1.00	0.97	0.00	0.98
Netherlands (J.P. Balkenende)	1.00	0.00	0.00	0.05	0.79	0.20
Poland (D. Tusk)	0.20	0.00	1.00	0.10	0.00	0.72
Portugal (J.M.D. Barroso)	0.00	1.00	0.00	0.03	0.00	0.98
Slovakia (R. Fico)	1.00	0.00	1.00	0.76	1.00	0.83
Spain (J.M. Aznar)	0.00	1.00	0.00	0.00	0.99	0.81
Spain (J.L.R. Zapatero)	1.00	0.00	1.00	0.96	0.61	0.87

Note: All scores reflect fuzzy sets, ranging from 1 (full set membership) to 0 (full set non-membership).

the benchmark of 0.90 consistency. This prompted one of the peer reviewers of the article to request an additional Chi-square test of association, which is not normally part of QCA but in this research setting made sense to also explore the relationship between upcoming elections and early withdrawal from a statistical perspective. This test showed a statistically significant difference in early withdrawal decisions among leaders who faced elections and those who did not. While 31 leaders faced elections during their tenure and their country's Iraq deployment, only two of these initiated a withdrawal in a two-month period before elections (Dominican President Mejia and Portuguese Prime Minister Santana Lopes).

The second step in the analysis is the construction of the *truth table*. Since the analysis entails five conditions, this results in a truth table with 32 rows (configurations of conditions). Of these, 25 rows were populated with empirical cases. Table 24.3 shows an abbreviated truth table with 6 rows and 14 cases. While it must be kept in mind that this merely presents a part of the complete truth table, it should suffice to illustrate the principles of QCA truth tables (for the complete truth table, see Mello (2020, 63)) and the accompanying online supplement. We can see that the top three rows consistently lead toward the outcome (with consistency levels above 0.89) and that the bottom three rows feature low consistencies. Hence, only the top three rows are used for the ensuing Boolean minimization (in addition to other rows not shown in this abbreviated table). On the left side of the truth table, we can see single letters that indicate the five conditions: leadership change (L), upcoming elections (E), leftist partisanship (P), low commitment (C), and fatalities (F). Each case is assigned to the row that best describes its configuration of conditions. For example, Spain (Zapatero) is located

Qualitative Comparative Analysis

in the second row, which reflects a new leader, no upcoming elections, leftist partisanship, low coalition commitment, and fatalities. This configuration is shared by Slovakia (Fico) and associated with a perfect consistency of 1, which indicates that membership in this row is a sufficient condition for membership in the outcome.

In the final step of the analysis, the truth table is minimized to gain a solution term for the outcome. It is generally recommended to derive all three solution terms (Schneider and Wagemann 2010), but researchers are – in principle – free to choose which of the solution terms they want to interpret and emphasize in their analysis.[10] This can vary, depending on the research aims and the level of complexity in a given study (especially the number of conditions included). Most often, the conservative solution will be too complex for meaningful interpretation. For my application, I chose the intermediate solution because I wanted to gain a more concise solution but also wanted to exclude some implausible counterfactuals (that is why I did not use the parsimonious solution).

Table 24.4 shows the solution paths toward early withdrawal.[11] There are different ways to summarize QCA solutions (cf. Rubinson 2019). The format displayed in Table 24.4 has the advantages that all conditions can be spelled out on the left side (rather than using acronyms and Boolean expressions), that all relevant measures of fit and all the cases are shown, and that the black and crossed-out circles (for the presence and absence of the respective condition) are more intuitive to read than Boolean notation. Hence, we can see that Path 1 entails the configuration of a new leftist leader without upcoming elections. This is shared by five leaders, as can be seen in the lower area ("covered cases"). *Uniquely covered cases* are those that are only covered by one single path of the solution. One downside of this notation is that the cases are represented by acronyms (to save space). Alternatively, one could, of course, also spell out the country names and leaders for a stand-alone table.

Table 24.4 further displays equifinality because four paths consistently lead toward the outcome. Each of these contains a different configuration of conditions, which also means that the paths and their underlying logic should be discussed separately in QCA study. The measures of fit below the paths show that all are highly consistent (scores close to 1) but their coverage varies quite a bit. Raw coverage indicates how much of the empirical evidence is accounted for, while unique coverage reflects only that part that is covered solely by the respective path. Hence, we can see that Path 2 has the highest raw coverage, but Path 1 has

Table 24.3 Truth Table for the Outcome Early Withdrawal (Abbreviated)

Conditions					Outcome			
L	E	P	C	F	W	N	Consistency	Leaders
0	0	0	0	1	1	3	1.00	Bulgaria (Sakskoburggotski), Netherlands (Balkenende), Denmark (A.F. Rasmussen)
1	0	1	1	1	1	2	1.00	Spain (Zapatero), Slovakia (Fico)
1	0	1	1	0	1	2	0.89	Italy (Prodi), Australia (Rudd)
0	1	0	1	1	0	3	0.25	Italy (Berlusconi), Australia (Howard), Spain (Aznar)
1	0	0	1	0	0	3	0.22	Estonia (Ansip), Poland (Tusk), Czech Republic (Topolánek)
0	1	0	1	0	0	1	0.17	Portugal (Barroso)

Note: L = leadership change, E = upcoming elections, P = leftist partisanship, C = low commitment, F = fatalities, W = early withdrawal.

the highest unique coverage. The bottom of the table reports the overall solution consistency (0.96) and coverage (0.76). This indicates that the solution is highly consistent, but it does not cover all cases, some of which may be accounted for with alternative explanations. We will return to this in the next step.

In addition to summarizing the QCA results as in Table 24.4, it is often a good idea to visualize the position of each case through a scatter plot (also known as XY plot). Figure 24.1 displays such a visualization for the 51 cases entailed in the study used for the empirical illustration. This was created with the R package "ggplot2" (Wickham 2016). The x-axis shows cases' fuzzy-set membership in the solution, and the y-axis shows membership in the outcome (early withdrawal). The plot also includes a diagonal line. This line separates cases with values that are equal to or higher for the outcome than for the solution ($Y \geq X$) from those that are equal to or lower for the outcome than for the solution ($Y \leq X$). Cases with equal values for the solution and the outcome are situated exactly on the diagonal line. In set-theoretic terms, a perfect sufficient condition (or perfectly sufficient solution, which may entail any number of configurations of conditions) is indicated if all cases are on or above the diagonal line. We can see that most cases in Figure 24.1 are located above the diagonal, but some cases are just below it, which means that these cases subtract from the overall solution consistency.[12] However, apart from the numerical estimate of consistency, it is also important to check for qualitative differences in cases' positions.

Qualitatively speaking, four types of cases exist, separated by the dashed lines that divide the plot into four squares. Cases in the bottom left hold neither membership in the

Table 24.4 Solution for the Outcome Early Withdrawal

	Solution Paths			
	1	2	3	4
Leadership change	●		⊗	⊗
Upcoming elections	⊗	⊗	⊗	⊗
Leftist partisanship	●		⊗	
Low commitment				●
Fatalities		●		
Consistency	0.92	0.99	0.98	0.98
Raw coverage	0.23	0.41	0.39	0.23
Unique coverage	0.15	0.10	0.10	0.04
Covered cases / uniquely covered cases (bold)	**AU2**	BG1	BG1	JP1
	ES2	DK1	DK1	NO1
	HU2	ES2	**HN1**	**NZ1**
	IT2	JP1	JP1	PH1
	SK2	**LV2**	**NI1**	
		NL1	NL1	
		PH1	NO1	
		RO2	PH1	
		SK2		
Solution consistency		0.96		
Solution coverage		0.76		

Note: Black circles indicate the presence of a condition, and crossed-out circles indicate its absence.

Qualitative Comparative Analysis

solution nor membership in the outcome. Hence, these can be largely considered *irrelevant cases* because they do not show the outcome of interest, nor do they feature configurations of conditions that are associated with the outcome. Conversely, cases in the top right hold membership both in the solution and in the outcome. These are *typical cases* for the relationship under study. The gray shaded area further defines cases that hold membership in the solution and the outcome, and which are also consistent with a set-theoretic relationship of sufficiency. However, the fact that several cases are just below the line should not be a reason for concern. It simply means that their membership in the solution (slightly) exceeds their membership in the outcome. Qualitatively, these should be treated in the same way as other cases in the top right corner. We can also see that there are two cases in the top left corner. These *unaccounted cases* are not part of the solution, but they still show the outcome we are interested in. This is not unusual because there can always be cases that require an alternative explanation. That said, if the number of unaccounted cases grows too large, then this should prompt the researcher to reconsider her research design (and possibly include another condition or reconceptualize one of the existing ones). Finally, the bottom right corner shows cases that hold membership in the solution, but which do not show the expected outcome. Hence, these are considered *deviant cases*. These pose a problem, because they directly challenge the assumed relationship between membership in the solution and the outcome. Empirically, this study entailed no deviant cases but two unaccounted cases, which are discussed in the study itself.

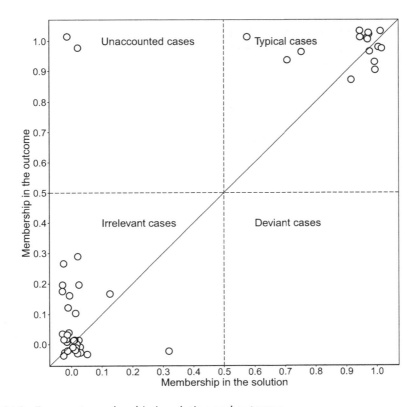

Figure 24.1 Fuzzy-set membership in solution and outcome.

397

Conclusion

While still being considered an emerging method in some corners, QCA has seen a vast increase in empirical applications in IR (Ide and Mello 2022) and also in the narrower field of FPA. It is likely that this trend will continue, not least due to a growing diversity in methodological approaches, move toward methodological pluralism and analytical eclecticism (Sil and Katzenstein 2010), and increase training opportunities across a broader spectrum of methods at summer schools, workshops, and graduate schools.[13]

That said, what are the method's strengths and limitations and how can new users avoid frequently made mistakes? The main asset of QCA is its ability to account for *causal complexity* – the identification of multiple paths toward the same outcome and combinations of conditions that jointly bring about the outcome. Another asset is the *rigorous analytical framework* which has been strengthened over the years of QCA's development and now presents a robust comparative approach to examine medium to large numbers of cases. This also shows in the increased functionality of the respective R packages, which now allow for a broad range of customization, depending on one's research aims (Duşa 2019; Oana, Schneider, and Thomann 2021). Additionally, robustness tests are becoming more and more standardized (Oana and Schneider 2021). For peer-reviewed publications, it is now more or less expected to conduct robustness tests, especially when the QCA study worked predominantly with quantitative data sets where calibration decisions can be difficult to justify.[14] Finally, it must be highlighted that despite its rigorous structure, QCA allows for *ample flexibility* in tailoring the analysis to the requirements of an individual research project. As such, the method can be used with qualitative and quantitative types of data, in small to large settings and with various forms of analytical steps and approaches (Rihoux and Ragin 2009; Schneider and Wagemann 2012; Mello 2017, 2021; Pagliarin, La Mendola, and Vis 2022).

But the method is not without limitations. The first limitation is empirical: to conduct a QCA, the researcher needs to have a certain number of cases and data on these cases. For new research phenomena or topics where data can be sensitive and hard to obtain (e.g., many issues in security policy), this can pose a hurdle that effectively undermines a comparison and may lead researchers to opt for a single case study or a paired comparison (Mello 2017). The second limitation relates to the analysis itself, which is sensitive to changes in the calibration of conditions and the selection of cases (Skaaning 2011; Oana and Schneider 2021). This means that researchers ought to pay close attention to their criteria for calibration and case selection. Analytical decisions must be justified and where alternatives are feasible, robustness tests should be conducted. Finally, even though QCA provides a rigorous comparative framework, its comparisons are inherently static. If researchers are interested in processes of decision-making and temporal aspects of policy, then these elements must either be incorporated at the research design level (Pagliarin and Gerrits 2020), or in combination with other methods such as *process tracing* (see van Meegdenburg in this volume). Indeed, multimethod research has been hailed as the new gold standard in the social sciences, even though there are quite different conceptions of what multimethod research entails (Seawright 2016; cf. Goertz 2017).

What are frequently made mistakes in QCA? Here, we can distinguish between conceptual errors at the research design stage and those committed during the analysis and the interpretation of the set-theoretic results (see also Rubinson et al. 2019). To begin with, QCA studies should aim to explore set relations and causal complexity. Researchers should highlight why they apply QCA and to which extent set relations and causal complexity are expected. An often-overlooked issue in research design is the relationship between cases and conditions. Simply put, the number of cases should generously exceed the number of conditions to have enough empirical material for all possible combinations of conditions (but this does not mean that all combinations must be filled empirically). As a rule of thumb, four cases per condition should be included in a study and even higher ratios are recommended when a study features more than five conditions (Mello 2021, 27). This means that studies with few cases should focus their research design on a select number of conditions, rather than aiming to cover all potentially relevant factors. When it comes to the analysis, one often-encountered issue are low coverage scores (e.g., in the range of 0.5/0.6 coverage, and even lower). Frankly, a coverage around 0.5 raises serious questions about a study's selection of conditions (because it indicates that a substantial share of the phenomenon of interest may be explained by alternative factors that were not included). Another important point concerns the selection of the solution term. As indicated above, researchers can choose which of the three different solution terms they want to focus on in their interpretation. However, each requires a thorough justification, which can relate to the research aims, theoretical expectations, the extent to which there is limited diversity, and the nature of the logical remainders. Finally, QCA deals in complexity, but its results should be presented in a parsimonious way. Here, transparency and clarity are key to make it unambiguous for readers (and reviewers) to grasp how a study achieved its results and how results were interpreted (Mello 2021, 191).

What are the prospects for QCA in FPA? As summarized in the literature review section, QCA has increasingly been used in research on foreign policy, and particularly in work on international security. From my perspective, several areas invite further exploration. First, due to its emphasis on a combinatorial logic, QCA should be fruitful as a method to use in combination with *leadership trait analysis* (LTA, see Brummer in this volume) or *operational code analysis* (OCA, see Schafer and Walker in this volume). This could be used, for instance, to explore comparative research questions about the behavior of leaders during crises and conflict (on *comparative foreign policy*, see Feng and He in this volume). To be sure, such an undertaking would require a tremendous data effort and sequential analytical steps, hence this may best be pursued collaboratively as part of a larger project. Second, due to its emphasis on theoretical integration and the combination of systemic and domestic-level variables, *neoclassical realism* appears to be a promising theoretical framework for set-theoretic applications in FPA (Davidson 2011; Meibauer 2021; Rosa and Cuppuleri 2021). At the time of writing, there is only a single study that embraces the combination of neoclassical realism and QCA (Dall'Agnol 2022), but with their inherent synergy such integrative approaches are bound to see wider application in future years.

Notes

1 A search on the Web of Science using the terms "qualitative comparative analysis" and "foreign policy" identifies 15 SSCI journal articles that empirically apply the method of QCA (as of May 11, 2022). The first of these was published in 2008, but the majority of the articles appeared throughout the last few years, showing an upward trajectory in publication trends.
2 This should not imply that statistical research cannot model causally complex relationships (for an exception, see Braumoeller 2003). For an empirical examination of "quantitative" and "qualitative" cultures, see Kuehn and Rohlfing (2022).
3 For a discussion of the mathematical transformation of raw data into calibrated data, see Ragin (2008). An illustration and further applied examples are given in Mello (2021).
4 To be precise, the consistency of a truth table row is calculated on the basis of all cases' set-membership scores for the respective configuration. With fuzzy sets, cases may also hold partial membership in a configuration (e.g., a fuzzy score of 0.1, as in being almost entirely outside the set) but their score still affects the calculation of consistency. This explains why consistency may not be "perfect" even

when all cases with membership above 0.5 (cases that are qualitatively considered to be inside the set) also show the outcome.
5 A comprehensive list of software is maintained on the COMPASSS website (which also hosts other QCA-related resources): https://compasss.org/software/.
6 A user-friendly introductory manual to QCA in R complements my textbook (Mello 2021). This can be accessed at: https://doi.org/10.7910/DVN/KYF7VJ.
7 This is an important difference to some statistical approaches, where a certain extent of missing data is expected. In QCA, complete data are required to proceed with the analysis.
8 On guidelines for using qualitative data in QCA, for instance when working with information from interviews or focus groups, see Pagliarin, La Mendola, and Vis (2022).
9 Further details on the calibration of these conditions can be found in the online supplement to Mello (2020), available at: https://doi.org/10.7910/DVN/8UWS1R.
10 For different perspectives on QCA solution terms and their interpretability, see, among others, Haesebrouck and Thomann (2021), Álamos-Concha et al. (2021), and Haesebrouck (2022).
11 A side-by-side comparison of all three solutions is provided in Table S5 in the online supplement to Mello (2020).
12 On the calculation of consistency and coverage, see Ragin (2006).
13 Regular courses and workshops on QCA are offered at the ECPR Summer School of Methods and Techniques, the FORS Summer School in Social Science in Lugano, and as part of the newly instituted MethodsNET. The COMPASSS website and newsletter provide regular updates on courses offered (see link above).
14 For examples on how such robustness tests can be documented, see Haesebrouck (2017a) and Ide et al. (2021). Meissner and Mello (2022) also apply the new robustness test protocol for QCA (Oana and Schneider 2021).

References

Álamos-Concha, Priscilla, Valérie Pattyn, Benoît Rihoux, Benjamin Schalembier, Derek Beach, and Bart Cambré. 2021. "Conservative Solutions for Progress: On Solution Types when Combining QCA with In-depth Process-Tracing." *Quality & Quantity* (3 August).
Böller, Florian. 2021. "Brakeman or Booster? Presidents, Ideological Polarization, Reciprocity, and the Politics of US Arms Control." *International Politics* (7 July).
Böller, Florian, and Marcus Müller. 2018. "Unleashing the Watchdogs: Explaining Congressional Assertiveness in the Politics of US Military Interventions." *European Political Science Review* 10 (4): 637–662.
Boogaerts, Andreas. 2018. "Beyond Norms: A Configurational Analysis of the EU's Arab Spring Sanctions." *Foreign Policy Analysis* 14 (3): 408–428.
Boogaerts, Andreas, and Edith Drieskens. 2020. "Lessons from the MENA Region: A Configurational Explanation of the (In)Effectiveness of UN Security Council Sanctions between 1991 and 2014." *Mediterranean Politics* 25 (1): 71–95.
Braumoeller, Bear F. 2003. "Causal Complexity and the Study of Politics." *Political Analysis* 11 (3): 209–233.
Brummer, Klaus, and Kai Oppermann. 2019. *Aussenpolitikanalyse*. Berlin: De Gruyter.
Caspersen, Nina. 2019. "Human Rights in Territorial Peace Agreements." *Review of International Studies* 45 (4): 527–549.
Cronqvist, Lasse. 2019. *Tosmana [Version 1.61]*. University of Trier.
Dall'Agnol, Augusto C. 2022. "The Diffusion of Military Power: A Neoclassical Realist Analysis." Paper presented at the ISA Annual Convention.
Davidson, Jason W. 2011. *America's Allies and War: Kosovo, Afghanistan, and Iraq*. New York: Palgrave Macmillan.
de Sá Guimarães, Feliciano, and Maria Hermínia Tavares de Almeida. 2017. "From Middle Powers to Entrepreneurial Powers in World Politics: Brazil's Successes and Failures in International Crises." *Latin American Politics and Society* 59 (4): 26–46.
Duşa, Adrian. 2019. *QCA with R. A Comprehensive Resource*. Cham: Springer.
Gerrits, Lasse, and Stefan Verweij. 2014. "Critical Realism as a Meta-Framework for Understanding the Relationships between Complexity and Qualitative Comparative Analysis." *Journal of Critical Realism* 12 (2): 166–182.

Goertz, Gary. 2017. *Multimethod Research, Causal Mechanisms, and Case Studies*. Princeton, NJ: Princeton University Press.
Goertz, Gary, and James Mahoney. 2012. *A Tale of Two Cultures: Qualitative and Quantitative Research in the Social Sciences*. Princeton, NJ: Princeton University Press.
Grynaviski, Eric, and Amy Hsieh. 2015. "Hierarchy and Judicial Institutions: Arbitration and Ideology in the Hellenistic World." *International Organization* 69 (3): 697–729.
Haesebrouck, Tim. 2017a. "EU Member State Participation in Military Operations: A Configurational Comparative Analysis." *Cambridge Review of International Affairs* 30 (2–3): 137–159.
———. 2017b. "NATO Burden Sharing in Libya: A Fuzzy Set Qualitative Comparative Analysis." *Journal of Conflict Resolution* 61 (10): 2235–2261.
———. 2018. "Democratic Participation in the Air Strikes Against Islamic State: A Qualitative Comparative Analysis." *Foreign Policy Analysis* 14 (2): 254–275.
———. 2022. "Relevant, Irrelevant, or Ambiguous? Toward a New Interpretation of QCA's Solution Types." *Sociological Methods & Research*.
Haesebrouck, Tim, and Eva Thomann. 2021. "Introduction: Causation, Inferences, and Solution Types in Configurational Comparative Methods." *Quality & Quantity* (July 29).
Haesebrouck, Tim, and Anouschka van Immerseel. 2020. "When Does Politics Stop at the Water's Edge? A QCA of Parliamentary Consensus on Military Deployment Decisions." *European Political Science Review* 12 (3): 371–390.
Heldt, Eugénia C., Patrick A. Mello, Anna Novoselova, and Omar Ramon Serrano Oswald. 2022. "When Do International Organizations Engage in Agency Slack? A Qualitative Comparative Analysis of United Nations Institutions." *Global Studies Quarterly* 2 (3): ksac035.
Hudson, Valerie M., and Benjamin S. Day. 2019. *Foreign Policy Analysis: Classic and Contemporary Theory*. Lanham: Rowman & Littlefield.
Ide, Tobias, and Patrick A. Mello. 2022. "QCA in International Relations: A Review of Strengths, Pitfalls, and Empirical Applications." *International Studies Review* 24 (1): 1–20.
Ide, Tobias, Miguel Rodriguez Lopez, Christiane Fröhlich, and Jürgen Scheffran. 2021. "Pathways to Water Conflict During Drought in the MENA Region." *Journal of Peace Research* 58 (3): 568–582.
Kaarbo, Juliet. 2022. "What Happened to Vladimir Putin?". International Affairs Blog. https://medium.com/international-affairs-blog/what-happened-to-vladimir-putin-5755addf2a15.
Kisangani, Emizet F., and Jeffrey Pickering. 2022. *African Interventions: State Militaries, Foreign Powers, and Rebel Forces*. New York: Cambridge University Press.
Kuehn, David, and Ingo Rohlfing. 2022. "Do Quantitative and Qualitative Research Reflect two Distinct Cultures? An Empirical Analysis of 180 Articles Suggests "no"." *Sociological Methods & Research* (31 March).
Mahoney, James. 2021. *The Logic of Social Science*. Princeton, NJ: Princeton University Press.
Meibauer, Gustav. 2021. "Neorealism, Neoclassical Realism and the Problem(s) of History." *International Relations* (29 July).
Meissner, Katharina L., and Patrick A. Mello. 2022. "The Unintended Consequences of UN Sanctions: A Qualitative Comparative Analysis." *Contemporary Security Policy* 43 (2): 243–273.
Mello, Patrick A. 2012. "Parliamentary Peace or Partisan Politics? Democracies' Participation in the Iraq War." *Journal of International Relations and Development* 15 (3): 420–453.
———. 2014. *Democratic Participation in Armed Conflict: Military Involvement in Kosovo, Afghanistan, and Iraq*. Basingstoke: Palgrave Macmillan.
———. 2017. "Qualitative Comparative Analysis and the Study of Non-State Actors." In *Researching Non-State Actors in International Security: Theory & Practice*, edited by Andreas Kruck and Andrea Schneiker, 123–142. Oxon: Routledge.
———. 2020. "Paths towards Coalition Defection: Democracies and Withdrawal from the Iraq War." *European Journal of International Security* 5 (1): 45–76.
———. 2021. *Qualitative Comparative Analysis: An Introduction to Research Design and Application*. Washington, DC: Georgetown University Press.
———. 2022. "Incentives and Constraints: A Configurational Account of European Involvement in the Anti-Daesh Coalition." *European Political Science Review* (24 February): 1–19.
Oana, Ioana-Elena, and Carsten Q. Schneider. 2018. "SetMethods: An Add-on R Package for Advanced QCA." *The R Journal* 10 (1): 507–533.
———. 2021. "A Robustness Test Protocol for Applied QCA: Theory and R Software Application." *Sociological Methods & Research* (26 August).

Oana, Ioana-Elena, Carsten Q. Schneider, and Eva Thomann. 2021. *Qualitative Comparative Analysis Using R: A Beginner's Guide*. New York: Cambridge University Press.

Oppermann, Kai, and Klaus Brummer. 2020. "Who Gets What in Foreign Affairs? Explaining the Allocation of Foreign Ministries in Coalition Governments." *Government and Opposition* 55 (2): 241–259.

Pagliarin, Sofia, and Lasse Gerrits. 2020. "Trajectory-Based Qualitative Comparative Analysis: Accounting for Case-Based Time Dynamics." *Methodological Innovations* online first (27 September) (doi:10.1177%2F2059799120959170).

Pagliarin, Sofia, Salvatore La Mendola, and Barbara Vis. 2022. "The "Qualitative" in Qualitative Comparative Analysis (QCA): Research Moves, Case-Intimacy and Face-to-Face Interviews." *Quality & Quantity*.

Pilster, Ulrich, Tobias Böhmelt, and Atsushi Tago. 2013. "Political Leadership Changes and the Withdrawal from Military Coalition Operations, 1946–2001." *International Studies Perspectives* 16 (4): 463–483.

Ragin, Charles C. 1987. *The Comparative Method: Moving Beyond Qualitative and Quantitative Strategies*. Berkeley, CA: University of California Press.

———. 2006. "Set Relations in Social Research: Evaluating Their Consistency and Coverage." *Political Analysis* 14 (3): 291–310.

———. 2008. *Redesigning Social Inquiry: Fuzzy Sets and Beyond*. Chicago, IL: University of Chicago Press.

Ragin, Charles, and Sean Davey. 2017. *fs/QCA [Version 3.0]*. Irvine, CA: University of California.

Rihoux, Benoît, and Charles C. Ragin, eds. 2009. *Configurational Comparative Methods: Qualitative Comparative Analysis (QCA) and Related Techniques*. Thousand Oaks, CA: Sage.

Rosa, Paolo, and Adriana Cuppuleri. 2021. "Dangerous dyads in the post-Soviet space: explaining Russia's military escalation decisions, 1992–2010." *Italian Political Science Review/Rivista Italiana di Scienza Politica* 51 (3): 355–372.

Rubenzer, Trevor. 2008. "Ethnic Minority Interest Group Attributes and U.S. Foreign Policy Influence: A Qualitative Comparative Analysis." *Foreign Policy Analysis* 4 (2): 169–185.

Rubinson, Claude. 2019. "Presenting Qualitative Comparative Analysis: Notation, Tabular Layout, and Visualization." *Methodological Innovations* 12 (2): 1–22.

Rubinson, Claude, Lasse Gerrits, Roel Rutten, and Thomas Greckhamer. 2019. Avoiding Common Errors in QCA: A Short Guide for New Practitioners.

Rutten, Roel. 2020. "Applying and Assessing Large-N QCA: Causality and Robustness from a Critical-Realist Perspective." *Sociological Methods & Research* (26 April): 1–21.

Schmitt, Olivier. 2018. *Allies that Count: Junior Partners in Coalition Warfare*. Washington, DC: Georgetown University Press.

Schneider, Carsten Q., and Claudius Wagemann. 2010. "Standards of Good Practice in Qualitative Comparative Analysis (QCA) and Fuzzy-Sets." *Comparative Sociology* 9 (3): 397–418.

———. 2012. *Set-Theoretic Methods for the Social Sciences: A Guide to Qualitative Comparative Analysis*. New York, NY: Cambridge University Press.

Seawright, Jason. 2016. *Multi-Method Social Science: Combining Qualitative and Quantitative Tools*. Cambridge: Cambridge University Press.

Sil, Rudra, and Peter J. Katzenstein. 2010. *Beyond Paradigms: Analytic Eclecticism in the Study of World Politics*. Basingstoke: Palgrave Macmillan.

Skaaning, Svend-Erik. 2011. "Assessing the Robustness of Crisp-set and Fuzzy-set QCA Results." *Sociological Methods & Research* 40 (2): 391–408.

Tago, Atsushi. 2009. "When Are Democratic Friends Unreliable? The Unilateral Withdrawal of Troops from the 'Coalition of the Willing'." *Journal of Peace Research* 46 (2): 219–234.

Treisman, Daniel. 2022. "Putin Unbound: How Repression at Home Presaged Belligerence Abroad." *Foreign Affairs* 101 (3): 40–53.

van Nieuwenhuizen, Simone. 2019. "Australian and People's Republic of China government conceptions of the international order." *Australian Journal of International Affairs* 73 (2): 181–197.

Wickham, Hadley. 2016. *ggplot2: Elegant Graphics for Data Analysis*. New York: Springer.

Part VI
Qualitative Methods and Historical Approaches

25
Process Tracing
An Analyticist Approach

Hilde van Meegdenburg

Introduction

This chapter develops process tracing (PT) as a method for Foreign Policy Analysis (FPA). It explains what it takes to conduct PT, trace a mechanism, and draw conclusions on that basis. Importantly, I develop a form of PT that is amendable to the more actor-centered and oftentimes, though not necessarily, interpretivist approaches to FPA (Houghton 2007; Hudson 2005). In the PT I propose there is space for *agency* and *contingency*. This means this chapter will not follow the dominant regularity understanding of PT because I hold the assumptions of generalizability that underlay it to be too rigid (e.g., Beach and Pedersen 2019; Bennett and Checkel 2015; George and Bennett 2005; Goertz 2017; Hall 2006; Mahoney 2015). Instead, I treat mechanisms as akin to Weberian ideal types: abstract constructs that are adduced from multiple concrete, contextually embedded, and largely *idiosyncratic instantiations* (e.g., Falleti and Lynch 2009; Guzzini 2017; Hedström and Swedberg 1998; Jackson 2006; McAdam, Tarrow, and Tilly 2004; Pouliot 2015; Robinson 2017).[1] As I will show, treating mechanisms as analytical constructs allows us to (a) study how a mechanism or concatenation of mechanisms led to a particular outcome; (b) assess how the mechanism(s) functioned in a given context; and (c) abstract from the specific instantiation(s) more general propositions about foreign policy making.

This chapter proceeds as follows. First, I argue that PT is a method. Although this may seem obvious, it has an important implication that is not always strictly observed: PT does not come with a particular philosophical ontology. As part of my discussion of *the regularity understanding* of PT, I will explain what this means and why it matters. Second, I introduce *an analyticist approach* to PT as a method for studying idiosyncratic cases by treating causal mechanisms as analytical constructs or ideal types. I address, in turn, mechanisms, concrete instantiations, and their portability and explain why this understanding of mechanisms is more amendable to FPA. To be sure, the argument is not that all PT or FPA should follow this approach. To the contrary, it is only to say that more actor-centered and interpretivist accounts may benefit from rethinking what mechanisms are and how they inform our understanding of processes and PT. Third, I provide an example based on my own work on foreign policy narratives and the use of Private Military and Security Contractors (PMSCs) by Denmark. Lastly, I offer a short conclusion that reflects on the benefits and challenges of following an analyticist approach to PT.

The Regularity Understanding of PT

Process tracing is demanding. Uncovering a *causal mechanism* or a *concatenation of multiple mechanisms* is a meticulous task. However, before continuing we have to establish what PT is and what it can do. One argument easy to agree on is that PT is a *method*—it is a systematic mode of inquiry that allows a researcher to draw inferences and further our knowledge of the world. That said, in this section I want to make one thing explicit: PT is not concerned, as Patrick Jackson put it, with "the definition of knowledge and the overall goal of empirical research" (Jackson 2016, 27). Put differently, PT does not adhere to any philosophical ontology and does not come with a set of prescribed assumptions about the empirical world and our access to it. PT offers a particular understanding of how outcomes come about—through processes and driven by mechanisms—but what a researcher believes a mechanism is, and how she believes a mechanism can be studied, is not a given. Yet, the particular philosophical position a researcher takes does shape what PT would look like and what conclusions can be drawn on its basis.

In the PT literature, the dominant (and largely positivist) understanding treats mechanisms as supporting regular associations. This *regularity understanding* of PT comes with a set of logical assumptions that are not well-suited for much of FPA. In what follows, I briefly discuss the regularity understanding of PT with an emphasis on the bounded generalizations that are inherent to it. After that, I explain why the road taken in this chapter differs.

In the regularity understanding, PT is applied to *test hypotheses* against a more or less *objective empirical reality* and to come to (moderate) *generalizations* (Beach and Pedersen 2019, 6; Bennett and Checkel 2015, 7; Collier 2011, 824; George and Bennett 2005, 207; Gerring 2004, 348; Goertz and Mahoney 2012, 101; Hall 2006, 27f.; Mayntz 2004, 241; see also Runhardt 2015, 1297). Although differences in emphases and points of contention exist within this group of authors, they understand PT as supporting *nomothetic research* aimed at uncovering the mechanism—understood as a causal pathway or a causally connected sequence of events—that underlies an otherwise regular association (Glennan 1996, 64). This logic is often referred to as the X → M → Y model whereby research is focused on studying the mechanism (M) that relates a trigger (X) to an outcome (Y; Mahoney 2015, 205; but see Waldner 2012; 2016 for a sustained critique on this depiction). The mechanism is generally taken to be the entire sequence between the trigger and the outcome (see Figure 25.1).

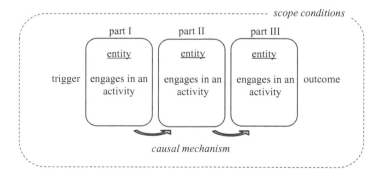

Figure 25.1 Schematic causal mechanism as understood in the regularity understanding.

To be sure, these process tracers do not draw (causal) conclusions on the basis of the observation of a cross-case regularity: their focus and conclusions regard the mechanism that connects the trigger to the outcome. However, the overall assumption is that mechanisms do sustain such regularities. Renate Mayntz summarized this position succinctly by arguing that "[s]tatements of mechanisms are accordingly *generalizing* causal propositions … [and mechanisms] 'are' sequences of causally linked events that occur repeatedly in reality if certain conditions are given" (2004, 241). Although critical of the *covering law* model of social science, her critique is not that law-like propositions are wrong but that their domain of application cannot be universal and should be specified through scope conditions or a "ceteris paribus clause" (ibid., 240; see also Glennan 1996, 54).

In this approach, scope conditions thus place limitations on the applicability of a theory. They define the socio-institutional context in which a mechanism can play out and create a "causally homogenous population" of cases—a group of sufficiently similar cases within which the causal relation is expected to hold true (Beach and Pedersen 2018, 838; Rohlfing 2012, 24; 44). PT, then, should be conducted on cases that are "representative" or "typical" of this broader class of cases because this allows a (moderate) generalization from the "studied case" to the "rest of the population" (Beach and Pedersen 2018, 838; see also Beach and Rohlfing 2018; Rohlfing 2014; Schneider and Rohlfing 2019). The regularity understanding thus argues that given certain conditions and the existence of causally important similarities a causal process-as-mechanism is a reoccurring phenomenon that produces the same (or at least a sufficiently similar) outcome every time it is triggered—that is, given the presence of conditions $X_1...X_n$ triggering mechanism M leads to outcome Y (see Figure 25.2).

A practical example can be taken from Benjamin Brast (2015). Brast studies the regional dimension of statebuilding and argues that interventions "will succeed in establishing a monopoly on large-scale violence if they enjoy the support of key regional actors" (ibid., 81). Brast's aim is "to build a theoretical framework applicable to current interventions" by "test[ing] the proposed theory on a [single] case" (ibid., 94). His X_1 is "liberal statebuilding intervention" and his triggering event is the start of regional cooperation. His outcome of interest (Y) is the establishment of a monopoly on violence. From a number of cases that have both X_1 and the trigger he selects one case, Sierra Leone, to test his hypotheses. He finds the expected relation holds and he is able to uncover the mechanism that sustains the relation (see ibid., 89). Subsequently, he argues that given X_1 and the trigger an equivalent mechanism should lead to a similar outcome in a defined set of similar cases—including Liberia and East Timor (ibid., 95). In short, he understands the discovered mechanism to underlie a bounded

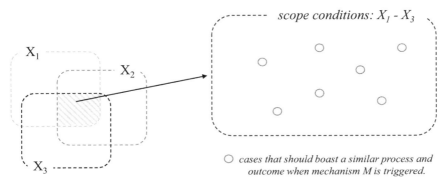

Figure 25.2 Scope conditions and generalization in the regularity understanding.

but regular association and his study offers a well-worked out and coherent example of what PT in this tradition would look like.

However, it is my conviction that this approach is too restrictive for much of FPA. Especially for the more actor-centered and interpretivist approaches, it is too deterministic (Jackson 2006, 33; 2014, 273; Pouliot 2007, 373).[2] Saying mechanisms underlie a bounded but regular association means we assume that actors, under a given set of conditions, will, by and large, act in similar ways bringing about similar outcomes. For instance, as John Owen argued in his mechanism-based approach to the democratic peace: "Liberals *will* trust states they consider liberal" and "agitate for [peaceful] policies" (Owen 1994, 103). This assumption is inherent to the regularity understanding and buttresses (and is buttressed by) the conceptions of *scope conditions*, *representative* and *typical cases*, and *generalizations*. And this assumption may work well for research that is neither interpretivist (and interested in contextually embedded meaning-making) nor particularly actor-centered. In that case, uncovering the mechanism that underlies a regular association adds significantly to our understanding of the world and the regularities we do observe. But if we want to account for or study agency or the potential of local meanings and meaning-making, then we have to allow contingency in our methods and the outcomes of processes. True agency—and therewith agential interpretations, (mis)calculations, understandings, assessments, meanings, ideas, emotions, creativity, and spontaneity—contradicts, at least in potential, regular associations (Jackson 2014, 270f.; Robinson 2017, 509). Agency introduces contingency. And taking agency seriously means our understanding of mechanisms should support "multifinality"—the idea that the same mechanism can produce different outcomes even under the same structural conditions (Guzzini 2017, 432).

If this is our understanding of agency and foreign policy making, then we need an approach to PT that accommodates that understanding. In what follows, I systematically introduce PT from the "analyticist tradition" (see Jackson 2016, 153ff.) treating mechanisms as analytical constructs or ideal types.[3]

An Analyticist Approach

When we apply PT to FPA, we are interested in the mechanisms that shape policy outcomes. We want to study *how* a given outcome came about. Moreover, to be scientifically interesting, PT should be both specific about the case at hand—how did *they* arrive at *that* decision?—and inform FPA more generally—what mechanisms were uncovered and are they applicable to a wider set of cases? In this section, I lay out an *analyticist approach* to PT that treats mechanisms as analytical constructs and that is interested in (a) studying how a mechanism or concatenation of mechanisms led to a particular outcome; (b) assessing how the mechanism(s) functioned in a given context; and (c) abstracting from the specific instantiation(s) more general propositions about foreign policy making. Following this approach, a mechanism is *an analytical construct that defines, in abstract terms, how a given set-up or entity transfers motion in identical or closely similar ways over a variety of situations* (partially adopted from McAdam, Tarrow, and Tilly 2004, 24). A distinction is made between the mechanism as abstract ideal type—the mechanism proper—and the concrete instantiations that exemplify it (Pouliot 2015, 238). Below, I first focus on the *mechanisms proper*, I then discuss *concrete instantiations*, and I close with a reflection on the *portability* of mechanisms.

Mechanisms. I treat mechanisms as analytical constructs and as akin to Weberian ideal types (Bengtsson and Hertting 2014, 717; Hedström and Swedberg 1998, 13; Jackson 2006, 43; 2014, 271; Pouliot 2007, 379; 2015, 238; Robinson 2017, 508). As such, a mechanism is an abstraction that captures the essence of a social phenomenon (Weber 2014 [1904], 124ff.).

First, mechanisms are distinct from the process. This argument resembles David Waldner's who also argues that it is generally not a single *mechanism* that defines the whole *process* (Waldner 2012, 65; 2016, 29f.; see also Robinson 2017, 508). Rather, a process typically comprises multiple mechanisms each with their own logic and contribution and each at their own position in the larger sequence of events. If PT studies the "cogs and wheels" of the social world (Elster 2006 [1989], 3), then the particular concatenation of cogs and wheels that brings about an outcome is the *process* and each piece of machinery, each cog and each wheel, is a *mechanism* with a number of typical characteristics that affords a particular flow, motion, or activity.

Second, mechanisms are abstractions drawn from multiple concrete yet diverse instantiations and, as such, are (scholarly) *constructs*. Take a "cog" as mechanism. In the abstract, a cog is a toothed wheel with the ability to transfer motion when spinning. This ideal typified description captures the most important characteristics (toothed wheel) and features (transfers motion when spinning) of cogs. It also distinguishes cogs from nuts, bolts, and wheels. Yet, what any existing cog looks like and what its function is in a process is an empirical question. There are metal cogs and ones carved out of wood, cogs that spur acceleration and cogs that produce a distinct sound upon every rotation. What all cogs have in common, however, are the ideal typical features that mark the abstraction. In fact, the abstract image is derived from the study of a (great) number of cogs and by *abstracting* from those concrete instantiations the characteristics of the mechanism proper—that is, the characteristics that the instantiations share and that are not part of their contextual setting (Pouliot 2015; 235). It is, moreover, abstraction that makes a mechanism a social construct (Robinson 2017, 508). Abstraction is the product of scholarly choice and interpretation. It is always based in what the researcher deems the "essential elements" of a situation to be and about deciding what causally relevant characteristics are to be included and what can be left out (Hedström and Swedberg 1998, 14; see also Goertz 2006, 27ff.). As such, while mechanisms are deduced from reality, they are "*not a depiction* of reality" (Weber 2014, 125). Moreover, through the continuous empirical study of distinct instantiations our understanding of the mechanism will, over time, be refined and amended. An ideal type in use is always an ideal type under construction as our understanding of the mechanism is constantly challenged, refined, adapted, or re-confirmed. As Weber noted, "all ideal typical constructions are transitory" (Weber 2014, 133). Finally, the fact that we can discuss and (dis)agree on the strengths and weaknesses of a given mechanism shows that it exists, *as construct*, in our (scholarly) discourse only. A mechanism is a "mental image" that "in its conceptual purity ... cannot be found empirically anywhere in reality" (ibid., 125; see also Pouliot 2007, 374).

Third, mechanisms are our "conceptual tools" (Weber 2014, 129). They are our "analytical" and "heuristic" devices (Hedström and Swedberg 1998, 13; Pouliot 2007, 374). We apply mechanisms to grasp, describe, and study reality. They allow us to compare or contrast cases as particular instantiations of "something" or "some-process" (McAdam, Tarrow, and Tilly 2004, 24; Robinson 2017, 508). Our abstract understanding of a cog allows us to recognize a cog when we see one and gives us the tools to compare and contrast one instantiation to others. Moreover, mechanisms allow us to summarize and communicate: *It was a case of a spinning cog transferring motion!* Their primary value is thus as heuristics and guides to research as we compare and contrast reality—concrete instantiations—to them (Weber 2014, 129). In fact, the empirical analysis of a mechanism-as-analytical construct is not about establishing its "truth value" or "accuracy". Instead, the relevant question is whether a given mechanism is *useful*—whether that mechanism affords an understanding and point of entrance for our studies (Hedström and Swedberg 1998, 15; Jackson 2014, 271; Pouliot 2015, 252).

But what, then, does a mechanism consist of? Similar to the regularity understanding, mechanisms should include entities that engage in activities (Machamer, Darden, and Craver 2000, 5). "Verbs have replaced nouns" and actors take the place of the passive descriptors that are central in variable-oriented research (McAdam, Tarrow, and Tilly 2004, 50). A cog (entity) may transfer motion when spinning (activity); a politician (entity) may vie for votes (activity); a parliamentary committee (entity) may arrive at a recommendation (activity); and so forth. Important however, rather than the methodological individualism espoused by some—which holds that social mechanisms are based in the individual decisions of discrete humans and should thus be studied at this level (Boudon 1998, 199; Hedström and Swedberg 1998, 11ff.; León-Medina 2017, 161; Little 1998, viii)—I see no objections to studying collective actors and macro-level processes without reverting to the individual-level. As McAdam, Tarrow and Tilly argued, limiting the method to "individual-level processes ... severely limit[s] our ability to interpret collective processes" (2004, 25; see also Falleti and Lynch 2009, 1149). Actors *can be* discrete human beings, and the focus of a study *can be* on how their position in a given social setting shaped a particular policy outcome, but it need not be.[4]

Concrete instantiations. As noted, an analyticist approach to PT differentiates between the abstract ideal type and the instantiations that inform it. This point can hardly be overemphasized. The description of the ideal type, like a good definition, can be short and focused. The instantiations—an instantiation being a mechanism's occurrence or manifestation in empirical reality—, however, are always contextually embedded, case specific, and often times part of a larger process. Concrete instantiations combine with their specific environments, whereby the environment (and potential other mechanisms) may either support, propel, constrain, or counteract their characteristic motion. "And", and this is an important distinction form the regularity understanding, "because mechanisms interact with the contexts in which they operate, the outcomes of the process cannot be determined a priori by knowing the type of mechanism that is at work" (Falleti and Lynch 2009, 1147; also see Jackson 2014, 274). Mechanisms are "multifinal"—the same mechanism can bring about different outcomes (Guzzini 2017, 432).

Take rational decision making as mechanism. We could define the ideal type as a decision based on the collection of information, the weighing of pros and cons of identified alternatives, and deciding for the best option. Whether we take an instrumental, bounded, or value-based understanding of rationality does not matter for the example. Now, let us say that rational decision making is ubiquitous. From this, it may be intuitively clear that every concrete instantiation is different. Each instantiation involves different actors, dealing with different questions, in a different setting. Logically, then, each outcome, each final decision, will also be case specific. Rational decision making can result in ordering food for dinner, in switching to online teaching in times of a pandemic, or in abstaining from voting on a resolution in the UN Security Council. However, although the concrete "outcome[s are] significantly different", the "mechanism is essentially the same" (McAdam, Tarrow, and Tilly 2004, 27). "On the fundamental level of mechanisms ... all are analogous" (Hedström and Swedberg 1998, 21) and the different cases, despite their differences, are "analytically equivalent" (Falleti and Lynch 2009, 1148). If we are interested in studying rational decision making, we could study each of these cases.

Of note is that the concrete instantiations are the empirical objects of study. To learn about a mechanism, we study its instantiations. Three related things are likely to be in focus of an empirical study.

First, the researcher would expose what the *particular instantiation* looked like. How did the typical characteristics manifest themselves in this case and how, if at all, did the mechanism's motion push the process forward? The analytical narrative should be more than a thick description. It should focus on the mechanism and its causal relevance and thus on those entities that pushed, shoved, and moved—that is, that engaged in activities. It should also explicate how those activities were relevant to the process: what did they change, bring about, or make (im)possible? Second, the researcher would study the functioning of the mechanism in its *specific context* and as part of a *specific process*. How did the socio-institutional setting in which the instantiation was embedded spur, change, or limit its typical motion? Third, a researcher would compare and contrast the instantiation to the ideal type and see if broader lessons about the mechanism and its functioning can be learned.

A hypothetical example: imagine a study on the use of a presidential veto in "Owncountry". To understand this instantiation, we have to look at the *process* of which it is part and the *socio-institutional context* in which it is embedded. Figure 25.3 provides a sketch of what such a hypothetical process, including multiple mechanisms, could look like. The process runs from the trigger—a public uprising in "Neighborland" and the immediate violent crackdown by Neighborland's authoritarian ruler—through three distinct mechanisms to the outcome—the freezing of the assets of Neighborland's leaders despite a parliamentary decision to, as always, not interfere with Neighborland's internal politics. The three identified mechanisms that conjoinedly shape the process are: "societal pressure" (Mechanism I); "parliamentary decision making" (Mechanism II); and "presidential veto and decree" (Mechanism III). The mechanisms run partly in parallel, partly in sequence, and, or at least so we may assume, what happens as part of one mechanism influences what happens in another.

Pending our research interests, we can approach this case differently. The principal investigator of a research project titled "*The (ir)rationality of presidential vetoes*" would probably zoom in on mechanism III, lay-bare how decision making functioned in this particular case, and how societal pressure shaped the decision. The conclusions would focus on what *this specific instantiation* reveals about the *mechanism proper* and its functioning in a specific context. Moreover, this instantiation is likely to be but one of multiple instantiations that will be compared and contrasted with the ultimate aim to learn about presidential vetoes more broadly. As McAdam, Tarrow, and Tilly noted, "mechanisms ... reappear in a wide variety of settings but in different sequences and combinations, hence with different collective

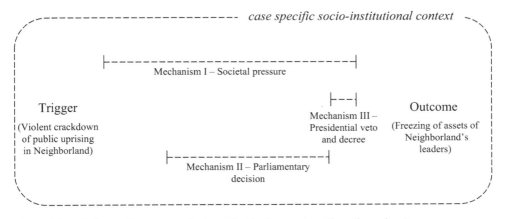

Figure 25.3 Schematic process of a hypothetical concatenation of mechanisms.

outcomes" and this invites us to study "[c]ommon properties across historically and culturally distinct settings" (2004, 23–24; see also Robinson 2017, 508). By contrasting multiple yet diverse instantiations, we can refine our understanding of the mechanism and learn about its (dis)functioning in distinct contexts.

Alternatively, a researcher may start from an empirical interest in the case: how can we explain that, after years of non-interference, Owncountry now froze all assets of the leadership of Neighborland? In this case, the researcher would study the *process* in its entirety. Either inductively, deductively, or as part of an iterative process they would uncover which mechanisms—which tools from our scientific toolbox—afford an understanding of the case. The three mechanisms would probably be of equal interest: how did Owncountry civil society come to protest the developments in Neighborland? How did parliament arrive at the decision to disregard Owncountry's civil society and continue politics as usual? And how did the president come to the alternate conclusion, veto parliament's bill, and issue a decree? The outcome of this study would be a thick, holistic explanation of the case. Yet the mechanisms, once specified, *guide* the research and the discussion of the findings. The researcher would draw on them to zoom in on causally relevant entities and activities and to show how the mechanisms combined and motioned the process forward. We would learn about the case-specific process and how this particular concatenation of mechanisms led to a particular outcome. But the study would also provide a basis to reflect on the abstract mechanisms and their typical characteristics and motions—that is, it allows us to draw broader inferences and (re)confirm, amend, or adjust our understanding of the ideal types.

Portability. Going back to the earlier given definition: a mechanism is an analytical construct that defines, in abstract terms, how a given set-up or entity transfers motion in identical or closely similar ways over a variety of situations. This definition should be largely explained by now. Only the portability—the "over a variety of situations"—can still be differentiated from the treatment of generalizations in the regularity understanding. As I argued, understanding mechanisms as supporting regular associations is too deterministic for much of FPA. It minimizes agency and assumes that actors, whether individual, small groups, or collective actors, will, by and large, act similarly under the same structural conditions. This assumption may be accurate enough for some research, but it is problematic for the more actor-centered and interpretivist approaches to FPA.

Understanding mechanisms as analytical constructs foregoes this problem. As analytical constructs, mechanisms can travel—they are "portable constructs" (Falleti and Lynch 2009, 1159)—but their portability lies in their abstraction (Guzzini 2017, 434; Pouliot 2015, 251). On *the abstract level of mechanisms*, general features, characteristic similarities, and typical motions can be discerned, contrasted, and analyzed. On this abstract level, mechanisms travel. On *the concrete level of instantiations*, however, we are likely to find mechanisms manifest differently. On this concrete level, instantiations are integrated into distinct processes and contexts and are explicitly expected not to be the same—neither as the ideal type nor as other instantiations. This allows us to talk, simultaneously, about the "principles of portability and indeterminacy" of mechanisms (Falleti and Lynch 2009, 1147). Mechanisms are portable in that we would expect the same mechanism to occur more frequently in reality. Yet, they are indeterminate in that we would expect the causally relevant characteristics to manifest and work differently in different situations, bringing about different outcomes. And it is exactly the acknowledgment of the indeterminacy of mechanisms on the one hand, and the contextual embeddedness of their instantiations on the other, that opens space for *idiosyncrasy, agency,* and *contingency* in analyticist PT.

In short, the outcome a mechanism produces cannot be determined *a priori*. Much depends on the creativity and agency of the actors involved as well as on the socio-institutional context in which it is embedded and the presence of other mechanisms that may allow, support, or counteract a mechanism's typical motion. This, perhaps, is what most distinguishes an analyticist approach from the regularity understanding. Where regularity-oriented researchers would have strong expectations about outcomes based on established or hypothesized scope conditions, analyticists would say they may know the *typical motions* of a mechanism but that they cannot know, in advance, how those motions did or will manifest themselves (if at all) in a particular instantiation. However, I believe that to be a strength of analyticist PT: by empirically studying contextually embedded instantiations, it *captures the idiosyncratic nature of cases* and encourages in-depth investigations; and by abstracting from the concrete instantiations more general lessons about the mechanism(s) proper, it *refines the conceptual tools* through which we approach and understand the world. Analyticist PT allows for variation and agency on the case level, while advancing our knowledge and understanding of the world by, bit by bit, explicating the different mechanisms that function in it on a more conceptual, abstract level.

In what follows, I explicate one such mechanism. In relation to state employment of Private Military and Security Contractors (PMSCs), I look at how narrative, and more particularly *discursive interventions*, shapes (produces) the boundaries of foreign policy. This means I zoom in on a mechanism that is itself part of a broader and ongoing process. A mechanism, moreover, that I hold to be ubiquitous: narrative and discursive interventions shape foreign policy throughout. Yet, each instantiation of the mechanisms will likely be different as narrative and discourse are always situated and shaped by the local socio-historical context in which they are embedded.

Denmark and the Decision not to Employ Private Military and Security Contractors

In this section, I show what understanding mechanisms as analytical constructs means for more actor-centered and interpretivist approaches to FPA. Personally, I conduct interpretivist research focusing on the narrative basis of foreign policy (see also Oppermann and Spencer in this volume). In what follows, I first elaborate the mechanism proper, I then show how this mechanism can be used to study a concrete instantiation, and I close by discussing the mechanism's portability.

The mechanism. The mechanism I present (based on what was an iterative and prolonged research process) is a double-barreled gun. It produces, simultaneously, two interrelated outcomes: a policy outcome and an identity outcome. The argument is that foreign policy making is based in *narratives*, in "the total collection of stories that we tell and that are told about us" (Ringmar 1996, 452; see also Subotić 2016, 612f.). It is essentially a mechanism of *justification* (Jackson 2006, 24). Based in the rhetorical tools and the understandings of reality that are available to them, actors, in justifying their positions, interpretations, and policy suggestions, narrate the world around them. They give meaning to other actors, events, and objects and they collectively demarcate what can be done in name of the *self*—the state (e.g., Browning 2008, 14; Doty 1993, 303; Guzzini 2012, 53; Jackson 2006, 24; Somers 1994, 614; Weldes 1996, 280). In this case, I am interested in how, by positioning (narrating) the self in relation to PMSCs, a state's collective identity and plausible courses of action, and therewith foreign policy, are simultaneously defined and plotted. The mechanism thus regards the narrative constitution of identity and foreign policy and the instantiation I address is the case of Denmark, 2001–2013.[5] Empirically, I draw on a mixture of parliamentary debates, newspaper articles, semi-structured interviews, government policy documents, statements by officials, think tank publications, and earlier scholarly work to show that the Danish narrative about PMSCs is simultaneously a narrative about Denmark and about the boundaries of foreign policy.

The instantiation. In Denmark, the use of PMSCs was, and is, controversial. The Danish Defense approached PMSCs with constraint and outsourcing remained limited (van Meegdenburg 2019, 30). This, despite the fact that commonly referenced post-Cold War functional pressures (van Meegdenburg 2015, 327ff.), also affected the Danish Defense (Mandrup 2013, 44). How can we explain this? Overall, the public debate on PMSCs in Denmark is marked by a taken-for-granted negativity—as if it is obvious that PMSCs should not be employed. The way PMSCs are narrated defines Denmark as a country that *does not do that* and makes policy suggestions to employ PMSCs difficult to rhetorically sustain and justify. In this case, the *narrators* (politicians and civil servants, but also journalists, pundits, ministries, and NGOs) are the entities and the activity they engage in is uttering of a discursive intervention. The outcome of interest is the parallel constitution of a state identity and foreign policy.

For instance, in June 2005, during a debate on the "In Larger Freedom" reform-plan for the United Nations, PMSCs came up (Folketinget 2005a). The exchange was between members of parliament Margrethe Vestager (*Radikale Venstre*, Danish Social Liberal Party, centrist) and Troels Lund Poulsen (*Venstre*, Denmark's Liberal Party, center-right). In an earlier position paper, the *Radikale Venstre* (RV) included the following suggestion: "Give the UN the opportunity—in acute cases where Member States fail—to engage (recognized) private military companies (PMCs) in peace operations until the regional organizations and the UN itself have the capacity to solve the peacekeeping/creative tasks" (Radikale Venstre 2003). During the debate, Poulsen referred to this position paper and asked Vestager why one would engage PMSCs; "would it not be better to make sure that it is countries that contribute"? Vestager's reply has three interesting components: (1) she stresses that "it is clear […] that the absolute best thing is that it is the countries that take responsibility […]. There can be no doubt about that"; (2) she acknowledges "this is a very controversial proposal"; and (3) she points out that much needs to pass before the option would be considered. Poulsen—who switches to calling PMSCs mercenaries ("*lejesoldater*")—subsequently asks Vestager what, then, would be examples of "reputable companies that have mercenaries"? Vestager answers she has no concrete examples and stresses, instead, that RV sees this as an emergency option when "big and principled things are at stake, such as genocide", and all other options have been exhausted. The conversation goes on for a bit. In reply to Kristian Pihl Lorentzen (also *Venstre*), Vestager notes that "naturally" democratic control over the execution of force must be ensured, but ends thereafter. The suggestion to explore PMSCs as an emergency option for the UN is not included in the final vote (Folketinget 2005b).

This exchange is not about Danish employment of PMSCs but about giving the UN the right to do so in extreme cases. However, the narrators do position Denmark in relation to PMSCs, leading to a number of interesting observations. For one, it may be noted that Poulsen switches to calling PMSCs "*lejesoldater*"—mercenaries. Like in English, this term has a more negative connotation but it is regularly used to refer to PMSCs (e.g., Høi 2007; Sangild 2009). Second, Vestager replies defensively and stresses the RVs agreement with shared values and priorities: states are—"naturally", "of course", "it is clear", "there can be no doubt about that"—the "preferred means of conflict resolution". And she notes the RV is aware the proposal is "very controversial". Lastly, as Vestager also brings up, it is noteworthy that Poulsen problematized this particular point from a document that contains 55 concrete suggestions—it clearly caught Poulsen's attention.

In the period under investigation, this was the only parliamentary exchange on the topic. Newspapers devoted some space to background stories—notably on Blackwater in the light of scandals and often referring to them as *lejesoldater*—but direct employment was not discussed. As my interviewees noted: "Well, we simply did not consider, I think, using [PMSCs] for anything" (Knudsen, interview).[6] "No one has talked about, debated, or even considered using defense contractors for, for instance, guard service … in Afghanistan. We don't do that" (Petersen, interview).[7] "We don't think like that" (Malm, interview).[8] Interviews, in this type of research, may be second-best sources because they do not probe the narrative itself but the interviewees' reflections on the practices and understandings that informed decisions (Pouliot 2007, 370). However, given triangulation, they can offer valuable insights. For one, Jes Rynkeby Knudsen explicated what remained implicit in the parliamentary debate in 2005. Reflecting on the "political view", he noted that "Denmark is clearly very cognizant of the fact that the monopoly on the use of force is a state monopoly … [it] is a state prerogative" (interview). Moreover, it is interesting to note that Rasmus Helveg Petersen and Major Kim Malm drew on an implicit understanding of "we"—Denmark—whereby that "we" explains why PMSCs are not employed: "we", because of who we are, because of what we stand for, "don't do that". As Nina Tannenwald argued, it is noteworthy when a particular norm (or taboo) is "a shared but 'unspoken' assumption of decisions makers" and when the justification for non-action simply notes that "because of who we are […] 'we just don't do things like this'" (1999, 440).

So what does the above tell us in terms of the mechanism I am interested in? How does Denmark, in narrating PMSCs and the Danish relation to PMSCs, (re-)produce, simultaneously, a particular identity and foreign policy? First, by referring to PMSCs as mercenaries an implicit sense of illegitimacy is contained in the debate. The use of the term (re-)establishes how Denmark thinks about and relates to PMSCs. At the same time, it demarcates a policy space. Poulsen shows this by asking which would be examples of "reputable companies that have mercenaries"? It becomes a contradiction in terms. Similarly, the questions and answers largely reproduce PMSCs as controversial actors: by saying the proposal is "very controversial", its controversiality is (re-)established. Overall, Denmark is narrated as a country that holds to the primacy of states, where PMSCs are controversial, and where employing PMSCs-cum-mercenaries is a rhetorical contradiction.

To be sure, this application zooms in on a specific instantiation of the mechanism. Earlier, however, I argued mechanisms are generally part of a larger process, often including multiple mechanisms. Two short observations in relation to that. First, other mechanisms were implicitly present. The newspaper articles referred to, for example, are part of the public narrative. Yet, the selection of "newsworthy stories" is itself a distinct mechanism. This mechanism runs partly in parallel, partly in sequence to the foreign policy narratives, and what happens as part of one mechanism influences what happens in the other—newspaper articles may influence parliamentary debates and debates may shape what is considered newsworthy. Therefore, even when not in focus, other mechanisms are generally present and (co-)shape what happens in the mechanism of interest. Whether those other mechanisms can and should be explicated depends on the interests and expertise of the researcher. Second, the way I understand it, foreign policy making is best conceived as an *ongoing* process revolving around continuous collective narratives that are temporarily "fixed" or "stabilized" in action—in policy outcomes (Bucher and Jasper 2017, 393; Jackson 2006, 15). As such, what we are dealing with is a sequence of instantiations of, essentially, the same mechanism.

Clearly, the above offers only a snapshot. Where space allows, we would want to display the collective narrative in full, tap into a multiplicity of sources and discursive interventions to show how a narrative reproduces or contests a given relation, and how that narrative, inherently and simultaneously, (re-)produces a space for legitimate policy and sets forth a particular understanding of the collective self. For now, I hope the above offers a sufficient illustration.

Portability. It should not come as a surprise when I say the above is but one instantiation of a mechanism that occurs frequently in reality. Although not explicitly conceptualized this way by all (but see Jackson 2006; Robinson 2017), different instantiations of this mechanism can be found throughout the FPA literature—including studies from the 1990s until today; studies focusing on countries from the North, East, South, and West; and studies focusing on the foreign policies of big and small states (Bacik and Afacan 2013; Browning 2008; Bucher and Jasper 2017; Campbell 1992; Communi 2010; Crawford 2002; Fofanova and Morozov 2013; Guzzini 2012; Hopf 2002; Jackson 2006; Krebs 2015; Ostermann 2019; Ringmar 1996b; Robinson 2017; Stengel 2020; Subotić 2016; Weldes 1996; Zehfuss 2001). Despite their differences, the above studies all argue that it is in and through narrative that a state's collective identity is defined and courses of action are plotted. The outcomes are wildly different: the USA as innocent and provoked to self-defense by the Soviet Union (Weldes 1996); Serbia as historically victimized and incomplete without Kosovo (Subotić 2016); and India as shifting between more secular and religious self-understandings and a less or more antagonistic foreign policy (Communi 2010). Yet, the mechanisms, the underlying motions, are essentially the same: in justifying policies, positions, and interpretations, actors (re-)produce both a state's identity and delimit the space for action. As such, the abstract mechanism is portable. We can apply this understanding of foreign policy narratives to contrast and compare different cases. The concrete instantiations, the concrete narratives and the concrete identities and foreign policies they produce, however, are always contextually embedded and can be understood only in their specific contexts.

Conclusion

This chapter argued that FPA that takes actors' interpretations, (mis)calculations, understandings, assessments, meaning-making, emotions, creativity, or spontaneity seriously—regardless of whether it is also interpretivist—would run into logical problems with the structural conditions that underpin generalizations in the regularity understanding of PT. Understanding mechanisms as analytical constructs foregoes these problems. Following an analyticist understanding, mechanisms are *portable* but *indeterminate* and therewith create space for *agency* and *contingency*. In short, a mechanism's abstract and ideal-typical motions are general and portable—they can be used to compare and contrast different instantiations across a multitude of case—, but its concrete manifestations, especially when shaped by human activity, are instantiation specific and indeterminate. Variation in outcomes does not prove a mechanism wrong, it simply shows that mechanisms can manifest differently in different contexts.

In fact, one of the major benefits of the analyticist approach is that it invites the researcher to truly study a case holistically and include in their final account all aspects, big and small, that were deemed causally relevant without compromising the portability of the mechanism. This is possible because the analyticist approach makes a clear distinction between the concrete and contextualized instantiations on the one hand, and the conceptual, theoretical, and ideal-typical mechanism that is derived from these instantiations on the other. This distinction dissolves the trade-off between inclusive and parsimonious accounts that haunts generalizations in the regularity understanding. It makes it possible to conduct both in-depth, thick, qualitative, situated, and, when wanted, interpretivist work *and* to abstract from that work elegant conclusions that may inform future research and refine our understanding of the workings of one or more of the mechanisms that shapes our world.

At the same time, this also constitutes a challenge. Although the implications of the differences between the regularity understanding and an analyticist approach are substantial, the actual differences are subtle. Especially since causal language can be employed, I would advise those who conduct analyticist PT to avoid using terms common to the regularity understanding. Instead of talking about scope, contextual, or structural *conditions* it would be better to talk about the (socio-institutional) *context* or, perhaps, the contextual *embeddedness* or *situatedness* of concrete instantiations. *Generalizability* can be named *portability*. When referring to a single empirical manifestation of the mechanism a *case* would be an *instantiation*. And a *causal mechanism* probably can be best qualified as the *abstract mechanism*, the *ideal-typified mechanism*, or, as I did, the *mechanism proper*. Of course, variations on this theme are possible but making a clear distinction in terminology would remind the reader of the distinctions in meaning—distinctions that are not, I like to emphasize, stylistic. Terms such as "causal mechanisms", "generalizability", and "scope conditions" come with pre-established meanings and those meanings are strongly informed by the (dominant) regularity understanding of PT. As such, I fear that lest terminology is clearly distinguished, well-explained, and used carefully and consistently, the analyticist process tracer may be misunderstood and perceived as incoherent.

In all, the above is not to say that *all* PT should follow an analyticist approach, or that PT that follows a regularity understanding is less valuable or insightful. To the contrary, it is simply to say that more actor-centered and interpretivist approaches to FPA, and social science in general, may benefit from rethinking what mechanisms are and how they inform our understanding of processes and outcomes.

Acknowledgments

This contribution and its open access publication are supported by a Marie Skłodowska-Curie Individual Fellowship under the European Union's Horizon 2020 research and innovation program, grant agreement No. 897274.

Notes

1. "Idiosyncratic" means specific, unique, or singular and the term "instantiation" refers to a discrete occurrence of the mechanism in reality—that is, an instantiation is a "case of" the mechanism.
2. See Beach and Pedersen (2019, 22ff.) for a discussion of ontological determinism in the regularity understanding.
3. I will use these two terms, "analytical construct" and "ideal type", synonymously.
4. Likewise, a study can assume actor rationality (thin or otherwise) and focus on path dependencies or other theoretical notions, but making these "the fundamental logic of action behind all social mechanisms" (Bengtsson and Hertting 2014, 714) unnecessarily essentializes human action and imports theory into a discussion about method.
5. These are the years Denmark was most actively involved in Afghanistan and Iraq.
6. Jes Rynkeby Knudsen, then Director of the Danish Military Manual on international law, interview by author, Copenhagen, 12.09.2012.

7 Rasmus Helveg Petersen, then defense spokesperson for the Radikale Venstre, interview by author, Copenhagen, 12.04.2012.
8 Major Kim Malm, then Finance and Budget Department of the Ministry of Defense, interview by author, Copenhagen, 12.11.2012.

References

All internet sources have last been accessed on 9 February 2022.

Bacik, Gökhan, and Isa Afacan. 2013. "Turkey Discovers Sub-Saharan Africa: The Critical Role of Agents in the Construction of Turkish Foreign-Policy Discourse." *Turkish Studies* 14 (3): 483–502.

Beach, Derek, and Rasmus B. Pedersen. 2018. "Selecting Appropriate Cases When Tracing Causal Mechanisms." *Sociological Methods & Research* 47 (4): 837–871.

———. 2019. *Process-Tracing Methods. Foundations and Guidelines*, 2nd ed. Ann Arbor, MI: University of Michigan Press.

Beach, Derek, and Ingo Rohlfing. 2018. "Integrating Cross-Case Analyses and Process Tracing in Set-Theoretic Research: Strategies and Parameters of Debate." *Sociological Methods & Research* 47 (1): 3–36.

Bengtsson, Bo, and Nils Hertting. 2014. "Generalization by Mechanism: Thin Rationality and Ideal-Type Analysis in Case Study Research." *Philosophy of the Social Sciences* 44 (6): 707–732.

Bennett, Andrew, and Jeffrey T. Checkel. 2015. "Process Tracing: From Philosophical Roots to Best Practices." In *Process Tracing: From Metaphor to Analytic Tool*, edited by Andrew Bennett and Jeffrey T. Checkel. Cambridge: Cambridge University Press, 3–37.

Boudon, Raymond. 1998. "Social Mechanisms without Black Boxes." In *Social Mechanisms. An Analytical Approach to Social Theory*, edited by Peter Hedström and Richard Swedberg. Cambridge: Cambridge University Press, 172–203.

Brast, Benjamin. 2015. "The Regional Dimension of Statebuilding Interventions." *International Peacekeeping* 22 (1): 81–99.

Browning, Christopher S. 2008. *Constructivism, Narrative and Foreign Policy Analysis: A Case Study of Finland*. Bern: Peter Lang.

Bucher, Bernd, and Ursula Jasper. 2017. "Revisiting 'Identity' in International Relations: From Identity as Substance to Identifications in Action." *European Journal of International Relations* 23 (2): 391–415.

Campbell, David. 1992. *Writing Security: United States Foreign Policy and the Politics of Identity*. Minneapolis, MN: University of Minnesota Press.

Collier, David. 2011. "Understanding Process Tracing." *Political Science & Politics* 44 (4): 823–830.

Commuri, Gitika. 2010. *Indian Identity Narratives and the Politics of Security*. Thousand Oaks, CA: Sage Publications.

Crawford, Neta C. 2002. *Argument and Change in World Politics. Ethics, Decolonization, and Humanitarian Intervention*. Cambridge: Cambridge University Press.

Doty, Roxanne Lynn. 1993. "Foreign Policy as Social Construction: A Post-Positivist Analysis of U.S. Counterinsurgency Policy in the Philippines." *International Studies Quarterly* 37 (3): 297–320.

Elster, Jon. 2006. *Nuts and Bolts for the Social Sciences*. Cambridge: Cambridge University Press.

Falleti, Tulia G., and Julia F. Lynch. 2009. "Context and Causal Mechanisms in Political Analysis." *Comparative Political Studies* 42 (9): 1143–1166.

Fofanova, Elena, and Viatcheslav Morozov. 2013. "Imperial Legacy and the Russian–Baltic Relations: From Conflicting Historical Narratives to a Foreign Policy Confrontation?" In *Identity and Foreign Policy: Baltic-Russian Relations and European Integration*, edited by Eiki Berg and Piret Ehin. New York: Routledge, 15–32.

Folketinget. 2005a. "F 13 Om at Styrke Og Reformere FN." *Parliament. 2004–2005. 2nd Session*, June 2. https://www.ft.dk/samling/20042/forespoergsel/F13/BEH1-45/forhandling.htm.

———. 2005b. "V 35 Om FNs Topmøde." *Parliament. 2004–2005. 2nd Session*, June 7. https://www.ft.dk/samling/20042/vedtagelse/V35/index.htm.

George, Alexander L, and Andrew Bennett. 2005. *Case Studies and Theory Development in the Social Sciences*. Cambridge, MA: MIT Press.

Gerring, John. 2004. "What Is a Case Study and What Is It Good For?" *American Political Science Review* 98 (2): 341–354.

Glennan, Stuart S. 1996. "Mechanisms and the Nature of Causation." *Erkenntnis* 44: 49–71.

Goertz, Gary. 2006. *Social Science Concepts: A User's Guide.* Princeton, NJ: Princeton University Press.
Goertz, Gary. 2017. *Multimethod Research, Causal Mechanisms, and Case Studies.* Princeton, NJ: Princeton University Press.
Goertz, Gary, and James Mahoney. 2012. *A Tale of Two Cultures. Qualitative and Quantitative Research in the Social Sciences.* Princeton, NJ, and Oxford: Princeton University Press.
Guzzini, Stefano. 2012. *The Return of Geopolitics in Europe? Social Mechanisms and Foreign Policy Identity Crises.* Cambridge: Cambridge University Press.
———. 2017. "Militarizing Politics, Essentializing Identities: Interpretivist Process Tracing and the Power of Geopolitics." *Cooperation and Conflict* 52 (3): 423–445.
Hall, Peter A. 2006. "Systematic Process Analysis: When and How to Use It." *European Management Review* 3 (1): 24–31.
Hedström, Peter, and Richard Swedberg. 1998. "Social Mechanisms: An Introductory Essay." In *Social Mechanisms. An Analytical Approach to Social Theory,* edited by Peter Hedström and Richard Swedberg. Cambridge: Cambridge University Press, 1–31.
Høi, Poul. 2007. "Dødens Drabanter." *Berlingske,* September 19. https://www.berlingske.dk/internationalt/doedens-drabanter.
Hopf, Ted. 2002. *Social Construction of International Relations: Identities and Foreign Policies, Moscow, 1955 and 1999.* Ithaca, NY: Cornell University Press.
Houghton, David. 2007. "Reinvigorating the Study of Foreign Policy Decision Making: Toward a Constructivist Approach." *Foreign Policy Analysis* 3 (1): 24–45.
Hudson, Valerie M. 2005. "Foreign Policy Analysis: Actor-Specific Theory and the Ground of International Relations." *Foreign Policy Analysis* 1 (1): 1–30.
Jackson, Patrick Thaddeus. 2006. *Civilizing the Enemy. German Reconstruction and The Invention of The West.* Ann Arbor, MI: University of Michigan Press.
———. 2014. "Making Sense of Making Sense. Configurational Analysis and the Double Hermeneutic." In *Interpretation and Method,* edited by Dvora Yanow and Peregrine Schwartz-Shea. New York: Routledge, 267–283.
———. 2016. *The Conduct of Inquiry in International Relations. Philosophy of Science and Its Implications for the Study of World Politics,* 2nd ed. Abingdon: Routledge.
Krebs, Ronald R. 2015. *Narrative and the Making of US National Security.* Cambridge: Cambridge University Press.
León-Medina, Francisco J. 2017. "Analytical Sociology and Agent-Based Modeling: Is Generative Sufficiency Sufficient?" *Sociological Theory* 35 (3): 157–178.
Little, Daniel. 1998. *Microfoundations, Method, and Causation: On the Philosophy of the Social Sciences.* New Brunswick: Transaction Publishers.
Machamer, Peter, Lindley Darden, and Carl F. Craver. 2000. "Thinking about Mechanisms." *Philosophy of Science* 67 (1): 1–25.
Mahoney, James. 2015. "Process Tracing and Historical Explanation." *Security Studies* 24 (2): 200–218.
Mandrup, Thomas. 2013. "Denmark: How Not If to Outsource Military Services." In *Commercialising Security in Europe,* edited by Anna Leander. New York: Routledge, 39–57.
Mayntz, Renate. 2004. "Mechanisms in the Analysis of Social Macro-Phenomena." *Philosophy of the Social Sciences* 34 (2): 237–259.
McAdam, Doug, Sidney Tarrow, and Charles Tilly. 2004. *Dynamics of Contention.* Cambridge: Cambridge University Press.
Meegdenburg, Hilde van. 2015. "What the Research on PMSCs Discovered and Neglected: An Appraisal of the Literature." *Contemporary Security Policy* 36 (2): 321–345.
———. 2019. "'We Don't Do That': A Constructivist Perspective on the Use and Non-Use of Private Military Contractors by Denmark." *Cooperation and Conflict* 54 (1): 25–43.
Ostermann, Falk. 2019. *Security, Defense Discourse and Identity in NATO and Europe. How France Changed Foreign Policy.* London and New York: Routledge.
Owen, John M. 1994. "How Liberalism Produces Democratic Peace." *International Security* 19 (2): 87–125.
Pouliot, Vincent. 2007. "'Sobjectivism': Toward a Constructivist Methodology." *International Studies Quarterly* 51 (2): 359–384.
———. 2015. "Practice Tracing." In *Strategies for Social Inquiry. Process Tracing From Metaphor to Analytic Tool,* edited by Andrew Bennett and Jeffrey T. Checkel. Cambridge: Cambridge University Press, 237–259.

Radikale Venstre. 2003. "FN i Forvandling Og Forandring." *Folketingets Udenrigsudvalg*, October 24. http://webarkiv.ft.dk/?/samling/20031/udvbilag/uru/almdel_bilag17.htm.

Ringmar, Erik. 1996. "On the Ontological Status of the State." *European Journal of International Relations* 2 (4): 439–466.

———. 1996b. *Identity, Interest and Action. A Cultural Explanation of Sweden's Intervention in the Thirty Years War*. Cambridge: Cambridge University Press.

Robinson, Corey. 2017. "Tracing and Explaining Securitization: Social Mechanisms, Process Tracing and the Securitization of Irregular Migration." *Security Dialogue* 48 (6): 505–523.

Rohlfing, Ingo. 2012. *Case Studies and Causal Inference: An Integrative Framework*. New York: Palgrave Macmillan.

———. 2014. "Comparative Hypothesis Testing Via Process Tracing." *Sociological Methods & Research* 43 (4): 606–642.

Runhardt, Rosa W. 2015. "Evidence for Causal Mechanisms in Social Science: Recommendations from Woodward's Manipulability Theory of Causation." *Philosophy of Science* 82 (5): 1296–1307.

Sangild, Rasmus. 2009. "Lejesoldaten." *Politiken*, March 1. https://global.factiva.com.

Schneider, Carsten Q., and Ingo Rohlfing. 2019. "Set-Theoretic Multimethod Research: The Role of Test Corridors and Conjunctions for Case Selection." *Swiss Political Science Review* 25 (3): 253–275.

Somers, Margaret R. 1994. "The Narrative Constitution of Identity: A Relational and Network Approach." *Theory and Society* 23 (5): 605–649.

Stengel, Frank A. 2020. *The Politics of Military Force. Antimilitarism, Ideational Change, and Post-Cold War German Security Discourse*. Ann Arbor, MI: University of Michigan Press.

Subotić, Jelena. 2016. "Narrative, Ontological Security, and Foreign Policy Change." *Foreign Policy Analysis* 12 (4): 610–627.

Tannenwald, Nina. 1999. "The Nuclear Taboo: The United States and the Normative Basis of Nuclear Non-Use." *International Organization* 53 (3): 433–468.

Waldner, David. 2012. "Process Tracing and Causal Mechanisms." In *The Oxford Handbook of Philosophy of Social Science*, edited by Harold Kincaid. Oxford: Oxford University Press, 65–84.

———. 2016. "Invariant Causal Mechanisms." *Qualitative & Multi-Method Research* 14 (1–2): 28–33.

Weber, Max. 2014. "The 'Objectivity' of Knowledge in Social Science and Social Policy." In *Max Weber. Collected Methodological Writings*, edited by Hans Henrik Bruun and Sam Whimster. Abingdon: Routledge, 100–138.

Weldes, Jutta. 1996. "Constructing National Interests." *European Journal of International Relations* 2 (3): 275–318.

Zehfuss, Maja. 2001. "Constructivism and Identity: A Dangerous Liason." *European Journal of International Relations* 7 (3): 315–348.

26
Interviews
Delphine Deschaux-Dutard

Introduction: Why Are Interviews a Well-Suited Method to Study Foreign Policy?

Social science research on foreign policy has grown increasingly in international academic research in the last decades. As the contemporary world order is more and more based on multilateralism and diplomatic exchanges, investigating foreign policy in the twenty-first century is not only pertinent but also indispensable. Yet as a very specific kind of state policy, as it often requires secrecy and can sometimes result in the use of force, foreign policy requires methodological reflexivity from the researcher. Accessing internal documents might be either very difficult in the foreign policy area, or subject to an authorization that would make it difficult to publish the research results. This is why interviews constitute a very good and original way of getting information in foreign policy studies. Methodologically speaking, it is interesting to study foreign policy as a public policy. A public policy can be defined as a set of practices and representations emanating from one or several state actors and which has a content, dedicated resources and is supposed to deliver outcomes. Furthermore, there is a relationship between the contents of public policies and the actors and mechanisms implementing them. Focusing on the study of foreign policy as a public policy logically means for the researcher that he/she focuses a large part of her investigation on the actors (Hudson 2005). Therefore, interviews represent an important research strategy in that matter to access these actors. Interviews constitute an interesting method to explain how foreign policy actors make sense of the world (Breuning 2007). Therefore, this chapter will focus on interviews and the methodological questions and challenges they raise for the study of foreign policy. Interviews constitute one of the main methods to investigate foreign policy: Potter (2010), indeed, identifies four main methods (archival research, content analysis, interviews, and focus groups). Researching foreign policy through the use of qualitative interviews represents a methodological challenge, as foreign policy is often characterized by secrecy and sensitivity of some issues. But interviews also give a very stimulating way of looking at the actors' practices and representations in this area. Thus, I will assess the advantages and precautions to be considered when relying on interviews for the study of foreign policy topics. After a brief literature review, I will first present the key terms and challenges of this method and illustrate them with an empirical application. Last but not least, the chapter will conclude with new trends and challenges for the future of interview-leading while studying foreign policy issues.

Literature Review

Interviews have become a rather classical method to investigate foreign policy in social science research works since the 1980s. Even though the previous privileged method had long been based on archives following the work of Graham Allison (Allison 1971) on the management of the Cuban Missile Crisis by the American government in 1962 and the following foundation of Foreign Policy Analysis (FPA) as a discipline (for a synthesis on the evolution of FPA, see Hudson and Day 2019), interviews have been more and more used since the 1980s either as an additional method or as a principal research method by researchers investigating foreign policy (see for instance Cohen 1986; Lequesne 1993; Ross 1995). If at first interviews were mostly used by social psychology researchers to investigate psychological trends developed by leaders in foreign policy (see Rasler et al. 1980), political science researchers have started to invest a lot of energy on this method with the development of the analysis of foreign policy as a public policy since the end of the Cold War, as I stated in the introduction of this chapter. As foreign policy has been increasingly studied as a public policy, the focus on its actors has made the use of interviews more and more accurate to study their representations and their practices of foreign policy across the world. This increasing use of interviews has been accompanied by the rise of the ethnographic method in FPA, as, for instance, in research on the European Commission (EU) (Ross 1995; Kuus 2013; Mérand 2021), on French foreign policy toward the EU (Lequesne 1993; Deschaux-Beaume 2008) or toward wider issues (Cohen 1986; Pouponneau 2013; Rieker 2017), on American foreign policy (see Kandel 2016 on the study of the role of the American Congress on Foreign policy), just to name a few. The last three decades have witnessed the normalization of interviews as an important investigation method in social science research on foreign policy.

Moreover, another trend linked to the development of this method is the increasing use of ethnography in the study of foreign policy issues (see also Neumann in this volume). The ethnographic method seems to be one of the most popular among young scholars working on defence questions, as it offers a unique access to this normally restrained field (2015). Christian Lequesne spent, for instance, more than 30 hours as an embedded researcher in the French Ministry of Foreign Affairs and in two French embassies between 2013 and 2014; Frédéric Mérand spent almost a year at the European Commission in two-month research stays between 2015 and 2019 (Mérand 2021; see also Kuus 2013). But some scholars also experiment with other techniques as focus groups, for instance (Carreiras and Castro 2012), participant observation (Ross 1995; Carreiras and Castro 2012; Schmitt 2015; Lequesne 2017; Mérand 2021) and, of course, archives (see Friedrich in this volume) when this is possible (Deschaux-Beaume 2011, 2013; Schmitt 2015) in order to enrich and triangulate the data collected through interviews. Another issue regarding the choice of methodology when investigating foreign policy issues is the comparative method (see also Feng and He in this volume). The foreign policy field could bring the profane researcher to think that each foreign policy milieu is quite similar to the others whatever country considered. But as any other social organization, each country's institutional organization of foreign policy has its organizational specificities. There again interviews are a well-suited methodology to better understand the domestic and international constraints weighing on foreign policy institutions and organizations when these institutions and organizations are studied in a comparative perspective (Kaarbo, Lantis, and Beasley 2002; Breuning 2007). A service or an office existing in a country does not necessarily exist as such in another country, as it is the case in my own research about the French and German political-military decision-making systems, for instance, as I show below. Another important element to take into account in the case of a multi-country comparison is that there may exist different rules surrounding the status of public speech held by state officials in each country, which may impact the content of authorized speech, this speech expressing a delegation of power to the member of the foreign policy institutions (Bourdieu 1982: 103–119). Not to mention the difficulty to master several languages, which is not limited to foreign policy comparative studies but applies in any comparative research.

Key Terms and Concepts, Methodology

Conducting research on foreign policy relying mainly on qualitative interviews can be tricky but also very stimulating, as foreign policy as a global practice can sometimes be considered as "'difficult environment',[...] a suspicious environment and yet not hermetic to research" (Cohen 1999: 17). How shall I reach foreign policy actors? Once reached, how can I be sure they will speak to the researcher? What are the precautions to consider while interviewing foreign policy elites? In this part, I first shortly explain why interviews are well-suited to investigate foreign policy issues, and then focus on three important topics to keep in mind while using qualitative interviews as the main research method for studies on foreign policy issues.

Interviews as the Main Method in Research on Foreign Policy Issues

Qualitative methods constitute a very fruitful way of enquiring the foreign policy field. Following Becker's comment that "if one wants to know society, one first has to know it first-hand" (Becker 2002: 44), qualitative methods relying on semi-directed interviews or ethnography (I come back to this point below) constitute a stimulating methodology to study foreign policy issues.[1] More precisely, in the case of a social science research on foreign policy in the widest sense, qualitative interviews correspond to two main uses: getting first-hand information to the extent that most of the time the researcher does not have an extensive access to internal documents, and having an interesting access to the actors in a research context where secrecy and a specific language often constitute an issue for the analyst (Deschaux-Beaume 2011, 2012).

Even when internal documents are accessible to a researcher (sometimes needing an authorization procedure when investigating defence issues, for instance), they often turn out to use an opaque technical jargon. Therefore, depending on the aim of the research, the question of the access to the foreign policy field is directly linked to the question of methodology. For instance, in my own research, as I wanted to analyse the practices and representations of French and German officers and diplomats regarding European defence policy, qualitative interviews turned out to be the only way of gaining access to genuine data. This characteristic appears to be specific to research on inaccessible or *difficult* social fields as the military or the police, for instance (Bogner and Menz 2005; Boumaza and Campana 2007). Qualitative interviews, may they be semi-structured, non-structured, or taking the form of focus groups, not only help the researcher get accustomed with the foreign policy field but also enable her to access the professional practices of the foreign policy actors and even propose a sociology of practices within the international arena (see Pouliot 2017a, b). I will explain below how I accessed defence actors.

Last but not least, the use of new communication technologies and social networks tend to imply a change in social practices. Research in social sciences aiming at explaining how contemporary state and organizations operate is more and more confronted with the evolution of the decision-making process in public administrations due to the introduction of new information and communication technologies and, more precisely, the mobile phone and the Internet (e.g., e-mails, Intranet). A growing part of the decision-making processes is actually informally performed via e-mails and conference calls in France as well as in Germany and in Brussels: "Electronic communication at the office, that is, the reception and sending of mails and documents via Intranet, has become a central element of the diplomatic service".[2] (Beuth, 2005: 124–125). The revolution of the mobile phone in the 1990s has accentuated this trend: every minister and his cabinet has the mobile number of their counterparts and maintain a permanent virtual dialogue. Therefore, diplomatic archives are made up of a mix of paper and electronic documents, which are even more difficult to access for a researcher. This makes interviews an accurate method to capture foreign policy representations and practices.

Once established that interviews are a useful method to investigate foreign policy issues, I still need to point four issues raised by the use of qualitative interviews in social science research works on foreign policy. I first shortly explain the difference between the types of interviews. Then, I explore the insider/outsider dilemma and analyse the question of accessing the research field and data in foreign policy studies. Third, I focus on the qualitative method as a specific researcher/interviewee interaction in the light of the defence sphere. Finally, I give a thought to the question of the publication of the results taking into account the frequent necessity of secret that lies at the heart of many foreign policy issues.

What Kind of Interviews?

The first practical issue raised by the choice for a research method based on interviews is for the researcher to determine what kind of interviews to choose. This choice depends not only on the research question, of course, but also on the kind of data the researcher wants to access. On the one hand, *structured interviews* and *semi-structured interviews* with one actor at a time are, for instance, well-suited to investigate the representations and practices of the foreign policy actors as well as getting precise information. Such interviews are usually quite long (from about 30 minutes to several hours). Structured interviews rely on an interview guideline that helps the researcher progress through its quest for information, whereas semi-structured interviews tend to alternate open questions with the free expression of the interviewees on a given topic. I personally mostly use semi-structured interviews, as they offer more flexibility for both the interviewee and researcher and have proven very fruitful to get information. They represent a very rewarding method, though the transcription of the material may take a long time and has to be taken into account in the research plan. *Focus groups*, on the other hand, are a way of leading collective interviews to investigate the interactions within a group of foreign policy actors. They might be interesting to complement individual interviews. But basing an entire research strategy on focus group interviews may be difficult as the main bias of focus group interviews is the self-censorship that some interviewees may apply when talking before the other actors. Yet focus group might help the researcher get accustomed to the foreign policy field, which raises the question of the insider/outsider dilemma.

The Insider/Outsider Dilemma: Should one *go Native*?

In any research project on foreign policy issues based mostly on qualitative interviews, an important methodological problem may arise: the problem of accessing the field, not only internal documents and grey literature but sometimes also persons when it comes to sensitive topics. Indeed, for the social science researcher, the foreign policy field raises the question of the social distance with her interviewees (see also Alles, Guilbaud and Lagrange 2016). This social asymmetry is actually conveyed by a specific language of their own:

> The special languages produced and reproduced by the specialist professions [. . .] are, as every discourse, the product of a compromise between an expressive interest and a censorship constituted by the structure of the very social field within which the discourse is produced and operated.
>
> *(Bourdieu 1982: 167–168)*

This *going native* approach is interested in the actors' discourse. It enables the analyst to access internal information if the research strategy is based on the following presupposition: the meaning the actor gives to his social action largely contributes to determine the formal aspects of this action. This leads the researchers to pay careful attention to the meaning the interviewees give to their action. Therefore, immersing oneself in the specific language and the social codes of one's interviewees can be very fruitful and can only happen by repeated contact with the research field, enabling the weaving of relations of mutual trust between the researcher and the person interviewed.

The question of introducing oneself to the field and raising trust among the foreign policy community becomes crucial. The access to the foreign policy field can be difficult for many reasons: the actors travel a lot and do not always have plenty of time for a consistent interview, some are reluctant to answer to a researcher when the topic is sensitive (as in the case of nuclear deterrence, for instance), the language used by the diplomatic actors can sometimes be difficult for people working outside the field, etc. Investigating the foreign policy field also regularly implies negotiation with the actors because of a common fear of secrecy-breaking toward externals. Therefore, a specific challenge needs to be taken into account by the researcher: if he/she wants to collect valid data, the researcher should not be perceived as an *intruder* in the social configuration within which he/she enquires, and this is particularly true in the foreign policy field, as it remains one of the core competences of modern states. Thus, it is very important to raise trust to access actors within the field.

The identification of the right persons to interview is another challenge. Several methods can be pursued here. At first, after having started with reading a lot of information on the research topic, the researcher can rely on press articles, administrative phone books, and organigrams. These sources are useful to identify well-known actors like heads of departments at ministries of foreign affairs or in embassies, for instance. But how to access less mediatized persons who are not known by the public? In that matter, as I could notice in my own practice, some contacts offer *open sesames*: the practice of name-dropping often happens to be fruitful as I show below.[3] This method of *snowballing* from an actor to other actors in the same field also helps the researcher develop trust, as the more actors he can speak to, the more he can be identified as a person to be trusted.

Another way of bringing interviews one step further is to rely on the ethnographic method (see also Neumann in this volume) consisting not only of interviews but also of embedded participation, recurrent observation, and interviews as explained above (see, for instance, Ross 1995; Neumann 2012; Schmitt 2015; Lequesne 2017; Mérand 2021).

Being well introduced in the foreign field is also quite important so as master the culture and technical language of the foreign policy professionals. But this insider strategy raises another dilemma, which I explore below in my section on the interview as a social interaction: how to keep distance once the researcher has gone native? The main answer is *reflexivity*. Reflexivity necessitates to "set the collected discourse in the institutional context where it has been enunciated to the extent that speech cannot sociologically exist independently from the institution giving it its social justification" (Bourdieu 1982: 71). This located discourse informs the researcher on the institution, its internal functioning, and its alive dimension but it also outlines a bias of the methodology based on qualitative interviews: the researcher has to be careful and keep this collected discourse at a distance. The interviewees cannot be assumed to be objective, as they are personally involved in the process the analyst is investigating: "often the memory of the actors is failing, they mix up dates and tend to reconstruct their role a posteriori" (Muller 2003: 94). On the side of the enquirer, the solution is to shrug off the myth of "objective truth" to replace it by "subjective and partial truths" that the researcher has to restore and confront so as to be able to make up his own point of view (Beaud and Weber 2003: 303). Another way to exert reflexivity is to consider interviews as a specific social interaction with the foreign policy field.

Interviews as a Social Interaction with the Foreign Policy Field

As any social science research constitutes a social interaction between the researcher and its terrain, research on foreign policy makes no exception. But in the case of this field, the question of social distance can take a peculiar importance. In the case of foreign policy, a social asymmetry is most of the time materialized through the use of a specific language. Moreover, social asymmetry between the researchers and its interviewees in the foreign policy field also relies on the fact that the researcher can sometimes be in a dominated social position (for instance while interviewing top diplomats or ministers). It is indeed important to rely on reflexivity and source triangulation as to consolidate the validity of the data produced through this specific interaction during the interviews with actors of the foreign policy community. Even though this asymmetry is not specific to the foreign policy field, as many fields investigated by social scientist necessitate the researcher to be able to "impose oneself to impressive actors" (see, for instance, Chamboredon et al. 1994), it is particularly palpable within the foreign policy community where many interviewees either hold a PhD (and sometimes several PhDs) and/or have attended the most prestigious universities in the world, which gives them a dominating social position and habitus within the European foreign policy and defence configuration.

Doing qualitative research by interviews on foreign policy issues, indeed, raises the question of the place of the speech producer within the field of speech production (Bourdieu 1982: 170 and fol.). This place takes a particular meaning bearing in mind the hierarchy principle within many foreign policy administrations. Often, intermediary actors (that is, actors who are not in a very high hierarchical position as a minister or the head of a department within an embassy, for instance) constitute precious interviewees: they hold a less media-related position and have few contacts with public opinion and journalists. It is also what Breuning underlines when saying that leaders are not alone while underlining the role of bureaucrats and administrations in foreign policy (Breuning 2007: 85ff.). As a matter of fact, they do not internalize censorship as much as the superior officials: "censorship [does not] impose its form onto [their] words" (Bourdieu 1982: 169) to the extent that they show less concern about their social image than members of the high hierarchy who hold political positions and are most exposed to the media. Moreover, conducting interviews with several members of the same department or service offers a way to guarantee a relatively better objectivity by cross-checking the collected data, even if this method may imply pedagogy from the researcher to explain why it is important for his/her research to talk with several colleagues of the same department, for instance (this pedagogy was mostly needed for my field research in Germany).

Another aspect of the specific social interaction at stake during interviews is linked to the gender issue. Qualitative interviewing is not only a way of getting data but also a complex social interaction between the researcher and the interviewee. Moreover, this interaction becomes more specific when one is a (young) woman investigating a mostly masculine environment like in military affairs (Arendell 1997). Even if the foreign policy field in many developed (and even developing) countries has been subject to feminization for the last decades, many interviewees are still white males aged between 35 and 60, depending on the foreign policy issue investigated. (It is particularly striking while investigating security and defence issues.) Thus, gender can become an issue while investigating the foreign policy field and conducting expert interviews (see Littig 2005). The attitude adopted toward a woman researcher comes close to being semi-fatherly or, sometimes, seductive. Reflexions have already been carried out on the topic (see Carreiras 2006; Carreiras and Castro 2012; Deschaux-Beaume 2008, 2011). A good way of handling this gender issue tends to stay in a professional position for the woman researcher and dress up in a rather formal manner, so that there is no room left for seductive interaction, at least during the interview itself.

To sum up, if the interview strategy is carefully tailored to the research design, it may not only be very fruitful for the researcher, as the collected data are most of the time quite rich, but it is also a way of interacting with the researcher's own field of investigation and to continue these interactions after the interviews so as to remain updated on the evolution of the field.

Empirical Illustration: Conducting Interviews Within the Foreign Policy Professional Community

To illustrate how interviews can be conducted in research on foreign policy issues, I will propose empirical examples derived from my PhD research practice and the research I have conducted since. My main research topic in the last decade has been the Common Security and Defence Policy (CSDP) within the EU and defence and foreign policy cooperation between France and Germany. During my PhD, I first envisaged a participant observation so as to get closer to my field by my application as an intern at the Delegation for Strategic Affairs of the French Ministry of Defence, which is a key department in the institutions elaborating the French positions on European defence. The application came back negative because of the impossibility of "making available the material and human resources necessary for this training".[4] The same request was made to the Brussels structures, resulting in the same reply. Under these conditions, in addition to a very thorough reading of the specialized literature on my research topic mixing official documents, websites, booklets of the institutions, and official declarations by foreign policy high profile actors (like ministers for instance), I rapidly chose to rely on qualitative semi-structured interviews to get first-hand data. Another, more epistemological reason confirmed us in my research strategy: qualitative enquiry in social sciences enables the researcher to have a direct connection to the social reality he/she aims at analysing (Marmoz 2001:19), even though this meant meeting the insider/outsider dilemma mentioned above.

In my research, qualitative interviews constituted not only a tool for the analysis of representations (in my case the influence of a European or pro-NATO strategy on the social representations of the French and German politico-military actors and diplomats' daily dealing with the construction and implementation of the CSDP) but also this method reveals nevertheless the social practices of the interviewees through their discourse on their practices. The implementation of interviews within the foreign policy field also raises peculiar methodological challenges that I will exemplify here.

Identifying the Actors and Mapping the Networks

A research approach based on foreign policy actors in several countries and in supranational arenas encompassing historical elements tends to complicate the enquiry phase. In my specific research, in order to analyse the construction and implementation of the CSDP as well as the representations and practices related to this policy among the French and German actors operating it, I had to reach the officers and diplomats who were working at putting on track the European defence project – that is the *historical actors* whose professional rotation frequency makes them quite difficult to reach. A second type of interviewees were the actors operating the CSDP daily once it was launched in 1999. It then appeared essential to map this network of actors both in France and in Germany so as to identify the relationships of interdependence and the interactions between them. I concretely had to find my way up this network so as to understand the similarities and divergences in the practices and representations of CSDP within this foreign policy multilateral community.

Empirically, I raised the following questions: who is a member of the network? Who is an outsider? Does the institutional structure match between Paris and Berlin? How do the members of the network cooperate? How does the network evolve through time and as Europeanization of foreign policy issues progresses? More precisely, the field's enquiry of my doctoral dissertation relied on 135 semi-directed interviews (based on an interview grid mixing open and closed, thematic and analytical questions) led in Paris, Berlin, and Brussels between 2005 and 2008 and relying on a snowballing technique aiming at cross-ruling the actors' networks. This technique was complemented by content analysis. The interviews were led in some of the following services with officers, civilian actors, and diplomats:[5]

- the Foreign Minister's cabinet in Paris and Berlin;
- the Defence Minister's cabinet in Paris and Berlin;
- the cabinets of the French President and the German Chancellor;
- different services of both ministers dealing with European military cooperation in Paris and Berlin;
- permanent representations of France and Germany in Brussels;
- the General Secretariat of the Council in Brussels;
- the CSDP organs in Brussels (Political and Security Committee, EU Military Staff, and EU Military Committee);
- NATO structures in Brussels.

Once the interviewees have been identified, the question of how to contact them arises. I chose to send them a manuscript letter explaining the aim of my research, the reason why I wanted to meet them and mentioned the financial support of the Ministry of Defence for my doctoral dissertation as a gate opener. This helped me in getting lots of positive replies to my mailing. In my most recent research, I also tend to contact my interviewees either by institutional e-mailing or by telephone but use the same pedagogy explaining why I need to interview them in the course of my research field. In some cases when the interviewees do not answer, it is useful either to relaunch the invitation after a couple of weeks, or to rely on colleagues to access them. As a matter of fact, I have several times noticed that some contacts offer *open sesames*: the practice of name-dropping can be very important not only among superior officials but also at the intermediary levels. For example, in my case, having interviewed a former French minister of foreign affairs several times helped get in touch with a former minister of foreign affairs in Germany and also some French and German diplomatic counsellors from the 1990s. The progressive integration and even the curiosity shown by some interviewees are largely favoured by word of mouth: the diplomatic and foreign affairs fields in most of the developed countries tend to function as a big family (Deschaux-Beaume 2011; Schmitt 2015). The actors dealing with CSDP daily in Paris, Berlin, and Brussels know one another well; they sometimes have been friends for years as some of them confessed, and have often followed either similar or sometimes the same professional training. Though turnover is quite regular,[6] a detailed study of this configuration shows that in fact the researcher often comes across the same contacts, who have evolved from one position to another in this social space. Once the actors of the foreign policy field have been identified, the implementation of the interviews still meets an important challenge: how to make sure that the interviewees will talk and that the researcher will collect valid data?

Making the Interviewees Talk: An Implementation Based on a Comprehensive Framework

If the researcher wants to collect valid data by relying on the method of interviews in the foreign policy field, he/she has to make sure that the actors will talk and give relevant information. Therefore, I empirically used three techniques. The first one was based on the construction of an interview questionnaire (or interview guide) to be able to manage the interview and keep it in the right direction. The questionnaire I used was structured into three main parts, and it performed two main functions: getting data and diverting any ready-to-serve discourse. To this end, I always started in a way that put the interviewees at ease: by asking them questions on their professional CV and the daily practices linked to their professional position. This strategy has many times revealed itself as fruitful because the interviewees had first to go back to their own curriculum before addressing the topic they were interviewed: this not only helped create a connection with the interviewees but also helped in understanding the professional logic underlying their evolution within the foreign policy community. Several times, the interviewees actually thanked us for this opportunity to talk about their curriculum and not only the very content of their daily job. As Lequesne explains (2017), diplomats also express the need for a better connection with society that can be provided by research interviews. This helps the researcher in creating a contact with the interviewees.

Once the connection has been created, the second part of the interview guide delves into the topic under investigation with semi-open questions involving long answers (and never yes or no answers!). The third part of the questionnaire usually leaves room for the interviewees to freely comment on the topic or add any missing dimension. With this kind of interview guide, I led interviews ranging from 30 minutes to three hours, and sometimes even several interviews with the same interviewee. I sometimes also contacted the interviewees later in case I needed more details on the information given. What has been striking in my research is that most of the interviewees did neither ask for the interview guide beforehand, nor did they ask to review the transcription of the interview. However, sending questionnaires beforehand and granting review requests is a perfectly acceptable practice. It is important to always cope with the interviewees' will, as the researcher in foreign policy needs to be seen as trustful in order to further investigate the field. The same applies for the use of a recording device. In my experience, most of the interviewees accepted my recording device. When this was not the case, I only relied on a notebook and tried to transcribe the interview as soon as possible once the interview was over, so as to be able to remember as many details as possible. Keeping the notebook close is always a good strategy, as some interviewees tend to say interesting things once the interview is over, while escorting the researcher back to the entrance, for instance.

The second technique I used was meant to avoid the illusion of the *scoop* by relying on cross-checking, which means that I tended to consider data as valid when it was triangulated with at least another source (and even more when possible). As a result, I have many times opted for a multiplication of interviews at different levels of the decision-making process (from the high-ranking officials and diplomatic actors down to the executing actors) so as to avoid a unilateral and official discourse and to cross the collected data and sources. Supplementing the words of the politico-military and diplomatic high representatives both in Paris and Berlin as well as in Brussels by interviews with actors on the ground provides access to the actual practices and the social interactions that are developing within CSDP. Moreover, leading interviews with several members of the same department constitutes a way to guarantee a relatively better objectivity, even though it does not equate to long-term immersion (see, for instance, Mérand 2021). This method implies pedagogy from the researcher, mostly when leading comparative research. This has been the case with many German interviewees in my own research: the co-signature principle (*Mitzeichnung*) in German administrative organizations supposes that every agent of a same service or department has the same information at their disposal to the extent that all the information is transmitted to everyone in the service. Therefore, multiplying the contacts with different agents in the same service was necessary to justify my request. Explaining the researcher's way of investigating also provides an efficient communication tool between the researcher and the interviewee and helps build mutual trust in their social interaction.

The third technique I relied on was the anonymization of the interviews, if requested by interviewees. Anonymization is a rather classical challenge for researchers working either on foreign policy or security issues (Deschaux-Beaume 2011; Deschaux-Dutard 2015; Schmitt 2015; Deschaux-Dutard and Borzillo 2020). Anonymizing the interviewees empirically means removing the information leading to a potential identification of the interviewee and only mentioning elements like the date of the interview and the general institution (but not the detailed department or service) while referencing the interviews in the research. When anonymizing military interviewees, it may be helpful to only keep their rank to better understand the scope of their speech. Yet anonymity can be a difficult issue in the foreign policy field as the number of interviewees on a given topic is not very wide and it may imply less efficiency in the researcher's effort to guarantee it. Therefore, a possible option may be the use of the Chatham House rule (formalized in 1927!) stating that participants to a conference (or here an interview) are free to use the information received, but neither the identity nor the affiliation of the speaker. Within the foreign policy field, confidentiality is often an important prerequisite, which calls for specific attention when the researcher archives the collected data. Thus, interviews within the foreign policy professional community bear fruitful promises but must be carried out with precautions more than in any other research field, given the specificity of the field and its relationship toward academic research between eagerness to show openness and difficulties of trust in some sensitive issues like terrorism or nuclear dissuasion, for instance (see Cohen 1999).[7]

Implementing Interviews as a Social Interaction: Is Research on Foreign Policy Gendered?

Last but not least, as in any social science research, the methodology of interviews in research on foreign policy issues also constitutes a social interaction between the researcher and its interviewees inasmuch as the interviewee is led to "answer for his speech" (Blanchet 1985: 113) by the way the analyst questions him. This social interaction is to be considered and analysed not only under its social dimension, as I explained earlier, but also with regard to the gender of the researcher in the present case. Qualitative interviewing is not only a way of getting data but also a full social interaction between the researcher and the interviewee. Analysing this social relationship actually consists in questioning the conditions of production of the *truth* expressed by the interviewees. This interaction becomes even more specific when one is a (young) woman investigating a rather masculine environment. Concerning my own practice and with regard to discussions with male and female colleagues also investigating this field, the gender of the analyst seems to weigh on the research interaction. Being a woman can actually be of help: because of the male dominance in the field, it is possible for the female researchers to ask *naïve* questions (mostly to military actors) enabling to obtain lots of information on the social practices and representations of the military and diplomatic actors (Deschaux-Beaume 2011). Yet this raises the question of playing with a sexist presumption that is, of course, problematic and may of course not be encouraged. When it comes to women interviewees in my own experience, I had many times the experience of a connection created by the belonging to the same generation and gender, which helped made the interviewees feel more at ease and even sometimes open up on more personal elements of their professional curriculum. Indeed, the politico-military environment in France as well as in Germany tends to be a very masculine environment: among my interviewees, fewer than 10% – both officers and diplomats – were women. Therefore, the female researcher can sometimes feel like a curiosity and an indulgent ear for the interviewees of this social field. A small number of interviewees even tend to confide more personally in the women researcher, expressing professional trouble or making observations that only the interview interaction makes possible. Yet when exchanging with other researchers, it also appears that gender can sometimes impede research when confronted with interviewees who tend to consider some topics as rather masculine (like in the case of nuclear deterrence in my own case, once interviewing a senior male diplomat in Paris). This is why the researcher needs to rely on reflexivity when using interviews as his/her principal research method.

Conclusion

Interviews constitute an interesting and fruitful method to investigate foreign policy issues not only because they enable the researcher to gain a direct access to the field in a context where more and more professional activity relies on digital technologies and Internet, but because it also enables to grasp the practices and representations of the foreign policy actors. Yet this method has limits and always has to be used with precautions and reflexivity. Therefore, it is important to triangulate the information and data with other sources or at least with several interviews, and to assess the discourse provided by the interviewees with a critical distance. Another limitation can be raised that is proper to the foreign policy and security field: the question of confidentiality. Once the data have been obtained, under what conditions can the researcher publish the results of the research (which is the aim of any research) when it comes to managing secret or restricted data? As I have shown here, the researcher has to guarantee the anonymization of the data so that the interviewees would not be recognized when the data are published. The research also needs to cope with the protection of individual data, such as the European General Directive on Data Protection (GDPR) in recent years.

The Covid-19 pandemic has had an important impact on research interviewees, and it is important to acknowledge this impact to finish this chapter. On the one hand, the digital technologies enable the researcher to carry on their professional activities by leading expert interviews with teleconferencing software. These digital tools are also time and money-saving, as the researcher does not have to travel to reach the interviewee. Leading virtual interviews, however, necessitates as much organization from the researcher as interviews lead in person. For instance, when leading an interview with a foreign policy actor located on another continent, it is important to take the time zone into account so as to avoid leading the interview in the middle of the night, for instance. It is also important to make sure that the researcher as well as the interviewee can speak freely via the virtual platform used, without being interrupted by either colleagues or family. Therefore, the researcher needs to explain the importance of the interview to its interviewees when the interviews are led virtually and put the interviewee at ease. One of the main advantages of virtual interviews is the possibility to record the interview, of course with the authorization of the interviewee, which can also save transcription time if the researcher uses software able to convert sound files into text.

Yet the use of these software raises some issues to be carefully considered: while face-to-face interviews take place in the professional environment of the interviewee where s/he has decided to dedicate the duration of the interview with the researcher, an interview led in remote mode can take place when the researcher and the interviewees are at home and can possibly be disturbed by their everyday life. Leading a virtual interview necessitates an important energy as the interviewee may not be entirely focused on the interview, contrary to an interview led in his office: he might be checking his professional mails in parallel for instance, or even be in charge of its family if the interview is to take place during special periods like lockdowns. Therefore, the researcher has to help the interviewee focus on the interview by preparing the interview guideline carefully. Virtual interviews also miss an important element of the method: the body language and facial expressions of the interviewee, which help relying on the interviewee's reaction to ask further questions or tackle sensitive topics. This is made difficult when the interview becomes virtual. Last but not least, relying on virtual tools also exposes both the research and the interviewees to the technical hazard (when the Internet connection collapses for instance) and to risks of breeching, as it happened during a virtual European Council of Defence Ministers when a journalist popped up on the screen. This shows that even though virtual tools offer interesting venues to lead research interviews in the future when the interviewee is far away for instance or has a very busy schedule, face-to-face interviews remain the most interesting method to grasp the complexity of foreign policy issues by interviewing foreign policy actors and making sense of today's world through the social interaction with them.

Notes

1 Samy Cohen incidentally underlines how much more fruitful than archives those interviews turn out to be in the defence field (Cohen 1999: 19).
2 My translation.
3 Samy Cohen states a similar assessment regarding his interviews with former French President Mitterrand. Cohen 1999: 24.
4 Letter from the Human Resources Office of the Delegation for Strategic Affairs, January 2007.
5 A complete table of the services where my interviews were conducted can be found in Deschaux-Beaume (2012).
6 A politico-military position is usually held for two to three years.
7 Here we don't mention the question of the potential re-use of data collected by interviews. For details on this topic, see Deschaux-Dutard and Borzillo 2020.

References

Allison, Graham. 1971. *The essence of decision. Explaining the Cuban missile crisis.* Boston, MA: Little Brown.
Alles, Delphine, Auriane Guilbaud, and Delphine Lagrange. 2016. –"L'entretien en relations internationales." In Méthodes de recherche en relations internationales, edited by Devin G. Guillaume. Paris: Presses de Sciences Po, 159–176.
Arendell, Terry. 1997. "Reflections on the researcher-researched relationship: A woman interviewing men." *Qualitative Sociology* 2 (3): 341–368.
Beaud, Stéphane, and Florence Weber. 2003. *Le guide de l'enquête de terrain. Produire et analyser des données ethnographiques.* Paris: La Découverte.
Becker, Howard. 2002. *Les ficelles du métier. Comment conduire sa recherche en sciences sociales.* Paris: La Découverte.
Beuth, Hans. 2005. "Regiert wird schriftlich." In *Auswärtiges amt, diplomatie als beruf*, edited by Enrico Brand and Christian Buck. Wiesbaden: VS Verlag für Sozialwissenschaften, 119–128.
Blanchet, Alain. 1985. *L'entretien dans les sciences sociales.* Paris: Dunod.
Bogner, Alexander, Menz, Wolfgang. 2005 [2002]. "*Expertenwissen und Forschungspraxis: Die modernisierungstheoretische und die methodische Debatte um die Experten. Zur Einführung in ein unübersichtliches Problemfeld.*" In *Das experteninterview, theorie, methode, anwendung*, edited by Alexander Bogner, Beate Littig, and Wolfgang Benz. Wiesbaden, VS Verlag für Sozialwissenschaften, 7–30.
Bourdieu, Pierre. 1982. *Ce que parler veut dire. L'économie des échanges linguistiques.* Paris: Fayard.
Boumaza Magali, and Aurélie Campana. 2007. "Enquêter en milieu difficile." *Revue Française de Sciences Politique* 57 (1): 5–25.
Breuning, Marijke. 2007. *Foreign policy analysis: A comparative introduction.* London: Palgrave.
Chamboredon, Hélène, Muriel Surdez, Fabienne Pavis, Laurent Willemez, Laurent. 1994. "S'imposer aux imposants. A propos de quelques obstacles rencontrés par les sociologues débutants dans la pratique et l'usage de l'entretien." *Genèses. Sciences Sociales et Histoire* 16: 114–132.
Carreiras, Helena. 2006. *Gender and the military: Women in the armed forces of western democracies.* London and New York: Routledge.
Carreiras, Helena, and Celsio Castro. eds. 2012. *Qualitative methods in military studies: Research experiences and challenges.* London and New York: Routledge.
Cohen, Samy. 1986. La monarchie nucléaire: Les coulisses de la politique étrangère sous la Ve République. Paris: Hachette.
Cohen, Samy. 1999. "Enquêtes au sein d'un 'milieu difficile': Les responsables de la politique étrangère et de défense." In L'art d'interviewer les dirigeants, edited by Samy Cohen. Paris: PUF, 17–50.
Deschaux-Beaume, Delphine. 2008. De l'Eurocorps à une armée européenne? Pour une sociologie historique de la politique européenne de sécurité et de défense (1991–2007). Doctoral Dissertation, Université Pierre Mendès-France-Grenoble II.
Deschaux-Beaume, Delphine. 2011. "Enquêter en milieu militaire: Stratégie qualitative et conduite d'entretiens dans le domaine de la défense." *Res Militaris* 1 (2), online: https://resmilitaris.net/vol-1-n-2-winter-spring-hiver-printemps-2011/.
Deschaux-Beaume, Delphine. 2012. "Investigating the military field: Qualitative research strategy and interviewing in the defence networks." *Current Sociology* 60 (1): 101–117.

Deschaux-Beaume, Delphine. 2013. "Studying the military in a qualitative and comparative perspective: Methodological challenges and issues." In Qualitative methods in military studies: Research experiences and challenges, edited by Helena Carreiras and Celsio Castro. London and New York: Routledge, 132–114.

Deschaux-Dutard, Delphine. 2015. "Stratégie qualitative et défense: L'entretien comme interaction sociale en milieu militaire." Les Champs de Mars (2): 42–49.

Deschaux-Dutard, Delphine, and Laurent Borzillo. 2020. "Secondary analysis of qualitative data in defence studies: Methodological opportunities and challenges." In Research methods in defence studies, edited by Delphine Deschaux-Dutard. London and New York: Routledge, 60–75.

Hudson, Valerie. 2005. "Foreign policy analysis: Actor-specific theory and the ground of international relations." *Foreign Policy Analysis* 1 (1): 1–30.

Hudson, Valerie, and Benjamin Day. 2019. Foreign policy analysis: Classic and contemporary theory. Lanham, MD: Rowman & Littlefield.

Kaarbo, Juliet, Jeffrey S. Lantis, and Ryan K. Beasley. 2002. "The analysis of foreign policy in comparative perspective." In 2012 Foreign policy in comparative perspective: Domestic and international influences on state behavior, edited by Juleit Kaarbo, Jeffrey S. Lantis, and Ryan K. Beasley. Thousand Oaks, CA: Cq Press, 1–23.

Kandel, Maya. 2016. "Le rôle du Congrès américain dans le processus de décision en politique étrangère: Les accords de Dayton." *Critique Internationale* 71 (2): 109–127.

Kuus, Merje. 2013. "Foreign policy and ethnography: A sceptical intervention." *Geopolitics*, 18 (1), 115–131.

Lequesne, Christian. 1993. Paris-Bruxelles. Comment se fait la politique européenne de la France. Paris: Presses de la Fondation Nationale des Sciences Politiques.

Lequesne, Christian. 2017. Ethnographie du Quai d'Orsay. Les pratiques des diplomates français. Paris: CNRS Éditions.

Littig, Beate. 2005 [2002]. "Interviews mit experten und expertinnen. Überlegung aus geschlechter-theoretischer Sicht." In Das experteninterview, theorie, methode, anwendung, edited by Alexander Bogner, Beate Littig, and Wolfgang Menz. Wiesbaden, VS Verlag für Sozialwissenschaften, 191–206.

Marmoz, Louis. 2001. "L'outil, l'objet et le sujet: Les entretiens de recherche, entre le secret et la connaissance." In L'entretien de recherche dans les sciences sociales et humaines. La place du secret, edited by Louis Marmoz. Paris: L'Harmattan, 11–68.

Mérand, Frédéric. 2021, Un sociologue à la commission européenne. Paris: Presses de Sciences Po.

Muller, Pierre. 2003. Les politiques publiques. Paris: PUF.

Neumann, Iver. 2012. At home with the diplomats. Ithaca, NY: Cornell University Press.

Potter, Philip. 2010. Methods of foreign policy analysis. In Oxford research encyclopedia of international studies, https://doi.org/10.1093/acrefore/9780190846626.013.34.

Pouliot, Vincent. 2017a. "La logique du praticable: Une théorie de la pratique des communautés de sécurité." *Études Internationales* 48 (2): 153–190.

Pouliot, Vincent. 2017b. L'ordre hiérarchique international. Paris: Presses de Sciences Po.

Pouponneau, Florent. 2013. "Luttes nationales et politique étrangère: Analyse d'un changement de la 'position de la France' dans la crise du nucléaire iranien." *Gouvernement et Action Publique* OL2: 461–486.

Rasler, Karen, William Thompson, and Kathleen Chester. 1980. "Foreign policy makers, personality attributes, and interviews: A note on reliability problems." *International Studies Quarterly* 24 (1): 47–66.

Rieker, Pernille. 2017. French foreign policy in a changing world: Practising Grandeur. London: Palgrave.

Ross, George. 1995. Jacques Delors and European integration. Oxford: Oxford University Press.

Schmitt, Olivier. 2015. "L'accès aux données confidentielles en milieu militaire: problèmes méthodologiques et éthiques d'un 'positionnement intermédiaire'." *Les Champs de Mars,* 2: 50–58.

27
Historical Analysis
Payam Ghalehdar

Introduction

A casual glance at this handbook demonstrates the variety of explanatory approaches and methods of inquiry that the study of foreign policy draws on. According to one scholar, this diversity has its share in making Foreign Policy Analysis (FPA), that is, the subfield of International Relations (IR) that is most directly dedicated to explaining and understanding both the processes and outcomes of foreign policy decision-making, not only the "most inchoate subfield of international relations," but also its "most challenging from the point of view of research design" (Stuart 2008, 577).[1] Among the various tools and approaches employed to shed light on foreign policy, the "historical method" has been argued to be a standard go-to means, which "a significant strand of FPA […] owes a great debt to" (Alden and Aran 2017, 4). Indeed, FPA studies rely heavily on history, both as an abundant well of empirical data, that is, an "objective array of facts" (Reus-Smit 2008, 400) for historical case studies, and by regarding history itself as a prominent shaper of foreign policy. This reality warrants a systematic engagement with historical analysis in FPA. But while IR writ large has experienced a sustained debate on the relationship between itself and history (see, for example, Elman and Elman 2001; Haber, Kennedy, and Krasner 1997), there is a dearth of discussion about the role and place of historical analysis in FPA.

The purpose of this chapter is to provide an introductory exploration of FPA engagement with history. More than a mere ordering exercise, its goal is to enable readers to get a better understanding of how history can be utilized in the service of furthering our understanding of foreign policy. As a tool, history can be leveraged both as an explanatory approach and as a data source for empirical inquiry. As an explanatory approach, history joins the group of *explanans*, that is, factors that are said to explain chosen outcomes. Approaches like historical institutionalism (Fioretos 2011; Rixen, Viola, and Zürn 2016) or learning (Breslauer and Tetlock 1991; Levy 1994; Nye 1987) are but two examples of how scholars have employed the basic notion that *history matters* in order to develop theoretical expectations for the nature and character of foreign policy and, more broadly speaking, international politics. As a data source for theory-guided empirical inquiry, on the other hand, history is a means for testing, supporting, refuting, or building theories and hypotheses. Based on an epistemological stance

DOI: 10.4324/9781003139850-33

that one author calls "pragmatic positivism" (Thies 2002, 353),[2] history can, for example, be utilized to expand the temporal scope of explanations, indeed serving as an abundant well of empirical data. Offering a comprehensive overview of the use of history as an approach and a data source in FPA, this chapter orders the existing literature and provides specific guidance on how to utilize historical analysis on the basis of historiographies and primary sources.

The outline of the chapter is as follows. As a basis for inquiring into the role of history in FPA, the next section presents a brief overview of different definitions of foreign policy and FPA. The second section reviews strands of FPA literature that engage with history, identifying two fundamental ways to deal with history – either as a data source or explanatory factor. The third section defines historical source material either as primary sources or historiographies, presents arguments for the use of each, and offers practical guidelines for their application in FPA. The fourth section concludes with the overview of the strengths of this approach and method.

Definitions of Foreign Policy

Before reviewing the role of history in FPA, a brief specification of what we mean by foreign policy and FPA is in order. Perhaps surprisingly, the field exhibits no consensus with respect to either term. Offering a useful working definition, Christopher Hill defines foreign policy as "the sum of official external relations conducted by an independent actor (usually but not exclusively a state) in international relations" (Hill 2016, 4). While this definition puts the focus on outputs and argues that "foreign (or health, or education) policy is about the effort to carry through some generally conceived strategy" (Hill 2016, 6), other definitions treat rules, that is, "guides to action" (Snyder, Bruck, and Sapin 2002, 74), as a second component of foreign policy in addition to action itself (Morin and Paquin 2018, 3). A third alternative suggests we turn away from focusing on action altogether. By drawing a conceptual distinction between action and decision, this definition favors a focus on decisions: some decisions "may never result in action," but while "leaving no action artifact, such decisions are as likely to be as important as decisions to act" and therefore deserve scrutiny (Hudson 2014, 5).

Disagreement regarding the nature of foreign policy extends to what FPA should explain. To some, the purpose of FPA is to explain discrete foreign policy choices undertaken by actors engaged in external relations. More specifically, this view considers explaining the adoption of a "given policy in certain conditions" as FPA's prime task, for example Norway's decision to join NATO but abstain from joining the European Union (EU) (Morin and Paquin 2018, 2). Explaining policy choices is, in the words of another scholar, "embraced by most foreign policy analysts" (Carlsnaes 2013, 304–305). Yet, others treat decision-making processes as the real explanandum of FPA. FPA pioneers like Richard Snyder, James Rosenau, and Harold and Margaret Spout argued that the "process of foreign policy making was at least as important, if not more important, than foreign policy as an output" (Hudson 2012, 17). Inspired by this view, the goal of FPA is to identify explanatory factors that influence "foreign policy decisionmaking and foreign policy decisionmakers" (Hudson 2014, 6). In other words, FPA should be explicitly focused on "human decisional behavior" (Stuart 2008, 576), which is premised on the notion that processes shape outcomes. After all, "an actor could arrive at different *outcomes* depending on the decision *process*" (Mintz and DeRouen 2010, 4; emphasis in original).

It is not the goal of this chapter to consolidate the field's subject of inquiry. Regardless of the different aims that FPA can serve, historical analysis constitutes a viable tool and explanatory approach no matter how foreign policy and the goals of FPA are defined.

History-focused explanations can be employed to shed light both on how rules of actions have changed, if foreign policy is defined as entailing rules of action, and on how actual foreign policy outputs have shifted over time. Similarly, if a process-oriented definition of FPA is adopted, historical case studies can reveal temporal variations in decision-making processes; if an outcome-focused definition is employed, historical analysis reveals how foreign policy choices have varied.

The Role of History in Foreign Policy Analysis

FPA literature features two fundamental types of engagement with history, treating history either as a data source or as an explanatory approach. The next two sub-sections present each of the two approaches in turn, highlighting their assumptions and differences.

History as a Data Source

The first sustained, if unreflective, engagement with history within FPA came during the onset of the *behavioral revolution* in the 1950s, a time when the social sciences approached their subject matters as a "second Nature" (Guilhot 2017, 9).[3] During that time, the Comparative Foreign Policy school (CFP) (see also Feng and He in this volume) set out to establish a general theory of foreign policy, one that would be constructed on the basis of gradually improving conceptualizations and growing collections of empirical data (Snyder, Bruck, and Sapin 2002, 29; see also Singer 1968). According to James Rosenau, an influential CFP scholar, so-called "pre-theories" would provide orientation regarding the relative explanatory weight of an ordered set of potential explanans for foreign policy decisions (Rosenau 2006, 172). In a subsequent step, new theories would specify causal relationships by drawing on ever more empirical data, thereby facilitating a move "to ever higher levels of generalization" (Ibid., 177). To systematize the empirical raw material needed for a general theory of foreign policy and to "develop a quantifiable unit of foreign policy interaction" (Potter 2017, 4), CFP scholars started to generate what they called *event data* (see also Raleigh and Kishi in this volume), that is, quantified information on specific historical foreign policy actions (Schrodt 1995, 146). Data were generated by content analysis, which led to the assignment of numerical scores to different types of events deemed relevant for theoretical analysis. Some of the event datasets created from the 1960s onward are still used by FPA and IR scholars today, with the *Correlates of War Project* being one of the most prominent ones.

Much of the impetus for the CFP approach was a unified opposition to qualitative approaches to the study of foreign policy. The CFP school gathered scholars who were "dissatisfied with the domination of case-studies and diplomatic history" (Smith 1983, 559). Indeed, in the words of leading CFP scholars of the 1960s, CFP was a "self-conscious effort to offset the non-cumulative, atheoretical, case-oriented study of foreign policy" (Rosenau, Burgess, and Hermann 1973, 122). For all its aversion to historical case studies, however, the quest to establish systematized quantitative data on foreign policy and to build a "GUT (grand unified theory) of all foreign policy behaviour for all nations for all time" necessitated an engagement with history (Hudson 2012, 22). The desire to include as many data points as possible encouraged CFP scholars to extend their datasets as far back as possible. The *International Crisis Behavior Project* launched in 1975, for example, had the end of World War I as its starting point (Potter 2017, 6).

First-generation FPA scholars engaged history based on an objectivist epistemology that treated the past as a treasure trove of foreign policy events waiting to be included in large, quantitative datasets. Underlying this quest was a Rankian view of history, that is, the view established by the nineteenth-century historian Leopold von Ranke that historians could accumulate value-free historical knowledge by uncovering objective facts of past times (Doran 2013, 4).[4] Generating quantitative datasets was predicated on the act of coding foreign policy events after the sifting of newspapers and other available sources, evidently involving human decisions, but the Rankian view of history left little room for acknowledging the potential impact of the scholar's interpretation of historical events (Hudson 2012, 22).[5] It would be a stretch to argue that the objectivist epistemology of first-generation FPA scholars necessitated a focus on objective material structures, that is, a materialist ontology. As David Houghton shows, there was a clear awareness on the part of CFP scholars of the subjective ways in which policymakers related to their environments and how culture informed their perceptions. While one could indeed claim that first-generation FPA popularized ontological "subjectivism" (Houghton 2007, 31–33), they nevertheless assumed that the social world could be studied just like the natural world, that is, from the perspective of an external observer. General knowledge could be obtained, so the argument went, because the scholar's findings would not interfere with the real-world conduct of foreign policy as its subject of inquiry (Neack, Hey, and Haney 1995, 3–5).

Apart from its objectivist epistemological commitments, the *event data* approach to history assumed, however implicitly, that accumulated lines of code represented independent foreign policy events. Used to construct general theories in which causal relationships between a set of explanatory factors and foreign policy events such as interstate crises were to be generated, causation was to be found between those factors and events, not between the events themselves. To be sure, Charles McClelland, the director of the *World Event/Interaction Survey Project* (WEIS), argued that policymakers' growth of experience was likely to have an impact on future state behavior and that past international crises were "part of the process of experimenting with and learning a 'new politics' of international relations" (McClelland 1961, 188). Yet, event datasets like McClelland's own WEIS, which treated collected data points as discrete units of state behavior (Lantis and Beasley 2017), did not repudiate the *independence assumption*, that is, the "idea that for each observation, the value of a particular variable is not influenced by its value in other observations" (Collier, Seawright, and Munck 2010, 43). To CFP scholars, context-independent causal factors produced foreign policy outcomes in a constant and regularized manner, leaving little room for causal interactions between the latter over time.

The Comparative Foreign Policy school declined in the 1970s (Smith 1986, 19–22), having reached a "dead end" (Hill 2016, 13), but its view of history has persisted. To be sure, its first commitment, that is, the epistemological commitment to the possibility of uncovering an objectively existing truth in the real world, has come under sustained attack from scholars who argue that "historians construct history" (Reus-Smit 2008, 403; see also Cello 2018, 240). According to this competing view, the narratives historians construct are a function of the importance they attach to specific historical events. To illustrate this point, E. H. Carr uses an analogy between facts and fish, arguing that "facts are available to the historian [...] like fish on the fishmonger's slab" and that the "historian collects them [facts], takes them home, and cooks and serves them in whatever style appeals to him" (Carr 1987, 9).[6] Reacting to such objections, FPA scholars with objectivist epistemological inclinations take inspiration from the originally behavioralist notion that objective facts exist, but concede that they require interpretation (Levy 2001, 51).

In terms of the *independence assumption*, that is, the second commitment of early FPA scholars regarding their treatment of history, persistence in the field is common, having crossed the divide between quantitative and qualitative approaches. A prominent example of qualitative FPA operating with the *independence assumption* is Rose McDermott's application of prospect theory to four US foreign policy decisions under Dwight D. Eisenhower and Jimmy Carter (McDermott 1998). In her analysis, McDermott engages in a "parallel demonstration of theory" (Ibid., 9), that is, the repeated application of theoretical expectations to disparate historical cases. The approach is not a "macrocausal analysis" (Ibid., 10), meaning that it is not concerned with the ways in which the four analyzed cases could exhibit potential causal links. Another example for the persistence of the *independence assumption* in FPA is the argument of Juliet Kaarbo, Jeffrey Lantis, and Ryan Beasley that "the search for regular and identifiable patterns" in foreign policy making remains the main goal of theorizing in FPA (Kaarbo, Lantis, and Beasley 2013, 5). The authors argue that, in principle, causal patterns and regularities can be abstracted from specific cases. Rather than treating history as contingent, the authors "assume that at least some of the same reasons behind Catherine the Great's Russian foreign policy in the eighteenth century might influence Dimitry Medvedev's Russian foreign policy in the twenty-first century" (Ibid., 4). In line with the *independence assumption*, causal influence is not to be detected between foreign policy outcomes, for example between different temporal periods of Russia's foreign policy, but between outcomes and patterns of underlying factors yet to be uncovered. Just like in quantitative approaches, history, according to this approach, is viewed as a well of empirical source material to be used for the construction of generalizable theories.

History as Explanation

Owing to its diversity, FPA features alternative views of history. Approaches based on feedback effects, learning, historical analogies, or historical institutionalism do not consider history as an objective source of data to be mined with quantitative or qualitative methods. Instead, such approaches confer to history the status of an explanatory factor, turning it from raw data into a genuine explanation for foreign policy. Feedback effects, defined as a "message about an actor's action, which a system sends back to that actor," have a bearing on decision-making, establishing a relationship between past and future behavior in "constant flows of actions and reactions spread over time" (Morin and Paquin 2018, 48). Although not explicitly dealing with history, scholars working on feedback effects stress how they can account for long-term dynamics in historical contexts (Gadinger and Peters 2016, 253). Rather than treating foreign policy decisions as isolated events, a "feedback analysis would [...] explore their linkages in a unified framework" (Ibid., 256). Viewed from this perspective, it is imperative to assess potential feedback effects in order to understand a given foreign policy outcome. David Dreyer, for example, traces "issue spirals" in bilateral relations between China and Vietnam in the 1970s as an explanation for the 1979 Sino-Vietnamese War, arguing that the war was the result of a "dynamic process in which tension increases as multiple issues accumulate" (Dreyer 2010, 298).

A second approach that treats history as an explanatory factor is learning. Defined as a "change of beliefs [...] or the development of new beliefs, skills, or procedures as a result of the observation and interpretation of experience" (Levy 1994, 283), the learning perspective allows for state leaders to draw inferences from the past and act upon them in the future. What exactly is learned from the past depends on the mental frames individuals apply to history, that is, their lenses through which they choose and interpret past events. While feedback loops are usually unintended by the actors involved, learning presupposes a more deliberate use of history. A recent study, for example, argues that "Germany is in a process of learning new leadership roles in the CFSP [Common Foreign and Security Policy]" as a reaction to the Russian annexation of Crimea in 2014 (Aggestam and Hyde-Price 2020, 10), a learning process that, judged from this perspective, arguably gained further momentum in the wake of the Russian invasion of Ukraine in 2022. While the study provides an example for the relevance of inferences drawn from the recent past, referenced events can also lie further in the past (see, for example, Bennett 1999). Closely linked to the learning perspective is the historical analogies perspective, the latter being a "principal device" to the former (Khong 1992, 6). Drawing on past experiences that serve as lessons for challenges at hand, historical analogies represent a third perspective of how history can have a discernible effect on foreign policymaking, for better or worse (Neustadt and May 1988, xiii). Analogies can be used either strategically to legitimize desired policies or, more earnestly, as mental shortcuts providing orientation in situations of uncertainty (Kaarbo and Kenealy 2017, 69). Either way, they exemplify how the invocation of history can influence important foreign policy decisions, for example the UK House of Commons' opposition to military involvement in Syria in 2012 based on invoked parallels to British involvement in the 2003 Iraq War (Ibid.).

Finally, historical institutionalism is among the most prominent theoretical perspective relying on history as an explanatory factor. Originally developed in comparative politics, this approach stresses the staying power of past institutional creation and decisions at what the approach calls *critical junctures*. Such decisions create positive feedback loops and path dependencies (Capoccia and Kelemen 2007; Pierson 2004). They leave their imprint on future behavior, becoming an impediment to policy change. At a deeper and more general level, the motivating concern of historical institutionalism is "to understand the processes by which institutions change or do not change" (Rixen and Viola 2016, 10), meaning that both change and continuity are the focus of this approach. Applied to the realm of foreign policy, historical institutionalism accounts for how past decisions influence today's foreign policy. Bryan Mabee, for example, employs the insights of the approach to explain the creation of the US National Security Council after the end of World War II and how the institution has managed to survive through reproducing itself in changing times (Mabee 2011). Another study shows how US Middle East policy is not solely driven by geopolitical considerations or powerful domestic lobbies, but rather by past US decisions in the 1970s that manifested support for Israel and were "entrenched and reproduced in subsequent US policymaking" (Dannreuther 2011, 189).

What sets explanatory approaches inspired by feedback effects, learning, analogies, or historical institutionalism apart from the view that history is a mere data source, is the shared notion that temporality matters. Taking the timing of events, their sequence, and their location within historical chains seriously militates against "analyses into which past developments are simply imported as an independent variable" (Hall 2003, 385-386). As such, such approaches relax the *independence assumption*, allowing for the possibility that events have a causal impact on later events. In a more fundamental sense, however, both views of history in FPA scholarship laid out in this section require a conscious use of historical source material, which is the focus of the next section.

Guidelines for Using Historiographies and Primary Sources

When it comes to historical source material, one can distinguish between two types – historiographies and primary sources. This section discusses the principal goal of historical engagement before laying out each type of historical sources and established guidelines for their respective use.

Case-Oriented versus Theory-Oriented Engagement

Engagement with history can be case-oriented or theory-oriented. Theory-oriented engagement with history utilizes history as a means to build new theories or to test them. In case-oriented engagement with history, in contrast, historical analysis aims at explaining specific decisions or cases. The disciplined-configurative approach, for example, which is a term borrowed from qualitative comparative research, is a tool that serves to explain specific historical configurations rather than to test general hypotheses against a particular case. As explanatory factors, it uses factors that have "general relevance" to a broader population, thereby relying on "general rules, but on complicated combinations of them" (Verba 1967, 114f). Yet, its main focus is on the historical case at hand, not the development and improvement of theory.[7] A prominent example for the use of the disciplined-configurative method is Deborah Larson's analysis of the perception of policymakers within the Truman administration toward the Soviet Union, in which she "mobilizes existing theories" to explain the origins of the US policy of containment but argues that the "results of the case study cannot disprove or prove the validity of the theory" (Larson 1985, 59).

Apart from the disciplined-configurative method, most qualitative approaches in FPA are theory-oriented, that is, they rely on historical source material to build and test foreign policy theories. The case study method, a prominent method in qualitative FPA, knows two alternative inferential perspectives: cross-case comparisons and within-case analysis.[8] Particularly with respect to the latter, which focuses on the analysis of causal paths within single cases (Goertz and Mahoney 2012, 89), scholars rely heavily on historical source material (on cross-case comparisons see Mello in this volume). The use of history introduces variation and provides a temporal perspective, making it an ideal source for process tracing (see also van Meegdenburg in this volume) and the congruence method, two within-case methods in small-N case study designs (George and Bennett 2005, 179). In fact, the link between historical analysis and process tracing, that is, the method that attempts to "study causal mechanisms in a single-case research design" (Beach and Pedersen 2013, 2), is so pronounced that Alexander George and Andrew Bennett title their book's chapter on process tracing "process-tracing and historical explanation" (2005, 205). This is not surprising. Process tracing, and to a lesser extent the congruence method, are data-heavy methods that require fine-grained empirical material, oftentimes with specific evidence regarding time and place, in order to facilitate the reconstruction of temporal sequences and causal chains. Historical sources can provide such evidence, giving FPA scholars more depth in data than contemporary sources.

Primary Sources versus Historiographies

To date, there is little explicit, practical guidance for FPA scholars on how to engage history in explanatory within-case analysis. A crucial question to ask is the type of source material that should be consulted for empirical analysis. In principle, there are two distinct types of historical sources: primary sources, that is, sources that may stem from archives and "provide direct or firsthand evidence about events, objects or persons," and secondary sources, that is, sources that involve "some kind of interpretation and analysis of events, conditions or experiences" (Munck, Møller, and Skaaning 2020, 340). History-friendly IR scholarship has debated whether IR scholars, and non-historians more broadly, should rely solely on the work of historians, that is, use secondary sources, or whether they should engage in archival research (see also Friedrich in this volume) and uncover primary sources themselves (Thies 2002, 358). Views are mixed. One FPA scholar argues for the latter, cautioning against relying exclusively on historians' work and noting that political scientists and historians have different priorities when reviewing historical sources. The narratives of historians, according to this view, are based on "intuitive theories," whereas political scientists are "more concerned with causal variables" linked to more general theories (Larson 2001, 337). Relying on the work of historians would, thus, import their research priorities into the building and testing of IR and FPA theories and thereby bias findings. Self-conducted archival research would remedy this risk, making "process tracing through archival research [...] a potent method of foreign policy analysis" as long as scholars are "more reflective, transparent, and strategic about [the] selective use of available documentation" (Darnton 2018, 123f).

According to skeptical voices concerning the demand that FPA scholars consult primary sources, archival research puts high demands on non-historians. It is especially for three reasons – lack of expertise, time constraints, and the inability to solve issues of selectivity – that these voices advocate for relying on already existing historiographies rather than self-conducted archival research. First, especially for inexperienced researchers, assessing what George and Bennett call the "evidentiary value of archival materials" can pose an insurmountable challenge (2005, 99). Even historians struggle with weighing the relative value of a given document in the wider context of foreign policy decision-making, let alone non-historians with less experience and proper training. Compounding the lack of expertise, non-historians engaging in archival research must be aware of a second potential issue, that is, time constraints. Pointing to the political scientist's likely selection of more than a single empirical case, Jack Levy, for example, argues that "it is simply not possible for a single scholar to engage in a thorough investigation of all available primary sources for each case" (2001, 60). Finally, redoing what historians do holds little promise of eliminating selectivity. While the risk of importing the historian's selective choice of primary sources would be remedied, selectivity would remain, stemming from the FPA scholar's own potential confirmation bias (Levy 2001, 60–61). Primary sources are oftentimes viewed as more reliable than secondary sources (Thies 2002, 358). Their use, however, presupposes great experience, an adequate time budget, and, perhaps most importantly, a sustained attention to the dangers of selectivity and bias.

As mentioned above, relying on secondary sources comes with its own difficulties and challenges. If one accepts the notion that historians create history, not uncover it (Lustick 1996, 613), the question of interpretation and the influence of what one author calls the historian's "synoptic judgment" become central (Schroeder 1997, 68). Selection bias, that is, an unjustifiable bias in the selection of historical sources that is likely to distort inferences drawn from the empirical evidence, is a risk that needs to be confronted. FPA scholars must be aware that the "historical 'facts' they abstract from historical accounts and organize and stylize for their own purposes are historians' selections and constructs" (Schroeder 1997, 71). Such awareness requires a good grasp of different historiographies of the subject matter one investigates. Historiography, in the words of Ian Lustick, "multiplies history, as each pattern in the latter produces the potential for many patterns in the former" (Lustick 1996, 605). The historiography of the Cold War, for example, features distinct historiographical strands. In tackling the origins of the confrontation between the United States and the Soviet Union, one tradition considers communism and Soviet expansionism as the main reason for the rift in the wartime alliance, while revisionist scholars instead hold capitalism and US economic interests responsible for the Cold War (Lebow 2001, 117; see also Saull 2012, 64). Awareness of these divergent historiographical traditions is central, lest we use historical narratives unreflectively.

Practical Guidelines for Engagement with Historiographies

Whether they choose primary or secondary sources, FPA scholars should follow a set of guidelines when engaging with history. Scholars who primarily rely on the work of historians rather than their own archival research should justify their selection of historiographies, present the breadth of alternative historiographies, prefer more recent historical accounts over older ones, and demonstrate awareness of the type of historical discipline they rely on. The following will elaborate on each of these four recommendations in turn.

First, to avoid the pitfalls of selectivity when it comes to historiographies, FPA scholars should be transparent with their source selection rationale. That means that the selection of historiographies for empirical within-case analysis should require as systematic and explicit a justification as the selection of empirical cases in case study research designs. In the words of Ian Lustick, qualitative historical FPA scholars should be encouraged to "direct explicit and systematic attention to historiography and to demonstrate self-consciousness in the selection of source material" (Lustick 1996, 614). One viable source selection strategy is to base one's empirical analysis on a historiographical strand "whose implicit theoretical assumptions [run] counter, or at least not parallel, to the theory entertained by the researcher" (Lustick 1996, 615; see also Møller and Skaaning 2021, 111–112).[9] Mirroring the choice of *hard cases* in case selection strategies (Rapport 2015), the logic of this selection strategy is to create a difficult test for the preferred theoretical explanation and thereby increase our confidence in the explanation on an unfavorable terrain of sources. FPA scholars, for example, who sift historical evidence for emotion-based foreign policy explanations, should avoid relying exclusively on historiographies that similarly stress the role of emotions in world politics (see, for example, Costigliola 2016).

Second, FPA scholars relying on historiographies should make the reader aware of the state of diversity in historical research on a given subject matter. If different historiographical strands are available, as for example in Cold War historiography, showing awareness of that diversity to readers enables the latter to better assess the author's historiographical selection. This strategy, called "explicit triage" (Lustick 1996, 616), facilitates replication and increases readers' confidence in the avoidance of selection bias. Third, scholars can include more recent historical accounts that are based on new primary evidence. What should be avoided is an exclusive focus on old accounts: it is paradoxical to "come across social scientists who freely base their empirical claims on historical research done 60 or 80 years ago, considering that they would very rarely (if ever) do so within their own field of study" (Møller and Skaaning 2021, 114). Through new historical accounts, scholars can take into account how the historical literature itself has progressed, making sure that a reliance on outdated or limited access to historical sources is avoided.

Finally, FPA scholars turning to historiographies should not only be aware of different historiographical strands, but also the turns within the discipline of history itself. For some, the go-to equivalent of IR (and FPA) scholarship in the discipline of history is diplomatic history, the field that involves the "study of elites, or rulers" (Haber, Kennedy, and Krasner 1997, 38). Despite methodological differences, both disciplines share epistemological commitments and are therefore, according to this view, "brothers under the skin" (Ibid., 43). Others disagree. Pointing to alternative subfields in the discipline of history, one author argues, for example, that IR scholars should not "quarantine international history from social history" and eschew assuming singular conceptions of history (Reus-Smit 2008, 402). Indeed, diplomatic history itself has undergone a transformation in which insights from cultural history, social history, and gender history have been incorporated in the subfield. This has led to a shift in focus from leaders and policymakers to the "interaction not just of governments but also of non-state actors, peoples, and transnational communities" (Brands 2017, 134f). Next to acquiring an awareness of these recent trends in the discipline of history, FPA scholars who rely on historiographies should be explicit about which subfield of history in the neighboring discipline they draw from. The choice should be guided by the type of research questions asked. Transparency in selecting a particular type of history helps readers assess the suitability of historiographies and, ultimately, the extent to which an empirical analysis is convincing.

Practical Guidelines for the Use of Primary Sources

Engagement with primary sources should similarly be governed by a set of guiding principles. Compared to the use of historiographies, the use of primary sources has not been at the center of discussions in FPA research (Larson 2001, 342–343). Creating awareness and discussing suitable ways to rely on primary documents, however, is no less warranted than in the case of historiographies. While it is generally accepted that archival documents have high evidentiary value, FPA scholars should always keep in mind that collections of primary sources, no matter how extensive and systematic they are, can only provide a selective glimpse into the inner workings of bureaucracies and their decisions. At best, the written record can approximate past foreign policy, it can never fully represent it.

To improve scholars' engagement with historical sources, the following guidelines facilitate a transparent and defensible use of such sources. First, scholars should be aware of the "general tendency to attach particular significance to an item that supports pre-existing or favored interpretation" (George and Bennett 2005, 99). Countering the risk of cherry-picking, it is key for scholars to grasp and represent the context of used sources. This can be done by a "few supplementary searches or robustness checks" (Darnton 2018, 116), that is, an explicit attempt to look for countervailing evidence in the wider context of available documents. If it can be demonstrated that inferences we draw from a selected document or group of documents are not a function of our selection, we can increase the reader's confidence in the justifiability of the selection and, ultimately, the conducted analysis. This is especially true for government documents that present a diverse set of policy options. Take, for example, US secretary of defense Donald Rumsfeld's July 2001 memo on Iraq to national security adviser Condoleezza Rice, in which Rumsfeld outlined three distinct future policy avenues for the United States: an end to the enforcement of no-fly zones in Iraq, a turn to regime change, or a diplomatic outreach to the Iraqi regime.[10] Ignoring the context of the document by, for example, singling out one of Rumsfeld's presented options without mentioning the others would be bad practice. Instead, one should point to the entirety of options presented even if the source of inference might be one particular option (see, for example, Ghalehdar 2021, 179).

Second, and relatedly, to convince readers of the evidentiary value of a chosen primary source, scholars should be aware of the purpose of the cited document and present it accordingly. Archival documents can contain evidence from behind the scenes of foreign policy decisions. Relying on the notion that private correspondence entails more genuine evidence than their public counterparts (Ibid., 19), however, does not free scholars from the responsibility of taking into account the underlying motivational context of a given document. Depending on whether a leader convenes a meeting with advisers to obtain information in preparation for an impending decision or to build consensus for a decision already taken privately, for example, should make a difference in how we judge the value of the written record of said meeting (George and Bennett 2005, 101). Evidently, judging the purpose of documents is no easy feat. Awareness of its importance, however, helps scholars critically assess evidence found in historical sources and the legitimacy of inferences drawn from it. Awareness can be built by familiarizing oneself with the policymaking process of the bureaucratic unit or organization in question and by gaining knowledge about the foreign policy makers involved in the decision-making process.

Finally, scholars conducting research involving historical sources should present the used material as transparently as possible. This means specifying the provenance of archival sources, ideally by providing not only the research site, but specific names or numbers of series, boxes, and folders (Darnton 2018, 111). To facilitate access to cited sources and ensure transparency on the process from evidence to inference, scholars can use "active citations," that is, "primary-source citations hyperlinked to the sources themselves" (Moravcsik 2010, 31).[11] More generally, if space limitations allow, scholars should present a brief overview of all the archival sites and other potential depositories they have consulted for a given study. This allows readers not only to gauge the depth of engagement with historical sources but also give them an idea of the "relevant population of documents from which a scholar sampled" (Darnton 2018, 112).

Conclusion

History and historical analysis play a vital in the study of foreign policy. The use of historical sources and history-based explanations are widely embedded in FPA. Even in the heyday of the behavioralist revolution, in which early FPA scholars eschewed historical case studies and considered them to be unscientific, FPA could not but rely on historical sources for the coding and quantification of foreign policy events. But while both quantitative and qualitative approaches use history, there is little systematic discussion nor necessary reflection on how to do it. Focusing on the use of historical source material both in terms of primary sources and historiographies, this chapter has presented several practical guidelines for FPA scholars who are open to a more conscious use of history for the testing and building of foreign policy theories.

There are good reasons to engage in historical analysis: if we consider history primarily as a data source, extending the time period under investigation allows us to test our theories against a wider scope of empirical observations; if we consider history as an explanatory factor for the making of foreign policy (see also Møller and Skaaning 2021, 104), engagement with history helps us uncover historical contingencies and gain a better understanding for the vagaries of different historical contexts. Following the practical guidelines presented here is a small step toward a more reflective engagement with history and, by extension, better FPA scholarship.

Notes

1 The denotation that Stuart uses for the field is "foreign-policy decision-making," which, according to some scholars, is a subfield of FPA focused on explaining decision-making processes rather than policy (Carlsnaes 2013, 310; 2012, 116).
2 Thies borrows the term from John Odell (2001, 162).
3 Note that the study of foreign policy outside of the field of FPA "has been around as long as there have been historians and others who have sought to understand why national leaders have made the choices they did regarding interstate relations," see (Hudson 2014, 15–16).
4 Ranke's other commitments, particularly his commitment to archival research and aversion to general theory (Doran 2013, 4), were not shared by FPA scholars of the behavioralist tradition.

5 Another potential issue was the selection of sources. The World Event/Interaction Survey Project, for example, relied on the New York Times as its sole source of data (Potter 2017, 5).
6 Cameron Thies similarly invokes E. H. Carr's analogy (2002, 353).
7 Alexander George and Andrew Bennett note that the disciplined-configurative approach can "contribute to theory testing." Its main focus, however, is on using "established theories to explain a case" (2005, 75).
8 As Ingo Rohlfing explains, the cross-case level is the level on which a causal effect is theorized and examined, while the within-case level is concerned with causal mechanisms and causal processes (also called "causal chains") (2012, 12).
9 Evidently, this strategy requires a good grasp of the debates within historical scholarship.
10 Rumsfeld to Rice, July 27, 2001, see https://library.rumsfeld.com/doclib/sp/293/2001-07-27%20To%20Condoleezza%20Rice%20re%20Iraq.pdf.
11 Note that apart from inserting hyperlinks, "active citations" involve annotations as a second important element.

References

Aggestam, Lisbeth, and Adrian Hyde-Price. 2020. "Learning to Lead? Germany and the Leadership Paradox in EU Foreign Policy." *German Politics* 29(1): 8–24.

Alden, Chris, and Amnon Aran. 2017. *Foreign Policy Analysis: New Approaches*. 2nd ed. London: Routledge.

Beach, Derek, and Rasmus B. Pedersen. 2013. *Process-Tracing Methods: Foundations and Guidelines*. Ann Arbor, MI: University of Michigan Press.

Bennett, Andrew. 1999. *Condemned to Repetition? The Rise, Fall, and Reprise of Soviet-Russian Military Interventionism, 1973–1996*. Cambridge, MA: MIT Press.

Brands, Hal. 2017. "The Triumph and Tragedy of Diplomatic History." *Texas National Security Review* 1(1): 133–143.

Breslauer, George, and Philip Tetlock. 1991. *Learning In U.S. And Soviet Foreign Policy*. Boulder, CO: Westview Press.

Capoccia, Giovanni, and R. Daniel Kelemen. 2007. "The Study of Critical Junctures: Theory, Narrative, and Counterfactuals in Historical Institutionalism." *World Politics* 59(3): 341–369.

Carlsnaes, Walter. 2012. "Actors, Structures, and Foreign Policy Analysis." In *Foreign Policy: Theories, Actors, Cases*, edited by Steve Smith, Amelia Hadfield and Tim Dunne. Oxford: Oxford University Press, 113–129.

Carlsnaes, Walter. 2013. "Foreign Policy." In *Handbook of International Relations*, edited by Walter Carlsnaes, Thomas Risse and Beth A. Simmons. London: Sage, 298–325.

Carr, E.H. 1987. *What is History?* 2nd ed. London: Penguin Books.

Cello, Lorenzo. 2018. "Taking History Seriously in IR: Towards a Historicist Approach." *Review of International Studies* 44(2): 236–251.

Collier, David, Jason Seawright, and Gerardo L. Munck. 2010. "The Quest for Standards: King, Keohane, and Verba's Designing Social Inquiry." In *Rethinking Social Inquiry: Diverse Tools, Shared Standards*, edited by Henry E. Brady and David Collier. Lanham, MD: Rowman & Littlefield, 33–63.

Costigliola, Frank. 2016. "Reading for Emotion." In *Explaining the History of American Foreign Relations*, edited by Frank Costigliola and Michael J. Hogan. Cambridge: Cambridge University Press, 356–373.

Dannreuther, Roland. 2011. "Understanding the Middle East Peace Process: A Historical Institutionalist Approach." *European Journal of International Relations* 17(2): 187–208.

Darnton, Christopher. 2018. "Archives and Inference: Documentary Evidence in Case Study Research and the Debate over U.S. Entry into World War II." *International Security* 42(3): 84–126.

Doran, Robert. 2013. "Choosing the Past: Hayden White and the Philosophy of History." In *Philosophy of History After Hayden White*, edited by Robert Doran. London: Bloomsbury.

Dreyer, David R. 2010. "One Issue Leads to Another: Issue Spirals and the Sino-Vietnamese War." *Foreign Policy Analysis* 6(4): 297–315.

Elman, Colin, and Miriam F. Elman. 2001. *Bridges and Boundaries: Historians, Political Scientists, and the Study of International Relations*. Cambridge, MA: MIT Press.

Fioretos, Orfeo. 2011. "Historical Institutionalism in International Relations." *International Organization* 65(2): 367–399.

Gadinger, Frank, and Dirk Peters. 2016. "Feedback Loops in a World of Complexity: A Cybernetic Approach at the Interface of Foreign Policy Analysis and International Relations Theory." *Cambridge Review of International Affairs* 29(1): 251–269.

George, Alexander L., and Andrew Bennett. 2005. *Case Studies and Theory Development in the Social Sciences*. Cambridge, MA: MIT Press.

Ghalehdar, Payam. 2021. *The Origins of Overthrow: How Emotional Frustration Shapes US Regime Change Interventions*. Oxford: Oxford University Press.

Goertz, Gary, and James Mahoney. 2012. *A Tale of Two Cultures: Qualitative and Quantitative Research in the Social Sciences*. Princeton, NJ: Princeton University Press.

Guilhot, Nicolas. 2017. *After the Enlightenment: Political Realism and International Relations in the Mid-Twentieth Century*. Cambridge: Cambridge University Press.

Haber, Stephen H., David M. Kennedy, and Stephen D. Krasner. 1997. "Brothers under the Skin - Diplomatic History and International Relations." *International Security* 22(1): 34–43.

Hall, Peter A. 2003. "Aligning Ontology and Methodology in Comparative Politics." In *Comparative Historical Analysis in the Social Sciences*, edited by James Mahoney and Dietrich Rueschemeyer. Cambridge: Cambridge University Press, 373–404.

Hill, Christopher. 2016. *Foreign Policy in the Twenty-First Century*. 2nd ed. New York: Palgrave Macmillan.

Houghton, David Patrick. 2007. "Reinvigorating the Study of Foreign Policy Decision Making: Toward a Constructivist Approach." *Foreign Policy Analysis* 3(1): 24–45.

Hudson, Valerie M. 2012. "The History and Evolution of Foreign Policy Analysis." In *Foreign Policy: Theories, Actors, Cases*, edited by Steve Smith, Amelia Hadfield and Tim Dunne. Oxford: Oxford University Press, 13–34.

Hudson, Valerie M. 2014. *Foreign Policy Analysis: Classic and Contemporary Theory*. 2nd ed. Lanham, MD: Rowman & Littlefield.

Kaarbo, Juliet, and Daniel Kenealy. 2017. "Precedents, Parliaments, and Foreign Policy: Historical Analogy in the House of Commons Vote on Syria." *West European Politics* 40(1): 62–79.

Kaarbo, Juliet, Jeffrey S. Lantis, and Ryan K. Beasley. 2013. "The Analysis of Foreign Policy in Comparative Perspective." In *Foreign Policy in Comparative Perspective: Domestic and International Influences on State Behavior*, edited by Ryan K. Beasley, Juliet Kaarbo, Jeffrey S. Lantis and Michael T. Snarr. Los Angeles, CA: Sage, 1–26.

Khong, Yuen Foong. 1992. *Analogies at War: Korea, Munich, Dien Bien Phu, and the Vietnam Decisions of 1965*. Princeton, NJ: Princeton University Press.

Lantis, Jeffrey S., and Ryan K. Beasley. 2017. "Comparative Foreign Policy Analysis." *Oxford Research Encyclopedia of Politics*. Oxford University Press. doi.org/10.1093/acrefore/9780190228637.013.398

Larson, Deborah W. 1985. *Origins of Containment: A Psychological Explanation*. Princeton, NJ: Princeton University Press.

Larson, Deborah W. 2001. "Sources and Methods in Cold War History: The Need for a New Theory-Based Archival Approach." In *Bridges and Boundaries: Historians, Political Scientists, and the Study of International Relations*, edited by Colin Elman and Miriam F. Elman. Cambridge, MA: MIT Press, 327–350.

Lebow, Richard Ned. 2001. "Social Science and History: Ranchers versus Farmers?" In *Bridges and Boundaries: Historians, Political Scientists, and the Study of International Relations*, edited by Colin Elman and Miriam F. Elman. Cambridge, MA: MIT Press, 111–135.

Levy, Jack S. 1994. "Learning and Foreign Policy: Sweeping a Conceptual Minefield." *International Organization* 48(2): 279–312.

Levy, Jack S. 2001. "Explaining Events and Developing Theories: History, Political Science, and the Analysis of International Relations." In *Bridges and Boundaries: Historians, Political Scientists, and the Study of International Relations*, edited by Colin Elman and Miriam F. Elman. Cambridge, MA: MIT Press, 39–83.

Lustick, Ian S. 1996. "History, Historiography, and Political Science: Multiple Historical Records and the Problem of Selection Bias." *American Political Science Review* 90(3): 605–618.

Mabee, Bryan. 2011. "Historical Institutionalism and Foreign Policy Analysis: The Origins of the National Security Council Revisited." *Foreign Policy Analysis* 7(1): 27–44.

McClelland, Charles A. 1961. "The Acute International Crisis." *World Politics* 14(1): 182–204.

McDermott, Rose. 1998. *Risk-Taking in International Politics: Prospect Theory in American Foreign Policy*. Ann Arbor, MI: University of Michigan Press.

Mintz, Alex, and Karl DeRouen. 2010. *Understanding Foreign Policy Decision Making*. Cambridge: Cambridge University Press.

Møller, Jørgen, and Svend-Erik Skaaning. 2021. "The Ulysses Principle: A Criterial Framework for Reducing Bias When Enlisting the Work of Historians." *Sociological Methods & Research* 50(1): 103–134.

Moravcsik, Andrew. 2010. "Active Citation: A Precondition for Replicable Qualitative Research." *PS: Political Science & Politics* 43(1): 29–35.

Morin, Jean-Frédéric, and Jonathan Paquin. 2018. *Foreign Policy Analysis: A Toolbox*. New York: Palgrave Macmillan.

Munck, Gerardo L., Jørgen Møller, and Svend-Erik Skaaning. 2020. "Conceptualization and Measurement: Basic Distinctions and Guidelines." In *The SAGE Handbook of Research Methods in Political Science and International Relations*, edited by Luigi Curini and Robert Franzese. Los Angeles, CA: Sage, 331–352.

Neack, Laura, Jeanne A.K. Hey, and Patrick J. Haney. 1995. "Generational Change in Foreign Policy Analysis." In *Foreign Policy Analysis: Continuity and Change in Its Second Generation*, edited by Laura Neack, Jeanne A.K. Hey and Patrick J. Haney. Englewood Cliffs, NJ: Prentice Hall, 1–15.

Neustadt, Richard E., and Ernest R. May. 1988. *Thinking In Time: The Uses Of History For Decision Makers*. New York: Free Press.

Nye, Joseph S. 1987. "Nuclear Learning and U.S.–Soviet Security Regimes." *International Organization* 41(3): 371–402.

Odell, John S. 2001. "Case Study Methods in International Political Economy." *International Studies Perspectives* 2(2): 161–176.

Pierson, Paul. 2004. *Politics in Time: History, Institutions, and Social Analysis*. Princeton, NJ: Princeton University Press.

Potter, Philip B.K. 2017. "Methods of Foreign Policy Analysis." *Oxford Research Encyclopedia of International Studies*. Oxford University Press. doi.org/10.1093/acrefore/9780190846626.013.34

Rapport, Aaron. 2015. "Hard Thinking about Hard and Easy Cases in Security Studies." *Security Studies* 24(3): 431–465.

Reus-Smit, Christian. 2008. "Reading History through Constructivist Eyes." *Millennium* 37(2): 395–414.

Rixen, Thomas, and Lora Anne Viola. 2016. "Historical Institutionalism and International Relations: Towards Explaining Change and Stability in International Institutions." In *Historical Institutionalism and International Relations*, edited by Thomas Rixen, Lora Anne Viola and Michael Zürn. Oxford: Oxford University Press, 3–34.

Rixen, Thomas, Lora Anne Viola, and Michael Zürn. 2016. *Historical Institutionalism and International Relations: Explaining Institutional Development in World Politics*. Oxford: Oxford University Press.

Rohlfing, Ingo. 2012. *Case Studies and Causal Inference: An Integrative Framework*. New York: Palgrave Macmillan.

Rosenau, James N. 2006. "Pre-Theories and Theories of Foreign Policy." In *The Study of World Politics: Theoretical and Methodological Challenges*, edited by James N. Rosenau. London: Routledge, 171–199.

Rosenau, James N., Philip M. Burgess, and Charles F. Hermann. 1973. "The Adaptation of Foreign Policy Research: A Case Study of an Anti-Case Study Project." *International Studies Quarterly* 17(1): 119–144.

Saull, Richard. 2012. "American Foreign Policy during the Cold War." In *US Foreign Policy*, edited by Michael Cox and Doug Stokes. New York: Oxford University Press, 59–81.

Schrodt, Philip A. 1995. "Event Data in Foreign Policy Analysis." In *Foreign Policy Analysis: Continuity and Change in Its Second Generation*, edited by Laura Neack, Jeanne A.K. Hey and Patrick J. Haney. Englewood Cliffs, NJ: Prentice Hall, 145–166.

Schroeder, Paul W. 1997. "History and International Relations Theory: Not Use or Abuse, but Fit or Misfit." *International Security* 22(1): 64–74.

Singer, David J. 1968. *Quantitative International Politics: Insights and Evidence*. New York: Free Press.

Smith, Steve. 1983. "Foreign Policy Analysis: British and American Orientations and Methodologies." *Political Studies* 31(4): 556–565.

Smith, Steve. 1986. "Theories of Foreign Policy: An Historical Overview." *Review of International Studies* 12(1): 13–29.

Snyder, Richard C., H.W. Bruck, and Burton Sapin. 2002. *Foreign Policy Decision-Making (Revisited)*. New York: Palgrave Macmillan.

Stuart, Douglas T. 2008. "Foreign-Policy Decision-Making." In *The Oxford Handbook of International Relations*, edited by Christian Reus-Smit and Duncan Snidal. New York: Oxford University Press, 576–593.

Thies, Cameron G. 2002. "A Pragmatic Guide to Qualitative Historical Analysis in the Study of International Relations." *International Studies Perspectives* 3(4): 351–372.

Verba, Sidney. 1967. "Some Dilemmas in Comparative Research." *World Politics* 20(1): 111–127.

28
Oral History
Michal Onderco

Introduction

Asking people about their recollections and experiences from the past is one of the most frequent human activities. We ask our grandmother how she fell in love with grandfather, we ask our parents about their recollections of momentous historical events they lived through. This is all our personal and simple version of oral history. We may know that our grandparents married in 1949, but that tells us little about their relationship.

In the study of foreign policy, we also often want to know in more detail about how individuals experienced momentous events, what guided their thinking, and how they interpreted the world. Furthermore, we may often lack basic information about *what happened* because the information may be not have been recorded, may still be classified, or is otherwise not accessible. This is where oral history may be of help.

The Oral History Association defines oral history as "a field of study and a method of gathering, preserving and interpreting the voices and memories of people, communities, and participants in past events" (Oral History Association n.a.). Oral history is a special type of interviewing (see also Deschaux-Dutard in this volume) that places the onus on individual participants, their memories, experiences, and recollections. The participant in oral history can be an ordinary person – indeed, the expansion of oral history as an accepted method has increased in the 1960s and 1970s as a reaction to the civil rights movement and the desire to give voice to "the other" (Hajek 2014). However, the participant in oral history can also be a person who is extraordinary for one or another reason – perhaps because they took part in a crucial meeting, led a department when a certain decision was made, or were at the table when critical resolutions were being negotiated. For foreign policy analysts, both types of persons might be relevant.

In mainstream Foreign Policy Analysis (FPA) scholarship (or International Relations (IR) more broadly), oral history is not a common method. Similarly, IR is not a field for oral historians: searching for the term "international relations" in the archive of the *Oral History Journal*, the leading field journal, leads to but a handful of hits, mainly book reviews. However, oral history offers scholars of foreign policy a unique way to explain phenomena by looking at how direct participants looked at them at the time. Compared with other interviewing methods, oral history recognizes more explicitly the process of co-creation of research between the researcher and the participant.

This chapter introduces oral history as a method for FPA, as well as its slight adjustment, which might be also attractive for foreign policy scholars – critical oral history. By the end of reading this chapter, you should know whether oral history is a suitable method for your research, how to design an oral history project, and where to look for more information in this field. Before continuing further, however, aspiring oral historians will be well advised to consult the work of Patricia Leavy (2011), whose *Oral History* is unparalleled in breadth and depth of advice on how to conduct a successful oral history project, although it is geared primarily to sociologists and some of the practical advice is by now dated. In this chapter, I wish to develop more specific recommendations and suggestions for FPA.

The second section of this chapter provides a literature review of some of the existing applications of oral history to the study of foreign policy. The third section looks at the key terms and concepts in both oral history and critical oral history, and it offers some methodological advice on how to conduct oral history interviews. The fourth section offers an illustration based on the research project which I conducted in 2015–2018 in the field of nuclear nonproliferation. The fifth section concludes with a look to the practical aspects related to organizing and designing an oral history project.

Literature Review

As mentioned in the introduction, oral history is a fairly exotic method in the study of foreign policy. Historians have for a long time used oral history to study subjects that are of interests to foreign policy scholars – for example, the experiences of soldiers during war (Hutching 2004, 2006). However, looking at FPA as such, we find that there have been only a number of projects that used oral history as the primary tool of data collection for the study of foreign policy. In these projects, we can distinguish between oral history projects in a traditional sense, oral history conferences, and critical oral history projects.

Traditional Oral History Projects

A major *traditional* oral history project was led by Sue Onslow in the framework of the *Commonwealth Oral History Project*.[1] This project offered a unique history of the Commonwealth since 1965 and provided a unique source of data on non-Western perspectives on the Commonwealth, especially on what the Commonwealth meant for former British colonies.

Two other important traditional oral history projects were related to Israel's national security. Magen and Gilboa (2014) and Ben Aharon (2020) used oral history to understand national security policy-making in Israel. While the former contribution focused on the domestic strategic communication and the relationship between the Israeli Security Agency and the media, the latter focused on the security establishment itself and the link between intelligence and foreign policy. These projects focused on oral history interviews undertaken with key participants (elites, in the language of social science methodology). As Ben Aharon (2020) explains, use of oral history helps us to understand the role of intelligence, often hidden from the public eye and publicly accessible documents, but also the institutional politics of relations between individual agencies.

Another traditional oral history project was done by Gardini (2012), who studied the foundation of Mercosur and the Argentine-Brazilian cooperation in 1985–1991. Gardini interviewed 60 elites, but he also collected archival documents and "cross-checked with one another and tested against available written diplomatic documents along with journalistic reports and other secondary sources" (Gardini 2012, 119–120). What Gardini did, however, is slightly outside the oral history territory. Gardini's study still delivers new, important insights into the foundation of Mercosur, which would otherwise not be found, such as the reasons why executives did not feel constrained by domestic institutional structures, and rather focused on building relations of trust between the country leaders.

In another project undertaken in Latin America, Patti (2014) interviewed participants in the Brazilian nuclear program since its inception. He showed that, contrarily to frequently argued narratives, there has never been a formal decision to pursue a nuclear weapon, and Brazilian military officials and scientists mainly played around with the technology to explore its possibilities. Patti's project is unusual, because he worked in his project with primary sources which the interviewees were asked to engage with, resembling critical oral history described at the end of this section.

Oral History Conferences

A particular type of oral history is one which brings together a number of participants in a conference to have them discuss one particular event. This set-up allows scholars to have participants confront one another with how they perceived the situation and whether similar considerations guided their thinking. In some history subfields, oral history conferences may also be called *witness seminars* (see eg Maas and Svorenčík 2016). Such conferences "bring together key participants of an important historical event to obtain a mix of different perspectives that may agree or disagree, but preferably lead to an exchange of memories that feed upon one another" (Maas and Svorenčík 2016, 3). In addition to direct participants, the conferences also often include academic participants. The academics' main goal is to advance discussions and ask questions – in a way, it may resemble a group interview. However, the academics might also be reduced to the role of observers, or those who provide some initial input for the discussion by the direct participants.

The oral history conference was the format for one of the first projects where oral history was used for FPA. In a series of conferences organized by James Blight, David Welch, and Bruce Allyn, American and Russian direct participants in the decision-making during the Cuban Missile Crisis came together to discuss the pivotal moment of the Cold War when, in 1962, the world almost experienced a nuclear war (Allyn, Blight, and Welch 1989; Blight and Welch 1989; Blight, Allyn, and Welch 1993). In these conferences, the individual participants discussed their roles in decision-making and in crafting of objectives. It was the first conference in which Russians and Americans met to discuss how they made decisions during this key episode of the Cold War. As Barkawi and Laffey (2006) remarked in a later review, these conferences, and books which stemmed from them, were the first ones to highlight the *Cuban* dimension of the Cuban Missile Crisis. Cuba was an actor in its own right in the Cuban Missile Crisis. Yet, the hitherto existing scholarship was fixed on the US and Soviet perspectives, hence forgetting the key Cuban participants. As Barkawi and Laffey (2006) make clear, the Cuban dimension would be hidden from the researchers if it was not for the Russian participants who insisted on including Cuban participants in the discussions.

Another prominent oral history conference focused on key elements of the end of Cold War (Wohlforth 2003). During a conference at Princeton in 1996, eight former top-level officials from the US and Soviet governments met to discuss the bilateral relationship between the superpowers in this period, the link between domestic politics and foreign policy, arms control, as well as the collapse of communism in Eastern Europe and the first Gulf War.

This conference was truly key for the scholarly understanding why Soviets did not use force to suppress the anti-Communist protests in Eastern Europe (as they had done two decades earlier), and how the understanding between the superpowers was built.

Critical Oral History (Conferences)

A slight twist on the oral history theme is provided by the format of *critical* oral history (conferences). Critical oral history (conferences) is different from other forms of oral history (conferences) in that they are supported by documentary basis. The archival document then offers an anchoring point for the discussion. Such debates lead to richer narratives, and often to a more comparative element (Schneider 2011). For example, participants may be asked whether similar documents were produced in their national setting (when dealing with, for instance, declassified national assessments); how certain documents were negotiated with their headquarters (when discussing certain resolutions); or how documents were perceived or received. Work with documents improves interaction and helps participants to stay focused.

The critical oral history conferences conducted in the framework of the Wilson Center's *History and Public Policy* project are particularly relevant in this category. Onslow and van Wyk (2013) conducted a critical oral history conference of the liberation struggle in post-1974 Southern Africa, bringing together the local, American, as well as Russian participants. This conference was one of the first when the former opponents met together to discuss their individual perceptions of the key moments of Cold War history in Southern Africa, and as such produced new insights into how different actors perceived one another in this period. Mallea, Spektor, and Wheeler (2015) conducted a critical oral history conference of the emergence of nuclear cooperation between Argentina and Brazil. This project produced the insight that at three major historical junctures, the Argentinian government chose not to engage in security dilemma dynamics, but instead opted for conciliatory steps emphasizing empathy and trust. As the three editors of that book make clear in their introductory note, the Cold War could have ended up very differently in Latin America if the Argentinian government chose a different path in each of these junctures. Onderco and Nuti (2020) used a critical oral history conference to study the indefinite extension of the Treaty on Nonproliferation of Nuclear Weapons (NPT). This project, for example, produced the finding that the famous *package* of extension actually emerged at the conference and that ahead of the conference, lobbying was the key strategy for all participants.

What these conferences have in common is that they gave participants opportunities to ground their discussions in archival documents. Hence, their views and perspectives were still at center-stage, but they had the same point of reference for their study. This framework works particularly well when the conference is accompanied by newly available data. However, as was done in the study by Onslow and van Wyk (2013), the format works well also when academic participants prepare background papers.

Key Terms and Concepts

The key assumption behind the use of oral history is that human memory stores things that are worth remembering (Thomson 2011). Memory is seen not as a passive depository of information, but as a tool which helps humans create meanings. Such meanings, recollections, and experiences are what a researcher is interested in when doing an oral history project. It is through the interaction with the interviewer that they come to live and become expressed. Hence, scholars who use oral history see research as a process and social knowledge as emerging from that process (Leavy 2011).

As Leavy argues, "oral history may tap into any combination of the following:

1   historical processes,
2   agency within shifting contexts, and
3   holistic understandings of life experiences" (Leavy 2011, 15).

It is usually less structured than in-depth interviews, but more structured than individual narratives produced based on a prompt (see also Oppermann and Spencer in this volume for more on narratives). Oral history interviews are also most of the time focused on "personal experiences; memories of events; attitudes, values, beliefs; opinions and perspectives" (Leavy 2011, 9). The whole process of oral history interviewing leaves the participant at center-stage, and the researcher is part of the co-creation of the research.

Indeed, this underlines the importance of the researcher in the process. In the same way as the defining categories for coding in a quantitative analysis involves the scholar, the conscious methodological choices done in undertaking an oral history project influence the outcomes. Oral history is, therefore, a method that requires self-reflection from the scholar conducting research.

Leavy (2011) invites researchers to be explicit not only about the motivation for the research but also about the research choices. In academic research, we often conduct research because we are intrinsically motivated to study a particular subject, but there are a number of other reasons why people select their research questions (Van Evera 1997). For instance, Hutching (2006, 2004) wrote her books on the experience of New Zealanders in various conflicts as a part of a government-sponsored project. Because the role of the researcher in the project is crucial, so is the explicitness about why we select certain research questions. The purpose of the research project can influence the focus of the questions, which may indeed explain why certain topics are discussed – and why certain topics are not.

The key criticism of oral history is similar to general criticism of interviewing. The most succinct encapsulation of this criticism was offered by historian Mark Kramer in his response to new findings on the Cuban Missile Crisis. In his letter to the editor of *International Security*, Kramer decries "failings and selectivity of memory (...) because the events transpired nearly 30 years ago and almost all of those who played any part (...) are now elderly" (Kramer 1990, 213). Kramer's criticism of the oral history of the Cuban Missile Crisis is a good example of the so-called traditional positivist criticism of oral history (Thomson 2011). This criticism focuses on failings of human memory and implicitly privileges written sources. Yet, written sources are, naturally, not without their own problems. In the same way as human memory is not fail-proof, the documentary sources we can access most of the time have been pre-sampled (often in ways we are not even aware of). For social scientists using oral history for social scientific purposes, fallibility of human memory is not a unique problem, but rather provides a challenge which is present elsewhere, too.

Other criticisms of oral history can be similarly challenged. Gardini (2012) created a catalogue of such criticisms. Next to forgetfulness, listed above, Gardini lists reticence, inaccuracy, and intrusion. Yet, none of them are unique to oral history. Reticence – the unwillingness of the respondents to be completely true – is also present in correspondence or official documents. Similarly, written documents can be inaccurate (whether willingly or not). Intrusion can lead to introduction of bias into interviews, but can be similarly introduced into written documents. Hence, the solution is not to throw away the oral history baby with the bathwater of potential bias, but to remedy these potential shortcomings in the research itself. For instance, one could prepare more probing questions, ask for more details, give respondents option not to answer certain questions or answer them off-record, or recruit a more diverse group of respondents. In the section below, I will discuss how this was done in a framework of one concrete project.

Empirical Illustration

To provide an illustration about how an oral history project might be executed, I use the example of the methodology applied to conduct research into the indefinite extension of the Treaty on Nonproliferation of Nuclear Weapons (NPT), which happened in 1995 (Onderco and Nuti 2020; Onderco 2021). This project aimed at illuminating how it was possible that the treaty was extended indefinitely, even though a majority of parties were opposed to it. The answers provided by the existing scholarship were unsatisfactory, and the question was ripe for research.

Motivation and Design

In devising the project, I opted for oral history as a research method not only because numerous sources were still classified but also because numerous aspects appeared undiscoverable and hence hidden from the researchers' eye. Ben Aharon (2020) has recently cited similar justifications for his use of oral history. In this project on the indefinite extension of the NPT, oral history was not the only source, but an additional source supplementing the archival research. The oral history part of the project included two parts – a set of traditional oral history interviews, and a critical oral history conference. In subsequent parts of the chapter, I will delve into both elements separately.

In designing the traditional oral history part of the project, I followed the guidelines suggested by Patricia Leavy (2011). At the outset, I conducted an extensive literature review of existing explanations for (and analyses of) the NPT's indefinite extension. Then, I created an interviewing frame, a list of questions for these semi-structured discussions. These questions were formulated on the basis of two factors: what was still unknown about the conference (on the basis of the secondary literature) and what factors could matter on the basis of extant IR theories. In formulating the questions, I focused on participants' views and perceptions in order to not only establish the factual basis but also understand better their individual and their nation's decision-making.[2]

The next step required me to identify the initial interviewees. To identify them, I created a list of the most important countries taking part in the NPT extension conference on the basis of the secondary literature (Rauf and Johnson 1995; Welsh 1995; Dhanapala and Rauf 2017; Dhanapala and Ryddel 2017). Based on the official list of the participants from the website of the United Nations, I identified the delegation leaders from these countries. Next to these direct participants, I have also put together a list of independent experts cited in the secondary literature and contacted them as well. I contacted these observers and academic experts because they approached the question before (most of them immediately after) and so they also had interesting observations to offer about the research question.

Parallel to these individual interviews, I also started preparing for the critical oral history conference, which took place at the end of the project. The preparation for the critical oral history conference included creating the set of topics to be discussed at the conference (focusing on those that were the most controversial or least known), selecting policy elite participants as well as academic participants, and taking care of the technical and logistical aspects of the conference.

Organizing Oral History Interviews

All interviewees were initially approached by email. In this email, I explained clearly who I am, what the purpose of the interview was, that the interviewee would be taped and later published, but also that they would have an opportunity to review the transcript prior to publication. At the start of every interview, each interviewee was again informed about the procedure and expressed again their agreement. It is important to note that this set-up includes a number of choices – for example, that I only taped the voice and not the video or that the respondents received the right to review the transcript. These choices were consciously made to give the respondents a greater feeling of control over the interview and less fear that any slip-ups would be recorded for posterity.

A reader might want to note here that it is important for the interviewee to know the respondents before – what kind of people are they, and how are they likely to react during the interview? In practice, this requires some prior preparation, for example reading some texts the respondent has written. But the respondent can also ask: "What kind of position was this person in?", "What was expected from them in this position?", "Are they used to interact with researchers?", "Would face-saving be important in their life?", "How much autonomy are they used to have?" One of the things I expected about diplomats as interviewees was that they wanted to be in control, as much as possible, because they were socialized in a profession that does not take slip-ups lightly. Therefore, I tried to give my respondents as much sense of control as possible. As Leavy (2011) suggests, it is generally a good idea to give the respondents a feeling of autonomy and freedom – participants will open up the most when they feel safe. Feeling of being in charge reinforces that feeling of safety.

The first interview took place in September 2016, and I soon realized two things. First, I suddenly received a long list of interviewee suggestions from the participants, an effect known as *snowballing* in social science methodology. I filtered those on the basis of their position in their delegations, privileging more senior members and participants who were involved more *hands-on*, simply because interviewing everyone was beyond my abilities. Second, it became obvious that even though the events discussed happened almost a quarter century earlier, the interviewees were not free (or did not feel it was appropriate) to discuss certain subjects. Therefore, I gave all interviewees an option to do a part of the interview "off-record". The off-record portions of the interviews were not taped, and hence also not transcribed. The off-record parts allowed me not only to build better rapport with the interviewees but also to have them provide a more colorful description of certain events or personalities. The transcript was clearly marked where the discussion went off-record. The transcripts of all of the interviews (except the off-the-record parts) can be found in the Digital Archive of the Wilson Center.[3]

Each interview was then transcribed by a student assistant. The student assistant also transcribed long pauses, laughter, or other emotional para-verbal reactions in order to keep the transcript as close as possible to the authentic interview. I reviewed each transcript and compared it against the audio recording. Once reviewed, each interviewee received the transcript for review, and 30 days to suggest any changes. Most of the interviewees used this opportunity to do minor changes (e.g., edit slightly some clumsy formulations). A handful of interviewees asked to review major portions – these were either excised completely (treated as off-record), or the edits were marked in the transcript.

All in all, I conducted in-depth oral history interviews with over 30 key diplomats. Whenever possible, I met them in person at the location of their choice. This made interviewees more at ease, reinforced their feeling of being in control, and also contributed to a more open atmosphere during the meeting. The locations were often restaurants or cafes, but also offices or homes. One interviewee preferred to visit me at home for an interview, and I made this possible. Whenever costs occurred (e.g., for a lunch or coffee), I bore those unless the interviewee insisted otherwise. In a small number of instances where in-person meeting was impossible due to the distance or cost, I reached out to the interviewees by phone or Skype, depending on where they resided and which options they felt more comfortable with.

All oral history interviews were semi-structured: in all of the interviews, I used the same basic interview script and the same basic questions. However, as it usually happens in elite interviews (and as is appropriate for oral history), we often wandered into other unexplored areas. Interviewees often wanted to share particular insights, or details they thought were important. An average interview lasted around two hours, but it was not uncommon to have much longer ones (the record was a four-hour interview). The shortest interview ended after 15 minutes, when the interviewee became fed up with my questions and shut the phone.

I then divided each interview into snippets (replies) which were then linked to the original questions, and marked if they contained information about a particular meeting, event, or a person. These snippets were then triangulated with other data sources to increase the reliability and validity of the research.

Organizing the Critical Oral History Conference

The critical oral history conference combined two features to make the oral history stronger: it brought together multiple participants who could share their insights (the *conference* part), and it provided declassified information to support the debate (the *critical* part).

In organizing the conference, a few rules were followed, which were based on the previous oral history conferences organized within the framework of the Nuclear Proliferation International History Project. The conference was focused on a particular time period and a set of events – from late 1994 till the end of the NPT extension conference in mid-May 1995, thus delimiting the scope of discussions very clearly. Naturally, the participants every now and then wandered off this time period, but best efforts were taken to ensure that the participants remained focused on this period.

To select the participants, I started with the list of interviewees for the oral history part of the project. I approached the senior delegation leaders from the most important countries (the five nuclear weapons states, Germany, South Africa, Egypt, Canada, the Netherlands) and the Conference President in May 2017. Almost all of them accepted. I could not secure a participation by a senior German diplomat as neither of them was willing or able to come to Rotterdam. I therefore invited Professor Harald Müller, a senior scientific advisor to the delegation, to join. However, in the end, three participants cancelled due to scheduling conflicts or logistics issues. In addition to the policy veterans, I invited ten academics to participate in the conference as observers and chairs. These were mainly a mix of scholars of nuclear weapons, proliferation, and history.

The conference took place over a period of two days (three days, starting with a dinner). It was divided into six thematic sessions, covering the main themes of discussions. During two days of discussions, the critical oral history conference explored six topics: the mood and expectations for the conference, hurdles for the agreement, overcoming the obstacles for agreement, *the Middle East question*,[4] the discussion about the origins of the final documents of the conference, and the discussion about the extension's impact.

One month ahead of the conference, the participants received a detailed information package which included – beyond the usual logistical details – a set of questions to think about for each thematic session, and an extensive document reader. Importantly, I did not distribute other participants' interviews to the policy veterans, in order to avoid grinding of axes (here I followed the suggestion made by Mallea, Spektor, and Wheeler 2015). The briefing packet was important because it gave participants something to chew on (mentally) in preparation for the conference. The documents that were circulated gave them an opportunity to refresh their memories as well as gave them an idea about what we were to discuss. Given that most of the participants were former leading diplomats, the feeling of being prepared for a meeting was very important for them.

Each thematic session took 90 minutes and was chaired by two chairs: me and another academic expert. The probing questions for thematic sessions were prepared in cooperation with the academic expert for each individual session. The conference was, similarly to oral history interviews, conducted entirely in English. This was, again, a conscious choice. Since all of the participants were former top-level diplomats, speaking English was easy for them. However, in other contexts, scholars should be mindful to choose a language in which participants are free to express themselves. This may mean that scholars may have to provide (and budget for) professional translation service (this was done, for example, by Mallea, Spektor, and Wheeler 2015). Conducting a multi-lingual oral history conference also means that the final output should be either published in multiple languages, or carefully translated, ideally by native speakers with in-depth knowledge of specific terminology.

Scholars who wish to prepare future oral history conferences should be mindful of the logistical and organizational burden. Organization of a three-day conference with a dozen former VIPs (including a former prime minister) took considerable time and effort (and money). Even the smallest details had to be planned: the hotel for participants, their transport, how the participants were to be seated, what was to be served for lunch (taking into account participants' dietary preferences and the fact that getting a warm lunch from a catering service is next to impossible at a reasonable cost in many countries). Even then some things could not be planned: one of the participants, for example, did not inform us that due to health issues, he was not able to walk more than 50m at a time, creating challenges on a car-free campus. These may appear as small issues, but during oral history conferences, time is scarce and events are tightly planned, hence it is important to foresee and plan for all sorts of eventualities.

After the conference, the recording of the two days of discussions was transcribed by a professional transcribing service. The transcription was then reviewed by me. Then, the draft was sent to the policy participants (but not to the academics). The participants were given 30 days to review their section of the transcript and suggest any changes. Most of them left but a handful of changes, usually misspellings of names, abbreviations, or idioms which we originally did not correctly catch. One participant wished to completely alter some of his statements – together with my co-editor, we allowed this, but marked in the transcript very clearly that the participant wished to retract his original statement and replace it with a different one. This solution allowed the participant to withdraw the statement, but signaled to the reader that this was done ex-post. The transcript of the conference, as well as detailed information about agenda and main lessons learnt was published by the Wilson Center (Onderco and Nuti 2020).

The critical oral history delivered the insights related not only to the preparation for the 1995 NPT Review and Extension Conference but also to the conduct of the conference itself. As mentioned above, one of the things that emerged from the meeting was not only that the *extension package* emerged only at the conference but also that in many Western countries, there was reluctance to offer any concessions (one of the respondents said that any idea of concessions was *verboten* [forbidden] in discussions of the Western group). We also learnt that at the conference itself, the domestic actors were very important – for example, the White House engaged in extensive lobbying. A South African participant in the critical oral history conference, Ambassador Abdul Minty, for example, spoke at great length about the bifurcation in the South African camp between the holdovers from the apartheid era and the political appointees of the African National Congress. The critical oral history also made clear that the Resolution on the Middle East was not a precondition for the extension (and hence not a part of the *extension package*), but it was a price for not calling a vote on the extension.

Conclusion

The key goal of this chapter was to explain to the reader what oral history is, how an oral history project can be designed, and where to look for more information about oral history. Oral history is a very strong tool when one is interested in individual's experiences, memories, attitudes, or perspectives. As such, it holds much promise for foreign policy analysts. Whenever a scholar is interested in research which gives the respondent a strong voice, oral history might be a very suitable method for research.

The method has also downsides. Because it relies on co-creation between the respondent and the academic, it is often seen as less reliable and reliant on memories (Hajek 2014). Regardless of whether such criticism is correct or not, a scholar must be aware that it might be raised by reviewers and editors. Triangulation with other sources offers a possible way out here, establishing plausibility with other courses.

There are also downsides of more practical nature. Conducting a successful oral history project takes time (to identify and conduct respondents, conduct interviews, and analyze them); it takes money (to purchase equipment or to travel to visit participants); it takes a very particular research mindset (for example, a researcher comfortable conducting interviews with strangers); but it also provides preparedness to battle bureaucracy (for example, institutional ethical reviews or data processing rules). These are but a few of potential issues that a researcher may encounter (this list is loosely based on advice presented by Hajek 2014).

In 2022, a researcher should not underestimate the legal aspects. With the entry into force of the General Data Protection Regulation (GDPR) in the EU, academic institutions have become much more concerned about the data processing, storage of personal information (where oral history interviews undoubtedly fall), as well as ethical aspects of research. Scholars who wish to embark on new oral history projects today should contact, in the early stages of the process, their institutions' ethical review board, legal counsel, the data protection officer, and a data steward.

One aspect which is often ignored in the broader oral history scholarship but which is of crucial importance is how the data are stored and shared. Also in social science today, there is a growing trend to make data "FAIR" – findable, accessible, interoperable, and reusable (Wilkinson et al. 2016). This means that scholars should share their data, including the oral history data. Sharing of qualitative data has been historically a touchy subject, but has been increasingly picked up in the discipline (Bishop and Kuula-Luumi 2017; Mannheimer et al. 2018).[5] For aspiring oral historians, the question of how the data could and should be shared, as well as how to incorporate different privacy and data protection issues in the research design, must be tackled at the start. Scholars should consider repositories, ideally such that give their data persistent identifiers that can be used across different platforms.

Before embarking on a new oral history project, researchers should not underestimate the costs such project may bring about. Interviewing participants in different countries can easily run into hundreds of Euros per trip, excluding the cost of the researcher's own time. Transcription of interviews is also costly, in terms of time and money. It might be tempting to overlook such costs in favor of automated transcription services powered by artificial intelligence. However, at the time of writing, transcripts produced by fully automated processes require extensive review and the time saved is limited, if any. Organizing an oral history conference may be even more expensive. Some of your participants might not be willing to fly economy class, and some might not even be willing to fly business (especially on long-haul). Other participants may have special needs which may create cost (such costs might be minuscule – for example, the extra cost of arranging a gluten-free vegan menu; but also major – it may happen that a former dignitary might have a resident nurse who travels along, effectively doubling the costs). You must consider whether your participants can travel by public transport from the airport, or what kind of hotel they would stay in. Technical solutions – such as recording the event – also bring about costs. An important starting point for an oral history project – whether a set of interviews, a conference, or both – is a deep and honest look at the budget, ideally with someone who has experience running conferences and workshops.

Last but certainly not the least, already at the start, one must be very clear about what the output of the project will be. How does the oral history square with the publication strategy of the project? How will the outputs look like? Will there be a book based on the interviews? If yes, how it will look like, and who will publish it? Scholars should be conscious that their research design choices are interlined with their broader research project including the publication strategy, and therefore they need to be thought about as a part of the whole.

Oral history is a great method for foreign policy scholars who wish to understand individual's experiences, memories, attitudes, and perspectives on foreign policy. Those who ultimately choose this method for their research will be impressed by the broad array of new insights they will gain. Yet, as all other choices, researcher needs to consider it as a part of the project. The research question should drive the choice of the method, not vice versa.

Acknowledgments

This chapter is based on a chapter in my habilitation thesis, defended at Sciences Po Paris in December 2020. I am very thankful to Christian Lequesne for his extensive comments on the earlier draft. My ideas about oral history are influenced by extensive discussions with Leopoldo Nuti and Matias Spektor, whom I thank for sharing their insights with me over the years.

Notes

1 The interviews can be found at https://commonwealthoralhistories.org/.
2 This approach was in line with the suggestions included in a seminal political science book on elite interviewing (Dexter 2006).
3 The interviews can be found at https://digitalarchive.wilsoncenter.org/collection/496/the-1995-npt-review-and-extension-conference.
4 The notion of the Middle East question refers to the establishment of the Weapons of Mass Destruction-Free Zone in the Middle East.
5 Researchers might be also interested in the transparency initiatives related to qualitative work, such as Annotation for Transparent Inquiry. See https://www.cambridge.org/core/services/authors/annotation-for-transparent-inquiry-ati.

References

Allyn, Bruce J., James G. Blight, and David A. Welch. 1989. "Essence of Revision: Moscow, Havana, and the Cuban Missile Crisis." *International Security* 14 (3): 136–172.

Barkawi, Tarak, and Mark Laffey. 2006. "The Postcolonial Moment in Security Studies." *Review of International Studies* 32 (2): 329–352.

Ben Aharon, Eldad. 2020. "Doing Oral History with the Israeli Elite and the Question of Methodology in International Relations Research." *The Oral History Review* 47 (1): 3–25.

Bishop, Libby, and Arja Kuula-Luumi. 2017. "Revisiting Qualitative Data Reuse: A Decade On." *Sage Open* 7 (1): 2158244016685136.

Blight, James G., Bruce J. Allyn, and David A. Welch. 1993. *Cuba on the Brink: Castro, the Missile Crisis, and the Soviet Collapse*. First edition. New York: Pantheon Books.

Blight, James G., and David A. Welch. 1989. *On the Brink: Americans and Soviets Reexamine the Cuban Missile Crisis*. First edition. New York: Hill and Wang.

Dexter, Lewis Anthony. 2006. *Elite and Specialized Interviewing (Ecpr Classics Series)*. Colchester: ECPR Press.

Dhanapala, Jayantha, and Tariq Rauf. 2017. *Reflections on the Treaty on the Non-Proliferation of Nuclear Weapons*. Stockholm: SIPRI.

Dhanapala, Jayantha, and Randy Ryddel. 2017. "Multilateral Diplomacy and the Npt: An Insider's Account." In *Reflections on the Treaty on the Non-Proliferation of Nuclear Weapons: Review Conferences and the Future of the Npt*, edited by Jayantha Dhanapala and Tariq Rauf. Stockholm: SIPRI, 5–133.

Gardini, Gian Luca. 2012. "In Defense of Oral History: Evidence from the Mercosur Case." *Journal of Politics in Latin America* 4 (1): 107–133.

Hajek, Andrea. 2014. *Oral History Methodology*. Available from http://methods.sagepub.com/case/oral-history-methodology.

Hutching, Megan, ed. 2004. *A Fair Sort of Battering: New Zealanders Remember the Italian Campaign*. Auckland: HarperCollins.

Hutching, Megan, ed. 2006. *Against the Rising Sun: New Zealanders Remember the Pacific War*. Auckland: Harper Collins.

Kramer, Mark. 1990. "Correspondence: Remembering the Cuban Missile Crisis: Should We Swallow Oral History?" *International Security* 15 (1): 212–218.

Leavy, Patricia. 2011. *Oral History*. Oxford and New York: Oxford University Press.

Maas, Harro, and Andrej Svorenčík. 2016. "A Witness Seminar on the Emergency of Experimental Economics." In *The Making of Experimental Economics*, edited by Andrej Svorenčík and Harro Maas. Cham: Springer, 1–18.

Magen, Clila, and Eytan Gilboa. 2014. "Communicating from within the Shadows: The Israel Security Agency and the Media." *International Journal of Intelligence and CounterIntelligence* 27 (3): 485–508.

Mallea, Rodrigo, Matias Spektor, and Nicholas J. Wheeler, eds. 2015. *The Origins of Nuclear Cooperation: A Critical Oral History of Argentina and Brazil*. Rio de Janeiro and Washington, DC: FGV and Wilson Center.

Mannheimer, Sara, Amy Pienta, Dessislava Kirilova, Colin Elman, and Amber Wutich. 2018. "Qualitative Data Sharing: Data Repositories and Academic Libraries as Key Partners in Addressing Challenges." *American Behavioral Scientist* 63 (5): 643–664.

Onderco, Michal. 2021. *Networked Nonproliferation: Making the Npt Permanent*. Stanford, CA: Stanford University Press.

Onderco, Michal, and Leopoldo Nuti, eds. 2020. *Extending the Npt*. Washington, DC: Woodrow Wilson International Center for Scholars.

Onslow, Sue, and Anna-Mart van Wyk, eds. 2013. *Southern Africa in the Cold War, Post-1974, Critical Oral History Conference Series*. Washington, DC: Woodrow Wilson International Center for Scholars.

Oral History Association. n.a. *Oral History: Defined*. Available from https://www.oralhistory.org/about/do-oral-history/.

Patti, Carlo, ed. 2014. *O Programa Nuclear Brasileiro: Uma História Oral*. São Paulo: Editora FGV.

Rauf, Tariq, and Rebecca Johnson. 1995. "After the Npt's Indefinite Extension: The Future of the Global Nonproliferation Regime." *The Nonproliferation Review* 3 (1): 28–42.

Schneider, William. 2011. "Interviewing in Cross-Cultural Settings." In *The Oxford Handbook of Oral History*, edited by Donald A. Ritchie. Oxford: Oxford University Press, 51–64.

Thomson, Alistair. 2011. "Memory and Remembering in Oral History." In *The Oxford Handbook of Oral History*, edited by Donald A. Ritchie. Oxford: Oxford University Press, 77–95.

Van Evera, Stephen. 1997. *Guide to Methods for Students of Political Science*. Ithaca, NY: Cornell University Press.

Welsh, Susan B. 1995. "Delegate Perspectives on the 1995 Npt Review and Extension Conference." *The Nonproliferation Review* 2 (3): 1–24.

Wilkinson, Mark D., Michel Dumontier, IJsbrand Jan Aalbersberg, Gabrielle Appleton, Myles Axton, Arie Baak, Niklas Blomberg, Jan-Willem Boiten, Luiz Bonino da Silva Santos, Philip E. Bourne, Jildau Bouwman, Anthony J. Brookes, Tim Clark, Mercè Crosas, Ingrid Dillo, Olivier Dumon, Scott Edmunds, Chris T. Evelo, Richard Finkers, Alejandra Gonzalez-Beltran, Alasdair J.G. Gray, Paul Groth, Carole Goble, Jeffrey S. Grethe, Jaap Heringa, Peter A.C. 't Hoen, Rob Hooft, Tobias Kuhn, Ruben Kok, Joost Kok, Scott J. Lusher, Maryann E. Martone, Albert Mons, Abel L. Packer, Bengt Persson, Philippe Rocca-Serra, Marco Roos, Rene van Schaik, Susanna-Assunta Sansone, Erik Schultes, Thierry Sengstag, Ted Slater, George Strawn, Morris A. Swertz, Mark Thompson, Johan van der Lei, Erik van Mulligen, Jan Velterop, Andra Waagmeester, Peter Wittenburg, Katherine Wolstencroft, Jun Zhao, and Barend Mons. 2016. "The Fair Guiding Principles for Scientific Data Management and Stewardship." *Scientific Data* 3 (1): 160018.

Wohlforth, William C., ed. 2003. *Cold War Endgame: Oral History, Analysis, Debates*. University Park, PA: Penn State University Press.

29
Archival Research
Anne Kerstin Friedrich

Introduction

> "Quod non est in actis, non est in mundo."
> ("What is not filed, is not in the world.")

This Roman proverb and principle of roman civil law equally applies to modern bureaucracies. As events and administrative processes are documented in archives, researchers follow the idea of administrative science that "People govern in writing" (Beuth 2005: 119). Archival analysis has a longstanding tradition in the social sciences. The preservation of events and political processes in written text is an important source to analyze foreign policy processes.

Archival analysis as a method includes the historical analysis (see also Ghalehdar in this volume) of documents in archives and can be combined with other methods of Foreign Policy Analysis (FPA), for example focused and structured comparison. In various national contexts, continuous research projects work on the historical processing of administrative files. In Germany, the *Akten zur Auswärtigen Politik der Bundesrepublik Deutschland* (AAPD) document the diplomatic history of the Federal Republic until 1990. In France, the *Documents diplomatiques françaises (DDF)* cover the period after the Second World War, as established by decree in 1983. The British edition is called *Documents on British Policy Overseas (DBPO)*.

In this chapter, I focus on diplomatic archives, as they serve, especially in states with a democratic and bureaucratic tradition, as a rich source of foreign policy documents that is continuously evolving. In general, the method can be used for different kinds of archives, including personal archives of politicians, organizational archives, or national archives such as the *Digital National Security Archive* (DNSA) located at George Washington University in Washington, D.C.

There is a huge potential in the digitization of diplomatic archives and big datasets as growing resources for archival research (Becker et al. 2021; see also Cujaj in this volume). To take archival research to the next level, large datasets can be analyzed with computer-based research methods, such as text as data (see Vignoli in this volume) or quantitative content analysis (see Friedrichs in this volume). Relevant material in the field of FPA can be found in libraries of foreign ministries, diplomats, and heads of state, often compiled in national and university archives. The diplomatic archives present a collection of official files of the political apparatus of the respective ministry of foreign affairs. Therefore, reports and memos of Ambassadors around the globe are not only well documented, first-hand sources for researchers, but also accessible for diplomats and interested public.

In this chapter, I further suggest combining archival research with theories of practice. As such, we can identify practices of specific groups of actors in foreign policy, for example, diplomats, following the definition of practices as social actions, for instance by analyzing categories such as representation, mandate, or scope of negotiation. Consequently, practices of individual professional groups, such as diplomats, can be extracted from written documents and compared from different perspectives, trying to limit personal biases. Finally, as the study of foreign policy includes various non-governmental actors, archives of NGOs or personal libraries can be analyzed.

As a precondition, categories of analysis must be determined by a specific research question for archival research. As *per se* the method is applicable and open to all kinds of questions in FPA, there is a significant need to narrow down and structure analytical categories. A tendency exists to link research questions to state-centric subjects, as official archives tend to be a rich source of state documents. Therefore, archival research is useful to study the implication of a bureaucratic organization of a specific country in the foreign policy process. Questions such as "What bureaucratic and political course did an issue take?" are subject to archival research methods. Furthermore, we can study processes of the exercise of authority ("Who exerted authority to issue directives on a particular issue?") or responsibility ("Who bears responsibility for a decision and who shaped the decision-making process?"). In addition, we can study questions on the macro level using archives, such as "To what extent does a country's bureaucratic organization affect foreign policy making?"

This chapter presents the method of archival research in foreign policy to demonstrate how the quality of studies is improved using direct, first-hand sources. After describing the state-of-the-art and application in empirical studies, key terms and concepts (material, truth, and reliability) are discussed. In this context, I will present methodological assumptions from the works of Hegel and Weber and their understanding of the state as a bureaucracy that is relevant to the modern concept of archival studies and the development of cases. The fourth section presents empirical illustrations of the method using the political archive of the German Foreign Office in a case study of Economic cooperation in agriculture in German Foreign Policy. Finally, the chapter concludes by discussing strengths and limitations and provides advice for first-time users.

Literature Review

When it comes to recent contributions, one must start at the first interconnections between FPA and archival research. Archival research is often applied by historians, also in the field of international studies. The goal of historical archival research is the study of one or several precise events by analyzing discourse, narratives, and thoughts. Traditionally, the domain of diplomatic studies has been explored by diplomatic historians and political biographers. Famous statesmen and diplomats, such as Ernest von Satow, Henry Kissinger, or Sir Harold Nicolson, described their activities as diplomats and often gave advice on the qualities of a good diplomat. Diplomats, by the original meaning, were archivists who dealt with official documents, called *diploma*. The original idea of diplomats is also reflected in Dom Jean Mabillions *De Re Diplomatica*, published in 1681, in which he describes diplomats as those judging the authenticity of charters and official documents in Benedictine archives. This historical perspective allows us to uncover the close link between diplomacy and archival studies.

However, the application of this method specifically for FPA has not been fully formalized but shows promising potential. In the 1950s and 1960s, diplomacy as a field of study has started to become theorized, contributing to the rise of International Relations (IR) theories (Potter 2010: 2). FPA was born out of the atheoretical nature of historically oriented diplomatic analysis and the analysis of decision makers. Often, political scientists rely on secondary sources and biographies produced by historians. This generates the problem of historiography (see also Ghalehdar in this volume), which means that historians produce a background narrative in order to introduce a representation of history for interpreting texts or artifacts. According to Ian S. Lustick (1996: 605), political scientists cannot rely on historical monographs from which theoretically neutral data can be elicited, but they must ponder on competing streams of historiography. This guides us toward archival research, or as often referred to, *diplomatic history*. Content-wise, diplomatic historians are studying events of foreign policy, such as summits and talks, as well as biographies of diplomats and foreign ministers. Foreign ministries remain in the lead to coordinate the government's foreign policy and deal with issues that play a role in domestic policy (Greenstock 2013). Diplomatic history has generally been limited to official archives, apart from oral traces and interviews, and, of course, diplomats' personal narratives (see also Onderco in this volume). Still, diplomatic history and IR theory are intertwined, starting both from rationalist assumptions of realism and empiricism – scientific historical knowledge about world order. Most importantly, however, Jack S. Levy notes that the research goals of political scientists and historians are different: historians are primarily concerned with the task of describing, explaining, and understanding individual events or temporally bounded series of events, while political scientists are interested in generalizing relationships (Elman and Elman 1997: 19). Advantages and disadvantages of archival research have been studied more recently by Deborah Welch Larson (2017) and by Trachtenberg (2006), Hill (1993), Larson (2001) as well as in Lustick's competing streams of historiography (1996).

> Besides all technological development of our time and the continuously growing importance of conference diplomacy and telephone calls, until nowadays people govern in writing.
>
> *(Möller et al. 2015: 50)*

As Horst Möller observes, even in our modern times written documents stay of uttermost importance for each administration. With this citation, Möller reveals the potential for the analysis of written historical sources for understanding foreign policy, based on the collection of written sources in administrative archives.

The epistemology of the discipline has been studied by various scholars in IR and history. As originally suggested by Michel Foucault and Jacques Derrida, Western states' rationalism has led to a desire to collect and store everything produced by the state (Derrida 1995; Foucault 2002). In the development toward a more formalized approach, the first attempts at merging case studies and datasets on historical events were time consuming and costly (see also Raleigh and Kishi in this volume). In most cases, thousands of newspaper articles of interactions between different states were analyzed through pre-defined codebooks or criteria. Original bases for diplomatic analysis, such as histories, documents, interviews, biographies, and memoirs, were often less easy to use as datasets for thorough, quantitative hypothesis testing. On the one hand, different versions and artifacts must be collected in different places to gather the complete puzzle of involved actors. On the other hand, handwritten sources require time-consuming transcription processes. However, with the digitization and easier accessibility of large datasets, as well as the development of behavioralist models of analysis, there is great potential in the rediscovery of diplomatic archives for analysis.

Benefits of Archival Research

What are the benefits of adopting this method to study foreign policy? First, archival research in FPA is a systematic method. Whereas archives consist of large piles of unprocessed documents, using a systematic approach in the method of archival research creates structure. The goals are to trace, compare, and categorize foreign policy. Second, the work with first-hand documents reduces bias. These consist of first-hand, eyewitness accounts by people who saw or participated in the historical events. As first-hand testimonies, reports and direct evidence, the study of original sources is a distinctive criterion for quality of research. Third, it can be combined with further methods to elaborate the research subject. While qualitative IR researchers of all theoretical strands have consistently engaged in archival research, the approach has not yet been systematically addressed in FPA. However, this method explicitly differentiates itself from diplomatic historians and narrative analysis. By choosing a FPA approach, archival research is not focused on explanation or tracing of events itself, but on tracing intra-ministerial processes of decision-making by analyzing archival documents of foreign ministries or other institutions.

Key Terms and Concepts, Methodology

Archival research is founded on text-based analysis that studies the written traces of past foreign policy processes based on original documents. This includes the comparison of various documents and a detailed analysis of annotations, signatures, and contextualization to retrace a political process. By reconstructing – what often also means deconstructing – a decision-making process in written traces, practices such as representation, mandate, or scope of negotiation can be revealed. By combining archival research with the study of practices, the method can be located in the agent-oriented and behavioralist understanding of foreign policy (Hudson 2005). This implicates that diplomacy, as well as other activities, is first of all a social practice. The diplomatic community in particular serves as an example for a community of practice, illustrating how practices produce structures, rules, and norms in a social setting (Adler & Pouliot 2011). Following Ole Sending, Vincent Pouliot, and Iver B. Neumann's concept of practices as "socially meaningful patterns of action" (Cornut & Pouliot 2015: 299), in the study of diplomacy, practices serve to operationalize the modus operandi of diplomats (Sending et al. 2015).

In this context, I suggest combining archival research further with the method of structured and focused comparison and computer-based, coded analysis. This improves the precision of the qualitative research design for practices. Following the ideas of Alexander L. George and Andrew Bennett (2005), case study analysis seeks to extract a maximum benefit for policy formulation, which remains a fundamental goal of FPA. Therefore, I follow an understanding of archival research as the study of specific scientific cases from which systematic lessons for foreign policy can be drawn, leading to identification of generalizable practices. The method increases explanatory value due to a precise case selection. A case consists of a certain foreign policy in a certain diplomatic community in a certain period. In addition to a specific research question, a well-defined and time-constrained focus is necessary to achieve the highest possible explanatory value. One could imagine focusing on specific events, such as summits or bilateral meetings, a certain policy, or certain actors to gain a higher explanatory value. As elaborated in the empirical section below, findings might range from a wide scope of independent decision-making authorities to a culture of influential power. For example, in the German case described later in this chapter, in modern forms of representation an enlarged authority of diplomats has been observed. Additionally, practices in Economic diplomacy were shaped by tensions between different ministries and responsibilities of leading directorates.

Methodological assumptions. Regarding methodology, archival research is based on Hegel's and Weber's understanding of the state as a bureaucracy in which administrative processes and political decisions can be traced. This includes written rules, an impersonal order, a clear division of labor, and a meritocratic principle (Weber 1980: 124–130). The written deposits of administrative action and procedure are files (Beck 2000: 67). Following Max Weber's theory of bureaucracy, described in *Economy and Society* (1921), the ideal administration is a legal-rational bureaucracy, following a steady process called *modernization*. Weber shared a consciousness of the German bureaucratic tradition based on Georg Wilhelm Friedrich Hegel's *Philosophy of Right* (1820), both sharing their conception of a powerful state in view of the Prussian administrative tradition. In-depth analysis of official files serves as one method to study "the paper trail that diplomats leave behind" and thus tell something about their deepest taken-for-granted ideas (Bjola and Kornprobst 2020: 90 ff.).

Archival research is based on textual analysis and is, therefore, dependent on textual formalization. The administrative language and the specific style of diplomatic *Notes* allows a precise analysis of foreign policy processes based on these texts. Starting with the structure, diplomatic archives are organized either by departments or by subjects. In the German Federal Foreign Office (FFO), for instance, one must study different organizational plans to understand the departmental organization of each period and therefore understand the location of the original source in the logics of the archive, which is revealing an organizational logic *per se*. It has proven to be especially efficient to look into *drafts to the direction* that are addressing secretaries of state and the foreign minister, and then identify the occurrence of topics related to the different fields of diplomacy.

Besides understanding the archival organizational structure, a differentiated knowledge of different sources and artifacts is necessary. Different versions of one document may exist in the different departments which signed or edited the file. These different versions of the very same document can reveal information about the intra-ministerial processes and policies. As explained by historians of the *Marburger Archivschule*, a renowned educational institution of the German state archives system and group of researchers in archival studies, file numbers or stamps may indicate to which departments a copy was sent in advance, allowing to trace the decision-making process (Beck 2000: 68). The challenge of archival research is to find, retroactively, all versions of the files. Further, we have to consider the category of diplomatic files called *diplomatic notes* sent from representations around the world, or *drafts to the direction*, which are used particularly within the foreign ministry itself. These documents might vary from one country to another, and they are highly formalized, being closely linked to the diplomatic culture and bureaucracy of a country.

As an example, in the preface of *Die Einheit*, Tim Geiger and Heike Amos (2015: 50 ff.) provide a useful guide to read files of the German political archive of the FFO. Accordingly, we must differentiate between different sources. Regarding FPA, the study of drafts to the direction are of uttermost importance, as they often contain instructions and are passing through the whole bureaucratic hierarchy. One can differentiate between *Informationsvorlagen* (drafts for information) and *Entscheidungsvorlagen* (drafts for decisions). When it comes to diplomatic correspondence, different telexes from headquarters of the FFO to the foreign diplomatic missions are called *Drahterlass* (often contain directives and instructions) or *Drahtbericht* (often of informative character). Whereas in past decades, most of the decrees and reports were sent via telegram, thus via wire, which corresponds to the German word "Draht", nowadays the correspondence is affected in a digitally secured system. They can further be classified by their group of recipients. Additionally, these telexes can be sorted by priority: *Cito* (urgent), *citissime* (very urgent), *citissime nachts* (as urgent as to inform the director at night), as shown in the example of a chemical contamination hazard in Mogadishu below (Figure 29.1).

The same priority system exists in the internal communication of the German FFO: *Normal* (NO, urgent), *Blitz* (BL, very urgent), *Blitz-Nachts* (BN, as urgent as to inform the director at night).

Further, we can analyze *Rotstrichinformationen*, which are red bars framing the document and indicating different degrees of confidentiality. Degrees of confidentiality are also indicated by stamps *streng geheim* (top secret), *geheim* (secret), *vertraulich* (confidential), and *nur für Dienstgebrauch* (NfD, only for official use).

Moreover, there are written notes, documenting all kind of matters. They can be useful records of conversations or telephone calls and therefore fix verbal conversations of interest to the analyst.

Additionally, general correspondence from the German FFO to diplomats is highly formalized. One can distinguish between *letters* and *notes*. Whereas letters are correspondence

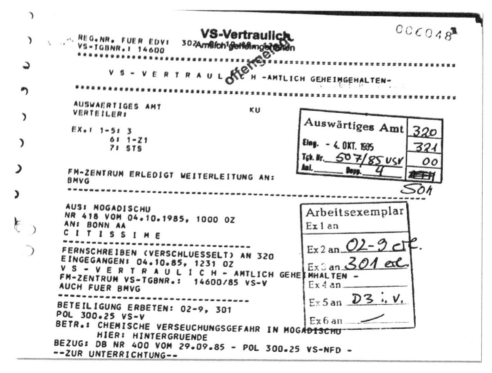

Figure 29.1 Telex 418 from Mogadischu on October 4th, 1985, see annotations "VS - vertraulich" (confidential) and "citissime" (very urgent).
Source: Politisches Archiv des Auswärtigen Amts, Doc. B 150-AAPD/247.

between two heads of state, the foreign ministers, or secretaries of state address other ambassadors in *Personalnoten* (diplomatic notes), *Verbalnoten* (verbal notes), or *Rundnoten* (circular notes). A *Démarche* or *Aide-memoire* is an informal record on official letterhead or a memorandum. A letter without any official signs is a *Non-paper* and often serves to explore positions. These documents are of particular interest in revealing positions and discretionary authority of different state officials and diplomats.

Another category of sources are memos or notebooks of ambassadors themselves, often conserved within diplomatic archives. They share *a posteriori* a more personal view on historical events – differing from the very formalized style of official documents.

Scope of analysis. Archival research in FPA shows great potential, as most bureaucratic states guarantee to record all official communications in their diplomatic archives. The main interest of a researcher applying archival research is to understand historical decisions by trace, compare, and categorize foreign policy. However, it has to be stated that archival research has a rather low predictive power for foreign policy due to the time gap in publication: A 30-year closure period occurs for most diplomatic documents worldwide before they are disclosed and made available to the general public. Combined with other methods, such as ethnography (see Neumann in this volume), the predictive power for foreign policy can be increased (Lequesne 2019). Recent findings from ethnography can be compared with historical findings of archival research to show the evolution of diplomatic practices over time.

Key terms and nature of official (diplomatic) files. Regarding the nature of official files, I will engage in *genetical* archival studies, analyzing the processual development of a document and therefore tracing decisions and positions. General diplomatic correspondence can be found in diplomatic conversations around the world (for a detailed overview of documents in the German FFO, see the material section). Diplomatic documents in France are called *Notes diplomatiques, Note verbale, Courrier formel (CF, circular letter), Aide-memoire,* and *Non-paper.* The United Kingdom Foreign and Commonwealth Office uses *Notes, Notes verbales, Collective note, Bouts de papier (speaking note), Démarches and Aide-memoire* or *Non-papers.* General diplomatic correspondence between a state and an international organization is also written in the form of letters or notes. Correspondence between states and the European Union (EU) is labeled as *COREUs* (CORrespondance EUropéenne). A very similar system can also be found in the United States Department of State with the *Note Verbale, Memorandum, Aide-Memoire, Pro Memoria, Note Diplomatique, Note Collective,* or *Circular Diplomatic Note.* Further, there exist *Letters* and *Congressional Letters.* The specific practices written down in diplomatic correspondence, following similar rules and codes to ensure communication between different countries, serves therefore as excellent material for the study of foreign policy.

Diplomatic Practices. When it comes to key terms for archival research, researchers can apply analytical categories to identify (diplomatic) practices within the primary sources. Following Jérémie Cornut and Vincent Pouliot, from a practice theory approach diplomacy can be defined as an "historically and culturally contingent bundle of practices that are analytically alike in their claim to represent, protect, negotiate, report and promote a given polity to the outside world" (Cornut & Pouliot 2015: 299). For a focused and structured comparison, hereinafter, findings on three categories will be extracted from primary sources: the practice of *discretionary authority,* the practice of *negotiation,* and the practice of *representation.* Diplomats, therefore, do not only need extensive knowledge in the areas of representation, negotiation, and communication, but each MFA embodies a set of practices linked to these skills. This historically and culturally contingent bundle of practices then forms a diplomatic apparatus of a country. The comparison of larger period of time allows to elaborate diplomatic practices.

Discretionary authority, as the power to decide on a matter, serves as one key pillar to understand practices of diplomacy in IR theory and in diplomatic studies (Adler-Nissen 2015: 284 ff.). Perceiving diplomacy from a relational perspective which includes governing, Paul Behrens points out to diplomatic interference and the law. This means, to govern is to make authoritative decisions that steer power toward what is understood to be the public interest (Behrens 2017: 5 ff.). If diplomacy, following James Der Derian's definition, consists of reducing the estrangement between diplomatic actors (mostly states), it also consists of many bureaucratic bargains and compromises inside the state (Lequesne 2017).

Second, following the relational approach, we can identify *practices of negotiation* from primary sources. When it comes to negotiations, these can be looked upon as the representation of the state's interest, which are conveyed through the diplomat's instructions and national positions. Therefore, diplomacy, including protocol and manners, keeps open a possibility of conversation, even in case of conflict (Warren 2006: 175).

In addition to the concept of discretionary authority, *representation* is a constituting practice of diplomacy. Representation can be defined as a main task of a diplomat according to international law (Art. 3 of Vienna Convention of 1961). According to Jennifer Mitzen, in the diplomatic sphere, representation has two meanings: First, the diplomat represents the state's interest in the sense of conveying a set of beliefs and preferences to other states. Second, diplomacy as representation can refer to how diplomatic practices embody the state on the world stage, making it possible for the state to appear to others as a social actor pushing interest and capable of negotiating (Mitzen 2015: 115). We can further differentiate between traditional tasks of representation and modern forms of representation.

The categorial framework is dependent on the research question and setting and interest of research and can be exchanged with different categories of analysis. For archival research, it is particularly important to fix a set of categories in advance to study the material in a structured way.

When it comes to the methodological understanding of truth, Holger Berwinkel describes the document flow of a diplomatic document in the following quote:

> On the way up, the document collects imposed notes from the intervening instances, with which it is endorsed, supplemented, modified or rejected, but without obscuring the original intention, because the original text of the draft remains.
>
> *(Berwinkel 2017: 264).*

Internal correspondence represents a qualitatively and quantitatively excellent transmission of diplomatic events and official state positions, allowing the reconstruction of the decision-making process within an authority (Berwinkel 2017: 263). However, in the study of historical documents, subjective bias, particularly linked to the author of the document, must always be considered. This subjectivity can be reduced by the research design and comparison. A statement with a high degree of truth can only be made by very precise reconstruction of the facts, for example, by comparing different files of different authors. There is still a chance that important events are not documented in writing, are missing, are not or will not be disclosed by state officials. Further, we have to consider a certain political orientation in documents and directives given by an administration at a certain time, influencing the structure and orientation of files. Berwinkel, for example, describes the development of the nature of German *Leitungsvorlagen* (drafts to the direction) as a part of administrative orders (ibid. 261). For example, the different styles of directives under different ministers of foreign affairs are referred to as a "clear, dispassionate formulation, strict sequences of thoughts, objective presentation of the facts, unreserved disclosure of all motives and careful consideration in expression and judgment" (Carstens 1971: 222) as the prevailing style of diplomatic correspondence since German Foreign Minister Hans-Dietrich Genscher.

Under consideration of the described pitfalls, it can be stated that the system of diplomatic correspondence and the intra-ministerial communication via documents is highly interrelated with essential decision-making processes of the ministry.

Concluding the archival studies section, the study of original documents bears a huge potential in order to analyze diplomatic practices, such as discretionary authority, the practice of negotiation, and the practice of representation. As specific practices – formalized in diplomatic correspondence – are following similar rules and codes to ensure communication between different countries, they serve as excellent study material on a worldwide scope. By choosing a FPA approach, archival research is focused on tracing intra-ministerial processes by analyzing archival documents of foreign ministries or other institutions. Whereas subjective bias, particularly linked to the author of the document, and disclosed and missing documents must always be considered, the research design and comparative cases can reduce subjectivity. As this process is bound to administrative rules and is documented, it presents a valuable, original source for reconstructing diplomatic practices.

Empirical Illustration

Empirical applications of the archival method may vary dependent on its combination with other methods chosen for a specific research project. One way of application is the study of specific foreign policy *fields*, such as demonstrated by Kim B. Olsen (2020) on the topic of economic sanctions as a form of diplomacy, looking into archives of the German and French Ministry of Foreign Affairs. Other applications might be to focus on *practices* and the bilateral relations of two countries, such as twinned cities between France and German as a diplomatic tool (Defrance 2021). For instance, in his introduction "Ministries of Foreign Affairs: A Crucial Institution Revisited" of *The Hague Journal of Diplomacy*, Christian Lequesne calls to launch more empirical research with a focus on contemporary diplomatic practices by comparative studies of MFAs. In general, he points to the need for "theories to explain relational ontology in the study of MFAs" (Lequesne 2020: 5).

Following the idea of combining archival research with practice theory, an internalist view on practices is necessary to qualify social actions as *social* by virtue of being constituted as meaningful within the internal domain of a practice (Adler and Pouliot 2011). Consequently, to study diplomatic practices, we need to study diplomatic drafts and papers defining the national interest, negotiation positions, and conversations between different agents of foreign ministries. Concretely, the following paragraphs demonstrate the steps involved in the application of archival research using practice theory. As an illustrative example, I will demonstrate the application of archival research in diplomacy with the use of practice theory by the following research question: "Under what conditions do discrepancies between representation and discretionary authority in diplomatic practices occur?" The issues raised are substantially linked to not only the question of the change of negotiation outcomes related to representation and authority but also the political influence of diplomats in the foreign policy-making process in the case of Economic cooperation in agriculture.

The application of archival research always starts with establishing an overview of accessible archives and sources and familiarization with the archival structure. Often, special permissions must be requested in advance to work in an archive. Researchers must check whether resources are available in digital form and if documents might be copied, photographed, or scanned. In some archives, only on-site work with the (declassified) documents is possible. Also, special rules regarding the number of documents accessed and availability have to be followed.

For example, to gain an understanding of the edition of Akten zur Auswärtigen Politik der Bundesrepublik Deutschland, a detailed overview of the development of the inventories has been provided by Ilse Dorothée Pautsch (2008). These editions consist of edited files, which have been worked on since 1990 under the lead of Horst Möller and can be seen as an international benchmark in the global editing of diplomatic files. To guarantee academic independence, the FFO transferred this task to the Institute of Contemporary History in Munich (IfZ), which established an editing group based in the Foreign Office, led by Ilse Dorothée Pautsch. She worked on the structure and history of the political archives located in Berlin.

> Since the temporal boundary is designed as a 'moving wall', one more volume of the AAPD will be available free of charge each year. Therefore, the Institute of Contemporary History is confident that in the future it will be able to make scientifically prepared files on the foreign policy of the Federal Republic of Germany available to an even larger public.
>
> *(Pautsch 2008: 39)*

The structure and profound analysis of archival documents requires a familiarization with the archive and archival structure. Especially when studying official documents, an overview of the ministerial structures and hierarchies is necessary to uncover the administrative journey a document has passed.

For example, in the case of Economic cooperation in agriculture in German Foreign Policy, documents can be analyzed linked to the Economy and trade policy. Looking at the organizational structure of the FFO after 1949 under Federal Minister of Foreign Affairs, Konrad Adenauer, one Directorate-General (DG) IV, named Trade Policy Directorate General, had two sub-departments, each with three sub-departments. Further, a state secretary was directly subordinated to the federal minister of foreign affairs. In the Political Directorate-General (II) further units are dealing with economic affairs. These are, for example, DG III (preparation of the peace settlement in the economic field), DG IV (Council of Europe), and DG VII (economy, Marshall Plan, international cooperation in the economic field). Later, DG IV continued to deal with issues of foreign economic policy, development policy, and European economic integration. The former Department 42 now became a separate subdepartment (42) with its own Department 422 for basic foreign economic policy issues. Basically, this organizational structure persisted until today.

The familiarization with the archive and archival structure enables the researcher to gain a proper overview of the available data and decide if the research question can be analyzed with the use of available material.

As a second step, I suggest defining the category of analysis. I recommend combining archival research with the method of structured, focused comparison to enhance methodological rigor. This is linked to the idea that by combining archival research with comparative analyses of multiple cases, generalizable practices can be identified. Following George and Bennett, this approach can minimize bias and over-generalization of results. The method is *structured* by testing the same hypothesis in every case study, thereby making systematic comparison and accumulation of the findings of the cases possible. The method is *focused* by analyzing only certain subjects within the cases (George and Bennett 2005). Categories for case comparison can reach different scopes and, therefore, determine the number and extent of each case. For example, different policies or diplomacy fields can be chosen in a least likely approach to compare different (foreign) policy fields. In diplomacy, these fields can also be observed in the bureaucratic structure of ministries of foreign affairs. I recommend choosing three to eight categories to narrow the scope of documents to analyze. Categories must be applicable to all documents, and in each country respectively. In the given example, the categories of *discretionary authority, negotiation,* and *representation* have been chosen to distill findings on diplomatic practices from documents dealing with agricultural policy in economic international cooperation.

By applying this array of categories to the entire chosen material from the archives, the researcher structures the research to draw analytical conclusions from the material.

In order to define a scope of material from which practices can be distilled, I recommend focusing on several case studies. When working with case studies, a pre-study of the historical context and policy field of the period is recommended. Therefore, news articles or yearbooks can be further sources to contextualize events and conduct an analysis taking into consideration historical circumstances. This is especially important in the field of foreign policy, where events in other countries might influence national decisions. Pre-studies also help to understand narratives and phrases used at the time, which can be misinterpreted without further contextualization. An excellent overview of foreign policy events on a yearly basis can be found on the websites of different diplomatic archives that inform on recently released material. A comprehensive list is published by the Office of the Historian[1] of the United States Administration, listing a guide to the accessibility of diplomatic archives around the world.

Once the theoretical case selection process has been finished, the latter is followed by a first review of original documents, confirming the availability and quality of material for each case selected. In this phase, the documents are read carefully. Further, different versions of one document may exist in the different departments which signed or edited the file. File numbers or stamps may indicate to which departments a copy was sent beforehand. The challenge is now to find retroactively all versions of the files to trace the process of a policy topic and identify practices linked to the process. To gain knowledge about the responsibilities and positions of different actors and departments, one can analyze the different signatures and annotations on the documents. This step leads to a detailed overview of the events and decision-making processes, the actors involved, and traces of practices in diplomacy.

Taking the example of Economic cooperation in agriculture in German Foreign Policy, the European Agricultural Conference, which took place in Paris in 1953, has been analyzed. In this case, the president of the German Farmers' Association, Hermes, was given authority to lead the negotiations at the European Conference to Organize Agricultural Markets.[2] In a letter from Ludwig Erhard, Minister of Economic Affairs at the time, the importance of two negotiators for the German Delegation is strengthened. Further, a close alignment and implication of a representative of the Ministry of Economic Affairs is requested, as the issues are linked to general politico-economical questions. The alignment of negotiation positions and support of the mandate given to representative Hermes is strengthened in another letter addressed to both the chancellor and the State Secretary Hallerstein by Prof. Ophüls, leading the Department of International and Supranational Organizations at the time. These correspondences underline the mandate for international trade negotiation for the German Delegation provided directly by Chancellor Adenauer.[3]

As a next step, transcription of archival material is necessary. As primary files and documents in archives exist mostly in a non-replicable form, a sort of working of the material is necessary. If archive material is analyzed on a computer-based system, a transcription of the archive material is necessary, using a software for qualitative content analysis, for instance. All documents, including annotations and headlines, must be transcribed in one unique format to analyze and code all written elements. This can be a challenging task, especially when it comes to handwritten notes and comments, which are important signs for procedural issues. Discussion on standards for transcription of documents are currently led by the *International Editors of Diplomatic Documents* (IEDD).[4] Further, abbreviations and receiver must be included in the transcript. Regarding instructions on transcription, various manuals are available; see, for example, Rehbein et al. (2004). Digitization of diplomatic material allows the analysis of larger datasets, already being transcribed. For example, a member of IEDD suggested to publish a series-wide corpus of documents as a database, rather than a collection of books meant to be read cover to cover.

The organization also provides an overview of elements of a diplomatic document,[5] as shown in Tables 29.1 and 29.2.

Documents also contain references to several kinds of *entities* relevant for the analysis:

With these steps of transcription, the researcher can pinpoint all relevant material, identify missing pieces, and judge on the further need for additional documents. Finally, by concluding this step all relevant material is ready for coding and analyzing.

Table 29.1 Elements of a Diplomatic Document Following Best Practices of the International Editors of Diplomatic Documents

Elements of a Diplomatic Document
Document type (e.g., memorandum, telegram)
Heading
Correspondence (sender, recipient)
Dateline (place, date)
Provenance
Classification and handling markings
Opener (e.g., salutation)
Subject lines
Body paragraphs, lists, tables
Closers (e.g., signatures)
Footnotes

Source: International Editors of Diplomatic Documents (IEDD).

Table 29.2 Entities of a Diplomatic Document Following Best Practices of the International Editors of Diplomatic Documents

Entities of a Diplomatic Document
People
Organizations
Places
Events
Agreements

Source: International Editors of Diplomatic Documents (IEDD).

The following Telex on the topic of monetary questions on the French-German summit of 1972 shows different elements mentioned above (Figures 29.2 and 29.3):

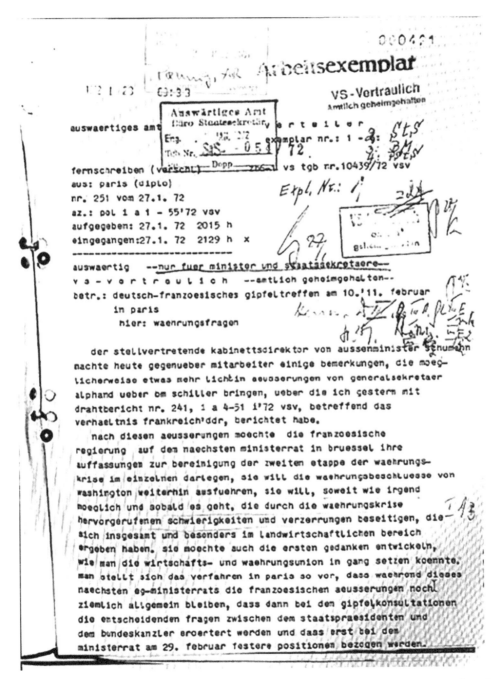

Figure 29.2 Telex on the topic of monetary questions on the French-German summit of 1972. *Source*: Politisches Archiv des Auswärtigen Amts, Doc. B 150-AAPD/628 (Part 1).

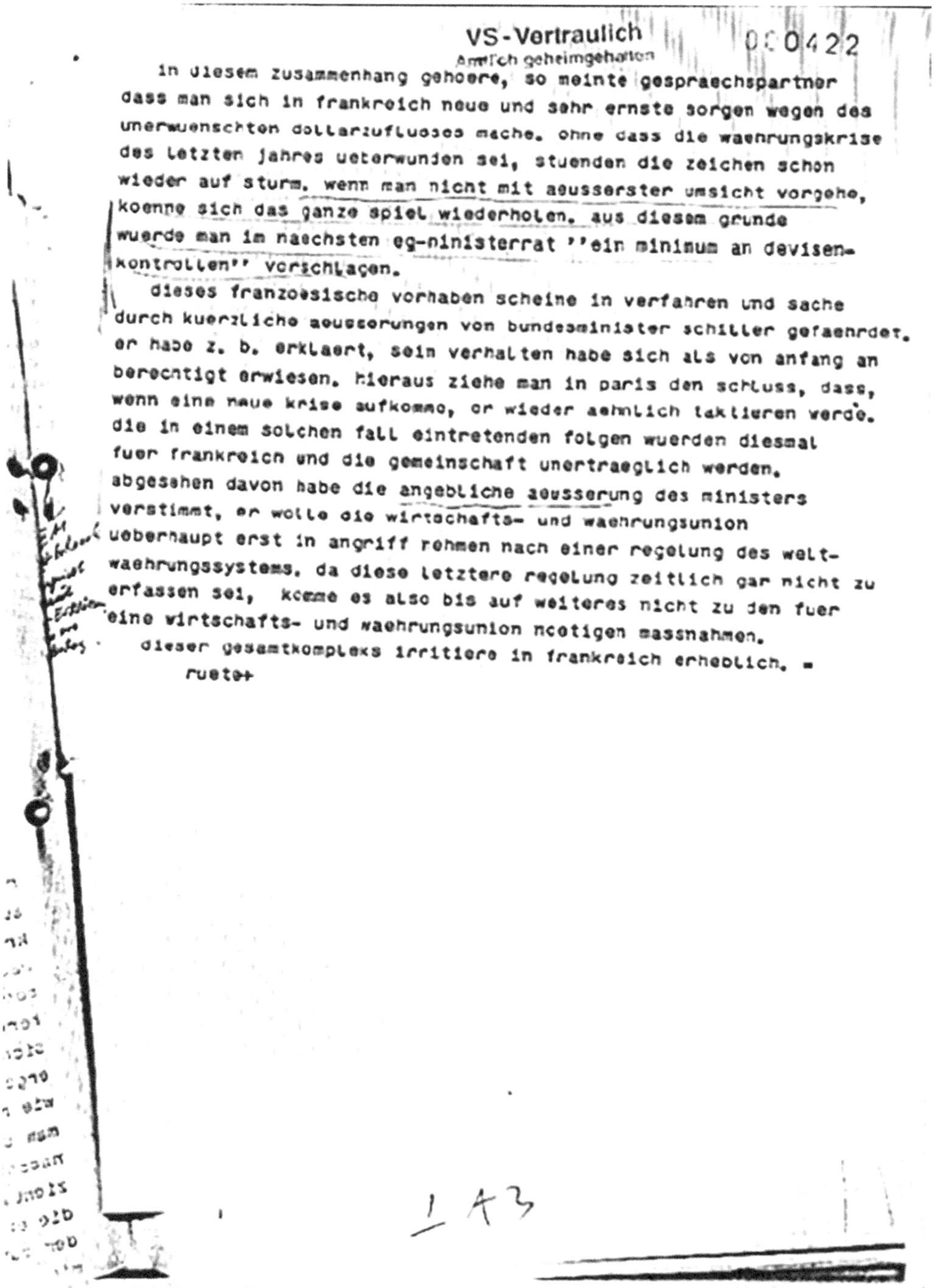

> VS-Vertraulich
> Amtlich geheimgehalten
>
> in diesem zusammenhang gehoere, so meinte gespraechspartner
> dass man sich in frankreich neue und sehr ernste sorgen wegen des
> unerwuenschten dollarzuflusses mache. ohne dass die waehrungskrise
> des letzten jahres ueberwunden sei, stuenden die zeichen schon
> wieder auf sturm. wenn man nicht mit aeusserster umsicht vorgehe,
> koenne sich das ganze spiel wiederholen. aus diesem grunde
> wuerde man im naechsten eg-ministerrat "ein minimum an devisen-
> kontrollen" vorschlagen.
>
> dieses franzoesische vorhaben scheine in verfahren und sache
> durch kuerzliche aeusserungen von bundesminister schiller gefaehrdet.
> er habe z. b. erklaert, sein verhalten habe sich als von anfang an
> berechtigt erwiesen. hieraus ziehe man in paris den schluss, dass,
> wenn eine neue krise aufkomme, er wieder aehnlich taktieren werde.
> die in einem solchen fall eintretenden folgen wuerden diesmal
> fuer frankreich und die gemeinschaft unertraeglich werden.
> abgesehen davon habe die angebliche aeusserung des ministers
> verstimmt, er wolle die wirtschafts- und waehrungsunion
> ueberhaupt erst in angriff nehmen nach einer regelung des welt-
> waehrungssystems. da diese letztere regelung zeitlich gar nicht zu
> erfassen sei, koenne es also bis auf weiteres nicht zu den fuer
> eine wirtschafts- und waehrungsunion noetigen massnahmen.
> dieser gesamtkomplex irritiere in frankreich erheblich. -
> rueter+

Figure 29.3 Telex on the topic of monetary questions on the French-German summit of 1972
Source: Politisches Archiv des Auswärtigen Amts, Doc. B 150-AAPD/628 (Part 2).

Based on the categories and practices linked to the research question, the transcribed material is now analyzed by applying the same coding scheme to all documents and therefore distilling traces of practices from the written documents. One helpful method proceeding in a structured manner can be Qualitative Comparative Analysis (see Mello in this volume). State of the art in relevant research projects today is qualitative data analysis with special-purpose software or computer-aided/assisted qualitative data analysis software, to provide support and systematization service for the interpretation work that continues to be carried out by the researchers themselves. For the development of a coding scheme, grounded theory can be helpful (Vollstedt & Rezat 2019). Mara Olekalns and Wendi L. Adair (2013: 313) provide an overview of different coding schemes for negotiation analysis in their *Handbook of Research on Negotiation*. As a negotiation-based coding scheme, the Cue-Response Negotiation Coding System of Donohue, Diez, and Hamilton serves as a good example for working with qualitative phrase coding, as it allows to code naturalistic negotiation interaction with a focus on confrontative, defensive, and integrative elements (Donohue 1984).

Once the selected material is chosen for each case study and the coding scheme has been established, the transcribed material is coded. Using *categories* and *codes*, all documents are analyzed in the same manner, assuring comparability and rigor. It is recommended to note missing categories and codes, as the process of coding improves in a repetitive manner and can – once the first case study is finished – be refined. The iterative process with several reviews of the original documents allows to refine precision of the categories and codes. The more a coding scheme gets refined, the more accurately the results serve for further analysis and categorization. Following the refinement of the coding scheme, the selected material is coded once again to apply new codes and refine the scope of analysis. By abductive reasoning, the aim is to achieve greater abstraction from the data material by bundling similar codes into superordinate categories.

Taking the example of Economic cooperation in agriculture in German Foreign Policy, the category *discretionary authority* can be analyzed by coding different practices. These can be traces of authority given to a diplomat, for example, an ambassador or a representative of a delegation by the chancellor or the minister of foreign affairs. The involvement of the chancellor is defined in the German Constitution by the *Richtlinienkompetenz* (Art. 65 GG). Nevertheless, the decision-making authority and formal jurisdiction over foreign policy as well as the bureaucratic resources and expertise that come with the MFA provide important agenda-setting powers and informational advantages. These can be linked to codes such as "involvement of a higher official", "alignment with further departments requested", or "mandate to lead negotiations", which are then translated into codes and identified in the material. One example is shown in the above-mentioned letter of Ludwig Erhard, mentioning the importance of two negotiators for the German Delegation, handing the authority to lead the negotiations at the European Conference to Organize Agricultural Markets to Hermes, president of the German Farmers' Association.

As another step, I suggest conducting an evaluation and comparison. It is important to state that the steps of coding and the steps of analysis require two different lectures of the document. Whereas the previous steps serve to structure and process the documents, the cases are not yet analyzed and interpreted. In the second lecture linked to the step of evaluation and comparison, an interpretative lecture is applied, linking the codes to the categories and interpreting them to answer the research question. Prevalent examples from the original documents may be cited in the study to sculpt the research. In addition to the detailed coding of the material and the formation of categories based on it, a summary case description is prepared for each case. Finally, comparisons of different categories for case studies are elaborated and serve as basis for the last step.

As a last step, the researcher conducts a deeper analysis and categorization of the chosen case studies, as illustrated on the example of Economic cooperation in agriculture in German Foreign Policy, putting together the pre-studies altogether and linking them to results of the coding analysis. The defined categories – discretionary authority, negotiation, and representation in our example – can be further elaborated in the cross-case analysis, allowing larger comparison between different diplomatic services and generalization in categories. Ideally, these categories are based on FPA theories and provide further explanatory empirical value to theories.

Concluding with the given example, the studied cases showed that the practice of diplomatic negotiations is closely linked to discretionary authority provided. This might range from a wide scope of independent decision-making authorities to a culture of influential power. In the given case, modern forms of representation and an enlarged authority of diplomats have been observed. Further, practices in Economic diplomacy were shaped by tensions between different ministries and responsibilities of leading directorates. The creation of permanent departments of specific representatives centralized responsibility. A change of competency or the centralization of the topic toward the chancellor impacts the scope of negotiation and representation in foreign policy issues. Further, the scope of discretionary authority and the relation between domestic and international politics have also been discovered as influential in the examples of economic cooperation about agriculture.

Conclusion

The specific strength of archival research is the work with primary sources allowing a first-hand view on original documents and foreign policy processes. Due to the increase of official records in the last century, the number of potential case studies and interesting foreign policy processes to be analyzed is increasing exponentially. Diplomatic archives serve as a rich and comprehensive source of scripted practices of diplomats as a community of practice. Archival studies can consequently reveal decision-making power and negotiation processes by following documentary paths. The recent democratization of information has resulted in a push toward greater accountability and transparency for government officials, including diplomats, that can be useful for archival analysis by publishing further material of public interest.

Recent trends in archival research are linked to an increasing number of registered official documents and stable conditions in growing national archives, which are often starting to be digitized. The method of archival research *per se* is not restricted in quantity or scope of analysis and can thus be combined with various other quantitative or qualitative methods. A whole new potential opens up with the digitization of archives, which make quantitative analyses easier to conduct and cross-country comparison easier to access. The digitization of material provides, therefore, an enormous research potential worldwide. In their best practices described above, the *Text Encoding Initiative* provides a *de facto* standard in the digital humanities for encoding text and is the format recommended by IEDD, adopted by diplomatic documentary editions for their text. Combining historical finding of archival research with ethnographic studies of diplomacy, for example through expert interviews of diplomats, guides us toward more recent foreign policy process. Several scholars of diplomatic studies, such as Christian Lequesne or Jan Melissen, call for research theorizing FPA in relation to diplomacy, among others regarding practices (Lequesne 2020; Melissen 2020: 219). Only a limited number of empirical studies based on deep archival research exists and must be conducted on a larger scope.

One critical point of archival research is still the lack of predictive capacity. With the faster indexing of archives and their digitization, it may be possible to conduct more timely research, which is, nevertheless, not valid for classified archives. As the most recent development, the accessibility and digitization of files makes archival research much easier and more accessible. Even if original paper files and the work with microfiche has its own charm, digital documents accelerate the visibility and availability of the process, as described by the International Editors of Diplomatic Documents in the following: "Harnessing the indisputable advantages of digital distribution without compromising the proud traditions of diplomatic documentary editing, a discipline rooted in print publishing" (IEDD 2021). IEDD provides recommendations and best practices for digital diplomatic documentary editions. On this point, large differences remain in the accessibility of archives. Whereas for example the United States' *Edition of Foreign Relations of the United States* (FRUS) or Switzerland's *Diplomatic Documents of Switzerland* have started to work on a comprehensive digitization of their archives, other countries have not even established a public accessible analogue structure of their diplomatic documents.

Potential problems and pitfalls for first-time use are particularly linked to the declassification and availability of original documents. Not all documents in all archives are seamlessly preserved and without a clear archival plan, it is impossible to rediscover specific files in miles of documents. Some countries face complex release processes for diplomatic documents. Another prerequisite is the nature of a regime. Following Max Weber's bureaucratic theory, one might argue that archival research of state processes is only applicable in democratic bureaucratic regimes, as they tend to textualize and archive traces of their governmental processes. In authoritarian regimes, accessibility or preservation of archives might not be given. Further, due to regulation, a 30-year closure of official diplomatic documents is existing in almost all Western archives. Due to a specific public interest, specific documents might be disclosed earlier, and the accessibility of archives is evolving, for example, through pressure from the U.S. Freedom of Information Act. Further, comparability might be an issue, resulting from a limited access to archives and partly incomplete documentation. Finally, a cross-country comparison needs travel funds and profound language skills for the analysis of first-hand sources, which are always written in the national language.

To conclude, the method of archival research and record management of official documents bears unimagined potential for FPA. Due to the exponential increase of records in national archives, this method contributes an important part to the understanding of FPA by studying primary sources and distilling practices of diplomats as a community of practice.

Notes

1. Office of the Historian of the United States, accessible under https://history.state.gov/countries/archives/all.
2. Political Archives of the German Federal Foreign Office, Documents 1953 Dok. 372.
3. Political Archives of the German Federal Foreign Office, Documents PA AA B10 – 773; PA AA B150 – D2; PA AA B10 – 733.
4. https://diplomatic-documents.org.
5. https://diplomatic-documents.org/best-practices/digital-editions/.

References

Note: All electronic sources have been last accessed on January 14, 2022.

Adler, Emanuel & Pouliot Vincent, eds. 2011. *International Practices*. Cambridge: Cambridge University Press.

Adler-Nissen, Rebecca. 2015. 'Relationalism or Why Diplomats Find International Relations Theory Strange'. In: Sending, Ole Jacob, Pouliot, Vincent, and Neumann, Iver B. (eds.), *Diplomacy and the Making of World Politics*. Cambridge: Cambridge University Press. pp. 284–308.

Beck, Lorenz Friedrich. 2000. Leistung und Methoden der Aktenkunde bei der Interpretation formalisierter Merkmale von historischem Verwaltungsschriftgut. In: Brübach, Nils Hg (ed.), *Der Zugang zu Verwaltungsinformationen. Transparenz als Archivische Dienstleistung*. Marburg: Archivschule, S. 67–7.

Becker, Irmgard, Thomas Henne, Niklas Konzen, Robert Meier, Kai Naumann, and Karsten Uhde, eds. 2021. E-Government und digitale Archivierung. Beiträge zum 23. Archivwissenschaftlichen Kolloquium der Archivschule Marburg.

Berwinkel, Holger. 2017. Leitungsvorlagen in Ministerien als aktenkundliche Kategorie. Ihre Bedeutung für die Bewertung, Erschließung und Auswertung des Archivgutes. *Archivalische Zeitschrift*, 95(1), 261–286. doi:10.7788/az-2017-950114.

Behrens, Paul, ed. 2017. *Diplomatic Law in a New Millennium*. Oxford: Oxford University Press.

Beuth, Heinrich Wilhelm. 2005. Regiert wird schriftlich. Bericht, Weisung und Vorlage. In: Brandt, Enrico und Buck, Christian, Hg (eds.), *Auswärtiges Amt. Diplomatie als Beruf*. 4. Auflage. Wiesbaden: Verlag für Sozialwissenschaften, pp. 119–128.

Bjola, Corneliu and Markus Kornprobst, Markus. 2018. *Understanding International Diplomacy: Theory, Practice and Ethics*. Abingdon, Oxon, New York, NY: Routledge.

Carstens, Karl. 1971. *Politische Führung. Erfahrungen im Dienst der Bundesregierung*. Stuttgart 1971.

Cornut, Jérémie and Pouliot, Vincent. 2015. "Practice Theory and the Study of Diplomacy: A Research Agenda." *Cooperation and Conflict*, 50(3), 297–315.

Defrance, Corine. 2021. « Städtepartnerschaften in Europa. Eine alternative Form der Diplomatie im Dienst der Annäherung und der Kooperation », In Roland Behrmann, Friedrich Huneke, Julia Oppermann. *Zeitenwende '45 – Aufbruch in ein neues Europa*, Wochenschau Verlag, pp. 52–66.

Derrida, Jaques and Prenowitz, Eric. 1995. Archive Fever: A Freudian Impression. *Diacritics*, 25(2), 9–63. https://doi.org/10.2307/465144.

Donohue, William et al. 1984. Coding Naturalistic Negotiation Interaction. S. 403-425. In: *Human Communication Research*, 10(3) (Spring 1984). p. 405 ff.

Elman, Colin and Elman, Miriam Fendius. 1997. "Diplomatic History and International Relations Theory: Respecting Difference and Crossing Boundaries." *International Security*, 22(1). https://doi.org/10.2307/2539324.

Foucault, Michel. 2002. *The Archaeology of Knowledge*. London: Routledge.

Geiger, Tim and Amos, Heike. 2015. In Möller, Horst, Pautsch, Ilse Dorothee, Schöllgen, Gregor, Wentker, Hermann, and Wirsching, Andreas. *Die Einheit inDas Auswärtige Amt, das DDR-Außenministerium und der Zwei-plus-Vier-Prozess*. Institut für Zeitgeschichte. Vandenhoeck & Ruprecht, Göttingen.

George, Alexander L. and Bennett, Andrew. 2005. *Case Studies and Theory Development in the Social Sciences*. Cambridge, MA: MIT Press.

Greenstock, Sir Jeremy. 2013. "The Bureaucracy: Ministry of Foreign Affairs, Foreign Service and other Government Departments." In: Cooper, Andrew, Heine, Jorge, Thakur, Ramesh (eds.), *The Oxford Handbook of Modern Diplomacy*. Oxford: Oxford University Press, pp. 106–121.

Hill, Michael R. 1993. *Archival Strategies and Techniques*. Beverly Hills: Sage Publications.

Hudson, Valerie. 2005. "Foreign Policy Analysis: Actor-Specific Theory and the Ground of International Relations." In *Foreign Policy Analysis*, pp. 1–30. https://Doi:10.1111/j.1743-8594.2005.00001.x.

International Committee of Editors of Diplomatic Documents. 2021. "Best Practices for Digital Diplomatic Documentary Editions." https://diplomatic-documents.org/best-practices/digital-editions/.

Larson, Deborah. 2001. Sources and Methods in Cold War History: The Need for a New Theory Based Archival Approach. In: Elman, Colin and Elman, Miriam Fendius (eds.), *Bridges and Boundaries: Historians, Political Scientists, and the Study of International Relations*. Cambridge: MIT Press, pp. 327–350.

———. 2017. Archival Research in Foreign Policy. Oxford Research Encyclopedia of Politics. https://doi.org/10.1093/acrefore/9780190228637.013.389.

Lequesne, Christian. 2017. *Ethnographie du Quai d'Orsay. Les Pratiques des Diplomates Français*. Paris: CNRS Editions.

———. 2019. '*Studying Diplomatic Practices through the Lens of Direct Observation*'. London: Sage Research Method Cases.

———. 2020. Ministries of Foreign Affairs: A Crucial Institution Revisited. *The Hague Journal of Diplomacy*, 15(1–2), 1–12. doi: https://doi.org/10.1163/1871191X-BJA10003

Lustick, Ian S. 1996. History, Historiography, and Political Science: Multiple Historical Records and the Problem of Selection Bias. *The American Political Science Review*, 90(3), 605–618. https://doi:10.2307/2082612

Melissen, Jan. 2020. Consular Diplomacy's First Challenge: Communicating Assistance to Nationals Abroad. *Asia Pac Policy Stud*. 7, 217– 228. https://doi.org/10.1002/app5.298.

Mitzen, Jennifer. 2015. "From Representation to Governing: Diplomacy and the Constitution of International Public Power." In: Sending, Ole Jacob, Pouliot, Vincent, Neumann, Iver B. (eds.), *Diplomacy and the Making of World Politics*. Cambridge: Cambridge University Press, pp. 111–139.

Möller, Horst et al. 2015. *Die Einheit : Das Auswärtige Amt, das DDR-Außenministerium und der Zwei-plus-Vier-Prozess*. Institut für Zeitgeschichte, Vandenhoeck & Ruprecht, Göttingen.

Olsen, Kim B. 2020. Diplomats, Domestic Agency and the Implementation of Sanctions: The MFAs of France and Germany in the Age of Geoeconomic Diplomacy. *The Hague Journal of Diplomacy*, 15(1–2), 126–154. doi: https://doi.org/10.1163/1871191X-BJA10001.

Olekalns, Mara and Adair, Wendi L. 2013. *Handbook of Research on Negotiation*. Cheltenham: Edward Elgar Publishing Ltd.

Pautsch, Ilse D. 2008. "Die Akten zur Auswärtigen Politik der Bundesrepublik Deutschland" – ein Arbeitsbericht über die Erschließung der Bestände des Politischen Archivs des Auswärtigen Amts, In Der Archivar. Zeitschrift für Archivwesen, 61. Jahrgang, Heft 1, February 2008, pp. 26–31.

Potter, Philip B.K. 2010. 'Methods of Foreign Policy Analysis.' In Oxford Research Encyclopedia of International Studies.

Rehbein, Jochen, Schmidt, Thomas, Meyer, Bernd, Watzke, Franziska, and Herkenrath, Annette. 2004. Handbuch für das Computergestützte Transkribieren nach HIAT. Arbeiten zur Mehrsprachigkeit. (56). http://www1.unihamburg.de/exmaralda/files/azm_56.pdf.

Sending, Ole Jacob, Pouliot, Vincent, and Neumann, Iver B., eds. 2015. *Diplomacy and the Making of World Politics*. Cambridge: Cambridge University Press.

Trachtenberg, Marc. 2006. *The Craft of International History*. Princeton and Oxford: Princeton Universtiy Press.

Vollstedt, Maike, and Rezat, Sebastian. 2019. An Introduction to Grounded Theory with a Special Focus on Axial Coding and the Coding Paradigm. In: Kaiser, G., Presmeg, N. (eds.), *Compendium for Early Career Researchers in Mathematics Education . ICME-13 Monographs*. Cham: Springer, https://doi.org/10.1007/978-3-030-15636-7_4.

Warren, Mark E. 2006. "What Should and Should Not be Said: Deliberating Sensitive Issues." *Journal of Social Philosophy*, 37(2), 2006: 163–181.

Weber, Max. 1980. *Wirtschaft und Gesellschaft : Grundriß der Verstehenden Soziologie*. Überarbeitete Fassung. Tübingen: Mohr (Paul Siebeck).

Images

Telex 418 from Mogadischu on October 4, 1985, see annotations "VS - vertraulich" (confidential) and "citissime" (very urgent). Source: Politisches Archiv des Auswärtigen Amts, Doc. B 150-AAPD/247. https://politisches-archiv.diplo.de/invenio/direktlink/5a126e97-4211-4d07-a3d8-a84e4bb8178d/

Telex on the topic of monetary questions on the French-German summit of 1972. Source: Politisches Archiv des Auswärtigen Amts, Doc. B 150-AAPD/628. https://politisches-archiv.diplo.de/invenio/direktlink/440c6312-5c2d-46c6-b9de-1e17bcee26e4/

Part VII
New Technology, Social Media, and Networks

30
Big Data Analysis
Sebastian Cujai

Introduction

In principle, researchers can draw on a wide range of existing data sets to analyze foreign policy issues. In practice, however, inherent limitations often become apparent. The underlying research questions determine the regional focus, the inclusion of actors, or the specification of the period under investigation and thereby constrain the availability of information. Furthermore, the aggregation of information fosters the loss of valuable context. As a result, new projects often require the collection of additional information. At the same time, new research questions continually arise requiring further information for their empirical investigation.

Against this background, the Big Data phenomenon appears to be a blessing. In recent decades, various developments in information and communication technology have contributed to increased availability of information. One of these technologies is the Internet, which significantly improves the collection and the sharing of existing data. Social network platforms are another development, where users can generate their individual content. However, data are increasingly created as a by-product of technological processes. One example is the collection of positioning data by GPS-enabled mobile phones. These developments provide us with information about different regions of the world that were previously unavailable on this scale (Cukier and Mayer-Schoenberger 2013). Foreign Policy Analysis (FPA) can benefit enormously from this knowledge base in the form of official and unofficial, digitized, and digitally created documents, photos, videos, and audio files.

Therefore, this chapter addresses the question of how these newly available data can be utilized for the analysis of states' foreign policy. I first provide a brief overview of different efforts to describe the Big Data phenomenon, followed by a definition of key features from a social science perspective. I then look at previous contributions that use these newly available data to examine foreign policy issues. Afterward, I briefly discuss both the methodological-technical challenges of handling large, unorganized data and the existing approaches in social sciences. Building on this, I present a technical implementation of an information retrieval model. This script-based program identifies potential relationships between different entities (e.g., politicians, dates, topics) in large, unorganized text collections and allows for a verification of these results based on a detailed text examination. By simplifying the access to specific information, this script-based program becomes an extremely helpful tool in various areas of data processing and analysis. Besides these methodological-technical aspects, I also consider further challenges in dealing with large, unorganized text collections. In the empirical illustration, I then use the presented approach to identify information on salient issues related to the escalation process of the Russian-Georgian conflict (2004–2008) from a large number of news reports (4,876 text documents).

Defining Big Data and Literature Review

Historically, the Big Data phenomenon is the result of breakthroughs in information and communication technology in the context of the information revolution. Following these advances, the scientific community faces an increasing volume of available data. As a result, natural sciences have been forced to move beyond the currently prevalent and established methods of data storage and manipulation (Kuiler 2014). In this context, the term Big Data first appears in 1998 within a computer science article (Grossman and Pedahzur 2020). The volume of the newly available data decisively shapes the current understanding of Big Data.

In one of the first definitions, Laney (2001) specifies three characteristics to describe these newly available data. First, they have a large *volume* (i.e., at least terabytes). Second, they are created at a high *rate* (i.e., in or near real-time). Third, they are extremely *diverse* in their shape (i.e., format, structure, semantic). In the following years, several researchers continued to develop the definition by adding new characteristics (Kitchin and McArdle 2016). In contrast, other authors refer to the limited applicability of broader definitions. Their different characteristics result from attributions by different scientific disciplines, making the definition less precise for each discipline. For instance, while the social sciences often use large data sets, these are often much smaller and less complex to process than the data sets used in the natural sciences. Therefore, the volume is a less central feature of Big Data from the perspective of the social sciences (Grossman and Pedahzur 2020). Against this backdrop, some authors argue for a specification of defining characteristics.

To this end, some authors assess the significance of already named Big Data characteristics for the social sciences. One central characteristic is the *variety* of the newly available data which, for example, becomes visible in the different formats of the information (Grossman and Pedahzur 2020, 232). This variety quickly becomes a challenge as soon as this diverse information is stored in an unstructured form as part of a larger data collection. The processing of these large, diversely composed data collections requires the application of powerful computer equipment and software applications (Earl 2018). Accordingly, Big Data in social sciences refers to the availability of large, diversely composed data requiring the use of technical tools for the systematic extraction of the embedded information.

A closer look at the literature shows that several political scientists have already used large, unorganized data and computational tools before the current debate on Big Data (Grossman and Pedahzur 2020). They used computer programs to automatically capture political events (see also Raleigh and Kishi in this volume) from textual data and categorize them into cooperative and conflictual actions of varying intensity (Azar 1984; McClelland and Hoggard 1969). Many authors use these event data sets in their studies on interstate relations (e.g., Fordham 2005; Kleinberg, Robinson, and French 2012; Ward and Rajmaira 1992; see also Raleigh and Kishi in this volume). From the 1990s onward, we witness the emergence of further computer programs to identify political events (Norris, Beieler, and Schrodt 2017; Schrodt and Gerner 1994), new schemes to code actions and their intensity (Bond et al. 2003;

Schrodt and Gerner 2004), and new event data sets building on these efforts (Althaus et al. 2019; Boschee et al. 2015). Likewise, the well-established *Correlates of War Project* optimizes the data collection process by using computer-based applications to reduce the workload of human coders (D'Orazio et al. 2014).

Besides the longstanding research on event data collection, some recent projects use large, unorganized data to examine foreign policy issues as well. The article by Zeitzoff et al. (2015) identifies key interest groups in the context of the Israeli-Iranian conflict using social media data and web blogs on Iran's nuclear program. O'Halloran et al. (2019) gather a large collection of texts and images from various sources (Twitter, Instagram, Flickr, Dabiq Magazine) to analyze violent extremist discourse in the context of the Islamic State. For their investigation, they apply a mixed-methods approach combining computational approaches with discourse analytical perspectives. Katagiri and Min (2019) investigate the credibility of public and private signals in interstate relations by digitalizing 10,000 declassified documents on U.S. decision-makers' assessments of Soviet propensity to use force in the context of the Berlin crisis from 1958 to 1963. Finally, data are quantified and analyzed through statistical methods. Trubowitz and Watanabe (2021) search for a solution to identify the threat perception of U.S. decision-makers in international relations. They collect news coverage of *The New York Times* from 1861 to 2017 via the news portal's application programming interface (API). Thereafter, they analyze the data with the help of semi-supervised machine learning models.

From a social science perspective, Big Data refers to data that require computer-assisted processing due to their size and diverse composition (Earl 2018; Grossman and Pedahzur 2020). As shown in this literature review, existing studies already employ various computer-assisted techniques for the collection and analysis of information on foreign policy phenomena. In this context, the authors often transform the information into highly structured data sets to perform the analysis. This procedure has the side effect of losing valuable context information. In the next section, I deal in more detail with the computational processing of large, unorganized data.

Key Terms, Concepts, and Methodology

In this section, I start with some general reflections regarding the handling of Big Data, before I take a closer look at the developments in FPA so far. Building on this, I present the implicit entity network approach as a useful supplement to existing techniques. Finally, I highlight further challenges in dealing with large, unorganized text collections.

In the context of Big Data, some authors observe the increasing investigation of social science issues by other disciplines such as computer science (King 2011). These investigators usually possess large amounts of unorganized data and modern analytic techniques, giving them an advantage in this research field (Diaz-Bone, Horvath, and Cappel 2020). Thus, computer-based text analysis tools emerge which identify topics, attitudes, and feelings. While these tools provide a great deal of support, it remains questionable whether they can replace human abilities for nuanced interpretation and subtle understanding of social context (Eldridge, Hobbs, and Moran 2018; Hesse et al. 2019). Therefore, many authors see an increased need for social science expertise in this context and advance two main arguments. First, the complexity of large, unorganized data collection hinders the identification of meaningful information. The use of theories, concepts, and hypotheses provides valuable guidance for data collection and analysis. Second, the emerging correlations do not necessarily imply causality. To interpret findings, social scientists have extensive knowledge about societal issues and processes (Grossman and Pedahzur 2020; Zwitter 2015). Accordingly, data processing requires social science as well as technical expertise to avoid reductionist or flawed explanations of social processes (Kitchin, 2014, 5).

In FPA, established and new techniques are used in dealing with large, unorganized data. A more recent approach is the use of text-as-data methods that quantify texts using computer-based applications (see also Vignoli in this volume). These programs typically parse the text into specific analytical units (e.g., paragraphs, sentences, or individual words). Afterward, they use statistical methods (e.g., frequency of occurrence) to analyze the quantified data (Welbers, Van Atteveldt, and Benoit 2017). Due to information aggregation, these approaches usually lose valuable context information.

As an alternative, I present a technical solution that uses a network approach to extract and explore information from large text collections. The script-based program identifies potential relationships between different entities (e.g., politicians, dates, topics) in large text collections and allows for a verification of these results based on a detailed text examination. This approach thereby combines the strengths of quantitative and qualitative approaches by uncovering both broad patterns and underlying details.

The complexity of large text collections requires technical solutions that harness such data for FPA. For this purpose, I draw on the extensive research on implicit entity networks (Spitz 2019; Spitz and Gertz 2016, 2018). The approach builds on the common assumption in distributional semantics that words in the environment of another word are directly related to it (see Firth 1962, 11). These relationships represent implicit networks within a text, which can be extracted automatically using a network approach.

Figure 30.1 illustrates the process of automated network extraction. After the creation of a large text collection, the approach looks at each text, treating each sentence as a unique set of words. Thereby, the algorithm searches for words that belong to a predefined category, called entities. These entities represent topics to which a special significance is attributed

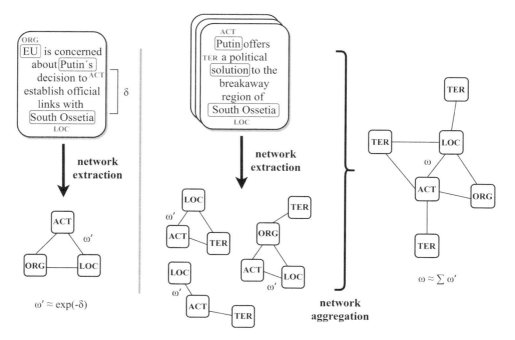

Figure 30.1 Information retrieval using implicit entity networks (see Spitz 2019).

in the context of the investigation (e.g., actors and locations). The identified words in the text document constitute the nodes of the network (e.g., "Putin" and "South Ossetia"). Afterward, the algorithm calculates the relationships between these nodes in two consecutive steps. First, the co-occurrence of words within the text is determined. Second, the model defines the weight of this connection (ω') by determining the distance between the occurring words (δ). The weight diminishes exponentially with the distance between the two words. The algorithm then repeats the described procedure for each document and thereby extracts the networks for all text documents. In the final step, the algorithm merges the networks from each text into one comprehensive network that contains all identified relationships in the text collection. This network also combines the weighting of the repeatedly occurring relationships (ω), revealing their relevance for the entire text collection (Spitz 2019, 35ff). The authors not only demonstrate the model's functionality using a text collection consisting of all English Wikipedia pages[1] but also emphasize the approach's applicability to other text forms (Spitz, Almasian, and Gertz 2017; Spitz and Gertz 2016).

The model was originally developed to identify events (Spitz and Gertz 2016). However, concerning its applicability for FPA, it is important to note that the underlying logic is not limited to this field of application. The network approach can uncover a wide variety of relationships and their relevance within any text collection. Therefore, the presented approach can be applied flexibly for different research questions.

For this purpose, the user can adjust settings at two points. The first option is via the composition of the document collection. In principle, this collection can contain any machine-readable text. The second possibility exists with the compilation of entities according to our research topic. After selecting central entities (e.g., state leaders), we can compile a word list that stands for the respective entities (e.g., Putin and Saakashvili).

For the compilation of entities and word lists, three approaches are thinkable. First, the researcher can proceed deductively by selecting concrete entities and the corresponding terms due to preliminary theoretical/conceptual considerations. Second, an inductive compilation of entities and word lists can be performed. For example, the researcher can choose terms from the text collection as the foundation for the entity-based word list. Third, it is also possible to select an iterative process as a hybrid form of the aforementioned approaches, allowing theoretical/conceptual considerations and inductive findings to complement each other. Certainly, the presented procedures always depend on whether the program is used for either an exploratory or a testing research approach.

The implementation of the implicit entity networks model was performed in the programming language R and focuses on the calculation of the entity networks.[2] The script-based programming relies on various R packages and benefits from the free access to these resources. The network extraction process takes place in several steps. In the following, I discuss the programming features for each step. The first step is to load the individual texts from the document collection into the program. The current version can only read plain text files (.txt). However, it is possible to read other common formats (e.g., .csv, .json) by extending the programming. When preparing the text documents, it is important to keep in mind that the algorithm identifies sentences by punctuation. This approach can cause errors as soon as dots appear within a sentence (e.g., in the case of dates), which are then interpreted as the end of the sentence. The program then offers two options for identifying entities. First, users can utilize the R package *openNLP* (Hornik 2019), which has a comprehensive dictionary containing word lists for different entities. With this option, they save time and effort by relying on predefined word lists for several entities. Second, users can create a customized dictionary, called a *gazetteer*. This dictionary contains an individually composed selection of entities and the corresponding word lists. Regardless of the choice, the used terms cannot consist of multiple words (e.g., European Union), because the algorithm regards them as unrelated due to the spaces in between. In the next step, the program identifies the implicit entity networks based on the already described model. Finally, the results are presented in tables and visualized with a graph. However, the graphical representation becomes unreadable with an increasing number of nodes and edges. Therefore, I prefer a tabular presentation of the weighted relations for further analysis.

Besides the methodological-technical aspects, there are further challenges when dealing with large, unorganized text collections. The first challenge is the acquisition of methodological and technical knowledge. Researchers can acquire this knowledge through advanced training programs. Thereby, the learning of programming skills is necessary to use common applications. In addition, social scientists require knowledge of essential web technologies (e.g., database management systems) as well as data collection techniques (Munzert et al. 2015). Alternatively, social scientists can establish collaborations with computer science to enhance their skills (Lazer et al. 2009). In recent years, we can observe the publication of many contributions that provide essential skills for handling large, unorganized data (Dalgaard 2008; Munzert et al. 2015; Urdinez and Cruz 2020). Furthermore, we are witnessing the emergence of computational social science as a new research field that investigates social behavior using computational methods and practices (see Alvarez 2016; Lazer et al. 2009; Salganik 2018). These developments considerably simplify the acquisition of required skills.

Another challenge arises from biases within the data occurring at various stages of data production. The coverage of news portals tends to be selective because their reports only offer an excerpt of all current political events. The location, the type, and the severity of the event are the main drivers influencing the likelihood of news coverage. In addition, the content may not necessarily be accurate or complete. Journalists often report from dangerous parts of the world. These circumstances complicate a precise representation of the local events. Their experiences also affect the interpretation of events, promoting unbalanced news coverage (Cook and Weidmann 2019; Weidmann 2015a). A similar effect can be observed regarding the data infrastructure of different service providers. The applied computer algorithms represent and prioritize certain worldviews, reproducing specific snippets of reality (Hesse et al. 2019; Kitchin 2014, 4f). This becomes apparent when looking at the APIs of some providers, which offer simplified access to their data inventories (Gonzalez-Bailon et al. 2012). An investigation of Twitter's API shows that the provided data neither correspond to the entire news inventory on the platform nor offer a representative sample (Morstatter et al. 2013). These results challenge the frequently held assumption that Big Data always implies a full data collection (Leonelli, 2014, 7). Data from social media platforms represent a special case because users proactively generate the content (Giest and Samuels 2020). This form of data generation encourages the conclusion that social media authors are a subset of the general public. But several observations disagree with this view. First, the usage of these platforms is not limited to citizens expressing their opinions. Companies, campaigns, and bots also use social media for their purposes (Keller et al. 2020; Zeitzoff, Kelly, and Lotan 2015). Second, the use of such platforms varies across the population. Some people lack the access or expertise to participate. Additionally, many users are rather passive, which means that a small group is responsible for a large part of the content (Hesse et al. 2019). A study of the 2009 German parliamentary election clearly shows that social media platforms like Twitter do not adequately reflect public opinion. The authors argue that the frequency of party references on Twitter can predict the electoral votes (Tumasjan et al. 2010). However, a closer look at their results shows that the small, but highly discussed, Pirate Party was mentioned in one-third of the Tweets, but it received only 2.1% of the electoral votes (Jungherr, Jürgens, and Schoen 2012).

These insights show that the given data are never absolute but shaped in many different ways (Dreier 2009, 16). This observation is not new but becomes relevant again due to the availability of new sources and data collections. Earl (2018), therefore, argues in favor of a reconsideration of already existing standards in social sciences. This includes that any research project that uses Big Data should address the production process of the used data. In addition, researchers should ask certain questions about the data material: from what is the data material a subset of? How complete is the material? Which information might be missing, intentionally or accidentally? What consequences does the data selection have for my results?

A further challenge is gaining access to the newly available data sources. Big Data is often owned by large private companies such as Twitter, Facebook, or news publishers. Given their economic value, access is often associated with costs. Using such data for research is then tied to the availability of financial resources. When funds are limited, other data collection strategies offer alternatives, such as web scraping or the usage of APIs (Diaz-Bone, Horvath, and Cappel 2020).[3] In this context, we need to consider legal standards in particular. Given my choice to use web scraping as data collection strategy in this contribution, I take a closer look at the prominent aspect of copyright issues. Due to the complex nature of this subject, the following insights are primarily intended to serve as a starting point for further inquiries.

The use of website content requires a closer look at the copyright regulations of the respective state. For example, the member states of the European Union have agreed on harmonization of digital copyright with the *Information Society Directive*, which aims to provide the greatest possible legal certainty for the various application fields (Schack 2017). As a result, the member states have established new laws regulating computer-assisted data collection for scientific purposes. In the case of Germany, the regulations now allow the systematic and automated duplication of data without the permission of the copyright holder, as long as this information is used for non-commercial research. However, this permission is limited to data that is unprotected by technical measures (e.g., robots.txt) and publicly accessible to third parties. Researchers can also make the collected data publicly available for collaborative research and peer review. However, they must completely delete the data after the research goal is achieved or the project is officially finished. Nevertheless, some institutions (e.g., libraries) are entitled to store all generated duplicates in an archive for non-commercial purposes (Hagemeier 2021). In other countries, such as the United States, the legal situation is less clear. Following the fair use principle, the U.S. copyright law is formulated as openly as possible to be able to react adequately to possible technological changes (Schack 2017). Given the cross-border accessibility of website content, the question of which legal text should be used arises. In principle, the *lex loci protectionis* says that the law of the state should be applied where the protection of intellectual property is requested. Because cross-border data traffic affects several legal systems, it is difficult to assign activities to a specific territory. In this case, it remains unclear which copyright law is applicable (RatSWD 2019, 48). Regarding variations within national regulations, Munzert et al. (2015, 278) review several legal disputes in the context of web scraping projects to get a better understanding of the legal situation. Their findings show that these disputes mostly involve cases where web scraping was used for commercial purposes. However, the authors conclude that the existing case law provides no clear guidance regarding the legality of web scraping procedures.

In light of the remaining lack of legal certainty, the informal rules of Munzert et al (2015, 285) are a very helpful orientation. After identifying interesting content on a website, we should start by checking the accessibility of the required information via an API. If no interface exists, there is still a possibility that the required information is already stored in a structured form. If this assumption turns out to be reasonable, we can ask the website owner for data access. After ruling out these possibilities, we access the robots.txt file in the website's root directory (e.g., www.nytimes.com/robots.txt). This file specifies what information we are allowed to duplicate. Finally, we should check the terms of use to determine if the operator explicitly prohibits the content's duplication via web scraping. If nothing speaks against the web scraping approach, it is necessary to pay attention to the existing etiquette regarding the implementation. It encourages us to remain identifiable during the web scraping process, to keep the collected material to a minimum, and to avoid bombarding the server with requests. Besides these practical implications, these direct or indirect access restrictions imply an enormous influence of data-producing companies over knowledge production (Diaz-Bone, Horvath, and Cappel 2020).

To sum up, the presented information retrieval approach extracts all relationships between predefined entities and weights them by relevance for the entire text collection. The identified relationships can be examined in the text to check interpretation and gain new insights. Due to its adaptability, the approach allows the researcher to customize the network extraction according to project-specific considerations. The script-based program provides all the basic features of the model. At the same time, the use of the R programming language offers the opportunity to make various extensions and revisions. Regarding the diverse challenges in dealing with large, unorganized data, we still observe a lack of technical knowledge that can easily be tackled through advanced training and cooperation with computer scientists. However, some challenges, such as data biases, are well known but still require our heightened attention. Despite the availability of large quantities of data, the access is hindered by financial or legal restrictions. These challenges should be considered when we plan to use large, unorganized text data for our projects.

Empirical Illustration

In the following section, I examine salient issues in the context of an interstate conflict escalation. In doing so, I draw on existing FPA research on issue salience (Oppermann and Viehrig 2011). As an example, I focus on the well-documented conflict between Russia and Georgia in the period from 2004 to 2008. For identifying salient conflict issues, I supplement highly aggregated event data with extracted information from a text collection. Before I begin with the information retrieval process, I discuss in more detail the applied theoretical concept, the data material, and the gazetteer's composition.

As mentioned before, we can draw on different data sets to analyze current foreign policy questions. One option is the use of structured and highly aggregated data sets. Conflict research has made great progress in capturing conflict events in recent decades. For example, the *Integrated Crisis Early Warning System* (ICEWS) data set is one potential source for information on events in interstate relations (Boschee et al. 2015). For the Russian-Georgian relations, I use the ICEWS data set to determine the dynamics in states' conflict actions and to identify periods where escalation can be observed.

Figure 30.2 shows the intensity trend of Russian-Georgian conflict actions over some time from 1995 to 2019. To create this intensity trend, I first identify all events in Russian-Georgian relations in the ICEWS data set that constitute a conflict action. Next, I draw on the CAMEO scale to determine the conflict action's intensity. This scale classifies conflict actions into 12 intensity levels in ascending order (Gerner, Schrodt, and Yilmaz 2009). Building on this,

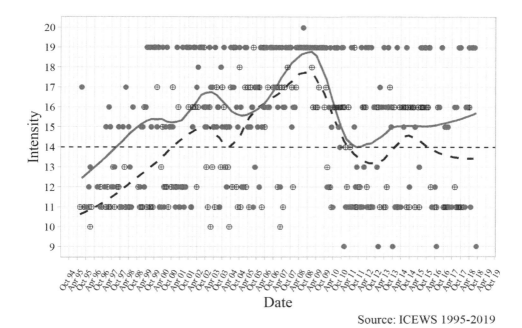

Figure 30.2 Intensity Trend of Russian and Georgian Conflict Actions from 1995 to 2019.

I generate the intensity trend of Russian-Georgian conflict actions. This choice is intended to uncover intentional state actions while excluding temporary interstate skirmishes. By looking at the trend line, we observe an escalation in the conflict actions of both states in the period from 2004 to 2008. When asking about the underlying conflict issue, the data set provides no further details. This is not surprising. Interstate relations are usually determined by multiple issues simultaneously (Diehl 1992). The extraction of such information is, thus, extremely complex.

Before I turn to the more technical aspects, I first consider several theoretical/conceptual aspects that guide the later information retrieval process. When measuring the salience of issues, a central question is: who attributes a high relevance to these issues (Black et al. 2011, 241). In line with the principal-agent approach (Przeworski 1999), the supporters' interest constitutes a crucial factor for the state leadership in determining the salience of an issue (Oppermann and Viehrig 2011, 7f). However, the decision-making process is built on the decision-makers' perceptions and their assessment of supporters' interest (McDermott 1998, 37). Accordingly, the current foreign policy most accurately reflects the perceived salience of an issue by state leaders. I, thus, identify salient issues by looking at the topics that are frequently mentioned in connection with the state leader's foreign policy.

To complement the existing event data, I draw on extensive reports from a Web-based news portal that promise more details about the context of interstate conflict events. In creating a text collection, we need to consider potential biases such as the selectivity problem (Cook and Weidmann 2019; Weidmann 2015b). One way of handling this problem is to collect texts from multiple news portals. However, I assume that salient issues are rarely absent from news coverage given their prominence. For this reason, I only select the Georgia-based news website *Civil Georgia* which offers extensive coverage of the Georgian-Russian conflict (Civil Georgia 2021). Before I start the data collection, I check the website for information about use restrictions (robots.txt and terms of use). After I could identify no restrictions, I start collecting the texts using a web scraping algorithm in R.[4] This script-based program runs a search query on the *Civil Georgia* website for the period from April 2004 till December 2008. Then, the program extracts the suggested news texts and saves them. After collecting the reports, I count 5,079 texts containing the terms "Russia" and "Georgia". In several steps, I filter the existing text collection to remove similar and irrelevant reports by using a script-based program. As already mentioned, the R application shows some peculiarities in its programming, so further preprocessing of the text data is required (e.g., adjustment of the date format or pairing of connected words). Finally, I have a document collection of 4,876 texts reflecting Russian-Georgian relations for the phase of conflict escalation.

In the next step, I create a gazetteer that contains the word lists for all used entities. I choose to create a gazetteer because this option gives me better control over the information retrieval. I only use three entities for the Gazetteer: Dates (DAT), actors (ACT), and terms (TER). The entity "terms" contains words that provide information about interstate affairs. Using an inductive approach, I identify all nouns in the document collection and then add all words to the list that occur more than 15 times. Thereafter, I delete words that reveal no further insights (e.g., titles, general descriptions). This inductive approach ensures that the unique characteristics of Russian-Georgian relations receive proper consideration. The entity "actors" consists of key decision-makers involved in the state's foreign policy (heads of state and government, foreign ministers, and defense ministers). This manually created list relies on available data in Wikipedia and includes the names, inauguration, and departure from office of the decision-makers. The entity "dates" includes the dates of all days within the period of investigation.

After the preparations are completed, the script-based program calculates the weighted relationships between the predefined entities. I then combine the saved results in a table, thus creating an overview of all identified weighted connections between entities. In addition,

Table 30.1 Selections of Identified Relations Sorted by Source Document or Weighting

Node1	Token1	Type1	Tode2	Token2	Type2	Weight	Doc_id	Documents
uid-23	burjanadze	ACT	uid-346	troops	TER	23.5	3266	Fears increase over …
uid-359	south_ossetia	TER	uid-48	baramidze	ACT	21.4	3266	Fears increase over …
uid-23	burjanadze	ACT	uid-300	peace	TER	45.3	3266	Fears increase over …
uid-190	accusation	TER	uid-357	26.10.2004	DAT	1	3266	Fears increase over …
uid-347	tskhinvali	TER	uid-48	baramidze	ACT	1.5	3266	Fears increase over …
uid-24	saakashvili	ACT	uid-359	south_ossetia	TER	626.7	1010	JCC on south_ossetia …
uid-24	saakashvili	ACT	uid-359	south_ossetia	TER	626.7	1013	Negotiators on south_ossetia…
uid-24	saakashvili	ACT	uid-359	south_ossetia	TER	626.7	1059	Saakashvili comments …
uid-24	saakashvili	ACT	uid-359	south_ossetia	TER	626.7	107	Russia sets deadline …
uid-24	saakashvili	ACT	uid-359	south_ossetia	TER	626.7	1097	Defense spending …

all news texts can be viewed where the relationships appear. Table 30.1 shows a sample of weighted relationships between the predefined words.

I now use this compilation for identifying salient issues in interstate relations. For this purpose, I first identify all connections between actors (ACT) and terms (TER) in the table. For the sake of clarity, I select only the state leadership of the two countries for further analysis. Then, I focus on the connections with the highest weights. I assume that this compilation of connections represents an adequate representation of salient issues in Russian-Georgian relations.

Figure 30.3 shows the 20 most frequently occurring topics in connection with the leadership of both states from 2004 to 2008. The visualization illustrates multiple overlaps among the state leaders. The frequency of the occurring relations suggests that the breakaway regions of South Ossetia and Abkhazia strongly shape Russian-Georgian relations. In addition, the frequent appearance of the United States points to an important external actor. Regardless of this first impression, many of the identified relations are abstract and require a closer background examination.

To learn more about the context of a specific relationship, I can consult the text where this connection occurs. However, the text size often hinders a quick overview. Therefore, I apply an algorithm that extracts only those sentences containing the searched relationship. As an example, I use this algorithm to get more information about the relationship between the actor "saakashvili" and the terms "south_ossetia" and "united_states". To give a better impression, Table 30.2 shows a selection of the identified sentences. The news snippets show that Saakashvili is striving for a solution regarding the breakaway region of South Ossetia throughout the entire period under investigation. The impression emerges that Saakashvili initially seeks a bilateral solution with Russia. In the following years, he looks for a domestic solution and increasingly involves international partners in the conflict resolution

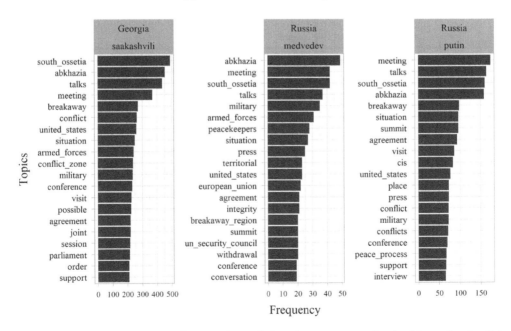

Figure 30.3 The most frequently occurring relations between state leadership and potential topics.

Table 30.2 A Selection of Identified Sentences[1]

Date	Sentences
01.06.2004	Georgian President Mikhail Saakashvili said that he held a phone conversation with his Russian counterpart, Vladimir Putin, on May 31 to discuss the situation in the breakaway region of **south_ossetia**.
30.07.2004	Moscow accused Tbilisi of escalating tensions in breakaway **south_ossetia** on July 30, amid conflicting reports over an exchange of fire near Tskhinvali, the capital of the self-styled republic.
26.01.2005	Georgian President Mikheil Saakashvili presented a vision for resolving the **south_ossetia** conflict at the PACE session in Strasbourg on January 26.
29.09.2006	President Saakashvili said in an address to the un_general_assembly on September 22 that Russia is annexing breakaway **south_ossetia** and Abkhazia.
28.03.2007	Tbilisi is intent on breaking the current peacekeeping and negotiating formats, resulting in the deterioration of the situation vis-a-vis Abkhazia and **south_ossetia**.
11.08.2008	Russia said it has sent troops deep into Georgian territory as far as Senaki, as part of its peace enforcement operation in **south_ossetia**.
10.07.2004	President Saakashvili held a phone conversation with **united_states** Secretary of State Colin Powell and **united_states** National Security Adviser Condoleezza Rice over recent crisis in Georgia.
13.05.2005	The issue of these military_base was discussed during the talks between Russian and **united_states** Presidents in Moscow on May 9.
04.06.2005	**United_states** President George W Bush held a phone conversation with his Georgian counterpart Mikheil Saakashvili on June 3 and discussed separatist conflicts and the recent deal with Russia over the withdrawal of military_base from Georgia, […].
28.11.2006	**United_states** President George W Bush said on November 28 that he has discussed Georgia with Russian counterpart Vladimir Putin during talks in Hanoi at the apec_summit this month.

[1] *The text snippets included in the table are from the text collection based on the extracted news stories from the Civil Georgia website (Civil Georgia 2021).*

process. Before the conflict escalates into an open military confrontation between Russia and Georgia, the Georgians increasingly appear disillusioned. Saakashvili's efforts are backed by the U.S. government which is proactively engaging in the conflict resolution process.

Besides the identification of salient conflict issues, the time of appearance is also important to connect the identified issues with the conflict trend. For this purpose, I assign the time of occurrence to the identified relations. The graphs show the time of appearance of the 10 most frequent relations (see Figure 30.4). The occurrence of the term "south_ossetia" remains constantly high over the entire period under investigation. According to this timeline, the breakaway region of South Ossetia is among the central interstate conflict issues. In contrast, Abkhazia, the other secessionist region, is mentioned far less frequently in connection with Saakashvili. This only changes with the military confrontation in 2008. The timing of the other relations offers further insights into the escalation dynamics. For example, we observe a frequent occurrence of the term "talks" in the first three years of Saakashvili's presidency, before this connection loses its relevance. This pattern supports my previous observation that the Georgian government increasingly becomes tired in its efforts to find a peaceful solution.

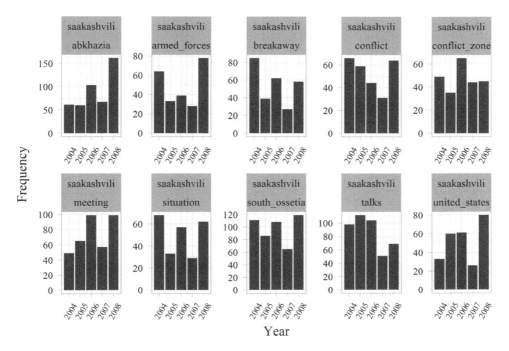

Figure 30.4 Appearances of relations over time.

In extracting information on salient issues in the Georgian–Russian conflict, the information retrieval approach proves to be very helpful. After extracting the weighted connections between predefined entities, the weightings suggest that South Ossetia is a central conflict issue for both state leaders. This interpretation is quickly verifiable by examining the text sections where these relations occur. The background review confirms my interpretation of the connection and reveals more information about the interstate conflict (e.g., the U.S. support of the Georgian government). Adding the time of appearance, we can also observe that South Ossetia, in particular, remains a salient issue for the Georgian side throughout the entire phase of conflict escalation. However, the contextual examination reveals a thematic overlap between terms linked to the Georgian leadership. These results suggest a need for more precision in the gazetteer's composition.

Conclusions

While volume is considered to be the defining feature of the newly available data, their diverse compilation represents a further critical factor for social scientists. These characteristics require the use of computer-assisted applications for information extraction. Therefore, learning fundamental programming skills is the first challenge in working with large, unorganized data. When looking for potential data sources, we see a wide range of platforms reporting on international relations. However, these platforms impose different restrictions (e.g., clauses in the terms of use, technical limitations) which hinder the data duplication for scientific purposes. Additionally, we have to consider the applicable copyright regulations. Besides these legal aspects, we also need to consider possible reporting biases.

Thus, the process of data collection is characterized by multiple considerations regarding methodological-technical knowledge, data access, and potential biases.

When dealing with large, unorganized text collections, researchers can flexibly apply the presented information retrieval approach according to their object of investigation. Searching for salient issues in interstate relations, I determine the text selection and the compilation of entities according to my theoretical/conceptual considerations. For example, I only select government officials for the entity "actors" who occupy a central position in the foreign policy decision-making process. After these preparations, the script-based program extracts all relationships between the predefined entities and weights them according to their relevance. In addition to this aggregated representation, the underlying information is still accessible for a background investigation. Building on this, the analysis of Russian-Georgian relations reveals strongly weighted relationships between state leaders and potential conflict issues, their temporal occurrence, and the underlying background. In this way, the script-based program assists the researcher in closing existing information gaps on salient conflict issues in highly aggregated event data sets.

Furthermore, the script-based program can be applied fruitfully to many other fields of data processing and analysis. To underline my argumentation with examples, I only present two possible ways of integrating the program into the research process. First, the application is suitable for a detailed case study in combination with established qualitative methods such as process tracing (see also van Meegdenburg in this volume). The program provides an overview of all relationships of interest within a topic-specific document collection, which facilitates a quick exploration of the case. In addition, the researcher can track interesting relationships in detail within the document. Second, the application simplifies the investigation of multiple explanatory factors for a larger number of cases by allowing the user to identify different relationships through the use of different entities. This option is particularly interesting for methods that assume complex causal relationships between multiple variables like Qualitative Comparative Analysis (see Mello in this volume).

However, the presented tool requires a high one-time technical effort, resulting from the creation of the document collection and the gazetteer. Therefore, the effort requires careful consideration of the benefits which are especially evident for larger projects or several thematically similar projects. In addition, it is important to note that the programming of the script-based program currently has some minor limitations. For example, the algorithm can only process one text format. However, these shortcomings can be quickly fixed with basic programming knowledge.

Currently, we observe the emergence of a new research field in the social sciences which develop the methodological-technical knowledge in dealing with large, unorganized data. On this path, considering the existing knowledge of the social sciences, we should explore a wide range of techniques to create a multifaceted, sophisticated toolbox for the demands of social science research.

Notes

1 4.6 million articles at the time of the data collection.
2 The R-script version of the code was implemented in a software project by Katja Hauser. The implementation can be accessed from the following repository. For further information, refer to the enclosed README file. https://github.com/katjahauser/ImplicitNetworksInR.
3 Web scraping describes a procedure for extracting specific information from websites to generate structured data for further processing (Khalil and Fakir 2017, 99). An API refers to the program

part of a software system that allows other programs to connect to the system. In my contribution, I especially refer to interfaces offered by web services (Munzert et al. 2015, 12, 259).
4 The R-scripts used here are available in the following data repository: https://osf.io/q9wkc/.

References

Note: All electronic sources have been last accessed on 30 November 2021.

Althaus, Scott, Joseph Bajjalieh, John Carter, Buddy Peyton, and Dan Shalmon. 2019. "Cline Center Historical Phoenix Event Data. Cline Center for Advanced Social Research. v1.1.0." University of Illinois at Urbana-Champaign. https://doi.org/10.13012/B2IDB-0647142_V1.

Alvarez, R. Michael, ed. 2016. *Computational Social Science: Discovery and Prediction*. Analytical Methods for Social Research. New York, NY: Cambridge University Press.

Azar, Edward E. 1984. "Conflict and Peace Data Bank (COPDAB), 1948-1978: Version 4." Inter-university Consortium for Political and Social Research. doi:10.3886/ICPSR07767.v4.

Black, Ryan C., Amanda C. Bryan, and Timothy R. Johnson. 2011. "An Actor-Based Measure of Issue Salience. Information Acquisition and the Case of the United States Supreme Court." In *Issue Salience in International Politics*, edited by Kai Oppermann and Henrike Viehrig, 241–257. Routledge Advances in International Relations and Global Politics 91. London ; New York: Routledge.

Bond, Doug, Joe Bond, Churl Oh, J. Craig Jenkins, and Charles Lewis Taylor. 2003. "Integrated Data for Events Analysis (IDEA): An Event Typology for Automated Events Data Development." *Journal of Peace Research* 40 (6): 733–745. doi:10.1177/00223433030406009.

Boschee, Elizabeth, Jennifer Lautenschlager, Sean O'Brien, Steve Shellman, James Starz, and Michael Ward. 2015. "ICEWS Coded Event Data." Harvard Dataverse. doi:10.7910/dvn/28075.

Civil Georgia. 2021. "Homepage." https://civil.ge/.

Cook, Scott J., and Nils B. Weidmann. 2019. "Lost in Aggregation: Improving Event Analysis with Report-Level Data." *American Journal of Political Science* 63 (1): 250–264. doi:10.1111/ajps.12398.

Cukier, Kenneth, and Viktor Mayer-Schoenberger. 2013. "The Rise of Big Data: How It's Changing the Way We Think About the World." *Foreign Affairs* 92 (3): 28–40.

Dalgaard, Peter. 2008. *Introductory Statistics with R*. 2nd ed. Statistics and Computing. New York: Springer-Verlag. doi:10.1007/978-0-387-79054-1.

Diaz-Bone, Rainer, Kenneth Horvath, and Valeska Cappel. 2020. "Social Research in Times of Big Data. The Challenges of New Data Worlds and the Need for a Sociology of Social Research." *Historical Social Research* 45 (3): 314–341. doi:10.12759/HSR.45.2020.3.314-341.

Diehl, Paul F. 1992. "What Are They Fighting For? The Importance of Issues in International Conflict Research." *Journal of Peace Research* 29 (3): 333–344. doi:10.1177/0022343392029003008.

D'Orazio, Vito, Steven T. Landis, Glenn Palmer, and Philip A. Schrodt. 2014. "Separating the Wheat from the Chaff: Applications of Automated Document Classification Using Support Vector Machines." *Political Analysis* 22 (02): 224–242. doi:10.1093/pan/mpt030.

Dreier, Volker. 2009. "Wissenschaftstheoretische Und Methodische Anmerkungen Zum Konzept Der Daten." In *Datenwelten: Datenerhebungen Und Datenbestände in Der Politikwissenschaft*, edited by Kai-Uwe Schnapp, Nathalie Behnke, and Joachim Behnke, 1. Aufl, 9–18. Forschungsstand Politikwissenschaft. Baden-Baden: Nomos.

Earl, Jennifer. 2018. "The Promise and Pitfalls of Big Data and Computational Studies of Politics." *Partecipazione e Conflitto* 11 (2): 484–496. doi:10.1285/I20356609V11I2P484.

Eldridge, Christopher, Christopher Hobbs, and Matthew Moran. 2018. "Fusing Algorithms and Analysts: Open-Source Intelligence in the Age of 'Big Data.'" *Intelligence and National Security* 33 (3): 391–406. doi:10.1080/02684527.2017.1406677.

Firth, John R. 1962. "A Synopsis of Linguistic Theory 1930-1955." In *Studies in Linguistic Analysis*, edited by Philological Society, Repr, 1–32. Special Volume of the Philological Society. Oxford: Blackwell.

Fordham, Benjamin O. 2005. "Strategic Conflict Avoidance and the Diversionary Use of Force." *The Journal of Politics* 67 (1): 132–153. doi:10.1111/j.1468-2508.2005.00311.x.

Gerner, Deborah, Philip A. Schrodt, and Ömür Yilmaz. 2009. "Conflict and Mediation Event Observations (CAMEO): An Event Data Framework for a Post-Cold War World." In *International Conflict Mediation: New Approaches and Findings*, edited by Jacob Bercovitch and Scott Sigmund Gartner, 287–304. New York: Routledge.

Giest, Sarah, and Annemarie Samuels. 2020. "'For Good Measure': Data Gaps in a Big Data World." *Policy Sciences* 53 (3): 559–569. doi:10.1007/s11077-020-09384-1.

Gonzalez-Bailon, Sandra, Ning Wang, Alejandro Rivero, Javier Borge-Holthoefer, and Yamir Moreno. 2012. "Assessing the Bias in Communication Networks Sampled from Twitter." *SSRN Electronic Journal*. doi:10.2139/ssrn.2185134.

Grossman, Jonathan, and Ami Pedahzur. 2020. "Political Science and Big Data: Structured Data, Unstructured Data, and How to Use Them." *Political Science Quarterly* 135 (2): 225–257. doi:10.1002/polq.13032.

Hagemeier, Stefanie. 2021. "UrhG § 60d Text Und Data Mining." In *Beck'scher Online Kommentar Urheberrecht*, edited by Hartwig Ahlberg, Horst-Peter Götting, and Anne Lauber-Rönsberg, 31st ed. https://beck-online.beck.de/Bcid/Y-400-W-BECKOKURHR-G-URHG-P-60D.

Hesse, Arielle, Leland Glenna, Clare Hinrichs, Robert Chiles, and Carolyn Sachs. 2019. "Qualitative Research Ethics in the Big Data Era." *American Behavioral Scientist* 63 (5): 560–583. doi:10.1177/0002764218805806.

Hornik, Kurt. 2019. *OpenNLP: Apache OpenNLP Tools Interface* (version 0.2-7, R package). https://CRAN.R-project.org/package=openNLP.

Jungherr, Andreas, Pascal Jürgens, and Harald Schoen. 2012. "Why the Pirate Party Won the German Election of 2009 or The Trouble With Predictions: A Response to Tumasjan, A., Sprenger, T. O., Sander, P. G., & Welpe, I. M. 'Predicting Elections With Twitter: What 140 Characters Reveal About Political Sentiment.'" *Social Science Computer Review* 30 (2): 229–234. doi:10.1177/0894439311404119.

Katagiri, Azusa, and Eric Min. 2019. "The Credibility of Public and Private Signals: A Document-Based Approach." *American Political Science Review* 113 (1): 156–172. doi:10.1017/S0003055418000643.

Keller, Franziska B., David Schoch, Sebastian Stier, and JungHwan Yang. 2020. "Political Astroturfing on Twitter: How to Coordinate a Disinformation Campaign." *Political Communication* 37 (2): 256–280. doi:10.1080/10584609.2019.1661888.

Khalil, Salim, and Mohamed Fakir. 2017. "RCrawler: An R Package for Parallel Web Crawling and Scraping." *SoftwareX* 6: 98–106. doi:10.1016/j.softx.2017.04.004.

King, Gary. 2011. "Ensuring the Data-Rich Future of the Social Sciences." *Science* 331 (6018): 719–721.

Kitchin, Rob. 2014. "Big Data, New Epistemologies and Paradigm Shifts." *Big Data & Society* 1 (1). doi:10.1177/2053951714528481.

Kitchin, Rob, and Gavin McArdle. 2016. "What Makes Big Data, Big Data? Exploring the Ontological Characteristics of 26 Datasets." *Big Data & Society* 3 (1). doi:10.1177/2053951716631130.

Kleinberg, Katja B., Gregory Robinson, and Stewart L. French. 2012. "Trade Concentration and Interstate Conflict." *The Journal of Politics* 74 (2): 529–540. doi:10.1017/s0022381611001745.

Kuiler, Erik W. 2014. "From Big Data to Knowledge: An Ontological Approach to Big Data Analytics." *Review of Policy Research* 31 (4): 311–318. doi:10.1111/ropr.12077.

Laney, Doug. 2001. "3D Data Management: Controlling Data Volume, Velocity, and Variety." *Meta Group*. https://www.bibsonomy.org/bibtex/742811cb00b303261f79a98e9b80bf49?lang=de.

Lazer, D., A. Pentland, L. Adamic, S. Aral, A.-L. Barabasi, D. Brewer, N. Christakis, et al. 2009. "Computational Social Science." *Science* 323 (5915): 721–723. doi:10.1126/science.1167742.

Leonelli, S. 2014. "What Difference Does Quantity Make? On the Epistemology of Big Data in Biology." *Big Data & Society* 1 (1). doi:10.1177/2053951714534395.

McClelland, Charles A., and Gary D. Hoggard. 1969. "Conflict Patterns in the Interactions Among Nations." In *International Politics and Foreign Policy: A Reader in Research and Theory*, edited by James N. Rosenau, 711–724. New York: The Free Press.

McDermott, Rose. 1998. *Risk-Taking in International Politics: Prospect Theory in American Foreign Policy*. Ann Arbor, MI: University of Michigan Press. doi:10.3998/mpub.15779.

Morstatter, Fred, Jürgen Pfeffer, Huan Liu, and Kathleen M. Carley. 2013. "Is the Sample Good Enough? Comparing Data from Twitter's Streaming API with Twitter's Firehose." *Proceedings of the International AAAI Conference on Web and Social Media* 7 (1). http://arxiv.org/abs/1306.5204.

Munzert, Simon, Christian Rubba, Peter Meißner, and Dominic Nyhuis. 2015. *Automated Data Collection with R: A Practical Guide to Web Scraping and Text Mining*. Chichester, West Sussex, United Kingdom: John Wiley & Sons Inc.

Norris, Clayton, John Beieler, and Philip A. Schrodt. 2017. "PETRARCH2: Another Event Coding Program." *The Journal of Open Source Software* 2 (9): 133. doi:10.21105/joss.00133.

O'Halloran, Kay L., Sabine Tan, Peter Wignell, John A. Bateman, Duc-Son Pham, Michele Grossman, and Andrew Vande Moere. 2019. "Interpreting Text and Image Relations in Violent Extremist

Discourse: A Mixed Methods Approach for Big Data Analytics." *Terrorism and Political Violence* 31 (3): 454–474. doi:10.1080/09546553.2016.1233871.

Oppermann, Kai, and Henrike Viehrig, eds. 2011. *Issue Salience in International Politics*. Routledge Advances in International Relations and Global Politics 91. London ; New York: Routledge.

Przeworski, Adam. 1999. "On the Design of the State: A Principal-Agent Perspective." In *Reforming the State. Managerial Public Administration in Latin America*, edited by Luiz Carlos Bresser Pereira and Peter Spink, 15–40. London: Lynne Rienner.

Rat Für Sozial- Und Wirtschaftsdaten (RatSWD). 2019. "Big Data in den Sozial-, Verhaltens- und Wirtschaftswissenschaften: Datenzugang und Forschungsdatenmanagement - Mit Gutachten 'Web Scraping in der unabhängigen wissenschaftlichen Forschung.'" *RatSWD Output Paper Series*. German Data Forum (RatSWD). doi:10.17620/02671.39.

Salganik, Matthew J. 2018. *Bit by Bit: Social Research in the Digital Age*. Princeton: Princeton University Press.

Schack, Haimo. 2017. "Das Neue UrhWissG – Schranken Für Unterricht, Wissenschaft Und Institutionen." *Zeitschrift Für Urheber- Und Medienrecht* 61 (11): 802–808.

Schrodt, Philip A., and Deborah J. Gerner. 1994. "Validity Assessment of a Machine-Coded Event Data Set for the Middle East, 1982-92." *American Journal of Political Science* 38 (3): 825–854. doi:10.2307/2111609.

———. 2004. "An Event Data Analysis of Third-Party Mediation in the Middle East and Balkans." *Journal of Conflict Resolution* 48 (3). SAGE Publications Inc: 310–330. doi:10.1177/0022002704264137.

Spitz, Andreas. 2019. "Implicit Entity Networks: A Versatile Document Model." doi:10.11588/heidok.00026328.

Spitz, Andreas, Satya Almasian, and Michael Gertz. 2017. "EVELIN: Exploration of Event and Entity Links in Implicit Networks." In *Proceedings of the 26th International Conference on World Wide Web Companion - WWW '17 Companion*, 273–277. Perth, Australia: ACM Press. doi:10.1145/3041021.3054721.

Spitz, Andreas, and Michael Gertz. 2016. "Terms over LOAD: Leveraging Named Entities for Cross-Document Extraction and Summarization of Events." In *Proceedings of the 39th International ACM SIGIR Conference on Research and Development in Information Retrieval - SIGIR '16*, 503–512. Pisa, Italy: ACM Press. doi:10.1145/2911451.2911529.

———. 2018. "Entity-Centric Topic Extraction and Exploration: A Network-Based Approach." In *Advances in Information Retrieval*, edited by Gabriella Pasi, Benjamin Piwowarski, Leif Azzopardi, and Allan Hanbury, 10772: 3–15. Cham: Springer International Publishing. doi:10.1007/978-3-319-76941-7_1.

Trubowitz, Peter, and Kohei Watanabe. 2021. "The Geopolitical Threat Index: A Text-Based Computational Approach to Identifying Foreign Threats." *International Studies Quarterly*. doi:10.1093/isq/sqab029.

Tumasjan, Andranik, Timm Sprenger, Philipp Sandner, and Isabell Welpe. 2010. "Predicting Elections with Twitter: What 140 Characters Reveal about Political Sentiment." *Proceedings of the International AAAI Conference on Web and Social Media* 4 (1). https://ojs.aaai.org/index.php/ICWSM/article/view/14009.

Urdinez, Francisco, and Andres Cruz. 2020. *R for Political Data Science: A Practical Guide*. Chapman & Hall/CRC the R Series. Boca Raton: Taylor and Francis.

Ward, Michael D., and Sheen Rajmaira. 1992. "Reciprocity and Norms in U.S.-Soviet Foreign Policy." *Journal of Conflict Resolution* 36 (2): 342–368. doi:10.1177/0022002792036002006.

Weidmann, Nils B. 2015a. "Communication, Technology, and Political Conflict: Introduction to the Special Issue." *Journal of Peace Research* 52 (3): 263–268. doi:10.1177/0022343314559081.

———. 2015b. "On the Accuracy of Media-Based Conflict Event Data." *Journal of Conflict Resolution* 59 (6): 1129–1149. doi:10.1177/0022002714530431.

Welbers, Kasper, Wouter Van Atteveldt, and Kenneth Benoit. 2017. "Text Analysis in R." *Communication Methods and Measures* 11 (4): 245–265. doi:10.1080/19312458.2017.1387238.

Zeitzoff, Thomas, John Kelly, and Gilad Lotan. 2015. "Using Social Media to Measure Foreign Policy Dynamics: An Empirical Analysis of the Iranian–Israeli Confrontation (2012–2013)." *Journal of Peace Research* 52 (3): 368–383. doi:10.1177/0022343314558700.

Zwitter, Andrej. 2015. "Big Data and International Relations." *Ethics & International Affairs* 29 (4): 377–389. doi:10.1017/S0892679415000362.

31
Analyzing Twitter
Andrea Schneiker

Introduction

In 2016, Twitter was "the most commonly used social network by foreign ministries" (DiPLO 2016) worldwide, according to the Swiss-Maltese NGO DiploFoundation. The 2020 *Twiplomacy* report finds that 98% of UN member states have a Twitter presence. Only the governments of "Laos, North Korea, Sao Tome and Principe and Turkmenistan" (Twiplomacy Report 2020) have not. Maybe the most widely known issue area when it comes to studying the use of social media by state actors in the context of Foreign Policy Analysis (FPA) is *digital diplomacy* (Bjola 2016a; Manor 2016). Yet, not only states but also international governmental organizations (Bjola/Zaiotti 2021; Goritz et al. 2020) and non-state actors (Joachim et al. 2018; Klausen 2015; Schneiker et al. 2019a) are using social media such as Twitter. It is therefore not surprising that an increasing number of scholars are turning to social media data when seeking to study foreign policy. Scholars have, for example, studied what information, ideas, and interests are communicated on Twitter (Zeitzoff et al. 2015), how actors seek to legitimize their actions and garner support for their actions (Bjola/Manor 2018; Manor/Crilley 2020), and the impact of the use of social media (Manor/Segev 2020). The latter is the most difficult question to answer: "What impact means in the digital context, how to capture it and how best to make use of it are questions that nevertheless remain poorly understood" (Bjola 2016b: 345). This chapter therefore spares out discussions about impact and impact measurements. Instead, it is interested in methods and methodologies to organize and classify big data available on social media.

Given the huge amount of data, scholars often need methods that allow them to structure, organize, or filter this data in order to, for example, identify links, connections, or patterns and/or to reduce data in such a way that it can subsequently be interpreted by qualitative means. Different methods can be used to filter or organize Twitter data, including network analysis, analyzing frequencies of words used (word clouds), and sentiment analysis.[1] Sentiment analysis is suited for studying Twitter data, because emotions are central to the functioning of Twitter. First, Twitter lends itself to emotionally charged messages. Given that a tweet can be posted without preparation from almost anywhere at any time makes tweeting "a highly impulsive activity" (Ott 2017: 61) that might result in emotionally charged messages. In addition, unlike face-to-face interaction, communication on Twitter takes place without people necessarily being physically present in the same place, which makes it easier to offend others and post something insulting (Ott 2017: 62). Second, "emotionally charged Twitter messages tend to be retweeted more often and more quickly compared to neutral ones" (Stieglitz/Dang-Xuan 2013: 217) and, hence, have a relatively higher outreach. Overall, Duncombe argues that "emotion is implicated in the power of this social media platform. [...] Twitter can both represent emotions and provoke emotions, which can play an important role in the escalation or de-escalation of conflict" (Duncombe 2019: 409). Furthermore, sentiment analysis lends itself to the study of foreign policy issues given the importance of emotions for foreign policy (analysis) (see chapter by Koschut in this volume). In light of the centrality of emotions for social media in general and for Twitter in particular, this chapter focuses on the merits and use of sentiment analysis for FPA. In this context, multiple challenges in terms of access and accessibility as well as the huge amount of data are discussed.

Sentiment analysis or opinion mining are commonly used as umbrella terms for "a process that automates mining of attitudes, opinions, views and emotions from text, speech, tweets, and database sources through Natural Language Processing" (Kharde/Sonawane 2016: 5). All these techniques have in common that they automatically classify text segments according to their evaluative expressions in terms of a positive or negative polarity on a predefined scale (Lucas et al. 2015; Pang/Lee 2008; Serrano-Guerrero et al. 2015). This being said, the main strength of sentiment analysis is its power to categorize large amounts of data (Bryman 2006).

In a first step, I will situate sentiment analysis with respect to other approaches used to classify Twitter data and provide a brief overview of how sentiment analysis has been applied thus far to study topics of relevance for FPA, before I elaborate on key terms, concepts, and challenges, as well as on the underlying methodology. Afterward, I will discuss the application of sentiment analysis before I end with some concluding remarks.

Although sentiment analysis is used in relation to issues that are of relevance to foreign policy scholars, the latter – thus far – rarely apply sentiment analysis when studying social media.[2] Hence, analyses referred to in the following have been often carried out by scholars coming from other fields than foreign policy, such as information technology (Cheong/Lee 2011) or computer science (Agarwal et al. 2018; Dahal et al. 2019), communication studies (Park et al. 2021), arts and culture (Cunliffe/Curini 2018), or business and economics (Georgiadou et al. 2020). Yet, as I will show, sentiment analysis of social media data has great potential for FPA.

Literature Review

Twitter data poses various challenges for researchers. One is the sheer amount of data. This is why researchers often use mainly quantitative methods to classify and organize the data.[3] One such technique is data mining. It is possible to categorize Twitter accounts based on parameters such as the number of followers or the average number of tweets issued per day. In a study on the marketing of private military and security companies (PMSCs) via Twitter, Schneiker et al. (2019a) used a data mining technique by carrying out a latent profile analysis (LPA) in order to identify different clusters of Twitter accounts and respective patterns of Twitter usage by PMSCs. This allowed to find out about the different ways in which PMSCs use Twitter. While some companies were found to promote their services, others were mainly monitoring what is said about them and yet others used Twitter to distract from what they are actually doing.

Another technique to categorize Twitter data is social network analysis. Scholars, for example, have analyzed communication networks around particular topics, that is, which groups of Twitter users post what type of content, which actors hold a central position in a network, and the interaction between different groups of users (e.g., Schuster et al. 2021; Williams et al. 2015; Zeitzoff et al. 2015). In their social network analysis of Twitter protests against the Australian government's secret surveillance programs on Indonesian political leaders, Chatfield et al. (2015: 124), for example, show that the Australian protest network is, contrary to the authors' expectations, bigger than the Indonesian one. Often, scholars combine social network analysis with text mining techniques (Zeitzoff et al. 2015). Text mining is an extension of data mining to textual data in terms of "attempts to extract meaningful information from unstructured textual data" (He et al. 2013: 465). Topic modeling, for example, can be used "to determine which topics are present and in what quantities" (Dahal et al. 2019; see also Lucas et al. 2015). Depending on the size of the sample and the number of coders, instead of using such an unsupervised machine learning technique, scholars can also manually code the tweets – or a portion of the sample – and carry out a quantitative content analysis to identify dominant topics (Collins et al. 2019). This was, for example, done by Danziger and Schreiber to find out what diplomatic topics are covered by the Twitter accounts of the foreign ministries of Israel, Russia, and Turkey (Danziger/Schreiber 2021). Based on either machine learning or manual coding techniques, it is possible to count the frequency of particular words, expressions, or group of words related to a particular topic (Al-Rawi/Groshek 2018). These can be presented, for example, in terms of word clouds (Dahal et al. 2019: 24).

Sentiment analysis is another text mining technique. Hence, sentiment analysis can be applied to analyze different sets of Twitter data on topics that are of relevance for FPA. Sentiment analysis allows to filter Twitter data in order to distil particular data and/or particular patterns of communication relevant to foreign policy. For example, in their analysis of online communication of the Islamic State (IS), Macnair and Frank used "[t]he words and phrases with the most extreme sentiment values [. . .] as a starting point for the identification of specific narratives that exist within online IS media" (Macnair/Frank 2018: 438). The IS, for example, presents its own fighters as strong and furious while its enemies are humiliated (Macnair/Frank 2018: 449–450). Others have used sentiment analysis in a similar way in order to identify security actors' self-representations (Schneiker et al. 2019a).

Sentiment analysis can also be used to measure opinions or attitudes regarding particular policies (Ceron et al. 2014), particular behavior such as heritage destruction by the IS (Cunliffe/Curini 2018), or topics such as climate change (Dahal et al. 2019), the Brexit negotiations (Georgiadou et al. 2020), refugee movements (Öztürk/Ayvaz 2018), or in order to find out about the needs of disaster-affected people (Ragini et al. 2018). Sentiment analysis also allows to study when and where social media activism on foreign policy issues and relevant sentiments expressed on Twitter spike most and whether this correlates with (which) real time events. Dahal et al., for example, in their analysis of tweets regarding climate change find that the public reaction on Twitter to "drastic political, weather, or social media events" is higher than in response to top-down events planned by advocacy organizations (Dahal et al. 2019: 23). But sentiment analysis does not provide an explanation for such findings. Yet, such findings allow to formulate new "why" research questions which, however, often require further qualitative analysis in order to be answered (Bennett 2015).

In some cases, sentiment analysis is used within comparative research designs, for example, to compare communication on Twitter with offline communication (Zeitzoff et al. 2015), with communication on other platforms such as Facebook (Park et al. 2021), with other media (Macnair/Frank 2018), across different languages (Öztürk/Ayvaz 2018), across countries (Dahal et al. 2019), or over time (Park et al. 2021). In some cases, sentiment analysis is combined with other methods such as data mining (Cheong/Lee 2011) and with other data, for example user metadata such as gender (Cheong/Lee 2011) or with geospatial location data, what Agarwal et al. label "geospatial sentiment analysis" (Agarwal et al. 2018; see also Georgiadou et al. 2020: 7). It is, for example, possible to

> clustering geographic location obtained from the Twitter message authors on a Google Maps 'mashup' to illustrate the locations of users who have contributed to chatter about a topic. This simply visualizes the location of users who have GPS geo-tagging capability (i.e. annotating tweets with exact geographic coordinates) on an overlay of the real topological map, making it easy to separate groups of users based on their immediate location at time of tweet broadcast.
>
> *(Cheong/Lee 2011: 52).*

Yet, this requires that Twitter users also use GPS (Georgiadou et al. 2020: 7). Sentiment analysis can also be combined with social network analysis. For example, Williams et al. show that different groups of Twitter users have very divergent opinions regarding climate change and that most of them only communicate with those who share their ideas (Williams et al. 2015). While this finding is consistent with other studies regarding the creation of homogeneous online communities or echo chambers (Sunstein 2007), other analysis combining social network and sentiment analysis yield more differentiated results. Studying the communication on Twitter of interest groups within "a defined issue community – American-Jewish organizations advocating on the issue of U.S.-Israel relations" (Osterbur/Kiel 2021: 195), Osterbur and Kiel find that while some groups tend to communicate within echo chambers, others, in turn, also reach out to opposing groups. The authors "conclude that organizations utilize Twitter strategically, incorporating a differentiated use of the interaction tools, depending on whether they are trying to reinforce a narrative or broadening their support base" (Osterbur/Kiel 2021: 210).

Some scholars consider sentiment analysis to be a policy relevant tool that can be used by political decision-makers. Data from sentiment analysis based on geospatial information, for example, are considered to be potentially useful for "homeland security authorities and law enforcement agencies to immediately chronicle and respond to terror threats" (Cheong/Lee 2011: 58) or for state militaries to carry out intelligence and surveillance, for example to predict behavior (Gray/Gordo 2014). Sentiment analysis can also be used to study the foreign policy narratives of governments and the reactions to those by domestic and foreign actors. Some, for example, consider that

> large-scale analysis of user sentiment can provide a platform that enables governments to grasp collective citizens' preferences towards specific negotiation processes such as Brexit, thus potentially bridging the informational gaps between decisionmakers and citizens in terms of preferred, and eventually winning, outcomes
>
> *(Georgiadou et al. 2020: 6)*

and even "propose, therefore, that the user sentiment on Twitter may potentially constitute a key part of future decision-making and negotiating strategies signalling most and least preferred negotiating outcomes and thus also pointing to their possible ramifications" (Georgiadou et al. 2020: 6).

Others, in contrast, posit that social media should not be equated with public opinion, because social media such as Twitter

> represent a field of communicative engagement among diverse sets of actors, only some of which are subsets of 'the public'. Straightforward attempts to use social media as an opinion poll will miss these important dynamics and may draw incorrect inferences.
> *(Zeitzoff et al. 2015: 380)*

Furthermore, actors can manipulate opinions shared on social media such as Twitter and engage in strategies of disinformation, defined as "the distribution, assertion, or dissemination of false, mistaken, or misleading information in an intentional, deliberate, or purposeful effort to mislead, deceive, or confuse" (Fetzer 2004: 231). One such strategy is the use of trolls: "paid and organised bloggers (both military and civilian) who disseminate propaganda and otherwise behave disruptively online to derail conversations in opposition to their own political agendas" (Boyte 2017: 92). These trolls can be used to spread positive stories not only about oneself but also for "hacking and smear campaigns" (Golovchenko et al. 2018: 980; see also Aro 2016: 129) in order to discredit others. The use of these strategies has been studied with respect to Russia (Aro 2016; Boyte 2017; Golovchenko et al. 2018; Gunitsky 2015; Jensen et al. 2019) but also with respect to the United States (Gray/Gordo 2014: 255). The Russian government is said to maintain at least one so-called troll farm, the Russian Internet Research Agency (IRA) (Park et al. 2021: 1–2), and is reported to have paid users "to post pro-regime message on websites and social media outlets" and to "'dislike' anti-regime videos on YouTube" (Gunitsky 2015: 45). Yet, sentiment analysis can also be employed to analyze such manipulation of "public opinion". Park et al. (2021), for example, carried out a sentiment analysis of tweets posted by the IRA. They studied the IRA's "emotion-based strategies on Twitter and in Facebook advertising" (Park et al. 2021: 2) for purposes of "manipulation of partisan and racial identities" (Park et al. 2021: 2) during the 2016 U.S. presidential election. But the caution that Zeitzoff et al. demand of researchers also results from the special nature of social media.

Key Terms and Concepts, Methodology

Social media are not neutral communication channels, but "political in and of themselves" (Jackson 2019: 521) and "the politics of social media [...] produces, reproduces, reinforces and shifts power and privilege" (Nahon 2016: 41). Social media are an "organizing agent" (Bennett/Segerberg 2012: 752) of communication that groups and classifies communication based on algorithms that follow commercial logics. Social media such as Twitter thereby trade participation for visibility. The reward system inherent in social media suggests that users are the more successful the more follower or friends their account has. In this sense, "[o]n social media platforms, the network is part of the content displayed" (Klinger/Svensson 2015: 1252). In this context, participation according to Bennett and Segerberg and drawing on Benkler (2006) "becomes self-motivating as personally expressive content is shared with, and recognized by, others who, in turn, repeat these networked sharing activities" (Bennett/Segerberg 2012: 753). Such "connective action" (Bennet/Segerberg 2012) does not require the "high levels of organizational resources and the formation of collective identities" (Bennett/Segerberg 2012: 739) that are necessary for analogue collective action:

> In this connective logic, taking public action or contributing to a common good becomes an act of personal expression and recognition or self-validation achieved by sharing ideas

and actions in trusted relationships. Sometimes the people in these exchanges may be on the other side of the world, but they do not require a club, a party, or a shared ideological frame to make the connection. In place of the initial collective action problem of getting the individual to contribute, the starting point of connective action is the self-motivated (though not necessarily self-centered) sharing of already internalized or personalized ideas, plans, images, and resources with networks of others.

(Bennett/Segerberg 2012: 752–753)

Hence, being part of a network may not only provide a "sense of belonging" (Milan 2015: 66), but it also requires the constant endorsement by others, what might result in self-referential and "self-reinforcing 'echo chambers'" (Williams et al. 2015). The creation of homogeneous online communities is also supported by the algorithms that social media platforms are based on. For instance, the news feed of Facebook and the trends in hashtags that Twitter displays are based on such algorithms that privilege "breaking news and viral content dissemination over long-term issues of interest" (Poell/van Dijck 2015: 531). In their analysis of Twitter data, Williams at al., for example, "show that social media discussion of climate change is characterised by strong attitude-based homophily and widespread segregation of users into like-minded communities" (Williams et al. 2015: 135). According to the authors,

> the public nature of communication on Twitter is likely to encourage users towards behaviors consistent with the image they wish to express. Following another user is a public decision to associate with and receive content from that user. Retweeting often implies (public) endorsement of either the individual tweet or its original author. Thus users are likely to follow/retweet others with views consistent with their own.
>
> *(Williams et al. 2015: 135)*

Therefore, it might be intriguing to combine sentiment analysis with other methods such as social network analysis (Zeitzoff et al. 2015) in order to find out whose communication is studied and to identify potential bias. In addition, given that joint "communication spaces" (Poell/van Dijck 2015: 533) are likely to consist of shared or even similar attitudes and opinions about a particular foreign policy topic, sentiment analysis allows to test relevant hypotheses and to identify potential outliers to the overall opinion shared within an online community.

Sentiment analysis allows to categorize or classify communication published on Twitter based on the attitudes or emotions that are expressed therein – or more precisely, that the underlying algorithm considers to be expressed therein. Often, sentiment analysis involves machine learning techniques that rely on dictionaries based on which a sentiment score is assigned to each word, then to combination of words, and finally to each sentence. It allows, for example, to identify attitudes toward a particular politician or a particular foreign policy. Although sentiment analysis is a quantitative method, it relies on some qualitative decisions to be made. Some of these decisions have to be taken due to the different challenges that Twitter poses for researchers.

The first challenge can be to identify the relevant actors that one seeks to study. Corporate actors might have various Twitter accounts. The U.S. Department of State, for example, has a main Twitter account and its different offices and sub-entities – such as the U.S. Mission to the International Organizations in Vienna, the U.S. Mission to the OSCE, the U.S. Mission to the AU, the Bureau of International Organization Affairs, and the U.S. Mission to the UN – do have their own Twitter accounts. In addition, individuals such as the U.S. Secretary of

State and the U.S. Department of State's Spokesperson do also have own Twitter accounts. The same person might have different accounts: an official and a private account, whereby – as the example of Donald Trump has shown – the categories of public and private blur as the private person might use a private account in an official capacity. Hence, scholars who seek to analyze, for example, the U.S. foreign policy based on Twitter first have to determine which accounts they consider to represent U.S. foreign policy actors. A researcher's decision on which social media account(s) to study may affect the result of the analysis. As a corporate actor might have "numerous Twitter accounts controlled by numerous agents, [Twitter] creates a perfect recipe for a public diplomacy operation that is unsystematic, indiscriminate, and ad-hoc" (Collins et al. 2019: 92). Hence, the narrative that foreign policy actors tell on social media might not be coherent (Manor 2016: 18). Analyzing different Twitter accounts of the same country allows scholars to study to what extent a foreign policy discourse of a state is coherent and whether the degree of coherence differs between different states or depending on the context. In their analysis of digital diplomacy under the Obama Administration, Collins et al., for example, come to the somehow counter-intuitive result that "U.S. digital diplomacy largely displayed a deliberate, disciplined, rational approach" (Collins et al. 2019: 92).

A second challenge is the huge amount of data available on Twitter. Generally, not all of this "data [is] relevant to the[...] topic of interest" (Sudulich et al. 2014: 10) of a research project. Some of the data on Twitter constitutes "non-relevant 'noise'" (Sudulich et al. 2014: 10). Identifying what is relevant information and deleting "noise" can be called "data cleaning" (Dahal et al. 2019: 3). Another challenge involves the "heterogeneous character of social media data" (Sudulich et al. 2014: 11). Very often tweets include not only texts but also pictures, animated gifs, videos, or hyperlinks that refer to other internet sites which may include a hybrid type of content as well. Furthermore, the limitation of 280 characters per tweet (before November 2017: 140 characters per tweet) leads to unorthodox ways of communication, including abbreviations or emojis, and thereby furthers a "lack of concern with proper grammar and style" (Ott 2017: 62). In addition, tweets often include not only alphabetic characters, but also signs like @ and hashtags (#) followed by names, words, or phrases that are "glued together". In addition, words may be deliberately misspelled (e.g., "yesssss" or "nooooo") and, last but not least, sentences are not necessarily separated by a punctuation mark, which makes it difficult to identify where a sentence ends. While in the beginning programs used for sentiment analysis required proper language to identify words and assign a score, relevant programs have evolved over time and some have been created explicitly for analyzing social media and allow to "detect sentiment from emojis and slang, which are important components of Twitter" (Georgiadou et al. 2020: 4; see also Dahal et al. 2018: 5; Hutto/Gilbert 2014). Depending on the program that is used, the various characteristics of tweets mentioned above might render an automated analysis by means of a software based on a standardized categorization of data difficult. Therefore, the data often require "preparation" (Dahal et al. 2019: 3) in terms of producing a text corpus consisting of words that can be identified as such by the program before the text can be processed. However, data cleaning and preparation is necessary not only for sentiment analysis but also for text mining in general (He et al. 2013: 466). This preparation as well as the above-mentioned cleaning might involve some interpretation of the data prior to being categorized.

In addition to these challenges that require some qualitative decisions, another challenge relates to accessing the data. This normally requires either a special software that downloads tweets and related information or money to buy relevant information from commercial entities who do the download. With respect to some processes, such as the 2022 war in Ukraine, scholars provide open access data sets for others (Chen/Ferrara 2022).[4] Relying on these data sets, however, does imply that researchers have to work with data that were collected according to particular criteria decided upon by others and that might not necessarily correspond to the research interest of those who seek to work with the data set. Access is also limited by the legal provisions of the social media platform that do, however, change over time. The data to be downloaded from Twitter can, for example, only cover a limited time span and/or number of tweets. The reproduction of the tweets is also limited by the platform. Hence, research on communication by public actors such as foreign ministries depends on rights granted by commercial entities.

Method and Empirical Illustration

In order to carry out a sentiment analysis, several steps are needed: data download, data cleaning, and data preparation. As a first step, the data that are about to be analyzed have to be downloaded from Twitter. Often, this is done by using the Twitter Stream Application Programming Interface (API, e.g., Williams et al. 2015; Georgiadou et al. 2020: 4). But data can also be bought from companies that do the download (Cunliffe/Curini 2018). Data can be downloaded based on users that are identified beforehand, that is, their accounts, and/or based on particular hashtags or catchwords. If the data are downloaded with reference to a particular topic, for example based on catchwords, it is possible that the data set includes tweets that refer to other topics than the one the researcher is interested in. The downloaded data have, therefore, to be consolidated or "cleaned" (Dahal et al. 2019: 24; Georgiadou et al. 2020: 4; Macnair/Frank 2018) by removing the "noise" (Sudulich et al. 2014: 9). For this purpose, a randomly composed subset of the overall sample can be examined manually to identify "false positives" (Dahal et al. 2019: 3). This is a qualitative element of the analysis since researchers have to determine which tweets do not relate to the topic under investigation. The identification of false positives generally takes place inductively, since it is difficult to know beforehand which unrelated topics will be included in the data set. In a study on the presentations of self and other of the PMSC Academi (that is now part of the Constellis Group) that we carried out (Schneiker et al. 2019b), we did, for example, search for tweets by users (other than Academi itself) that referred to the PMSC by downloading tweets that contained the word "Academi" or one of the company's previous names ("Blackwater" or "Xe"). Yet, when manually examining a random sample of 1000 tweets out of the downloaded data in order to identify the "noise", we noticed that not all tweets that we had collected referred to the PMSC Academi. Some tweets referred to completely other things that were of no interest to our study, such as the popular TV series *Game of Thrones*. In a next step, the false positives are removed "from the entire dataset programmatically" (Dahal et al. 2019: 3) along with their respective retweets (Schneiker et al. 2019b).

Data cleaning can also involve the identification of bot or spam accounts and the removal of respective tweets, because such users "can greatly influence the analysis especially temporally" (Dahal et al. 2019: 4). Bots can be defined as "a social media account controlled at least in part through software" (Botometer 2022). The detection of bot users can be done based on a calculation of the "number of duplicate tweets per user" (Dahal et al. 2019: 4) in order to see whether some users' daily activity exceeds those of others. In their sentiment analysis on Tweets related to global climate change, Dahal et al. identified one user who posted "more than five times as many tweets as the second highest tweeter" which is why this particular "user was determined to be [a] [...] bot user, and it was [...] removed" (Dahal et al. 2019: 4). It is also possible to use particular tools to identify bots. The botometer, for example, calculates the likelihood that an account is a bot based on a broad range of parameters such as "the account's profile, friends, social network structure, temporal activity patterns" (Botometer 2022). Depending on the context, what might be more difficult to determine than a bot is whether a Twitter account is "covertly managed by government agents to manipulate the public" (Golovchenko et al. 2018: 987), that is, by trolls. This was a difficulty encountered by Golovchenko et al. (2018) in their analysis of Russian Twitter accounts when studying the communication regarding "the downing of the Malaysian Airlines Flight 17 (MH17) in the Ukrainian war zone in 2014" (Golovchenko et al. 2018: 977). The authors relied on a list of human-controlled Twitter profiles linked to the IRA that was published by the United States Congress (Golovchenko et al. 2018: 987).[5] In addition to the verification of accounts and depending on the software that is used for the subsequent analysis, it can also be necessary to remove non-English tweets if the software is only trained to code English words (Chambers et al. 2015: 67–69; Dahal et al. 2019: 23).

A variety of software exists that allows to carry out sentiment analysis.[6] Relevant software generally involves machine learning techniques (Kharde/Sonawane 2016). These often rely on dictionaries based on which a sentiment score is assigned to each word, then to combinations of words, and finally to each sentence. Sentiment, in this sense, "refers to the valence or arousal of emotion automatically detected in a piece of text and whether (or how much) it is positive or negative, thus making an evaluative judgment of attitude or opinion in the posts expressed" (Park et al. 2021: 10). Some programs use three-level scales (neutral, positive, negative/objective) (Chambers et al. 2015: 69; Dahal et al. 2019: 23) while others, such as the open-source software Stanford NLP from the Stanford Natural Language Processing Group,[7] use a five-level scale ranging from 0 to 4 with 0 being very negative, 1 negative or fairly negative, 2 neutral, 3 positive or fairly positive, and 4 very positive (Serrano-Guerrero et al. 2015: 23). A positive score of 3 is, for example, assigned by the program to the word *good* and a neutral score of 2 to the word *book*. Together the combination of the two words, that is *good book* expresses then a very positive sentiment and would therefore be assigned the highest positive score of 4 by the program (Schneiker et al. 2019b).

Depending on the software that is chosen, the data set has to be prepared so that the program can make sense of the tweets. The Stanford NLP that we used as well as other programs had been developed for the study of offline communication such as newspaper articles or parliamentary speeches. They, therefore, are based on dictionaries that include formally correct expression, grammar, and punctuation and, hence, work best with or even require correct formal language. Given that tweets have some particularities that distinguish them from other types of written language (see above), they pose challenges for the classification of text by this type of automated programs. Therefore, Twitter data sets generally have to be revised or "prepared" (Dahal et al. 2019: 3; Kharde/Sonawane 2016: 7; Macnair/Frank 2018: 445) to ensure smooth processing of the data. It might be necessary, for example, to remove the @-username references and the #-signs and to separate the words used for a hashtag from each other (Macnair/Frank 2018: 445). Furthermore, the colloquial language often used in tweets can cause difficulties for an automated analysis. Therefore, it might be necessary to, for example, remove repeated letters such as in *nooooo* and to replace these words with the correctly spelled version, in this case *no* (Macnair/Frank 2018: 445) and to expand the most commonly used abbreviations (e.g., replacing *ive* with *I have*).[8]

A key advantage of such machine learning approaches is their ability to construct patterns from a limited amount of data and to then apply these patterns to new data. Although machine learning techniques can produce very good results, they can be time-consuming (Schneiker et al. 2019b: 194). If no ready-made program for an automated analysis is available

(Hutto/Gilbert 2014; Kharde/Sonawane 2016), the programs used for sentiment analysis require training before they can be used to classify the overall data set (Chambers et al. 2015). Therefore, a certain number of tweets out of the data set is manually coded (see Socher et al. 2013) before it is used to train the program until a sufficient accuracy level is reached (Schneiker et al. 2019b: 196). In our project, two trained individuals manually coded 1,000 tweets from our sample by assigning sentiment scores before we trained the program to code the tweets (Schneiker et al. 2019b).

As to the results of our analysis of the self-representation of PMSCs, the majority of tweets posted by Academi were generally evaluated as being positive in tone, but the data set also included some tweets that the program classified as highly negative. This raised the following question: why would Academi post tweets with a negative sentiment? This seems counter-intuitive if we assume that PMSCs use Twitter to promote their services and to boost their image (Joachim et al. 2018). In order to answer this question, we examined the tweets classified as "very negative" in more detail. We saved all of these tweets in one text file and analyzed a random sample of 1,000 tweets by means of a qualitative content analysis (Schneiker et al. 2019b).

Based on this analysis, the negative classification of some of the Academi tweets can at least partially be attributed to the security-related context in which PMSCs operate and the associated vocabulary used by the companies to promote their services. PMSCs such as Academi publish security-related information that the program we used considered to be negative on the basis of the words included in the messages (Schneiker et al. 2019b). For example, the following tweet by Academi was classified as very negative by the program: "We have a variety of training options for civilians and individuals: pistols, shotguns, rifles – we have it all!" Although the negative classification of the words "pistols, shotguns, rifles" led to the overall classification of the whole sentence as very negative, it can be assumed that this tweet was meant as promotion for Academi's services and, therefore, seen from the company's perspective, has a positive meaning. Similar, in their sentiment analysis of IS media, Macnair and Frank used the "the identification of the most positive and negative words […] as a starting point for the identification of specific ideological narratives" (Macnair/Frank 2018: 449). They also find that posts including words with a negative sentiment value, such as "slaughter" and "terrorized" are used to promote the IS, because they imply "strength and fury" (Macnair/Frank 2018: 449–450). Such false negatives (as well as false positives) are not uncommon when carrying out a sentiment analysis, because the automated programs relying on algorithms have problems to take into account the context and/or have difficulties in identifying ironic, sarcastic, or sardonic meaning (Dahal et al. 2019: 6). Yet, this can be mitigated by the prior manual coding (Ceron et al. 2014; Cunliffe/Curini 2018).

Conclusion

While already in 2012 the Israeli Defense Forces (IDF) used a Twitter account to announce their airstrikes against Hamas targets in the Gaza Strip, the latest war in Ukraine in 2022 has demonstrated that social media and especially Twitter are used by conflict parties for a variety of purposes, for example to spread a particular narrative about the war and to garner support (Feldstein 2022). While foreign policy scholars have studied social media and especially Twitter in the context of digital diplomacy, they have yet to explore the full potential of studying Twitter in order to learn something about foreign policy.

While Twitter data can be analyzed based on a variety of methods, this chapter has discussed the merits and use of sentiment analysis of Twitter data for FPA. It has shown that the method's main strength is its filter function: it can, for example, detect dominant narratives or outliers. This allows, for example, to test hypothesis about actors' communication or self-presentation on Twitter or on others' opinions about a particular actor or topic. However, in order to explain the results, those then generally need further qualitative research in order to make sense of them and/or to interpret the findings. Yet, sentiment analysis of Twitter data is still rarely used in FPA.

Sentiment analysis poses some challenges for researchers, the first of which is the access to the data and the ability and rights to download it in order to make it available for an analysis. Second, given the multitude of accounts, including troll accounts, scholars have to determine which accounts to include into the analysis. Third, scholars have to clean up the data set and remove irrelevant tweets or those that cannot be analyzed (for example due to language issues) from the data set. Fourth, the data have to be prepared so that it can be analyzed.

While the first software programs to carry out sentiment analysis were originally designed for offline text corpora, more and more sophisticated programs have been specifically designed to analyze social media data. Hence, the method of sentiment analysis is evolving as is the data that it seeks to capture. Taking into account that tweets increasingly include gifs, pictures, or videos, because this "significantly increase[s] the chances they will be favorited (recognized), and/or retweeted (amplified)" (Collins et al. 2019:93), some are already extending sentiment analysis to include visuals as well (Jindal/Aron 2022).

All in all, studying Twitter in the context of FPA acknowledges that "information is an important foreign policy tool" (Fisher et al. 2022: 1). Yet, scholars have to take into account the particular production logics of information available on social media such as Twitter. Not only do the algorithms underlying the social media platforms affect the communication that is taking place and its dynamics, but actors also might seek to manipulate communication by using, for example, trolls or bots.

Notes

1. On working with textual data, see also the chapters on quantitative content analysis, big data, and text as data in this handbook.
2. For a use of sentiment analysis of non-social media data in FPA, see, for example, Fisher et al. (2022).
3. In cases of relatively small samples, scholars also categorize tweets by manually coding them in terms of a qualitative content analysis (Schneiker 2019). Jezierska, for example, does so in order to analyze how Sweden implements its feminist foreign policy through digital diplomacy (Jezierska 2021).
4. https://github.com/echen102/ukraine-russia, 21 March 2022.
5. https://democrats-intelligence.house.gov/uploadedfiles/exhibit_b.pdf, 21 March 2022.
6. For an overview of 15 open-access software to carry out sentiment analysis, see Serrano-Guerrero et al. (2015).
7. The framework is available online at http://nlp.stanford.edu. Alternatives include the Apache Software Foundation Mahout (http://mahout.apache.org) and its Spark framework (http://spark.apache.org/mllib).
8. For a more detailed description of how we proceeded, see Schneiker et al. (2019b).

References

Note: All electronic sources have been last accessed on 5 May 2022.

Agarwal, Amit, Ritu Singh and Durga Toshniwal. 2018. "Geospatial sentiment analysis using Twitter data for UK-EU referendum" *Journal of Information and Optimization Sciences*, 39(1): 303–317. London: Taylor & Francis.

Al-Rawi, A. and J. Groshek. 2018. "Jihadist propaganda on social media: An examination of ISIS related content on Twitter." *International Journal of Cyber Warfare and Terrorism*, 8(4): 1–15. Pennsylvania: IGI Global.

Aro, Jessikka. 2016. "The cyberspace war: Propaganda and trolling as warfare tools" *European View*, 15:121–132, DOI: 10.1007/s12290-016-0395-5.

Benkler, Yochai. 2006. *The Wealth of Networks: How Social Production Transforms Markets and Freedom*. New Haven, CO and London: Yale University Press.

Bennett, Andrew. 2015. "Found in translation: Combining discourse analysis with computer assisted content analysis" *Journal of International Studies*, 43(3): 984–997. Cambridge: Cambridge University Press.

Bennett, W. Lance and Alexandra Segerberg. 2012. "The logic of connective action" *Information, Communication & Society*, 15(5): 739–768. London: Routledge.

Bjola, Corneliu. 2016a. "Digital diplomacy – The state of the art" *Global Affairs*, 2(3): 297–299. London: Taylor & Francis.

———. 2016b. "Getting digital diplomacy right: What quantum theory can teach us about measuring impact" *Global Affairs*, 2(3): 343–353. London: Taylor & Francis.

Bjola, Corneliu and Ruben Zaiotti. 2021. *Digital Diplomacy and International Organisations. Autonomy, Legitimacy and Contestation*. London: Routledge.

Botometer. 2022. https://botometer.osome.iu.edu/faq#contact, 21 March 2022.

Boyte, K.J. 2017. "An analysis of the social-media technology, tactics, and narratives used to control perception in the propaganda war over Ukraine" *Journal of Information Warfare*, 16(1): 88–111.

Bryman, Alan. 2006. "Integrating quantitative and qualitative research: How is it done?" *Qualitative Research*, 6: 97–113. Thousand Oaks, CA: SAGE Publications.

Ceron, Andrea, Luigi Curini, Stefano M. Iacus and Giuseppe Porro. 2014. "Every tweet counts? How sentiment analysis of social media can improve our knowledge of citizens' political preferences with an application to Italy and France" *New Media and Society*, 16(2): 340–358. Thousand Oaks, CA: SAGE Publications.

Chambers, Nathanael, Victor Bowen, Ethan Genco, Xisen Tian, Eric Young, Ganesh Harihara, and Eugene Yang. 2015. *Identifying Political Sentiment between Nation States with Social Media*, Proceedings of the 2015 Conference on Empirical Methods in Natural Language Processing, Association for Computational Linguistics, Lisbon, Portugal, 17–21 September, 65–75. Available from https://aclanthology.org/D15-1007.pdf.

Chatfield, Akemi Takeoka, Christopher G. Reddick and Uuf Brajawidagda. 2015. "Government surveillance disclosures, bilateral trust and Indonesia–Australia cross-border security cooperation: Social network analysis of Twitter data" *Government Information Quarterly*, 32: 118–128. Amsterdam: Elsevier.

Chen, Emily and Emilio Ferrara. 2022. *Tweets in Time of Conflict: A Public Dataset Tracking the Twitter Discourse on the War Between Ukraine and Russia*, https://arxiv.org/abs/2203.07488, 21 March 2022.

Cheong, Marc and Vincent C.S. Lee. 2011. "A microblogging-based approach to terrorism informatics: Exploration and chronicling civilian sentiment and response to terrorism events via Twitter" *Information System Frontiers*, 13: 45–59. Berlin: Springer.

Collins, Stephen D., Jeff R. DeWitt and Rebecca K. LeFebvre. 2019. "Hashtag diplomacy: Twitter as a tool for engaging in public diplomacy and promoting US foreign policy" *Place Branding and Public Diplomacy*, 15: 78–96. London: Palgrave Macmillan.

Corneliu Bjola and Ilan Manor. 2018. "Revisiting Putnam's two-level game theory in the digital age: Domestic digital diplomacy and the Iran nuclear deal" *Cambridge Review of International Affairs*, 31(1): 3–32. Cambridge: Cambridge University Press.

Cunliffe, Emma and Luigi Curini. 2018. "ISIS and heritage destruction: A sentiment analysis" *Antiquity*, 92(364): 1094–1111. Cambridge: Cambridge University Press.

Dahal, Biraj, A.P. Sathish Kumar and Zhenlong Li. 2019. "Spatiotemporal topic modeling and sentiment analysis of global climate change tweets" *Social Network Analysis and Mining*, 9(24). Wien: Springer.

Danziger, Roni and Mia Schreiber. 2021. "Digital diplomacy: Face management in MFA Twitter accounts" *Policy and Internet*, 13(4): 586–605. New Jersey: Wiley Blackwell.

Diplo. 2016. *Social Media Factsheet of Foreign Ministries*, last modified 23 March 2016. Available from https://www.diplomacy.edu/blog/infographic-social-media-factsheet-foreign-ministries/.

Duncombe, Constance. 2019. "The politics of Twitter: Emotions and the power of social media" *International Political Sociology*, 13: 409–429.

Feldstein, Steven. 2022. *Russia's War in Ukraine Is a Watershed Moment for Internet Platforms*, 03 March 2022. https://carnegieendowment.org/2022/03/03/russia-s-war-in-ukraine-is-watershed-moment-for-internet-platforms-pub-86569, 21 March 2022.

Fetzer, James H. 2004. "Disinformation: The use of false information." *Minds and Machines* 14: 231–240.

Fisher, Scott, Graig R Klein, Juste Codjo. 2022. "Focusdata: Foreign Policy through Language and Sentiment" *Foreign Policy Analysis*, 18(2). April 2022, orac002, DOI: 10.1093/fpa/orac002.

Georgiadou, Elena, Spyros Angelopoulos and Helen Drake. 2020. "Big data analytics and international negotiations: Sentiment analysis of Brexit negotiating outcomes" *International Journal of Information Management*, 51(102048).

Golovchenko, Yevgeniy, Mareike Hartmann and Rebecca Adler-Nissen. 2018. "State, media and civil society in the information warfare over Ukraine: Citizen curators of digital disinformation" *International Affairs*, 94: 5: 975–994. DOI: 10.1093/ia/iiy148.

Goritz, Alexandra, Johannes Schuster, Helge Jörgens and Nina Kolleck. 2020. "International Public Administrations on Twitter: A Comparison of Digital Authority in Global Climate Policy" *Journal of Comparative Policy Analysis: Research and Practice* 24(3): 271–295.

Gray, Chris Hables and Ángel J. Gordo. 2014. "Social Media in Conflict. Comparing Military and Social-Movement Technocultures" *Cultural Politics*, 10(3): 251–261. DOI: 10.1215/17432197-2795645.

Gunitsky, Seva. 2015. "Corrupting the cyber-commons: Social media as a tool of autocratic stability" *Perspectives on Politics*, 13(1): 42–54.

He, Wu, Shenghua Zha and LingLi. 2013. "Social media competitive analysis and text mining: A case study in the pizza industry" *International Journal of Information Management*, 33: 464–472.

Hutto, C.J. and Eric Gilbert. 2014. *VADER: A Parsimonious Rule-based Model for Sentiment Analysis of Social Media Text*, Proceedings of the Eighth International AAAI Conference on Weblogs and Social Media, 8(1), 216–225. Available from https://ojs.aaai.org/index.php/ICWSM/article/view/14550.

Jackson, Susan T. 2019. "A turning IR landscape in a shifting media ecology: The state of IR literature on new media" *International Studies Review*, 21: 518–534.

Jensen, Benjamin, Brandon Valeriano and Ryan Maness. 2019. "Fancy bears and digital trolls: Cyber strategy with a Russian twist" *Journal of Strategic Studies*, 42(2): 212–234. DOI: 10.1080/01402390.2018.1559152.

Jezierska, Katarzyna. 2021. "Incredibly loud and extremely silent: Feminist foreign policy on Twitter" *Cooperation and Conflict*. DOI: 10.1177/00108367211000793.

Jindal, Kanika and Rajni Aron. 2022. Sentiment Analysis of Twitter Images Through Novel Sequential Attention-Based Deep Metric Network. In: Mandal, J.K., Buyya, R., De, D. (eds) *Proceedings of International Conference on Advanced Computing Applications*. Advances in Intelligent Systems and Computing, vol 1406. Springer, Singapore. https://doi.org/10.1007/978-981-16-5207-3_24.

Joachim, Jutta, Marlen Martin, Henriette Lange, Andrea Schneiker and Magnus Dau. 2018. "Twittering for talent: Private military and security companies between business and military branding" *Contemporary Security Policy*, 39(2): 298–316.

Kharde, Vishal A. and Sonawane, Sheetal. 2016. "Sentiment Analysis of Twitter Data: A Survey of Techniques" *International Journal of Computer Applications*, 139(11): 5–15.

Klausen, J. 2015. "Tweeting the Jihad: Social media networks of western foreign fighters in Syria and Iraq." *Studies in Conflict and Terrorism*, 38(1): 1–22.

Klinger, Ulrike and Jakob Svensson. 2015. "The emergence of network media logic in political communication: A theoretical approach" *New Media & Society*, 17(8): 1241–1257.

Lucas, Christopher, Richard A. Nielsen, Margaret E. Roberts, Brandon M. Stewart, Alex Storer, and Dustin Tingley. 2015. "Computer-assisted text analysis for comparative politics" *Political Analysis*, 23(2): 254–277.

Macnair, Logan and Richard Frank. 2018. "The mediums and the messages: Exploring the language of Islamic State media through sentiment analysis" *Critical Studies on Terrorism*, 11(3): 438–457.

Manor, Ilan. 2016. "Are we there yet: Have MFAs realized the potential of digital diplomacy? Results from a cross-national comparison" *Diplomacy and Foreign Policy*, 1(2): 1–110.

Manor, Ilan and Elad Segev. 2020. "Social media mobility: Leveraging Twitter networks in online diplomacy" *Global Policy*, 11(2): 233–244.

Manor, Ilan and Rhys Crilley. 2020. "The mediatisation of MFAs: diplomacy in the new media ecology" *The Hague Journal of Diplomacy*, 15: 66–92.

Milan, Stefania. 2015. "Mobilizing in Times of Social Media. From Politics of Identity to a Politics of Visibility" In *Critical Perspectives on Social Media and Protest. Between Control and Emancipation* edited by Lina Dencik und Oliver Leistert. London: Rowman & Littlefield International, 53–70.

Nahon, Karine. 2016. "Where There is Social Media There is Politics" In *The Routledge Companion to Social Media and Politics* edited by Axel Bruns, Gunn Enli, Eli Skogerbo, Anders Olof Larsson and Christian Christensen. London and New York: Routledge, 39–55.

Megan Osterbur and Christina Kiel. 2021. "Tweeting in echo chambers? Analyzing Twitter discourse between American Jewish interest groups" *Journal of Information Technology & Politics*, 18(2): 194–213, DOI: 10.1080/19331681.2020.1838396.

Ott, Brian L. 2017. "The age of Twitter: Donald J. Trump and the politics of debasement." *Critical Studies in Media Communication*, 34(1): 59–68.

Öztürk, Nazan and Serkan Ayvaz. 2018. "Sentiment analysis on Twitter: A text mining approach to the Syrian refugee crisis" *Telematics and Informatics*, 35(1): 136–147.

Pang, Bo and Lillian Lee. 2008. "Opinion mining and sentiment analysis" *Foundations and Trends in Information Retrieval*, 2(1–2): 1–135.

Park, Soyoung, Sharon Strover, Jaewon Choi and Schnell MacKenzie. 2021. "Mind games: A temporal sentiment analysis of the political messages of the Internet Research Agency on Facebook and Twitter" *New Media & Society*: 1–22. https://doi.org/10.1177/14614448211014355

Poell, Thomas and José van Dijck. 2015. Social Media and Activist Communication. In *The Routledge Companion to Alternative and Community Media* edited by C. Atton. London: Routledge, 527–537.

Ragini, Rexiline J., Rubesh P.M. Anand and Vidhyacharan Bhaskar. 2018. "Big data analytics for disaster response and recovery through sentiment analysis" *International Journal of Information Management*, 42: 13–24.

Schneiker, Andrea. 2019. "Telling the story of the superhero and the anti-politician as president: Donald Trump's branding on Twitter" *Political Studies Review*, 17(3): 210–223.

Schneiker, Andrea, Magnus Dau, Jutta Joachim, Marlen Martin and Henriette Lange. 2019a. "Hiding in plain sight: Private military and security companies' use of Twitter as a distraction tool" *Media, War & Conflict*, 12(4): 483–503.

———. 2019b. "How to Analyze Social Media? Assessing the Promise of Mixed-Methods Designs for Studying the Twitter Feeds of PMSCs" *International Studies Perspectives*, 20: 188–200.

Schuster, Johannes, Helge Jörgens and Nina Kolleck. 2021. "The rise of global policy networks in education: analyzing Twitter debates on inclusive education using social network Analysis" *Journal of Education Policy*, 36(2): 211–231.

Serrano-Guerrero, Jesus, Jose A. Olivas, Francisco P. Romero and Enrique Herrera-Viedma. 2015. "Sentiment analysis: A review and comparative analysis of web services" *Information Sciences*, 311: 18–38.

Socher, Richard, Alex Perelygin, Jean Y. Wu, Jason Chuang, Christopher D. Manning, Andrew Y. Ng, and Christopher Potts. 2013. *Recursive Deep Models for Semantic Compositionality Over a Sentiment Treebank*, Proceedings of the 2013 Conference on Empirical Methods in Natural Language Processing, Association for Computational Linguistics, Seattle, Washington, 18–21 October, 1631–1642. Available from https://aclanthology.org/D13-1170.pdf.

Stieglitz, Stefan and Linh Dang-Xuan. 2013. "Emotions and information diffusion in social media-sentiment of microblogs and sharing behavior" *Journal of Management Information Systems*, 29(4): 217–247.

Sudulich, Laura, Matthew Wall, Rachel Gibson, Marta Cantijoch and Stephen Ward. 2014. "Introduction: The Importance of Method in the Study of the 'Political Internet.'" In *Analyzing Social Media Data and Web Networks* edited by Marta Cantijoch, Rachel Gibson and Stephen Ward. London: Palgrave Macmillan, 1–21.

Sunstein, Cass R. 2007. Republic.com 2.0. Princeton, NJ: Princeton University Press.

Twiplomacy. 2020. *Twiplomacy Study 2020*, last modified 20 March 2020. Available from https://twiplomacy.com/blog/twiplomacy-study-2020/.

Williams, Hywel T.P., James R. McMurray, Tim Kurz and F. Hugo Lambert. 2015. "Network analysis reveals open forums and echo chambers in social media discussions of climate change" *Global Environmental Change*, 32: 126–138.

Zeitzoff, Thomas, John Kelly and Gilad Lotan. 2015. "Using social media to measure foreign policy dynamics: An empirical analysis of the Iranian–Israeli confrontation (2012–2013)" *Journal of Peace Research*, 52(3): 368–383.

32
Discourse Network Analysis
Franz Eder

Introduction

Most work on foreign policy is (still) concerned with the role of (powerful) individuals, small-groups, governments, and bureaucracies, and of structural forces on the international level (Brummer et al. 2019b, 3). From a methodological point of view, these approaches apply only a limited number of well-established instruments from the social sciences' toolbox, such as archival research, classical content analysis, interviews, or focus groups (Potter 2017, 1). Kaarbo (2019, 220), therefore, criticizes that although there has been quite a lot of innovation within Foreign Policy Analysis (FPA), the discipline as such has not evolved much since the 1980s.

Discourse Network Analysis (DNA), the approach outlined in this chapter, builds upon recent theoretical developments in FPA (Kaarbo 1996; Kaarbo and Beasley 2008; Kaarbo 2015; Oppermann, Kaarbo, and Brummer 2017; Brummer et al. 2019a), caused by the trends of globalization and internationalization (Liftin 2000; Ansell and Torfing 2019). It profits from the insights of the *domestic turn* (Kaarbo 2015, 189; Lake 2013, 571; Brummer et al. 2019b, 2) in IR and the methodological innovations of the discipline ever since (Zeitzoff, Kelly, and Lotan 2015; de Graaf and van Apeldoorn 2019; Ingenhoff, Calamai, and Sevin 2021). As I will argue, DNA has the potential to considerably contribute to the theoretical and methodological advancement of FPA. From a theoretical perspective, the approach rests on four basic assumptions. First, foreign policy is a policy field as contested as any other public policy. Second, actors are "communicative agents" (Checkel 2008, 76; Kaarbo 2015, 201) that discursively seek to promote their ideas and beliefs in this policy arena. Third, every individual or organization that participates in this debate with a speech act in the form of a statement/claim is conceived as an actor. Finally, actors seek to form coalitions of like-minded to either uphold or change the current status quo.

Hence, DNA focuses on both the *content* (i.e., the discursive dimension of a political discourse) and the *process* (the coordinative dimension) of a political debate (Schmidt 2008, 303). DNA links FPA to the discursive turn in political science by referring to concepts such as Political Claims Theory (PCT) (Koopmans and Statham 1999), Discourse Coalition Theory (DCT) (Hajer 1993, 2005), and the Advocacy Coalition Framework (ACF) (Sabatier 1988, 1998; Sabatier and Weible 2007). Methodologically, DNA proceeds in two stages: first, determining the individual preferences of actors by applying qualitative content analysis to their speech acts (from sources such as speeches, interviews, position papers, or newspaper articles) to detect statements/claims toward a certain policy problem; second, aggregating these statements into a network using social network analysis and observing the evolution of this network over time.

Overall, adopting DNA to the study of foreign policy brings four benefits with it. First, theoretically, DNA links FPA to public/domestic politics by conceiving the realm of foreign policy as a policy field like any other. In this field, not only individual characteristics, group-dynamics, or systematic factors influence a state's foreign policy, but also domestic political processes and a variety of actors on different levels of analysis seek to influence policy outcomes. DNA integrates all these factors into a single and coherent framework of analysis. Second, methodologically, the approach brings together second- and third-generation FPA methods by combining qualitative content analysis and social network analysis (Potter 2017). Scholars can apply DNA to both classical FPA puzzles (i.e., approaches where multiple actors seek to influence policy outcomes in a complex interplay, like group decision-making or bureaucratic politics) and to contemporary approaches that conceive of FPA as a special form of public policy.

Third, DNA contributes to the discussion of continuity and change in foreign policy (Haesebrouck and Joly 2020) by considering foreign policy decision-making as a dynamic discourse that proceeds in sequences of statements. Finally, DNA contributes to the discussion of agency and structure in FPA (Carlsnaes 1992), that is the discussion of actors' abilities to shape and shove structural forces (in this case discourses) and how these forces influence actors in return. Overall, DNA allows us to answer research questions such as "How did the domestic political contestation of policy X in country Y contribute to the overall change of X?" (focus on the process of policy change); "Which actors and what coalitions were the driving forces in (not) changing policy X in country Y"? (focus on foreign policy actors and their interactions); or "What were the central arguments for changing policy X in country Y and how have these arguments changed and reinforced each other over time?" (focus on the content and dynamics of a debate).

To outline the approach, and to demonstrate its applicability and usefulness for the study of foreign policy, this chapter proceeds in four steps. First, I will review the literature and trace the development of DNA from an approach in public policy to its recent application in FPA. In the second step, I will discuss the theoretical and methodological basics of DNA. In the third step, I will illustrate the application of DNA by outlining a series of parliamentary debates in the British House of Commons in the run-up to the Iraq War of 2003. The data for the analysis, the final coding of statements, and the code for reproducing the results of this investigation are freely available on Github (https://github.com/franzeder/dna-example). In the fourth and final step, I will conclude the chapter and make suggestions for future research.

Literature Review

DNA originated in the late 2000s with the works of Schneider, Janning, Leifeld, and Malang, who investigated the role of political networks in public policy (Janning et al. 2009). The overall goal of this research programme was to evaluate the benefits of social network analysis for the study of political processes, especially in the realm of public policy, and to determine its applicability to this policy field. Philip Leifeld then advanced and formalized the approach in his PhD thesis on German pension politics (Leifeld 2016, 2013), laying the foundations for DNA's development into a promising tool for grasping the content and dynamics of policy debates.

Ever since, scholars have applied DNA in a variety of cases and have thereby contributed to a vivid research community and the emergence of four interdependent streams of research. Studies in the *first stream* apply DNA to cases from the field of public policy, and they further develop and refine the approach. The DNA provides the framework for analysing public policies in different geographical regions and diverse political systems, such as energy policies (Rinscheid 2015), software patents, and property rights in Europe (Leifeld and Haunss 2012), agricultural policies in Brazil (Ghinoi, Wesz Junior, and Piras 2018), or health policies in the UK (Buckton et al. 2019; Hilton et al. 2020). All these studies underline the usefulness of the approach for both displaying the content of a policy debate and visualizing the attempt of policy actors to influence the policy process in their favour by building coalitions of like-minded.

In contrast to these contributions, studies in the *second stream* seek to methodologically advance DNA. On the one hand, they move forward from sole description to inference (Leifeld 2018). The goal of these contributions is to identify "the generative mechanisms behind policy debates" (Leifeld 2020, 181), and to uncover the structural causes of continuity and change in such debates (see also van Meegdenburg in this volume). On the other hand, these studies move beyond the qualitative analysis of political claims and apply natural language processing, such as machine learning, for a supervised classification of statements (Haunss et al. 2020; Lapesa et al. 2020).

A steadily increasing number of studies in the *third stream* apply DNA to policies that are transnational in character. These studies bridge the divide between domestic public policies and the international arena. Most of these studies investigate the dynamics of political debates in the field of climate change and the regulation of carbon dioxide in the United States (Fisher, Leifeld, and Iwaki 2013; Fisher, Waggle, and Leifeld 2013; Kukkonen, Ylä-Anttila, and Broadbent 2017; Fisher and Leifeld 2019) or Italy (Ghinoi and Steiner 2020). Others investigate international financial politics (Haunss 2017) or migration (Wallaschek 2020). The contributions in this stream have demonstrated how to successfully integrate actors from different levels of analysis into a single and coherent framework for analysing political processes. Furthermore, they have underlined that policy debates are increasingly becoming transnational and *pluricentric*, with a variety of actors seeking to participate.

The *fourth and final stream* is the most recent one and seeks to apply DNA to the realm of foreign and security policy. Eder (2019) refers to DNA for analysing instances of group decision-making in the Bush cabinet in course of the run-up to the Iraq War of 2003. He applies the approach to public speeches and interviews of key decision-makers. Instead of indirectly inferring hasty concurrence-seeking from the presence of antecedent conditions or from final symptoms of groupthink, he is able to visualize non-public decision-making in group settings. Thereby, he unveils concurrence-seeking mechanisms and contributes to the methodological advancement of groupthink (see also Barr and Mintz in this volume). Troy (2019) also refers to DNA, displaying 80 years of papal human rights discourse against the backdrop of global developments. He determines the central figure in this discourse (i.e., Pope John Paul II) and characterizes Pope Francis I as a crucial transformer of the debate. The influence of different feminist perspectives on Canada's foreign policy is in the focus of interest in the study of Morton, Muchiri, and Swiss (2020). They seek to understand how and which feminist perspectives impact Canadian foreign policy and its implementation in various fields. Finally, Eder, Libiseller, and Schneider (2021) discuss how domestic politics, especially government-opposition dynamics and the perception of political opportunities, determine a country's foreign and security policy in the case of counter-terrorism. Applying DNA, they conclude that this policy field "is highly politicised and contested and resembles any other 'normal' policy field in democratic societies" (Eder, Libiseller, and Schneider 2021, 172).

This last and most recent stream of research has demonstrated the potential of applying DNA to the study of foreign and security policy. On the following pages, I will outline the basic foundations of the approach and elaborate why scholars should consider this method more seriously when investigating the foreign policy decision-making of states. As I will demonstrate, DNA allows scholars to investigate the content and the dynamics of a debate, and display the actors and coalitions as the carriers of these political debates that either cause foreign policy to change or to remain in the status quo.

Key Terms and Concepts, Methodology

DNA is a promising approach for the analysis of foreign policy because it enables researchers to tackle the analytical challenges of contemporary developments in global affairs: first, the blurring line between domestic and international politics; and second, the increasing trend of the contestation of (foreign) policies in this globalized world (Zürn 2014; Wagner et al. 2018; Haesebrouck and Mello 2020). First, as Liftin (2000, 239) observes, the "increased economic, social, and ecological interdependence means that domestic . . . politics are less insulated than ever from the international system". But it is not only the dynamics and the actors on the international level that interfere in domestic politics. Also, the international arena becomes a place where domestic political actors articulate and defend their preferences. Especially when it comes to the change of the status quo on the international level, the causes for this change are often to be found on the domestic, not the international level (Haesebrouck and Joly 2020, 6). A state's external affairs, hence, is not the sole realm of unilateral government action (Ansell and Torfing 2019, 141) anymore, but has become a playground for a plethora of actors and a number of coalitions with transnational character. Fisher and Leifeld (2019, 470) describe this phenomenon as "polycentric governance" in the sense that "multiple actors from different parts of a system interact to produce decentralised outcomes". This development is not only true for *soft* foreign policy issues like social, environmental, or maybe even financial policies, but also for classical *hard* foreign policy issues and security affairs.

Second, these policy decisions increasingly become contested. Executive decision-makers or government coalitions, for example, can disagree about a foreign policy because they respond differently to the domestic and international environment (Oppermann, Kaarbo, and Brummer 2017, 458). Also, representatives from civil society and other actors (e.g., interest groups or media) become part of the political debates that influence foreign policy decision-making. It is this domestic contestation and the derived political realignments of power and interests from it that cause change on the international level (Haesebrouck and Joly 2020, 6–7). Hence, Brummer et al. (2019b, 2) conclude that foreign policy becomes "more similar to (and intertwined with) 'ordinary' public policies".

Political debates are the *visible* manifestation of this contestation. DNA conceives of actors as "communicative agents" (Kaarbo 2015, 201) and as the central drivers in these debates. Actors make political claims or issue statements, understood as the verbal expression for or against a certain (aspect of a) policy (Leifeld 2018, 301). Actors do so, to learn about each other's positions, to reduce uncertainty (Leifeld 2014, 2), and to collectively mobilize support for their policy preferences (Koopmans and Statham 1999, 204). This debate, understood as a political discourse, is characterized by two elements: first, it is dynamic because actors repeatedly participate in the debate by issuing statements; second, it is relational, because actors refer to others in their statements (Leifeld 2014, 1). The debate, hence, is the "interactive process of conveying ideas" (Schmidt 2008, 303) via statements. These statements are instrumental and have a signalling function that is directed toward a certain target audience

(Leifeld 2018, 301–302). Furthermore, the debate's discourse comprises two elements: its content, and the interactive process – it is about what people say to each other, and how they say it. The process itself is characterized by a coordinative and a communicative function. The former is directed toward other policy actors with the aim of allying with or differentiating from them. The latter is directed toward an interested public that can join the debate and become actors by supporting or opposing other actors' statements (Schmidt 2008, 303–305).

This conception of political debates as instrumental discourses goes along with Hajer's concept of discourse coalitions (Hajer 1993, 2005). According to DCT, two or more discourse coalitions (i.e., alliances of communicative agents that share a high number of statements) group around common storylines (i.e., collections of statements that make up a certain discourse) and thereby seek to influence policies (Leifeld and Haunss 2012, 384).

From here, it is only a small step to the Advocacy Coalition Framework (ACF) (Sabatier 1988, 1998; Sabatier and Weible 2007). ACF is a theoretical framework for the analysis of public policy that is the theoretical backbone of DNA and that can also be utilized for the analysis of FP. Similar to PCT and comparable to DCT, ACF argues that actors issue statements and group themselves into "coalitions of competing policy beliefs" (Leifeld 2013, 170) to further their preferences and to enforce their policy conceptions. These coalitions are centred around actors' normative beliefs and policy core beliefs (Kukkonen, Ylä-Anttila, and Broadbent 2017, 715), which explains why these coalitions are quite stable and often polarized over time, and why policies only change when external shocks or new information through processes of learning disturb this equilibrium (Leifeld 2013, 170–171).

Although the ACF and DNA were originally conceptualized for the study of public policy, they are also applicable to the realm of foreign policy and bring several benefits with it. With the conception of actors' statements as materializations of individual beliefs and as the source of their policy preferences, these concepts directly fit into FPA's tradition of focusing on individuals and their belief systems. However, ACF and DNA extend the conception of who is an actor in foreign policy. Any person, group, or organization that participates in a debate, and that gets referred to by others in their statements, becomes a discursive agent (Pierce and Hicks 2019, 68–69). Hence, it is not up to the observer to decide who is an actor or not. Only by analysing debate contributions (i.e., statements), individuals, groups, and organizations that speak and get heard become actors, no matter whether they are government officials or ordinary citizens. Besides this integration of often overlooked actors into FPA, these approaches also contribute to a better understanding of continuity and change in foreign policies. They allow us to trace the dynamics of a debate and show, who is able to initiate change at which point in time (Kaarbo 2019, 226).

Methodologically, DNA proceeds in two stages and uses a combination of qualitative content analysis and social network analysis for grasping the statements of actors and relating them to each other (Leifeld 2013, 169). The data basis for this analysis are texts from various sources that are openly available. In the first stage, researchers look for actors' statements in these texts and annotate them using a coding-scheme (Leifeld 2018, 304). Statements must be made public by actors to be instrumental in a discourse (Leifeld 2018, 301). Hence, we can refer to a variety of textual data, such as newspaper articles, parliamentary speeches or testimonies, interviews, or position papers, to search for statements. The final decision as to which text formats are the most suitable for determining political claims depends on the discursive arena we seek to investigate.

These texts are then annotated using a category-based coding-scheme. We can either deductively or inductively (Bauer 2000; Schreier 2014) develop these codes or combine both approaches. Deductively generated codes are developed top-down, inspired by theoretical

Discourse Network Analysis

assumptions researchers seek to verify. In contrast to that, inductively generated codes are developed during the process of coding itself. Combining both approaches is a common and promising procedure because it allows scholars to both test their theoretical assumptions and ensure at the same time that no categories are overlooked.

This coding-scheme is then used to code statements that are the basic units of analysis in DNA. Statements comprise four variables (Leifeld 2018, 304–305): actors, concepts, agreement, and time stamps. An actor is any person or organization that speaks in a debate. Concepts are political claims (henceforth claims) that either support or oppose policies, policy instruments, or certain actions in a policy process (see also Lapesa et al. 2020, 144). Agreement refers to the extent of agreement or opposition of an actor toward a claim. This variable can either be dichotomous (i.e., agree – 1 or disagree – 0) or lie within a certain range (e.g., from −5 to +5). Time stamp is a temporal variable that specifies the date and time of a statement and allows the construction of dynamic networks. So, for example, the statement of Prime Minister Tony Blair "if Saddam [Hussein, FE] continues to fail to co-operate, force should be used" is coded as follows: "T Blair" (= actor), "Cabinet" (= organization), "22 – war" (= claim), "yes" (= agreement), "18 March 2002" (= time stamp).

Unlike Foucauldian discourse analysis that ultimately seeks to unveil power relations, the overall aim of the second stage of DNA is to transform the generated data (i.e., the sum of coded statements) into a two-mode network (a bipartite graph), also known as an affiliation network of actors (or organizations) and claims (for the mathematical details of this transformation, see Leifeld, Gruber, and Bossner 2019) that allows us to display the content, dynamics, and drivers of political debates. In this affiliation network (see Figure 32.1), every actor referring to a certain claim is displayed as an actor-node with an edge, linking the actor to the specific claim-node. This graph then allows us to gain insights into the content of the debate (the sum of claim-nodes) and who carries these claims (the actor nodes) (Leifeld 2018, 306).

In the next step, we are able to transform this two-mode affiliation network into a one-mode congruence (or conflict) network of actors or claims (see Figure 32.2). This transformation assumes that networks are "belief similarity networks of actors" (Leifeld 2013, 170) in the sense that "the more concepts [(i.e., claims), FE] two actors agree (or both disagree) on, the more similar they are in terms of preferences on concepts in the discourse" (Leifeld 2013, 174). Hence, actor congruence networks are networks that link actors to each other by edges,

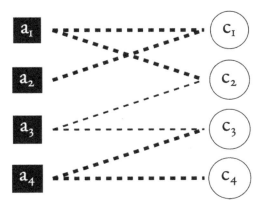

Figure 32.1 Affiliation network with actors (a) agreeing to certain claims (c). The edgeweights (displayed by the line width) provide information about the extent of agreement towards claims.

whenever these actors share the same claim by either both agreeing or both disagreeing to it. Claim congruence networks, on the other hand, are networks that display the edges between claims, whenever actors refer to the same claim in the same direction (i.e., both agreeing or both disagreeing). The same logic applies to conflict networks that display actors or claims, where actors have different attitudes toward claims (e.g., one actor agrees to a claim, the other one disagrees). One can, of course, also combine both, concurrence and conflict networks, with the subtraction mode, where agreements and disagreements are added up. So, for example, when two actors agree to a claim two times, and one time they disagree to the same claim, the overall value of agreement is +1.

So consequently, the more often actors refer to the same claim, the larger the edge-weight between these actors becomes. Hence, the edge-weight becomes a measurement of similarity in the discourse (Leifeld 2013, 175). To cope with the fact that some actors in a debate are supposed to speak more often than others (e.g., government officials receive more space in newspaper articles than ordinary citizens), we apply normalization (Leifeld 2013, 176; 2018, 310–313; Fisher and Leifeld 2019, 476) to control for this phenomenon by setting the mentioning of claims by actors in relation to their overall possibilities to mention claims in the first place.

The time stamp variable of statements is useful to display dynamic networks (see Figure 32.3). In this case, networks are drawn by grouping statements into certain time periods (e.g., statements of the same day, the same month, or the same year). "[M]odelling the development of political debates as dynamic networks may enable us to identify recurring mechanisms that drive the development of political debates" (Haunss et al. 2020, 326). Hence, dynamic networks are essential tools to understand the continuity and change of policies.

Finally, we can refer to various network measurements to better describe the characteristics of the overall discourse network and the discourse coalitions within it. Three of these measurements are especially helpful in the context of DNA: density, centrality, and various community detection algorithms. First, density describes the fraction of the maximum number of possible edges between nodes that is present in a network. By doing so, density gives an impression how connected nodes in a network really are (Newman 2010, 134–135).

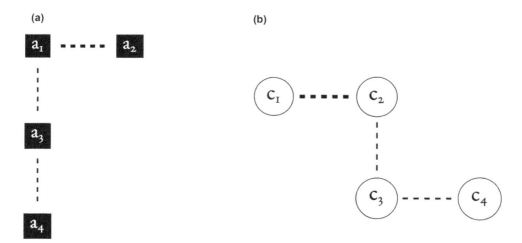

Figure 32.2 Congruence networks. (a) Actor-congruence network. (b) Claim-congruence network

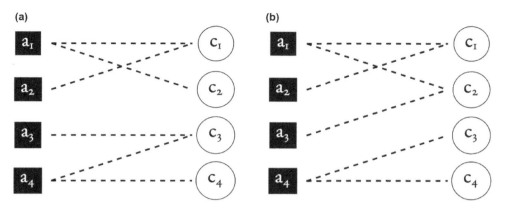

Figure 32.3 Dynamic affiliation network. (a) Network at t_0. (b) Network at t_1

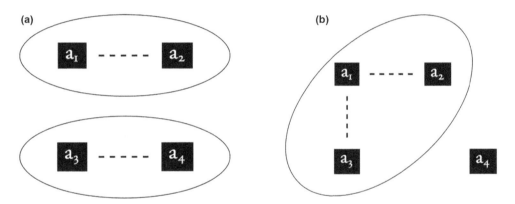

Figure 32.4 Dynamic actor congruence network.

The value for density ranges between 0 (there are no edges in a network, so that not a single node is linked to at least one other node) and 1 (the maximum number of edges is present because every node is connected to every other node). Thereby, density gives us information about the degree of interaction in a network. The higher the number of nodes and edges between these nodes in a network is, the more likely it is that a variety of claims and a greater number of actors support these claims in a debate.

Second, centrality measures give answers to the question as to which nodes are the most important in a network, either because they have the most links to other nodes (degree centrality), are connected to other important nodes (eigenvector centrality), are closely linked to other nodes in terms of distance (closeness centrality), or because they are strategically situated between other nodes (betweenness centrality) and thereby have a high social capital and hence power (Newman 2010, 168–193). These measurements allow us to detect the central carriers of a debate. These are the nodes that link different groups to each other and contribute to the establishment of a solid majority for the continuity or the change of an existing policy.

Third, community detection algorithms like modularity-maximization, hierarchical clustering, or betweenness-approaches are concepts that group nodes into clusters or communities of like-minded nodes, because they share a higher number of similarities than other nodes (Newman 2010, 357–358 and 371–391). These approaches, therefore, are the preferred measurements to group actors into discourse coalitions and to make them visible (see, for example, Figure 32.4).

To summarize this section, DNA proceeds in two steps. First, the statements of actors are coded using qualitative content analysis and a deductively and/or inductively developed coding-scheme. Second, these statements are then used to build affiliation- and congruence-networks that allow us to gain more insights into the content, dynamics, and structure of the debate over time. By applying different sorts of network measurements, we are able to describe the characteristics of, and to detect powerful nodes in the network.

Empirical Illustration

To illustrate the application of DNA, I will investigate the debates in the House of Commons on the UK's participation in the Iraq War in 2003. As this analysis will show, three central elements influenced the UK's decision to invade Iraq. First, the cabinet of Prime Minister (PM) Blair successfully implemented a discursive strategy in early 2003 that lay the focus of the threat storyline on humanitarian issues, and thereby diverted opponents of the war to publicly more difficult to comprehend claims such as questions of international law. Second, the path-dependency of the discourse in late 2002 (i.e., the extensive reference to the threat of force) narrowed the decision corridor in early 2003, and almost forced the PM and his cabinet to take the war route, if they did not want to lose their credibility. Finally, the support of the Conservative party, and especially of its leadership, was essential for PM Blair to balance the opposition from within his own Cabinet (Robin Cook, Leader of the House of Commons and Clare Short, Secretary of State for International Development resigned from the Cabinet over this question) and especially from backbenchers of his own party, and to secure a solid majority for the war resolution. The data for the analysis, the final coding of statements, and the code for reproducing the results of this investigation are freely available at https://github.com/franzeder/dna-example. There, readers will also find a more detailed discussion of the coding-scheme and additional graphs that are not used in this chapter due to page-limitation.

Why is the case of the UK's debate on its participation in the Iraq War in 2003 a good example for demonstrating the use of DNA? This debate, that dominated much of the House of Common's debates in late 2002 and early 2003, was one of the most controversial foreign policy debates in the UK since 1945 (Bluth 2004, 871) and "a defining moment in UK foreign policy" (Hoggett 2005, 418). Also in the UK, domestic politics increasingly interferes in foreign policy and requires a greater say in this policy area (Strong 2015, 605). Although PM Blair refused to hold a debate on this issue in the first half of 2002, he was finally forced by serious opposition within his own party (Kennedy-Pipe and Vickers 2007, 206) to debate the matter publicly, preventing to lose his party's support and reducing the risk of being overthrown (Strong 2015, 608–610). This debate was a turning point in the political history of the UK because it started a process that finally took away the royal prerogative from the PM to deploy military assets as s/he likes, and established a new parliamentary prerogative that military deployments need domestic legitimacy and a parliamentary resolution (Strong 2015, 604–605; Mello 2017). Prime ministers, therefore, are in need of a solid majority in parliament to legitimize the use of force in foreign policy domestically. Thus, this process of coalition-building in the parliamentary setting is a perfect example for illustrating the application of DNA.

I collected the statements of Members of Parliament (MPs) in the House of Commons from 12 debates on ten different days in the period from 16 April 2002 through 18 March 2003. To extract these statements and to display the various storylines and the overall discourse coalitions, I developed a coding-scheme as a mix of mainly deductively derived claims (from the secondary literature), complemented by inductively generated claims during coding. In total, 22 claims were used to code 1,166 statements of 161 persons (i.e., MPs), from nine organizations (i.e., parties in the House of Commons and the Cabinet).[1]

Following the secondary literature and a close reading of these debates, three strands (i.e., different storylines) dominated the overall discourse; that is, (1) the nature of the Iraqi threat, (2) the policies to address these threats, and (3) the overall goals of the UK's policy toward Iraq and the Middle East. First, decision-makers feverishly argued in the threat storyline whether Iraq and the regime of Saddam Hussein posed an imminent threat to the UK (Bluth 2004, 871), an overall threat to the world (Hoggett 2005, 423), or only a threat to the Middle East. Furthermore, the actors disagreed whether this threat emanated from the possible possession and use of weapons of mass destruction (WMD), Iraq's supposed link to international terrorism, or its ballistic missile programme (Bluth 2004, 884; Kennedy-Pipe and Vickers 2007, 211). Another claim that MPs raised in their contributions was the humanitarian issue (Hoggett 2005, 418; Kennedy-Pipe and Vickers 2007, 211) and the threat of Saddam Hussein to his own people (Bluth 2004, 884). Finally, speakers warned of the threat to the international order if Iraq did not obey the United Nations (UN) Security Council resolutions (Bluth 2004, 871), and feared the consequence of unilateralism, should the United States decide to go alone (Bluth 2004, 875).

Based on this threat storyline, MPs introduced a second policy-means storyline, presenting their policy preference to tackle these threats. In this storyline they either proposed regime change, the use of force (i.e., war), containment and deterrence, arms inspections, disarmament, sanctions, the threat of force (i.e., all options are on the table), diplomacy or the involvement of the UN Security Council, or a combination of these claims, to address the challenges.

Finally, decision-makers presented in the policy-goals storyline the overall aims the UK sought to achieve. That is to uphold a close alliance with the United States (Doig and Phythian 2005, 369; Kennedy-Pipe and Vickers 2007, 209), to reintegrate Iraq into the international community, to democratize the country, and to stabilize the whole region.

I divided the data into two phases: Phase one, starting from 16 April 2002, when PM Blair accepted to discuss the matter in Parliament until the end of 2002; Phase two, the remaining debates in 2003, until the final debate on 18 March 2003. Figures 32.5 and 32.6 display the overall agreement and disagreement of actors toward the claims in the whole debate, and thus allow us to gain insight into the discursive content of the debate. As these figures demonstrate, there was a solid consensus in 2002 that the alleged Iraqi WMD-programme (04 – WMD) posed a threat, that Saddam Hussein was a threat to his own people (07 – humanitarian), and that disarmament was the preferred measure to tackle this threat (25 – disarmament) by enforcing inspections (24 – inspections) via the United Nations (29 – United Nations). Actors also agreed that there was no imminent threat (01 – imminent), and hence war (22 – war) was mostly conceived not an option. However, actors unanimously agreed that the threat of force (27 – all options) should be applied to increase the pressure on the Iraqi regime to comply with the demands of the international community.

This discourse radically changed in 2003. War (22 – war) became the dominant claim used by actors in the debate. This measure was fiercely debated, and the discourse was polarized along it. There was, however, a dominant use and solid consensus of the moral argument

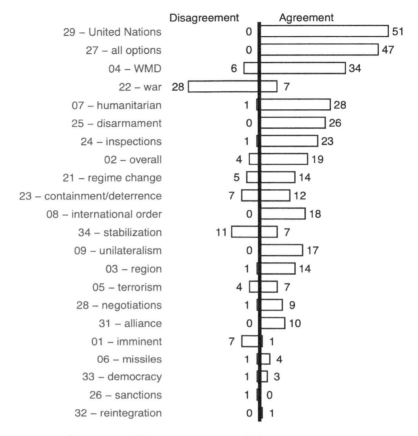

Figure 32.5 Overall agreement/disagreement toward claims in 2002.

that Iraq and Hussein posed a humanitarian threat (07 – humanitarian) that was supported by both proponents and opponents of war. The usefulness of inspections (24 – inspections) and of containment/deterrence (23 – containment/deterrence) was as contested as the conception of Iraq as an imminent threat (01 – imminent). However, actors agreed that there was a serious danger for the international community (08 – international order) if the threat of force (27 – all options) was toothless, and if Iraq would not be punished if it did not comply with the Security Council's resolutions. This result underlines the argumentation of Strong (2015, 884–885) that by focusing on moral issues (i.e., Iraq as a threat to humanity), proponents of the war gained the upper-hand in the debate. Furthermore, the extensive use of the claim "27 – all options" in 2002 created some kind of a path-dependency for the proponents of war. By referring to this claim, they lured themselves into a *rhetorical trap* and were finally "forced to honor ... [their, FE] commitments in order to protect their credibility and reputation" (Schimmelfennig 2001, 77).

Figure 32.7 displays the affiliation network of the most active speakers (i.e., those with ten or more statements in the debate) and their positions (agreement = black edges, rejection = grey edges) toward four central claims, that is "01 – imminent", "22 – war", "23 – containment/deterrence", and "24 – inspections". This graph shows a clear discursive strategy of the cabinet (especially PM Tony Blair and Foreign and Commonwealth Secretary Jack Straw) to

Discourse Network Analysis

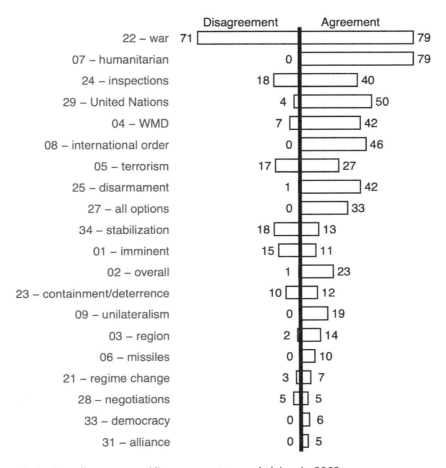

Figure 32.6 Overall agreement/disagreement toward claims in 2003.

warn of an imminent threat emanating from Iraq, calls for war as the final measure to tackle this threat, and questions the effectiveness of containment, deterrence, and inspections to cope with these challenges (see also Strong 2015, 878). The cabinet received support by influential frontbenchers of both the Labour and the Conservative parties, first and foremost Iain Duncan Smith (Leader of the Opposition and Leader of the Conservative Party) and Michael Ancram (Shadow Secretary of State for Foreign and Commonwealth Affairs, Conservative Party). Opposition came mostly from the Liberal Democrats and Labour backbenchers (see also Bluth 2004, 887, 880).

Figures 32.8 and 32.9, showing the respective congruence networks of both periods, underline this observation. In 2002, the majority of actors stuck together very closely, by referring to similar claims and united in opposition to war as a policy option. As Figure 32.8 also demonstrates, already in 2002, PM Blair (accompanied by another cabinet member and Tory MPs) deviated from this anti-war discourse. Figure 32.9 finally shows that the PM and his cabinet (high edge betweenness of PM Blair and Foreign Secretary Straw) were successful in convincing a majority of MPs that war is a necessary evil. Hence, the discourse in 2003 is characterized by two opposing discourse coalitions – one coalition in favour and one against war as viable option.

527

Franz Eder

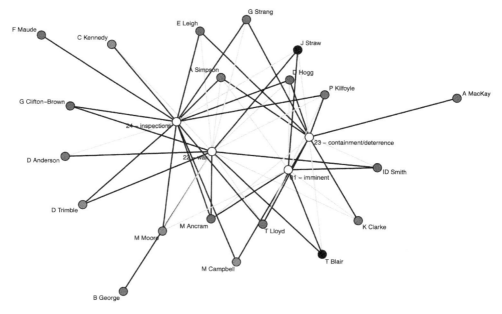

Figure 32.7 Affiliation network of most active speakers and central claims. Black edges indicate agreement with, grey edges indicate rejection of a claim.

Figure 32.8 Congruence network between most active speakers via shared claims in 2002.

Discourse Network Analysis

Figure 32.9 Congruence network between most active speakers via shared claims in 2003.

Figure 32.10 is a different perspective on this polarization process. This graph clusters organizations (i.e., parties) according to their overall positions toward the four central claims mentioned before and displays these organizations as distinctive branches. Organizations of the same branch or subbranch are ideologically closer than organizations of different branches. The interesting point here is, that the Cabinet's discourse in the debate resembled the discourse of the Conservative party (i.e., the major opposition). In contrast, Labour's discourse (i.e., the discourse of PM's own party) shared more of the claims the Liberal Democrats (i.e., the major opposition to war) applied in their storylines.

529

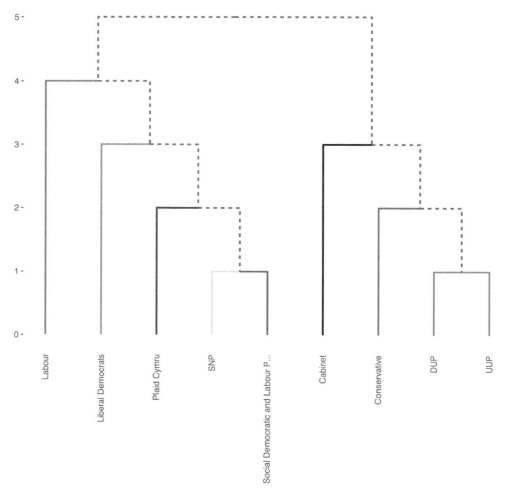

Figure 32.10 Dendrogram of organizations and their distance to each other via shared claims in 2003.

This observation underlines the fact that although the PM was able to secure a solid majority in the House of Commons for a war resolution, backbenchers from his own party opposed this resolution, whereas the Conservative Party and its leadership mainly supported the Cabinet's approach. As a close reading of the debate contributions shows, it was the Conservative's general attitude to support military measures in external affairs and to give the executive the leap of faith in such decisions that guaranteed PM Blair and his cabinet a solid majority for radically changing its policies toward Iraq and allowing the UK to enter the war in 2003.

As this empirical illustration exemplifies, DNA allows us to uncover the discursive strategies of actors to gain the upper-hand in the discursive battle. Furthermore, it gives insights into the dynamics of these debates and shows at which points in time, crucial changes of the status quo happened that finally contributed to the introduction of new policies.

Conclusion

With this chapter, I introduced DNA as a promising method for the analysis of foreign policy decision-making. I first traced the evolution of DNA from an instrument in the analysis of public policy to its recent application in transnational politics and finally in FPA. I then argued that DNA is so promising because it enables researchers to tackle the analytical challenges of contemporary developments in global affairs, such as the blurring of line between domestic and international politics, and the trend of contesting foreign policy in the domestic political arena, as well as in the global public sphere. DNA helps us to make these debates of contestation visible, and it thus allows us to better understand the content and the dynamics of discourses that influence foreign policy decision-making in one way or the other. I then showed how DNA proceeds in two stages: first, gathering statements of actors by applying qualitative content analysis; second, by linking these statements in networks using social network analysis. Finally, I demonstrated the applicability of DNA by analysing the debates in the House of Commons on UK's participation in the Iraq War in 2003.

As this chapter demonstrated, the strength of DNA lies in its capacity to make political debates – understood as central elements in foreign policy decision-making – visible. Hence, it allows scholars to integrate political processes on the domestic level of analysis into the study of foreign policy, and to link FPA as a discipline more closely to other fields, first and foremost public policy.

However, there are also limitations to this approach that researchers should be aware of. First, DNA is only able to grasp and display the content and dynamics of political contestation that are openly visible. Decision-making behind closed doors, or in isolated political systems with hardly any public discourse, is difficult to analyse with this approach due to the lack of openly available data. Second, explanations of foreign policy decision-making are multifactorial (Hudson 2005, 2). Hence, the analysis of the political contestation of foreign policy by applying DNA can only contribute to a better understanding of the discursive strategies and the dynamics that result in policies.

In addition, first-time users should focus on three aspects that are crucial for the successful application of DNA. First, they should thoroughly think which discursive arena and what textual data are appropriate to satisfy their specific research interests. Second, first-time users should develop and test the coding-scheme on a small sample of the data, to ensure that the scheme is both appropriate for the analysis of the texts, and that the coders apply it consistently. Third and finally, first-time users should comprehend the basics of social network analysis – that is, understanding what the concept of nodes and edges mean, what centrality measurements are and what they tell us about a network, and how to detect communities in a social network – for applying its techniques adequately and for being able to use the whole potential of the various measures for their analyses.

Concluding, further research should focus on two elements. First, scholars should increasingly apply DNA in combination with different approaches from FPA, especially for the analysis of small-group decision-making, bureaucratic politics, or international diplomacy. Second, quantitative text analysis should investigate the possibilities of (semi) automatically coding and classifying statements. This would address one of the main obstacles for researchers to apply DNA – the time and cost-intensive first stage of coding.

Acknowledgement

The University of Innsbruck supported this open access publication through its Open Access Funding Programme.

Note

1 For more information on the coding, please have a look at https://github.com/franzeder/dna-example.

References

Ansell, Christopher, and Jacob Torfing. 2019. 'The Network Approach and Foreign Policy.' In Foreign Policy as Public Policy? Promises and Pitfalls, edited by Klaus Brummer, Sebastian Harnisch, Kai Oppermann, and Diana Panke, 139–170. Manchester: Manchester University Press.

Bauer, Martin W. 2000. 'Classical Content Analysis: a Review.' In Qualitative Researching with Text, Image and Sound: A Practical Handbook, edited by Martin W. Bauer and George Gaskell, 131–151. Los Angeles, CA: SAGE.

Bluth, Christoph. 2004. 'The British Road to War: Blair, Bush and the Decision to Invade Iraq.' International Affairs 80 (5): 871–892. https://doi.org/10.1111/j.1468-2346. 2004.00423.x.

Brummer, Klaus, Sebastian Harnisch, Kai Oppermann, and Diana Panke, eds. 2019a. Foreign Policy as Public Policy? Promises and Pitfalls. Manchester: Manchester University Press.

———. 2019b. 'Introduction: Foreign Policy as Public Policy.' In Foreign Policy as Public Policy? Promises and Pitfalls, edited by Klaus Brummer, Sebastian Harnisch, Kai Oppermann, and Diana Panke, 1–18. Manchester: Manchester University Press.

Buckton, Christina H., Gillian Fergie, Philip Leifeld, and Shona Hilton. 2019. 'A Discourse Network Analysis of UK Newspaper Coverage of the "Sugar Tax" Debate before and after the Announcement of the Soft Drinks Industry Levy.' BMC Public Health 19 (490): 1–14. https://doi.org/10.1186/s12889-019-6799-9.

Carlsnaes, Walter. 1992. 'The Agency-Structure Problem in Foreign Policy Analysis.' International Studies Quarterly 36 (3): 245–270. https://doi.org/10.2307/2600772.

Checkel, Jeffrey T. 2008. 'Constructivism and Foreign Policy.' In Foreign Policy: Theories, Actors, Cases, edited by Steve Smith, Amelia Hadfield, and Tim Dunne, 71–82. Oxford: Oxford University Press.

de Graaf, Nana, and Bastiaan van Apeldoorn. 2019. 'The Transnationalist US Foreign-policy Elite in Exile? A Comparative Network Analysis of the Trump Administration.' Global Networks 21 (2): 238–264. https://doi.org/10.1111/glob.12265.

Doig, Alan, and Mark Phythian. 2005. 'The National Interest and the Politics of Threat Exaggeration: The Blair Government's Case for War against Iraq.' The Political Quarterly 76 (3): 368–376. https://doi.org/10.1111/j.1467-923X.2005.00695.x.

Eder, Franz. 2019. 'Making Concurrence-Seeking Visible: Groupthink, Discourse Networks, and the 2003 Iraq War.' Foreign Policy Analysis 15 (1): 21–42. https://doi.org/10.1093/fpa/orx009.

Eder, Franz, Chiara Libiseller, and Bernhard Schneider. 2021. 'Contesting Counterterrorism: Discourse Networks and the Politicisation of Counter-Terrorism in Austria.' Journal of International Relations and Development 24 (1): 171–195. https://doi.org/10.1057/s41268-020-00187-8.

Fisher, Dana R., and Philip Leifeld. 2019. 'The Polycentricity of Climate Policy Blockage.' Climatic Change 155 (4): 469–487. https://doi.org/10.1007/s10584-019-02481-y.

Fisher, Dana R., Philip Leifeld, and Yoko Iwaki. 2013. 'Mapping the Ideological Networks of American Climate Politics.' Climate Change 116 (3): 523–545. https://doi.org/10. 1007/s10584-012-0512-7.

Fisher, Dana R., Joseph Waggle, and Philip Leifeld. 2013. 'Where Does Political Polarization Come From? Locating Polarization Within the U.S. Climate Change Debate.' American Behavioral Scientist 5 (1): 70–92. https://doi.org/10.1177/0002764212463360.

Ghinoi, Stefano, and Bodo Steiner. 2020. 'The Political Debate on Climate Change in Italy: A Discourse Network Analysis.' Politics and Governance 8 (2): 215–228. https://doi.org/10.17645/pag.v8i2.2577.

Ghinoi, Stefano, Valedemar João Wesz Junior, and Simone Piras. 2018. 'Political Debates and Agricultural Policies: Discourse Coalitions Behind the T creation of Brazil's Pronaf.' Land Use Policy 76:68–80. https://doi.org/10.1016/j.landusepol.2018.04.039.

Haesebrouck, Tim, and Jeroen Joly. 2020. 'Foreign Policy Change: From Policy Adjustments to Fundamental Reorientations.' Political Studies Review online first:1–10. https://doi.org/10.1177/1478929920918783.

Haesebrouck, Tim, and Patrick A. Mello. 2020. 'Patterns of Political Ideology and Security Policy.' *Foreign Policy Analysis* 16 (4): 565–586. https://doi.org/10.1093/fpa/oraa006.

Hajer, Maarten A. 1993. 'Discourse Coalitions and the Institutionalization of Practice: The Case of Acid Rain in Britain.' In The Argumentative Turn in Policy Analysis and Planning, edited by Frank Fisher and John Forester, 43–76. Durham, NC and London: Duke University Press.

———. 2005. The Politics of Environmental Discourse: Ecological Modernization and the Policy Process. Oxford: Oxford University Press.

Haunss, Sebastian. 2017. '(De-)Legitimating Discourse Networks: Smoke without Fire?' In Capitalism and Its Legitimacy in Times of Crisis, edited by Steffen Schneider, Henning Schmidtke, Sebastian Haunss, and Jennifer Gronau, 191–220. Cham: Palgrave MacMillan.

Haunss, Sebastian, Jonas Kuhn, Sebastian Padó, Andre Blessing, Nico Blokker, Erenay Dayanik, and Gabriella Lapesa. 2020. 'Integrating Manual and Automatic Annotation for the Creation of Discourse Network Data Sets.' *Politics and Governance* 8 (2): 326– 339. https://doi.org/10.17645/pag.v8i2.2591.

Hilton, Shona, Christina H. Buckton, Tim Henrichsen, Gillian Fergie, and Philip Leifeld. 2020. 'Policy Congruence and Advocacy Strategies in the Discourse Networks of Minimum Unit Pricing for Alcohol and the Soft Drinks Industry Levy.' *Addiction* 115 (2): 2303–2314. https://doi.org/10.1111/add.15068.

Hoggett, Paul. 2005. 'Iraq: Blair's Mission Impossible.' *British Journal of Politics and International Relations* 7 (3): 418–428. https://doi.org/10.1111/j.1467-856X.2005. 00195.x.

Hudson, Valerie. 2005. 'Foreign Policy Analysis: Actor-Specific Theory and the Ground of International Relations.' *Foreign Policy Analysis* 1 (1): 1–30. https://doi.org/10. 1111/j.1743-8594.2005.00001.x.

Ingenhoff, Diana, Giada Calamai, and Efe Sevin. 2021. 'Key Influencers in Public Diplomacy 2.0: A Country-Based Social Network Analysis.' *Social Media + Society* online first: 1–12. https://doi.org/10.1177/2056305120981053.

Janning, Frank, Philip Leifeld, Thomas Malang, and Volker Schneider. 2009. 'Diskursnetzwerkanalyse. Überlegungen zur Theoriebildung und Methodik.' In Politiknetzwerke: Modelle, Anwendungen und Visualisierungen, edited by Volker Schneider, Frank Janning, Philip Leifeld, and Thomas Malang, 59–92. Wiesbaden: Springer VS.

Kaarbo, Juliet. 1996. 'Power and Influence in Foreign Policy Decision Making: The Role of Junior Coalition Partners in German and Israeli Foreign Policy.' *International Studies Quarterly* 40 (4): 501–530. https://doi.org/10.2307/2600889.

———. 2015. 'A Foreign Policy Analysis Perspective on the Domestic Politics Turn in IR Theory.' *International Studies Review* 17 (2): 189–216. https://doi.org/10.1111/ misr.12213.

Kaarbo, Juliet. 2019. 'Conclusion: The Promise and Pitfalls of Studying Foreign Policy as Public Policy.' In Foreign policy as public policy? Promises and Pitfalls, edited by Klaus Brummer, Sebastian Harnisch, Kai Oppermann, and Diana Panke, 218–231. Manchester: Manchester University Press.

Kaarbo, Juliet, and Ryan K. Beasley. 2008. 'Taking It to the Extreme: The Effect of Coalition Cabinets on Foreign Policy.' *Foreign Policy Analysis* 4 (1): 67–81. https://doi.org/10.1111/ j.1743-8594.2007.00058.x.

Kennedy-Pipe, Caroline, and Rhiannon Vickers. 2007. '"Blowback" for Britain?: Blair, Bush, and the War in Iraq.' *Review of International Studies* 33 (2): 205–221. https://doi.org/10.1017/ S0260210507007474.

Koopmans, Ruud, and Paul Statham. 1999. 'Political Claims Analysis: Integrating Protest Event and Political Discourse Approaches.' *Mobilization: An International Journal* 4 (1): 203–221. https://doi.org/10.17813/maiq.4.2.d759337060716756.

Kukkonen, Anna, Tuomas Ylä-Anttila, and Jeffrey Broadbent. 2017. 'Advocacy Coalitions, Beliefs and Climate Change Policy in the United States.' *Public Administration* 95 (3): 713–729. https://doi.org/10.1111/padm.12321.

Lake, David A. 2013. 'Theory is Dead, Long Live Theory: The end of the Great Debates and the Rise of Eclecticism in International Relations.' *European Journal of International Relations* 19 (3): 567–587. https://doi.org/10.1177/1354066113494330.

Lapesa, Gabriella, Andre Blessing, Nico Blokker, Erenay Dayanik, Sebastian Haunss, Jonas Kuhn, and Sebastian Padó. 2020. 'Analysis of Political Debates through Newspaper Reports: Methods and Outcomes.' *Datenbank Spektrum* 20 (2): 143–153. https://doi.org/10.1007/s13222-020-00344-w.

Leifeld, Philip. 2013. 'Reconceptualizing Major Policy Change in the Advocacy Coalition Framework: A Discourse Network Analysis of German Pension Politics.' *The Policy Studies Journal* 41 (1): 169–198. https://doi.org/10.1111/psj.12007.

———. 2014. 'Polarization of Coalitions in an Agent-Based Model of Political Discourse.' *Computational Social Networks* 1 (7): 1–22. https://doi.org/10.1186/s40649-0140007-y.

———. 2016. Policy Debates as Dynamic Networks: German Pension Politics and Privatization Discourse. Frankfurt a. M. and New York, NY: Campus.

———. 2018. 'Discourse Network Analysis: Policy Debates as Dynamic Networks.' In The Oxford Handbook of Political Networks, edited by Jenniger Nicoll Victor, Alexander H. Montgomery, and Mark Lubell, 301–325. Oxford: Oxford University Press.

Leifeld, Philip. 2020. 'Policy Debates and Discourse Network Analysis: A Research Agenda.' *Politics and Governance* 8 (2): 180–183. https://doi.org/10.17645/pag. v8i2.3249.

Leifeld, Philip, Johannes Gruber, and Felix Rolf Bossner. 2019. Discourse Network Analyzer Manual. https://github.com/leifeld/dna/releases/download/v2.0-beta.24/dnamanual.pdf: Github.

Leifeld, Philip, and Sebastian Haunss. 2012. 'Political Discourse Networks and the Conflict over Software Patents in Europe.' *European Journal of Political Research* 51 (3): 382– 409. https://doi.org/10.1111/j.1475-6765.2011.02003.x.

Liftin, Karen T. 2000. 'Advocacy Coalitions Along the Domestic-Foreign Frontier: Globalization and Canadian Climate Change.' *Policy Studies Journal* 28 (1): 236–252. https://doi.org/10.1111/j.1541-0072.2000.tb02026.x.

Mello, Patrick A. 2017. 'Curbing the Royal Prerogative to Use Military Force: The British House of Commons and the Conflicts in Libya and Syria.' *West European Politics* 40 (1): 80–100. https://doi.org/10.1080/01402382.2016.1240410.

Morton, Sam E., Judyannet Muchiri, and Liam Swiss. 2020. 'Which Feminism(s)? For Whom? Intersectionality in Canada's Feminist International Assistance Policy.' *International Journal* 75 (3): 329–348. https://doi.org/10.1177/0020702020953420.

Newman, M.E.J. 2010. Networks: An Introduction. Oxford: Oxford University Press.

Oppermann, Kai, Juliet Kaarbo, and Klaus Brummer. 2017. 'Introduction: Coalition Politics and Foreign Policy.' *European Political Science* 16 (4): 457–462. https://doi.org/10.1057/s41304-016-0064-9.

Pierce, Jonathan J., and Katherine C. Hicks. 2019. 'Foreign Policy Applications of the Advocacy Coalition Framework.' In Foreign Policy as Public Policy? Promises and Pitfalls, edited by Klaus Brummer, Sebastian Harnisch, Kai Oppermann, and Diana Panke, 65–90. Manchester: Manchester University Press.

Potter, Philip B.K. 2017. 'Methods of Foreign Policy Analysis.' Oxford Research Encyclopedia of International Studies, no. 5 August, 1–20. https://doi.org/10.1093/ acrefore/9780190846626.013.34.

Rinscheid, Adrian. 2015. 'Crisis, Policy Discourse, and Major Policy Change: Exploring the Role of Subsystem Polarization in Nuclear Energy Policymaking.' *European Policy Analysis* 1 (2): 34–37. https://doi.org/10.18278/epa.1.2.3.

Sabatier, Paul A. 1988. 'An Advocacy Coalition Framework of Policy Change and the Role of Policy-Oriented Learning Therein.' *Policy Sciences* 21 (2/3): 129–168.

———. 1998. 'The Advocacy Coalition Framework: Revisions and Relevance for Europe.' *Journal of Public Policy* 5 (1): 98–130.

Sabatier, Paul A., and Christopher M. Weible. 2007. 'The Advocacy Coalition Framework.' In Theories of the Policy Process, edited by Paul A. Sabatier, 189–220. Cambridge, MA: Westview Press.

Schimmelfennig, Frank. 2001. 'The Community Trap: Liberal Norms, Rhetorical Action, and the Eastern Enlargement of the European Union.' *International Organization* 55 (1): 47–80. https://doi.org/10.1162/002081801551414.

Schmidt, Vivien. 2008. 'Discursive Institutionalism: The Explanatory Power of Ideas and Discourse.' *Annual Review of Political Science* 11: 303–326. https://doi.org/10.1146/ annurev.polisci.11.060606.135342.

Schreier, Margit. 2014. 'Qualitative Content Analysis.' In The SAGE Handbook of Qualitative Data Analysis, edited by Uwe Flick, 170–183. London: SAGE.

Strong, James. 2015. 'Why Parliament Now Decides on War: Tracing the Growth of the Parliamentary Prerogative through Syria, Libya and Iraq.' *British Journal of Politics and International Relations* 17 (4): 604–622. https://doi.org/10.1111/1467856X.12055.

Troy, Jodok. 2019. 'The Papal Human Rights Discourse: The Difference Pope Francis Makes.' *Human Rights Quarterly* 41 (1): 66–90. https://doi.org/10.1353/hrq.2019. 0003.

Wagner, Wolfgang, Anna Herranz-Surrallés, Juliet Kaarbo, and Falk Ostermann. 2018. 'Party Politics at the Water's Edge: Contestation of Military Operations in Europe.' *European Political Science Review* 10 (4): 537-563. https://doi.org/10.1017/S1755773918000097.

Wallaschek, Stefan. 2020. 'The Discursive Construction of Solidarity: Analysing Public Claims in Europe's Migration Crisis.' *Political Studies* 68 (1): 47–92. https://doi. org/10.1177/0032321719831585.

Zeitzoff, Thomas, John Kelly, and Gilad Lotan. 2015. 'Using Social Media to Measure Foreign Policy Dynamics: An Empirical Analysis of the Iranian–Israeli Confrontation (2012–2013).' *Journal of Peace Research* 52 (3): 368–383. https://doi.org/10.1177/ 0022343314558700.

Zürn, Michael. 2014. 'The Politicization of World Politics and Its Effects: Eight Propositions.' *European Political Science Review* 6 (1): 47–71. https://doi.org/10.1017/S1755773912000276.

33
Text as Data
Valerio Vignoli

Introduction

Texts are a fundamental source of data in the study of foreign policy. The main reason is that the subject of analysis is ultimately the interaction between actors who mostly express themselves through language: heads of states make speeches, international organizations release statements, and NGOs draft reports. Therefore, researchers in the field often rely on texts to capture agents' beliefs, preferences, and intentions. In most cases, foreign policy scholars have analyzed these texts through qualitative methods such as discourse and narrative analysis (see Koschut, Ostermann and Sjöstedt, or Oppermann and Spencer in this volume). These approaches strongly value how the individual scholar interprets the text and its nuances. In turn, they require careful and thoughtful reading of all the textual material considered as useful for the purposes of the research. This endeavor becomes increasingly challenging as the amount of text to be read increases.

Nowadays, we indeed live in a world where we have an unprecedented quantity of readily available textual contents. Thanks to the diffusion of digital technologies, researchers can access and collect a multitude of textual documents in a short span of time. Moreover, the range of texts of interest has also increased: other than *traditional documents* such as speeches and newspaper articles, the web offers also new type of texts such as social media posts. This poses a challenge for foreign policy scholars: how is it possible to analyze all relevant data on a certain research topic? Reading and manually coding documents is a time-consuming effort. When we deal with thousands (if not millions) of documents, it becomes simply unfeasible.

The rise and evolution of automated text analysis methods in the last two decades has been fostered by the intention to address this issue. In fact, these quantitative methods allow scholars to automatically extract meaningful information from a large number of texts. To do so, the researcher is asked to treat *text as data* rather than as text, that is, transforming unstructured into structured data. Such data are subsequently analyzed through statistical techniques. In contrast to many qualitative methods, quantitative text analysis methods produce numeric estimates that quantify the concept of interest. The fact that the process of features extraction is completely automated is also a distinctive aspect. A wide range of methods of text as data, such as Wordfish or Structural Topic Model, have been developed across the years to perform different tasks, including measuring variation in actors' positions and attention for different topics. For instance, they can be used to address questions such as "how do states' positions on climate change differ?" or "how does the US Department of State examine human rights violations in allied states?"

Various scholars have already surveyed the state of the art about these methods, underlining their characteristics, aims, and standard procedures (Grimmer and Stewart 2013; Wilkerson and Casas 2017; Benoit 2020). This chapter is different from these works as it focuses on how methods of texts as data have been employed in the field of International Relations (IR) and the sub-field of Foreign Policy Analysis (FPA). Therefore, the characteristics of these techniques will be explained through various examples applied to the study of foreign policy. Subsequently, this chapter will assess the potentialities and challenges that automated text analysis methods present in the context of the discipline.

On the one hand, as it was suggested, they contribute to the study of foreign policy, offering the opportunity for scholars to extract features from large bodies of text. Such features can be used to gauge relevant concepts in the discipline that have been previously measured in different ways. On the other hand, the paucity of large sets of textual documents has inhibited the use of these methods in the field this far. There is admittedly a problem of data availability. Diplomatic documents are often secreted or not easily accessible; international institutions tend to have less intense activities and, consequently, produce fewer documents with respect to domestic counterparts (e.g., national parliaments). Still, the study of foreign policy would benefit from stronger efforts to collect large sets of textual data that require to be analyzed through automated text analysis methods.

Key Terms and Concepts: Text as Text versus Text as Data

Text, both in its written and spoken form, is not originally meant to be analyzed through statistical methods. It aims to communicate authors' beliefs, ideas, concerns, and so on. A diplomat speaking at the UN General Assembly does not even remotely think that a scholar may count the number of times s/he uses a specific word. As Benoit (2020, 463) claims, "texts start to become data when we record it for reference or analysis and this process involves imposing some abstraction or structure that exists outside the text itself". He follows by pointing out that "absent the imposition of this structure, the text remains *informative* – we can read it and understand (in some form) what it means – but it does not provide a form of *information*" (emphasis in the original). In other words, raw text, that is, text in its original form, can be employed as a source of data. Qualitative methods of text analysis fruitfully do that. However, it is only when we convert it to a format suitable to be described and analyzed through statistical tools that we treat that as if it was (quantitative) data.

The flipside of this process of transforming "words into numbers" is that we completely lose our chance to understand our texts of interests (defined as *corpus* in the jargon) in their original form.[1] They are stripped of their original structure: that series of words taking a certain meaning according to their semantics and context, occasionally interrupted by punctuation marks and ordered according to syntactic rules, forming sentences connected between each other in a (presumedly) sensible way is definitively gone. We are left with what is known as a *document-feature matrix* (or, alternatively, *document term matrix*): the usual starting point for analyzing text as data. Table 33.1 presents a school example of a document-feature matrix. In the columns you can find three words (w) occurring in our corpus, while in the lines the three documents composing our corpus (d). The numbers in the cells represent the frequency with which a word w occurs in document d. For instance, w1 occurs 0 times in d1, once in d2, and twice in d3.

Table 33.1 Example of a Document-Feature Matrix

	w1	w2	w3
d1	0	2	1
d2	1	1	2
d3	2	0	0

Such matrixes represent an incomplete and incorrect approximation of the texts. In fact, the matrix does not take into account the word order nor their meaning. Consider, for instance, the sentences "Germany attacks Russia" and "Russia attacks Germany". They clearly convey opposite messages. However, they contain the same words and, therefore, they will contribute in the same manner to shaping the document-feature matrix. This is defined as a *Bag of Words* approach to texts: all the words are extrapolated of their context and put without any need for order in a matrix, similarly to a cluttered bag. Furthermore, during the transformation of corpora into a document-feature matrix, the words lose their meaning. For instance, the word itself "mean" is polysemic (multiple meanings): it is a synonym of "instrument", an adjective with a negative connotation, and a verb's infinite form. To sum up, when we treat text as data, we should be aware about all that is lost in the process.

That must not lead us to discard text as data methods as flawed. In fact, automated text analysis methods are not designed to interpret texts but rather to obtain information from a large quantity of them. This can be thought as a process of *data mining*, in which we have to mine a cave (our large body of texts) in order to extract nuggets of gold (a synthetic description and analysis of the texts themselves). In this light, we should interpret the claim that "all quantitative models of language are wrong – but some of them are useful" (Grimmer and Stewart 2013, 269). On one side, treating text as data inherently involves the imposition of what Benoit (2020, 265) defines as a "semantic violence" to our raw texts, occurring in the moment when we transform them into a document-feature matrix. On the other side, it is also true that such a violence is perpetrated in the name of the "higher purpose of enabling more systematic large-scaled inference" (Benoit 2020, 265). It is up to the researcher to judge if the advantages of such an approach outweigh the drawbacks.

A Classification of Text as Data Methods

As it was already suggested in the introduction, multiple automated text analysis methods were developed across the years to perform different tasks in various ways. Therefore, the choice of one method over another should be mostly driven by the scholar's research question and aims. In this section, an overview of the most well-known methods of text as data is presented. They are divided into four groups, according to their task and the extent of inputs given by the researcher in the process of analysis (see Table 33.2).

On one side, we can distinguish between *classification methods* and *scaling methods*: while the former aim at classifying texts in one or more categories, the latter are designed to measure actors' position in an ideological space. Classification methods are designed for dealing with a very large quantity of texts as they amplify the human capacity to place documents in a category.[2] Therefore, if the number of documents to classify is small enough to make the effort feasible for the researcher, there is little point in using them. To the contrary, in scaling methods, the quality of the documents is more important than the quantity. Since the aim is locating actors on a dimension, we must for instance be sure and that the language employed

Table 33.2 Categories of Automated Text Analysis and Some Examples

	Supervised	*Unsupervised*
Classification	Naive Bayes, Support vector machines	K-means clustering, Latent Dirichlet allocation
Scaling	Wordscores, Class affinity	Wordfish, Correspondence analysis

reflects that dimension. On the other side, we distinguish between *supervised techniques* and *unsupervised techniques*. Supervised techniques need a fundamental input from the researcher in some form. Unsupervised methods formulate their estimates (almost) entirely on the basis of the content of the documents themselves. The kind of input changes between classification and scaling methods: while in the former it consists in the classification of a portion of the documents, in the latter it refers to the *a priori* identification of the dimension of interest. As a consequence of the lack of input, validation of the estimates – the assessment of how effectively a measure captures the concept of interest – becomes even more important in unsupervised methods.

Various platforms and programming languages are available to apply text as data methods. R and Python are the most frequently used by researchers: Political Scientists tend to prefer the former; scholars interested in Natural Language Processing (NLP), that field between linguistic and computer science aiming to teach machines how to analyze language, tend to prefer the latter. R works using *packages*, which are extensions containing codes, data, and documentations. Quanteda (Quantitative Analysis of Textual Data) is by far the most well-known package to process large quantity of texts and analyze them through several text as data techniques that are implemented within the package (Benoit et al. 2018). Python's counterparts for packages are called *libraries*: chunks of usable codes to be used in the project to perform specific tasks. Natural Language Toolkit (NLTK) and Spacy are probably the most used packages in Python to perform NLP tasks: while NLTK is a more general and basic platform, also suited for manipulating texts, Spacy is designed for advanced tasks, mostly associated with supervised machine learning classification.[3]

Qualitative Methods

Before starting to list and describe texts and data methods, it is important to clarify which methods of textual analysis are not methods of text as data. Interpretivist methods, including (critical) discourse analysis (see also Ostermann and Sjöstedt in this volume), do not belong to this category. As already suggested, the reason is that these methods do not treat text as data but rather employ raw text to interpret them. These methods focus less on the description of the text itself but more on the underlying dynamics of power in a specific social context that produced that text.

Qualitative Content Analysis consists in the extraction of features from text but cannot be considered as a text as data method either (Krippendorff 2018). What divides content analysis from text as data methods is that that the process is not automated but in most cases relies on the judgment of the individual researcher.[4] Such reliance presents both advantages and disadvantages. On the one hand, it allows to capture the nuances contained in the original texts, exploiting the researcher's own expertise and capacity to interpret the text. On the other hand, the measures produced through manual hand-coding are subject to a serious replication issue. In fact, a different researcher, with a different background and different beliefs, might code the same sentence in a significantly different way. Not even the most detailed coding guideline can guarantee full replicability of the results.[5] By automating the process of features extraction, text as data methods have the advantage of having an almost absolute level of replicability.[6]

Dictionary Methods

There is some controversy instead on whether to include dictionary analysis in the list of text as data methods. On the one hand, Grimmer and Stewart (2013) believe that it is a part of the category. In fact, dictionary analysis places texts into categories in a completely automated manner. On the other hand, Benoit (2020) defines it as a "hybrid" between qualitative and quantitative methods of text analysis. The reason is the high extent of human discretion in the process of analysis.

Dictionary analysis employs the relative frequency of a word or a group of words to measure the presence and extent of pre-defined categories across texts. It can be used to perform various tasks such as assessing the tone and the presence of topics in the document of interests. Researchers can rely on ready-made generic dictionaries, elaborated by linguists and psychologists, attributing scores to words on the basis of their tone. However, scholars have cautioned against the application of general dictionaries in specific contexts, as word meanings can change dramatically (Loughran and McDonald 2016). For instance, Leadership Trait Analysis and Operational Code Analysis make use of peculiar dictionaries designed to investigate foreign policy leaders' personality and beliefs (Hermann 2005; Schafer and Walker 2006, see Brummer or Schafer and Walker in this volume).[7] Such dictionaries have themselves turned into a point of reference for other scholars employing this method in their works.

However, in many cases, researchers create *ad hoc* dictionaries for their own purposes. For example, Hauenstein and Joshi (2020) build a dictionary based on most frequent words in a series of UN Security Council resolutions targeting states that signed a Comprehensive Peace Agreement (CPA) to investigate their approach toward these countries. Wagner (2020) investigates the justification for military interventions across different countries through the relative frequency of specific words associated with different topics such as multilateralism and national interest.

The point is that, sooner or later, someone must compose these dictionaries, and their content is inherently debatable. Some may believe that one word is lacking; others that a different word is superfluous. Some may think that the score attributed to a certain word is too high, while others think that is too low. Such extent of unavoidable disagreement in designing dictionaries is the reason why dictionary analysis may not be regarded as a text as data method in a narrow sense of the term.

Supervised Classification Methods

The idea underpinning supervised classification methods is that the researcher codes only a portion of a corpus and that the machine replicates such coding on all the remaining documents. Therefore, the first step in the process consists in selecting and then labeling a subset, the *training set*, into defined categories. That means, for instance, codifying a document as being connotated by a positive or negative sentiment. As the name suggests, a training set serves to *train* the algorithm, making it learn the relationship between words in the texts and labels. Such knowledge is then used by the machine to infer the previously unknown labels of documents in the *test set*. Provided that the model effectively performs the classification task, then it can be applied on the out-of-sample remaining documents (Grimmer and Stewart 2013).

There are various procedures and parameters to perform the validation of this classification. The best practice consists in iteratively splitting the training sets in smaller samples and testing how the model predicts the categories of the texts already classified by the researcher. This completely automated process is called *cross validation*. The machine calculates various parameters to evaluate the model performance, including accuracy (the proportion of correctly classified documents), recall (what proportion of instances a given category the document correctly identified), and precision (how many times the documents were classified correctly in a category, against the number of false positives). The *F-score* is the aggregate of recall and precision scores. The higher the scores in these metrics, the better the performance of the model is.

Various supervised classifying algorithms exist: Naïve Bayes (Pang et al. 2002), Support Vector Machines (SVM) (Joachims 1999), random forests (Fang and Zhan 2015), and neural networks (Lai et al. 2015). We should select the algorithm that allows to perform the classification task in the most effective way on our data, as indicated by the just mentioned metrics. This also entails the comparison of multiple techniques and their performances through cross validation. If performances are rather similar, it is recommendable to choose the computationally most efficient method. In an empirical application, Boucher and Thies (2019) use a Naïve Bayes machine learning algorithm to categorize over 600 thousand tweets on foreign trade posted by President Donald Trump's supporters. They show that most of them contained a populist rhetoric. This result highlights that the way a leader frames a foreign policy issue has an impact on how his/her electorate sees it. The article can also be considered as an example of how a concept associated with constructivism such as "framing" could be explored through machine learning techniques.

Unsupervised Classification Methods

A similar classification task can also be performed without having to manually annotate a portion of the corpus, thereby avoiding human input in the process. Indeed, unsupervised machine learning methods learn the underlying features of texts without explicitly imposing categories of interest (Grimmer and Stewart 2013). These methods exploit the occurrence and co-occurrence of words across the documents to divide them into groups. This is the principle behind *K-means clustering methods*, a series of unsupervised classification techniques. They are designed to partition the set of documents into k non overlapping groups (clusters) in a way that maximizes the difference between groups and minimizes the difference within them (Benoit 2020). For example, they may automatically distinguish between US presidents' foreign policy speeches according to whether the president is a Republican or a Democrat.

As already said, validation is particularly important in unsupervised methods. However, in contrast with supervised classification methods, there is no standard procedure to validate results: both qualitative and quantitative tests may be performed. One possibility in the previous examples could be comparing the estimates with existing literature and experts' judgment. Another one is examining the words that contributed the most to locate a document in a specific cluster.

The machine learning classification models presented this far are designed to categorize documents as belonging to no more than a single category. However, complex texts such as speeches and reports can be thought of as a mixture of multiple categories, or rather, topics. Unsupervised topic models estimate the presence of these topics across texts without the use of a dictionary. They provide a relatively simple parametric model describing the relationship between clusters of co-occurring words representing topics and their relationship to documents which contain them in relative proportions (Benoit 2020).

The only input that topic models demand from the researcher is the number of expected topics composing the documents in the corpus. The selection of this figure may be driven by elements such as theoretical considerations and the characteristics of the documents contained in the corpus. However, there are also some empirical tests facilitating this choice. The most common one suggests the scholar the number of topics that simultaneously maximizes the semantic coherence and exclusivity of the topics themselves. With semantic coherence, we refer to the fact that the words that identify a topic the most tend to co-occur across documents. With exclusivity, we mean instead that the words that identify a topic are different from the ones identifying another topic. Furthermore, the researcher is asked to engage in an effort of topic validation. Detecting patterns across a series of words that are most associated with each topic and inspecting documents to find evidence of topic occurrence are considered as standard practices to perform this task.

Latent Dirichlet Allocation (LDA) arguably constitutes the most widely used topic model in political science (Blei 2003). LDA assumes that documents are a mixture of topics with each word within a given document belonging to exactly one topic. It "recreates" the documents in the corpus by adjusting the relative importance of topics in documents and words in topics iteratively. To put it simply, this model tries to figure out what topics would create the documents included in the corpus. Applying LDA on a corpus of high-level climate change conference speeches, Bagozzi (2015) argues that restricting the number of countries to developed countries would reduce the dimensionality (number of topics) of the debate, thereby increasing cooperation. Schönfeld et al. (2018) employ LDA to analyze the UN Security Council debates over war in Afghanistan between 2001 and 2007, producing valid estimates that fluctuate in a sensible manner following key events in the conflict. Hanania (2021) uses this method to examine variation in international norms as expressed in UN Security Council resolution, finding an increasing attention toward humanitarian concerns after the end of the Cold War.

Structural Topic Model (STM) is an evolution of LDA presenting two modifications (Roberts et al. 2014). First, STM assumes that topics can be potentially correlated between each other. Second, it takes into account the impact of covariates explaining topical prevalence in the estimation process. Bagozzi and Berliner (2018) employ STM to analyze a corpus containing all US State Department's human rights reports from 1976 to 2012, extracting measures of attention for different violations. They use these measures as dependent variables in regression models to show that reports regarding US allies devote more attention to serious human rights violation such as torture and less to "minor" ones like electoral frauds. As the author points out in the paper, topic models present a significant advantage in highlighting attention for violation of human rights report with respect to manual hand-coding: they are not subject to individual authors' interpretations as well as changes in the definitions and perceptions that occurred over time.

In their study of civil-military relationship in Russia, Stewart and Zukhov (2008) provide an interesting example of combining supervised and unsupervised classification methods. First, they apply the expressed agenda model – another unsupervised topic model (Grimmer 2010) – on their corpus of 8,000 statements made by Russian military and political elites between 1998 and 2008 to uncover the presence of a wider set of topics regarding the use of force. Subsequently, they code 300 texts, distinguishing between those showing conservative and activist stances, and train a model that replicates the annotation on the remaining documents. The authors find that Russian military elite are more hesitant than political elites to embrace an interventionist foreign policy but tend to be more activist in considering force as an instrument of foreign policy. This article shows how automated text analysis methods and specifically, topic models can be used to infer foreign policy leaders' and bureaucracies' perceptions, a longstanding FPA concern.

Supervised Scaling Methods

As suggested, scaling methods are designed to perform a completely different task than classification methods. While the latter estimates document membership in one or more categories, the former estimates positions in a latent dimension such as left-right or pro/anti-war. *Wordscores* is the par excellence supervised scaling method (Laver et al. 2003).[8] The supervised element in Wordscores consists of the *a priori* definition of the dimension. This is identified relying on two *reference (or virgin) texts* that are assumed to provide representations of distinct positions in the dimension. After the author has attributed a numerical value to such positions, Wordscores generates a score for each of the words based on its frequency across reference texts. Finally, the positions of all the remaining texts are the product of the occurrence of such words within them. In other words, Wordscores learns word association with two contrasting reference classes and then combines these word frequencies in texts whose positions are known to estimate positions with respect to reference classes (Benoit 2020).

Carmody et al. (2020) use Wordscores to extract a measure of African states' closeness to China from speeches in the United Nations General Debate, using Chinese and American speeches as reference texts to identify the dimension. They employ the measure as a dependent variable to find that, surprisingly, increasing trade exchanges does not make African states align more with China in terms of general foreign policy. However, it does make a difference when it comes to voting on human rights. Wordscores' strength lies in its easy implementation, simplicity, and reliance on known reference texts (Egerod and Klemmensen 2020). But the last aspect is a double-edged sword. In fact, in some cases, the researcher cannot (or does not want to) rely on appropriate reference texts. For instance, let us imagine that instead of examining closeness to China, we want to investigate the disagreement within African states on global politics priorities and there is no consensus in the literature about which states are keener to focus on development. In this situation, the researcher is not able to identify solid reference texts. Therefore, it is advisable to use an unsupervised scaling method.

Unsupervised Scaling Methods

Wordfish is the most well-known unsupervised scaling method (Slapin and Proksch 2008). Wordfish is unsupervised in the sense that the dimension is not defined *ex ante*.[9] Therefore, in contrast with Wordscores, it is not necessary to identify any sort of reference text. Wordfish assumes that the occurrence of the words across documents is drawn from a Poisson distribution: one in which the probability of observing the event is not correlated with the probability of the previous event.[10] Such distribution of word frequencies is obtained by combining a parameter (*beta*) capturing the importance of a word to distinguish between documents with another parameter representing the position on the latent dimension, conditioned by both word and feature fixed effects (Benoit 2020). In practice, words that occur frequently in all documents do not meaningfully contribute to shape the actors' position and receive a score in the beta parameter close to zero. Contrarily, those that occur in a more heterogenous manner discriminate across the documents, receiving either more positive or more negative scores. The sum of these scores weighted by the other fixed-effect parameters produces the final position.

The estimates extracted by scaling methods must be carefully validated *ex post* by the researcher, together with the actors' position along it. One standard practice consists in comparing the extracted positions with similar positions obtained through other methods such as manual hand-coding or expert surveys, if available. The validation process is even more relevant in the case of Wordfish, since, unlike with supervised methods, the dimension of interest was not known beforehand. But this is not its only downside. In fact, while the performance of both these scaling methods worsens as the extent of language diversity in the corpus (number of unique words) increases and document length decreases, Wordfish is more sensitive to these factors than Wordscores (Egerod and Klemmensen 2020). Furthermore, by allowing to attribute different scores to the same reference texts or changing reference texts, Wordscores allows to estimate positions on multiple dimensions from the same texts. In fact, Chelotti et al. (2022) are able to extract two measures of distance between the EU and Russia and the EU and the US, respectively, in the UN assembly by simply changing the reference texts.

Despite these challenges, Wordfish has found considerable application in the study of foreign policy. Genovese (2014) employs it to estimate states' positions on climate change negotiations, finding substantial variation between developed countries and developing countries with the latter focusing more on international cooperation. Vignoli (2020) chooses Wordfish to extract Italian parties' positions on military interventions and then uses it as a dependent variable in a regression model, showing a consensus between center-left and center-right parties on the issue. Barnum and Lo (2020) estimate states' positions about Nuclear Proliferation Treaty (NPT), defying the argument that disagreement between Non-Nuclear Weapon States (NNWS) and Nuclear Weapons State (NWS) has increased over time. Interestingly, they correlate the Wordfish estimates with the proportions of disarmament and non-proliferation topics in the same documents produced by a topic model in order to validate them.

However, Wordfish is not the only existing unsupervised scaling method. *Correspondence Analysis* (Greenacre 2017) shares its same approach as it aims at locating actors in a space. It presents both advantages and disadvantages with respect to Wordfish. On one side, Correspondence Analysis allows to identify more than one dimension. One the other side, being a non-parametric technique, it does not provide estimates of uncertainty. Correspondence Analysis has found extensive applications partly thanks to its computational simplicity. Baturo et al. (2017) apply it to the analysis of debates in the UN General Assembly. The results show a certain extent of validity since allied countries (US and UK) tend to have more similar positions over time than non-allied countries (US and Russia).

New Frontiers: Semi-Supervised Models and Word-Embeddings

The text as data methods presented this far are arguably the most established in the field of Political Science. However, research is in constant evolution as innovative and more sophisticated sets of techniques emerging are developed. Two of them are particularly promising and, consequently, deserve more attention.

The first one is the group of *semi-supervised learning models*. As the name suggests, these approaches collocate in the middle between supervised and unsupervised methods through the employment of *seed words*, a non-dictionary like list of words that should nevertheless improve the performance of the models. *Seeded LDA* is a variant of standard LDA in which the seed words are used to weight a prior distribution of topics (Lu et al. 2011). Curini and Vignoli (2021) employ it to investigate the arguments employed by parties in Italy to support or criticize military interventions. *Newsmap* (Watanabe 2018) is instead a model for geographical classification combining seed words with a Naïve Bayes classifier. Trubowitz and Watanabe (2021) extract a plausible measure of threat against the US, analyzing summaries from *New York Times* articles with this technique. Watanabe and Zhou (2020) compare these two semi-supervised methods, applying them to a corpus of the UN General Assembly documents.

Word-embedding models also represent a very interesting way forward for the research in the field (Mikolov 2013). A word-embedding is a distributed representation for text that allows words that have similar meaning to have a similar representation. Word-embeddings are based on the same *distributional hypothesis* as other semantic models such as topic models. Each word is represented as a real-valued vector in a pre-defined vector space. Therefore, a first major difference when compared to the bag of words approach is that instead of being represented by just one number, in a word-embeddings framework each word in the corpus is mapped to a vector of real numbers, in the order of tens/hundreds of dimensions. To put it simply, these models provide a way to connect words to their usage (Benoit 2020). Employing a word-embeddings model in their analysis of the aforementioned corpus of speeches at the UN, Gurciullo and Mikhaylov (2017) construct an index of semantic centrality that its cross-time variation well mirrors historical developments: for example, interest in Nuclear Proliferation has decreased after the end of the Cold War.

Potentialities and Challenges for the Study of Foreign Policy

The potentialities of text as data methods in the study of foreign policy are twofold. First, text as data methods promise to provide a more comprehensive approach to test theories and arguments with respect to qualitative text analysis techniques. As it was suggested, these automated techniques enable the researcher to extract features from a large number of documents in a relatively short amount of time. In theory, this can prevent us from being forced to pick only a small portion of a potentially much larger universe of documents and having to find justification for the case selection. We should always bear in mind that such an advantage comes often at the expense of the destruction of the texts themselves and their nuances. At the same time, quantitative analysis, when it is rigorously performed, has a value in itself. In particular, quantitative analysis guarantees a substantially higher level of replicability in the result that it produces. As it was noted, all text as data methods, and especially those with a form of supervision, entail a fundamental input from the scholar. However, once such input is given, the process of extractions of the estimates is completely automated and, consequently, replicable.

Second, text as data methods allow the researcher to develop innovative measures to capture relevant concepts for the study of foreign policy. In one way or another, all the techniques described produce a numeric variable measuring some attributes of the documents, whether it is a position (scaling methods), the emphasis on a topic (topic models), or the belonging to a particular category (classification methods). These numeric values can gauge concepts that attracted considerable theoretical and empirical attention from foreign policy scholars. For example, as already suggested, Trubowitz and Watanabe (2021) elaborate a measure of threat, which is a fundamental concept in the field. When other existing measures of the same concept are available, it is worthwhile to look for correlation with the ones obtained through text as data methods. As it was noted, this is a standard practice of validation, especially for the measures extracted with unsupervised techniques. For instance, Barnum and Lo (2020) validate their country's position on the NPT showing their correlation with existing measures of foreign policy preferences as taken from voting preferences in the UN General Assembly as elaborated by Bailey et al. (2017). On the other side, it is interesting to investigate cases in which the correlation with existing measures is not convincingly strong. For instance, Gurciullo and Mikhaylov (2017) find substantial discrepancies in countries' closeness to the US as measured through UN General Assembly debates and votes. That can be attributed to higher constraints involved in the voting process.

The main challenge in the application of text as data methods in the study of foreign policy concerns the selection of suitable and appropriate corpora, in terms of quantity and quality of the documents. The problem of quantity can be mainly attributed to two elements distinguishing international from domestic politics. First, the activities of international organizations are often less structured than the ones of domestic political institutions. Especially among democratic states, there are a set of institutions where political actors frequently and regularly meet, discuss, and decide, such as national parliaments. The consequence of such an intense activity is the production of a constant and vast number of documents over time. At the international level, we hardly find institutions having such a constant and intense activity.[11] For instance, from 1949, only 30 NATO summits occurred at irregular intervals. Second, the same national governments that are eager to present their results to the public can be very reluctant to speak about their foreign policy strategy as this would give an advantage to other countries. In turn, many documents relative to foreign policy are often kept secret, and only in some cases, they get published after a few years following the occurrence of the events they refer to. For instance, only at the end of 1990s, the Central Intelligence Agency (CIA) declassified documents revealing plans to execute Communist leaders in Guatemala in 1954 as part of a broader effort to engineer a coup in the country. The lower extent of activity within international institutions and the secrecy of states' foreign policymaking have negative repercussions on the amount of the texts that researchers can use in their analyses. As we suggested, classification methods are particularly made to deal with a large quantity of texts.

At the same time, it is fair to admit that IR and FPA scholars have made this far a limited effort to build corpora from existing institutional sources. The UN library contains over a million documents but to date it has generated only three comprehensive datasets. The UN General Debate (UNGD) corpus is probably the most well-known and utilized at this moment (Baturo et al. 2017). It contains 7,314 statements made by country representatives at the UNGD, the one that inaugurates each session of the General Assembly, between 1970 and 2014. During these debates, UN Member States tend to present their views about the main issues of international politics and, therefore, these documents represent a valuable source to estimate their preferences. Various authors have already performed different analysis using text as data methods (Gurciullo and Mikhaylov 2017; Carmody et al. 2020; Watanabe and Zhou 2020; Chelotti et al. 2022). The PeaceKeeping Operations Corpus (PKOC) is also constructed using UN material as a source (Amicarelli and Di Salvatore 2021). The PKOC is composed of 1,455 reports drafted by UN Secretary General covering 68 missions between 1994 and 2020. In addition, Hanania (2021) collects all the UN Security Council resolutions approved between 1946 and 2017 in a corpus containing 2,397 documents. However, it goes without saying that further corpora can be built with UN online resources. The Freedom of Information Archive database represents instead a unique effort to gather state-level diplomatic documents (Connelly et al. 2020). It contains over 3 million foreign policy-related texts, mostly regarding the US, but also covering the UK and Brazil.

However, institution and state-level documents and reports do not exhaust the possible list of sources from which a corpus suited for text as data methods can be built. Trubowitz and Watanabe (2021) show that it is possible to address foreign policy-related research questions through newspaper articles. Furthermore, nowadays posts on social media such as Twitter and Facebook are important sources to explore international actors' stances and communication strategies. For example, Boucher and Thies (2019) employ Twitter posts to explore the use of populist narratives to articulate foreign policy positions by President Trump and his supporters (see also Schneiker in this volume).

The linguistic heterogeneity of the documents that a researcher in foreign policy may deal with is a second challenge for the application of text as data methods. First, this issue is associated to the fact that documents may be written in different languages. For example, a scholar may want to rely on European heads of states' statements about the Iraq War to estimate their respective country's position on the issue. A problem may rise in the sense that these documents are not all in the same language and the researcher does not speak all of them. However, De Vries et al. (2018) show how texts translated with Google Translate do not produce substantially different document-feature matrices. Furthermore, Proksch et al. (2019) demonstrate that translating dictionaries through the same platform do not introduce large biases in the estimates. In other words, the bag of words approach makes it possible to use automated form of translation without affecting the results of the analysis. That said, it is always recommendable to employ original texts, if that is possible.

Linguistic heterogeneity refers also to the presence of a high extent of peculiar words even in documents sharing many characteristics in common such as topic, audience, and authorship. For example, Bagozzi and Berliner (2018) highlight that US State Department country reports on human rights violations contain a number of references that are associated with the countries themselves. To give an example, documents about human rights violations in Egypt are expected to contain several mentions to the capital "Cairo" and to former president Hosni Mubarak. Such a considerable level of heterogeneity in word usage is a problem especially for unsupervised methods that base their estimates entirely on the (co)occurrence of words. We might end up with estimates reflecting the country to which the document refers to rather than variation in the object of interest. The same authors address this issue through a standard practice of pre-processing: keep only those words that occur in a certain percentage of texts. This is an appropriate strategy to avoid rare and country-specific words to bias our estimates. However, such country-specific words may also be useful for us to recognize to which country a document refers to if we do not know beforehand. As it was suggested, Watanabe (2018) designed *Newsmap* with this objective in mind: recognizing to which country a text belongs on the basis of its features.

Conclusion

In the last decade, text as data methods have significantly contributed to the methodological advancement of Political Science. A number of different techniques have been successfully applied to address various research questions. The interest on text as data techniques has constantly grown over the years and it will probably continue to grow in the next years. It is possible that, by the time this chapter is published, brand-new techniques or new applications of existing ones will have appeared in the scene.

Against this background, it is worth pointing out that IR and FPA scholars have this far exploited such techniques in their works to a much lower extent than their colleagues in Comparative Politics. While it is true that the employment of quantitative methods is generally less spread in our field, the limited interest for text as data methods can be attributed to objective obstacles in terms of availability of appropriate set of texts for the use of text as data methods. However, this should not be taken as a reason for not investing time and resources in building new corpora and analyzing them through the most up-to-date techniques. As said, text as data methods have much to offer to the study of foreign policy. In fact, they enable the researcher to conduct a systematic analysis of a large amount of textual data. The information extracted can be used to test (and question) existing theories and address measurement issues. To sum up, text as data methods represent an extremely innovative and effective instrument to study foreign policy.

Acknowledgments

The author would like to thank Luigi Curini and Giovanni Pagano for their useful comments and suggestions on earlier drafts of the chapter.

Notes

1. Some text as data methods such as those using word embeddings allow to take into consideration the semantic context of a word.
2. Classification models can also be employed to create some measures of actors' positions on some scale. However, this is not their original purpose.
3. Link to NLTK: https://www.nltk.org. Link to Spacy: https://github.com/explosion/spaCy.
4. Some qualitative content analysis methods involve (partial) machine coding.
5. The Comparative Manifesto Project (CMP) is arguably the most known and articulated project of manual hand-coding in the field of Political Science (Klingemann et al. 2006). Mikhaylov et al. (2012) show "serious and systemic problems" with the CMP dataset and coding process.
6. Some supervised machine-learning classification algorithms may present slightly different results across replications.
7. Operational Code Analysis not only counts the frequency of specific words but also employs other metrics in the process, such as variance in word usage.
8. Perry and Benoit (2017) recently introduced a new variant of Wordscores called *Class affinity*.
9. The only input given by the researcher pertains to the direction of the dimension: what a positive and negative score substantively means.
10. The name of the distribution comes from its inventor, the mathematician Simeon-Denis Poisson (1781–1840). Wordfish probably derives its name from the fact that "poisson" in French means "fish".
11. With the notable exceptions of a few United Nations (General Assembly and Security Council) and EU (European Parliament, European Council) bodies.

References

All online sources have been last checked for availability on 22 May 2022.

Amicarelli, Elio and Jessica Di Salvatore. 2021. "Introducing the Peace Keeping Operations Corpus (PKOC)". *Journal of Peace Research*, 0022343320978693.

Bagozzi, Benjamin E. 2015. "The Multifaceted Nature of Global Climate Change Negotiations." *The Review of International Organizations* 10 (4): 439–464.

Bagozzi, Benjamin. E. and Daniel Berliner. 2018. "The Politics of Scrutiny in Human Rights Monitoring: Evidence from Structural Topic Models of US State Department Human Rights Reports." *Political Science Research and Methods* 6 (4): 661–677.

Bailey, Michael. A., Anton Strezhnev, and Erik Voeten. 2017. "Estimating Dynamic State Preferences from United Nations Voting Data." *Journal of Conflict Resolution* 61 (2): 430–456.

Barnum, Miriam and James Lo. 2020. "Is the NPT Unraveling? Evidence from Text Analysis of Review Conference Statements." *Journal of Peace Research* 57 (6): 740–751.

Baturo, Alexander, Niheer Dasandi, and Slava J. Mikhaylov. 2017. "Understanding State Preferences with Text as Data: Introducing the UN General Debate Corpus." *Research & Politics* 4 (2), https://doi.org/10.1177/2053168017712821.

Benoit, Ken. 2020. "Text as Data: An Overview." In *The SAGE Handbook of Research Methods in Political Science and International Relations*, edited by Luigi Curini and Robert Franzese. London: SAGE, 461–497.

Benoit, Ken, Kohei Watanabe, Haiyan Wang, Paul Nulty, Adam Obeng, Stefan Müller, and Akitaka Matsuo. 2018. "Quanteda: An R Package for the Quantitative Analysis of Textual Data." *Journal of Open Source Software* 3 (30): 774.

Blei, David M., Andrew Y. Ng, and Michael I. Jordan. 2003. "Latent Dirichlet Allocation." *The Journal of Machine Learning Research* 3: 993–1022.

Boucher, Jean-Cristophe and Cameron G. Thies. 2019. "'I am a Tariff Man': The Power of Populist Foreign Policy Rhetoric under President Trump." *The Journal of Politics* 81 (2): 712–722.

Carmody, Padraig, Niheer Dasandi, and Slava Jankin Mikhaylov. 2020. "Power Plays and Balancing Acts: The Paradoxical Effects of Chinese Trade on African Foreign Policy Positions." *Political Studies*, 68 (1), 224–246.

Chelotti, Nicola, Niheer Dasandi, and Slava Jankin Mikhaylov (2022). "Do Intergovernmental Organizations Have a Socialization Effect on Member State Preferences? Evidence from the UN General Debate." *International Studies Quarterly*, 66 (1), https://academic.oup.com/isq/article/66/1/sqab069/6347693.

Connelly, Matthew J., Raymond Hicks, Robert Jervis, Arthur Spirling, and Clara H. Suong. 2020. "Diplomatic Documents Data for International Relations: The Freedom of Information Archive Database." *Conflict Management and Peace Science* 38 (6): 762–781.

Curini, Luigi and Valerio Vignoli. 2021. "Committed Moderates and Uncommitted Extremists: Ideological Leaning and Parties' Narratives on Military Interventions in Italy." *Foreign Policy Analysis* 17 (3), https://doi.org/10.1093/fpa/orab016.

De Vries, Eric, Martijn Schoonvelde, and Gijs Schumacher. 2018. "No Longer Lost in Translation: Evidence that Google Translate Works for Comparative Bag-of-Words Text Applications." *Political Analysis* 26 (4): 417–430.

Egerod, Benjamin C.K. and Robert Klemmensen. 2020. "Scaling Political Positions from Text: Assumptions, Methods and Pitfalls." In *The SAGE Handbook of Research Methods in Political Science and International Relations*, edited by Luigi Curini and Robert Franzese. London: SAGE, 498–521.

Fang, Xing and Justin Zhan. 2015. "Sentiment Analysis Using Product Review Data." *Journal of Big Data* 2 (1): 1–14.

Genovese, Federica. 2014. "States' Interests at International Climate Negotiations: New Measures of Bargaining Positions." *Environmental Politics* 23 (4): 610–631.

Greenacre, Michael. 2017. *Correspondence Analysis in Practice*. Chapman and Hall: crc.

Grimmer, Justin. 2010. "A Bayesian Hierarchical Topic Model for Political Texts: Measuring Expressed Agendas in Senate Press Releases." *Political Analysis* 18 (1): 1–35.

Grimmer, Justin and Brandon M. Stewart. 2013. "Text as Data: The Promise and Pitfalls of Automatic Content Analysis Methods for Political Texts." *Political Analysis* 21 (3): 267–297.

Gurciullo, Stefano and Slava J. Mikhaylov. 2017. "Detecting Policy Preferences and Dynamics in the UN General Debate with Neural Word Embeddings." In *International Conference on the Frontiers and Advances in Data Science (FADS)* (pp. 74–79). IEEE.

Joachims, Thorsten. 1999. *Svmlight: Support Vector Machine. SVM-Light Support Vector Machine*. http://svmlight.joachims.org/. University of Dortmund, available from https://www.researchgate.net/profile/Thorsten-Joachims/publication/243763293_SVMLight_Support_Vector_Machine/links/5b0eb5c2a6fdcc80995ac3d5/SVMLight-Support-Vector-Machine.pdf

Hanania, Richard. 2021. "The Humanitarian Turn at the UNSC: Explaining the Development of International Norms Through Machine Learning Algorithms." *Journal of Peace Research* 58 (4): 655–670.

Hauenstein, Matthew and Madhav Joshi. 2020. "Remaining Seized of the Matter: UN Resolutions and Peace Implementation." *International Studies Quarterly* 64 (4): 834–844.

Hermann, Margaret G. 2005. "Assessing Leadership Style: A Trait Analysis." In *The Psychological Assessment of Political Leaders*, edited by Jerrold M. Post. Ann Arbor, MI: University of Michigan Press, 178–212.

Klingemann, Hans-Dieter, Andrea Volkens, Judith Bara, Judith, Ian Budge, and Michael D. McDonald. 2006. *Mapping Policy Preferences II: Estimates for Parties, Electors, and Governments in Eastern Europe, European Union, and OECD 1990-2003*, vol. 2. Oxford University Press on Demand.

Krippendorff, Klaus. 2018. *Content Analysis: An Introduction to its Methodology*. London: SAGE.

Lai, Siwei, Liheng Xu, Kang Liu, and Jjun Zhao. 2015. "Recurrent Convolutional Neural Networks for Text Classification." In *Twenty-Ninth AAAI Conference on Artificial Intelligence*.

Laver, Michael, Ken Benoit, and John Garry. 2003. "Extracting Policy Positions from Political Texts Using Words as Data." *American Political Science Review* 97 (2): 311–331.

Loughran, Tim and Bill McDonald. 2016. "Textual Analysis in Accounting and Finance: A Survey." *Journal of Accounting Research* 54 (4): 1187–1230.

Lu, Bin, Myle Ott, Claire Cardie, and Benhamin K. Tsou. 2011. "Multi-Aspect Sentiment Analysis with Topic Models." In *2011 IEEE 11th International Conference on Data Mining Workshops* (pp. 81–88). IEEE.

Mikhaylov, Slava, Michael Laver, and Ken Benoit. 2012. "Coder Reliability and Misclassification in the Human Coding of Party Manifestos." *Political Analysis* 20 (1): 78–91.

Mikolov, Tomas, Ilya Sutskever, Kai Chen, Greg S. Corrado, and Jeffrey Dean. 2013. "Distributed Representations of Words and Phrases and Their Compositionality." In *Advances in Neural Information Processing Systems* (pp. 3111–3119). Available from https://proceedings.neurips.cc/paper/2013/file/9aa42b31882ec039965f3c4923ce901b-Paper.pdf.

Pang, Bo, Lillian Lee, and Shivakumar Vaithyanathan. 2002. "Thumbs Up? Sentiment Classification Using Machine Learning Techniques." *arXiv preprint cs/0205070*.

Perry, Patrick O. and Ken Benoit. 2017. "Scaling Text with the Class Affinity Model." *arXiv preprint arXiv:1710.08963*.

Proksch, Sven-Oliver, Will Lowe, Jens Wäckerle, and Stuart Soroka. 2019. "Multilingual Sentiment Analysis: A New Approach to Measuring Conflict in Legislative Speeches." *Legislative Studies Quarterly* 44 (1): 97–131.

Roberts, Margaret E., Brandon M. Stewart, Dustin Tingley, Caroline Lucas, Jetson Leder-Luis, Shana K. Gadarian, Bethany Albertson, and David G. Rand. 2014. "Structural Topic Models for Open-Ended Survey Responses." *American Journal of Political Science* 58 (4): 1064–1082.

Schafer, Mark and Stephen G. Walker, eds. 2006. *Beliefs and Leadership in World Politics: Methods and Applications of Operational Code Analysis*. New York and Houndmills: Palgrave Macmillan.

Schönfeld, Mirco, Steffen Eckhard, Ronny Patz, and Hilde van Meegdenburg. 2018. "Discursive Landscapes and Unsupervised Topic Modeling in IR: A Validation of Text-as-Data Approaches through a New Corpus of UN Security Council Speeches on Afghanistan." *arXiv preprint arXiv:1810.05572*.

Slapin, Jonathan B. and Sven-Oliver Proksch. 2008. "A Scaling Model for Estimating Time-Series Party Positions from Texts." *American Journal of Political Science* 52 (3): 705–722.

Stewart, Brandon M. and Yuri M. Zhukov. 2009. "Use of Force and Civil–Military Relations in Russia: An Automated Content Analysis." *Small Wars & Insurgencies* 20 (2): 319–343.

Trubowitz, Peter and Kohei Watanabe. 2021. "The Geopolitical Threat Index: A Text-Based Computational Approach to Identifying Foreign Threats." *International Studies Quarterly* 65 (3), https://doi.org/10.1093/isq/sqab029.

Vignoli, Valerio. 2020. "Where Are the Doves? Explaining Party Support for Military Operations Abroad in Italy." *West European Politics* 43 (7): 1455–1479.

Wagner, Wolfgang. 2020. *The Democratic Politics of Military Interventions: Political Parties, Contestation, and Decisions to Use Force Abroad*. Oxford: Oxford University Press.

Watanabe, Kohei. 2018. "Newsmap: A Semi-Supervised Approach to Geographical News Classification." *Digital Journalism* 6 (3): 294–309.

Watanabe, Kohei and Yuan Zhou. 2020. "Theory-Driven Analysis of Large Corpora: Semisupervised Topic Classification of the UN Speeches." *Social Science Computer Review*, doi: 10.1177/0894439320907027.

Wilkerson, John and Andreu Casas. 2017. "Large-Scale Computerized Text Analysis in Political Science: Opportunities and Challenges." *Annual Review of Political Science* 20: 529–544.

34
Conflict Event Data
Clionadh Raleigh and Roudabeh Kishi

Introduction

Conflict event data and analysis now constitute an ever greater share of the main evidence base for political violence studies. This is a major advancement for the study of conflict, which has long been characterized by national-level studies which obscure the specifics of conflicts, or individual state or conflict studies that can have limited generalizability. Event data allow researchers a great depth and breadth of options to explore, analyze, and predict conflict patterns – exploring research questions such as *In what ways has conflict shifted subnationally?*, or *Which actors are responsible for which types of violence?* Questions ranging from *Where are conflict prevention policies most effective at mitigating violence?* to *What explains the differences in escalation and diffusion rates amongst non-state armed groups?* can only be answered using event data, and specifically event data that capture the range of violence that occurs in and across states.

Several conflict event data projects – such as the *Armed Conflict Location and Event Data Project* (ACLED), the Uppsala Conflict Data Program's *Georeferenced Event Dataset* (UCDP GED), and the *Global Database of Events, Language, and Tone* (GDELT), to name a few – are now available for use, yet they differ significantly in their scope, catchment, and depth. In this chapter, we review the basics of event data collection, and in doing so, suggest that the main differences in data projects are in how each prioritizes conflicts and event types. To use or compare individual events, the instability in countries, or the pattern and trajectories of conflict patterns, requires a keen awareness of what the dataset is designed to capture, and what narratives on violence it supports and refutes. For the most part, the current distinctions in datasets are due to the working definition of *political violence* and the associated *catchment* of events that datasets purport to collect, and the sourcing of how to gather information on those events.

In this review, we concentrate on datasets that have global coverage, although few actually cover each state in the world and instead cover states where conflict has breached a threshold set by the data project. Different data projects capture different spectrums of conflict events, with some focusing just on conflict events meeting a certain level of lethality, or conflict that involves state forces specifically, while others might have a broader remit, capturing everything from the early stages of a movement, such as peaceful demonstrations, to the most lethal, such as acts of genocide against civilians.

In line with a dataset's catchment, the sourcing strategy for data projects can be equally broad or narrow. Often, event datasets have chosen to rely heavily, if not exclusively, on international, English-based media to capture information. This is due to the availability of these media, and the consistency in their reporting. Datasets focused on an individual country often rely on a single national media source, over time, to record conflict events therein. Indeed, adding new sources can create issues of consistency; however, avoiding doing so sacrifices thoroughness for consistency. Data collectors ought to consider a wider breadth of sources than solely those which are the easiest to access and most consistent, with any concerns mitigated by careful sourcing methodologies so as to not distort the pattern of conflict on the ground.

Further to the distinctions in current datasets referenced above, there are several advancements that are being developed around the collection of event data; these are primarily in the areas of automation and artificial intelligence (AI), specifically through machine learning. There are, however, multiple pitfalls to such methods that create difficult distortions and unreliable patterns about current and future conflict. We will review these in light of necessary advancements in efficiency and coverage.

Limitations of National- and Temporally-Aggregated Datasets

For most conflict questions and contexts, national- and temporally-aggregated datasets offer poor choices for information. Most conflicts are not national but take place on the subnational level and within a limited part of that country (Raleigh et al. 2010). An average conflict arena – even a nationally relevant civil war – may only occur in 15% of a state's territory. In these cases, using national-level variables to explain or describe a non-national phenomenon is problematic: it either extends the unique characteristics of the conflict space nationwide or distorts the characteristics through aggregation.

Further, countries are often beset by multiple types of conflicts, and these can be markedly different in terms of size, targets, agents, intentions, and proliferation (Raleigh, 2014). Using an aggregate measure could subsume low levels of violence (e.g., riots) and highly lethal ones (e.g., acts of genocide) into a national total, and hence distort the risks, intensity, and severity of violence in that country. This is a point that the Foreign Policy Analysis (FPA) literature has long considered, with recent developments in the International Relations (IR) literature also coming to similar conclusions regarding the important role of factors such as domestic politics (Kaarbo, 2015).

Conflict of all forms can occur in ways that defy national boundaries as a useful container. It can occur between countries, within countries, or even with high levels of violence in countries that are otherwise not experiencing traditional forms of armed conflict. National indices often pick specific forms of conflict to prioritize and measure, and in doing so, ignore the levels of violence that fail to reach arbitrary thresholds. There is a further tendency to prioritize conflict dyads that are more relevant and present in past violent contexts than those in current contexts – such as civil wars, which have declined as other forms of political violence have increased. Without considering a spectrum of political violence, data projects can miss significant and growing trends in conflict within states.

Similar issues are present in temporal aggregations. When conflict is aggregated annually, much of the volatility and change is erased. Conflicts go through periods of sharp increases and decreases, often related to the changes in the political environment, other violent actors, or internal fragmentation and cohesion. However, an annual tally aggregates risks and patterns that enhance, mitigate, or explain variations in conflict trajectories. These annual tallies distort information rather than elucidate it.

In summation, disorder does not present as the same in every space. Only by taking an expansive view of its modalities can a data project seek to accurately account for its occurrence and patterns. By using the most disaggregated, reliable information, projects can present researchers with information without purposeful distortions. This transcends the differences between national and event datasets, and instead questions: *What is political violence in this era?* This is an especially important question now, as multiple forms of political violence are present and increasing. Spaces where political violence is high but dismissed as *criminal* or difficult to categorize – such as in Mexico and Brazil – should be given equal coverage to more *traditional* conflict spaces – like Afghanistan or the Democratic Republic of Congo. Given existing and developing patterns of instability across the world, it is critical for researchers to consider the modality of unrest in high-income states; the differences in communal violence across identity groups; and the presence and range of armed, organized groups in democratic states. Using event data is a crucial step in properly understanding, modeling, and responding to such diverse forms of conflict and disorder.

Comparing Researcher-Led and Machine-Based Event Datasets

There are a variety of event datasets that are publicly available. Projects such as ACLED (Raleigh et al. 2010); UCDP-GED (Sundberg and Melander, 2013); GDELT (Leetaru and Schrodt, 2013); the *Integrated Crisis Early Warning System* (ICEWS) dataset (Boschee et al. 2018, 2020); and the *Global Terrorism Database* (GTD) (LaFree and Dugan, 2007) are all common sources of event data, used to study conflict in its various forms.

However, these projects vary in a number of ways, such as (1) how the data are collected, either as researcher-led projects or as machine automated projects; (2) the inclusion criteria for what does and does not constitute a relevant event to be coded, thus defining what conflict does and does not look like according to the dataset; (3) the sources used to collect events; (4) the review process; and more. These differences lead to variation in how usable, valid, and accurate each dataset is. With the recent push toward the further use of automation and AI in making conflict data collection faster and more cost effective, this chapter focuses on the comparison between researcher-led data collection (with ACLED used as an example therein) and machine-based data collection (with the two most prominent automated datasets, GDELT and ICEWS, used as examples therein). The following sections outline the catchments, inclusion criteria, and methodologies of those data projects.

Machine-Based Datasets

Most machine-based, automated data projects that capture events related to conflict are updated quite regularly, as they benefit from the automated procurement and review of source information. In addition to the gains in speed such processes allow for, the cost of running such projects is also minimal since paid researchers need not be hired to maintain data collection. For example, GDELT and ICEWS are the primary machine-based, automated data projects that capture events related to conflict. GDELT originated in 2014 and produces data that cover a temporal range from 1979 to the present; data are updated as often as every 15 minutes, meaning that the dataset is constantly evolving (i.e., there is no *authoritative* version of the dataset to which to refer). ICEWS, meanwhile, launched in 2008; its publicly available data on the Harvard Dataverse cover 1995 to the present, with data released weekly as of 2020.

Catchment and Inclusion Criteria. Most machine-based data projects rely on automated searches based on the *Conflict and Mediation Event Observations* (CAMEO) coding system (Schrodt, 2012). Such is the case for both GDELT and ICEWS. Under this system, events are recorded as *actions* being carried out by one actor toward another, grouped into categories – capturing both conflict/hostility and mediation/cooperation. This system captures a large range of events of broad types, such as "consult," "fight," "reduce relations," or "express intent to cooperate." Within each class are specific events. For example, one event under the "fight" class is "fight with small arms and light weapons." In addition to these categorizations, events are also scored on intensity – known as the Goldstein Scale of Intensity – ranging in value from −10 to +10 based on the level of hostility/cooperation.

In addition to providing data on the event type using the CAMEO code system, both GDELT and ICEWS also code information about actor names, intensity, and location information. Within such data projects, data are collected based on a dictionary of phrases used to capture and sort text into its relevant event type; actor information is then gathered from that text (i.e., which actor took that action, and against whom). The CAMEO codebook highlights that over 15,000 phrases are searched for, forming the backbone of the data that can be gathered by such projects (Schrodt, 2012, p. 3). The inclusion criterion for such machine-automated datasets is therefore the search itself. This leads to the potential for variation in the actual types of events that are gathered. Rather than relying on clear conceptualizations and subsequent operationalizations of event types based on research, expertise, and context, the use of a word allows for its incorporation into the data as an event type.

For example, one CAMEO code event type (code: 202) is "engage in mass killings." The CAMEO codebook defines this as the "Kill[ing of] a substantial number of people, typically with the intention of ridding a territory of a particular group of people" (Schrodt, 2012, p. 89). However, there is no clear definition of what "substantial" means in practice – it could mean three fatalities or 3,000 fatalities. Further, the automation relies on the text used by the source itself. For example, all events labeled as "massacres" are coded under this category, "even if the language may be politicized" (Boschee et al. 2015c, p. 118). If events are described as massacres or mass killings, they are likely to end up in GDELT or ICEWS as such, despite potential large variation across cases as they actually occurred. ICEWS notes that, "the use of this code in these cases reflects the severity of the language used and/or the extremity of the violence employed" (Boschee et al. 2015c, p. 118). Because ICEWS and GDELT do not report fatalities, but rather rely on the Goldstein Scale for Intensity, it becomes difficult to sort through events to understand which events substantively fit in with the concept and which events were simply labeled as such. In sum, the combination of a broad and machine-based inclusion criteria and methodology can produce a collection of event data that are not guided by concepts and strict standards, but rather by the language used to describe them.

Review Processes. Automated datasets often have little to no intervention for quality control or review by researchers, given that most such projects do not employ a team of research staff. Often, if and what review process exists for these automated datasets is not clear. ICEWS and GDELT are no exception. For example, ICEWS provides one assessment document, "BBN ACCENT Event Coding Evaluation" that addresses how many of its events were correctly assigned to their broadest event class. This document outlines the precision of each event type as of 2015 (Boschee et al. 2015a). Whether this process is repeated at all, or regularly, is unknown, but the inclusion of incorrect events suggests that such review is not regularly occurring. For example, an article in ICEWS records the leader of the Movement for Democratic Change

(MDC), Thokozani Khupe, as having physically assaulted "Men (Zimbabwe)"; in reality, the original article notes how Khupe was giving a speech decrying sexual and gender harassment in Zimbabwe (Zana, 2018). In another example from GDELT, Jammu Martyr's Day commemorating the 1947 massacre in Jammu and Kashmir in India (Kashmir Media Service, 2018) was coded as "engaging in mass violence" in 2018 between Pakistan and an unidentified army in India. This event incorrectly notes that mass violence is occurring in a contentious region, and can have quite negative ramifications in analysis using these data.

Further error is introduced if duplicates are not removed. ICEWS notes that "duplicate stories from the same publisher, same headline, and same date are generally omitted," but that "duplicate stories across multiple publishers (as is the case in syndicated new stories) are permitted" (Boschee et al. 2015b). GDELT checks for duplicates across all source documents during the 15-minute window in which an event first appears, limiting the flagging of duplicate events to only a 15-minute period. Events that make international headlines will get updated repeatedly as more details become available in the aftermath of the event, and when the event is reported in a different form or by different media. Such duplicates can obscure true trends in conflict patterns.

Sourcing. The sources of information are also crucial, especially given that only information which is reported can be coded at all. Within automated data projects, sourcing can often be limited to certain language(s) only, and often does not rely on a set source list.

For example, to gather data, ICEWS relies on " . . . about 6000 sources . . . many of [which] are aggregators of hundreds of other sources" (Ward et al, 2013) in English, Spanish, Portuguese, and Arabic, sharing its source for each event. While a broader range of languages than English alone is a step in the right direction, limiting coverage to four languages alone means that a great deal of local media is missed, and multiple stories with varied descriptions of the same event are aggregated. GDELT, meanwhile, claims to trawl hundreds of thousands of sources in numerous languages, providing the URL used to pull and create each event. It provides no list of sources and notes how its number of sources grows daily. While a wider range of sources can be very useful, the lack of a consistent source list means that artificial spikes might be observed in the data – that is, the addition of new sources can result in the addition of new events, resulting in a spike in events when one might not exist in reality.

In sum, machine-automated data projects, such as GDELT and ICEWS, can make event data collection faster – allowing for data updates in real-time; and the costs associated with such projects can be considerably low since tasks are automated and do not require the employment of researchers (who would need to be paid). However, despite such benefits, the outputs produced by such projects come with severe limitations that can (at best) distort and (at worst) render conclusions drawn from analysis useless. Such projects use an inclusion criterion – and in turn produce a catchment – that is based on broad definitions and keywords. Their methodology relies on internet trawling for those keywords, not clear and careful operationalizations that allow for consistency within event types. Finally, a lack of review and minimal duplication checking leads to a final dataset that inflates its event counts, leads to the inclusion of irrelevant or incorrect events, and inflates the intensity of events and conflicts.

Researcher-Led Datasets

Researcher-based data projects vary considerably from machine-based, automated data projects. There is also more variance among researcher-led datasets than among different machine-based datasets as automation limits and streamlines collection processes while researcher-based projects are staffed with teams of researchers able to make specific decisions about catchments, inclusion criteria, review processes, sourcing, etc. The *researcher*-led aspect produces considerable, critical variance in event data output, as we demonstrate in our comparison of ACLED and others. ACLED is the most widely used real-time data and analysis source on political violence and protests across the world, capturing a wide range of event types related to conflict. It originated in 2005 and produces data that cover a temporal range from 1997 to the present, with different temporal coverage across different geographic regions; data are publicly available via its website and API, with data released weekly. It has set the standard for researcher-led collections, and continues to develop methodologies of coding and sourcing to accurately capture the spectrum of political disorder as it occurs globally.

Catchment and Inclusion Criteria. The key difference in researcher-led data begins with the project's research agendas and organizational mandates. Some projects consider only conflict which meets certain thresholds of lethality, such as UCDP-GED, or codes only terrorism as a subset of conflict, such as GTD. ACLED's agenda is to capture disorder and conflict as it manifests across the world, and its catchment is therefore political violence and demonstration events. Political violence is defined as the use of force by a group with political motivations or objectives, which can include replacing an agent or system of government; the protection, harassment, or repression of identity groups, the general population, and political groups/organizations; the destruction of safe, secure, public spaces; elite competition; contests to wield authority over an area or community; and mob violence (ACLED, 2021).

A broad catchment is useful for conflict and foreign policy analysts as modern conflict is best categorized on a spectrum of armed, active organization. A state or international military body with an armed, hierarchical order can engage with all other conflict agents, be present across a territory, or be expected to be perpetually active; rebel organizations seek to address national-level power disparities; militias are *hired* and objectives are closely tied to political patrons; community armed groups provide specific security services on a club good basis; cartels require territorial and population control to engage in an extensive economic racket; violent mobs respond to community threats with targeted violence before disbanding, largely emerging in areas with poor police presence and trust; and rioters emerge to quickly create disorder before reconstituting or fading quickly. The underlying theme to these groups and forms of conflict are that they are all organized to varying degrees in a defined time and space to pursue political objectives, and many arm themselves to do so. As a result, their event forms, intensity, and frequency differ extensively.

This spectrum can, in turn, be populated by incidents which have been categorized as event types and/or into sub-categories therein, each involving specific actors. Ideally, such categorization, definitions, and coding structure allow for extensive aggregation and disaggregation based on event type, agents, and types of groups, in addition to geography, intensity, severity, time, and context. Such flexibility allows for maximal use by analysts working with event data. This is the case with ACLED, which includes event types and sub-event types therein (ACLED, 2021), along with distinct, named actors grouped into broad categories that acknowledge groups' larger agendas and organizational structures.

Review Processes. Unlike automated datasets, researcher-led data projects benefit from having full research teams who are involved in quality control or review. Some researcher-led projects collect information and review before publishing on an annual basis, while others might integrate review into more frequent publication schedules, instead building on mechanisms to account for new information which may come to light, requiring an event to be updated. ACLED abides by the latter and is hence a *living dataset*. Data are published on a weekly release schedule; this timing is designed to harness the most accurate and available information and allows for near real-time monitoring by users. It is also the basis for a robust and reliable early warning system. Despite the frequent publication schedule, prior to publication, ACLED data still go through multiple rounds of review to account for inter-coder, intra-coder, and inter-code reliability that together allow for cross-context comparability. This regular oversight ensures the accuracy of events, and the avoidance of false positives and duplicates. Oversight continues after data are published: as more information comes to light, corrections and updates are uploaded to the dataset, though ensuring that event IDs remain constant so as to allow users to update their information regularly with ease.

Open, continual, and transparent reviews and discussions of collection processes are imperative as this benefits both data developers and user communities. Users whose research is affected by coding decisions should be informed about how these choices are made, and how they will impact analysis. This is important as even similar conflicts in different regions can be fundamentally distinct, and methodological decisions are hence ongoing and so ought to be publicized to inform users upon implementation. Offering a depository of information from which to make informed choices about event data forms and comparisons is a necessary feature of modern projects. While automated data projects are not able to provide such details, especially as automated coding does not always abide by such rules, researcher-led projects are able to be more transparent. ACLED, for example, publishes codebooks, training, and explanatory materials, while also making methodology documents on a range of significant and specific issues openly accessible. Such methodological transparency ensures that coding remains standardized across countries, conflicts, and researchers. In addition to documentation, being accessible to users to address questions is also a boon for users; in that vein, the ACLED team remains accessible, with questions from users regularly received and addressed.

Sourcing. The breadth and depth of sourcing are the most critical determinants of what version of reality is relayed in conflict data projects. Two central issues pervade conflict data collection efforts: (1) which combination of media and other information sources can be relied upon, and (2) how to develop a sourcing profile for each unique context that takes into account both the conflict and the media landscape in order to allow for the best and most reliable coverage.

Further, targeted supplementation of key periods or access to new sources of information means that coverage is always being strengthened (ACLED, 2020). There are tradeoffs for changing sources and methodologies to capture changing circumstances. The number or types of sources alone will not guarantee that data are more reliable. All sources contain some biases – ranging from propaganda to specific focuses on certain actors or regions. Simply including *more* sources merely reproduces these variables on a larger scale, and does not yield more reliable data. Furthermore, every context has unique variables to consider, such as geography, freedom of the press, and types of violence. Again, not taking such nuance into account means that simply increasing the number and types of sources will simply perpetuate these patterns. One must take into account the variation in types of violence, available sources, and potential biases in order to curate a sourcing strategy that is effective in capturing local conflict dynamics. Such strategies often involve relying on a mix of traditional and new media (for example, see Dowd et al., 2020); drawing on media in local languages (beyond English alone in contexts where English is not the primary language); and prioritizing local media, so as to neither miss conflict occurring in more remote places that foreign correspondents have difficulty accessing nor miss smaller events which the audiences of international media care less to read. (For more on biases, see Miller et al., 2022.)

ACLED employs such a wide and deep sourcing net, with sources of information being country- and context-specific – collecting reports in over 100 distinct languages, and from over 13,600 sources ranging from national newspapers to local radio, coded by a team of researchers who often live and work in the environments they cover, and hence benefit from local context and language knowledge. ACLED privileges local and subnational sources, and hence sourcing often includes local conflict observatories, especially as extensive and accurate information sourcing requires local partners and media in local languages.

The optimum constellation of sources to capture the full range of conflict varies across countries. Consider the example of Syria: Figure 34.1 notes coverage by source type, depicting the differences that can be seen both geographically (across governorates) and by violence type. The map depicts traditional media on the left, which includes media outlets like Shaam News, for example. Its coverage focuses on the capital, Damascus, and surrounding Rural Damascus, in the southwest and on the very active Hama province in the west. The vast majority of information capturing the war against the Islamic State is missed from multiple traditional sources, as the activity is largely occurring outside of the areas well-covered by these media. Information from a wide range of sources beyond traditional media alone – which makes up ACLED's sourcing profile for its Syrian coverage – is reflected in the map on the right; the majority of this information comes from local partners and sources.

Different sources of information may also privilege the reporting of different types of information. For example, in Syria, national media may best capture explosions and remote violence, which are prolific in the Syrian context. But local partners and other media can improve on that catchment and uniquely capture small-scale battles, violence against civilians, protests, riots, and large-scale arrests by state forces. To develop such sourcing profiles, one must conduct extensive testing in order to determine the optimum constellation of sources that offers the most complete picture of the conflict with minimal duplication in types of events reported (De Bruijne and Raleigh, 2017).

In sum, researcher-led data projects sacrifice turnaround times, and tend to cost more to run given the required staffing of researchers, but are much more reliable in what they produce. The catchment and inclusion criteria of such projects is more robust and transparent; review processes exist and are well-documented; and sourcing can be considerably more nuanced and expansive.

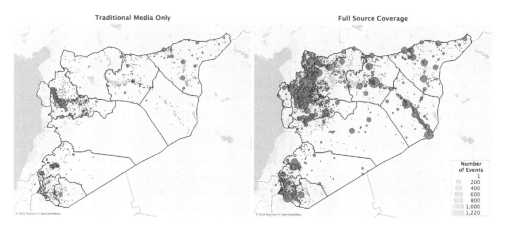

Figure 34.1 Conflict in Syria in 2017 by source type.

A standard *one-size-fits-all* approach to data collection and event coding is not a suitable or adequate response to the variability of modern conflict. Each country and the unique risks that it faces must be regularly reviewed by country experts to ensure that data accurately reflect the most reliable information available. Event data methodologies for manual, researcher-led data collection are able to make such revisions and adapt to best practices in order to ensure reliable and consistent data collection. ACLED, for example, regularly engages in such rigorous review – benefitting both from a team of researchers based around the world with local context knowledge, as well as from a vast network of local partner organizations based around the globe.

How information is collected is one of the primary cleavages between event-based datasets – specifically when comparing automated, machine-based projects with researcher-led ones. The latter, as explored above, tends to be more reliable, consistent, and accurate (free of mass duplicates and false positives), though this comes at a higher cost than automated projects which need not be bounded by finite resources.

The discrepancy is also impacted by the fact that automated datasets do not benefit from close human oversight, meaning inclusion into the dataset is not overseen and duplicates and false positives can skew trends. Errors of false positives and duplicates are not benign in datasets, and it is not the case that automated datasets capture trends correctly on the aggregate. Rather, the result of rampant false positives and duplicates is the depiction of trends – such as an increase in a certain type of violence, or more lethality – that is not there. This can have serious ramifications for users and analysts who depend on accurate reporting of real events rather than false or manufactured trends. The trajectories of this violence too can be skewed as a result of the same trends.

Additional characteristics, including physical geography and intensity, are critical considerations for data generators and analysts. How precisely a dataset seeks to address the who, what, when, and where of conflict data will have drastic effects on analysis. Consider the implications for using centroids (i.e., the center point of a country) rather than specific locations for a conflict location when source materials are not explicit about where something happened. This is a common occurrence in machine-based datasets. Imprecision can create conflicts where no such violence occurs. This matters for practitioners: if an agency seeks to provide relief, assess the danger to its staff and to the civilian population, or engage in early warning, conflicts that appear in areas in which they are not present have serious implications. Furthermore, given that many conflict studies use location to discern the different causal explanations for subnational violence, arbitrary violence locations are a serious mistake and will bias analysis.

Different Data Lead to Different Conclusions

Differences in methodologies – specifically in catchment, inclusion criteria, review processes, and sourcing – can all contribute to how different datasets come to distinct conclusions: Where are civilians at most risk? Which countries are experiencing the most conflict? The following section explores these differences.

Geographies and Scales of Conflict

When looking at broad trends in conflict in 2019 (as a common year of coverage across the data projects reviewed here), the different datasets come to different conclusions regarding which countries were most violent. According to GDELT, in 2019 the US experienced the largest number of relevant events, with 720,407 events of "other conventional force," 422,654 events of "small arms/light weapons fights," and 191,835 "other unconventional force" events. In fact, comparing across countries, GDELT comes to the conclusion that the US has more recorded events of "other conventional force" than other countries, including India and Syria – countries with active and ongoing civil conflicts. In comparison, India topped the list of overall activity for both ICEWS and ACLED – though ACLED recorded over twice as many events; states experiencing large-scale conflicts – like Afghanistan and Syria – also made ICEWS' top five list as home to the most conflict events, though again with ten times fewer events relative to ACLED.

Such trends vary even further when considering specific types of violence. Conventional military force, for example, can be explored within the GDELT dataset by looking at the "fight" subset of events; these events are consistent with the use of conventional military force, blockades or movement restrictions, territory occupations, small arms and light weapons fights, artillery and tank fights, aerial weapons usage, and ceasefire violations (although not all types are necessarily included in the data). Using these data, the conclusion is that the US was home to more conventional military force than any other country in 2019, with event totals higher than the next nine highest countries combined.

Within the CAMEO system, used by machine-based datasets, there is tremendous variation in the countries where conventional force was applied and how intense that conflict was. Looking at the same trends explored above with the ICEWS dataset, the US is once again near the top of the list – though ICEWS records more such events in India, Syria, Palestine, and Afghanistan. Conclusions around the scales of conflict also vary greatly by dataset. For example, according to GDELT, the US was home to over one million events; in comparison, ICEWS records 570 events.

Across both GDELT and ICEWS, there are countries included in the "top 25" list of "most violent through conventional force" that did not experience any conventional fighting on their territory. These include France, Germany, Canada, and the United Kingdom. These incorrect conclusions are stark especially when considering the relatively low ranking – or absence – of countries with large-scale conflicts in 2019, such as Yemen, which is absent from GDELT altogether, and ranked 22nd by ICEWS; or Somalia, again absent from GDELT altogether, and ranked 14th by ICEWS, though still behind Australia and the US.

In short, simple conclusions on which foreign policy analysts might need to rely, and which countries ought to be prioritized when considering where to invest resources to combat conflict, will vary greatly depending on which dataset is used. More worrying is that the conclusions from some of these datasets – notably the machine-based ones – are knowingly incorrect, pointing to locales that are not home to large-scale conflicts. False positives in the data result in skewing trends, and hence conclusions, immensely.

An analyst may ask whether event numbers matter in the absolute or relative sense. In 2019, ICEWS recorded 3,427 events in India. Comparing this number with trends captured by GDELT, this would put ICEWS' India intensity on par with GDELT's Trinidad and Tobago, ranked 113th most violent in 2019. In addition to presenting a skewed depiction of the state of conflict, casual users would be hard-pressed to explain what accounts for the variation across the two projects. More concerning are comparisons of scale *within* datasets. For example, GDELT records 151,456 events of conventional fighting in Syria in 2019 – less than eight times the number recorded in the US despite the former being an active war zone. Not only do the rankings here (i.e., the US being more violent than Syria) raise questions, but also the magnitude of this difference (i.e., eight times more violent) leaves the user wondering how to interpret conclusions.

Conflict Event Data

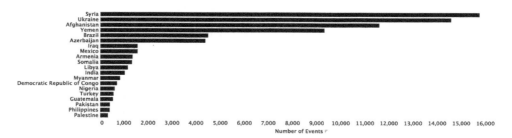

Figure 34.2 Top 20 Countries exhibiting conventional force in 2019, per ACLED data.

A foreign policy analyst relying on GDELT or ICEWS, if asked which countries in 2019 experienced the most conventional fighting, or which countries were at risk of continuing with conventional conflicts, might argue that India is a greater priority than countries like Syria, Afghanistan, or Yemen. They would also find that the US is a hotspot for such fighting, and if they relied on GDELT data, that it far outpaced all other countries around the world in the intensity of the violence experienced. Moreover, if asked about the intensity of conflict across all countries, a reliable count of violent events would be elusive. Overall, they would find conflict patterns that do not reflect an empirical reality – making foreign policy conclusions meaningless.

In contrast, a foreign policy analyst asking the same research questions though relying on ACLED data would come to different conclusions. According to ACLED, the countries with the highest rates of conventional force[1] in 2019 include Syria, Ukraine, Afghanistan, Yemen, Brazil, Azerbaijan, Iraq, and Mexico (see Figure 34.2). Each country noted is actively embroiled in conflicts over territory, facing insurgencies, experiencing high degrees of gang and cartel violence, and more. Moreover, the composition of the countries experiencing such conflict according to ACLED is validated by outside sources relying on qualitative research by experts, such as the Council on Foreign Relations. Finally, the violence in these countries is collected systematically, and reflects event counts that are categorized and aggregated in a systematic way across conflicts; it is not a count of media mentions but of comparable conflict incidents. For this reason, the information available allows for in-depth analysis of the contexts and change in each country, and between countries experiencing similar or different forms of instability.

Threats to Civilians

Similar differences can be seen when exploring trends regarding the threat to civilians. While battles and conventional fighting pose clear risks to civilians, foreign policy analysts are often curious about other forms of civilian risk, such as unconventional mass violence, mass expulsions, mass killings, ethnic cleansing, and the use of weapons of mass destruction. The CAMEO classification system has similar categories, yet they are not clearly defined and it is not clear how many deaths constitute a mass killing; what distinguishes an ethnic cleansing from a mass expulsion; or even what the boundaries between conventional and unconventional are.

Nevertheless, looking at unconventional mass violence through the lens of GDELT's data, the US again remains the country where civilians are at greatest risk, with 2,395 recorded mass killings, 1,292 instances of ethnic cleansing, and 90 instances of mass expulsion in 2019.

Not only are such conclusions known to be false, a foreign policy analyst relying on data from GDELT would come to the conclusion that American civilians face higher risk than groups such as the Uyghur minority in China, who are facing an active ethnic cleansing campaign. According to GDELT, however, only 264 ethnic cleansing events were recorded in China in 2019 – nearly five times fewer than what was recorded in the US.

According to ICEWS, unconventional mass violence in 2019 looks very different. GDELT only recorded mass killings, ethnic cleansings, and mass expulsion events in 2019; ICEWS records mass killings, ethnic cleansings, chemical/biological/radiological weapons, and nuclear weapons use that same year. In regards to these events, ICEWS records occurrences in 17 states – a smaller number of countries relative to GDELT. The intensity of those events also vary, with a maximum of six events in the most prolific country (Japan); notably, all six were specifically nuclear weapon attacks. Users of the data, however, will likely remember that such nuclear attacks did not happen in 2019, though media did reference the World War II bombings of Hiroshima and Nagasaki that year.

Again, a foreign policy analyst relying on GDELT or ICEWS to understand risk to civilians might prioritize places like the US or Japan, as opposed to places like China. In contrast, a foreign policy analyst asking the same research questions though relying on ACLED data would come to different conclusions. ACLED finds that in 2019, Mexico, Brazil, India, the Philippines, Syria, Nigeria, and the Democratic Republic of the Congo are most violent for civilians. Again, the countries here reflect what a foreign policy analyst likely would expect to see: countries with war zones and active targeting of local populations are not necessarily experiencing similar types of conflict, but regardless of the modality, the impact on civilians is systemically and robustly collected and verified. For example, Mexico was noted as having its "murder rate [hit] record high in 2019" (Al Jazeera, 2020). Brazil, ranked second, similarly was noted as being in "complete chaos" due to gang violence in 2019 (Kaiser, 2019).

What explains these disparities? The automated trawling by machine-based projects can inflate event counts, especially in which there is little to no checking for duplicate events. In cases where such trawling is done more often – such as in GDELT, which publishes data every 15 minutes – the dramatically different event counts, even relative to other projects that rely on the same CAMEO coding system, does not inspire confidence in the conclusions. The inflated number of events is driven largely by countries that produce many of the news articles that are trawled, such as the US – which can, in turn, also explain why the US features so prominently in GDELT's rankings.

Concluding Thoughts on Event Data and Their Future

The most useful conflict data will present conflict environments as complex and multifaceted, volatile, and fractured. Although there has been tremendous growth in and attention toward event-level data, national and yearly aggregated datasets are still dominant in public use. A review of articles in three of the top political science journals focused on conflict – the *Journal of Conflict Resolution*, the *Journal of Peace Research*, and *Conflict Management and Peace Science* – reveals that less than a quarter (approximately 22%) of the articles published in the past five years rely on event data.

As event data use begins to rise, it is important to remember that not all conflict datasets offer equal levels of coverage, depth, usability, and content. A review of the catchment, inclusion criteria, review processes, and sourcing of researcher-led compared with machine-based conflict event datasets suggests that the pitfalls of automation are too many to simply use these data without significant reservations. The promises of increased automation, and indeed advancements into AI, are not realized because of issues with accuracy, patterns, and thoroughness. Instead, complex conflicts are rendered one dimensional, and reporting, media schedules, and interest determine how and whether conflict events are captured. As event data projects will provide the bulk of information for conflict analysis and early warning in the future, it is important to take stock of our conclusions.

Data Collection and Oversight

A rigorous researcher is the best way to ensure reliable, consistent, and accurate events are coded that are not false positives. Researcher-led datasets generate fewer false positives and maintain oversight mechanisms to review potential events according to an established methodology. At ACLED, for example, regardless of the multiple systems used to source information, researchers, reviewers, and experts have the final say in the coding of events, and these practices ensure that the coding process remains carefully regulated and updated as necessary. Machine-based datasets are still being refined and are not yet at the point where they can be used as accurate representations of reality. In this current stage, the rate of false positives prevents their use for analysis of dynamics, agents, impacts, and spaces of violence. Due to the rate of duplicates, automated datasets are more accurately interpreted as a measure of media interest in a story and the frequency of reporting on various conflicts, rather than as a source for the details of conflicts themselves. It is not appropriate to use these event datasets to present trends, maps, or distributions of violence in a country.

Inclusion

Inclusion criteria should allow for accurate representations of conflict, while being flexible to how conflict dynamics have changed. Who is considered a relevant and legitimate actor in conflict is pre-determined by the mandate of each dataset; the definitions, catchment, and categorization are hence critical, as they tell a user who and what is likely to be included. In turn, the rules of inclusion determine how and in what detail one understands violence. Limiting coverage by arbitrary thresholds can obscure low-level violence, violence linked to unidentified perpetrators, and other forms of conflict – all of which can distort results; this can be true of both machine-based and researcher-led datasets. ACLED, for example, does not employ such thresholds, while other researcher-led datasets do.

Coverage and Classification

Clear, coherent, and correct classifications are important for users because conflicts are not homogenous: conflict events differ in their frequency, sequences, and intensity. Event types that reflect the variation of modalities common across conflicts and contentious periods are basic, central components of insightful and useful analysis. Without capturing the spectrum of conflict, datasets can distort the truth about the distribution of instability and their impact on civilians and state security.

Usability and Transparency

Datasets must be useful and useable if they are to be relied upon for regular analysis, and users should be able to access every detail of how conflict data are coded and collected. Usability is closely tied to straightforward, consistent inclusion criteria and clear methodology. Near real-time data require the ability to capture low-level events, seek accurate sources of triangulation, and have a robust checking and updating system, which allow for evaluation and monitoring of ongoing and past projects, politics, and strategies.

Sourcing

Extensive sourcing – including from local partners and media in local languages – provides the most thorough and accurate information on conflict, as well as the most accurate presentation of the risks that citizens and civilians experience in their homes and communities. A wide and deep net of sourcing is integral when gathering information.

Acknowledgments

The Horizon 2020 ERC grant 726504 provided some funding for this work.

Note

1 ACLED does not rely on CAMEO codes. For a comparison to machine-based datasets which do rely on such codes, the following ACLED sub-event types are reviewed here to capture conventional force: armed clashes (including those with territorial transfer), airstrikes, drone strikes, shelling, artillery, or missile attacks.

References

ACLED. "FAQs: ACLED Sourcing Methodology". *ACLED 2020*. Accessed 15 December 2021. https://acleddata.com/acleddatanew/wp-content/uploads/dlm_uploads/2020/02/FAQs_ACLED-Sourcing-Methodology.pdf.

ACLED. "Armed Conflict Location & Event Data Project (ACLED) Codebook". *ACLED 2021*. Accessed 15 December 2021. https://acleddata.com/acleddatanew/wp-content/uploads/2021/11/ACLED_Codebook_v1_January-2021.pdf.

Al Jazeera. 2020. "Mexico Murder Rate Hits Record High in 2019". January 8. https://www.aljazeera.com/news/2020/1/21/mexico-murder-rate-hits-record-high-in-2019.

Boschee, Elizabeth, Jennifer Lautenschlager, Sean O'Brien, Steve Shellman, James Starz, and Michael Ward. 2015a. "BBN ACCENT Event Coding Evaluation.updated v01.pdf". *ICEWS Coded Event Data*. Accessed 5 August 2021. https://doi.org/10.7910/DVN/28075/GBAGXI, Harvard Dataverse, V30 https://dataverse.harvard.edu/file.xhtml?persistentId=doi:10.7910/DVN/28075/GBAGXI&version=30.0.

Boschee, Elizabeth, Jennifer Lautenschlager, Sean O'Brien, Steve Shellman, James Starz, and Michael Ward. 2015b. "ICEWS Coded Event Data Read Me.pdf". *ICEWS Coded Event Data*. Accessed 5 August 2021. https://doi.org/10.7910/DVN/28075/1GGS5G, Harvard Dataverse, V30.

Boschee, Elizabeth, Jennifer Lautenschlager, Sean O'Brien, Steve Shellman, James Starz, and Michael Ward. 2015c. "ICEWS Expanded CAMEO Annotation Guidelines.pdf". *ICEWS Coded Event Data*. Accessed 5 August 2021. https://doi.org/10.7910/DVN/28075/SODSMT, Harvard Dataverse, V30 https://dataverse.harvard.edu/file.xhtml?persistentId=doi:10.7910/DVN/28075/SODSMT&version=30.0.

Boschee, Elizabeth, Jennifer Lautenschlager, Sean O'Brien, Steve Shellman, and James Starz. 2018. *ICEWS Weekly Event Data*. Harvard Dataverse. https://doi.org/10.7910/DVN/QI2T9A.

Boschee, Elizabeth, Jennifer Lautenschlager, Sean O'Brien, Steve Shellman, James Starz, and Michael Ward. 2020. *ICEWS Coded Event Data*. Harvard Dataverse. https://dataverse.harvard.edu/dataset.xhtml?persistentId=doi:10.7910/DVN/28075.

De Bruijne, Kars, and Clionadh Raleigh. 2017. "Reliable Data on the Syrian Conflict by Design." *ACLED*. https://www.acleddata.com/wp-content/uploads/2018/05/PilotReport_March2018_FINAL-1.pdf.

Dowd, Caitriona, Patricia Justino, Roudabeh Kishi, and Gauthier Marchais. 2020. "Comparing 'New' and 'Old' Media for Violence Monitoring and Crisis Response: Evidence from Kenya." *Research & Politics* 7 (3): 75–92.

Kaiser, Anna Jean. 2019. "It's Complete Chaos: Brazilian State Overwhelmed By Gang Violence." *The Guardian*, January 9. https://www.theguardian.com/world/2019/jan/09/brazil-ceara-violence-fortaleza-gangs-bolsonaro.

Kaarbo, Juliet. 2015. "A Foreign Policy Analysis Perspective on the Domestic Politics Turn in IR Theory." *International Studies Review* 17 (2): 189–216.

Kashmir Media Service. 2018. "Jammu Martyrs' Day Tomorrow". *Kashmir Media Service*, November 5. https://kmsnews.org/news/2018/11/05/jammu-martyrs-day-tomorrow/.

LaFree, Gary, and Laura Dugan. 2007. "Introducing the Global Terrorism Database." *Terrorism and Political Violence* 19 (2): 181–204.

Leetaru, Kalev, and Philip A Schrodt. 2013. GDELT: Global Data on Events, Location, and Tone. *ISA Annual Convention*. http://citeseerx.ist.psu.edu/viewdoc/download;jsessionid=98ACB9D-85020D6E2EBB8AF185AB93479?doi=10.1.1.686.6605&rep=rep1&type=pdf.

Miller, Erin, Roudabeh Kishi, Clionadh Raleigh, and Catriona Dowd. 2022. "An Agenda for Addressing Bias in Conflict Data." *Scientific Data* 9: 593, https://doi.org/10.1038/s41597-022-01705-8.

Raleigh, Clionadh. 2014. "Political Hierarchies and Landscapes of Conflict Across Africa." *Political Geography* 42 (1): 92–103.

Raleigh, Clionadh, Andrew Linke, Håvard Hegre, and Joakim Karlsen. 2010. "Introducing ACLED: An Armed Conflict Location and Event Dataset: Special Data Feature." *Journal of Peace Research* 47 (5): 651–660.

Schrodt, Philip. 2012. *Cameo: Conflict and Mediation Event Observations Event and Actor Codebook*. Pennsylvania State University. Accessed 5 August 2021. https://parusanalytics.com/eventdata/cameo.dir/CAMEO.Manual.1.1b3.pdf.

Sundberg, Ralph, and Erik Melander. 2013. "Introducing the UCDP Georeferenced Event Dataset." *Journal of Peace Research* 50 (4): 523–532.

Ward, Michael D., Andreas Beger, Josh Cutler, Matthew Dickenson, Cassy Dorff, and Ben Radford. 2013. *Comparing GDELT and ICEWS Event Data*, 15 October. Accessed 15 December 2021. https://www.researchgate.net/profile/Andreas-Beger/publication/303211430_Comparing_GDELT_and_ICEWS_event_data/links/57f7d9bb08ae886b89836115/Comparing-GDELT-and-ICEWS-event-data.pdf.

Zana, Jabulani. 2018. "Chamisa Power Quest: Cult Following and Deception." *The Herald*, August 8. https://www.pressreader.com/zimbabwe/the-heralzimbabwe/20180808/282011853182722.

Index

Note: **Bold** page numbers refer to tables; *italic* page numbers refer to figures.

Acharya, A. 53
ACLED *see* Armed Conflict Location and Event Data (ACLED)
actorless threats 203
actor-specific approach 7, 10, 51, 291, 294–295, 302
Adair, W.L. 477
Adams, D. 47
Adduci, M. 83
Adler, E. 52, 101, 109, 151, 466, 471
Adler-Nissen, R. 58, 180, 470
Advocacy Coalition Framework (ACF) 520
affiliation network *521, 523*, 526, *528*
agency 53, 88, 102, 189, 405, 408, 416
Agnew, J. 82, 83, 85, 89, 93
Aharon, B. 451, 455
Akten zur Auswärtigen Politik der Bundesrepublik Deutschland (AAPD) 463
Allan, B.B. 105
Allison, G. 422
Allison, G.T. 298–300
Almond, G.A. 295
anthropomorphization 31–33
antipreneurs 53
applicatory contestation 56
Aran, A. 135
archival research 464–466
Arena, P. 356
Armed Conflict Location and Event Data (ACLED) 13
associative networks 74
audience 108
Auspurg, K. 343
Australia **250**, 251, 387, **393, 394, 395**, 504, 560
autocracy 341
automated machine coding 310
automated text analysis 135, 535–548, **539**
Avdan, N. 341, 342, 347, 349, 350

BACE *see* belief in the ability to control events (BACE)
Bagozzi, B.E. 542, 547
Bailey, M. 545
Baldwin, D. 258
Barkawi, T. 452
Barnett, M. 46
Barnhart, J.N. 380
Barnum, M. 544, 545
Baturo, A. 544
Becker, D. 103
belief in the ability to control events (BACE) 240
beliefs 22–26, 53, 69, 92, 119, 123, 126, 190, 206, 208, 213–214, 238, 255–263, 311, 354–355, 359–360, 364–365, 377, 439, 470, 516, 520
Beltyokova, S. 10
Bennett, A. 441, 442, 444, 472, 506
Benoit, K. 537, 538, 540
Berliner, D. 542, 547
between-subject designs 341, 348–349
big data (analysis) 4, 12, 147, 463, 485–498, 502
Bils, P. 356
binary role theory 190
Bleiker, R. 173
Bloomfield, A. 53
Böller, F. 387
Boolean minimization 389–390
Boomgaarden, H. 135
Boucher, J-C. 541, 547
bounded rationality 256; *see also* rationalism
Bourdieu, P. 43
Brast, B. 407
Brazil 87, 224–234, 451–452, 546
Breuning, M. 10, 34, 193, 195
Bruck, H. 338
Brummer, K. 6, 10, 90, 241, 386

Bueno de Mesquita, E. 356
Buhaug, H. 87
Bulgaria 230, **393**, **394**, **395**
bureaucracy 46–47, 74, 464, 467
Busby, J. 345

Campbell, D.T. 30, 102, 345
Canada 58, 71, 224–234, 518
Cantir, C. 192
Carmody, P. 543
Carnegie, A. 356
Carson, A. 356
Carter Administration 91–92
Carter, J. 91, 92, 439
cascading activation model 219, 222
case selection 296, 298, 300, 398, 473, 545
case study 70, 189–190, 194, 196–198, 264, 272, 293, 296–301, 385, 398, 435, 437, 441, 443, 465–466, 472–473
Casey, S. 90
causal asymmetry 385, 388
causal complexity 385, 387–388
causal emplotment 120
causal story 104
causality 24–25, 28, 92, 104, 325, 385, 387–388, 438, 487
causation *see* causality
Chaban, N. 10
Chatfield, A.T. 504
chemical weapons (CW) 58–62
Chen, M. 83
Chi, S-H. 83
China (People's Republic) 61, 92, 119, 128, 134, 139, 144, 146, 147, 203, 207, 260, 293, 296–298, 314, 439, 543, 562
Chinese Communist Party (CCP) 139–147, 203, 207, 260, 297–298, 543, 562
circles of recognition 26
civilizing missions 84
class affinity 548
classification methods 538–539
Clifford, J. 45
closed-ended questions 375
CNN effect 153
co-constitution 190
coding 75, 90, 110, 121–124, 127, 135, 147, 173, 194–195, 198, 219, 239–240, 242, 244, 251, 264, 307, 310–313, 318, 375, 392, 438, 474, 477, 504, 511, 520–521, 524–525, 531, 536, 539–540, 542, 544, 554, 556, 557, 563
Coe, A.J. 356
cognition 86, 88, 120, 133, 169, 173–174, 177–178, 203–206, 221, 255–257, 259–261, 263–265, 276, 294, 338–339, 357, 366, 375
cognitive geopolitics 86, 90, 93
Cohn, C. 69
collective identities *see* identity

common conjecture 360–361
Common Security and Defence Policy (CSDP) 427
comparative case approach 119, 155, 196–198, 214, 296–298
comparative foreign policy (CFP) 291–303, 322, 437–438
comparative method approach 300–302, 386, 422
comparative methods 7, 10–11, 23, 69–70, 133, 187, 191, 219, 239–240, 251, 291–303, 307, 309, 317, 321–333, 385–399, 422–423, 430, 440–441, 504, 547
comparative theory approach 298–300; *see also* case selection
Composite Indicator of National Capability (CINC) 263
Comprehensive Peace Agreement (CPA) 540
computer-assisted text analysis (CATA) 310
conceptual complexity (CC) 240
Con-Div dynamic 271
confidence interval 325–326, *331*
Conflict and Peace Data Bank (COPDAB) 292
conflict event data 551–552
congruence networks 521–522, *522–523*, 527, *528, 529*
conjoint (design, experiments) 342–343, 347–348, 350
conjunctural causation 385
constructivism 6, 21–22, 26–33, 51–52, 57, 62, 86, 101, 108–109, 127–128, 150, 170, 173, 178, 193, 294
content analysis 90, 121, 138, 193–195, 242, 255–257, 306–318, 428, 437, 474, 511, 517, 520, 539, 541
contest success function (CSF) 87
contestation 3, 51–62, 74, 121, 126, 154, 192–197, 310, 317, 386, 517, 519, 531
contingency 32, 55, 107, 156, 171, 204, 215, 277, 280–281, 350, 405, 408, 412, 416, 439, 469
convenience sample 344–345, 349, 378
Cook, T.D. 345
coordination game 361
Copenhagen School *see* securitization (theory)
Correlates of War Project (COW) 292, 308, 437, 487
counterfactuals 212–213, 356, 389–390, 395
covariate balance across 346
covering law model 407
COW *see* Correlates of War Project (COW)
Cox, M. 101–102
Criekemans, D. 86
Critical Discourse Analysis (CDA) 108
critical geopolitics 85–86
cross validation 541
cross-sectional designs 376–377
CSDP *see* Common Security and Defence Policy (CSDP)

Culpepper, P.D. 135
Curini, L. 544
cycle-grid model 57
Czech Republic 32, **393**, **394**, **395**

D'Ignazio, C. 75
da Vinha, L. 9
Dalby, S. 82
data availability 133, 194, 264, 537
data cleaning 508–509
data mining 503–505, 538
dataset 219, 292, 321–323, 324, 326–328, 385, 437–438, 463, 465–466, 474, 546, 551–564
de la Blache, P.V. 88
de Vries, E. 547
democratic corporatist model 221
Denmark **393**, **394**, **395**, 413–416
dependent variable (DV) 259–261, 263, 265, 296–297, 303, 324–332, 339, 542–544
Derrida, J. 465
Deschaux-Dutard, D. 11–12
Devetak, R. 86
dictionary methods 138, 310, 489, 540, 554
Dietrich, S. 344, 380
Diez, T. 103
diplomatic documents 452, 469–474, **474**
diplomatic notes 467
discourse analysis 28, 56, 73–74, 88–89, 101–110, 118, 151, 168–180, 521
discourse network analysis (DNA) 516–531
discretionary authority 470–478
discursive nodal points (DNPs) 106
distrust of others (DIS) 240
Documents on British Policy Overseas (DBPO) 463
domestic role contestation 192
don't know/no opinion (DKNO) 375–376
Doty, R.L. 102, 105
Drahterlass 468

Earl, J. 491
Eder, F. 12, 105, 120, 517–518, 524, 532
Egypt 208, 301, 547
Elias, N. 43
elite samples 344–345
emotion discourse analysis 168–180
empty signifiers 109
endowment effect 208
Enloe, C. 69
Entman, R.M. 133, 135–137, 219, 222
epistemology 45, 72–74, 85, 104–105, 128, 308, 427, 435–438, 443, 465
equifinality 385, 388, 395
Essex School 108
Estonia **393**, **394**, **395**
ethnography 4, 7, 9, 39–47, 422–423, 425, 478

EU Migration Crisis **225**, *227, 228,* **229, 230,** *231–233*
European Union (EU) 224–226, 229, 469, 491
event data 437
expected utility 357
experiments 125, 206–207, 300–301, 338–350, 356, 370–373, 376–378

Facebook 135, 491, 504–507, 546
factorial assignment 342
faded frames 137
FAIR *see* findable, accessible, interoperable, and reusable (FAIR)
fake news 4
Fariss, C. 87
Fattah, K. 170
Fearon, J.D. 355, 356
Federal Foreign Office (FFO) 467
feminism 4, 6–7, 43–44, 67–76, 102, 246, 518
Feng, H. 10, 260
fieldwork 39–47, 73, 75–76
Fierke, K.M. 170
findable, accessible, interoperable, and reusable (FAIR) 459
Finnemore, M. 52
Fisher, D.R. 519
Fleischmann, L. 135
Flint, C. 82, 84, 88
focal points 220
focus groups 424
formal validation 56
Foster, D. 245
Foucault, M. 45, 103–104, 107–108, 164, 465
Fox, C. 10
frame analysis (frames) 25, 52, 59–61, 71, 106, 109, 133–147, 151, 193, 196, 204, 207, 219–222, 228–229, 233–235, 439, 541
framing moves 106
France 55–56, 61, 106, 298–299, 427–431, 463, 469
Friedrichs, G.M. 309, 311, 312, 314, 316, 317
Futák-Campbell, B. 135

game theory 260, 263–264, 354–366
Gardini, G.L. 451, 452, 454
Gates, S. 87
Gaullism 106
gazetteer 489
GDPR *see* General Data Protection Regulation (GDPR)
GEE *see* generalized estimation equation model (GEE)
gender 43, 62, 67–76, 85, 102, 152, 208, 238, 246, 248–249, 251, 324, 328–329, **329, 330,** 332, 339, 376, 427, 431, 443, 555
General Data Protection Regulation (GDPR) 432, 459

Index

generalized estimation equation (GEE) model 87
Germany 29, 84, 103, 104–105, 124, 126, 156–163, 173, 174, 297, 298–299, 361, 423–431, 463–478, 490
Genovese, F. 544
geographical codes 90
geopolitics 3, 28
George, A. 257–259
Ghalehdar, P. 12, 90, 151, 444, 463, 465
Ghraib, A. 152, 153, 160
Gilboa, E. 451
Goemans, H. 356
Goldstein, J. 24, 27, 103, 220
Gottman, J. 82
governmentality 103
Gray, C. 82
Greussing, E. 135
Grimmer, J. 540
Gross Stein, J. 10, 293
group decision-making 269–286, *270*, 339, 386, 517–518, 531
groupthink 212, 269–286, 518
Guimarães, F. 190, 196, 197
Guisinger, A. 372, 380
Gurciullo, S. 546
Gusterson, H. 46
Guzzini, S. 8, 104, 408, 410

habitual validation 56
habitus 32, 43, 426
Haesebrouck, T. 400, 519
Hallin, D. 220
Hanania, R. 546
Hansel, M. 195
Hansen, L. 152, 153
Hardt, H. 344
Harnisch, S. 191, 309, 311, 314, 316
Heck, A. 152, 153
hegemony (discourse) 85, 88, 104–110, 119, 162
hegemony (U.S.) 69, 297, 299
Heinrich, T. 343
He, K. 10, 260
Henshaw, A. 9, 76, 246
Hermann, C. 338, 437
Hermann, M.G. 239, 242, 338
hermeneutics xxiii, 44, 104, 110, 163, 179
heteronormative views 72
heteroskedasticity 327
high inference analysis 233–234, *234*
Hinz, T. 343
historical analysis 12, 90, 435–445
historical institutionalism 435, 439–440
Hobolt, S. 347
Hofmann, S. 34, 323
Hollis, M. 189
Holsti, K.J. 187–191, 193–195
Holsti, O. 256, 257

homo economicus 357
homoskedasticity 327
Hopf, T. 27, 28, 31, 105
Hudson, V.M. 6–7, 51, 187, 193, 292, 294, 322, 386
Hughes, M.M. 72
human preset coding 310–311
Hungary 230, 313
Hurley, M. 76
Hutching, M. 454
Hymans, J. 308, 309, 311, 313, 314, 316, 317

ICEWS *see* Integrated Crisis Early Warning System (ICEWS)
iconographic analysis 154–155
Ide, T. 386
ideal type 104, 125, 179, 256, 405, 408–412
ideas 21–34, 51, 52, 101, 103–104, 109, 153, 173, 198, 224, 300, 355, 360, 408, 467, 516, 537
identity 11, 21–22, 26–34, 53, 75–76, 102–104, 106, 123, 150, 152–154, 161, 168–174, 177, 292, 297, 300–301, 307–317, 387, 413–416
identity crisis 30, 32
IDF *see* Israeli Defense Forces (IDF)
IEDD *see* International Editors of Diplomatic Documents (IEDD)
IGB *see* in-group bias (IGB)
implicit entity networks *488,* 489
in-group bias (IGB) 240
independence assumption 438–440
India 87, 195, 224–234, 416, 555, 560–562
individualism xxi, 6–7, 21–22, 24, 109, 328, 410
Instagram 487
instrumental rationality *see* rationalism
Integrated Crisis Early Warning System (ICEWS) 492
interaction effect 204, 214, 260, 325
intermediate solution 390, 395
internal validity 340–345
International Crisis Behavior Project (ICB) 292
International Editors of Diplomatic Documents (IEDD) 474
International Monetary Fund (IMF) 298
international organizations (IO) 11, 40, 56, 239, 259, 328–329, 469, 546
Interpretive Policy Analysis 102
interpretivist process-tracing 32; *see also* process tracing
intersectionality 69, 72
intersubjectivity 25, 46, 103, 105, 107, 109–110, 120, 126, 128, 170, 174, 176, 177, 306
intertextuality 105, 119, 122, 125–126, 174
interviews 42, 46, 70, 75–76, 156, 171, 195, 242, 249, 261–262, 377–378, 421–432, 451–452, 454–459
Iran 92, 212, 260, 263, **315**

Iran nuclear deal *see* Joint Comprehensive Plan of Action (JCPOA)
Israel 91, 134–135, 208, **272–273**, 315, 344, 451
Israeli Defense Forces (IDF) 511
Italy 32, **393**, **394**, **395**, 544

Jackson, P.T. 7, 104–105, 108, 406–408, 413
Janis, I.L. 269, 270
Joint Comprehensive Plan of Action (JCPOA) 117, 125–128, **273**, 274, 282, 284
Jones, M. 88
Jones, R. 88

K-means clustering methods 541
Kaarbo, J. 34, 51–52, 55, 291, 295, 299, 308, 385, 439, 516, 519
Kaplan, O. 380
Kastner, S. 297
Katagiri, A. 487
Katzenstein, P.J. 27, 398
Kazazis, C. 263
Keller, J.W. 245
Kelly, P. 89
Kenix, L.J. 10
Keohane, R.O 24, 27
Kertzer, J.D. 345, 372, 377
Kim, C. 134
King, G. 346, 347
Kishi, R. 13, 292, 303, 318, 322, 437, 465, 486
Kissinger, H.A. 21, 22, 26, 28, 30, 31
Klein, L.F. 75
Kleinberg, K. 11, 23, 205, 377
Klotz, A. 27
Kobayashi, Y. 343
Koschut, S. 9, 174, 503
Krasner, S.D. 23
Kratochwil, F. 24
Kurki, M. 103
Kuus, M. 40, 42, 422
Kydd, A.H. 355

Laclau, E. 107–109, 171
Lacoste, Y. 93
Laffey, M. 25, 452
Laney, D. 486
large-N statistics 7, 255, 260, 300, 323, 385
Larsen, H. 103
Larson, D. 465
Latent Dirichlet Allocation (LDA) 542
LDA *see* Latent Dirichlet Allocation (LDA)
leadership styles 238–242, 246, **247**, 249, **250**, 540
Leadership Trait Analysis (LTA) 238–251, 399, 540
leadership traits 240–244, **241**, **243**, **244**
Leavy, P. 451, 454, 455, 456
Leeper, T. 347

Leifeld, P. 519
Leites, N. 255, 259
Leventoğlu, B. 355
liberal international order (LIO) 3, 62, 146
liberalism 21–22, 151, 169, 177, 219, 295, 408
limited information 211, 357, *360*, 364, *364*
Lo, J. 544, 545
logistic regression 327, 330–331
low inference analysis 226–233
loss aversion 205–208, 345
LTA *see* Leadership Trait Analysis (LTA)
Lujala, P. 87
Lupton, D.L. 342, 345, 348, 349, 350
Lustick, I.S. 465

machine learning 214, 303, 487, 504, 507, 510, 518, 539, 541, 552
Magen, C. 451
Malinowski, B. 39
Mälksoo, M. 32
Mallea, R. 453, 458
Mamadouh, V. 84
Mancini, P. 220
March, J.G. 43
Marcus, G. 45
Markowitz, J. 87
Marxism 25, 84, 108, 295
Mauss, M. 43
MAXQDA 123, 127, 138–139
McCarthy, D.R. 108
McGlen, N.E. 69
Mead, G.H. 188, 191, 192
Mead, M. 42, 43
medium-N statistics 198, 387
Meernik, J.D. 263, 264
Meirowitz, A. 356
Mello, P.A. 11, 162, 195, 303, 325, 386, 391–397, 399–400, 441, 498
mental maps 90–92
metaphors 106, 109, 152, 172, 173, 175
methodological pluralism 7, 73, 75, 294, 398
Mexico 224–234, 553
middle powers 74
MIDs *see* militarized international disputes (MIDs)
Mikhaylov, S.J. 546
militarized international disputes (MIDs) 87, 259
Min, E. 487
Mintz, A. 7, 10, 212, 269–273, 281, 339, 436, 518
mise-en-scène 155
mixed-methods approach 73, 151, 300–303, 487
model intercept 324, 329
Mokry, S. 9, 110
Möller, M. 195
Montgomery, J. 347
Morgan, K.L. 346
Morgenthau, H.J. 169

Morin, J-F. 8
Morrow, J.D. 355, 365
Morton, S.E. 518
Mouffe, C. 108, 109, 171
Muchiri, J. 518
Müller, M. 89, 387
Mullers, B. 39
multi-methods approach 300
multi-sited field work 42
multicollinearity 327
multilevel regression 327–328
multiple linear regression 325–327
multimodal frame analysis 151
Munzert, S. 491
Murray, M. 297
Mutz, D. 347

Nalebuff, B. 355
narrative entrepreneurs 121
narratives (narrative analysis) xxi, 29–32, 46, 69, 73–74, 85, 88–89, 92, 106, 108–109, 117–129, 133, 135, 150–151, 154, 169, 179, 189, 194–196, 308, 314, 375, 405, 411, 413–416, 438, 442, 453–454, 465–466, 473, 504–505, 508, 511–512, 547, 551
Nash Equilibrium 355, 357, 360–363
national identity conceptions (NICs) 308, **313**
national role conceptions (NRCs) 187–189, 192–193, 197, 301, 309
National Security Council (NSC) 279–281, 400
nationalism 169, 309, 311, 314, 316, **316**
NATO (North Atlantic Treaty Organization) 70, 76, 102–103, 106, 160, 174–178, 260, 387, 428, 546
Natural Language Processing (NLP) 510, 518, 539
Natural Language Toolkit (NLTK) 539
negative predictions 104
neo-neo synthesis 23
neoclassical realism 152, 399
neoliberal institutionalism 23
neopositivism xxii, 24, 104
Netherlands **393, 394,** 395
Neuendorf, K. 307
Neumann, I. 9, 29, 102, 109, 179, 466
New Zealand **250**, 251, 454
NGO see non-governmental organizations (NGO)
Nicholls, T. 135
Nieman, M.D. 301, 302
Niezen, R. 39
Niklasson, B. 75
nomothetic research 406
non-governmental organizations (NGO) 40, 42, 179, 464, 502, 536
non-probability sample 344
norm contestation 51–62
norm life cycle model 52

norm saboteurs 53
norm validation 56
normativity 23–25, 54, 56–61, 71–72, 74–75, 105, 371, 520
Nuclear Non-Proliferation Treaty (NPT) 453, 455–459, 544–545
null hypothesis 24, 27, 324–326, 346
Nussio, E. 380
Nuti, L. 453
NVivo 123, 138
Nye, J.S. 293
Nyhan, B. 347

O'Brien, D.Z. 70
O'Halloran, K.L. 487
O'Loughlin, B. 118
O'Loughlin, J. 83, 88
Oktay, S. 11, 202, 325, 327–328, 346, 388
Olekalns, M. 477
OLS see ordinary least squares (OLS); statistical analysis
Olsen, J.P 43
Olsen, K.M. 471
Onderco, M. 12, 453, 465
Onslow, S. 453
ontological (in)security 21–22, 27, 30–33, 206, 312
ontology xxi, 8, 21–22, 24, 27, 30–34, 54, 72–73, 85, 103, 110, 127, 206, 312, 405–406, 417, 438, 471
Operational Code Analysis (OCA) 238, 255–265, 308, 399, 540
operationalization 24, 54, 136, **136**, 187, 219, 223, 262, 333, 466, 554–555
Oppermann, K. 29, 74, 104, 106, 109, 117, 119, 121–128, 151, 179, 194–195, 386, 454, 492–493, 516, 519, 536
oral history 92, 450–460
Orchard, P. 9
ordinary least squares (OLS) 321, 324–325, 346
Ostermann, F. 102–104, 106, 108, 110, 120–121, 135, 323
Ó Tuathail, G. 82, 89
out-of-equilibrium beliefs 365
overconfidence 205, 208

panel surveys 377
Panofsky, E. 154, 155
Paquin, J. 8
Partial-Credit Model 224
patriarchy 69, 72
Patti, C. 452
Pautsch, I.D. 472
Paxton, P.M. 72
Pearson, M. 297
Pemantle, R. 347
People's Republic of China (PRC) see China (People's Republic)

perception 74, 86, 90, 123, 128, 153, 155, 191, 202–203, 206, 218–236, 238, **241**, 293, 298, 308, 339–343, 348–350, 441, 453, 455, 487, 493, 518, 542
Perfect Bayesian Equilibrium (PBE) 364, *364*
Però, D. 39
p-hacking 326
Pham, P. 347
Pickering, S. 85
Pizzorno, A. 26, 31
PMCs *see* private military companies (PMCs)
PMSCs *see* private military and security contractors (PMSCs)
Poland 177, **315**, **393**, **394**, **395**
polarized pluralist model 221
political geography 82–93
politicization 3, 152, 212, 213
polycentric governance 519
Polythink model 269–286
Portugal **393**, **394**, **395**
Posen, B.R. 298–300
positivism 72, 85, 102, 127–128, 295, 308, 406, 436, 454
post-positivism 85, 88, 104–105, 128, 308
poststructuralism 21, 26–33, 45, 108
Potter, P. 421
Pouliot, V. 105, 109, 408–409, 415, 424, 466, 469
Powell, R. 355, 356
practice (theory) 23–33, 42, 46–47, 51, 54–58, 62, 69, 71–72, 88, 101, 104–105, 108–109, 169, 171, 204, 415, 421–424, 429, 464, 466–467, 469, 471–473, 477–478
predication 105–106
prediction 28, 104, 136, 208, 222, 256, 258, 261–263, 299, 321, 324–327, 329–332, 345, 370–371, 373, 376, 469, 479, 541
presuppositions 105, 425
Prisoner's Dilemma 362, *362*
private military and security companies (PMSCs) 405, 413, 503, 511
private military companies (PMCs) 414
process tracing (PT) 32, 92, 196, 198, 309, 405–417, 441–442
Profiler Plus 240, 242, 249, 261, 262, 264
Proksch, S-O. 547
Psychological Characteristics of Leaders (PsyCL) 262
public opinion (survey) 119, 121, 125, 135, 339, 344, 370–380, 426, 490, 506
Pütz, M. 135
p-value 326

Qualitative Comparative Analysis (QCA) 11, 385–399, 441
Quanteda 539
Quantitative Content Analysis (QuantCA) 242, 255, 306–318, 504

R2P *see* Responsibility to Protect (R2P)
Ragin, C.C. 386, 389, 398, 399–400
Raleigh, C. 13, 292, 303, 322, 437, 465, 486, 552–553
random assignment 338–341, 348, 350, 377
random probability sample 344
Rasch Measurement Model (RMM) 218, 223–226
Rasch Rating Scale Model 223–224
rationalism xxii, 21–33, 86, 465
realism xxii, 6, 22–23, 87, 152, 295, 299, 301, 355; *see also* scientific realism
Rector, C. 297
reflexivity xxii, 29, 31–32, 110, 421, 426, 431, 432
regime theory 24
regression 321–333, 343, 346–347, **348**, 542, 544; *see also* logistic regression; multilevel regression
regularity theory of causation 11, 387, 400, 405–408, 410, 416–417; *see also* causality
Rehbein, J. 474
reliability 12, 110, 195, 224, 239, 251, 256, 259, 306–307, 310, 374, 379, 457, 557, 559, 563
Renshon, J. 300–302
repeated cross-sectional designs 377
research programs 9, 26, 163, 188, 255, 264, 291–292, 294–295, 302, 323, 517
Responsibility to Protect (R2P) 53, 55, 58–61, 161
rhetoric 74, 119, 134, 136–137, 142–144, 161, 171, 413, 415, 526, 541
Rhodes, B. 60, 283, 284
Rihoux, B. 6, 386, 398–399
Riles, A. 39
RMM *see* Rasch Measurement Model (RMM)
Rohlfing, I. 7, 399, 407, 446
role conflict 193, 196
role contestation 192–193, 197
role dissonance 193
role enactment 190–193, 195–197
role expectations 191–192, 196, 312
role socialization 192
role theory 187–198, 264, 301, 309
Roselle, L. 118
Rosenau, J.N. 292–293, 322, 436–437
R-squared (R^2) 326
Rubin, D.B. 346
Ruggie, J.G. 24
Russia 9, 32, 53, 61, 106, 174–178, 188, 192, 255, 260, 279, 281, **315**, 388, 439–440, 452–453, 506, 510, 542
Russia-Georgia War 12, 486, 492–497, **493**, **496**

sampling 45, 121, 175, *225*, 226–230, 232–233, 249, **250**, 251, 260–261, 265, 301, 306, 317, 326–328, 340–346, **348**, 349, 363–364, 370, 373, 375–377, 378–380, 454, 490, 504, 531, 540–541

Sapignoli, M. 39
Sapin, B. 338
Sarkees, M.R. 69
Sartori, A.E. 356
scaling methods 310, 538–539, 543–544, 545
Schafer, M. 23, 89–90, 194, 242, 255
Schia, N.N. 42
Schlag, G. 152, 153
Schneider, C.Q. 386–387, 407
Schneiker, A. 53
scientific realism xxii, 104
Secor, A. 84
securitization (theory) 31–32, 85, 107–108
securitizing move 107
semi-structured interviews 424, 427, 455
semi-supervised learning models 544–545; sentiment analysis 214, 503–508, 509–511, 512
Sharpe, J. 84
Shih, C. 189
Shore, C. 39
Siedschlag, A. 8
signaling 23, 212, 355–356, 360
Sikkink, K. 52
Simon, H.A. 194
situatedness 42–46, 174, 413, 417
Sjöstedt, R. 9, 101, 103, 107
Skalski, P.D. 307
Skjelsbæk, I. 74
Slovakia **393**, **394**, **395**
small-N qualitative method 6, 198, 264, 298, 300, 441
Smith, G. 260
Smith, K.E. 246
Smith, S. 189, 292, 293
Snyder, R. 338
social constructivism *see* constructivism
social media 4, 12, 109, 135, 487, 490, 502–504, 506–509, 511–512, 536, 546
Social Sciences Citation Index (SSCI) 4
socialization game 192
sociological theory 25
solution concept 355–356, 360, 366
solution terms 390, 395, 399
South Africa 27, 224–234, 459
Soviet Union 89, 122, 172, 193, 207, 294, 299, 416, 441–442
Spain **393**, **394**, **395**
Spaniel, W. 356
spatial analysis 87
Spencer, A. 9, 106, 195
Spektor, M. 453, 458
spiral model 355
Stahl, B. 9, 128, 154, 170, 179
standard error 325–326, **329**, **330**
Statham, A. 188
statistical analysis 222, 259, 300, 301, 321–333, 343, 347

statistical significance 228–229, 326, 329, 330, 314, 394
stereotypes, stereotyping 72, 153, **241**, 246, 248–249, **278**, **282**, 283, **285**
Stewart, B.M. 540, 542
Stimmer, A. 54
storytelling (storylines) 45, 46, 104, 106, 117, 118, 120–123, **121**, 125, 128, 179, 358, 520, 524–525, 529
strategic narratives 118–119
stratified sample 344
structural role theory 188, 189–190, 192
Structural Topic Model (STM) 542–543
structured interviews 424
Stryker, S. 188
Stuart, E.A. 347
Subgame Perfect Equilibrium (SPE) 363, *363*
subject positioning 106
sunk cost experiment 301
supervised classification methods 540–541
supervised scaling methods 543
Support Vector Machines (SVM) 541
survey experiments 125, 377–378
surveys 42, 193, 197, 205–206, 223–224, 292, 308, 317, 328, 339–345, 347–349, 370–380, 392, 438, 544
Swedlund, H.J. 344
Swiss, L. 518
symbolic technologies 103

Tal-Shir, E. 281
Tarar, A. 355
TASK *see* task focus or orientation focus (TASK)
task focus or orientation focus (TASK) 240
temporal emplotment 120, 123
text-based analysis 90, 102, 108, 150, 170–172, 175, 467–479, 486, 504, 520, 531, 536–537, 539
Thies, C.G. 8, 192, 197, 301, 302, 547
Thomann, E. 387, 391, 398, 400
Thomas, M. 90
threat assessment 202–215
Tilley, J. 347
time horizons theory 299
Tomz, M. 341, 344, 345
Torres, M. 347
Towns, A. 75
Trachtenberg, M. 465
transcription 261, 424, 430, 456, 458, 466, 473–474, 477
treatment 136, 321, 339–342, 346–350, 377–378, 390
trolls (troll farm) 506, 510, 512
Troy, J. 518
Trubowitz, P. 545, 546
truth table 389–390, 394–395, **395**
Tryggestad, T.L. 74
Turkey 30, 103, 239, 246

574

Twitter 490–491, 502–512, 546, 547
Tyson, S.A. 356

UK (United Kingdom) 55, 59, 61, 102, 122, 125, 206, 209–211, 224–234, 236, **250**, 262, **272, 273,** 279, 298–299, 440, 469, 524–530
uniformity pressures 275, 283, 327
unit of analysis 261–263, 292, 324, 327
unsupervised classification methods 541–543
unsupervised scaling methods 543–544
USA (United States of America) 59–61, 72, 171, 203, 206–207, 209–211, **250**, 260, **272, 273,** 297, 299, 328, 378–379, 416, 442, 444, 469, 479, 491, 495, **496**, 525
Usher, N. 219, 222
utilitarianism 21–23, 25, 27

validity 55–56, 62, 110, 194–195, 297–298, 300–301, 303, 306–307, 340, 343–348, 350, 378, 426, 457, 544
value rationality 25
van Meegdenburg, H. 32, 92, 123, 196, 398, 414, 441, 498, 518
Van Wyk, A-M. 453
Vaynman, J. 356
Verbs In Context System (VICS) 255, 257–261, 264–265
vertical role contestation 192–193
VICS *see Verbs In Context System*
Vignoli, V. 323, 536, 544
vision of itself 26, 33
visual analysis 150–163, 179

Wagemann, C. 386–387, 395, 398
Wagner, R.H. 355, 366
Wagner, W. 3, 323, 519, 540

Walker, S.G. 189, 191, 255, 257, 260, 294, 308
Ward, S. 296, 297
Watanabe, K. 487, 545, 546, 547
Webb, C. 341, 342, 347, 349, 350
Weber, C. 69
Weeks, J. 341, 344, 345
Wehner, L.E. 195, 196
WEIS *see* World Event/Interaction Survey (WEIS)
Weldes, J. 25, 27, 28, 30
Wheeler, N.J. 453, 458
White, H. 46
Wiener, A. 8, 9, 23, 53–58, 62
Windhoek Declaration 70
Wish, N.B. 189
Wisken, L. 54
within-subject designs 341–342
witness seminars 452
Wojczewski, T. 103
Wolfers, A. 169
Wolford, S. 11, 25, 356, 359, 361
Women, Peace, and Security (WPS) 70
Woods, M. 88
word-embedding models 545
World Event/Interaction Survey (WEIS) 292
World Trade Organization (WTO) 298
Wright, J. 90
Wright, K.A.M. 76
Wright, S. 39
Wu, C. 356

Yang, Y.E. 241
Yarhi-Milo, K. 344, 345

Zeitzoff, T. 487
Zhukov, Y.M. 542

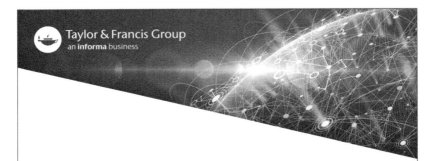